CASES AND MATERIALS
ON
INTERNATIONAL LAW

AUSTRALIA AND NEW ZEALAND
The Law Book Company Ltd.
Sydney : Melbourne : Perth

CANADA AND U.S.A.
The Carswell Company Ltd.
Agincourt, Ontario

INDIA
N. M. Tripathi Private Ltd.
Bombay
and
Eastern Law House Private Ltd.
Calcutta *and* Delhi
M.P.P. House
Bangalore

ISRAEL
Steimatzky's Agency Ltd.
Jerusalem : Tel Aviv : Haifa

MALAYSIA : SINGAPORE : BRUNEI
Malayan Law Journal (Pte.) Ltd.
Singapore

PAKISTAN
Pakistan Law House
Karachi

CASES AND MATERIALS
ON
INTERNATIONAL LAW

By

D. J. HARRIS, LL.M., PH.D.

*Professor of Public
International Law at the
University of Nottingham*

THIRD EDITION

LONDON
SWEET & MAXWELL
1983

First Edition........ 1973
Second Impression. 1976
Second Edition...... 1979
Third Edition........ 1983
Second Impression. 1986

Published in 1983 by
Sweet & Maxwell Limited of
11 *New Fetter Lane, London.*
Computerset by MFK Typesetting Ltd.,
Saffron Walden, Essex.
Printed in Scotland

British Library Cataloguing in Publication Data

Harris, D. J. (David John), *1938–*
  Cases and materials on international law.—3rd ed.
  1. International law—Cases   2. International
  law—Sources
  I. Title
  341'.0268   JX68

ISBN 0-421-29270-9
ISBN 0-421-29280-6 Pbk

PREFACE

Much has happened since the second edition. UNCLOS III has finally made port. Hopefully, its epic voyage has been worthwhile. The United Kingdom has been at war, and the Falkland factor has had its effect on the teaching of international law. The United Kingdom has changed its recognition policy and its law of sovereign immunity has been developed further. The International Law Commission has adopted more draft articles on state responsibility and the awards in the *Liamco* and *B.P.* cases, which have now been published, offer further evidence of the complexities of the law of expropriation. The International Court of Justice has decided the *Hostages Case*. The European Court of Human Rights has been very active so that it is now not easy to keep the section on the European Convention on Human Rights within reasonable bounds. The United Nations Covenants on Human Rights, particularly that on Civil and Political Rights, also demand more attention. Inevitably, room has had to be made to allow for these developments. In particular, some British recognition cases which may no longer be of such importance as previously have been omitted. The section on United Nations Peacekeeping Forces has also been reduced.

Permission has been sought and obtained in respect of the extracts used in this third edition. I wish to thank those writers, or their representatives, who have given me permission to include extracts from their writings. I wish also to thank the following publishers and institutions for giving me permission to print extracts from publications in which they have copyright: American Society of International Law; Cambridge University Press; Clarendon Press; Columbia University Press; Council of Europe; Hague Academy of International Law; Alfred A. Knopf Inc.; Longmans; David McKay Inc.; Manchester University Press; Martinus Nijhoff; Phaedon Press; Praeger Publishers Inc.; A. W. Sitjhoff; United Nations; United States Government Printing Office. In addition, I am grateful to the American Society of International Law and the authors concerned for permission to reprint passages from *The Future of the International Court of Justice*, published by Oceana Publications Inc. I wish to thank the publishers for their assistance during the preparation of the third edition. I am also extremely grateful to my colleague Rod Edmunds for compiling the tables and index.

It is hoped that the book is up-to-date to December 1982. It has been possible to include materials and comment beyond this date in some cases.

Department of Law,   D. J. HARRIS
University of Nottingham,
February 1983

CONTENTS

TABLE OF CASES

*[Page references in **bold** type indicate extracts of the case.]*

TABLE OF STATUTES

*[Page references in **bold** type indicate extracts of the statute.]*

UNITED KINGDOM

UNITED STATES

OTHER COUNTRIES

TABLE OF TREATIES

*[Page references in **bold** type indicate extracts of the treaty; 'n' is an abbreviation for footnote.]*

TABLE OF OTHER DOCUMENTS

*[Page references in **bold** type indicate extracted material; 'n' is an abbreviation for footnote]*

GENERAL ASSEMBLY RESOLUTIONS

SECURITY COUNCIL RESOLUTIONS AND CONSENSUS STATEMENTS

MISCELLANEOUS

TABLE OF ABBREVIATIONS

A.D.	Annual Digest of Public International Law Cases.
A.J.C.L.	American Journal of Comparative Law.
A.J.I.L.	American Journal of International Law.
Annuaire Français	Annual Français de Droit International.
Austr. Y.B.I.L.	Australian Yearbook of International Law.
B.D.I.L.	British Digest of International Law.
B.F.S.P.	British and Foreign State Papers.
B.P.I.L.	British Practice in International Law.
B.Y.I.L.	British Yearbook of International Law.
Brierly	The Law of Nations, 6th Ed., 1963.
Brownlie	Principles of Public International Law, 3rd Ed., 1979.
Cal. West. I.L.J.	California Western International Law Journal.
C.Y.I.L.	Canadian Yearbook of International Law.
C.D.E.C.H.R.	Collection of Decisions of the European Commission of Human Rights.
Col.Jo.Trans.Law	Columbia Journal of Transnational Law.
Col.L.R.	Columbia Law Review.
C., Cd., Cmd., Cmnd.	U.K. Command Papers.
C.M.L.R.	Common Market Law Reports.
C.M.L.Rev.	Common Market Law Review.
C.P.U.K.I.L.	Contemporary Practice of the U.K. in International Law.
C.E.	Council of Europe.
C.L.P.	Current Legal Problems.
De Visscher	Theory and Reality in Public International Law, 3rd Ed., 1960 (Translation by Corbett).
D.R.E.C.H.R.	Decisions and Reports of the European Commission of Human Rights.
Ed.	Editor.
E.T.S.	European Treaty Series.
Eur. Court H.R.	European Court of Human Rights.
G.A.O.R.	General Assembly Official Records.
Ga.J.I.C.L.	Georgia Journal of International and Comparative Law.
Hackworth	Digest of International Law, 8 vols. (1940–44).
Hague Recueil	Recueil des cours de l'Academie de droit international.
H.Rts Jo.	Human Rights Journal.
H.R.L.J.	Human Rights Law Journal.
H.Rts Q.	Human Rights Quarterly.
J.A.L.C.	Journal of Air Law and Commerce.
J.O.	Official Journal of the European Communities.

Jo.I.C.J.	Journal of the International Commission of Jurists.
Jo.W.T.L.	Journal of World Trade Law.
I.C.L.Q.	International and Comparative Law Quarterly.
Int.Conc.	International Conciliation.
I.L.C.	International Law Commission.
I.L.Q.	International Law Quarterly.
I.L.R.	International Law Reports.
I.L.M.	International Legal Materials.
Int.Leg.	Hudson, International Legislation, 9 vols. (1931–50).
Int.Org.	International Organisation.
Int.Rel.	International Relations.
Lauterpacht, *Development*	The Development of International Law by the International Court, 1958.
L. & C.P.	Law and Contemporary Problems.
L.N.T.S.	League of Nations Treaty Series.
L.N.O.J.	League of Nations Official Journal.
Malloy	Treaties, Conventions, etc., between the U.S.A. and Other Powers, 4 vols. (1776–1937).
McNair	International Law Opinions, 3 vols. (1956).
McNair, *Treaties*	The Law of Treaties, 2nd Ed., 1961.
Moore	Digest of International Law, 8 vols. (1906).
Moore, *Int.Arb.*	International Arbitrations, 5 vols. (1898).
Neth.I.L.R.	Netherlands International Law Review.
N.I.L.Q.	Northern Ireland Legal Quarterly.
N.Y.U.J.I.L.P.	New York University Journal of International Law and Politics.
N.Y.U.L.R.	New York University Law Review.
N.Z.T.S.	New Zealand Treaty Series.
Oppenheim, Vol. 1	International Law, Vol. 1, 8th Ed., 1955.
Proc.A.S.I.L.	Proceedings of the American Society of International Law.
Rec.Acad.	See Hague Recueil, above.
R.I.A.A.	United Nations Reports of International Arbitral Awards.
Rev.I.C.J.	Review of the International Commission of Jurists.
S.A.L.J.	South African Law Journal.
S.A.Y.B.I.L.	South African Yearbook of International Law.
Schwarzenberger	International Law, Vol. 1, 3rd Ed., 1957.
S.C.O.R.	Security Council Official Records.
Trans.Grot. Soc.	Transactions of the Grotius Society.
U.K.M.I.L.	U.K. Materials on International Law.
U.K.T.S.	U.K. Treaty Series.
U.N.T.S.	United Nations Treaty Series.
U.S.Dept. State Bull.	U.S. Department of State Bulletin.
U.S.D.I.L.	U.S. Digest of International Law.
U.S.For.Rel.	Foreign Relations of the U.S.
U.S.T.S.	U.S. Treaty Series.

U.S.T.I.A.S.	U.S. Treaties and Other International Agreements.
Verzijl	Jurisprudence of the World Court, 2 Vols., 1965, 1966.
Virg.Jo.I.L.	Virginia Journal of International Law.
Wash.L.R.	Washington Law Review.
Whiteman	Digest of International Law, 14 vols (1963–70).
Wisc.L.R.	Wisconsin Law Review.
Y.B.E.C.H.R.	Yearbook of the European Convention on Human Rights.
Y.B.I.L.C.	Yearbook of the International Law Commission.
Y.B.W.A.	Yearbook of World Affairs.
Z.A.O.R.V.	Zeitschrift für Ausländisches Offentliches Recht und Völkerrecht.

CHAPTER 1

INTRODUCTION[1]

1. *INTERNATIONAL LAW AS "LAW"*

BRIERLY, THE LAW OF NATIONS

Waldock (6th ed., 1963), pp. 41–42, 68–76

LAW can only exist in a society, and there can be no society without a system of law to regulate the relations of its members with one another. If then we speak of the "law of nations," we are assuming that a "society" of nations exists, and the assumption that the whole of the civilized world constitutes in any real sense a single society or community is one which we are not justified in making without examination. In any case the character of the law of nations is necessarily determined by that of the society within which it operates, and neither can be understood without the other.

The law of nations had its origin among a few kindred nations of western Europe which, despite their frequent quarrels and even despite the religious schism of the sixteenth century, all had and were all conscious of having a common background in the Christian religion and the civilization of Greece and Rome. They were in a real sense a society of nations. But the rise of the modern state system undermined the tradition of the unity of Christendom, and eventually gave rise to those sentiments of exclusive nationalism which are rife in the world today. It is true that side by side with this development there has been an immense growth of the factors that make states mutually dependent on one another. Modern science has given us vastly increased facilities and speed of communications, and modern commerce has created demands for the commodities of other nations which even the extravagances of modern economic nationalism are not able to stifle. If human affairs were more wisely ordered, and if men were clearer-sighted than they are in seeing their own interests, it might be that this interdependence of the nations would lead to a strengthening of their feelings of community. But their interdependence is mainly in material things, and though material bonds are necessary, they are not enough without a common social consciousness; without that they are as likely to lead to friction as to friendship. Some sentiment of shared responsibility for the conduct of a common life is a necessary element in any society, and the necessary force behind any system of law; and the strength of any legal system is proportionate to the strength of such a sentiment. . . .

[1] In addition to the writings from which passages are printed in this Chapter, see Carlston, *Law and Organisation in World Society* (1962); Falk, *The Status of Law in International Society* (1970); Jenks, *The Common Law of Mankind* (1958); *ibid. Law in the World Community* (1967); Jennings (1958) 34 B.Y.I.L. 334; Kaplan and Katzenbach, *The Political Foundations of International Law* (1961); Lissitzyn, *International Law Today and Tomorrow* (1965), first published as *International Conciliation*, No. 543, March 1963; McDougal, 82 *Hague Recueil* 133 (1953–II); Merrills, *Anatomy of International Law* (2nd ed., 1981); Mosler, 140 *Hague Recueil* 1 (1974–IV); Schwarzenberger, *The Frontiers of International Law* (1962); De Visscher, *passim*; Corbett, *The Growth of World Law* (1971).

1

It has often been said that international law ought to be classified as a branch of ethics rather than of law. The question is partly one of words, because its solution will clearly depend on the definition of law which we choose to adopt; in any case it does not affect the value of the subject one way or the other, though those who deny the legal character of international law often speak as though "ethical" were a depreciatory epithet. But in fact it is both practically inconvenient and also contrary to the best juristic thought to deny its legal character. It is inconvenient because if international law is nothing but international morality, it is certainly not the whole of international morality, and it is difficult to see how we are to distinguish it from those other admittedly moral standards which we apply in forming our judgments on the conduct of states.[2] Ordinary usage certainly uses two tests in judging the "rightness" of a state's act, a moral test and one which is somehow felt to be independent of morality. Every state habitually commits acts of selfishness which are often gravely injurious to other states, and yet are not contrary to international law; but we do not on that account necessarily judge them to have been "right." It is confusing and pedantic to say that both these tests are moral. Moreover, it is the pendantry of the theorist and not of the practical man; for questions of international law are invariably treated as legal questions by the foreign offices which conduct our international business, and in the courts, national or international, before which they are brought; legal forms and methods are used in diplomatic controversies and in judicial and arbitral proceedings, and authorities and precedents are cited in argument as a matter of course. It is significant too that when a breach of international law is alleged by one party to a controversy, the act impugned is practically never defended by claiming the right of private judgment, which would be the natural defence if the issue concerned the morality of the act, but always by attempting to prove that no rule has been violated. . . .[3]

If, as Sir Frederick Pollock[4] writes, and as probably most competent jurists would today agree, the only essential conditions for the existence of law are the existence of a political community, and the recognition by its members of settled rules binding upon them in that capacity, international law seems on the whole to satisfy these conditions. . . .[5]

The best view is that international law is in fact just a system of customary law, upon which has been erected, almost entirely within the last two generations, a superstructure of "conventional" or treaty-made law, and some of its chief defects are precisely those that the history of law teaches us to expect in a customary system. It is a common mistake to suppose that of these the most conspicuous is the frequency of its violation. Violations of law are rare in all customary systems, and they are so in international law. . . . For the law is normally observed because, as we shall see, the demands that it makes on states

---

[2] *Ed., e.g.* the legality and morality of the ill-treatment of nationals are for the most part to be judged by different standards: see below, p. 470.

[3] *Ed.* See, *e.g.* the British justification for the invasion of Suez, below, p. 667, and the Argentinian justification for the invasion of the Falkland Islands, below, p. 661.

[4] *First Book of Jurisprudence*, p. 28.

[5] *Ed.* In *The Outlook for International Law* (1944), p. 5, Brierly writes: "The best evidence for the existence of international law is that every actual state recognises that it does exist and that it is itself under obligation to observe it. States may often violate international law, just as individuals often violate municipal law, but no more than individuals do states defend their violations by claiming that they are above the law."

are generally not exacting, and on the whole states find it convenient to observe it. . . . But the weakness of the international law lies deeper than any mere question of sanctions. It is not the existence of a police force that makes a system of law strong and respected, but the strength of the law that makes it possible for a police force to be effectively organized. The imperative character of law is felt so strongly and obedience to it has become so much a matter of habit within a highly civilized state that national law has developed a machinery of enforcement which generally works smoothly, though never so smoothly as to make breaches impossible. If the imperative character of international law were equally strongly felt, the institution of definite international sanctions would easily follow.

A customary system of law can never be adequate to the needs of any but a primitive society, and the paradox of the international society is that, whilst on the material side it is far from primitive, and therefore needs a strong and fairly elaborate system of law for the regulation of the clashes to which the material interdependence of different states is constantly giving rise, its spiritual cohesion is, as we have already seen, weak, and as long as that is so the weakness will inevitably be reflected in a weak and primitive system of law.[6]

Among the most serious shortcomings of the present system are the rudimentary character of the institutions which exist for the making and the application of the law, and the narrow restrictions on its range. . . . There is no legislature to keep the law abreast of new needs in the international society; no executive power to enforce the law; and although certain administrative bodies have been created, these, though important in themselves, are far from being adequate for the mass of business which ought to be treated today as of international concern. There exist also convenient machinery for the arbitration of disputes and a standing court of justice, but the range of action of these is limited because resort to them is not compulsory.[7]

The restricted range of international law is merely the counterpart of the wide freedom of independent action which states claim in virtue of their sovereignty. . . . Law will never play a really effective part in international relations until it can annex to its own sphere some of the matters which at present lie within the "domestic jurisdictions" of the several states. . . .[8]

It is a natural consequence of the absence of authoritative law-declaring machinery that many of the principles of international law, and even more the detailed application of accepted principles, are uncertain. But on the whole the layman tends to exaggerate this defect. It is not in the nature of any law to

[6] *Ed. cf.* Corbett, *Law in Diplomacy* (1959), pp. 273–274: "What is principally missing is the measure of agreement on supreme common values, the sense of community, loyalty, and mutual tolerance which within the State make compulsory institutions bearable. The reserved domain and the whole legal concept of sovereignty correspond to the fact that the State remains in the hearts and minds of men the highest center of human authority and chief guardian of the most treasured values . . . the State continues to be for practical purposes the chief end of man. So long as this is so, whatever their covenants or declarations, governments will not assume in practice a position of general subjection to a law of nations."

[7] *Ed.* See Chap. 12, below.

[8] *Ed.* Matters within the "domestic jurisdiction" of a state are matters not regulated by international law so that a state is free to act in its discretion. They are numerous and varied. They range from the kind of government (democratic, totalitarian) a state has, to the treatment of nationals (but not of aliens) in most respects, to cruelty to cats. For the concept in the UN Charter, see below, p. 694.

provide mathematically certain solutions of problems which may be presented to it; for uncertainty cannot be eliminated from law so long as the possible conjunctions of facts remain infinitely various. Although therefore the difference between international law and the law of a state in this respect is important it is one of degree and not of kind, and it tends to be reduced as the practice of resorting to international courts, which are able to work out the detailed practical implication of general principles, becomes more common.[9] The difficulty of formulating the rules of international law with precision is a necessary consequence of the kinds of evidence upon which we have to rely in order to establish them. . . .

Brierly then discusses the international law attitude to the legality of war.[10]

Whether from a review of all these shortcomings we ought to conclude that international law is a failure depends upon what we assume to be its aim. It has not failed to serve the purposes for which states have chosen to use it; in fact it serves these purposes reasonably well. . . . the practice of international law proceeds on much the same lines as that of any other kind of law, with the foreign offices taking the place of the private legal adviser[11] and exchanging arguments about the facts and the law, and later, more often than is sometimes supposed, with a hearing before some form of international tribunal. The volume of this work is considerable, but most of it is not sensational. . . . That does not mean that the matters to which it does relate are unimportant in themselves; often they are very important to particular interests or individuals. But it means that international law is performing a useful and indeed a necessary function in international life in enabling states to carry on their day-to-day intercourse along orderly and predictable lines. That is the role for which states have chosen to use it and for that it has proved a serviceable instrument.

Notes

1. *Ubi societas ibi ius.* Is there an international society with a sufficient sense of community to allow one realistically to expect a more than fragmentary system of international law? Or are the attitudes and interests of the Communist countries, the Western powers and the Third World too diverse to allow this? What does Brierly think? Note the following view of De Visscher[12]:

It is therefore pure illusion to expect from the mere arrangement of inter-State relations the establishment of a community order; this can find a solid foundation only in the development of the true international spirit in men. . . . There will be no international community so long as the political ends of the State overshadow the human ends of power.

Is De Visscher unduly pessimistic? Even if states do shrink from surrendering the sovereignty they need to surrender to extend significantly the "range of international

---

[9] *Ed.* This is optimistic. On the dearth of cases before the World Court, see below, p. 746. The lack of cases interpreting the increasing number of "law-making" treaties (see below, p. 39) presents a problem. In municipal law, a new statute that raises questions of interpretation is soon taken to court for a ruling. Unfortunately, that is unlikely to happen in international law. An outstanding exception is the European Convention on Human Rights, the meaning of which is gradually being established by the jurisprudence of the Strasbourg authorities: see below, Chap. 9. It would be helpful, for example, to have a court construe Article 2(4) of the UN Charter, see below, p. 641.

[10] See below, Chap. 11.

[11] *Ed.* See Merillat, ed., *Legal Advisers and Foreign Affairs* (1964), and Vallat, *International Law and the Practitioner* (1966).

[12] De Visscher, pp. 89, 94. See also Mosler, *loc. cit.* at p. 1, n. 1, above, pp. 17–47.

law" and permit its enforcement, are there now at least some signs of the recognition by states of more common interests and of more accommodation of the interests of individuals? Consider this again when having read the materials in this casebook.

2. *The Austinian Handicap.* Is international law "law" is a standard sherry party question. Its sometimes irritating persistence is very largely the responsibility of John Austin, an English jurist of the first part of the nineteenth century and a familiar friend of any student who has taken a course in jurisprudence. He defined laws "properly so-called" as commands and "positive law," which he regarded as the "appropriate matter of jurisprudence," as the commands of a sovereign.[13] A sovereign he defined as a person who received the habitual obedience of the members of an independent political society and who, in turn, did not owe such obedience to any other person. Rules of international law did not qualify as rules of "positive law" by this test and, not being commands of any sort, were placed by Austin in the category of "laws improperly so-called." This uncompromising and unhappily phrased rejection of international law's claim to be law of the same order as municipal law[14] has, to this day, upset international lawyers and placed them on the defensive. Although international law is still not "law" according to Austin's test, most international lawyers would at least dispute that that test is more helpful than certain others by which international law could be said to be "law."[15]

3. *The "Law Habit."* No writer would seem to dissent from the view expressed by Brierly that, in terms of the number, as opposed to the political importance, of the occasions on which international law is complied with, it is more honoured in the observance than in the breach. Jessup,[16] for example, takes Brierly's view:

> Wars, breaches of treaties, oppression of the weak by the strong, are the headlines of the daily press and of the history textbooks. The superficial observer has not noted the steady observance of such treaties as that under which letters are carried all over the world at rates fixed by the Universal Postal Union. He ignores the fact that there is scarcely an instance in two hundred years in which an ambassador has been subjected to suit in courts of the country where he is stationed. . . . The superficial observer has not read the hundreds of decisions handed down by international courts called Mixed Claims Commissions, which have awarded money damages duly paid by the defendant states. . . . He may be unfamiliar with the extent to which international law has been incorporated in national law and has thus secured an enforcement agency through the ordinary governmental machinery of the national states. . . . One of the wisest and most experienced of them all, John Bassett Moore, has recorded his observation that on the whole international law is as well observed as national law. The Director of the Yale Institute of International Studies has recently remarked that those "who make light of treaty commitments in general seem to ignore the fact that the vast majority of such engagements are continuously, honestly, and regularly observed even under adverse conditions and at considerable inconvenience to the parties." . . . The record proves that there is a "law habit" in international relations. It is not immaterial to add that the instances in which judgments of international tribunals have been flouted are so rare that the headline-reader may well place them in the man-bites-dog category.[17]

---

[13] See *The Province of Jurisprudence Determined* (1832), Lectures I, V and VI. A recent edition is that edited by Hart in 1954.

[14] This is the term used in international law to refer to the law of a state.

[15] For the view that the question whether international law is "law" is a verbal one not worth bothering with: see Glanville Williams (1945) 22 B.Y.I.L. 146 at p. 163. See also Hart, *The Concept of Law* (1961), pp. 209–210.

[16] *A Modern Law of Nations* (1948), pp. 6–8.

[17] Nantwi, *The Enforcement of International Judicial Decisions and Arbitral Awards in Public International Law* (1966), Chap. IV, records only a few cases, constituting but a very small proportion of the whole, in which the losing state has not complied with the decision or

Although there is clearly some merit to the "law habit" view, might it not, to some extent, be misleading? What has to be emphasised as strongly is that a state can usually flout international law if it wants to and get away with it. How relevant also is a comparison of the number or percentage of violations of municipal and international law? The point about a train robber is that if there is a good case against him and if his whereabouts are known he will be punished. The U.S.S.R. has yet to be arraigned for intervening unlawfully in Afghanistan in 1979[18] and the United Kingdom got away with its import surcharge in violation of the EFTA Treaty in 1965.

But are we asking too much of international law? Are we expecting it to be effective often in disputes in which we would not imagine law to apply, or at least not to be in the forefront, within a state because of the political importance of the problem?

Note also, by way of apology for international law, the following statement. Writing of the North Atlantic Treaty,[19] Katz[20] suggests:

> When such a treaty is negotiated and signed, none of the participating states contemplates that its future course under the treaty will be governed exclusively or primarily by technical juridical procedures or patterns of analysis. No participating state considers itself to have acquired a right to demand that the course of conduct of the other participating states should be so determined. The relevant procedures are diplomatic, and the relevant intellectual canons are the canons of political thought— with something added. The addition is a sense of law. In the language of lawyers, Article 5 of the North Atlantic Treaty constitutes a formal statement of policy, a formal declaration of purpose or declaration of intent, upon which the participating states are entitled reciprocally to rely subject to the limitations inherent in the nature of such a declaration. Article 5 neither expresses nor was intended to express a contractual obligation in the strict legal sense. It does nevertheless express an obligation. The obligation is diplomatic, reinforced by what I call a sense of law.

MORGENTHAU, POLITICS AMONG NATIONS[21]

(5th ed., 1973), pp. 290–291.

The great majority of the rules of international law are generally observed by all nations without actual compulsion, for it is generally in the interest of all nations concerned to honor their obligations under international law. A nation will hesitate to infringe upon the rights of foreign diplomats residing in its capital; for it has an interest, identical with the interests of all other nations, in the universal observance of the rules of international law which extend their protection to its own diplomatic representatives in foreign capitals as well as to the foreign diplomats in its own capital. A nation will likewise be reluctant to disregard its

---

award. All of the decisions and opinions of the P.C.I.J. were followed; those of the I.C.J. have been less effective: see below, p. 747. It is true, of course, that jurisdiction is voluntary so that the parties are predisposed (although this is not necessarily true of cases brought under the "optional clause": see below, p. 718) to accept the ruling made (note that one of the rulings of the I.C.J. not complied with was that against Albania in the *Corfu Channel Case* which had initially been brought before the Court very much against its will: see below, p. 713) and that the percentage of disputes between states referred to the Court is minute.

[18] See below, p. 652.

[19] Below, p. 672.

[20] *The Relevance of International Adjudication* (1968), pp. 53–54. And see Dean Acheson's comment on the role of law in the Cuban missile crisis, below, p. 660.

[21] See also on sanctions, Kunz, 54 A.J.I.L. 324 (1960), and Schwebel, ed., *The Effectiveness of International Decisions* (1971).

obligations under a commercial treaty, since the benefits that it expects from the execution of the treaty by the other contracting parties are complementary to those anticipated by the latter. It may thus stand to lose more than it would gain by not fulfilling its part of the bargain. This is particularly so in the long run, since a nation that has the reputation of reneging on its commercial obligations will find it hard to conclude commercial treaties beneficial to itself.

Most rules of international law formulate in legal terms such identical or complementary interests. It is for this reason that they generally enforce themselves, as it were, and that there is generally no need for a specific enforcement action. In most cases in which such rules of international law are actually violated despite the underlying community of interests, satisfaction is given to the wronged party either voluntarily or in consequence of adjudication. . . .

Thus the great majority of rules of international law are generally unaffected by the weakness of its system of enforcement, for voluntary compliance prevents the problem of enforcement from arising altogether. The problem of enforcement becomes acute, however, in that minority of important and generally spectacular cases, particularly important in the context of our discussion, in which compliance with international law and its enforcement have a direct bearing upon the relative power of the nations concerned. In those cases . . . considerations of power rather than of law determine compliance and enforcement.

FITZMAURICE, THE FOUNDATIONS OF THE AUTHORITY OF INTERNATIONAL LAW AND THE PROBLEM OF ENFORCEMENT

(1956) 19 M.L.R. 1

With regard to the actual position concerning the enforceability of the international legal system, there has always been a respectable body of international lawyers that has both considered enforceability to be a necessary characteristic of any system of law, properly so called, and has also believed that international law possessed this characteristic, even if only in a rough and rudimentary form. Oppenheim, for instance, whose treatise may be cited because it constitutes so very much the practitioner's Bible, so to speak, . . . defines law as

> a body of rules for human conduct within a community which, by common consent of this community, shall be enforced by external power [8th ed., p. 10, para. 5].

. . . so great a modernist as Kelsen seems, in one of his latest works, *Principles of International Law,* published in 1952, to incline towards a similar view. He says, on page 5 of this work, that

> . . . law is a coercive order. It provides for socially organised sanctions, and these can be clearly distinguished from a religious order on the one hand and a merely moral order on the other hand. As a coercive order, the law is that specific social technique which consists in the attempt to bring about the desired social conduct of men through the threat of a measure of coercion which is to be taken in case of . . . legally wrong conduct.

Later, on page 14 of the same work, Kelsen points out that in decentralized societies (and the international society is such a society), enforcement of the law is accomplished through the application of the principle of self-help. The legal order leaves the enforcement function to the individuals injured by a delict or illegality. . . .

Eventually—see particularly pages 18–39 of the book—Kelsen appears to reach the conclusion that, judged by these tests, international law is true law because, broadly speaking, it provides sanctions, such as the adoption of reprisals, war, and the use of force generally, and makes the employment of these sanctions lawful as a counter-measure against a legal wrong, but unlawful in all other cases. . . .

Without necessarily subscribing fully to all these views, it can fairly be said that up to a comparatively recent date, war, and the use of force generally, did constitute in some sense a recognised method of enforcing international law; or, more accurately, a means whereby in the last resort a dispute between States as to their rights could be settled. It was a means of settlement or enforcement analogous in the international field to the "blood feud" or "ordeal by battle" or single combat, by which, in a more primitive stage of national societies, disputes between individuals or groups were settled—and it has always been the case, and still is, that the international society tends to reflect national society at an earlier stage of development. . . .

There is no need to retail the steps by which, in the period following on the first world war, up to date, war has, by a series of measures, been divested of its former basic legitimacy. . . .

Now this is, of course, very well, and greatly to be welcomed: no one would wish it otherwise. But it has given rise to one curious and perhaps unforeseen consequence—for in so far as war, or the use of force, was a means, however crude, by which an injured State could assert or defend its legal rights, as the case might be—then the position now is that international law is less enforceable today then it ever has been in the whole of its history—for nothing definite or certain has been put in the place of force as a means of settlement. . . .

It must be concluded that although the international order may have made [through Chapter VII of the U.N. Charter[22]] some attempt at progress in repressing or countering that particular type of illegality that consists in armed aggression or breach of the peace, it has not yet made much progress in the enforcement of international rights and obligations generally, or of international law as such. It now frowns on self-help, without, however, as yet having put anything in its place. It is obvious that such a situation is unsatisfactory. Fortunately, there can be set against it not only the fact that international law has never, in practice, been more than partly dependent for its authority[23] on the possibility of its physical enforcement, but also the principle that no system of law depends, or can, in the last resort, depend for its authority solely on the chances of enforcement. If it did, it could never in practice be enforced. The assumed certainty of enforcement in the national society masks the fact that, in general, the law does not have to be enforced, not so much because it is

[22] *Ed.* See below, Chap. 11.
[23] *Ed.* The author states elsewhere in the article that this is "a term here used in the sense of prestige."

taken for granted that it would be, but because it commands in practice the general assent or tolerance of the community.

The real foundation of the authority of international law resides similarly in the fact that the States making up the international society recognise it as binding upon them, and, moreover, as a system that *ipso facto* binds them *as* members of the society, irrespective of their individual wills.

THE NAULILAA CASE

Portugal *v.* Germany (1928)

Portuguese-German Mixed Arbitral Tribunal: De Meuron; Guex; Fazy. 2 R.I.A.A. 1012.
Translation

In October 1914, when Portugal was a neutral state during the First World War, three members of a party of German soldiers and officials lawfully in the Portuguese colony of Angola were killed by Portuguese soldiers as a result of a misunderstanding. Germany subsequently retaliated by sending a military force into Angola which destroyed property including the fort at Naulilaa. In this case, Portugal claimed reparation for damage attributable to the German action. Germany argued that it was a lawful reprisal.

Award of the Tribunal

The most recent doctrine, especially German doctrine, defines a reprisal as follows:

A reprisal is an act of self-help (*selbsthilfehandlung*) by the injured state, responding—*after an unsatisfied demand*—to an act contrary to international law committed by the offending state. It has the effect of suspending momentarily, in relations between the two states, the observance of the rule of international law in question. It is *limited* by common human experience and the rules of good faith, applicable in the relations between two states. *It would be illegal in the absence of a prior act contrary to international law justifying it.* Its object is to effect reparation from the offending state for the offense or a return to legality by the avoidance of further offenses.

This definition does not demand that reprisals remain *proportionate* to the offense. On this point writers, unanimous until a few years ago, have begun to differ. The majority see, in a certain proportion between the offense and the reprisal, a necessary condition for the lawfulness of the latter. Others, among the more modern, no longer insist on this. International law, as it is now developing in the light of the experience of the last war, certainly tends to limit the notion of lawful reprisals and to prohibit excesses. . . .

The first condition—*sine qua non*—for the right to exercise reprisals is a *justification* furnished by a previous act contrary to international law. This condition—which is recognised in the German argument—is lacking, which would by itself defeat the defense invoked by the German Government.

Even if the arbitrators had found, on the part of the Portuguese authorities, an act contrary to international law capable in principle of justifying a reprisal, the German argument ought nevertheless to be rejected for two other reasons, either of which is decisive.

1. A reprisal is only lawful when preceded by an unsatisfied *demand*. The use of force is only justified if absolutely necessary. . . .

2. The necessity of a *proportion* between the reprisal and the offense would appear to be recognised in the German reply. Even if one admitted that international law does not require that a reprisal should be approximately in proportion to the offense, one should certainly consider as excessive and illegal, a reprisal out of all proportion to the act justifying it. Now, in this case . . . there has been evident disproportion between the Naulilaa incident and the six acts of reprisals which have followed it.

Notes

1. The *Naulilaa Case* has now to be read in the light of the developments mentioned by Fitzmaurice[24] and considered in detail later[25] limiting the use of force. An example of the use of economic force as a sanction that would probably still be lawful nearly arose in connection with the *Corfu Channel Case*.[26] It would seem that the British Government were prepared to act against Albanian assets in the United Kingdom when Albania failed to pay the damages awarded against it by the International Court of Justice in that case but were unable to find any.[27]

2. Sanctions available to a state in international law by way of self-help include acts of retorsion as well as reprisals. Acts of retorsion are acts which, although unfriendly, are, unlike reprisals, not illegal under international law. Whether the term "retorsion" can be applied only to unfriendly but lawful acts in retaliation for acts of a similar kind or whether it also covers such acts taken against acts unlawful under international law is, curiously, not clear. In either case, there can be no doubt that lawful retaliation against such unlawful acts is permitted.[28]

3. In a few areas (most noticeably in the protection of the property of aliens and cases of diplomatic and sovereign immunity) municipal courts enforce international law. The problem is that the national understanding of international law which they enforce may not be that common to state practice as a whole.

4. So far as sanctions organised through the international community are concerned, the main ones are those within the power of the United Nations.[29] They are of limited scope and, in so far as they are exercisable by the Security Council, are subject to the "veto." Friedmann[30] argues that in the "international law of co-operation," which operates in areas in which states participate in activities furthering common state interests through international organisations or otherwise, a sanction of exclusion from the benefits of such activities is available. He gives as an example the power of the World Bank to grant or withhold development funds:

> . . . if a borrowing state were to confiscate, without compensation and in a discriminatory manner, the property of foreign investors . . . it would find itself excluded from participation in further development aid.[31]

[24] Above, p. 7.
[25] Below, Chap. 11.
[26] Below, p. 380. On the legality of the use of economic coercion not as a sanction, but to influence policy, see below, p. 642.
[27] *Hansard*, H.C., Vol. 488, col. 981, June 6, 1951.
[28] On reprisals, see the Commentary to the ILC Draft Articles on State Responsibility, Y.B.I.L.C., 1979, II (Part Two), pp. 115–122.
[29] See below, Chap. 12.
[30] *The Changing Structure of International Law* (1964), p. 88.
[31] *Ibid.* p. 91. Note that the U.K. Government managed in 1972 to postpone at least consideration of Tanzanian loan proposals by the World Bank on the ground that Tanzania had not paid adequate compensation for British property it had nationalised: *The Times,* January 28, 1972, p. 21.

As Friedmann suggests, the national interest of the defaulting state in continued participation must be at least as great as that in the course of action that caused it to default for such a sanction to be effective. When Indonesia withdrew from the United Nations in 1965 it left those United Nations specialised agencies from which it "did not have much benefit" but remained a member of the World Health Organisation which was conducting a malaria campaign in Indonesia at the time.[32] Political pressures, such as those at work in the *Certain Expenses* case in the United Nations,[33] may also prevent the application of such sanctions in some cases.

5. How do the sanctions available in international law differ from those in any developed system of municipal law? What improvements in the former are (i) desirable; (ii) reasonable to expect?

2. THE DEVELOPMENT OF INTERNATIONAL LAW

(i) GENERALLY

Modern international law has its origins in the Europe of the sixteenth and seventeenth centuries. Although communities of states regulated by law had previously existed in Europe (*e.g.* in Greece) and elsewhere (*e.g.* in India), it is, for reasons apparent from subsequent world history, the law created to govern the diplomatic, commercial, military and other relations of the society of Christian states forming the Europe of that time that provides the basis for the present law. Although the writers[34] who recorded (and, to a large extent, invented) this early "Law of Nations"[35] may have regarded it as having universal application, it was for many generations really no more than the Public Law of Europe. International law was first extended beyond Europe at the end of the eighteenth and at the beginning of the nineteenth centuries to the states that succeeded the rebel European colonies of North and South America respectively. By the mid-nineteenth century, Turkey had been accepted as the first non-Christian subject of international law. By 1914, increasing European penetration into Asia had led to the "admission," though scarcely on terms of equality,[36] of other such subjects, including Persia, China and Japan. It was the advent in 1920 of the League of Nations, membership of which was open to "any" state (Article 1, Covenant), that, as much as any other single event, marked the beginning of the present situation in which international law applies automatically to all states whatever their location or character. Since that time, the community of states has more then doubled in number.

Other changes of great importance too have occurred in the present century. Resort to war has been made illegal and a system of collective enforcement of peace and security has been initiated—though not very successfully—through the United Nations in place of self-help. The change in the balance of interests and values in the world community resulting first from the emergence of Communist states and then from the independence since 1945 of colonial and similar territories has had an effect in shaping or reshaping some international law rules. The demise of Oppenheim's doctrine that

---

[32] *The Times,* January 19, 1965, p. 8. This, of course, was a case of voluntary withdrawal, but the attitude might well be adopted in cases of expulsion too.

[33] See below, p. 704.

[34] See below, p. 50.

[35] The term "international law" would appear to have been coined later by Bentham (1748–1832).

[36] A system of capitulations, which in some cases lasted well into the present century, commonly applied by which European nationals present in the territory of the capitulating state were subject not to its local law or courts, but were subject instead to their national law administered in the territory of the capitulating state by their national consular courts.

"States solely and exclusively are the subject of International Law"[37] is also evident. The growth of public international organisations in particular bears witness to this. If other claimants still have very limited personality, it is nonetheless the case that inter-state treaties are increasingly concerned with the "trans-national" affairs, to use Jessup's terminology,[38] of private individuals and companies. Of great importance is the increase in the subject-matter of international law to cover what Friedmann has called "the international law of co-operation."[39] The development of the law of human rights is a notable aspect of this more positive, community-minded kind of law. Science too has had considerable impact. It has added two new territorial areas—outer space and the deep sea-bed—for which international law rules are required, and it has produced nuclear weapons, which have revised thinking about some existing rules and caused the introduction of new ones.

(ii) NEW STATES[40]

HENKIN, HOW NATIONS BEHAVE

(2nd ed., 1979), pp. 121–127. Some footnotes omitted

We are frequently reminded that international law was the product of European civilization. . . . One might expect, then, that this law would not survive the decline of Europe's dominance, surely would not govern a society of nations most of which were not European, not Christian, not imperialist, not capitalist, which did not participate in the development of the law, and whose interests were different from those of the nations that shaped the law. In fact, however, international law has survived and would not be unrecognizable to our parents and teachers in the law and in diplomacy. The new nations raised the theoretical difficulties which have long troubled jurists as to why newborn nations should be bound by pre-existing law.[41] Some of those nations spoke and speak suspiciously of white, colonial law and have proclaimed the need for revolutionary transformations. Many indeed have challenged particular principles. But all were eager to enter international society and to accept its law.[42]

The reasons why new nations accepted international law are not difficult to perceive. They came into an established system accepted by all nations, including the revolutionary governments and the many small powers which had supported their struggle for self-determination. Acceptance into that society as an independent equal was the proof and crown of their successful struggle, and international law provided the indispensable framework for living in that society. They adopted traditional forms in international trade and the growing co-operation for welfare of which they have been the principal beneficiaries, and early in their young history they have had to invoke international law in

---

[37] Oppenheim (1st ed., 1905), Vol. I, para. 13. Para. 13 now reads, in its 8th ed., "States are the principal subjects of International Law."

[38] See Jessup, *Transnational Law* (1956), pp. 15–16.

[39] See the extract, below, p. 17.

[40] See also Castañeda 15 Int.Org. 38 (1961); Falk, 118 *Hague Recueil* 1 (1966–II); Higgins, *Conflict of Interests: International Law in a Divided World* (1965); Sinha, 14 I.C.L.Q. 121 (1965).

[41] *Ed.* See below, p. 84.

[42] Even the hostile reaction following the decision of the International Court of Justice in the South West Africa case did not represent any rejection of traditional law. It struck primarily at the Court rather than at international law. . . .

their disputes, among themselves or with others—on the Indus River and in Kashmir, between India and Bangladesh, on the definition of the continental shelf. . . .

The explosion of new states. . . has made it yet more difficult to make new law. It has been long established that law of universal applicability can be made only by universal agreement or acquiescence; the likelihood of general agreement decreases, of course, as the number of nations who must agree increases. New univeral customary law, then, may become a rarity. . . . The multilateral convention, then, has become the principal form of general law-making, but already experience suggests that universality (or general acceptance) will be hard to come by. . . . General agreement may be possible only to codify accepted basic principles and practices, or perhaps to adopt some general, imprecise, and ambiguous standards to which time and experience may give some agreed content. (One may wonder whether even the Charter of the United Nations, hardly an instrument of legal precision, could be universally adopted today.) Regional law and law for other, smaller groupings may be the new law of the future, with universality a distant hope that we must learn not to expect or even desire.

The reluctance to make new law and the difficulties of making it do not apply equally to unmaking or remaking old law. Whatever the theory, new nations can in fact have a sharp impact on thc law by collective "massive resistance," especially where older states are reluctant to insist on the old law. . . . Customary law cannot long retain validity if a substantial number of states reject it. . . .

In several particular respects, however, the new nations, especially as they joined with other developing states and emerged as the Third World, have created new law in their image and interest. The Third World has succeeded where it was united and determined, had the full support of the Communist World, and had some support or sympathy, at least not resistance, among Western powers. They have succeeded in making that new law in the face of the principle of unanimity, by reinterpreting universal agreements (*e.g.* the UN Charter), by overwhelming or silencing or even disregarding remaining opposition, especially through the use of UN resolutions. To date, the changes they have achieved in international law have been limited and special, but some see more radical transformation ahead. . . .

The success of Third World countries in virtually ending colonialism and racism, their solidarity on economic issues and their ability to extend that solidarity to other issues, on which enough of them feel strongly, have stirred dreams or fears that they might try to eliminate or erode the principle of unanimity in favor of more law-making by majority. Increasingly, they have been encouraged to seek new institutions based essentially on "one state-one vote" and majority rule (*e.g.* the proposed International Sea-bed Authority); to eliminate special voting rights (like the veto in the UN Security Council); to increase the matters subject to majority vote, *e.g.* in UN General Assembly resolutions. They have effectively exploited other procedures, for example, decision by "consensus."[43] The developed majority perhaps originally saw in that change protection against being overwhelmed by top-sided majority votes, but in time the drives for consensus, where the Third World largely agreed,

[43] *Ed.* On the attempt at "consensus" in the drafting of the 1982 Convention on the Law of the Sea, see below, p. 286.

began to weigh heavily on would-be dissenters not to dissent. And resolutions in the United Nations and other multilateral bodies have begun to weigh more heavily in the law-making process.

Notes

1. On the same theme, see also Anand, below, p. 743.

2. For instances of the impact of the "new nations" upon international law, see the General Assembly Declaration on the Granting of Independence to Colonial Countries and Peoples,[44] the Vienna Covention of the Law of Treaties[45] (which was the first of the "law-making" treaties prepared by the International Law Commission in the drafting of which the "new nations" participated fully) and the 1982 Convention on the Law of the Sea.[46] Note also the impact they have had in the debate over the rules on the treatment of aliens[47] and the rules concerning the use of force.[48]

(iii) THE SOVIET VIEW[49]

TUNKIN, CO-EXISTENCE AND INTERNATIONAL LAW

95 *Hague Recueil* 1 at pp. 51 *et seq.* (1958–III). Some footnotes omitted

. . . Soviet international lawyers are of unanimous opinion that general international law, regulating relations between all the States irrespective of their social systems, not only can exist, but has good prospects of progressive development.

. . . the opinion is often expressed in the western international law literature of recent years that in the present day division of the world into two diametrically different systems, general international law is going to disintegrate into separate regional systems or at least that the ground on which it may exist has become narrower. This conclusion usually proceeds from a completely erroneous assumption that every law, and therefore international law as well, is based on a community of ideology. . . .

Difference of ideologies has always existed. True, this difference at present is profound. But when States agree on recognition of this or that norm as a norm of international law they do not agree on problems of ideology. They do not try to agree on such problems, for instance, as what is international law, what is its social foundation, its sources, what are the main characteristics of a norm of this law, etc. They do agree on rules of conduct. . . .

[44] Below, p. 95.
[45] Below, Chap. 10.
[46] Below, Chap. 7.
[47] Below, Chap. 8.
[48] Below, Chap. 11.
[49] For the Soviet view of international law as expressed by Soviet writers, see also Kozhevnikov, ed., *International Law* (1961). The contributions to this textbook are by Soviet international lawyers. It contains a lot of vigorous, polemical broadsides at "bourgeois" theories. And see Tunkin, *Theory of International Law,* published in Russian (1970) (English translation by Butler (1974)) and *ibid.,* 147 *Hague Recueil* 1 (1975–IV). For Western commentaries, see Baade, *The Soviet Impact on International Law* (1964); Corbett, *op. cit.* at p. 3, n. 6, above, Chap. III; Friedmann, *op. cit.* at p. 10, n. 30, above, pp. 327–340; Grzybowski, *Soviet Public International Law* (1970). For the position of Mainland China, see Chiu, 60 A.J.I.L. 245 (1966); Cohen, ed., *China's Practice of International Law* (1972); Cohen & Chiu, *People's China and International Law* (1974), 2 vols; Kim, 72 A.J.I.L. 317 (1978).

It is true that the Soviet Union did not accept all the norms which at the time of her emergence were considered as norms of general international law. But the Soviet Union refused to recognize only reactionary norms such as norms relating to colonial domination, spheres of influence, etc. V. I. Lenin said "We reject all provisions sanctioning international robbery and oppression, but all provisions relating to good neighbourly relations we willingly accept, we cannot reject them." These words express the attitude of the socialist State to international law in general.

It is not therefore inaccurate to assert that with the appearance of the Soviet State some norms of the then general international law, rejected by the Soviet State, ceased to be norms of general international law, but it is of importance to add that this limitation took place at the expense of reactionary norms of international law. As to democratic norms of general international law, the Soviet Union never rejected them. . . .

The Soviet Union and now also other socialist States have consistently fought and are continuing to fight for the introduction into general international law of new principles and norms, which are of vital importance for strengthening international peace and developing friendly co-operation between States (prohibition of the use of force in international relations, the principle of self-determination, the principle of peaceful co-existence; efforts for introducing into international law norms concerning the reduction of armaments, the prohibition of nuclear weapons, etc.). . . .

The new States of Asia and Africa, which have come into existence as a result of gaining independence by the colonial peoples, also as a rule support democratic norms of general international law and their progressive development and are taking an active part in the efforts to introduce into international law new democratic principles and norms. . . . The most important of these new principles is the principle of prohibition of the use of force in international relations. . . . The starting of war constitutes, according to contemporary general international law, the gravest breach of international law involving, side by side with the responsibility of a State which resorts to such war, also personal responsibility of the perpetrators of the war.

One of the most important developments in the field of international law in the period of co-existence has been the emergence of the principle of self-determination of nations.[50] As is well known, the inception of this principle took place in the time of bourgeois revolutions. . . .

Now we find the principle of self-determination of peoples in the Charter of the United Nations and it is to be considered as a principle of general international law (Arts. 1, 55, 76 of the Charter). . . .

A new page in the development of general international law constitutes the principle of peaceful co-existence. This principle is in fact at the very basis of the United Nations. Really, this world organization was instituted to comprise the States of both systems, and to ensure their peaceful co-existence. . . .

The principle of peaceful co-existence has been confirmed in many bilateral and multilateral international documents, such as the well-known Chou En-lai/Nehru Declaration of June 1954, Final Communiqué of the Bandung Conference of April 1955, Resolution of the General Assembly of December 14, 1957, etc.

---

[50] *Ed.* See below, p. 95.

The principle of peaceful co-existence includes the obligation for each State to use only peaceful means and methods in its relations with other States, to develop friendly relations with other States, to follow such a foreign policy as would contribute to strengthening peaceful co-existence, and to refrain from any action which might endanger peaceful relations between States. The principle of peaceful co-existence goes far beyond the principle of non-aggression. It requires that States not only should refrain from the threat or use of force in international relations, but also from pursuing a policy which might eventually lead to war.

The process of creating new progressive principles and norms of international law is continuing. Vital significance should be attached to the formation of international law norms concerning the reduction of armaments and the banning of nuclear weapons, the use of which is contrary to already-existing principles of international law, to the efforts to secure a universally recognized definition of aggression, universal recognition of norms prohibiting war propaganda, etc.

At the same time we witness the continued development and strengthening of the old democratic principles and norms of international law: the principles of respect for State sovereignty, non-interference in internal affairs, equality of States, and others.

Notes

1. A key feature of the Soviet view of international law is its emphasis upon state sovereignty. Thus the Soviet Branch of the International Law Association stated in its report to the Association's 1962 Conference[51]:

> Sovereignty and modern international law are integrally inter-linked and one is impossible without the other. It is not sovereignty that runs counter to the interests of consolidating international law, but disregard for the sovereignty of other states that undermines the foundations of modern international law and cripples it.

This emphasis upon state sovereignty is apparent, for example, in the U.S.S.R.'s opposition to compulsory judicial procedures for the settlement of disputes arising under the Vienna Convention on the Law of Treaties 1969[52] and its refusal to accept the compulsory jurisdiction of the International Court of Justice.[53] It also explains the primacy given by Soviet writers to treaties, not custom, as "the principal means of creating norms of international law" in "contemporary conditions."[54]

2. *Is* "peaceful co-existence" a principle of international law? Would you agree with the following comment by Lapenna[55]:

> Co-existence is not a legal principle, but a necessary premise for the existence and operation of international law?

3. On socialist international law (applying to socialist states *inter se*), see below, p. 22.

[51] I.L.A., *Report of the 50th Conference,* Brussels (1962), p. 357.
[52] See below, p. 632.
[53] See below, p. 720.
[54] Tunkin, *loc. cit.* at p. 14, above, p. 25. Custom continues to be recognised as a (less important) source. The same author also notes that UN resolutions "are playing a larger and larger role in the process of forming norms of international law"; 147 *Hague Recueil* 1, 41 (1975–IV).
[55] 12 I.C.L.Q. 737 (1963). See also Hazard, 57 A.J.I.L. 88 (1953) and McWhinney, *Peaceful Co-existence and Soviet-Western International Law* (1964), *passim.*

4. When reading opinions written by Soviet judges on the International Court of Justice, consider whether their approach is significantly different from that of their colleagues.[56]

(iv) THE INTERNATIONAL LAW OF CO-OPERATION

FRIEDMANN, THE CHANGING STRUCTURE OF INTERNATIONAL LAW

(1964), pp. 60 *et seq.* Some footnotes omitted

The changing structure of contemporary international relations is reflected in more diversified patterns of modern international law. Just as modern international relations are no longer essentially a matter of diplomatic interstate relations, but affect groups and individuals and reach into many domains of social and economic life, so modern international law moves on different levels. . . .

First, there is the traditional sphere of diplomatic interstate relations, represented by the classical system of international law. These rules aim at the peaceful co-existence of all states regardless of their social and economic structure. . . .

To this traditional sphere of diplomatic existence and the corresponding rules of international law, modern needs and developments have added many new areas expressing the need for positive co-operation which has to be implemented by international treaties and in many cases permanent international organisations. . . .

To the extent, however, that international law expands from what is essentially a set of rules of abstention, to organised international co-operation, it becomes more sensitive to the divergencies of internal systems, as expressed in their political ideology, their legal structure and their economic organisation. The building of "co-operative" international law proceeds today on different levels of universality, depending on the extent of the common interests and values that bind the participants. Certain types of the new international law are developing today on the universal level, because they reflect universal interests of mankind. Others, depending on a more closely knit community of values and purposes, proceed on a more restrictive level of international organisation, mostly of a regional pattern (notably in the West European Communities). The borderline between the two groups is not an absolute one, and it will obviously shift in accordance with changing political configurations. It represents nevertheless a fairly definite and important division in the processes of international legal development. . . .

In the present phase of international society, attempts at legal regulation on a universal level occur principally in three spheres: the international organisation of security from physical annihilation by war, the international organisation of certain aspects of communications, health and welfare, the tentative beginning to control the conservation of resources by international co-operation and organisation.

---

[56] For an example in this casebook, see the opinion of Judge Krylov in the *Corfu Channel Case,* below, p. 383.

While in theory such fields as the protection of human rights, as formulated in the United Nations Declaration of Human Rights of December 1948, is a universal concern of mankind, in fact, the disparity of standards, systems and values is too great to make an effective international organisation possible in this field. . . .

In other fields, too, such as the assimilation of corporate laws, anti-trust laws, patent laws, the closer community of the six European nations joined in the European Economic Community has proceeded to a level of international legal co-operation not presently attainable in the world at large. . . .

The recognition that the structure of international society has undergone some basic changes, and that, correspondingly, international law is now developing on several levels, one continuing the traditional international law of diplomatic co-existence, and the other two implementing the quest for both universal and regional international co-operation and organisation must lead to a far-reaching reorientation in our conceptions of the science and study of contemporary international law.

Some of the new tasks and dimensions of international law were discernible in the inter-war period. This is true of the gradual extension, since the end of the First World War, of international law to new subject-matters, or of the impact of new principles of state organisation and especially of the growing state control over economic activities, on the traditional system of international law. But the horizontal expansion of international law, towards non-western states and civilisations, with differing cultural backgrounds and differing stages of economic development, as well as the vertical extension of international law, from states to public and private groupings, as participants in the international legal process, are essentially, though not entirely, phenomena of the world as it emerged from the Second World War.

Shortly after the last World War, Maurice Bourquin[57] pointed out that the subject-matter of international law is not enclosed in "immovable boundaries." . . : He pointed to the rapidly expanding number of fields affected by international legal regulations, such as labour, human rights, education, science, refugee assistance, civil aviation, communications, agriculture, international money and banking matters, and on the other hand, to the increasing participation of technical, scientific and other experts in the process of international law and diplomacy. He characterised the entire development as one of both quantitative and qualitative renovation of international law. . . .

The shift in the structure of international law has been vividly formulated by Wilfred Jenks[58]:

. . . [T]he emphasis of the law is increasingly shifting from the formal structure of the relationship between States and the delimitation of their jurisdiction to the development of substantive rules on matters of common concern vital to the growth of an international community and to the individual well-being of the citizens of its member States. We shall also find that as the result of this change of emphasis the subject-matter of the law increasingly includes cross-frontier relationships of individuals, organisations and corporate bodies which call for appropriate legal regulation on an international basis. . . .

[57] . . . 70 *Hague Recueil* (1947) 331, at pp. 359 *et seq.*
[58] Jenks, *The Common Law of Mankind* (1958), p. 17.

CHAPTER 2

THE SOURCES OF INTERNATIONAL LAW[1]

1. *GENERALLY*

See Article 38(1), Statute of the International Court of Justice[2]

SCHWARZENBERGER, INTERNATIONAL LAW

(3rd ed., 1957), Vol. 1, pp. 26–27. Footnote omitted

This paragraph [Art. 38(1)] deals with two different issues. Sub-paragraphs (*a*)–(*c*) are concerned with the pedigree of the rules of international law. In sub-paragraph (*d*), some of the means for the determination of alleged rules of international law are enumerated.

In order to enable the World Court to apply any asserted rule of international law, it must be shown that it is the product of one, or more, of three law-creating processes: treaties, international customary law or the general principles of law recognised by civilised nations. The significance of this enumeration lies in its exclusiveness. It rules out other potential law-creating processes such as natural law, moral postulates or the doctrine of international law. Conversely, the Court is bound to take into consideration any asserted rule which bears the hall-mark of one of these three law-creating processes. It is immaterial whether such a rule is also claimed as their own by any of the various brands of natural law, has its origin in considerations of humanity, or is postulated by the standards of civilisation.

This interpretation of paragraph 1 of Article 38 is further strengthened by the following paragraph.[3] The power of the Court to decide a case *ex aequo et bono*, that is to say, to ignore rules which are the product of any of the above three law-creating agencies and to substitute itself as a law-creating agency, depends on agreement of the parties to a dispute. In other words, such power must itself rest on a rule created by one of the three normal law-creating processes, in this case, a treaty.

In terms of a more conventional terminology, sub-paragraphs (*a*)–(*c*) of paragraph 1 of Article 38 of the Statute of the World Court deal with the three formal sources of international law to which the Court may resort and exclude material sources as such.[4] In view of the ambiguity of the metaphor "source" and the inclination towards self-aggrandisement which this metaphor appears to foster among some of these "sources" of international law, it has been found advisable to eliminate the use of this term.

By way of contrast to the law-creating processes, sub-paragraph (*d*) of paragraph 1 of Article 38 refers to decisions of judicial institutions and the

---

[1] See Fitzmaurice, *Symbolae Verzijl*, p. 153 and Parry, *The Sources and Evidence of International Law* (1965).
[2] Appendix I, below.
[3] *Ed.* Article 38(2).
[4] *Ed.* For the view that treaties are not a formal source of law, see Fitzmaurice, below, p. 38.

teachings of the most highly qualified publicists as "subsidiary means for the determination of rules of law." It follows that principal means for the determination of rules of law must exist. In close leaning on this text, these principal and subsidiary means of evidence are called law-determining agencies. Each of these is composed of more or less fallible human beings, and these cannot be taken to be passive agents who merely reflect true international law as it were in a faithful mirror. This term, therefore, is also meant to bring out the unavoidable subjective and formative element which all these agencies have in common. Whereas, in the case of the law-creating processes, the emphasis lies on the forms by which any particular rule of international law is created, in the case of the law-determining agencies it is on how an alleged rule is to be verified.

Notes

1. Article 38 follows the wording of the same Article in the Statute of the Permanent Court of International Justice (which preceded the International Court of Justice as the primary court of the international community[5]), except that the words "whose function is to decide in accordance with international law such disputes as are submitted to it" are inserted in paragraph 1. The original text was drafted in 1920 by an Advisory Committee of Jurists appointed by the League of Nations.[6] Although they were concerned to draft a text relating directly only to the functioning of the P.C.I.J., Article 38 is generally accepted as a correct statement of the sources of international law.

2. *Classification of sources.* The distinction between "formal" and "material" sources to which Schwarzenberger refers was explained by Salmond[7] in the following terms:

> A formal source is that from which a rule of law derives its force and validity. . . . The material sources, on the other hand, are those from which is derived the matter, not the validity of the law. The material source supplies the substance of the rule to which the formal source gives the force and nature of law.

For example, a rule will be legally binding if it meets the requirements of a custom, which is a formal source of international law, and its substance will be indicated by state practice, which is the material source of custom. The term *evidence* is then used in the sense that diplomatic correspondence, for example, is evidence of state practice.

3. *Order of application.*[8] When drafting the original text of Article 38, the Advisory Committee of Jurists considered a proposal that it should state that the sources listed should be considered by the Court "in the undermentioned order"[9] (*i.e.* the order (*a*) to (*d*) in which they now appear). Opposing the proposal, M. Ricci-Busatti (Italy) is reported as saying:

> These words were not only superfluous, but they might also suggest the idea that the judge was not authorised to draw upon a certain source, for instance point 3,[10] before having applied conventions and customs mentioned respectively in points 1 and 2. That would be a misinterpretation of the Committee's intentions.[11]

In response, the President of the Committee, Baron Descamps (Belgium), remarked, however, that:

---

[5] The term World Court is commonly used to refer to each of these Courts.

[6] For a record of the Committee's work, see Permanent Court of International Justice, Advisory Committee of Jurists, *Procés verbaux of the Proceedings of the Committee* (June 16–July 24, 1920, L.N. Publication, 1920).

[7] Salmond, *Jurisprudence* (7th ed., 1924), para. 44.

[8] See Akehurst (1974–75) 47 B.Y.I.L. 273.

[9] *Loc. cit.* at n. 6 above, p. 344.

[10] *Ed.* General principles of law.

[11] *Ed. Ibid.* p. 337.

there was a natural classification. If two States concluded a treaty in which the solution of the dispute could be found, the Court must not apply international custom and neglect the treaty.[12] If a well-known custom exists, there is no occasion to resort to a general principle of law. We shall indicate an order of natural *précellence*, without requiring in a given case the agreement of several sources.[13]

M. Ricci-Busatti held to his opinion. He said:

> if the expression "*ordre successif*" [undermentioned order] only meant that a convention should be considered before, for instance, customary law, it is unnecessary. It is a fundamental principle of law that a special rule goes before general law. This expression also seems to fail to recognise that these various sources may be applied simultaneously, and also that the nature of each source differs.[14]

Agreement with M. Ricci-Busatti was expressed by other members and the statement was omitted.[15]

2. CUSTOM[16]

See the *Lotus Case*, below, p. 212, and the *Anglo-Norwegian Fisheries Case*, below, p. 289. These cases are important to an understanding of the nature of custom and the extracts printed later in these materials should be read at the same time as those from the two cases extracted in this section.

ASYLUM CASE[17]

Columbia v. Peru

I.C.J. Reports 1950, p. 266

After an unsuccessful rebellion in Peru in 1948, a warrant was issued for the arrest on a criminal charge arising out of the rebellion of one of its leaders, Haya de la Torre, a Peruvian national. He was granted asylum by Colombia in its Peruvian Embassy in Lima. Colombia sought, and Peru refused, a safe conduct to allow Haya de la Torre out of the country. Colombia brought this case against Peru, asking the Court to rule, *inter alia*, that:

> Colombia, as the state granting asylum, is competent to qualify the offence[18] for the purposes of the said asylum.[19]

It argued for such a ruling on the basis of both treaty provisions and "American international law in general." In the following extract, the Court considered the latter basis for the Colombian argument.

---

[12] *Ed.* This must now be read subject to the rules concerning *jus cogens*: see below, p. 616.
[13] *Ibid.*
[14] *Ibid.*
[15] *Ibid.* p. 338.
[16] See Akehurst (1974–75) 47 B.Y.I.L. 1; Corbett (1925) 6 B.Y.I.L. 20; De Visscher, pp. 144–163; Jenks, *The Prospects of International Adjudication* (1964), Chap. 5; Kopelmanas (1937) 18 B.Y.I.L. 127; Kunz, 47 A.J.I.L. 662 (1953); Lauterpacht, *Development*, pp. 368–393; Wolfke, *Custom in Present International Law* (1964); D'Amato, *The Concept of Custom in International Law* (1971); Thirlway, *International Customary Law and Codification* (1972).
[17] See Briggs, 45 A.J.I.L. 728 (1951).
[18] *i.e.* to characterise the offence—in this case to say whether it was a political offence or not.
[19] I.C.J. Rep. 1950 at p. 273.

Judgment of the Court

The Colombian Government has finally invoked "American international law in general." In addition to the rules arising from agreements which have already been considered, it has relied on an alleged regional or local custom peculiar to Latin-American States.

The Party which relies on a custom of this kind must prove that this custom is established in such a manner that it has become binding on the other Party. The Colombian Government must prove that the rule invoked by it is in accordance with a constant and uniform usage practised by the States in question, and that this usage is the expression of a right appertaining to the State granting asylum and a duty incumbent on the territorial State. This follows from Article 38 of the Statute of the Court, which refers to international custom "as evidence of a general practice accepted as law."

. . . the Colombian Government has referred to a large number of cases in which diplomatic asylum was in fact granted and respected. But it has not shown that the alleged rule of unilateral and definitive qualification was invoked or . . . that it was, apart from conventional stipulations, exercised by the States granting asylum as a right appertaining to them and respected by the territorial State as a duty incumbent on them and not merely for reasons of political expediency. The facts brought to the knowledge of the Court disclose so much uncertainty and contradiction, so much fluctuation and discrepancy in the exercise of diplomatic asylum and in the official views expressed on various occasions, there has been so much inconsistency in the rapid succession of conventions on asylum, ratified by some States and rejected by others, and the practice has been so much influenced by considerations of political expediency in the various cases, that it is not possible to discern in all this any constant and uniform usage, accepted as law, with regard to the alleged rule of unilateral and definitive qualification of the offence.

The Court cannot therefore find that the Colombian Government has proved the existence of such a custom. But even if it could be supposed that such a custom existed between certain Latin-American States only, it could not be invoked against Peru which, far from having by its attitude adhered to it, has, on the contrary, repudiated it by refraining from ratifying the Montevideo Conventions of 1933 and 1939, which were the first to include a rule concerning the qualification of the offence in matters of diplomatic asylum.

Notes

1. *General and Local Customs.* As the Court recognised in this case, although Article 38(1)(*b*) refers to "a general" practice, it allows for local (or regional) customs amongst a group of states or just two states[20] in their relations *inter se* as well as for general customs binding upon the international community as a whole. Local customs may supplement or derogate from general customary international law (subject to such rules of *jus cogens* as may exist[21]). A new and important kind of local custom may be Socialist International Law which, according to a leading Soviet writer, "is coming to replace contemporary general international law" in the relations of socialist states. Tunkin writes:

---

[20] Such a custom was found to exist between India and Portugal in the *Right of Passage Case*, below, p. 198.

[21] See below, p. 616.

. . . contemporary general international law cannot impede the creation of local international legal norms which by their social content are distinct from norms of general international law. In co-relation with general international law, the international legal principles of socialist internationalism are just such local principles.

The principles of proletarian internationalism and other socialist norms arising in relations between countries of the socialist camp are international legal principles and norms of a new, higher type of international law—a socialist international law, the basis of which is being formed in relations among states of the socialist system and which is coming to replace contemporary general international law.[22]

The "principles of proletarian internationalism" to which Tunkin refers "have been recognised by all states of the world system of socialism" as international legal principles.[23] One such principle is that of intervention by socialist states in the affairs in any one of them to preserve socialism.[24]

The Court's description of custom as a "constant and uniform usage, accepted as law" has been accepted by most writers[25] as being applicable to *general* customs (which are by far the more numerous and important) as well as *local* ones.

2. *State Practice.* By "usage" the Court means a usage that is to be found in the practice of states.[26] The International Law Commission included the following in a non-exhaustive list[27] of the forms that state practice may take: treaties, decisions of international and national courts, national legislation,[28] diplomatic correspondence, opinions of national legal advisers and the practice of international organisations.[29] Other categories listed by Brownlie[30] are policy statements, press releases, official manuals on legal questions (*e.g.* manuals of military law), executive decisions and practices, orders to naval forces, etc., and comments by governments on drafts produced by the International Law Commission.

In his judgment in the *Anglo-Norwegian Fisheries Case*[31] Judge Read said in respect of state practice and with particular reference to the facts of the case before him:

This cannot be established by citing cases where coastal States have made extensive claims, but have not maintained their claims by the actual assertion of sovereignty over trespassing foreign ships. Such claims may be important as starting points, which, if not challenged, may ripen into historic title in the course of time. The only convincing evidence of State practice is to be found in seizures, where the coastal State asserts its sovereignty over the water in question by arresting a foreign ship and by maintaining its position in the course of diplomatic negotiation and international arbitration.

How far should Judge Read's emphasis upon "action rather than words" be carried? Should statements of a legal position such as may be found in national legislation or in the debates or voting records of the General Assembly be ignored? Although acts in

---

[22] Tunkin, *Theory of International Law, loc. cit.* at p. 14, n. 49, above, p. 444. *cf. ibid.* 147 *Hague Recueil* 106–107 (1975–IV).

[23] *Ibid.* p. 433.

[24] *Ibid.* p. 434. See further below, p. 652.

[25] But see D'Amato, *op. cit.* at p. 21, n. 16, above, Chap. 8.

[26] On the question whether the practice of other international persons may contribute to the development of custom, see below, p. 124.

[27] Y.B.I.L.C., 1950, II, pp. 368–372.

[28] The term "legislation" was used "in a comprehensive sense . . . No form of regulatory disposition effected by a public authority is excluded": *loc. cit.* at n. 26, above, p. 370.

[29] "Records of the cumulating practice of international organisations may be regarded as evidence of customary international law with reference to States relations to the organisations": *loc. cit.* at n. 25, above, p. 372. On the role of UN General Assembly Resolutions, see below, p. 50.

[30] Brownlie, p. 4.

[31] I.C.J. Rep. 1951, at p. 191.

support of a claim may be "the only convincing evidence" where the claim is challenged by the acts of another state, abstract statements of a legal position have been recognised as being of value in other cases, as the extract from the *North Sea Continental Shelf Cases* below (para. 75) shows.

On the need to take care in assessing the significance of a state's acts or pronouncements, Brierly[32] states:

> There are multifarious occasions on which persons who act or speak in the name of a state do acts or make declarations which either express or imply some view on a matter of international law. Any such act or declaration may, so far as it goes, be some evidence that a custom, and therefore that a rule of international law, does or does not exist; but of course its value as evidence will be altogether determined by the occasion and the circumstances. States, like individuals, often put forward contentions for the purpose of supporting a particular case which do not necessarily represent their settled or impartial opinion.

Unfortunately,[33] evidence of state practice is not as available as it should be to permit considered opinions on many questions of customary international law. At present, only the practice of the United States is available in a comprehensive and up-to-date form.[34] There are also very useful, but less extensive, Digests of French, Italian and Swiss practice.[35] A British Digest is being prepared which, when complete, will provide a full record of British practice from 1860–1960.[36] The practice of other states is less generally available.[37] A lot of evidence of state practice is available to the public at the time that it comes into being in such sources as parliamentary papers, law reports and newspapers. Much of it (for example, diplomatic correspondence and other confidential government papers), is, however, subject to rules such as those in the United Kingdom under which government records are not available to the public until 30 years (formerly 50) have elapsed.[38]

---

[32] Brierly, p. 4.

[33] Anyone who has spent time sifting through records of state practice may not agree with the use of this word.

[34] See the *Digests of International Law* edited successively by Wharton (3 vols., 1887), Moore (8 vols., 1906), Hackworth (8 vols., 1940–44) and Whiteman (14 vols., 1963–70), and the annual volumes of *Digest of United States Practice in International Law* (1973–). There is also the *U.S. Foreign Relations and Official Opinions of the Attorneys-General of the U.S.* series of documents.

[35] *Répertoire de la pratique française en matière de droit international public* (7 vols., 1962–72); *Italian Practice in International Law* (1971–); and *Répertoire Suisse de Droit International* (1975–).

[36] Parry, ed., *British Digest of International Law*. The Digest is divided into Phases I (1860–1914) and II (1915–60). So far Vols. 2b, 5, 6, 7 and 8 of Phase I have been published. Other very useful, but less complete, digests of British practice are Smith, *Great Britain and the Law of Nations* (2 vols., 1932, 1935); McNair, *International Law Opinions* (3 vols., 1956); and E. Lauterpacht, *British Practice in International Law* (B.P.I.L.) (1963–67). The last of these was preceded by *Contemporary Practice of the United Kingdom in the Field of International Law*, which was first published as a series of occasional articles in the I.C.L.Q. covering the years 1956–59 and which was first published separately in 1962. *United Kingdom Materials in International Law* (U.K.M.I.L.), edited by Marston, published annually (1978–) in the B.Y.I.L. is a valuable new source. The *Digest of the Diplomatic Correspondence of the European States* in the *Fontes Juris Gentium* series includes that of Great Britain for the years 1856–78. There is also the *British and Foreign State Papers* series of documents.

[37] A large number of other European states have plans for national digests: see Green, 19 I.C.L.Q. 118 (1970). The increasing number of national *Yearbooks* on international law is also making recent evidence more readily available.

[38] Public Records Act 1967.

NORTH SEA CONTINENTAL SHELF CASES[39]

Federal Republic of Germany *v.* Denmark; Federal Republic of Germany *v.*
The Netherlands

I.C.J. Reports 1969, p. 3

A number of bilateral agreements had been made drawing lateral or median lines
delimiting the North Sea continental shelves[40] of adjacent and opposite states, including
two lateral line agreements between the Netherlands and the Federal Republic of
Germany (1964) and Denmark and the Federal Republic of Germany (1965). Each of
these last two agreements, however, did no more than draw a dividing line for a short
distance from the coast beginning at the point at which the land boundary of the two
states concerned was located. Further agreement had proved impossible. Special agreements were concluded between the Netherlands and the Federal Republic of Germany
and between Denmark and the Federal Republic of Germany referring the problem to
the I.C.J. In each special agreement the question put to the Court was:

> What principles and rules of international law are applicable to the delimitation as
> between the Parties of the areas of the continental shelf in the North Sea which
> appertain to each of them beyond the partial boundary [already] determined . . .?

The two cases were joined by the Court. Denmark and the Netherlands argued that the
"equidistance-special circumstances principle" in Article 6(2) of the 1958 Geneva
Convention on the Continental Shelf[41] applied. The Federal Republic of Germany
denied this and proposed "the doctrine of the just and equitable share." The reason for
the Federal Republic's opposition to the "equidistance-special circumstances principle"
was that the principle has the effect, as the Court pointed out,[42] on a concave coastline
such as that shared by the three states concerned of giving the state in the middle—in
this case West Germany—a smaller continental shelf than it might otherwise obtain.
    The Court rejected the West German proposal. After rejecting also the Danish and
Dutch argument that Article 6(2) stated or crystallised customary international law at
the time of its adoption, it continued:

Judgment of the Court

70. The Court must now proceed to the last stage in the argument put forward
on behalf of Denmark and the Netherlands. This is to the effect that even if
there was at the date of the Geneva Convention no rule of customary international law in favour of the equidistance principle, and no such rule was
crystallised in Article 6 of the Convention, nevertheless such a rule has come
into being since the Convention, partly because of its own impact, partly on the
basis of subsequent State practice,—and that this rule, being now a rule of
customary international law binding on all States, including therefore the
Federal Republic, should be declared applicable to the delimitation of the
boundaries between the Parties' respective continental shelf areas in the North
Sea.

71. In so far as this contention is based on the view that Article 6 of the
Convention has had the influence, and has produced the effect, described, it

---

[39] See Nelson, 35 M.L.R. 52 (1972).
[40] On the law of the continental shelf, see below, p. 354.
[41] Below, p. 357.
[42] I.C.J. Rep. 1969 at p. 17.

clearly involves treating that Article as a norm-creating provision which has constituted the foundation of, or has generated a rule which, while only conventional or contractual in its origin, has since passed into the general *corpus* of international law, and is now accepted as such by the *opinio juris*, so as to have become binding even for countries which have never, and do not, become parties to the Convention. There is no doubt that this process is a perfectly possible one and does from time to time occur: it constitutes indeed one of the recognised methods by which new rules of customary international law may be formed. At the same time this result is not lightly to be regarded as having been attained.

72. It would in the first place be necessary that the provision concerned should, at all events potentially, be of a fundamentally norm-creating character such as could be regarded as forming the basis of a general rule of law. Considered *in abstracto* the equidistance principle might be said to fulfil this requirement. Yet in the particular form in which it is embodied in Article 6 of the Geneva Convention, and having regard to the relationship of that Article to other provisions of the Convention, this must be open to some doubt. In the first place, Article 6 is so framed as to put second the obligation to make use of the equidistance method, causing it to come after a primary obligation to effect delimitation by agreement. Such a primary obligation constitutes an unusual preface to what is claimed to be a potential general rule of law. Without attempting to enter into, still less pronounce upon any question of *jus cogens*,[43] it is well understood that, in practice, rules of international law can, by agreement, be derogated from in particular cases, or as between particular parties—but this is not normally the subject of any express provision, as it is in Article 6 of the Geneva Convention. Secondly the part played by the notion of special circumstances relative to the principle of equidistance as embodied in Article 6, and the very considerable, still unresolved controversies as to the exact meaning and scope of this notion, must raise further doubts as to the potentially norm-creating character of the rule. Finally, the faculty of making reservations to Article 6, while it might not of itself prevent the equidistance principle being eventually received as general law, does add considerably to the difficulty of regarding this result as having been brought about (or being potentially possible) on the basis of the Convention: for so long as this faculty continues to exist, and is not the subject of any revision brought about in consequence of a request made under Article 13 of the Convention—of which there is at present no official indication—it is the Convention itself which would, for the reasons already indicated, seem to deny to the provisions of Article 6 the same norm-creating character as, for instance, Articles 1 and 2 possess.

73. With respect to the other elements usually regarded as necessary before a conventional rule can be considered to have become a general rule of international law, it might be that, even without the passage of any considerable period of time, a very widespread and representative participation in the convention might suffice of itself, provided it included that of States whose interests were specially affected. In the present case however, the Court notes that, even if allowance is made for the existence of a number of States to whom participation in the Geneva Convention is not open, or which, by reason for instance of being land-locked States, would have no interest in becoming parties

43 *Ed.* See below, p. 616.

to it, the number of ratifications and accessions so far secured is, though respectable, hardly sufficient. That non-ratification may sometimes be due to factors other than active disapproval of the Convention concerned can hardly constitute a basis on which positive acceptance of its principles can be implied. The reasons are speculative, but the facts remain.

74. As regards the time element, the Court notes that it is over ten years since the Convention was signed, but that it is even now less than five since it came into force in June 1964, and that when the present proceedings were brought it was less than three years, while less than one had elapsed at the time when the respective negotiations between the Federal Republic and the other two Parties for a complete delimitation broke down on the question of the application of the equidistance principle. Although the passage of only a short period of time is not necessarily, or of itself, a bar to the formation of a new rule of customary international law on the basis of what was originally a purely conventional rule, an indispensable requirement would be that within the period in question, short though it might be, State practice, including that of States whose interests are specially affected, should have been both extensive and virtually uniform in the sense of the provision invoked—and should moreover have occurred in such a way as to show a general recognition that a rule of law or legal obligation is involved.

75. The Court must now consider whether State practice in the matter of continental shelf delimitation has, subsequent to the Geneva Convention, been of such a kind as to satisfy this requirement. . . . Some fifteen cases have been cited in the course of the present proceedings, occurring mostly since the signature of the 1958 Geneva Convention, in which continental shelf boundaries have been delimited according to the equidistance principle—in the majority of the cases by agreement, in a few others, unilaterally—or else the delimitation was foreshadowed but has not yet been carried out . . . even if these various cases constituted more than a very small proportion of those potentially calling for delimitation in the world as a whole, the Court would not think it necessary to enumerate or evaluate them separately, since there are, *a priori*, several grounds which deprive them of weight as precedents in the present context.

76. . . . Over half the States concerned, whether acting unilaterally or conjointly, were or shortly became parties to the Geneva Convention, and were therefore presumably, so far as they were concerned, acting actually or potentially in the application of the Convention. From their action no inference could legitimately be drawn as to the existence of a rule of customary international law in favour of the equidistance principle. As regards those States, on the other hand, which were not, and have not become parties to the Convention, the basis of their action can only be problematical and must remain entirely speculative. Clearly, they were not applying the Convention. But from that no inference could justifiably be drawn that they believed themselves to be applying a mandatory rule of customary international law. There is not a shred of evidence that they did and . . . there is no lack of other reasons for using the equidistance method, so that acting, or agreeing to act in a certain way, does not of itself demonstrate anything of a juridical nature.

77. The essential point in this connection—and it seems necessary to stress it—is that even if these instances of action by non-parties to the Convention were much more numerous than they in fact are, they would not, even in the

aggregate, suffice in themselves to constitute the *opinio juris*—for, in order to achieve this result, two conditions must be fulfilled. Not only must the acts concerned amount to a settled practice, but they must also be such, or be carried out in such a way, as to be evidence of a belief that this practice is rendered obligatory by the existence of a rule of law requiring it. The need for such a belief, *i.e.* the existence of a subjective element, is implicit in the very notion of the *opinio juris sive necessitatis*. The States concerned must therefore feel that they are conforming to what amounts to a legal obligation. The frequency, or even habitual character of the acts is not in itself enough. There are many international acts, *e.g.* in the field of ceremonial and protocol, which are performed almost invariably, but which are motivated only by considerations of courtesy, convenience or tradition, and not by any sense of legal duty.

78. In this respect the Court follows the view adopted by the Permanent Court of International Justice in the *Lotus Case*,[44] as stated in the following passage, the principle of which is, by analogy, applicable almost word for word, *mutatis mutandis*, to the present case (P.C.I.J., Series A, No. 10, 1927, at p. 28):

> Even if the rarity of the judicial decisions to be found . . . were sufficient to prove . . . the circumstance alleged . . . it would merely show that States had often, in practice, abstained from instituting criminal proceedings, and not that they recognised themselves as being obliged to do so; for only if such abstention were based on their being conscious of having a duty to abstain would it be possible to speak of an international custom. The alleged fact does not allow one to infer that States have been conscious of having such a duty; on the other hand . . . there are other circumstances calculated to show that the contrary is true.

Applying this dictum to the present case, the position is simply that in certain cases—not a great number—the States concerned agreed to draw or did draw the boundaries concerned according to the principle of equidistance. There is no evidence that they so acted because they felt legally compelled to draw them in this way by reason of a rule of customary law obliging them to do so—especially considering that they might have been motivated by other obvious factors. . . .

81. The Court accordingly concludes that if the Geneva Convention was not in its origins or inception declaratory of a mandatory rule of customary international law enjoining the use of the equidistance principle for the delimitation of continental shelf areas between adjacent States neither has its subsequent effect been constitutive of such a rule; and that State practice up-to-date has equally been insufficient for the purpose. . . .

Having thus found that neither of the approaches argued for by the parties was a part of international law, the Court then proceeded to spell out the customary international law principles and rules that did apply "as between States faced with an issue concerning the lateral delimitation of adjacent continental shelves." . . .

85. It emerges from the history of the development of the legal régime of the continental shelf . . . that the essential reason why the equidistance method is not to be regarded as a rule of law is that, if it were to be compulsorily applied in all situations, this would not be consonant with certain basic legal notions which . . . have from the beginning reflected the *opinio juris* in the matter of

---

[44] *Ed.* See below, p. 212.

delimitation; those principles being that delimitation must be the object of agreement between the States concerned, and that such agreement must be arrived at in accordance with equitable principles. . . .

88.. . . Whatever the legal reasoning of a court of justice, its decisions must by definition be just, and therefore in that sense equitable. Nevertheless, when mention is made of a court dispensing justice or declaring the law, what is meant is that the decision finds its objective justification in considerations lying not outside but within the rules, and in this field it is precisely a rule of law that calls for the application of equitable principles. . . .

91. Equity does not necessarily imply equality. There can never be any question of completely refashioning nature, and equity does not require that a State without access to the sea should be allotted an area of continental shelf, any more than there could be a question of rendering the situation of a State with an extensive coastline similar to that of a State with a restricted coastline. Equality is to be reckoned within the same plane, and it is not such natural inequalities as these that equity could remedy. But in the present case there are three States whose North Sea coastlines are in fact comparable in length and which, therefore, have been given broadly equal treatment by nature except that the configuration of one of the coastlines would, if the equidistance method is used, deny to one of these States treatment equal or comparable to that given the other two. . . .

101. For these reasons, THE COURT, by eleven votes to six,[45] finds that, in each case,

(A) the use of the equidistance method of delimitation not being obligatory as between the Parties; and

(B) there being no other single method of delimitation the use of which is in all circumstances obligatory;

(C) the principles and rules of international law applicable to the delimitation as between the Parties . . . are as follows:

(1) delimitation is to be effected by agreement in accordance with equitable principles, and taking account of all the relevant circumstances, in such a way as to leave as much as possible to each Party all those parts of the continental shelf that constitute a natural prolongation of its land territory into and under the sea, without encroachment on the natural prolongation of the land territory of the other;

(2) if, in the application of the preceding sub-paragraph, the delimitation leaves to the Parties areas that overlap, these are to be divided between them in agreed proportions or, failing agreement, equally, unless they decide on a régime of joint jurisdiction, user, or exploitation for the zones of overlap or any part of them;

(D) in the course of the negotiations, the factors to be taken into account are to include:

(1) the general configuration of the coasts of the Parties, as well as the presence of any special or unusual features;

---

[45] The judges in the majority were President Bustamente y Rivero; Judges Sir Gerald Fitzmaurice, Jessup, Sir Muhammad Zafrulla Khan, Padilla Nervo, Forster, Gros, Ammoun, Petrén and Onyeama; Judge ad hoc Mosler. Vice-President Koretsky; Judges Tanaka, Morelli, Bengzon and Lachs; Judge ad hoc Sørensen dissented.

(2) so far as known or readily ascertainable, the physical and geological structure, and natural resources, of the continental shelf areas involved;

(3) the element of a reasonable degree of proportionality, which a delimitation carried out in accordance with equitable principles ought to bring about between the extent of the continental shelf areas appertaining to the coastal State and the length of its coast measured in the general direction of the coastline, account being taken for this purpose of the effects, actual or prospective, of any other continental shelf delimitations between adjacent States in the same region.[46]

DISSENTING OPINION OF JUDGE TANAKA. To decide whether these two factors [usage and *opinio juris*] in the formative process of a customary law exist or not, is a delicate and difficult matter. The repetition, the number of examples of State practice, the duration of time required for the generation of customary law cannot be mathematically and uniformly decided. Each fact requires to be evaluated relatively according to the different occasions and circumstances.
. . . what is important in the matter at issue is not the number or figure of ratifications of and accessions to the Convention or of examples of subsequent State practice, but the meaning which they would imply in the particular circumstances. We cannot evaluate the ratification of the Convention by a large maritime country or the State practice represented by its concluding an agreement on the basis of the equidistance principle, as having exactly the same importance as similar acts by a land-locked country which possesses no particular interest in the delimitation of the continental shelf.

Next, so far as. . . *opinio juris sive necessitatis* is concerned, it is extremely difficult to get evidence of its existence in concrete cases. This factor, relating to international motivation and being of a psychological nature, cannot be ascertained very easily, particularly when diverse legislative and executive organs of a government participate in an internal process of decision-making in respect of ratification or other State acts. There is no other way than to ascertain the existence of *opinio juris* from the fact of the external existence of a certain custom and its necessity felt in the international community, rather than to seek evidence as to the subjective motives for each example of State practice, which is something which is impossible of achievement. . . .

DISSENTING OPINION OF JUDGE LACHS. Delay in the ratification of and accession to multilateral treaties is a well-known phenomenon in contemporary treaty practice . . . experience indicates that in most cases [it is] caused by factors extraneous to the substance and objective of the instrument in question.
. . . [This] indicates that the number of ratifications and accessions cannot, in itself, be considered conclusive with regard to the general acceptance of a given instrument.

In the use of the Convention on the Continental Shelf, there are other elements that must be given their due weight. In particular, thirty-one States came into existence during the period between its signature (June 28, 1958) and its entry into force (June 10, 1964), while thirteen other nations have since

[46] The parties agreed upon the delimitation of their continental shelves *inter se* on the basis of the Court's judgment by treaties made in 1971: for texts, see *Yearbook of the I.C.J.* (1970–71), pp. 118 *et seq.*

acceded to independence. Thus the time during which these forty-four States could have completed the necessary procedure enabling them to become parties to the Convention has been rather limited, in some cases very limited. Taking into account the great and urgent problems each of them had to face, one cannot be surprised that many of them did not consider it a matter of priority. This notwithstanding, nine of those States have acceded to the Convention. Twenty-six of the total number of States in existence are moreover land-locked and cannot be considered as having a special and immediate interest in speedy accession to the Convention (only five of them have in fact acceded).

Finally, it is noteworthy that about seventy States are at present engaged in the exploration and exploitation of continental shelf areas.

It is the above analysis which is relevant, not the straight comparison between the total number of States in existence and the number of parties to the Convention. It reveals in fact that the number of parties to the Convention on the Continental Shelf is very impressive, including as it does the majority of States actively engaged in the exploration of continental shelves.

. . . in the world today an essential factor in the formation of a new rule of general international law is to be taken into account: namely that States with different political, economic and legal systems, States of all continents, participate in the process. No more can a general rule of international law be established by the fiat of one or of a few, or—as it was once claimed—by the consensus of European States only. . . .

All this leads to the conclusion that the principles and rules enshrined in the Convention, and in particular the equidistance rule, have been accepted not only by those States which are parties to the Convention on the Continental Shelf, but also by those which have subsequently followed it in agreements, or in their legislation, or have acquiesced in it when faced with legislative acts of other States affecting them. This can be viewed as evidence of a practice widespread enough to satisfy the criteria for a general rule of law.

For to become binding, a rule or principle of international law need not pass the test of universal acceptance. This is reflected in several statements of the Court, *e.g.*: "generally . . . adopted in the practice of States" (*Fisheries, Judgment*, I.C.J. Reports 1951, p. 128). Not all States have . . . an opportunity or possibility of applying a given rule. The evidence should be sought in the behaviour of a great number of States, possibly the majority of States, in any case the great majority of the interested States. . . .

Dissenting Opinion of Judge ad hoc Sørensen. I agree, of course, that one should not lightly reach the conclusion that a convention is binding upon a non-contracting State. But I find it necessary to take account of the fact—to which the Court does not give specific weight—that the Geneva Convention belongs to a particular category of multilateral conventions, namely those which result from the work of the United Nations in the field of codification and progressive development of international law, under Article 13 of the Charter. . . .

According to classic doctrine. . . [the] practice [necessary to establish a rule of customary international law] must have been pursued over a certain length of time. There have even been those who have maintained the necessity of "immemorial usage." In its previous jurisprudence, however, the Court does not seem to have laid down strict requirements as to the duration of the usage or practice which may be accepted as law. In particular, it does not seem to have drawn any conclusion in this respect from the ordinary meaning of the word "custom" when used in other contexts. . . . The possibility has thus been reserved of recognising the rapid emergence of a new rule of customary law based on the recent practice of States. This is particularly important in view of the extremely dynamic process of evolution in which the international community is engaged at the present stage of history.[47] Whether the mainspring of this evolution is to be found in the development of ideas, in social and economic factors, or in new technology, it is characteristic of our time that new problems and circumstances incessantly arise and imperatively call for legal regulation. In situations of this nature, a convention adopted as part of the combined process of codification and progressive development of international law may well constitute, or come to constitute the decisive evidence of generally accepted new rules of international law. The fact that it does not purport simply to be declaratory of existing customary law is immaterial in this context. The convention may serve as an authoritative guide for the practice of States faced with the relevant new legal problems, and its provisions thus become the nucleus around which a new set of generally recognised legal rules may crystallise. The word "custom," with its traditional time connotation, may not even be an adequate expression for the purpose of describing this particular source of law.

. . . The adoption of the Geneva Convention on the Continental Shelf was a very significant element in the process of creating new rules of international law in a field which urgently required legal regulation. . . . No State which has exercised sovereign rights over its continental shelf in conformity with the provisions of the Convention has been met with protests by other States. . . .

I do not find it necessary to go into the question of the *opinio juris*. This is a problem of legal doctrine which may cause great difficulties in international adjudication. In view of the manner in which international relations are conducted, there may be numerous cases in which it is practically impossible for one government to produce conclusive evidence of the motives which have prompted the action and policy of other governments. Without going into all aspects of the doctrinal debate on this issue, I wish only to cite the following passage by one of the most qualified commentators on the jurisprudence of the Court. Examining the conditions of the *opinio necessitatis juris* Sir Hersch Lauterpacht writes:

> Unless judicial activity is to result in reducing the legal significance of the most potent source of rules of international law, namely, the conduct of States, it would appear that the accurate principle on the subject consists in regarding all uniform conduct of Governments (or, in appropriate cases, abstention therefrom) as evidencing the *opinio necessitatis juris* except when it is shown that the conduct in question was not accompanied by any such intention. (Sir Hersch Lauterpacht: *The Development of International Law by the International Court*, London 1958, p. 380.)

---

[47] *Ed.* Judge Lachs took the same view in his Opinion. He gave the following example of the "rapid emergence" of a customary rule: " . . . the first instruments that man sent into outer space traversed the airspace of States and circled above them in outer space, yet the launching States sought no permission, nor did the other States protest. This is how the freedom of movement into outer space, and in it, came to be established and recognised as law within a remarkably short period of time" (p. 230).

Applying these considerations to the circumstances of the present cases, I think that the practice of States referred to above may be taken as sufficient evidence of the existence of any necessary *opinio juris*.

In my opinion, the conclusion may therefore safely be drawn that as a result of a continuous process over a quarter of a century, the rules embodied in the Geneva Convention on the Continental Shelf have now attained the status of generally accepted rules of international law.

That being so, it is nevertheless necessary to examine in particular the attitude of the Federal Republic of Germany with regard to the Convention. In the *Fisheries Case* the Court said that the ten-mile rule would in any event "appear to be inapplicable as against Norway inasmuch as she has always opposed any attempt to apply it to the Norwegian coast" (I.C.J. Reports 1951, p. 131). Similarly, it might be argued in the present cases that the Convention on the Continental Shelf would be inapplicable as against the Federal Republic, if she had consistently refused to recognise it as an expression of generally accepted rules of international law and had objected to its applicability as against her. But far from adopting such an attitude, the Federal Republic has gone quite a long way towards recognising the Convention. It is part of the whole picture, though not decisive in itself, that the Federal Republic signed the Convention in 1958, immediately before the time-limit for signature under Article 8. More significant is the fact that the Federal Republic has relied on the Convention for the purpose of asserting her own rights in the continental shelf. . . . This attitude is relevant, not so much in the context of the traditional legal concepts of recognition, acquiescence or estoppel, as in the context of the general process of creating international legal rules of universal applicability. At a decisive stage of this formative process, an interested State, which was not a party to the Convention, formally recorded its view that the Convention was an expression of generally applicable international law. This view being perfectly well founded, that State is not now in a position to escape the authority of the Convention.

It has been asserted that the possibility, made available by Article 12, of entering reservations to certain articles of the Convention, makes it difficult to understand the articles in question as embodying generally accepted rules of international law. . . . In my view, the faculty of making reservations to a treaty provision has no necessary connection with the question whether or not the provision can be considered as expressing a generally recognised rule of law. To substantiate this opinion it may be sufficient to point out that a number of reservations have been made to provisions of the Convention on the High Seas, although this Convention, according to its preamble, is "generally declaratory of established principles of international law." Some of these reservations have been objected to by other contracting States, while other reservations have been tacitly accepted. The acceptance, whether tacit or express, of a reservation made by a contracting party does not have the effect of depriving the Convention as a whole, or the relevant article in particular, of its declaratory character. It only has the effect of establishing a special contractual relationship between the parties concerned within the general framework of the customary law embodied in the Convention. Provided the customary rule does not belong to the category of *jus cogens*, a special contractual relationship of this nature is not invalid as such. Consequently, there is no incompatibility between the faculty of making reservations to certain articles of the Convention on the Continental

Shelf and the recognition of that Convention or the particular articles as an expression of generally accepted rules of international law.

Notes

1. The *North Sea Continental Shelf Cases*, which are the most recent of the relatively few cases in which the World Court has discussed in any detail the requirements for the existence of a rule of customary international law, were concerned with a question of increasing importance as the process of codifying and developing international law by multilateral treaties continues, *viz.* the role of such treaties as state practice and hence as a material source of customary international law binding upon parties and non-parties alike.[48]

Why, in the opinion of the Court, would Denmark's and the Netherlands' task have been easier if they had been arguing that the rules in Articles 1 or 2 of the Continental Shelf Convention (instead of that in Article 6) had become a part of customary international law? Since states may contract out of a rule of customary international law in their relations *inter se*, should it matter whether a treaty rule which is claimed to be a custom is one to which reservations are permitted? Does the Court's judgment indicate whether bilateral (as well as multilateral) treaties may be evidence of state practice? Is it possible that in some cases it may be precisely because the rights and duties set out in a treaty are not a part of customary international law that the parties feel the need to make it?[49]

2. As well as setting down rules on the particular question of the role of treaties as a material source of custom, the Court's judgment, and those of several of the judges who gave separate opinions, throws light on the nature of customary international law in other respects also. For example, it recognises that there is no precise length of time during which a practice must exist; the position is simply that it must be followed long enough to show that the other requirements of a custom are met.

3. The Court's approach to the question of the number and kind of states whose practice has to be established is also instructive. It demonstrates that a practice does not have to be followed by all states for it to be the basis of a general custom.

In the course of considering whether there was sufficient evidence of state practice to justify the conclusion that the doctrine of the continental shelf was a part of general customary international law, Lauterpacht[50] states:

> . . . assuming here that we are confronted with the creation of new international law by custom, what matters is not so much the number of states participating in its creation and the length of the period within which that change takes place, as the relative importance, in any particular sphere, of states inaugurating the change. In a matter closely related to the principle of the freedom of the seas the conduct of the two principal maritime Powers—such as Great Britain and the United States—is of special importance. With regard to the continental shelf and submarine areas generally these two states inaugurated the development and their initiative was treated as authoritative almost as a matter of course from the outset.

On the same question, note also the following comment by De Visscher,[51] who, after adopting the analogy by which the growth of a custom is likened to that of a path across land, continues:

> Among the users are always some who mark the soil more deeply with their footprints than others, either because of their weight, which is to say their power in

---

[48] See on this question Baxter, 129 *Hague Recueil* 25 (1970–71), and, for a different view, D'Amato, *op. cit.* at p. 21, n. 16, above, Chap. 5.
[49] See the *Lotus Case*, below, p. 212.
[50] (1950) 27 B.Y.I.L. 376 at p. 394.
[51] De Visscher, p. 155.

this world, or because their interests bring them more frequently this way. Thus it happens that the great Powers, after imprinting a definite direction upon a usage, make themselves its guarantors and defenders. Their role, which was always decisive in the formation of customary international law, is to confer upon usages that degree of effectiveness without which the legal conviction, condition of general assent, would find no sufficient basis in social reality. Many customs owe their origin wholly to decisions or acts of great Powers which by their repetition or sequence, and above all by the idea of order that finally grows out of them, have little by little lost their personal, contingent, in a word political character and taken on that of a custom in process of formation. The strong impulse given by the United States, from the end of the eighteenth century on, to the development of the law of neutrality may be cited as an example.

Which states' practice, if any, should be given particular weight when considering (a) the general customary international law concerning outer space and (b) whether the rule concerning the making of reservations to multilateral treaties has been changed?

4. *Opinio juris sive necessitatis*. As the Court indicates in its judgment (para. 77), the second requirement of a custom—acceptance that it is binding in law—is necessary to distinguish it from a rule of international comity,[52] which is a rule based upon a consistent practice in the relations of states which is not accompanied by a feeling of legal obligation. The saluting by a ship at sea of another ship flying a different flag is an example. Another example—which may now have been translated into a rule of customary international law[53]—has been the rule by which the goods of a diplomatic agent and his family are immune from customs duty.

As the judgments of Judges Tanaka and Sørensen stress, it is often difficult to discover the necessary *opinio juris* because the reason underlying a state's adoption or acceptance of a particular practice is not clear. In this connection, the suggestion by Judge Sørensen (following Lauterpacht) that *opinio juris* may be presumed to exist if a uniform practice is proven is helpful. The judgment of the Court (para. 78), however, adopts a stricter approach.

Another difficulty with *opinio juris* is that the first states to adopt a new practice are supposed to be acting on the basis that it is binding even as they do so. It was this that Lauterpacht[54] had in mind when he referred to:

> the mysterious phenomenon of customary international law which is deemed to be a source of law only on condition that it is in accordance with law.

Would it be correct to say that in the early days of the formation of a new rule the state or states adopting the practice either do not think about whether it is binding or, if they are thinking about its significance in the development of international law, put it forward more as an "offer," which other states can accept or reject, rather than as something which they are convinced is already binding? On this view, the feeling of obligation, if it arises at all, arises only later when there has been general adoption or acceptance of the practice or "offer."

5. What if one state, or just a few states, protest at a practice? Can it, or they, prevent it from establishing a custom? Judge Tanaka, in his dissenting opinion in the *South West Africa Cases, Second Phase*,[55] stated:

> the answer must be in the negative for the reason that Article 38, paragraph 1(*b*), of the Statute does not exclude the possibility of a few dissidents for the purpose of the creation of a customary international law and that the contrary view of a particular

---

[52] Note that national courts sometimes use the term "international comity" as a synonym for international law: see Akehurst (1972–1973) 46 B.Y.I.L. 145, at pp. 214–216.

[53] See Articles 36 and 37, Vienna Convention on Diplomatic Relations 1961, below, p. 264.

[54] *Loc. cit.* at p. 34, n. 50, above, p. 395.

[55] I.C.J. Rep. 1966 at p. 291.

State or States would result in the permission of obstruction by veto, which could not have been expected by the legislator who drafted the said Article.

Does the *Anglo-Norwegian Fisheries Case*[56] indicate, as Judge Sørensen suggests, that although a dissenting state may not by itself prevent a rule from coming into being, that a state will not be bound by the rule if it maintains its dissent throughout the rule's formative period? Would any state, for example, that were to have protested consistently from 1957 (when the first satellite was launched) onwards against the passage of satellites through its airspace, now be bound by any change in the law affecting the upper limit of a state's airspace that may have resulted from the general acquiescence by states in the passage of satellites over their territory? And what was the effect of the consistent opposition by France to any rule prohibiting nuclear tests on the high seas during the 1960s and early 1970s? Is France bound by any such rule that developed?[57]

6. What is the effect of dissent by a state *after* a custom has been established? Can this by itself affect the application of the custom to the dissenting state? In answering this question, does it matter whether the dissenting state was in existence or not at the time that the custom came into being?[58] Can the dissent of one state bring down a custom if it is coupled with that of others? If so, there is clearly a stage when states leading an assault upon a custom are, although participating in an accepted law-changing process, delinquents.[59] Another intrinsic weakness in the customary international law-making process is that, in some cases, *e.g.* that concerning the breadth of the territorial sea,[60] the change from one rule of customary international law to another is unacceptably slow with an interim period of considerable uncertainty.[61]

7. For the purpose of the formation of rules of customary international law, consent is commonly indicated by state practice not in the form of positive statements or other action approving the practice in question, but of acquiescence. This MacGibbon[62] describes as "silence or absence of protest in circumstances which generally call for a positive reaction signifying an objection." For example, if the law concerning airspace has been changed as a result of the use of satellites, the practice of all but the states participating in satellite launching has consisted mostly of acquiescence in this sense. As the *Anglo-Norwegian Fisheries Case*[63] shows, acquiescence cannot be established unless a state has actual or constructive knowledge of the claim being made. How strict a standard did the Court apply in that case in finding that the United Kingdom did have knowledge of the Norwegian claims? Would you agree with Johnson's comment that:

> under the Court's formulation, it would seem that ignorance as to another State's legislation on territorial waters, however excusable, can be fatal, and that States may neglect at their own risk, to study each other's statute-books?[64]

---

[56] Below, p. 289. See also the final paragraph of the extract from the *Asylum Case* quoted above, p. 21.

[57] See below, p. 322. See also the position of developed states in respect of the majority view within the UN on expropriation: see below, pp. 422 *et seq.*

[58] See below, p. 84.

[59] What, for example, was the legal position of Iceland in the late 1950s when it insisted upon a 12 miles exclusive fishing zone off its coasts—something that was questionable then but clearly lawful now (partly because of Iceland's efforts)? What was Iceland's position in the 1970s when it claimed, again to the tune of protest by other states, an exclusive fishing zone of 50 miles? See below, p. 347. Note also Canada's exclusion of I.C.J. jurisdiction precisely because of the doubtful legality of its Arctic pollution laws (see below, p. 721).

[60] See below, p. 287.

[61] See Friedmann, below.

[62] (1954) 31 B.Y.I.L. 143. See also MacGibbon (1957) 33 B.Y.I.L. 115. On the meaning of protest, see below, pp. 169–170. See also p. 600, below.

[63] See below, p. 289.

[64] 1 I.C.L.Q. 145, 166 (1952).

FRIEDMANN, THE CHANGING STRUCTURE OF INTERNATIONAL LAW

(1964), pp. 121–123. Footnote omitted

Custom, the major instrument of law-making in any primitive society, has been, until recently, the principal source of law-making in international society. . . .

It is an obvious reflection of the radically different character and methods of international relations in our time that custom can no longer be as predominant or important a source of law as it was in the formative period of international law. . . . custom is too clumsy and slow moving a criterion to accommodate the evolution of international law in our time, and the difficulties are increased as the number of subjects of the law of nations swells from a small club of Western Powers to 120 or more "sovereign" states. More importantly, custom is an unsuitable vehicle for international "welfare" or "co-operative" law.[65] The latter demands the positive regulation of economic, social, cultural and administrative matters, a regulation that can only be effective by specific formulation and enactment. . . . Even in some of the domains of classical international law, as in the various aspects of the Law of the Sea, multilateral conventions arising out of preparatory work of international legal bodies and international conferences, tend to displace custom.

Yet it would be wrong to dismiss custom too easily as a source of international law of continuing importance. There is today a frequent interplay between the growth or modification of custom, the formulation of such developments by international law, recording bodies, such as the International Law Commission or the International Law Institute, and the eventual "codification" of such custom in a law-making treaty. The interplay is well demonstrated by the evolution of the doctrine of the Continental Shelf. As an articulate doctrine or state practice it hardly goes back further than the Truman Proclamation of 1945. This led to a rapid succession and multiplication of similar claims to the exclusive exploitation of sea bed resources of the Continental Shelf by other states, to a great deal of theoretical discussion, International Law Commission drafts, and the eventual adoption of the doctrines of the Continental Shelf by the Geneva Convention of 1958, only thirteen years after it was first articulated by the United States. It is possible to argue that, even before the adoption of the Continental Shelf Convention by the Geneva Conference, the essentials of the principle, *i.e.* the exclusive right of a coastal state to exploit the sea bed resources of a continental shelf, at least down to a depth of 200 metres, had become so universally accepted by state practice that it could be regarded as a new custom.

Note
Note also the following comments by De Visscher.[66] On the one hand, he points to a merit of customary international law:

> What gives international custom its special value and its superiority over conventional institutions, in spite of the inherent imprecision of its expression, is the fact that, developing by spontaneous practice, it reflects a deeply felt community of law. Hence the density and stability of its rules.

[65] *Ed.* See above, p. 17.
[66] De Visscher, pp. 161–162.

On the other hand, like Friedmann, he points out a new weakness:

> Malleable as it is, custom can neither establish itself, nor evolve and so remain a source of living law, when, owing to the rapidity with which they follow each other or to their equivocal or contradictory character, State activities cease to crystallise into "a general practice accepted as law." Acceleration of history, and above all diminishing homogeneity in the moral and legal ideas that have long governed the formation of law—such, in their essential elements, are the causes that today curtail the development of customary international law.

3. *TREATIES*[67]

FITZMAURICE, SOME PROBLEMS REGARDING THE FORMAL SOURCES OF INTERNATIONAL LAW

Symbolae Verzijl (1958), p. 153. Some footnotes omitted

Considered in themselves, and particularly in their inception, treaties are, formally, a source of obligation rather than a source of law. In their contractual aspect,[68] they are no more a source of law than an ordinary private law contract; which simply creates rights and obligations. . . . In this connexion, the attempts which have been made to ascribe a law-making character to *all* treaties irrespective of the character of their content or the number of the parties to them, by postulating that some treaties create "particular" international law and others "general," is of extremely dubious validity. There is really no such thing as "particular" international treaty law, though there are particular international treaty rights and obligations. The only "law" that enters into these is derived, not from the treaty creating them—or from any treaty—but from the principle *pacta sunt servanda*—an antecedent general principle of law. The law is that the obligation must be carried out, but the obligation is not, in itself, law. . . . A statute is always, *from its inception*, law: a treaty may reflect, or lead to, law but, *particularly* in its inception, is not, as such, "law." . . . True, where it reflects (*e.g.* codifies) existing law, non-parties may conform to the same rules, but they do so by virtue of the rules of general law thus reflected in the treaty, not by virtue of the treaty itself. In that sense, the treaty may be an instrument in which the law is conveniently stated, and evidence of what it is, but it is still not itself the law—it is still formally not a source of law but only evidence of it. Where a treaty is, or rather becomes, a *material* source of law, because the rules it contains come to be generally regarded as representing rules of universal applicability, it will nevertheless be the case that when non-parties apply or conform to these rules, this will be because the rules are or have become rules of general law. . . .

---

[67] See Jenks, *op cit.* at p. 21, n. 16, above, pp. 92–98; McNair, *Treaties*, Appendix I; Starke (1946) 23 B.Y.I.L. 341.

[68] It may be recalled that in the *Reservations to the Genocide Convention Case*, the jointly dissenting Judges (Guerrero, McNair, Read and Hsu Mo), speaking of the so-called "law-making" general multilateral convention, pointed out that the circumstance "that this activity is often described as 'legislative' or 'quasi-legislative,' must not obscure the fact that the legal basis of these conventions, and the essential thing that brings them into force, is the common consent of the parties"—(I.C.J. Rep. 1951, p. 32).

This position is equally true, strictly speaking, of *parties* to the treaty also. If the treaty reflects (codifies) existing law, then, in applying it, the parties merely conform to general law obligations already valid for them. . . .

The position is the same, even as regards parties to a treaty, in those cases where the treaty does not reflect existing law but leads to the emergence of a new general rule of law. Before that occurs, the parties apply the treaty, not as law, but as an obligation *inter se* which antecedent general law respecting treaties compels them to carry out because they have undertaken to do so. If the treaty rule does eventually pass into general law, its formal source *as law* . . . is clearly custom or practice—*i.e.* its adoption into general customary law. The parties, in applying it, are no doubt also (or still) applying the treaty: but, as they would now be bound to apply it even if there were no treaty (or if the treaty, *quâ instrument*, had lapsed or the party concerned had formally "denounced," or given notice of withdrawal from it), its legal basis as *law* is clearly not the treaty, although it retains a treaty basis of *obligation* so far as the parties *inter se* are concerned. . . .

Notes

1. There are an increasing number of multilateral treaties to which a large number of states are parties which lay down general rules of conduct for the parties to them. The Vienna Convention on Diplomatic Relations 1961[69] is a good example. They are sometimes referred to as "law-making treaties" or "international legislation." Such terms are probably sufficiently useful to justify their retention even though they are strictly inaccurate. Note also that, in the past at least, the Great Powers have, in effect, legislated for other states by treaty on a number of occasions. Thus the Final Act of the Congress of Vienna 1815, *inter alia*, made Switzerland a neutral state and provided for free navigation on certain international rivers. Note also the report of the Commission of Jurists in the *Aaland Islands Case*.[70]

2. It scarcely needs adding that whatever dignity treaties may lose by not being "a formal source of law," in practice they are a very, and increasingly, important source of a state's rights and duties. Note also the Soviet point of view:

> . . . the main sources of International Law are international treaties and international custom. Of these, the first is the most important.[71]

3. Imagine that State A agrees with State B by treaty that it will hand over to B certain war criminals, including X, if they should enter A. X, a national of State C, enters A as the ambassador of C to A. A hands him over to B. C claims that A has thereby violated a customary international law rule concerning the treatment of diplomatic representatives. Assuming that there is a customary rule concerning the treatment of diplomatic representatives that C can rely on, would A be able to rely on its treaty obligation towards B as a defence to any claim by C? If A had not handed X over, could B have claimed successfully against A for the breach of a treaty obligation? Should a treaty be interpreted as being consistent with customary international law in the absence of clear wording to the contrary?

---

[69] See below, p. 264. The 1949 Red Cross (Geneva) Conventions (over 140 parties), see below, p. 638, and the UN Charter (in respect of its law-making provisions, *e.g.* Art. 2(4)), see below, p. 641, are other examples.
[70] Below, p. 81. On the juridical nature of such treaties and of treaties such as the Suez Canal Convention 1888 and the Antarctic Treaty 1959, see below, p. 608.
[71] Kozhevnikov, *loc. cit.* at p. 14, n. 49, above, p. 12. See further Tunkin, *loc. cit.* at p. 23, n. 22, above, pp. 21–23.

4. GENERAL PRINCIPLES OF LAW[72]

WALDOCK, GENERAL COURSE ON PUBLIC INTERNATIONAL LAW

106 *Hague Recueil* 54 (1962–II). Some footnotes omitted

On one side there are jurists like Verdross,[73] who say that Article 38 has the effect of incorporating "natural law" in international law and even claim that positive rules of international law are invalid if they conflict with natural law. At the other extreme are jurists like Guggenheim,[74] and Tunkin,[75] who maintain that paragraph (c) adds nothing to what is already covered by treaties and custom; for these authorities hold that general principles of national law are part of international law only to the extent that they have been adopted by States in treaties or recognised in State practice. In between stand the majority of jurists. . . . They take the line that general principles recognised in national law constitute a reservoir of principles which an international judge is authorised by Article 38 to apply in an international dispute, if their application appears relevant and appropriate in the different context of inter-State relations.

The *travaux préparatoires* of Article 38 and the decisions of international tribunals support the position taken by the majority. . . .

The Court, it must be admitted, has shown restraint in its recourse to "general principles of national law" as authority for its own pronouncements, although individual judges have been less reluctant to invoke them as support for their opinions.[76] Even when apparently relying on this source of law, the Court has not infrequently either referred also to customary law or left it ambiguous as to whether it was speaking of a general principle of national or international law.

. . . The main spheres in which these principles have been held to apply have been either the general principles of legal liability and of reparation for breaches of international obligations or the administration of international justice. . . . For example, in the *Chorzow Factory Case*[77] the Permanent Court described the principle, that a party cannot take advantage of its own wrong, as a principle "generally accepted in the jurisprudence of international arbitration, as well as by municipal courts"; and at a later stage of the same case[78] the Court said that "it is a general conception of law that every violation of an engagement involves an obligation to make reparation," and it went on to speak of restitution and damages. . . .

As to the administration of justice, there are a number of references to "general principles of law" in connection with questions of jurisdiction, procedure, evidence or other aspects of the judicial process. Thus, speaking in the *Corfu Channel Case*[79] of circumstantial evidence, the International Court said:

---

[72] See Cheng, *General Principles of Law Applied by International Courts and Tribunals* (1953); Fitzmaurice (1953) 30 B.Y.I.L. 1; Friedmann, *op. cit.* at p. 17, above, Chap. 12; H. C. Gutteridge, 38 Trans. Grot. Soc. 125 (1952); Jenks, *op. cit.* at p. 21, n. 16, Chap. 6.

[73] See Rec. Acad. 1935, II, pp. 204–206; and R.G.D.I.P. 1938, pp. 44–52.

[74] *Traité de droit international public*, I, p. 152.

[75] Rec. Acad. 1958, III, pp. 25–26.

[76] *Ed.* See, *e.g.* Judge Lauterpacht's opinion in the *Norwegian Loans Case*, below, p. 726.

[77] (1927) A/9, at p. 31.

[78] (1928) A/17, p. 29.

[79] I.C.J. Rep. 1949 at p. 18.

"this indirect evidence is admitted in all systems of law, and its use is recognised by international decisions. . . ."

In inter-State relations, however, the Court has shown little disposition to transport into international law substantive doctrines or institutions of national law; as distinct from principles of legal liability and reparation. . . .

The correct conclusion, it seems to me, to draw from the practice of the Court may well be that it treats the "common law" which it is authorised to apply under Article 38, paragraphs (b) and (c), very much as a single corpus of law. In this corpus customary law enormously predominates and most of the law applied by the Court falls within it. But paragraph (c) adds to this corpus—very much in the way actually intended by its authors—a flexible element which enables the Court to give greater completeness to customary law and in some limited degree to extend it.

. . . as Lord McNair pointed out in the *South-West Africa Case*,[80] it is never a question of importing into international law private law institutions "lock, stock and barrel," ready made and fully equipped with a set of rules. It is rather a question of finding in the private law institutions indications of legal policy and principles appropriate to the solution of the international problem in hand. It is not the concrete manifestations of a principle in different national systems—which are anyhow likely to vary—but the general concept of law underlying them that the international judge is entitled to apply under paragraph (c).

Accordingly, the question arises as to what basic conditions must be satisfied before a principle qualifies to be considered "a general principle of law recognised by civilised nations." The phrase "civilised nations" now has an antiquated look. The intention in using it, clearly, was to leave out of account undeveloped legal systems so that a general principle present in the principal legal systems of the world would not be disqualified from application in international law merely by reason of its absence from, for example, the tribal law of a backward people. . . . Accordingly, we are quite safe in construing "the general principles of law recognised by civilised nations" as meaning to-day simply the general principles recognised in the legal systems of independent States.

The number of independent States, we know, has doubled since 1920, and is now over one hundred. Does this mean that today a principle has to pass the test of a hundred legal systems and that in this legal tower of Babel no principle will ever be able to qualify for application under paragraph (c)? Two considerations, it is thought, permit us to be reassured on this point.

First, by the accidents of history, some of the principal European systems of law have penetrated over large areas of the globe, mixing in greater or less degree with the indigenous law and often displacing it in just those spheres of law in which we have seen that international law has most readily borrowed from domestic law. In consequence, there is a much larger unity in the fundamental concepts of the legal systems of the world today than there might otherwise have been. . . .

Secondly, it was never intended under paragraph (c) that proof should be furnished of the manifestation of a principle in every known legal system considered to be civilised; and certainly it has never been the practice of the Court or of arbitral tribunals to insist upon proof of the widespread manifesta-

[80] I.C.J. Rep. 1950 at p. 148.

tions of a principle or to indulge in elaborate comparative studies of the legal systems of the world. Truth to tell, arbitral tribunals, which usually consist of one, three or five judges, have probably done no more in most cases than take into account their own knowledge of the principles of the systems in which the arbitrators were themselves trained, and these would usually have been Roman law, Common law, or Germanic systems.

Notes

1. In the course of discussion by the Advisory Committee of Jurists on Article 38(1)(c), Lord Phillimore (Great Britain), who, with Mr. Root (U.S.A.), was the author of that provision, pointed out that:

> the general principles referred to. . . were those which were accepted by all nations *in foro domestico*, such as certain principles of procedure, the principle of good faith, and the principle of *res judicata*, etc.[81]

He later said that by "general principles" he meant "Maxims of law."[82] In the same discussion the President of the Committee, Baron Descamps (Belgium), stated that the draft that became Article 38(1)(c) "was necessary to meet the possibility of a nonliquet."[83]

2. Commenting on Tunkin's approach to Article 38(1)(c), Waldock[84] states:

> . . . Probably, the chief difficulty Soviet jurists feel about paragraph (c) is the possibility that it opens up of the development of international law by judicial action instead of exclusively by States.

Consider when reading the cases in these materials whether the Court has taken much advantage of the scope that Article 38(1)(c) gives for judicial legislation.[85] Would it be true to say that the Court has used such "straws" of state practice as it has been able to find to build a custom at least as often as it has relied upon general principles?

3. Fitzmaurice[86] suggests:

> A rule answers the question "what": a principle in effect answers the question "why."

Has the World Court followed this distinction in its practice?

4. In addition to the jurisprudence of the World Court referred to by Waldock, see the statement by the International Court of Justice in the *South West African Cases* (*Second Phase*) on the "*actio popularis*" (known to certain legal systems, but not a general principle of law).[87]

ABU DHABI ARBITRATION

Sheikh of Abu Dhabi *v.* Petroleum Development (Trucial Coast) Ltd. (1951)

1 I.C.L.Q. 247 (1952); 18 I.L.R. 144 (1951)

The case concerned a dispute over the interpretation of the terms of an oil concession contract. It was submitted to arbitration in accordance with the contract. The sole

---

[81] *Loc. cit.* at p. 20, n. 6, above, p. 335.   [82] *Ibid.*

[83] *Ibid.* at p. 336. *i.e.* the possibility that a court or tribunal could not decide a case because of a "gap" in the law.

[84] *Loc. cit.* at p. 40, above, p. 68.

[85] For examples of the use to which general principles might be put, see Friedmann, *op. cit.* at p. 17, above, Chap. 12.

[86] 92 *Hague Recueil* 1, 7 (1957–II).   [87] I.C.J. Rep. 1966, p. 6.

arbitrator—Lord Asquith, a Lord of Appeal in Ordinary—had to decide first upon the law governing the contract. According to Clause 17, the parties "declare that they base their work in the Agreement on goodwill and sincerity of belief and on the interpretation of this Agreement in a fashion consistent with reason."

LORD ASQUITH OF BISHOPSTONE. The terms of that clause [Clause 17] invite, indeed prescribe, the application of principles rooted in the good sense and common practice of the generality of civilised nations—a sort of "modern law of nature." I do not think that on this point there is any conflict between the parties.

But, albeit English municipal law is inapplicable *as such*, some of its rules are in my view so firmly grounded in reason, as to form part of this broad body of jurisprudence—this "modern law of nature." For instance, . . . the English rule which attributes paramount importance to the actual language of the written instrument in which the negotiations result seems to me no mere idiosyncrasy of our system, but a principle of ecumenical validity. Chaos may obviously result if that rule is widely departed from; and if, instead of asking what the words used mean, the inquiry extends at large to what each of the parties meant them to mean, and how and why each phrase came to be inserted.

The same considerations seem to me to apply to the principle *expressio unius est exclusio alterius* . . . confined within its proper borders it seems to me mere common sense. . . .

Much more dubious to my mind is the application to this case of certain other English maxims relied on by one or the other party in this case. For instance, . . . the rule that grants by a sovereign are to be construed against the grantee. The latter is an English rule which owes its origin to incidents of our own feudal polity and royal prerogative which are now ancient history; and its survival, to considerations which, though quite different, seem to have equally little relevance to conditions in a protected State of a primitive order on the Persian Gulf. . . .

Note

The *Abu Dhabi Arbitration* was one between a state and a foreign company concerning the application of a contract between them. It was provided for by the contract itself. In such arbitrations, the arbitrator is, expressly or impliedly, frequently instructed to apply "general principles of law" and not the municipal law of the contracting state or any other municipal law. See further on such contracts the *Texaco Case*, below, p. 434. In that case, the Arbitrator concluded that the French law of administrative contracts did not state general principles of law.

THE DIVERSION OF WATER FROM THE MEUSE CASE

Netherlands *v.* Belgium (1937)

P.C.I.J. Reports, Series A/B, No. 70, pp. 76–77

INDIVIDUAL OPINION OF JUDGE HUDSON. What are widely known as principles of equity have long been considered to constitute a part of international law, and as such they have often been applied by international tribunals. . . . A sharp division between law and equity, such as prevails in the administration of justice in some States, should find no place in international jurisprudence; even in some national legal systems, there has been a strong tendency towards the fusion of law and equity. Some international tribunals are expressly directed by the *compromis* which control them to apply "law and equity." See the *Cayuga Indians Case*, Nielsen's Report of the United States—British Claims Arbitration (1926), p. 307. Of such a provision, a special tribunal of the Permanent Court of Arbitration said in 1922 that "the majority of international lawyers seem to agree that these words are to be understood to mean general principles of justice as distinguished from any particular systems of jurisprudence." Proceedings of the United States—Norwegian Tribunal (1922), p. 141. Numerous arbitration treaties have been concluded in recent years which apply to differences "which are justiciable in their nature by reason of being susceptible of decision by the application of the principles of law or equity." Whether the reference in an arbitration treaty is to the application of "law and equity," or to justiciability dependent on the possibility of applying "law or equity," it would seem to envisage equity as a part of law.

The Court has not been expressly authorised by its Statute to apply equity as distinguished from law. . . . Article 38 of the Statute expressly directs the application of "general principles of law recognised by civilised nations," and in more than one nation principles of equity have an established place in the legal system. The Court's recognition of equity as a part of international law is in no way restricted by the special power conferred upon it "to decide a case *ex aequo et bono*, if the parties agree thereto." . . . It must be concluded, therefore, that under Article 38 of the Statute, if not independently of that Article, the Court has some freedom to consider principles of equity as part of the international law which it must apply.

It would seem to be an important principle of equity that where two parties have assumed an identical or a reciprocal obligation, one party which is engaged in a continuing non-performance of that obligation should not be permitted to take advantage of a similar non-performance of that obligation by the other party. The principle finds expression in the so-called maxims of equity which exercised great influence in the creative period of the development of the Anglo-American law. Some of these maxims are, "Equality is equity"; "He who seeks equity must do equity." It is in line with such maxims that "a court of equity refuses relief to a plaintiff whose conduct in regard to the subject-matter of the litigation has been improper." . . . A very similar principle was received into Roman Law. . . . This conception was the basis of Articles 320 and 322 of the German Civil Code, and even where a code is silent on the point Planiol states the general principle that "*dans tout rapport synallagmatique, chacune des deux parties ne peut exiger la prestation qui lui est due que si elle offre elle-même d'exécuter son obligation.*" . . .

Notes[88]

1. What does Judge Hudson understand by "equity"? Is it an undefined idea of fairness or justice? Does he regard it as a formal source of international law?

2. Arbitral tribunals have sometimes been given terms of reference of the sort referred to by Judge Hudson. The British-Mexican Claims Commission of 1926 was instructed to act "in accordance with the principles of justice and equity."[89] This was because:

[88] On equity in international law, see Cheng, 8 C.L.P. 185 (1955), and Jenks, *op cit.* at p. 21, n. 16, above, Chap. 7.
[89] British-Mexican Convention 1926, Art. 2, 5 R.I.A.A. 8.

it is the desire of Mexico *ex gratia* fully to compensate the injured parties, and not that her responsibility should be established in conformity with the general principles of International Law.[90]

Note that tribunals given such instructions have not infrequently had occasion to formulate and apply rules of international law and their awards are often quoted as authority for such rules.[91]

3. In the *Rann of Kutch Arbitration* (*India* v. *Pakistan*),[92] the Tribunal stated:

As both Parties have pointed out, equity forms part of international law; therefore the Parties are free to present and develop their cases with reliance on principles of equity.[93]

The Tribunal then, applying the international law rules concerning the acquisition of territory "and with due regard to what is fair and reasonable as to details,"[94] decided on the boundary between the two parties in the disputed area. In respect of one part of it the Tribunal stated:

The two deep inlets on either side of Nagar Parkar will constitute the territory of Pakistan . . . it would be inequitable to recognise these inlets as foreign territory. It would be conducive to friction and conflict. The paramount consideration of promoting peace and stability in this region compels the recognition and confirmation that this territory, which is wholly surrounded by Pakistan territory, also be regarded as such.[95]

In the *Damage to Portuguese Colonies in South Africa Arbitration*,[96] the Tribunal, having decided that it was required to apply international law, recited the contents of Article 38 of the Statute of the P.C.I.J. as being applicable and continued:

Finally, in the absence of rules of international law applicable to the case, the arbitrators consider that they should fill the gap by deciding in accordance with the principles of equity, while keeping within the spirit of international law, applied by analogy, and taking account of its evolution.

Note also the recent application of "equitable principles" as the content of a customary rule in the *Continental Shelf Cases*,[97] the use of "equity" in the *Barcelona Traction Case*,[98] and the search for an "equitable solution derived from the applicable law" in the *Fisheries Jurisdiction Cases*.[99]

4. *Natural Law* played an important part in the development of international law in its early years. According to the positivist approach, however, it is at best a material source of international law today. The following passage from the *North American Dredging Company Case*[1] is a forceful statement of the positivist point of view:

The law of nature may have been helpful, some three centuries ago, to build up a new law of nations, and the conception of inalienable rights of men and nations may have exercised a salutary influence, some one hundred and fifty years ago, on the develop-

---

[90] *Ibid.*
[91] See, *e.g.* the *Eschauzier Claim*, 5 R.I.A.A. 207 (1931).
[92] 50 I.L.R. 2.
[93] *Ibid.* p. 18.
[94] *Ibid.* p. 519. Opinion of the Umpire (Mr. Lagergren).
[95] *Ibid.* p. 520. Opinion of the Umpire (Mr. Lagergren).
[96] 2 R.I.A.A. 1013 at p. 1016 (1928). Translation.
[97] Above, p. 25. *cf.* in the same context, the *Continental Shelf* (*Tunisia* v. *Libya*) *Case*, below, p. 359 and the *English Channel Arbitration*, below, p. 360.
[98] Below, p. 453.
[99] Below, p. 346.
[1] 4 R.I.A.A. 26 (1926).

ment of modern democracy on both sides of the ocean; but they have failed as a durable foundation of either municipal or international law and cannot be used in the present day as substitutes for positive municipal law, on the one hand, and for positive international law, as recognised by nations and governments through their acts and statements, on the other hand.

Fitzmaurice, however, argues that some general principles of law in the sense of Article 38(1)(c),

> involving inherently necessary principles of natural law, are such as to cause natural law, at any rate in that aspect of it that relates to these principles, to be a formal, not merely a material, source of law.[2]

He gives a number of examples, including the rule *pacta sunt servanda*, the

> rule that a State or government cannot plead the provisions or deficiencies of its own internal laws or constitution as a ground or excuse for non-compliance with its international obligations

and

> rules of the type which assert that a State cannot plead its own wrong as a ground of non-compliance, or plead impossibility of performance arising from a situation it has itself brought about.[3]

5. *JUDICIAL DECISIONS*

SCHWARZENBERGER, INTERNATIONAL LAW

(3rd ed., 1957), Vol. I, pp. 30 *et seq.* Some footnotes omitted

It may be asked why the views expressed by international judges in their official capacity should carry greater weight than if contained in private studies. The answer certainly cannot be derived in the international field from the principle of *stare decisis*. Nevertheless, it appears advisable not to overestimate the difference between the binding and persuasive authority of judgments. A perusal of the practice of the World Court will reveal remarkable consistency in its judgments. It certainly did not hesitate to refer to, and to quote from, its previous judgments and advisory opinions. Yet the true answer lies first in the greater degree of responsibility and care that the average lawyer shows when he deals in a judicial capacity with real issues as compared with private comments on such issues or the discussion of hypothetical cases. There is a world of difference between practising shooting with dummy ammunition at a wooden target and firing in earnest with live ammunition at a living target. In addition, where a case is argued by experienced counsel from two or more angles, and where the court is composed of members with widely differing legal training and experience, it is more likely that an all-round view of the matter will be taken than where the same topic is turned over by a writer in the isolation of his study or even discussed with colleagues. . . .

Nevertheless, even the World Court is but an element of a law-determining agency[4]—and, be it recalled, of a subsidiary law-determining agency—and,

---

[2] *Loc. cit.* at p. 19, n. 1, above, p. 174.
[3] *Ibid.* pp. 164–165.
[4] *Ed.* For the meaning of this term, see above, p. 19.

therefore, should not be sacrosanct against sympathetic, but searching criticism. The persuasive character of its judgments and advisory opinions depends on the fullness and cogency of the reasoning offered. It is probably not accidental that the least convincing statements on international law made by the International Court of Justice excel by a remarkable economy of argument. In view of the element of compromise that is the price of any majority decision, this is not surprising. Exactly for this reason, the minority opinions of judges who could not square it with their judicial conscience to join the "compact majority" are especially precious and, in some cases, may constitute evidence of a kind which has at least the same, or even higher, intrinsic value than any particular majority opinion. At this point, the autonomy of the Doctrine of international law must necessarily assert itself. It then becomes the task of a writer to state without fear or favour why he considers any particular judicial pronouncements appear to err, for instance, on the side of either excessive caution or daring.

Municipal courts are not quite in the same category as international courts and tribunals. In the case of the judgments of the courts of some countries it may be justifiable to praise them in the terms in which Chancellor Kent spoke of the decisions of English courts and, especially, of the decisions of the English High Court of Admiralty:

> In the investigation of the rules of the modern law of nations, particularly with regard to the extensive field of maritime capture, reference is generally and freely made to the decisions of the English courts. . . . They contain more intrinsic argument, more full and precise details, more accurate illustrations, and are of more authority than the loose dicta of elementary writers.[5]

Yet there are countries in which the independence of the judiciary from the executive is not so much cherished as in countries in which the rule of law in the Western sense is recognised. Furthermore, the judges of municipal courts are more likely to suffer from subconscious national bias than a body of international judges drawn from all quarters of the globe. It is very much easier for the latter to guard against this most dangerous type of "inarticulate major premise." . . .

Notes

1. For the common lawyer, the most striking feature of the role of international courts and tribunals, and one of which he constantly needs to remind himself, is that cases do not make law. Article 59 of the Statute of the International Court of Justice, for example, provides that "the decision of the Court has no binding force except between the parties and in respect of that particular case." In taking this approach, international law follows the civil law tradition. Yet although judgments do not constitute a formal source of law, those of the World Court at least play a larger part in the development of international law than theory might suggest. State practice seldom points so clearly in one direction as to leave the Court no discretion in its formulation of a custom.[6] Quite often it is non-existent, sparse or contradictory so that the Court is thrust into the speculative realm of general principles and analogy to decide a case. In other words, the

[5] Kent's *Commentaries on American Law* (1896), Vol. I, pp. 69–70.
[6] For an extreme case where the Court's law-making role would be patent, note the controversy concerning the standard to apply to the treatment of the property of aliens: see below, Chap. 8. Note also the difficulties the Court had in the *Fisheries Jurisdiction Cases*: below, p. 346.

World Court, as any other international court or tribunal, is by no means the mechanical recorder of law that might be supposed, a fact which becomes important in assessing the contribution of the Court because of the undoubted influence that its pronouncements have on subsequent state practice. The impact of the judgments and opinions in the *Anglo-Norwegian Fisheries*,[7] *Reservations*[8] and *Reparation Cases*,[9] for example, bears ample witness to this influence.[10] Note also Judge Azevedo's view in the *Asylum Case*[11]:

> It should be remembered. . . that the decision in a particular case has deep repercussions, particularly in international law, because views which have been confirmed by that decision acquire quasi-legislative value, in spite of the legal principle to the effect that the decision has no binding force except between the parties and in respect of that particular case (Statute, art. 59).

2. International courts and tribunals not only do not make law; they are also not bound by their previous decisions as to the law which they apply. But despite this absence of a doctrine of binding precedent, the World Court, as Schwarzenberger makes clear, does tend to follow or feel the need to distinguish its own jurisprudence.[12] It relies very heavily upon this jurisprudence and only occasionally refers to that of other courts or tribunals. Often the Court will cite only its own case law for a proposition and not bother to refer to state practice supporting it.[13] Other international courts[14] and tribunals[15] that decide more than one case tend naturally to build up a consistent jurisprudence too. Although there is no hierarchy of courts, the World Court is indisputably pre-eminent and its judgments and advisory opinions are highly persuasive for other international courts and tribunals.[16] The persuasiveness of the pronouncements of international courts and tribunals apart from the World Court for any other international court or tribunal depends very much, as Schwarzenberger suggests, upon their intrinsic merits.[17]

3. Among the many examples of judicial decisions of municipal courts discussing and applying rules of international law, see the cases below on state and diplomatic immunity.[18]

---

[7] Below, p. 289.

[8] Below, p. 582.

[9] Below, p. 114.

[10] One exceptional instance of a ruling by the Court *not* finding general acceptance is that in the *Lotus Case* on criminal jurisdiction in respect of collisions at sea: see below, p. 212. The Court's "preferential rights" doctrine in the *Fisheries Jurisdiction Cases*, below, p. 346, has not been adopted in the 1982 Convention on the Law of the Sea: see below, p. 353.

[11] I.C.J. Rep. 1950 at p. 232.

[12] See, *e.g.* the Court's treatment of its earlier jurisprudence in the *Barcelona Traction Case*, below, p. 453. Note, in particular, the way in which the Court distinguishes the *Nottebohm Case*. Would it in fact be correct to say that the Court was there making use of the distinction between *ratio decidendi* and *obiter dicta*, which does not formally exist in international law?

[13] See Kearney, in Gross, ed., *The Future of the International Court of Justice* (1976), Vol. II, 610, at p. 698.

[14] *e.g.* the European Court of Human Rights: see Chap. 9, below.

[15] *e.g.* the Mexican Claims Commissions of the 1920s and 1930s: see the cases in Chap. 8, below.

[16] Note, however, the restricted reading in the *Flegenheimer Case*, below, p. 449, of the I.C.J.'s judgment in the *Nottebohm Case*.

[17] Thus the European Commission of Human Rights felt itself quite free in the *Nielsen Case*, 2 *Y.B. E.C.H.R.* 412, to disagree with the tribunal in the *Salem Case*, below, p. 451.

[18] Below, Chap. 6.

6. *WRITERS*

PARRY, THE SOURCES AND EVIDENCES OF INTERNATIONAL LAW

(1965), pp. 103–105

In the Court's Statute "the teachings of the most highly qualified publicists" are assigned the same subsidiary status, whatever that may be, as judicial decisions. Upon a long view, there would seem to be no legal order wherein the publicist—a peculiar term—has played a greater part than international law. Grotius is the father of the law of nations. And . . . at the beginning of the last century, all States seemed to rely heavily on Vattel. Indeed both the books and the opinions of the nineteenth century seem often to resemble catalogues of the praises of famous men. "Hear also what Hall sayeth. Hear the comfortable words of Oppenheim" is an incantation which persists even into this century.

The credit is to be given to Judge Jessup[19] for finding a truly devastating example of the opposite point of view, that of the Court of Admiralty, expressed in the case of *The Renard*[20] in 1778. . . . The question was how long a prize must be in the captor's hands for the original property in her to be divested. Opposing counsel offered opposing opinions of Grotius and Bynkershoek. And the Court "observed that there was something ridiculous in the decisive way each lawyer, as quoted, had given his opinion. Grotius might as well have laid down, for a rule, twelve hours, as twenty-four; or forty-eight, as twelve. A pedantic man in his closet dictates the law of nations; everybody quotes, and nobody minds him. The usage is plainly as arbitrary as it is uncertain; and who shall decide, when doctors disagree? Bynkershoek, as is natural to every writer or speaker who comes after another, is delighted to contradict Grotius. . . ."

It is difficult not to see truth as well as humour in this. And it is also no doubt true that, as the body of judicial decisions increases, the authority of the commentator is diminished. . . . The literature of international law, to which the majority of the World Court at least pays scant lip-service, possesses evident defects. One of the most frequent charges brought against it is that it displays a great deal of national bias. The charge is probably exaggerated. The fact is that international lawyers are inevitably municipal lawyers first of all. The law, furthermore, is inevitably a somewhat conservative training. The writers of one country thus reflect their national legal tradition and technique rather than any national political viewpoint. . . .

Notes

1. *The current role of writers*. Wolfke,[21] a Polish writer, describes the role of writers today as consisting in the:

> analysis of facts and opinions and in drawing conclusions on binding customary rules and on trends of their evolution. Such conclusions, like all generalisations of this kind, involve unrestricted supplementation by introducing elements lacking and hence, a creative factor. Further, by attracting attention to international practice and

[19] *Transnational Law* (1956), p. 11.
[20] Hay & M. 222.
[21] *Loc. cit.* at p. 21, n. 16, above, pp. 79–80.

appraising it, the writers indirectly influence its further evolution, and hence the development of customs. At present, the influence of doctrine on the formation of international law in general is certainly rather behind the scenes and anonymous. To disregard it would, however, be to say the least, unjustified.

2. *Their earlier role.* The contribution of writers was a much more important one in the formative period of international law. They were largely responsible for establishing the basic idea that there was such a thing as law governing the relations between states. In addition, they exercised a much more creative role in the determination of particular rules of law than would be possible today. Their statements of the law were derived by deduction from natural law principles, by analogy from Roman law, and by generalisation from what state practice they could find, as well as, occasionally, from more bizarre sources such as the writings of Homer. It was after Grotius (1583–1645) that writers became polarised into one of three schools: the "naturalists," of whom Pufendorf (1632–94) is the most well known, who based international law on natural law; the "positivists," such as Bynkershoek (1673–1743), who based it on the consent of states evidenced in state practice; and the "eclectics" or "Grotians," including Vattel (1714–67), who, like Grotius, relied on both. By the nineteenth century, most writers were positivists, reflecting the general change of attitude to natural law thinking. By that time also, as their adoption of positivism ensured, the role of writers had declined to its present state.

3. For a less charitable view of the objectivity of writers than that of Parry, note the following comment by the Arbitrator (Huber) in the *Spanish Zones of Morocco Claims*[22]:

> It is true that the great majority of writers show a very marked tendency to restrict the responsibility of States. Their doctrines, however, are frequently politically inspired and represent a natural reaction against unjustified intervention in the affairs of certain nations.

7. *GENERAL ASSEMBLY RESOLUTIONS*[23]

JOHNSON, THE EFFECT OF RESOLUTIONS OF THE GENERAL ASSEMBLY OF THE UNITED NATIONS

(1955–56) 32 B.Y.I.L. 97

Many Resolutions of the General Assembly, such as those concerned with the internal working of the United Nations Organisation, have a full "legal effect" in that they are binding upon both the Members and the organs of the Organisation.[24] These Regulations create obligations and legal situations which did not exist before. There is also nothing to prevent Members incurring binding legal obligations by the act of voting for Resolutions in the General Assembly, provided there is a clear intention to be so bound. "Recommendations" of the General Assembly addressed to Members who have voted against them have, however, a "legal effect" only in the sense that they may constitute a

[22] 2 R.I.A.A. 615, at p. 640 (1925). Translation.
[23] See Asamoah, *The Legal Significance of the Declarations of the General Assembly of the United Nations* (1966); Cheng, 5 Indian J.I.L. 23 (1965); Detter, *Law Making by International Organisations* 1965, pp. 211–214; Falk, 60 A.J.I.L. 782 (1966); Skubiszewski, *Recueil d'études de droit international en hommage à Paul Guggenheim* (1968), p. 508.
[24] *Ed., e.g.* resolutions on the budget of the UN: Article 17(1), UN Charter.

"subsidiary means for the determination of rules of law" capable of being used by an international court. They are not in themselves sources of law. Their value, even as means for the determination of rules of international law, depends upon the degree of objectivity surrounding the circumstances in which they were adopted. In particular, it depends upon the extent to which they can be regarded as expressions of "juridical conscience" of humanity as a whole rather than of an incongruous or ephemeral political majority.

Notes

1. In December 1963, the General Assembly adopted unanimously a resolution declaring the "legal principles" governing activities in outer space.[25] The debates on the resolution contain some comments on the question of the significance as a source of law of General Assembly resolutions that formulate general rules of conduct for states. In the Legal Sub-Committee of the Committee on the Peaceful Uses of Outer Space, the United Kingdom representative stated:

> Although, as stated by the U.S.S.R. delegation, resolutions of the General Assembly were not—save in the exceptional cases provided for in the Charter—binding upon Member States, a resolution, if adopted unanimously, would be most authoritative and would have some advantages over an agreement in view of the possibility that all states might not accede to an agreement or that delays in ratification or failure to ratify might considerably reduce its scope.[26]

The United States representative stated:

> Some delegations had argued that only an international agreement signed by Governments would be legally binding. International agreements were not, however, the only sources of law. As stated in Article 38 of the Statute of the International Court of Justice, decisions of international tribunals and the growth of customary law as evidenced by State practice should also be taken into consideration. When a General Assembly resolution proclaimed principles of international law—as resolution 1721 (XVI)[27] had done—and was adopted unanimously, it represented the law as generally accepted in the international community.[28]

The Italian representative said:

> In international law, rules were binding primarily because States considered themselves bound by such rules, whatever their origin. From that viewpoint, recommendations of the General Assembly undoubtedly had binding force. In any case, recommendations of the General Assembly had the function of identifying, and even of eliciting participation in the formation of, the rules exacted by the awareness of the international community to certain basic needs—an awareness which was the primary and fundamental source of international law.[29]

In the First Committee of the General Assembly, the French representative said:

> While supporting the principles set forth in the draft declaration,[30] he wished to stress that the latter could not be looked on as more than a statement of intention; legal

---

[25] See below, p. 190. Resolution 1962 (XVIII) was specifically called a "Declaration of *Legal Principles* Governing the Activities of States in the Exploration and Use of Outer Space" (italics added).

[26] U.N. Doc. A/AC.105/C.2/SR.17, p. 9.

[27] *Ed.* This was the 1961 precursor of the 1963 Declaration: see below, p. 190.

[28] U.N. Doc. A/AC.105/C.2/SR.20, pp. 10–11.

[29] U.N. Doc. A/AC.105/C.2/SR.20, p. 7.

[30] *Ed. i.e.* that in the 1963 Resolution.

obligations *stricto sensu* could only flow from international agreements, and an international law of outer space had yet to be created.[31]

The U.S.S.R. representative said:

The United States representative had said that in his Government's view the legal principles contained in the draft declaration reflected international law as accepted by the Members of the United Nations and that the United States for its part intended to respect them. The Soviet Union, in its turn, undertook also to respect the principles enunciated in the draft declaration[32] if it were adopted unanimously.[33]

Do the opinions of states thus expressed support Johnson's conclusions? Do they treat the *resolutions* themselves as a source of law or do they see the views of states in voting for or against them as instances of state practice indicative of custom in the normal way in which any state practice contributes to custom?

2. Parry[34] states:

. . . it is exceedingly difficult to resist the impression that the content of international law is very different now from what it was commonly understood to be at the beginning of the life of the United Nations—even after the entry into force of the Charter. Numerous factors no doubt have contributed to the change. But among these the resolutions of the General Assembly would seem to have been of no little importance. It would not seem, moreover, that the effect of these resolutions can be explained away, as it were, or rather brought under the accepted categories of the sources of international law, by any argument that they are only binding for the States which vote in favour of them. . . . The matter may be sufficiently tested by reference to the General Assembly's resolution of 1960 concerning "colonialism."[35] . . . Can even the nine abstaining members deny that the law of territorial sovereignty has been, or must be, re-written as a result of that resolution? And must not even the 89 States which voted in favour of it concede that its disguise as an interpretation of the Charter, and therefore as existing law, is an exceedingly thin one?

3. The 1974 Charter of Economic Rights and Duties of States[36] was adopted by the General Assembly by 120 votes to six with ten abstentions. For the identity of the states abstaining or voting against the Charter, see below, p. 429, n. 55. Does the rule it contains on expropriation state customary international law?[37] One needs to consider whether the intention of states was to formulate political or legal rules as well as their voting records to answer this question.

8. *CODIFICATION AND PROGRESSIVE DEVELOPMENT OF INTERNATIONAL LAW*[38]

Note

The codification of international law has been the subject of public and private action at various levels since the late nineteenth century. Before the First World War notable success was achieved by the Hague Conventions of 1899 and 1907, resulting from the Hague Conferences of the same years, on the laws of war and neutrality. Between the

---

[31] U.N. Doc. A/C.1/SR.1345, para. 17.
[32] See n. 30 above.
[33] U.N. Doc. A/C.1/SR.1342, para. 17.
[34] *Op. cit.* at p. 19, n. 1, above, pp. 21–22.
[35] *Ed.* Resolution 1514 (XV), below, p. 95.
[36] Below, p. 429.   [37] See the *Texaco Case*, below, p. 434.
[38] See Briggs, *The International Law Commission* (1965); Gross, 19 Int.Org. 537 (1965); Jennings, 13 I.C.L.Q. 385 (1964); Lauterpacht, 49 A.J.I.L. 16 (1955); Rosenne (1960) 36 B.Y.I.L. 104; *ibid.* (1965) 19 Y.B.W.A. 183; Stone, 57 Col.L.R. 16 (1957).

two world wars, the League of Nations sponsored a Codification Conference at The Hague in 1930 which was prepared for in optimistic mood and which examined the law of nationality, territorial waters and state responsibility. It was a great disappointment when agreement proved possible only on certain aspects of the law of nationality.

In 1946, with the major part of international law still to be found in the uncollated practice of states, the General Assembly, acting under Article 13 of the Charter of the United Nations,[39] established the International Law Commission. The Commission was given the function of promoting the "progressive development" and "codification" of international law. By "progressive development" is meant "the preparation of draft conventions on subjects which have not yet been regulated by international law or in regard to which the law has not yet been sufficiently developed in the practice of States."[40] "Codification" means "the more precise formulation and systematisation of rules of international law in fields where there already has been extensive State practice, precedent and doctrine."[41] On the relationship in practice between these two objectives, Judge ad hoc Sørensen, in his dissenting opinion in the *North Sea Continental Shelf Cases*, states:

> It has come to be generally recognised, however, that this distinction between codification and progressive development may be difficult to apply rigorously to the facts of international legal relations. Although theoretically clear and distinguishable, the two notions tend in practice to overlap or to leave between them an intermediate area in which it is not possible to indicate precisely where codification ends and progressive development begins. The very act of formulating or restating an existing customary rule may have the effect of defining its contents more precisely and removing such doubts as may have existed as to its exact scope or the modalities of its application. The opportunity may also be taken of adapting the rule to contemporary conditions, whether factual or legal, in the international community. On the other hand, a treaty purporting to create new law may be based on a certain amount of State practice and doctrinal opinion which has not yet crystallised into customary law.[42]

A number of multilateral conventions now in force are the result of the Commission's work. The established procedure is for the Commission to prepare a set of draft articles which are submitted to states for their comments. The United Nations may then decide to call an international conference for the adoption of a convention based on the Commission's draft. For example, the four 1958 Geneva Conventions on the Law of the Sea,[43] the 1961 Vienna Convention on Diplomatic Relations,[44] the 1969 Vienna Convention on the Law of Treaties[45] and the 1978 Vienna Convention on Succession of States in Respect of Treaties[46] all result from the Commission's work. Projects at present under way within the Commission concern state succession in respect of matters other than treaties, state responsibility, the status of the diplomatic courier and the diplomatic bag, jurisdictional immunity of states and international liability for injurious consequences arising out of acts not prohibited by international law. Other work done by the Commission has included the formulation of (1) a Draft Declaration on Rights and Duties of States (1949)[47]; (2) the Principles of International Law recognised in the Charter of the Nuremberg Tribunal and in the Judgment of the Tribunal (1950)[48]; (3) a

[39] Appendix I, below.
[40] Article 15, Statute of the I.L.C.
[41] *Ibid.*
[42] I.C.J. Rep. 1969 at pp. 242–243.
[43] Below, Chap. 7.
[44] Below, Chap. 7.
[45] Below, Chap. 10.
[46] Below, p. 634.
[47] See below, p. 57.
[48] Below, p. 560.

Draft Code of Offences against the Peace and Security of Mankind (1954)[49]; and (4) Model Rules on Arbitral Procedure (1958).[50]

In his *Survey of International Law in Relation to the Work of Codification of the International Law Commission*,[51] Lauterpacht suggested that the texts prepared by the International Law Commission

> would be at least in the category of writings of the most qualified publicists.[52]

The Commission is composed of 34 members "who shall be persons of recognised competence in international law."[53] Members are elected by the General Assembly[54] which "shall bear in mind that. . . in the Commission as a whole representation of the main forms of civilisation and of the principal legal systems of the world should be assured."[55] Members sit as individuals and not as representatives of their Governments. In 1965, one Member wrote:

> Most of the original members of the Commission elected in 1948 were not professional diplomats. . . . Today the Commission is different. Of its present twenty-five members, seventeen [approximately] . . . are professional diplomats, and, of these, seven or eight are Legal Advisers of their respective Foreign Offices, and several others are Legal Advisers of Delegations in New York. This is an interesting development which signifies quite eloquently the raising of the level of official interest in codification and the importance which is now attached on official levels to the preparatory work undertaken by the International Law Commission.[56]

Consider when examining those areas of law (primarily the law of the sea, the law of diplomatic relations and the law of treaties) that have been made the subject of "law-making" treaties whether there are disadvantages as well as advantages in codifying international law and whether, on balance, it is worthwhile. Consider also whether an unsuccessful attempt at codification leaves the law in a worse state than it would be if no attempt had been made.

---

[49] G.A.O.R. 9th Session, Supp., p. 11. See Johnson, 4 I.C.L.Q. 445 (1955).
[50] Y.B.I.L.C., 1958, II, p. 83.
[51] E. Lauterpacht, ed., *International Law, being the collected papers of Hersch Lauterpacht* (1970), Vol. I, p. 445, reprinted from UN Doc. A/CN.4/1/Rev. 1, February 10, 1949.
[52] *Ibid.* p. 465.
[53] Article 2, Statute of the I.L.C.
[54] Article 3, *ibid.*
[55] Article 8, *ibid.*
[56] Rosenne, *loc. cit.* at p. 52, n. 38, above, p. 188.

CHAPTER 3

INTERNATIONAL LAW AND MUNICIPAL LAW

1. *MONISM AND DUALISM*

FITZMAURICE, THE GENERAL PRINCIPLES OF INTERNATIONAL LAW CONSIDERED FROM THE STANDPOINT OF THE RULE OF LAW

92 *Hague Recueil* 5 at pp. 70–80 (1957–II). Some footnotes omitted

THIS controversy [between monism and dualism] turns on whether international law and internal law are two separate legal orders, existing independently of one another—and, if so, on what basis it can be said that either is superior to or supreme over the other; or whether they are both part of the same order, one or other of them being supreme over the other *within that order*. The first view is the dualist view, the second the monist. . . . [A] radical view of the whole subject may be propounded to the effect that the entire monist-dualist controversy is unreal, artificial and strictly beside the point, because it assumes something that has to exist for there to be any controversy at all—and which in fact does not exist—namely a *common field* in which the two legal orders under discussion both simultaneously have their spheres of activity. . . . In order that there can be controversy about whether the relations between two orders are relations of *co-ordination* between self-existent independent orders, or relations of *subordination* of the one to the other, or of the other to the one—or again whether they are part of the same order, but both subordinate to a superior order—it is necessary that they should both be purporting to be, and in fact be, applicable in the same field—that is, to the same set of relations and transactions. For instance . . . it would be idle to start a controversy about whether the English legal system was superior to or supreme over the French or *vice-versa*, because these systems do not pretend to have the same field of application. . . . There is indeed no basis on which it is even possible to start an argument, because, although these legal systems may in a certain sense come into conflict in particular cases, thus giving rise to problems of what is called Conflict Law, or Private International Law, each country has its own conflict rules whereby it settles such problems arising before its own Courts. Ultimately therefore, there can be no conflict between any two systems *in the domestic field*, for any apparent conflict is automatically settled by the domestic conflict rules of the forum. Any conflict between them in the international field, that is to say on the inter-governmental plane, would fall to be resolved by international law, because in that field international law is not only supreme, but in effect the only system there is. Domestic law does not, as such, apply at all in the international field. But the supremacy of international law in that field exists, not because of any inherent supremacy of international law as a category over national law as a category, but for other reasons. It is, rather, a supremacy of exactly the same order as the supremacy of French law in France, and of English law in England—*i.e.* a supremacy not arising from *content*, but from the field of operation—not because the law is *French* but because the place, the field, is *France*. The view here suggested is neither dualist nor monist. It is precisely the view put forward in the following passage from Anzilotti,[1] who is often miscalled a dualist in this respect:

> It follows from the same principle that there cannot be conflict between rules belonging to different juridical orders, and, consequently, in particular between international and internal law. To speak of conflict between international law and internal law is as inaccurate as to speak of conflict between the laws of different States: in reality the existence of a conflict between norms belonging to different juridical orders cannot be affirmed except from a standpoint outside both the one and the other.

The logic of this cannot be contraverted, and in actual fact, the necessity for a common field of operation as the basis of any discussion as to the relations between two legal orders, is recognised by modern protagonists of the monist-dualist controversy. This can be seen from the following sentence in an article by a writer of the monist school,[2] reading: "Two normative systems with binding force *in the same field* must form part of the same order"—[italics added]. This may be true, or at least it is capable of discussion, if the two orders in question *are* binding in the same field, but not otherwise. Consider again a sentence such as the following one, taken from one of the most eminent and justly celebrated modern exponents of the positivist-monist view[3]: "International law and national law cannot be mutually different and mutually independent systems . . . if . . . both systems are considered to be valid for the same space and at the same time." Everything here depends of course on the "if"—which surely assumes the very point that has to be proved. What calls for question is precisely the phrase "valid for the same space at the same time." Had this passage said "valid simultaneously for the same class of relations," it would not have been open to question, though only because international and national law do not in fact govern the same set of relations. To say this is not to deny the validity of the monist view, but only its relevance in this particular connexion. Equally, the relevance of the dualist view is denied.[4] Recognising, as they evidently do, that only relations between legal orders that operate in the same field can usefully and meaningfully be discussed, the protagonists of the monist-dualist controversy seem to be driven to trying to *create* the necessary common field—though it is more particularly the monists who seek to do this, since the dualists can rest quite content with the existence of two orders, provided they operate in separate fields. The endeavour to create a common field takes the form in effect of denying the existence or reality of the State, or reducing it to the sum total of the individuals composing it. For instance, the same eminent authority, evidently aware of the difficulty that must arise unless there is a common field, has suggested the following solution[5]:

---

[1] *Corso di diritto internazionale*. This passage is translated from the French translation by Gidel, p. 57.

[2] J. G. Starke, "Monism and Dualism in the Theory of International Law" in *British Year Book* (1936) at p. 74.

[3] Professor Kelsen, *The Principles of International Law*, Rinehart (1952), p. 404. *Ed.* Now see 2nd ed., 1967, p. 553.

[4] If either view were relevant, the monist would seem preferable, but only on the basis that there is a legal order, natural law, behind and above both domestic and international law, which affirms the supremacy of international law. . . .

[5] Kelsen, *op cit.* . . . *ibid. Ed.* Now see 2nd ed., 1967, p. 544.

The mutal independence of international and national law is often substantiated by the alleged fact that the two systems regulate different subject matters. National law, it is said, regulates the behaviour of individuals, international law the behaviour of States. We have already shown that the behaviour of States is reducible to the behaviour of individuals representing the State. Thus the alleged difference in subject matter between international and national law cannot be a difference between the kinds of subjects whose behaviour they regulate. . . .

Formally, therefore, international and domestic law as *systems* can never come into conflict. What may occur is something strictly different, namely a conflict of *obligations*, or an inability for the State *on the domestic plane* to act in the manner required by international law. The supremacy of international law in the international field does not in these circumstances entail that the judge in the municipal courts of the State must override local law and apply international law. Whether he does or can do this depends on the local law itself, and on what legislative or administrative steps can be or are taken to deal with the matter. The supremacy of international law in the international field simply means that if nothing can be or is done, the State will, on the international plane, have committed a breach of its international law obligations, for which it will be internationally responsible, and in respect of which it cannot plead the condition of its domestic law by way of absolution. International law does not therefore in any way purport to govern the content of national law in the national field—nor does it need to. It simply says—and this is all it needs to say—that certain things are not valid according to international law, and that if a State in the application of its domestic law acts contrary to international law in these respects, it will commit a breach of its international obligations.

Notes
1. How would you distinguish between Fitzmaurice's view and that of the dualist?
2. Consider when examining the cases in the remainder of this chapter whether the international and municipal courts and tribunals that decided them show any awareness of the monist-dualist controversy.

2. *MUNICIPAL LAW IN INTERNATIONAL LAW*[6]

DRAFT DECLARATION ON RIGHTS AND DUTIES OF STATES 1949

Y.B.I.L.C., 1949, 286, 288

The Draft Declaration was prepared by the International Law Commission. The United Nations General Assembly noted it and commended it to members and jurists as a "notable and substantial contribution towards the progressive development of international law and its codification": Resolution 375 (IV), G.A.O.R., 4th Session, *Resolutions*, p. 66.

Article 13

Every state has the duty to carry out in good faith its obligations arisng from treaties and other sources of international law, and it may not invoke provisions in its constitution or its laws as an excuse for failure to perform this duty.

[6] See Jenks, *The Prospects of International Adjudication* (1964), Chap. 9.

Note

There is ample judicial and arbitral authority for the rule that a state cannot rely upon its municipal law to avoid its international law obligations. For example, in the *Alabama Claims Arbitration*,[7] the Tribunal rejected the British argument that because its constitutional law was not such as to provide it with the power to interfere with the private construction and sailing of the ships concerned, Great Britain had not violated its obligations as a neutral in the United States Civil War by allowing the construction and sailing to occur:

> . . . the government of Her Britannic Majesty cannot justify itself for a failure in due diligence on the plea of insufficiency of the legal means of action which it possessed.

EXCHANGE OF GREEK AND TURKISH POPULATIONS CASE

Advisory Opinion. P.C.I.J. Reports, Series B, No. 10, p. 20 (1925)

Referring to Article 18 of the Treaty of Lausanne 1923, by which the parties undertook "to introduce in their respective laws such modifications as may be necessary with a view to ensuring the execution of the present Convention," the Court stated:

Opinion of the Court

This clause . . . merely lays stress on a principle which is self-evident, according to which a State which has contracted valid international obligations is bound to make in its legislation such modifications as may be necessary to ensure the fulfilment of the obligations undertaken.

Notes

1. If State A and State B make a treaty by which each agrees to allow the nationals of the other into its territory on terms better than those required by customary international law, and if State A fails to make the necessary changes in its local law to allow the admission of the nationals of State B on the terms agreed, has State A violated international law if no national of State B has tried to obtain, and been refused, admission under the treaty?[8]

2. If, contrary to customary international law, State A claims jurisdiction to board ships on the high seas flying the flag of another state and gives its navy power under its municipal law so to act, does it *thereby* violate international law?[9]

BRAZILIAN LOANS CASE

France *v.* Brazil (1929)

P.C.I.J. Reports, Series A, No. 21, pp. 124–125

The question in this case was one of the interpretation of certain Brazilian Government Loans, some bonds of which were held by French nationals. The Loans were governed by Brazilian law. The Court ruled that it had jurisdiction under Article 38 of its Statute to decide cases such as the one before it involving disputes between states which turned not upon international law but the interpretation of municipal law. In the following

---

[7] Moore, 1 Int.Arb. 495 at p. 656 (1872).

[8] See Fitzmaurice, *loc. cit.* at p. 55, above, pp. 89–90; McNair, *Treaties*, p. 100; Schwarzenberger, p. 614.

[9] See Fitzmaurice, *loc. cit.* at n. 8, above.

passage the Court considered how it should go about interpreting municipal law when called upon to do so. The Agreement between the parties referring the case to the Court read in part: "In estimating the weight to be attached to any municipal law of either country which may be applicable to the dispute, the Permanent Court of International Justice shall not be bound by the decisions of the respective courts" (Article VI).

Judgment of the Court

Though bound to apply municipal law when circumstances so require, the Court, which is a tribunal of international law, and which, in this capacity, is deemed itself to know what this law is, is not obliged also to know the municipal law of the various countries. All that can be said in this respect is that the Court may possibly be obliged to obtain knowledge regarding the municipal law which has to be applied. And this it must do, either by means of evidence furnished it by the Parties or by means of any researches which the Court may think fit to undertake or to cause to be undertaken.

Once the Court has arrived at the conclusion that it is necessary to apply the municipal law of a particular country, there seems no doubt that it must seek to apply it as it would be applied in that country. It would not be applying the municipal law of a country if it were to apply it in a manner different from that in which that law would be applied in the country in which it is in force.

It follows that the Court must pay the utmost regard to the decisions of the municipal courts of a country, for it is with the aid of their jurisprudence that it will be enabled to decide what are the rules which, in actual fact, are applied in the country the law of which is recognised as applicable in a given case. If the Court were obliged to disregard the decisions of municipal courts, the result would be that it might in certain circumstances apply rules other than those actually applied; this would seem to be contrary to the whole theory on which the application of municipal law is based.

Of course, the Court will endeavour to make a just appreciation of the jurisprudence of municipal courts. If this is uncertain or divided, it will rest with the Court to select the interpretation which it considers most in conformity with the law. . . . As the Court has already observed in the judgment in the case of Serbian loans,[10] it would be a most delicate matter to do so, in a case concerning public policy—a conception the definition of which in any particular country is largely dependant on the opinion prevailing at any given time in such country itself—and in a case where no relevant provisions directly relate to the question at issue. Such are the reasons according to which the Court considers that it must construe Article VI of the Special Agreement to mean that, while the Court is authorised to depart from the jurisprudence of the municipal courts, it remains entirely free to decide that there is no ground for attributing to the municipal law a meaning other than that attributed to it by that jurisprudence.

Notes

1. If a nationalisation statute enacted by State A were alleged to be contrary to international law by State B before an international court or tribunal and if the dispute turned upon the meaning of the compensation provision in the statute, how would the court or tribunal go about interpreting that provision (a) if the statute had not been

[10] *Ed.* P.C.I.J. Rep., Series A, No. 20, p. 46 (1929).

construed by State A's courts; (b) if it had been construed by them but State B alleged that the court in the case in which this was done had failed to follow a binding precedent that would have led it to a different conclusion?

2. Note the reliance on the municipal law concept of the company in the *Barcelona Traction Case*.[11]

3. *INTERNATIONAL LAW IN MUNICIPAL LAW*[12]

(i) THE UNITED KINGDOM[13]

(a) *Customary International Law*

TRIQUET v. BATH

(1764) 3 Burr. 1478. Court of King's Bench

In this case, in which the defendant, a domestic servant of the Bavarian Minister to Great Britain, successfully claimed diplomatic immunity, Lord Mansfield discussed the position of international law in English law.

LORD MANSFIELD. This privilege of foreign ministers and their domestic servants depends upon the law of nations. The Act of Parliament of 7 Ann. c. 12,[14] is declaratory of it.

. . . the Act was not occasioned by any doubt "whether the law of nations, particularly the part relative to public ministers, was not part of the law of England; and the infraction, criminal; nor intended to vary, an iota from it."

I remember in a case before Lord Talbot, of *Buvot* v. *Barbuit*[15] upon a motion to discharge the defendant (who was in execution for not performing a decree), "because he was agent of commerce, commissioned by the King of Prussia, and received here as such"; the matter was very elaborately argued at the Bar; and a solemn deliberate opinion given by the Court. These questions arose and were discussed. . . . "What was the rule of decision: the Act of Parliament; or, the law of nations." Lord Talbot declared a clear opinion; "That the law of nations, in its full extent was part of the law of England." . . .

I remember, too, Lord Hardwicke's declaring his opinion to the same effect; and denying that Lord Chief Justice Holt ever had any doubt as to the law of nations being part of the law of England, upon the occasion of the arrest of the Russian Ambassador [which had led to the Act of Anne].

Notes

Triquet v. *Bath* and *Buvot* v. *Barbuit* are two of the cases commonly cited in support of the view that English law adopts the "incorporation" approach to the reception of customary international law as part of common law. For a description of the "incorporation" approach, and of the rival "transformation" approach, see Lord Denning in the *Trendtex Case*, below, p. 258.

[11] Below, p. 453.
[12] See Morgenstern (1950) 27 B.Y.I.L. 42 and Seidl-Hohenveldern, 12 I.C.L.Q. 88 (1963).
[13] See Fawcett, *The British Commonwealth in International Law* (1963), Chap. 2; Holdsworth, *Essays in Law and History* (1946), pp. 260–272; Jenks, *op cit.* at p. 21, n. 16, above, Chap. 13; Lauterpacht, 25 Trans.Grot.Soc. 51 (1939).
[14] *Ed.* Diplomatic Privileges Act 1708.
[15] *Ed.* (1737) Cases t. Talbot 281.

R. v. KEYN

(1876) 2 Ex.D. 63. Court for Crown Cases Reserved

The *Franconia*, a German ship, collided with the *Strathclyde*, a British ship, at a point in the English Channel within three miles of the English coast. The defendant, the German captain of the *Franconia*, was prosecuted at the Central Criminal Court for the manslaughter of a passenger on board the *Strathclyde* who died as a result of the collision. The defendant was found guilty, but the question whether an English court had jurisdiction to try the case was reserved for the Court for Crown Cases Reserved[16] which decided, by seven votes to six, that it did not. The following is an extract from the judgment of Cockburn C.J. who was one of the judges in the majority.

COCKBURN C.J. On board a foreign ship on the high seas, the foreigner is liable to the law of the foreign ship only. It is only when a foreign ship comes into the ports or waters of another state that the ship and those on board become subject to the local law. These are the established rules of the law of nations. They have been adopted into our own municipal law, and must be taken to form part of it.

. . . Unless, therefore, the accused, Keyn, at the time the offence of which he has been convicted was committed, was on British territory or on board a British ship, he could not be properly brought to trial under English law, in the absence of express legislation.

On the question whether the three mile belt of sea surrounding Great Britain was British territory in English law, Cockburn C.J. ruled first that it was not such according to "the ancient law of England."[17] He then considered whether it had become such because of a rule of customary international law to that effect. After concluding that the opinions of writers on the width of sea over which jurisdiction could be exercised and on the nature of any such jurisdiction was conflicting, Lord Cockburn continued:

. . . even if entire unanimity had existed . . . the question would still remain, how far the law as stated by the publicists had received the assent of the civilized nations of the world. . . . To be binding, the law must have received the assent of the nations who are to be bound by it. This assent may be express, as by treaty or the acknowledged concurrence of governments, or may be implied from established usage. . . . Nor, in my opinion, would the clearest proof of unanimous assent on the part of other nations be sufficient to authorize the tribunals of this country to apply, without an Act of Parliament, what would practically amount to a new law. In so doing we should be unjustifiably usurping the province of the legislature. The assent of nations is doubtless sufficient to give the power of parliamentary legislation in a matter otherwise within the sphere of international law; but it would be powerless to confer without such legislation a jurisdiction beyond and unknown to the law, such as that now insisted on, a jurisdiction over foreigners in foreign ships on a portion of the high seas.

When I am told that all other nations have assented to such an absolute dominion on the part of the littoral state, over this portion of the sea, as that their ships may be excluded from it, and that, without any open legislation, or notice to them or their subjects, the latter may be held liable to the local law, I

---

[16] The case was argued twice. On the first occasion a court of six judges was equally divided.
[17] 2 Ex.D. 174.

ask, first, what proof there is of such assent as here asserted; and, secondly, to what extent has such assent been carried? a question of infinite importance, when, undirected by legislation, we are called upon to apply the law on the strength of such assent. . . .

Lord Cockburn examined the evidence of treaties and of usage and concluded that in neither case was it clear.

It may well be, I say again, that—after all that has been said and done in this respect—after the instances which have been mentioned of the adoption of the three-mile distance, and the repeated assertion of this doctrine by the writers on public law, a nation which should now deal with this portion of the sea as its own, so as to make foreigners within it subject to its law, for the prevention and punishment of offences, would not be considered as infringing the rights of other nations. But I apprehend that as the ability so to deal with these waters would result, not from any original or inherent right, but, from the acquiescence of other states, some outward manifestation of the national will, in the shape of open practice or municipal legislation, so as to amount, at least constructively, to an occupation of that which was before unappropriated, would be necessary to render the foreigner, not previously amenable to our general law, subject to its control. That such legislation, whether consistent with the general law of nations or not, would be binding on the tribunals of this country—leaving the question of its consistency with international law to be determined between the governments of the respective nations—can of course admit of no doubt. The question is whether such legislation would not, at all events, be necessary to justify our Courts in applying the law of this country to foreigners under entirely novel circumstances in which it has never been applied before.

It is obviously one thing to say that the legislature of a nation may, from the common assent of other nations, have acquired the full right to legislate over a part of that which was before high sea, and as such common to all the world; another and very different thing to say that the law of the local state becomes thereby at once, without anything more, applicable to foreigners within such part, or that, independently of legislation, the Courts of the local state can proprio vigore so apply it. The one position does not follow from the other; and it is essential to keep the two things, the power of Parliament to legislate, and the authority of our Courts, without such legislation, to apply the criminal law where it could not have been applied before, altogether distinct, which, it is evident, is not always done. It is unnecessary to the defence, and equally so to the decision of the case, to determine whether Parliament has the right to treat the three-mile zone as part of the realm consistently with international law. That is a matter on which it is for Parliament itself to decide. It is enough for us that it has, so far as to be binding upon us, the power to do so. The question is whether, acting judicially, we can treat the power of Parliament to legislate as making up for the absence of actual legislation. I am clearly of opinion that we cannot, and that it is only in the instances in which foreigners on the seas have been made specifically liable to our law by statutory enactment that the law can be applied to them.

Finally, on the question of the location of the offence, Cockburn C.J. ruled that although the defendant's action had had its effect on board the *Strathclyde*, the offence of manslaughter could not be said to have been committed there so as to give an English court jurisdiction over it.[18]

Pollock B. and Field J. concurred in the judgment of Cockburn C.J. Kelly C.B., Bramwell J.A., Lush J., and Sir Robert Phillimore gave concurring judgments. Lord Coleridge C.J., Brett and Amphlett JJ.A., Grove, Denman, and Lindley JJ., gave dissenting judgments.

Notes

1. *R.* v. *Keyn* was reversed by the Territorial Waters Jurisdiction Act 1878, the preamble to which reads: "Whereas the rightful jurisdiction of Her Majesty, her heirs and successors, extends *and always has extended* over the open seas adjacent to the coasts of the United Kingdom and of all other parts of Her Majesty's dominions to such a distance as is necessary for the defence and security of such dominions. . . . "[19]

2. Is Cockburn C.J.'s judgment, which is the leading one among those given by the judges in the majority, consistent with the "incorporation" approach to the reception of customary international law? Or does it support the "transformation" approach, according to which only such rules of international law are a part of the municipal law of a state as are actually adopted by a state's courts or legislature in their or its discretion? Did any rule of English constitutional law influence Cockburn C.J. in his judgment?[20] Note the following comment on Lord Cockburn's judgment by Lauterpacht[21]:

. . . it cannot be said that this judgment amounts to a rejection of the rule that international law is a part of the law of England. Writers seem to forget that the main issue of the controversy in the case was not the question whether a rule of international law can be enforced without an Act of Parliament; what *was* in dispute was the existence and the extent of a rule of international law relating to jurisdiction in territorial waters.

3. Which view of the relationship between international and municipal law does the "transformation" approach support?

WEST RAND CENTRAL GOLD MINING CO. v. R.

[1905] 2 K.B. 391. King's Bench Division

The South African Republic seized gold, the property of the suppliant, a British company, in a manner allegedly contrary to the law of the Republic. When Great Britain annexed the Republic in 1900, a petition of right was brought against the Crown to recover the gold or compensation for its loss. Upon the Crown's demur, the court rejected the suppliant's contention that a conquering state was liable in international law for the financial obligations of its predecessor. It was therefore not required to rule upon the argument that the alleged rule was a part of English law. Nonetheless, Lord Alverstone, delivering the opinion of the court, made the following comments.

LORD ALVERSTONE C.J. It is quite true that whatever has received the common consent of civilised nations must have received the assent of our country, and that to which we have assented along with other nations in general may properly be called international law, and as such will be acknowledged and

---

[18] See Beckett (1927) 8 B.Y.I.L. 108.
[19] Italics added.
[20] See Brownlie, pp. 46–47.
[21] *Private Law Sources and Analogies of International Law* (1927), p. 76, footnote. See also *Pianka* v. *The Queen* [1979] A.C. 107 (P.C.).

applied by our municipal tribunals when legitimate occasion arises for those tribunals to decide questions to which doctrines of international law may be relevant. But any doctrine so invoked must be one really accepted as binding between nations, and the international law sought to be applied must, like anything else, be proved by satisfactory evidence, which must shew either that the particular proposition put forward has been recognised and acted upon by our own country, or that it is of such a nature, and has been so widely and generally accepted, that it can hardly be supposed that any civilised State would repudiate it. . . . *Barbuit's Case*,[22] *Triquet* v. *Bath*,[23] and *Heathfield* v. *Chilton*[24] are cases in which the Courts of law have recognised and have given effect to the privilege of ambassadors as established by international law. But the expressions used by Lord Mansfield when dealing with the particular and recognised rule of international law on this subject, that the law of nations forms part of the law of England, ought not to be construed so as to include as part of the law of England opinions of text-writers upon a question as to which there is no evidence that Great Britain has ever assented, and a fortiori if they are contrary to the principles of her laws as declared by her Courts. The cases of *Wolff* v. *Oxholm*[25] and *Rex* v. *Keyn*[26] are only illustrations of the same rule— namely, that questions of international law may arise, and may have to be considered in connection with the administration of municipal law.

Notes

1. What explanation of *R.* v. *Keyn* does this case support?[27] If a "proposition put forward has been recognised and acted upon by our own country," is this sufficient to establish it as a rule of customary international law for the purpose of its application by an English court? Would it be sufficient to establish it as such for the purpose of its application by an international court or tribunal?

2. Would Lord Alverstone permit the incorporation of a customary rule that was contrary to existing common law? In *Chung Chi Cheung* v. *The King*,[28] Lord Atkin, delivering the opinion of the Privy Council, stated:

> It must always be remembered that, so far, at any rate, as the Courts of this Country are concerned, international law has no validity save in so far as its principles are accepted and adopted by our own domestic law. There is no external power that imposes its rule upon our own code of substantive law or procedure.

> The Courts acknowledge the existence of a body of rules which nations accept amongst themselves. On any judicial issue they seek to ascertain what the relevant rule is, and having found it, they will treat it as incorporated into the domestic law, so far as it is not inconsistent with rules enacted by statutes *or finally declared by* their tribunals.

Lord Atkin then considered and applied the international law rules on state immunity in respect of public ships.

Lord Denning quoted the first sentence of the above passage from Lord Atkin's speech when following the "transformation" approach in *Thakrar* v. *Secretary of State for the Home Office*.[29] Lord Denning changed his mind in *Trendtex Trading Corp.* v.

[22] *Ed., i.e. Buvot* v. *Barbuit,* above, p. 60, n. 15.   [23] *Ed.* Above, p. 60.
[24] 4 Burr. 2016.
[25] (1817) 6 M. & S. 92.
[26] *Ed.* Above, p. 61.
[27] See Westlake (1906) 22 L.Q.R. 14.
[28] [1939] A.C. 160 at pp. 167–168. Italics added.
[29] See the extract below, p. 406.

Central Bank of Nigeria[30] where he adopted the "incorporation" approach. The problem in the *Trendtex* case was whether the doctrine of precedent applies to rules of English law that incorporate rules of customary international law so that a change in international law can only be recognised by the English courts within the limits of that doctrine.[31] The majority in that case—Lord Denning M.R. and Shaw L.J.—thought that there was an exception to the doctrine of precedent so that, for example, the Court of Appeal could apply a new rule of international law even though there were Court of Appeal decisions to the contrary based upon the rule's predecessor. Stephenson L.J. considered that the Court of Appeal's earlier decisions were binding upon it in the usual way. In *Thai-Europe Tapioca Service Ltd.* v. *Govt. of Pakistan*[32] two other members of the Court of Appeal—Lawton and Scarman L.JJ.—had earlier taken the same view as Stephenson L.J. Scarman L.J. stated:

> I think that it is important to realise that a rule of international law, once incorporated into our law by decisions of a competent court, is not an inference of fact but a rule of law. It therefore becomes part of our municipal law and the doctrine of *stare decisis* applies as much as to that as to a rule of law with a strictly municipal provenance.[33]

3. *Prize courts.* These constitute a special case. In accordance with international law, prize claims arising out of the capture of ships in war are heard before prize courts. These are courts set up by maritime states. Although municipal courts, they administer the (customary and treaty) international law of prize. In *The Zamora*,[34] the Judicial Committee of the Privy Council held that a British prize court had to apply that law even though it conflicted with an order in council. Such a court would, however, be bound by a British statute.[35]

MORTENSEN v. PETERS

(1906) 8 F. (J.) 93. Court of Justiciary. Scotland

The Fishery Board for Scotland issued a byelaw under the Herring Fishery (Scotland) Act 1889 making it an offence ("no person . . . shall") to fish by beam or otter trawling in the Moray Firth, part of which is more than three miles from the nearest point of land.[36] By the Sea Fisheries Regulation (Scotland) Act 1895, s.10(4), "any person" who fished by beam or otter trawling in contravention of that byelaw was subject to a fine or imprisonment. The appellant was a Dane and the master of a Norwegian ship. He was convicted in a Scottish court of the above offence for otter trawling at a place covered by the byelaw but beyond the three mile limit. His appeal against conviction was dismissed unanimously by a full bench of 12 judges.

LORD JUSTICE-GENERAL (LORD DUNEDIN). . . . It is not disputed that if the appellant had been a British subject in a British ship he would have been rightly convicted. . . .

I apprehend that the question is one of construction, and of construction only. In this Court we have nothing to do with the question of whether the Legislature has or has not done what foreign powers may consider a usurpation in a question with them. Neither are we a tribunal sitting to decide whether an

[30] See the extract below, p. 258.
[31] See Morgenstern, *loc. cit.* at p. 60, n. 12, above, pp. 80–82.
[32] [1975] 1 W.L.R. 1485.
[33] *Ibid.* p. 1495.
[34] [1916] 2 A.C. 77.
[35] *Ibid.* p. 93.
[36] The Firth as defined by statute was a little over 70 miles wide at its mouth.

Act of the Legislature is *ultra vires* as in contravention of generally acknowledged principles of international law. For us an Act of Parliament duly passed by Lords and Commons and assented to by the King, is supreme, and we are bound to give effect to its terms. The counsel for the appellant advanced the proposition that statutes creating offences must be presumed to apply only (1) to British subjects; and (2) to foreign subjects in British territory; and that short of express enactment their application should not be further extended. The appellant is admittedly not a British subject, which excludes (1); and he further argued that the *locus delicti*, being in the sea beyond the three-mile limit, was not within British territory; and that consequently the appellant was not included in the prohibition of the statute. Viewed as general propositions the two presumptions put forward by the appellant may be taken as correct. This, however, advances the matter but little, for like all presumptions they may be redargued,[37] and the question remains whether they have been redargued on this occasion.

The first thing to be noted is that the prohibition here, a breach of which consitutes the offence, is not an absolute prohibition against doing a certain thing, but against doing it in a certain place. Now, when the Legislature, using words of admitted generality—"It shall not be lawful," etc., "Every person who," etc.—conditions an offence by territorial limits, it creates, I think, a very strong inference that it is, for the purposes specified, assuming a right to legislate for that territory against all persons whomsoever. This inference seems to me still further strengthened when it is obvious that the remedy to the mischief sought to be obtained by the prohibition would be either defeated or rendered less effective if all persons whosoever were not affected by the enactment. . . .

It is said by the appellant that all this must give way to the consideration that International Law has firmly fixed that a *locus* such as this is beyond the limits of territorial sovereignty, and that consequently it is not to be thought that in such a place the Legislature could seek to affect any but the King's subjects.

It is a trite observation that there is no such thing as a standard of international law extraneous to the domestic law of a kingdom, to which appeal may be made. International law, so far as this Court is concerned, is the body of doctrine regarding the international rights and duties of states which has been adopted and made part of the law of Scotland. Now, can it be said to be clear by the law of Scotland that the *locus* here is beyond what the legislature may assert right to affect by legislation against all whomsoever for the purpose of regulating methods of fishing?

I do not think I need say anything about what is known as the three-mile limit. It may be assumed that within the three miles the territorial sovereignty would be sufficient to cover any such legislation as the present. It is enough to say that that is not a proof of the counter proposition that outside the three miles no such result could be looked for. The *locus* although outside the three-mile limit, is within the bay known as the Moray Firth, and the Moray Firth, says the respondent, is *intra fauces terrae*. Now, I cannot say that there is any definition of what *fauces terrae* exactly are. But there are at least three points which go far to shew that this spot might be considered as lying therein.

1. The dicta of the Scottish institutional writers seem to shew that it would be no usurpation, according to the law of Scotland, so to consider it. . . .

---

[37] *Ed., i.e.* rebutted.

2. The same statute[38] puts forward claims to what are at least analogous places. If attention is paid to the schedule appended to section 6, many places will be found far beyond the three-mile limit—*e.g.* the Firth of Clyde near its mouth. I am not ignoring that it may be said that this in one sense is proving *idem per idem*, but none the less I do not think the fact can be ignored.

3. There are many instances to be found in decided cases where the right of a nation to legislate for waters more or less landlocked or landembraced, although beyond the three-mile limit, has been admitted. . . .

It seems to me therefore, without laying down the proposition that the Moray Firth is for every purpose within the territorial sovereignty, it can at least be clearly said that the appellant cannot make out his proposition that it is inconceivable that the British Legislature should attempt for fishery regulation to legislate against all and sundry in such a place. And if that is so, then I revert to the considerations already stated which as a matter of construction made me thing that it did so legislate. . . .

LORD KYLLACHY. . . . This Court is of course not entitled to canvass the power of the Legislature to make the enactment. The only question open is as to its just construction. . . .

Now dealing, first, with the point of construction—the question as to what the statutory enactment means—it may probably be conceded that there is always a certain presumption against the Legislature of a country asserting or assuming the existence of a territorial jurisdiction going clearly beyong limits established by the common consent of nations—that is to say, by international law. . . . But then it is only a presumption, and as such it must always give way to the language used if it is clear, and also to all counter presumptions which may legitimately be had in view in determining, on ordinary principles, the true meaning and intent of the legislation. Express words will of course be conclusive, and so also will plain implication.

The concurring judgments of Lord Johnston and Lord Salvesen are omitted.

Notes

1. In reality the trawler of which the appellant was captain was British financed, controlled and crewed.[39] It had been given a foreign master and registration in the hope of circumventing the Fishery Board's regulations. Shortly after *Mortensen* v. *Peters*, a number of other successful prosecutions of Norwegian masters of foreign ships occurred. In some cases the convicted men went to prison rather than pay a fine. They were released, however, after protests by Norway. In March, 1907, a Foreign Office spokesman stated in the House of Commons: "The Act of Parliament as interpreted by the High Court of Justiciary is in conflict with international law."[40] In 1909, Parliament tried another approach. It enacted the Trawling in Prohibited Areas Prevention Act which prohibited the landing in the United Kingdom of fish caught contrary to the legislation applied in *Mortensen* v. *Peters*.

2. Is it possible that Lord Dunedin might have decided the case differently if there had been no argument at all for saying that the Moray Firth was *intra fauces terrae*? If so, why? Because the statute would then have conflicted with the customary international

---

[38] *Ed.* Herring Fishery (Scotland) Act 1889.
[39] See Fulton, *The Sovereignty of the Sea* (1911), p. 722.
[40] *Hansard*, H.C., Vol. 170, col. 472. March 4, 1907.

law on freedom of fishing on the high seas, or because of a presumption that Parliament will not legislate contrary to international law?

3. A statute may sometimes incorporate a rule of customary international law by reference. For example, section 7 of the Territorial Waters Jurisdiction Act 1878 defines the "territorial waters of Her Majesty's Dominions" as "such part of the sea . . . as is deemed by international law to be within the territorial sovereignty of Her Majesty."[41]

(b) *Treaties*[42]

THE PARLEMENT BELGE

(1878–79) 4 P.D. 129. Probate, Divorce and Admiralty Division

SIR ROBERT PHILLIMORE. In the month of February, 1878, the owners of the steam-tug *Daring* served a writ on board the steamship *Parlement Belge* against the owners of that vessel and her freight, in which they claimed the sum of 3500 l. for damage, arising out of a collision which occurred between that vessel and the steam-tug *Daring* on the 14th of February 1878, off Dover. . . .

The Attorney General has appeared and filed what is called an "information and protest" . . .

By this protest it is in substance contended that this steamship *Parlement Belge* is not amenable to the process of this Court, first, on the ground that she is the property of the King of the Belgians, and at the time of collision was controlled and employed by him. Secondly, that her Majesty the Queen, by a convention with the King of the Belgians,[43] has placed this packet-boat in the category of a public ship of war. . . .

. . . the plaintiffs in this suit have a statutable right of action against the *Parlement Belge*, unless that vessel be of that privileged class which is not amenable to a court of law.

The burden of proving that she does belong to this class lies upon the defendant. . . .

The *Parlement Belge* is a packet conveying certain mails and carrying a considerable commerce, officered, as I have said, by Belgian officers and flying the Belgian pennon.

Can such a vessel so employed be entitled to the privileges of a public ship of war? . . .

Upon the whole, I am of opinion that neither upon principle, precedent, nor analogy of general international law, should I be warranted in considering the *Parlement Belge* as belonging to that category of public vessels which are exempt from process of law and all private claims.

I now approach the consideration of the second question. . . .

It is admitted that this convention has not been confirmed by any statute; but it has been contended on the part of the Crown both that it was competent to her Majesty to make this convention, and also to put its provisions into operation without the confirmation of them by parliament. The plaintiffs admit the former, but deny the latter of these propositions.

---

[41] See also *Post Office* v. *Estuary Radio Ltd.* [1968] 2 Q.B. 740 (C.A.).
[42] See Mann, 44 Trans.Grot.Soc. 29 (1958–59).
[43] *Ed.* A postal convention of 1876.

The power of the Crown to make treaties with foreign states is indisputable. [Blackstone is quoted on the prerogative power to make treaties.] . . .

Blackstone must have known very well that there were a class of treaties the provisions of which were inoperative without the confirmation of the legislature; while there were others which operated without such confirmation. The strongest instance of the latter, perhaps, which could be cited is the Declaration of Paris in 1856, by which the Crown in the exercise of its prerogative deprived this country of belligerent rights, which very high authorities in the state and in the law had considered by be of vital importance to it. But this declaration did not affect the private rights of the subject; and the question before me is whether this treaty does affect private rights, and therefore required the sanction of the legislature.

The authority of Chancellor Kent was relied on. That learned writer observes:

> Treaties of peace, when made by the competent power, are obligatory upon the whole nation. If the treaty requires the payment of money to carry it into effect, and the money cannot be raised but by an Act of the legislature, the treaty is morally obligatory upon the legislature to pass the law, and to refuse it would be a breach of public faith. Kent's Comm. Vol. i. p. 166 (ed. 1873).

And he further observes:

> There can be no doubt that the power competent to bind the nation by treaty may alienate the public domain and property by treaty. . . .

If the Crown had power without the authority of parliament by this treaty to order that the *Parlement Belge* should be entitled to all the privileges of a ship of war, then the warrant, which is prayed for against her as a wrong-doer on account of the collision, cannot issue, and the right of the subject, but for this order unquestionable, to recover damages for the injuries done to him by her is extinguished.

This is a use of the treaty-making prerogative of the Crown which I believe to be without precedent, and in principle contrary to the laws of the constitution. Let me consider to what consequences it leads. If the Crown without the authority of parliament, may by process of diplomacy shelter a foreigner from the action of one of her Majesty's subjects who has suffered injury at his hands, I do not see why it might not also give a like privilege of immunity to a number of foreign merchant vessels or to a number of foreign individuals. The law of this country has indeed incorporated those portions of international law which give immunity and privileges to foreign ships of war and foreign ambassadors; but I do not think that it has therefore given the Crown authority to clothe with this immunity foreign vessels, which are really not vessels of war, or foreign persons, who are not really ambassadors.

Let me say one word more in conclusion. Mr. Bowen, in his very able speech, dwelt forcibly upon the wrong which would be done to this packet if, being invited to enter ports of this country with the privileges of a ship of war, she should find them denied to her. I acknowledge the hardship, but the remedy, in my opinion, is not to be found in depriving the British subject without his consent, direct or implied, or his right of action against a wrong-doer, but by the agency of diplomacy, and proper measures of compensation and arrangement, between the Governments of Great Britain and Belgium. I must allow the warrant of arrest to issue.

Notes

1. The decision was reversed by the Court of Appeal[44] on the ground that, contrary to the ruling of Sir Robert Phillimore, the immunity sought was available at customary international law and hence at common law. The ruling at first instance on the effect of a treaty in English law is still good law.

2. In *Porter* v. *Freudenberg*,[45] the Court of Appeal had to consider whether "the old rule (not peculiar to English law, though it has been more prominent in England than elsewhere) that an alien enemy's rights of action are suspended during the war"[46] had been abrogated by the 1907 Hague Convention on Land Warfare. The court ruled, *as a matter of construction of the Convention*, that it had not done so. It is possible to read the judgment as meaning that the Convention *could* have had this effect without statutory implementation as an exercise of the prerogative if it had been appropriately worded.

ATT.-GEN. FOR CANADA v. ATT.-GEN. FOR ONTARIO

[1937] A.C. 326. Judicial Committee of the Privy Council

The Dominion Parliament of Canada legislated to implement certain international labour conventions. On appeal from the Supreme Court of Canada, the Judicial Committee advised that the legislation was *ultra vires* the Dominion Parliament; that legislative competence on the subject concerned vested in the legislatures of the Provinces. The following statement of principle was made by Lord Atkin in the course of delivering the Committee's opinion.

LORD ATKIN. It will be essential to keep in mind the distinction between (1.) the formation, and (2.) the performance, of the obligations constituted by a treaty, using that word as comprising any agreement between two or more sovereign States. Within the British Empire there is a well-established rule that the making of a treaty is an executive act, while the performance of its obligations, if they entail alteration of the existing domestic law, requires legislative action. Unlike some other countries, the stipulations of a treaty duly ratified do not within the Empire, by virtue of the treaty alone, have the force of law. If the national executive, the government of the day, decide to incur the obligations of a treaty which involve alteration of law they have to run the risk of obtaining the assent of Parliament to the necessary statute or statutes. To make themselves as secure as possible they will often in such cases before final ratification seek to obtain from Parliament an expression of approval. But it has never been suggested, and it is not the law, that such an expression of approval operates as law, or that in law it precludes the assenting Parliament, or any subsequent Parliament, from refusing to give its sanction to any legislative proposals that may subsequently be brought before it. Parliament, no doubt, as the Chief Justice points out, has a constitutional control over the executive: but it cannot be disputed that the creation of the obligations undertaken in treaties and the assent to their form and quality are the function of the executive alone. Once they are created, while they bind the State as against the other contracting parties, Parliament may refuse to perform them and so leave the State in default.

---

[44] (1880) 5 P.D. 197.

[45] [1915] 1 K.B. 857. See McNair (1928) 9 B.Y.I.L. 59.   [46] *Ibid.* p. 877.

In a unitary State whose Legislature possesses unlimited powers the problem is simple. Parliament will either fulfil or not treaty obligations imposed upon the State by its executive. The nature of the obligations does not affect the complete authority of the Legislature to make them law if it so chooses. But in a State where the Legislature does not possess absolute authority, in a federal State where legislative authority is limited by a consitutional document, or is divided up between different Legislatures in accordance with the classes of subject-matter submitted for legislation, the problem is complex. The obligations imposed by treaty may have to be performed, if at all, by several Legislatures; and the executive have the task of obtaining the legislative assent not of the one Parliament to whom they may be responsible, but possibly of several Parliaments to whom they stand in no direct relation. The question is not how is the obligation formed, that is the function of the executive; but how is the obligation to be performed, and that depends upon the authority of the competent Legislature of Legislatures.

Notes

On the treaty-making power within the United Kingdom, see below, p. 574. On the question whether individuals may rely in the English courts upon provisions in treaties concluded by the United Kingdom as the basis for a claim, see *Rustomjee* v. *R.*, below, p. 400.

I.R.C. v. COLLCO DEALINGS LTD

[1962] A.C. 1. House of Lords

Section 4(2) of the Finance (No. 2) Act 1955, states: "Where a person entitled under any enactment to an exemption from income tax which extends to dividends on shares becomes entitled to receive a dividend on . . . shares . . . to which [this] . . . section applies," such exemption shall not apply to that dividend. The appellant Irish company was entitled to an exemption of the kind described. In this case, in trying to avoid the effect of section 4(2), the appellant argued that its application to an Irish company would be contrary to a 1926 Double Taxation Agreement between the United Kingdom and Eire.

VISCOUNT SIMONDS. It was [argued] . . . that to apply section 4(2) to the appellant company would create a breach of the 1926 and following agreements, and would be inconsistent with the comity of nations and the established rules of international law: the subsection must, accordingly, be so construed as to avoid this result.

My Lords, the language that I have used is taken from a passage at p. 148 of the 10th edition of "Maxwell on the Interpretation of Statutes" which ends with the sentence: "But if the statute is unambiguous, its provisions must be followed even if they are contrary to international law." It would not, I think, be possible to state in clearer language and with less ambiguity the determination of the legislature to put an end in all and every case to a practice which was a gross misuse of a concession. What, after all, is involved in the argument of the appellant? It is nothing else than that, when Parliament said "under any enactment," it meant "any enactment except . . ." But it was not found easy to state precisely the terms of the exception. The best that I could get was "except an enactment which is part of a reciprocal arrangement with a sovereign foreign state." It is said that the plain words of the statute are to be disregarded and these words arbitrarily inserted in order to observe the comity of nations and the established rules of international law. I am not sure upon which of these highsounding phrases the appellant company chiefly relies. But I would answer that neither comity nor rule of international law can be invoked to prevent a sovereign state from taking what steps it thinks fit to protect its own revenue laws from gross abuse, or to save its own citizens from unjust discrimination in favour of foreigners. To demand that the plain words of the statute should be disregarded in order to do that very thing is an extravagance to which this House will not, I hope, give ear.

I am well aware that there are cases—many were cited to your Lordships—in which the principle stated in Maxwell has been applied, though less often, I think, upon an appeal to comity of nations than to rules of international law. But each case must be judged in its own context, and I know of no cases in which at the same time the words of a statute were unambiguously clear and it was sought to vary them upon grounds which could not be justified by broad considerations of justice or expediency, nor could be supposed to commend themselves to that sovereign power whose citizens relied on them.

The appeal was dismissed unanimously. The opinions of Lords Morton, Reid, Radcliffe and Guest are omitted.

R. v. CHIEF IMMIGRATION OFFICER, ex p. BIBI

[1976] 1 W.L.R. 979. Court of Appeal

The case concerned the application by immigration officers of Immigration Rules made under the Immigration Act 1971. It was argued for the applicant (a person who was seeking admission to the United Kingdom as the wife of a Commonwealth citizen already in the United Kingdom) that the Rules should be interpreted and applied by immigration officers in accordance with the right to family life in Article 8, European Convention on Human Rights. The following extract concerns this point only.

LORD DENNING. The position as I understand it is that if there is any ambiguity in our statutes, or uncertainty in our law, then these courts can look to the Convention as an aid to clear up the ambiguity and uncertainty, seeking always to bring them into harmony with it. Furthermore, when Parliament is enacting a statute, or the Secretary of State is framing rules, the courts will assume that they had regard to the provisions of the Convention, and intended to make the enactment accord with the Convention: and will interpret them accordingly. But I would dispute altogether that the Convention is part of our law. Treaties and declarations do not become part of our law until they are made law by Parliament.[47] I desire, however, to amend one of the statements I made in the *Bhajan Singh* case [1976] Q.B. 198, 207. I said then that the immigration officers ought to bear in mind the principles stated in the Convention. I think that would be asking too much of the immigration officers. They cannot be expected to know or to apply the Convention. They must go simply

---

[47] *Ed.* Lord Denning had said in *Birdi* v. *Secretary of State for Home Affairs* (unreported, but referred to in *R.* v. *Secretary of State for Home Affairs, Ex p. Bhajan Singh* [1976] Q.B. 198), that if an Act of Parliament contradicted the European Convention "I might be inclined to hold it invalid." Lord Denning recanted on this in *Ex. p. Bhajan Singh.*

by the immigration rules laid down by the Secretary of State, and not by the Convention.

I may also add this. The Convention is drafted in a style very different from the way which we are used to in legislation. It contains wide general statements of principle. They are apt to lead to much difficulty in application: because they give rise to much uncertainty. They are not the sort of thing which we can easily digest. Article 8 is an example. It is so wide as to be incapable of practical application. So it is much better for us to stick to our own statutes and principles, and only look to the Convention for guidance in case of doubt.

Notes

1. Roskill and Geoffrey Lane L.JJ. agreed with Lord Denning on the question whether immigration officers should take the European Convention on Human Rights into account in exercising their powers under the Rules. In *R. v. Secretary of State for the Home Department, ex parte Phansopkar*,[48] Scarman L.J. had said in a similar case (after referring to Magna Carta):

> This hallowed principle of our law is now reinforced by the European Convention for the Protection of Human Rights 1950 *to which it is now the duty of our public authorities in administering the law*, including the Immigration Act 1971, and of our courts in interpreting and applying the law, including the Act, to have regard.[49]

This was thought by Roskill and Geoffrey Lane L.JJ. in *ex p. Bibi* to go too far.

2. In *Waddington v. Miah*,[50] Lord Reid, speaking for the whole House of Lords, said (when considering whether an offence created under the Immigration Act 1971 was intended to operate retrospectively) that in view of the Universal Declaration of Human Rights (Article 11)[51] and the European Convention on Human Rights (Article 7)[52] "it is hardly credible that any government department would promote or that Parliament would pass retrospective criminal legislation."

3. In *Cassell v. Broome*,[53] Lord Kilbrandon stated that:

> . . . since all commercial publication is undertaken for profit, one must be watchful against holding the profit motive to be sufficient to justify punitive damages: to do so would be seriously to hamper what must be regarded, at least since the European Convention [on Human Rights] was ratified, as a constitutional right to free speech.

Was Lord Kilbrandon suggesting that the European Convention should be taken into account by judges in developing the common law?[54]

SALOMON v. COMMISSIONERS OF CUSTOMS AND EXCISE

[1967] 2 Q.B. 116. Court of Appeal

The Court was required to interpret an ambiguous provision in the Customs and Excise Act 1952. The Act, drafted in Parliament's own language, was intended to implement the 1950 Convention on the Valuation of Goods for Customs Purposes, a treaty to

---

[48] [1976] Q.B. 606 (C.A.).
[49] *Ibid.* p. 626. Italics added.
[50] [1974] 1 W.L.R. 683 at p. 694.
[51] Below, p. 535.
[52] Below, p. 474.
[53] [1972] A.C. 1027 at p. 1133 (H.L.).
[54] See, however, Sir Robert Megarry V.C. in *Malone v. MPC* [1979] Ch. 344. On the relationship between EEC law and that of member states, see Lasok and Bridge, *An Introduction to the Law and Institutions of the European Communities* (3rd ed., 1982), Chaps. 10–12.

which a number of European states were parties. The Convention was not included as a Schedule to the Act, or anywhere referred to in it. The question arose whether recourse could be had to the treaty to interpret the statute.

DIPLOCK L.J. Where, by a treaty, Her Majesty's Government undertakes either to introduce domestic legislation to achieve a specified result in the United Kingdom or to secure a specified result which can only be achieved by legislation, the treaty, since in English law it is not self-operating, remains irrelevant to any issue in the English courts until Her Majesty's Government has taken steps by way of legislation to fulfil its treaty obligations. Once the Government has legislated, which it may do in anticipation of the coming into effect of the treaty, as it did in this case, the court must in the first instance construe the legislation, for that is what the court has to apply. If the terms of the legislation are clear and unambiguous, they must be given effect to, whether or not they carry out Her Majesty's treaty obligations, for the sovereign power of the Queen in Parliament extends to breaking treaties (see *Ellerman Lines* v. *Murray*)[55] . . . and any remedy for such a breach of an international obligation lies in a forum other than Her Majesty's own courts. But if the terms of the legislation are not clear but are reasonably capable of more than one meaning, the treaty itself becomes relevant, for there is a prima facie presumption that Parliament does not intend to act in breach of international law, including therein specific treaty obligations; and if one of the meanings which can reasonably be ascribed to the legislation is consonant with the treaty obligations and another or others are not, the meaning which is consonant is to be preferred. . . .

It has been argued that the terms of an international convention cannot be consulted to resolve ambiguities or obscurities in a statute unless the statute itself contains either in the enacting part or in the preamble an express reference to the international convention which it is the purpose of the state to implement. The judge seems to have been persuaded that *Ellerman Lines etc.* v. *Murray etc.* was authority for this proposition. But, with respect, it is not. The statute with which that case was concerned did not refer to the convention. The case is authority only for the proposition for which I have already cited it. . . . I can see no reason in comity or common sense for imposing such a limitation upon the right and duty of the court to consult an international convention to resolve ambiguities and obscurities in a statutory enactment. If from extrinsic evidence it is plain that the enactment was intended to fulfil Her Majesty's Government's obligations under a particular convention, it matters not that there is no express reference to the convention in the statute. One must not presume that Parliament intends to break an international convention merely because it does not say expressly that it is intending to observe it. Of course the court must not merely guess that the statute was intended to give effect to a particular international convention. The extrinsic evidence of the connection must be cogent.

Lord Denning L.J. and Russell L.J. delivered concurring judgments.

Notes

1. On the duty to interpret a statute or order in council that is intended to implement a treaty so as to give effect to the treaty if the language of the statute or order allows, see

[55] [1931] A.C. 126. (H.L.)

also *Post Office* v. *Estuary Radio Ltd.*[56] and *Benin* v. *Whimster.*[57] What if an ambiguous statute is inconsistent with a treaty which it is *not* intended to implement? What does *Ex p. Bibi*, above, suggest?

2. In *Buchanan* v. *Babco*,[58] the Carriage of Goods by Road Act 1965, s.1, provided that the English (but not the other, French) authentic text of the multilateral 1956 Convention on the Contract for the International Carriage of Goods by Road, which text was included as a Schedule to the Act, should have the force of law in the United Kingdom. Indicating the rules of interpretation that should apply in the interpretation of the English text of the Convention as a part of English law, Lord Wilberforce[59] stated:

> I think that the correct approach is to interpret the English text, which after all is likely to be used by many others than British businessmen, in a normal manner, appropriate for the interpretation of an international convention, unconstrained by technical rules of English law, or by English legal precedent, but on broad principles of general acceptation. . . . Moreover, it is perfectly legitimate . . . to look for assistance, if assistance is needed, to the French text. . . . There is no need to impose a preliminary test of ambiguity [before doing so].

3. In *Fothergill* v. *Monarch Airlines*,[60] the Carriage by Air Act 1961, s.1, enacted that the 1929 Warsaw Convention for the Unification of Certain Rules regarding Air Transport should have the force of law in the United Kingdom. The two (French and English) authentic texts were scheduled to the Act. Interpreting the word "damage" (*avarie*) in the Convention to include loss of, as well as injury to, goods, the House of Lords held that recourse could be had to the *travaux préparatoires* of the Convention to interpret it. Lord Wilberforce[61] stated:

> These cases [of recourse to *travaux préparatoires*] should be rare, and only where two conditions are fulfilled, first, that the material involved is public and accessible, and, secondly, that the travaux préparatoires clearly and indisputably point to a definite legislative intention.

Lord Diplock[62] thought that "an English court should have regard to any material which those delegates [drafting the treaty] themselves had thought would be available to clear up any possible ambiguities or obscurities." Lord Scarman[63] agreed with Lord Wilberforce and, emphasising the need for uniformity of interpretation, pointed out that the courts of most other states would look to the *travaux préparatoires*.

(ii) THE UNITED STATES[64]

HEAD MONEY CASES: EDYE v. ROBERTSON

112 U.S. 580 (1884). U.S. Supreme Court

It was argued in this case that an Act of Congress conflicted with earlier U.S. treaties and that therefore it was invalid. The Court, which was unanimous, found no such

---

[56] [1968] 2 Q.B. 740 (C.A.).
[57] [1976] Q.B. 297 (C.A.).
[58] [1978] A.C. 141 (H.L.).
[59] *Ibid.* p. 152.   [60] [1981] A.C. 251.
[61] *Ibid.* p. 278. Lord Fraser considered that recourse could not be had to the *travaux* in this case because they had not been sufficiently well published to the persons whose rights were affected: *ibid.* p. 287.
[62] *Ibid.* p. 283.
[63] *Ibid.* p. 294.
[64] On the position in Israel, see the *Eichmann* Case, below, p. 224

conflict on the facts of the case but nonetheless made the following statement of principle.

MR. JUSTICE MILLER (FOR THE COURT). A treaty is primarily a compact between independent Nations. . . . But a treaty may also contain provisions which confer certain rights upon the citizens or subjects of one of the Nations residing in the territorial limits of the other, which partake of the nature of municipal law, and which are capable of enforcement as between private parties in the courts of the country. . . . The Constitution of the United States [Article VI] places such provisions as these in the same category as other laws of Congress by its declaration that "This Constitution and the laws made in pursuance thereof, and all treaties made or which shall be made under authority of the United States, shall be the supreme law of the land." A treaty, then, is a law of the land as an Act of Congress is, whenever its provisions prescribe a rule by which the rights of the private citizen or subject may be determined. And when such rights are of a nature to be enforced in a court of justice, that court resorts to the treaty for a rule of decision for the case before it, as it would to a statute.

But even in this aspect of the case, there is nothing in this law which makes it irrepealable or unchangeable. The Constitution gives it no superiority over an Act of Congress in this respect, which may be repealed or modified by an Act of a later date. . . .

In short, we are of opinion that, so far as a treaty is made by the United States with any foreign Nation can become the subject of judicial cognisance in the courts of this country, it is subject to such Acts as Congress may pass for its enforcement, modification or repeal.

SEI FUJII v. CALIFORNIA

242 P. 2d 617 (1952). 19 I.L.R. 312 (1952). Supreme Court of California

GIBSON C.J. Plaintiff, an alien Japanese . . . appeals from a judgment declaring that certain land purchased by him in 1948 had escheated to the state. There is no treaty between this country and Japan which confers upon plaintiff the right to own land, and the sole question presented on this appeal is the validity of the California alien land law.

It is first contended that the land law has been invalidated and superseded by the provisions of the United Nations Charter pledging the member nations to promote the observance of human rights and fundamental freedoms without distinction as to race. Plaintiff relies on statements in the preamble and in Articles 1, 55 and 56 of the Charter.[65] . . .

It is not disputed that the charter is a treaty, and our federal Constitution provides that treaties made under the authority of the United States are part of the supreme law of the land and that the judges in every state are bound thereby. U.S.Const., art. VI. A treaty, however, does not automatically supersede local laws which are inconsistent with it unless the treaty provisions are self-executing. In the words of Chief Justice Marshall: A treaty is "to be regarded in courts of justice as equivalent to an act of the Legislature, whenever it operates

---

[65] *Ed.* Appendix I, below.

of itself, without the aid of any legislative provision. But when the terms of the stipulation import a contract—when either of the parties engages to perform a particular act, the treaty addresses itself to the political, not the judicial department; and the Legislature must execute the contract, before it can become a rule for the court." *Foster* v. *Neilson*, 1829, 2 Pet. 253, 314, 7 L.Ed. 415.

In determining whether a treaty is self-executing courts look to the intent of the signatory parties as manifested by the language of the instrument, and if the instrument is uncertain, recourse may be had to the circumstances surrounding its execution. See *Foster* v. *Neilson*. . . . In order for a treaty provision to be operative without the aid of implementing legislation and to have the force and effect of a statute, it must appear that the formers of the treaty intended to prescribe a rule that, standing alone, would be enforceable in the courts. See Head Money Cases [*Edye* v. *Robertson*].[66] . . .

It is clear that the provisions of the preamble and of Article 1 of the charter which are claimed to be in conflict with the alien land law are not self-executing. They state general purposes and objectives of the United Nations Organisation and do not purport to impose legal obligations on the individual member nations or to create rights in private persons. . . . Although the member-nations have obligated themselves [in Article 55 and 56] to co-operate with the international organisation in promoting respect for, and observance of, human rights, it is plain that it was contemplated that future legislative action by the several nations would be required to accomplish the declared objectives, and there is nothing to indicate that these provisions were intended to become rules of law for the courts of this country upon the ratification of the charter.

The language used in Articles 55 and 56 is not the type customarily employed in treaties which have been held to be self-executing and to create rights and duties in individuals. For example, the treaty involved in *Clark* v. *Allen*, 331 U.S. 503, 507–508 . . . relating to the rights of a national of one country to inherit real property located in another country, specifically provided that "such national shall be allowed a term of three years in which to sell the [property] . . . and withdraw the proceeds . . ." free from any discriminatory taxation. . . . In other instances treaty provisions were enforced without implementing legislation where they prescribed in detail the rules governing rights and obligations of individuals or specifically provided that citizens of one nation shall have the same rights while in the other country as are enjoyed by that country's own citizens. *Bacardi Corp.* v. *Domenech*, 311 U.S. 150, *Asakura* v. *City of Seattle*, 265 U.S. 332, 340.

It is significant to note that when the framers of the charter intended to make certain provisions effective without the aid of implementing legislation they employed language which is clear and definite and manifests that intention. [The Court referred to Articles 104 and 105.[67]] . . . In *Curran* v. *City of New York*, 191 Misc. 229, 77 N.Y.S. 2d 206, 212, these articles were treated as being self-executory.

We are satisfied, however, that the charter provisions relied on by plaintiff were not intended to supersede existing domestic legislation, and we cannot hold that they operate to invalidate the alien land law.[68]

---

[66] *Ed.* See above, p. 75. [67] *Ed.* Appendix I, below.

[68] *Ed.* This ruling by the Court, which reversed that of the California Court of Appeals, was unanimous. The Court, nonetheless, decided the case in favour of the plaintiff on another ground.

Notes

1. As far as customary international law is concerned, the following general statement by Gray J. in *The Paquete Habana*[69] applies:

International law is part of our law, and must be ascertained and administered by the Courts of Justice of appropriate jurisdiction, as often as questions of right depending upon it are duly presented for their determination.

In that case, the United States Supreme Court found and applied a customary rule of international law exempting coastal fishing vessels from capture as prize of war.

2. *Treaties and Executive Agreements*. In *Asakura* v. *City of Seattle*,[70] in which a conflict was alleged (but not found) between a 1911 treaty and a 1921 city ordinance, the U.S. Supreme Court stated: "The rule established by it [the treaty] cannot be rendered nugatory in any part of the United States by Municipal ordinances or state laws." In *Johnson* v. *Browne*,[71] the U.S. Supreme Court, in holding that certain federal statutory provisions had not been repealed by treaty, stated: "Repeals by implication are never favoured, and a later treaty will not be regarded as repealing an earlier statute by implication unless the two are absolutely incompatible and the statute cannot be enforced without antagonising the treaty." In *Cook* v. *U.S.*,[72] the U.S. Supreme Court noted that "a treaty will not be abrogated or modified by a later [federal] statute unless such purpose on the part of the Congress has been clearly expressed."

In addition to "treaties," which are made by the President with the advice and consent of the Senate,[73] the U.S. may also enter into "executive agreements" which are made by the President acting alone.[74] Both types of agreements are treaties for the purposes of international law. In *U.S.* v. *Pink*[75] the Supreme Court stated: "A treaty is a Law of the Land under the supremacy clause (Art. VI, cl. 2) of the Constitution. Such international compacts and agreements as the Litvinoff Assignment [an executive agreement] have a similar dignity." Whereas subsequent federal legislation will override an executive agreement, it is not clear whether an executive agreement will supersede prior federal legislation.[76] In *Territory of Hawaii* v. *Ho*[77] the Supreme Court of the Territory of Hawaii held that an executive agreement overrode a subsequent inconsistent law of the Territory.

4. *THE EXECUTIVE CERTIFICATE*

Notes

1. *British practice*. Oppenheim[78] states: "It is the practice of British Courts to accept as conclusive statements of the Foreign Office relating to certain categories of questions of fact in the field of international affairs. These include: (a) the question whether a foreign State or Government has been recognised by the United Kingdom either *de facto* or *de jure*, (b) the question whether recognition has been granted to conquest by another State or to other changes of territorial title, and, generally, whether certain

---

[69] 175 U.S. 677 (1900).
[70] 265 U.S. 332 at p. 341 (1924).
[71] 205 U.S. 309 at p. 321 (1907).
[72] 288 U.S. 102 at pp. 119–120 (1933).
[73] U.S. Constitution, Article II, Section 2.
[74] See below, p. 575.
[75] 315 U.S. 203 at p. 230 (1942).
[76] See *Maria Jeritza Seery* v. *U.S.*, 127 F.Supp. 601 (1955) (U.S. Court of Claims) (Cert. denied, 359, U.S. 943 (1959)) and *U.S.* v. *Guy W. Capps Inc.*, 204 F. 2d 655 (1953) (U.S. Court of Appeals, 4th Circuit). See also Erades and Gould, *International Law and Municipal Law in the Netherlands and in the United States* (1961), pp. 388–390 and 459–460.
[77] 41 Hawaii 565 (1957); 26 I.L.R. 557.
[78] Oppenheim, Vol. I, para. 357a.

territory is under the sovereignty of one foreign State or another; (c) the sovereign status of a foreign State or its monarch, (d) the commencement and termination of a state of war against another country, (e) the question whether a state of war exists with a foreign country or between two foreign countries, (f) the existence of a case for reprisals in maritime war, (g) the question whether a person is entitled to diplomatic status and (h) the existence or extent of British jurisdiction in a foreign country."

The "practice" of the courts, which has only become established in the present century,[79] has been confirmed by statute in two important areas. A Foreign Office certificate is "conclusive evidence" on matters of diplomatic and state immunity under the Diplomatic Privileges Act 1964, s.7, below, p. 280, and the State Immunity Act 1978, s.21, below, p. 251.[80] On the uncertain position concerning certificates respecting the recognition of governments, see below, p. 135.

2. In *The Fagernes*,[81] in which the Court of Appeal asked for and received from the Attorney-General a statement on the question whether a point in the Bristol Channel was regarded by the Crown as British territory, Atkin L.J. stated:

> What is the territory of the Crown is a matter of judicial notice. The Court has, therefore, to inform itself from the best material available. . . . Any definite statement from the proper representative of the Crown as to the territory of the Crown must be treated as conclusive.

Lawrence L.J. took the same position. Bankes L.J. was of the opinion that a statement by the Crown was persuasive but not binding. In *Post Office* v. *Estuary Radio Ltd.*,[82] the Court of Appeal followed the approach of Atkin and Lawrence L.JJ. In *Duff Development Co.* v. *Govt. of Kelantan* [1924] A.C. 797 (H.L.), Lord Sumner based the conclusive nature of certificates upon the "best evidence" rule and, to a lesser degree, the "one voice" doctrine, *i.e.* the doctrine that the courts and the executive should follow the same approach on matters of foreign affairs.

The following statement by Sir Francis Vallat,[83] Legal Adviser to the Foreign Office, suggests another reason why the courts should accept a certificate:

> It is believed that the test of a true certificate is not whether the facts are peculiarly within the knowledge of the Foreign Office or such as the Foreign Office may reasonably be expected to know or which the Foreign Office ought to know in the conduct of its business, but the presence of some element of recognition by Her Majesty's Government.[84] The logic of this position is sound. On matters of pure fact the view of the Foreign Office must be based on the type of evidence normally used to prove facts before a Court, and it is such evidence rather than the certificate that ought in general to be produced before the Court. When, however, it comes to a matter of recognition, there is no source which can state with equal authority what is or is not recognised by the Government.

---

[79] See Lyons (1946) 23 B.Y.I.L. 240.
[80] See also s.1(7) of the Deep Sea Mining (Temporary Provisions) Act 1981, below, p. 370.
[81] [1927] P. 311, 324.
[82] [1968] 2 Q.B. 740.
[83] *International Law and the Practitioner* (1966), p. 54.
[84] *cf. Spinney* v. *Royal Ins. Co.* [1980] 1 Lloyd's Rep. 406 (Q.B.).

CHAPTER 4

PERSONALITY

1. *GENERALLY*

O'CONNELL, INTERNATIONAL LAW

(2nd ed., 1970), Vol. I, pp. 80–82

IT is clear that the word "person" is used to refer to one who is a legal actor, but that it is of no assistance in ascertaining who or what is competent to act. Only the rules of law can determine this, and they may select different entities and endow them with different legal functions, so that it is a mistake to suppose that merely by describing an entity as a "person" one is formulating its capacities in law. . . .

The correct questions should be: (a) Do the rules of international law establish that this claimant to capacity has the capacity which it claims? (b) What exactly is the capacity which it claims and which is allowed to it, or in other words, just what sorts of legal relations may this entity enter into? If the claimant to capacity is a novelty there will be, of course, no rule of international law on the subject at all until it appears and asserts itself, whereupon there arises question (c), should the entity be recognised as having the capacity which it claims to have? Recognition here means acquiescence in the claim by the other parties to international actions. . . .

Capacity implies personality, but always it is capacity *to do those particular acts*. Therefore "personality" as a term is only short-hand for the proposition that an entity is endowed by international law with legal capacity. But entity A may have capacity to perform acts X and Y, but not act Z, entity B to perform acts Y and Z but not act X, and entity C to perform all three.

2. *STATES*[1]

(i) GENERALLY

MONTEVIDEO CONVENTION ON RIGHTS AND DUTIES OF STATES 1933

165 L.N.T.S. 19; U.S.T.S. 881; 4 Malloy 4807; 28 A.J.I.L., Supp., 75 (1934)

Article I

The State as a person of international law should possess the following qualifications: (a) a permanent population; (b) a defined territory; (c) government; and (d) capacity to enter into relations with other States.

---

[1] See Crawford, *The Creation of States in International Law* (1979) and Marek, *Identity and Continuity of States in Public International Law* (2nd ed., 1968).

Notes

1. The Montevideo Convention was adopted by the 7th International Conference of American States. Fifteen Latin American states and the United States are parties to it. The Convention is commonly accepted as reflecting, in general terms, the requirements of statehood at customary international law. There is some evidence, however, to suggest that these requirements, which are concerned solely with the effectiveness of the entity claiming the rights and duties of a state, have recently been supplemented by others—independence achieved (i) in accordance with the principle of self-determination,[2] and (ii) not in the pursuance of racist policies[3]—of a political or moral character.[4] The term "state" may be given a different meaning for the purposes of a particular treaty.[5] The status of protected states is considered separately below, p. 93, as is the role of recognition by other states in the attainment of international personality by a state, below, p. 125.

2. *Population and territory.* There is no lower limit to the size of a state's population and territory. Nauru, for example, has less than 10,000 inhabitants and is only eight square miles in area. The Vatican City has even fewer permanent residents and, whatever domain it may have elsewhere, has less than 100 acres on earth.[6]

There is ample evidence in state practice and in judicial and arbitral decisions to show that to be a state it is not necessary for an entity to have exactly defined or undisputed boundaries, either at the time that it comes into being or subsequently. Israel, for example, is undoubtedly a state although its borders have never been settled.[7] In *Deutsche Continental Gas-Gesellschaft* v. *Polish State*[8] the German-Polish Mixed Arbitral Tribunal said:

> In order to say that a State exists and can be recognised as such . . . it is enough that . . . [its] territory has a sufficient consistency, even though its boundaries have not yet been accurately delimited.

3. *Government.* One of the preliminary questions which arose in the *Aaland Islands* case was the date on which Finland became a state. Finland had been a part of the Russian Empire until the Russian Revolution. When the new Soviet Government issued a manifesto proclaiming the right of all peoples within the Russian Empire to self-determination, the Finnish Diet, or Parliament, declared Finland's independence on December 4, 1917. This was recognised by the Soviet Government but there was opposition within Finland by those, including a section of the army, who continued to support the old Russian régime and to reject the idea of independence. As a result, violence broke out and for a time the government of the new state was able to maintain order only with the help of Soviet troops. The Report of the International Committee of Jurists appointed to consider the case reads (in a passage which bears upon "independence" as well as "government" as requirements of statehood):

> In the midst of revolution and anarchy, certain elements essential to the existence of a State, even some elements of fact, were lacking for a fairly considerable period. Political and social life was disorganised; the authorities were not strong enough to assert themselves; civil war was rife; further, the Diet, the legality of which had been

---

[2] See the Southern Rhodesia case, below, p. 91.

[3] See the Transkei case, below, p. 88.

[4] See Crawford, *op. cit.* at p. 80, n. 1, above, pp. 106 and 226. Crawford also suggests that independence obtained by the use of force contrary to Article 2(4) of the UN Charter may in some cases not give rise to statehood: *ibid.* p. 118; see also, below, pp. 91–92.

[5] On its meaning in the UN Charter, see Higgins, *The Development of International Law through the Political Organs of The United Nations* (1963), pp. 11–57.

[6] See further below, p. 124. On "mini" states generally, see de Smith, *Microstates and Micronesia* (1970).

[7] See below, pp. 176 *et seq.*

[8] (1929) 5 A.D. 11 at p. 15.

disputed by a large section of the people, had been dispersed by the revolutionary party, and the Government had been chased from the capital and forcibly prevented from carrying out its duties; the armed camps and the police were divided into two opposing forces, and Russian troops, and after a time Germans also, took part in the civil war between the inhabitants and between the Red and White Finnish troops. It is, therefore, difficult to say at what exact date the Finnish Republic, in the legal sense of the term, actually became a definitely constituted sovereign State. This certainly did not take place until a stable political organisation had been created, and until the public authorities had become strong enough to assert themselves throughout the territories of the State without the assistance of foreign troops. It would appear that it was in May 1918, that the civil war ended and that the foreign troops began to leave the country, so that from that time onwards it was possible to re-establish order and normal political and social life, little by little.[9]

Was the Republic of the Congo (now Zaïre) a state in July 1960 when law and order broke down immediately following its independence?[10] State practice suggests that the requirement of a "stable political organisation" in control of the territory of the state does not apply during a civil war (*e.g.* the Spanish Civil War) after a state has established itself.

4. For a list of most of the states in the international community, who now total over 160, see the list of members of the United Nations, Appendix II, below. Other states are Switzerland, Nauru, Tonga, Kiribati, Tuvalu, the European "ministates" of Liechtenstein,[11] Monaco,[12] San Marino[12] and the Vatican City[13]; Territories the legal status of which is disputed include South West Africa/Namibia,[14] the Transkei,[15] Taiwan[16] and North and South Korea.[17]

5. *The Federal Republic of Germany (West Germany) and the German Democratic Republic (East Germany).*[18] On June 5, 1945, France, the United Kingdom, the United States and the U.S.S.R., "acting by authority of their respective Governments and in the interests of the United Nations," assumed "supreme authority with respect to Germany, including all the powers possessed by the German Government, the High Command and any state, municipal, or local government or authority."[19] It was expressly stated that the assumption of the above powers "does not effect the annexation of Germany."[20] On the same day, a Four Power Statement provided:

(i) In the period when Germany is carrying out the basic requirements of unconditional surrender, supreme authority in Germany will be exercised, on instructions from their Governments, by the Soviet, British, United States, and French Commanders-in-Chief, each in his own zone of occupation, and also jointly, in matters affecting Germany as a whole. The four Commanders-in-Chief will together con-

[9] L.N.O.J., Special Supp. No. 3, p. 3 (1920).
[10] See below, p. 697.
[11] See below, p. 92.
[12] Monaco and San Marino are states with close treaty relations with France and Italy respectively: see O'Connell, *International Law* (2nd ed., 1970), Vol. I, pp. 290–291.
[13] See above, p. 81 and below, p. 124. Andorra is not a state, but, by a 1278 treaty, "a 'fief' under the joint suzerainty of the President of the French Republic and the Bishop of Urgel (Spain)": 1 Whiteman 277.
[14] See below, p. 103.
[15] See below, p. 88.
[16] See below, p. 84.
[17] See below, p. 682.
[18] See Mann, 16 I.C.L.Q. 760 (1967). On the status of Berlin, see Bathhurst (1962) 38 B.Y.I.L. 255.
[19] 1 Whiteman 325.
[20] *Ibid.*

stitute the Control Council. Each Commander-in-Chief will be assisted by a political adviser.

(ii) The Control Council whose decisions shall be unanimous, will ensure appropriate uniformity of action by the Commanders-in-Chief in their respective zones of occupation and will reach agreed decisions on the chief questions affecting Germany as a whole.[21]

With regard to foreign affairs the Four Powers acted jointly for Germany (e.g. in making treaties on its behalf) through their Foreign Offices. The United States Department of State analysed the nature of the government of Germany at this time as follows:

While the Hitler government and the Doenitz government had disappeared, there was from the time of the conquest a military government of the Allies, distinct from the governments of their respective countries though unilaterally receiving instructions from those countries. The relationship was analogous to that of the governor of a protectorate and his home government. The governments of the United Kingdom, of France, of the United States and of the Soviet Union were neither individually nor collectively the government of Germany. There was a distinct government of Germany, even though it was not German in personnel or origin.[22]

Disagreement among the Four Powers caused the breakdown of the Allied Control system in 1948. In 1949, the Western Allies transferred most of their powers to the Bonn Government of the Federal Republic of Germany (F.R.G.) and the U.S.S.R. acted similarly in creating the German Democratic Republic (G.D.R.). In 1954, the U.S.S.R. declared the G.D.R. to be a sovereign state. The Western Allies responded as follows:

This statement [by the U.S.S.R.] . . . does not alter the actual situation in the Soviet Zone. The Soviet Government still retains effective control there. The three governments represented in the Allied High Commission will continue to regard the Soviet Union as the responsible power for the Soviet Zone of Germany. These governments do not recognize the sovereignty of the East German régime which is not based on free elections, and do not intend to deal with it as a government. They believe that this attitude will be shared by other states, who, like themselves, will continue to recognize the Government of the Federal Republic as the only freely elected and legally constituted government in Germany.[23]

In 1955, the Western Allies granted full sovereign powers to the Federal Republic of Germany subject to retained powers concerning the making of a peace treaty.[24]

In 1972, the F.R.G. and the G.D.R. recognised each other by treaty as sovereign states.[25] In 1973, both states were admitted to the United Nations and the Western Occupying Powers recognised and entered into diplomatic relations with the G.D.R. At the time of the signature of the 1972 treaty, the F.R.G. indicated unilaterally that "this treaty does not conflict with the political objective of the Federal Republic of Germany to work for a state of peace in Europe in which the German nation will recover its unity in free self-determination."[26] In a joint Four Power Declaration,[27] the Occupying Powers indicated acceptance of the 1972 treaty and affirmed the continuance of their rights and responsibilities as occupying powers.

[21] *Ibid.* p. 326.
[22] *Ibid.* p. 333.
[23] *Ibid.* p. 337.
[24] See the 1952 Convention on Relations between the Three Powers and the F.R.G., U.K.T.S. 10 (1959), Cmnd. 653; 331 U.N.T.S. 327.
[25] 1972 Treaty on the Bases of Relations between the F.R.G. and the G.D.R., 12 I.L.M. 16 (1973).
[26] Letter of December 21, 1972, from Mr. Bahr (F.R.G.) to Mr. Kohl (G.D.R.); *Keesings Archives*, p. 25707.
[27] Declaration of November 9, 1972; *Keesings Archives*, p. 25623.

6. An entity is not a state if it declines to be one, as in the case of Taiwan (Formosa). Both the Peking and Taiwan Governments claim to be the one government of the one state of China, with Taiwan as a part of it. This situation developed after the 1949 revolution, following which the defeated Nationalist Government withdrew to Taiwan, *cf.* below, p. 138. In 1972, a joint communiqué[28] was issued by the Governments of the People's Republic and the United States after President Nixon's visit to Peking in which it was agreed that Taiwan was a part of China and that the question of the government of China was an internal matter, a position from which the Taiwan Government would not dissent. Crawford[29] suggests that Taiwan's "status is that of a consolidated local *de facto* government in a civil war situation" and that, although not a state, it has a "limited status in international law" by which it can make treaties and otherwise commit the state of China in respect of the territory which it effectively controls.

7. It is accepted that a new state is automatically bound by international law upon attaining statehood.[30] Is this because it is deemed to consent to its being so bound? Or is it because there is a rule that says that it shall be so bound? If the latter is the case, why is that rule binding upon it? Is a new state's position different from that of an individual born into a state and automatically subject to its laws?[31]

(ii) INDEPENDENCE

AUSTRO-GERMAN CUSTOMS UNION CASE

Advisory Opinion. P.C.I.J. Reports, Series A/B, No. 41 (1931)

By a Protocol of 1931 Austria and Germany reached preliminary agreement on a customs union establishing free trade between the two states. The proposed union "caused such disturbance in international relations that it is no exaggeration to speak of a European crisis."[32]

Article 88 of the Treaty of Saint-Germain 1919 provided:

> The independence of Austria is inalienable otherwise than with the consent of the Council of the League of Nations. Consequently, Austria undertakes in the absence of the consent of the said Council to abstain from any act which might directly or indirectly or by any means whatever compromise her independence. . . .

A Protocol of 1922 concerning the economic independence of Austria in particular was to the same effect. The Council of the League of Nations asked the P.C.I.J. whether Austria would be acting contrary to these provisions if it went ahead with the proposed union. The Court advised, by eight votes to seven, that the union would be incompatible with the Protocol of 1922. Seven judges in the majority also thought that it would be contrary to Article 88 of the Treaty of Saint-Germain. The following extracts are limited to the Court's discussion of the nature of independence as applied to states. It has been

---

[28] 11 I.L.M. 443, 445 (1972). *cf.* the British statement, *Hansard*, H.C., Vol. 833, Col. 32. March 13, 1972. See also the Foreign Office statement in *Reel* v. *Holder*, below, p. 150. The U.S.A. continued to recognise the Taiwan Government as the Government of China until 1979, see below, p. 132.

[29] *Op. cit.* at p. 80, n. 1, above, pp. 149–150. See also *Luigi Monta of Genoa* v. *Cechofracht Co. Ltd.*, below, at p. 148.

[30] This is subject to any effect that recognition has; see below, pp. 125 *et seq*. Although new post-colonial states have objected to particular areas of international law and argue for different rules in those areas, they do not reject the system as a whole.

[31] See Brierly, p. 52; Fitzmaurice, *loc. cit.* at p. 19, n. 1, above, pp. 165–167; Kelsen, *Principles of International Law* (2nd ed., 1967), p. 247. See further, p. 375 below.

[32] Fachiri (1932) 13 B.Y.I.L. 68.

argued that in its assessment of the situation the Court placed as much emphasis upon the likelihood of a political union occurring as a further, separate step after the establishment of the proposed customs union as it did upon the customs union itself.[33]

Opinion of the Court

. . . irrespective of the definition of the independence of States which may be given by legal doctrine or may be adopted in particular instances in the practice of States, the independence of Austria, according to Article 88 of the Treaty of Saint-Germain, must be understood to mean the continued existence of Austria within her present frontiers as a separate State with sole right of decision in all matters economic, political, financial or other with the result that that independence is violated, as soon as there is any violation there, either in the economic, political, or any other field, these different aspects of independence being in practice one and indivisible. . . .

By "alienation," as mentioned in Article 88, must be understood any voluntary act by the Austrian State which would cause it to lose its independence or which would modify its independence in that its sovereign will would be subordinated to the will of another Power or particular group of Powers, or would even be replaced by such will.

SEPARATE OPINION OF JUDGE ANZILOTTI[34] . . . the independence of Austria within the meaning of Article 88 is nothing else but the existence of Austria, within the frontiers laid down by the Treaty of Saint-Germain, as a separate State and not subject to the authority of any other State or group of States. Independence as thus understood is really no more than the normal condition of States according to international law; it may also be described as *sovereignty* (*suprema potestas*), or *external sovereignty*, by which is meant that the State has over it no other authority than that of international law.

The conception of independence, regarded as the normal characteristic of States as subjects of international law, cannot be better defined than by comparing it with the exceptional and, to some extent, abnormal class of States known as "dependent States." These are States subject to the authority of one or more States. The idea of dependence therefore necessarily implies a relation between a superior State (suzerain, protector, etc.) and an inferior or subject State (vassal, *protégé*, etc.); the relation between the State which can legally impose its will and the State which is legally compelled to submit to that will. Where there is no such relation of superiority and subordination, it is impossible to speak of dependence within the meaning of international law.

It follows that the legal conception of independence has nothing to do with a State's subordination to international law or with the numerous and constantly increasing states of *de facto* dependence which characterise the relation of one country to other countries.

It also follows that the restrictions upon a State's liberty, whether arising out of ordinary international law or contractual engagements, do not as such in the least affect its independence. As long as these restrictions do not place the State under the legal authority of another State, the former remains an independent State however extensive and burdensome those obligations may be.

[33] See Borchard, 25 A.J.I.L. 711 at p. 715 (1931).
[34] Judge Anzilotti was one of the seven judges in the majority who found the proposed union incompatible with Art. 88 of the Treaty of Saint-Germain as well as with the Protocol of 1922.

This is obviously the standpoint of the Treaty of Saint-Germain when it proclaims the independence of Austria despite the many serious restrictions it imposes upon her freedom in the economic, military and other spheres. These restrictions do not put Austria under the authority of the other contracting States, which means that Austria is an independent State within the meaning of international law. . . .

Notes

1. When the Montevideo Convention[35] refers to "capacity to enter into relations with other states" as a requirement of statehood it is referring to independence as that term is understood in Judge Anzilotti's opinion, *i.e.* independence in law from the authority of any other state (and hence the capacity in law to conduct relations with other states).

2. In the *North Atlantic Coast Fisheries Case* (1910),[36] the Permanent Court of Arbitration rejected a United States submission in the following terms: ". . . to hold that the United States, the grantee of the fishing right, has a voice under the treaty granting the right in the preparation of fishing legislation, involves recognition of a right in that country to participate in the internal legislation of Great Britain and her Colonies and to that extent would reduce these countries to a state of dependence." Elsewhere, dealing with the same submission, the Court stated: ". . . the exercise of such a right of consent by the United States would predicate an abandonment of independence in this respect by Great Britain. . . ."[37]

3. In the *Wimbledon Case*[38] the Permanent Court of International Justice stated: "No doubt any convention creating an obligation of this kind places a restriction upon the exercise of the sovereign rights of the State, in the sense that it requires them to be exercised in a certain way. But the right of entering into international engagements is an attribute of State sovereignty."

4. Units within a *federal state* may or may not be allowed by the federal constitution to conduct their own foreign affairs. If, and to the extent that, they are allowed to do so, such units are regarded by international law as having international personality. For example, the Republics of the U.S.S.R. are all entitled in law to conduct their own foreign affairs and two of them—Byleorussia and the Ukraine—have to a small extent done so.[39] Such units are not states but international persons *sui generis*.

5. See further on legal independence, the materials on protected states, below, p. 93.

FRENCH INDEMNITY OF 1831

Moore, 5 Int.Arb. 4447 at p. 4472

France paid the U.S. compensation to be distributed among U.S. nationals in respect of certain damage caused during the Napoleonic Wars. Some claims were made that related to injuries apparently caused by Holland and Denmark and the question arose whether France was responsible for them. The report of the U.S. Commission that distributed the compensation was supplemented by notes by Commissioner Kane indicating the general principles upon which the Commission had relied. The following extract from these notes concerns the above question.

---

[35] Above, p. 80.
[36] Scott, *Hague Court Reports* 141 at p. 170.
[37] *Ibid.* p. 167.
[38] P.C.I.J. Reports, Series A, No. 1, p. 25 (1923).
[39] See Dolan, 4 I.C.L.Q. 629 (1955). Both of the Republics mentioned are members of the UN, see below, Appendix II. See also Art. 32 of the Basic Law of the F.R.G. on the treaty-making power of the West German *Länder*.

1. Holland, after some ten years of political changes, during which though nominally independent she was tributary to all the projects of France, had received in the month of June 1806, a king of the Napoleon family. . . . The form of distinct sovereignties was presented to the public eye; but the energies of the Dutch people were directed more than ever to the advancement of the imperial policy. At last, in the concluding month of 1809, a new crisis approached. At a moment when the finances of Holland were in a state of extreme embarrassment, she was required to destroy her commerce with foreign nations, which formed the principal source of her revenues. Louis ventured to remonstrate. . . . He was reminded in reply, that the country of which he was sovereign was a French conquest, and that 'his highest and imprescriptible duties were to the imperial crown;' . . .

The tenth article of the [Franco-Dutch] treaty of 16th March 1810 was as follows: 'All merchandize, which has arrived in American vessels in the ports of Holland since the 1st of January 1809, shall be placed under sequestration, and shall belong to France, to be disposed of according to circumstances and to the political relations with the United States.' . . .

It was for the value of these cargoes, that reclamations were made before the commissioners. The brief account which has been given of the political condition of Holland from the year 1809 till it was formally merged in the French empire [in July 1810], sufficiently explains the reason for allowing them. Holland was already a dependent kingdom, and Louis a merely nominal sovereign. The treaty was a form; in substance it was an imperial decree.

2. The spoliations to which Denmark ministered were of a different character. . . .

It may be, that the conduct of King Frederic was dictated by his anxiety to conciliate the favour of the French emperor; or perhaps he was moved by the portion of the spoil which might fall into his hands: we had nothing to do with his motives or his fears. The act was his own: the kingdom of Denmark was then, as now, independent. . . .

This then is the broad distinction between the cases of Holland and Denmark. The former was a nominal, the latter an actual sovereignty. The intervention of one was merely formal, and was exacted by force; the other was the voluntary pander to French avidity.

Notes

1. As this case suggests, there may come a point where *factual* dependence by one state upon another is so great that it is really no more than a "puppet" state and will not be treated as meeting the requirement of independence. Lauterpacht proposed the following:

The first condition of statehood is that there must exist a government actually independent of that of any other State. . . . If a community, after having detached itself from the parent State, were to become, legally or actually, a satellite of another State, it would not be fulfilling the primary condition of independence and would not accordingly be entitled to recognition as a State.[40]

He gave "Manchukuo" as an example of an entity that was not a state according to this test. "Manchukuo" came into being after Japan invaded Manchuria, a province of

[40] Lauterpacht, *Recognition in International Law* (1948), pp. 26–29.

China, in 1931.[41] The following year Japan recognised "Manchukuo" as an independent state. Its territory was that of Manchuria. The League of Nations sent the Lytton Commission to "Manchukuo" to discover the facts. The Commission reported:

> In the "Government of Manchukuo," Japanese officials are prominent and Japanese advisers are attached to all important Departments. Although the Premier and his Ministers are all Chinese, the heads of the various Boards of General Affairs, which, in the organisation of the new State, exercise the greatest measure of actual power, are Japanese. At first they were designated as advisers, but recently those holding the most important posts have been made full Government officials on the same basis as the Chinese. . . . They are doubtless not under the orders of the Tokyo Government, and their policy has not always coincided with the official policy either of the Japanese Government or of the Headquarters of the Kwantung Army. But in the case of all-important problems, these officials and advisers, some of whom were able to act more or less independently in the first days of the new organisation, have been constrained more and more to follow the direction of Japanese official authority. This authority, in fact, by reason of the occupation of the country by its troops, by the dependence of the "Manchukuo Government" on those troops for the maintenance of its authority both internally and externally, in consequence, too, of the more and more important role entrusted to the South Manchuria Railway Company in the management of the railways under the jurisdiction of the "Manchukuo Government," and finally by the presence of its consuls, as liaison agents, in the most important urban centres, possesses in every contingency the means of exercising an irresistible pressure.[42]

The Commission did not pronounce upon the specific question whether "Manchukuo" was an independent state. In the light of the Commission's Report, on February 24, 1933, the League of Nations Assembly resolved that "the sovereignty over Manchuria belongs to China."[43] By 1939, only El Salvador, Germany, Hungary, Italy and Japan had recognised "Manchukuo." Manchuria was returned to China after the Second World War. Was it at any time an independent state according to the *Customs Union Case*? Suppose that at the present time an existing state were to come under the influence of another state to such an extent (in a military, economic, or other sense) that the other state could dictate the composition of its Government and its policies? Would that state continue to be independent for the purposes of statehood?[44] Was Czechoslovakia in 1969?[45] Or is Afghanistan now?[46]

2. In 1976, South Africa, in pursuance of its homelands or bantustan policy, granted independence to the Transkei, the homeland of the Xhosa people.[47] Legal sovereignty over the Transkei was transferred to the new African Government. It is in full control in law of the internal and external affairs of the Transkei, although provision is made for appeals from the Transkei Supreme Court to be heard by the Appellate Division of the Supreme Court of South Africa. The Transkeian nationality arrangements have given rise to disputes between South African and the Transkei Government (which broke off diplomatic relations with South Africa between 1978 and 1980 because of them and of

---

[41] See 1 Hackworth 333–338.

[42] L.N.Doc. C. 663. M 320. 1932, VII.

[43] L.N.O.J. Special Supp. No. 112, p. 75. On the Stimson Doctrine of Non-Recognition, which was prompted by the "Manchukuo" situation, see below, p. 172.

[44] See the discussion in Marek, *loc. cit.* at p. 80, n. 1, above, pp. 162–180. On the relative nature of the independence of states, see Hart, *The Concept of Law* (1961), pp. 215–221.

[45] See below, p. 652.

[46] See below, p. 652.

[47] Other homelands have been given their independence also: Bophuthatswana (1977), Venda (1979), and Ciskei (1981).

related problems of migrant labour). By those arrangements Xhosa or Sotho speaking South African citizens lost that citizenship and were made Transkeian citizens, even though they lived in South Africa. As a result, about half of the citizens of the Transkei are former South African citizens who continue to live and work in South Africa. The Transkei receives considerable economic aid (approximately 90 per cent. of its total revenue) from South Africa. On October 26, 1976, the United Nations General Assembly, by a vote of 134 to 0, with 1 abstention,

> (i) *Strongly condemns* the establishment of bantustans as designed to consolidate the inhuman policies of *apartheid*, to destroy the territorial integrity of the country, to perpetuate white minority domination and to dispossess the African people of South Africa of their inalienable rights;
> (ii) *Rejects* the declaration of "independence" of the Transkei and declares it invalid;
> (iii) *Calls upon* all Governments to deny any form of recognition to the so-called independent Transkei and to refrain from having any dealings with the so-called independent Transkei or other bantustans;
> (iv) *Requests* all States to take effective measures to prohibit all individuals, corporations and other institutions under their jurisdiction from having any dealings with the so-called independent Transkei or other bantustans.[48]

No state has recognised the Transkei as a state, apart from South Africa. One interpretation of state practice in the matter is that "the Transkei, as an entity created directly pursuant to a fundamentally illegal policy of *apartheid*, is for that reason, and irrespective of its degree of formal or actual independence, not a State."[49] If the non-recognition of the Transkei by the international community is interpreted in this way (and not, under a constitutive theory of recognition, as a collective policy decision not to recognise an entity that meets the requirements of statehood), there will come a time when, if the Transkei and other independent homelands survive the pressure of non-recognition, the same problem as arises with the illegal but successful acquisition of territory will have to be faced. In that context, international law has ultimately "faced the facts" and, by a process of general recognition, acknowledged the changed situation.[50]

BRITISH RECOGNITION OF THE FORMER SPANISH COLONIES IN LATIN AMERICA

Smith, *Great Britain and the Law of Nations* (Vol. I, 1932), p. 149

In 1808, following the invasion of Spain by France, the Spanish colonies in Latin America successfully rebelled. After a while, the question of their recognition by other

---

[48] G.A. Resn., G.A.O.R., 31st Session, Supp. 39, p. 10. The U.S.A. abstained; although agreeing with the recommendation that the Transkei not be recognised, it considered the resolution too strongly worded in other respects. In 1981, the Security Council condemned the independence of the Ciskei as "totally invalid" and called on "all Governments to deny any form of recognition to the so-called independent bantustans": 19 *UN Chronicle*, February 1982, p. 42.

[49] Crawford, *op. cit.* at p. 80, n. 1, above, p. 226.

[50] See the extract from Jennings, below, p. 174. Problems arise in such a case immediately upon independence. Who, for example, has jurisdiction over foreign vessels passing through the waters off the Transkeian coast? Who may give permission for flight over the Transkei or for the entry of individuals into it? Note that the travel documents issued by the Transkeian Government "are not acceptable for U.K. immigration control purposes as evidence of identity and nationality or as valid passports": *Hansard*, H.L., Vol. 407, cols. 154–155. March 17, 1980; *U.K.M.I.L. 1980* (1980) 51 B.Y.I.L. 368.

states arose. Great Britain's decision to recognise certain of them, taken only after considerable hesitation in a delicate political situation, was announced and justified in the following dispatch of December 31, 1824, from Canning which the British Minister in Madrid was instructed to read to the Spanish Minister.

In looking at the present situation of Mexico and Columbia, and comparing it with that of Spain, every impartial judgment will be convinced of the utter hopelessness of the success of any attempt to bring those Provinces again under subjection to the Mother Country; nor can it be denied that a much longer continuance of so large a portion of the Globe without any recognized existence, or any definite connexion with the Governments of Europe, whose subjects are in daily intercourse with them, must be productive of the greatest embarrassments to such Governments, and greatly injurious to the Interests of their Subjects, as well as to the General Commercial Interests of the World. . . .

In Peru, a struggle is still maintained in behalf of the Mother Country. With regard to Peru, therefore, a just consideration for the rights of Spain, and for the chance, whatever it may be, of the practical assertion of them, forbids any interference on the part of His Majesty's Government. . . .

With Mexico and Columbia, . . . His Majesty. . . has been pleased to decide that measures should be taken forthwith for negotiating Commercial Treaties. The effect of such Treaties, when severally ratified by His Majesty, will be a Diplomatick Recognition of the 'De facto' Governments of those three Countries. . . .

On March 25, 1825, Canning answered Spanish protests against the British decision in the following dispatch to the Spanish Minister in London.

To come now to the second charge against Gt. Britain: the alleged violation of general international Law. . . .

To continue to call that a possession of Spain, in which all Spanish occupation and power had been actually extinguished and effaced, could render no practical service to the Mother Country;—but it would have risked the peace of the World. For all political communities are responsible to other political communities for their conduct:—that is, they are bound to perform the ordinary international duties, and to afford redress for any violation of the rights of others by their citizens or subjects.

Now, either the Mother Country must have continued responsible for acts over which it could no longer exercise the shadow of a control; or the Inhabitants of those countries, whose independent political existence was, in fact, established, but to whom the acknowledgement of that independence was denied, must have been placed in a situation in which they were either wholly irresponsible for their actions, or were to be visited for such of those actions as might furnish ground of complaint to other Nations, with the punishment due to Pirates and Outlaws.

If the former of these alternatives, the total irresponsibility of unrecognized States—be too absurd to be maintained; and if the latter—the treatment of their Inhabitants as Pirates and Outlaws be too monstrous to be applied, for any indefinite length of time, to a large portion of the habitable Globe:—no other choice remained for Gt. Britain, or for any other Country having intercourse with the Spanish American Provinces but to recognize, in due time, their political existence as States, and thus to bring them within the pale of those rights and duties, which civilized Nations are bound mutually to respect, and are entitled reciprocally to claim from each other. . . .

Notes

1. These are cases of the seizure of independence by force. The United States had taken its decision to recognise the Spanish colonies in 1822. It explained that "the Government of the United States, far from consulting the dictates of a policy questionable in its morality, yielded to an obligation of duty of the highest order by recognising as independent states nations which, after deliberately asserting their right to that character, have maintained and established it against all the resistance which had been, or could be brought to oppose it."[51] Oppenheim states that:

> no hard and fast rule can be laid down as regards the time when it can be said that a State created by revolution has established itself safely and permanently. Indication of such safe and permanent establishment may be found either in the fact that the revolutionary State has utterly defeated the mother-State, or that the mother-State has ceased to make efforts to subdue the revolutionary State, or even that the mother-State, in spite of its efforts, is apparently incapable of bringing the revolutionary State back under its sway. . . . Recognition by the mother-State is conclusive proof of the fact that the new State has finally established its independence.[52]

2. In 1965, Southern Rhodesia, a British self-governing colony, declared its independence. The rebel Smith Government sought in this way to continue white rule in Rhodesia. This would inevitably have given way to black majority rule if the normal constitutional progress towards independence had been allowed to take its course. The United Kingdom continued to claim sovereignty and applied economic and political sanctions short of the use of armed force to re-assert its authority. The United Nations Security Council imposed a comprehensive régime of economic sanctions upon the rebel Government and "[called] upon all states not to recognise this illegal racist minority régime."[53] No state recognised Southern Rhodesia as a state. After guerrilla warfare, a political settlement was reached that led to independence in 1980 for Zimbabwe in accordance with the principle of self-determination. Thereupon, Security Council sanctions were terminated. From 1965 onwards, Southern Rhodesia could claim to have met the requirements of statehood in the Montevideo Convention. The Southern Rhodesian case may, however, indicate that an additional requirement of statehood has evolved, *viz.* that independence be achieved in accordance with the principle of self-determination.[54]

3. What if independence is seized by force by rebels with the assistance of another state contrary to Article 2(4), United Nations Charter or to the principle of non-intervention, as to which, see below, Chap. 11. Crawford[55] suggests:

[51] I Moore 86.

[52] Oppenheim, Vol. I, para. 72. Oppenheim states in a footnote: "Thus the recognition of the United States by France in 1778 was precipitate. [*Ed.* British armed resistance continued until Yorktown in 1781.] But when in 1782 Great Britain herself recognised the independence of the United States, other States could accord recognition too without giving offence to Great Britain": *ibid.* p. 129, n. 2.

[53] See below, p. 690. The General Assembly similarly called upon "all states not to recognise any form of independence in Southern Rhodesia without the prior establishment of a government based on majority rule in accordance with General Assembly resolution 1514 (XX)": G.A. Resn. 2379 (XXVI), October 28, 1968: 7 I.L.M. 1401 (1968). The resolution was adopted by 92 votes to 2, with 17 abstentions.

[54] *cf.* Crawford, *op. cit.* at p. 80, n. 1, above, p. 106. On the principle of self-determination, see below, p. 95. See further the discussion of the situation concerning the Transkei, above, p. 88.

[55] *Op. cit.* at p. 80, n.1 above, p. 118. Footnote omitted. This is one of a list of conclusions that "are to some extent *de lege ferenda.*" On the rule as to title to illegally obtained territory, see below, p. 172.

Illegality of intervention in aid of independence of a self-determination unit does not then, as a matter of law, impair the status of the local unit. On the other hand, *semble*, where a State illegally intervenes in and foments the secession of part of a metropolitan State, other States are under the same duty of non-recognition as in the case of illegal annexation of territory. An entity created in violation of the rules relating to the use of force in such circumstances will not be regarded as a State.

Thus, Indian assistance to Bangladesh, although arguably illegal, did not impair the latter's statehood given that Bangladesh was, in Crawford's view, a unit to which the principle of self-determination applied.[56] The Turkish Federated State of Cyprus could not claim to be a state, supposing that Turkey's intervention in 1974 was illegal, unless it too was a self-determination unit.[57] Would the same sentence of the above extract apply to the case of "Manchukuo"?[58] Such cases do not often arise in practice; most commonly the aggressor annexes the territory itself.

ADMISSION OF LIECHTENSTEIN TO THE LEAGUE OF NATIONS[59]

Report of the 5th Committee to the First Assembly of the L.N., December 6, 1920.
1 Hackworth 48–49

Liechtenstein sought admission to the League of Nations. Membership was open to "any fully self-governing State, Dominion or Colony . . . provided that it shall give effective guarantees of its sincere intention to observe its international obligations, and shall accept such regulations as may be prescribed by the League in regard to its military, naval and air forces and armaments."[60] The application was rejected in view of the following Report.

The Government of the Principality of Liechtenstein has been recognised *de jure* by many states. It has concluded a number of Treaties with various States. . . .

The Principality of Liechtenstein possesses a stable Government and fixed frontiers. . . .

There can be no doubt that juridically the Principality . . . is a sovereign State, but by reason of her limited area, small population and her geographical position, she has chosen to depute to others some of the attributes of sovereignty. For instance she has contracted with other Powers for the control of her Customs, the administrations of her Posts, Telegraphs and Telephone Services, for the diplomatic representation of her subjects in foreign countries, other than Switzerland and Austria, and for final decisions in certain judicial cases.

Liechtenstein has no army.

For the above reasons, we are of opinion that the Principality of Liechtenstein could not discharge all the international obligations which would be imposed upon her by the Covenant.

---

[56] *Ibid.* p. 117. For the facts, see below, p. 650.
[57] On the Turkish invasion of Cyprus, see below, p. 655.
[58] On "Manchukuo," see above, p. 87.
[59] On the status of Liechtenstein, see Kohn, 61 A.J.I.L. 547 (1967).
[60] Article 1(2), L.N. Covenant.

Note

Liechtenstein has not applied for membership of the United Nations. In 1949, it was allowed to become a party to the Statute of the International Court of Justice,[61] which is open only to "states," despite some opposition. The Byleorussian representative in the General Assembly is reported as saying:

It [Liechtenstein] had formed a customs union with Switzerland, which country took care of Liechtenstein's post and telegraph service and its diplomatic representation . . . it must be considered a dependent State and therefore [not eligible].[62]

Liechtenstein was a party to the *Nottebohm Case*[63] in 1955.

(iii) PROTECTED STATES, ETC.

BATY, PROTECTORATES AND MANDATES

(1921–22) 3 B.Y.I.L. 109

[In the nineteenth century] Europe was coming into official and formal contact with Africa and Asia: that is, with peoples whose civilisation is very different from that of Europe. These peoples could neither be ignored as States or treated quite on the footing of ordinary States. The formula which was found convenient to express the relations between them and the State which wished to exploit their resources was that of Protection. And this meant Protection . . . involving a certain measure of control, and a definite diminution (if not a total deprivation) of sovereignty . . . in many cases it involved the loss of control over foreign relations and the almost inevitable disappearance of the protected State from the list of States known to international law. Of this kind of Oriental arrangement, the States of Khiva,[64] Zanzibar, Madagascar, Tonquin,[65] Tunis may be cited as examples . . . [Protection was also] . . . to afford a forum for dealing with the tribes of Africa who enjoyed not a different civilisation, but no civilisation. Their chiefs entered into treaties of "protection," which not only amounted to the resignation of all independent status, but are universally recognised as such. . . . Either an African protectorate means nothing, or it means annexation.[66]

NATIONALITY DECREES IN TUNIS AND MOROCCO CASE

Advisory Opinion. P.C.I.J. Reports, Series B, No. 4, p. 27 (1923)

Opinion of the Court

The extent of the powers of a protecting State in the Territory of a protected State depends, first, upon the Treaties between the protecting State and the

[61] See Article 93(2), UN Charter, Appendix I, below.
[62] G.A.O.R., 4th Session, 6th Committee, 174th Meeting, p. 215. Was it at all surprising that Byleorussia should have been the member to have raised this point?
[63] Below, p. 442. See also the *Gerliczy Case*, Hudson, 4 *World Court Reports* 495.
[64] *Ed.* In Asia. Now a part of the Uzbek S.S.R. in the U.S.S.R.
[65] *Ed.* Tongking. Now a part of Vietnam.
[66] *Ed.* Examples in former British Africa were Northern Rhodesia (Zambia) and Nyasaland (Malawi). As Batty suggests, it would be incorrect to think of any residual statehood vesting in the peoples of these colonial protectorates.

protected State establishing the Protectorate, and, secondly, upon the conditions under which the Protectorate has been recognised by third Powers as against whom there is an intention to rely on the provisions of these treaties. In spite of common features possessed by Protectorates under international law, they have individual legal characteristics resulting from the special conditions under which they were created, and the stage of their development.

RIGHTS OF NATIONALS OF THE UNITED STATES IN MOROCCO CASE

U.S. v. France

I.C.J. Reports 1952, p. 176

Judgment of the Court

It is not disputed by the French Government that Morocco, even under the Protectorate, has retained its personality as a State in international law. . . .

Under this Treaty [the Treaty of Fez 1912, establishing the protectorate], Morocco remained a sovereign State but it made an arrangement of a contractural nature whereby France undertook to exercise certain sovereign powers in the name and on behalf of Morocco, and, in principle, all of the international relations of Morocco. France, in the exercise of this function, is bound not only by the provisions of the Treaty of Fez, but also by all treaty obligations to which Morocco had been subject before the Protectorate and which have not since been terminated or suspended by arrangement with the interested States. . . .

[The Court concluded that certain treaties made by France for Morocco under the Treaty of Fez] must therefore be regarded as agreements made by a protecting Power, within the scope of its authority, touching the affairs of and intending to bind the protected State. . . . In these circumstances, it is necessary to hold that these arrangements bound and enured to the benefit of Morocco. . . .

Notes

1. How does the status of Liechtenstein[67] differ from that of Morocco under the Treaty of Fez? Note that Western Samoa, which became independent in 1962, agreed by a 1962 Treaty of Friendship[68] with New Zealand that the latter should assist Western Samoa in the conduct of its foreign relations but:

in such a manner as will in no way impair the rights of the Government of Western Samoa to formulate its own foreign policies.

Cyprus has been accepted as a state despite the right of intervention in its affairs allowed to its guaranteeing powers.[69]

2. *Protected states* are a dying species which few seem anxious to preserve. Remaining examples include the British protected state of Brunei[70] and the Indian protected state of Bhutan in the Himalayas.[71]

[67] See above, p. 92.   [68] N.Z.T.S. 5 (1962).
[69] See below, p. 655. On the British sovereign bases in Cyprus, see below, p. 197.
[70] Brunei will cease to be a protected state on December 31, 1983.
[71] Article 2 of the 1949 Treaty of Friendship between India and Bhutan, 157 B.F.S.P. 214, reads: "The Government of India undertakes to exercise no interference in the internal

(iv) SELF-DETERMINATION[72]

Note

The principle of self-determination is a controversial one. It has a long history in international relations as a reason for the cession of territory from one state to another and for the use of plebiscites to establish the wishes of the inhabitants in this connection. Under the United Nations Charter, it has been the cornerstone of the General Assembly's decolonisation policy of the 1960s and 1970s. The controversy has concerned the principle's status in international law and its meaning. It was not a part of international law before the United Nations Charter.[73] Soviet[74] and third world writers[75] now regard it as such, as do an increasing number of western writers.[76] Schwarzenberger argues that it "is a formative principle of great potency, but not part and parcel of international customary law."[77] The evidence of the following materials suggests that in the colonial field the point may have been reached where the principle has generated a rule of international law by which the political future of a colonial or similar non-independent territory should be determined in accordance with the wishes of its inhabitants.[78] The 1966 International Covenants on Human Rights[79] give the principle a legal application on a wider front (not limited to the colonial situation) as a matter of treaty law, although precisely what the Covenant provisions entail is not clear.[80] The materials in this section are limited to political self-determination. Economic self-determination is considered in Chapter 8.

DECLARATION ON THE GRANTING OF INDEPENDENCE TO COLONIAL TERRITORIES AND PEOPLES[81]

G.A. Resn. 1514 (XV). December 14, 1960. G.A.O.R. 15th Sess., Supp. 16, p. 66

The General Assembly . . . Declares that

1. The subjection of peoples to alien subjugation, domination and exploitation constitutes a denial of fundamental human rights, is contrary to the Charter of the United Nations and is an impediment to the promotion of world peace and co-operation;

---

administration of Bhutan. On its part the Government of Bhutan agrees to be guided by the advice of the Government of India in regard to its external relations." Bhutan was admitted to the UN in 1971. On "associated states" under the West Indies Act 1967, of which only one (St. Kitts-Nevis) remains, see Broderick, 13 I.C.L.Q. 368 (1968).

[72] See Bowett, 1966 Proc.A.S.I.L. 129; Emerson, 65 A.J.I.L. 459 (1971); *idem*, 1966 Proc.A.S.I.L. 135; Rigo Sureda, *The Evolution of the Right of Self-determination* (1973); Umozurike, *Self-determination in International Law* (1972).

[73] See the report of the International Committee of Jurists in the *Aaland Islands* case, L.N.O.J., Special Supp. No. 3, p. 5 (1920), and Oppenheim, Vol. I, para. 219.

[74] See, *e.g.* Vyshinsky, *The Law of the Soviet State* (1948), p. 349.

[75] See, *e.g.* Nawaz, 1965 Duke L.J. 82.

[76] See, *e.g.* Brownlie, p. 577, and Higgins, *The Development of International Law through the Political Organs of the United Nations* (1963), p. 103.

[77] *Manual of International Law* (6th ed., 1976), p. 59.

[78] On the legality of the use of force to repress a war of national liberation, *i.e.* one aimed at realising the right of self-determination, or to assist it, see below, p. 649.

[79] See below, p. 541.

[80] See Cassesse, in Henkin, ed., *The International Bill of Rights* (1981), Chap. 4.

[81] The resolution was adopted by 89 votes to 0, with nine abstentions. The abstaining states were Australia, Belgium, Dominican Republic, France, Portugal, South Africa, Spain the U.K. and the U.S.A.

2. All peoples have the right to self-determination; by virtue of that right they freely determine their political status and freely pursue their economic, social and cultural development;

3. Inadequacy of political, economic, social or education preparedness should never serve as a pretext for delaying independence;

4. All armed action or repressive measures of all kinds directed against dependent peoples shall cease in order to enable them to exercise peacefully and freely their right to complete independence, and the integrity of their national territory shall be respected;

5. Immediate steps shall be taken, in Trust and Non-Self-Governing Territories or all other territories which have not yet attained independence, to transfer all powers to the peoples of those territories, without any conditions or reservations, in accordance with their freely expressed will and desire, without any distinction as to race, creed or colour, in order to enable them to enjoy complete independence and freedom.

6. Any attempt aimed at the partial or total disruption of the national unity and the territorial integrity of a country is incompatible with the Purposes and Principles of the Charter of the United Nations;

7. All States shall observe faithfully and strictly the provisions of the Charter of the United Nations, the Universal Declaration of Human Rights and the present Declaration on the basis of equality, non-interference in the internal affairs of all States, and respect for the sovereign rights of all peoples and their territorial integrity.

Notes

1. The 1960 Declaration, which has been the continual point of reference in the General Assembly's decolonisation practice,[82] builds upon Articles 1, 55 and 56 of the Charter[83] and has been supplemented by the 1970 Programme of Action for the Full Implementation of the Declaration[84] and the 1970 Declaration on Principles of International Law.[85]

2. Resolution 1514 does not state that title to colonial and similar non-independent territory that is not in accord with the wishes of its people is invalid. The position is instead that "immediate steps" should be taken to achieve independence in accordance with the principle of self-determination. Resolution 1514 proposes self-determination within existing colonial boundaries (para. 6). The post-colonial states in particular have taken the view that it would be too disruptive of international stability to allow self-determination within those boundaries for minorities (*e.g.* the Biafrans in Nigeria[86]).

3. In 1963, the General Assembly established a committee to assist it in the implementation of Resolution 1514. The Committee has been variously known as the Decolonisation Committee and the Special Committee of 24. It is composed of the number of representatives of United Nations Member States indicated by its name.

[82] See, *e.g.* the General Assembly resolution on Namibia, below, p. 105.
[83] Appendix I, below.
[84] G.A. Resn. 2621 (XXV), G.A.O.R., 25th Session, Supp. 16, p. 10. See also G.A. Resn. 1541 (XV), G.A.O.R., 15th Session, Supp. 16, p. 29.
[85] Appendix III, below.
[86] See below, p. 127.

WESTERN SAHARA CASE[87]

Advisory Opinion. I.C.J. Reports 1975, p. 12

Western Sahara was colonised by Spain in 1884 and remained until recently a Spanish colony known as the Spanish Sahara. Its population of less than 100,000 consists of Saharan tribesmen, mostly nomads. It is rich in phosphates, in the production of which it is an important competitor of Morocco in the international phosphates industry. In 1966, the General Assembly indicated that the decolonisation of the territory should occur on the basis of the right to self-determination as expressed in General Assembly Resolution 1514 (XV) and invited Spain, in consultation with the neighbouring states of Mauritania and Morocco, to "determine at the earliest possible date . . . the procedures for the holding of a referendum under United Nations auspices with a view to enabling the indigenous population of the territory to exercise freely its right to self-determination."[88] After much delay, Spain agreed to hold a referendum of the people in the Spanish Sahara under United Nations supervision in 1975. At this point, King Hassan, who had previously supported the application of the principle of self-determination to the Spanish Sahara, claimed the territory for Morocco on the basis of "historic title" predating Spain's colonisation of the territory. Mauritania made a similar, overlapping claim. On the initiative of these two states, the General Assembly requested in 1974 an opinion from the Court on the following questions:

I Was Western Sahara (Rio de Oro and Sakiet El Hamra) at the time of colonisation by Spain a territory belonging to no one (*terra nullius*)? If the answer to the first question is in the negative,

II What were the legal ties between this territory and the Kingdom of Morocco and the Mauritanian entity?

In the course of considering whether it should give the requested opinion, the Court found it necessary "to recall briefly the basic principles governing the decolonisation policy of the General Assembly," which it did in the following extract. Further extracts from the Court's opinion are printed below, pp. 165 and 740.

Opinion of the Court

54. The Charter of the United Nations, in Article 1, paragraph 2, indicates, as one of the purposes of the United Nations: "To develop friendly relations among nations based on respect for the principle of equal rights and self-determination of peoples . . ." This purpose is further developed in Articles 55 and 56 of the Charter. Those provisions have direct and particular relevance for non-self-governing territories, which are dealt with in Chapter XI of the Charter. As the Court stated in its Advisory Opinion of 21 June 1971 on *The Legal Consequences for States of the Continued Presence of South Africa in Namibia (South West Africa) notwithstanding Security Council Resolutions 276 (1970)*:

. . . the subsequent development of international law in regard to non-self-governing territories, as enshrined in the Charter of the United Nations, made the principle of self-determination applicable to all of them (*I.C.J. Reports* 1971, p. 31).

[87] See Shaw (1978) 49 B.Y.I.L. 119.
[88] G.A. Resn. 2229 (XXI), G.A.O.R., 21st Session, Supp. 16, p. 72.

55. The principle of self-determination as a right of peoples, and its application for the purpose of bringing all colonial situations to a speedy end, were enunciated in the Declaration on the Granting of Independence to Colonial Countries and Peoples, General Assembly resolution 1514 (XV). . . . The above provisions, in particular paragraph 2, thus confirm and emphasize that the application of the right of self-determination requires a free and genuine expression of the will of the peoples concerned.

56. The Court had occasion to refer to this resolution in the above-mentioned Advisory Opinion of 21 June 1971. Speaking of the development of international law in regard to non-self-governing territories, the Court there stated:

> A further important stage in this development was the Declaration on the Granting of Independence to Colonial Countries and Peoples (General Assembly resolution 1514 (XV) of 14 December 1960), which embraces all peoples and territories which "have not yet attained independence." (*I.C.J. Reports* 1971, p. 31).

It went on to state:

> . . . the Court must take into consideration the changes which have occurred in the supervening half-century, and its interpretation cannot remain unaffected by the subsequent development of law, through the Charter of the United Nations and by way of customary law (*ibid.*).

The Court then concluded:

> In the domain to which the present proceedings relate, the last fifty years, as indicated above, have brought important developments. These developments leave little doubt that the ultimate objective of the sacred trust was the self-determination and independence of the peoples concerned. In this domain, as elsewhere, the *corpus iuris gentium* has been considerably enriched, and this the Court, if it is faithfully to discharge its functions, may not ignore. (*Ibid.* pp. 31 *et seq.*).

57. General Assembly resolution 1514 (XV) provided the basis for the process of decolonization which has resulted since 1960 in the creation of many States which are today Members of the United Nations. It is complemented in certain of its aspects by General Assembly resolution 1541 (XV), which has been invoked in the present proceedings. The latter resolution contemplates for non-self-governing territories more than one possibility, namely:

(*a*) emergence as a sovereign independent State;
(*b*) free association with an independent State; or
(*c*) integration with an independent State.

At the same time, certain of its provisions give effect to the essential feature of the right of self-determination as established in resolution 1514 (XV). Thus principle VII of resolution 1541 (XV) declares that: "Free association should be the result of a free and voluntary choice by the Peoples of the territory concerned expressed through informed and democratic processes." Again, principle IX of resolution 1541 declares that:

> Integration should have come about in the following circumstances:
>
> (*b*) The integration should be the result of the freely expressed wishes of the territory's peoples acting with the full knowledge of the change in their

status, their wishes having been expressed through informed and democratic processes, impartially conducted and based on universal adult suffrage. The United Nations could, when it deems it necessary, supervise these processes.

58. General Assembly resolution 2625 (XXV), "Declaration on Principles of International Law concerning Friendly Relations and Co-operation among States in accordance with the Charter of the United Nations"[89] . . . mentions other possibilities besides independence, association or integration. But in doing so it reiterates the basic need to take account of the wishes of the people concerned . . .

59. The validity of the principle of self-determination, defined as the need to pay regard to the freely expressed will of peoples, is not affected by the fact that in certain cases the General Assembly has dispensed with the requirement of consulting the inhabitants of a given territory. Those instances were based either on the consideration that a certain population did not constitute a "people" entitled to self-determination or on the conviction that a consultation was totally unnecessary, in view of special circumstances.

SEPARATE OPINION OF JUDGE DILLARD.[90] At the broadest level there is the problem of determining whether the right of self-determination in the context of non-self-governing territories can qualify as a norm of contemporary international law. . . .

As is well known [this] . . . problem has elicited conflicting views which, in terms of opposing poles, may be described as follows. At one extreme is the contention that even if a particular resolution of the General Assembly is not binding, the cumulative impact of many resolutions when simlar in content, voted for by overwhelming majorities and frequently repeated over a period of time may give rise to a general *opinio juris* and thus constitute a norm of customary international law. According to this view, this is the precise situation manifested by the long list of resolutions which, following in the wake of resolution 1514 (XV), have proclaimed the principle of self-determination to be an operative right in the decolonization of non-self-governing territories.

At the opposite pole are those who, resisting generally the law-creating powers of the General Assembly, deny that the principle has developed into a "right" with corresponding obligations or that the practice of decolonization has been more than an example of a usage dictated by political expediency or convenience and one which, in addition, has been neither constant nor uniform.

I need not dwell on the theoretical aspects of this broad problem which, as everyone knows, commands an immense literature. Suffice it to call attention to the fact that the present Opinion is forthright in proclaiming the existence of the "right" in so far as the present proceedings are concerned.

This is made explicit in paragraph 56 and is fortified by calling into play two dicta in the *Namibia* case (*I.C.J. Reports* 1971, p. 31) to which are added an analysis of the numerous resolutions of the General Assembly dealing in general with its decolonization policy. . . .

The pronouncements of the Court thus indicate, in my view, that a norm of international law has emerged applicable to the decolonization of those non-self-governing territories which are under the aegis of the United Nations.

[89] *Ed.* Appendix III, below.
[90] Judge Dillard concurred in the Court's Opinion.

It seemed hardly necessary to make more explicit the cardinal restraint which the legal right of self-determination imposes. That restraint may be captured in a single sentence. It is for the people to determine the destiny of the territory and not the territory the destiny of the people. Viewed in this perspective it becomes almost self-evident that the existence of ancient "legal ties" of the kind described in the Opinion, while they may influence some of the projected procedures for decolonization, can have only a tangential effect in the ultimate choices available to the people. This in turn fortifies the view, expressed earlier, that the first conclusion in paragraph 162 of the Opinion[91] is of limited significance.

Notes

1. The General Assembly took note "with appreciation"[92] of the Court's opinion.

2. The history of the *Western Sahara* case after the Court's opinion (of October 16, 1975) shows that the principle of self-determination may not always be adhered to despite the wishes of the General Assembly.[93] On November 4, 1975, Morocco, which had interpreted the Court's opinion (quite wrongly) as recognising its claim to the territory, began its "Green (*i.e.* peaceful) March" into Western Sahara. The March was made by about 200,000 unarmed civilians. On November 6, the Security Council, which had earlier vainly called for "restraint and moderation"[94] on the part of the states concerned (including Algeria, which was backing the claims of Polisario—the independence movement of the Saharans—against Morocco and Mauritania) adopted a resolution deploring the March and calling for its termination.[95] This did not occur until a week or so later, after tripartite talks between Spain, Morocco and Mauritania had led to an agreement between the three states whereby Western Sahara would be divided between Morocco (two-thirds) and Mauritania (one-third) and Spain would retain a 35 per cent. interest in the phosphates industry.

In December 1975, following the tripartite agreement, the General Assembly adopted two resolutions which are difficult to reconcile. In the first[96] (the "Algerian" resolution), it requested Spain to take immediate steps to enable the Saharans to exercise their right of self-determination and made no reference to the tripartite agreement. In the second[97] (the "Moroccan" resolution), it took note of the tripartite agreement (thereby appearing to recognise the arrangement for the future of Western Sahara which it proposed) and requested the interim administration established in the territory by Spain to take the necessary steps to realise the self-determination of the inhabitants. In February 1976, Spain withdrew from the territory and Morocco and Mauritania took over in accordance with the tripartite agreement. No steps towards self-determination have been taken. The United Nations Secretary General refused an invitation to attend the ceremony witnessing the change over of power. In 1981, the General Assembly "re-affirmed the inalienable right of the people of Western Sahara to self-determination and independence."[98] Polisario has declared the independence of Western Sahara and continues to wage a guerrilla war.

3. Another recent case of lack of respect for the principle of self-determination by a neighbouring state is that of *East Timor*.[99] East Timor, which was a Portuguese colony,

[91] Printed below, pp. 166–167.
[92] G.A. Resn. 3458A (XXX), G.A.O.R., 30th Session, Supp. 34, p. 116.
[93] See Franck, 70 A.J.I.L. 694 (1976).
[94] S.C. Resn. 377 (1975), *Resolutions and Decisions*, 1975, p. 8.
[95] S.C. Resn. 380 (1975), *Resolutions and Decisions*, 1975, p. 9.
[96] G.A. Resn. 3458A (XXX), *loc. cit.* at n. 92 above.
[97] G.A. Resn. 3458B (XXX), G.A.O.R., 30th Session, Supp. 34, p. 117.
[98] G.A. Resn. 36/46, November 24, 1981.
[99] See Elliott, 27 I.C.L.Q. 238 (1978).

shares an island with Indonesia. In 1974, Indonesia and Australia agreed that the best solution for the security of the region when Portugal relinquished the territory would be for it to join Indonesia. An independence movement within East Timor—Fretilin—opposed this solution. In August 1975, it used force to seize control over the territory from Portugal and declared its independence. In December 1975, Indonesia invaded East Timor and defeated the Fretilin forces, although a guerrilla war continues. Later in the same month the General Assembly[1] and the Security Council[2] called upon Indonesia to withdraw and upon all states to allow the people of East Timor to decide their own future. Indonesia has not withdrawn and claims sovereignty over the territory.

4. The Committee of 24 and the General Assembly have not applied Resolution 1514 in the usual way in the case of *Gibraltar*. In 1964, after Spain had raised the question of its status, the Committee of 24 reached a consensus inviting Spain and the United Kingdom to conduct "conversations in order to find . . . a negotiated solution, in keeping with the provisions of Resolution 1514 (XV) taking duly into account the opinions expressed by members of the Committee and bearing in mind the interests of the population of the territory."[3] The request for a "negotiated solution" was unusual, as were the references to "the opinions expressed by members of the Committee" (which were not unanimous) and the "interests" (not the wishes) of the inhabitants. The Committee of 24 also rejected the 1967 referendum held by the United Kingdom of residents of Gibraltar on their political future.[4] The Committee and the General Assembly have taken the view that the wishes of the current population should not be paramount in the case of Gibraltar because it is an imported, colonial population, replacing the earlier, largely Spanish population which left the territory at the time of its capture in the early eighteenth century.[5] The emphasis has been upon paragraph 6 of the Resolution 1514 which has been viewed as having retroactive effect, back to the time when Gibraltar was captured from Spain.[6]

5. As noted above, p. 95, the 1966 Covenants do not limit the principle of self-determination to the colonial situation. It seems unlikely that they reflect customary international law in this respect. On the question of self-determination for *minorities* such as the Scots, the Welsh, the French Canadians, the Kurds (in Iraq), the Nagas (in India), and the Somalis (in Kenya) in existing states and for *majorities* in non-democratic states, there is little evidence in United Nations or other state practice to suggest that the right to self-determination applies outside of the colonial or similar context. Note, however, that the General Assembly has accepted that the Palestinians[7] and the inhabitants of South Africa[8] are "peoples" with a right to self-determination.

---

[1] G.A. Resn. 3485 (XXX), G.A.O.R., 30th Session, Supp. 34, p. 118. The Resolution was adopted by 72 votes to 10 with 43 abstentions.

[2] S.C. Resn. 384 (1975), *Resolutions and Decisions*, 1975, p. 10. The resolution was adopted unanimously.

[3] Cmnd. 2632, p. 14. See also G.A. Resn. 2070 (XX), G.A.O.R., 20th Session, Supp. 14, p. 58.

[4] See Cmnd. 3735, p. 15. The result of the referendum was that 12,138 wanted Gibraltar to remain in association with the U.K.; 44 wanted it to become a part of Spain.

[5] Following the occupation of the territory by the British, Gibraltar was populated during the 18th century by Genoese, Maltese, Moroccans, British and others.

[6] The Committee of 24 and the General Assembly have adopted the same approach to the similar *Falkland Islands* case, with Argentina and the U.K. being invited to seek a negotiated solution: G.A. Resn. 2065 (XX), G.A.O.R., 20th Session, Supp. 14, p. 57. Almost all of the small civilian population of the island (under 2,000) are British subjects who have settled there since 1833 and who strongly favour retaining their association with the U.K.: see further below, p. 171.

[7] See, *e.g.* G.A. Resn. ES-7/2, G.A.O.R., 7th Emergency Session, Supp. 1, p. 3.

[8] See, *e.g.* G.A. Resn. 33/24, G.A.O.R., 33rd Session, Supp. 45, p. 137.

3. *MANDATED AND TRUST TERRITORIES*

Notes

1. After the First World War, the League of Nations solution to the problem of the future of the overseas possessions of the defeated states of Germany and Turkey was to place them under mandate. Article 22 of the Covenant of the League reads:

> To those colonies and territories which as a consequence of the late war have ceased to be under the sovereignty of the States which formerly governed them and which are inhabited by peoples not yet able to stand by themselves under the strenuous conditions of the modern world, there should be applied the principle that the well-being and development of such peoples form a sacred trust of civilisation and that securities for the performance of this trust should be embodied in this Covenant.
>
> The best method of giving practical effect to this principle is that the tutelage of such peoples should be entrusted to advanced nations who by reason of their resources, their experience or their geographical position can best undertake this responsibility, and who are willing to accept it, and that this tutelage should be exercised by them as Mandatories on behalf of the League.

Three categories of mandate were devised, "A," "B" and "C." Territories were placed within them according to their stage of development as follows: "A" mandates—Iraq (Mandatory, Great Britain), Palestine and Transjordan (Great Britain), Syria and Lebanon (France); "B" mandates, British Cameroons (Great Britain), French Cameroons (France), Ruanda Urundi (Belgium), Tanganyika (Great Britain), British Togoland (Great Britain), French Togoland (France); "C" mandates, Nauru (Great Britain, Australia and New Zealand), New Guinea (Australia), Pacific Islands north of the Equator (Japan), South West Africa (South Africa), Western Samoa (New Zealand). The "C" mandates were the least developed. The Mandatories were given powers of administration and responsibilities that varied according to the category of mandate. In no case was sovereignty transferred to the mandatory.

2. When the United Nations replaced the League of Nations after the Second World War the system of mandates was replaced by a trusteeship system,[9] which was inspired by the same problem and the same ideal. All of the former mandated territories were placed under the system by their mandatories (who were then appointed the administering authorities in the same territories) with the exception of (1) those territories—Iraq, Syria, Lebanon and Palestine (now Israel and Jordan)—which had become or were soon to become independent; (2) the islands in the Pacific north of the Equator (which were taken from the former mandatory—Japan—and made into a "strategic trust area" (because of their significance for purposes of defence[10]) administered by the United States; and (3) South West Africa. Somaliland was also made a trust territory and administered as such for a ten year period from 1950 until 1960 by Italy, from whom it had been taken after the Second World War. No new area has been voluntarily placed under the trusteeship system.[11] All of the trust territories have now become independent states, or parts of such states, with the exception of the Pacific Islands north of the Equator. These, as a "strategic trust area," are subject to a special supervisory régime operated by the Security Council.[12]

---

[9] See Chaps. XII and XIII UN Charter, Appendix I, below.

[10] This was calculated by reference to the experience of the Second World War.

[11] On the temporary UN administration of West Irian, a former Dutch colony, for a few months in 1962–63 pending its transfer to Indonesian administration and its exercise of the right to self-determination, see Higgins, *UN Peace-Keeping 1946–67* (1970), Vol. II, pp. 124 *et seq.*

[12] In 1982, the Trusteeship Council noted the intention of the U.S. to seek the termination of the Trusteeship Agreement soon and its replacement by a status for the islands of free association with the U.S.A.

3. *South West Africa/Namibia*.[13] South West Africa, or Namibia, is a territory of small population but great economic and political importance. Although twice as large as the United Kingdom, it has a population (according to a 1976 estimate) of only 852,000 people. Nearly half of these (386,000) are members of the Ovambo tribe. The remainder are mostly whites (99,000) or members of other African tribes. The territory has rich diamond and uranium deposits which are mined by South African, British, and other foreign interests. It lies between South and Black Africa.

In 1950, after South Africa had declined to place South West Africa under the trusteeship system, the United Nations General Assembly asked the International Court of Justice for its advice on the status of the territory following the demise of the League of Nations and its effective replacement by the United Nations. In the *International Status of South West Africa Case*,[14] the Court advised:

unanimously

> that South West Africa is a territory under the international Mandate assumed by the Union of South Africa on December 17, 1920; . . .

by twelve votes to two,

> that the Union of South Africa continues to have the international obligations stated in Article 22 of the Covenant of the League of Nations and in the Mandate for South West Africa as well as the obligation to transmit petitions from the inhabitants of that Territory, the supervisory functions to be exercised by the United Nations, to which the annual reports and the petitions are to be submitted, and the reference to the Permanent Court of International Justice to be replaced by a reference to the International Court of Justice, in accordance with Article 7 of the Mandate and Article 37 of the Statute of the Court;

unanimously,

> that the provisions of Chapter XII of the Charter are applicable to the Territory of South West Africa in the sense that they provide a means by which the Territory may be brought under the Trusteeship System;

and by eight votes to six,

> that the provisions of Chapter XII of the Charter do not impose on the Union of South Africa a legal obligation to place the Territory under the Trusteeship System; . . .

unanimously,

> that the Union of South Africa acting alone has not the competence to modify the international status of the Territory of South West Africa, and that the competence to determine and modify the international status of the Territory rests with the Union of South Africa acting with the consent of the United Nations.

On the basis of this opinion, the United Nations took up the supervisory functions that had previously been exercised by the League, although its competence to do so has never been accepted by South Africa which has consistently refused to co-operate. In two later opinions in the 1950s, the Court advised that decisions by the General Assembly on questions relating to reports and petitions concerning South West Africa were "important questions" for the purposes of its voting rules[15] and that the oral

[13] See Dugard, ed., *The South West Africa/Namibia Dispute* (1973), and Slonim, *South West Africa and the United Nations* (1973).
[14] I.C.J.Rep. 1950, p. 128 at pp. 143–144.
[15] *Voting Procedures on Questions relating to Reports and Petitions concerning the Territory of South West Africa Case*, I.C.J.Rep. 1955, p. 67.

hearing by the United Nations of petitioners from South West Africa was constitutional.[16]

As African nationalism gathered force in the 1960s, resort to the Court was had again, this time in two cases, brought by Ethiopia and Liberia, against South Africa under the mandate—the *South West Africa Cases*[17]—and not in a request for an advisory opinion. A judgment on the merits in these cases would have been binding in law upon South Africa. In fact, the Court, by the casting vote of the President,[18] rejected the claims on the basis that the applicant states had no legal right or interest in them. There was therefore no ruling upon the merits. The Court distinguished between "conduct" and "special interests" provisions in the mandate. Whereas members of the League of Nations, such as the applicants, were granted rights under the latter (*e.g.* in respect of the freedom of movement of missionaries in South West Africa), the former (which, it was alleged, had been infringed in this case by, for example, South Africa's introduction of *apartheid* into the territory and its failure to promote the welfare of its inhabitants) gave rise to obligations *vis-à-vis* the League alone, which only the League could enforce.

The question whether the applicants had "any legal right or interest" in the cases was one upon which South Africa did not present argument during the hearing on the merits. In 1962, when the Court had ruled that it had jurisdiction to hear the cases,[19] South Africa's third preliminary objection to the jurisdiction of the Court had been that the cases did not involve:

> a "dispute" as envisaged by Article 7 . . . in that no material interests of . . . Ethiopia and/or Liberia . . . are involved . . .[20]

The Court had rejected this objection as follows:

> . . . the manifest scope and purport of the provisions of this Article indicate that the Members of the League were understood to have a legal right or interest in the observance by the Mandatory of its obligations both towards the inhabitants of the Mandated Territory, and towards the League of Nations and its Members.[21]

The 1966 judgment, in effect, reversed this ruling.

The Court that heard the cases on the merits in 1966 was differently composed from that which had heard them in 1962 at the preliminary objections stage. This was partly because elections to the Court had taken place in the meantime and partly for other reasons. Of the three judges who were members of the Court in 1966 who did not participate in the hearing on the merits, Judge Ammoun had been appointed (to replace Judge Badawi who had died) too late to do so, Judge Bustamente y Rivero was ill, and Judge Sir Zafrullah Khan recused himself because of his interest in the case (he had been asked by the applicant states to sit as an ad hoc judge in the cases before his appointment to the Court). He would appear to have done so against his own wishes at

---

[16] *Admissibility of Hearings of Petitioners by the Committee on South West Africa Case*, I.C.J.Rep. 1956, p. 23.

[17] I.C.J.Rep. 1966, p. 6. Of the extensive literature on the cases, see Cheng, 20 C.L.P. 181 (1967); Dugard, 83 S.A.L.J. 429 (1966); Falk, 21 Int.Org. 1 (1967); Friedmann, 6 Col.Jo.Trans..Law 1 (1967); Higgins, 42 Int. Affairs 573 (1966); Johnson 3 Int.Rel. 157 (1967); Landis, 52 Cornell L.Q. 627 (1967); and Reisman, 7 Virg. Jo. I.L. 1 (1966).

[18] The judges in the majority were President Sir Percy Spender; Judges Winiarski, Spiropoulos, Sir Gerald Fitzmaurice, Morelli and Gros; Judge ad hoc van Wyk. The dissenting judges were Vice-President Wellington Koo; Judges Koretsky, Tanaka, Jessup, Padilla Nervo and Forster; Judge ad hoc Mbanefo.

[19] *South West Africa Cases, Preliminary Objections*, I.C.J.Rep. 1962, p. 319.

[20] *Ibid*. p. 327.

[21] *Ibid*. p. 342.

the request of the Court.[22] Eight judges of the Court and the two ad hoc judges participated at both stages of the proceedings. All of these who were in the minority in 1962 were in the majority in 1966 and vice versa.

It is possible to argue for and against the Court's distinction between "conduct" and "special" provisions of the mandate and the Court's freedom to change its mind on the question of the "legal interest" of the applicant states. The difference between the two groups within the Court was basically one of judicial philosophy, turning upon a preference for a teleological or a positivist approach (see para. 91, judgment).[23] The 1966 majority may have been concerned about the wisdom of giving a judgment on the merits that would have had considerable political implications and might (if it went against South Africa) have proved unenforceable.[24] The effect of its failure to rule on the merits (particularly after its 1962 judgment) upon its standing in a large part of the international community has to be weighed against such a consideration. The Court's judgment angered a majority of the General Assembly to the point that its Fourth Committee refused to approve a financial appropriation for the Court[25] and the next election of judges was affected by the wish of African states to achieve a more sympathetic court.[26]

GENERAL ASSEMBLY RESOLUTION 2145 (XXI)[27]

October 27, 1966. G.A.O.R., 21st Sess., suppl. 16, p. 2

The General Assembly

1. *Reaffirms* that the provisions of General Assembly resolution 1514 (XV) are fully applicable to the people of the Mandated Territory of South West Africa and that, therefore, the people of South West Africa have the inalienable right to self-determination, freedom and independence in accordance with the Charter of the United Nations;

2. *Reaffirms further* that South West Africa is a territory having international status and that it shall maintain this status until it achieves independence;

3. *Declares* that South Africa has failed to fulfil its obligations in respect of the administration of the Mandated Territory and to ensure the moral and material well-being and security of the indigenous inhabitants of South West Africa and has, in fact, disavowed the Mandate;

4. *Decides* that the Mandate conferred upon His Britannic Majesty to be exercised on his behalf by the Government of the Union of South Africa is therefore terminated, that South Africa has no other right to administer the

---

[22] See UN Doc. A/638B. On the recusal of judges, see below, p. 708.

[23] *cf.* Dugard, *op. cit.* at p. 103, n. 13, p. 357, above, and the writers he cites. See also the dissenting opinion of Judge Tanaka at a point where he is discussing the continuance of the power of supervision of the mandate after the demise of the League: ". . . the difference of opinions on the questions before us in the final instance attributed to the difference between two methods of interpretation: teleological or sociological and conceptional or formalistic": I.C.J.Rep. 1966, p. 276.

[24] See Falk, *op. cit.* at p. 104, n. 17, above, p. 20.

[25] Dugard, *op. cit.* at p. 103, n. 13, above, p. 378.

[26] In November 1966, the retiring Judges Bustamante y Rivero (Peruvian), Sir Percy Spender (Australian), Spiropoulos (Greek), and Winiarski (Polish) were replaced by Judges Bengzon (Philippino), Lachs (Polish), Oneyeama (Nigerian), and Petrén (Swedish).

[27] Adopted by 114 votes to two (Portugal, South Africa), with three abstentions (France, Malawi and the U.K.).

Territory and that henceforth South West Africa comes under the direct responsibility of the United Nations;

5. *Resolves* that in these circumstances the United Nations must discharge those responsibilities with respect to South West Africa; . . .

Note

The United Nations Council for Namibia.[28] In 1967, the General Assembly established the United Nations Council for Namibia (then South West Africa[29]) to administer the territory and to prepare it for independence.[30] The Council, which is responsible to the Assembly, consists of 31 United Nations Member States. It is assisted by a Commissioner for Namibia, an international civil servant responsible to the Council.[31] The Council's first act was to try to enter the territory it was supposed to govern, but the South African authorities predictably refused to let it in. Since then, the Council has had its headquarters in New York. It has a regional office in Lusaka in Zambia. The Council's work has consisted of representing Namibian interests in international organisations[32] and at international conferences, raising funds for and administering the United Nations Fund for Namibia, acting to achieve compliance with the Namibia opinion (below), and consulting with governments on matters concerning Namibia. Travel and identity documents issued to Namibians by the Council are recognised by most states.[33] In 1976, the United Nations Institute for Namibia was established in Lusaka to plan for Namibian independence and to train its future civil service.

LEGAL CONSEQUENCES FOR STATES OF THE CONTINUED PRESENCE OF SOUTH AFRICA IN NAMIBIA (SOUTH WEST AFRICA) NOTWITHSTANDING SECURITY COUNCIL 276 (1970)

Advisory Opinion. I.C.J. Reports 1971, p. 16

Following upon the General Assembly's decision to terminate the mandate, the Security Council called upon South Africa to withdraw from Namibia (Resolutions 264 (1969) and 269 (1969)). When South Africa failed to do so, the Council adopted Resolution 276 (1970), the key terms of which are quoted in para. 108 of the Court's Opinion. When South Africa still did not act, the Council requested in July 1970 an advisory opinion on the following question: "What are the legal consequences for states of the continued presence of South Africa in Namibia, notwithstanding Security Council resolution 276 (1970)?" After confirming its earlier jurisprudence to the effect that the mandate had survived the demise of the League and that the United Nations had taken over the League's supervisory role, the Court continued:

---

[28] See Hermann, 13 C.Y.B.I.L. 306 (1975).

[29] In 1968, South West Africa was renamed Namibia by the General Assembly "in accordance with the desires of its people": G.A. Resn. 2372 (XXII), G.A.O.R., 22nd Session, Supp. 16A.

[30] G.A. Resn. 2248 (S-V), G.A.O.R., 5th Special Session, Supp. 1, p. 1. The resolution was adopted by 85 votes to two (Portugal and South Africa), with 30 abstentions. The Council took over from an ad hoc Committee for South West Africa established by G.A. Resn. 2145 (XXI). The U.K. does not "recognise the Council of Namibia's claim to be the administering authority of Namibia or to take decisions binding upon the international community," the General Assembly having lacked the constitutional authority to establish it: *Hansard*, H.L., Vol. 408, col. 758. April 23, 1980.

[31] The present Commissioner is Mr. Mishra (Indian).

[32] On the participation of Namibia in international organisations, see Osieke (1980) 51 B.Y.I.L. 189.

[33] See Engers, 65 A.J.I.L. 571 (1971).

Opinion of the Court

90. The Mandatory Powers while retaining their mandates assumed, under Article 80 of the Charter, *vis-à-vis* all United Nations Members, the obligation to keep intact and preserve, until trusteeship agreements were executed, the rights of other States and of the peoples of mandated territories, which resulted from the existing mandate agreements and related instruments, such as Article 22 of the Covenant and the League Council's resolution of 31 January 1923 concerning petitions. The mandatory Powers also bound themselves to exercise their functions of administration in conformity with the relevant obligations emanating from the United Nations Charter, which member States have undertaken to fulfil in good faith in all their international relations.

91. One of the fundamental principles governing the international relationship thus established is that a party which disowns or does not fulfil its own obligations cannot be recognized as retaining the rights which it claims to derive from the relationship.

94. In examining this action [resolution 2145 (XXI)] of the General Assembly it is appropriate to have regard to the general principles of international law regulating termination of a treaty relationship on account of breach. For even if the mandate is viewed as having the character of an institution,[34] as is maintained, it depends on those international agreements which created the system and regulated its application. As the Court indicated in 1962 "this Mandate, like practically all other similar Mandates" was "a special type of instrument composite in nature and instituting a novel international régime. It incorporates a definite

agreement . . ." (*I.C.J. Reports* 1962, p. 331). The Court stated conclusively in that Judgment that the Mandate ". . . in fact and in law, is an international agreement having the character of a treaty or convention" (*I.C.J. Reports* 1962, p. 330). The rules laid down by the Vienna Convention on the Law of Treaties concerning termination of a treaty relationship on account of breach (adopted without a dissenting vote) may in many respects be considered as a codification of existing customary law on the subject. In the light of these rules [see Article 60(3), below, p. 619], only a material breach of a treaty justifies termination. . . .

95. General Assembly resolution 2145 (XXI) determines that both forms of material breach had occurred in this case. By stressing that South Africa "has in fact, disavowed the Mandate," the General Assembly declared in fact that it had repudiated it. The resolution in question is therefore to be viewed as the exercise of the right to terminate a relationship in case of a deliberate and persistent violation of obligations which destroys the very object and purpose of that relationship.

96. It has been contended that the Covenant of the League of Nations did not confer on the Council of the League power to terminate a mandate for misconduct of the mandatory and that no such power could therefore be exercised by the United Nations, since it could not derive from the League greater powers than the latter itself had. For this objection to prevail it would be necessary to show that the mandates system, as established under the League,

---

[34] *Ed.* The I.C.J. had called it a "new institution" in its 1950 Opinion: I.C.J.Rep. 1950 at p. 132.

excluded the application of the general principle of law that a right of termination on account of breach must be presumed to exist in respect of all treaties,
except as regards provisions relating to the protection of the human person
contained in treaties of a humanitarian character (as indicated in Art. 60, para.
5, of the Vienna Convention). The silence of a treaty as to the existence of such
a right cannot be interpreted as implying the exclusion of a right which has its
source outside of the treaty, in general international law, and is dependent on
the occurrence of circumstances which are not normally envisaged when a
treaty is concluded. . . .

102. In a further objection to General Assembly resolution 2145 (XXI) it is
contended that it made pronouncements which the Assembly, not being a
judicial organ, and not having previously referred the matter to any such organ,
was not competent to make. Without dwelling on the conclusions reached in the
1966 Judgment in the *South West Africa* contentious cases, it is worth recalling
that in those cases the applicant States, which complained of material breaches
of substantive provisions of the Mandate, were held not to "possess any separate
self-contained right which they could assert . . . to require the due performance
of the Mandate in discharge of the 'sacred trust'" (*I.C.J. Reports* 1966, pp. 29
and 51). On the other hand, the Court declared that: " . . . any divergences of
view concerning the conduct of a mandate were regarded as being matters that
had their place in the political field, the settlement of which lay between the
mandatory and the competent organs of the League" (*ibid.* p. 45). To deny to a
political organ of the United Nations which is a successor of the League in this
respect the right to act, on the argument that it lacks competence to render what
is described as a judicial decision, would not only be inconsistent but would
amount to a complete denial of the remedies available against fundamental
breaches of an international undertaking.

103. The Court is unable to appreciate the view that the General Assembly
acted unilaterally as party and judge in its own cause. In the 1966 Judgment in
the *South West Africa Cases*, referred to above, it was found that the function to
call for the due execution of the relevant provisions of the mandate instruments
appertained to the League acting as an entity through its appropriate organs.
The right of the League "in the pursuit of its collective, institutional activity, to
require the due performance of the Mandate in discharge of the 'sacred trust'",
was specifically recognized (*ibid.* p. 29). Having regard to this finding, the
United Nations as a successor to the League, acting through its competent
organs, must be seen above all as the supervisory institution, competent to
pronounce, in that capacity, on the conduct of the mandatory with respect to its
international obligations, and competent to act accordingly. . . .

105. General Assembly resolution 2145 (XXI), after declaring the termination of the Mandate, added in operative paragraph 4 "that South Africa has no
other right to administer the Territory." This part of the resolution has been
objected to as deciding a transfer of territory. That in fact is not so. The
pronouncement made by the General Assembly is based on a conclusion,
referred to earlier, reached by the Court in 1950:

> The authority which the Union Government exercises over the Territory is
> based on the Mandate. If the Mandate lapsed, as the Union Government
> contends, the latter's authority would equally have lapsed. (*I.C.J. Reports*
> 1950, p. 133.)

This was confirmed by the Court in its Judgment of 21 December 1962 in the *South West Africa Cases* (Ethiopia v. South Africa; Liberia v. South Africa) (*I.C.J. Reports* 1962, p. 333). Relying on these decisions of the Court, the General Assembly declared that the Mandate having been terminated "South Africa has no other right to administer the Territory." This is not a finding on facts, but the formulation of a legal situation. For it would not be correct to assume that, because the General Assembly is in principle vested with recommendatory powers, it is debarred from adopting, in specific cases within the framework of its competence, resolutions which make determinations or have operative design.

106. By resolution 2145 (XXI) the General Assembly terminated the Mandate. However, lacking the necessary powers to ensure the withdrawal of South Africa from the Territory, it enlisted the co-operation of the Security Council by calling the latter's attention to the resolution, thus acting in accordance with Article II, paragraph 2, of the Charter. . . .

108. Resolution 264 (1969) [of the Security Council], in paragraph 3 of its operative part, calls upon South Africa to withdraw its administration from Namibia immediately. Resolution 269 (1969), in view of South Africa's lack of compliance, after recalling the obligations of Members under Article 25 of the Charter, calls upon the Government of South Africa, in paragraph 5 of its operative part, "to withdraw its administration from the territory immediately and in any case before 4 October 1969." The preamble of resolution 276 (1970) reaffirms General Assembly resolution 2145 (XXI) and espouses it, by referring to the decision, not merely of the General Assembly, but of the United Nations "that the Mandate of South West Africa was terminated." In the operative part, after condemning the non-compliance by South Africa with General Assembly and Security Council resolutions pertaining to Namibia, the Security Council declares, in paragraph 2, that "the continued presence of the South African authorities in Namibia is illegal" and that consequently all acts taken by the Government of South Africa "on behalf of or concerning Namibia after the termination of the Mandate are illegal and invalid." In paragraph 5 the Security Council "*Calls upon* all States, particularly those which have economic and other interests in Namibia, to refrain from any dealings with the Government of South Africa which are inconsistent with operative paragraph 2 of this resolution."

109. . . . The Security Council, when it adopted these resolutions, was acting in the exercise of what it deemed to be its primary responsibility, the maintenance of peace and security, which, under the Charter, embraces situations which might lead to a breach of the peace. (Art. 1, para. 1.) . . .

110. As to the legal basis of the resolution, Article 24 of the Charter vests in the Security Council the necessary authority to take action such as that taken in the present case. The reference in paragraph 2 of this Article to specific powers of the Security Council under certain chapters of the Charter does not exclude the existence of general powers to discharge the responsibilities conferred in paragraph 1. Reference may be made in this respect to the Secretary-General's Statement, presented to the Security Council on 10 January, 1947, to the effect that "the powers of the Council under Article 24 are not restricted to the specific grants of authority contained in Chapters VI, VII, VIII and XII . . . the Members of the United Nations have conferred upon the Security Council powers commensurate with its responsibility for the maintenance of peace and

security. The only limitations are the fundamental principles and purposes found in Chapter I of the Charter."

111. As to the effect to be attributed to the declaration contained in paragraph 2 of resolution 276 (1970), the Court considers that the qualification of a situation as illegal does not by itself put an end to it. It can only be the first, necessary step in an endeavour to bring the illegal situation to an end.

112. It would be an untenable interpretation to maintain that, once such a declaration had been made by the Security Council under Article 24 of the Charter, on behalf of all member States, those Members would be free to act in disregard of such illegality or even to recognize violations of law resulting from it. When confronted with such an internationally unlawful situation, Members of the United Nations would be expected to act in consequence of the declaration made on their behalf. The question therefore arises as to the effect of this decision of the Security Council for States Members of the United Nations in accordance with Article 25 of the Charter.

113. It has been contended that Article 25 of the Charter applies only to enforcement measures adopted under Chapter VII of the Charter. It is not possible to find in the Charter any support for this view. Article 25 is not confined to decisions in regard to enforcement action but applies to "the decisions of the Security Council" adopted in accordance with the Charter. Moreover, that Article is placed, not in Chapter VII, but immediately after Article 24 in that part of the Charter which deals with the functions and powers of the Security Council. If Article 25 had reference solely to decisions of the Security Council concerning enforcement action under Articles 41 and 42 of the Charter, that is to say, if it were only such decisions which had binding effect, then Article 25 would be superfluous, since this effect is secured by Articles 48 and 49 of the Charter.

114. It has also been contended that the relevant Security Council resolutions are couched in exhortatory rather than mandatory language and that, therefore, they do not purport to impose any legal duty on any State nor to affect legally any right of any State. The language of a resolution of the Security Council should be carefully analysed before a conclusion can be made as to its binding effect. In view of the nature of the powers under Article 25, the question whether they have been in fact exercised is to be determined in each case, having regard to the terms of the resolution to be interpreted, the discussion leading to it, the Charter provisions invoked and, in general, all circumstances that might assist in determining the legal consequences of the resolution of the Security Council.

115. Applying these tests, the Court recalls that in the preamble of resolution 269 (1969), the Security Council was "*Mindful* of its responsibility to take necessary action to secure strict compliance with the obligations entered into by States Members of the United Nations under the provisions of Article 25 of the Charter of the United Nations." The Court has therefore reached the conclusion that the decisions made by the Security Council in paragraphs 2 and 5 of resolutions 276 (1970), as related to paragraph 3 of resolution 264 (1969) and paragraph 5 of resolution 269 (1969), were adopted in conformity with the purposes and principles of the Charter and in accordance with its Articles 24 and 25. The decisions are consequently binding on all States Members of the United Nations, which are thus under obligation to accept and carry them out.

116. In pronouncing upon the binding nature of the Security Council deci-

sions in question, the Court would recall the following passage in its Advisory Opinion of 11 April 1949 on *Reparation for Injuries Suffered in the Service of the United Nations*:

"The Charter has not been content to make the Organization created by it merely a centre 'for harmonizing the actions of nations in the attainment of these common ends' (Article 1, para. 4). It has equipped that centre with organs, and has given it special tasks. It has defined the position of the Members in relation to the Organization by requiring them to give it every assistance in any action undertaken by it (Article 2, para. 5), and to accept and carry out the decisions of the Security Council." (*I.C.J. Reports* 1949, p. 178.)

Thus when the Security Council adopts a decision under Article 25 in accordance with the Charter, it is for member States to comply with that decision, including those members of the Security Council which voted against it and those Members of the United Nations who are not members of the Council. . . .

117. . . . A binding determination made by a competent organ of the United Nations to the effect that a situation is illegal cannot remain without consequence. Once the Court is faced with such a situation, it would be failing in the discharge of its judicial functions if it did not declare that there is an obligation, especially upon Members of the United Nations, to bring that situation to an end. . . .

118. South Africa, being responsible for having created and maintained a situation which the Court has found to have been validly declared illegal, has the obligation to put an end to it. It is therefore under obligation to withdraw its administration from the Territory of Namibia. By maintaining the present illegal situation, and occupying the Territory without title, South Africa incurs international responsibilities arising from a continuing violation of an international obligation. It also remains accountable for any violations of its international obligations, or of the rights of the people of Namibia. The fact that South Africa no longer has any title to administer the Territory does not release it from its obligations and responsibilities under international law towards other States in respect of the exercise of its powers in relation to this Territory. Physical control of a territory, and not sovereignty or legitimacy of title, is the basis of State liability for acts affecting other States.

119. The member States of the United Nations are, for the reasons given in paragraph 115 above, under obligation to recognize the illegality and invalidity of South Africa's continued presence in Namibia. They are also under obligation to refrain from lending any support or any form of assistance to South Africa with reference to its occupation of Namibia, subject to paragraph 125 below.

120. The precise determination of the acts permitted or allowed—what measures are available and practicable, which of them should be selected, what scope they should be given and by whom they should be applied—is a matter which lies within the competence of the appropriate political organs of the United Nations acting within their authority under the Charter. Thus it is for the Security Council to determine any further measures consequent upon the decisions already taken by it on the question of Namibia. . . .

121. The Court will in consequence confine itself to giving advice on those

dealings with the Government of South Africa which, under the Charter of the United Nations and general international law, should be considered as inconsistent with the declaration of illegality and invalidity made in paragraph 2 of resolution 276 (1970), because they may imply a recognition that South Africa's presence in Namibia is legal.

122. For the reasons given above, and subject to the observations contained in paragraph 125 below, member States are under obligation to abstain from entering into treaty relations with South Africa in all cases in which the Government of South Africa purports to act on behalf of or concerning Namibia. With respect to existing bilateral treaties, member States must abstain from invoking or applying those treaties or provisions of treaties concluded by South Africa on behalf of or concerning Namibia which involve active intergovernmental co-operation. With respect to multilateral treaties, however, the same rule cannot be applied to certain general conventions such as those of a humanitarian character, the non-performance of which may adversely affect the people of Namibia. It will be for the competent international organs to take specific measures in this respect.

123. Member States, in compliance with the duty of non-recognition imposed by paragraphs 2 and 5 of resolution 276 (1970), are under obligation to abstain from sending diplomatic or special missions to South Africa including in their jurisdiction the Territory of Namibia, to abstain from sending consular agents to Namibia, and to withdraw any such agents already there. They should also make it clear to the South African authorities that the maintenance of diplomatic or consular relations with South Africa does not imply any recognition of its authority with regard to Namibia.

124. The restraints which are implicit in the non-recognition of South Africa's presence in Namibia and the explicit provisions of paragraph 5 of resolution 276 (1970) impose upon member States the obligation to abstain from entering into economic and other forms of relationship or dealings with South Africa on behalf of or concerning Namibia which may entrench its authority over the Territory.

125. In general, the non-recognition of South Africa's administration of the Territory should not result in depriving the people of Namibia of any advantages derived from international co-operation. In particular, while official acts performed by the Government of South Africa on behalf of or concerning Namibia after the termination of the Mandate are illegal and invalid, this invalidity cannot be extended to those acts, such as, for instance, the registration of births, deaths and marriages, the effects of which can be ignored only to the detriment of the inhabitants of the Territory.

126. As to non-member States, although not bound by Articles 24 and 25 of the Charter, they have been called upon in paragraphs 2 and 5 of resolution 276 (1970) to give assistance in the action which has been taken by the United Nations with regard to Namibia. In the view of the Court, the termination of the Mandate and the declaration of the illegality of South Africa's presence in Namibia are opposable to all States in the sense of barring *erga omnes* the legality of a situation which is maintained in violation of international law: in particular, no State which enters into relations with South Africa concerning Namibia may expect the United Nations or its Members to recognize the validity or effects of such relationship, or of the consequences thereof. The Mandate having been terminated by decision of the international organization

in which the supervisory authority over its administration was vested, and South Africa's continued presence in Namibia having been declared illegal, it is for non-member States to act in accordance with those decisions. . . .

130. It is undisputed, and is amply supported by documents annexed to South Africa's written statement in these proceedings, that the official governmental policy pursued by South Africa in Namibia is to achieve a complete physical separation of races and ethnic groups in separate areas within the Territory. . . .

131. Under the Charter of the United Nations, the former Mandatory had pledged itself to observe and respect, in a territory having an international status, human rights and fundamental freedoms for all without distinction as to race. To establish instead, and to enforce, distinctions, exclusions, restrictions and limitations exclusively based on grounds of race, colour, descent or national or ethnic origin which constitute a denial of fundamental human rights is a flagrant violation of the purposes and principles of the Charter. . . .

133. For these reasons,

THE COURT IS OF OPINION. . . .

by 13 votes to 2,[35]

(1) that, the continued presence of South Africa in Namibia being illegal, South Africa is under obligation to withdraw its administration from Namibia immediately and thus put an end to its operation of the Territory;

by 11 votes to 4,[36]

(2) that States Members of the United Nations are under obligation to recognize the illegality of South Africa's presence in Namibia and the invalidity of its acts on behalf of or concerning Namibia, and to refrain from any acts and in particular any dealings with the Government of South Africa implying recognition of the legality of, or lending support or assistance to, such presence and administration;

(3) that it is incumbent upon States which are not Members of the United Nations to give assistance, within the scope of subparagraph (2) above, in the action which has been taken by the United Nations with regard to Namibia. . . .

Notes

1. See also the dissenting opinion of Judge Sir Gerald Fitzmaurice who considered that the General Assembly lacked the power to terminate the mandate. Whereas the Court's conclusion that there was such a power was not unexpected, its opinion that the Security Council could act in respect of Namibia by "decisions" that were binding upon Member States of the United Nations under Article 25 of the Charter was surprising. Although the Court has on other occasions applied a doctrine of implied powers to United Nations constitutional law,[37] it had been previously thought that the Security

---

[35] The judges in the majority were President Sir Zafrullah Khan; Vice-President Ammoun; Judges Padilla Nervo, Forster, Bengzon, Petrén, Lachs, Onyeama, Dillard, Ignacio-Pinto, de Castro, Morozov and Jimenez de Aréchaga. Judges Sir Gerald Fitzmaurice and Gros dissented.

[36] Judges Petrén and Onyeama joined the dissenting judges.

[37] See below, p. 704.

Council could only take Article 25 "decisions" when engaged in enforcement action under Chapter VII.[38] The Court's opinion draws a distinction between member and non-member states; the Security Council's resolutions on Namibia do not create *legal* obligations for the latter, although it is "incumbent upon" them to help.

2. The Court's Opinion was accepted by the Security Council which once again called upon South Africa to withdraw from Namibia and called upon other states to act in accordance with the terms of the Opinion.[39]

3. In 1972, the Secretary General of the United Nations, with a mandate from the Security Council,[40] had talks with the interested parties in Namibia and with the South African Government but without any satisfactory outcome. Since then, the Security Council has adopted several further resolutions calling upon South Africa to withdraw from Namibia,[41] but despite changes in the internal government structure, South Africa remains in overall control. A draft resolution before the Security Council in 1981 that asked the Council to impose a mandatory arms embargo on South Africa was vetoed by France, the United Kingdom and the United States.[42] In 1978, South Africa agreed in principle to Namibian independence and negotiations have been conducted between it and the Five Western "Contact" Powers (Canada, France, F.R.G., U.K., and the U.S.A.) since then to achieve this on a basis of elections supervised by the UN.[43] A problem exists in respect of Walvis Bay which is Namibia's main port. Although administered as a part of Namibia since 1919, it is a former British colony which was never a part of the mandated territory and became South African territory upon its independence in 1910. South Africa has indicated its intention not to surrender Walvis Bay.

4. *OTHER LEGAL PERSONS*

(i) PUBLIC INTERNATIONAL ORGANISATIONS[44]

REPARATION FOR INJURIES SUFFERED IN THE SERVICE OF THE UNITED NATIONS CASE

Advisory Opinion, I.C.J. Reports 1949, p. 174

On September 17, 1948, Count Bernadotte, a Swedish national, was killed, allegedly by a private gang of terrorists, in the new city of Jerusalem. The new city was then in Israeli possession.[45] Count Bernadotte was the Chief United Nations Truce Negotiator in the area. In the course of deciding what action to take in respect of his death, the United Nations General Assembly sought the advice of the I.C.J. Israel was admitted to the United Nations on May 11, 1949, shortly after the Court gave its opinion.

---

[38] See Dugard, 88 S.A.L.J. 463, 467 (1971). See, however, Higgins, 21 I.C.L.Q. 270, 275–286 (1972).

[39] S.C.Resn. 301 (1971), *Resolutions and Decisions* (1971), p. 7.

[40] S.C. Resn. 309 (1972), *id.*, 1972, p. 4.

[41] See, *e.g.* S.C. Resn. 385 (1976), *id.*, 1976, p. 8.

[42] *UN Chronicle,* June 1981, p. 5.

[43] See S.C.Resn. 435 (1978), *Resolutions and Decisions*, 1978, p. 13.

[44] See Bowett, *The Law of International Institutions* (4th ed., 1982); Hardy (1961) 37 B.Y.I.L. 516; Parry (1949) 26 B.Y.I.L. 108; Wright, 43 A.J.I.L. 509 (1949). There are also many *private* international organisations (*e.g.* the Inter-Parliamentary Union), the members of which are normally private individuals or bodies, although states do participate in some cases.

[45] For a summary of events in the Middle East in 1947–1949, see below, p. 176.

Opinion of the Court

The first question asked of the Court is as follows:

In the event of an agent of the United Nations in the performance of his duties suffering injury in circumstances involving the responsibility of a State, has the United Nations, as an Organisation, the capacity to bring an international claim against the responsible *de jure* or *de facto* government with a view to obtaining the reparation due in respect of the damage caused (*a*) to the United Nations, (*b*) to the victim or to persons entitled through him? . . .

The subjects of law in any legal system are not necessarily identical in their nature or in the extent of their rights, and their nature depends upon the needs of the Community. Throughout its history, the development of international law has been influenced by the requirements of international life, and the progressive increase in the collective action of States has already given rise to instances of action upon the international plane by certain entities which are not States. This development culminated in the establishment in June 1945 of an international organisation whose purposes and principles are specified in the Charter of the United Nations. But to achieve these ends the attribution of international personality is indispensable.

The Charter has not been content to make the Organisation created by it merely a centre "for harmonising the actions of nations in the attainment of these common ends" (Article 1, para. 4). It has equipped that centre with organs, and has given it special tasks. It has defined the position of the Members in relation to the Organisation by requiring them to give it every assistance in any action undertaken by it (Article 2, para. 5), and to accept and carry out the decisions of the Security Council; by authorising the General Assembly to make recommendations to the Members; by giving the Organisation legal capacity and privileges and immunities in the territory of each of its Members; and by providing for the conclusion of agreements between the Organisation and its Members. Practice—in particular the conclusions of conventions to which the Organisation is a party—has confirmed the character of the Organisation, which occupies a position in certain respects in detachment from its Members, and which is under a duty to remind them, if need be, of certain obligations. It must be added that the Organisation is a political body, charged with political tasks of an important character, and covering a wide field namely the maintenance of international peace and security, the development of friendly relations among nations, and the achievement of international co-operation in the solution of problems of an economic, social, cultural or humanitarian character (Article 1); and in dealing with its Members it employs political means. The "Convention on the Privileges and Immunities of the United Nations" of 1946 creates rights and duties between each of the signatories and the Organisation (see in particular, Section 35). It is difficult to see how such a convention could operate except upon the international plane and as between parties possessing international personality.

In the opinion of the Court, the Organisation was intended to exercise and enjoy, and is in fact exercising and enjoying, functions and rights which can only be explained on the basis of the possession of a large measure of international personality and the capacity to operate upon an international plane. It is at present the supreme type of international organisation, and it could not carry out the intentions of its founders if it was devoid of international personality. It must be acknowledged that its Members, by entrusting certain functions to it, with the attendant duties and responsibilities, have clothed it with the competence required to enable those functions to be effectively discharged.

Accordingly, the Court has come to the conclusion that the Organisation is an international person. That is not the same thing as saying that it is a State, which it certainly is not, or that its legal personality and rights and duties are the same as those of a State. Still less is it the same thing as saying that it is "a super-State," whatever that expression may mean. It does not even imply that all its rights and duties must be upon the international plane, any more than all the rights and duties of a State must be upon that plane. What it does mean is that it is a subject of international law and capable of possessing international rights and duties, and that it has capacity to maintain its rights by bringing international claims.

The next question is whether the sum of the international rights of the Organisation comprises the right to bring the kind of international claim described in the Request for this Opinion. That is a claim against a State to obtain reparation in respect of the damage caused by the injury of an agent of the Organisation in the course of the performance of his duties. Whereas a State possesses the totality of international rights and duties recognised by international law, the rights and duties of an entity such as the Organisation must depend upon its purposes and functions as specified or implied in its constituent documents and developed in practice. The functions of the Organisation are of such a character that they could not be effectively discharged if they involved the concurrent action, on the international plane, of fifty-eight or more[46] Foreign Offices, and the Court concludes that the Members have endowed the Organisation with capacity to bring international claims when necessitated by the discharge of its functions. . . .

. . . It cannot be doubted that the Organisation has the capacity to bring an international claim against one of its Members which has caused injury to it by a breach of its international obligations towards it. The damage specified in Question I (*a*) means exclusively damage caused to the interests of the Organisation itself, to its administrative machine, to its property and assets, and to the interests of which it is the guardian. It is clear that the Organisation has the capacity to bring a claim for this damage. As the claim is based on the breach of an international obligation on the part of the Member held responsible by the Organisation, the Member cannot contend that this obligation is governed by municipal law, and the Organisation is justified in giving its claim the character of an international claim.

When the Organisation has sustained damage resulting from a breach by a Member of its international obligations, it is impossible to see how it can obtain reparation unless it possesses capacity to bring an international claim. It cannot be supposed that in such an event all the Members of the Organisation, save the defendant State must combine to bring a claim against the defendant for the damage suffered by the Organisation.

In dealing with the question of law which arises out of Question I (*b*) . . . The only legal question which remains to be considered is whether, in the course of

---

[46] *Ed.* Now over 150.

bringing an international claim of this kind, the Organisation can recover "the reparation due in respect of the damage caused . . . to the victim. . . ."

The traditional rule that diplomatic protection is exercised by the national State does not involve the giving of a negative answer to Question I (b).

In the first place, this rule applies to claims brought by a State. But here we have the different and new case of a claim that would be brought by the Organisation.

In the second place, even in inter-State relations, there are important exceptions to the rule, for there are cases in which protection may be exercised by a State on behalf of persons not having its nationality.[47]

In the third place, the rule rests on two bases. The first is that the defendant State has broken an obligation towards the national State in respect of its nationals. The second is that only the party to whom an international obligation is due can bring a claim in respect of its breach. This is precisely what happens when the Organisation, in bringing a claim for damage suffered by its agent, does so by invoking the breach of an obligation towards itself. Thus, the rule of the nationality of claims affords no reason against recognizing that the Organisation has the right to bring a claim for the damage referred to in Question I (b). On the contrary, the principle underlying this rule leads to the recognition of this capacity as belonging to the Organisation, when the Organisation invokes, as the ground of its claim, a breach of an obligation towards itself.

Nor does the analogy of the traditional rule of diplomatic protection of nationals abroad justify in itself an affirmative reply. It is not possible, by a strained use of the concept of allegiance, to assimilate the legal bond which exists, under Article 100 of the Charter, between the Organisation on the one hand, and the Secretary-General and the staff on the other, to the bond of nationality existing between a State and its nationals.

The Court is here faced with a new situation. The questions to which it gives rise can only be solved by realizing that the situation is dominated by the provisions of the Charter considered in the light of the principles of international law. . . .

The Charter does not expressly confer upon the Organisation the capacity to include, in its claim for reparation, damage caused to the victim or to persons entitled through him. The Court must therefore begin by enquiring whether the provisions of the Charter concerning the functions of the Organisation, and the part played by its agents in the performance of those functions, imply for the Organisation power to afford its agents the limited protection that would consist in the bringing of a claim on their behalf for reparation for damage suffered in such circumstances. Under international law, the Organisation must be deemed to have those powers which, though not expressly provided in the Charter, are conferred upon it by necessary implication as being essential to the performance of its duties. This principle of law was applied by the Permanent Court of International Justice to the International Labour Organisation in its Advisory Opinion No. 13 of July 23rd, 1926 (Series B., No. 13, p. 18) and must be applied to the United Nations.

[47] *Ed.* The Court is probably referring to cases of protected persons, alien members of a state's armed forces and alien crew members of a state's merchant ships. It is also possible to avoid the application of the nationality rule by treaty. See Schwarzenberger, pp. 592–596.

Having regard to its purposes and functions already referred to, the Organisation may find it necessary, and has in fact found it necessary, to entrust its agents with important missions to be performed in disturbed parts of the world. Many missions, from their very nature, involve the agents in unusual dangers to which ordinary persons are not exposed. For the same reason, the injuries suffered by its agents in these circumstances will sometimes have occurred in such a manner that their national State would not be justified in bringing a claim for reparation on the ground of diplomatic protection, or, at any rate, would not feel disposed to do so. Both to ensure the efficient and independent performance of these missions and to afford effective support to its agents, the Organisation must provide them with adequate protection. . . .

In order that the agent may perform his duties satisfactorily, he must feel that this protection is assured to him by the Organisation, and that he may count on it. To ensure the independence of the agent, and, consequently, the independent action of the Organisation itself, it is essential that in performing his duties he need not have to rely on any other protection than that of the Organisation (save of course for the direct and immediate protection due from the State in whose territory he may be). In particular, he should not have to rely on the protection of his own State. If he had to rely on that State, his independence might well be comprised, contrary to the principle applied by Article 100 of the Charter. And lastly, it is essential that—whether the agent belongs to a powerful or to a weak State; to one more affected or less affected by the complications of international life; to one in sympathy or not in sympathy with the mission of the agent—he should know that in the performance of his duties he is under the protection of the Organisation. This assurance is even more necessary when the agent is stateless. . . .

The obligations entered into by States to enable the agents of the Organisation to perform their duties are undertaken not in the interest of the agents, but in that of the Organisation. When it claims redress for a breach of these obligations, the Organisation is invoking its own right, the right that the obligations due to it should be respected. On this ground, it asks for reparation of the injury suffered, for "it is a principle of international law that the breach of an engagement involves an obligation to make reparation in an adequate form;" as was stated by the Permanent Court in its Judgment No. 8 of July 26th, 1927 (Series A., No. 9, p. 21). In claiming reparation based on the injury suffered by its agent, the Organisation does not represent the agent, but is asserting its own right, the right to secure respect for undertakings entered into towards the Organisation.

Having regard to the foregoing considerations, and to the undeniable right of the Organisation to demand that its Members shall fulfil the obligations entered into by them in the interest of the good working of the Organisation, the Court is of the opinion that in the case of a breach of these obligations, the Organisation has the capacity to claim adequate reparation, and that in assessing this reparation it is authorised to include the damage suffered by the victim or by persons entitled through him.

The question remains whether the Organisation has "the capacity to bring an international claim against the responsible *de jure* or *de facto* government with a view to obtaining the reparation due in respect of the damage caused (*a*) to the United Nations, (*b*) to the victim or to persons entitled through him" when the defendant State is not a member of the Organisation.

In considering this aspect of Question I (*a*) and (*b*), it is necessary to keep in mind the reasons which have led the Court to give an affirmative answer to it when the defendant State is a Member of the Organisation. It has now been established that the Organisation has capacity to bring claims on the international plane, and that it possessed a right of functional protection in respect of its agents. Here again the Court is authorised to assume that the damage suffered involves the responsibility of a State, and it is not called upon to express an opinion upon the various ways in which that responsibility might be engaged. Accordingly the question is whether the Organisation has capacity to bring a claim against the defendant State to recover reparation in respect of that damage or whether, on the contrary, the defendant State, not being a member, is justified in raising the objection that the Organisation lacks the capacity to bring an international claim. On this point, the Court's opinion is that fifty States,[48] representing the vast majority of the members of the international community, had the power, in conformity with international law, to bring into being an entity possessing objective international personality and not merely personality recognised by them alone, together with capacity to bring international claims. . . .

The Court answered Question I (*a*), unanimously, and I (*b*), by 11 votes to 4,[49] in the affirmative.

Question II is as follows:

"In the event of an affirmative reply on point I (*b*), how is action by the United Nations to be reconciled with such rights as may be possessed by the State of which the victim is a national?"

The affirmative reply given by the Court on point I (*b*) obliges it now to examine Question II. When the victim has a nationality, cases can clearly occur in which the injury suffered by him may engage the interest both of his national State and of the Organisation. In such an event, competition between the State's right of diplomatic protection and the Organisation's right of functional protection might arise, and this is the only case with which the Court is invited to deal.

In such a case, there is no rule of law which assigns priority to the one or to the other, or which compels either the State or the Organisation to refrain from bringing an international claim.

. . . The Court sees no reason why the parties concerned should not find solutions inspired by goodwill and common sense, and as between the Organisation and its Members it draws attention to their duty to render "every assistance" provided by Article 2, paragraph 5, of the Charter.

Although the bases of the two claims are different, that does not mean that the defendant State can be compelled to pay the reparation due in respect of the damage twice over. International tribunals are already familiar with the problem of a claim in which two or more national States are interested, and they know how to protect the defendant State in such a case.[50]

---

[48] *Ed.*, *i.e.* the 50 states that participated in the San Francisco Conference in 1945 at which the UN Charter was drafted.

[49] The judges in the majority were President Basdevant; Vice-President Guerrerro; Judges Alvarez, Fabela, Zoričić, de Visscher, Sir Arnold McNair, Klaestad, Read, Hsu Mo and Azevedo. Judges Hackworth, Winiarski, Badawi Pasha and Krylov dissented.

[50] *Ed.* See below, p. 450.

The risk of competition between the Organization and the national State can be reduced or eliminated either by a general convention or by agreements entered into in each particular case. There is no doubt that in due course a practice will be developed, and it is worthy of note that already certain States whose nationals have been injured in the performance of missions undertaken for the Organisation have shown a reasonable and co-operative disposition to find a practical solution.

The question of reconciling action by the Organisation with the rights of a national State may arise in another way; that is to say, when the agent bears the nationality of the defendant State.

The ordinary practice whereby a State does not exercise protection on behalf of one of its nationals against a State which regards him as its own national, does not constitute a precedent which is relevant here. The action of the Organisation is in fact based not upon the nationality of the victim but upon his status as agent of the Organisation. Therefore it does not matter whether or not the State to which the claim is addressed regards him as its own national, because the question of nationality is not pertinent to the admissibility of the claim.

In law, therefore, it does not seem that the fact of the possession of the nationality of the defendant State by the agent constitutes any obstacle to a claim brought by the Organisation for a breach of obligations towards it occurring in relation to the performance of his mission by that agent.

The Court answered Question II by 10 votes to 5.[51]

Notes

1. In the light of the opinion in the *Reparation Case*, the United Nations General Assembly authorised the Secretary-General to seek reparation from Israel in connection with the death of Count Bernadotte.[52] In 1950, Israel paid the sum requested by the Secretary-General "as reparation for the damages borne by the United Nations."[53]

2. What advice do you think the Court would have given on (i) a claim by the United Nations to exercise sovereignty over territory; (ii) a claim against the United Nations by a state in respect of the breach of a treaty?

3. Might the Court's opinion on the United Nations right to bring a claim against a non-member have been different if the United Nations had had only six members? How do you reconcile the United Nations "objective international personality" with the rule that treaties (*e.g.* the United Nations Charter) cannot create obligations for third states without their consent?[54]

4. Bowett[55] states:

Whilst . . . specific acknowledgment of the possession of *international* personality is extremely rare, it is permissible to assume that most organisations created by a multilateral inter-governmental agreement will, so far as they are endowed with functions on the international plane, possess some measure of international personality in addition to the personality within the system of municipal law of the members which all the agreements on privileges and immunities (and often the basic constitutions) provide for. Possession of such international personality will normally involve, as a consequence, the attribution of power to make treaties, of privileges and immunities, of power to undertake legal proceedings: it will also pose a general problem of dissolution, for in the nature of things, the personality of all such organisations can be brought to an end.

[51] The five dissenting judges were the four who dissented on Question I (*b*) and one other (unknown).
[52] Resolution 365 (IV); G.A.O.R., 4th Session, *Resolutions*, p. 64.
[53] U.N. Doc. A/1347.
[54] See Schwarzenberger, pp. 128–130.   [55] *Op. cit.* at p. 114, n. 44, above, p. 339.

5. Peaslee[56] lists over 100 public international organisations, the majority of which have come into existence since the Second World War. They range from organisations of universal membership and general competence, such as the United Nations, to regional ones with specialised functions, such as NATO.

6. With regard to the European Communities[57] the European Coal and Steel Community (ECSC) is expressly accorded "in international relations . . . the legal capacity it requires to perform its functions and attain its objectives."[58] The Treaty of Rome contains no such general provision but does authorise the European Economic Community (EEC) to make tariff and trade agreements with "third countries" in the implementation of the Community commercial policy[59] and to make association agreements with "a third state, a union of states or an international organisation."[60] Similarly, the European Atomic Energy Authority (EURATOM) "may, within the limits of its powers and jurisdiction, enter into obligations by concluding agreements or contracts with a third state, an international organisation or a national of a third state."[61] All three Communities have in fact made agreements with third states or countries and with international organisations which can be classified as treaties for international law purposes. The Communities are probably competent to exercise diplomatic relations also.[62] At present they exercise the right of passive legation by receiving and accrediting representatives from states.[63] In February 1972, the six original members of the Community and the United Kingdom agreed to extend diplomatic recognition to Bangladesh. It was decided not to make a single joint announcement of recognition, to avoid the impression that diplomatic recognition is a communities affair.[64] Similar steps to co-ordinate the foreign policy actions of Member States have occurred since then.

(ii) INDIVIDUALS[65]

LAUTERPACHT, SURVEY OF INTERNATIONAL LAW IN RELATION TO THE WORK OF CODIFICATION OF THE INTERNATIONAL LAW COMMISSION

Memorandum prepared for the U.N. Secretariat, U.N. Doc. A/CN.4/1/Rev. 1, February 10, 1949, pp. 19–20. Reprinted in E. Lauterpacht (ed.), *International Law being the Collected Papers of Hersch Lauterpacht* (1970, 445), Vol. I at pp. 469–471

27. The question of the subjects of international law has, in particular in the last twenty-five years, ceased to be one of purely theoretical importance and it is

[56] *International Governmental Organisations*, Parts I–V (3rd ed., 1974).
[57] On their external relations, see Kapteyn and Verloren van Themat, *Introduction to the Law of the European Communities* (1973), Chap. XI; Lasok and Bridge, *An Introduction to the Law and Institutions of the European Communities* (3rd ed., 1982), pp. 39–47; and Parry and Hardy, *EEC Law* (2nd ed., 1981), Chap. 29–31.
[58] Art. 6, ECSC Treaty 1951, Cmnd. 4863.   [59] Art. 113(3), EEC Treaty 1957, Cmnd. 4864.
[60] Art. 238, *ibid*. See Hunnings, in Bathurst *et al.*, eds., *Legal Problems of an Enlarged European Community* (1972), Chap. 10; and Leopold, 26 I.C.L.Q. 54 (1977). See also *Re the European Road Transport Agreement* [1971] C.M.L.R. 335.
[61] Art. 101, EURATOM Treaty, Cmnd. 4865.   [62] See Feld, 43 *Texas L.R.* 891 (1965).
[63] Over 70 states have missions, usually at ambassador level, accredited to the Communities. As far as the right of active legation is concerned, the Commission of the Communities has delegations accredited to the U.S.A., Tokyo, Ottawa and Latin America (in Caracas) and to certain international organisations. The Communities have observer status in the UN General Assembly and have participated in international conferences.
[64] See Twitchett, in Twitchett, ed., *Europe and the World* (1976), p. 27.
[65] See Brownlie, 11 I.C.L.Q. 701 (1962); Gormley, *The Procedural Status of the Individual before International and Supernational Tribunals* (1966); Korowicz, 50 A.J.I.L. 533 (1956); Lauterpacht, 63 L.Q.R. 438 (1947) and 64 L.Q.R. 97 (1948); Nørgaard, *The Position of the Individual in International Law* (1962).

now probable that in some respects it requires authoritative international regulation. Practice has abandoned the doctrine that States are the exclusive subjects of international rights and duties. Although the Statute of the International Court of Justice adheres to the traditional view that only States can be parties to international proceedings,[66] a number of other international instruments have recognised the procedural capacity of the individual. This was the case not only in the provisions of the Treaty of Versailles relating to the jurisdiction of the Mixed Arbitral Tribunals, but also in other treaties such as the Polish-German Convention of 1922 relating to Upper Silesia in which—as was subsequently held by the Upper Silesian Mixed Tribunal—the independent procedural status of individuals as claimants before an international agency was recognised even as against the State of which they were nationals.[67]

28. In the sphere of substantive law, the Permanent Court of International Justice recognised, in the advisory opinion relating to the postal service in Danzig,[68] that there is nothing in international law to prevent individuals from acquiring directly rights under a treaty provided that this is the intention of the contracting parties. A considerable number of decisions of municipal courts tendered subsequently to the advisory opinion of the Permanent Court expressly affirmed that possibility.

29. In the field of customary international law the enjoyment of benefits of international law by individuals as a matter of right followed from the doctrine, accepted by a growing number of countries, that generally recognised rules of the law of nations form part of the law of the land.[69] In the sphere of duties imposed by international law the principle that the obligations of international law bind individuals directly regardless of the law of their State and of any contrary order received from their superiors was proclaimed in the Charter annexed to the Agreement of 8 August 1945, providing for the setting up of the International Military Tribunal at Nürnberg as well as in the Charter of the International Military Tribunal at Tokyo of 19th January 1946.[70] That principle was fully affirmed in the judgment of the Nürnberg Tribunal as flowing from the imperative necessity of making international law effective. The Tribunal said: "Crimes against international law are committed by men, not by abstract entities, and only by punishing individuals who commit such crimes can the provisions of international law be enforced".[71] It was reaffirmed in the resolution of the General Assembly of 11 December, 1946, expressing adherence to the principles of the Nürnberg Charter and Judgment. . . .[72]

30. On a different plane the Charter of the Nürnberg Tribunal—and the judgment which followed it—proclaimed the criminality of offences against humanity, i.e. of such offences against the fundamental rights of man to life and liberty, even if committed in obedience to the law of the State.[73] To that extent, in a different sphere, positive law has recognised the individual as endowed, under international law, with rights the violation of which is a criminal act. The

[66] Ed. See below, p. 711.
[67] Ed. See *Steiner and Gross* v. *Polish State*, 4 A.D. 291 (1927–28).
[68] Ed. P.C.I.J.Rep., Series B, No. 11 (1925).
[69] See above, Chap. 3.
[70] See below, p. 555.
[71] See below, p. 558.
[72] See below, p. 560.
[73] See below, p. 555.

repeated provisions of the Charter of the United Nations in the matter of human rights and fundamental freedoms are directly relevant in this connection.[74]

Notes

1. The "procedural capacity of the individual" has more recently been recognised before the Court of Justice of the European Communities[75] and in treaties on human rights.[76] For a recent example of a treaty imposing duties upon individuals, see the International Convention on Civil Liability for Oil Pollution Damage 1969.[77]

2. For the most part, however, the individual remains an object, not a subject, of international law whose most important characteristic for international law purposes is his nationality. It is this, for example, that determines which state (his national state) may protect him against the extravagances of another (if he is stateless normally no state may do so) and, more ominously, places him within the domestic jurisdiction, and hence the discretionary treatment, of his national state. It is nationality also that decides whether an individual can benefit from treaty guarantees that a state secures for its "nationals."

3. On the juridical nature of some kinds of agreements between states and large companies, see below, p. 439.

(iii) OTHER ENTITIES

NANNI v. PACE AND THE SOVEREIGN ORDER OF MALTA

8 A.D. 2 (1935–37). Italian Court of Cassation

The Order, the official title of which is the Sovereign Military Order of St. John of Jerusalem, of Rhodes, and of Malta, was established during the Crusades as a nursing brotherhood and military organisation directed against the Moslems. In 1309, the Order conquered the Island of Rhodes, which it then ruled until 1522 when it was ejected by the Ottoman Empire. In 1530, the Order moved to Malta which had been given to it by Emperor Charles V. This it ruled until 1798 when the island was taken by Napoleon. The Order established its headquarters in Rome in 1834. Since that time it has performed work of a humanitarian character for the poor and the sick. In the present case, which raised the question of the personality of the Order in Italian law, the Court examined its history and status in international law.

Judgment of the Court

With the recognition of the Church and of the Byzantine Empire, the Order established, after the conquest of territory of its own, its independence and sovereignty. . . . The Grand Master was recognised as Sovereign Head of Rhodes with all the attributes of such a position, which included . . . the right of active and passive legation together with the right of negotiating directly with other States and of making conventions and treaties. . . . Such attributes of sovereignty and independence have not ceased, in the case of the Order, at the present day—at least not from the formal point of view in its relations with the Italian State. Nor has its personality in international law come to an end

---

[74] See below, p. 532.
[75] See, *inter alia*, Art. 173, EEC Treaty 1957, Cmnd. 4864.
[76] See below, Chap. 9.
[77] Below, p. 343.

notwithstanding the fact that as a result of the British occupation of Malta such personality cannot be identified with the possession of territory. . . . With regard to this second aspect of the matter it is enough to point out that the modern theory of the subjects of international law recognises a number of collective units whose composition is independent of the nationality of their constituent members and whose scope transcends by virtue of their universal character the territorial confines of any single State. It must be admitted that only States can contribute to the formation of international law as an objective body of rules—States as international entities which are territorially identifiable. This is so because the fulfilment of this latter requirement makes them the principal objects and creators of such rules. But it is impossible to deny to other international collective units a limited capacity of acting internationally within the ambit and the actual exercise of their own functions with the resulting international juridical personality and capacity which is its necessary and natural corollary. In accordance with these doctrines, such personality was never denied to the Holy See even before the Lateran Treaty of February 11, 1929, and it is unanimously conceded to the League of Nations, although it is neither a State, nor a super-State, nor a Confederation of States. It is equally conceded to certain international administrative unions.

Notes

1. The Order maintains diplomatic relations with over 40 states.[78] Is its practice as to, for example, the extent of diplomatic immunity relevant to the formation of customary international law in the way that state practice is? What about the practice of the United Nations with regard, for example, to treaties it has made with states or other public international organisations? Does that contribute to the customary international law of treaties?

2. *The Holy See and the Vatican City.* Graham[79] states:

> The view seems to be dominant today . . . that the Holy See does, in fact, enjoy international personality. Furthermore, this personality of the Holy See is distinct from the personality of the State of Vatican City. One is a non-territorial institution, and the other a state. The papacy as a religious organ is a subject of international law and capable of international rights and duties.
>
> . . . The fact that the Holy See is a non-territorial institution is no longer regarded as a reason for denying it international personality. The papacy can act in its own name in the international community. It can enter into legally binding conventions known as concordats. In the world of diplomacy the Pope enjoys the rights of active and passive legation. He can send and receive representatives who are public ministers in the sense of international law.

The Lateran Treaty of February 11, 1929, between Italy and the Holy See reads:

> *Article 2.* Italy recognises the sovereignty of the Holy See in the international domain as an attribute inherent in its nature, in accordance with its traditions and with the requirements of its mission in the world. . . .
>
> *Article 4.* The Exclusive sovereignty and jurisdiction of the Holy See over the City of the Vatican which Italy recognises, implies the consequence that no

[78] O'Connell (1976–77) 48 B.Y.I.L. 433. On the Order generally, see Farran, 3 I.C.L.Q. 217 (1954) and 4 I.C.L.Q. 308 (1955). The U.K. does not maintain diplomatic relations with the Order.

[79] *Vatican Diplomacy: a Study of Church and State on the International Plane* (1959), pp. 186, 201. See also Kunz, 46 A.J.I.L. 308 (1952).

interference on the part of the Italian government may be there manifested, and that there will be no other authority than that of the Holy See.[80]

5. RECOGNITION OF STATES AND GOVERNMENTS[81]

BRIERLY, THE LAW OF NATIONS

(6th ed., 1963), p. 138

The legal significance of recognition is controversial. According to one view it has a 'constitutive' effect; through recognition only and exclusively a state becomes an international person and a subject of international law.[82] But there are serious difficulties in this view. The status of a state recognized by state A but not recognized by state B, and therefore apparently both an 'international person' and not an 'international person' at the same time, would be a legal curiosity. Perhaps a more substantial difficulty is that the doctrine would oblige us to say that an unrecognized state has neither rights nor duties at international law, and some of the consequences of accepting that conclusion might be startling. We should have to say, for example, that an intervention, otherwise illegal, would not have been illegal in Manchukuo,[83] or that if Manchukuo had been involved in war, she would have been under no legal obligation to respect the rights of neutrals. Non-recognition may certainly make the enforcement of rights and duties more difficult than it would otherwise be, but the practice of states does not support the view that they have no legal existence before recognition.[84]

The better view is that the granting of recognition to a new state is not a 'constitutive' but a 'declaratory' act; it does not bring into legal existence a state which did not exist before. A state may exist without being recognized, and if it does exist in fact, then, whether or not it has been formally recognized by other states, it has a right to be treated by them *as* a state. The primary function of recognition is to acknowledge as a fact something which has hitherto been uncertain, namely the independence of the body claiming to be a state, and to declare the recognizing state's readiness to accept the normal consequences of that fact, namely the usual courtesies of international intercourse. It is true that the present state of the law makes it possible that different states should act on different views of the application of the law to the same state of facts. This does not mean that their differing interpretations are all equally correct, but only that there exists at present no procedure for determining which are correct and which are not. The constitutive theory of recognition gains most of its plausibility from the lack of centralized institutions in the system, and it treats this lack not as an accident due to the stage of development which the law has so

---

[80] Peaslee, 3 *Constitutions of Nations* (3rd ed., rev. 1968) Pt. 2, pp. 1187–1188.

[81] See Blix, 130 *Hague Recueil* 587 (1970–II); Briggs, 43 A.J.I.L. 113 (1949); Chen, *The International Law of Recognition* (1951); Lauterpacht, *Recognition in International Law* (1947).

[82] Oppenheim, *International Law* (8th ed., 1955), Vol. I, § 71.

[83] *Ed.* see above, p. 88.

[84] See on this point Jaffé, *Judicial Aspects of Foreign Relations*, at p. 98. When Jewish airmen shot down British aeroplanes over Egypt in January 1949 the British Government at once informed the government of the Jewish state, which at that time Britain had not recognized, that they would demand compensation.

far reached, but as an essential feature of the system. It is in fact one more relic of absolutist theories of state sovereignty.

In practice non-recognition does not always imply that the existence of the unrecognized state is a matter of doubt. States have discovered that the granting or withholding of recognition can be used to further a national policy; they have refused it as a mark of disapproval, as nearly all of them did to Manchukuo; and they have granted it in order to establish the very independence of which recognition is supposed to be a mere acknowledgement, as when in 1903 the United States recognized Panama only three days after it had revolted from Colombia or when in 1948 the United States recognized Israel within a few hours of its proclamation of independence.[85]

Notes

1. The declaratory theory is adopted by most modern writers. It is also supported by arbitral practice. In particular, the *Tinoco Case*, below, p. 132, suggests that recognition is simply evidence (to be discounted if politically biased) that the international law requirements are met. State practice confirms this in the sense that states do not refrain from bringing claims under international law against unrecognised states or governments.[86] Although the extract from Brierly is expressed in terms only of the recognition of states, it is clear that the declaratory theory applies to the recognition of governments too. The 1951 Morrison statement of British practice, below, p. 129, supposes that there is a legal duty to grant recognition when the necessary requirements are met. This approach, which is not repeated in the 1980 British statement, below, p. 127, has never found favour with other states.[87] The United States, for example, has consistently maintained that recognition is a "high political act."[88] The position would seem to be that it is a discretionary act with evidential value in law.

[85] In regard to the recognition of Israel, Mr. W.R. Austin, the representative of the United States on the Security Council, asserted the political character of the act of recognition in the most unequivocal terms: "I should regard it as highly improper for me to admit that any country on earth can question the sovereignty of the United States of America in the exercise of that high political act of recognition of the *de facto* status of a state. Moreover, I would not admit here, by implication or by direct answer, that there exists a tribunal of justice or of any other kind, anywhere, that can pass upon the legality or the validity of that act of my country" (*New York Times*, May 19, 1948).

[86] See the example given by Brierly, at n. 85, above, and the U.S.A. response to the seizure of the *Pueblo* by North Korea, which the U.S.A. did not recognise, below, p. 332. In 1957, the U.K. claimed compensation from the unrecognised Taiwan Government for damage done to British vessels by its forces: see *C.P.U.K.I.L.* 1957, 6 I.C.L.Q. 507 (1957). In 1954, the U.S.A. claimed under international law against the unrecognised Government of the Chinese People's Republic for the killing of U.S.A. nationals when a commercial aircraft was shot down by a Chinese military aircraft: see 2 Whiteman 651. Arab states regard Israel as governed by international law although they do not (except for Egypt since 1979) recognise it as a state. See also the 1948 U.K. statement in the next note.

[87] The 1951 statement was influenced by Lauterpacht, *Recognition in International Law* (1947), p. 6, who argued that there was a duty on the part of states to grant recognition in the absence of an international body competent to do so. Lauterpacht also thought that recognition so granted was constitutive. This view was not clearly adopted in the 1951 statement. In 1948, the U.K. adopted a declaratory approach in the UN: ". . . the existence of a state should not be regarded as depending upon recognition but on whether in fact it fulfils the conditions which create a duty for recognition"; UN Doc. A/CN.4/2, p. 53, quoted in Crawford, *op. cit.* at p. 80, n. 1, p. 16.

[88] See, *e.g.* the extract from Brierly, above. *cf.* the following statement by the UN Secretariat when considering the question of the representation of members in the UN (UN Doc. S/1466; S.C.O.R., 5th Year, Supp. for January/May 1950, p. 19): "The recognition of a new state, or a new government of an existing state, is a unilateral act which the recognizing government can grant or withhold. It is true that some legal writers have argued forcibly that when a new

2. On May 30, 1967, Biafra declared its independence of Nigeria, of which it had constituted the Eastern Region. Its war of independence was unsuccessful and Biafra surrendered to the Nigerian Federal Government on January 12, 1970. It is now once again fully a part of Nigeria. Five States—Tanzania, Gabon, Ivory Coast, Zambia and Haiti—recognised it as an independent state during the rebellion, although no state entered into formal diplomatic relations. What effect did these recognitions have in law according to the declaratory and constitutive theories?[89]

3. *Modes of recognition.* Recognition of states or of governments may occur expressly or by implication. There is no precise catalogue of acts that imply recognition.[90] Entry into diplomatic relations clearly implies it, as, normally, does the making of a bilateral treaty arranging for commercial or other relations. The crucial question is that of intention. Participation in an international conference with a state or government will not indicate recognition if it is made clear that it is not intended to have this effect. Thus, in 1954, when the Foreign Ministers of France, the United Kingdom, the United States and the U.S.S.R. proposed the Geneva Conference to discuss Korea and Indochina and invited the Government of the People's Republic of China, the two Koreas and "other interested states," they added: "It is understood that neither the invitation to, nor the holding of, the above mentioned conference shall be deemed to imply diplomatic recognition in any case where it has not already been accorded."[91]

BRITISH PRACTICE ON THE RECOGNITION OF GOVERNMENTS[92]

Statement by the Foreign Secretary (Lord Carrington), *Hansard*, H.L., Vol. 408, Cols. 1121–1122. April 28, 1980; U.K.M.I.L. 1979 (1980) 51 B.Y.I.L. 367. *cf.* the statement by the Lord Privy Seal (Sir Ian Gilmour), *ibid.* H.C., Vol. 983, W.A. Cols. 277–279. April 25, 1980.

. . . we have conducted a re-examination of British policy and practice concerning the recognition of Governments. This has included a comparison with the practice of our partners and allies. On the basis of this review we have decided that we shall no longer accord recognition to Governments. The British Government recognise States in accordance with common international doctrine.

Where an unconstitutional change of régime takes place in a recognised State, Governments of other States must necessarily consider what dealings, if any, they should have with the new régime, and whether and to what extent it qualifies to be treated as the Government of the State concerned. Many of our partners and allies take the position that they do not recognise Governments

government, which comes into power through revolutionary means, enjoys, with a reasonable prospect of permanency, the habitual obedience of the bulk of the population, other states are under a legal duty to recognize it. However, while states may regard it as desirable to follow certain legal principles in according or withholding recognition, the practice of States shows that the act of recognition is still regarded as essentially a political decision, which each state decides in accordance with its own free appreciation of the situation."

[89] See Ijalaye, 65 A.J.I.L. 551 (1971).

[90] Apparently, even the sale of blankets may suffice. In 1962, the question arose of the sale to the Republican Government to the Yemen, which had recently come into being by revolution and which had not been recognized by the British Government, of 50,000 surplus blankets. The Lord Privy Seal stated in Parliament: "We could not sell them to the Yemeni republican authorities without recognizing the republican government": *Hansard*, H.C., Vol. 669, Cols. 1253–1254. December 19, 1962; *C.P.U.K.I.L.* 1962, p. 152.

[91] Communiqué on the 1954 Berlin Conference dated February 18, 1954, *Documents on American Foreign Relations* (1954) p. 219.

[92] See Davidson, 32 N.I.L.Q. 22 (1981) and Symmons, 1981 P.L. 249.

and that therefore no question of recognition arises in such cases. By contrast, the policy of successive British Governments has been that we should make and announce a decision formally 'recognising' the new Government.

This practice has sometimes been misunderstood, and, despite explanations to the contrary, our 'recognition' interpreted as implying approval. For example, in circumstances where there might be legitimate public concern about the violation of human rights by the new régime, or the manner in which it achieved power, it has not sufficed to say that an announcement of 'recognition' is simply a neutral formality.

We have therefore concluded that there are practical advantages in following the policy of many other countries in not according recognition to Governments. Like them, we shall continue to decide the nature of our dealings with régimes which come to power unconstitutionally in the light of our assessment of whether they are able of themselves to exercise effective control of the territory of the State concerned, and seem likely to continue to do so.

Notes

1. This statement is concerned solely with the recognition of new revolutionary governments in existing states. Governments that come into office constitutionally (*e.g.* by election) in existing states require no recognition in international law. New states (and hence their governments) will, as the statement indicates, continue to be recognised expressly, or formally, "in accordance with common international doctrine." The effect of the statement is that the United Kingdom has abandoned the practice of expressly recognising revolutionary governments; recognition is to be inferred instead from the "dealings" that the United Kingdom has with the claimant.[93] The new approach is reminiscent of the Estrada doctrine[94] adopted by Mexico in the 1930s and is in line with the practice of an increasing number of other states, including the United States and EEC States.[95] Galloway[96] summarises state practice as follows:

> In each region [of the world] the movement is towards deemphasizing or completely eliminating the recognition issue. However, it is doubtful that the recognition question will be eliminated in the foreseeable future because, in a significant minority of cases, nations consider the political factors strong enough to make an issue of recognition. This desire to deemphasize recognition in the majority of cases has resulted in the adherence of over thirty states to the Estrada Doctrine, but with the proviso that in certain situations they grant recognition based on political considerations.[97] The desire to deemphasize recognition also affects the adherence of well over thirty other states to an ad hoc policy based on political considerations in which recognition is usually downplayed and finessed by the euphemism that relations are continuing, or that relations are being resumed. Taken together, the two approaches account for over 75 of the states included in this study.

2. The 1980 statement does not basically change the criteria upon which the United Kingdom had previously followed in deciding whether to recognise a government and which will continue to be relied upon when deciding whether to have "dealings" with it. These were stated by the Foreign Secretary (Mr. Morrison) in 1951:

[93] The Foreign Secretary's statement and other parliamentary pronouncements say, in keeping with the universal trend towards minimising the role of recognition, that Governments will not be recognised at all. It seems more accurate to regard the move as one from express to implied recognition.
[94] See 2 Whiteman 85.
[95] On U.S. practice, see below, p. 131.
[96] *Recognizing Foreign Governments* (1978), p. 138.
[97] *Ed.* See the express recognition of the Chinese Government in 1979, below, p. 132.

. . . it is international law which defines the conditions under which a Government should be recognised *de jure* or *de facto* and it is a matter of judgment in each particular case whether a régime fulfils the conditions. The conditions under international law for the recognition of a new régime as the *de facto* Government of a State are that the new régime has in fact effective control over most of the State's territory and that this control seems likely to continue. The conditions for the recognition of a new régime as the *de jure* Government of a State are that the new régime should not merely have effective control over most of the State's territory, but that it should, in fact, be firmly established. His Majesty's Government consider that recognition should be accorded when the conditions specified by international law are, in fact, fulfilled and that recognition should not be given when these conditions are not fulfilled. The recognition of a Government *de jure* or *de facto* should not depend on whether the character of the régime is such as to command His Majesty's Government's approval.[98]

The effectiveness of a government is, of course, a *sine qua non* of recognition of an entity as the government of a state; recognition of an entity before it has become effective is "premature" and intervention in a state's affairs contrary to international law.[99]

The 1951 statement was supplemented in subsequent parliamentary pronouncements. In 1970, the Joint Under-Secretary for Foreign Affairs (Mr. Foley) stated in the House of Commons that the "normal criteria" employed by the British Government are:

that the new Government enjoy, with a reasonable prospect of permanence, the obedience of the mass of the population, and have effective control of much the greater part of the territory of the State concerned.[1]

In 1967, a Foreign Office spokesman listed the same criteria, but added that due account had to be taken of "special circumstances relating to any specific instance, including any United Nations or other international action."[2] Commenting upon the recognition by the United Kingdom of the Kadar Government established in Hungary after the 1956 uprising had been suppressed, the Joint Under-Secretary of State for Foreign Affairs (The Earl of Gosford) said:

. . . Her Majesty's Government . . . have, in common with other Western nations with representatives already in Budapest, continued to maintain a diplomatic mission there and to accept a Hungarian mission in London. Generally speaking, Her Majesty's Government's policy in the matter of recognition of Governments is to face facts and to acknowledge *de facto* a Government which has effective control of the territory within its jurisdiction, and of the inhabitants within that territory.[3]

3. The 1980 statement differs from that of 1951 in that (i) there is no mention of *de jure* and *de facto* governments and (ii) the words "of themselves" (*i.e.* without outside assistance) are added.[4] The question of the recognition of a government as the *de facto* government only arises where there are two competing governments in being. In most cases, the situation is quickly resolved and the question is simply one of recognising the revolutionary government as the new government if the revolution has succeeded. Even where the struggle continues for some time, the United Kingdom has tended in recent

---

[98] *Hansard*, H.C., Vol. 485, cols. 2410–2411. March 21, 1951.
[99] *cf.* above, p. 91, on the premature recognition of new states.
[1] *Hansard*, H.C., Vol. 799, col. 23. April 6, 1970.
[2] *Hansard*, H.C., Vol. 742 W.A. cols. 6–7. February 27, 1967.
[3] *Hansard*, H.L., Vol. 204, col. 755. July 4, 1957.
[4] It seems likely that the gloss placed upon the 1951 statement in the 1967 and 1970 statements quoted above remains intact.

years to wait until matters have sorted themselves out rather than grant interim recognition to a revolutionary movement as the *de facto* government of the territory it controls. Thus in the case of Cambodia in the 1970s, the only step taken was to withdraw recognition from the established government as the *de jure* government and grant it to the revolutionary Pol Pot government in 1976 once the latter had reached the capital and was in full control. The latter was not recognised as a *de facto* government as it gradually gained control of the countryside. It seems likely that, where two governments remain in being, the United Kingdom will henceforth have "dealings" with only one government, even though another government is in control of a part of the state's territory. The words "of themselves" in the 1980 statement reflect a later stage in the Cambodian case, as does the passage in the statement about the "violation of human rights" and the possibility of misunderstandings. The Pol Pot government, which had ill-treated the Cambodian population badly, was replaced by force in 1979 by the Heng Samrin government with the military assistance of Vietnam. In October 1979, the British Government declined to withdraw recognition from the former and to recognise the latter instead. It declined to do so (even though it acknowledged that the latter had "control of the greater part of the territory of Cambodia") for the reason that there was "no other Government which satisfies the criteria for recognition which have been applied by successive British Governments." This would seem to have been a reference to the dependence of the Heng Samrin Government upon Vietnamese support. The British Government stressed that its continued recognition of Pol Pot was not to be taken as "approval of . . . the enormity of Pol Pot's human rights violations."[5] By December, the position had changed:

> When we came to power last May, Pol Pot's Government held a dwindling proportion of the territory in Cambodia. Since September that proportion has further dwindled though of course Pol Pot's forces continue to resist. As the House is aware, our normal criteria require us to accord recognition to a Government who enjoy, with a reasonable prospect of permanence, the obedience of the mass of the population and the effective control of much the greater part of the country. . . .
>
> It will therefore come as no surprise to the House if I say that we can no longer regard Pol Pot as leading an effective Government in Cambodia. By the same token, however, the dependence of the so-called Heng Samrin régime on the Vietnamese occupation army is complete; there is no reason to doubt that without the presence of the occupation troops it would be swept away by resurgent Cambodian nationalism. I therefore make it very clear that we emphatically do not recognise any claim by Heng Samrin. Our position is that there is no Government in Cambodia whom we can recognise. This position is shared by the United States and by some of our leading friends in Europe.[6]

4. Despite the United Kingdom's adoption of a "face the facts" approach, it may sometimes have been swayed by politics in its judgment. Note, for example, the non-recognition of the German Democratic Republic as a state before 1973[7] and the continued non-recognition of North Korea.[8] Again, the United Kingdom "Government's position remains to recognise *de facto* the incorporation of the Baltic States [Latvia, Lithuania, and Estonia] into the Soviet Union but to withhold full recognition."[9] It was also noticeable that the United Kingdom recognised the new Obote

[5] *Hansard*, H.C., Vol. 972, cols. 31–34; *ibid.* W.A., col. 268. October 25, 1979; *U.K.M.I.L.* 1979; (1979) 50 B.Y.I.L. 296.

[6] *Hansard*, H.C. Vol. 975, col. 723. December 6, 1979.

[7] See above, p. 82, and below, p. 141. See also Greig, 83 L.Q.R. 96 at pp. 128–130 (1967).

[8] See Re *Al-Fin Corporation's Patent*, below, p. 148. South Korea is recognised.

[9] *Hansard*, H.C., Vol. 970, W.A., Col. 461. July 17, 1979; *U.K.M.I.L.* (1979) 50 B.Y.I.L. 293 (1979). The Baltic states were independent states between the two World Wars but were occupied by the U.S.S.R. and incorporated into its territory in 1940.

Government in Uganda in 1979 while the Tanzanian troops that had brought it to power were still in the country, when at the same time the Heng Samrin Government in Cambodia was refused recognition because of Vietnamese support.[10]

5. In practice, the question of the recognition of governments that have come into being by unconstitutional means in existing states is more common than that of the recognition of new states. As far as the first question is concerned, it is important to distinguish between recognition of a government as the government that can act for a state for international law purposes and entry into diplomatic relations with that government. The latter implies the former, but the former does not require the latter. A not uncommon situation is that in which one government terminates its diplomatic relations with another as an act of retorsion.[11] This by itself does not affect recognition.

U.S. PRACTICE ON THE RECOGNITION OF GOVERNMENTS

1977 U.S. Department of State statement, 77 U.S. Dept. of State Bull. 462 (1977); [1977] U.S.D.I.L. 19

. . . when the revolutionary French Government took power in 1792, Thomas Jefferson, our first Secretary of State, instructed the U.S. envoy in Paris to deal with it because it had been "formed by the will of the nation substantially declared."

Throughout most of the 19th century, the United States recognized stable governments without thereby attempting to confer approval. U.S. recognition policy grew more complex as various Administrations applied differing criteria for recognition and expressed differently the reasons for their decisions. For example, Secretary of State William Seward (1861–69) added as a criterion the government's ability to honour its international obligations; President Rutherford Hayes (1877–81) required a demonstration of popular support for the new government; and President Woodrow Wilson (1913–21) favored using recognition to spread democracy around the world by demanding free elections.

Other criteria have been applied since then. These include the degree of foreign involvement in the government as well as the government's political orientation, attitude toward foreign investment, and treatment of U.S. citizens, corporations, and government representatives.

One result of such complex recognition criteria was to create the impression among other nations that the United States approved of those governments it recognized and disapproved of those from which it withheld recognition. This appearance of approval, in turn, affected our decisions in ways that have not always advanced U.S. interests. In recent years, U.S. practice has been to deemphasize and avoid the use of recognition in cases of changes of governments and to concern ourselves with the question of whether we wish to have diplomatic relations with the new governments.

The Administration's policy is that establishment of relations does not involve approval or disapproval but merely demonstrates a willingness on our part to conduct our affairs with other governments directly.

---

[10] See Symmons, *loc. cit.* at p. 127, n. 92, above, p. 250, referring to a letter by Mr. Evan Luard, in *The Guardian*, October 5, 1979.

[11] *e.g.* the U.K. broke off diplomatic relations with Albania as an act of retorsion in 1946 and has yet to restore them. It also broke off relations with Argentina in 1982 over the Falklands Islands War. Guatemala has broken off diplomatic relations with the U.K. over Belize. These, and Cambodia, are the only states recognised by the U.K. with which the U.K. has no diplomatic relations.

Notes

1. As the statement indicates, "the United States Government has quietly moved to the Estrada Doctrine" so that "the significance of recognition has faded away."[12] Thus, on the question of the recognition of the Taraki Government in Afghanistan in 1978, the U.S. Government stated that "the question of recognition under the formulation of the last few years doesn't arise *per se*. . . . The important question is not recognition. The question is whether diplomatic relations continue. . . ."[13] On the latter point, it was stated:

> "The Government of the United States of America assumes that the Government of the Democratic Republic of Afghanistan will continue to honour and support the existing treaties and international agreements in force between our two states. On that assumption, it is the intention of the U.S. Government . . . to maintain diplomatic relations. . . ."[14]

Note, however, that Governments of the United States and China did expressly agree "to recognise each other and to establish diplomatic relations" as of 1979.[15]

2. On the criterion qualifying a government to be treated as the government of a state, the U.S. would appear to have moved to a simple test of effective control. In 1977, Deputy Secretary of State Christopher[16] stated:

> We maintain diplomatic relations with many governments of which we do not necessarily approve. The reality is that, in this day and age, coups and other unscheduled changes of government are not exceptional developments. Withholding diplomatic relations from these régimes, after they have obtained effective control, penalizes us. It means that we forsake much of the chance to influence the attitudes and conduct of a new régime. . . . Isolation may well bring out the worst in the new government.

3. On the criteria applying to the recognition of states, in 1976 the United States Department of State stated[17]:

> In the view of the United States, international law does not require a state to recognize another entity as a state; it is a matter for the judgment of each state whether an entity merits recognition as a state. In reaching this judgment, the United States has traditionally looked to the establishment of certain facts. These facts include effective control over a clearly-defined territory and population; and organized governmental administration of that territory; and a capacity to act effectively to conduct foreign relations and to fulfill international obligations. The United States has also taken into account whether the entity in question has attracted the recognition of the international community of states.

TINOCO ARBITRATION

Great Britain *v*. Costa Rica (1923)

Sole Arbitrator: William H. Taft, President of the United States Supreme Court,
1 R.I.A.A. 369

In 1917, Tinoco ousted the Government of Costa Rica by force. Elections were held and "[f]or a full two years Tinoco and the legislative assembly under him peaceably

---

[12] Baxter, 72 A.J.I.L. 875, 876 (1978).
[13] Department of State spokesman, May 1, 1978: 72 A.J.I.L. 879 (1978).
[14] U.S. Embassy in Kabul statement, May 6, 1978, 72 A.J.I.L. 879 (1978).
[15] Joint Communiqué, U.S. Government and the Government of the People's Republic of China: 73 A.J.I.L. 277 (1979). At the same time, the U.S.A. withdrew its recognition of the Government of Taiwan as the Government of the one state of China.
[16] Speech at Occidental College, June 11, 1977 [1977] U.S. D.I.L.
[17] 72 A.J.I.L. 337 (1978).

administered the affairs of the Government of Costa Rica." (*ibid.* p. 379). In 1919, Tinoco was ousted in his turn and the new Government repudiated certain obligations undertaken by the Tinoco Government towards British nationals. In the course of ruling upon the claims brought by Great Britain on the basis of these obligations, the arbitrator discussed the question of recognition.

TAFT C.J. I must hold that from the evidence . . . the Tinoco government was an actual sovereign government.

But it is urged that many leading Powers refused to recognize the Tinoco government, and that recognition by other nations is the chief and best evidence of the birth, existence and continuity of succession of a government. Undoubtedly recognition by other Powers is an important evidential factor in establishing proof of the existence of a government in the society of nations. What are the facts as to this? The Tinoco government was recognized by . . . [20 states]. . . .

The non-recognition by other nations of a government claiming to be a national personality, is usually appropriate evidence that it has not attained the independence and control entitling it by international law to be classed as such. But when recognition *vel non* of a government is by such nations determined by inquiry, not into its *de facto* sovereignty and complete governmental control, but into its illegitimacy or irregularity of origin,[18] their non-recognition loses something of evidential weight on the issue with which those applying the rules of international law are alone concerned. What is true of the non-recognition of the United States in its bearing upon the existence of a *de facto* government under Tinoco for thirty months is probably in a measure true of the non-recognition by her Allies in the European War. Such non-recognition for any reason, however, cannot outweigh the evidence disclosed by this record before me as to the *de facto* character of Tinoco's government, according to the standard set by international law. . . .

It is further objected by Costa Rica that Great Britain by her failure to recognize the Tinoco government is estopped now to urge claims of her subjects dependent upon the acts and contracts of the Tinoco government. . . . The contention here . . . precludes a government which did not recognize a *de facto* government from appearing in an international tribunal in behalf of its nationals to claim any rights based on the acts of such government.

To sustain this view a great number of decisions in English and American courts are cited to the point that a municipal court cannot, in litigation before it, recognize or assume the *de facto* character of a foreign government which the executive department of foreign affairs of the government of which the court is a branch has not recognized. . . . But such cases have no bearing on the point before us. Here the executive of Great Britain takes the position that the Tinoco government which it did not recognize, was nevertheless a *de facto* government that could create rights in British subjects which it now seeks to protect. Of course, as already emphasized, its failure to recognize the *de facto* government can be used against it as evidence to disprove the character it now attributes to that government, but this does not bar it from changing its position. Should a

---

[18] *Ed.* The Arbitrator is here referring to the "constitutionality" test of recognition introduced as U.S. policy by President Wilson in 1913 which made "the coming into power of a new government by constitutional means a prerequisite of recognition, particularly with respect to the Central American Republics": 2 Whiteman 69. The test was abandoned by 1931.

case arise in one of its own courts after it has changed its position doubtless that court would feel it incumbent upon it to note the change in its further rulings.

. . . It may be urged that it would be in the interest of the stability of governments and the orderly adjustment of international relations, and so a proper rule of international law, that a government in recognizing or refusing to recognize a government claiming admission to the society of nations should thereafter be held to an attitude consistent with its deliberate conclusion in this issue. Arguments for and against such a rule occur to me; but it suffices to say that I have not been cited to text writers of authority or to decisions of significance indicating a general acquiescence of nations in such a rule. Without this, it cannot be applied here as a principle of international law.

Note

This case concerned the recognition of governments. On the recognition of states, in *Deutsche Continental Gas-Gesellschaft* v. *Polish State*[19] the German-Polish Mixed Arbitral Tribunal stated: ". . . according to the opinion rightly admitted by the great majority of writers on international law, the recognition of a State is not constitutive but merely declaratory. The State exists by itself (*par lui-même*) and the recognition is nothing else than a declaration of this existence, recognised by the States from which it emanates."

INTERNATIONAL REGISTRATION OF TRADE-MARK (GERMANY) CASE

28 I.L.R. 82. Federal Supreme Court of the Federal Republic of Germany, 1959

The case concerned the 1883 Paris Convention for the Protection of International Property and the Supplementary 1934 Madrid Arrangement to which Germany had been a party before the Second World War. In 1956, the German Democratic Republic gave notice that both treaties were "again applicable" in its territory. In the course of ruling that a trademark originating in the G.D.R. and registered under the Convention was, despite the G.D.R.'s announcement, not entitled to protection in the Federal Republic of Germany, the Court stated:

Judgment of the Court

The Contracting Parties which are already bound by a multilateral convention can be bound by the accession of another State entity only to the extent that the latter is a subject of international law *as far as they themselves are concerned*. If, and to thé extent that, in the territory of the Soviet zone of Occupation there exists *factual* sovereign power, the exercise of this power does not, as such, automatically create an organisational entity which must be treated as a new subject of international law. Any entity which exists *in fact* requires, in addition, the *recognition* of its existence in some form—which need not be considered in detail here. In relation to other States which do not recognise it as a subject of international law, such an entity cannot be a party to a treaty, let alone become a party merely by a unilateral declaration, as, *e.g.* by accession to a multilateral convention, thus conferring upon itself the status of a subject of international law in relation to States which do not recognise it. As the Federal Republic of Germany has not recognised the so-called German Democratic Republic as a State and a subject of international law capable of acceding to an international agreement, "accession" by the so-called Democratic Republic to the Madrid

[19] 5 A.D. 11 at p. 15 (1929).

Arrangement would be incapable of having any legal effect *vis à vis* the German Federal Republic.

Note

In contrast with the *Tinoco Arbitration*, this national court decision follows the constitutive theory.

6. THE EFFECT OF RECOGNITION IN MUNICIPAL LAW

Note

Before the 1980 statement, the practice of the British courts when called upon to recognise the law or capacity to act of a foreign state or government was to seek and regard as conclusive a Foreign Office certificate.[20] In this context, recognition was constitutive. The position remains unchanged in respect of the recognition of states. A certificate would still be sought and followed on the facts of the *Carl Zeiss Case*, below, p. 141. When asked about the effect of the 1980 statement on legal proceedings concerning new revolutionary governments, the Foreign Secretary (Lord Carrington) replied:

> In future cases where a new régime comes to power unconstitutionally our attitude on the question whether it qualifies to be treated as a Government, will be left to be inferred from the nature of the dealings, if any, which we may have with it, and in particular on whether we are dealing with it on a normal Government to Government basis.[21]

This delphic response does not rule out the possibility that the Foreign Office would reply to a request for information from the courts, indicating what dealings (including diplomatic relations) the United Kingdom has with the Government concerned. It remains to be seen whether the courts will, consistently with the "one voice" doctrine, seek such information or whether they will go their own way and apply their own test, probably that of effectiveness.[22] In either event, the problems of retroactivity which are dealt with in some of the cases in this section[23] will still arise. The difficulties resulting from the co-existence of *de jure* and *de facto* governments[24] will not, unless (i) the United Kingdom Government decides under its new approach to have dealings with more than one government at the same time or (ii) the courts, going their own way, find and take into account the fact that different governments are in effective control of different parts of the territory of a state.

LUTHER v. SAGOR

[1921] 1 K.B. 456; [1921] 3 K.B. 532. King's Bench Division; Court of Appeal

In 1920, the defendant company bought a quantity of wood from the new Soviet Government of the U.S.S.R. The plaintiff Russian company claimed title to the wood on the ground that it had come from a factory in the U.S.S.R. that had been owned by it before being nationalised by a 1919 decree of the Soviet Government. The plaintiff argued, *inter alia*,[25] that the decree should not be recognised by an English court because the Soviet Government had not been recognised by the United Kingdom.

---

[20] See Lord Reid's speech in the *Carl Zeiss Case*, below, p. 141.

[21] *Hansard*, H.L., Vol. 409, Cols. 1097–1098; *U.K.M.I.L.* 1980; (1980) 51 B.Y.I.L. 368.

[22] *cf.* the *Re Al-Fin Case* below, p. 148. Note also the recent dicta on the status of unrecognised governments in the *Carl Zeiss* and *Hesperides Cases*, below, pp. 141 and 147.

[23] *Luther* v. *Sagor*, the *Civil Air Transport Case* and the *Gdynia Amerika Case*.

[24] See, *e.g. Haile Selassie* v. *Cable and Wireless Ltd. (No. 2)* [1939] 1 Ch. 182 (C.A.).

[25] It also argued that the decree was confiscatory.

ROCHE J. The attitude proper to be adopted by a Court of this country with regard to foreign governments or powers I understand to be as follows. . . . If a foreign government, or its sovereignty, is not recognized by the Government of this country the Courts of this country either cannot, or at least need not, or ought not, to take notice of, or recognize such foreign government or its sovereignty. This negative proposition is . . . established and recognised by the judgment of Kay J. in *Republic of Peru* v. *Dreyfus*.[26] . . . In the *City of Berne* v. *Bank of England*[27] the question at issue was the right of an unrecognized foreign government to maintain a suit, but Lord Eldon's judgment is, I think, an authority for the general proposition I have stated. . . .

This being the law which must guide and direct my decision, I have to consider whether and in what sense the Government represented by M. Krassin in this matter is recognized by His Majesty's Government. . . .

Roche J. then read a letter from the Foreign Office dated November 20th, 1920.

Gentlemen,

I am directed by Earl Curzon of Kedleston . . . to inform you that for a certain limited purpose His Majesty's Government has regarded Monsieur Krassin as exempt from the process of the Courts, and also for the like limited purpose His Majesty's Government has assented to the claim that that which Monsieur Krassin represents in this Country is a State Government of Russia, but that beyond these propositions the Foreign Office has not gone, nor moreover do these expressions of opinion purport to decide difficult, and it may be very special questions of law upon which it may become necessary for the Courts to pronounce. I am to add that His Majesty's Government has never officially recognised the Soviet Government in any way.

It was said on behalf of the defendants that these communications were vague and ambiguous. I should rather say that they were guarded, but as clear as the indeterminate position of affairs in connection with the subject-matter of the communications enabled them to be . . . I am not satisfied that His Majesty's Government has recognized the Soviet Government as the Government of a Russian Federative Republic or of any sovereign state or power. I therefore am unable to recognize it, or to hold it has sovereignty, or is able by decree to deprive the plaintiff company of its property.

Roche J. gave judgment for the plaintiffs. The defendants appealed to the Court of Appeal.

Court of Appeal

BANKES L.J. Upon the evidence which was before the learned judge I think that his decision was quite right. . . .

In this Court the appellants asked leave to adduce further evidence . . . It consisted of two letters from the Foreign Office dated respectively April 20 and 22, 1921. The first is . . . in these terms: "I am . . . to inform you that His Majesty's Government recognize the Soviet Government as the de facto Government of Russia." The letter of April 22 . . . contains (inter alia) the

[26] 38 Ch.D., at pp. 357, 358 and 359.
[27] 9 Ves. 347.

statement that the Provisional Government came into power on March 14, 1917, that it was recognized by His Majesty's Government as the then existing Government of Russia, and that the Constituent Assembly remained in session until December 13, 1917, when it was dispersed by the Soviet authorities.[28] . . .

Under these circumstances the whole aspect of the case is changed, and it becomes necessary to consider matters which were not material in the Court below. The first is a question of law of very considerable importance—namely, what is the effect of the recognition by His Majesty's Government in April, 1921, of the Soviet Government as the de facto Government of Russia upon the past acts of that Government, and how far back, if at all, does that recognition extend.

. . . counsel have been unable to refer the Court to any English authority. Attention has been called to three cases decided in the Supreme Court of the United States: *Williams* v. *Bruffy*[29]; *Underhill* v. *Hernandez*[30]; and *Oetjen* v. *Central Leather Co.*[31] In none of these cases is any distinction attempted to be drawn in argument between the effect of a recognition of a government as a de facto government and a recognition of a government as a government de jure, nor is any decision given upon that point; nor, except incidentally, is any mention made as to the effect of the recognition of a government upon its past acts. The mention occurs in two passages, one in the judgement of . . . Fuller C.J. in *Underhill* v. *Hernandez*.[32] He says, in speaking of civil wars: "If the party seeking to dislodge the existing government succeeds, and the independence of the government it has set up is recognized, then the acts of such government from the commencement of its existence are regarded as those of an independent nation." These are weighty expressions of opinion on a question of international law. Neither learned judge cites any authority for his proposition. Each appears to treat the matter as one resting on principle. On principle the views put forward by these learned judges appear to me to be sound, though there may be cases in which the Courts of a country whose government has recognized the government of some other country as the de facto government of that country may have to consider at what stage in its development the government so recognized can, to use the language to which I have already referred of those learned judges, be said to have "commenced its existence." No difficulty of that kind arises in the present case, because, upon the construction which I place upon the communication of the Foreign Office to which I have referred, this Court must treat the Soviet Government, which the Government of this country has now recognized as the de facto Government of Russia, as having commenced its existence at a date anterior to any date material to the dispute between the parties to this appeal.

. . . The Government of this country having . . . recognized the Soviet Government as the Government really in possession of the powers of sovereignty in Russia, the acts of that Government must be treated by the

---

[28] The Provisional Government came into being after the "February Revolution" of 1917, as a result of which the Tsar abdicated. It was led first by Prince Lvov and then by Kerensky. After the "October Revolution" of the same year, the Provisional Government was replaced by the Soviet Government, *i.e.* the Bolshevik Government led by Lenin.

[29] 96 U.S. 176.

[30] 168 U.S. 250.

[31] 246 U.S. 297.

[32] 168 U.S. 253. *Ed.* The other was in the judgment of Field J. in *Williams* v. *Bruffy*.

Courts of this country with all the respect due to the acts of a duly recognized foreign sovereign state.

. . . From the letter from the Foreign Office addressed to Messrs. Linklater of April 22, 1921, it appears that the Soviet authorities dispersed the then Constituent Assembly on Decemer 13, 1917, from which date I think it must be accepted that the Soviet Government assumed the position of the sovereign Government and purported to act as such.

WARRINGTON L.J. I should have thought that in principle recognition would be retroactive at any rate to such date as our Government accept as that by which the government in question in fact established its authority. It appears from the letter of the Foreign Office dated April 22, 1921, that that date is anterior to any of the events material to the present case.

Scrutton L.J. delivered a concurring judgment. Appeal allowed.

CIVIL AIR TRANSPORT INC. v. CENTRAL AIR TRANSPORT CORPORATION[33]

[1953] A.C. 70, Judicial Committee of the Privy Council

On October 1, 1949, the Government of the People's Republic of China, which had by then obtained control over most of the Chinese mainland, proclaimed itself the Government of China. Its predecessor, the Nationalist Government, withdrew from the mainland and, on December 9, established its headquarters on the island of Taiwan (Formosa). The United Kingdom Government continued to recognise the Nationalist Government as the *de jure* government of China until midnight on January 5–6, 1950, when it recognised the Government of the People's Republic instead. By September 1949, Nationalist Government employees had flown to Hong Kong 40 aircraft that formed part of the fleet of the respondents, a Chinese state enterprise at that time still under the control of the Nationalist Government. On December 12, 1949, the Nationalist Government sold the aircraft to a United States partnership which resold them to the appellant United States corporation. In the meantime, on November 12, 1949, the respondents and their assets were declared by the People's Republic to be their property. At about the same time, the majority of the respondents' employees in Hong Kong defected from the Nationalist Government and took physical control of the aircraft in Hong Kong for the People's Republic Government. This they retained in defiance of a Hong Kong court injunction.

In this case, the appellants appealed to the Judicial Committee against a decision of the Appellate Court of Hong Kong dismissing their claim to a declaration that the aircraft were their property and holding instead that the ownership and right to possession of the aircraft were in the People's Republic Government. An Order in Council provided that it would be no bar to jurisdiction in any case concerning the aircraft that a foreign state was impleaded.

LORD SIMON, FOR THE JUDICIAL COMMITTEE. Her Majesty's Government in the United Kingdom is the sovereign government of Hong Kong, and the effect of the above replies [by the Foreign Office to questions on the status of the rival governments] is to establish that, at any rate in the courts of Hong Kong

[33] See Johnson (1952) 29 B.Y.I.L. 464 and Mann, 16 M.L.R. 226 (1953).

and in the present appeal, the former Nationalist Government must be regarded as the sole de jure sovereign government of China up to midnight of January 5–6, 1950; that the present Communist Government was not the de jure government until that time; and that, while the Foreign Office, in its answer of March 13, 1950, acknowledged that from October 1, 1949, onwards the de facto government of those parts of China in which the Nationalist Government had ceased to be in effective control was the Communist Government, H.M. Government had not announced or communicated their recognition of the Communist Government as the de facto government over any part of China before they recognized the Communist Government as the de jure government of China on January 5–6, 1950.

. . . the validity of the transaction [for the sale of the aircraft] must be judged as at the date when it was entered into, and not in the light of subsequent events, which might have turned out differently. On December 12, 1949, the Nationalist Government was the de jure government of China, of which C.A.T.C. was an organ, and therefore the property in these aeroplanes was in the Nationalist Government. The machines had been moved to Hong Kong two months before, and it was open to their owners to sell them, and thereby to pass the property in them to the purchasers.

. . . At the same time, their Lordships must not be understood to reject the possibility of our courts refusing, in a conceivable case, to recognize the validity of the disposal of State property by a government on the eve of its fall, e.g. by a despot, who knows that previous recognition is just being withdrawn, where it is clear that his purpose was to abscond with the proceeds, or to make away with State assets for some private purpose. . . .

Subsequent recognition de jure of a new government as the result of successful insurrection can in certain cases annul a sale of goods by a previous government. If the previous government sells goods which belong to it but are situated in territory effectively occupied at the time by insurgent forces acting on behalf of what is already a de facto new government, the sale may be valid if the insurgents are afterwards defeated and possession of the goods is regained by the old government. But if the old government never regains the goods and the de facto new government becomes recognized by H.M. Government as the de jure government, purchasers from the old government will not be held in Her Majesty's courts to have a good title after that recognition.

Primarily, at any rate, retroactivity of recognition operates to validate acts of a de facto government which has subsequently become the new de jure government, and not to invalidate acts of the previous de jure government. It is not necessary to discuss ultimate results in the hypothetical case when before the change in recognition both governments purport to deal with the same goods. The crucial question under this branch of the analysis in the present appeal is whether anything that happened in Hong Kong to these aeroplanes at the instigation of or on behalf of the de facto Communist Government before the change of recognition on January 5–6, 1950, is retrospectively validated, so that the title conferred by the contract of December 12, 1949, is extinguished.

It might be too wide a proposition to say that the retroactive effect of de jure recognition must in all cases be limited to acts done in territory of the government so recognized, for the case of a ship of the former government taken possession of by insurgents on the high seas and brought into a port which is under the control of the de facto government would have to be considered (see

Banco de Bilbao v. *Sancha*[34]). But the actual question now to be answered concerns chattels in the British colony of Hong Kong which at the time of the sale belonged to the Nationalist Government. Whatever the degree of physical control over these chattels maintained by the defecting ex-employees, this control was in defiance of the injunction granted by the Supreme Court of Hong Kong on November 24. Moreover, if these persons could be regarded as acting on behalf of the de facto Communist Government, their action would be a direct infringement of the Representation of Foreign Powers (Control) Ordinance of November 4, 1949, and would be a criminal offence by the law of Hong Kong. This Ordinance provided that no person should "function on behalf of any foreign Power" without the consent of the governor, and "foreign Power" was defined to include "the government whether legal or de facto of any foreign State." The governor gave no consent. In such circumstances the action of those who illegally took control of these aeroplanes cannot give ground for the principle of retroactivity.

". . . My opinion therefore upon this aspect of the case is that the Central People's Government could not show any superior title or right to possession; nor can it rely upon any rights arising out of actual possession acquired in the way it was; therefore it had no possession which could bring into effect the doctrine of retroactivity. That doctrine, I think, relates to the acts of a government which has already acquired jurisdiction through possession and cannot include the actual act of taking possession if that act be wrongful. On this point I hold therefore that the ordinary principle of continuity was not displaced by any consideration of retroactivity and that it follows that the Nationalist Government was entitled to possession of and had jurisdiction over the aeroplanes."

Their Lordships agree with the argument and conclusions of Gould J. on this point.

The trial judge attached importance to the announcement of October 1, 1949, the authors of which proclaimed themselves to be the government of China, and to the decree issued on that date purporting in the name of that government to dismiss the ministers of the Nationalist Government. Their Lordships cannot accept the view that this is any reason for saying "that as from October 1, 1949, these aircraft were owned by the Central People's Government." They adopt on this point the opinion of Gould J., who observed: "The purported dismissal on October 1, 1949, of the ministers of the Nationalist Government . . . can only be deemed effective within the territory and as regards assets from time to time in the control of the People's Government. Elsewhere, and so long as the Nationalist Government retained de jure recognition, such a decree could have no effect."

For the above reasons, their Lordships have reached the conclusion that the appeal should be allowed.

Lord Normand, Lord Oaksey, Lord Reid and Sir Lionel Leach also sat in this case.

Notes

1. What if it had been the Government of the People's Republic of China that had purported to sell the aircraft in Hong Kong on December 12? What if, as in the actual case, it were the Nationalist Government, but the aircraft had been in Mainland China on December 12?

[34] [1938] 2 K.B. 176.

2. *Gydnia Ameryka Linie Zeglugowe Spolka Akcyjna* v. *Boguslawski*[35] concerned the Polish Government in Exile in London during the Second World War. This Government was then recognised by the United Kingdom as the *de jure* government of Poland. Although it had no control over Polish territory during the War, it did have control over that part of the Polish merchant fleet that had avoided capture by Germany. On June 28, 1945, a new communist Provisional Government established itself with *de facto* control of Polish territory. At midnight on July 5–6, 1945, the United Kingdom withdrew its recognition of the London Government and recognised the Provisional Government as the *de jure* government of Poland instead. Just before this, on July 3, the competent Minister of the London Government, Mr. K, acting under powers conferred by Polish law not revoked by the Provisional Government, offered certain Polish seamen compensation (to be paid by their employers) should they wish to leave their employment rather than continue to serve under the jurisdiction of the Provisional Government. The two respondents in this case accepted the offer. When their employers, the appellants, refused to pay, they sought to recover the compensation offered through the English courts. The appellants argued that the recognition by the British Government of the Provisional Government had retroactive effect so that acts of the London Government ceased to have effect in Polish law (which, the House of Lords held, governed the case) from June 28, 1945, when the Provisional Government established itself in Poland. There was consequently, it was argued, no duty on the part of the appellants to make the payments required by Mr. K. The argument was rejected and the appeal dismissed unanimously. Lord Reid stated:

> There is ample authority for the proposition that the recognition by the British Government of a new government of a foreign country has at least this effect. It enables and requires the courts of this country to regard as valid not only acts done by the new government after its recognition but also acts done by it before its recognition in so far as those acts related to matters under its control at the time when the acts were done. But there appears to be no English authority which goes beyond that. I do not accept the argument for the appellants that this necessarily or logically involves antedating for all purposes the withdrawal of the recognition of the old government. I do not see anything strange or even difficult in our saying that we still recognize that the old government was the Government of Poland up to midnight of July 5–6 but that we also now accept the validity of certain acts done by the new government before that time and while it was still unrecognized by us. Apart from the distinction between recognition de jure and recognition de facto which does not affect this case, we cannot recognize two different governments of the same country at the same time, and the British Government did not in fact recognize both the old and the new government at the time. But I do not think that it is inconsistent with this principle to say that the recognition of the new government has certain retroactive effects, but that the recognition of the old government remains effective down to the date when it was in fact withdrawn. I can see that there might be difficulties if the old government had purported before withdrawal of recognition to take some action with regard to matters already under the control of the new government, but that does not arise in this case.[36]

CARL ZEISS STIFTUNG v. RAYNER AND KEELER LTD. (No. 2)

[1967] 1 A.C. 853. House of Lords

C.Z.S. is a German charitable foundation that makes optical instruments. Under its constitution, it is run by a Special Board. After the First World War, the Board was the

---

[35] [1953] A.C. 11.
[36] *Ibid.* 44–45.

Minister of Education of Thuringia, a state within Germany. In 1945, Thuringia became part of the Russian Zone of Occupied Germany. In 1949, the U.S.S.R. handed over government of its Zone to the German Democratic Republic.[37] In 1952, the G.D.R. reorganised its local government and Thuringia ceased to exist. The Special Board of C.Z.S., under the new arrangements, became the Council of Gera.

In this case, C.Z.S., acting through its new Board, brought a claim in the English courts. In these interlocutory proceedings, the defendants, now the respondents, asked that the claim be dismissed because it had been brought without the proper authority of the appellants. The requested order was denied by Cross J. but granted by the Court of Appeal after an argument based upon recognition had been put to that court for the first time in the case. The argument was that as the United Kingdom had not recognised the G.D.R. the new Special Board, having been created by the G.D.R., could not be recognised by an English court. The House of Lords unanimously reversed the Court of Appeal's ruling on appeal.

LORD REID. Shortly stated, the respondent's case is that we are bound to have regard to the basis on which the Democratic Republic purports to act, and that as Her Majesty's Government has never granted recognition de jure or de facto to that Republic or its Government, we must refuse to recognise as effective all legislation emanating from it, and all acts done under such legislation. For reasons which I shall give later I do not think that that is right, but first I shall explain why, if it were right, it would be decisive of the point I am now dealing with.

. . . If the respondents' argument based on non-recognition is well founded, then it must follow that British courts cannot recognise either the existence of the Council of Gera or the validity of anything done by it, and in particular cannot recognise any authority given by it for the raising of the present action. . . .

In the normal case a law is made either by the sovereign directly or by some body entitled under the constitution of the country to make it or by some person or body to which the sovereign has delegated authority to make it. On the other hand, there are many cases where laws have been made against the will of the sovereign by persons engaged in a rebellion or revolution: then until such persons or the government which they set up have been granted de facto recognition by the Government of this country, their laws cannot be recognised by the courts of this country, but after de facto recognition such laws will be recognised. So far there is no difficulty. But the present case does not fit neatly into any of these categories. We are considering whether the law of 1952 under which the Council of Gera was set up can be recognised by our courts and therefore we must ascertain what was the situation in East Germany in 1952.

It is a firmly established principle that the question whether a foreign state ruler or government is or is not sovereign is one on which our courts accept as conclusive information provided by Her Majesty's government: no evidence is admissible to contradict that information.[38]

. . . In the present case the Court of Appeal twice received . . . information from the Foreign Secretary. First on September 16, 1964, it was stated: "Her Majesty's Government has not granted any recognition de jure or de facto to (a)

---

[37] See above, p. 82.
[38] *Ed.* Lord Reid cited *Duff Development Co. Ltd.* v. *Kelantan Government* [1924] A.C. 797 (H.L.) as authority.

the 'German Democratic Republic' or (b) its 'Government,' " and secondly on November 6, 1964, a further answer was given. . . .

In my opinion, this latter answer is decisive on the question which I am now considering and I must therefore quote the relevant question and the relevant parts of the answer or certificate given by the Foreign Secretary. The question was:

What (a) states or (b) governments or (c) authorities (if any) have since July 1, 1945, up to the present date been recognised by Her Majesty's Government as (a) entitled to exercise or (b) exercising governing authority in the area of Germany outside the zones allocated to the Governments of the United Kingdom, the United States of America and the French Republic by the protocol of September 12, 1944, and the agreement of July 26, 1945, concluded between the Governments of the said states and the Union of Soviet Socialist Republics. Has such recognition been de jure or de facto.

The relevant parts of the certificate are as follows:

The area of Germany to which the question is understood to refer comprises (a) the zone of occupation allocated to the Union of Soviet Socialist Republics under the protocol of September 12, 1944, and the agreement of July 26, 1945, as modified by the protocol of the proceedings of the Berlin Conference of August 2, 1945, and (b) the 'Greater Berlin' area. The question is understood not to relate to the areas of Germany placed under Soviet or Polish administration in pursuance of the aforesaid protocol of August 2, 1945.

(a) From the zone allocated to the Union of Soviet Socialist Republics Allied forces under the Supreme Allied Commander, General Eisenhower, withdrew at or about the end of June, 1945. Since that time and up to the present date Her Majesty's Government have recognised the state and Government of the Union of Soviet Socialist Republics as de jure entitled to exercise governing authority in respect of that zone. In matters affecting Germany as a whole, the states and Governments of the French Republic, the United Kingdom of Great Britain and Northern Ireland, the United States of America and the Union of Soviet Socialist Republics were jointly entitled to exercise governing authority. In the period from August 30, 1945, to March 20, 1948, they did exercise such joint authority through the Control Council for Germany. Apart from the states, Governments and Control Council aforementioned, Her Majesty's Government have not recognised either de jure or de facto any other authority purporting to exercise governing authority in or in respect of the zone. Her Majesty's Government, however, regard the aforementioned Governments as retaining rights and responsibilities in respect of Germany as a whole. . . .

The purpose of a certificate is to provide information about the status of foreign governments and states and therefore the statement that since June, 1945, "Her Majesty's Government have recognised the state and Government of the Union of Soviet Socialist Republics as de jure entitled to exercise governing authority in respect of that zone" cannot merely mean that Her Majesty's Government have granted this recognition so as to leave the courts of this country free to receive evidence as to whether in fact the U.S.S.R. are still entitled to exercise governing authority there. The courts of this country are no more entitled to hold that a sovereign, still recognised by our Government, has ceased in fact to be sovereign de jure, than they are entitled to hold that a government not yet recognised has acquired sovereign status. So this certificate requires that we must take it as a fact that the U.S.S.R. have been since 1954 and still are de jure entitled to exercise that governing authority. The certificate makes no distinction between the period before and the period after the German Democratic Republic was set up. So we are bound to hold that the setting up of that Republic made no difference in the right of the U.S.S.R. to exercise governing authority in the zone. And it must follow from that that the U.S.S.R. could at any time lawfully bring to an end the German Democratic Republic and its Government and could then resume direct rule of the zone. But that is quite inconsistent with there having in fact been any abdication by the U.S.S.R. of its rights when the German Democratic Republic was set up.

The judgment of the Court of Appeal appears to me to be based on the view that the courts of this country can and must accept the position that the U.S.S.R. have recognised the German Democratic Republic as an independent sovereign state. . . .

But the learned judges of the Court of Appeal do not appear to have had their attention directed to the true import of the certificate of the Secretary of State. The U.S.S.R. may have purported to confer independence or sovereignty on the German Democratic Republic but, in my judgment, that certificate clearly requires us to hold that, whatever the U.S.S.R. may have purported to do, they did not in fact set up the German Democratic Republic as a sovereign or independent state. If they retained their right to govern its territory, they could not possibly have done so; and the certificate requires us to hold that they did retain that right.

If we are bound to hold that the German Democratic Republic was not in fact set up as a sovereign independent state, the only other possibility is that it was set up as a dependent or subordinate organisation through which the U.S.S.R. is enitled to exercise indirect rule. I do not think that we are concerned to inquire or to know to what extent the U.S.S.R. in fact exercise their right of control. . . .

It was argued that the present case is analogous to cases where subjects of an existing sovereign have rebelled and have succeeded in gaining control of a part of the old sovereign's dominions. When they set up a new government in opposition to the de jure sovereign that new government does not and cannot derive any authority or right from the de jure sovereign, and our courts must regard its acts and the acts of its organs or officers as nullities until it has established and consolidated its position to such an extent as to warrant our government according de facto recognition of it. . . .

Lord Reid referred to *Luther* v. *Sagor*, above, p. 135, as an example of this situation and approved of the first instance and the Court of Appeal judgments in that case.

But the present case is essentially different. The German Democratic Republic was set up by the U.S.S.R. and it derived its authority and status from the Government of the U.S.S.R. So the only question could be whether or not it was set up as a sovereign state. But the certificate of our Government requires us to hold that it was not set up as a sovereign state because it requires us to hold that the U.S.S.R. remained de jure sovereign and therefore did not voluntarily transfer its sovereignty to the Democratic Republic. And, if the Democratic

Republic did not become a sovereign state at its inception, there is no suggestion that it has at any subsequent time attempted to deprive the U.S.S.R. of rights which were not granted to it at its inception. The courts of this country must disregard any declarations of the Government of the U.S.S.R. in so far as they conflict with the certificate of Her Majesty's Secretary of State, and we must therefore hold that the U.S.S.R. set up the German Democratic Republic, not as a sovereign state, but as an organisation subordinate to the U.S.S.R. If that is so, then mere declarations by the Government of the Democratic Republic that it is acting as the government of an independent state cannot be regarded as proof that its initial status has been altered, and we must regard the acts of the German Democratic Republic, its government organs and officers as acts done with the consent of the Government of the U.S.S.R. as the government entitled to exercise governing authority.

It appears to me to be impossible for any de jure sovereign governing authority to disclaim responsibility for acts done by subordinate bodies which it has set up and which have not attempted to usurp its sovereignty. So, in my opinion, the courts of this country cannot treat as nullities acts done by or on behalf of the German Democratic Republic. De facto recognition is appropriate—and, in my view, is only appropriate—where the new government have usurped power against the will of the de jure sovereign. I would think that where a sovereign has granted independence to a dependency any recognition of the new state would be a recognition de jure. . . .

I am reinforced in my opinion by a consideration of the consequences which would follow if the view taken by the Court of Appeal were correct. Counsel for the respondents did not dispute that in that case we must not only disregard all new laws and decrees made by the Democratic Republic or its Government, but we must also disregard all executive and judicial acts done by persons appointed by that Government because we must regard their appointments as invalid. The result of that would be far-reaching. Trade with the Eastern Zone of Germany is not discouraged. But the incorporation of every company in East Germany under any new law made by the Democratic Republic or by the official act of any official appointed by its Government would have to be regarded as a nullity, so that any such company could neither sue nor be sued in this country. And any civil marriage under any such new law, or owing its validity to the act of any such official, would also have to be treated as a nullity, so that we should have to regard the children as illegitimate. And the same would apply to divorces and all manner of judicial decisions, whether in family or commercial questions. And that would affect not only status of persons formerly domiciled in East Germany but property in this country the devolution of which depended on East German law.

It was suggested that these consequences might be mitigaged if the courts of this country could adopt doctrines which have found some support in the United States of America.[39] . . . In the view which I take of the present case, it is unnecessary to express any opinion whether it would be possible to adopt any similar solutions in this country, if the need should ever arise.

LORD WILBERFORCE. My Lords, if the consequences of non-recognition of the East German "government" were to bring in question the validity of its

---

[39] See Lord Wilberforce, below.

legislative acts, I should wish seriously to consider whether the invalidity so brought about is total, or whether some mitigation of the severity of this result can be found. As Locke said: "A government without laws is, I suppose, a mystery in politics, inconceivable to human capacity and inconsistent with human society," and this must be true of a society—at least a civilised and organised society—such as we know to exist in East Germany. In the United States some glimmerings can be found of the idea that non-recognition cannot be pressed to its ultimate logical limit, and that where private rights, or acts of everyday occurrence, or perfunctory acts of administration are concerned (the scope of these exceptions has never been precisely defined) the courts may, in the interests of justice and common sense, where no consideration of public policy to the contrary has to prevail, give recognition to the actual facts or realities found to exist in the territory in question. These ideas began to take shape on the termination of the Civil War (see *U.S.* v. *Insurance Companies*), and have been developed and reformulated, admittedly as no more than dicta, but dicta by judges of high authority, in later cases. I mention two of these, *Sokoloff* v. *National City Bank* and *Upright* v. *Mercury Business Machines Co. Inc.*, a case which was concerned with a corporate body under East German law. Other references can be found conveniently assembled in Professor D. P. O'Connell's International Law (1965) vol. I, pp. 189 *et seq*. No trace of any such doctrine is yet to be found in English law, but equally, in my opinion, there is nothing in those English decisions, in which recognition has been refused to particular acts of non-recognised governments, which would prevent its acceptance or which prescribes the absolute and total invalidity of all laws and acts flowing from unrecognised governments. In view of the conclusion I have reached on the effect to be attributed to non-recognition in this case,[40] it is not necessary here to resort to this doctrine but, for my part, I should wish to regard it as an open question, in English law, in any future case whether and to what extent it can be invoked. . . .

Lords Hodson, Guest and Upjohn delivered concurring speeches.

Notes[41]

1. In 1967, the Home Secretary stated in Parliament:

As Her Majesty's Government do not recognise the East German régime, passports issued by that régime are not acceptable as travel documents for the purpose of journeys to the United Kingdom.[42]

Was this consistent with the reasoning in the *Carl Zeiss* case (which preceded the statement)?

2. Lords Reid and Wilberforce referred to certain United States cases in which the position of an unrecognised government had been considered. In the American Civil War case of *U.S.* v. *Insurance Companies*,[43] the United States Supreme Court applied the following rule:

All the enactments of the *de facto* Legislatures in the insurrectionary States during the war, which were not hostile to the Union or to the authority of the General Government and which were not in conflict with the Constitution of the United

---

[40] *Ed.* That the G.D.R. was acting as the delegate of the U.S.S.R., the *de jure* sovereign.
[41] See Greig, *loc. cit.* at p. 130, n. 7, above.
[42] *Hansard*, H.C., Vol. 744, W.A. col. 19. April 4, 1967.
[43] 89 U.S. 99 at p. 103 (1974).

States, or of the States, have the same validity as if they had been enactments of legitimate Legislatures.

In *Sokoloff* v. *National City Bank*,[44] Cardozo J., in the New York Court of Appeals, proposed as the correct test, without having to apply it on the facts of the case, that an unrecognised government which has established itself in control of its state's territory could have its acts and decrees recognised:

if violence to fundamental principles of justice or to our own public policy might otherwise be done.

In *Upright* v. *Mercury Business Machines Co. Inc.*,[45] in which, as in the *Carl Zeiss Case*, the acts of a public institution of the G.D.R. were in issue, the New York Supreme Court stated:

A foreign government, although not recognised by the political arm of the United States Government, may nevertheless have *de facto* existence which is juridically cognisable. The acts of such a *de facto* government may affect private rights and obligations arising either as a result of activity in, or with persons or corporations within, the territory controlled by such *de facto* government.

Yet by no means all of the judicial practice in courts in the United States is in favour of some degree of recognition of the acts of an unrecognised government. In *The Maret*,[46] for instance, in the United States Third Circuit Court of Appeals, it was stated: "When the fact of non-recognition of a foreign sovereign and non-recognition of its decrees by our Executive is demonstrated as in the case at bar, the courts of this country may not examine the effect of decrees of the unrecognised foreign sovereign and determine rights in property . . . upon the basis of those decrees."

3. *Hesperides Hotels* v. *Aegean Holidays Ltd.*[47] concerned two hotels owned by the Greek Cypriot plaintiffs which were being run by Turkish Cypriots with the approval of the Turkish Cypriot administration which has governed the part of Cyprus in which the hotels were located since the armed invasion of Cyprus by Turkey in 1974. The plaintiffs' action in trespass was rejected by the Court of Appeal for lack of jurisdiction on the basis of English conflict of law rules. Addressing the fact that the United Kingdom continues to recognise the pre-invasion constitutional government of Cyprus as the *de jure* government of the whole of Cyprus and does not recognise the Turkish administration *de jure* or *de facto* (and had produced to the court a certificate to this effect), Lord Denning stated *obiter dicta*:

If it were necessary to [do so] . . . I would unhesitatingly hold that the courts of this country can recognise the laws or acts of a body which is in effective control of a territory even though it has not been recognised by Her Majesty's Government *de jure* or *de facto*: at any rate, in regard to the laws which regulate the day to day affairs of the people, such as their marriages, their divorces, their leases, their occupations, and so forth; and furthermore that the courts can receive evidence of the state of affairs so as to see whether the body is in effective control or not.[48]

See also *Adams* v. *Adams*,[49] in which a divorce decree made by a Rhodesian judge appointed by the unrecognised Smith Government was not recognised by an English court because the decree was not valid under the legal system which continued to be applicable in Southern Rhodesia under United Kingdom Law.

---

[44] 239 N.Y. 158 at p. 165 (1924). The case concerned the Soviet Government in Russia which was not recognised by the U.S.A. until 1933.
[45] 213 N.Y.S. 2d 417 at p. 419 (1961). See Lubmann, 62 Col.L.R. 275 (1962).
[46] 145 F.2d 431 at p. 442 (1944).
[47] [1978] Q.B. 205 (C.A.). The matter was not discussed in the House of Lords: [1979] A.C. 508.
[48] [1978] Q.B. at 218.   [49] [1971] P. 188.

Re AL-FIN CORPORATION'S PATENT[50]

[1970] Ch. 160. (Chancery Division)

Section 24(1) of the Patents Act 1949 allows a patentee an extension of his patent if he has suffered loss "by reason of hostilities between His Majesty and any foreign state." In this case, the applicants sought an extension under section 24(1) in respect of loss suffered during the Korean War between 1950 and 1953. The Comptroller-General rejected the application partly on the ground that the Korean War did not come within section 24(1) because North Korea, not having been recognised by the United Kingdom, was not a "foreign state." The applicants sought a ruling on this question. The Court had before it a letter from the Foreign Office which read:

> 3. I am to inform you that between June 25, 1950 and July 27, 1953, His/Her Majesty's Government did not recognise the existence of an independent sovereign state in the area of Korea north of the 38th parallel either de facto or de jure, and did not recognise any authority exercising control in that area as a Government either de facto or de jure.
>
> 4. So far as the existence of authorities is concerned, this is considered to be a question of fact but Her Majesty's Government are aware that between June 25, 1950 and July 27, 1953, there were certain authorities styling themselves "The Government of the Democratic People's Republic of Korea" exercising control over the above-mentioned area.
>
> 5. I am to add that, in providing the above information the Foreign Office is expressing no view as to whether there were "hostilities between His Majesty and any foreign state" within the meaning of section 24 of the Patents Act 1949, which is regarded as a question for determination by the court on the basis of all the relevant evidence and in the light of the true interpretation of the Statute.

GRAHAM J. The question depends primarily on the proper construction of section 24, and the difference between the parties may be succinctly stated as follows: Must the section be read as if the words "recognised as such by Her Majesty" were included after the words "any foreign state" in subsection (1), or is it correct to read the section in a broader sense without the necessity for the qualification of recognition?

Mr. MacCrindle argued that the court is not here construing a contract between parties but ascertaining the intention of the legislature which is an arm of state. . . .

Mr. Dillon, on the other hand, for the applicants argued that the obvious intention of the section was to give a right to an extension for loss where the applicant could show that hostilities between this country and another country had occasioned such loss, and that the definition of "state" should certainly not be limited in such a way that it depended on the technical fact of recognition. . . .

In support of his argument he cited the authority of *Luigi Monta of Genoa* v. *Cechofracht Co. Ltd.* [1956] 2 Q.B. 552. In that case the question was whether the ship had complied with

> any orders or directions . . . given by the government of the nation under whose flag the vessel sails . . . or by any other government . . . and com-

[50] See Merrills, 20 I.C.L.Q. 476 (1971).

pliance with any such orders or directions shall not be deemed to be a variation, and delivery in accordance with such orders or directions shall be a fulfilment of the contract voyage and the freight shall be paid accordingly.

The ship was intercepted and ordered by a general who said he came from "the government of Formosa" to discharge her cargo in that country, and did so. On a case stated by the umpire it was held by Sellers J., see pp. 564, 565 and 566, that the question to be decided was very different from a decision on a question of immunity or other question dependent on recognition, and that there was no such rule of law restricting the evidence to be considered to that provided by the Foreign Office, or which precluded the umpire from finding that there was a government in Formosa on all the evidence which was adduced. He held, on p. 564, that

the qualities or character required by the body giving the order or on whose behalf it was given or purported to be given must, therefore, include essentially the exercise of full executive and legislative power over an established territory.

Mr. Dillon also referred to the Foreign Enlistment Act 1870, sections 4 and 30, which makes it clear that the legislature was well aware that for the purposes of that Act a "foreign state" was not dependent on recognition. . . .

Although it is true that the *Luigi Monta* case is one dealing with the construction of a clause in a charterparty and Mr. MacCrindle is entitled to draw some distinction between the construction of such a document and of a statute, nevertheless the general principle must be that the true intention of the document, whether it be a commercial document or a statute, is to be ascertained. . . .

Applying these principles to section 24, I have no hesitation in holding that the phrase "any foreign state," although of course it includes a foreign state which has been given Foreign Office recognition, is not limited thereto. It must at any rate include a sufficiently defined area of territory over which a foreign government has effective control. Whether or not the state in question satisfies these conditions is a matter primarily of fact in each case. . . .

In the present case, apart from paragraph 4 of the Foreign Office Certificate, there is the evidence of Mr. Frank in his affidavit of April 24, 1968, which satisfies me, see paragraphs 22 to 25 in particular, that at the relevant time North Korea had a defined territory over which a government had effective control and that His late Majesty was engaged in hostilities with this state albeit his troops were under the command and formed part of the United Nations' forces fighting in the area.

I hold therefore that North Korea was a foreign state within the meaning of section 24. . . .

Notes

1. As this case shows, the English courts adopt a different approach (looking to the intention of the draftsman) when interpreting the phrases "state" or "government" in a statute or other document from that which they have, until now, adopted (relying upon an executive certificate) when recognising the law or the capacity to act of a foreign state or government.

2. In *Reel* v. *Holder*[51] the Court of Appeal was "simply concerned with the interpretation of the rules of the IAAF [the International Amateur Athletic Federation]" and not "with international law or with sovereignty" when asked to decide whether Taiwan was a "country" within the meaning of the IAAF rules (held that it was). *cf. Spinney's Royal Ins. Co.*[52] (Certificate not sought on question whether hostilities in Lebanon constituted "civil war" for insurance purposes).

[51] [1981] 1 W.L.R. 1226 (C.A.), *per* Lord Denning M.R.
[52] [1980] 1 Lloyd's Rep. 406 (Q.B.).

CHAPTER 5

TERRITORY

1. *TITLE TO TERRITORY*[1]

(i) OCCUPATION AND PRESCRIPTION

ISLAND OF PALMAS CASE[2]

The Netherlands *v*. U.S. (1928)

Permanent Court of Arbitration. Sole Arbitrator: Huber. 2 R.I.A.A. 829

As a result of the Spanish-American War of 1898, Spain ceded the Philippines to the United States by the Treaty of Paris of that year. In 1906, a United States official visited the island of Palmas (or Miangas), which the United States believed to be a part of the territory ceded to it, and found, to his surprise, a Dutch flag flying there. Palmas lies about 50 miles southeast of Cape San Augustin on the island of Mindanao. It is two miles long and less than a mile wide. In 1928, it had a population of less than 1,000 and was of negligible economic, military or other importance. Nonetheless, the Netherlands and the United States referred the question of sovereignty over the island to arbitration.

Award of the Arbitrator

Sovereignty in the relations between States signifies independence. Independence in regard to a portion of the globe is the right to exercise therein, to the exclusion of any other State, the functions of a State. The development of the national organisation of States during the last few centuries and, as a corollary, the development of international law, have established this principle of the exclusive competence of the State in regard to its own territory in such a way as to make it the point of departure in settling most questions that concern international relations. . . . The fact that the functions of a State can be performed by any State within a given zone is . . . precisely the characteristic feature of the legal situation pertaining in those parts of the globe which, like the high seas or lands without a master, cannot or do not yet form the territory of a State.

. . . If a dispute arises as to the sovereignty over a portion of territory, it is customary to examine which of the States claiming sovereignty possesses a title—cession, conquest, occupation, etc.—superior to that which the other State might possibly bring forward against it. However, if the contestation is based on the fact that the other Party has actually displayed sovereignty, it cannot be sufficient to establish the title by which territorial sovereignty was validly acquired at a certain moment; it must also be shown that the territorial sovereignty has continued to exist and did exist at the moment which for the decision of the dispute must be considered as critical. This demonstration

---

[1] See Jennings, *The Acquisition of Territory in International Law* (1963).
[2] See Jessup, 22 A.J.I.L. 735 (1938).

consists in the actual display of State activities, such as belongs only to the territorial sovereign.

Titles of acquisition of territorial sovereignty in present-day international law are either based on an act of effective apprehension, such as occupation or conquest, or, like cession, presuppose that the ceding and the cessionary Powers or at least one of them, have the faculty of effectively disposing of the ceded territory. In the same way natural accretion can only be conceived of as an accretion to a portion of territory where there exists an actual sovereignty capable of extending to a spot which falls within its sphere of activity. It seems therefore natural that an element which is essential for the constitution of sovereignty should not be lacking in its continuation. So true is this, that practice, as well as doctrine, recognizes—though under different legal formulae and with certain differences as to the conditions required—that the continuous and peaceful display of territorial sovereignty (peaceful in relation to other States) is as good as a title. The growing insistence with which international law, ever since the middle of the 18th century, has demanded that the occupation shall be effective would be inconceivable, if effectiveness were required only for the act of acquisition and not equally for the maintenance of the right. If the effectiveness has above all been insisted on in regard to occupation, this is because the question rarely arises in connection with territories in which there is already an established order of things. Just as before the rise of international law, boundaries of lands were necessarily determined by the fact that the power of a State was exercised within them, so too, under the reign of international law, the fact of peaceful and continuous display is still one of the most important considerations in establishing boundaries between States.

Territorial sovereignty, as has already been said, involves the exclusive right to display the activities of a State. This right has as corollary a duty: the obligation to protect within the territory the rights of other States, in particular their right to integrity and inviolability in peace and in war, together with the rights which each State may claim for its nationals in foreign territory. Without manifesting its territorial sovereignty in a manner corresponding to circumstances, the State cannot fulfil this duty. . . .

Although municipal law, thanks to its complete judicial system, is able to recognize abstract rights of property as existing apart from any material display of them, it has none the less limited their effect by the principles of prescription and the protection of possession. International law, the structure of which is not based on any super-State organisation, cannot be presumed to reduce a right such as territorial sovereignty, with which almost all international relations are bound up, to the category of an abstract right, without concrete manifestations. . . .

Manifestations of territorial sovereignty assume, it is true, different forms, according to conditions of time and place. Although continuous in principle, sovereignty cannot be exercised in fact at every moment on every point of a territory. The intermittence and discontinuity compatible with the maintenance of the right necessarily differ according as inhabited or uninhabited regions are involved, or regions enclosed within territories in which sovereignty is incontestably displayed or again regions accessible from, for instance, the high seas. It is true that neighbouring States may by convention fix limits to their own sovereignty, even in regions such as the interior of scarcely explored continents where such sovereignty is scarcely manifested, and in this way each may prevent the other from any penetration of its territory. The delimitation of Hinterland may also be mentioned in this connection.

If, however, no conventional line of sufficient topographical precision exists or if there are gaps in the frontiers otherwise established, or if a conventional line leaves room for doubt, or if, as *e.g.* in the case of an island situated in the high seas, the question arises whether a title is valid *erga omnes*, the actual continuous and peaceful display of State functions is in case of dispute the sound and natural criterion of territorial sovereignty. . . .

The *title alleged by the United States of America* as constituting the immediate foundation of its claim is that of *cession*, brought about by the Treaty of Paris, which cession transferred all rights of sovereignty which Spain may have possessed . . . concerning the island of Palmas (or Miangas).

It is evident that Spain could not transfer more rights than she herself possessed . . . the United States bases its claim, as successor of Spain, in the first place on *discovery*. . . .

It is admitted by both sides that international law underwent profound modifications between the end of the Middle Ages and the end of the 19th century, as regards the rights of discovery and acquisition of uninhabited region or regions inhabited by savages or semi-civilized peoples. Both Parties are also agreed that a juridical fact must be appreciated in the light of the law contemporary with it, and not of the law in force at the time when a dispute in regard to it arises or falls to be settled. The effect of discovery by Spain is therefore to be determined by the rules of international law in force in the first half of the 16th century. . . .

If the view most favourable to the American arguments is adopted—with every reservation as to the soundness of such view—that is to say, if we consider as positive law at the period in question the rule that discovery as such, *i.e.* the mere fact of seeing land, without any act, even symbolical, of taking possession, involved *ipso jure* territorial sovereignty and not merely an "inchoate title," a *jus ad rem*, to be completed eventually by an actual and durable taking of possession within a reasonable time, the question arises whether sovereignty yet existed at the critical date, *i.e.* the moment of conclusion and coming into force of the Treaty of Paris.

As regards the question which of different legal systems prevailing at successive periods is to be applied in a particular case (the so-called intertemporal law), a distinction must be made between the creation of rights and the existence of rights. The same principle which subjects the act creative of a right to the law in force at the time the right arises, demands that the existence of right, in other words its continued manifestation, shall follow the conditions required by the evolution of law. International law in the 19th century, having regard to the fact that most parts of the globe were under the sovereignty of States members of the community of nations, and that territories without a master had become relatively few, took account of a tendency already existing and especially developed since the middle of the 18th century, and laid down the principle that occupation, to constitute a claim to territorial sovereignty, must be effective, that is, offer certain guarantees to other States and their nationals. It seems therefore incompatible with this rule of positive law that there should be regions which are neither under the effective sovereignty of a State, nor without a master, but which are reserved for the exclusive influence of one State, in virtue solely of a title of acquisition which is no longer recognized by existing law, even if such a title ever conferred territorial sovereignty. For these reasons, discovery alone, without any subsequent act, cannot, at the present time suffice to prove sovereignty over the Island of Palmas (or Miangas); and in so far as there is no sovereignty, the question of an abandonment properly speaking of sovereignty by one State in order that the sovereignty of another may take its place does not arise.

If on the other hand the view is adopted that discovery does not create a definitive title of sovereignty, but only an "inchoate" title, such a title exists, it is true, without external manifestation. However, according to the view that has prevailed at any rate since the 19th century, an inchoate title of discovery must be completed within a reasonable period by the effective occupation of the region claimed to be discovered. This principle must be applied in the present case, for the reasons given above in regard to the rules determining which of successive legal systems is to be applied (the so-called intertemporal law). Now, no act of occupation nor, except as to a recent period, any exercise of sovereignty at Palmas by Spain has been alleged. But even admitting that the Spanish title still existed as inchoate in 1898 and must be considered as included in the cession under Article III of the Treaty of Paris, an inchoate title could not prevail over the continuous and peaceful display of authority by another State; for such display may prevail even over a prior, definitive title put forward by another State . . .

In the last place [in examining the United States arguments] there remains to be considered *title arising out of contiguity* . . . it is impossible to show the existence of a rule of positive international law to the effect that islands situated outside territorial waters should belong to a State from the mere fact that its territory forms the *terra firma* (nearest continent or island of considerable size). Not only would it seem that there are no precedents sufficiently frequent and sufficiently precise in their bearing to establish such a rule of international law, but the alleged principle itself is by its very nature so uncertain and contested that even Governments of the same State have on different occasions maintained contradictory opinions as to its soundness. The principle of contiguity, in regard to islands, may not be out of place when it is a question of allotting them to one State rather than another, either by agreement between the Parties, or by a decision not necessarily based on law; but as a rule establishing *ipso jure* the presumption of sovereignty in favour of a particular State, this principle would be in conflict with what has been said as to territorial sovereignty and as to the necessary relation between the right to exclude other States from a region and the duty to display therein the activities of a State. Nor is this principle of contiguity admissible as a legal method of deciding questions of territorial sovereignty; for it is wholly lacking in precision and would in its application lead to arbitrary results. This would be especially true in a case such as that of the island in question, which is not relatively close to one single continent, but forms part of a large archipelago in which strict delimitations between the different parts are not naturally obvious.

There lies, however, at the root of the idea of contiguity one point which must be considered also in regard to the Island of Palmas (or Miangas). It has been explained above that in the exercise of territorial sovereignty there are necessarily gaps, intermittence in time and discontinuity in space. This phenomenon will be particularly noticeable in the case of colonial territories, partly uninhabited or as yet partly unsubdued. The fact that a State cannot prove display of sovereignty as regards such a position of territory cannot forthwith be interpreted as showing that sovereignty is inexistent. Each case must be appreciated in accordance with the particular circumstances. . . .

As regards groups of islands, it is possible that a group may under certain circumstances be regarded as in law, a unit, and that the fate of the principal part may involve the rest. Here, however, we must distinguish between, on the one hand, the act of first taking possession, which can hardly extend to every portion of territory, and, on the other hand, the display of sovereignty as a continuous and prolonged manifestation which must make itself felt through the whole territory.

As regards the territory forming the subject of the present dispute, it must be remembered that it is a somewhat isolated island, and therefore a territory clearly delimited and individualised. It is moreover an island permanently inhabited, occupied by a population sufficiently numerous for it to be impossible that acts of administration could be lacking for very long periods. The memoranda of both Parties assert that there is communication by boat and even with native craft between the Island of Palmas (or Miangas) and neighbouring regions. The inability in such a case to indicate any acts of public administration makes it difficult to imagine the actual display of sovereignty, even if the sovereignty be regarded as confined within such narrow limits as would be supposed for a small island inhabited exclusively by natives. . . .

The Court then examined the argument put by the Netherlands.

The Netherlands found their claim to sovereignty essentially on the title of peaceful and continuous display of State authority over the island. Since this title would in international law prevail over a title of acquisition of sovereignty not followed by actual display of State authority, it is necessary to ascertain in the first place, whether the contention of the Netherlands is sufficiently established by evidence, and, if so, for what period of time.

In the opinion of the Arbitrator the Netherlands have succeeded in establishing the following facts:

a. The Island of Palmas (or Miangas) is identical with an island designated by this or a similar name, which has formed, at least since 1700, successively a part of two of the native States of the Island of Sangi (Talautse Isles).

b. These native States were from 1677 onwards connected with the East Indian Company, and thereby with the Netherlands,[3] by contracts of suzerainty, which conferred upon the suzerain such powers as would justify his considering the vassal State as a part of his territory.

c. Acts characteristic of State authority exercised either by the vassal State or by the suzerain Power in regard precisely to the Island of Palmas (or Miangas) have been established as occurring at different epochs between 1700 and 1898, as well as in the period between 1898 and 1906.

The acts of indirect or direct display of Netherlands sovereignty at Palmas (or Miangas), especially in the 18th and early 19th centuries are not numerous, and

---

[3] *Ed.* Elsewhere the Arbitrator commented on the nature of the acts of the Dutch East India Company as follows: "[They] must, in international law, be entirely assimilated to acts of the Netherlands State itself. From the end of the 16th till the 19th century, companies formed by individuals and engaged in economic pursuits (Chartered Companies), were invested by the State to whom they were subject with public powers for the acquisition and administration of colonies."

there are considerable gaps in the evidence of continuous display. But apart from the consideration that the manifestations of sovereignty over a small and distant island, inhabited only by natives, cannot be expected to be frequent, it is not necessary that the display of sovereignty should go back to a very far distant period. It may suffice that such display existed in 1898, and had already existed as continuous and peaceful before that date long enough to enable any Power who might have considered herself as possessing sovereignty over the island, or having a claim to sovereignty, to have, according to local conditions, a reasonable possibility for ascertaining the existence of a state of things contrary to her real or alleged rights.

It is not necessary that the display of sovereignty should be established as having begun at a precise epoch; it suffices that it had existed at the critical period preceding the year 1898. It is quite natural that the establishment of sovereignty may be the outcome of a slow evolution, of a progressive intensification of State control. This is particularly the case, if sovereignty is acquired by the establishment of the suzerainty of a colonial Power over a native State, and in regard to outlying possessions of such a vassal state.

Now the evidence relating to the period after the middle of the 19th century makes it clear that the Netherlands Indian Government considered the island distinctly as a part of its possessions and that, in the years immediately preceding 1898, an intensification of display of sovereignty took place.

Since the moment when the Spaniards, in withdrawing from the Moluccas in 1666, made express reservations as to the maintenance of their sovereign rights, up to the contestation made by the United States in 1906, no contestation or other action whatever or protest against the exercise of territorial rights by the Netherlands over the Talautse (Sangi) Isles and their dependencies (Miangas included) has been recorded. The peaceful character of the display of Netherlands sovereignty for the entire period to which the evidence concerning acts of display relates (1700–1906) must be admitted.

There is moreover no evidence which would establish any act of display of sovereignty over the island by Spain or another Power, such as might counterbalance or annihilate the manifestations of Netherlands sovereignty. As to third Powers, the evidence submitted to the Tribunal does not disclose any trace of such action, at least from the middle of the 17th century onwards. These circumstances, together with the absence of any evidence of a conflict between Spanish and Netherlands authorities during more than two centuries as regards Palmas (or Miangas), are an indirect proof of the exclusive display of Netherlands sovereignty.

This being so, it remains to be considered first whether the display of State authority might not legally be defective and therefore unable to create a valid title of sovereignty, and secondly whether the United States may not put forward a better title to that of the Netherlands.

As to the conditions of acquisition of sovereignty by way of continuous and peaceful display of State authority (so-called prescription), some of which have been discussed in the United States Counter-Memorandum, the following must be said:

The display has been open and public, that is to say that it was in conformity with usages as to exercise of sovereignty over colonial States. A clandestine exercise of State authority over an inhabited territory during a considerable length of time would seem to be impossible. . . .

The conditions of acquisition of sovereignty by the Netherlands are therefore to be considered as fulfilled. It remains now to be seen whether the United States as successors of Spain are in a position to bring forward an equivalent or stronger title. This is to be answered in the negative.

The title of discovery, if it had not been already disposed of by the Treaties of Munster and Utrecht would, under the most favourable and most extensive interpretation, exist only as an inchoate title, as a claim to establish sovereignty by effective occupation. An inchoate title however cannot prevail over a definite title founded on continuous and peaceful display of sovereignty.

The title of contiguity, understood as a basis of territorial sovereignty, has no foundation in international law.

The title of recognition by treaty does not apply, because even if the Sangi States, with the dependency of Miangas, are to be considered as "held and possessed" by Spain in 1648, the rights of Spain to be derived from the Treaty of Munster [1648] would have been superseded by those which were acquired by the Treaty of Utrecht [1714]. Now if there is evidence of a state of possession in 1714 concerning the island of Palmas (or Miangas), such evidence is exclusively in favour of the Netherlands. But even if the Treaty of Utrecht could not be taken into consideration, the acquiescence of Spain in the situation created after 1677 would deprive her and her successors of the possibility of still invoking conventional rights at the present time.

The Netherlands title of sovereignty, acquired by continuous and peaceful display of State authority during a long period of time going probably back beyond the year 1700, therefore holds good. . . .

For these reasons the Arbitrator, in conformity with Article I of the Special Agreement of January 23, 1925, decides that: the Island of Palmas (or Miangas) forms in its entirety a part of Netherlands territory.

Notes

1. The Award in the *Palmas Case* is of outstanding importance in the law on the acquisition of title to territory because of its full and scholarly treatment of such basic matters as the nature of territorial sovereignty and because of the emphasis placed upon the effect of a "continuous and peaceful display of State authority." As to the latter, the case indicates very clearly that the state that can show such "a display of State authority" in the period leading up to the "critical date" (*i.e.* the date on which the location of territorial sovereignty is decisive) can defeat any other claim whatever its basis. It has, however, to be a "peaceful" display of such authority, *i.e.* one without protest by interested states of the sort that prevents prescription, and of sufficient duration to establish a prescriptive title.[4] Thus, a state which exercises continuous and peaceful governmental possession has a title by way of occupation if the territory was previously *res nullius* and by way of prescription if it was not.

2. *Territorial Sovereignty*. The meaning of territorial sovereignty was discussed by France in its pleadings in the *Nationality Decrees in Tunis and Morocco Case*.[5] There M. A. de La Pradelle stated:

. . . territory is neither an object nor a substance; it is a framework. What sort of framework? The framework within which the public power is exercised . . . territory as such must not be considered, it must be regarded as the external, ostensible sign of the sphere within which the public power of the state is exercised.[6]

[4] See below, pp. 169–170.
[5] P.C.I.J.Rep., Series B, No. 4 (1923).
[6] *Ibid*. Series C, No. 2, pp. 106, 108.

3. *Title by Discovery*. On the possibility of obtaining title by discovery, Keller, Lissitzyn and Mann,[7] referring to the years 1400–1800, state:

Throughout this lengthy period, no state appeared to regard mere discovery, in the sense of "physical" discovery or simple "visual apprehension," as being in any way sufficient *per se* to establish a right of sovereignty over, or a valid title to, *terra nullius*. Furthermore, mere disembarkation upon any portion of such regions—or even extended penetration and exploration therein—was not regarded as sufficient itself to establish such a right or title . . . the formal ceremony of taking of possession, the symbolic act, was generally regarded as being wholly sufficient *per se* to establish immediately a right of sovereignty over, or a valid title to, areas so claimed and did not require to be supplemented by the performance of other acts, such as, for example, "effective occupation." A right or title so acquired and established was deemed good against all subsequent claims set up in opposition thereto unless, perhaps, transferred by conquest or treaty, relinquished, abandoned, or successfully opposed by continued occupation on the part of some other state.

4. On the relevance of contiguity, see also the *Western Sahara* case, below, p. 165. When the Arbitrator in the *Palmas Case* refers to "the delimitation of Hinterland,"[8] he has the Hinterland doctrine of the period of colonial expansion in mind. The doctrine was expressed as follows by the British Law Officers in 1885:

[T]he general principle is, that if a national has made a settlement it has a right to assume sovereignty over all the adjacent vacant territory, which is necessary to the integrity and security of the Settlement.[9]

5. *Intertemporal Law*. Commenting upon Huber's conception of intertemporal law, Jessup[10] wrote:

Assume that State A in a certain year acquires Island X from State B by a treaty of peace after a war in which A is the victor. Assume Island X is a barren rocky place, uninhabited and desired by A only for strategic reasons to prevent its fortification by another Power. Assume that A holds Island X, but without making direct use of it, for two hundred years. At the end of that time suppose that the development of international morality has so far progressed as to change the previous rule of international law and that the new rule is that no territory may be acquired by a victor from a vanquished at the close of a war. Under the theory of "intertemporal law" as expounded, it would appear that A would no longer have good title to Island X but must secure a new title upon some other basis or in accordance with the new rule. Such a retroactive effect of law would be highly disturbing. Every state would constantly be under the necessity of examining its title to each portion of its territory in order to determine whether a change in the law had necessitated, as it were, a reacquisition.

As noted below, p. 170, conquest is no longer a valid means of acquiring title to land. An extension of the doctrine of intertemporal law from a requirement that title must be valid in accordance with the law in force at the time at which it is claimed to have been established to one by which the validity of title must also be constantly updated as the international law bases for title change would, as Jessup suggests, be extremely disruptive. For the effect of such an extension on the Falkland Islands situation, see below, p. 171.

6. In the special agreement by which the *Palmas Case* was submitted to arbitration, the arbitrator was instructed to determine whether the island formed "a part of

---

[7] *Creation of Rights of Sovereignty through Symbolic Acts* 1400–1800 (1938), pp. 148–149.
[8] Above, p. 153.
[9] 1 *McNair* 292.
[10] *Loc. cit.* at p. 151, n. 10, above, p. 135.

Netherlands territory or of territory belonging to the United States of America." Could he, with these instructions, have decided that the island was *res nullius* or that a third state had title to it? Was his ruling in favour of the Netherlands binding upon third states? Is an arbitral award, in effect, a further means of acquiring title?[11]

7. The Arbitrator's reliance upon the acts of the Dutch East India Company as evidence of the exercise of authority by the Netherlands makes it relevant to point out the different situation in respect of the acts of individuals unauthorised to act for the state of which they are nationals. In the *Anglo-Norwegian Fisheries Case*, Judge Sir Arnold McNair stated that "the independent activity of private individuals is of little value unless it can be shown that they have acted in pursuance of a licence or some other authority received from their Governments or that in some other way their Governments have asserted jurisdiction through them."[12] A somewhat related question arose in the mid-nineteenth century when the Sultan of Borneo ceded Sarawak to Sir James Brooke, a British subject. In 1853, the Law Officers of the Crown were asked by the Foreign Office "whether it would be proper for Her Majesty's Government to recognise Sir James Brooke, as independent ruler or Sovereign of the Foreign State of Sarawak."[13] They replied that this was entirely a question of policy. As a question of *British Constitutional Law*, the report continued, "it is legally competent to Her Majesty to permit one of Her Subjects to assume the Sovereignty of a Foreign state, and to recognize him as such. Without such permission from the Crown, a Subject cannot acquire independent Sovereignty; the latter position being inconsistent with the allegiance which he owes to his own Sovereign. . . ."[14]

CLIPPERTON ISLAND CASE[15]

France v. Mexico (1931)

Arbitrator: King Victor Emmanuel III of Italy. 26 A.J.I.L. 390 (1932)

Award of the Arbitrator

In fact, we find, in the first place, that on November 17, 1858, Lieutenant Victor Le Coat de Kerwéguen, of the French Navy, commissioner of the French Government, while cruising about one-half mile off Clipperton,[16] drew up, on board the commercial vessel *L'Amiral*, an act by which, conformably to the orders which had been given to him by the Minister of Marine, he proclaimed and declared that the sovereignty of the said island beginning from that date belonged in perpetuity to His Majesty the Emperor Napoleon III and to his heirs and successors. During the cruise, careful and minute geographical notes were made; a boat succeeded, after numerous difficulties, in landing some members of the crew; and on the evening of November 20, after a second unsuccessful attempt to reach the shore, the vessel put off without leaving in the island any sign of sovereignty. Lieut. de Kerwéguen officially notified the accomplishment of his mission to the Consulate of France at Honolulu, which made a like communication to the Government of Hawaii. Moreover, the same consulate had published in English in the journal *The Polynesian*, of Honolulu,

---

[11] See Brownlie, pp. 127–128.
[12] I.C.J.Rep. 1951 at p. 184.
[13] 1 *McNair* 21.
[14] *Ibid.*   [15] See Dickinson, 27 A.J.I.J. 130 (1933).
[16] *Ed.* Clipperton is "a low coral lagoon reef, less than three miles in diameter, situated in the Pacific Ocean . . . some 670 miles south-west of Mexico": Dickinson, *loc. cit.* at n. 15 above, p. 131.

on December 8, the declaration by which French sovereignty over Clipperton had already been proclaimed.

Thereafter, until the end of 1887 no positive and apparent act of sovereignty can be recalled either on the part of France or on the part of any other Powers. The island remained without population, at least stable, and no administration was organized there. A concession for the exploitation of guano[17] beds existing there, which had been approved by the Emperor on April 8, 1958, in favor of a certain Mr. Lockart, and which had given rise to the expedition of Lieut. de Kerwéguen, had not been followed up, nor had its exploitation been undertaken on the part of any other French subjects.

Towards the end of 1897 . . . France stated . . . that three persons were found in the island collecting guano . . . and that they had, on the appearance of the French vessel, raised the American flag. Explanations were demanded on this subject from the United States, which responded that it had not granted any concession to the said company and did not intend to claim any right of sovereignty over Clipperton . . .

About a month after this act of surveillance had been accomplished by the French Navy . . . Mexico, ignoring the occupation claimed by France and considering that Clipperton was territory belonging to her for a long time, sent to the place a gun-boat, *La Democrata*, which action was caused by the report, afterwards acknowledged to be inaccurate, that England had designs upon the island. A detachment of officers and marines landed from the said ship December 13, 1897, and again found the three persons who resided on the island at the time of the preceding arrival of the French ship. It made them lower the American flag and hoist the Mexican flag in its place. Of the three individuals above mentioned, two consented to leave the island, and the third declared his wish to remain there, and in fact remained there until an unknown date. After that the *Democrata* left on December 15.

On January 8, France, having learned of the Mexican expedition, reminded that Power of its rights over Clipperton. . . .

According to Mexico, Clipperton Island, which had been given the name of the famous English adventurer who, at the beginning of the 18th century, used it as a place of refuge, was none other than Passion Island . . . that this island had been discovered by the Spanish Navy and, by virtue of the law then in force, fixed by the Bull of Alexander VII,[18] had belonged to Spain, and afterwards, from 1836, to Mexico as the successor state of the Spanish state.

But according to the actual state of our knowledge, it has not been proven that this island . . . had been actually discovered by the Spanish navigators. . . . However, even admitting that the discovery had been made by Spanish subjects, it would be necessary, to establish the contention of Mexico to prove that Spain not only had the right, as a state, to incorporate the island in her possessions, but also had effectively exercised the right. But that has not been demonstrated at all. . . .

Consequently, there is ground to admit that, when in November, 1858,

---

[17] *Ed.* Guano is a fertiliser made from the excrement of sea birds, particularly some that nest on islands off the coast of South America. Its discovery in the nineteenth century led to a sort of "Guano-rush."

[18] *Ed.* This was the Papal Bull *Inter Caetera* of 1493 by which a remarkably generous Pope gave to Spain all land discovered or to be discovered west of a line 100 miles west of the Azores and Cape Verde not in the possession of any Christian king.

France proclaimed her sovereignty over Clipperton, that island was in the legal situation of *territorium nullius*, and, therefore, susceptible of occupation.

The question remains whether France proceeded to an effective occupation, satisfying the conditions required by international law for the validity of this kind of territorial acquisition. In effect, Mexico maintains . . . that the French occupation was not valid, and consequently her own right to occupy the island which must still be considered as *nullius* in 1897.

In whatever concerns this question, there is, first of all, ground to hold as incontestable, the regularity of the act by which France in 1858 made known in a clear and precise manner, her intention to consider the island as her territory.

On the other hand, it is disputed that France took effective possession of the island, and it is maintained that without such a taking of possession of an effective character, the occupation must be considered as null and void.

It is beyond doubt that by immemorial usage having the force of law, besides the *animus occupandi*, the actual, and not the nominal, taking of possession is a necessary condition of occupation. This taking of possession consists in the act, or series of acts, by which the occupying state reduces to its possession the territory in question and takes steps to exercise exclusive authority there. Strictly speaking, and in ordinary cases, that only takes place when the state establishes in the territory itself an organization capable of making its laws respected. But this step is, properly speaking, but a means of procedure to the taking of possession, and, therefore, is not identical with the latter. There may also be cases where it is unnecessary to have recourse to this method. Thus, if a territory, by virtue of the fact that it was completely uninhabited, is, from the first moment when the occupying state makes its appearance there, at the absolute and undisputed disposition of that state, from that moment the taking of possession must be considered as accomplished, and the occupation is thereby complete. . . .

The regularity of the French occupation has also been questioned because the other Powers were not notified of it. But it must be observed that the precise obligation to make such notification is contained in Art. 34 of the [1885] Act of Berlin[19] . . . which . . . is not applicable to the present case. There is good reason to think that the notoriety given to the act, by whatever means, sufficed at the time, and that France provoked that notoriety by publishing the said act in the manner above indicated.

It follows from these premises that Clipperton Island was legitimately acquired by France on November 17, 1858. There is no reason to suppose that France has subsequently lost her right by *derelictio*, since she never had the *animus* of abandoning the island, and the fact that she has not exercised her authority there in a positive manner does not imply the forfeiture of an acquisition already definitively perfected.

FOR THESE REASONS, we decide, as arbiter, that the sovereignty over Clipperton Island belongs to France, dating from November 17, 1858.

Notes

1. This is a classic case of obtaining title to *res nullius* by occupation. What amount of authority does it suggest has to be exercised over an uninhabited island to establish possession?

[19] *Ed.* This required a party to the Act that took possession of land on the coast of Africa to notify the other parties that it had done so.

2. In the *Eastern Greenland Case*,[20] Norway "officially confirmed" its "taking possession" of Eastern Greenland, an uncolonised part of the island, by a declaration of July 10, 1931. Denmark, which had colonies elsewhere in Greenland and which claimed sovereignty over the whole of the island, asked the Permanent Court of International Justice to declare that the Norwegian declaration was invalid.

Although Denmark had not colonised Eastern Greenland, the Court found sufficient evidence of its claim and of exercise of state authority over the area during many centuries to show that it had established title to it at the "critical date," *viz.* July 10, 1931, when Norway made its claim. In recent history, this evidence consisted, from 1814 to 1915, of treaties applying to Greenland as a whole (which showed Denmark's "will and intention to exercise sovereignty"), the granting of concessions for trading, etc., in Eastern Greenland and legislation establishing the width of the territorial sea. From 1915 to 1931, it consisted of steps by Denmark to have its title to Greenland recognised by other states as well as various acts of administration and legislation. During both periods, Norwegian expeditions had sometimes wintered in Eastern Greenland and a wireless station and other buildings had been erected. Denmark had protested against the erection of the wireless station. The Court found this evidence sufficient to establish Denmark's sovereignty over the years indicated. Finally, the Court stressed the relative nature of the test to be applied in establishing occupation:

> It is impossible to read the records of the decisions in cases as to territorial sovereignty without observing that in many cases the tribunal has been satisfied with very little in the way of the actual exercise of sovereign rights, provided that the other State could not make out a superior claim. This is particularly true in the case of claims to sovereignty over areas in thinly populated or unsettled countries.[21]

The Court itself added to this jurisprudence by emphasising the absence of any other claim to Greenland prior to 1931.

MINQUIERS AND ECREHOS CASE[22]

France *v.* U.K.

I.C.J. Reports 1953, p. 47

Judgment of the Court

By Article I of the Special Agreement, signed on December 29th, 1950, the Court is requested:

> to determine whether the sovereignty over the islets and rocks (in so far as they are capable of appropriation) of the Minquiers and Ecrehos groups[23] respectively belongs to the United Kingdom or the French Republic.

Having thus been requested to decide whether these groups belong either to France or to the United Kingdom, the Court has to determine which of the Parties has produced the more convincing proof of title to one or the other of these groups, or to both of them. By the formulation of Article I the Parties have excluded the status of *res nullius* as well as that of *condominium*.

---

[20] P.C.I.J.Rep., Series A/B, No. 53 (1933). See the discussion of this case in the *Western Sahara Case*, below, p. 165.

[21] *Ibid.* p. 46.

[22] Fitzmaurice (1955–56) 32 B.Y.I.L. 20–76; Johnson, 3 I.C.L.Q. 189 (1954); Wade, 40 Trans.Grot.Soc. 97 (1954).

[23] *Ed.* These are in the English Channel, near Guernsey.

In Article II the Parties have stated their agreement as to the presentation of the Pleadings "without prejudice to any question as to the burden of proof," a question which it is for the Court to decide. Having regard to the position of the Parties, both claiming sovereignty over the same territory, and in view of the formulation of the task of the Court in Article I, and the terms of Article II, the Court is of the opinion that each Party has to prove its alleged title and the facts upon which it relies. . . .

Both Parties contend that they have respectively an ancient or original title to the Ecrehos and the Minquiers, and that their title has always been maintained and was never lost. The present case does not therefore present the characteristics of a dispute concerning the acquisition of sovereignty over *terra nullius*.

The United Kingdom Government derives the ancient title invoked by it from the conquest of England in 1066 by William, Duke of Normandy. By this conquest England became united with the Duchy of Normandy, including the Channel Islands, and this union lasted until 1204 when King Philip Augustus of France drove the Anglo-Norman forces out of Continental Normandy. But his attempts to occupy also the Islands were not successful, except for brief periods when some of them were taken by French forces. On this ground the United Kingdom Government submits the view that all of the Channel Islands, including the Ecrehos and the Minquiers, remained, as before, united with England and that this situation of fact was placed on a legal basis by subsequent Treaties concluded between the English and French Kings . . .

The French Government derives the original title invoked by it from the fact that the Dukes of Normandy were the vassals of the Kings of France, and that the Kings of England after 1066, in their capacity as Dukes of Normandy, held the Duchy in fee of the French Kings. . . .

The Court considers it sufficient to state as its view that even if the Kings of France did have an original feudal title also in respect of the Channel Islands, such a title must have lapsed as a consequence of the events of the year 1204 and following years.[24] Such an alleged original feudal title of the Kings of France in respect of the Channel Islands could today produce no legal effect, unless it had been replaced by another title valid according to the law of the time of replacement. What is of decisive importance, in the opinion of the Court, is not indirect presumptions deduced from events in the Middle Ages, but the evidence which relates directly to the possession of the Ecrehos and Minquiers groups. . . .

The Parties have further discussed the question of the selection of a "critical date" for allowing evidence in the present case. The United Kingdom Government submits that, though the Parties have for a long time disagreed as to the sovereignty over the two groups, the dispute did not become "crystallized" before the conclusion of the Special Agreement of December 29th, 1950, and that therefore this date should be considered as the critical date, with the result that all acts before that date must be taken into consideration by the Court. The French Government, on the other hand, contends that the date of the Convention of 1839 should be selected as the critical date, and that all subsequent acts must be excluded from consideration.

---

[24] *Ed*. The Duchy of Normandy was dismembered after Anglo-Norman forces had been driven out of Normandy in 1204.

At the date of the [fishery] Convention of 1839, no dispute as to the sovereignty over the Ecrehos and Minquiers groups had yet arisen. The Parties had for a considerable time been in disagreement with regard to the exclusive right to fish oysters, but they did not link that question to the question of sovereignty over the Ecrehos and the Minquiers. In such circumstances there is no reason why the conclusion of that Convention should have any effect on the question of allowing or ruling out evidence relating to sovereignty. A dispute as to sovereignty over the groups did not arise before the years 1886 and 1888, when France for the first time claimed sovereignty over the Ecrehos and the Minquiers respectively. But in view of the special circumstances of the present case, subsequent acts should also be considered by the Court, unless the measure in question was taken with a view to improving the legal position of the Party concerned. In many respects activity in regard to these groups had developed gradually long before the dispute as to sovereignty arose, and it has since continued without interruption and in a similar manner. In such circumstances there would be no justification for ruling out all events which during this continued development occurred after the years 1886 and 1888 respectively. . . .

The Court examined evidence of sovereignty in respect of the Ecrehos presented by each party. In the course of considering the evidence produced by the United Kingdom relating to the nineteenth century, the Court stated that it "attaches, in particular, probative value to the acts which relate to the exercise of jurisdiction and local administration and to legislation."[25] The Court concluded unanimously as follows:

The Court, being now called upon to appraise the relative strength of the opposing claims to sovereignty over the Ecrehos in the light of the facts considered above, finds that the Ecrehos group in the beginning of the thirteenth century was considered and treated as an integral part of the fief of the Channel Islands which were held by the English King, and that the group continued to be under the dominion of that King, who in the beginning of the fourteenth century exercised jurisdiction in respect thereof. The Court further finds that British authorities during the greater part of the nineteenth century and in the twentieth century have exercised State functions in respect of the group. The French Government, on the other hand, has not produced evidence showing that it has any valid title to the group. In such circumstances it must be concluded that the sovereignty over the Ecrehos belongs to the United Kingdom.

The Court then examined the evidence relating to the Minquiers group and reached the same conclusion.

For these reasons, the Court, unanimously,[26] finds that the sovereignty over the islets and rocks of the Ecrehos and Minquiers groups, in so far as these islets and rocks are capable of appropriation, belongs to the United Kingdom.

[25] It referred to the exercise of criminal jurisdiction, the holding of inquests, the collection of taxes and to a British Treasury Warrant of 1875 including the "Ecrehos Rocks" within the Port of Jersey.

[26] The Court consisted of Vice-President (and acting President) Guerrero; President Sir Arnold McNair; Judges Alvarez, Basdevant, Hackworth, Winiarski, Klaestad, Badawi, Read, Hsu Mo, Levi Carneiro and Armand-Ugon.

Notes

1. What was the basis for title in this case?

2. Why was the critical date in this case the date of the special agreement submitting it to the Court when it was held to be earlier than this in the *Palmas Case*?

3. Although the pleadings in the case contain lengthy attempts by both parties to trace their title to the islands over many centuries (which must have taken a lot of time and trouble!), the Court decided the case on the basis of recent evidence of the exercise of state authority. Does this confirm the approach taken by the Arbitrator in the *Palmas Case*?

WESTERN SAHARA CASE

Advisory Opinion, I.C.J.Rep. 1975, p. 12

The background to the request for an opinion in this case and the questions put to the Court are indicated above, p. 97. In the course of argument, Morocco claimed that it had had "legal ties" (see Question II put to the Court) with Western Sahara amounting to sovereignty at the time of its colonisation by Spain in 1884. The following extract concerns the Court's treatment of that claim, prefaced by an extract from the Court's answer to Question I. It ends with the general conclusion to the Court's Opinion.

Opinion of the Court

79. Turning to Question 1 . . . a determination that Western Sahara was a "*terra nullius*" at the time of colonization by Spain would be possible only if it were established that at that time the territory belonged to no one in the sense that it was then open to acquisition through the legal process of "occupation."

80. Whatever differences of opinion there may have been among jurists, the State practice of the relevant period [1884] indicates that territories inhabited by tribes or peoples having a social and political organization were not regarded as *terrae nullius*. It shows that in the case of such territories the acquisition of sovereignty was not generally considered as effected unilaterally through "occupation" of *terra nullius* by original title but through agreements concluded with local rulers . . . such agreements with local rulers, whether or not considered as an actual "cession" of the territory, were regarded as derivative roots of title, and not original titles obtained by occupation of *terrae nullius*.

81. In the present instance, the information furnished to the Court shows that at the time of colonization Western Sahara was inhabited by peoples which, if nomadic, were socially and politically organized in tribes and under chiefs competent to represent them. . . . In its Royal Order of 26 December 1884, far from treating the case as one of occupation of *terra nullius*, Spain claimed that the King was taking the Río de Oro under his protection on the basis of agreements which had been entered into with the chiefs of the local tribes: . . .

90. [In respect of Question II], Morocco's claim to "legal ties" with Western Sahara at the time of colonization by Spain has been put to the Court as a claim to ties of sovereignty on the ground of an alleged immemorial possession of the territory. . . .

91. In support of this claim Morocco refers to a series of events stretching back to the Arab conquest of North Africa in the seventh century A.D., the evidence of which is, understandably, for the most part taken from historical works. . . . Stressing that during a long period Morocco was the only independent State which existed in the north-west of Africa, it points to the geographical contiguity of Western Sahara to Morocco and the desert character of the territory. In the

light of these considerations, it maintains that the historical material suffices to establish Morocco's claim to a title based "upon continued display of authority" (*loc cit.*, p. 45) on the same principles as those applied by the Permanent Court in upholding Denmark's claim to possession of the whole of Greenland [see above p. 162].

92. This method of formulating Morocco's claims to ties of sovereignty with Western Sahara encounters certain difficulties. As the Permanent Court stated in the case concerning the *Legal Status of Eastern Greenland*, a claim to sovereignty based upon continued display of authority involves "two elements each of which must be shown to exist: the intention and will to act as sovereign, and some actual exercise or display of such authority" . . . True, the Permanent Court recognized that in the case of claims to sovereignty over areas in thinly populated or unsettled countries, "very little in the way of actual exercise of sovereign rights" (*ibid.* p. 46) might be sufficient in the absence of a competing claim. But, in the present instance, Western Sahara, if somewhat sparsely populated, was a territory across which socially and politically organized tribes were in constant movement and where armed incidents between these tribes were frequent. In the particular circumstances . . . the paucity of evidence of actual display of authority unambiguously relating to Western Sahara renders it difficult to consider the Moroccan claim as on all fours with that of Denmark in the *Eastern Greenland* case. Nor is the difficulty cured by introducing the argument of geographical unity or contiguity. In fact, the information before the Court shows that the geographical unity of Western Sahara with Morocco is somewhat debatable, which also militates against giving effect to the concept of contiguity. Even if the geographical contiguity of Western Sahara with Morocco could be taken into account in the present connection, it would only make the paucity of evidence of unambiguous display of authority with respect to Western Sahara more difficult to reconcile with Morocco's claim to immemorial possession.

93. In the view of the Court, however, what must be of decisive importance in determining its answer to Question II is not direct inferences drawn from events in past history but evidence directly relating to effective display of authority in Western Sahara at the time of its colonization by Spain and in the period immediately preceding that time (cf. *Minquiers and Ecrehos, Judgment, I.C.J. Reports* 1953, p. 57). As Morocco has also adduced specific evidence relating to the time of colonization and the period preceding it, the Court will now consider that evidence. . . .

The Court then examined this evidence and found that, although there was evidence of *personal* allegiance owed by Saharan tribes to Morocco, there was no *political* authority of the sort associated with sovereignty. The Court also rejected the Moroccan claim that its sovereignty over Western Sahara had been recognised by the international community.

162. The materials and information presented to the Court show the existence, at the time of Spanish colonization, of legal ties of allegiance between the Sultan of Morocco and some of the tribes living in the territory of Western Sahara. They equally show the existence of rights, including some rights relating to the land, which constituted legal ties between the Mauritanian entity,[27] as

---

[27] *Ed.* No question of ties amounting to sovereignty in 1884 arose in the case of the "Mauritanian Entity" because it was not then a state.

understood by the Court, and the territory of Western Sahara. On the other hand, the Court's conclusion is that the materials and information presented to it do not establish any tie of territorial sovereignty between the territory of Western Sahara and the Kingdom of Morocco or the Mauritanian entity. Thus the Court has not found legal ties of such a nature as might affect the application of resolution 1514 (XV) in the decolonization of Western Sahara and, in particular, of the principle of self-determination through the free and genuine expression of the will of the peoples of the Territory (*cf.* paragraphs 54–59 above[28]).

163. For these reasons . . .

THE COURT IS OF OPINION,

with regard to Question I,

unanimously,

that Western Sahara (Río de Oro and Sakiet El Hamra) at the time of colonization by Spain was not a territory belonging to no one (*terra nullius*),

with regard to Question II,

by 14 votes to 2,[29]

that there were legal ties between the territory and the Kingdom of Morocco of the kinds indicated in paragraph 162 of this Opinion.

by 15 votes to 1,[30]

that there were legal ties between this territory and the Mauritanian entity of the kinds indicated in paragraph 162 of this Opinion.

CHAMIZAL ARBITRATION

U.S. *v.* Mexico (1911)

International Boundary Commission: La Fleur, Presiding Commissioner: Mills, U.S. Commissioner, Puga, Mexican Commissioner. 5 A.J.I.L. 782 (1911)

By a treaty of 1848, the Rio Grande was made, for part of its length, the boundary between the United States and Mexico. By 1911, the river had changed its course leaving a tract of land of about 600 acres—the Chamizal Tract—between the old and the new beds of the river on the United States side of the new bed over which both states claimed sovereignty. The Commission decided that the part of the Tract that had resulted from a gradual process of accretion belonged to the United States but that the part of it that had resulted from a flood in 1864 belonged to Mexico. The case was decided on the basis of the relevant treaty provisions; an argument based upon prescription was, however, put by the United States and examined by the Commission in the following passage. The United States Commissioner, who dissented from the Commission's decision, concurred in its treatment of this argument.

Opinion of the Commission

. . . it is contended that the Republic of Mexico is estopped from asserting the national title over the territory known as "El Chamizal" by reason of the

[28] Above, pp. 97–99.

[29] The judges in the majority were President Lachs; Vice-President Ammoun; Judges Forster, Gros, Bengzon, Petrén, Onyeama, Dillard, Ignacio Pinto, de Castro, Morozov, Jiménez de Aréchaga, Sir Humphrey Waldock and Nagendra Singh. Judge Ruda and Judge ad hoc Boni dissented.

[30] Only judge ad hoc Boni dissented.

undisturbed, uninterrupted, and unchallenged possession of said territory by the United States of America since the Treaty of Guadalupe Hidalgo.

Without thinking it necessary to discuss the very controversial question as to whether the right of prescription invoked by the United States is an accepted principle of the law of nations, in the absence of any convention establishing a term of prescription, the commissioners are unanimous in coming to the conclusion that the possession of the United States in the present case was not of such a character as to found a prescriptive title. Upon the evidence adduced it is impossible to hold that the possession of El Chamizal by the United States was undisturbed, uninterrupted and unchallenged from the date of the Treaty of Guadalupe Hidalgo in 1848 until the year 1895, when, in consequence of the creation of a competent tribunal to decide the question, the Chamizal case was first presented. On the contrary it may be said that the physical possession taken by citizens of the United States and the political control exercised by the local and federal governments, have been constantly challenged and questioned by the Republic of Mexico, through its accredited diplomatic agents. . . . From . . . [1867] until the negotiation of the Convention of 1884, a considerable amount of diplomatic correspondence is devoted to the very question, and the Convention of 1884 was an endeavour to fix the rights of the two nations with respect to the changes brought about by the action of the waters of the Rio Grande.

The very existence of that convention precludes the United States from acquiring by prescription against the terms of their title and, as has been pointed out above, the two republics have ever since the signing of that convention treated it as a source of all their rights in respect of accretion to the territory on one side or the other of the river.

Another characteristic of possession serving as a foundation for prescription is that it should be peaceable. . . .

It is quite clear from the circumstances . . . that however much the Mexicans may have desired to take physical possession of the district, the result of any attempt to do so would have provoked scenes of violence and the Republic of Mexico cannot be blamed for resorting to the milder forms of protest contained in its diplomatic correspondence.

In private law, the interruption of prescription is effected by a suit, but in dealings between nations this is of course impossible, unless and until an international tribunal is established for such a purpose. In the present case, the Mexican claim was asserted before the International Boundary Commission within a reasonable time after it commenced to exercise its functions, and prior to that date the Mexican Government had done all that could be reasonably required of it by way of protest against the alleged encroachment.

Under these circumstances the Commissioners have no difficulty in coming to the conclusion that the plea of prescription should be dismissed.

Notes

1. See also the extract from the *Anglo-Norwegian Fisheries Case*, below p. 289.

2. In the *Frontier Land Case*,[31] Belgium and the Netherlands disputed sovereignty over certain plots of land in the area of the border between them. The Court stated:

[31] I.C.J.Rep. 1959, p. 209.

The final contention of the Netherlands is that if sovereignty over the disputed plots was vested in Belgium by virtue of the Boundary Convention [of 1843], acts of sovereignty exercised by the Netherlands since 1843 have established sovereignty in the Netherlands. This is a claim to sovereignty in derogation of title established by treaty. . . . The question for the Court is whether Belgium has lost its sovereignty, by non-assertion of its rights and by acquiescence in acts of sovereignty alleged to have been exercised by the Netherlands at different times since 1843.[32]

The Court examined the evidence and concluded that Belgian sovereignty had not been extinguished. The Court here would seem to be accepting that title may be established by prescription. The same conclusion is implicit in the *Palmas* case, above, p. 151. In the *Right of Passage Case*[33] Judge Moreno Quintana, in his dissenting opinion, stated that the reasoning in the majority opinion "implies, by definition, a recognition that territorial sovereignty can be acquired by prescription, a private law institution which I consider finds no place in international law."[34]

3. In the *British Guiana* v. *Venezuela Boundary Arbitration*[35] the arbitrators were instructed by their treaty terms of reference as follows:

Adverse holding or prescription during a period of 50 years shall make a good title.

4. Writers distinguish between acquisitive and extinctive prescription in international law, the latter being based upon the rule that a claim must be brought within a reasonable period of time. As to the former, which is the type of prescription being considered in this section, most writers accept that it can be a basis for title. Hall[36] states:

Title by prescription arises out of a long continued possession, where no original source of proprietary right can be shown to exist, or where possession in the first instance being wrongful, the legitimate proprietor has neglected to assert his right, or has been unable to do so.

Johnson[37] states:

"Acquisitive prescription" is the means by which, under international law, legal recognition is given to the right of a state to exercise sovereignty over land or sea territory in cases where that state has, in fact, exercised its authority in a continuous, uninterrupted, and peaceful manner over the area concerned for a sufficient period of time, provided that all other interested and affected states (in the case of land territory the previous possessor, in the case of sea territory neighbouring states and other states whose maritime interests are affected) have acquiesced in this exercise of authority. Such acquiescence is implied in cases where the interested and affected states have failed within a reasonable time to refer the matter to the appropriate international organization or international tribunal or—exceptionally in cases where no such action was possible—have failed to manifest their opposition in a sufficiently positive manner through the instrumentality of diplomatic protests. The length of time required for the establishment of a prescriptive title on the one hand, and the extent of the action required to prevent the establishment of a prescriptive title on the other hand, are invariable matters of fact to be decided by the international tribunal before which the matter is eventually brought for adjudication.

The same writer also states:

. . . as Verykios[38] . . . said, a [diplomatic] protest not followed up by other action becomes in time "academic" and "useless." The other action that was formerly

---

[32] *Ibid*. p. 227.
[33] I.C.J.Rep. 1960, p. 6. See the extract below, p. 198.
[34] *Ibid*. p. 88.
[35] 92 B.F.S.P. 160 (1899–1900).
[36] *International Law* (8th ed., 1924) (Pearce Higgins), p. 143.
[37] (1950) 27 B.Y.I.L. 332 at pp. 353–354.
[38] Ed. *La prescription en droit international* (1934).

required was forceful opposition of some sort. Since 1919 it was, where possible, reference of the matter to the League of Nations or the Permanent Court of International Justice. Since 1945 it has been, where possible, reference of the matter to the United Nations or to the International Court of Justice . . . the advent of this new machinery for settling international disputes has largely altered the role of the protest in the matter of acquisitive prescription. The result is that the diplomatic protest is of reduced significance and is certainly not now the principal method of interrupting prescription. A protest since 1919 can be said to have amounted to no more than a temporary bar.[39]

Brownlie[40] disagrees with the view that "protest must be followed by steps to use available machinery for the settlement of international disputes." He states:

If acquiescence is the crux of the matter (and it is believed that it is) one cannot dictate what its content is to be. . . .

5. See further on prescription, the note on Gibraltar, below, p. 177.

(ii) CONQUEST

Notes

1. Conquest was a recognised and important basis for title until the early years of this century. It is now well established that the "territory of a state shall not be the object of acquisition by another state resulting from the threat or use of force" contrary to Article 2(4), United Nations Charter: 1970 Declaration on Principles of International Law, section on the principle on the use of force, paragraph 10, Appendix II, below. As the 1928 Briand-Kellogg Pact and the United Nations Charter have outlawed the use of armed force, see below, Chap. 11, so the law of conquest has declined to the point where it provides, under the doctrine of intertemporal law, justification only for the titles acquired before the force used to obtain them was declared illegal by customary international law. An interesting question is whether a state that acts in self-defence to repel armed force used against it contrary to Article 2(4) can acquire any territory of the aggressor which it occupies during hostilities. (See, *e.g.* the Middle East situation below, p. 175) Akehurst[41] refers to the wording of the 1970 Declaration (paragraph referred to above) in support of the view that it cannot:

In these words, the Declaration makes a significant distinction between military occupation and acquisition of territory. Military occupation is unlawful only if it results from the use of force in contravention of the Charter; *any* threat or use of force, whether it is in contravention of the Charter or not, invalidates acquisition of territory.

Jennings[42] argues for the same conclusion:

. . . the suggestion that the state that does not resort to force unlawfully, *e.g.* resorts to war in self-defence, may still acquire a title by conquest . . . though not infrequently heard, is to be regarded with some suspicion. It seems to be based upon a curious assumption that, provided a war is lawful in origin, it goes on being lawful to whatever lengths it may afterwards be pursued. The grave dangers of abuse inherent in any such notion are obvious . . . Force used in self-defence . . . must be proportionate to the threat of immediate danger, and when the threat has been averted the plea of self-defence can no longer be available . . . it would be a curious law of self-

---

[39] *Loc. cit.* at n. 37 above, p. 346.
[40] Brownlie, p. 161.
[41] *A Modern Introduction to International Law* (4th ed., 1982), p. 147. Footnote omitted.
[42] *Op cit.* at p. 151, n. 1, above, p. 55. Footnote omitted.

defence that permitted the defender in the course of his defence to seize and keep the resources and territory of the attacker.

2. *The Falkland Islands*.[43] The Falkland Islands are a British Crown Colony. Sovereignty over them is also claimed by Argentina, which calls them the Malvinas. According to British sources, they were first sighted by a British sea captain in 1592. Argentina claims that they were discovered earlier in the same century by Spanish explorers. The first recorded landing was by a British sea captain in 1690. The first settlement on the previously uninhabited islands was made by the French on East Falkland in 1764. When Spain (which based its claim mainly on the Papal Bull *Inter Caetera*, as to which, see above p. 160) objected, France sold the settlement to Spain in 1766. In the meantime, Great Britain had established a settlement on West Falkland in 1765. This was taken by Spain by force in 1770. After British protests, it was handed back the following year, but with Spanish claims to sovereignty over the Malvinas expressly reserved. In 1774, the British settlement was abandoned for reasons of economy. A metal plaque claiming sovereignty over the Islands for King George III was left behind. The Spanish later removed the plaque and razed the remaining buildings to the ground. The Spanish thereafter continued to occupy the Malvinas until 1811. In 1820, Argentina which had obtained its independence from Spain in 1816, laid claim to the Malvinas and in the next decade established a new settlement there. (The Islands had been left uninhabited by Spain during the Napoleonic wars and the American wars of independence.) In 1831, the Argentinian governor arrested three American ships for breach of seal fishing regulations, whereupon the United States, which regarded the islands as *res nullius*, sent a warship which demilitarised the Argentinian settlement. Great Britain did not protest at the Argentinian claim in 1820; it did protest at the appointment of a Governor in 1829. In 1833, it took the Falkland Islands by force and has remained in possession of them ever since. Negotiations have occurred between Argentina and the United Kingdom from time to time since the question of the status of the islands was raised by Argentina in the "Committee of 24" in 1965,[44] but without success. On the Argentinian invasion in 1982, see below, p. 661. The island's exclusive economic zone is important for fishing purposes and *could* contain commercially viable deposits of oil and gas.[45] Does the United Kingdom have title to the islands? Although conquest is not a good basis for title now, it was in 1833. Unless Huber's interpretation of the doctrine of intertemporal law, above, p. 158, is followed, Argentine protest since 1833[46] would not affect the British claim based upon conquest. In any event, there has almost certainly been general recognition, as to which, see below, p. 174, of British title since 1833. Neither Argentina nor the United Kingdom have referred the dispute to the I.C.J.[47] On the application of the principle of self-determination, see above, pp. 95 *et seq*.

During the Falkland Islands War, Argentina claimed (see below, p. 662) sovereignty also over South Georgia and the South Sandwich Islands, which are about 800 and 1,000 miles to the east of the Falklands respectively. They were both discovered, landed upon and formally annexed by Captain Cook in 1775 for Great Britain, and have been administered by it ever since. Argentina claimed sovereignty over South Georgia (but not the South Sandwich Islands) in 1925, but this claim was rejected by the United Kingdom. Apart from the taking of South Georgia by force during the 1982 war, these islands have never been occupied by Spain.

[43] See Goebel, *The Struggle for the Falklands* (1927); Metford, 44 *International Affairs* 463 (1968); Northedge, 7 Int. Rel. 2167 (1982). On the Argentinian Claim, see *Rev. I.C.J.*, No. 28, p. 25 (1982).

[44] See above, p. 101, n. 6.

[45] See the Shackleton Economic Survey of the Falkland Islands (1976), Vol. I, pp. 174 *et seq*.

[46] For details of such protest, see *Rev. I.C.J.*, No. 28 at p. 32 (1982).

[47] See Minister of State for Foreign Affairs (Lord Belstead), *Hansard*, H.L., Vol. 429, col. 399. April 19, 1982.

THE STIMSON DOCTRINE OF NON-RECOGNITION

1 Hackworth 334

On January 7, 1932, the United States Secretary of State for Foreign Affairs (Stimson) sent a note to the Japanese and Chinese Governments, from which the following extract is taken. It was occasioned by the invasion of Manchuria by Japan and the establishment by the latter of the "puppet state" of "Manchukuo."[48]

The American Government deems it to be its duty to notify both the Imperial Japanese Government and the Government of the Chinese Republic that it can not admit the legality of any situation de facto nor does it intend to recognize any treaty or agreement entered into between those Governments, or agents thereof, which may impair the treaty rights of the United States or its citizens in China, including those which relate to the sovereignty, the independence, or the territorial and administrative integrity of the Republic of China, or to the international policy relative to China, commonly known as the open-door policy; and that it does not intend to recognize any situation, treaty, or agreement which may be brought about by means contrary to the convenants and obligations of the Pact of Paris of August 27th, 1928, to which treaty both China and Japan, as well as the United States, are parties.

Note
On March 11, 1932, the Assembly of the League of Nations resolved that "it was incumbent upon the Members of the League of Nations not to recognise any situation, treaty or agreement which may be brought about by means contrary to the Covenant of the League of Nations, or the Pact of Paris."[49] This, however, proved the high-water mark of the Stimson Doctrine. It was applied by some states upon the invasion of Ethiopia in 1935 and in response to German and Russian invasions shortly afterwards but is no longer invoked under this name. It has reappeared in the 1970 Declaration on Principles of International Law, section on the principle on the use of force, paragraph 10, Appendix III, below. Article 11 of the Draft Declaration on Rights and Duties of States[50] similarly reads:

Every State has the duty to refrain from recognising any territorial acquisition by another State acting in violation of Article 9 [prohibiting resort to war as an instrument of national policy and the threat or use of force contrary to Article 2(4) of the United Nations Charter.[51]]

THE INVASION OF GOA[52]

S.C.O.R., 16th Yr., 987th and 988th Meetings, December 18, 1961

On December 17–18, 1961, India invaded the Portuguese territories of Goa, Dañao and Diu on the Indian subcontinent. On December 18, Portugal asked the Security Council of the United Nations "to put a stop to the contemnable act of aggression of the Indian Union, ordering an immediate cease-fire and the withdrawal forthwith from Portuguese territories of Goa, Dañao and Diu of all the invading forces of the Indian Union."[53] A

---

[48] See above, p. 87.
[49] L.N.O.J., Special Supp. No. 101, pp. 87, 88 (1932).
[50] Y.B.I.L.C., 1949, II, pp. 286, 288. On the Draft Declaration, see p. 57.
[51] Appendix I, below.
[52] See Wright, 56 A.J.I.L. 617 (1962).   [53] U.N.Doc. S/5030.

draft resolution rejecting the Portuguese complaint was rejected by the Security Council by seven votes to four. A second draft resolution recalling the terms of Articles 2(3), (4) of the Charter and calling both for the immediate cease-fire and for the withdrawal by India of its forces was vetoed by the U.S.S.R. The following are extracts from the Security Council debate.

987th Meeting

46. MR. JHA (INDIA). I have already said that this is a colonial question, in the sense that part of our country is illegally occupied by right of conquest by the Portuguese. The fact that they have occupied it for 450 years is of no consequence because, during nearly 425 or 430 years of that period we really had no chance to do anything because we were under colonial domination ourselves. But during the last fourteen years, from the very day when we became independent, we have not ceased to demand the return of the peoples under illegal domination to their own countrymen, to share their independence, their march forward to their destiny. I would like to put this matter very clearly before the Council: that Portugal has no sovereign right over this territory. There is no legal frontier—there can be no legal frontier—between India and Goa. And since the whole occupation is illegal as an issue—it started in an illegal manner, it continues to be illegal today and it is even more illegal in the light of resolution 1514 (XV)—there can be no question of aggression against your own frontier, or against your own people, whom you want to keep liberate.

47. That is the situation that we have come to face. If any narrow-minded, legalistic considerations—considerations arising from international law as written by European law writers—should arise, those writers were, after all, brought up on the atmosphere of colonialism. I pay all respect due to Grotius, who is supposed to be the father of international law, and we accept many tenets of international law. They are certainly regulating international life today. But the tenet which says, and which is quoted in support of colonial Powers having sovereign rights over territories which they won by conquest in Asia and Africa is no longer acceptable. It is the European concept and it must die. It is time, in the twentieth century that it died. . . .

72. MR. STEVENSON (UNITED STATES OF AMERICA.) Let it be perfectly clear what is at stake here; it is the question of the use of armed force by one State against another and against its will, an act clearly forbidden by the Charter. We have opposed such action in the past by our closest friends as well as by others. We opposed it in Korea in 1950, in Suez and in Hungary in 1956 and in the Congo in 1960. And we do so again in Goa in 1961. . . .

75. But what is at stake today is not colonialism; it is a bold violation of one of the most basic principles in the United Nations Charter, stated in these words from Article 2, paragraph 4: . . .[54]

76. We realize fully the depths of the differences between India and Portugal concerning the future of Goa. We realize that India maintains that Goa by right should belong to India. Doubtless India would hold, therefore, that its action is aimed at a just end. But, if our Charter means anything, it means that States are obliged to renounce the use of force, are obligated to seek a solution of their

---

[54] *Ed*. Appendix I, below.

differences by peaceful means, are obligated to utilize the procedures of the United Nations when other peaceful means have failed.

988th Meeting

77. Mr. Jha (India). . . . We are criticized here by various delegations which say, "Why have you used force? The Charter absolutely prohibits force"; but the Charter itself does not completely eschew force, in the sense that force can be used in self-defence, for the protection of the people of a country—and the people of Goa are as much Indians as the people of any other part of India.[55] We cannot accept any other position.

78. If the use of force is a mockery—and many representatives have said that it is not internationally moral—if that is so, I would say that all freedom movements, all independent countries which have attained freedom through violent movements, should also come in that category. If fighting a colonial Power is immoral I am afraid the existence of many States around this table becomes immoral. The use of force, in all circumstances, is regrettable but so far as the achievement of freedom is concerned, when nothing else is available, I am afraid that it is a very debatable proposition to say that force cannot be used at all. . . .

79. . . . I have said that we accept international law . . . International law is not a static institution. It is developing constantly. If international law would be static, it would be dead driftwood, if it did not respond to the public opinion of the world. And it is responding every day, whether we like it or not General Assembly resolution 1514 (XV),[56] which has been referred to here and elsewhere very frequently, is the embodiment of that great leap forward in the public opinion of the world on these matters. There can be no getting away from that. Just as the process of decolonization is irreversible and irresistible, the embodiment of the principles in resolution 1514 (XV), which has been accepted by virtually every member around this table, is irresistible. One cannot go behind that now. That is the new dictum of international law.

Note

India remains in control of the territories taken in 1961. Portugal recognised Indian title to them in 1974. Who had title to them between 1961 and 1974 in international law? Is the attitude of Portugal or of other states relevant? On the dispute over the legality of external *material* support given by a state to a "people" that is waging its own war of national liberation, see below p. 649. Jennings,[57] starting with the assumption that a state cannot now obtain title to territory by action contrary to Article 2(4) of the United Nations Charter, suggests the following approach to the sort of problem exemplified by the Goan situation:

> The traditional procedure by which the law is adjusted to fact—by which indeed, the law when occasion requires may seem to embrace illegality—is the procedure of recognition. In the present context recognition is apt not only because title is *ex hypothesi* a matter that concerns States in general, but also because the principal effect of the change in the law concerning force, is to make the use of force itself a matter of concern to States generally and not only to the States immediately in-

---

[55] *Ed.* According to a 1950 census, of the 650,000 people living in Goa, 800 were European, 316 were of mixed descent and the rest were Indian: *Hansard,* H.C., Vol. 651, col. 1129. December 19, 1961.

[56] Above, p. 95.   [57] *Op. cit.* at p. 151, n. 1, above, p. 62.

volved. This is a reversal of the previous position in regard to the use of force, when it could be said that "the validity of the title of the subjugating State does not depend upon recognition on the part of other States. Nor is a mere protest of a third State of any legal weight."[58]

SECURITY COUNCIL RESOLUTION ON THE MIDDLE EAST, NOVEMBER 22, 1967[59]

Security Council Resolution 242 (XXII), S.C.O.R., 22nd Yr., *Resolutions and Decisions* 1967, p. 8

The Security Council

Expressing its continuing concern with the grave situation in the Middle East,

Emphasizing the inadmissibility of the acquisition of territory by war and the need to work for a just and lasting peace in which every State in the area can live in security,

Emphasizing further that all Member States in their acceptance of the Charter of the United Nations have undertaken a commitment to act in accordance with Article 2 of the Charter,

1. Affirms that the fulfilment of Charter principles requires the establishment of a just and lasting peace in the Middle East which should include the application of both the following principles:

(i) Withdrawal of Israeli armed forces from territories occupied in the recent conflict;

(ii) Termination of all claims or states of belligerency and respect for and acknowledgment of the sovereignty, territorial integrity and political independence of every State in the area and their right to live in peace within secure and recognized boundaries free from threats or acts of force;

2. Affirms further the necessity

(*a*) For guaranteeing freedom of navigation through international waterways in the area;

(*b*) For achieving a just settlement of the refugee problem;

(*c*) For guaranteeing the territorial inviolability and political independence of every State in the area, through measures including the establishment of demilitarized zones;

3. Requests the Secretary-General to designate a Special Representative to proceed to the Middle East to establish and maintain contacts with the States concerned in order to promote agreement and assist efforts to achieve a peaceful and accepted settlement in accordance with the provisions of this resolution;

4. Requests the Secretary-General to report to the Security Council on the progress of the efforts of the Special Representative as soon as possible.

Notes

1. Resolution 242 (XXII) was made under Chapter VI of the United Nations Charter.[60] It is therefore not binding upon member states. The term "territories" in paragraph 1(i) was left purposely vague (*some* territories (if so, which)? All?)

[58] Oppenheim, *International Law* (8th ed.), Vol. 1, p. 573.
[59] See Rosenne, 33 L. & C.P. 44 (1968) and Wright, *ibid.* 5.
[60] See the U.K. representative (Lord Caradon), U.N. Doc. S/PV. 1379, para. 6. The resolution was adopted unanimously.

2. The history behind Resolution 242 (XXII) may be summarized as follows.[61] In 1947, the United Kingdom gave notice to the United Nations that it was withdrawing forthwith from Palestine, a territory it had administered as mandatory.[62] The General Assembly recommended on November 29, 1947[63] that Palestine should be partitioned into separate Arab and Jewish states subject to provision for economic union. This was acceptable to the Zionists but not to the Palestinian Arabs. On May 14, 1948, Israel unilaterally declared itself an independent state. It was immediately attacked by neighbouring Arab states, whom it defeated. During 1949, armistice agreements were made, with the assistance of the United Nations, between Israel and each of its neighbours. Under these, Israel retained considerably more territory than it would have had under the 1947 plan for partition. In 1956, after frequent violations of the armistice agreements on all sides, Israel invaded the Egyptian Sinai Peninsula but later withdrew to the 1949 armistice line on the recommendation of the General Assembly.[64] In the "Six Day War" of June 1967, Israel again invaded the Sinai Peninsula, this time as far as the East Bank of the Suez Canal in the West and the Straits of Tiran in the South. It also invaded the West Bank of the River Jordan (Jordanian territory); that part of the city of Jerusalem[65] which it had not previously occupied (also Jordanian); and the strategically important Golan Heights in Syria.

Hostilities broke out again in the Yom Kippur War[66] of October 1973. On October 6, Egypt and Syria launched simultaneous attacks upon Israeli forces in the Sinai Peninsula and the Golan Heights respectively. When a cease-fire was finally achieved on October 24, Egypt had retaken about 400 square miles of its territory in the Sinai Peninsula to the east of the Suez Canal, but had lost about the same amount of territory to Israel on the West Bank of the Canal. In the Golan Heights area, Syria had been forced back to within 20 miles of Damascus after initial successes. The cease-fire was preceded by Security Council Resolution 338 (1973)[67] which, in addition to calling for a cease-fire, read as follows:

The Security Council . . .

2. Calls upon the parties concerned to start immediately after the cease-fire the implementation of Security Council Resolution 242 (1967) in all of its parts;
3. Decides that immediately and concurrently with the cease-fire, negotiations shall start between the parties concerned under appropriate auspices aimed at establishing a just and durable peace in the Middle East.

In 1979, Egypt and Israel made a Treaty of Peace[68] by which Egypt recognised Israel as a state and Israel returned the Sinai Peninsula to Egypt. No such treaty has been made between Israel and other Arab states, but by a 1974 Israeli-Syrian disengagement agreement, Israel withdrew from all of the areas taken in the 1973 war and from some of those taken by it in 1967. A buffer zone was established which was to be patrolled by the United Nations Disengagement Observation Force (UNDOF).[69] Otherwise attempts to negotiate a final settlement of the Arab/Israeli dispute in accordance with Resolutions 242 (1967) and 338 (1973) have been unsuccessful. A major stumbling block is the

---

[61] See Cattan, *Palestine and International Law* (1973); Feinberg, *The Arab-Israeli Conflict in International Law* (1970); *id., Studies in International Law with Special Reference to the Arab-Israeli Conflict* (1979).
[62] See above, p. 102.
[63] G.A. Resn. 181 (II).
[64] See below, p. 667.
[65] On the status of Jerusalem, see Jones, 33 L. & C.P. 169 (1968) and Wright, *ibid.* p. 5 at pp. 15–16.
[66] The attacks were launched on Yom Kippur, the most sacred Jewish holy day.
[67] *Resolutions and Decisions*, 1973, p. 10.
[68] For the text, see *Keesings Archives*, p. 29942.
[69] On UNDOF, see below, p. 697.

question of the Palestinian Arabs, who number approximately 3,250,000.[70] Nearly half of these live in Israel; the remainder live in Israeli-occupied territory or surrounding Arab states. They are represented by the Palestinian Liberation Organisation (PLO). According to the Palestine National Charter 1964 (as affirmed in 1977),[71] they regard Palestine, with the boundaries it had during the British mandate, as "an indivisible territorial unit"[72] and as "the homeland of the Palestinian Arab people."[73] They claim "the legal right to their homeland and have the right to determine their destiny after achieving the liberation of their country in accordance with their wishes and entirely of their own will and accord."[74]

Israel continues to hold much of the territory it gained in 1967, including the West Bank of the Jordan, the Golan Heights, and the part of Jerusalem occupied by it then. Since 1967, it has acted to incorporate this new territory into Israel in law[75] and has established Israeli settlements in it. In a series of resolutions, the Security Council has declared such action to be illegal and called for the dismantlement of settlements.[76]

(iii) CESSION

OPPENHEIM, INTERNATIONAL LAW

Vol. I (8th ed., 1955). Some footnotes omitted

213. Cession of State territory is the transfer of sovereignty over State territory by the owner-State to another State. . . .

215. . . . As far as the Law of Nations is concerned, every State as a rule can cede a part of its territory to another State, or by ceding the whole of its territory can even totally merge in another State. However, since certain parts of State territory, as for instance rivers and the maritime belt, are inalienable appurtenances of the land, they cannot be ceded without a piece of land.

216. The only form in which a cession can be effected is an agreement embodied in a treaty between the ceding and the acquiring State. Such treaty may be the outcome of peaceable negotiations or of war, and the cesssion may be made with or without compensation. . . .

Note

Gibraltar.[77] Like the Falkland Islands,[78] Gibraltar is a British Crown Colony. In 1704, it was captured from Spain by a British/Dutch expedition during the War of Spanish Succession. It was later ceded by Spain to Great Britain after the latter had lost the War. Article X of the Treaty of Utrecht 1713 reads:

> The Catholic King does hereby, for himself, his heirs and successors, yield to the Crown of Great Britain the full and entire property of the town and castle of Gibraltar, together with the port, fortifications, and forts thereunto belonging; and

---

[70] This estimate was made by the PLO in 1976.
[71] Reprinted in *Keesings Archives*, p. 28385.
[72] Article 2.
[73] Article 1. On the principle of self-determination, see above p. 95.
[74] Article 3.
[75] The Israeli courts have recognised the "united Jerusalem" as an "inseparable part of Israel": *Hanzalis* v. *Greek Orthodox Patriarchate Religious Court* (1969) 48 I.L.R. 93, 98.
[76] See, *e.g.* S.C. Resn. 465 (1980), *Resolutions and Decisions* (1980), p. 5. See also the 1976 Security Council Consensus Statement, 13 *UN Monthly Chronicle* (December 1976), p. 5.
[77] See Fawcett, 43 Int. Affairs 236 (1967).
[78] See above, p. 171.

he gives up the said property to be held and enjoyed absolutely with all manner of right for ever, without any exception or impediment whatsoever. . . .[79]

In 1963, Spain raised the question of the status of Gibraltar before the United Nations "Committee of 24." The following year the Committee reached a consensus by which it invited Spain and the United Kingdom to conduct "conversations in order to find . . . a negotiated solution."[80] During the resulting discussions, the following positions were established.[81] Spain argued that Article X granted to Great Britain "a British military base installed in Spain," not sovereignty over the territory of Gibraltar.[82] The United Kingdom disputed this limited reading of Article X.[83] Spain contended that the United Kingdom had no claim to Gibraltar based on conquest because its seizure in 1704 was not in the name of Great Britain but on behalf of a possible King of Spain—the Pretender to the Spanish Crown, Archduke Charles of Austria—and by an allied force, not an exclusively British one.[84] The United Kingdom reserved its opinion on this question.[85] Spain claimed that certain "neutral ground" to the North of the Rock proper was not included in Article X. The United Kingdom denied this and, in the alternative, claimed a prescriptive title:

> "Her Majesty's Government do not accept that the ground between the Gibraltar frontier fence and the foot of the Rock is Spanish sovereign territory. . . . The whole of the territory has in any case been under exclusive British jurisdiction since at least 1838, by which time British sentries were established along the line of the present frontier fence. . . .
>
> Notwithstanding occasional protests concerned with specific issues such as the construction by Britian of permanent works on the ground, successive Spanish Governments have, in the view of Her Majesty's Government, demonstrated their acquiescence in these developments and forfeited any title which they may at one time have possessed to the area concerned. Nor has the Spanish Government ever sought to have the matter referred to an international tribunal."[86]

Spain denied that a prescriptive title had been established[87]:

> In addition to prescription being a debatable and vague institution, both in judicial decisions and in doctrine . . . in order that prescription may produce legal effects it is necessary to take into account the behaviour of both the interested parties; in other words, the indifference or tacit abandonment on the part of one side, and the occupation as owner on the part of the other. And that is something that has certainly not occurred here. The Spanish Government has continually declared that its acts of tolerance did not imply any extension of the concessions made in the Treaty of Utrecht, and the Government of Great Britain has repeatedly assured it that in their actions there was no intention of altering the "status quo ante." Consequently it is not possible to speak to any legitimization of the British presence in part of the neutral ground, by reason of the long series of Spanish protests and refusals which have been made uninterruptedly from 1713 down to the present day.

---

[79] 28 C.T.S. 325.

[80] Cmnd. 2632, p. 14. See also G.A. Resn. 2070 (XX), G.A.O.R., 20th Session, Supp. 14, p. 59.

[81] For a U.K. record of the discussion, see Cmnd. 3131.

[82] *Ibid.* p. 8.

[83] *Ibid.* p. 53.

[84] *Ibid.* p. 8.

[85] *Ibid.* p. 53.

[86] *Ibid.* p. 62. Does the refusal by Spain to refer the question of title to Gibraltar to the I.C.J., as suggested by the U.K. in 1966, indicate acquiescence? See Fawcett, *loc. cit.* at p. 177, n. 77, above, pp. 240–241.

[87] *Ibid.* pp. 27–28.

Spain also claimed sovereignty over Gibraltar's territorial sea. The 1966 (and subsequent) negotiations have proved unsuccessful and the issue remains unresolved. Spain continues to press for the return of Gibraltar, but the United Kingdom continues to refuse.

Is a title based upon a cession made by a defeated state to a victorious state in 1713 still valid? How does the doctrine of inter-temperoral law[88] affect the position? Would such a cession be valid if it were to occur now? On the validity of treaties by which one state cedes territory to another after a war or other use of force contrary to Article 2(4), United Nations Charter, see below, p. 615. What is the relevance of the principle of self-determination?[89]

(iv) ACCRETION AND AVULSION

Note

A state may also attain sovereignty over new land as a result of natural forces. This may happen slowly (accretion), for example, by the gradual movement of a river bed or suddenly (avulsion), for example, by the creation of an island in territorial waters by volcanic action.[90]

(v) NEW STATES

Note

Which, if any, of the means of acquiring territorial sovereignty considered in the above materials applies or apply when a new state emerges, either by revolution or, as in the case of many former colonial territories since the Second World War, by peaceful means? Do these means apply only to the acquisition of additional territory by an existing state, so that the emergence of a new state is to be considered solely by reference to the criteria of statehood considered in Chapter 4?[91]

2. *POLAR REGIONS*[92]

(i) ANTARCTICA[93]

NEW ZEALAND'S CLAIM TO THE ROSS DEPENDENCY[94]

1 Hackworth 457

The following correspondence concerned Admiral Byrd's second expedition to the Antarctic in 1934. The United Kingdom learnt that a post office was to be established at the expedition's base in the Ross Dependency; that special stamps had been issued for use there; and that certain expedition members had been sworn in to act as United States postmasters. The United Kingdom protested that "such acts could not be regarded otherwise than as infringing the British sovereignty and New Zealand administrative rights in the dependency. . . ." The following exchange then occurred.

---

[88] See above, p. 158.
[89] See above, p. 95.
[90] See further, Oppenheim, Vol. I, pp. 563–566.
[91] See Jennings, *op cit.* at p. 151, n. 1, above, pp. 7–9.
[92] See Mouton, 107 *Hague Recueil* 169 (1962–III).
[93] See Hayton, 54 A.J.I.L. 349 (1960).
[94] See Auburn, *The Ross Dependency* (1972).

Note from the United States Secretary of State to the British Ambassador, November 14, 1934

It is understood that His Majesty's Government in New Zealand bases its claim of sovereignty on the discovery of a portion of the region in question. . . . in the light of long established principles of international law . . . I cannot admit that sovereignty accrues from mere discovery unaccompanied by occupancy and use.

Note from the British Ambassador to the United States Secretary of State, December 27, 1934

1. . . . The supposition that the British claim to sovereignty over the Ross Dependency is based on discovery alone, and, moreover on the discovery of only a portion of the region, is based on a misapprehension of the facts of the situation.

2. The Dependency was established and placed under New Zealand Administration by an Order in Council of 1923 in which the Dependency's geographical limits were precisely defined. Regulations have been made by the Governor General of New Zealand in respect of the Dependency and the British title has been kept up by the exercise in respect of the Dependency of administrative and governmental powers, *e.g.* as regards the issue of whaling licences and the appointment of a special officer to act as magistrate for the Dependency.

3. As I had the honour to state in my note No. 33 of January 29th last, His Majesty's Government in New Zealand recognize the absence of ordinary postal facilities in the Dependency and desire therefore to facilitate as far as possible the carriage of mail by United States authorities to and from the Byrd Expedition. As regards Mr. Anderson's present mission, they understand that he is carrying letters to which are, or will be, affixed special stamps printed in the United States and that these stamps are to be cancelled and date-stamped on board the Expedition's vessel. They also understand that these stamps are intended to be commemorative of the Byrd Expedition and have been issued as a matter of philatelic interest.

4. In the above circumstances His Majesty's Government in New Zealand have no objection to the proposed visit of Mr. Anderson. They must, however, place it on record that, had his mission appeared to them to be designed as an assertion of United States sovereignty over any part of the Ross Dependency or as a challenge to British sovereignty therein, they would have been compelled to make a protest.

Notes

1. Antarctica is a land mass covered with ice. At certain points (*e.g.* the Ross Ice Shelf), permanently frozen sea adjoins it. Beyond the land mass and the shelf ice there is a large area of sea that is frozen in some seasons and navigable in others. Official claims to sectors of Antarctica have been made by Argentina, Australia, Chile, France, New Zealand, Norway and the United Kingdom.[95] The only major sector not officially claimed is Marie Byrd Land. Admiral Byrd discovered it and claimed it for the United States, but his claim was not officially adopted. The United States does not recognise

[95] For maps of Antarctica with the sectors marked, see the article by Mouton and Hayton referred to above, p. 179 n. 92 and n. 93.

the claim of any other state and has proposed the internationalisation of the whole area. The claimant states would appear to recognise each others claims,[96] except that the Argentinian and Chilean sectors overlap with each other, as does each with that of the United Kingdom. In 1955, the United Kingdom instituted proceedings before the International Court of Justice by unilateral application asking the Court to rule on the disputes resulting from this situation between the United Kingdom, on the one hand, and Argentina and Chile, on the other.[97] The applications met with no response from Argentina and Chile and the Court struck them off its list in 1956. Did they nonetheless serve a useful purpose from the standpoint of the United Kingdom?[98] In its applications, the United Kingdom claimed sovereignty over its sector on the basis of "historic British discoveries" followed by "the long-continued and peaceful display of British sovereignty from the date of those discoveries onwards in, and in regard to, the territories concerned.[99]

2. A sector is established by enclosing an area within a line of latitude and two lines of longitude to the point at which the latter lines converge at the South Pole. Thus, applying this method in two stages, the United Kingdom sector, the British Antarctic Territory, consists of "all islands and territories whatsoever which . . . are situated south of the 60th parallel of the south latitude between the 20th degree of west longitude and the 80th degree of west longitude."[1]

ANTARCTIC TREATY 1959[2]

U.K.T.S. 97 (1961), Cmnd. 1535, 402 U.N.T.S. 71; A.J.I.L. 477 (1960)

Article 1

1. Antarctica shall be used for peaceful purposes only. There shall be prohibited, *inter alia*, any measures of a military nature, such as the establishment of military bases and fortifications, the carrying out of military manoeuvres, as well as the testing of any type of weapons.

2. The present treaty shall not prevent the use of military personnel or equipment for scientific research or for any other peaceful purpose. . . .

Article 4

1. Nothing contained in the present treaty shall be interpreted as:

(a) a renunciation by any Contracting Party of previously asserted rights of or claims to territorial sovereignty in Antarctica;

(b) a renunciation or diminution by any Contracting Party of any basis of claim to territorial sovereignty in Antarctica which it may have whether as a result of its activities or those of its nationals in Antarctica, or otherwise;

---

[96] See, *e.g.* the implied mutual recognition of claims by France and by Commonwealth states in the exchange of notes of October 25, 1938, Cmd. 5900.

[97] I.C.J. Pleadings, *Antarctica Cases (U.K.* v. *Argentina; U.K.* v. *Chile).*

[98] On the role of protest, see above, pp. 169–170.

[99] *Loc. cit.* at n. 97, above, p. 74.

[1] S.I. 1972 No. 400. Waldock (1948) 25 B.Y.I.L. 311, 328 states that the area "does not seem to have been framed in pursuance of any specal sector doctrine. The sector was merely the most convenient geographical definition of the numerous islands and continental territory claimed. . . ."

[2] The Treaty entered into force on June 23, 1961. The following 27 states are the parties to it: Argentina, Australia, Belgium, Brazil, Bulgaria, Chile, Czechoslovakia, Denmark, France, GDR, GFR, Italy, Japan, Netherlands, New Zealand, Norway, Papua New Guinea, Peru, Poland, Romania, South Africa, Spain, U.K., U.S., U.S.S.R. and Uruguay.

(c) prejudicing the position of any Contracting Party as regards its recognition or non-recognition of any other State's right of or claim or basis of claim to territorial sovereignty in Antarctica.

2. No acts or activities taking place while the present treaty is in force shall constitute a basis for asserting, supporting or denying a claim to territorial sovereignty in Antarctica or create any rights of sovereignty in Antarctica. No new claim, or enlargement of an existing claim, to territorial sovereignty in Antarctica shall be asserted while the present treaty is in force.

Article 5

1. Any nuclear explosions in Antarctica and the disposal there of radioactive waste material shall be prohibited. . . .

Article 6

The provisions of the present treaty shall apply to the area south of 60° South Latitude, including all ice shelves, but nothing in the present treaty shall prejudice or in any way affect the rights, or the exercise of the rights, of any state under international law with regard to the high seas within that area.

Article 7

1. In order to promote the objectives and ensure the observance of the provisions of the present treaty, each Contracting Party whose representatives are entitled to participate in the meetings referred to in Article 9 of the treaty[3] shall have the right to designate observers to carry out any inspection provided for by the present article. . . .

Article 8

1. In order to facilitate the exercise of their functions under the present treaty, and without prejudice to the respective positions of the Contracting Parties relating to jurisdiction over all other persons in Antarctica, observers designated under paragraph 1 of Article 7 and scientific personnel exchanged under subparagraph 1(b) of Article 3 of the treaty, and members of the staffs accompanying any such persons, shall be subject only to the jurisdiction of the Contracting Party of which they are nationals in respect of all acts or omissions occurring while they are in Antarctica for the purpose of exercising their functions.

2. Without prejudice to the provisions of paragraph 1 of this article, and pending the adoption of measures in pursuance of subparagraph 1(e) of Article 9, the Contracting Parties concerned in any case of dispute with regard to the exercise of jurisdiction in Antarctica shall immediately consult together with a view to reaching a mutually acceptable solution.

Notes

1. What is the effect of Art. 4 of the Treaty for states not parties to it?[4]
2. Although the Treaty has worked well so far, the question of the exploitation of

---

[3] *Ed., i.e.* the 12 original signatories.
[4] On treaties establishing objective legal régimes, see below, p. 608.

natural resources (fish, oil and minerals) when the Treaty expires in 1991 is causing increasing concern.

(ii) THE ARCTIC

Notes

1. In 1956, the Canadian Minister of Northern Affairs and National Resources stated:

We have never subscribed to the sector theory in application to the ice. We are content that our sovereignty exists over all the Arctic Islands. There is no doubt about it and there are no difficulties concerning it. . . . We have never upheld a general sector theory. To our mind the sea, be it frozen or in its natural liquid state, is the sea; and our sovereignty exists over the lands and over our territorial waters.[5]

In 1970, the Canadian Government stated in correspondence with the United States:

Canada's sovereignty over the islands of the Arctic archipelago is not, of course, in issue. . . . With respect to the waters of the Arctic archipelago, the position of Canada has always been that these waters are regarded as Canadian.[6]

2. In 1926, the U.S.S.R. claimed "sovereignty over all territory, discovered or undiscovered, lying in the Arctic Ocean north of the coast of the Soviet Union to the North Pole, between meridian 32° 4'35" east of Greenwich and meridian 168° 49'30" west of Greenwich."[7] This has been understood by one Soviet commentator to refer to the polar pack ice as well as to land,[8] but the Soviet Government itself may not go so far.[9] Norway[10] and the United States[11] have opposed the use of the sector principle in the Arctic.

3. On the question of territorial sovereignty over ice, note the following two conflicting opinions. The Soviet writer Lakhtine[12] states:

We are of the opinion that floating ice should be assimilated legally to open polar seas, whilst ice formations that are more or less immovable should enjoy a legal status equivalent to polar territory. Polar States acquire sovereignty over them within the limits of their sectors of attraction.

The American writer Balch[13] states:

Ice, unlike the water of the high seas, is a solid substance upon which mankind can build habitations and live for an indefinite period of time. . . . In that sense it might be urged that men might permanently occupy the ice cover of the Polar Sea. But the ice at the North Pole is never at rest. It is in continual motion. It moves slowly in a direction from Bering's Strait towards the Atlantic Ocean. Consequently any habitation fixed upon it would be continually moving. And such possible occupation would be too precarious and shifting to and fro to give any one a good title. And so the rules of the Law of Nations that recognise the freedom of the high seas, would seem to apply naturally to a moving and shifting substance like the North Polar Sea ice at all points beyond the customary three-mile limit from the shore.

---

[5] 1956 Debates, H.C., Canada, Vol. 7, p. 6955. See Head, 9 McGill L.J. 200 (1963).
[6] 9 I.L.M. 607 at p. 613 (1970).
[7] 1 Hackworth 461.
[8] Lakhtine, 24 A.J.I.L. 703, 712 (1930).
[9] See Pharand, *The Law of the Sea of the Arctic* (1973), p. 170.
[10] 1 Hackworth 463.
[11] *Ibid.* pp. 463–464.
[12] *Loc. cit.* at n. 8 above, p. 712.
[13] 4 A.J.I.L. 265–266 (1910).

3. AIRSPACE[14]

CHICAGO CONVENTION ON INTERNATIONAL CIVIL AVIATION 1944[15]

U.K.T.S. 8 (1953), Cmd. 8742; 15 U.N.T.S. 295

Article 1

The contracting States recognize that every State has complete and exclusive sovereignty over the air space above its territory.

Article 2

For the purposes of this Convention the territory of a State shall be deemed to be the land areas and territorial waters adjacent thereto under the sovereignty, suzerainty, protection or mandate of such State.

Article 3

(a) This Convention shall be applicable only to civil aircraft, and shall not be applicable to state aircraft.

(b) Aircraft used in military, customs and police services shall be deemed to be state aircraft.

(c) No state aircraft of a contracting State shall fly over the territory of another State or land thereon without authorization by special agreement or otherwise, and in accordance with the terms thereof.

(d) The contracting States undertake, when issuing regulations for their state aircraft, that they will have due regard for the safety of navigation of civil aircraft.

Article 5

Each contracting State agrees that all aircraft of the other contracting States, being aircraft not engaged in scheduled international air service, shall have the right, subject to the observance of the terms of this Convention, to make flights into or in transit non-stop across its territory and to make stops for non-traffic purposes without the necessity of obtaining prior permission, and subject to the right of the State flown over to require landing. Each contracting State nevertheless reserves the right, for reasons of safety of flight, to require aircraft desiring to proceed over regions which are inaccessible or without adequate air navigation facilities to follow prescribed routes, or to obtain special permission for such flights.

Such aircraft, if engaged in the carriage of passengers, cargo, or mail for remuneration or hire on other than scheduled international air services, shall also, subject to the provisions of Article 7, have the privilege of taking on or discharging passengers, cargo, or mail, subject to the right of any State where

---

[14] See Cheng, *The Law of International Air Transport* (1962), and Johnson, *Rights in Air Space* (1965).

[15] The Convention entered into force on April 4, 1947. On May 1, 1978 there were 142 contracting parties, including the U.K.

such embarkation or discharge takes place to impose such regulations, conditions or limitations as it may consider desirable.

Article 6

No scheduled international air service may be operated over or into the territory of a contracting State, except with the special permission or other authorization of that State, and in accordance with the terms of such permission or authorization.

Article 17

Aircraft have the nationality of the State in which they are registered.

Article 18

An aircraft cannot be validly registered in more than one State, but its registration may be changed from one State to another.

Article 19

The registration or transfer of registration of aircraft in any contracting State shall be made in accordance with its laws and regulations.

Notes

1. Article 1 of the Chicago Convention reflects a rule of customary international law that developed rapidly in the first part of this century. An example of the violation of airspace of great political importance occurred in the *U-2 Incident*.[16] On May 1, 1960, a U-2, a United States high altitude reconnaisance aircraft, was shot down at a height of 20,000 metres over Soviet territory. The aeroplane had taken off from Pakistan and was scheduled to land in Finland after taking aerial photographs while over Soviet territory. The U.S.S.R. protested at the flight. The United States did not try to justify its action in terms of international law or protest at the shooting down or of the subsequent trial of the pilot.

2. Unlike the law of the territorial[17] sea, the law concerning airspace does not allow a right of innocent passage. Is there a good reason for this distinction? On the law applying to the entry by an aircraft of one state into the airspace of another in distress or by mistake, note the following suggestions by Lissitzyn.[18]

(1) Intruding aircraft must obey all reasonable orders of the territorial sovereign, including orders to land, to turn back, or to fly on a certain course, unless prevented by distress or *force majeure*. . . .

(2) In its efforts to control the movements of intruding aircraft the territorial sovereign must not expose the aircraft and its occupants to unnecessary or unreasonably great danger—unreasonably great, that is, in relation to the reasonably apprehended harmfulness of the intrusion.

(3) Intruding aircraft, whether military or not, and whatever the cause of the intrusion, are generally not entitled to the special privileges and immunities customarily accorded to foreign warships. They and their occupants may be

---

[16] See Lissitzyn, 56 A.J.I.L. 135 (1962) and Wright, 54 A.J.I.L. 836 (1960).

[17] But see the right of transit passage through international straits in the 1982 Law of the Sea Convention, below, p. 312.

[18] Lissitzyn, 47 A.J.I.L. 559 (1953). The author discusses cases of foreign aircraft being shot down over East European states.

penalized by the territorial sovereign for an intrusion not privileged by reason of distress or mistake. . . .

(4) . . . there is no right of entry for all foreign aircraft, state or civil, when such entry is due to distress not deliberately caused by persons in control of the aircraft and there is no reasonably safe alternative. . . . Foreign aircraft and their occupants may not be subjected to penalties or to unnecessary detention by the territorial sovereign for entry under such circumstances or for entry caused by mistake, at least when the distress or mistake has not been due to negligence chargeable to the persons in control of the aircraft.

3. In 1952, the Council of the International Civil Aviation Organisation (ICAO) defined a "scheduled international air service" (see Article 5 and 6, Chicago Convention) as "a series of flights that possesses all the following characteristics: (a) it passes through the airspace over the territory of more than one State; (b) it is performed by aircraft for the transport of passengers, mail or cargo for remuneration, in such a manner that each flight is open to use by members of the public; (c) it is operated, so as to serve traffic between the same two or more points, either (i) according to a published timetable, or (ii) with flights so regular and frequent that they constitute a recognisably systematic series."[19]

4. Contrast Article 17 of the Chicago Convention with Article 5 of the High Seas Convention 1958 on the nationality of ships.[20] The latter contains a "genuine link" requirement, as in the *Nottebohm Case*.[21]

CHICAGO INTERNATIONAL AIR SERVICES TRANSIT AGREEMENT 1944[22]

U.K.T.S. 8 (1953) Cmd. 8742, 171 U.N.T.S. 387

Article 1

1. Each contracting State grants to the other contracting States the following freedoms of the air in respect of scheduled international air services.

(1) The privilege to fly across its territory without landing;

(2) The privilege to land for non-traffic purposes. . . .

Notes

1. The Chicago International Air Services Transit Agreement is known as the "Two Freedoms" Agreement. More ambitious was the Chicago International Air Transport Agreement 1944[23] which guarantees "Five Freedoms" for its parties. These are the two in the "Two Freedoms" Agreement plus the following:

(3) the privilege to put down passengers, mail or cargo taken on in the territory of the State whose nationality the aircraft possesses; (4) The privilege to take on passengers, mail and cargo destined for the territory of the State whose nationality the aircraft possesses; (5) The privilege to take on passengers, mail and cargo destined for the territory of any other contracting State and the privilege to put down passengers, mail and cargo coming from any such territory.[24]

[19] *Definition of a Scheduled International Air Service*, ICAO Doc. 7278-C/841 (May 10, 1952), p. 3.
[20] See below, p. 323.
[21] See below, p. 442.
[22] The agreement entered into force on January 30, 1945. There are 95 contracting parties, including the U.K.
[23] 171 U.N.T.S. 387; 149 B.F.S.P. 1. The Agreement entered into force on February 8, 1945.
[24] Art. 5.

The "Five Freedoms" Agreement has not been widely ratified and, since the withdrawal of the United States in 1947, it has not been of great significance.[25]

2. The exclusion of scheduled flights from the multilateral arrangements of the 1944 Chicago Convention and the failure of the "Five Freedoms" Agreement has led to a network of bilateral and other less extensive multilateral agreements. It is largely upon the basis of such agreements that international scheduled flights occur.

4. OUTER SPACE[26]

TREATY ON PRINCIPLES GOVERNING THE ACTIVITIES OF STATES IN THE EXPLORATION AND USE OF OUTER SPACE, INCLUDING THE MOON AND OTHER CELESTIAL BODIES 1967[27]

U.K.T.S. 10 (1968) Cmnd. 3519; 610 U.N.T.S. 205

Article 1

The exploration and use of outer space, including the moon and other celestial bodies, shall be carried out for the benefit and in the interests of all countries, irrespective of their degree of economic or scientific development, and shall be the province of all mankind.

Outer space, including the moon and other celestial bodies, shall be free for exploration and use by all States without discrimination of any kind, on a basis of equality and in accordance with international law, and there shall be free access to all areas of celestial bodies.

There shall be freedom of scientific investigation in outer space, including the moon and other celestial bodies, and States shall facilitate and encourage international co-operation in such investigation.

Article 2

Outer space, including the moon and other celestial bodies, is not subject to national appropriation by claim of sovereignty, by means of use or occupation, or by any other means.

Article 3

States Parties to the Treaty shall carry on activities in the exploration and use of outer space, including the moon and other celestial bodies, in accordance with international law, including the Charter of the United Nations, in the interest of maintaining international peace and security and promoting international co-operation and understanding.

[25] See Johnson, *op. cit.* at p. 184, n. 14, above p. 65. The U.K. has not become a party to it. There are 12 contracting parties.
[26] See Fawcett, *International Law and the Uses of Outer Space* (1968); Jenks, *Space Law* (1965); Lay and Taubenfeld, *The Law Relating to the Activities of Man in Space* (1970); McDougal, Lasswell and Vlasic, *Law and Public Order in Space* (1963); Matte, *Aerospace Law* (1969); Lachs, *The Law of Outer Space* (1972); Kish, *The Law of International Spaces* (1973); Reijnen, *Legal Aspects of Outer Space* (1976).
[27] The treaty entered into force on October 10, 1967. There are 84 contracting parties, including the U.K., the U.S. and the U.S.S.R. For discussion of the treaty, see Darwin (1967) 42 B.Y.I.L. 278; Goedhuis, 15 Neths.I.L.R. 17 (1968) and Cheng, 95 *Journal du Droit International* 532 (1968).

Article 4

States Parties to the Treaty undertake not to place in orbit around the Earth any objects carrying nuclear weapons or any other kinds of weapons of mass destruction, install such weapons on celestial bodies, or station such weapons in outer space in any other manner.

The moon and other celestial bodies shall be used by all State Parties to the Treaty exclusively for peaceful purposes. The establishment of military bases, installations and fortifications, the testing of any type of weapons and the conduct of military manoeuvres on celestial bodies shall be forbidden. The use of military personnel for scientific research or for any other peaceful purposes shall not be prohibited. The use of any equipment or facility necessary for peaceful exploration of the moon and other celestial bodies shall also not be prohibited.

Article 5

States Parties to the Treaty shall regard astronauts as envoys of mankind in outer space and shall render to them all possible assistance in the event of accident, distress, or emergency landing on the territory of another State Party or on the high seas. When astronauts make such a landing, they shall be safely and promptly returned to the State of registry of their space vehicle.

In carrying on activities in outer space and on celestial bodies, the astronauts of one State Party shall render all possible assistance to the astronauts of other State Parties.

State Parties to the Treaty shall immediately inform the other States Parties to the Treaty or the Secretary-General of the United Nations of any phenomena they discover in outer space, including the moon and other celestial bodies, which could constitute a danger to the life or health of astronauts.

Article 6

States Parties to the Treaty shall bear international responsibility for national activities in outer space, including the moon and other celestial bodies, whether such activities are carried on by governmental agencies or by non-governmental entities, and for assuring that national activities are carried out in conformity with the provisions set forth in the present Treaty. The activities of non-governmental entities in outer space, including the moon and other celestial bodies, shall require authorization and continuing supervision by the appropriate State Party to the Treaty. When activities are carried on in outer space, including the moon and other celestial bodies, by an international organization, responsibility for compliance with this Treaty shall be borne both by the international organization and by the States Parties to the Treaty participating in such organization.

Article 7

Each State Party to the Treaty that launches or procures the launching of an object into outer space, including the moon and other celestial bodies, and each State Party from whose territory or facility an object is launched, is internationally liable for damage to another State Party to the Treaty or to its natural or judicial persons by such object or its component parts on the Earth, in air space or in outer space, including the moon and other celestial bodies.

Article 8

A State Party to the Treaty on whose registry an object launched into outer space is carried shall retain jurisdiction and control over such object, and over any personnel thereof, while in outer space or on a celestial body. Ownership of objects launched into outer space, including objects landed or constructed on a celestial body, and of their component parts, is not affected by their presence in outer space or on a celestial body or by their return to the Earth. Such objects or component parts found beyond the limits of the State Party to the Treaty on whose registry they are carried shall be returned to that State Party, which shall, upon request, furnish identifying data prior to their return.

Article 9

In the exploration and use of outer space, including the moon and other celestial bodies, State Parties to the Treaty shall be guided by the principle of co-operation and mutual assistance and shall conduct all their activities in outer space, including the moon and other celestial bodies, with due regard to the corresponding interests of all other States Parties to the Treaty. States Parties to the Treaty shall pursue studies of outer space, including the moon and other celestial bodies, and conduct exploration of them so as to avoid their harmful contamination and also adverse changes in the environment of the Earth resulting from the introduction of extra-terrestrial matter and, where necessary, shall adopt appropriate measures for this purpose. If a State Party to the Treaty has reason to believe that an activity or experiment planned by it or its nationals in outer space, including the moon and other celestial bodies, would cause, potentially harmful interference with activities of other States Parties in the peaceful exploration and use of outer space, including the moon and other celestial bodies, it shall undertake appropriate international consultations before proceeding with any such activity or experiment. A State Party to the Treaty which has reason to believe that an activity or experiment planned by another State Party in outer space, including the moon and other celestial bodies, would cause potentially harmful interference with activities in the peaceful exploration and use of outer space, including the moon and other celestial bodies, may request consultation concerning the activity or experiment.

Article 10

In order to promote international co-operation in the exploration and use of outer space, including the moon and other celestial bodies, in conformity with the purposes of this Treaty, the States Parties to the Treaty shall consider on a basis of equality any requests by other States Parties to the Treaty to be afforded an opportunity to observe the flight of space objects launched by those States.

The nature of such an opportunity for observation and the conditions under which it could be afforded shall be determined by agreement between the States concerned.

Article 11

In order to promote international co-operation in the peaceful exploration and use of outer space, States Parties to the Treaty conducting activities in outer space, including the moon and other celestial bodies, agree to inform the Secretary-General of the United Nations as well as the public and the international scientific community, to the greatest extent feasible and practicable, of the nature, conduct, locations and results of such activities. On receiving the said information, the Secretary-General of the United Nations should be prepared to disseminate it immediately and effectively.

Article 12

All stations, installations, equipment and space vehicles on the moon and other celestial bodies shall be open to representatives of other States Parties to the Treaty on a basis of reciprocity. Such representatives shall give reasonable advance notice of a projected visit, in order that appropriate consultations may be held and that maximum precautions may be taken to assure safety and to avoid interference with normal operations in the facility to be visited.

Notes

1. Acting through the United Nations and greatly helped by the common interest of the United States and the U.S.S.R., the international community has been remarkably quick in agreeing upon the basic legal principles governing activities in outer space.[28] The 1967 Treaty builds upon a number of General Assembly resolutions on space law, particularly Resolutions 1721 (XVI),[29] 1884 (XVIII)[30] and 1962 (XVIII).[31] Resolution 1884 (XVIII) is reproduced in substance in the first paragraph of Article 4 of the Treaty; the various principles stated in the other two resolutions form the basis of Articles 1–3 and 5–9. All three resolutions were adopted unanimously. For support for the view that they state rules of customary international law, see above, p. 51.

2. Note the following criticism of the 1967 Treaty by Fawcett[32]:

> In the Outer Space Treaty we have then a rigidly contractual instrument, in essence a bilateral arrangement between the principal space-users. Apart from its provisions for partial demilitarisation of outer space, tracking and inspection, it does little or nothing to elaborate or secure the principles already set out in General Assembly Resolutions. It may even be that this ill-constructed and precarious instrument is a retrograde step. For in the wise words of Dr. Jenks, written before the conclusion of the Outer Space Treaty[33]: "The authority of the Declaration of Legal Principles may be expected to grow with the passage of years. While it is somewhat less than a treaty it must already be regarded as rather more than a statement of custom."

> Though Resolution 1962 (XVIII) is for the most part a declaration, not of rules of international law, but of directive principles, it may like other similar General Assembly Resolutions, be regarded as forming part of an international *ordre public*, to which States should strive to make their policies conform. . . .

---

[28] One measure of the importance of a legal régime for outer space is that there are over 5,000 satellites and other objects in outer space.

[29] G.A.O.R., 16th Session, Supp. 17, p. 6 (1961).

[30] G.A.O.R., 18th Session, Supp. 15, p. 13 (1963).

[31] *Ibid*. p. 15 (1963).

[32] *Op. cit*. at p. 187, n. 26, above, pp. 15–16.

[33] *Op. cit*. at p. 187, n. 26, above, p. 185.

3. *Article* 2 of the Treaty establishes that territory in outer space, like the high seas, is not subject to sovereignty. It is well known that states have reconnaissance satellites used for military spying purposes; these are not prohibited by *Article* 4.[34] Does *Article* 4 prohibit the passage of ballistic missiles through outer space?[35] *Article* 5 (and to some extent *Article* 8) is supplemented by the Agreement on the Rescue of Astronauts, the Return of Astronauts and the Return of Objects launched into Outer Space 1968.[36] *Article* 6 tackles the problem of imputability[37] in respect of any liability that may arise from space activities. Who is responsible under it for the acts or omissions of any private space activities (*e.g.* by a telecommunications company)? Does the Treaty imagine the possibility of activities by an international organisation (*e.g.* the European Space Agency)? On damage resulting from space activities, *Article* 7 indicates when liability may arise on the part of a state or international organisation responsible under Article 6. It has been supplemented by the 1972 Convention on International Liability for Damages caused by Space Objects, see below, note 5. *Article* 8 gives the state of registry jurisdiction over space objects and persons on them, but does not indicate the extent to which this is exclusive.[38] The best analogy is with the rules concerning ships.[39]

4. By Resolution 1721 (XVI),[40] the General Assembly called upon "states launching objects into orbit to furnish information promptly to the Committee on the Peaceful Uses of Outer Space . . . for the registration of launching" and requested the Secretary General "to maintain a public registry of the information furnished." This voluntary system has not been wholly satisfactory and has been supplemented, for the parties to it, by the 1975 Convention on Registration of Objects launched into Outer Space.[41] Launching states must register every launch, indicating its purpose, on a public register kept by the Secretary General.

5. The 1972 Liability Convention[42] establishes *strict* liability (subject to *Article VI*) for damage caused by a space object to persons or property on the surface of the earth or to an aircraft in flight (*Article II*) and *fault* liability for damage to other space objects in flight and to persons in them (*Article III*). It establishes joint and several liability in the case of a joint launch (*Article VI*). Local remedies need not be exhausted before a claim is brought (*Article XI*). A claim in respect of damage to individuals is brought by a national state in the first instance, although the place where the damage occurs or where the individual is a resident may act if the national state fails to do so (*Article VIII*). If a claim cannot be settled diplomatically, it will be determined by a mixed claims commission established at the request of either party (*Article XIV*). The compensation due

> Shall be determined in accordance with international law, and the principles of justice and equity, in order to provide such reparation in respect of the damage as will restore the person . . . on whose behalf the claim is brought to the condition which would have existed if the damage had not occurred. (*Article XII*).

No upper limit to the amount of compensation is set. There have been a number of instances recorded of débris or parts of space objects falling to earth but no claims have

---

[34] See Goedhuis, 27 I.C.L.Q. 576 (1978). The American *Samos* satellites provided Israel with important information about Egyptian military installations in hostilities in the Middle East.

[35] See Darwin, *loc. cit.* at p. 187, n. 27, above, p. 284.

[36] U.K.T.S. 56 (1969), Cmnd. 3997; 63 A.J.I.L. 382 (1969). The Agreement entered into force on December 3, 1968. There are 78 contracting parties, including the U.K., the U.S., and the U.S.S.R. See Cheng, 23 Y.B.W.A. 185 (1969) and Hall, 63 A.J.I.L. 197 (1968).

[37] As to imputability generally in international law, see below, p. 384.

[38] See Czabati, *The Concept of State Jurisdiction in International Space* (1971).

[39] See below, p. 324.

[40] *Loc. cit.* at p. 190, n. 29, above.

[41] 14 I.L.M. 43 (1975). In force. On December 31, 1981, there were 30 contracting parties, including the U.K., the U.S. and the U.S.S.R.

[42] 10 I.L.M. 965 (1971). In force. There were 69 contracting parties, including the U.K. See Foster, 10 C.Y.I.L. 137 (1972).

resulted so far. A part of Sputnik IV weighing 20 lbs that fell on Manitowoc, Wisconsin, in 1962 was handed back to the U.S.S.R. at a meeting of the United Nations Committee on the Peaceful Uses of Outer Space.[43] In 1969, some Russian débris broke a kitchen window in Southend. On January 24, 1978, a malfunctioning Russian satellite, powered by a small nuclear reactor weighing about 100 lb, broke up over Canada and came down in a remote part of the North-West Territories. Moderate radiation was reported from the débris located.[44] Damage of a more far-reaching kind of the sort that may result from experiments conducted in space (for example, affecting the climate or the atmosphere) is the subject of a very limited undertaking in *Article XXI*.

6. *The Moon Treaty*.[45] The 1979 Agreement Governing the Activities of States on the Moon and other Celestial Bodies[46] repeats, clarifies and supplements the 1967 Outer Space Treaty. Most significantly, it deals with the question of natural resources. Article 11 reads:

1. The moon[47] and its natural resources are the common heritage of mankind, which finds its expression in the provisions of this Agreement and in particular in paragraph 5 of this article. . . .

2. The moon is not subject to national appropriation by any claim of sovereignty, by means of use or occupation, or by any other means.

3. Neither the surface nor the subsurface of the moon, nor any part thereof or natural resources in place, shall become property of any State, international intergovernmental or non-governmental organization, national organization or non-governmental entity or of any natural person. The placement of personnel, space vehicles, equipment, facilities, stations and installations on or below the surface of the moon, including structures connected with its surface or subsurface, shall not create a right of ownership over the surface or the subsurface of the moon or any areas thereof. The foregoing provisions are without prejudice to the international régime referred to in paragraph 5 of this article.

4. States Parties have the right to exploration and use of the moon without discrimination of any kind, on a basis of equality and in accordance with international law and the terms of this Agreement.

5. States Parties to this Agreement hereby undertake to establish an international régime, including appropriate procedures, to govern the exploitation of the natural resources of the moon as such exploitation is about to become feasible. . . .

7. The main purposes of the international régime to be established shall include: . . .

(d) An equitable sharing by all States Parties in the benefits derived from those resources, whereby the interests and needs of the developing countries, as well as the efforts of those countries which have contributed either directly or indirectly to the exploration of the moon, shall be given special consideration.

This adds to the 1967 Treaty by establishing that the natural resources of celestial bodies are, like those of the deep sea-bed, the "common heritage of mankind" and, as such, to be exploited, when technical and commercial considerations permit, in accordance with an international régime. Cheng[48] suggests that, although Article 11(5)

[43] A/AC. 105/PV. 15, pp. 33–34 (1962), noted in Lay and Taubenfeld, *op. cit.* at p. 187, n. 26, above, p. 137, where a number of similar incidents are listed.

[44] *The Times*, January 24, 1978, and January 31, 1978. Any claim resulting from damage caused by the operation of Skylab will be dealt with under the 1972 Liability Convention, to which the U.S. is a party: *Hansard*, H.C., Vol. 969, W.A. Col. 657. July 5, 1979.

[45] See Cheng, 33 C.L.P. 213 (1980).

[46] 18 I.L.M. 1434 (1979). The Agreement requires five parties to enter into force. As at December 31, 1981, there were three. The U.K. was not a party.

[47] The Convention provisions "relating to the moon shall also apply to other celestial bodies within the solar system, other than the earth": Article 11(1) Agreement.

[48] *Loc. cit.* at n. 45, above, pp. 231–232. On the disagreement concerning a deep sea-bed moratorium, see below, p. 365.

imposes an obligation to negotiate in good faith to establish the proposed international régime, if no such régime can be agreed upon, the Agreement imposes no moratorium upon unilateral exploitation by the contracting parties.

The Agreement clarifies Article 2 of the 1967 Treaty by providing that when carrying out scientific investigations a party has "the right to collect and remove from the moon[49] samples of its minerals and other substances" (Article 6(2)). It also confirms (Article 11(3)) what is implicit in the characterisation of celestial bodies as *res extra commercium* in Article 2 of the 1967 Treaty, *viz.* that private property rights (as well as state sovereignty) may not be acquired over territory or natural resources in outer space, subject, in the case of the latter, to the international régime to be established.

7. The treaties on outer space which have been adopted so far are the work of the United Nations Committee on the Peaceful Uses of Outer Space, a body established in 1958 (the as an *ad hoc* committee) and composed of 53 states. The Committee now has under consideration questions of the control of remote sensing of the earth (particularly of natural resources) by satellite; the control of direct television broadcasting by satellite[50]; the boundary between air and outer space; and the use of nuclear power sources in outer space.

McMAHON, LEGAL ASPECTS OF OUTER SPACE

(1962) 38 B.Y.I.L. 339. Some footnotes omitted

One school of thought interprets airspace in terms of aerodynamic lift and maintains that a State may only claim sovereignty over the height up to which aircraft can ascend. Such height would be no more than about 20 miles.[51]

The merits of such a common-sense approach are quite evident. However, it fails to offer a sufficiently precise criterion for drawing the line in airspace and is rendered less useful by such hybrid craft as the X-15 which possess characteristics of both aircraft and spacecraft and can attain a height of up to 47 miles. It is also unlikely that States will be content to restrict their claims to sovereignty to 20 miles when they might claim substantially more without unduly interfering with the exploration of outer space by other States.

A number of other writers, invoking what they call the natural principle of interpretation, maintain that airspace is synonymous with atmospheric space and includes any space where air is to be found. As there are traces of air in the atmosphere up to 10,000 miles it would be quite consistent, on the basis of this approach, for States to claim sovereignty up to 10,000 miles. . . .

A third approach, representing an even more exaggerated view than the one above, maintains that State sovereignty extends *usque ad infinitum*. Such a view may be more accurately characterized as *usque ad absurdum*. . . .

[49] See above, n. 47 on the meaning of "moon."

[50] On these questions, see Dalfen, 10 C.Y.I.L. 186 (1972). See also on the use of satellites for broadcasting, the 1971 Agreement relating to INTELSAT, 10 I.L.M. 909 (1971) and the 1974 Brussels Convention relating to the Distribution of Programme-carrying Signals Transmitted by Satellite, 13 I.L.M. 1444 (1974). The 2nd UN Conference on Outer Space in 1982 made no recommendations on the above questions.

[51] The height up to which an aircraft ascends would usually be about 12 miles. However, see "Draft Code of Rules on the Exploration and Uses of Outer Space," in *David Davies Memorial Institute of International Studies* (1962), p. 6: "As far as the performance of existing conventional aircraft is a guide to the definition of airspace, the ram jet which makes more efficient use of such air as is available can 'breathe' at greater heights than jet—or piston-engined—aircraft, but 25 miles is probably the outside limit of effective aerodynamic lift."

One or two writers, proceeding by analogy to the law of the sea, suggest the drawing of several lines rather than one. It has been proposed that a State should exercise full sovereignty up to the height to which aircraft can ascend; that then there should be a second area, of up to 300 miles, designated as a contiguous zone and allowing for a right of transit through this zone for all non-military flight instrumentalities; and that finally there should be outer space, free to all. More recently it has been suggested that there be established a neutral zone between the upper limits of airspace and the lower limits of outer space to be known as 'Neutralia' in which the right of innocent passage would be recognized. Such an attempt to divide space up into sectors and zones would seem to be too impractical and artificial to commend itself.

A more sensible approach would seem to be the suggestion that a State should only exercise sovereignty over that area whose boundary is the lowest altitude at which an artificial satellite may be put in orbit at least once around the earth. It would seem that the maximum altitude required to do this would be between 70 and 100 miles. The advantage of such an approach is that it takes cognizance of State practice since the launching of the first sputnik, recognizes the legality of those satellites already in orbit and may easily be reconciled with claims to sovereignty up to the height of aerodynamic lift or even up to 70 miles.

A number of other proposals, suggesting more or less arbitrary criteria, have also been advanced. One may note the suggestion that sovereignty should extend as far out as the subjacent State could exercise effective control; that the boundary should be fixed at an altitude approximating to lift or drag; that the sovereignty ceiling should be the line where an object travelling at 25,000 feet per second loses its aerodynamic lift and centrifugal force takes over (the so-called Karman jurisdiction line which would extend up to about 53 miles); and finally that instead of drawing a demarcation line between airspace and outer space there should only be one doctrine, namely freedom of all-inclusive space subject to agreed restrictions.

Most of the above theories presuppose that a demarcation line must be drawn somewhere in space and the problem is to determine where. However, as an alternative, it has been suggested that States should concentrate on the regulation of activities in space, regardless of the location of those activities. The possibility of such an approach was referred to as early as June 1959 by the United Nations *Ad Hoc* Committee on the Peaceful Uses of Outer Space: 'There was also discussion as to whether or not further experience might suggest a different approach, namely, the desirability of basing the legal régime governing outer space activities primarily on the nature and type of particular space activities.'[52] Of course, the difficulty here is to reach an agreement concerning those activities which are to be permitted and those which are forbidden; such an agreement will be difficult to reach on account of the almost insuperable technical obstacles in disengaging the civil from the military uses of space vehicles. Secondly, even if such an agreement were reached, it could only be enforced by establishing some form of inspection system. In other words, the whole question merely becomes another facet of the disarmament problem.

Notes

1. The boundary between airspace and outer space has yet to be defined. The question was purposely not dealt with in the seminal General Assembly resolutions and

[52] *Report of the* Ad Hoc *Committee on the Peaceful Uses of Outer Space*, U.N. Doc. A/4141, July 14, 1959, p. 68.

in the 1967 treaty. The Committee on the Peaceful Uses of Outer Space now has the question under active consideration.[53] The principle of free and equal use of outer space must mean that there is a limit to national sovereignty at some point. It is also significant that states have not protested at the passage of satellites over their territory.[54] This might mean only the acceptance of a right of innocent passage, but this is unlikely.

2. The "perigee" approach, by which the limit of airspace would be the lowest perigee of an orbiting satellite, would appear to be the most likely one to be accepted. It would, in the light of recent studies, probably set the limit at a lower height—between 50 and 60 miles—than that indicated by McMahon.[55]

5. RIGHTS IN FOREIGN TERRITORY[56]

NORTH ATLANTIC FISHERIES ARBITRATION

U.S. v. Great Britain (1910)

Permanent Court of Arbitration: Lammasch; de Savornin Lohman; Gray; Drago; Fitzpatrick. 11 R.I.A.A. 167

By a treaty of 1818, Great Britain and the United States agreed that "the inhabitants of the said United States shall have forever, in common with the subjects of His Britannic Majesty, the liberty to take fish of every kind on that part of the Southern coast of Newfoundland . . . [then described]" (Art. 1). A dispute arose over Great Britain's competence under the treaty to regulate fishing by United States nationals exercising the liberty granted by it. In the following passage, the Tribunal considered a United States argument that the liberty amounted to a servitude.

Award of the Tribunal

It is contended by the United States: . . .

That the liberties of fishery granted to the United States constitute an International servitude in their favour over the territory of Great Britain, thereby involving a derogation from the sovereignty of Great Britain, the servient State, and therefore Great Britain is deprived, by reason of the grant, of its independent right to regulate the fishery.

The Tribunal is unable to agree with this contention:
(*a*) Because there is no evidence that the doctrine of International servitudes was one with which either American or British Statesmen were conversant in 1818, no English publicists employing the term before 1818, and the mention of it in Mr. Gallatin's report being insufficient;
(*b*) Because a servitude in the French law, referred to by Mr. Gallatin, can, since the Code, be only real and cannot be personal (Code Civil, Art. 686);
(*c*) Because a servitude in International law predicates an express grant of a sovereign right and involves an analogy to the relation of a *praedium dominans*

---

[53] See the 1976 Report of the Committee on the Peaceful Uses of Outer Space, G.A.O.R., 31st Session, Supp. 20, para. 25.
[54] *cf.* the dissenting opinion of Judge Lachs in the *North Sea Continental Shelf Cases*, above, p. 32, n. 47. And see Fawcett, *op. cit.* at p. 187, n. 26, above, p. 22.
[55] See the UN Secretariat background papers on the subject: A/AC.105/C.2/7 and A/AC.105/C.2/7/Add.1.
[56] See Reid, *International Servitudes* (1932) and Vali, *Servitudes in International Law* (2nd ed., 1958).

and a *praedium serviens*; whereas by the Treaty of 1818 one State grants a liberty to fish, which is not a sovereign right, but a purely economic right, to the inhabitants of another State;

(*d*) Because the doctrine of international servitude in the sense which is now sought to be attributed to it orginated in the peculiar and now obsolete conditions prevailing in the Holy Roman Empire of which the *domini terrae* were not fully sovereigns . . .

(*e*) Because this doctrine being but little suited to the principle of sovereignty which prevails in States under a system of constitutional government such as Great Britain and the United States, and to the present International relations of Sovereign States, has found little, if any, support from modern publicists. It could therefore in the general interest of the Community of Nations, and of the Parties to this Treaty, be affirmed by this Tribunal only on the express evidence of an International contract;

(*f*) Because even if these liberties of fishery constituted an International servitude, the servitude would derogate from the sovereignty of the servient State only in so far as the exercise of the rights of sovereignty by the servient State would be contrary to the exercise of the servitude right by the dominant State. Whereas it is evident that, though every regulation of the fishery is to some extent a limitation, as it puts limits to the exercise of the fishery at will, yet such regulations as are reasonable and made for the purpose of securing and preserving the fishery and its exercise for the common benefit, are clearly to be distinguished from those restrictions and "molestations," the annulment of which was the purpose of the American demands formulated by Mr. Adams in 1782, and such regulations consequently cannot be held to be inconsistent with a servitude;

(*g*) Because the fishery to which the inhabitants of the United States were admitted in 1783, and again in 1818, was a regulated fishery . . .

(*h*) Because the fact that Great Britain rarely exercised the right of regulation in the period immediately succeeding 1818 is to be explained by various circumstances and is not evidence of the non-existence of the right;

(*i*) Because the words "in common with British subjects" tend to confirm the opinion that the inhabitants of the United States were admitted to a regulated fishery;

(*j*) Because the statute of Great Britain, 1819, which gives legislative sanction to the Treaty of 1818, provides for the making of "regulations with relation to the taking, drying and curing of fish by inhabitants of the United States in 'common.'"

Notes

1. Does the Court's award give any support to the view that international law recognises servitudes or, in English law terms easement and profits? Does the extract from *The Wimbledon* case, below p. 201? For Brierly,[57] the position is as follows:

Its [a servitude's] essential characteristic is that it is a right *in rem*, that is to say, it is exercisable not only against a particular owner of the servient tenement but against any successor to him in title, and not only by a particular owner of the dominant

[57] Brierly, p. 191. See also McNair (1925) 6 B.Y.I.L. 111.

tenement but also by his successors in title. It is, of course, quite common that a state should acquire rights of one kind or another over the territory of another state, the right, for example, to have an airfield or free port facilities, but ordinarily at least such rights are merely right *in personam* like any other treaty-created right; they do not in any way resemble servitudes. The test of an international servitude can only be, on the analogy of private law, that the right should be one that will survive a change in the sovereignty of either of the two states concerned in the transaction. There is no real evidence that any such right exists in the international system.

2. In the *Aaland Islands Case*,[58] Sweden argued that the provisions in the General Treaty of Peace of 1856 between France, Great Britain and Russia demilitarising the Islands created a servitude binding upon Finland, which had succeeded Russia as the territorial sovereign.

The International Commission of Jurists which reported on the case stated that "the existence of international servitudes, in the true technical sense of the term, is not generally admitted."[59] Nevertheless, it managed to hold that the demilitarisation provisions were binding upon Finland:

> The provisions were laid down in European interests. They constituted a special international status relating to military considerations, for the Aaland Islands. It follows that until these provisions are duly replaced by others, every State interested has the right to insist upon compliance with them.[60]

Earlier the Commission had noted:

> . . . the Powers have, on many occasions since 1815, and especially at the conclusion of peace treaties, tried to create true objective law, a real political status the effects of which are felt outside the immediate circle of contracting parties.[61]

3. A recent example of one state being granted rights in the territory of another is found in the 1960 Treaty Concerning the Establishment of the Republic of Cyprus[62] between Greece, Turkey and Great Britain, on the one hand, and Cyprus, on the other hand, which permits the present British military bases in Cyprus. Annex B[63] reads:

> The Government of the United Kingdom shall have the right to continue to use, without restriction or interference, the Sites in the territories of the Republic of Cyprus listed in Schedule A. . . .

4. In the nineteenth century, China agreed to lease, while retaining sovereignty, several parts of its territory to Western Powers. For example, in 1898 it agreed by treaty[64] to lease to Great Britain the New Territories on the Chinese mainland adjacent to the island of Hong Kong for a period of 99 years. The island of Hong Kong is a British Crown Colony that was ceded by China to Great Britain by the 1842 Treaty of Nanking[65] after the Opium War. See also the 1860 Treaty of Peking[66] by which China ceded Kowloon, on the mainland opposite the island of Hong Kong, to Great Britain.

---

[58] L.N.O.J., Special Supp. No. 3, p. 3 (1920).
[59] *Ibid.* p. 16.
[60] *Ibid.* p. 19.
[61] *Ibid.* p. 17.
[62] U.K.T.S. 4 (1961), Cmnd. 1252; 382 U.N.T.S. 8.
[63] s.1(1).
[64] 90 B.F.S.P. 17.
[65] 30 B.F.S.P. 389.
[66] 50 B.F.S.P. 10.

RIGHT OF PASSAGE CASE[67]

Portugal v. India

I.C.J. Reports 1960, p. 6

Judgment of the Court

In [its] Application the Government of the Portuguese Republic states that the territory of Portugal in the Indian Peninsula is made up of the three districts of Goa, Daman and Diu.[68] It adds that the district of Daman comprises, in addition to its littoral territory, two parcels of territory completely surrounded by the territory of India which constitutes enclaves: Dadra and Nagar-Aveli. It is in respect of the communications between these enclaves and Daman and between each other that the question arises of a right of passage in favour of Portugal through Indian territory, and of a correlative obligation binding upon India. The Application states that in July 1954, contrary to the practice hitherto followed, the Government of India, in pursuance of what the Application calls "the open campaign which it has been carrying on since 1950 for the annexation of Portuguese territories," prevented Portugal from exercising this right of passage. This denial by India having been maintained, it has followed, according to the Application, that the enclaves of Dadra and Nagar-Aveli have been completely cut off from the rest of the Portuguese territory, the Portuguese authorities thus being placed in a position in which it became impossible for them to exercise Portuguese rights of sovereignty there. . . .

Portugal claims a right of passage . . . to the extent necessary for the exercise of its sovereignty over the enclaves, subject to India's right of regulation and control of the passage claimed, and without any immunity in Portugal's favour. It claims further that India is under obligation so to exercise its power of regulation and control as not to prevent the passage necessary for the exercise of Portugal's sovereignty over the enclaves. . . .

With regard to Portugal's claim of a right of passage as formulated by it on the basis of local custom, it is objected on behalf of India that no local custom could be established between only two States. It is difficult to see why the number of States between which a local custom may be established on the basis of long practice must necessarily be larger than two. The Court sees no reason why long continued practice between two States accepted by them as regulating their relations should not form the basis of mutual rights and obligations between the two States. . . .

The Court . . . concludes that, with regard to private persons, civil officials and goods in general there existed during the British and post-British periods a constant and uniform practice allowing free passage between Daman and the enclaves. This practice having continued over a period extending beyond a century and a quarter unaffected by the change in regime in respect of the intervening territory which occurred when India became independent, the Court is, in view of all the circumstances of the case, satisfied that that practice

---

[67] See Krenz, *International Enclaves and Rights of Passage* (1961); E. Lauterpacht, 44 Trans.Grot.Soc. 313, 352–6 (1958–59); 2 Verzijl 368.

[68] *Ed*. On the subsequent annexation of these territories by India, see above, p. 172.

was accepted as law by the Parties and has given rise to a right and a correlative obligation. . . .

As regards armed forces, armed police and arms and ammunition, the position is different. . . .

The Court is, therefore, of the view that no right of passage in favour of Portugal involving a correlative obligation on India has been established in respect of armed forces, armed police, and arms and ammunition. The course of dealings established between the Portuguese and the British authorities with respect to the passage of these categories excludes the existence of any such right. The practice that was established shows that, with regard to these categories, it was well understood that passage could take place only by permission of the British authorities. This situation continued during the post-British period.

Portugal also invokes general international custom, as well as the general principles of law recognized by civilized nations, in support of its claim of a right of passage as formulated by it. Having arrived at the conclusion that the course of dealings between the British and Indian authorities on the one hand and the Portuguese on the other established a practice, well understood between the Parties, by virtue of which Portugal had acquired a right of passage in respect of private persons, civil officials and goods in general, the Court does not consider it necessary to examine whether general international custom or the general principles of law recognized by civilized nations may lead to the same result.

As regards armed forces, armed police and arms and ammunition, the finding of the Court that the practice established between the Parties required for passage in respect of these categories the permission of the British or Indian authorities, renders it unnecessary for the Court to determine whether or not, in the absence of the practice that actually prevailed, general international custom or the general principles of law recognized by civilized nations could be relied upon by Portugal in support of its claim to a right of passage in respect of these categories.

The Court is here dealing with a concrete case having special features. Historically the case goes back to a period when, and relates to a region in which, the relations between neighbouring States were not regulated by precisely formulated rules but were governed largely by practice. Where therefore the Court finds a practice clearly established between two States which was accepted by the Parties as governing the relations between them, the Court must attribute decisive effect to that practice for the purpose of determining their specific rights and obligations. Such a particular practice must prevail over any general rules. . . .

Having found that Portugal had in 1954 a right of passage over intervening Indian territory between Daman and the enclaves in respect of private persons, civil officials and goods in general, the Court will proceed to consider whether India has acted contrary to its obligation resulting from Portugal's right of passage in respect of any of these categories. . . .

The events that took place in Dadra on 21–22 July 1954 resulted in the overthrow of Portuguese authority in that enclave. This created tension in the surrounding Indian territory. Thereafter all passage was suspended by India. India contends that this became necessary in view of the abnormal situation which had arisen in Dadra and the tension created in surrounding Indian territory. . . .

In view of the tension then prevailing in intervening Indian territory, the Court is unable to hold that India's refusal of passage to the proposed delegation and its refusal of visas to Portuguese nationals of European origin and to native Indian Portuguese in the employ of the Portuguese Government was action contrary to its obligation resulting from Portugal's right of passage. Portugal's claim of a right of passage is subject to full recognition and exercise of Indian sovereignty over the intervening territory and without any immunity in favour of Portugal. The Court is of the view that India's refusal of passage in those cases was, in the circumstances, covered by its power of regulation and control of the right of passage of Portugal.

For these reasons,

THE COURT, . . . by eleven votes to four,
finds that Portugal had in 1954 a right of passage over intervening Indian territory between the enclaves of Dadra and Nagar-Aveli and the coastal district of Daman and between these enclaves, to the extent necessary for the exercise of Portuguese sovereignty over the enclaves and subject to the regulation and control of India, in respect of private persons, civil officials and goods in general;
    by eight votes to seven,
finds that Portugal did not have in 1954 such a right of passage in respect of armed forces, armed police, and arms and ammunition;
    by nine votes to six,
finds that India has not acted contrary to its obligations resulting from Portugal's right of passage in respect of private persons, civil officials and goods in general.[69]

Note

Was the right of passage acknowledged by the Court one that would survive a transfer of title to the territory to which it applied? The Court's judgment was based upon local custom. Does it have any relevance for similar situations, such as that of land-locked states—*e.g.* Lesotho (surrounded entirely by the one state of South Africa) and Austria (surrounded by several states)—that seek access by land to the sea[70] or that of West Berlin?[71] Writing about freedom of transit across another state's territory generally, Lauterpacht[72] states:

> The operative principle, it is believed, is that States, far from being free to treat the establishment or regulation of routes of transit as a substantial derogation from their sovereignty which they are entirely free to refuse, are bound to act in this matter in the fulfilment of an obligation to the community of which they form a part. It is a principle formulated by Grotius over three hundred years ago in the following words: "Similarly also lands, rivers, and any part of the sea that has become subject to the ownership of a people, ought to be open to those who, for legitimate reasons, have

[69] It is not clear how every judge voted.
[70] See the 1958 High Seas Convention, Art. 3, and the 1982 Convention on the Law of the Sea, below, p. 320. See also the 1965 Convention on Transit Trade of Land-Locked States, 597 U.N.T.S. 3; 4 I.L.M. 957. On December 31, 1981, the latter was in force for 30 contracting parties. The U.K. was not a party.
[71] See Bathurst, *loc. cit.* at p. 82, n. 18, above, pp. 293–305.
[72] E. Lauterpacht, *loc. cit.* at n. 198, above, p. 313.

need to cross them; as, for instance, if a people . . . desires to carry on commerce with a distant people. . . ."[73]

On that view [Grotius's], there exists in customary international law a right to free or innocent passage for purposes of trade, travel and commerce over the territory of all States—a right which derives from the fact of the existence of the international community and which is a direct consequence of the interdependence of States.

THE WIMBLEDON CASE[74]

France, Italy, Japan and the U.K. *v.* Germany (1923)

P.C.I.J. Reports, Series A, No. 1

The Kiel Canal is cut through what is now the Federal Republic of Germany and links the Baltic and North Seas. Article 380 of the Treaty of Versailles of 1919 reads: "The Kiel Canal and its approaches shall be maintained free and open to the vessels of commerce and of war of all nations at peace with Germany on terms of entire equality." The Court discussed the effect of Article 380 on the legal status of the Canal in the following passage.

Judgment of the Court

The Court considers that the terms of article 380 are categorical and give rise to no doubt. It follows that the canal has ceased to be an internal and national navigable waterway, the use of which by the vessels of states other than the riparian state is left entirely to the discretion of that state, and that it has become an international waterway intended to provide under treaty guarantee easier access to the Baltic for the benefit of all nations of the world. . . .

In order to dispute in this case, the right of the S.S. "Wimbledon" to free passage through the Kiel Canal under the terms of Article 380, the argument has been urged upon the Court that this right really amounts to a servitude by international law resting upon Germany and that, like all restrictions or limitations upon the exercise of sovereignty, this servitude must be construed as restrictively as possible and confined within its narrowest limits, more especially in the sense that it should not be allowed to affect the rights consequent upon neutrality in an armed conflict. The Court is not called upon to take a definite attitude with regard to the question, which is moreover of a very controversial nature, whether in the domain of international law, there really exist servitudes analogous to the servitudes of private law. Whether the German Government is bound by virtue of a servitude or by virtue of a contractual obligation undertaken towards the Powers entitled to benefit by the terms of the Treaty of Versailles, to allow free access to the Kiel Canal in time of war as in time of peace to the vessels of all nations, the fact remains that Germany had to submit to an important limitation of the exercise of the sovereign rights which no one disputes that she possesses over the Kiel Canal. This fact constitutes a sufficient reason for the restrictive interpretation, in case of doubt, of the clause which

---

[73] *De Jure Belli ac Pacis*, II, 2, 13, as translated in *Classics of International Law* (1925), pp. 196–197.

[74] On international canals generally, see Baxter, *The Law of International Waterways* (1964), and Lee, 33 L. & C.P. 158 (1968).

produces such a limitation. But the Court feels obliged to stop at the point where the so-called restrictive interpretation would be contrary to the plain terms of the article and would destroy what has been clearly granted.

CONVENTION RESPECTING FREE NAVIGATION OF THE SUEZ CANAL 1888[75]

C. 5623; 79 B.F.S.P. 18; 3 A.J.I.L., Supp., 123 (1909)

Article 1

The Suez Maritime Canal shall always be free and open, in time of war as in time of peace, to every vessel of commerce or of war, without distinction of flag.

Consequently, the High Contracting Parties agree not in any way to interfere with the free use of the Canal, in time of war as in time of peace.

The Canal shall never be subjected to the exercise of the right of blockade.

Article 4

The Maritime Canal remaining open in time of war as a free passage, even to the ships of war of belligerents, according to the terms of Article 1 of the present Treaty, the High Contracting Parties agree that no right of war, no act of hostility, nor any act having for its object to obstruct the free navigation of the Canal, shall be committed in the Canal and its ports of access, as well as within a radius of 3 marine miles from those ports, even though the Ottoman Empire should be one of the belligerent Powers. . . .

Article 10

Similarly, the provisions of Articles 4, 5, 7 and 8 shall not interfere with the measures which His Majesty the Sultan and His Highness the Khedive, in the name of His Imperial Majesty, and within the limits of the Firmans granted, might find it necessary to take for securing by their own forces the defence of Egypt and the maintenance of public order.

In case His Imperial Majesty the Sultan, or His Highness the Khedive, should find it necessary to avail themselves of the exceptions for which this Article provides, the Signatory Powers of the Declaration of London shall be notified thereof by the Imperial Ottoman Government.

It is likewise understood that the provisions of the four Articles aforesaid shall in no case occasion any obstacle to the measures which the Imperial Ottoman Government may think it necessary to take in order to insure by its own forces the defence of its other possessions situated on the eastern coast of the Red Sea.

---

[75] The original parties were Austria-Hungary, France, Germany, Great Britain, Italy, the Netherlands, Russia, Spain and the Ottoman Empire.

Article 11

The measures which shall be taken in the cases provided for by Articles 9 and 10 of the present Treaty shall not interfere with the free use of the Canal. In the same cases, the erection of permanent fortifications contrary to the provisions of Article 8 is prohibited.

Article 14

The High Contracting Parties agree that the engagements resulting from the present Treaty shall not be limited by the duration of the Acts of Concession of the Universal Suez Canal Company.

Notes

1. The Suez Canal was built by the Suez Canal Company in accordance with concession agreements made between the Company and the Sultan of Turkey in the 1850s, at a time when Egypt was a part of the Ottoman Empire. Under the terms of these agreements, the Company was to operate the Canal for ninety-nine years from the time that it opened (1869). At the termination of this period, the Egyptian Government was to "take the place of the company and to enter into full possession of the canal." In July 1956, Egypt nationalised the Suez Canal Company and assumed control of the Canal. In August 1956, a conference of 22 interested states was held in London. A proposal supported by 18 of them called for the "efficient and dependable operation, maintenance and development of the Canal as a free, open and secure international waterway in accordance with the principles of the Convention of 1888."[76] On September 26, 1956, the United States Secretary of State for Foreign Affairs (Mr. Dulles) said:

> We believe that the treaty of 1888 internationalises, you might say, the right of use of the canal. It creates a sort of an easement across Egyptian territory, of which we believe the beneficiaries of the treaty as well as the parties to the treaty have the right to make use. And we believe they are also entitled to organise to exercise the right of use and, generally, their rights under the treaty.[77]

In a Declaration made on April 24, 1957, Egypt stated:

> It remains the unaltered policy and firm purpose of the Government of Egypt to respect the terms and the spirit of the Constantinople Convention of 1888 and the rights and obligations arising therefrom. The Government of Egypt will continue to respect, observe and implement them.[78]

2. By the 1977 Panama Canal Treaty[79] between Panama and the United States, sovereignty over the Panama Canal Zone was transferred from the United States to Panama, but the United States will continue to operate and have the right to defend the Canal, with increasing Panamanian involvement, until the termination of the treaty in 1999. Thereupon, Panama will assume full responsibility for the Canal itself. The Canal "shall remain . . . open to peaceful transit by the vessels of all nations on terms of entire equality."[80]

---

[76] 3 Whiteman 1103.

[77] *Ibid.* 1102.

[78] 51 A.J.I.L. 673 (1957). On Egypt's acceptance of the I.C.J.'s compulsory jurisdiction concerning Suez Canal disputes, see 51 A.J.I.L. 675 (1957).

[79] 72 A.J.I.L. 225 (1978).

[80] Article 2 of the 1977 Treaty concerning the Permanent Neutrality and Operation of the Panama Canal, *ibid.* p. 238, which accompanies the main treaty. The canal is declared to be "permanently neutral": Article 1.

6. *INTERNATIONAL PROTECTION OF THE ENVIRONMENT*[81]

STOCKHOLM DECLARATION ON THE HUMAN
ENVIRONMENT 1972[82]

Report of the U.N. Conference on the Human Environment, U.N. Doc. A/CONF. 48/14;
11 I.L.M. 1416 (1972)

Principle 21

States have, in accordance with the Charter of the United Nations and the
principles of international law, the sovereign right to exploit their own resources
pursuant to their own environmental policies, and the responsibility to ensure
that activities within their jurisdiction or control do not cause damage to the
environment of other States or of areas beyond the limits of national
jurisdiction.

Principle 22

States shall co-operate to develop further the international law regarding
liability and compensation for the victims of pollution and other environmental
damage caused by activities within the jurisdiction or control of such States to
areas beyond their jurisdiction.

Notes

1. The Stockholm Declaration was adopted by the United Nations Conference on the
Human Environment held at Stockholm in 1972. It was adopted by acclamation by the
113 participating states.[83] It contains 26 principles which provide the basis of an
international policy for the protection and improvement of the environment, of which
Principles 21 and 22 directly concern international law. Its potential significance in the
environmental field has been compared with that which the Universal Declaration on
Human Rights has come to have in respect of human rights.[84] Principle 21 states, as a
matter of current international law, the right of a state to exploit its own natural
resources and its duty not to cause harm to others or to places outside of its territory in
the course of their exploitation. The *Trail Smelter* case (below) gives some idea of the
content of this duty. Principle 22 imposes an obligation (*quaere* a legal one) to co-
operate to develop the duty further. Areas "beyond the limits of national jurisdiction"
include the high seas and Antarctica.

2. The Stockholm Declaration was accompanied by an Action Plan consisting of 109
recommendations on action that should be taken to protect and improve man's environment. In 1972 the United Nations established a United Nations Environment
Programme (UNEP) to carry out the Action Plan and to take such other initiatives and
action as might seem appropriate.[85] The Governing Council of the Programme

[81] See Barros and Johnston, *The International Law of Pollution* (1974); Gormley, *Human
Rights and the Environment* (1976); Schneider, *World Public Order of the Environment*,
(1979); Teclaff and Utton, eds., *International Environmental Law* (1974). For a comprehensive collection of treaties and documents, see Rüster and Simma, eds., *International
Protection of the Environment*, Vols. I–XXVII (1975–82).
[82] See Sohn, 14 Harvard I.L.J. 423 (1973).
[83] The U.S.S.R. and other communist states did not attend because the G.D.R. was not invited.
[84] Sohn, *loc. cit.* at n. 82 above, p. 515.
[85] G.A. Resn. 2997 (XXVII). See Bacon, 12 C.Y.I.L. 255 (1974) and Gardner, 26 Int.Org. 237
(1972).

(composed of 58 United Nations members) is responsible for determining questions of general policy; the Environment Secretariat administers the programme; the Environment Fund, based on voluntary contributions, finances the action taken to implement it; and the Environmental Co-ordinating Board links the work of the Programme with that of other United Nations bodies. A number of initiatives have already been taken, including the 1976 Vancouver Conference on Human Settlements, which resulted in the 1976 Declaration on Human Settlements.[86]

TRAIL SMELTER ARBITRATION

U.S. *v.* Canada (1938 and 1941)

Arbitral Tribunal: Hostie, Chairman; Warren, U.S. member; Greenshields, Canadian member; 3 R.I.A.A. 1905

A Canadian company began smelting lead and zinc at the beginning of the century at Trail, on the Columbia River about 10 miles from the border between the two countries on the Canadian side. In the 1920s, the company stepped up production and by 1930 over 300 tons of sulphur, containing considerable quantities of sulphur dioxide, were being emitted daily. Some of the fumes were being carried down the Columbia River valley and across into the United States where they were allegedly causing considerable damage to land and other interests in the state of Washington. After negotiations between the two countries, Canada agreed that the case should be referred to the International Joint Commission. This is a body established by the two countries by the Boundary Waters Treaty of 1909[87] with jurisdiction over problems concerning their common water boundaries. It is a notable early example of one kind of standing administrative body that can be of use in controlling international air or water pollution. The Commission reported in 1931 that damage had indeed occurred and assessed it at $350,000. Canada, which had not disputed the question of liability, agreed to pay this amount. But the smelter at Trail continued to operate and the question whether damage had been caused after 1931 for which compensation should be paid was raised and referred, this time, to arbitration. The United States claimed about $2 million compensation. In 1938, the Tribunal allowed the claim in part, awarding $78,000 compensation in respect of damage caused between 1930 and 1937. The Tribunal was also asked—Question 2—"whether the Trail Smelter should be required to refrain from causing damage in the State of Washington in the future and, if so, to what extent?" It is this question that is considered in the following extract.

1941 *Report of the Tribunal*

The first problem which arises is whether the question should be answered on the basis of the law followed in the United States or on the basis of international law.[88] The Tribunal, however, finds that this problem need not be solved here as the law followed in the United States in dealing with the quasi-sovereign rights of the States of the Union, in the matter of air pollution, whilst more definite, is in conformity with the general rules of international law.

Particularly in reaching its conclusions as regards this question as well as the

---

[86] U.N.Doc. A/CONF.70/15, p. 2.
[87] 3 Malloy 2607.
[88] *Ed.* The Tribunal was instructed to apply "the law and practice followed in dealing with cognate questions in the United States of America as well as international law and practice." It was also to "give consideration to the desire of the high contracting parties to reach a solution just to all parties concerned."

next, the Tribunal has given consideration to the desire of the high contracting parties "to reach a solution just to all parties concerned."

As Professor Eagleton puts it (*Responsibility of States in International Law* (1928), p. 80): "A State owes at all times a duty to protect other States against injurious acts by individuals from within its jurisdiction." A great number of such general pronouncements by leading authorities concerning the duty of a State to respect other States and their territory have been presented to the Tribunal. . . . But the real difficulty often arises rather when it comes to determine what, *pro subjecta materie*, is deemed to constitute an injurious act.

A case concerning, as the present one does, territorial relations, decided by the Federal Court of Switzerland between the Cantons of Soleure and Argovia, may serve to illustrate the relativity of the rule. Soleure brought a suit against her sister State to enjoin use of a shooting establishment which endangered her territory. The court, in granting the injunction, said: "This right (sovereignty) excludes . . . not only the usurpation and exercise of sovereign rights (of another State) . . . but also an actual encroachment which might prejudice the natural use of the territory and the free movement of its inhabitants." As a result of the decision, Argovia made plans for the improvement of the existing installations. These, however, were considered as insufficient protection by Soleure. The Canton of Argovia then moved the Federal Court to decree that the shooting be again permitted after completion of the projected improvements. This motion was granted. "The demand of the Government of Soleure," said the court, "that all endangerment be absolutely abolished apparently goes too far." The court found that all risk whatever had not been eliminated, as the region was flat and absolutely safe shooting ranges were only found in mountain valleys; that there was a federal duty for the communes to provide facilities for military target practice and that "no more precautions may be demanded for shooting ranges near the boundaries of two Cantons than are required for shooting ranges in the interior of a Canton." (R. O. 26, I, p. 450, 451; R. O. 41, I, p. 137; see D. Schindler, "The Administration of Justice in the Swiss Federal Court in Intercantonal Disputes," *American Journal of International Law*, Vol. 15 (1921), pp. 172–174.)

No case of air pollution dealt with by an international tribunal has been brought to the attention of the Tribunal nor does the Tribunal know of any such case. The nearest analogy is that of water pollution. But, here also, no decision of an international tribunal has been cited or has been found.

There are, however, as regards both air pollution and water pollution, certain decisions of the Supreme Court of the United States which may legitimately be taken as a guide in this field of international law, for it is reasonable to follow by analogy, in international cases, precedents established by that court in dealing with controversies between States of the Union or with other controversies concerning the quasi-sovereign rights of such States, where no contrary rule prevails in international law and no reason for rejecting such precedents can be adduced from the limitations of sovereignty inherent in the Constitution of the United States. . . .

The Tribunal, therefore, finds that the above decisions, taken as a whole, constitute an adequate basis for its conclusions, namely, that, under the principles of international law, as well as of the law of the United States, no State has the right to use or permit the use of its territory in such a manner as to cause injury by fumes in or to the territory of another or the properties or persons therein, when the case is of serious consequence and the injury is established by clear and convincing evidence.

The decisions of the Supreme Court of the United States which are the basis of these conclusions are decisions in equity and a solution inspired by them, together with the régime hereinafter prescribed, will, in the opinion of the Tribunal, be "just to all parties concerned," as long, at least, as the present conditions in the Columbia River Valley continue to prevail.

Considering the circumstances of the case, the Tribunal holds that the Dominion of Canada is responsible in international law for the conduct of the Trail Smelter. Apart from the undertakings in the Convention, it is, therefore, the duty of the Government of the Dominion of Canada to see to it that this conduct should be in conformity with the obligation of the Dominion under international law as herein determined.

The Tribunal, therefore, answers Question No. 2 as follows: (2) So long as the present conditions in the Columbia River Valley prevail, the Trail Smelter shall be required to refrain from causing any damage through fumes in the State of Washington; the damage herein referred to and its extent being such as would be recoverable under the decisions of the courts of the United States in suits between private individuals. The indemnity for such damage should be fixed in such manner as the Governments, acting under Article XI of the Convention, should agree upon.

Notes

1. The Tribunal was further asked by the parties, in the light of its answer to Question 2, "what measures or régime, if any, should be adopted and maintained by the Trail Smelter?" In answer to this further question, the Tribunal, with the assistance of technical experts, laid down a régime for the future operation of the Smelter aimed at reducing pollution to an acceptable level. The following comment by Read,[89] who was closely concerned with the case, on the effect of this régime is of interest:

> The capital cost of complying with the régime was of the order of twenty million dollars: pre-war costs when a million dollars meant a lot of money. Fortunately for the economic life of the south-eastern part of British Columbia, in which the Trail Smelter was the most important factor, it was a private enterprise and not a government department. Notwithstanding the enormous capital expenditure and intermittent interruption of the metallurgical operations imposed, in perpetuity, by the régime of control, the Consolidated Mining and Smelting Company succeeded in selling the products of its smoke abatement programme for substantial profit. In order to comply with the régime, the Company was compelled to remove from the smoke cloud at the stacks more sulphur dioxide than was taken from the stacks of all other smelters of the North American Continent combined.

2. Note also the further comment by the same writer on the reason why the claim was presented as one of injury to the United States directly, through damage to its territory, and not as one of injury to it indirectly, through injury to the property of United States nationals:

> The third difficulty—the technical rules of international law governing the presentation of claims—was overcome by avoiding the format of the ordinary claims convention. The problem presented to the Tribunal for solution was not the problem of damage or injury to this, that or the other person in the State of Washington. It was the problem of damage caused in the State of Washington, regardless of who was

[89] 1 C.Y.I.L. 213 at p. 221 (1963).

hurt. Damage was not related to persons, and the problems of national character of claims and pursuit of national remedies became irrelevant.[90]

3. Like common law nuisance, the rule in the *Trail Smelter* case founds liability on unreasonable interference with the enjoyment of land. An example of state practice that accords with the *Trail Smelter* rule occurred in 1961 when Mexico complained of smells reaching its territory from stockyards owned privately and located on the United States side of the border. The United States reply was in terms not of absence of liability in international law but of recent steps that had been taken by the companies concerned to bring the situation under control.[91] See also the reference in the *Corfu Channel* case[92] (in a context of liability for not warning of the presence of dangerous objects on one's territory) to "every state's obligation not to allow knowingly its territory to be used for acts contrary to the rights of other states." And see the *Gut Dam Arbitration*,[93] in which a U.S.-Canadian agreement by which Canada agreed to pay compensation in respect of any damage caused by raising the level of a dam across the international boundary on the St. Lawrence river was interpreted and applied to compensate all United States nationals who suffered property damage by flooding and erosion, not just those in the immediate area.

4. The problem of air pollution was recognised in the 1979 Convention on Long-Range Transboundary Air Pollution.[94] This defines air pollution (Article 1) as

"the introduction by man, directly or indirectly, of substances or energy into the air resulting in deleterious effects of such a nature as to endanger human health, farm living resources and ecosystems and material property and impair or interfere with amenities and other legitimate uses of the environment."

The Convention does not tackle the issue of liability for pollution across state borders. Instead, the parties "shall, by means of exchanges of information, consultation, research and monitoring, develop without undue delay policies and strategies" to combat air pollution (Article 2).

A current example of air pollution of an international character is the "acid rain" that falls in Norway causing fish to die and metal to corrode. It is believed to come from sulphur fumes emitted by industry in the United Kingdom and the Federal Republic of Germany and carried across the North Sea by wind. Could this situation give rise to responsibility in international law?

5. The law of nuisance has been supplemented in English law by legislative and administrative controls of a preventive and enforcement character which have proved much more effective. Is there an analogy here that international law could make use of? Might it be that the best way to treat localised cross-border pollution is by particular treaty régimes establishing enforcement machinery appropriate to the facts?[95] Is there a case for treating the question of pollution on a human rights basis controlling internal as well as cross-border pollution? Does the Stockholm Declaration go this far?

6. The rule in the *Trail Smelter* case can probably be applied to river pollution too. Certainly the principle *sic utere tuo ut alienum non laedas* which underlies it is applicable to river pollution as it is to air pollution. The Helsinki Rules on the Uses of International Rivers adopted by the International Law Association in 1966,[96] which were understood by the Association to state customary international law, define "water pollution" as

---

[90] *Ibid.* p. 224.
[91] 6 Whiteman 256.
[92] I.C.J.Rep. 1949, p. 4 at p. 22.
[93] 8 I.L.M. 118 (1969).
[94] 18 I.L.M. 1442 (1979). Not in force. The Convention requires 24 parties to enter into force. On December 31, 1981, there were 12. The U.K. was not a party.
[95] *cf.* the machinery in the *Trail Smelter* case.
[96] Report of the 52nd Conference of the International Law Association, Helsinki (1966), pp. 477 *et seq.*

"any detrimental change resulting from human conduct in the natural composition, content or quality of the waters." (Article IX.) Article X, then states the following rule:

1. Consistent with the principle of equitable utilisation of the waters of an international drainage basin, a state

(a) must prevent any new form of water pollution or any increase in the degree of existing water pollution in an international drainage basin which would cause substantial injury in the territory of a co-basin state, and

(b) should take all reasonable measures to abate existing water pollution in an international drainage basin to such an extent that no substantial damage is caused in the territory of a co-basin state.

In the *Lake Lanoux* arbitration,[97] Spain complained that France had violated a treaty by diverting a river in French territory before it entered Spain. The Tribunal found no violation of the Treaty because Spain could not show that the effect of the diversion had been detrimental to it in any way. In considering on what sort of ground Spain could have had a good claim based upon the diversion, the Tribunal stated: "It could have been argued that the works would bring about an ultimate pollution of the waters of the Carol or that the returned waters would have a chemical composition or a temperature or some characteristic which could injure Spanish interests."[98]

7. On the control of sea pollution by oil see below, p. 338. See also Article 9 of the Outer Space Treaty 1967, above, p. 189.

8. On pollution from radio-active fallout, see the Nuclear Test Ban Treaty.[99] See also the 1954 American-Japanease incident in the Pacific.[1]

9. The International Law Commission has under consideration the question of international liability for injurious consequences arising out of acts not prohibited by international law, which is concerned to a large extent with the law of the environment.[2]

---

[97] (1957) 24 I.L.R. 101.
[98] *Idem.* p. 123.
[99] *Loc. cit.* at p. 322, n. 33, below.
[1] See below, p. 322.
[2] See, most recently, the Third Report of the Special Rapporteur (Quentin-Baxter), U.N.Doc. A/CN.4/360 (1982).

CHAPTER 6

STATE JURISDICTION

1. *INTRODUCTORY NOTE*[1]

STATE jurisdiction is the power of a state under international law to govern persons and property by its municipal law. It includes both the power to prescribe rules (prescriptive jurisdiction) and the power to enforce them (enforcement jurisdiction). The latter includes both executive and judicial powers of enforcement. Jurisdiction may be concurrent with the jurisdiction of other states or it may be exclusive. It may be civil or criminal. The rules of state jurisdiction identify the persons and the property within the permissible range of a state's law and its procedures for enforcing that law. They are not concerned with the content of a state's law except in so far as it purports to subject a person to it or to prescribe procedures to enforce it. International organisations have jurisdiction in the above sense to a limited extent (*e.g.* over employees). The European Communities are unusual in the degree of jurisdiction they have over individuals and companies through their powers of regulation and decision making.[2]

2. *CRIMINAL*[3] *JURISDICTION*

DICKINSON, INTRODUCTORY COMMENT TO THE HARVARD RESEARCH DRAFT CONVENTION ON JURISDICTION WITH RESPECT TO CRIME 1935

29 A.J.I.L., Supp., 443 (1935)

An analysis of modern national codes of penal law and penal procedure, checked against the conclusions of reliable writers and the resolutions of international conferences or learned societies, and supplemented by some exploration of the jurisprudence of national courts, discloses five general

---

[1] See Akehurst (1972–73) 46 B.Y.I.L. 145; Jennings, 32 *Nordisk Tidsskrift for International Ret*. 209 (1962); *ibid*. (1957) 33 B.Y.I.L. 146; Johnson, in David Davies Memorial Institute of International Studies, *Report of International Law Conference* (1962) p. 32; Mann, 111 *Hague Recueil* 1 (1964–I).

[2] On the "supra-national" character of the ECSC especially, see Robertson, *European Institutions* (3rd ed., 1973), pp. 156–160.

[3] Opinions differ on the extent of civil jurisdiction. Mann suggests that international law requires a "substantial connection" before civil jurisdiction can be exercised: see the extract below, p. 232. Brownlie states that "[e]xcessive and abusive assertion of civil jurisdiction could lead to international responsibility or protests at *ultra vires* acts." He argues that "as civil jurisdiction is ultimately reinforced by procedures of enforcement involving criminal sanctions, there is in principle no great difference between problems created by assertion of civil and criminal jurisdiction over aliens": *Brownlie*, p. 299. In contrast, Akehurst states that "[i]n practice, the assumption of jurisdiction by a State does not seem to be subject to any requirement that the defendant or the facts of the case need have any connection with that State; and this practice seems to have met with acquiescence by other States": *loc. cit.* at n. 1 above, p. 176. On the dispute concerning the extra-territorial application of U.S. anti-trust law (which is partly civil), see Jennings (1957) 33 B.Y.I.L. 146 and Oliver, 51 A.J.I.L. 380 (1957). See also the Report on the 51st Conference of the International Law Association, 1964, pp. 304 *et seq.*

principles on which a more or less extensive penal jurisdiction is claimed by states at the present time. These five general principles are: first, the territorial principle, determining jurisdiction by reference to the place where the offence is committed; second, the nationality principle, determining jurisdiction by reference to the nationality or national character of the person committing the offence; third, the protective principle, determining jurisdiction by reference to the national interest injured by the offence; fourth, the universality principle, determining jurisdiction by reference to the custody of the person committing the offence; and fifth, the passive personality principle, determining jurisdiction by reference to the nationality or national character of the person injured by the offence. Of these five principles, the first is everywhere regarded as of primary importance and of fundamental character. The second is universally accepted, though there are striking differences in the extent to which it is used in the different national systems. The third is claimed by most states, regarded with misgivings in a few, and generally ranked as the basis of an auxiliary competence. The fourth is widely, though by no means universally, accepted as the basis of an auxiliary competence, except for the offence of piracy, with respect to which it is the generally recognized principle of jurisdiction. The fifth, asserted in some form by a considerable number of states and contested by others, is admittedly auxiliary in character and is probably not essential for any state if the ends served are adequately provided for on other principles.

Notes
1. The Harvard Research Draft Convention of 1935 was the product of the unofficial work of a number of American international lawyers. It is not binding upon any state as a treaty and it is not state practice. Nonetheless, both in so far as it is intended to reflect customary international law and in its suggestions *de lege ferenda,* it is of considerable value because of the thorough study of state practice that preceded it. The Draft Convention adopts the first four of the principles listed in the above extract from the Introductory Comment, all of which were thought to be permitted by international law.[4] The passive personality principle, the permissibility of which was thought to be doubtful,[5] was omitted.

Where more than one state has jurisdiction on a basis permitted by international law, it seems that each state is free to exercise prescriptive jurisdiction when it wishes and that priority to exercise enforcement jurisdiction depends solely upon custody. Even a state with territorial jurisdiction, which is the form of jurisdiction the most firmly rooted in state practice, has no prior claim over another state having custody of a person and relying on some extra-territorial basis for jurisdiction. Two possible limitations upon a state's freedom to exercise enforcement jurisdiction are suggested by the Harvard Draft Convention. The first follows from the idea of double jeopardy. Article 13 of the Harvard Research Draft Convention reads:

> In exercising jurisdiction under this Convention, no state shall prosecute or punish an alien after it is proved that the alien has been prosecuted in another State for a crime requiring proof of substantially the same acts or omissions and has been acquitted on the merits, or has been convicted and undergone the penalty imposed, or having been convicted, has been pardoned.

The Commentary refers to considerable support for such a limitation in municipal law.[6] Article 13 does not protect nationals. On this point, the Commentary reads:

[4] 29 A.J.I.L. Supp. 480, 519, 556, 563–564 (1935).
[5] *Ibid.* p. 579.
[6] *Ibid.* pp. 602 *et seq.*

"In the present state of international law . . . it would seem inappropriate for a convention on jurisdiction with respect to crime to incorporate limitations upon a State's authority over its nationals."[7] Secondly, a somewhat similar problem arises when a person is placed in a position where under the law of State A he is required to do something which he is prohibited from doing under the law of State B. On this, Article 14 of the Harvard Research Draft Convention reads:

" . . . no state shall prosecute or punish an alien for an act which was required of that alien by the law of the place where the alien was at the time of the act or omission."

The Commentary acknowledges that there were "few precedents" in municipal law for Article 14; it was included as "eminently desirable and just."[8] Like Article 13, Article 14 does not apply to nationals.

2. *The Nationality Principle.* The Commentary to the Draft Convention reads:

The competence of the State to prosecute and punish its nationals on the sole basis of their nationality is based upon the allegiance which the person charged with crime owes to the State of which he is a national. . . . The States which derive their jurisprudence from the civil law assert a competence which is substantially more comprehensive than that exercised by States influenced by the English common law, but all make some use of the principle. . . . The principle that jurisdiction may be founded either upon nationality at the time of the offence or upon nationality at the time of the prosecution appears to be supported by such legislation as has dealt specifically with the question. If international law permits a state to regard the accused as its national, its competence is not impaired or limited by the fact that he is also a national of another State. . . . It is indisputable also that nothing in international law precludes a State from prosecuting and punishing one of its juristic persons for a crime committed outside of its territory.[9]

In English law, some of the small number of offences for which a national can be prosecuted for committing abroad can equally be seen as being based upon the idea of protection (*e.g.* treason[10] and offences under the Official Secrets Acts,[11]) but others (*e.g.* murder,[12] manslaughter[12] and bigamy[13]) cannot. The nationality principle is also relied upon in English law to give an English court jurisdiction "where any person, being a British subject, is charged with having committed any offence . . . on board . . . any foreign ship to which he does not belong. . . ."[14]

THE LOTUS CASE

France *v.* Turkey (1927)

P.C.I.J. Reports, Series A, No. 10

Judgment of the Court

According to the special agreement, the Court has to decide the following questions:

[7] *Ibid.* p. 613.   [8] *Ibid.* p. 616.   [9] *Ibid.* pp. 519 *et seq.*
[10] *R.* v. *Casement* [1917] 1 K.B. 98.
[11] Official Secrets Act 1911, s.10; Official Secrets Act 1970, s.8(1).
[12] Offences against the Person Act 1861, s.9.
[13] Offences against the Person Act 1861, s.57.
[14] Merchant Shipping Act 1894, s.686(1), which was interpreted in *R.* v. *Kelly* [1982] A.C. 665 (H.L.) as giving jurisdiction to hear charges under the Criminal Damage Act 1971, which otherwise has no extra-territorial effect, against three U.K. citizens for damage caused by them as passengers on board a Danish North Sea ferry on the high seas. See Hirst, [1982] Crim. L.R. 496.

"(1) Has Turkey, contrary to Article 15 of the Convention of Lausanne of July 24th, 1923, respecting conditions of residence and business and jurisdiction, acted in conflict with the principles of international law—and if so, what principles—by instituting, following the collision which occurred on August 2nd, 1926, on the high seas between the French steamer *Lotus* and the Turkish steamer *Boz-Kourt* and upon the arrival of the French steamer at Constantinople—as well as against the captain of the Turkish steamship—joint criminal proceedings in pursuance of Turkish law against M. Demons, officer of the watch on board the *Lotus* at the time of the collision, in consequence of the loss of the *Boz-Kourt* having involved the death of eight Turkish sailors and passengers?[15]

"(2) Should the reply be in the affirmative, what pecuniary reparation is due to M. Demons, provided, according to the principles of international law, reparation should be made in similar cases?" . . .

3. The prosecution was instituted because the loss of the *Boz-Kourt* involved the death of eight Turkish sailors and passengers. It is clear, in the first place, that this result of the collision constitutes a factor essential for the institution of the criminal proceedings in question; secondly, it follows from the statements of the two Parties that no criminal intention has been imputed to either of the officers responsible for navigating the two vessels; it is therefore a case of prosecution for involuntary manslaughter. . . .

. . . Article 15 of the Convention of Lausanne of July 24th, 1923,[16] . . . is as follows:

"Subject to the provisions of Article 16, all questions of jurisdiction shall, as between Turkey and the other contracting Powers, be decided in accordance with the principles of international law."

. . . The French Government contends that the Turkish Courts, in order to have jurisdiction, should be able to point to some title to jurisdiction recognized by international law in favour of Turkey. On the other hand, the Turkish Government takes the view that Article 15 allows Turkey jurisdiction whenever such jurisdiction does not come into conflict with a principle of international law.

The latter view seems to be in conformity with the special agreement itself, No. 1 of which asks the Court to say whether Turkey has acted contrary to the principles of international law and, if so, what principles. . . .

This way of stating the question is also dictated by the very nature and existing conditions of international law.

International law governs relations between independent States. The rules of law binding upon States therefore emanate from their own free will as expressed in conventions or by usages generally accepted as expressing principles of law and established in order to regulate the relations between these co-existing independent communities or with a view to the achievement of common aims. Restrictions upon the independence of States cannot therefore be presumed.

---

[15] *Ed.* M. Demons was a French national. Both accused were convicted.
[16] *Ed.* Before the First World War, Turkey had been subject to a régime of capitulations (see p. 11, n. 36, above). The purpose of Article 15 was to recognise that Turkey had become a full and equal member of the international community.

Now the first and foremost restriction imposed by international law upon a State is that—failing the existence of a permissive rule to the contrary—it may not exercise its power in any form in the territory of another State. In this sense jurisdiction is certainly territorial; it cannot be exercised by a State outside its territory except by virtue of a permisive rule derived from international custom or from a convention.[17]

It does not, however, follow that international law prohibits a State from exercising jurisdiction in its own territory, in respect of any case which relates to acts which have taken place abroad, and in which it cannot rely on some permissive rule of international law. Such a view would only be tenable if international law contained a general prohibition to States to extend the application of their laws and the jurisdiction of their courts to persons, property and acts outside their territory, and if, as an exception to this general prohibition, it allowed States to do so in certain specific cases. But this is certainly not the case under international law as it stands at present. Far from laying down a general prohibition to the effect that States may not extend the application of their laws and the jurisdiction of their courts to persons, property and acts outside their territory, it leaves them in this respect a wide measure of discretion which is only limited in certain cases by prohibitive rules. . . .

This discretion left to States by international law explains the great variety of rules which they have been able to adopt without objections or complaints on the part of other States. . . .

. . . Having regard to the terms of Article 15 and to the construction which the Court has just placed upon it, this [the French] contention would apply in regard to civil as well as to criminal cases, and would be applicable on conditions of absolute reciprocity as between Turkey and the other contracting Parties; in practice, it would therefore in many cases result in paralyzing the action of the courts, owing to the impossibility of citing a universally accepted rule on which to support the exercise of their jurisdiction. Nevertheless, it has to be seen whether the foregoing considerations really apply as regards criminal jurisdiction, or whether this jurisdiction is governed by a different principle: this might be the outcome of the close connection which for a long time existed between the conception of supreme criminal jurisdiction and that of a State, and also by the especial importance of criminal jurisdiction from the point of view of the individual.

Though it is true that in all systems of law the principle of the territorial character of criminal law is fundamental, it is equally true that all or nearly all of these systems of law extend their action to offences committed outside the territory of the State which adopts them, and they do so in ways which vary from State to State. The territoriality of criminal law, therefore, is not an absolute principle of international law and by no means coincides with territorial sovereignty.

This situation may be considered from two different standpoints corresponding to the points of view respectively taken up by the Parties. According to one of these standpoints, the principle of freedom, in virtue of which each State may

---

[17] *Ed.* An example of a convention by which each party permits the other parties to exercise jurisdiction within its territory is the NATO Status of Forces Agreement 1951, U.K.T.S. 3 (1955), Cmd. 9363, by which each party is permitted to exercise jurisdiction over its forces stationed in the territory of the other parties.

regulate its legislation at its discretion, provided that in so doing it does not come in conflict with a restriction imposed by international law, would also apply as regards law governing the scope of jurisdiction in criminal cases. According to the other standpoint, the exclusively territorial character of law relating to this domain constitutes a principle which, except as otherwise expressly provided, would *ipso facto,* prevent States from extending the criminal jurisdiction of their courts beyond their frontiers; the exceptions in question, which include for instance extra-territorial jurisdiction over nationals and over crimes directed against public safety, would therefore rest on special permissive rules forming part of international law.

Adopting, for the purposes of the argument, the standpoint of the latter of these two systems, it must be recognized that, in the absence of a treaty provision, its correctness depends upon whether there is a custom having the force of law establishing it. The same is true as regards the applicability of this system—assuming it to have been recognized as sound—in the particular case. It follows that, even from this point of view, before ascertaining whether there may be a rule of international law expressly allowing Turkey to prosecute a foreigner for an offence committed by him outside Turkey, it is necessary to begin by establishing both that the system is well-founded and that it is applicable in this particular case. Now, in order to establish the first of these points, one must, as has just been seen, prove the existence of a principle of international law restricting the discretion of States as regards criminal legislation.

Consequently, whichever of the two systems described above be adopted, the same result will be arrived at in this particular case: the necessity of ascertaining whether or not under international law there is a principle which would have prohibited Turkey, in the circumstances of the case before the Court, from prosecuting Lieutenant Demons. . . .

The arguments advanced by the French Government, other than those considered above, are, in substance, the three following:

(1) International law does not allow a State to take proceedings with regard to offences committed by foreigners abroad, simply by reason of the nationality of the victim; and such is the situation in the present case because the offence must be regarded as having been committed on board the French vessel.

(2) International law recognizes the exclusive jurisdiction of the State whose flag is flown as regards everything which occurs on board a ship on the high seas.

(3) Lastly, this principle is especially applicable in a collision case.

As regards the first argument . . . the Court does not think it necessary to consider the contention that a State cannot punish offences committed abroad by a foreigner simply by reason of the nationality of the victim. For this contention only relates to the case where the nationality of the victim is the only criterion on which the criminal jurisdiction of the State is based. Even if that argument were correct generally speaking—and in regard to this the Court reserves its opinion—it could only be used in the present case if international law forbade Turkey to take into consideration the fact that the offence produced its effects on the Turkish vessel and consequently in a place assimilated to Turkish territory in which the application of Turkish criminal law cannot be challenged, even in regard to offences committed there by foreigners. But no such rule of international law exists. No argument has come to the knowledge of the Court from which it could be deduced that States recognize themselves to be under an obligation towards each other only to have regard to the place where the author of the offence happens to be at the time of the offence. On the contrary, it is certain that the courts of many countries, even of countries which have given their criminal legislation a strictly territorial character, interpret criminal law in the sense that offences, the authors of which at the moment of commission are in the territory of another State, are nevertheless to be regarded as having been committed in the national territory, if one of the constituent elements of the offence, and more especially its effects, have taken place there. French courts have, in regard to a variety of situations, given decisions sanctioning this way of interpreting the territorial principle. Again, the Court does not know of any cases in which governments have protested against the fact that the criminal law of some country contained a rule to this effect or that the courts of a country construed their criminal law in this sense. Consequently, once it is admitted that the effects of the offence were produced on the Turkish vessel, it becomes impossible to hold that there is a rule of international law which prohibits Turkey from prosecuting Lieutenant Demons because of the fact that the author of the offence was on board the French ship. Since, as has already been observed, the special agreement does not deal with the provision of Turkish law under which the prosecution was instituted, but only with the question whether the prosecution should be regarded as contrary to the principles of international law, there is no reason preventing the Court from confining itself to observing that, in this case, a prosecution may also be justified from the point of view of the so-called territorial principle.

Nevertheless, even if the Court had to consider whether Article 6 of the Turkish Penal Code[18] was compatible with international law, and if it held that the nationality of the victim did not in all circumstances constitute a sufficient basis for the exercise of criminal jurisdiction by the State of which the victim was a national, the Court would arrive at the same conclusion for the reasons just set out. For even were Article 6 to be held incompatible with the principles of international law, since the prosecution might have been based on another provision of Turkish law which would not have been contrary to any principle of international law, it follows that it would be impossible to deduce from the mere fact that Article 6 was not in comformity with those principles, that the prosecution itself was contrary to them. The fact that the judicial authorities may have committed an error in their choice of the legal provision applicable to the particular case and compatible with international law only concerns municipal law and can only affect international law in so far as a treaty provision enters into account, or the possibility of a denial of justice arises.

[18] *Ed.* Article 6 reads:
> "Any foreigner who, apart from the cases contemplated by Article 4, commits an offence abroad to the prejudice of Turkey or of a Turkish subject, for which offence Turkish law prescribes a penalty involving loss of freedom for a minimum period of not less than one year, shall be punished in accordance with the Turkish Penal Code provided that he is arrested in Turkey. The penalty shall however be reduced by one third and instead of the death penalty, twenty years of penal servitude shall be awarded . . .
> If the offence committed injures another foreigner, the guilty person shall be punished at the request of the Minister of Justice, in accordance with the provisions set out in the first paragraph of this article, provided however that: (1) the article in question is one for which Turkish law prescribes a penalty involving loss of freedom for a minimum period of three years; (2) there is no extradition treaty or that extradition has not been accepted either by the government of the locality where the guilty person has committed the offence or by the government of his own country."

It has been sought to argue that the offence of manslaughter cannot be localized at the spot where the mortal effect is felt; for the effect is not intentional and it cannot be said that there is, in the mind of the delinquent, any culpable intent directed towards the territory where the mortal effect is produced. In reply to this argument it might be observed that the effect is a factor of outstanding importance in offences such as manslaughter, which are punished precisely in consideration of their effects rather than of the subjective intention of the delinquent. But the Court does not feel called upon to consider this question, which is one of the interpretation of Turkish criminal law. It will suffice to observe that no argument has been put forward and nothing has been found from which it would follow that international law has established a rule imposing on States this reading of the conception of the offence of manslaughter.

The second argument put forward by the French Government is the principle that the State whose flag is flown has exclusive jurisdiction over everything which occurs on board a merchant ship on the high seas.

It is certainly true that—apart from certain special cases which are defined by international law—vessels on the high seas are subject to no authority except that of the State whose flag they fly. In virtue of the principle of the freedom of the seas, that is to say, the absence of any territorial sovereignty upon the high seas, no State may exercise any kind of jurisdiction over foreign vessels upon them. Thus, if a war vessel, happening to be at the spot where a collision occurs between a vessel flying its flag and a foreign vessel, were to send on board the latter an officer to make investigations or to take evidence, such an act would undoubtedly be contrary to international law.

But it by no means follows that a State can never in its own territory exercise jurisdiction over acts which have occurred on board a foreign ship on the high seas. A corollary of the principle of the freedom of the seas is that a ship on the high seas is assimilated to the territory of the State of the flag of which it flies, for, just as in its own territory, that State exercises its authority upon it, and no other State may do so. All that can be said is that by virtue of the principle of the freedom of the seas, a ship is placed in the same position as national territory; but there is nothing to support the claim according to which the rights of the State under whose flag the vessel sails may go farther than the rights which it exercises within its territory properly so called. It follows that what occurs on board a vessel on the high seas must be regarded as if it occurred on the territory of the State whose flag the ship flies. If, therefore, a guilty act committed on the high seas produces its effects on a vessel flying another flag or in foreign territory, the same principles must be applied as if the territories of two different States were concerned, and the conclusion must therefore be drawn that there is no rule of international law prohibiting the State to which the ship on which the effects of the offence have taken place belongs, from regarding the offence as having been committed in its territory and prosecuting, accordingly, the delinquent.

This conclusion could only be overcome if it were shown that there was a rule of customary international law which, going further than the principle stated above, established the exclusive jurisdiction of the State whose flag was flown. The French Government has endeavoured to prove the existence of such a rule, having recourse for this purpose to the teachings of publicists, to decisions of municipal and international tribunals, and especially to conventions which, whilst creating exceptions to the principle of the freedom of the seas by permitting the war and police vessels of a State to exercise a more or less extensive control over the merchant vessels of another State, reserve jurisdiction to the courts of the country whose flag is flown by the vessel proceeded against.

In the Court's opinion, the existence of such a rule has not been conclusively proved.

In the first place, as regards teachings of publicists, and apart from the question as to what their value may be from the point of view of establishing the existence of a rule of customary law, it is no doubt true that all or nearly all writers teach that ships on the high seas are subject exclusively to the jurisdiction of the State whose flag they fly. But the important point is the significance attached by them to this principle; now it does not appear that in general, writers bestow upon this principle a scope differing from or wider than that explained above and which is equivalent to saying that the jurisdiction of a State over vessels on the high seas is the same in extent as its jurisdiction in its own territory. On the other hand, there is no lack of writers who, upon a close study of the special question whether a State can prosecute for offences committed on board a foreign ship on the high seas, definitely come to the conclusion that such offences must be regarded as if they had been committed in the territory of the State whose flag the ship flies, and that consequently the general rules of each legal system in regard to offences committed abroad are applicable.

In regard to precedents, it should first be observed that, leaving aside the collision cases which will be alluded to later, none of them relates to offences affecting two ships flying the flags of two different countries, and that consequently they are not of much importance in the case before the Court. The case of the *Costa Rica Packet*[19] is no exception, for the prauw on which the alleged depredations took place was adrift without flag or crew, and this circumstance certainly influenced, perhaps decisively, the conclusion arrived at by the arbitrator.

On the other hand, there is no lack of cases in which a State has claimed a right to prosecute for an offence, committed on board a foreign ship, which it regarded as punishable under its legislation. Thus Great Britain refused the request of the United States for the extradition of John Anderson, a British seaman who had committed homicide on board an American vessel, stating that she did not dispute the jurisdiction of the United States but that she was entitled to exercise hers concurrently.[20] This case, to which others might be added, is relevant in spite of Anderson's British nationality, in order to show that the principle of exclusive jurisdiction of the country whose flag the vessel flies is not universally accepted.

---

[19] *Ed. Great Britain v. The Netherlands* (1897) Moore, 5 Int.Arb. 4948. Crew from the *Costa Rica Packet*, a British merchant ship, boarded a derelict prauw (a Malayan vessel) on the high seas and took goods (mostly gin and brandy, from which the crew became drunk) from it. When the *Costa Rica Packet* entered a Dutch port in the East Indies, the captain was arrested on charges relating to the seizure of the goods. He was later released without being brought to trial. The Arbitrator (Martens) held that the Netherlands had no jurisdiction to act as it had done—only the flag state of the *Costa Rica Packet* had—and awarded damages against it.

[20] *Ed.* See the official correspondence of 1879 in 1 Moore 932.

The cases in which the exclusive jurisdiction of the State whose flag was flown has been recognized would seem rather to have been cases in which the foreign State was interested only by reason of the nationality of the victim, and in which, according to the legislation of that State itself or the practice of its courts, that ground was not regarded as sufficient to authorize prosecution for an offence committed abroad by a foreigner.

Finally, as regards conventions expressly reserving jurisdiction exclusively to the State whose flag is flown, it is not absolutely certain that this stipulation is to be regarded as expressing a general principle of law rather than as corresponding to the extraordinary jurisdiction which these conventions confer on the state-owned ships of a particular country in respect of ships of another country on the high seas. Apart from that, it should be observed that these conventions relate to matters of a particular kind, closely connected with the policing of the seas, such as the slave trade, damage to submarine cables, fisheries, etc., and not to common-law offences. Above all it should be pointed out that the offences contemplated by the conventions in question only concern a single ship; it is impossible therefore to make any deduction from them in regard to matters which concern two ships and consequently the jurisdiction of two different States. . . .

It only remains to examine the third argument advanced by the French Government. . . .

In this connection, the Agent for the French Government has drawn the Court's attention to the fact that questions of jurisdiction in collision cases, which frequently arise before civil courts, are but rarely encountered in the practice of criminal courts. He deduces from this that, in practice, prosecutions only occur before the courts of the State whose flag is flown and that that circumstance is proof of a tacit consent on the part of States and, consequently, shows what positive international law is in collision cases.

In the Court's opinion, this conclusion is not warranted. Even if the rarity of the judicial decisions to be found among the reported cases were sufficient to prove in point of fact the circumstance alleged by the Agent for the French Government, it would merely show that States had often, in practice, abstained from instituting criminal proceedings, and not that they recognized themselves as being obliged to do so; for only if such abstention were based on their being conscious of having a duty to abstain would it be possible to speak of an international custom. The alleged fact does not allow one to infer that States have been conscious of having such a duty; on the other hand, as will presently be seen, there are other circumstances calculated to show that the contrary is true.

So far as the Court is aware there are no decisions of international tribunals in this matter; but some decisions of municipal courts have been cited. Without pausing to consider the value to be attributed to the judgments of municipal courts in connection with the establishment of the existence of a rule of international law, it will suffice to observe that the decisions quoted sometimes support one view and sometimes the other. . . .

On the other hand, the Court feels called upon to lay stress upon the fact that it does not appear that the States concerned have objected to criminal proceedings in respect of collision cases before the courts of a country other than that the flag of which was flown, or that they have made protests: their conduct does not appear to have differed appreciably from that observed by them in all cases of concurrent jurisdiction. This fact is directly opposed to the existence of a tacit consent on the part of States to the exclusive jurisdiction of the State whose flag is flown, such as the Agent for the French Government has thought it possible to deduce from the infrequency of questions of jurisdiction before criminal courts. It seems hardly probable, and it would not be in accordance with international practice, that the French Government in the *Ortigia* v. *Oncle-Joseph Case*[21] and the German Government in the *Ekbatana* v. *West-Hinder Case*[22] would have omitted to protest against the exercise of criminal jurisdiction by the Italian and Belgian Courts, if they had really thought that this was a violation of international law. . . .

The conclusion at which the Court has therefore arrived is that there is no rule of international law in regard to collision cases to the effect that criminal proceedings are exclusively within the jurisdiction of the State whose flag is flown. . . .

FOR THESE REASONS. The Court, gives, by the President's casting vote—the votes being equally divided[23]—judgment to the effect [that the answer to the first question was in the negative].

DISSENTING OPINION OF JUDGE MOORE.[24] . . . the countries by which the claim [to jurisdiction based upon the passive personality principle] has been espoused are said to have adopted the "system of protection."

What, we may ask, is this system? In substance, it means that the citizen of one country, when he visits another country, takes with him for his "protection" the law of his own country and subjects those with whom he comes into contact to the operation of that law. In this way an inhabitant of a great commercial city, in which foreigners congregate, may in the course of an hour unconsciously fall under the operation of a number of foreign criminal codes. This is by no means a fanciful supposition; it is merely an illustration of what is daily occurring, if the "protective" principle is admissible. It is evident that this claim is at variance not only with the principle of the exclusive jurisdiction of a State over its own territory, but also with the equally well-settled principle that a person visiting a foreign country, far from radiating for his protection the jurisdiction of his own country, falls under the dominion of the local law and, except so far as his government may diplomatically intervene in case of a denial of justice, must look to that law for his protection.

No one disputes the right of a State to subject its citizens abroad to the operations of its own penal laws, if it sees fit to do so. This concerns simply the citizen and his own government, and no other government can properly inter-

---

[21] *Ed.* 12 *Journal du Droit International* 286 (1885).

[22] *Ed.* 41 *Journal du Droit International* 1327 (1914).

[23] *Ed.* President Huber; Judges de Bustamante, Oda, Anzilotti, Pessôa; and National Judge Feizi-Daim voted for the Court's judgment. Former President Loder; Vice-President Weiss; and Judges Lord Finlay, Nyholm, Moore and Altimira dissented.

[24] On his reading of the special agreement by which the case was referred to the Court, Judge Moore found it necessary to consider whether Article 6 of the Turkish Criminal Code, with its reliance on the passive personality (or "protective") principle, was consistent with international law. It was his conclusion on this question that led to his dissent. Note that by "protective principle" the judge means the "passive personality principle" not the protective principle discussed below, p. 230.

fere. But the case is fundamentally different where a country claims either that its penal laws apply to other countries and to what takes place wholly within such countries or, if it does not claim this, that it may punish foreigners for alleged violations, even in their own country, of laws to which they were not subject.

In the discussions of the present case, prominence has been given to the case of the editor Cutting, a citizen of the United States, whose release was demanded when he was prosecuted in Mexico, under a statute precisely similar in terms to Article 6 of the Turkish Penal Code, for a libel published in the United States to the detriment of a Mexican. It has been intimated that this case was "political," but an examination of the public record (*Foreign Relations of the United States*, 1887, p. 751; *idem*, 1888, II, pp. 1114, 1180) shows that it was discussed by both Governments on purely legal grounds, although in the decision on appeal, by which the prisoner was discharged from custody, his release was justified on grounds of public interest.[25] In its representations to the Mexican Government, the Government of the United States, while maintaining that foreigners could not be "protected in the United States by their national laws," and that the Mexican courts might not, without violating international law, "try a citizen of the United States for an offence committed and consummated in his own country, merely because the person offended happened to be a Mexican," pointed out that it nowhere appeared that the alleged libel "was ever circulated in Mexico so as to constitute the crime of defamation under the Mexican law," or "that any copies were actually found . . . in Mexico." The United States thus carefully limited its protest to offences "committed and consummated" within its territory; and, in conformity with this view, it was agreed in the extradition treaty between the two countries of February 22nd, 1889, that except in the case of "embezzlement or criminal malversation of public funds committed within the jurisdiction of either Party by public officers or depositaries," neither Party would "assume jurisdiction in the punishment of crimes committed exclusively within the territory of the other." (Moore, *Digest of International Law*, II, pp. 233, 242.)[26]

Notes

1. On the approach of the Court to the question whether France had to prove a limitation upon Turkey's jurisdiction or whether Turkey had to prove a rule giving it jurisdiction, Brierly[27] states:

. . . their reasoning was based on the highly contentious metaphysical proposition of the extreme positivist school that the law emanates from the free will of sovereign independent States, and from this premiss they argued that restrictions on the independence of States cannot be presumed. Neither, it may be said, can the absence of restrictions; for we are not entitled to deduce the law applicable to a specific state of facts from the mere fact of sovereignty or independence. Further, the reasoning of the majority seems to imply that the process by which the international principles of penal jurisdiction have been formed is by the imposition of certain limitations on an

[25] *Ed.* Cutting had been convicted by the trial court. An appeal court ordered his release because "the offended party . . . has withdrawn from the action": see U.S.For.Rel., 1887, pp. 766–767.

[26] *Ed.* Mexico regarded itself as justified in using the passive personality principle: see the inclosure to the letter from Mr. Romero to Mr. Bayard, August 30, 1886, *ibid.* pp. 957 *et seq.*

[27] (1928) 44 L.Q.R. 154 at 155–156.

originally unlimited competence, and this is surely historically unsound. The original conception of law was personal, and it was only the rise of the modern territorial State that subjected aliens—even when they happened to be resident in a State not their own—to the law of that State. International law did not start as the law of a society of States each of omnicompetent jurisdiction, but of States possessing a personal jurisdiction over their own nationals and later acquiring a territorial jurisdiction over resident non-nationals. If it is alleged that they have now acquired a measure of jurisdiction over non-resident non-nationals, a valid international custom to that effect should surely be established by those who allege it.

2. What does the Court mean when it says that the "territoriality of criminal law . . . is not an absolute principle of international law and by no means coincides with territorial sovereignty?"[28]

3. *The territorial principle.* On the question whether the offence could be said to have been committed on Turkish territory to establish Turkish jurisdiction on a territorial basis, Judge Moore agreed with the Court:

> . . . it appears to be now universally admitted that, where a crime is committed in the territorial jurisdiction of one State as the direct result of the act of a person at the time corporeally present in another State, international law, by reason of the principle of constructive presence of the offender at the place where his act took effect, does not forbid the prosecution of the offender by the former State, should he come within its territorial jurisdiction.[29]

Consistent with this approach, the Harvard Research Draft Convention proposed that a State be allowed territorial jurisdiction when a crime is committed "in whole or in part" within its territory.[30] A crime is committed "in part" within the territory when any essential constituent element is consummated there.[31] The Commentary to the Draft Convention reads: "The text of the present article conforms to the modern trend by combining the subjective and objective applications of the territorial principle."[32] According to the "subjective application," a crime occurs in a State when it is "commenced within the State but completed or consummated [in the sense of a constituent element occurring] abroad."[33] The "objective" application is to the effect that it does so in the reverse situation.[34] Thus if X, in state A, shoots and kills Y, in state B, an offence is probably committed (depending upon the constituent elements of murder and related offences in the criminal law of the two states) in each state. In *D.P.P.* v. *Doot*[35] the respondents were aliens convicted of conspiracy to import cannabis resin into the United Kingdom. The agreement amounting to the conspiracy had been made abroad before the respondents were arrested in England while in the course of carrying it out. The House of Lords held that the English courts had jurisdiction in the case under English law because the offence continued to occur in England while steps were being taken to carry out the purpose of the conspiracy. This was so even though the agreement had already been made—and hence the constituent elements of the crime completed—abroad. Referring to the question of jurisdiction in the case according to international law, Lord Wilberforce stated:

> the present case involves "international elements"—the accused are aliens and the conspiracy was initiated abroad—but there can be no question here of any breach of any rules of international law if they are prosecuted in this country. Under the objective territorial principle (I use the terminology of the Harvard Research in International Law) or the principle of universality (for the prevention of the trade in

---

[28] Above, p. 214.   [29] P.C.I.J. Rep., Series A, No. 10, p. 73.
[30] Article 3. See the facts in *R.* v. *Keyn*, above, p. 61.
[31] 29 A.J.I.L. Supp. 495 (1935).
[32] *Ibid*. p. 494. *cf.* Lord Diplock in *Treacy* v. *D.P.P.* [1971] A.C. 537 (H.L.).
[33] *Ibid*. p. 484.   [34] *Ibid*. p. 488.   [35] [1973] A.C. 807 (H.L.).

narcotics falls within this description[36]) or both, the courts of this country have a clear right, if not a duty, to prosecute in accordance with our municipal law.

Would you agree with Lord Wilberforce's application of the territorial principle?[37] Would the protective principle apply?[38]

The Court's application of the territorial principle in the *Lotus* case was based upon the view that a ship, like an aircraft, is to be treated as part of a state's territory for jurisdictional purposes.[39] Lord Finlay took a different view in his dissenting opinion. For him, a ship was not "territory"; it was instead a "moving chattel" of a "very special nature" for which the relevant jurisdictional rule was that "[c]riminal jurisdiction for negligence causing a collision is in the courts of the country of the flag, provided that if the offender is of a nationality different from that of his ship, the prosecution may alternatively be in the courts of his own country."[40]

In *R. v. Bates*,[41] the defendant was charged with an offence under the Firearms Act 1937 committed on Rough's Tower, a wartime gun platform on which he was living and located seven miles off the coast of Harwich. The charge was dismissed because "the jurisdiction of the Admiral did not apply to an artificial structure not being a ship and . . . the Firearms Act was intended to operate only within 'the ordinary territorial limits' and on British ships."[42]

4. *The passive personality principle.* This was rejected by all of the six dissenting judges. The Commentary to the Harvard Draft Convention in 1935 lists over twenty States that, in one form or another, made, or proposed to make, use of the "passive personality" principle.[43] It had, however, "been vigorously opposed in Anglo-American countries" and, of the five principles "having substantial support in contemporary national legislation," it was "the most difficult to justify in theory."[44] The principle was not included in the Draft Convention. What are the objections to it? Why is it less acceptable than jurisdiction based upon the nationality of the alleged criminal? Might it be argued that, in some cases at least, the more States that may exercise jurisdiction over an alleged criminal the better in the interest of the administration of justice?

5. The ruling of the Court on the question of jurisdiction in cases of collisions on the high seas is contradicted by the 1958 High Seas Convention.[45] The latter probably now reflects customary international law.

ATTORNEY-GENERAL OF THE GOVERNMENT OF ISRAEL v. EICHMANN[46]

District Court of Jerusalem (1961) 36 I.L.R. 5

The accused, who had German nationality,[47] was the Head of the Jewish Office of the German Gestapo. He was the administrator in charge of "the final solution"—the

[36] See below, p. 232.
[37] See Akehurst, *loc. cit.* at p. 210, n. 1, above, p. 154.   [38] See below, p. 230.
[39] *cf. R. v. Brixton Prison Governor, ex p. Minervini* [1959] 1 Q.B. 155 (Q.B. Div.Ct.) (Norwegian ship "territory" on which a crime could be committed in the sense of the British-Norwegian extradition treaty; "territory" in the treaty meant "jurisdiction.")
[40] P.C.I.J.Rep., Series A, No. 10, p. 53.
[41] Unreported case before Essex Assizes; summarised in U.K.M.I.L. 1978; (1978) 49 B.Y.I.L. 393.
[42] *Ibid.*   [43] 29 A.J.I.L., Supp., p. 578 (1935).
[44] *Ibid.* p. 579.   [45] Article 11(2), below, p. 326.
[46] See Fawcett (1962) 38 B.Y.I.L. 181; Green, 23 M.L.R. 507 (1960); Papadatos, *The Eichmann Trial* (1964); Schwarzenberger, 15 C.L.P. 248 (1962); Silving, 55 A.J.I.L. 307 (1961).
[47] This at least was claimed by his counsel in Jerusalem: Rosen, ed., *Six Million Accusers* (1962), p. 301. He was born in Germany of German parents and taken to live in Austria as a boy. He entered Argentina with a refugee passport issued by the Red Cross under the false name of Ricardo Klement.

policy that led to the extermination of between 4,200,000 and 4,600,000 Jews in Europe.[48] Eichmann was found in Argentina in 1960 by persons who were probably agents of the Israeli Government[49] and abducted to Israel without the knowledge of the Argentinian Government.[50] There he was prosecuted under the Israeli Nazi and Nazi Collaborators (Punishment) Law of 1951 for war crimes, crimes against the Jewish people, the definition of which was modelled upon the definition of genocide in the Genocide Convention 1948,[51] and crimes against humanity.[52] War crimes were punishable under the 1951 Act if "done, during the period of the Second World War, in an enemy country"; other crimes within the Act were punishable if "done, during the period of the Nazi regime, in an enemy country." He was convicted and sentenced to death. His appeal to the Supreme Court of Israel was dismissed.[53] His ashes "were scattered over the Mediterranean waters—lest they defile Jewish soil."[54]

Judgment of the Court

8. Learned defence counsel . . . submits:

(a) that the Israel Law, by imposing punishment for acts done outside the boundaries of the State and before its establishment, against persons who were not Israel citizens, and by a person who acted in the course of duty on behalf of a foreign country ("Act of State") conflicts with international law and exceeds the powers of the Israel Legislature. . . .

10. . . . The law in force in Israel resembles that in force in England in [its application of International Law]. . . .

Our jurisdiction to try this case is based on the Nazi and Nazi Collaborators (Punishment) Law, an enacted Law the provisions of which are unequivocal. The Court has to give effect to a law of the Knesset,[55] and we cannot entertain the contention that this Law conflicts with the principles of international law. . . .

11. We have, however, also considered the sources of international law . . . and have failed to find any foundation for the contention that Israel law is in conflict with the principles of international law. . . .

12. The abhorrent crimes defined in this Law are not crimes under Israel law alone. These crimes, which struck at the whole of mankind and shocked the conscience of nations, are grave offences against the law of nations itself (*delicta juris gentium*).[56] Therefore, so far from international law negating or limiting the jurisdiction of countries with respect to such crimes, international law is, in the absence of an International Court, in need of the judicial and legislative organs of every country to give effect to its criminal interdictions and to bring the criminals to trial. The jurisdiction to try crimes under international law is universal.

[48] This estimate is that of Reitlinger in *The Final Solution* (1953), Appendix I.
[49] Even supposing they were not, Israel would appear to have adopted their acts.
[50] Note that there was no extradition treaty between Argentina and Israel.
[51] See below, p. 561.
[52] These were defined as " . . . any of the following acts: murder, extermination, enslavement, starvation or deportation and other inhumane acts committed against any civilian population, and persecution on national, racial, religious or political grounds."
[53] The Supreme Court Judgment is at 36 I.L.R. 277. The Supreme Court affirmed the reasoning of the trial court.
[54] Sachar, *A History of the Jews* (1967), p. 467.
[55] *Ed.* The Israeli Parliament.
[56] *Ed.* On crimes against international law, see below, p. 376. On genocide, in particular, see below, p. 561.

13. This universal authority, namely the authority of the *forum deprehensionis* (the court of the country in which the accused is actually held in custody), was already mentioned in the Corpus Juris Civilis (see C.3, 15, *ubi de criminibus agi oportet*) and the towns of northern Italy had already in the Middle Ages followed the practice of trying specific types of dangerous criminals (*banniti, vagabundi, assassini*) who happened to be within their area of jurisdiction, without regard to the place in which the crimes in question were committed. . . . Maritime nations have also since time immemorial acted on the principle of universal jurisdiction in dealing with pirates, whose crime is known in English law, *piracy jure gentium*. . . .

The Court quoted from a number of authors[57] who take the view that "crimes against international law" generally or war crimes in particular give rise to universal jurisdiction. It then considered an objection to its jurisdiction based upon Article 6 of the Genocide Convention 1948[58]:

22. . . . It is clear that Article 6, like all other articles which determine the conventional obligations of the contracting parties, is intended for cases of genocide which will occur in the future after the ratification of the treaty or the adherence thereto by the State or States concerned. It cannot be assumed, in the absence of an express provision in the Convention itself, that any of the conventional obligations, including Article 6, will apply to crimes which had been perpetrated in the past. It is of the nature of conventional obligations, as distinct from confirmation of existing principles, that unless another intention is implicit, their application is *ex nunc* and not *ex tunc*. . . . We must . . . draw a clear distinction between the first part of Article I, which lays down that "the Contracting Parties confirm that genocide, whether committed in time of peace or in time of war, is a crime under international law"—a general provision which confirms a principle of customary international law "binding on States, even without any conventional obligation"—and Article 6, which comprises a special provision undertaken by the contracting parties with regard to the trial of crimes that may be committed in the future. Whatever may be the purport of this latter obligation within the meaning of the Convention (and in the event of differences of opinion as to the interpretation thereof, each contracting party may, under Article 9, appeal to the International Court of Justice), it is certain that it constitutes no part of the principles of customary international law, which are also binding outside the conventional application of the Convention.

23. Moreover, even with regard to the conventional application of the Convention, it is not to be assumed that Article 6 is designed to limit the jurisdiction of countries to try crimes of genocide by the principle of territoriality. Without entering into the general question of the limits of municipal criminal jurisdiction, it may be pointed out that no one disputes that customary international law does not prohibit a State from trying its own citizens for offences they have committed abroad. . . . Had Article 6 meant to provide that those accused of genocide shall be tried *only* by "a competent tribunal of the State in the territory of which the act was committed" (or by an "international court" which has not been constituted), then that article would have foiled the

---

[57] These included Hyde, *International Law* (2nd ed., 1947), Vol. I, p. 804, and Cowles, 33 *California L.R.* 177 (1945).

[58] See below, p. 561.

very object of the Convention to prevent genocide and inflict punishment therefor. . . .

The Court rejected the defenses of *nullem crimen sine lege, nulla poena sine lege* and "act of state," relying on the reasoning of the International Military Tribunal at Nuremberg.[59]

30. . . . The State of Israel's "right to punish" the accused derives, in our view, from two cumulative sources: a universal source (pertaining to the whole of mankind), which vests the right to prosecute and punish crimes of this order in every State within the family of nations; and a specific or national source, which gives the victim nation the right to try any who assault its existence.

This second foundation of criminal jurisdiction conforms, according to accepted terminology, to the protective principle (*compétence réelle*). In England, which until very recently was considered a country that does not rely on such jurisdiction (see also *Harvard Research in International Law*, "Jurisdiction with respect to Crime," 1935, A.J.I.L., vol. 35 (Suppl.), 544) it was said in *Joyce* v. *Director of Public Prosecutions* [1946] A.C. 347, 372:

> The second point of appeal . . . was that in any case no English court has jurisdiction to try an alien for a crime committed abroad. . . . There is, I think, a short answer to this point. The statute in question deals with the crime of treason committed within or . . . without the realm: . . . No principle of comity demands that a state should ignore the crime of treason committed against it outside its territory. On the contrary a proper regard for its own security requires that all those who commit that crime, whether they commit it within or without the realm, should be amenable to its laws.[60]

Oppenheim-Lauterpacht, op. cit., vol. 1, S. 147, p. 333, says that the penal jurisdiction of the State includes "crimes injuring its subjects or serious crimes against its own safety." Most European countries go much further than this (see Harvard Research, loc. cit., pp. 546 et seq.).

31. Dahm says in his *Zur Problematik des Voelkerstrafrechts* (1956), p. 28, that the protective principle is not confined to those foreign offences that threaten the "vital interests" of the State, and goes on to explain (pp. 38–39) in his reference to the "immanent limitations" of the jurisdiction of the State, a departure from which would constitute an "abuse" of its sovereignty, [that]

> Penal jurisdiction is not a matter for everyone to exercise. It requires a 'linking point' (*Anknuepfungspunkte*), a legal connection that links the punisher with the punished. The State may, in so far as international law does

---

[59] See below, p. 555.

[60] *Ed.* Lord Jowitt L.C. The accused, William Joyce, was charged with treason under the Treason Act 1351 for having made propaganda broadcasts to the U.K. from Germany for the German Government. Although Joyce had spent his adult life in England, the accused was a U.S. citizen born in the U.S.A. of Irish parents who had emigrated there and become naturalised U.S. nationals. Apart from the "point of appeal" referred to above, it was also contended that the accused did not owe allegiance to the Crown and hence could not be guilty of treason. The House of Lords accepted that allegiance was necessary to the offence but found that the accused, as holder of a British passport in his name still in force at the time of his broadcasts, was entitled to protection by the Crown and, therefore, owed the Crown allegiance. This was so even though the passport had been obtained by fraud. See Lauterpacht, 9 C.L.J. 330 (1947).

not contain rules to the contrary, punish only persons and acts *which concern it more than they concern other States.* . . .

The Court cited other writers in support of the "linking point" doctrine.[61]

33. . . . The "linking point" between Israel and the accused (and for that matter any person accused of a crime against the Jewish people under this Law) is striking in the case of "crime against the Jewish people," a crime that postulates an intention to exterminate the Jewish people in whole or in part. . . .

34. The connection between the State of Israel and the Jewish people needs no explanation.

35. . . . This crime very deeply concerns the "vital interests" of the State of Israel, and under the "protective principle" this State has the right to punish the criminals. In terms of Dahm's thesis, the acts referred to in this Law of the State of Israel "concern it more than they concern other States," and therefore according also to this author there exists a "linking point." The punishment of Nazi criminals does not derive from the arbitrariness of a country "abusing" its sovereignty but is a legitimate and reasonable exercise of a right of penal jurisdiction.

A people which can be murdered with impunity lives in danger, to say nothing of its "honour and authority" (Grotius). . . .

36. Defence counsel contended that the protective principle cannot apply to this Law because that principle is designed to protect only an existing State, its security and its interests, whereas the State of Israel did not exist at the time of the commission of the said crimes. In his submission the same applies to the principle of "passive personality" which stems from the protective principle, and of which some States have made use through their penal legislation for the protection of their citizens abroad. Counsel pointed out that in the absence of a sovereign Jewish State at the time of the catastrophe the victims of the Nazis were not citizens of the State of Israel when they were murdered.

In our view learned Counsel errs when he examines the protective principle in this retroactive Law according to the time of the commission of the crimes, as is usual in the case of an ordinary law. This Law was enacted in 1950, to be applied to a specified period which had terminated five years before its enactment. The protected interests of the State recognized by the protective principle is in this case the interest existing at the time of the enactment of the Law, and we have already dwelt on the importance of the moral and defensive task which this Law is designed to fulfil in the State of Israel. . . .

39. We should add that the well-known judgment . . . in the *Lotus Case*[62] ruled that the principle of territoriality does not limit the power of a State to try crimes and, moreover, that any argument against such power must point to a specific rule in international law which negates that power. We have followed this principle which, so to speak, shifts the "onus of proof" upon him who pleads against jurisdiction, but have preferred to base ourselves on positive reasons for upholding the jurisdiction of the State of Israel.

40. The second contention of learned defence counsel was that the trial of the accused in Israel following upon his kidnapping in a foreign land, is in conflict with international law and takes away the jurisdiction of this Court.

---

[61] See also Mann, *loc. cit.* at p. 215, n. 1, above, pp. 49–51.   [62] *Ed.* Above, p. 212.

. . . with reference to the circumstances of the arrest of the accused and his transfer to Israel, the Republic of Argentina . . . lodged a complaint with the Security Council of the United Nations, which resolved on June 23, 1960, as follows (Doc. S/4349) . . . :

The Security Council,
Having examined the complaint that the transfer of Adolf Eichmann to the territory of Israel constitutes a violation of the sovereignty of the Argentine Republic,
Considering that the violation of the sovereignty of a Member State is incompatible with the Charter of the United Nations,
Mindful of the universal condemnation of the persecution of the Jews under the Nazis and of the concern of people in all countries that Eichmann should be brought to appropriate justice for the crimes of which he is accused, . . .
1. Declares that acts such as that under consideration, which affect the sovereignty of a Member State and therefore cause international friction, may, if repeated, endanger international peace and security;
2. Requests the Government of Israel to make appropriate reparation in accordance with the Charter of the United Nations and the rules of international law;
3. Expresses the hope that the traditionally friendly relations between Argentina and Israel will be advanced.

Pursuant to this Resolution the two Governments reached agreement on the settlement of the dispute between them, and on August 3, 1960, issued the following joint communique:

The Governments of Argentina and Israel, animated by a desire to give effect to the resolution of the Security Council of June 23, 1960, in so far as the hope was expressed that the traditionally friendly relations between the two countries will be advanced, resolve to regard as closed the incident which arose out of the action taken by citizens of Israel, which infringed the fundamental rights of the State of Argentina.[63] . . .

41. It is an established rule of law that a person being tried for an offence against the laws of a State may not oppose his trial by reason of the illegality of his arrest or of the means whereby he was brought within the jurisdiction of that State. The courts in England, the United States and Israel have constantly held that the circumstances of the arrest and the mode of bringing of the accused into the territory of the State have no relevance to his trial, and they have consistently refused in all instances to enter upon an examination of these circumstances. . . .

In *Ex parte Elliott* [1949] 1 All E.R. 373, the Court heard an application for habeas corpus by a British soldier who had deserted his unit in 1946, was arrested in Belgium in 1948 by two British military officers accompanied by two Belgian police officers, was transferred by the British military authorities to England and was there held in custody pending his trial for desertion. Counsel for the applicant pleaded *inter alia,* that the British authorities in Belgium had

---

[63] *Ed*. Earlier, Argentina had "requested appropriate reparation for the act, namely the return of Eichmann, for which it set a time limit of one week, and the punishment of those guilty of violating Argentine territory": U.N. Doc. S/4336.

no power to arrest the applicant and that he was arrested contrary to Belgian law. Lord Goddard dismissed the application, saying in his judgment (at p. 376):

> . . . If a person is arrested abroad and he is brought before a court in this country charged with an offence which that court has jurisdiction to hear, it is no answer for him to say, he being then in lawful custody in this country: "I was arrested contrary to the laws of the State of A or the State of B where I was actually arrested." He is in custody before the court which has jurisdiction to try him. What is it suggested that the court can do? The court cannot dismiss the charge at once without its being heard. He is charged with an offence against English law, the law applicable to the case.

42. That principle is also acknowledged in Palestine case law. . . .

In Afouneh v. Attorney-General, Cr.A. 14/42, (1942) 9 P.L.R. 63,[64] the Supreme Court [stated]:

> In our opinion, the law is correctly stated in volume 4 of Moore's *Digest of International Law*, at p. 311 . . . :
> "Where a fugitive is brought back by kidnapping, or by other irregular means, and not under an extradition treaty, he cannot, although an extradition treaty exists between the two countries, set up in answer to the indictment the unlawful manner in which he was brought within the jurisdiction of the court. It belongs exclusively to the government from whose territory he was wrongfully taken to complain of the violation of its rights."[65] . . .

48. The Anglo-Saxon rule has been accepted by Continental jurists as well. . . . [66]

49. Criticism of English and American case law from the point of view of international law has been levelled by Dickinson, "Jurisdiction Following Seizure or Arrest in Violation of International Law," in (1934) 28 *American*

---

[64] *Ed*. 10 A.D. 327, at p. 328 (1941–42).

[65] *Ed*. Moore relied on *Ker* v. *Illinois*, 119 U.S. 436 (1886), as his authority for this proposition. In that case, an agent acting for the state of Illinois went to Peru with a warrant for the extradition of Ker under the extradition treaty between the U.S.A. and Peru. At the time, Peru was at war with Chile and most of Peru, including Lima, was in Chilean hands. In this confused situation, the agent approached the Chilean military authorities in Lima and, with their assistance, obtained custody of Ker and took him back to Illinois. No approach was made to the Peruvian Government, which was still in existence in retreat, and no recourse was had to the extradition treaty. Peru did not protest against the agent's action or against Ker's trial. The U.S. Supreme Court ruled that Ker's trial was not contrary to the U.S. constitution. For the view that the case involved no violation of Peruvian territorial sovereignty because the Chilean military authorities were competent, in the situation prevailing at the time, to surrender Ker, see Fairman, 47 A.J.I.L. 678 (1953).

[66] *Ed*. See, *e.g.* (after the *Eichmann* case) the decision of the French Court of Cassation (Criminal Chamber) in *Re Argoud* (1964) 45 I.L.R. 90. The accused, a French national, who had been sentenced to death *in absentia* by a French military court for his part in insurrectionist activities and against whom a warrant for arrest was outstanding in respect of subsequent similar conduct, was arrested in Paris after being found there, bound and gagged, following a "tip off." He had been abducted in Munich and brought to Paris by persons who, for the purposes of argument, were taken to be French agents. After noting that the Federal Republic of Germany would have a claim to reparation and that no such claim had been presented, the Court ruled that the illegality of the accused's abduction did not rob it of jurisdiction.

Journal of International Law, 231, and Morgenstern, "Jurisdiction in Seizures Effected in Violation of International Law," in (1952) 29 *British Year Book of International Law*, 265. See also Lauterpacht in (1948) 64 *Law Quarterly Review*, 100, note (14). It is not for us to enter into this controversy between international jurists, but we would draw attention to two important points for this case: (1) the critics admit that the established rule is as summarized above; (2) in the case before us the controversy is immaterial.

. . . [Dickinson] suggests the following provision, in Harvard Research (p. 653) for which he is responsible, as part of the "Draft Convention on Jurisdiction with Respect to Crime":

> Article 16. Apprehension in Violation of International Law. In exercising jurisdiction under this Convention, no State shall prosecute or punish any person who has been brought within its territory or a place subject to its authority by recourse to measures in violation of international law or international convention *without first obtaining the consent of the State or States whose rights have been violated by such measures.* (Emphasis is ours.)

. . . He proposes this article *de lege ferenda* to ensure "an additional and highly desirable sanction for international law" (p. 624). . . .

50. . . . the question of the violation of international law by the manner in which the accused was brought into the territory of a country arises at the international level, namely, the relations between the two countries concerned alone, and must find its solution at such level. . . .

By the joint decision of the Governments of Argentina and Israel of August 3, 1960 . . . the country whose sovereignty was violated has waived its claims, including the claim for the return of the accused, and any violation of international law which might have been involved in the "incident" in question has been "cured." According to the principles of international law no doubt can therefore be cast on the jurisdiction of Israel to bring the accused to trial after August 3, 1960. After that date, no cause remained, in respect of a violation of international law, which could have served to support a plea against his trial in Israel.

Notes

1. *Protective principle.* The Harvard Research found that most, if not all, states used this principle to a greater or lesser extent. Great Britain and the United States used it less than most other states.[67] The Commentary to the Harvard Research Draft Convention suggested that use of the protective principle was justifiable as a basis for jurisdiction because of "the inadequacy of most national legislation punishing offences committed within the territory against the security, integrity and independence of foreign states."[68] It also stated:

> In view of the fact that an overwhelming majority of States have enacted such legislation (*i.e.* legislation relying on the protective principle), it is hardly possible to conclude that such legislation is necessarily in excess of competence as recognised by contemporary international law.[69]

[67] For its use in English law, see, *e.g.* the *Joyce* case, above, p. 226; *Molvan* v. *Attorney-General for Palestine* [1948] A.C. 351 (P.C.); the Prevention of Oil Pollution Act 1971, s.12, see below p. 342, n. 27; and the Criminal Jurisdiction Act 1975 (giving Northern Irish courts jurisdiction over listed offences committed in Ireland across the border).

[68] 29 A.J.I.L. Supp. 552 (1935).   [69] *Ibid.* p. 556.

An example of the general acceptance of the protective principle is found in the doctrine of the contiguous zone.[70] Would the principle allow State A to exercise criminal jurisdiction over the officials of State B in respect of their actions in the execution of an unfriendly policy (*e.g.* a trade embargo) of State B towards State A?[71] Who has the final word as to the danger to a state's security, etc.? The state concerned?

2. Was Israel justified in relying on the protective principle to prosecute the accused in the *Eichmann Case* for acts committed *before* Israel came into being?[72]

3. *Universality principle.* In addition to *piracy*,[73] the Harvard Research Draft Convention proposes jurisdiction just on the basis of custody in the following situations:

Article 10:

(*a*) When committed in a place not subject to its authority but subject to the authority of another state, if the act or omission which constitutes the crime is also an offence by the law of the place where it was committed, if surrender of the alien for prosecution has been offered to such other state or states and the offer remains unaccepted, and if prosecution is not barred by lapse of time under the law of the place where the crime was committed. The penalty imposed shall in no case be more severe than the penalty prescribed for the same act or omission by the law of the place where the crime was committed.

(*b*) When committed in a place not subject to the authority of any state,[74] if the act or omission which constitutes the crime is also an offence by the law of a state of which the alien is a national, if surrender of the alien for prosecution has been offered to the state or states of which he is a national and the offer remains unaccepted, and if prosecution is not barred by lapse of time under the law of a state of which the alien is a national. The penalty imposed shall in no case be more severe than the penalty prescribed for the same act or omission by the law of a state of which the alien is a national.

(*c*) When committed in a place not subject to the authority of any state, if the crime was committed to the injury of the state assuming jurisdiction, or of one of its nationals, or of a corporation or juristic person having its national character.

(*d*) When committed in a place not subject to the authority of any state and the alien is not a national of any state.

The Commentary to the Convention justifies this Article as being necessary to prevent offenders escaping punishment. The Commentary cites the adoption, in some form, of the rule in Article 10(*a*) by a number of states; it could find very little evidence of legislative claims to jurisdictional competence founded upon Article 10(*b*)–(*d*). Does Article 6 of the Turkish Penal Code[75] adopt in part the approach used in Article 10?

On universality jurisdiction in respect of *war crimes,* the British Manual of Military Law[76] reads:

War crimes are crimes *ex jure gentium* and thus triable by the courts of all States. . . . British military courts have jurisdiction outside the United Kingdom over war crimes committed . . . by . . . persons of any nationality. . . . It is not necessary that the victim of the war crime should be a British subject.[77]

---

[70] See below, p. 331.
[71] *cf.* Greig, *International Law* (2nd ed., 1976), p. 389.
[72] See 29 A.J.I.L. Supp. 558 (1935).
[73] See below, p. 327.
[74] *Ed., e.g.* outer space, the high seas (other than on a ship flying the flag of a state), an unoccupied island.
[75] Above, p. 216, n. 18.
[76] Part III, 1958, para. 637.
[77] On war crimes, see below, p. 555.

The United Nations War Crimes Commission[78] stated:

> . . . the right to punish war crimes . . . is possessed by any independent State whatsoever, just as is the right to punish the offence of piracy.

Is the analogy with piracy a sound one?[79]

Each of the four 1949 Geneva Red Cross Conventions[80] contains the following provision on jurisdiction:

> The High Contracting Parties undertake to enact any legislation necessary to provide effective penal sanctions for persons committing, or ordering to be committed, any of the grave breaches of the present Convention defined in the following Article.
>
> Each High Contracting Party shall be under the obligation to search for persons alleged to have committed, or to have ordered to be committed, such grave breaches and shall bring such persons, regardless of their nationality, before their own courts. . . .
>
> Each High Contracting Party shall take measures necessary for the suppression of all acts contrary to the provisions of the present Convention other than the grave breaches defined in the following Article.[81]

For the explanation given by the International Military Tribunal at Nuremberg of its jurisdiction, see below, p. 556.

Universality jurisdiction has also been provided in a number of treaties on matters of general international concern including, recently, drug-trafficking,[82] hi-jacking[83] and the sabotage of aircraft,[84] *apartheid*,[85] and attacks upon diplomats.[86] It is not clear whether any of them state rules of customary international law. The evidence is strongest in the case of hi-jacking.

4. On the "linking point" doctrine of jurisdiction (see para. 31, judgment), note the following suggestion by Mann,[87] who was considering both civil and criminal jurisdiction:

> The conclusion, then, is that a State has (legislative) jurisdiction, if its contact with a given set of facts is so close, so substantial, so direct, so weighty, that legislation in respect of them is in harmony with international law and its various aspects (including the practice of States, the principles of non-interference and reciprocity and the demands of inter-dependence). A merely political, economic, commercial or social interest does not in itself constitute a sufficient connection. Whether another State has an equally close or a closer, or perhaps the closest, contact, is not necessarily an

---

[78] 15 *War Crimes Reports* 26 (1949).

[79] See Carnegie (1963) 39 B.Y.I.L. 402, 421.

[80] U.K.T.S. 39 (1958), Cmnd. 550; 75 U.N.T.S. 3.

[81] See, *e.g.* Article 49, Convention I. "Grave offences" include such offences as "extensive destruction and appropriation of property, not justified by military necessity and carried out unlawfully and wantonly" where directed against persons protected by the Conventions concerned: see, *e.g.* Article 50, Convention I.

[82] Single Convention on Narcotic Drugs 1961, Article 36(2)(iv), U.K.T.S. 34 (1965), Cmnd. 2354; 520 U.N.T.S. 204. See also Lord Wilberforce in *D.P.P.* v. *Doot*, above, p. 222.

[83] Hague Convention for the Suppression of Unlawful Seizure of Aircraft 1970, Article 4, below, p. 237.

[84] Montreal Convention for the Suppression of Unlawful Acts against the Safety of Civil Aviation 1971, Article 5, *loc. cit.* at p. 240, n. 17, below.

[85] Convention on the Suppression and Punishment of the Crime of Apartheid 1973, Articles II–IV, *loc. cit.* at p. 561, n. 64, below.

[86] Convention on the Prevention and Punishment of Crimes against Internationally Protected Persons including Diplomats 1973, Article 2, *loc. cit.* at p. 421, n. 19, below.

[87] *Loc cit.* at p. 210, n. 1, above, pp. 49–51.

irrelevant question, but cannot be decisive where the probability of concurrent jurisdiction is conceded. . . .

It may be said that the test advocated in these pages would substitute vagueness for certainty. This would be formidable criticism if the principles of jurisdiction in fact were at present defined with certainty. . . .

Finally, from the point of view of the progressive evolution of international law it would no doubt be desirable if the principle of exclusivity would come to be accepted for the purpose of jurisdiction, if, in other words, by common consent jurisdiction in respect of a given set of acts were exercised by one State only. Such a development cannot even begin while the doctrine of jurisdiction is embedded in the procrustean law of territoriality. It is, however, likely to be promoted by a doctrine which bases jurisdiction upon closeness of connection.

5. *A fair trial.* It is clear that Eichmann was given a scrupulously fair hearing. Might it nonetheless be argued that, in terms of justice not only being done but being seen to be done, a court other than an Israeli court should have tried Eichmann?[88]

6. *Illegally obtained custody.*[89] In the *Savarkar Case,*[90] an Indian who was being returned to India from Great Britain under the Fugitive Offenders Act 1881 escaped and swam ashore in Marseilles harbour. A French policeman arrested him and handed him over to the British policeman who had come ashore in pursuit. Although the French police in Marseilles had been informed of the presence of Savarkar on board, the French policeman who made the arrest thought that he was handing back a member of the crew who had committed an offence on board. France alleged a violation of its territorial sovereignty and asked for the return of Savarkar to it as restitution. The Permanent Court of Arbitration decided in favour of Great Britain for the following reasons:

> . . . it is manifest that the case is not one of recourse to fraud or force in order to obtain possession of a person who had taken refuge in foreign territory, and that there was not, in the circumstances of the arrest and delivery of Savarkar to the British authorities and of his removal to India, anything in the nature of a violation of the sovereignty of France, and that all those who took part in the matter certainly acted in good faith and had no thought of doing anything unlawful . . . while admitting that an irregularity was committed by the arrest of Savarkar and by his being handed over to the British police, there is no rule of international law imposing, in circumstances such as those which have been set out above, any obligation on the Power which has in its custody a prisoner, to restore him because of a mistake committed by the foreign agent who delivered him up to that Power.[91]

In the *Lawler Incident,*[92] in 1860, a convict escaped from prison in Gibraltar. He was arrested by a British warder across the border in Spain and taken back to Gibraltar without Spanish consent. The British Law Officers advised:

> A plain breach of international law having occurred, we deem it to be the duty of the State, into whose territory the individual, thus wrongfully deported, was conveyed, to restore the aggrieved State, upon its request to that effect, as far as possible, to its original position.[93]

---

[88] It would seem that one state with territorial jurisdiction, Poland, offered to try Eichmann: Fawcett, *loc. cit.* at p. 223, n. 46, above p. 206.

[89] See Cardozo, 55 A.J.I.L. 127 (1961); Evans (1964) 40 B.Y.I.L. 77; O'Higgins (1960) 36 B.Y.I.L. 279.

[90] Scott, *Hague Court Reports,* p. 275.

[91] *Ibid.* p. 279.

[92] 1 McNair 78.

[93] *Ibid.*

Fawcett[94] suggests the following limitation upon the duty to return:

> . . . it might perhaps be said, in the case of irregular capture and removal for trial of a criminal *jure gentium*, that the State, from which he is taken, may only demand his reconduction if two conditions are satisfied: that that State is the *forum conveniens* for his trial, and that it declares an intention to put him on trial. If these conditions are not satisfied, then the State must accept reparation in another form, since otherwise the interest of justice would be defeated.

The same author[95] also points out that in the *Corfu Channel Case*,[96] the International Court of Justice allowed evidence to be introduced, and subsequently relied upon that evidence in its judgment, that had been obtained by a British minesweeping exercise which the Court had ruled to be a violation of Albanian territorial sovereignty.

3. *HIJACKING*[97]

Note

When hijacking[98] became a problem in the 1960s, it was soon realised that the customary international law rules on criminal jurisdiction did not (or did not sufficiently clearly) give states wide enough jurisdiction to deal with offenders and that extradition arrangements were inadequate.[99] The 1963 Tokyo Convention (below), which was concerned with the long-standing problem of jurisdiction over all crimes aboard aircraft, made some modest improvements. Since then, hijacking has become so widespread and so urgent a problem that states have taken the time to agree in the 1970 Hague and 1971 Montreal Conventions (below) to more effective, tailor-made rules. Even so, the "political offence" side of most[1] hijackings, as well as the usual considerations of state sovereignty, have prevented the adoption of rules imposing an obligation to exercise jurisdiction in any particular case or to extradite the offender.[2]

TOKYO CONVENTION ON OFFENCES AND CERTAIN OTHER ACTS COMMITTED ON BOARD AIRCRAFT 1963[3]

U.K.T.S. 126 (1969), Cmnd. 4230

Article 1

1. This Convention shall apply in respect of:

(a) offences against penal law;

---

[94] Fawcett, *loc. cit.* at p. 223, n. 46, above, pp. 99–200.
[95] *Ibid.* p. 201.　　　　　　　　　　　　　　　　　　　　　　　[96] Below, p. 380.
[97] See, from a large literature, Agrawala, *Aircraft Hijacking and International Law* (1973), Akehurst, 14 Indian J.I.L. 81 (1974); Joyner, *Aerial Hijacking as an International Crime* (1974); McWhinney, ed., *Aerial Piracy and International Law* (1971); Poulantzas, 18 Neth.I.L.R. 25 (1971); Shubber (1968–69) 43 B.Y.I.L. 193; *ibid.* 22 I.C.L.Q. 687 (1973); and White, 6 Rev.I.C.J. 38 (1971).
[98] The term "hijacking" comes from the call—"Hi Jack"—used when illegal liquor was seized from bootleggers during Prohibition in the U.S.
[99] There is no obligation to extradite in customary international law and most states will not extradite in the absence of bilateral or multilateral extradition treaty obligations governing the case. Extradition treaties normally prohibit the return of political offenders, *i.e.* offenders who commit an offence for a political purpose or who are sought for political reasons (although the definition of a political offence is a matter of debate).
[1] Some hijackings, of course, are purely criminal or crackpot activities.
[2] See, however, the European Convention on the Suppression of Terrorism 1977, *loc. cit.* at p. 239, n. 10, below.
[3] The Convention entered into force in 1969. On December 31, 1981, there were 106 contracting parties, including the U.K. For a discussion of the Convention, see Shubber, *Jurisdiction over Crimes on Board Aircraft* (1973), and Boyle and Pulsifier, 30 J.A.L.C. 305 (1964).

(b) acts which, whether or not they are offences, may or do jeopardize the safety of the aircraft or of persons or property therein or which jeopardize good order and discipline on board.

2. Except as provided in Chapter III,[4] this Convention shall apply in respect of offences committed or acts done by a person on board any aircraft registered in a Contracting State, while that aircraft is in flight or on the surface of the high seas or of any other area outside the territory of any State.

3. For the purposes of this Convention, an aircraft is considered to be in flight from the moment when power is applied for the purpose of take-off until the moment when the landing run ends.

4. This Convention shall not apply to aircraft used in military, customs or police services.

Article 3

1. The State of registration of the aircraft is competent to exercise jurisdiction over offences and acts committed on board.

2. Each Contracting State shall take such measures as may be necessary to establish its jurisdiction as the State of registration over offences committed on board aircraft registered in such State.

3. This Convention does not exclude any criminal jurisdiction exercised in accordance with national law.

Article 4

A Contracting State which is not the State of registration may not interfere with an aircraft in flight in order to exercise its criminal jurisdiction over an offence committed on board except in the following cases:

(a) the offence has effect on the territory of such State;
(b) the offence has been committed by or against a national or permanent resident of such State;
(c) the offence is against the security of such State;
(d) the offence consists of a breach of any rules or regulations relating to the flight or manoeuvre of aircraft in force in such State;
(e) the exercise of jurisdiction is necessary to ensure the observance of any obligation of such State under a multilateral international agreement.

Article 16

1. Offences committed on aircraft registered in a Contracting State shall be treated, for the purpose of extradition, as if they had been committed not only in the place in which they have occurred but also in the territory of the State of registration of the aircraft.

2. Without prejudice to the provisions of the preceding paragraph, nothing in this Convention shall be deemed to create an obligation to grant extradition.

Article 17

In taking any measures for investigation or arrest or otherwise exercising jurisdiction in connection with any offence committed on board an aircraft the

---

[4] *Ed.* This sets out the powers of the aircraft commander.

Contracting States shall pay due regard to the safety and other interests of air navigation and shall so act as to avoid unnecessary delay of the aircraft, passengers, crew or cargo.

Notes

1. After languishing with few ratifications for several years, the Tokyo Convention quickly came into force as hijackings became common in the late 1960s.

2. Although the state of registration, which will normally have the greatest interest in prosecution, is specifically listed in Article 3 as having jurisdiction, its jurisdiction is not exclusive or given priority. The interest that other states may have in a case is recognised by Article 3(3), with the qualification that, with one exception, the Convention does not extend the jurisdiction which their "national law" may claim beyond the limits set by customary international law. The exception is in Article 4, which applies only to the exercise of *executive* jurisdiction while the aircraft is in flight. The Convention imposes no obligation to extradite (Article 16).

HAGUE CONVENTION FOR THE SUPPRESSION OF UNLAWFUL SEIZURE OF AIRCRAFT 1970[5]

U.K.T.S. 39 (1972), Cmnd. 4956; 10 I.L.M. 133 (1971)

Article 1

Any person who on board an aircraft in flight:
(a) unlawfully, by force or threat thereof, or by any other form of intimidation, seizes, or exercises control of, that aircraft, or attempts to perform any such act, or
(b) is an accomplice of a person who performs or attempts to perform any such act
commits an offence (hereafter referred to as "the offence").

Article 2

Each Contracting State undertakes to make the offence punishable by severe penalties.

Article 3

1. For the purposes of this Convention, an aircraft is considered to be in flight at any time from the moment when all its external doors are closed following embarkation until the moment when any such door is opened for disembarkation. In the case of a forced landing, the flight shall be deemed to continue until the competent authorities take over the responsibility for the aircraft and for persons and property on board.

2. This Convention shall not apply to aircraft used in military, customs or police services.

3. This Convention shall apply only if the place of take-off or the place of actual landing of the aircraft on board which the offence is committed is situated outside the territory of the State of registration of that aircraft; it shall be immaterial whether the aircraft is engaged in an international or domestic flight. . . .

[5] The Convention entered into force in 1971. On December 31, 1981, there were 115 contracting parties, including the U.K. Hijacking is made an offence in English law by the Hijacking Act 1971.

5. Notwithstanding paragraphs 3 and 4 of this Article, Articles 6, 7, 8 and 10 shall apply whatever the place of take-off or the place of actual landing of the aircraft, if the offender or the alleged offender is found in the territory of a State other than the State of registration of that aircraft.

Article 4

1. Each Contracting State shall take such measures as may be necessary to establish its jurisdiction over the offence and any other act of violence against passengers or crew committed by the alleged offender in connection with the offence, in the following cases:

(a) when the offence is committed on board an aircraft registered in that State;
(b) when the aircraft on board which the offence is committed lands in its territory with the alleged offender still on board;
(c) when the offence is committed on board an aircraft leased without crew to a lessee who has his principal place of business or, if the lessee has no such place of business, his permanent residence, in that State.

2. Each Contracting State shall likewise take such measures as may be necessary to establish its jurisdiction over the offence in the case where the alleged offender is present in its territory and it does not extradite him pursuant to Article 8 to any of the States mentioned in paragraph 1 of this Article.

3. This Convention does not exclude any criminal jurisdiction exercised in accordance with national law.

Article 6

1. Upon being satisfied that the circumstances so warrant, any Contracting State in the territory of which the offender or the alleged offender is present, shall take him into custody or take other measures to ensure his presence. The custody and other measures shall be as provided in the law of that State but may only be continued for such time as is necessary to enable any criminal or extradition proceedings to be instituted.

2. Such State shall immediately make a preliminary enquiry into the facts.

3. Any person in custody pursuant to paragraph 1 of this Article shall be assisted in communicating immediately with the nearest appropriate representative of the State of which he is a national.

4. When a State, pursuant to this Article, has taken a person into custody, it shall immediately notify the State of registration of the aircraft, the State mentioned in Article 4, paragraph 1(c), the State of nationality of the detained person and, if it considers it advisable, any other interested States of the fact that such person is in custody and of the circumstances which warrant his detention. The State which makes the preliminary enquiry contemplated in paragraph 2 of this Article shall promptly report its findings to the said States and shall indicate whether it intends to exercise jurisdiction.

Article 7

The Contracting State in the territory of which the alleged offender is found shall, if it does not extradite him, be obliged, without exception whatsoever and whether or not the offence was committed in its territory, to submit the case to its competent authorities for the purpose of prosecution.

Those authorities shall take their decision in the same manner as in the case of any ordinary offence of a serious nature under the law of that State.

Article 8

1. The offence shall be deemed to be included as an extraditable offence in any extradition treaty existing between Contracting States. Contracting States undertake to include the offence as an extraditable offence in every extradition treaty to be concluded between them.

2. If a Contracting State which makes extradition conditional on the existence of a treaty receives a request for extradition from another Contracting State with which it has no extradition treaty, it may at its option consider this Convention as the legal basis for extradition in respect of the offence. Extradition shall be subject to the other conditions provided by the law of the requested State.

3. Contracting States which do not make extradition conditional on the existence of a treaty shall recognize the offence as an extraditable offence between themselves subject to the conditions provided by the law of the requested State.

4. The offence shall be treated, for the purpose of extradition between Contracting States, as if it had been committed not only in the place in which it occurred but also in the territories of the States required to establish their jurisdiction in accordance with Article 4, paragraph 1.

Article 9

1. When any of the acts mentioned in Article 1(a) has occurred or is about to occur, Contracting States shall take all appropriate measures to restore control of the aircraft to its lawful commander or to preserve his control of the aircraft.

2. In the cases contemplated by the preceding paragraph, any Contracting State in which the aircraft or its passengers or crew are present shall facilitate the continuation of the journey of the passengers and crew as soon as practicable, and shall without delay return the aircraft and its cargo to the persons lawfully entitled to possession.

Notes

1. Article 1 indicates the "offence" which contracting parties must make a part of their law to comply with the establishment of jurisdiction requirement in Article 4. Prior to the Convention, few states had a separate offence of hijacking; hijackers could only be prosecuted for assault, etc. It was understood during the drafting of Article 1 that the "aircraft" hijacked need not be registered in a contracting party for the Convention to apply.[6] The "severe penalties" requirement of Article 2 was introduced when agreement on a minimum sentence proved impossible.[7] The definition of "in flight" in Article

---

[6] Shubber, 22 I.C.L.Q. 701 (1973).

[7] The U.K. Hijacking Act 1971 imposes a life sentence. The U.S. Anti-Hijacking Act 1974 carries a death or life imprisonment sentence where death results from hijacking and a 20-year sentence otherwise.

3 is wider and easier to apply than that in the Tokyo Convention. Article 4 requires a state to "establish its jurisdiction" (*i.e.* create the offence of hijacking in its criminal law, etc.), but not actually to exercise it. Articles 6 and 7 indicate all that a state has to do in a particular case. "Any other act of violence" in Article 4 would include assault or a killing. There is no order of priority among the grounds for jurisdiction listed in Article 4(1). The third (Article 4(1)(*c*)) was added to meet the "dry leasing" situation, where an aircraft is leased without its crew and where, therefore, the state of registration may have less interest in prosecuting than it normally does.[8] Note the use and extension (beyond nationality) of the passive personality principle in Article 4(1)(*c*).[9] Article 4(2) establishes "universality" jurisdiction for hijacking (but not associated acts of violence) as a "safety net" to catch the person who escapes from, or is allowed to leave, a state with jurisdiction under Article 4(1). Article 8 makes hijacking an extraditable offence in present and future extradition treaties and practice between contracting parties but does not create an obligation to extradite which does not otherwise exist in such treaties and practice. Thus if hijacking is inserted by Article 8(1) into an existing extradition treaty that (as is common) allows a state to refuse extradition in the case of a "political offence" or where the offender is a national, the exception will apply to hijacking too.[10]

In 1978, at the Bonn Economic Summit, it was agreed that "in cases where a country refuses the extradition or prosecution of those who have hijacked an aircraft and/or does not return such aircraft," action would be taken to cease all flights to and from that country and its airlines.[11]

2. *The Dawson's Field Hijacking.* The most ambitious hijacking to date was probably that in September 1970 when Palestinian arab guerrillas successfully hijacked three civil airliners and forced them to land at the Dawson's Field airstrip in Jordan. The airliners were registered in Switzerland, the United Kingdom and the United States and belonged to Swissair, B.O.A.C., and T.W.A. respectively. The passengers and crew numbered over 400 and were of diverse nationality. The airliners were blown up. The passengers and crew were released in stages after detention for some time, in return for the release of a number of Palestinian arab guerrillas (including Leila Khaled) held by the police in London. The hijackers went their way into various countries. Supposing the states involved were parties to the Hague Convention, which of them would have jurisdiction to arrest and punish the hijackers if the incident were to occur now? Would the Convention apply retroactively to grant jurisdiction now over the incident when it actually occurred?[12]

Another (in)famous hijacking was that leading to the *Entebbe Incident*.[13] Did Uganda have jurisdiction under the Convention there?[14] Supposing it had an extradition treaty with Israel (which was, and is, not the case), would Uganda have been obliged to return the hijackers?

3. Hijacking of aircraft was condemned in 1970 shortly after Dawson's Field by a General Assembly Resolution[15]:

---

[8] White, *loc. cit.* at p. 234, n. 97, above, p. 40.

[9] *cf.* Article 4, Tokyo Convention.

[10] See, however, the European Convention on the Suppression of Terrorism 1977, E.T.S. No. 97; Cmnd. 7390. In force 1978. On November 15, 1982, there were 13 contracting parties, including the U.K. The Convention provides that defined terrorist activities shall not be regarded as political offences so as to prevent extradition. The Suppression of Terrorism Act 1978 brings U.K. extradition law into line with the Convention.

[11] U.K.M.I.L. 1978; (1978) 49 B.Y.I.L. 423. The states agreeing to do this were Canada, France, the F.R.G., Italy, Japan, the U.K. and the U.S.

[12] On the retroactive operation of treaties, see below, p. 592.

[13] See below, p. 669.

[14] Both Israel and Uganda were parties.

[15] G.A. Resn. 2645 (XXV), 9 I.L.M. 1288 (1970). The resolution was adopted by 105 votes to 0, with 8 abstentions. See also S.C.Resn. 286 (1970), *Resolutions and Decisions* 1970, p. 16.

The General Assembly, . . . recognizing that such acts jeopardize the lives and safety of the passengers and crew and constitute a violation of their human rights, . . .

1. *Condemns,* without exception whatsoever, all acts of aerial hijacking or other interference with civil air travel, whether originally national or international, through the threat or use of force, and all acts of violence which may be directed against passengers, crew and aircraft engaged in, and air navigation facilities and aeronautical communications used by, civil air transport;

2. *Calls upon* States to take all appropriate measures to deter, prevent or suppress such acts within their jurisdiction, at every stage of the execution of those acts, and to provide for the prosecution and punishment of persons who perpetrate such acts, in a manner commensurate with the gravity of those crimes, or, without prejudice to the rights and obligations of States under existing international instruments relating to the matter, for the extradition of such persons for the purpose of their prosecution and punishment;

3. *Declares* that the exploitation of unlawful seizure of aircraft for the purpose of taking hostages is to be condemned;

4. *Declares further* that the unlawful detention of passengers and crew in transit or otherwise engaged in civil air travel is to be condemned as another form of wrongful interference with free and uninterrupted air travel;

5. *Urges* States to the territory of which a hijacked aircraft is diverted to provide for the care and safety of its passengers and crew and to enable them to continue their journey as soon as practicable and to return the aircraft and its cargo to the persons lawfully entitled to possession.

Could it be argued that aerial hijacking, even in the short space of time since it has become a serious problem, has been placed by customary international law on the same footing as piracy on the high seas,[16] *i.e.* it is conduct in respect of which all states may exercise criminal jurisdiction under their law on a universality basis?

4. *The sabotage of aircraft.* The placing of bombs in aircraft and other acts of sabotage endangering both their safety and that of persons on board is a separate but related problem. The 1971 I.C.A.O. Montreal Convention for the Suppression of Unlawful Acts against the Safety of Civil Aviation[17] tackles it by means of rules as to jurisdiction and extradition similar to those in the Hague Convention.

5. Similar rules as to jurisdiction have also been included in the 1979 International Convention against the Taking of Hostages,[18] which is aimed at international terrorism. The Convention offence of "hostage-taking" which each party must incorporate into its law, is defined in Article 1(1):

Any person who seizes or detains and threatens to kill, to injure or to continue to detain another person . . . in order to compel a third party, namely, a State, an international intergovernmental organization, a natural or juridical person, or a group of persons, to do or abstain from doing any act as an explicit or implicit

---

[16] See below, p. 330.

[17] U.K.T.S. 10 (1974), Cmnd. 5524; 10 I.L.M. 1151. In force 19. On June 30, 1982, there were 115 contracting parties, including the U.K. The U.K. Protection of Aircraft Act 1973 gives effect to it.

[18] 18 I.L.M. 1456 (1979). The Convention requires 22 parties to enter into force. On December 31, 1981, there were 17. The U.K. was not a party. The U.K. Taking of Hostages Act 1982 gives affect to it. See also the 1973 Convention on the Prevention and Punishment of Crimes against Internationally Protected Persons, below, p. 421. On International terrorism generally, see Evans and Murphy, ed., *Legal Aspects of International Terrorism* (1978).

condition for the release of the hostage commits the offence of taking of hostages . . . within the meaning of this Convention.

Parties must either consider the prosecution of offenders found within their territory or extradite them.

4. *STATE IMMUNITY*[19]

Note

The following materials are concerned with the question whether a state can be impleaded before the courts of another state without its consent. There used formerly to be a rule of absolute immunity. In this century socialist states and others have come to engage in trading activities (acts *iure gestionis*) as well as exercising the public functions traditionally associated with states (acts *iure imperii*). As a result, most states now follow in their practice a doctrine of restrictive immunity by which a foreign state is allowed immunity for acts *iure imperii* only. The bulk of this practice consists of municipal court decisions. A recent study[20] shows that the courts of the great majority of states in which the matter has been considered in recent years now favour the doctrine of restrictive immunity; this is particularly true of the courts of the industrialised western world in which most of the cases have arisen.[21] The same study also considers state practice in the form of national legislation and treaties. New legislation, such as the United States Foreign Sovereign Immunities Act 1976[22] and the United Kingdom State Immunity Act 1978, below, p. 247, invariably applies the restrictive immunity doctrine, as do the two main multilateral treaties on the subject, *viz.* the 1926 Brussels Convention for the Unification of Certain Rules relating to the Immunity of State Owned Vessels[23] and the 1972 European Convention on State Immunity.[24] The 1926 Convention places "[s]eagoing vessels owned or operated by States, cargoes owned by them, and cargoes and passengers carried on Government vessels" on the same footing as private vessels (Articles 1 and 2). Article 3 then states the following exception:

The provisions of the two preceding articles shall not be applicable to ships of war, Government yachts, patrol vessels, hospital ships, auxiliary vessels, supply ships, and

[19] See Dunbar, 132 *Hague Recueil* 197 (1971–I); Johnson, 6 Austr. Y.B.I.L. 1 (1978); Lauterpacht (1951) 28 B.Y.I.L. 220; Sinclair, 167 *Hague Recueil* 113 (1980)–II); Sucharitkul, *State Immunities and Trading Activities in International Law* (1959); *ibid.* 149 *Hague Recueil* 87 (1976–I).

[20] 4th Report on Jurisdictional Immunities of States and their Property, 1982, prepared for the I.L.C. by its Special Rapporteur (Sucharitkul), UN Doc. A/CN.4/357, pp. 35 *et seq.* See also the survey in Sinclair, *op cit.* at n. 19 above, Chap. II.

[21] Courts following the restrictive immunity doctrine include those in Argentina, Austria, Belgium, Egypt, F.R.G., France, Italy, Netherlands, Pakistan, U.K. and the U.S. The courts in Chile and, possible Brazil, still keep to the absolute immunity doctrine.

[22] 15 I.L.M. 1388 (1976). See Brower, Bistline and Loomis, 73 A.J.I.L. 200 (1979) and Delaume, 71 A.J.I.L. 399 (1977).

[23] Cmnd. 7800; 176 L.N.T.S. 199; Hudson, 3 Int. Leg. 1837. In force 19. On June 30, 1982, there were 27 parties to the Convention and to its 1934 Protocol, Hudson, 6 Int. Leg. 868. The U.K. was a party. 12 states have become parties since 1949. See Thommen, *Legal Status of Government Merchant Ships in International Law* (1962).

[24] ETS No. 74; 11 I.L.M. 470 (1972). In force 1976. On November 15, 1982, there were five contracting parties, including the U.K. The 1972 Protocol, *ibid.* which had received four ratifications by that date, was not in force (five ratifications needed). The U.K. had not ratified it. The U.K. Foreign Office has stated that the 1972 Convention reflects "with sufficient accuracy general State practice in the field of Sovereign immunity": see Sinclair, *op. cit.* at 19 above, p. 258, n. 443. On the Convention, see Sinclair, 22 I.C.L.Q. 254 (1973), and the Explanatory Report in Cmnd. 5081.

other craft owned or operated by a State, and used at the time a cause of action arises exclusively on Governmental and non-commercial service, and such vessels shall not be subject to seizure, attachment or detention by any legal process, nor to judicial proceedings in rem.

The 1972 European Convention allows immunity except in certain listed categories of cases. The extensive bilateral treaty practice strongly supports a restrictive immunity approach as well. It is particularly interesting to note that the U.S.S.R. which supports absolute immunity in its executive pronouncements, has agreed to restrictive immunity in the many bilateral treaties to which it is a party.[25] The indications are that the International Law Commission will do the same in the draft articles on state immunity which it is preparing.[26] O'Connell suggests that in the current situation

> the most that can be said of customary international law is that it enjoins immunity from the judicial process only in respect of governmental activities that pertain to administration, and does not compel it in respect of other activities which are more truly commercial than administrative.[27]

Adoption of the restrictive immunity approach introduces the problem of classifying acts as *iure gestionis* or *iure imperii*. Other problems (which exist whether absolute or restrictive immunity is preferred) lie in deciding (i) which of the many governmental entities (*e.g.* public corporations) that claim to act for a state qualify for immunity and (ii) whether a state may be indirectly impleaded.

The following materials in this section examine the doctrine of state (or sovereign)[28] immunity largely as it applies in United Kingdom law.

THE SCHOONER EXCHANGE v. McFADDON

7 *Cranch* 116 (1812). U.S. Supreme Court

A French naval vessel put into Philadelphia for repairs after a storm. The libellants, who sought possession of the vessel, claimed that it was in reality the schooner *Exchange,* an American ship which they owned and which had been seized by France on the high seas in 1810 in accordance with a Napoleonic decree. The United States Attorney-General filed a suggestion to the effect that the Court should refuse jurisdiction on the ground of sovereign immunity.

MARSHALL C.J., FOR THE COURT: The jurisdiction of the nation within its own territory is necessarily exclusive and absolute. It is susceptible of no limitation not imposed by itself. . . .

This full and absolute territorial jurisdiction being alike the attribute of every sovereign, and being incapable of conferring extra-territorial power, would not seem to contemplate foreign sovereigns nor their sovereign rights as its objects. One sovereign being in no respect amenable to another, and being bound by obligations of the highest character not to degrade the dignity of his nation, by placing himself or its sovereign rights within the jurisdiction of another, can be supposed to enter a foreign territory only under an express license, or in the

---

[25] See the 4th Report for the I.L.C., *op. cit.* at p. 242, n. 20, above, p. 65.

[26] *Ibid.*

[27] *International Law*, Vol. I (2nd ed., 1970), p. 841.

[28] These terms tend to be used interchangeably, although, as Sinclair points out, *op. cit.* at p. 241, n. 19, above, p. 197, "[s]overeign immunity in the strict sense of the term should be taken to refer to the immunity which a personal sovereign or Head of State enjoys when present in the territory of another State."

confidence that the immunities belonging to his independent sovereign station, though not expressly stipulated, are reserved by implication, and will be extended to him.

This perfect equality and absolute independence of sovereigns, and this common interest impelling them to mutual intercourse, and an interchange of good offices with each other, have given rise to a class of cases in which every sovereign is understood to waive the exercise of a part of that complete exclusive territorial jurisdiction, which has been stated to be the attribute of every nation.

1st. One of these is admitted to be the exemption of the person of the sovereign from arrest or detention within a foreign territory. . . .

2d. A second case, standing on the same principles with the first, is the immunity which all civilised nations allow to foreign ministers. . . .

3d. A third case in which a sovereign is understood to cede a portion of his territorial jurisdiction is, where he allows the troops of a foreign prince to pass through his dominions. . . .

When private individuals of one nation spread themselves through another as business or caprice may direct, mingling indiscriminately with the inhabitants of that other, or when merchant vessels enter for the purposes of trade, it would be obviously inconvenient and dangerous to society, and would subject the laws to continual infraction, and the government to degradation, if such individuals or merchants did not owe temporary and local allegiance, and were not amenable to the jurisdiction of the country. Nor can the foreign sovereign have any motive for wishing such exemption. His subjects thus passing into foreign countries are not employed by him, nor are they engaged in national pursuits. Consequently there are powerful motives for not exempting persons of this description from the jurisdiction of the country in which they are found, and no one motive for requiring it. The implied license, therefore, under which they enter can never be construed to grant such exemption.

But in all respects different is the situation of a public armed ship. She constitutes a part of the military force of her nation; acts under the immediate and direct command of the sovereign; is employed by him in national objects. He has many and powerful motives for preventing those objects from being defeated by the interference of a foreign state. Such interference cannot take place without affecting his power and his dignity. The implied license, therefore, under which such vessel enters a friendly port, may reasonably be construed, and it seems to the court ought to be construed, as containing an exemption from the jurisdiction of the sovereign within whose territory she claims the right of hospitality. . . .

The Court found that the vessel in question was exempt from United States jurisdiction.

Notes

1. The doctrine is justified by Marshall C.J. on the basis of the equality, independence, and dignity of states. To the same effect, the maxim *par in parem non habet imperium* (an equal has no authority over an equal) is commonly invoked. Marshall C.J. marries the doctrine with that of the absolute jurisdiction of the territorial sovereign by assuming the latter's implied consent.

2. Although the move away from absolute to restricted immunity is now well established, state practice does not suggest that sovereign immunity should be abolished altogether. Note, however, that Lord Denning expressed an opinion in *Rahimtoola* v.

Nizam of Hyderabad[29] which could be used to support such a development (although Lord Denning did not go so far himself):

> It is more in keeping with the dignity of a foreign sovereign to submit himself to the rule of law than to claim to be above it, and his independence is better ensured by accepting the decisions of courts of acknowledged impartiality than by arbitrarily rejecting their jurisdiction. In all civilised countries there has been a progressive tendency towards making the sovereign liable to be sued in his own courts; notably in England by the Crown Proceedings Act, 1947. Foreign sovereigns should not be in any different position. There is no reason why we should grant to the departments or agencies of foreign Governments an immunity which we do not grant our own, provided always that the matter in dispute arises within the jurisdiction of our courts and is properly cognizable by them.

VICTORY TRANSPORT INC. v. COMISARIA GENERAL DE ABASTECIMENTOS Y TRANSPORTES

336 F. 2d 354; cert. denied, 381 U.S. 934 (1965); 35 I.L.R. 110. U.S. Court of Appeals, 2d Circuit, 1964

The appellants, Comisaria General de Abastecimentos y Transportes, were a branch of the Spanish Government. They chartered a ship from the respondent American company for the transportation of wheat under a charter agreement that provided for arbitration in New York. The respondent took a case to arbitration under the agreement but were met by a defence of sovereign immunity. The appellants appealed against a decision of a United States Federal District Court rejecting this defence.

SMITH, CIRCUIT JUDGE, FOR THE COURT.

. . . In 1952 our State Department, in a widely publicized letter from Acting Legal Adviser Jack B. Tate to the Acting Attorney-General Phillip B. Perlman, announced that the Department would generally adhere to the restrictive theory of sovereign immunity, recognizing immunity for a foreign State's public or sovereign acts (*jure imperii*) but denying immunity to a foreign State's private or commercial acts (*jure gestionis*). 26 *Dept. State Bull.* 984 (1952) . . . But the 'Tate letter' offers no guide-lines or criteria for differentiating between a sovereign's private and public acts. Nor have the courts or commentators suggested any satisfactory test. Some have looked to the nature of the transaction, categorizing as sovereign acts only activity which could not be performed by individuals. While this criterion is relatively easy to apply, it oft-times produces rather astonishing results, such as the holdings of some European courts that purchases of bullets or shoes for the army, the erection of fortifications for defense, or the rental of a house for an embassy, are private acts . . . Furthermore, this test merely postpones the difficulty, for particular contracts in some instances may be made only by States.[30] Others have looked to the purpose of the transaction, categorizing as *jure imperii* all activities in which the object of performance is public in character. But this test is even more unsatisfactory, for conceptually the modern sovereign always acts for a public

---

29 [1958] A.C. 379, at p. 418 (P.C.).

30 For example, any individual may be able to purchase a boat, but only a sovereign may be able to purchase a battleship. Should the purchase of a yacht be equated with the purchase of a battleship?

purpose . . . Functionally the criterion is purely arbitrary and necessarily involves the court in projecting personal notions about the proper realm of State functioning . . .

The purpose of the restrictive theory of sovereign immunity is to try to accommodate the interest of individuals doing business with foreign Governments in having their legal rights determined by the courts, with the interest of foreign Governments in being free to perform certain political acts without undergoing the embarrassment or hindrance of defending the propriety of such acts before foreign courts. Sovereign immunity is a derogation from the normal exercise of jurisdiction by the courts and should be accorded only in clear cases. Since the State Department's failure or refusal to suggest immunity is significant, we are disposed to deny a claim of sovereign immunity that has not been 'recognized and allowed' by the State Department unless it is plain that the activity in question falls within one of the categories of strictly political or public acts about which sovereigns have traditionally been quite sensitive. Such acts are generally limited to the following categories:

(1) internal administrative acts, such as expulsion of an alien;
(2) legislative acts, such as nationalization;
(3) acts concerning the armed forces;
(4) acts concerning diplomatic activity;
(5) public loans.

We do not think that the restrictive theory adopted by the State Department requires sacrificing the interests of private litigants to international comity in other than these limited categories. Should diplomacy require enlargement of these categories, the State Department can file a suggestion of immunity with the court. Should diplomacy require contraction of these categories, the State Department can issue a new or clarifying policy pronouncement.

The Comisaría General's chartering of the appellee's ship to transport a purchase of wheat is not a strictly public or political act. Indeed, it partakes far more of the character of a private commercial act than a public or political act.

The charter party has all the earmarks of a typical commercial transaction. It was executed for the Comisaría General by 'El Jefe del Servicio Commercial,' the head of its commercial division. The wheat was consigned to and shipped by a private commercial concern. And one of the most significant indicators of the private commercial nature of this charter is the inclusion of the arbitration clause. . . .

Even if we take a broader view of the transaction to encompass the purchase of wheat pursuant to the Surplus Agricultural Commodities Agreement to help feed the people of Spain, the activity of the Comisaría General remains more in the commercial than political realm. Appellant does not claim that the wheat will be used for the public services of Spain; presumptively the wheat will be resold to Spanish nationals. Whether the Comisaría General loses money or makes a profit on the sale, this purchasing activity has been conducted through private channels of trade. Except for United States financing, permitting payment in pesetas, the Comisaría General acted much like any private purchaser of wheat.

Our conclusion that the Comisaría General's activity is more properly labelled an act *jure gestionis* than *jure imperii* is supported by the practice of those countries which have adopted the restrictive theory of sovereign immunity. Thus the Commercial Tribunal of Alexandria declined to grant immunity to this same Spanish instrumentality in a more difficult case—a suit arising from the Comisaría's purchase of rice to help feed the people of neutral Spain during wartime.[30a]. . . Though there are a few inconsistencies, the courts in those countries which have adopted the restrictive theory have generally considered purchasing activity by a State instrumentality, particularly for resale to nationals, as commercial or private activity.

Finally, our conclusion that the Comisaría General's claim of sovereign immunity should be denied finds support in the State Department's communication to the Court in *New York and Cuba Mail S.S. Co.* v. *Republic of Korea*, 132 F.Supp. 684, 685 (S.D.N.Y. 1955). There the Republic of Korea was allegedly responsible for damaging a ship while assisting in the unloading of a cargo of rice for distribution without charge to its civilian and military personnel during the Korean War. Though suggesting that Korean property was immune from attachment, the State Department refused to suggest immunity 'inasmuch as the particular acts out of which the cause of action arose are not shown to be of a purely governmental character.' If the wartime transportation of rice to civilian and military personnel is not an act *jure imperii, a fortiori* the peacetime transportation of wheat for presumptive resale is not an act *jure imperii*. . . .

The order of the District Court is affirmed.

Notes

1. This extract concerns the difficult question which arises if a restrictive immunity doctrine is adopted, *viz.* by what criterion does one distinguish acts *iure imperii* and acts *iure gestionis?* Although some guidance is given in the 1972 European Convention, see below, p. 252, the matter has been considered mostly by national courts which have not always adopted the same approach. *cf.* the *Victory* case with the earlier cases cited in the judgment in it and with the *I Congreso* and the *Trendtex* cases, below, pp. 254 and 258 respectively. Another influential judgment, which was referred to approvingly in both the *I Congreso* and *Trendtex* cases, is that of the West German Constitutional Court in the *Claim Against the Empire of Iran* (1963) 45 I.L.R. 57. There the Court rejected a plea of immunity in respect of a claim for the cost of repairs to the Iranian Embassy in Cologne. The court stated (p. 80):

The distinction between sovereign and non-sovereign State activities cannot be drawn according to the purpose of the State transaction and whether it stands in a recognizable relation to the sovereign duties of the State. For, ultimately, activities of State, if not wholly then to the widest degree, serve sovereign purposes and duties, and stand in a still recognizable relationship to them. Neither should the distinction depend on whether the State has acted commercially. Commercial activities of States are not different in their nature from other non-sovereign State activities.

As a means for determining the distinction between acts *jure imperii* and *jure gestionis* one should rather refer to the nature of the State transaction or the resulting legal relationships, and not to the motive or purpose of the State activity. It thus depends on whether the foreign State has acted in exercise of its sovereign authority, that is in public law, or like a private person, that is in private law. . . .

The qualification of State activity as sovereign or non-sovereign must in principle be made by national (municipal) law, since international law, at least usually, contains no criteria for this distinction. . . .

[30a] *Egyptian Delta Rice Mills Co.* v. *Comisaria General de Madrid, Annual Digest* 12 (1943–45), p. 103 at p. 104.

The general rule of international law according to which immunity from municipal jurisdiction is granted to foreign States for their sovereign activities does not become bereft of content and lose its character as a rule of law through the national law determining the distinction between acts *jure imperii* and acts *jure gestionis*. Its more precise content derives rather from the national law applicable at any given time. It is not unusual for rules of international law to refer to national law. . . . In this way, for example, certain rights and duties of States depend, according to customary international law and international treaty law, on the nationality of a person. Acquisition and loss of nationality are, however, determined in principle by national law.

Finally, it cannot be of decisive importance that the reference to national law theoretically gives the national legislature the possibility of influencing the scope of the rule of international law through a corresponding formulation of the national law. . . . An improper form of law by the national legislature could . . . be opposed by the recognized international law principle of good faith.

It must be admitted that the application of general international law is made more difficult, and the desired uniformity of law is hindered, if the nature of the State activity determines the distinction between sovereign and non-sovereign acts and national law determines their qualification. The disadvantage is, however, mitigated in that international law restrictions set limits for the qualification of a State activity as an act *jure gestionis* by the national law.

National law can only be employed to distinguish between a sovereign and non-sovereign activity of a foreign State in so far as it cannot exclude from the sovereign sphere, and thus from immunity, such State dealings as belong to the field of State authority in the narrow and proper sense, according to the predominantly-held view of States. In this generally recognizable field of sovereign activity are included transactions relating to foreign affairs and military authority, the legislature, the exercise of police authority, and the administration of justice.

2. *The United States Restatement of the Law (Second): Foreign Relations Law*[31] similarly states that, as in the case of nationality law, international law leaves a large discretion to national law: "In considering what is commercial activity the standard to be applied is that of the state exercising jurisdiction . . . [but] a state must not apply its own standard in an unreasonable manner."

STATE IMMUNITY ACT 1978[32]

(1978, c. 33)

1.—(1) A State is immune from the jurisdiction of the courts of the United Kingdom except as provided in the following provisions of this Part of this Act.

(2) A court shall give effect to the immunity conferred by this section even though the State does not appear in the proceedings in question.

2.—(1) A State is not immune as respects proceedings in respect of which it has submitted to the jurisdiction of the courts of the United Kingdom.

(2) A State may submit after the dispute giving rise to the proceedings has arisen or by a prior written agreement; but a provision in any agreement that it is to be governed by the law of the United Kingdom is not to be regarded as a submission. . . .

---

[31] 1965, para. 69, note a.
[32] See Bowett, (1978) 37 C.L.J. 193; Delaume, 73 A.J.I.L. 185 (1979); Lewis, *State and Diplomatic Immunity*, 1980; Mann (1979) 50 B.Y.I.L. 43; Sinclair, *op. cit.* at p. 241, n. 19 above, pp. 257–265; White, 42 M.L.R. 72 (1979).

3.—(1) A State is not immune as respects proceedings relating to—

(*a*) a commercial transaction entered into by the State; or

(*b*) an obligation of the State which by virtue of a contract (whether a commercial transaction or not) falls to be performed wholly or partly in the United Kingdom.

(2) This section does not apply if the parties to the dispute are States or have otherwise agreed in writing; and subsection (1)(*b*) above does not apply if the contract (not being a commercial transaction) was made in the territory of the State concerned and the obligation in question is governed by its administrative law.

(3) In this section "commercial transaction" means

(*a*) any contract for the supply of goods or services;

(*b*) any loan or other transaction for the provision of finance and any guarantee or indemnity in respect of any such transaction or of any other financial obligation; and

(*c*) any other transaction or activity (whether of a commercial, industrial, financial, professional or other similar character) into which a State enters or in which it engages otherwise than in the exercise of sovereign authority;

but neither paragraph of subsection (1) above applies to a contract of employment between a State and an individual.

4.—(1) A State is not immune as respects proceedings relating to a contract of employment between the State and an individual where the contract was made in the United Kingdom or the work is to be wholly or partly performed there. . . .[32a]

5. A State is not immune as respects proceedings in respect of—

(*a*) death or personal injury; or

(*b*) damage to or loss of tangible property,

caused by an act or omission in the United Kingdom.

6.—(1) A State is not immune as respects proceedings relating to—

(*a*) any interest of the State in, or its possession or use of, immovable property in the United Kingdom; or

(*b*) any obligation of the State arising out of its interest in, or its possession or use of, any such property.

(2) A State is not immune as respects proceedings relating to any interest of the State in movable or immovable property, being an interest arising by way of succession, gift or bona vacantia.

(3) The fact that a State has or claims an interest in any property shall not preclude any court from exercising in respect of it any jurisdiction relating to the estates of deceased persons or persons of unsound mind or to insolvency, the winding up of companies or the administration of trusts.

[32a] s.4(2)(*a*) provides that s.4 does not apply if "at the time when the proceedings are brought the individual is a national of the state concerned." See *Sengupta* v. *Republic of India, The Times*, November 8, 1982 (successful plea of immunity in claim for unfair dismissal by Indian national employed at Indian embassy).

(4) A court may entertain proceedings against a person other than a State notwithstanding that the proceedings relate to property—

(*a*) which is in the possession or control of a State; or

(*b*) in which a State claims an interest,

if the State would not have been immune had the proceedings been brought against it or, in a case within paragraph (*b*) above, if the claim is neither admitted nor supported by prima facie evidence.

7. A State is not immune as respects proceedings relating to—

(*a*) any patent, trade-mark, design or plant breeders' rights belonging to the State and registered or protected in the United Kingdom or for which the State has applied in the United Kingdom;

(*b*) an alleged infringement by the State in the United Kingdom of any patent, trade-mark, design, plant breeders' rights or copyright; or

(*c*) the right to use a trade or business name in the United Kingdom.

8.—(1) A State is not immune as respects proceedings relating to its membership of a body corporate, an unincorporated body or a partnership which—

(*a*) has members other than States; and

(*b*) is incorporated or constituted under the law of the United Kingdom or is controlled from or has its principal place of business in the United Kingdom,

being proceedings arising between the State and the body or its other members or, as the case may be, between the State and the other partners. . . .

9.—(1) Where a State has agreed in writing to submit a dispute which has arisen, or may arise, to arbitration, the State is not immune as respects proceedings in the courts of the United Kingdom which relate to the arbitration.

(2) This section has effect subject to any contrary provision in the arbitration agreement and does not apply to any arbitration agreement between States.

10.—(1) This section applies to—

(*a*) Admiralty proceedings; and

(*b*) proceedings on any claim which could be made the subject of Admiralty proceedings.

(2) A State is not immune as respects—

(*a*) an action in rem against a ship belonging to that State; or

(*b*) an action in personam for enforcing a claim in connection with such a ship,

if, at the time when the cause of action arose, the ship was in use or intended for use for commercial purposes.[33]

(3) Where an action in rem is brought against a ship belonging to a State for enforcing a claim in connection with another ship belonging to that State, subsection (2)(*a*) above does not apply as respects the first-mentioned ship unless, at the time when the cause of action relating to the other ship arose, both ships were in use or intended for use for commercial purposes.

(4) A State is not immune as respects—

(*a*) an action in rem against a cargo belonging to that State if both the cargo and the ship carrying it were, at the time when the cause of action arose, in use or intended for use for commercial purposes; or

---

[33] *Ed.* s.17(1) states that "commercial purposes" means "purposes of such transactions or activities as are mentioned in s.3(3)."

(*b*) an action in personam for enforcing a claim in connection with such a cargo if the ship carrying it was then in use or intended for use as aforesaid.

(5) In the foregoing provisions references to a ship or cargo belonging to a State include references to a ship or cargo in its possession or control or in which it claims an interest; and, subject to subsection (4) above, subsection (2) above applies to property other than a ship as it applies to a ship.

(6) Sections 3 to 5 above do not apply to proceedings of the kind described in subsection (1) above if the State in question is a party to the Brussels Convention and the claim relates to the operation of a ship owned or operated by that State, the carriage of cargo or passengers on any such ship or the carriage of cargo owned by that State on any other ship.

11. A State is not immune as respects proceedings relating to its liability for—

(*a*) value added tax, any duty of customs or excise or any agricultural levy; or
(*b*) rates in respect of premises occupied by it for commercial purposes.

13.—(1) No penalty by way of committal or fine shall be imposed in respect of any failure or refusal by or on behalf of a State to disclose or produce any document or other information for the purposes of proceedings to which it is a party.

(2) Subject to subsections (3) and (4) below—

(*a*) relief shall not be given against a State by way of injunction or order for specific performance or for the recovery of land or other property; and
(*b*) the property of a State shall not be subject to any process for the enforcement of a judgment or arbitration award or, in an action in rem, for its arrest, detention or sale.

[s.13(3) provides that s.13(2) does not apply if the State consents.]

(4) Subsection 2(*b*) above does not prevent the issue of any process in respect of property which is for the time being in use or intended for use for commercial purposes; but, in a case not falling within section 10 above, this subsection applies to property of a State party to the European Convention on State Immunity only if—

(*a*) the process is for enforcing a judgment which is final within the meaning of section 18(1)(*b*) below and the State has made a declaration under Article 24 of the Convention; or
(*b*) the process is for enforcing an arbitration award.

14.—(1) The immunities and privileges conferred by this Part of this Act apply to any foreign or commonwealth State other than the United Kingdom; and references to a State include references to—

(*a*) the sovereign or other head of that State in his public capacity;
(*b*) the government of that State; and
(*c*) any department of that government,

but not to any entity (hereafter referred to as a "separate entity") which is distinct from the executive organs of the government of the State and capable of suing or being sued.

(2) A separate entity is immune from the jurisdiction of the courts of the United Kingdom if, and only if—

(a) the proceedings relate to anything done by it in the exercise of sovereign authority; and
(b) the circumstances are such that a State (or, in the case of proceedings to which section 10 above applies, a State which is not party to the Brussels Convention) would have been so immune.

(3) If a separate entity (not being a State's central bank or other monetary authority) submits to the jurisdiction in respect of proceedings in the case of which it is entitled to immunity by virtue of subsection (2) above, subsections (1) to (4) of section 13 above shall apply to it in respect of those proceedings as if references to a State were references to that entity.

(4) Property of a State's central bank or other monetary authority shall not be regarded for the purposes of subsection (4) of section 13 above as in use or intended for use for commercial purposes; and where any such bank or authority is a separate entity subsections (1) to (3) of that section shall apply to it as if references to a State were references to the bank or authority.

(5) Section 12 above applies to proceedings against the constituent territories of a federal State; and Her Majesty may by Order in Council provide for the other provisions of this Part of this Act to apply to any such constituent territory specified in the Order as they apply to a State.

(6) Where the provisions of this Part of this Act do not apply to the constituent territory by virtue of any such Order subsections (2) and (3) above shall apply to it as if it were a separate entity.

20.—(1) Subject to the provisions of this section and to any necessary modifications, the Diplomatic Privileges Act 1964[34] shall apply to—

(a) a sovereign or other head of State;
(b) members of his family forming part of his household; and
(c) his private servants,

as it applies to the head of a diplomatic mission, to members of his family forming part of his household and to his private servants.

(2) The immunities and privileges conferred by virtue of subsection (1)(a) and (b) above shall not be subject to the restrictions by reference to nationality or residence mentioned in Article 37(1) or 38 in Schedule 1 to the said Act of 1964. . . .

(5) This section applies to the sovereign or other head of any State on which immunities and privileges are conferred by Part I of this Act and is without prejudice to the application of that Part to any such sovereign or head of State in his public capacity.

21. A certificate by or on behalf of the Secretary of State shall be conclusive evidence on any question—

(a) whether any country is a State for the purposes of Part I of this Act, whether any territory is a constituent territory of a federal State for those purposes or as to the person or persons to be regarded for those purposes as the head or government of a State; . . .

---

[34] *Ed.* Below, p. 279.

Notes

1. The Act came into force on November 22, 1978; it does not have retrospective effect.[35] At common law, the British courts had abandoned the doctrine of absolute immunity, in *The Philippine Admiral* [1977] A.C. 373 (J.C.) (actions *in rem*) and *Trendtex Trading Corpn.* v. *Central Bank of Nigeria* [1977] Q.B. 529 (C.A.) (actions in personam), just before the 1978 Act was enacted. Although there may yet be cases to be decided on the basis of common law, the materials in this section concentrate on the new statutory law; earlier cases are referred to only to illustrate the meaning of the present law.

2. The Act was introduced partly to permit ratification of the 1926 Brussels Convention and the 1972 European Convention, see above, p. 241, and certain of the complications in its text result from this objective. The Act was also a response to the fear in the City that the United Kingdom would increasingly lose business to other jurisdictions if it did not offer better legal security for persons trading with states.[36] The Act applies to all foreign states, except for the provisions about the recognition of judgments (ss.18–9) which apply only to parties to the 1972 European Convention.

3. The pattern of the Act (like that of the 1972 European Convention), is to provide for general immunity (s.1(1)), subject to a list of exceptions (ss.2–11) which accord with the doctrine of restrictive immunity. Most of the exceptions are limited by requirements linking the case with the United Kingdom (*e.g.* the contract to be performed in the United Kingdom: section 3(1)(*b*)). These are aimed at compliance with the rules limiting the jurisdiction of states in customary international and hence assisting in the execution of judgments against states that are impleaded.

4. Section 2(2) reverses the rule in *Kahan* v. *Pakistan Federation* [1951] 2 K.B. 1003 (C.A.) by which submission to jurisdiction could only be made before the court and not by prior written agreement. It is quite common for a waiver of immunity to be included in a loan or other financial agreement. A state is deemed to have waived its immunity if it institutes proceedings, or intervenes, or takes any step in the proceedings (s.2(3)).

5. The definition of "commercial transactions" in section 3(3) covers *all* contracts and financial transactions of the kinds listed in section 3(*a*)(*b*); there is no need for the court to consider the difficult question whether they result from the "exercise of sovereign authority." They are, by definition, "commercial transactions." Hence neither the purpose for which the goods or services are wanted nor the fact that the contract or loan is one that could only be made by a governmental entity is relevant. A contract for the supply of cement for an army barracks (*Trendtex* case, below, p. 258) or of military equipment (or of technicians to train soldiers to use it) would come within section 3(3)(*a*). A loan to or by a Government would similarly fall within section 3(3)(*b*), as would the letter of credit in the *Trendtex* case. In the case of "any other transaction or activity" in the sense of section 3(3)(*c*), a court will have to decide whether it results from "an exercise of sovereign authority." On the distinction between acts *iure imperii* and *iure gestionis*, see p. 246, above. In such cases, the United Kingdom courts are likely to look to the approach developed in the *Trendtex* and *I Congreso* cases, below, pp. 258 and 254 respectively. Mann[37] argues that the word "activity" allows claims in tort to be brought against a state where they do not result from an "exercise of sovereign authority." Thus a claim in libel, such as that in *Krajina* v. *Tass Agency*, below, p. 261, n. 48, could not be met by a defence of state immunity unless the tort was committed "in the exercise of sovereign authority." For another example of an "activity" that would probably come within section 3(3)(*c*), see the facts of *U.S.* v. *Dolfus Mieg*, next note. Section 3(1)(*b*) adds to section 3(1)(*a*) by denying immunity in certain non-"commercial transaction" cases in contract.

---

[35] s.23. Exceptionally, s.12 (service of process and judgments in default of appearance) applies retrospectively.

[36] See Lord Hailsham L.C., *Hansard*, H.L., Vol. 389, col. 1502. March 16, 1978.

[37] *Op. cit.* p. 247, n. 32, above, p. 52. This is in addition to tort claims allowed by ss.5–6.

6. Section 6(4) deals with indirect impleading, *i.e.* the situation in which proceedings are brought against someone other than the state but which concern property within a state's ownership, possession, or control. A defence of state immunity is allowed in such a case under section 6(4) only if the defence would be available if the proceedings had been brought against the state itself. Under the Act, therefore, the plaintiff would still not have succeeded in respect of the 51 gold bars in *U.S.* v. *Dolfus Mieg* [1952] A.C. 582 (H.L.). In that case, the plaintiffs claimed, as owners, the return of gold bars deposited by certain Governments with the Bank of England under a contract of bailment, including 51 bars still in the Bank vaults. Although the proceedings were brought against the Bank, a plea of immunity was upheld because the foreign Governments concerned had an immediate right to possession under the contract of bailment and would have been indirectly impleaded had the case gone ahead. Since the bars (which had been taken from the plaintiffs by the German authorities in the Second World War, then recovered by American forces, and finally placed in the possession of the Allied Governments of France, the United Kingdom and the United States, pending restitution proceedings) had undoubtedly been deposited with the Bank by those Governments "in the exercise of sovereign authority," section 3(3)(c) would apply so that immunity would now be available to the American and French Governments if sued themselves in a United Kingdom court.

The *prima facie* evidence requirement in an "interest" case inserted at the end of section 6(4) confirms *Juan Ismael and Co.* v. *Indonesian Govt.* [1955] A.C. 72 (H.L.).

7. Section 13 lists certain procedural privileges which apply whether or not the state is entitled to state immunity on the facts of the case. Most significantly, in the absence of a state's consent, (i) a *Mareva* injunction[38] is not available to prevent property being taken out of the jurisdiction pending litigation and (ii) a state's property may not be used for the enforcement of a judgment against it unless it is property that is "for the time being in use or intended for use for commercial purposes."[39] On the attachment of ships, see section 10. These limitations are consonant with the distinction between immunity from jurisdiction and immunity from execution, it being generally accepted that the dignity of states and good international relations mean that immunity from compulsory execution can less easily be dispensed with than jurisdictional immunity.[40] Such an explanation may not satisfy a claimant who wins judgment against a state but is unable to enforce it. On the special position of central banks, see below, p. 264.

8. Section 14: see the notes to the *Trendtex* case, below, p. 258.

9. Section 20: The 1978 Act applies to a sovereign or other head of state acting in his *public* capacity. Section 20 provides that such a person in his *private* capacity is, together with his family and servants, entitled to the privileges accorded to the head of a diplomatic mission, etc., under the Diplomatic Privileges Act 1964, below, p. 279. Previously, the position of a sovereign in his personal capacity was regulated by common law.

10. Section 21(a) is consistent with *Duff Development Co.* v. *Kelantan* [1924] A.C. 797(H.L.) The statements *obiter dicta* in that case to the effect that if the Foreign Office did not respond to a request for a certificate the courts would have taken their own decision presumably still apply.

---

[38] See *Mareva Compania Naviera* v. *International Bulkcarriers* [1975] 2 Lloyd's Rep. 509 (C.A.).

[39] For the meaning of "commercial purposes," see p. 249, n. 33, above.

[40] On the rule by which states are immune from execution in international law, see Crawford, 75 A.J.I.L. 820 (1981). The 1972 European Convention on State Immunity, Article 20, obliges parties to execute judgments against them in the courts of other parties.

I CONGRESO DEL PARTIDO[41]

[1981] 3 W.L.R. 329 House of Lords

In 1973, Cubazucar, a Cuban state trading enterprise, contracted to sell sugar to a Chilean company. One shipment made under the contract was carried on the *Playa Larga*—a ship flying the Cuban flag, owned by the Cuban Government and operated by Mambisa, a second Cuban state trading enterprise. Such enterprises are legally independent of the Government and not a department of Government under Cuban law; it was not claimed in argument that they attracted sovereign immunity. The cargo was being discharged in Valparaiso when the socialist Allende Government in Chile was overthrown by the right-wing Pinochet Government, of which Cuba disapproved. Thereupon, the *Playa Larga* left Valparaiso on orders from Mambisa (acting on instructions from the Cuban Government) without discharging the remainder of its cargo, which was later sold to someone else in Cuba. A second shipment under the contract was carried on the *Marble Islands*—a ship then flying the Somali flag and owned by a Liechtenstein company which had been chartered by Mambisa for use by Cubazucar. The *Marble Islands*, which was on the high seas on its way to Valparaiso when the *coup d'état* occurred in Chile, was ordered by Mambisa, on Cuban Government instructions, to sail to North Vietnam. During the journey, it became a Cuban ship owned by the Cuban Government. On arrival in Haiphong, the cargo was (i) sold by the master, on behalf of Mambisa, to Alimport, a third Cuban state trading enterprise, and (ii) donated by the latter to the North Vietnamese people. Both of these actions were taken in accordance with Cuban Government instructions.

In this case, the owners of the cargoes of the two ships brought proceedings *in rem* against the Cuban Government for breach of contract (for non-delivery) and in tort (for detinue or conversion). The *I Congreso*, another ship owned by the Cuban Government, was arrested in British waters on the application of the plaintiffs, and the claims were then brought against the Government in the English High Court. The Cuban Government entered a defence of state immunity. The defence was upheld by Goff J. and by a divided two man Court of Appeal (in which Waller L.J. and Lord Denning M.R. voted for and against immunity respectively). The plaintiffs appealed to the House of Lords. The case was governed by the common law preceding the 1978 Act.

LORD WILBERFORCE. On the basis of these cases [*The Philippine Admiral* [1977] A.C. 373 and *Trendtex Trading Corp.* v. *Central Bank of Nigeria*, below, p. 258] . . . I have no doubt that the "restrictive" doctrine should be applied to the present case. . . . The issue is as to the limits of the doctrine. . . .

The limitation . . . under the so called "restrictive theory," arises from the willingness of states to enter into commercial, or other private law, transactions with individuals. It appears to have two main foundations: (a) It is necessary in the interest of justice to individuals having such transactions with states to allow them to bring such transactions before the courts. (b) To require a state to answer a claim based upon such transactions does not involve a challenge to or inquiry into any act of sovereignty or governmental act of that state. It is, in accepted phrases, neither a threat to the dignity of that state, nor any interference with its sovereign functions. . . .

The appellants contend that we have here (I take the case of *Playa Larga* for the present . . .) a commercial transaction, *viz.*, a trading vessel, owned by the Republic of Cuba, carrying goods, under normal commercial arrangements.

[41] See Fox (1982) 98 L.Q.R. 94.

Any claim arising out of this situation is, they assert, a claim of private law, and it is irrelevant that the purpose, for which the act giving rise to the claim was committed, may have been of a political character (sc. briefly, to break off trading relations with a state, Chile, with which Cuba was not friendly). . . .

In my opinion this argument, though in itself generally acceptable, burkes, or begs, the essential question, which is "what is the relevant act?" It assumes that this is the initial entry into a commercial transaction and that this entry irrevocably confers upon later acts a commercial, or private law, character. . . .

In many cases the process of deciding upon the character of the relevant act presents no difficulty. In *The Philippine Admiral* [1977] A.C. 373, once it was accepted that the contract for goods, the obligation to repay disbursements, and the charterparty, were of a trading or commercial character, the breach of these obligations was clearly within the same area, none the less because committed by a state. . . .

In other situations it may not be easy to decide whether the act complained of is within the area of non-immune activity or is an act of sovereignty wholly outside it. The activities of states cannot always be compartmentalised into trading or governmental activities; and what is one to make of a case where a state has, and in the relevant circumstances, clearly displayed, both a commercial interest and a sovereign or governmental interest? To which is the critical action to be attributed?

. . . Under the "restrictive" theory the court has first to characterise the activity into which the defendant state has entered. Having done this, and (assumedly) found it to be of a commercial, or private law, character, it may take the view that contractual breaches, or torts, prima facie fall within the same sphere of activity. It should then be for the defendant state to make a case (*cf. Juan Ysmael*)[42] that the act complained of is outside that sphere, and within that of sovereign action. . . .

The conclusion which emerges is that in considering, under the "restrictive" theory, whether state immunity should be granted or not, the court must consider the whole context in which the claim against the state is made, with a view to deciding whether the relevant act(s) upon which the claim is based, should, in that context, be considered as fairly within an area of activity, trading or commercial, or otherwise of a private law character, in which the state has chosen to engage, or whether the relevant act(s) should be considered as having been done outside that area, and within the sphere of governmental or sovereign activity. . . .

(a) *Playa Larga* . . . The appellants are certainly able to show, as a starting point, that this vessel was engaged in trade with the consent, if not with the active participation, of the Republic of Cuba. . . . The question is whether the acts which gave rise to an alleged cause of action were done in the context of the trading relationship, or were done by the government of the Republic of Cuba acting wholly outside the trading relationship and in exercise of the power of the state. . . . In my opinion it must be answered on a broad view of the facts as a whole and not upon narrow issues as to Cuba's possible contractual liability. I do not think that there is any doubt that the decision not to complete unloading at Valparaiso, or to discharge at Callao, was a political decision taken by the government of the Republic of Cuba for political and non-commercial

---

[42] *Ed*. See above, p. 253.

reasons. . . . The change of government in Chile, and the events at Santiago in which the Cuban Embassy was involved, provoked a determination on the part of the government of Cuba to break off and discontinue trading relations with Chile. There may also have been concern for the safety of *Playa Larga* at Valparaiso. . . .

Does this call for characterisation of the act of the Republic of Cuba in withdrawing *Playa Larga* and denying the cargo to its purchasers as done "jure imperii?" In my opinion it does not. Everything done by the Republic of Cuba in relation to *Playa Larga* could have been done, and, so far as evidence goes, was done, as owners of the ship: it exercised, and had no need to exercise, sovereign powers. It acted, as any owner of the ship would act, through Mambisa, the managing operators. It invoked no governmental authority. . . .

It may well be that those instructions [to Mambisa] would not have been issued, as they were, if the owner of *Playa Larga* had been anyone but a state: it is almost certainly the case that there was no commercial reason for the decision. But these consequences follow inevitably from the entry of states into the trading field. If immunity were to be granted the moment that any decision taken by the trading state were shown to be not commercially, but politically, inspired, the "restrictive" theory would almost cease to have any content and trading relations as to state-owned ships would become impossible. It is precisely to protect private traders against politically inspired breaches, or wrongs, that the restrictive theory allows states to be brought before a municipal court. It may be too stark to say of a state "once a trader always a trader": but, in order to withdraw its action from the sphere of acts done jure gestionis, a state must be able to point to some act clearly done jure imperii. Though, with much hesitation, I feel obligated to differ on this issue from the conclusion of the learned judge, I respectfully think that he well put this ultimate test [1978] Q.B. 500, 528:

> " . . . it is not just that the purpose or motive of the act is to serve the purposes of the state, but that the act is of its own character a governmental act, as opposed to an act which any private citizen can perform."

As to the *Playa Larga*, therefore, I find myself in agreement with Lord Denning M.R. and would allow the appeal.

(b) *Marble Islands* . . . I can find no basis on which it can be said that the cargo owners entered into any business relationship with the Republic of Cuba. There can be no doubt, as subsequent events showed, that *Marble Islands* continued to be operated by Mambisa, and though the ownership of *Marble Islands* by the Republic of Cuba is a factor to be considered, what is decisive on the question of immunity is what the Republic of Cuba did as regards the cargo when the ship arrived at Haiphong. . . .

The arrangements for the sale of the sugar are then discussed.

The Republic of Cuba never entered into these operations. The captain did not purport to act on its behalf. . . . Its actions were confined to directing transfer of the sugar to North Vietnam, and to the enactment of Law No. 1256 [which froze and blocked Chilean assets]. All of this was done in a governmental capacity: any attack upon its actions must call in question its acts as a sovereign state.

. . . I cannot agree that there was ever any purely commercial obligation upon the Republic of Cuba or any binding commercial obligation: the republic never assumed any such obligation; it never entered the trading area; the cargo owners never entered into a commercial relation with it. I agree that the purpose, above, is not decisive but it may throw some light upon the nature of what was done. The acts of the Republic of Cuba were and remained in their nature purely governmental. The fact is, that if any wrong (contractually or delictually) was done as regards the cargo it was done by Mambisa . . . in my opinion . . . the acts complained of as regards the Republic of Cuba were acts jure imperii and so covered by immunity. I would dismiss the *Marble Islands* appeal.

LORD DIPLOCK.

Although agreeing with Lord Wilberforce that the restrictive immunity doctrine should apply and that no immunity should be allowed in respect of the *Playa Larga*, Lord Diplock disagreed with him in respect of the *Marble Islands*:

The right asserted by the master to discharge and sell the perishable cargo in Haiphong is . . . fairly and squarely based on private law (jus gestionis), the contractual terms contained in the bills of lading and the Commercial Code in force in Cuba. There is no suggestion that the cargo had been requisitioned by the Cuban government jure imperii nor is there any mention of the Law No. 1256. . . .

So all that was done in Haiphong in November to Iansa's sugar laden on *Marble Islands* was done upon the instructions of the Cuban government in purported reliance upon Mambisa's rights in private law (jus gestionis) and not upon any jus imperii of the Cuban state itself. It was only after the property in the sugar had been purportedly transferred to Alimport under the terms of the sale contract by delivery of the warehouse warrants that the sugar was then handed over by Alimport as a gift by the state of Cuba to the government of Vietnam.

So the legal position of the Cuban government after October 13, 1973, was that it then acquired the ownership of a trading vessel *Marble Islands* then in mid-Pacific engaged in carrying cargo belonging to Iansa upon a voyage which the master claimed was authorised by a power to deviate contained in the bill of lading under which the cargo had been shipped. Mambisa from being demise charterer of *Marble Islands* had become managing operator of the vessel on behalf of the Cuban government, and legal possession of the cargo laden on her passed from Mambisa as former disponent owner to the Cuban government itself which in terms of English law became the "bailee" of Iansa's sugar. Thereafter, as the evidence discloses, everything that was done by the master was done on the express directions of the Cuban government; the Director and Senior Legal Adviser of the Ministry of Merchant Marine and Ports being sent to Haiphong in November to supervise what the master did there and the legal form and nature of the steps he took. . . .

Unless the master's assertions in the documents that the discharge and sale of the cargo was authorised by the bills of lading was right in law, the facts to which I have particularly referred would disclose in English law a prima facie case of conversion of the cargo by the Cuban government as bailee when the master sold and delivered it to Alimport on the instructions of the government in purported exercise of rights under private law. The relevant transaction, *viz.* the discharge and sale of the cargo to Alimport at Haiphong was, as it seems to me, deliberately treated by the Cuban government as being effected under private law and not in the exercise of any sovereign powers.

For these reasons I for my part would allow the appeal in the case of the *Marble Islands* as well as in the case of the *Playa Larga.*

Lord Edmund Davies delivered a speech agreeing wholly with Lord Wilberforce. Lords Keith and Bridge agreed with Lord Wilberforce, except that they agreed with Lord Diplock that the appeal should also be allowed in respect of the *Marble Islands* as well as the *Playa Larga.* The claim of immunity was therefore disallowed in respect of both ships.

Appeal allowed.

Notes

1. The State Immunity Act 1978 would govern the facts of the case if they were to occur now. Does section 3 allow of the same kind of reasoning as that adopted by the House of Lords? Can one, that is, look to the nature of the act complained of (the act in breach of contract, or of conversion, etc.)? Or must one look only to the nature of the transaction or activity in respect of which it occurs (as would previously seem to have been the approach at common law)? In the latter case, was there a "commercial transaction" entered into by Cuba in the case of the *Marble Islands*?

2. A pre-1978 Act case that would be decided the same way on its facts under the Act was *Planmount Ltd.* v. *Republic of Zaire* [1981] 1 All E.R. (Q.B.). In that case, a builder sued the defendant for the balance of monies due under a contract for repair work done to the official residence of the ambassador of Zaire in London. A defence of state immunity was rejected at common law (the 1978 Act not being in force), Lloyd J. relying upon the *Trendtex* case. *cf.* the facts of the *Claim against the Empire of Iran*, above, p. 246.

TRENDTEX TRADING CORP. v. CENTRAL BANK OF NIGERIA[43]

[1977] Q.B. 529. Court of Appeal

In 1975, the Central Bank of Nigeria issued a letter of credit in favour of the plaintiffs, a Swiss company, for the price of cement to be sold by the plaintiffs to an English company which had secured a contract with the Nigerian Government to supply it with cement for the construction of an army barracks in Nigeria. When, under instructions from the Nigerian Government (which was taking steps to extricate itself from the Nigerian Cement Scandal created by its predecessor Government),[43a] the bank refused to honour the letter of credit, the plaintiffs brought an action *in personam* against the bank in the English High Court. The bank successfully claimed sovereign immunity before Mr. J. Donaldson. The plaintiffs appealed.

LORD DENNING M.R. The Central Bank of Nigeria claims that it cannot be sued in this country on the letter of credit; because it is entitled to sovereign immunity. . . . The doctrine of sovereign immunity is based on international

---

[43] See Markensis (1977) C.L.J. 211 and White, 26 I.C.L.Q. 674 (1977).

[43a] Huge quantities of cement had been ordered from different sources—far more than Nigeria needed or the port of Lagos could handle. The new Nigerian Government took steps similar to those taken in this case against suppliers in other cases, leading to comparable court proceedings in the U.S.A. and the F.R.G.: see 16 I.L.M. 469 (1977). A doctrine of restrictive immunity was applied against the defendant's claim of state immunity in those cases also.

law. . . . Like all rules of international law, this rule is said to arise out of the consensus of the civilized nations of the world. . . .

To my mind this notion of a consensus is a fiction. . . . The courts of every country differ in their application of it. Some grant absolute immunity. Others grant limited immunity, with each defining the limits differently. . . . Yet this does not mean that there is no rule of international law on the subject. . . . It is, I think, for the courts of this country to define the rule as best they can, seeking guidance from the decisions of the courts of other countries, from the jurists who have studied the problem, from treaties and conventions and, above all, defining the rule in terms which are consonant with justice rather than adverse to it. . . .

Responding to the fact that in *The Parlement Belge* (1880) 5 P.D. 197 the Court of Appeal had adopted as common law a rule of absolute immunity in reliance upon the customary international law then in force, Lord Denning continued:

A fundamental question arises for decision: what is the place of international law in our English law? One school of thought holds to the doctrine of incorporation. It says that the rules of international law are incorporated into English law automatically and considered to be part of English law unless they are in conflict with an Act of Parliament. The other school of thought holds to the doctrine of transformation. It says that the rules of international law are not to be considered as part of English law except insofar as they have been already adopted and made part of our law by the decisions of the judges, or by Act of Parliament, or long established custom. The difference is vital when you are faced with a change in the rules of international law. Under the doctrine of incorporation, when the rules of international law change, our English law changes with them. But, under the doctrine of transformation, the English law does not change. It is bound by precedent.

. . . As between these two schools of thought, I now believe that the doctrine of incorporation is correct. Otherwise I do not see that our courts could ever recognise a change in the rules of international law. . . . International law does change, and the courts have applied the changes without the aid of any Act of Parliament. Thus, when the rules of international law were changed (by the force of public opinion) so as to condemn slavery, the English courts were justified in applying the modern rules of international law. . . . Again, the extent of territorial waters varies from time to time according to the rule of international law current at the time, and the courts will apply it accordingly: see *R. v. Kent Justices, ex parte Lye.*[44]

. . . Seeing that the rules of international law have changed—and do change—and that the courts have given effect to the changes without any Act of Parliament, it follows to my mind inexorably that the rules of international law, as existing from time to time, do form part of our English law. It follows, too, that a decision of this court, as to what was the ruling of international law 50 or 60 years ago, is not binding on this court today. International law knows no rule of stare decisis. If this court today is satisfied that the rule of international law on a subject has changed from what it was 50 or 60 years ago, it can give effect to that change, and apply the change in our English law, without waiting for the House of Lords to do it.

---

[44] [1967] 2 K.B. 153, at pp. 173, 189; [1967] 1 All E.R. 560, at pp. 564, 574.

After reviewing the evidence and concluding that international law had changed to a doctrine of restrictive immunity, Lord Denning continued:

In one respect already the Privy Council have abandoned the absolute theory and accepted the restrictive theory. It is in respect of actions *in rem*: see *Philippine Admiral (Owners)* v. *Wallem Shipping (Hong Kong) Ltd.*[45] But, unfortunately, the Privy Council seem to have thought that the absolute theory still applied to actions *in personam*. They said: "It is no doubt open to the House of Lords to decide otherwise but it may fairly be said to be at the least unlikely that it would do so." That is a dismal forecast. It is out of line with the good sense shown in the rest of the opinion of the Privy Council. . . . Such reasoning is of general application. It covers actions *in personam*. In those actions too, the restrictive theory is more consonant with justice. So it should be applied to them. . . .

It was suggested that the original contracts for cement were . . . for the building of barracks for the army. On this account it was said that the contracts of purchase were acts of a governmental nature—*jure imperii* and not of a commercial nature—*jure gestionis*. They were like a contract of purchase of boots for the army. But I do not think this should affect the question of immunity. If a government department goes into the market places of the world and buys boots or cement—as a commercial transaction—that government department should be subject to all the rules of the market place. The seller is not concerned with the purpose to which the purchaser intends to put the goods.

There is another answer. The plaintiffs here are not suing on the contracts of purchase. They are claiming on the letter of credit which is an entirely separate contract. . . . The letter of credit was issued in London through a London bank in the ordinary course of commercial dealings. It is completely within the territorial jurisdiction of our courts. I do not think it is open to the government of Nigeria to claim sovereign immunity in respect of it. . . .

If we are still bound to apply the doctrine of absolute immunity, there is, even so, an important question arising on it. The doctrine grants immunity to a foreign government or its department of state or any body which can be regarded as an "alter ego or organ" of the government. . . . In some countries the government departments conduct all their business through their own offices—even ordinary commercial dealings—without setting up separate corporations or legal entities. In other countries they set up separate corporations or legal entities which are under the complete control of the department, but which enter into commercial transactions, buying and selling goods, owning and chartering ships, just like any ordinary trading concern. This difference in internal arrangements ought not to affect the availability of immunity in international law. A foreign department of state ought not to lose its immunity simply because it conducts some of its activities by means of a separate legal entity. It was so held by this court in *Baccus SRL* v. *Servicio Nacional del Trigo.*[46]

Another problem arises because of the internal laws of many countries which grant immunities and privileges to their own organisations. Some organisations can sue, or be sued, in their courts. Others cannot. In England we have had for

[45] [1976] 2 W.L.R. 214, at p. 233; [1976] 1 All E.R. 78, at pp. 95, 96.
[46] [1957] 1 Q.B. 438; [1956] 3 All E.R. 715.

centuries special immunities and privileges for "the Crown," a phrase which has been held to cover many governmental departments and many emanations of government departments but not nationalised commercial undertakings: see *Tamlin* v. *Hannaford*.[47] The phrase "the Crown" is so elastic that under the Crown Proceedings Act 1947, the Treasury has issued a list of government departments covered by the Act. It includes even the Forestry Commission. It cannot be right that international law should grant or refuse absolute immunity, according to the immunities granted internally. I would put on one side, therefore, our cases about the privileges, prerogatives and exceptions of "the Crown."

It is often said that a certificate by the ambassador, saying whether or not an organisation is a department of state, is of much weight, though not decisive: see *Krajina* v. *Tass Agency*.[48] But even this is not to my mind satisfactory. What is the test which the ambassador is to apply? In the absence of any test, an ambassador may apply the test of control, asking himself: is the organisation under the control of a minister of state? On such a test, he might certify any nationalised undertaking to be a department of state. He might certify that a press agency or an agricultural corporation (which carried out ordinary commercial dealings) was a department of state, simply because it was under the complete control of the government.

I confess that I can think of no satisfactory test except that of looking to the functions and control of the organisation. I do not think that it should depend on the foreign law alone. I would look to all the evidence to see whether the organisation was under government control and exercised governmental functions. That is the way in which we looked at it in *Mellenger* v. *New Brunswick Development Corpn.* [1971] 1 W.L.R. 604 (C.A.) . . .

At the hearing we were taken through the Act of 1958 under which the Central Bank of Nigeria was established, and the amendments to the Act by later decrees. All the relevant provisions were closely examined; and we had the benefit of expert evidence on affidavit which was most helpful.[49] The upshot of it all may be summarised as follows. (1) The Central Bank of Nigeria is a central bank modelled on the Bank of England. (2) It has governmental functions in that it issues legal tender; it safeguards the international value of the currency; and it acts as banker and financial adviser to the government. (3) Its affairs are under a great deal of government control in that the Federal Executive Council may overrule the board of directors on monetary and banking policy and on internal administrative policy. (4) It acts as banker for other banks in Nigeria and abroad, and maintains accounts with other banks. It acts as banker for the states within the Federation, but has few, if any, private customers.

[47] [1950] 1 K.B. 18; [1949] 2 All E.R. 327.
[48] [1949] 2 All E.R. 274. In this case, the plaintiff sought damages for an alleged libel in a newspaper published by the defendant. The latter was described in the Russian statute establishing it as "the central information organ of the U.S.S.R." and as enjoying "all the rights of a legal person." The Ambassador of the U.S.S.R. to the U.K. certified that the defendant was "a department of state of the Soviet State . . . exercising the rights of a legal entity." The Court of Appeal held, unanimously, that the defendant was a department of state and entitled to immunity as such under the doctrine of absolute immunity. The Ambassador's certificate, although not conclusive, had sufficiently established this.
[49] *Ed.* This spoke of the bank as the agent of the Government and as being under its control; it did not refer to the bank as a Department of Government.

In these circumstances I have found it difficult to decide whether or not the Central Bank of Nigeria should be considered in international law a department of the Federation of Nigeria, even though it is a separate legal entity. But, on the whole, I do not think it should be.

SHAW L.J. Whether a particular organisation is to be accorded the status of a department of government or not must depend on its constitution, its powers and duties and its activities. . . . The bank is, in the first place, a statutory corporation whose personality, powers and legal attributes are determined by the Central Bank of Nigeria Act 1958. . . . Nowhere in that legislation is it called anything but a bank; . . . The 52 sections of the principal Act . . . contain no direct indication that the bank is a department of the government and there are many indications which deny it that status. The very name has a commercial ring. Its powers do not identify it with the government and in some respects preclude identification with the government. . . .

Apart from these matters there is an important practical consideration. . . . Those who contemplate entering into transactions with bodies which may be in a position to claim sovereign immunity are entitled at least to the opportunity of assessing any special risk which may arise. How can they know that such a risk lurks in dealing with a body which assumes a guise and bears a title appropriate to a commercial or financial institution? . . . There is no rule of law which demands this; but where the issue of status trembles on a fine edge, the absence of any positive indication that the body in question was intended to possess sovereign status and its attendant privileges must perforce militate against the view that it enjoys that status or is entitled to those privileges. This is especially the case where the opportunity to define the status of the institution concerned in clear and express terms has existed from the very inception, or indeed conception, of that institution—as in this case.

. . . It is clear enough that the bank was the subserving agent of the government in a variety of activities but this is not in my judgment adequate to constitute it as an organ or department of government. I cannot find in the constitution of the bank or in the functions it performs or in the activities it pursues or in all those matters looked at together any compelling or indeed satisfactory basis for the conclusion that it is so related to the Government of Nigeria as to form part of it. Accordingly I would hold that the bank is not entitled to the immunity which it claims. . . .

Shaw L.J. then, like Lord Denning, applied the restrictive doctrine of immunity and found that it did not allow immunity on the facts. In the course of doing so, he made the following comments on the incorporation-transformation argument.

However, the argument continues in this way. When once a rule of international law has been recognised and adopted and applied by an English court a transformation of the English law is brought about whereby the adopted rule becomes part of the corpus of English law. Thenceforth it cannot be changed save by a decision of a higher court than that which first applied it or else by legislation. This was the view expressed by a majority [Lawton and Scarman L.J.J.] of the Court of Appeal in *Thai-Europe Tapioca Service Ltd.* v. *Government of Pakistan* [1975] 1 W.L.R. 1485 . . . It is with diffidence that I venture to suggest that there may be a flaw in the reasoning which led to their conclusion as to the application of the principle of stare decisis. . . . May it not be that the true principle as to the application of international law is that the English courts must at any given time discover what the prevailing international rule is and apply that rule? . . .

What *is* immutable is the principle of English law that the law of nations (not what *was* the law of nations) must be applied in the courts of England. The rule of stare decisis operates to preclude a court from overriding a decision which binds it in regard to a particular rule of (international) law, it does not prevent a court from applying a rule which did not exist when the earlier decision was made if the new rule has had the effect in international law of extinguishing the old rule. The judgment in *The Parlement Belge*, 5 P.D. 197 cannot be a binding authority as to what form the doctrine of sovereign immunity would take a century after the judgment was delivered. . . .

Lawton L.J. expressed concern as to the possible prejudice which might result to those engaged in international trade if changes in international law brought about ipso facto corresponding changes in the law of England. But even the law of England changes quite apart from what may be happening to international law. Moreover, changes in rules of international law do not come about abruptly; and changes will not be recognised in an English court without convincing support. Those engaged in world commerce will not be insensible to the incidence of such changes over the years. Lastly there must be a greater risk of confusion if precepts discarded outside England by a majority (or perhaps all) of civilised states are preserved as effective in the English courts in the sort of judicial aspic.

Notes

1. The appeal was allowed unanimously. Stephenson L.J. agreed with the other two judges on the status of the Bank and that international law had changed to a doctrine of restrictive immunity. Unlike the other two, however, Stephenson L.J. (like the majority in the *Tapioca* case) felt himself bound by precedent to follow the doctrine of absolute immunity.

2. The current rule indicating whose acts are to be treated as state acts attracting immunity is in 1978 Act, section 14, above, p. 250. A department of government under a foreign state's law is entitled to immunity in respect of its acts even though it has a separate legal personality under that law. This is consistent with *Baccus* v. *S.R.L. Servicio Nacional del Trigo* [1957] 1 Q.B. 438 (C.A.) in which the plaintiff Italian company and the defendants made a contract for the sale of rye which contained an arbitration clause giving jurisdiction over disputes arising under the contract to the English High Court. The plaintiffs initiated proceedings under the clause but the defendants pleaded state immunity on the ground that, although formed as a separate legal person under Spanish law, they were nonetheless a Department of State of the Spanish Government. The Court of Appeal (Jenkins and Parker L.JJ., Singleton L.J. dissenting) upheld this plea in reliance upon affidavit evidence from the Spanish ambassador and a Spanish legal expert to the effect that the defendants were in Spanish law a Department of the Spanish Ministry of Agriculture. Although the same conclusion (that the defendants attracted immunity as a department of government) would be reached under section 14, immunity would nonetheless not be allowed on the facts of the case because the contract was a "commercial transaction": section 3(3)(*a*).

In the *Trendtex* case, the Court of Appeal looked not only to Nigerian law but also to the functions of the bank and its relationship with the Government when deciding whether it should be classified as a department of government. Section 14 would seem to limit itself to the first of these considerations. (If so, it is open to the criticism which Lord Denning makes, *viz.* that differences in "internal arrangements ought not to affect the availability of immunity in international law.") State trading agencies of the sort typical of socialist countries would thus qualify as departments of state if they are classified as such under the local law, but not otherwise.[50] The Cuban agencies in the *I Congreso* case above, p. 254, would not qualify. Nor would United Kingdom public corporations such as the Post Office and the Civil Aviation Authority. It seems likely that, when applying section 14, the courts will continue to rely upon expert evidence and the affidavits of ambassadors to establish the legal status of an entity as they had done at common law: see the *Trendtex* case, the *Baccus* case and the *Krajina* case.

3. A "separate entity" under section 14 (*i.e.* one that is not a department of state but that is capable of being sued) is not entitled to state immunity unless it is acting "in the exercise of sovereign authority."[51] Here again (as when interpreting section 3(3)(*c*)) the courts will have to develop their own distinction between acts *iure imperii* and acts *iure gestionis*: see above, p. 252. Sinclair[52] suggests that certain of the functions of a body such as the Civil Aviation Authority (*e.g.* the licensing of carriers) might qualify for immunity.

4. Under section 14(5) the "constituent territories of a federal state" do not qualify for immunity under the Act unless and to the extent that an Order in Council is made to the contrary in respect of particular territories.[53] To this extent, the decision in *Mellenger* v. *New Brunswick Development Corp.* [1971] 1 W.L.R. 604 (C.A.) Canadian Province of New Brunswick entitled to immunity) is reversed.

5. In the *Trendtex* case, the plaintiffs were granted a *Mareva* injunction ordering that assets held by the bank in a bank account in London remain within the jurisdiction pending the outcome of the case. As a result of section 14(4), such an injunction could not be granted. The United States Foreign Sovereign Immunities Act 1976, s.1611, contains a similar provision which was justified as follows:

> "If execution could be levied on such funds without an explicit waiver, deposit of foreign funds in the U.S. might be discouraged. Moreover, execution against the reserves of foreign states could cause significant foreign relations problems."[54]

Note that section 14(4) means that, unlike other state property, the property of a central bank is not subject to execution *even if it is being used, etc., for commercial purposes*. Section 14(4) also grants central banks the other procedural privileges allowed by section 13, as to which see above, p. 253. These limitations tend to undermine the effectiveness of the restrictive immunity doctrine as applied to central banks.

5. *DIPLOMATIC IMMUNITY*[55]

VIENNA CONVENTION ON DIPLOMATIC RELATIONS 1961[56]

U.K.T.S. 19 (1965), Cmnd. 2565; 500 U.N.T.S. 95; 55 A.J.I.L. 1064 (1961)

The States Parties to the present Convention, . . .

Realizing that the purpose of such privileges and immunities is not to benefit individuals but to ensure the efficent performance of the functions of diplomatic missions as representing States,

---

[50] Note, however, the good faith and other international law controls on claims of state immunity suggested in the *Claim against the Emperor of Iran*, above, p. 246.

[51] *cf.* the approach of the I.L.C. in respect of state responsibility above, p. 385.

[52] *Op. cit.* at p. 241 n. 19, above, p. 259.

[53] One Order in Council has been made so far, for the constituent territories of Austria; S.I. 1979 No. 457.

[54] Explanatory Memorandum to the Act, quoted in *Hispano Americana Mercantil* v. *Central Bank of Nigeria* [1979] 2 Lloyd's Rep. 277 (C.A.).

[55] See Denza, *Diplomatic Law* (1976); Hardy, *Modern Diplomatic Law* (1967); Wilson, *Diplomatic Privileges and Immunities* (1967); Young (1964) 40 B.Y.I.L. 141.

[56] The Convention entered into force on April 24, 1964. On December 31, 1981, there were 137 contracting parties, including the U.K. See Kerley, 56 A.J.I.L. 88 (1962).

Affirming that the rules of customary international law should continue to govern questions not expressly regulated by the provisions of the present Convention,

Have agreed as follows:

Article 1

For the purpose of the present Convention, the following expressions shall have the meanings hereunder assigned to them:

(a) the 'head of the mission' is the person charged by the sending State with the duty of acting in that capacity;

(b) the 'members of the mission' are the head of the mission and the members of the staff of the mission;

(c) the 'members of the staff of the mission' are the members of the diplomatic staff, of the administrative and technical staff and of the service staff of the mission;

(d) the 'members of the diplomatic staff' are the members of the staff of the mission having diplomatic rank;

(e) a 'diplomatic agent' is the head of the mission or a member of the diplomatic staff of the mission;

(f) the 'members of the administrative and technical staff' are the members of the staff of the mission employed in the administrative and technical service of the mission[57];

(g) the 'members of the service staff' are the members of the staff of the mission in the domestic service of the mission[58];

(h) a 'private servant' is a person who is in the domestic service of a member of the mission and who is not an employee of the sending State;

(i) the 'premises of the mission' are the buildings or parts of buildings and the land ancillary thereto, irrespective of ownership, used for the purposes of the mission including the residence of the head of the mission.

Article 9

1. The receiving State may at any time and without having to explain its decision, notify the sending State that the head of the mission or any member of the diplomatic staff of the mission is *persona non grata* or that any other member of the staff of the mission is not acceptable. In any such case, the sending State shall, as appropriate, either recall the person concerned or terminate his functions with the mission. A person may be declared *non grata* or not acceptable before arriving in the territory of the receiving State. . . .

Article 22

1. The premises of the mission shall be inviolable. The agents of the receiving State may not enter them, except with the consent of the head of the mission.

2. The receiving State is under a special duty to take all appropriate steps to protect the premises of the mission against any intrusion or damage and to prevent any disturbance of the peace of the mission or impairment of its dignity.

---

[57] *Ed., e.g.* archivists, clerical and secretarial staff, translators.
[58] *Ed., e.g.* Chauffeurs, porters, kitchen staff.

3. The premises of the mission, their furnishings and other property thereon and the means of transport of the mission shall be immune from search, requisition, attachment or execution.

Article 23

[Exemption from taxes on the premises of the mission.]

Article 24

The archives and documents of the mission shall be inviolable at any time and wherever they may be.

Article 25

The receiving State shall accord full facilities for the performance of the functions of the mission.

Article 26

Subject to its laws and regulations concerning zones entry into which is prohibited or regulated for reasons of national security, the receiving State shall ensure to all members of the mission freedom of movement and travel in its territory.

Article 27

1. The receiving State shall permit and protect free communication on the part of the mission for all official purposes. In communicating with the Government and the other missions and consulates of the sending State, wherever situated, the mission may employ all appropriate means, including diplomatic couriers and messages in code or cipher. However, the mission may install and use a wireless transmitter only with the consent of the receiving State.

2. The official correspondence of the mission shall be inviolable. Official correspondence means all correspondence relating to the mission and its functions.

3. The diplomatic bag shall not be opened or detained.

4. The packages constituting the diplomatic bag must bear visible external marks of their character and may contain only diplomatic documents or articles intended for official use. . . .

Article 29

The person of a diplomatic agent shall be inviolable. He shall not be liable to any form of arrest or detention. The receiving State shall treat him with due respect and shall take all appropriate steps to prevent any attack on his person, freedom or dignity.

Article 30

1. The private residence of a diplomatic agent shall enjoy the same inviolability and protection as the premises of the mission.

2. His papers, correspondence and, except as provided in paragraph 3 of Article 31, his property, shall likewise enjoy inviolability.

Article 31

1. A diplomatic agent shall enjoy immunity from the criminal jurisdiction of the receiving State. He shall also enjoy immunity from its civil and administrative jurisdiction, except in the case of:

(*a*) a real action[58a] relating to private immovable property situated in the territory of the receiving State, unless he holds it on behalf of the sending State for the purposes of the mission;

(*b*) an action relating to succession in which the diplomatic agent is involved as executor, administrator, heir or legatee as a private person and not on behalf of the sending State;

(*c*) an action relating to any professional or commercial activity exercised by the diplomatic agent in the receiving State outside his official functions.

2. A diplomatic agent is not obliged to give evidence as a witness.

3. No measures of execution may be taken in respect of a diplomatic agent except in the cases coming under sub-paragraphs (*a*), (*b*) and (*c*) of paragraph 1 of this Article, and provided that the measures concerned can be taken without infringing the inviolability of his person or of his residence.

4. The immunity of a diplomatic agent from the jurisdiction of the receiving State does not exempt him from the jurisdiction of the sending State.

Article 32

1. The immunity from jurisdiction of diplomatic agents and of persons enjoying immunity under Article 37 may be waived by the sending State.

2. Waiver must always be express.

3. The initiation of proceedings by a diplomatic agent or by a person enjoying immunity from jurisdiction under Article 37 shall preclude him from invoking immunity from jurisdiction in respect of any counter-claim directly connected with the principal claim.

4. Waiver of immunity from jurisdiction in respect of civil or administrative proceedings shall not be held to imply waiver of immunity in respect of the execution of the judgment, for which a separate waiver shall be necessary.

Article 34

[Exemption from taxation of diplomatic agents.]

Article 36

[Exemption from customs duties for the mission and diplomatic agents and their families.]

Article 37

1. The members of the family of a diplomatic agent forming part of his household shall, if they are not nationals of the receiving State, enjoy the privileges and immunities specified in Articles 29 to 36.

[58a] A "real action" does not include an action *in personam* to enforce obligations under a lease (*e.g.* to permit entry to effect repairs); the concept, which is otherwise unknown to English law, may refer to actions in which the ownership or possession of real property is in issue: *Intpro Properties Ltd.* v. *Sauvel* [1983] 1 All E.R. 658 (Q.B.D.).

2. Members of the administrative and technical staff of the mission, together with members of their families forming part of their respective households, shall, if they are not nationals of or permanently resident in the receiving State, enjoy the privileges and immunities specified in Articles 29 to 35, except that the immunity from civil administrative jurisdiction of the receiving State specified in paragraph 1 of Article 31 shall not extend to acts performed outside the course of their duties. They shall also enjoy the privileges specified in Article 36, paragraph 1, in respect of articles imported at the time of first installation.

3. Members of the service staff of the mission who are not nationals of or permanently resident in the receiving State shall enjoy immunity in respect of acts performed in the course of their duties, exemption from dues and taxes on the emoluments they receive by reason of their employment and the exemption contained in Article 33 [concerning social security provisions].

4. Private servants of members of the mission shall, if they are not nationals of or permanently resident in the receiving State, be exempt from dues and taxes on the emoluments they receive by reason of their employment. In other respects, they may enjoy privileges and immunities only to the extent admitted by the receiving State. However, the receiving State must exercise its jurisdiction over those persons in such a manner as not to interfere unduly with the performance of the functions of the mission.

Article 38

1. Except insofar as additional privileges and immunities may be granted by the receiving State, a diplomatic agent who is a national of or permanently resident in that State shall enjoy only immunity from jurisdiction, and inviolability, in respect of official acts performed in the exercise of his functions.

2. Other members of the staff of the mission and private servants who are nationals of or permanently resident in the receiving State shall enjoy privileges and immunities only to the extent admitted by the receiving State. However, the receiving State must exercise its jurisdiction over those persons in such a manner as not to interfere unduly with the performance of the functions of the mission.

Article 39

1. Every person entitled to privileges and immunities shall enjoy them from the moment he enters the territory of the receiving State on proceeding to take up his post or, if already in its territory, from the moment when his appointment is notified to the Ministry of Foreign Affairs or such other ministry as may be agreed.

2. When the functions of a person enjoying such privileges and immunities have come to an end, such privileges and immunities shall normally cease at the moment when he leaves the country, or on expiry of a reasonable period in which to do so, but shall subsist until that time, even in case of armed conflict. However, with respect to acts performed by such a person in the exercise of his functions as a member of the mission, immunity shall continue to subsist. . . .

Article 40

1. If a diplomatic agent passes through or is in the territory of a third State, which has granted him a passport visa if such visa was necessary, while proceed-

ing to take up or return to his post, or when returning to his own country, the third State shall accord him inviolability and such other immunities as may be required to ensure his transit or return. The same shall apply in the case of any members of his family enjoying privileges or immunities who are accompanying the diplomatic agent, or travelling separately to join him or to return to their country.

2. In circumstances similar to those specified in paragraph 1 of this Article, third States shall not hinder the passage of members of the administrative and technical or service staff of a mission, and of members of their families, through the territories.

3. Third States shall accord to official correspondence and other official communications in transit, including messages in code or cipher, the same freedom and protection as is accorded by the receiving State. They shall accord to diplomatic couriers, who have been granted a passport visa if such visa was necessary, and diplomatic bags in transit the same inviolability and protection as the receiving State is bound to accord.

4. The obligations of third States under paragraphs 1, 2 and 3 of this Article shall also apply to the persons mentioned respectively in those paragraphs, and to official communications and diplomatic bags, whose presence in the territory of the third State is due to *force majeure*.

Article 41

1. Without prejudice to their privileges and immunities, it is the duty of all persons enjoying such privileges and immunities to respect the laws and regulations of the receiving State. They also have a duty not to interfere in the internal affairs of that State. . . .

3. The premises of the mission must not be used in any manner incompatible with the functions of the mission as laid down in the present Convention or by other rules of general international law or by any special agreements in force between the sending and the receiving State.

Article 47

1. In the application of the provisions of the present Convention, the receiving State shall not discriminate as between States.

2. However, discrimination shall not be regarded as taking place:

(a) where the receiving State applies any of the provisions of the present Convention restrictively because of restrictive application of that provision to its mission in the sending State;

(b) where by custom or agreement States extend to each other more favourable treatment than is required by the provisions of the present Convention.

Notes

1. The Convention was adopted at the United Nations Conference on Diplomatic Intercourse and Immunities in Vienna in 1961.[59] The Conference based its work upon

---

[59] For the Conference Records, see *U.N. Conference on Diplomatic Intercourse and Immunities, Vienna*, March 2–April 15, 1961, *Official Records*, Vols. I and II, 1962, U.N. Docs. A/CONF.20/14 and A/CONF.20/14 Add. 1.

Draft Articles prepared by the International Law Commission.[60] Optional Protocols concerning the Acquisition of Nationality[61] and the Compulsory Settlement of Disputes[62] were also adopted. It is not stated in the Convention whether or not it was intended to be declaratory of the customary international law existing in 1961. As far as the law concerning diplomatic immunity is concerned, it is probably correct to regard it as a combination of codification and progressive development. It would seem both to incorporate clearly established rules (see the *U.S. Diplomatic and Consular Staff in Tehran Case*, below, p. 276) and to fill in gaps or to spell out rules where practice was uncertain or inconsistent. Whether the Convention, so far as it engages in progressive development, has yet had sufficient impact upon the attitudes and practice of states to have affected customary international law is impossible to say. What is clear is that its impact upon the legal rights and duties of states has already been great because of the very large number of states that have ratified it.

The above extracts from the Convention concern the immunity, inviolability and protection afforded to the premises of the mission, to certain property relating to the mission's functioning[63] and to certain persons representing states diplomatically or concerned with such representation. Immunity and inviolability overlap to some extent (see Article 22(1)(3), Vienna Convention for example). The former term is applied mainly to jurisdictional immunity, *i.e.* immunity from the process of the courts, and to immunity from taxes. The latter is concerned mainly with questions of trespass.

2. *Jurisdictional immunity.* Article 37(2) of the Convention, on the immunities of administrative and technical staff, was the subject of disagreement at Vienna.[64] Several states have made reservations agreeing to allow the immunity granted by it only on condition of reciprocity and several others have made reservations not accepting it at all[65]; some other states, including the United Kingdom, have deposited objections to reservations of the latter kind.[65] Note that the International Law Commission had appreciated in its Commentary that Article 37(2) would be an example of "progressive development":

(2) It is the general practice to accord to members of the diplomatic staff of a mission the same privileges and immunities as are enjoyed by heads of mission, and it is not disputed that this is a rule of international law. But beyond this there is no uniformity in the practice of States in deciding which members of the staff of a mission shall enjoy privileges and immunities. Some States include members of the administrative and technical staff among the beneficiaries, and some even include members of the service staff. . . .

(4) In view of the differences in State practice, the Commission had to choose between two courses: either to work on the principle of a bare minimum, and stipulate that any additional rights to be accorded should be decided by bilateral agreement; or to try to establish a general and uniform rule based on what would appear to be necessary and reasonable.

(5) A majority of the Commission favoured the latter course, believing that the rule proposed would represent a progressive step.

(6) The Commission differentiated between members of the administrative and technical staff on the one hand, and members of the service staff on the other.

[60] Y.B.I.L.C., 1958, II, p. 89.

[61] 500 U.N.T.S. 223. Entered into force in 1964. On December 31, 1981, there were 39 contracting parties. The U.K. was not a party.

[62] *Ibid.* 241. Entered into force in 1964. On December 31, 1981, there were 51 contracting parties, including the U.K.

[63] The rules on the availability and immunity of such premises and property are rules of *state,* rather than *diplomatic,* immunity. They are included here for convenience.

[64] See *op. cit.* at n. 59, above, Vol. I, 32nd and 33rd Meetings, pp. 193–201.

[65] For the reservations and objections to them, see *Multilateral Treaties in Respect of which the Secretary-General Performs Depositary Functions*, U.N. Doc. ST/LEG/SER. D/5, pp. 49–53.

(7) As regards persons belonging to the administrative and technical staff, it took the view that there were good grounds for granting them the same privileges and immunities as members of the diplomatic staff. . . .

(8) The reasons relied on may be summarized as follows. It is the function of the mission as an organic whole which should be taken into consideration, not the actual work done by each person. Many of the persons belonging to the services in question perform confidential tasks which, for the purposes of the mission's function, may be even more important than the tasks entrusted to some members of the diplomatic staff. An ambassador's secretary or an archivist may be as much the repository of secret or confidential knowledge as members of the diplomatic staff. Such persons equally need protection of the same order against possible pressure by the receiving State.[66]

Would a "diplomatic agent" who negligently injured a pedestrian while driving his car on holiday in the receiving state be entitled to claim immunity under the Convention in respect of any civil or criminal proceedings arising therefrom? Would a code clerk or a cook employed in an embassy be entitled to do so in the same situation? Would the wife or private employee of any of the above be entitled to do so?[67] Might the nationality or the place of permanent residence of the person claiming immunity in any of the above cases be relevant?

Article 40 of the Convention was interpreted in *R.* v. *Guildhall Magistrates Court, ex parte Jarrett-Thorpe.*[68] The applicant was the husband of the counsellor to the Sierra Leone Embassy in Rome. His wife travelled to London to buy furnishings for the Rome Embassy. It was intended that the applicant would join her later for the purpose of travelling back to Rome with her and to help with her luggage. It was not intended that he should enter the United Kingdom for any other purpose. When he arrived in the United Kingdom, the applicant received a message to the effect that his wife had already left for Rome. While he was waiting for a flight to Rome the applicant was arrested by the police at Heathrow in connection with criminal proceedings pending against him in London.

Mr. Justice Lawton held that Article 40 applied so that the applicant was entitled to immunity. The court rejected the argument that Article 40 only applied to diplomatic agents and members of their families when they were in transit between the sending state and the receiving state.

3. *Waiver of immunity.* A resolution adopted at Vienna recommended:

that the sending State should waive the immunity of members of its diplomatic mission in respect of civil claims of persons in the receiving State when this can be done without impeding the performance of the functions of the mission, and that, when immunity is not waived, the sending State should use its best endeavours to bring about a just settlement of the claims.[69]

The following is a 1952 statement of British practice, based upon "the principle that diplomatic immunity is accorded not for the benefit of the individual in question, but for the benefit of the State in whose service he is, in order that he may fulfil his diplomatic duties with the necessary independence":

. . . when a dispute arises between a person living in this country and a person possessing diplomatic immunity here and the dispute cannot be settled directly between the parties, it is commonly reported to the Foreign Office and the Foreign

---

[66] Y.B.I.L.C., 1958, II, pp. 101–102.
[67] On the status of the family of a diplomatic agent, see O'Keefe, 25 I.C.L.Q. 329 (1976).
[68] *The Times*, October 5, 1977. (Q.B.Divl. Court).
[69] U.N.Doc. A/CONF. 20/14, Add. 1, v. 90.

Office then approaches the diplomatic mission concerned with the request that the Head of the Mission will either waive the immunity of the member of his staff so that the dispute can be decided in the ordinary way in the courts or that the matter should be decided by a private arbitration conducted under conditions which are fair to both sides. Such requests are commonly acceded to, and the cases where this approach has not brought about a proper settlement of the matter have generally been cases where, owing to delay, the foreign diplomat in question has already left the country before the matter can be dealt with, a delay which is generally due to a failure of the party who thinks he is injured to approach the Foreign Office promptly. If a case arose where the foreign mission concerned was neither willing to waive immunity nor to persuade the foreign diplomat to accept a reasonable arbitration and the foreign diplomat remained in this country, the Foreign Office would in the circumstances feel obliged, unless there were exceptional features in the case, to inform the foreign mission concerned that this individual could no longer be accepted as a person holding a diplomatic immunity appointment in this country.

If a person possessing diplomatic immunity is alleged to have committed a criminal offence and there is a prima facie case which, in the ordinary way, would lead to the institution of a prosecution, the Foreign Office approaches the foreign mission concerned and, unless the offence is such that it is considered that an admonition by the Head of the Mission is sufficient, the Foreign Office requests a waiver of immunity in order that the case may be tried, on the footing that, if the immunity is not waived, it may be impossible for the Foreign Secretary to continue to accept the individual concerned as a person possessing diplomatic status in this country.[70]

Note that is a six month period in 1980, 25,112 fixed penalty motor car notices were cancelled in London because of claims of diplomatic immunity.[71]

4. *Inviolability of the premises of the mission.* An amendment[72] to the Convention to require the head of a mission to:

co-operate with the local authorities in case of fire, epidemic or other extreme emergency

was not adopted at Vienna. In the International Law Commission it had been suggested that

[i]t was hardly conceivable that a head of mission would fail to co-operate . . . in an emergency[73]

and that the sanction of declaring him *persona non grata* would be available if he did.[74] Commenting upon an incident in 1929, when French officials entered the Soviet Embassy in Paris after allegations that persons were being detained and might be executed there, Sibert argues that the intervention was consistent with international law:

because no civilised state could permit a foreign legation to be made a place of imprisonment, or, *a fortiori*, a place of execution.[75]

In the *Sun Yat Sen* Incident, in 1896, a Chinese national who was not in any way connected with the Chinese Embassy in London was kept there against his will. A writ of habeas corpus was refused by Wright J.

---

[70] Interdepartmental Committee on State Immunities, *Report on Diplomatic Immunity*, Cmnd. 8460, pp. 3–4. The statement still represents British practice.
[71] *Hansard*, H.C. Vol. 985, W.A., Col. 871. June 6, 1980. In 1979, criminal prosecutions in 284 cases (including cases of violence against the person, sexual offences and shoplifting) were not pursued because of claims of diplomatic immunity: *ibid.*
[72] U.N. Doc. A/CONF. 20/c.1 L.129.
[73] Y.B.I.L.C., 1958, I, 129 (Mr. Amado).   [74] *Ibid.* p. 130 (Mr. Bartos).
[75] *Traité de Droit International Public*, Vol. II, 1951, p. 24. Translation.

because I doubt the propriety of making any order or granting any summons against a foreign legation.[76]

Nonetheless, the

Chinese Minister was officially called upon to release his prisoner, and did so.[77]

The British Government referred to the detention as "an abuse of . . . diplomatic privilege" and a "flagrant . . . violation of municipal and international law."[78] It added that

if persisted in or repeated, it would justify the use of whatever measures might be necessary for the liberation of the captive, and a demand for the immediate departure from this country of any persons responsible for his imprisonment.[79]

Denza[80] considers the problem of "abuse" as follows:

Article 22 thus leaves absolute the inviolability of the premises of the mission. In the last resort however a receiving State which is sufficiently sure of the evidence of abuse which it will find will probably take the risk of acting in breach of the Article if it believes its essential security to be at risk. In 1973 for example the Iraqi Ambassador was called to the Pakistan Ministry of Foreign Affairs and told that arms were being brought into Pakistan under diplomatic immunity and that there was evidence that they were being stored at the Embassy of Iraq. The Ambassador refused permission for a search. In the presence of the Ambassador a raid on the Embassy by armed policemen then took place and huge consignments of arms were found to be stored in crates. The Pakistan Government then sent a strong protest to the Iraq Government, declared the Iraqi Ambassador and an attaché *persona non grata* and recalled their own Ambassador. In this case the forcible entry could be justified *ex post facto* because of the clear breach by Iraq of the duty in paragraph 3 of Article 41 not to use the premises of the mission in any manner incompatible with the functions of the mission. But such an entry could be justified only in an extreme case of abuse.

The question of *diplomatic asylum* within the premises of a mission was purposely not discussed at Vienna. According to British practice at the turn of the century:

[i]t is in no way necessary for the discharge of an Ambassador's duty that his house should be an asylum for persons charged with crime of any description, and no such privilege can be asserted. . . .[81]

But, according to the same practice, asylum is allowed in certain exceptional cases:

. . . the practice of harbouring political refugees is an objectionable one and should be resorted to only from motives of humanity in cases of instant or imminent personal peril. In such cases the refugee should not be allowed to communicate with his partisans from the shelter of His Majesty's Legation and should be removed the moment he is no longer exposed to summary treatment at the hands of his pursuers.

Protection must, of course, sometimes be afforded to British subjects in time of danger but this is an wholly different matter from harbouring political refugees who are citizens or subjects of the country. In cases where British subjects have committed an offence against the local laws and have sought refuge in His Majesty's

---

[76] 1 McNair 85. The person detained gave notice of his plight by placing a slip of paper in a bread roll which he then threw on to the street below through the bars of his window: Viscount Alverstone, *Recollections of Bar and Bench* (1914), pp. 168–169.

[77] 1 McNair 88.

[78] *Ibid.* p. 86.

[79] *Ibid.* p. 87.

[80] *Op. cit.* at p. 264, p. 55, above, p. 84. Footnote omitted.

[81] Law Officer's Report of 1896, 2 McNair 76. This is still British practice.

Legation they should be given up only to the competent authorities and on satisfactory guarantees being given that they will still receive proper treatment and a fair deal. . . .[82]

The Harvard Research Draft Convention on Diplomatic Privileges and Immunities 1932[83] reads:

Article 6. A sending state shall not permit the premises occupied or used by its mission or by a member of its mission to be used as a place of asylum for fugitives from justice.

Although the granting of diplomatic asylum has been common practice in Latin American states and is regulated by treaties between them, it would not seem that any rules of customary American international law have developed.[84] Diplomatic asylum has been granted elsewhere. Cardinal Mindszenty, for example, took refuge in the United States Embassy in Budapest after the failure of the Hungarian Uprising in 1956 and remained there until 1970 when he was allowed to leave the country to take up residence in Rome. Ronning[85] states:

The only generalization which seems at all acceptable is that the practice of states in this regard is not based upon any generally recognized *right of asylum* so far as general international law is concerned. Instead, it is a *de facto* result of the fact that international law accords to the various accredited diplomatic officers certain well-recognized immunities from local jurisdiction, such as immunity of their official residences and offices from invasion by local authorities. Humanitarian, political or other motives may lead to the original grant of asylum but once the refugee is inside the legation the territorial state is faced with an insoluble dilemma. Assuming the state of refuge will not surrender the refugee, the territorial state can apprehend him only by violating the immunity of the diplomatic premises or, possibly, by breaking diplomatic relations. The fact is that such extreme measures are considered too high a price to pay for apprehension of the refugee.

5. *Protection of the premises of the mission.* The "special duty" to protect the premises of the mission set out in Article 22 of the Convention is well established in customary international law and is very important at the present time when such premises prove convenient settings for political demonstrations. See the *U.S. Diplomatic and Consular Staff in Iran case*, below, p. 276. See also an incident in 1965 when the United States Embassy in Moscow was attacked by students; the U.S.S.R. expressed regret, indicated stricter measures of protection and agreed to pay compensation for property damage.[86]

The duty extends, under Article 30, to the private residence of a diplomatic agent and was interpreted in this context in *Agbor* v. *Metropolitan Police Commissioner*.[87] There, a dispute arose over the occupation of a flat in a house in London owned by the Nigerian Government and used to house diplomatic agents. Shortly after Biafra purported to secede from Nigeria, a Biafran family managed to gain possession of the flat while its next official tenant was awaited. At the request of the Nigerian Government, the family was evicted by the police. The court was asked in the application before it to allow the family to return to the flat pending a decision by it on the right of possession. The application was granted because the flat was not at the time the residence of a diplomatic agent. Lord Denning added that even if it had been he was

---

[82] Sir E. Grey to H.M. Minister in Haiti, May 30, 1913, 7 B.D.I.L. 922. The exception probably covers all cases, whether political or not.
[83] 26 A.J.I.L. Suppl. 19 (1932).
[84] See the *Asylum Case*, I.C.J.Rep. 1950, p. 266.
[85] *Diplomatic Asylum* (1965), p. 22.
[86] 7 Whiteman 387. On state responsibility for the actions of mobs, see below, p. 418.
[87] [1969] 1 W.L.R. 703. (C.A.).

not at all satisfied that the [Diplomatic Privileges] Act of 1964 gives to the executive any right to evict a person in possession who claims as of right to occupation of the premises. It enables the police to defend the premises against intruders. But not to turn out people who are in possession and claim as of right to be there.[88]

6. *Freedom of communication*. Before the 1961 Convention, "it was certainly accepted international practice, and probably international law," that the receiving state had a right of challenge in respect of the diplomatic bag.[89] It could, that is, ask for permission to inspect its contents. The sending state could either allow this to happen, or not send the bag. Article 27(3) requires that the bag be allowed through without inspection. Reservations to the Convention insisting upon a power of inspection have been made,[90] but have met with protest by other parties. Article 27 does not prohibit electronic scanning of the diplomatic bag. This would seem to be a practice followed by some receiving states, although it "would not necessarily pick up a weapon in a diplomatic bag."[91]

A remarkable incident (concerned this time with inviolability of correspondence) occurred in 1964 when an Israeli national was found drugged, bound and gagged at Rome airport in a trunk marked "diplomatic mail" that was being sent by the Egyptian mission to Cairo. Italy protested that the international law of diplomatic immunity had been violated. It declared one first secretary at the Egyptian Embassy *persona non grata* and expelled two others. The Egyptian Ambassador deplored the incident and claimed ignorance of it.[92]

The question of the status of the diplomatic courier and the diplomatic bag is at present under consideration by the International Law Commission.[93]

7. *The basis for diplomatic immunity*. In its commentary on its Draft Articles the International Law Commission stated:

(1) Among the theories that have exercised an influence on the development of diplomatic privileges and immunities, the Commission will mention the "exterritoriality" theory, according to which the premises of the mission represent a sort of extension of the territory of the sending State; and the "representative character" theory, which bases such privileges and immunities on the idea that the diplomatic mission personifies the sending State.

(2) There is now a third theory which appears to be gaining ground in modern times, namely, the "functional necessity" theory, which justifies privileges and immunities as being necessary to enable the mission to perform its functions.

(3) The Commission was guided by this third theory in solving problems on which practice gave no clear pointers, while also bearing in mind the representative character of the head of the mission and of the mission itself.[94]

In *Radwan* v. *Radwan*[95] it was held that the Egyptian consulate in London was not a part of the territory of the United Arab Republic so that a divorce obtained there was not obtained "in any country outside the British Isles" for the purposes of the Recogni-

---

[88] *Ibid.* p. 707. Salmon L.J. agreed, *ibid.* p. 710.
[89] Denza, *op. cit.* at p. 264, n. 55, above, p. 225. The diplomatic bag consists of packages, sacks, or possible trunks and is usually sent in the custody of a diplomatic courier, although some times entrusted to the safe keeping of the aircraft's captain.
[90] By Kuwait and Bahrein.
[91] *Hansard*, H.C., Vol. 985, Col. 1219. June 2, 1980; U.K.M.I.L. 1980; (1980) 51 B.Y.I.L.419.
[92] *Keesings Archives*, p. 20580. In 1980 £500,000 worth of cannabis was found in diplomatic baggage bound for the Moroccan Embassy in London when a crate marked "household effects" split open at Harwich; *The Times*, June 13, 1980.
[93] See, most recently, the 3rd Report of the Special Rapporteur (Yankov) UN Doc.A/CN./359. June 12, 1982.
[94] Y.B.I.L.C., 1958, II, pp. 94–95.
[95] [1973] Fam. 24.

tion of Divorces and Legal Separations Act 1971. After reviewing the literature on the subject, which he found rejected the extraterritoriality theory, Cumming-Bruce J. referred to the Vienna Convention:

> If it was the view of the high contracting parties that the premises of missions were part of the territory of the sending state, that would undoubtedly be formulated and it would have been quite unnecessary to set out the immunities in the way in which it has been done.[96]

8. *Article* 47. Why does the question of "a restrictive application" of the Convention arise? Why isn't there one legally correct application of the Convention, as there would be of a municipal law statute?

US DIPLOMATIC AND CONSULAR STAFF IN TEHRAN CASE[97]

U.S. *v.* Iran

I.C.J. Reports 1980, p. 3

On November 4, 1979, several hundred Iranian students and other demonstrators took possession of the United States Embassy in Tehran by force. They did so in protest at the admission of the deposed Shah of Iran into the United States for medical treatment. The demonstrators were not opposed by the Iranian security forces who "simply disappeared from the scene." United States consulates elsewhere in Iran were similarly occupied. The demonstrators were still in occupation when the present judgment was given. They had seized archives and documents and continued to hold 52 United States nationals. (Women and black people had been released.) Fifty were diplomatic or consular staff; two were private citizens. In an earlier judgment,[98] the Court had indicated interim measures at the request of the United States. In the present judgment, the Court ruled on the United States request for a declaration that Iran had infringed a number of treaties, including the 1961 and 1963 Vienna Conventions of Diplomatic and Consular Relations respectively. It also asked for a declaration calling for the release of the hostages, the evacuation of the Embassy and consulates, the punishment of the persons responsible and the payment of reparation. In April 1980, while the case was pending, United States military forces entered Iran by air and landed in a remote desert area in the course of an attempt to rescue the hostages. The attempt was abandoned because of equipment failure. United States military personnel were killed in an air collision as the units withdrew. No injury was done to Iranian nationals or property.

Judgment of the Court

The events which are the subject of the United States' claims fall into two phases . . .

57. The first . . . covers the armed attack on the United States Embassy by militants on 4 November 1979.

58. No suggestion has been made that the militants, when they executed their attack on the Embassy, had any form of official status as recognized "agents" or

---

[96] *Ibid.* p. 34.
[97] See Gross, 74 A.J.I.L. 395 (1980).
[98] I.C.J.Rep. 1979, p. 7. The Court called mainly for the vacation of the Embassy and other premises; the release of the hostages; and the restoration of full diplomatic protection. In 1979 the Security Council called upon Iran to release the hostages: S.C. Resn. 457 (1979), *Resolutions and Decisions*, 1979, p. 24.

organs of the Iranian State. Their conduct in mounting the attack, overrunning the Embassy and seizing its inmates as hostages cannot, therefore, be regarded as imputable to that State on that basis. . . .

61. [This] . . . does not mean that Iran is, in consequence, free of any responsibility in regard to those attacks; for its own conduct was in conflict with its international obligations. By a number of provisions of the Vienna Conventions of 1961 and 1963, Iran was placed under the most categorical obligations, as a receiving State, to take appropriate steps to ensure the protection of the United States Embassy and Consulates, their staffs, their archives, their means of communication and the freedom of movement of the members of their staffs. . . .

62. . . . In the view of the Court, the obligations of the Iranian Government here in question are not merely contractual obligations established by the Vienna Conventions of 1961 and 1963, but also obligations under general international law.

63. The facts . . . establish to the satisfaction of the Court that on 4 November 1979 the Iranian Government failed altogether to take any "appropriate steps" to protect the premises, staff and archives of the United States' mission against attack by the militants, and to take any steps either to prevent this attack or to stop it before it reached its completion. They also show that on 5 November 1979 the Iranian Government similarly failed to take appropriate steps for the protection of the United States Consulates at Tabriz and Shiraz. In addition they show, in the opinion of the Court, that the failure of the Iranian Government to take such steps was due to more than mere negligence or lack of appropriate means. . . .

67. This inaction of the Iranian Government by itself constituted clear and serious violation of Iran's obligations to the United States under the provisions of Article 22, paragraph 2, and Articles 24, 25, 26, 27 and 29 of the 1961 Vienna Convention on Diplomatic Relations, and Articles 5 and 36 of the 1963 Vienna Convention on Consular Relations. Similarly, with respect to the attacks of the Consulates at Tabriz and Shiraz, the inaction of the Iranian authorities entailed clear and serious breaches of its obligations under the provisions of several further articles of the 1963 Convention on Consular Relations . . .

69. The second phase of the events . . . comprises the whole series of facts which occurred following the completion of the occupation of the United States Embassy by the militants, and the seizure of the Consulates at Tabriz and Shiraz. The occupation having taken place and the diplomatic and consular personnel of the United States' mission having been taken hostage, the action required of the Iranian Government by the Vienna Conventions and by general international law was manifest. Its plain duty was at once to make every effort, and to take every appropriate step, to bring these flagrant infringements of the inviolability of the premises, archives and diplomatic and consular staff of the United States Embassy to a speedy end, to restore the Consulates at Tabriz and Shiraz to United States control, and in general to re-establish the status quo and to offer reparation for the damage.

70. No such step was, however, taken by the Iranian authorities. . . .

73. The seal of official government approval was finally set on this situation by a decree issued on 17 November 1979 by the Ayatollah Khomeini. His decree began with the assertion that the American Embassy was "a centre of espionage and conspiracy" and that "those people who hatched plots against our Islamic

movement in that place do not enjoy international diplomatic respect." He went on expressly to declare that the premises of the Embassy and the hostages would remain as they were until the United States had handed over the former Shah for trial and returned his property to Iran. . . .

74. . . . The approval given to these facts by the Ayatollah Khomeini and other organs of the Iranian State, and the decision to perpetuate them, translated continuing occupation of the Embassy and detention of the hostages into acts of that State. The militants, authors of the invasion and jailers of the hostages, had now become agents of the Iranian State for whose acts the State itself was internationally responsible. . . .

77. . . . these facts constituted breaches additional to those already committed of [the provisions of the 1961 Convention already infringed, as well as breaches of Article 22(1)(3) of that Convention and of Article 33 of the 1963 Convention.]

91. . . . Wrongfully to deprive human beings of their freedom and to subject them to physical constraint in conditions of hardship is in itself manifestly incompatible with the principles of the Charter of the United Nations, as well as with the fundamental principles enunciated in the Universal Declaration of Human Rights. But what has above all to be emphasized is the extent and seriousness of the conflict between the conduct of the Iranian State and its obligations under the whole corpus of the international rules for which diplomatic and consular law is comprised, rules the fundamental character of which the Court must here again strongly affirm.

92. . . . The frequency with which at the present time the principles of international law governing diplomatic and consular relations are set at naught by individuals or groups of individuals is already deplorable. But this case is unique and of very particular gravity because here it is not only private individuals or groups of individuals that have disregarded and set at naught the inviolability of a foreign embassy, but the government of the receiving State itself. . . . Such events cannot fail to undermine the edifice of law carefully constructed by mankind over a period of centuries, the maintenance of which is vital for the security and well-being of the complex international community of the present day, to which it is more essential than ever that the rules developed to ensure the ordered progress of relations between its members should be constantly and scrupulously respected.

93. . . . the Court . . . cannot let pass without comment the incursion into the territory of Iran made by United States military units on 24–25 April 1980 . . . No doubt the United States Government may have had understandable preoccupations with respect to the well-being of its nationals held hostage in its Embassy for over five months. No doubt also the United States Government may have had understandable feelings of frustration at Iran's long-continued detention of the hostages, notwithstanding two resolutions of the Security Council as well as the Court's own Order of 15 December 1979 calling expressly for their immediate release. Nevertheless . . . the Court cannot fail to express its concern in regard to the United States' incursion into Iran. . . . the Court was in course of preparing the present judgment adjudicating upon the claims of the United States against Iran when the operation of 24 April 1980 took place. The Court therefore feels bound to observe that an operation undertaken in those circumstances, from whatever motive, is of a kind calculated to undermine respect for the judicial process in international relations and

to recall that in paragraph 47, 1 B, of its Order of 15 December 1979 the Court had indicated that no action was to be taken by either party which might aggravate the tension between the two countries.

94. At the same time, however, the Court must point out that neither the question of the legality of the operation of 24 April 1980, under the Charter of the United Nations and under general international law, nor any possible question of responsibility flowing from it, is before the Court.

95. For these reasons, THE COURT, . . . By thirteen votes to two,[99]

Decides that the Islamic Republic of Iran has violated obligations owed by it to the United States of America under international conventions in force between the two countries, as well as under long-established rules of general international law; . . .

Note

The Court also decided (i) unanimously, that Iran "must immediately take all steps to redress the situation resulting from the events of November 4, 1979," including the release of the hostages and the return of the premises, documents, etc., to the United States and (ii), by 12 votes to 3,[1] that Iran was "under an obligation to make reparation" to the United States. Iran, which had declined to participate in the proceedings, did not comply with the Court's judgment in any respect. The hostages were ultimately released in January 1981 as a result of a negotiated settlement with the United States.

DIPLOMATIC PRIVILEGES ACT 1964

(1964, c. 81)

1. The following provisions of this Act shall, with respect to the matters dealt with therein, have effect in substitution for any previous enactment or rule of law.

2.—(1) Subject to section 3 of this Act, the Articles set out in Schedule 1 to this Act[2] . . . shall have the force of law in the United Kingdom . . .

(3) For the purposes of Article 32 a waiver by the head of the mission of any State or any person for the time being performing his functions shall be deemed to be a waiver by that State. . . .

3.—(1) If it appears to Her Majesty that the privileges and immunities accorded to a mission of Her Majesty in the territory of any State, or to persons connected with that mission, are less than those conferred by this Act on the mission of that State or on persons connected with that mission, Her Majesty may by an Order in Council withdraw such of the privileges and immunities so conferred from the mission of that State or from such persons connected with it as appears to Her Majesty to be proper. . . .

4. If in any proceedings any question arises whether or not any person is entitled to any privilege or immunity under this Act a certificate issued by or under the authority of the Secretary of State stating any fact relating to that question shall be conclusive evidence of that fact.

[99] The judges in the majority were President Sir Humphrey Waldock; Vice-President Elias; Judges Forster, Gros, Lachs, Nagendra Singh, Ruda, Mosler, Oda, Ago, El-Erian, Sette-Camara and Baxter. Judges Morozov and Tarazi dissented.
[1] Judge Lachs joined the dissenting judges.
[2] *Ed.* Articles 1, 22–24, 27–40, Vienna Convention.

7.—(1) Where any special agreement or arrangement between the Government of any State and the Government of the United Kingdom in force at the commencement of this Act provides for extending—

(*a*) such immunity from jurisdiction and from arrest or detention, and such inviolability of residence, as are conferred by this Act on a diplomatic agent; or

(*b*) such exemption from customs duties, taxes and related charges as is conferred by this Act in respect of articles for the personal use of a diplomatic agent;

to any class of person, or to articles for the personal use of any class of person, connected with the mission of that State, that immunity and inviolability or exemption shall so extend, so long as that agreement or arrangement continues in force. . . .

EMPSON v. SMITH

[1966] 1 Q.B. 426. Court of Appeal

In 1963, the plaintiff brought a county court action against the defendant for breach of a tenancy agreement. The action was stayed after the Ministry of Commonwealth Relations had certified that the defendant was an administrative officer employed by the High Commissioner for Canada.[3] In December 1964, an application by the plaintiff, made in August 1964, to have the stay removed was heard by the County Court, together with an application by the defendant, made in November 1964, to have the writ dismissed as a nullity. By that time the Diplomatic Privileges Act had come into force, on October 1, 1964. The County Court granted the defendant's application. The plaintiff appealed to the Court of Appeal.

DIPLOCK L.J.: [The 1964] Act makes radical amendments in the previously existing law on diplomatic privileges and immunity and in particular draws a distinction between the immunities enjoyed by "members of the diplomatic staff" and "members of the administrative and technical staff" of a mission. Section 4 of that Act provides that a certificate issued by or under the authority of the Secretary of State shall be conclusive evidence of any fact relevant to any person's entitlement to any privilege or immunity. A further certificate dated October 20, 1964, was issued under that Act certifying that the defendant was on October 1, and had continued to be, a member of the administrative and technical staff of the Diplomatic Mission of Canada in the United Kingdom.

When the action was commenced in March 1963, the defendant was entitled under section 1(1)(*a*) of the Act of 1952 "to the like immunity from suit and legal process as is accorded to members of the official staff of an envoy of a foreign sovereign power." He was thus entitled so long as he remained en poste to complete immunity from civil suit in the United Kingdom, both as respects acts done in his official capacity on behalf of his government and as respects acts done in his private capacity. . . .

---

[3] The certificate was issued under the Diplomatic Immunities (Commonwealth Countries and Republic of Ireland) Act 1952, s.1(1), as amended by the Diplomatic Privileges Act 1964, Sched. 2, which gives the missions of the Commonwealth countries listed the same immunities as those of other states.

If the defendant had applied before the passing of the Diplomatic Privileges Act 1964, to have the plaintiff's action dismissed there would have been no answer to his application. But he delayed until November, 1964. By that date his right to immunity from civil suit had been curtailed by that Act which applies to the United Kingdom the provisions of the Vienna Convention on Diplomatic Relations, 1961, contained in the Schedule to the Act. By the combined effect of articles 31 and 37 of the Convention as a member of the administrative and technical staff of the mission his immunity from the civil jurisdiction of the courts of the United Kingdom does not extend to acts performed outside the course of his duties. Whether he is entitled to immunity in any particular suit no longer depends solely upon his status but also upon the subject-matter of the suit.

It is elementary law that diplomatic immunity is not immunity from legal liability but immunity from suit. If authority is needed for this it is to be found in *Dickinson* v. *Del Solar* [4] . . . Statutes relating to diplomatic immunity from civil suit are procedural statutes. The Diplomatic Privileges Act, 1964, is in my view clearly applicable to suits brought after the date on which that statute came into force in respect of acts done before that date. If, therefore, the plaintiff had issued her plaint after October 1, 1964, instead of before, the action could not have been dismissed upon the ground of diplomatic privilege unless and until the court had determined the issue: whether or not the defendant's acts alleged by the plaintiff to constitute her cause of action against him were acts performed outside the course of his duties. It is, to say the least, arguable that acts done by the defendant in relation to his tenancy of his private residence in London were performed by him outside the course of his duties. But this issue is one which can be decided only upon evidence. It has not yet been considered, for the deputy county court judge found it unnecessary to go into it. He dismissed the plaintiff's action upon other grounds. He took the view that "the proceedings were a nullity at the time they were commenced, they are not affected by the 1964 Act which came into operation subsequently."

The deputy county court judge did not refer to section 3 of the Diplomatic Privileges Act, 1708 [5] but counsel for the defendant has in this court relied strongly upon it in support of the proposition that Mrs. Empson's plaint was void ab initio. The Act of Anne . . . has been repeatedly held to be declaratory of the common law, and must therefore be construed according to the common law of which the law of nations must be deemed a part . . . it was decided in *Re Suarez* [6] that notwithstanding that Act a writ issued in the High Court against an ambassador was not void ab initio. If it were it would, indeed, be impossible for the privilege ever to be waived for, as was decided in *Kahan* v. *Pakistan*

---

[4] [1930] 1 K.B. 376, 380. *Ed. cf. Shaw* v. *Shaw* [1979] Fam. 62 (C.A.): petition for divorce presented by a wife when her husband was a diplomatic agent could not be struck out on the basis of diplomatic immunity after he had ceased to be such.

[5] s.3 reads: "And to prevent the like insolences for the future be it further declared by the authority aforesaid that all writs and processes that shall at any time hereafter be sued forth or prosecuted whereby the person of any ambassador or other publick minister of any foreign prince or state authorized and received as such by her Majesty her heirs or successors or the domestick or domestick servant of any such ambassador or other publick minister may be arrested or imprisoned or his or their goods or chattels may be distrained seized or attached shall be deemed and adjudged to be utterly null and void to all intents constructions and purposes whatsoever."

[6] [1918] 1 Ch. 176.

Federation[7] there can be no effective waiver until the court is actually seised of the proceedings. The waiver is an undertaking given not to the other party to the proceedings but to the court itself. It can effectively be given only after the proceedings have commenced. *Kahan's* case was one of state immunity, but it is well settled that diplomatic immunity is governed by the same principles for it is claimed by the head of the mission on behalf of his state.

It follows therefore that until steps were taken to set it aside or to dismiss the action the plaintiff's plaint was no nullity: it was a valid plaint. If the defendant had, with the permission of his High Commissioner, appeared to it before October 1, 1964, the procedural bar to the hearing would have been removed. So, too, if the defendant had ceased to be en poste while the plaint was still outstanding the action could then have proceeded against him. I can see no reason in logic or the law of nations why the position should be any different when the procedural bar has been removed by Act of Parliament—particularly when that Act of Parliament gives statutory effect to an international convention, by which sovereign states have mutually waived in part immunities for members of the staff of their foreign missions to which they were formerly entitled by the law of nations.

In holding, in my view, incorrectly, that the proceedings were a nullity at the time they were commenced, the deputy county court judge founded himself upon a passage in the judgment of Lord Parker C.J. in *Reg.* v. *Madan*[8] in which he referred to the proceedings being "null and void unless and until there is a valid waiver which, as it were, would bring the proceedings to life and give jurisdiction to the court." Lord Parker was clearly not using the words "null and void" in a precise sense for what is null and void is not a phoenix, there are no ashes from which it can be brought to life. In that case he was concerned only with waiver as removing the procedural bar of diplomatic immunity. His words should not be read that *only* waiver can, as it were, bring the proceedings to life. The removal of the procedural bar from any other cause will have the same effect.

I am therefore of opinion that the deputy county court judge was wrong in dismissing the action as he did.[9] . . .

Appeal allowed.

Notes[10]

1. Would the question whether the breach of the tenancy agreement by the defendant was an act "performed outside the course of" his duties have been a question of *fact* with which an executive certificate could have dealt and upon which such a certificate would have been conclusive under s.4 of the Diplomatic Privileges Act?

2. *Empson* v. *Smith* indicates one respect in which the 1964 Act changes the previous English law on diplomatic immunity. Have the following pre-1964 rules also been changed:

   (a) That a diplomatic agent can claim immunity in a civil action for the payment of rates on his private residence?[11]

---

[7] [1951] 2 K.B. 1003; [1951] 2 T.L.R. 697, C.A.
[8] [1961] 2 Q.B. 1, 7.
[9] Sellers and Danckwerts L.JJ. delivered concurring judgments.
[10] See Buckley, (1965–66) 41 B.Y.I.L. 321.
[11] *Parkinson* v. *Potter* (1885) 16 Q.B.D. 152.

    (b) That a diplomatic agent can claim immunity in a civil action concerning his private commercial activities?[12]

    (c) That a British subject accredited as a diplomatic agent to a foreign mission in the United Kingdom has immunity from distraint of goods for non-payment of rates unless the contrary has been indicated by the British Government when he is received?[13]

    (d) That immunity can be deemed to have been waived by entry of appearance in an action?[14]

3. In *Engelke* v. *Musmann*[15] Lord Phillimore, obiter dicta, defined an ambassador's family for the purposes of immunity as "his wife and his children if living with him." In *Re C (An Infant)*[16] Harman J., considering whether the son of a person entitled to immunity was himself entitled to it, ruled that the test was whether "he is ordinarily resident with, or is under his father's control."[17] Are these statements consistent with the 1964 Act?

British Foreign Office practice is to treat a diplomat's "family" as "including the spouse and minor children [under 18], and certain other persons in exceptional circumstances." In practice, the "exceptional" cases fall into three categories:

    (a) a person who fulfils the social duties of hostess to the diplomatic agent (for example the sister of an unmarried diplomat or the adult daughter of a widowed diplomat);

    (b) the parent of a diplomat living with him and not engaged in paid employment on a permanent basis; and

    (c) the child of a diplomat living with him who has attained majority but is not engaged in paid employment on a permanent basis. Students are included in this category provided that they reside with the diplomat at least during vacations."[18]

4. *Reciprocity.* Sections 3 and 7 of the 1964 Act follow from Article 47 of the Convention which recognises that immunity may be based upon reciprocity. The United Kingdom has reciprocal arrangements under s.7(1)(a) with three states.[19] The arrangement with the U.S.S.R. reads in part " . ... members of the staff of Her Majesty's Embassy in Moscow below the rank of attaché (apart from those who are Soviet nationals), their wives and families, the personal servants of the Ambassador and servants employed in the Embassy Offices (again, apart from those who are Soviet nationals) will henceforth enjoy immunity from personal arrest or other legal process and from the civil and criminal jurisdiction of the Soviet courts and inviolability of residence, provided that the corresponding categories of the staff of the Soviet Embassy in London continue to enjoy these same immunities."[20] The United Kingdom has arrangements under s.7(1)(b) with nine states.[21]

---

[12] *Taylor* v. *Best* (1854) 14 C.B. 487.
[13] *MacCartney* v. *Garbutt* (1890) 24 Q.B.D. 368.
[14] *Dickinson* v. *Del Solar* [1930] 1 K.B. 376.
[15] [1928] A.C. 433.
[16] [1959] 1 Ch. 363.
[17] *Ibid.* p. 367.
[18] Denza, *op. cit.* at p. 264, n. 55, above, p. 225.
[19] Bulgaria, Czechoslavakia and the U.S.S.R.
[20] Note from the Foreign Office to the Soviet Ambassador in London, April 20, 1956, 1964 B.P.I.L., pp. 226, 227. The arrangements were justified by the British Under Secretary of State for Foreign Affairs as follows: " . . . the threat of legal proceedings, in other words, blackmail, is a weapon which can be and is used to subvert members of diplomatic missions in some countries,"*Hansard*, H.C. Vol. 697, col. 1362. July 1, 1964.
[21] Belgium, Bulgaria, France, Federal Republic of Germany, Indonesia, Luxembourg, Netherlands, Poland, United States. E. Lauterpacht suggests that the arrangements made under s.7(1)(a) and (b) are not regarded as treaties by the parties: 1964 B.P.I.L., p. 226.

CHAPTER 7

THE LAW OF THE SEA

1. *INTRODUCTORY NOTE*[1]

THE law of the sea was the subject of the first completed attempt of the International Law Commission to place a large segment of international law on a multilateral treaty basis. Four Conventions resulting from its work[2] were produced by the first and second Geneva Conferences on the Law of the Sea of 1958[3] and 1960.[4] They are the Geneva Conventions on the Territorial Sea and the Contiguous Zone,[5] on the High Seas,[6] on the Continental Shelf[7] and on Fishing and Conservation of the Living Resources of the High Seas.[8] All four have entered into force and have been ratified by a large, though not overwhelming, number of states.[9]

The High Seas Convention is said in its Preamble to be "generally declaratory of established principles of international law."[10] No such claim is made for any of the other Conventions and it is clear that they are a mixture of "codification" and "progressive development" in the sense of the terms of reference of the International Law Commis-

---

[1] See Alexander, ed., *The Law of the Sea* (1967); Bowett, *The Law of the Sea* (1967); Churchill, Nordquist, and Lay, eds., *New Directions in the Law of the Sea*, Vols. I–VI (1973–77); Nordquist and Simmonds, eds., *ibid.* Vols. VII–XI (1980–81); Colombos, *The International Law of the Sea* (6th ed., 1967); Dupuy, *The Law of the Sea* (1974); Friedmann, *The Future of the Oceans* (1971); McDougal & Burke, *The Public Order of the Oceans* (1962); Oda, *The Law of the Sea in Our Time—I: New Developments* 1966–75 (1977); Smith, *The Law and Custom of the Sea* (3rd ed., 1959); Zacklin, *The Changing Law of the Sea* (1974).

[2] In 1956 the Commission submitted to the U.N. General Assembly 73 *Draft Articles Concerning the Law of the Sea*, together with a Commentary upon them: for the text of the Draft Articles and the Commentary, see Y.B.I.L.C., 1956, II, pp. 256 *et seq*.

[3] See *U.N. Conference on the Law of the Sea, Geneva*, February 24–April 27, 1958, *Official Records*, Vols. I–VII; U.N.Doc. A/CONF. 13/37–43. (Referred to in this chapter as *1958 Sea Conference Records*.)

[4] See *2nd U.N. Conference on the Law of the Sea, Geneva*, March 17–April 26, 1960, *Official Records*, U.N.Doc. A/CONF. 19/8 and 9. See Dean, 54 A.J.I.L. 751 (1960).

[5] U.K.T.S. 3 (1965); Cmnd. 2511; 516 U.N.T.S. 205; 52 A.J.I.L. 834 (1958).

[6] U.K.T.S. 5 (1963); Cmnd. 1929; 450 U.N.T.S. 82; 52 A.J.I.L. 842 (1958).

[7] U.K.T.S. 39 (1964); Cmnd. 2422; 499 U.N.T.S. 311; 52 A.J.I.L. 858 (1958).

[8] U.K.T.S. 39 (1966); Cmnd. 3208; 599 U.N.T.S. 285; 52 A.J.I.L. 851 (1958).

[9] The Territorial Sea Convention entered into force on September 10, 1964; there are 46 contracting parties. The High Seas Convention entered into force on September 20, 1962; there are 57 contracting parties. The Continental Shelf Convention entered into force on June 11, 1964; there are 54 contracting parties. The Fisheries Convention entered into force on March 20, 1966; there are 36 contracting parties. The number of contracting parties in each case is that on December 31, 1981. The U.K. is a party to all four Conventions. The Conference also adopted an Optional Protocol on the Compulsory Settlement of Disputes, U.K.T.S. 60 (1963), Cmnd. 2112; 450 U.N.T.S. 169; 52 A.J.I.L. 862 (1958). This entered into force on September 30, 1962; it has 38 contracting parties, including the U.K. On the Conventions, see Dean, 52 A.J.I.L. 607 (1958); Fitzmaurice, 8 I.C.L.Q. 73 (1959); Jessup, 59 Col.L.R. 234 (1959); Sorensen, *The Law of the Sea*, Int.Conc., No. 520 (1958).

[10] Note that there are some provisions of the Convention, *e.g.* Article 15 on piracy (below, p. 327), that are clearly instances of "progressive development" of the law and not "codification."

sion.[11] It is often difficult to be sure within which of these two categories a particular rule falls and whether, if within the latter, practice has so developed since its adoption at Geneva that it now states a rule of customary international law. The *North Sea Continental Shelf Cases*[12] have shown that it must not be too readily assumed that a treaty provision even in a "law-making" treaty states a rule of customary international law.

Although the Geneva Conventions were a considerable achievement, they were not perfect. In particular, they did not contain a rule on the basic question of the width of the territorial sea or on the related question of the fishing rights, if any, of coastal states beyond their territorial sea. They also have been overtaken by events, both scientific and political. The development of new techniques for underwater exploitation of oil and other mineral resources has made it necessary to reconsider the régime of the continental shelf and to establish a régime for the deep sea-bed. Concern for the conservation of fishing resources and the prevention of pollution has grown and has led to general approval of an approach based upon control by the coastal state over wide areas of the sea adjacent to its coastline. State practice on the width of the territorial sea has changed, again in favour of the coastal state and with consequential problems for innocent passage and overflight. Archipelagic and land-locked states have pressed their claims for better treatment. These, and other considerations, including the fact that most post-colonial states had had no say in the drafting of the Geneva Conventions of 1958,[13] led to the decision to call a Third United Nations Conference on the Law of the Sea (UNCLOS III).[14]

After nine long years of negotiation,[15] the Conference adopted the 1982 Convention on the Law of the Sea.[16] The Convention, which will enter into force after 60 ratifications or accessions (Article 308), covers in its 320 articles and nine annexes all of the ground of the four 1958 Conventions and more. Many of its provisions repeat verbatim or in essence those of the Geneva Conventions. Some contain different or more detailed rules on matters covered by them. Others, most strikingly those on the exclusive economic zone and the deep sea-bed, spell out new legal régimes. The main changes or additions are the acceptance of a 12 mile territorial sea; provision for transit passage through international straits; increased rights for archipelagic and land-locked states; stricter control of marine pollution; further provision for fisheries conservation; acceptance of a 200 mile exclusive economic zone for coastal states; changes in the continental shelf régime; and provision for the development of deep sea-bed mineral resources. The Convention contains machinery for the settlement of disputes arising under it, including an International Tribunal for the Law of the Sea, with its seat at Hamburg (Article 287 and Annex VI). A considerable achievement is the provision for the *compulsory* judicial settlement or arbitration of most kinds of disputes that may arise under the Convention, at the request of just one of the parties to the dispute (Article

---

[11] See above, p. 53.

[12] See above, p. 25.

[13] 86 states participated in the 1958 Conference; over 150 states participated in UNCLOS III.

[14] On the Conference, see Ganz, 26 I.C.L.Q. 1 (1977); Oxman, 71 A.J.I.L. 247 (1977); Stevenson and Oxman, 68 A.J.I.L. 1 (1974); *ibid.* 69 A.J.I.L. 1 and 763 (1975); Oxman, 71 A.J.I.L. 247 (1977); *ibid.* 72 A.J.I.L. 57 (1978); *ibid.* 73 A.J.I.L. 1 (1979); *ibid.* 74 A.J.I.L. 1 (1980); *ibid.* 75 A.J.I.L. 211 (1981); *ibid.* 76 A.J.I.L. 1 (1982).

[15] The records of debates and documents of the Conference are published in *Third U.N. Conference on the Law of the Sea: Official Records*, Vols. I–, 1975–, 13 vols. published so far. Referred to in this Chapter as *UNCLOS III Records*. The records are less useful than usual because most of the drafting was done at informal meetings for which there is no official record of debates.

[16] U.N.Doc. A/CONF. 62/122; 21 I.L.M. 1261 (1982).

286).[17] The 1958 Conventions make no such provision; the Optional Protocol that accompanies these Conventions is all that drafting Conferences normally achieve.

The Convention is a remarkable document in that none of its particular provisions were voted upon. Articles were drafted in the working Committees and presented as stating the common, predominant, or accepted view, with the complete text of the Convention seen as an intricate and delicately balanced bargain between the different interests of the participating states. States opposed to provision A were prepared to accept it either in return for the inclusion of provision B or in the interest of an agreed régime for the law of the sea that taken as a whole was acceptable. The intention was that the complete text would be adopted by the same process of consensus too. The thought was that general acceptance of the complete package would increase its chances of ratification and strengthen its claim to be regarded as "instant" customary international law. In the event, this expectation was not realised. At the eleventh hour, the newly elected United States Government asked for time to review the draft text and, when it was unable to obtain all of the changes (almost entirely in respect of the deep sea-bed) that it wanted, requested a vote. The Convention was then adopted, in accordance with traditional Conference practice, by a majority vote.[18] The fact that the United States voted against the Convention and that certain other maritime states abstained is not a good omen for its future, particularly for the deep sea-bed régime.[19] Even so, and allowing for the *North Sea Continental Shelf Cases*, it seems likely that state practice will confirm or come to accept *many* of the particular Convention rules (whether those duplicating or building upon the 1958 Conventions or those adding to them) as being binding as custom. But it must be borne in mind that the consensus favouring the inclusion of a particular rule *as a part of the overall package* may mask opposition to the rule taken by itself. A number of provisions in the area of the more traditional law of the sea, as well as the acceptance of compulsory judicial and arbitral settlement, were, for example, concessions by developing states to which acceptance of the deep sea-bed régime was a necessary counterweight. Paradoxically, the attempt at consensus may, in the event, have hindered the development of customary international law in some cases. Had each provision been voted upon, the presence or absence of genuine agreement would have been more evident and, in some cases, further efforts to obtain a compromise text that was generally acceptable at this more particular level might have borne fruit.

In view of the likelihood that the 1958 Conventions will remain the source of the rules binding upon most maritime states for some time to come,[20] the materials in the present chapter are based upon them so far as they apply with references being made to the 1982

---

[17] Exceptionally, some kinds of disputes concerning the exercise by a coastal state of its sovereign rights, powers, and jurisdiction are not subject to compulsory jurisdiction: Article 297. In addition a contracting state or party may make a declaration excluding certain other kinds of disputes (territorial sea, continental shelf, exclusive economic zone boundary disputes; disputes concerning military activities; and disputes before the Security Council) from compulsory jurisdiction: Article 298.

[18] The vote was 130 to 4, with 17 abstentions. Israel, Turkey, the U.S., and Venezuela voted against. Seven West European states (Belgium, the F.R.G., Italy, Luxembourg, the Netherlands, Spain and the U.K.), eight East European States (Bulgaria, Byelorussia, Czechoslovakia, the G.D.R., Hungary, Poland, Ukraine, and the U.S.S.R.), Mongolia, and Thailand abstained.

[19] Since the vote, the U.S. has confirmed that it *will not* sign the Convention and the U.S.S.R. has indicated that it *will*.

[20] When the 1982 Convention enters into force, a complicated set of treaty relations will result, with the 1958 Conventions continuing in force for the states parties to them and not parties to the 1982 Convention. The 1958 Conventions will govern states parties to both the 1958 and the 1982 Conventions in their relations with states parties to the 1958 Conventions only. The 1982 Convention will replace completely the 1958 Conventions for the parties to both. See Article 311, 1982 Convention.

Convention when it proposes changes or developments. The 1982 Convention is made the basis for the sections on the exclusive economic zone and the deep sea-bed.

2. *THE TERRITORIAL SEA*[21]

(i) SOVEREIGNTY IN THE TERRITORIAL SEA

GENEVA CONVENTION ON THE TERRITORIAL SEA AND THE CONTIGUOUS ZONE 1958

See the references above, p. 284, n. 5

Article 1

1. The sovereignty of a state extends, beyond its land territory and its internal waters, to a belt of sea adjacent to its coast, described as the territorial sea.

2. This sovereignty is exercised subject to the provisions of these articles and to other rules of international law.

Article 2

The sovereignty of a coastal state extends to the airspace over the territorial sea as well as to its bed and subsoil.

Notes

1. There can be little doubt that the above rules, which are repeated in the 1982 Convention (Article 2), represent customary international law. The "other rules of international law" referred to in Article 1(2) presumably include both customary rules (*e.g.* concerning the treatment of aliens) and treaty obligations (*e.g.* concerning navigation at sea).

2. In the *Grisbadarna Case*,[22] the Permanent Court of Arbitration held that when certain land territory was ceded to Sweden "the radius of maritime territory constituting an inseparable appurtenance of this land territory must have automatically formed a part of this cession." Judge Sir Arnold McNair, in his dissenting opinion in the *Anglo-Norwegian Fisheries Case*,[23] stated: "International law does not say to a State: 'You are entitled to claim territorial waters if you want them.' No maritime state can refuse them. International law imposes upon a maritime State certain obligations and confers upon it certain rights arising out of the sovereignty which it exercises over its maritime territory."

(ii) WIDTH OF THE TERRITORIAL SEA

CONVENTION ON THE LAW OF THE SEA 1982

Loc. cit. at p. 284, n. 16, above.

Article 3

Every State has the right to establish the breadth of its territorial sea up to a limit not exceeding 12 nautical miles,[24] measured from baselines determined in accordance with this Convention.

[21] The term "territorial sea" is interchangeable with "territorial waters."
[22] *Norway* v. *Sweden, Hague Court Reports*, 121, at p. 127 (1909).
[23] I.C.J. Rep. 1951, 116, at p. 160. [24] *Ed.* A nautical mile is 1·1508 statute miles.

Notes

1. Lack of agreement prevented the inclusion in the 1958 Territorial Sea Convention of a rule on the width of the territorial sea. This absence of agreement reflected the uncertainty which has existed in customary international law for a number of years. It is arguable that at the turn of the century there was a rule of general application, originating for some states and writers in the distance from the coastline that a cannon could fire (and hence protect[25]), by which the territorial sea was three miles in width (the "cannon shot" rule). State practice now does not support such a rule or any other that specifies a single distance as the width of the territorial sea. Most coastal states claim from three to 12 miles; some states claim more. Information available in 1978[26] showed that 16 states claimed three miles[27]; nine claimed from four to 10 miles[28]; 75 claimed 12 miles[29] and 24 claimed more than that.[30] Compared with earlier figures,[31] these show a rapid swing from three miles to 12 miles as the width most commonly claimed. At UNCLOS III, Ecuador argued for a 200-miles territorial sea but found little support.[32] The 1982 Convention probably states the present customary international law position. Agreement upon a 200-mile exclusive economic zone[33] takes away much of the argument for a territorial sea wider than 12 miles.

2. The extension of the territorial sea to 12 miles has important consequences for the right of innocent passage for ships; it also affects aircraft, which have no right of innocent passage through the territorial sea. The following factors, referred to by the United States representative at Geneva in 1958, are worth bearing in mind:

> One of the merits of the three mile limit was that it was safest for shipping. Many landmarks still used for visual piloting by small craft were not visible at a range of 12 miles; only 20 per cent. of the world's lighthouses had a range exceeding that distance; radar navigation was of only marginal utility beyond twelve miles; and many vessels (which frequently did not wish to enter the territorial sea) did not carry sufficient cable or appropriate equipment to anchor at the depths normally found outside the 12-mile limit. In addition, any extension of the breadth of the territorial sea would mean an increase in the cost of patrolling the larger area. In the case of a country with a long coast-line, extension of the territorial sea from three to 12 miles would entail additional expenditure of perhaps hundreds of millions of dollars annually. One further objection to extending the territorial sea was that, in time of war, a neutral State would have greater difficulty in safeguarding the broader belt of territorial waters against the incursions of ships of belligerents.[34]

[25] See the preamble to the Territorial Waters Jurisdiction Act 1978, above, p. 63.

[26] FAO figures published in Nordquist and Simmonds, *op. cit.* at p. 284, n. 1, above, Vol. X, p. 472.

[27] These included Australia, Belgium, Chile, F.R.G., G.D.R., Ireland, Jordan, the Netherlands, Singapore, the U.K. and the U.S.A.

[28] These included Israel (6 miles); Finland, Norway and Sweden (4); and Yugoslavia (10).

[29] These included most Afro-Asian States, most of the Soviet Bloc, most Latin American states, and most Arab States. Western states such as Canada, France, Italy, Japan and New Zealand also claimed 12 miles, as did China.

[30] The distances claimed ranged from 15 to 200 miles. 200 miles were claimed by seven Latin American states (Argentina, Brazil, Ecuador, El Salvador, Panama, Peru, and Uruguay) and seven African states (Benin, Congo, Ghana, Guinea, Liberia, Sierra Leone, and Somalia). It is not clear to what extent these are claims to full territorial sovereignty. The Argentinian claim, for example, allows passage through and over the 200 miles claimed for ships *and aircraft*: see 6. I.L.M. 663 (1967).

[31] Figures produced by the UN Secretariat for the 1960 Conference showed that 22 states claimed 3 miles; 18 claimed 4–10 miles; 11 claimed 12 miles; and 2 claimed more than 12 miles: 4 Whiteman 21. 1973 FAO figures showed 21 claims to 3 miles and 56 claims to 12 miles.

[32] See *UNCLOS III Records*, Vol. IV, pp. 75–80.

[33] See below, p. 346.   [34] *1958 Sea Conference Records*, Vol. III, p. 26.

Note also the following comment by the representative of Byelorussia at the 1960 Geneva Conference:

The main objective of the champions of the six-mile limit (the 1960 Canadian/United States proposal) was to obtain for their naval forces unconditional, so-called legitimate, access to foreign waters close to coasts in which they were interested for strategic or political reasons.[35]

Clearly, if passage through the territorial sea by warships in order to check on a coastal state's security or of demonstrating a state's "presence" as a form of political pressure is not an exercise of the right of innocent passage,[36] the wider the territorial sea the less the sea can be used effectively for such purposes.

(iii) DELIMITATION OF THE TERRITORIAL SEA

ANGLO-NORWEGIAN FISHERIES CASE[37]

U.K. v. Norway

I.C.J. Reports 1951, p. 116

A Norwegian Decree of 1935 delimited Norway's "Fishery Zone" (by which was meant its territorial sea) along almost 1000 miles of coastline north of latitude 66° 28.8' North. The Zone, which the United Kingdom agreed was, as a matter of historic title, four (not three) miles wide, was measured not from the low-water mark at every point along the coast (as is the normal practice) but from straight baselines linking the outermost points of land (sometimes "drying rocks" above water only at high-tide) along it. The preamble to the Decree justified this system on grounds of "well-established national titles of right," "the geographical conditions prevailing on the Norwegian coasts," and "the safeguard of the vital interests of the inhabitants of the northernmost parts of the country." The first of these grounds related to the use of straight baselines in Norwegian decrees of 1869 and 1889 (though for different parts of the coastline totalling only 89 miles) and acquiescence in that use by other states. The "geographic conditions" were that the coastline concerned is deeply indented by *fiords* and *sunds* (sounds) and, for part of its length south of North Cape, is fronted by a fringe of islands and rocks (the *skjærgaard*) that is difficult to separate from the mainland. The third ground is explained in the Court's statement that "[i]n these barren regions the inhabitants of the coastal zone derive their livelihood essentially from fishing." By using straight baselines Norway enclosed waters within its territorial sea that would have been high seas, and hence open to foreign fishing, if it had used the low-water mark line. Several baselines were over 30 miles long; the longest was 44 miles long.[38] In this case, the United Kingdom challenged the legality of Norway's straight baseline system and the choice of certain baselines used in applying it. The question was important for British fishing interests. Norwegian enforcement of its system had given rise to disputes involving British fishing vessels.

Judgment of the Court

The Court has no difficulty in finding that, for the purpose of measuring the breadth of the territorial sea, it is the low-water mark as opposed to the high-

---

[35] U.N.Doc. A/CONF. 19/C.1/SR.17, p. 13.
[36] See below, p. 308.
[37] See Johnson, 1 I.C.L.Q. 145 (1952) and Waldock (1951) 28 B.Y.I.L. 114.
[38] For a map showing the baselines, see Waldock, *loc. cit.* at n. 37, above, p. 115.

water mark, or the mean between two tides, which has generally been adopted in the practice of States. This criterion is the most favourable to the coastal State and clearly shows the character of territorial waters as appurtenant to the land territory. The Court notes that the Parties agree as to this criterion, but that they differ as to its application.

The Parties also agree that in the case of a low-tide elevation (drying rock) the outer edge at low water of this low-tide elevation may be taken into account as a base-point for calculating the breadth of the territorial sea. . . .

The Court finds itself obliged to decide whether the relevant low-water mark is that of the mainland or of the "skjærgaard." Since the mainland is bordered in its western sector by the "skjærgaard" which constitutes a whole with the mainland, it is the outer line of the "skjærgaard," which must be taken into account in delimiting the belt of Norwegian territorial waters. This solution is dictated by geographic realities.

Three methods have been contemplated to effect the application of the low-water mark rule. The simplest would appear to be the method of the *tracé parallèle*, which consists of drawing the outer limit of the belt of territorial waters by following the coast in all its sinuosities. This method may be applied without difficulty to an ordinary coast, which is not too broken. Where a coast is deeply indented and cut into, as is that of Eastern Finnmark, or where it is bordered by an archipelago such as the "skjærgaard" along the western sector of the coast here in question, the base-line becomes independent of the low-water mark, and can only be determined by means of a geometric construction. In such circumstances the line of the low-water mark can no longer be put forward as a rule requiring the coast line to be followed in all its sinuosities. Nor can one characterize as exceptions to the rule the very many derogations which would be necessitated by such a rugged coast; the rule would disappear under the exceptions. Such a coast, viewed as a whole, calls for the application of a different method; that is, the method of base-lines which, within reasonable limits, may depart from the physical line of the coast.[39]

It is true that the experts of the Second Sub-Committee of the Second Committee of the 1930 Conference for the codification of international law formulated the low-water mark rule somewhat strictly ("following all the sinuosities of the coast"). But they were at the same time obliged to admit many exceptions relating to bays, islands near the coast, groups of islands. In the present case this method of the *tracé parallèle*, which was invoked against Norway in the Memorial, was abandoned in the written Reply, and later in the oral argument of the Agent of the United Kingdom Government. Consequently, it is no longer relevant to the case. "On the other hand," it is said in the Reply, "the *courbe tangente*—or, in English, 'envelopes of arcs of circles'— method is the method which the United Kingdom considers to be the correct one."

The arcs of circles method, which is constantly used for determining the position of a point or object at sea, is a new technique in so far as it is a method for delimiting the territorial sea. This technique was proposed by the United States delegation at the 1930 Conference for the codification of international law. Its purpose is to secure the application of the principle that the belt of territorial waters must follow the line of the coast. It is not obligatory by law, as

---

[39] *Ed.* These last two sentences are a revised translation by the I.C.J. Registry of the authoritative French text: see Y.B.I.L.C., 1956, II, p. 267.

was admitted by Counsel for the United Kingdom Government in his oral reply. . . .

The principle that the belt of territorial waters must follow the general direction of the coast makes it possible to fix certain criteria valid for any delimitation of the territorial sea; these criteria will be elucidated later. The Court will confine itself at this stage to noting that, in order to apply this principle, several States have deemed it necessary to follow the straight baselines method and that they have not encountered objections of principle by other States. This method consists of selecting appropriate points on the low-water mark and drawing straight lines between them. This has been done, not only in the case of well-defined bays, but also in cases of minor curvatures of the coast line where it was solely a question of giving a simpler form to the belt of territorial waters.

It has been contended, on behalf of the United Kingdom, that Norway may draw straight lines only across bays. The Court is unable to share this view. If the belt of territorial waters must follow the outer line of the "skjærgaard," and if the method of straight base-lines must be admitted in certain cases, there is no valid reason to draw them only across bays, as in Eastern Finnmark, and not also to draw them between islands, islets and rocks, across the sea areas separating them, even when such areas do not fall within the conception of a bay. It is sufficient that they should be situated between the island formations of the "skjærgaard," *inter fauces terrarum*.

In the opinion of the United Kingdom Government, Norway is entitled, on historic grounds, to claim as internal waters all fjords and sunds which have the character of a bay. . . .

By "historic waters" are usually meant waters which are treated as internal waters but which would not have that character were it not for the existence of an historic title. . . . In its [the United Kingdom's] opinion Norway can justify the claim that these waters are . . . internal on the ground that she has exercised the necessary jurisdiction over them for a long period without opposition from other States, a kind of *possessio longi temporis*, with the result that her jurisdiction over these waters must now be recognized although it constitutes a derogation from the rules in force. . . . But the United Kingdom Government concedes this only on the basis of historic title; it must therefore be taken that that Government has not abandoned its contention that the ten-mile rule is to be regarded as a rule of international law.

In these circumstances the Court deems it necessary to point out that although the ten-mile rule has been adopted by certain States both in their national law and in their treaties and conventions, and although certain arbitral decisions have applied it as between these States, other States have adopted a different limit. Consequently, the ten-mile rule has not acquired the authority of a general rule of international law.

In any event the ten-mile rule would appear to be inapplicable as against Norway inasmuch as she has always opposed any attempt to apply it to the Norwegian coast.

The Court now comes to the question of the length of the base-lines drawn across the waters lying between the various formations of the "skjærgaard." Basing itself on the analogy with the alleged general rule of ten miles relating to bays, the United Kingdom Government still maintains on this point that the length of straight lines must not exceed ten miles.

In this connection, the practice of States does not justify the formulation of any general rule of law. The attempts that have been made to subject groups of islands or coastal archipelagoes to conditions analogous to the limitations concerning bays (distance between the islands not exceeding twice the breadth of the territorial waters, or ten or twelve sea miles), have not got beyond the stage of proposals.

Furthermore, apart from any question of limiting the lines to ten miles, it may be that several lines can be envisaged. In such cases the coastal State would seem to be in the best position to appraise the local conditions dictating the selection.

Consequently, the Court is unable to share the view of the United Kingdom Government, that "Norway, in the matter of base-lines, now claims recognition of an exceptional system." As will be show later, all that the Court can see therein is the application of general international law to a specific case. . . .

It does not at all follow that, in the absence of rules having the technically precise character alleged by the United Kingdom Government, the delimitation undertaken by the Norwegian Government in 1935 is not subject to certain principles which make it possible to judge as to its validity under international law. The delimitation of sea areas has always an international aspect; it cannot be dependent merely upon the will of the coastal State as expressed in its municipal law. Although it is true that the act of delimitation is necessarily a unilateral act, because only the coastal State is competent to undertake it, the validity of the delimitation with regard to other States depends upon international law.

In this connection, certain basic considerations inherent in the nature of the territorial sea, bring to light certain criteria which, though not entirely precise, can provide courts with an adequate basis for their decisions, which can be adapted to the diverse facts in question.

Among these considerations, some reference must be made to the close dependence of the territorial sea upon the land domain. It is the land which confers upon the coastal State a right to the waters off its coasts. It follows that while such a State must be allowed the latitude necessary in order to be able to adapt its delimitation to practical needs and local requirements, the drawing of base-lines must not depart to any appreciable extent from the general direction of the coast.

Another fundamental consideration, of particular importance in this case, is the more or less close relationship existing between certain sea areas and the land formations which divide or surround them. The real question raised in the choice of base-lines is in effect whether certain sea areas lying within these lines are sufficiently closely linked to the land domain to be subject to the regime of internal waters. This idea, which is at the basis of the determination of the rules relating to bays, should be liberally applied in the case of a coast, the geographical configuration of which is as unusual as that of Norway.

Finally, there is one consideration not to be overlooked, the scope of which extends beyond purely geographical factors: that of certain economic interests peculiar to a region, the reality and importance of which are clearly evidenced by a long usage.

Norway puts forward the 1935 Decree as the application of a traditional system of delimitation, a system which she claims to be in complete conformity with international law. The Norwegian Government has referred in this connection to an historic title, the meaning of which was made clear by Counsel for Norway at the sitting on October 12th, 1951: "The Norwegian Government does not rely upon history to justify exceptional rights, to claim areas of sea which the general law would deny; it invokes history, together with other factors, to justify the way in which it applies the general law." This conception of an historic title is in consonance with the Norwegian Government's understanding of the general rules of international law. In its view, these rules of international law take into account the diversity of facts and, therefore, concede that the drawing of base-lines must be adapted to the special conditions obtaining in different regions. In its view, the system of delimitation applied in 1935, a system characterized by the use of straight lines, does not therefore infringe the general law: it is an adaptation rendered necessary by local condition.

The Court examined the Norwegian system.

The Court . . . finds that this system was consistently applied by Norwegian authorities. . . .

The Court considers that too much importance need not be attached to the few uncertainties or contradictions, real or apparent, which the United Kingdom Government claims to have discovered in Norwegian practice. They may be easily understood in the light of the variety of the facts and conditions prevailing in the long period which has elapsed since 1812, and are not such as to modify the conclusions reached by the Court. . . .

From the standpoint of international law, it is now necessary to consider whether the application of the Norwegian system encountered any opposition from foreign States.

Norway has been in a position to argue without any contradiction that neither the promulgation of her delimitation Decrees in 1869[40] and in 1889, nor their application, gave rise to any opposition on the part of foreign States. Since, moreover, these Decrees constitute, as has been shown above, the application of a well-defined and uniform system, it is indeed this system itself which would reap the benefit of general toleration, the basis of an historical consolidation which would make it enforceable as against all States.

The general toleration of foreign States with regard to the Norwegian practice is an unchallenged fact. For a period of more than sixty years the United Kingdom Government itself in no way contested it. . . . It would appear that it was only in its Memorandum of July 27th, 1933, that the United Kingdom made a formal and definite protest on this point.

The United Kingdom Government has argued that the Norwegian system of delimitation was not known to it and that the system therefore lacked the notoriety essential to provide the basis of an historic title enforceable against it. The Court is unable to accept this view. . . .

The notoriety of the facts, the general toleration of the international community, Great Britain's position in the North Sea, her own interest in the question, and her prolonged abstention would in any case warrant Norway's enforcement of her system against the United Kingdom.

---

[40] *Ed.* France, which had been in dispute with Norway on a related matter, did ask for an explanation of the 1869 Decree. Norway replied, arguing that the enactment was lawful, and France "did not pursue the matter": I.C.J. Rep. 1951, p. 136.

The Court is thus led to conclude that the method of straight lines, established in the Norwegian system, was imposed by the peculiar geography of the Norwegian coast; that even before the dispute arose, this method had been consolidated by a constant and sufficiently long practice, in the face of which the attitude of governments bears witness to the fact that they did not consider it to be contrary to international law.

The question now arises whether the Decree of July 12th, 1935, which in its preamble is expressed to be an application of this method, conforms to it in its drawing of the base-lines, or whether, at certain points, it departs from this method to any considerable extent. . . .

The Norwegian Government admits that the base-lines must be drawn in such a way as to respect the general direction of the coast and that they must be drawn in a reasonable manner. . . .

The delimitation of the Lopphavet basin has also been criticized by the United Kingdom. . . . The Lopphavet basin constitutes an ill-defined geographic whole. It cannot be regarded as having the character of a bay. It is made up of an extensive area of water dotted with large islands which are separated by inlets that terminate in the various fjords. The base-line has been challenged on the ground that it does not respect the general direction of the coast.[41] It should be observed that, however justified the rule in question may be, it is devoid of any mathematical precision. In order properly to apply the rule, regard must be had for the relation between the deviation complained of and what, according to the terms of the rule, must be regarded as the *general* direction of the coast. Therefore, one cannot confine oneself to examining one sector of the coast alone, except in a case of manifest abuse. . . . In the case in point, the divergence between the base-line and the land formations is not such that it is a distortion of the general direction of the Norwegian coast.

Even if it were considered that in the sector under review the deviation was too pronounced, it must be pointed out that the Norwegian Government has relied upon an historic title clearly referable to the waters of Lopphavet. . . . The Court considers that, although it is not always clear to what specific areas they apply, the historical data produced . . . lend some weight to the idea of the survival of traditional rights reserved to the inhabitants of the Kingdom over fishing grounds included in the 1935 delimitation, particularly in the case of Lopphavet. Such rights, founded on the vital needs of the population and attested by very ancient and peaceful usage, may legitimately be taken into account in drawing a line which, moreover, appears to the Court to have been kept within the bounds of what is moderate and reasonable. . . .

For these reasons, the Court . . . finds by ten votes to two[42] that the method employed for the delimitation of the fisheries zone by the Royal Norwegian Decree of July 12, 1935, is not contrary to international law; and by eight votes

---

[41] *Ed.* The baseline across the Lopphavet basin is 44 miles long. One of the points from which it is drawn is a drying rock 18 miles from the next point, which is also a drying rock.

[42] The judges in the majority were President Basdevant; Vice-President Guerrero; Judges Alvarez, Hackworth, Winiarski, Zoričić, de Visscher, Klaestad, Badawi Pasha and Hsu Mo. The dissenting judges were Judges Sir Arnold McNair and Read. Judge Hackworth voted with the majority on both rulings solely on the basis that Norway had established an historic title.

to four,[43] that the base-lines fixed by the said Degree in application of this method are not contrary to international law.

Notes

1. The judgment in the case was greeted with dismay by British commentators who felt that it did not do justice to the not insignificant body of state practice on the questions in issue.[44] Although, as those commentators suggest, it may have been an example of judicial legislation, the judgment has undoubtedly been accepted by states and now almost certainly reflects customary international law on most points.[45]

2. *Measurement of the outer limit of the territorial sea.* The two methods discussed by the Court for finding the outer limit of the territorial sea are the *tracé parallèle* and the arcs of circles (*courbe tangente*) methods. The former, which is apparently not used in practice,[46] involves drawing a line parallel to the baseline. The line is established by projections the width of the territorial sea from every point along the baseline made outwards in the general direction of the coast. The method is difficult to apply with exactness on any irregular stretch of coastline. With regard to the latter, which Judge Read, disagreeing with the Court, thought was not new but "the way in which the coastline rule has been applied in the international practice of the last century and a half,"[47] Waldock[48] states:

> To apply the rule you take a pair of dividers (compasses) opened to give a three-mile measurement and then draw a three-mile arc either from the land towards the given position at sea or from the position at sea towards the nearest points of land. If the arcs fall short, the position at sea is not within territorial waters. . . . That this was the procedure found in state practice is demonstrated by the fact that very few states indeed ever drew either the outer limit of their territorial waters or their base-line. Without a precise delimitation of territorial waters, the only possible course is to determine the outer limit by taking three-mile arcs from the land. . . . It is nothing but the application to territorial waters of the method used by seamen the world over for measuring distances at sea. . . .

Although easier to apply than the *tracé parallèle* method, the "arcs of circles" method may still lead to awkward pockets of high seas on exceptionally irregular coastlines.[49] It remains the standard method used by mariners in applying the low-water mark baseline, which also remains the baseline used by states along regular coastlines.

3. *Straight baselines.* Did the Court find for Norway because its system for the delimitation of its territorial sea was permitted by customary international law or because, although not permitted by it, Norway had established an historic title?[50] Or both? How long and how irregular does a coastline have to be for the Court's straight baseline approach to be applicable? Is it, where applicable, obligatory or can a state still use the low-water mark method instead? What is the precise relevance of economic factors in the Court's approach? Do they permit a state to be bolder than it might otherwise be in choosing its base points? As far as bays are concerned, might economic factors there too justify a longer closing line than would otherwise be permissible? Does

---

[43] Judge Hsu Mo joined the dissenting judges. It is not clear who the fourth dissenting judge was.

[44] See the articles by Johnson and Waldock cited above, p. 289, n. 37.

[45] Note the different rule in Territorial Sea Convention, Article 4(3), p. 296 below, on drying rocks, or low-tide elevations.

[46] Waldock, *loc. cit.* at p. 289, n. 37, above, pp. 134–135.

[47] I.C.J. Rep. 1951, at p. 192.

[48] *Loc. cit.* at p. 289, n. 37, above, pp. 134–135.

[49] For a proposal made some years ago by the U.S. to prevent such pockets arising, see Boggs, 24 A.J.I.L. 541, at p. 547 (Fig. 6) (1924).

[50] See further on "historic waters," the *Continental Shelf* (*Tunisia* v. *Libya*) *Case*, below, p. 359.

the Court set any upper limit in terms of miles to the length of a straight baseline or of a closing line for a bay?

GENEVA CONVENTION ON THE TERRITORIAL SEA AND THE CONTIGUOUS ZONE 1958

See the references above, p. 284, n. 5

Article 3

Except where otherwise provided in these articles, the normal baseline for measuring the breadth of the territorial sea is the low-water line along the coast as marked on large-scale charts officially recognized by the coastal state.

Article 4

1. In localities where the coastline is deeply indented and cut into, or if there is a fringe of islands along the coast in its immediate vicinity, the method of straight baselines joining appropriate points may be employed in drawing the baseline from which the breadth of the territorial sea is measured.

2. The drawing of such baselines must not depart to any appreciable extent from the general direction of the coast, and the sea areas lying within the lines must be sufficiently closely linked to the land domain to be subject to the regime of internal waters.

3. Baselines shall not be drawn to and from low-tide elevations, unless lighthouses or similar installations which are permanently above sea level have been built on them.

4. Where the method of straight baselines is applicable under the provisions of paragraph 1, account may be taken, in determining particular baselines, of economic interests peculiar to the region concerned, the reality and the importance of which are clearly evidenced by a long usage.

5. The system of straight baselines may not be applied by a state in such a manner as to cut off from the high seas the territorial sea of another state.

6. The coastal state must clearly indicate straight baselines on charts, to which due publicity must be given.

Article 5

1. Waters on the landward side of the baseline of the territorial sea form part of the internal waters of the state.

2. Where the establishment of a straight baseline in accordance with Article 4 has the effect of enclosing as internal waters areas which previously had been considered as part of the territorial sea or of the high seas, a right of innocent passage, as provided in Articles 14 to 23, shall exist in those waters.

Article 6

The outer limit of the territorial sea is the line every point of which is at a distance from the nearest point of the baseline equal to the breadth of the territorial sea.

Article 7

1. This article relates only to bays the coasts of which belong to a single state.

2. For the purposes of these articles, a bay is a well-marked indentation whose penetration is in such proportion to the width of its mouth as to contain landlocked waters and constitute more than a mere curvature of the coast. An indentation shall not, however, be regarded as a bay unless its area is as large as, or larger than, that of the semi-circle whose diameter is a line drawn across the mouth of that indentation.

3. For the purpose of measurement, the area of an indentation is that lying between the low-water mark around the shore of the indentation and a line joining the low-water marks of its natural entrance points. Where, because of the presence of islands, an indentation has more than one mouth, the semi-circle shall be drawn on a line as long as the sum total of the lengths of the lines across the different mouths. Islands within an indentation shall be included as if they were part of the water area of the indentation.

4. If the distance between the low-water marks of the natural entrance points of a bay does not exceed twenty-four miles, a closing line may be drawn between these two low-water marks, and the waters enclosed thereby shall be considered as internal waters.

5. Where the distance between the low-water marks of the natural entrance points of a bay exceeds twenty-four miles, a straight baseline of twenty-four miles shall be drawn within the bay in such a manner as to enclose the maximum area of water that is possible with a line of that length.

6. The foregoing provisions shall not apply to so-called "historic" bays, or in any case where the straight baseline system provided for in Article 4 is applied.

Article 8

For the purpose of delimiting the territorial sea, the outermost permanent harbour works which form an integral part of the harbour system shall be regarded as forming part of the coast.

Article 9

Roadsteads which are normally used for the loading, unloading and anchoring of ships, and which would otherwise be situated wholly or partly outside the outer limit of the territorial sea, are included in the territorial sea. The coastal state must clearly demarcate such roadsteads and indicate them on charts together with their boundaries, to which due publicity must be given.

Article 10

1. An island is a naturally-formed area of land, surrounded by water, which is above water at high tide.

2. The territorial sea of an island is measured in accordance with the provisions of these articles.

Article 11

1. A low-tide elevation is a naturally-formed area of land which is surrounded by and above water at low-tide but submerged at high tide. Where a low-tide

elevation is situated wholly or partly at a distance not exceeding the breadth of the territorial sea from the mainland or an island, the low-water line on that elevation may be used as the baseline for measuring the breadth of the territorial sea.

2. Where a low-tide elevation is wholly situated at a distance exceeding the breadth of the territorial sea from the mainland or an island, it has no territorial sea of its own.

Article 12

1. Where the coasts of two states are opposite or adjacent to each other, neither of the two states is entitled, failing agreement between them to the contrary, to extend its territorial sea beyond the median line every point of which is equidistant from the nearest points on the baselines from which the breadth of the territorial seas of each of the two states is measured. The provisions of this paragraph shall not apply, however, where it is necessary by reason of historic title or other special circumstances to delimit the territorial seas of the two states in a way which is at variance with this provision.

2. The line of delimitation between the territorial seas of two states lying opposite to each other or adjacent to each other shall be marked on large-scale charts officially recognized by the coastal states.

Article 13

If a river flows directly into the sea, the baseline shall be a straight line across the mouth of the river between points on the low-tide line of its banks.

Notes

1. *Baselines*. The 1958 Convention follows the approach of the International Court of Justice in the *Anglo-Norwegian Fisheries Case*. It differs only in requiring (Article 4(3)) that low-tide elevations be permanently above sea level to be used as the beginning of a straight baseline; Article 4(5), (6) supplement the judgment. The use of straight baselines is not compulsory where Article 4 applies. Applying Article 4, the United Kingdom now uses straight baselines from Cape Wrath to the Mull of Kintyre on the west coast of Scotland.[51] The result is to enclose as internal waters areas of water between the Outer Hebrides and the mainland which, when a low-water mark baseline was used, were high seas. Because of this result, the right of innocent passage in Article 5(2) applies. Other states that now use straight baselines include Cambodia, Guinea, Iceland and Venezuela.[52] On their use by archipelagic states, see below, p. 300.

The 1982 Convention (Arts. 5, 8, 4, 12, 15 and 9) repeats almost exactly nearly all of the provisions of the 1958 Convention (Arts. 3, 5, 6, 9, 12 and 13 respectively) on baselines. It retains Article 4 too (1982 Convention, Art. 7), but adds to the end of Article 4(4) the words "or except in instances where the drawing of baselines to and from such elevations has received general international recognition" (1982 Convention, Art. 7(4)). It also adds an additional paragraph to Article 4 (1982 Convention, Art. 7(2)) on deltas:

Where because of the presence of a delta and other natural conditions the coastline is highly unstable, the appropriate points may be selected along the furthest seaward extent of the low-water line and, notwithstanding subsequent regression of the low-water line, the straight baselines shall remain effective until changed by the coastal State in accordance with this Convention.

[51] Territorial Waters Order in Council 1964, Article 3, S.I. 1965, Part III, s.2, p. 6452A.
[52] 4 Whiteman 21–35.

The 1982 Convention (Art. 11) similarly retains but supplements Article 8, 1958 Convention by the following final sentence: "Offshore installations and artificial islands shall not be considered as permanent harbour works." The 1982 Convention adds a new provision (Art. 14) making it clear that a "coastal state may determine baselines in turn by any of the methods provided for in the foregoing articles to suit different conditions."

2. *Bays.*[53] On the closing line for bays, the Second Sub-Committee of the Second Committee of the 1930 Hague Codification Conference proposed a closing line of 10 miles.[54] The International Law Commission at one stage proposed a closing line of 25 miles, but later reduced it to 15. It explained in its Commentary:

> The proposal to extend the closing line to 25 miles had found little support; a number of Governments stated that, in their view, such an extension was excessive. By a majority, the Commission decided to reduce the 25 miles figure, proposed in 1955, to 15 miles. While appreciating that a line of 10 miles had been recognised by several Governments and established by international conventions, the Commission took account of the fact that the origin of the 10 mile line dates back to a time when the breadth of the territorial sea was much more commonly fixed at 3 miles than it is now.[55]

The 24 miles rule was inserted in the Convention at Geneva.[56] On the relation between the 24 miles rule and customary international law, the following statement in 1963 by the United States Secretary of State on the status of Bristol Bay off the coast of Alaska is of interest:

> Although the Convention is not yet in force . . . it must be regarded in view of its adoption (at Geneva) by a large majority of the States of the world as the best evidence of international law on the subject at the present time. This is particularly so in view of the rejection by the International Court of Justice in the *Anglo-Norwegian Fisheries Case* of the so-called 10-mile rule previously considered as international law by the United States and other countries. . . . Since the line drawn . . . [across the Bay] is over 162 miles long . . . there is no basis in international law . . . for Alaska's claim . . . unless these waters can be considered an "historic bay."[56a]

The 1982 Convention (Art. 10) repeats Article 7 of the Territorial Sea Convention. As to *bays bordered by more than one state*, Colombos[57] states:

> There exists a good deal for controversy on the subject, but the correct view is that territorial waters should follow the sinuosities of the coast . . . subject to any special agreement. . . .

An example of such a bay is the controversial Gulf of Aqaba in the Red Sea which is bordered by the states of Egypt, Israel, Jordan and Saudi Arabia.[58] Neither the 1958 nor the 1982 Conventions govern such bays or *historic bays*.

As to the latter, when in 1957, the U.S.S.R. claimed Peter the Great Bay off its Asian coast as internal waters, a number of states protested. The United Kingdom's note read:

> Her Majesty's Government can find no evidence that the Bay in question is an historic Bay in the technical sense of the term . . . and consider that this action of

---

[53] See Bouchez, *The Regime of Bays in International Law* (1964), and Strohl, *The International Law of Bays* (1963).
[54] L.N.Doc. C. 351 (b). M. 145 (b). 1930. V, p. 217.
[55] Y.B.I.L.C., 1956, II, p. 269.
[56] *1958 Sea Conference Records*, Vol. III, p. 146.
[56a] 2 I.L.M. 528 (1963).
[57] *Loc. cit.* at p. 284, n. 1, above, p. 188.
[58] On the right of passage through the Gulf, see below, p. 312.

drawing a closing line of 102 miles in length has no foundation in international law. . . . [59]

Historic bays undoubtedly may exist at customary international law. Thus in *El Salvador* v. *Nicaragua*,[60] the Central American Court of Justice held that the Gulf of Foncesa, which is surrounded by Nicaragua, Honduras and El Salvador and which is about 19 miles across at its mouth, was "an historic bay possessed of the characteristics of a closed sea." In 1974, the U.S.A. protested at a claim by Libya that a part of the Gulf of Sirte was Libyan internal or territorial waters as a "violation of international law."[61] The Gulf did not "meet the international law standards of past open, notorious and effective exercise of authority, and acquiesence of foreign nations necessary to be regarded historically as Libyan internal or territorial waters."[62]

See also on bays, *Post Office* v. *Estuary Radio Ltd.*[63]

3. *Islands.*[64] A case of an island being created by natural forces was the creation of Surtsey by volcanic activity in 1963 in Icelandic territorial waters. Would land which is permanently above the sea as a result of dredging operations be an island under the Territorial Sea Convention? Why can a lighthouse built on a low-tide elevation be the end of a baseline for measuring the territorial sea (Art. 3(3)) when it cannot be treated as an island under the Convention? Note that structures used in connection with work on or in the continental shelf are expressly stated by the 1958 Continental Shelf Convention not to be islands.[65] Small islands have become more important in recent years because of the possibility of exploiting oil and gas resources in the sea-bed surrounding them.

The 1982 Convention (Art. 121) repeats the definition of an island and the rule about its territorial sea, but restricts the circumstances in which it may have an exclusive economic zone or continental shelf, see below p. 353. Article 6 of the 1982 Convention adds the following rule about island baselines:

> In the case of islands situated on atolls or of islands having fringing reefs, the baseline for measuring the breadth of the territorial sea is the seaward low-water line of the reef, as shown by the appropriate symbol on charts officially recognised by the coastal State.

4. *Archipelagos.* In 1957, Indonesia announced that its territorial sea would hence-forth be "measured from straight baselines connecting the outermost points of the islands of the Republic of Indonesia."[66] The waters within the baselines would be "national waters subject to the absolute sovereignty of Indonesia," except that the "peaceful passage of foreign vessels would be guaranteed as long as and in so far as it is not contrary to the sovereignty of the Indonesian state or harmful to her security."[67] A number of states, including the United Kingdom,[68] protested. The International Law Commission felt itself unable, for lack of information, to reach any conclusion on the

---

[59] 5 C.P.U.K.I.L., in 7 I.C.L.Q. 112 (1958).
[60] 11 A.J.I.L. 674 (1917).
[61] 68 A.J.I.L. 510 (1974).
[62] *Ibid*. In 1981, two Libyan military aircraft were shot down when they attacked U.S. military aircraft engaged in exercises in the disputed area of the Gulf. See also on historic bays, 68 A.J.I.L. 107 (1974) and the *Continental Shelf (Tunisia* v. *Libya) Case*, p. 359, below.
[63] [1968] 2 Q.B. 740 (C.A.).
[64] See Bowett, *The Legal Régime of Islands in International Law* (1979) and Symmons, *The Maritime Zones of Islands in International Law* (1979). See also Papadakis, *The International Regime of Artificial Islands* (1977).
[65] Article 5(4) below, p. 356.
[66] 4 Whiteman 284. The Philippines had made a similar announcement in 1955; *ibid*. p. 282. Sørensen, *Varia Juris Gentium* (1959), p. 315.
[67] 4 Whiteman 284.
[68] See *Hansard*, H.C., Vol. 582, col. 1185. February 19, 1958.

question of a special rule for archipelagos. Does the *Anglo-Norwegian Fisheries Case* provide any basis for a rule of customary international law on archipelagos by analogy? What is the consequence of the absence of a special rule for archipelagos in the Territorial Sea Convention for the parties to it?

The 1982 Convention contains provisions allowing the use of straight baselines by archipelagic states (but not by continental states with archipelagos).[69] These read in part (Art. 47):

> 1. An archipelagic state may draw straight archipelagic baselines joining the outermost points of the outermost islands and drying reefs of the archipelago provided that within such baselines are included the main islands and an area in which the ratio of the area of the water to the area of the land, including atolls, is between one to one and nine to one.
>
> 2. The length of such baselines shall not exceed 100 nautical miles, except that up to three per cent. of the total number of baselines enclosing any archipelago may exceed that length, up to a maximum length of 125 nautical miles.
>
> 3. The drawing of such baselines shall not depart to any appreciable extent from the general configuration of the archipelago.

The archipelagic waters thus enclosed are within the territorial sovereignty of the archipelagic state (1982 Convention, Art. 49), but are subject to the Convention right of innocent passage (1982 Convention, Art. 52), and to the right of archipelagic sea lanes passage (Art. 53, *ibid.*). The latter is comparable to the right of transit passage through straits: see below p. 312.

(iv) Jurisdiction over Foreign Ships in the Territorial Sea

CORFU CHANNEL CASE (MERITS)

U.K. *v.* Albania

I.C.J. Reports 1949, p. 4

The facts of the case, so far as they concern the Albanian counter-claim, are indicated in the following extract from the Court's judgment. See also the further extract from the judgment below[70] on the United Kingdom's claim for compensation for damage caused by mines to the *Saumarez* and the *Volage* during their passage through the Corfu Channel on October 22, 1946.

Judgment of the Court

In the second part of the Special Agreement, the following question is submitted to the Court:

> "(2) Has the United Kingdom under international law violated the sovereignty of the Albanian People's Republic by reason of the acts of the Royal Navy in Albanian waters on the 22nd October and on the 12th and 13th November 1946 and is there any duty to give satisfaction?" . . .

[69] Article 46 reads: "For the purposes of this Convention: (a) 'Archipelagic State' means a State constituted wholly by one or more archipelagos and may include other islands; (b) 'Archipelago' means a group of islands, including parts of islands, interconnecting waters and other natural features which are so closely interrelated that such islands, waters and other natural features form an intrinsic geographical, economic and political entity, or which historically have been regarded as such."

[70] p. 380.

On May 15th, 1946, the British cruisers *Orion* and *Superb*, while passing southward through the North Corfu Channel, were fired at by an Albanian battery in the vicinity of Saranda. . . .

The United Kingdom Government at once protested to the Albanian Government, stating that innocent passage through straits is a right recognized by international law. There ensued a diplomatic correspondence in which the Albanian Government asserted that foreign warships and merchant vessels had no right to pass through Albanian territorial waters without prior notification to, and the permission of, the Albanian authorities. . . .

It was in such circumstances that these two cruisers together with the destroyers *Saumarez* and *Volage* were sent through the North Corfu Strait on . . . [October 22, 1946].

The Court will now consider the Albanian contention that the United Kingdom Government violated Albanian sovereignty by sending the warships through this Strait without the previous authorization of the Albanian Government.

It is, in the opinion of the Court, generally recognized and in accordance with international custom that States in time of peace have a right to send their warships through straits used for international navigation between two parts of the high seas without the previous authorisation of a coastal State, provided that the passage is *innocent*. Unless otherwise prescribed in an international convention, there is no right for a coastal State to prohibit such passage through straits in time of peace.

The Albanian Government does not dispute that the North Corfu Channel is a strait in the geographical sense; but it denies that this Channel belongs to the class of international highways through which a right of passage exists, on the grounds that it is only of secondary importance and not even a necessary route between two parts of the high seas, and that it is used almost exclusively for local traffic to and from the ports of Corfu and Saranda.

It may be asked whether the test is to be found in the volume of traffic passing through the Strait or in its greater or lesser importance for international navigation. But in the opinion of the Court the decisive criterion is rather its geographical situation as connecting two parts of the high seas and the fact of its being used for international navigation. Nor can it be decisive that this Strait is not a necessary route between two parts of the high seas, but only an alternative passage between the Ægean and the Adriatic Seas. It has nevertheless been a useful route for international maritime traffic. . . .

One fact of particular importance is that the North Corfu Channel constitutes a frontier between Albania and Greece, that a part of it is wholly within the territorial waters of these States, and that the Strait is of special importance to Greece by reason of the traffic to and from the port of Corfu.

Having regard to these various considerations, the Court has arrived at the conclusion that the North Corfu Channel should be considered as belonging to the class of international highways through which passage cannot be prohibited by a coastal State in time of peace.

On the other hand, it is a fact that the two coastal States did not maintain normal relations, that Greece had made territorial claims precisely with regard to a part of Albanian territory bordering on the Channel, that Greece had declared that she considered herself technically in a state of war with Albania, and that Albania, invoking the danger of Greek incursions, had considered it necessary to take certain measures of vigilance in this region. The Court is of opinion that Albania, in view of these exceptional circumstances, would have been justified in issuing regulations in respect of the passage of warships through the Strait, but not in prohibiting such passage or in subjecting it to the requirement of special authorization.

For these reasons the Court is unable to accept the Albanian contention that the Government of the United Kingdom has violated Albanian sovereignty by sending the warships through the Strait without having obtained the previous authorization of the Albanian Government.

In these circumstances, it is unnecessary to consider the more general question, much debated by the Parties, whether States under international law have a right to send warships in time of peace through territorial waters not included in a strait.

The Albanian Government has further contended that the sovereignty of Albania was violated because the passage of the British warships on October 22nd, 1946, was not an *innocent passage*. . . .

It is shown by the Admiralty telegram of September 21st . . . that the object of sending the warships through the Strait was not only to carry out a passage for purposes of navigation, but also to test Albania's attitude. . . . The legality of this measure taken by the Government of the United Kingdom cannot be disputed, provided that it was carried out in a manner consistent with the requirements of international law. . . . The Government of the United Kingdom was not bound to abstain from exercising its right of passage, which the Albanian Government had illegally denied.

It remains, therefore, to consider whether the *manner* in which the passage was carried out was consistent with the principle of innocent passage and to examine the various contentions of the Albanian Government in so far as they appear to be relevant.

The Court found, contrary to Albania's contention, that the warships were neither in combat formation nor manoeuvering and that there were no soldiers on board.

. . . The guns were . . . "trained fore and aft, which is their normal position at sea in peace time, and were not loaded." . . . In the light of this evidence, the Court cannot accept the Albanian contention that the position of the guns was inconsistent with the rules of innocent passage.

In the . . . telegram of October 26th, the Commander-in-Chief reported that the passage "was made with ships at action stations in order that they might be able to retaliate quickly if fired upon again." In view of the firing from the Albanian battery on May 15th, this measure of precaution cannot, in itself, be regarded as unreasonable. But four warships—two cruisers and two destroyers—passed in this manner, with crews at action stations, ready to retaliate quickly if fired upon. They passed one after another through this narrow channel, close to the Albanian coast, at a time of political tension in this region. The intention must have been, not only to test Albania's attitude, but at the same time to demonstrate such force that she would abstain from firing again on passing ships. Having regard, however, to all the circumstances of the case, as described above, the Court is unable to characterize these measures taken by the United Kingdom authorities as a violation of Albania's sovereignty.

. . . In a report of the commander of *Volage*, dated October 23rd, 1946—a report relating to the passage on the 22nd—it is stated: "The most was made of the opportunities to study Albanian defences at close range. . . ."

With regard to the observations of coastal defences made after the explosions, these were justified by the fact that two ships had just been blown up and that, in this critical situation, their commanders might fear that they would be fired on from the coast, as on May 15th.

Having thus examined the various contentions of the Albanian Government in so far as they appear to be relevant, the Court has arrived at the conclusion that the United Kingdom did not violate the sovereignty of Albania by reason of the acts of the British Navy in Albanian waters on October 22nd, 1946.

In addition to the passage of the United Kingdom warships on October 22nd 1946, the second question in the Special Agreement relates to the acts of the Royal Navy in Albanian waters on November 12th and 13th, 1946. This is the minesweeping operation called "Operation Retail". . . .

The United Kingdom Government does not dispute that "Operation Retail" was carried out against the clearly expressed wish of the Albanian Government. It recognizes that the operation had not the consent of the international mine clearance organizations, that it could not be justified as the exercise of a right of innocent passage, and lastly that, in principle, international law does not allow a State to assemble a large number of warships in the territorial waters of another State and to carry out minesweeping in those waters. The United Kingdom Government states that the operation was one of extreme urgency, and that it considered itself entitled to carry it out without anybody's consent.

. . . the explosions of October 22nd, 1946, in a channel declared safe for navigation, and one which the United Kingdom Government, more than any other government, had reason to consider safe, raised quite a different problem from that of a routine sweep carried out under the orders of the mine clearance organizations. These explosions were suspicious; they raised a question of responsibility.

Accordingly, this was the ground on which the United Kingdom Government chose to establish its main line of defence. According to that Government, the *corpora delicti* must be secured as quickly as possible, for fear they should be taken away, without leaving traces, by the authors of the minelaying or by the Albanian authorities. This justification took two distinct forms in the United Kingdom Government's arguments. It was presented first as a new and special application of the theory of intervention, by means of which the State intervening would secure possession of evidence in the territory of another State, in order to submit it to an international tribunal and thus facilitate its task.

The Court cannot accept such a line of defence. The Court can only regard the alleged right of intervention as the manifestation of a policy of force, such as has, in the past, given rise to most serious abuses and such as cannot, whatever be the present defects in international organization, find a place in international law. Intervention is perhaps still less admissible in the particular form it would take here; for, from the nature of things, it would be reserved for the most powerful States, and might easily lead to perverting the administration of international justice itself.

The United Kingdom Agent, in his speech in reply, has further classified "Operation Retail" among methods of self-protection or self-help. The Court cannot accept this defence either. Between independent States, respect for territorial sovereignty is an essential foundation of international relations. The

Court recognizes that the Albanian Government's complete failure to carry out its duties after the explosions, and the dilatory nature of its diplomatic notes, are extenuating circumstances for the action of the United Kingdom Government. But to ensure respect for international law, of which it is the organ, the Court must declare that the action of the British Navy constituted a violation of Albanian sovereignty.

This declaration is in accordance with the request made by Albania through her Counsel, and is in itself appropriate satisfaction.

The method of carrying out "Operation Retail" has also been criticized by the Albanian Government, the main ground of complaint being that the United Kingdom, on that occasion, made use of an unnecessarily large display of force, out of proportion to the requirements of the sweep. The Court thinks that this criticism is not justified. It does not consider that the action of the British Navy was a demonstration of force for the purpose of exercising political pressure in Albania. The responsible naval commander, who kept his ships at a distance from the coast, cannot be reproached for having employed an important covering force in a region where twice within a few months his ships had been the object of serious outrages.

For these reasons, the Court, . . . by fourteen votes to two,[71] gives judgment [for the United Kingdom in respect of the passage on October 22nd, 1946] and, unanimously, gives judgment [for Albania in respect of the minesweeping of November 13th, 1946].

GENEVA CONVENTION ON THE TERRITORIAL SEA AND THE CONTIGUOUS ZONE 1958

See the references above, p. 284, n. 5

Sub-section A.[72] Rules applicable to all ships.

Article 14

1. Subject to the provisions of these articles, ships of all states, whether coastal or not, shall enjoy the right of innocent passage through the territorial sea.

2. Passage means navigation through the territorial sea for the purpose either of traversing that sea without entering internal waters, or of proceeding to internal waters, or of making for the high seas from internal waters.

3. Passage includes stopping and anchoring, but only insofar as the same are incidental to ordinary navigation or are rendered necessary by *force majeure* or by distress.

4. Passage is innocent so long as it is not prejudicial to the peace, good order or security of the coastal state. Such passage shall take place in conformity with these articles and with other rules of international law.

---

[71] The Judges in the majority were Acting President Guerrero; President Basdevant; Judges Alvarez, Fabela, Hackworth, Winiarski, Zoričić, de Visscher, Sir Arnold McNair, Klaestad, Badawi Pasha, Read and Hsu Mo; Judge ad hoc Ečer. Judges Krylov and Azevedo dissented.

[72] *i.e.* subsection A of Section III of Part 1 of the Convention.

5. Passage of foreign fishing vessels shall not be considered innocent if they do not observe such laws and regulations as the coastal state may make and publish in order to prevent these vessels from fishing in the territorial sea.

6. Submarines are required to navigate on the surface and to show their flag.

Article 15

1. The coastal state must not hamper innocent passage through the territorial sea.

2. The coastal state is required to give appropriate publicity to any dangers to navigation, of which it has knowledge, within its territorial sea.

Article 16

1. The coastal state may take the necessary steps in its territorial sea to prevent passage which is not innocent.

2. In the case of ships proceeding to internal waters, the coastal state shall also have the right to take the necessary steps to prevent any breach of the conditions to which admission of those ships to those waters is subject.

3. Subject to the provisions of paragraph 4, the coastal state may, without discrimination amongst foreign ships, suspend temporarily in specified areas of its territorial sea the innocent passage of foreign ships if such suspension is essential for the protection of its security. Such suspension shall take effect only after having been duly published.

4. There shall be no suspension of the innocent passage of foreign ships through straits which are used for international navigation between one part of the high seas and another part of the high seas or the territorial sea of a foreign state.

Article 17

Foreign ships exercising the right of innocent passage shall comply with the laws and regulations enacted by the coastal state in conformity with these articles and other rules of international law and, in particular, with such laws and regulations relating to transport and navigation.

Sub-section B. Rules applicable to merchant ships.

Article 18

1. No charge may be levied upon foreign ships by reason only of their passage through the territorial sea.

2. Charges may be levied upon a foreign ship passing through the territorial sea as payment only for specific services rendered to the ship. These charges shall be levied without discrimination.

Article 19

1. The criminal jurisdiction of the coastal state should not be exercised on board a foreign ship passing through the territorial sea to arrest any person or to conduct any investigation in connexion with any crime committed on board the ship during its passage, save only in the following cases:

(*a*) If the consequences of the crime extend to the coastal state; or

(*b*) If the crime is of a kind to disturb the peace of the country or the good order of the territorial sea; or

(*c*) If the assistance of the local authorities has been requested by the captain of the ship or by the consul of the country whose flag the ship flies; or

(*d*) If it is necessary for the suppression of illicit traffic in narcotic drugs.

2. The above provisions do not affect the right of the coastal state to take any steps authorized by its laws for the purpose of an arrest or investigation on board a foreign ship passing through the territorial sea after leaving internal waters.

3. In the cases provided for in paragraphs 1 and 2 of this article, the coastal state shall, if the captain so requests, advise the consular authority of the flag state before taking any steps, and shall facilitate contact between such authority and the ship's crew. In cases of emergency this notification may be communicated while the measures are being taken.

4. In considering whether or how an arrest should be made, the local authorities shall pay due regard to the interests of navigation.

5. The coastal state may not take any steps on board a foreign ship passing through the territorial sea to arrest any person or to conduct any investigation in connexion with any crime committed before the ship entered the territorial sea, if the ship, proceeding from a foreign port, is only passing through the territorial sea without entering internal waters.

Article 20

1. The coastal state should not stop or divert a foreign ship passing through the territorial sea for the purpose of exercising civil jurisdiction in relation to a person on board the ship.

2. The coastal state may not levy execution against or arrest the ship for the purpose of any civil proceedings, save only in respect of obligations or liabilities assumed or incurred by the ship itself in the course or for the purpose of its voyage through the waters of the coastal state.

3. The provisions of the previous paragraph are without prejudice to the right of the coastal state, in accordance with its laws, to levy execution against or to arrest, for the purpose of any civil proceedings, a foreign ship lying in the territorial sea, or passing through the territorial sea after leaving internal waters.

Sub-section C. Rules applicable to government ships other than warships.

Article 21

The rules contained in Sub-sections A and B shall also apply to government ships operated for commercial purposes.

Article 22

1. The rules contained in Sub-section A and in Article 18 shall apply to government ships operated for non-commercial purposes.

2. With such exceptions as are contained in the provisions referred to in the preceding paragraph, nothing in these articles affects the immunities which such ships enjoy under these articles or other rules of international law.

Sub-section D. Rule applicable to warships.[73]

Article 23

If any warship does not comply with the regulations of the coastal state concerning passage through the territorial sea and disregards any request for compliance which is made to it, the coastal state may require the warship to leave the territorial sea.

Notes

1. *Vessels entitled to innocent passage.* In 1896, the British Law Officers referred to "an accepted principle of international law that the innocent passage of merchant vessels for the purposes of navigation should be permitted through territorial waters."[74] With regard to *warships*, in the *Corfu Channel Case* the Court limited itself to a consideration of their position in respect of passage through international straits. In 1956, the International Law Commission proposed a Draft Article which permitted coastal states to make the passage of warships "subject to previous authorisation or notification."[75] In its Commentary, the Commission stated that since "a number of States do require previous notification or authorisation" it could not "dispute the right of States to take such a measure."[76] At Geneva, the Draft Article, which was intended to precede that which became Article 23 of the Convention, was rejected without a replacement text being inserted.[77] In this situation, is there a right of innocent passage for warships under the Territorial Sea Convention? Note the wording, "all ships" preceding Article 14 and the reference to "submarines" in it. When ratifying the Convention, the U.S.S.R. reserved "the right to establish procedures for the authorisation of the passage of foreign warships through its territorial waters."[78] If "a number of states" still require authorisation of passage, what is the customary international law position? In 1967 the British Foreign Secretary, in response to the question "what steps are being taken to prevent the deliberate violation of British territorial waters off Gibraltar by Spanish warships?" stated in Parliament:

[73] There is no definition of "warship" in the Territorial Sea Convention. There is one in Article 8(2) of the High Seas Convention, below, p. 326, which was the one proposed by the I.L.C. for all of its Draft Articles: see Y.B.I.L.C., 1956, II, p. 280. It is based upon Articles 3 and 4 of the Hague Convention on the Conversion of Merchantships into Warships 1907, U.K.T.S. 11 (1910), Cd. 5115; 2 A.J.I.L., Suppl., 1933 (1908). For the definition in the 1982 Convention, see below, p. 326, n. 52.

[74] 1 McNair 343. Italics added.

[75] Article 24, I.L.C. Draft Articles.

[76] Y.B.I.L.C., 1956, II, p. 277. In 1978, there were at least 17 states that required prior notification, including the U.S.S.R., China, and India. Most of the legislation was adopted in the 1970s: see *Hansard*, H.L., Vol. 388, cols. 846–847. February 1, 1978; U.K.M.I.L. 1978; 49 B.Y.I.L. 395 (1978).

[77] An amendment to the Commission's text to omit "authorisation or" was carried by the Plenary Session by 45 votes to 27, with six abstentions. The text as thus amended was then voted on as a whole and failed to obtain the necessary two-thirds majority (the vote was 43 in favour, 24 against, with 12 abstentions): *1958 Sea Conference Records*, Vol. II, pp. 67–68.

[78] 4 Whiteman 416. Similar reservations were made by a number of other East European states and by Colombia. Some states have objected to these reservations: U.N.Doc. ST/LEG/SER.D/5, p. 374.

Under international law Spanish and other warships enjoy the right of innocent passage through Gibraltar's territorial sea. Exercise of this right is subject to compliance with the local regulations and with normal navigational practice.[79]

The 1982 Convention also contains no provision expressly allowing or denying a right of innocent passage for warships. Several attempts were made to add a provision requiring prior notification and authorisation, but it proved impossible to obtain the necessary consensus.[80] Like the 1958 Convention, the 1982 Convention has a heading "all ships" before the articles on innocent passage and requires "submarines" to navigate on the surface.[81] Article 30, 1982 Convention, which otherwise repeats Article 23, 1958 Convention, adds the word "immediately" after "leave the territorial sea." Article 31, 1982 Convention is a new provision:

> The flag State shall bear international responsibility for any loss or damage to the coastal State resulting from the non-compliance by a warship or other government ship operated for non-commercial purposes with the laws and regulations of the coastal State concerning passage through the territorial sea or with the provisions of this Convention or other rules of international law.

2. *Meaning of innocent passage.* The definition of passage in Article 14, Territorial Sea Convention, is developed in the 1982 Convention (Art. 18) as follows:

> 1. Passage means navigation through the territorial sea for the purpose of:
> (a) Traversing that sea without entering internal waters or calling at a roadstead or port facility outside internal waters; or
> (b) Proceeding to or from internal waters or a call at such roadstead port facility.
> 2. Passage shall be continuous and expeditious. However, passage includes stopping and anchoring, but only in so far as the same are incidental to ordinary navigation or are rendered necessary by *force majeure* or distress or for the purpose of rendering assistance to persons, ships or aircraft in danger or distress.

Is the right of innocent passage in Article 14, Territorial Sea Convention, the same in scope as that applied by the Court in the *Corfu Channel Case*?[82] Were the British warships that swept the Corfu Channel for mines on November 13, 1946, engaged in "passage" in the sense of Article 14? Were those that earlier went through the Channel on October 22, 1946, to test Albanian reaction?[83] If in the latter case they were, was their passage "innocent" according to Article 14? Would it have been if they had been taking arms to a state which was then at war with Albania? Note that the draft proposed by the International Law Commission, for which Article 14(4) was substituted at Geneva, read: "Passage is innocent so long as a ship does not use the territorial sea for committing any acts prejudical to the security of the coastal state . . ."[84] Suppose a merchant ship of State A wishes to pass through the territorial sea of State B at a time when the nationals of State B are inclined to demonstrate against State A. Could State B

---

[79] *Hansard*, H.C., Vol. 754, Written Answers, Col. 20. November 13, 1967; B.P.I.L. 1967, p. 95. The U.K. interprets the 1958 and the 1982 Conventions as allowing innocent passage for warships: *Hansard, loc. cit.* at n. 76, above.

[80] See Oxman, 75 A.J.I.L. 235 (1981). The 1982 Convention took the text of the 1958 Convention as its starting point.

[81] Article 20, 1982 Convention, which adds "other underwater vehicles" to submarines for this purpose.

[82] Although that case was only concerned with the innocent passage of warships through international straits, it seems permissible to regard the Court's understanding of the nature of innocent passage as of general application.

[83] Is the distinction between motive and intention for the purpose of *mens rea* in criminal law helpful here?

[84] Article 15(3) of the I.L.C. Draft Articles. The definition of "passage" in Article 15(2) of the Draft Articles was the same as that adopted in Article 14(2) of the Convention.

exclude the ship if it feared demonstrations against it? Would it matter whether the captain of the ship knew that demonstrations were likely to occur or intended to provoke them? Does non-compliance with the second sentence of Article 14(5) render passage non-innocent? If not, so that the sanction of exclusion (Art. 16) is not applicable, what juridiction may a coastal state exercise over the ship?[85]

After adapting the same general definition of "innocent" as Article 14, the 1982 Convention (Art. 19(2)) adds the following list of prejudicial activities:

Passage of foreign ship shall be considered to be prejudicial to the peace, good order or security of the coastal State if in the territorial sea it engages in any of the following activities:

(a) Any threat or use of force against the sovereignty, territorial integrity or political independence of the coastal State, or in any other manner in violation of the principles of international law embodied in the Charter of the United Nations;

(b) Any exercise or practice with weapons of any kind;

(c) Any act aimed at collecting information to the prejudice of the defence or security of the coastal State;

(d) Any act of propaganda aimed at affecting the defence or security of the coastal State;

(e) The launching, landing or taking on board of any aircraft;

(f) The launching, landing or taking on board of any military device;

(g) The loading or unloading of any commodity, currency or person contrary to the custom, fiscal, immigration or sanitary laws and regulations of the coastal State;

(h) Any act of wilful and serious pollution, contrary to this Convention[86];

(i) Any fishing activities;

(j) The carrying out of research or survey activities;

(k) Any act aimed at interfering with any systems of communication or any other facilities or installations of the coastal State;

(l) Any other activity not having a direct bearing on passage.

Note that non-innocent passage is limited (contrast 1958 Convention, Art. 14) to conduct "in the territorial sea." The 1982 Convention omits Article 14(5), 1958 Convention, which makes passage not in compliance with fishing regulations non-innocent. In the 1982 Convention, "fishing activities" render passage non-innocent (Art. 19(2)(i)), but non-compliance with fishing regulations generally does not.

3. *Hampering innocent passage.* The 1982 Convention (Art. 24) expands Article 15(1) of the Territorial Sea Convention as follows:

1. The coastal State shall not hamper the innocent passage of foreign ships through the territorial sea except in accordance with this Convention. In particular, in the application of this Convention or of any laws or regulations adopted in conformity with this Convention, the coastal State shall not:

(a) Impose requirements on foreign ships which have the practical effect of denying or impairing the right of innocent passage; or

(b) discriminate in form or in fact against the ships of any State or against ships carrying cargoes to, from or on behalf of any State.

2. The coastal state shall give appropriate publicity to any danger to navigation, of which it has knowledge, within its territorial sea.[87]

[85] The same questions arise in respect of Article 17 of the Territorial Sea Convention.

[86] In 1974, it was stated in Parliament by a government spokesman that a ship passing through U.K. territorial waters with a view to dumping something in those waters would not be engaged in innocent passage; H.C., Standing Committee B, May 7, 1974, p. 38. Large oil tankers flying flags of convenience cannot without more be denied innocent passage: *Hansard*, H.L., Vol. 390, Col. 1799. April 26, 1978; U.K.M.I.L. 1978; 49 B.Y.I.L. 396 (1978).

[87] Article 18 of the 1958 Convention (no charges for passage) is repeated in the 1982 Convention (Art. 26) but is now in the section of the Convention applying to "all ships."

4. *Laws governing passage*. The 1982 Convention contains much more detailed provisions on the laws and regulations that a coastal State may make governing passage, than the equivalent Article 17, Territorial Sea Convention does. The 1982 Convention reads:

Article 21

1. The coastal State may adopt laws and regulations, in conformity with the provisions of this Convention and other rules of international law, relating to innocent passage through the territorial sea, in respect of all or any of the following:

(a) The safety of navigation and the regulation of maritime traffic;

(b) The protection of navigational aids and facilities and other facilities or installations;

(c) The protection of cables and pipelines;

(d) The conservation of the living resources of the sea;

(e) The prevention of infringement of the fisheries laws and regulations of the coastal State;

(f) The preservation of the environment of the coastal State and the prevention, reduction and control of pollution thereof;

(g) Marine scientific research and hydrographic surveys;

(h) The prevention of infringement of the custom, fiscal, immigration or sanitary laws and regulations of the coastal State.

2. Such laws and regulations shall not apply to the design, construction, manning or equipment of foreign ships unless they are giving effect to generally accepted international rules or standards.

3. The coastal State shall give due publicity to all such laws and regulations.

4. Foreign ships exercising the right of innocent passage through the territorial sea shall comply with all such laws and regulations and all generally accepted international regulations relating to the prevention of collisions at sea.

Article 22

1. The coastal State may, where necessary having regard to the safety of navigation, require foreign ships exercising the right of innocent passage through its territorial sea to use such sea lanes and traffic separation schemes as it may designate or prescribe for the regulation of the passage of ships.

2. In particular, tankers, nuclear-powered ships and ships carrying nuclear or other inherently dangerous or noxious substances or materials may be required to confine their passage to such sea lanes.

3. In the designation of sea lanes and the prescription of traffic separation schemes under this article, the coastal State shall take into account:

(a) The recommendations of the competent international organization;

(b) Any channels customarily used for international navigation;

(c) The special characteristics of particular ships and channels; and

(d) The density of traffic.

4. The coastal State shall clearly indicate such sea lanes and traffic separation schemes on charts to which due publicity shall be given.

Article 23

Foreign nuclear-powered ships and ships carrying nuclear or other inherently dangerous or noxious substances shall, when exercising the right of innocent passage through the territorial sea, carry documents and observe special precautionary measures established for such ships by international agreements.

5. *Passage through International Straits*. The right of innocent passage through many international straits is guaranteed by treaty. Passage through the Bosphorus and the Dardanelles, for example, is guaranteed by the Treaty of Montreux 1936.[88] The right applies to merchant[89] ships flying any flag.

The *Corfu Channel Case* was concerned with passage through straits that lead from one part of the high seas to another. Suppose straits lead from the high seas into a bay which is wholly within the territorial sea of two or more states bordering it? The Straits of Tiran in the Red Sea, for example, lead into the Gulf of Aqaba, which is about 17 miles wide at its widest point and which is bordered by Egypt, Israel, Jordan and Saudi Arabia. If the claims to a 12 mile territorial sea of both Egypt and Saudi Arabia, which border the Gulf at its mouth and along most of its length, are valid, none of the Gulf is high seas. In that case, have ships bound for Israel and Jordan, which each have short stretches of coastline at the landward end of the Gulf, a right of innocent passage through it?[90] See Article 16(4), Territorial Sea Convention.[91] Note that Israel is a party to the Territorial Sea Convention, but that the other three states are not. In 1967, the decision of the United Arab Republic (now Egypt) to prevent Israeli and other ships carrying strategic material to Israel from passing through the Straits of Tiran was the *casus belli* of the "Six Day War." At the time of the closure, the British Prime Minster was reported as saying: "It is the view of Her Majesty's Government . . . that the Straits of Tiran must be regarded as an international waterway through which the vessels of all nations have a right of passage."[92] The Security Council Resolution of November 22, 1967,[93] setting out a basis for the settlement of the Arab-Israeli conflict, refers to the need to guarantee "freedom of navigation through international waterways in the area."

The question of passage through international straits has become more important as states have widened their territorial seas. The English Channel and the Straits of Gibraltar, for example, are not more than 24 miles wide at their narrowest points.[94] The 1982 Convention accordingly contains detailed provisions allowing a new right of *transit passage* through an international strait within the territorial sea of one or more coastal states,[95] including the following:

Article 37

This section applies to straits which are used for international navigation between one part of the high seas or an exclusive economic zone and another part of the high seas or an exclusive economic zone.

Article 38

1. In straits referred to in article 37, all ships and aircraft enjoy the right of transit passage, which shall not be impeded; except that, if the strait is formed by an island of a State bordering the strait and its mainland, transit passage shall not apply if there exists

---

[88] U.K.T.S. 30 (1937) Cmnd. 5551; 173 L.N.T.S. 213; 31 A.J.I.L., Supp., 1 (1937). There are 10 parties, including Turkey, the U.K. and the U.S.S.R.

[89] On the more limited rules for warships, see Articles 8–22, Treaty of Montreux.

[90] The water-line across the Straits of Tiran is about seven miles long. It is interrupted by the island of Tiran which is about three miles from the Egyptian side of the Straits and 4 miles from the Saudi Arabian side. The only navigable channel is on the Egyptian side of the island. See Gross, 53 A.J.I.L. 564 (1959); *ibid*. 33 L & C.P. 123 (1968); Selak, 52 A.J.I.L. 660 (1958).

[91] Above, p. 306.

[92] U.N.Doc. 5/PV 1342, p. 20. May 23, 1967.

[93] Above, p. 175.

[94] There are over 100 such straits: see Ganz, *loc. cit.* at p. 285, n. 14 above, p. 7.

[95] See Burke, 52 Wash. L.R. 193 (1977); Moore, 74 A.J.I.L. 77 (1980); Reisman, *ibid*. p. 48.

seaward of the island a route through the high seas or through an exclusive economic zone of similar convenience with respect to navigational and hydrographical characteristics.

2. Transit passage means the exercise in accordance with this Part of the freedom of navigation and overflight solely for the purpose of continuous and expeditious transit of the strait between one part of the high seas or an exclusive economic zone and another part of the high seas or an exclusive economic zone. However, the requirement of continuous and expeditious transit does not preclude passage through the strait for the purpose of entering, leaving or returning from a State bordering the strait, subject to the conditions of entry to that State.

3. Any activity which is not an exercise of the right of transit passage through a strait remains subject to the other applicable provisions of this Convention.

Article 39

1. Ships and aircraft, while exercising the right of transit passage, shall:

(a) proceed without delay through or over the strait;

(b) refrain from any threat or use of force against the sovereignty, territorial integrity or political independence of States bordering the strait, or in any other manner in violation of the principles of international law embodied in the Charter of the United Nations;

(c) refrain from any activities other than those incident to their normal modes of continuous and expeditious transit unless rendered necessary by *force majeure* or by distress; . . .

The right of *transit passage* in the 1982 Convention has no counterpart in the 1958 Convention. The wording "used for international navigation" in Article 37 of the 1982 Convention follows the wording of the judgment in the *Corfu Channel Case* (and that of 1958 Convention, Art. 16(4)). The right does not apply (i) to straits "in which passage is regulated in whole or in part by long-standing international conventions in force [*e.g.* the Treaty of Montreux] specifically relating to such straits" (Art. 35(c)); (ii) to a strait through which there exists "a route through the high seas or through an exclusive economic zone of similar convenience with respect to navigational and hydrographical characteristics" (Art. 36); (iii) in the "island" situation described in Article 38(1); and (iv) to straits between a part of the high seas or an exclusive economic zone and the territorial sea of a foreign state. In (iii) and (iv), the ordinary right of innocent passage through the territorial sea under Article 19 of the 1982 Convention applies, except that that right cannot be suspended where the passage is through an international strait (1982 Convention, Art. 45).

The right of *transit passage* through international straits is more generous than the right of innocent passage through other parts of the territorial sea in both the 1958 and 1982 Conventions.[96] It expressly allows passage by aircraft including, it seems, military aircraft—"all . . . aircraft" (Art. 38(1)); "state aircraft" (Art. 39(3))—and it appears to allow underwater transit by submarines (no provision comparable to 1982 Convention, Art. 20, above, p. 309, on innocent passage). There are also fewer Covention restrictions on conduct during passage (see Arts. 39–41) and less power is given to the coastal state to regulate passage (see Arts. 41, 42) than is the case with innocent passage. The right of transit passage probably allows passage by warships, as in the case of the previously established customary international law right of innocent passage through international straits (*Corfu Channel Case*).

6. *Civil and criminal jurisdiction over foreign merchant ships.* According to some commentators, the use of the word "should," as opposed to "may," in Article 19(1) of

---

[96] Although the reason for this is that the right of transit passage was prompted by the extension of the territorial sea into waters in which freedom of the high seas formerly applied, the right applies over the whole of the territorial sea.

the Territorial Sea Convention indicates that the rule it contains is one of comity and not of law.[97] The International Law Commission had proposed "may."[98] The wording was changed at Geneva on the suggestion of the United States, which explained its suggestion as follows:

> It was the practice of most states not to arrest or conduct criminal investigations on board foreign ships passing through their territorial waters save in the instances mentioned in sub-paragraphs *a, b* and *c*, but the declaration in the Commissions text that "A State may not take any steps . . . " was a departure from the doctrine of international law that the coastal State had unlimited criminal jurisdiction within its territorial seas.[99]

The United States also successfully proposed the use of "should" in place of "may" in Article 20 for the same reason.[1] Note, however, that in both cases the United States full proposal was "should, generally." The word "generally" was deleted in the First Committee in respect of Article 20[2] and in the Plenary Meetings in respect of Article 19.[3] At least one delegate opposing that word would seem to have thought that its exclusion had the effect of confirming that a coastal state "*could* not stop a ship for the purpose of exercising its *civil* jurisdiction in respect of an individual on board."[4] This uncertainty is parallelled by a difference in state practice between that of common law and civil law states. Generally, common law states follow the rules in Articles 19 and 20 in practice as rules of comity whereas civil law states regard them as binding in law.

In *Pianka* v. *The Queen*,[5] the appellants, United States citizens, had been given clearance to head from a Jamaican port to Montego Bay in Jamaica in their United States registered motor boat. The next night they were discovered in Jamaican territorial waters with a large quantity of the drug ganja on board. Their appeal in these proceedings against conviction by a Jamaican court, *inter alia*, for illegal possession of the drug in Jamaican territorial waters was unsuccessful. A part of their defence was that their arrest conflicted with Article 19 of the Territorial Sea Convention (which had been incorporated by statute into Jamaican law). The Jamaican Court of Appeal rejected this defence[6]:

> ". . . even if the "Star Baby" was not bound for Montego Bay . . . but rather was making for the high seas this was not in right of innocent passage through the territorial sea for the appellants had received into their possession while on the territorial sea a dangerous drug, the possession and conveyance of which were prohibited under the criminal law . . . of Jamaica, and its receipt and conveyance by the appellants in that event was prejudicial to the good order of Jamaica. The consequences of the crime, therefore, extended to Jamaica and additionally was such as to disturb the good order of the territorial sea. That being so, and these being within the exceptions contained in art. 19, there was no contravention of art. 19 in seeking to invoke the criminal jurisdiction of the court."

The Privy Council upheld the Court of Appeal judgment on the application of Article 19, adding only that "these provisions [of that Article] should receive a liberal construc-

---

[97] See Fitzmaurice, *loc. cit.* at p. 284, n. 9, above, p. 104, and Lee, 55 A.J.I.L. 77, 83–86 (1961). But see McDougal and Burke, *loc. cit.* at p. 284, n. 1, above, p. 300. The French text, which, like the English, is one of five authoritative texts, uses "devrait."

[98] Y.B.I.L.C., 1956, II, p. 274.

[99] *1958 Sea Conference Records*, Vol. III, p. 81.

[1] *Ibid.* p. 82.

[2] *Ibid.* p. 125.

[3] *Ibid.* Vol. I, p. 66.

[4] M. Petrén (Sweden), *ibid.* p. 125. Italics added. He was discussing Article 20, in particular.

[5] [1979] A.C. 107 (P.C.).

[6] (1975) 24 W.I.R. 285, 292–293.

tion" and that the case could have been dealt with under Article 19(1)(d) because Jamaica was a party to the 1961 Single Convention on Narcotic Drugs[7] which covers ganja. Would Article 19(2) have provided another way of deciding the case?[8]

In the *David*,[9] the facts were that the *David*, a Panamanian merchant ship, was arrested in 1925 in the territorial sea of the Panama Canal Zone, within the territorial jurisdiction of the United States, in connection with civil proceedings against it concerning a collision that had occurred in 1923. The United States-Panama General Claims Commission rejected Panama's claim that the arrest had been contrary to international law. It said: "There is no clear pre-ponderance of authority to the effect that such vessels [foreign merchant vessels] when passing through territorial waters are exempt from civil arrest. In the absence of such authority, the Commission cannot say that a country may not under the rules of international law, assert the right to arrest on civil process merchant ships passing through its territorial waters."[10] The Panamanian Commissioner (Alfaro), dissenting, stated:

> It is proper to point out also that the claimant does not maintain that absolute immunity exists from the jurisdiction of the littoral authorities; that it does not allege, for example, lack of jurisdiction in the case of an offense committed within territorial waters in the course of innocent passage, although some writers deny jurisdiction even in such cases. The claimant also accepts that the ship is obliged to comply with orders and maritime regulations which contribute to the safety of navigation, or that are of a sanitary or police character. The claimant maintains only that in case of a civil action growing out of a collision occurring previously beyond the jurisdiction of the littoral authorities, the latter were without jurisdiction later to interfere with the passage of the same ship by means of a civil suit not affecting in any way territorial sovereign interests.[11]

Presumably "the consequences of the crime extend to the coastal state" (Art. 19(1)(a), 1958 Convention) in such cases as smuggling, illegal immigration, pollution and violations of security laws. Would it do so just because the perpetrator or the victim "of the crime" (which presumably refers to a crime under the law of the coastal state) on board a foreign ship is a national of the coastal state? The International Law Commission's draft of Article 19(1)(a) read "beyond the ship." It was changed to "to the coastal state" at Geneva. Does the wording finally adopted exclude the coastal state's jurisidiction in cases of collisions between two ships neither of which is flying its flag?[12] What if the effect, as in some cases of pollution, is felt only in the territorial sea and not on land or in inland waters? On the meaning of the terms "peace" and "good order," which also appear in Article 14(4), see the cases on jurisdiction over foreign ships in internal waters immediately below. Are the limitations upon the coastal state's jurisdiction in Articles 19 and 20 limitations upon executive enforcement jurisdiction only, or are they limitations on other forms of jurisdiction too? Would, for example, a prosecution under the Territorial Waters Jurisdiction Act 1878 in the circumstances of *R. v. Keyn* be prohibited by Article 19 of the Convention?[13]

The 1982 Convention (Arts. 27 and 28 respectively) follows Articles 19 and 20, Territorial Sea Convention very closely. Like them, it uses "should" and not "may." It adds "or psychotropic substances" to "narcotic drugs" in Article 19(1)(d), Territorial Sea Convention.

---

[7] *Loc. cit.* at p. 232, n. 82, above.
[8] *cf.* Crawford (1978) 49 B.Y.I.L. 262.
[9] 6 R.I.A.A. 382 (1933).
[10] *Ibid.* p. 384.
[11] *Ibid.* p. 386.
[12] See McDougal and Burke, *loc. cit.* at p. 284, n. 1, above, p. 300.
[13] See above, p. 61.

(v) JURISDICTION OVER FOREIGN SHIPS IN INTERNAL WATERS[14]

R. v. ANDERSON

11 Cox's Criminal Cases 198. Court of Criminal Appeal. 1868

The defendant, a United States national, was found guilty by the Central Criminal Court of manslaughter on board a British merchant ship of which he was a crew member. The offence was committed on the River Garonne in France some 300 yards from shore when the ship was on its way to Bordeaux. The defendant appealed on the ground that the Court had lacked jurisdiction to try him.

BOVILL C.J.: There is no doubt that the place where the offence was committed was within the territory of France, and that the prisoner was therefore subject to the laws of France, which the local authorities of that realm might have enforced if so minded; but at the same time, in point of law, the offence was also committed within British territory, for the prisoner was a seaman on board a merchant vessel, which, as to her crew and master, must be taken to have been at the time under the protection of the British flag, and, therefore, also amenable to the provisions of the British law. It is true that the prisoner was an American citizen, but he had with his own consent embarked on board a British vessel as one of the crew. Although the prisoner was subject to the American jurisprudence as an American citizen, and to the law of France as having committed an offence within the territory of France, yet he must also be considered as subject to the jurisdiction of British law, which extends to the protection of British vessels, though in ports belonging to another country. From the passage in the treatise of Ortolan[15] . . . it appears that, with regard to offences committed on board of foreign vessels within the French territory, the French nation will not assert their police law unless invoked by the master of the vessel, or unless the offence leads to a disturbance of the peace of the port. . . . The place where the offence was committed was in a navigable part of the river below bridge, and where the tide ebbs and flows, and great ships do lie and hover. An offence committed at such a place, according to the authorities, is within the Admiralty jurisdiction, and it is the same as if the offence had been committed on the high seas. On the whole I come to the conclusion that the prisoner was amenable to the British law, and that the conviction was right.

BYLES J.: I am of the same opinion. . . . A British ship is, for the purposes of this question, like a floating island; and, when a crime is committed on board a British ship, it is within the jurisdiction of the Admiralty Court, and therefore of the Central Criminal Court, and the offender is as amenable to British law as if he had stood on the Isle of Wight and committed the crime. . . .

Channel B. and Lush J. delivered concurring judgments.

[14] See Charteris (1920–21) 1 B.Y.I.L. 45 and Jessup, *The Law of Territorial Waters and Maritime Jurisdiction* (1927), pp. 144–194. On the right of entry into foreign ports, see Lowe, 14 San Diego L.R. 597 (1977).
[15] *Règles internationales et diplomatie de la mer*, Vol. I (4th ed., 1864), pp. 269–271.

WILDENHUS'S CASE

120 U.S. 1. U.S. Supreme Court. 1887

W., a Belgian crew member of a Belgian merchant ship, was found guilty by an American state court of the murder of another Belgian crew member on board the ship when it was docked in the port of Jersey City, New York. It was argued in this application for habeas corpus that, under a consular convention of 1880 between Belgium and the United States, the United States court had lacked jurisdiction. The application was rejected by the United States Supreme Court.

WAITE C.J. It is part of the law of civilized nations that when a merchant vessel of one country enters the ports of another for the purposes of trade, it subjects itself to the law of the place to which it goes, unless by treaty or otherwise the two countries have come to some different understanding or agreement. . . . As the owner has voluntarily taken his vessel for his own private purposes to a place within the dominion of a government other than his own, and from which he seeks protection during his stay, he owes that government such allegiance for the time being as is due for the protection to which he becomes entitled.

From experience, however, it was found long ago that it would be beneficial to commerce if the local government would abstain from interfering with the internal discipline of the ship and the general regulation of the rights and duties of the officers and crew towards the vessel or among themselves. And so by comity it came to be generally understood among civilized nations that all matters of discipline and all things done on board which affected only the vessel or those belonging to her, and did not involve the peace or dignity of the country, or the tranquillity of the port, should be left by the local government to be dealt with by the authorities of the nation to which the vessel belonged as the laws of that nation or the interests of its commerce should require. But if crimes are committed on board of a character to disturb the peace and tranquillity of the country to which the vessel has been brought, the offenders have never by comity or usage been entitled to any exemption from the operation of the local laws for their punishment, if the local tribunals see fit to assert their authority. Such being the general public law on this subject, treaties and conventions have been entered into by nations having commercial intercourse, the purpose of which was to settle and define the rights and duties of the contracting parties with respect to each other in these particulars, and thus prevent the inconvenience that might arise from attempts to exercise conflicting jurisdictions. . . .

The Treaty [now before the Court] is part of the supreme law of the United States, and has the same force and effect in New Jersey that it is entitled to elsewhere. If it gives the Consul of Belgium exclusive jurisdiction over the offense which it is alleged has been committed within the territory of New Jersey, we see no reason why he may not enforce his rights under the Treaty by writ of *habeas corpus* in any proper court of the United States. This being the case, the only important question left for our determination is whether the thing which has been done—the disorder that has arisen—on board this vessel is of a nature to disturb the public peace, or, as some writers term it, the "public repose" of the people who look to the State of New Jersey for their protection. If the thing done—"the disorder," as it is called in the Treaty—is of a character to affect those on shore or in the port when it becomes known, the fact that only those on the ship saw it when it was done, is a matter of no moment. Those who are not on the vessel pay no special attention to the mere disputes or quarrels of the seamen while on board, whether they occur under deck or above. Neither do they as a rule care for anything done on board which relates only to the discipline of the ship, or to the preservation of order and authority. Not so, however, with crimes which from their gravity awaken a public interest as soon as they become known, and especially those of a character which every civilized nation considers itself bound to provide a severe punishment for when committed within its own jurisdiction. In such cases inquiry is certain to be instituted at once to ascertain how or why the thing was done, and the popular excitement rises or falls as the news spreads and the facts become known. It is not alone the publicity of the act, or the noise and clamor which attends it, that fixes the nature of the crime, but the act itself. If that is of a character to awaken public interest when it becomes known, it is a "disorder" the nature of which is to affect the community at large, and consequently to invoke the power of the local government whose peoples have been disturbed by what was done. The very nature of such an act is to disturb the quiet of a peaceful community, and to create, in the language of the Treaty, a "disorder" which will "disturb tranquility and public order on shore on in the port." The principle which governs the whole matter is this: Disorders which disturb only the peace of the ship or those on board are to be dealt with exclusively by the sovereignty of the home of the ship, but those which disturb the public peace may be suppressed, and, if need be, the offenders punished by the proper authorities of the local jurisdiction. It may not be easy at all times to determine to which of the two jurisdictions a particular act of disorder belongs. Much will undoubtedly depend on the attending circumstances of the particular case, but all must concede that felonious homicide is a subject for the local jurisdiction, and that if the proper authorities are proceeding with the case in a regular way the consul has no right to interfere to prevent it. That, according to the petition for the *habeas corpus*, is this case.

Notes

1. Is the rule limiting the criminal enforcement jurisdiction of the state of the port in these cases one of comity or one of law?[16]

2. In the *Eisler Case*,[17] in 1949, Eisler was arrested and taken off a Polish ship at Southampton for extradition to the United States. Poland protested "on the ground that Eisler was a political refugee entitled under international law to asylum and protection under the Polish flag, and that a state's jurisdiction over territorial and national waters did not entitle the state to arrest persons on board a foreign vessel for the purpose of extradition to a third state."[18] The British Government is reported as rejecting Poland's argument for the following reason:

> it would mean . . . that States could grant to persons on board their merchant or passenger ships in foreign ports or waters the same asylum that a State can grant to persons on its territory. It was, however, quite contrary to the practice of States to recognize any principle of asylum in connexion with merchant ships, and the Polish Government had refused it in the case of offences committed by persons who

---

[16] *cf.* the materials on jurisdiction in the territorial sea, above, pp. 301 *et seq.*
[17] Jennings (1949) 26 B.Y.I.L. 468.
[18] *Ibid.*

subsequently went on board a foreign ship in a Polish port. The absence of any right to grant asylum on board merchant ships sprang from a universally recognized principle of international law that a merchant ship in the ports or roadsteads of another country falls under the jurisdiction of the coastal State.[19]

What if the Polish ship in question had been stopped for the purpose of arresting Eisler while it was passing through British territorial waters?

3. On criminal jurisdiction over foreign warships in port, see *The Schooner Exchange* v. *McFaddon*.[20]

In 1977, while H.M.S. *Danae* was in Rio de Janeiro on a goodwill visit, some junior ratings invited Ronald Biggs, the Great Train Robber and a United Kingdom citizen, on board. When it was discovered who he was, Mr. Biggs was asked to leave the ship. Later the question was asked in Parliament why he had not been arrested. The following Government explanation was given:

> Since Mr. Biggs did not commit an offence while on board HMS "Danae" the only powers under which he could have been arrested would have been the powers of "citizen's arrest" under the provisions of the Criminal Law Act 1967. The relevant provisions of this Act, however, apply only to England and Wales.
>
> Whilst one of Her Majesty's ships in a foreign port has extra-territoriality—that is, it is immune from local jurisdiction and enforcement of local laws—it is not correct to regard it as floating United Kingdom territory, and all laws of the United Kingdom do not necessarily apply to all persons on board that ship. The relevant provisions of the Criminal Law Act are such an example.[21]

3. *THE HIGH SEAS*

(i) FREEDOM OF THE HIGH SEAS

GENEVA CONVENTION ON THE HIGH SEAS 1958

See the references above, p. 284, n. 6

Article 1

The term "high seas" means all parts of the sea that are not included in the territorial sea or in the internal waters of a state.

Article 2

The high seas being open to all nations, no state may validly purport to subject any part of them to its sovereignty. Freedom of the high seas is exercised under the conditions laid down by these articles and by the other rules of international law. It comprises, *inter alia*, both for coastal and non-coastal states:

(1) Freedom of navigation;
(2) Freedom of fishing;
(3) Freedom to lay submarine cables and pipelines;
(4) Freedom to fly over the high seas.

---

[19] *The Times*, June 9, 1949, p. 3.
[20] Above, p. 242.
[21] *Hansard*, H.C., Vol. 930, W.A., col. 450. April 29, 1977.

These freedoms, and others which are recognized by the general principles of international law, shall be exercised by all states with reasonable regard to the interests of other states in their exercise of the freedom of the high seas.

Article 3

1. In order to enjoy the freedom of the seas on equal terms with coastal states, states having no seacoast should have free access to the sea. To this end states situated between the sea and a state having no seacoast shall by common agreement with the latter and in conformity with existing international conventions accord:

(*a*) To the state having no seacoast, on a basis of reciprocity free transit through their territory and
(*b*) To ships flying the flag of that state treatment equal to that accorded to their own ships, or to the ships of any other states, as regards access to seaports and the use of such ports.

2. States situated between the sea and a state having no seacoast shall settle, by mutual agreement with the latter, and taking into account the rights of the coastal state or state of transit and the special conditions of the state having no seacoast, all matters relating to freedom of transit and equal treatment in ports, in case such states are not already parties to existing international conventions.

Notes

1. *Freedom of the High Seas.* Articles 1 and 2 of the High Seas Convention undoubtedly reflect customary international law. "Freedom of fishing" must now be read subject to the coastal state's exclusive fishing or economic zone.[22] Other freedoms recognised by the "general principles of international law" include the freedom to conduct scientific research (recognised in the 1982 Convention[23]) and the freedom to use the high seas for weapon testing and naval exercises. To the last of these freedoms should be added the freedom to observe the naval exercises of other states. Whiteman records:

> When a Soviet "electronics ship," supposedly operating as a Soviet trawler, cruised through a Polaris submarine test area off Long Island in April 1960 . . . Rear Admiral Charles C. Kirkpatrick . . . emphasised at a Pentagon news conference that, since the ship was in international waters at all times, the Soviet ship remained unmolested . . . "We are a legal people and abide by international law," he said . . . As reported, it was explained by an officer present that the Soviet ship with its electronic gear could monitor radio information for "hundreds of miles."[24]

States sometimes use the high seas to make a show of strength off the coast of other states. The 1982 Convention limits the use of the high seas to "peaceful purposes" (Article 88). The United Kingdom Government takes the view that rocket and other weapons testing on the high does not contravene this provision.[25] Another freedom

---

[22] See below, p. 346.
[23] Article 87(1)(*f*), 1982 Convention. It was also mentioned as an example by the I.L.C.: Y.B.I.L.C., 1956, II, p. 278.
[24] 4 Whiteman, 516–517.
[25] *Hansard*, H.L., Vol. 388, col. 842. February 1, 1978; U.K.M.I.L. 1978; (1978) 49 B.Y.I.L. 397.

listed by the 1982 Convention is the "freedom to construct artificial islands and other installations permitted under international law. . . ." [26]

2. *Land-Locked States.* In addition to Article 3, see the Convention on Transit Trade of Land-Locked States 1965,[27] The 1982 Convention has stronger and more detailed provisions on the transit trade of land-locked states (of which there are about 30) and their access to the high seas for other purposes than does the High Seas Convention.[28]

NUCLEAR TESTS IN THE PACIFIC

Hansard, H.C., Vol. 568, Written Answers, cols. 27–29. April 2, 1957

The United Kingdom conducted nuclear tests on the high seas near Christmas Island, a British island in the Pacific, from 1956–58. When a Japanese fishermen's organisation objected to plans for hydrogen bomb tests in 1957, the United Kingdom replied through its Ambassador in Tokyo as follows:

The tests will be high air bursts which will not involve heavy fall-out. Extensive safety precautions have been taken. A 'danger area' has been declared for the period 1st March to 1st August and all shipping and aircraft have been warned to keep clear of this area. The warning has been issued far in advance so that people should be clearly aware of the position. No permanently inhabited island lies within the danger area. Weather stations, weather ships and meteorological reconnaissance flights by aircraft will provide continuous meteorological information during the period of the tests. Provided persons stay outside the danger area they have nothing to fear. The temporary use of areas outside territorial waters for gunnery or bombing practice has, as such, never been considered a violation of the principles of freedom of navigation on the high seas. The present site has been carefully chosen because it lies far from inhabited islands and avoids as far as possible shipping and air routes. It is incidentally some 4,000 miles from Japan. . . .

In regard to publicity which has been given to the suggestion that the tests will involve a loss to Japanese fishing interests, it has to be borne in mind that, owing to their great distance from Japan these are not traditional fishing grounds for Japanese fishermen. Any Japanese fishermen who may now regularly visit this area, have only done so in the last three or four years. Ample warning has been given of the danger area, so enabling any fishermen who may have planned to visit the area to make alternative arrangements. In all the circumstances envisaged for the tests there should be no contamination of fish.

Her Majesty's Government have declared that if any claim is received for damage or loss said to have been incurred as a result of these tests, it will be carefully examined and Her Majesty's Government's attitude will depend on the facts in each particular case. . . .

In conclusion I am to state that, in Her Majesty's Government's view, it is impossible to consider the question of stopping nuclear tests without having regard to the wider problem of preventing war in general, including of course nuclear war.

---

[26] Article 87(1)(*d*).
[27] *Loc. cit.* at p. 200, n. 70 above.
[28] Articles 124–132, 1982 Convention. See Caflisch (1978) 49 B.Y.I.L. 71. As to the rights of land-locked states in the exclusive economic zone, see Article 69, 1982 Convention.

Notes

1. In 1954, radiation from hydrogen bomb tests conducted by the United States on the high seas in the area of the Eniwetok Atoll in the Strategic Trust Territory administered by the United States[28a] caused the death of a Japanese fisherman and caused injury to other Japanese fishermen, to some inhabitants of the Rongelap Atoll within the Territory and to some United States nationals.[29] The tests took place in a danger zone, within which shipping was advised not to go, of 50,000 square miles. Both the Japanese fishing vessel concerned and the Rongelap Atoll were outside this zone. They were affected because the force of the explosion had been miscalculated and because of a sudden change of wind. The United States gave medical and other assistance and paid monetary compensation. In the case of the Japanese nationals, the compensation, which was for personal injuries and for economic loss resulting from the contamination of Japanese fishing catches, was expressly stated to be *ex gratia*. At the time of a later test series in 1958, the United States took the following legal position:

> The high seas have long been used by the nations of the world for naval manoeuvres, weapons tests, and other matters of this kind. Such measures no doubt result in some inconvenience to other users of the high seas but they are not proscribed by international law.[29a]

When plans for the 1958 United States tests were announced, Japan stated that it was "greatly concerned" and expressed the view that "the United States Government has the responsibility of compensating for economic losses that may be caused by the establishment of a danger zone and for all losses and damages that may be inflicted on Japan and the Japanese people as a result of the nuclear tests."[30] Japan did not refer expressly to international law. On July 2, 1958, a United States national entered the danger zone in a yacht as a protest. He was prosecuted under United States law applying to United States nationals only. Could the United States have legislated to have excluded an alien? Could the national state of an alien injured by radiation in a danger zone successfully claim compensation under international law if the alien (a) deliberately ignores the warning or (b) is unaware of it?

An amendment to what became Article 2 of the High Seas Convention proposed by the U.S.S.R., which was conducting most of its nuclear tests in Siberia,[31] to make nuclear testing on the high seas a violation of the Convention was not voted upon at Geneva; instead the Conference adopted the proposal of India that the matter should be referred to the General Assembly "for appropriate action."[32] In 1963, the Nuclear Test Ban Treaty[33] was signed and came into force. This prohibits the testing of nuclear weapons, *inter alia*, on the high seas. France, which is not a party to the Treaty, continued to conduct tests in the South Pacific until 1973 when it completed its final series of tests in the atmosphere.[34] The 1972 and 1973 tests were the subject of protests by several states and led to the *Nuclear Tests Cases*.[35] These were brought by Australia

---

[28a] See above, p. 102.

[29] See generally 4 Whiteman 553 *et seq*. See also McDougal and Schlei, 64 Yale L.J. 648 (1955) ("for" the legality of the tests) and Margolis, 64 Yale L.J. 629 (1955) ("against" their legality).

[29a] 4 Whiteman 595.

[30] *Ibid*. pp. 585–586.

[31] But some were conducted in the Barents Sea: *ibid*. p. 574.

[32] Resolution on Nuclear Tests on the High Seas, *1958 Sea Conference Records*, Vol. II, p. 24, p. 101 (text).

[33] U.K.T.S. 3 (1964), Cmnd. 2245; 480 U.N.T.S. 43. In force 1963. 111 contracting parties on June 30, 1982, including the U.K.

[34] For a discussion of the legality of these tests, see Mercer, (1968) N.Z.L.J. 405–408, 418–421 and Swan, 9 Melb.U.L.R. 296 (1973–74).

[35] I.C.J. Rep. 1974, p. 253 (*Australia* v. *France*); I.C.J. Rep. 1974, p. 457 (*New Zealand* v. *France*).

and New Zealand against France. The cases were taken off the Court's list without a decision being given on the merits when France announced that it would not conduct further tests after 1973; despite argument to the contrary by the applicant states, the Court found that their claims no longer had any object.[36] The applicants had asked the court for a declaration that the carrying out of further nuclear tests in the South Pacific was not consistent with international law.[37]

2. In order to develop its long range missiles, the United States found it necessary to arrange for test sites in the territory of other states[38] in the Atlantic area and to fire the missiles over the high seas. One writer records:

> None of the missiles . . . carry warheads, atomic or otherwise; they are loaded with concrete blocks instead. A missile weighing many tons can, however, do considerable damage . . . accidents can occur, as in the case of the errant flight of a Snark into the wilds of Brazil in December 1956. . . . Thus far no official complaints from other governments, comparable to those voiced in and out of the United Nations with respect to the nuclear weapons testing, have apparently been made to the government of the United States. . . .[39]

In 1960, the U.S.S.R. announced that the descent stage of a rocket being developed for space flight would be brought down in the Pacific and addressed a "request" that an identified area be not entered for a month.[40] United States practice in this matter is as follows:

> At NASA's request, the United States Naval Oceanographic Office issues a Notice to Mariners (NOTAM) concerning the landing area of each manned spacecraft. the NOTAM, disseminated through customary shipping communication channels, specifies the projected time and coordinates of the landing.
> There have been no instances of ships of any nationality disregarding the NOTAMS. United States law prohibits ships of American registry from entering the reserved area.[41]

(ii) NATIONALITY OF SHIPS

GENEVA CONVENTION ON THE HIGH SEAS 1958

See references above, p. 284, n. 6

Article 4

Every state, whether coastal or not, has the right to sail ships under its flag on the high seas.

Article 5

1. Each state shall fix the conditions for the grant of its nationality to ships, for the registration of ships in its territory, and for the right to fly its flag. Ships have the nationality of the state whose flag they are entitled to fly. There must exist a

---

[36] See below, p. 571. France began testing again in 1981.
[37] This was specifically the Australian request; for the similar New Zealand request, see I.C.J. Rep. 1974, p. 460.
[38] The United Kingdom, for example, agreed to a U.S. base in the Bahamas. See generally 4 Whiteman 619–623.
[39] Reiff, *The United States and the Treaty Law of the Sea* (1959), p. 371.
[40] 4 Whiteman 624.
[41] Letter from NASA, dated October 13, 1972.

genuine link between the state and the ship; in particular, the state must effectively exercise its jurisdiction and control in administrative, technical and social matters over ships flying its flag.

2. Each state shall issue to ships to which it has granted the right to fly its flag documents to that effect.

Article 6

1. Ships shall sail under the flag of one state only and, save in exceptional cases expressly provided for in international treaties or in these articles, shall be subject to its exclusive jurisdiction on the high seas. A ship may not change its flag during a voyage or while in a port of call, save in the case of a real transfer of ownership or change in registry.

2. A ship which sales under the flags of two or more states, using them according to convenience, may not claim any of the nationalities in question with respect to any other state, and may be assimilated to a ship without nationality.

Article 7

The provisions of the preceding articles do not prejudice the question of ships employed on the official service of an intergovernmental organization flying the flag of the organization.

Notes

1. Ships are deemed to have a nationality for international law purposes.[42] Normally, a ship is registered under the law of a particular state and is then, under that state's law, both entitled to fly its flag and deemed to have its nationality. Before the *Nottebohm Case*,[43] a ship's nationality thus accorded by a state by its unilateral decision was accepted in international law as being that of the ship for international law purposes such as jurisdiction and state responsibility.[44] As a result of the *Nottebohm Case*, concerning the nationality of individuals for the purpose of diplomatic protection in international law, the International Law Commission inserted a "genuine link" requirement in its Draft Articles and the requirement was adopted at Geneva in Article 5 of the High Seas Convention. As to the position at customary international law in the light of the High Seas Convention, Jessup states that "the law is in the process of development; the most that can be said is that, in the light of the court's opinion in the *Nottebohm Case*, it is probable that if the issue were presented to it, the tribunal would sustain the link theory in its application to the nationality of ships."[45]

2. Does the lack of a "genuine link" render the ship stateless?[46] What is the significance of "in particular" in Article 5? Could other factors such as the nationality of the individual or company (or the interests behind it) owning the ship to be taken into account? Would a ship that was in every sense linked with its flag state cease to have a "genuine link" with that state if the latter failed effectively to enforce, for example, regulations concerning safety and conditions of work on board? It is clear that it would not do so under the 1982 Convention. There the text of Article 5(1) of the High Seas Convention is retained (Art.91(1)) except that the wording "in particular" onwards in

---

[42] See Myers, *The Nationality of Ships* (1972).
[43] See below, p. 442.
[44] See Watts (1957). 33 B.Y.I.L. 52.
[45] *Loc. cit.* at p. 284, n. 9, above, p. 256.
[46] For criticism of Article 5 because of the uncertainty, and hence the threat of instability, that it introduces into the law, see McDougal and Burke, *op. cit.* at p. 284, n. 1, above, Chap. 8.

the final sentence of Article 5(1) is omitted and re-appears in a later and quite separate provision (Art. 94) imposing duties on the flag states in respect of "administrative, technical and social matters" and safety at sea (*cf.* High Seas Convention, Art. 10).

3. The introduction of the "genuine link" requirement was prompted by the use of "flags of convenience." Of these, Sørenson[47] writes:

> This liberty [to grant nationality] has, however, been used by certain states, in particular Liberia and Panama and to a certain extent Honduras and Costa Rica as well, to enact "liberal" registration laws allowing for the registration even of ships owned and operated by foreigners. . . . Out of the total increase [of tonnage] since 1939, 43 per cent. has gone to these countries, which, at the end of 1957, had about 15·5 per cent. of world tonnage under their flags. . . . It is estimated that over 80 per cent. of the tonnage under flags of convenience is owned either by United States interests, in particular the large oil companies, or by persons of Greek origin supported to a certain extent by United States capital.
>
> Owners register their ships in such countries for various reasons. Taxation is very low, or practically non-existent. Operating costs are lower because the legislation and collective agreements on wages, labour conditions, and social security of the traditionally maritime countries do not apply. Lack of adequate administrative machinery, especially inspection services, means that the countries concerned are unable to enforce effectively such laws and regulations as they may have enacted with respect to safety standards, accommodation and protection of crews, and so forth.

In its advisory opinion in the *IMCO Case*,[48] the International Court of Justice advised that the term "largest ship-owning nations" in the IMCO Constitution (Art. 28(*a*)) referred to registered tonnage and not beneficially owned tonnage. On this basis, it advised that Liberia and Panama should have been elected to membership of the Maritime Safety Committee of IMCO. The Court limited itself to the particular issue of treaty interpretation before it and did not consider the question of the nationality of ships and flags of convenience generally.

4. A ship is not prohibited from sailing without a flag. If it does so, however, it is, for the purpose of protection at least, treated as the equivalent of a stateless person. Thus, in *Naim Molvan* v. *Att.-Gen. for Palestine*,[49] the Judicial Committee of the Privy Council stated,

> No question of comity nor of any breach of international law can arise if there is no State under whose flag the vessel sails. . . . having no [flag] . . . the *Asya* could not claim the protection of any State nor could any State claim that any principle of international law was broken by her seizure.

Nonetheless the State of which the owner of a ship without a flag was a national could intervene on the ground of injury to a national's property.[50]

(iii) JURISDICTION ON THE HIGH SEAS[51]

GENEVA CONVENTION ON THE HIGH SEAS 1958

See the references at p. 284, n. 6, above

Article 8

1. Warships on the high seas have complete immunity from the jurisdiction of any state other than the flag state.

---

[47] *Loc. cit.* at p. 284, n. 1, pp. 202–203. See generally Bozcek, *Flags of Convenience* (1962).
[48] I.C.J. Rep. 1960, p. 150.   [49] [1948] A.C. 351 at pp. 369–370.
[50] See below, Chap. 8.   [51] See Van Zwanenberg, 10 I.C.L.Q. 785 (1961).

2. For the purposes of these articles, the term "warship" means a ship belonging to the naval forces of a state and bearing the external marks distinguishing warships of its nationality, under the command of an officer duly commissioned by the government and whose name appears in the Navy List, and manned by a crew who are under regular naval discipline.[52]

Article 9

Ships owned or operated by a state and used only on governmental non-commercial service shall, on the high seas, have complete immunity from the jurisdiction of any other state other than the flag state.

Article 10

1. Every state shall take such measures for ships under its flag as are necessary to ensure safety at sea with regard *inter alia* to:

   (*a*) The use of signals, the maintenance of communications and the prevention of collisions;
   (*b*) The manning of ships and labour conditions for crews taking into account the applicable international labour instruments;
   (*c*) The construction, equipment and seaworthiness of ships.

2. In taking such measures each state is required to conform to generally accepted international standards and to take any steps which may be necessary to ensure their observance.

Article 11

1. In the event of a collision or of any other incident of navigation concerning a ship on the high seas, involving the penal or disciplinary responsibility of the master or of any other person in the service of the ship, no penal or disciplinary proceedings may be instituted against such persons except before the judicial or administrative authorities either of the flag state or of the state of which such person is a national.

2. In disciplinary matters, the state which has issued a master's certificate or a certificate of competence or licence shall alone be competent, after due legal process, to pronounce the withdrawal of such certificates, even if the holder is not a national of the state which issued them.

3. No arrest or detention of the ship, even as a measure of investigation, shall be ordered by any authorities other than those of the flag state.

Article 12

1. Every state shall require the master of a ship sailing under its flag, insofar as he can do so without serious danger to the ship, the crew or the passengers:

---

[52] Article 29, 1982 Convention reads: For the purposes of this Convention, "warship" means a ship belonging to the armed forces of a State bearing the external marks distinguishing such ships of its nationality, under the command of an officer duly commissioned by the government of the State and whose name appears in the appropriate service list or its equivalent, and manned by a crew which is under regular armed forces discipline.

(*a*) To render assistance to any person found at sea in danger of being lost;

(*b*) To proceed with all possible speed to the rescue of persons in distress if informed of their need of assistance, insofar as such action may reasonably be expected of him;

(*c*) After a collision to render assistance to the other ship, her crew and her passengers and, where possible, to inform the other ship of the name of his own ship, her port of registry and the nearest port at which she will call.

2. Every coastal state shall promote the establishment and maintenance of an adequate and effective search and rescue service regarding safety on and over the sea and—where circumstances so require—by way of mutual regional arrangements co-operate with neighbouring states for this purpose.

Article 13

Every state shall adopt effective measures to prevent and punish the transport of slaves in ships authorized to fly its flag, and to prevent the unlawful use of its flag for that purpose. Any slave taking refuge on board any ship, whatever its flag, shall *ipso facto* be free.

Article 14

All states shall co-operate to the fullest possible extent in the repression of piracy on the high seas or in any other place outside the jurisdiction of any state.

Article 15

Piracy consists of any of the following acts:

(1) Any illegal acts of violence, detention or any act of depredation, committed for private ends by the crew or the passengers of a private ship or a private aircraft, and directed:

(*a*) On the high seas, against another ship or aircraft, or against persons or property on board such ship or aircraft;

(*b*) Against a ship, aircraft, persons or property in a place outside the jurisdiction of any state;

(2) Any act of voluntary participation in the operation of a ship or of an aircraft with knowledge of facts making it a pirate ship or aircraft;

(3) Any act of inciting or of intentionally facilitating an act described in sub-paragraph 1 or sub-paragraph 2 of this article.

Article 16

The acts of piracy, as defined in Article 15, committed by a warship, government ship or government aircraft whose crew has mutinied and taken control of the ship or aircraft are assimilated to acts committed by a private ship.

Article 17

A ship or aircraft is considered a pirate ship or aircraft if it is intended by the persons in dominant control to be used for the purpose of committing one of the acts referred to in Article 15. The same applies if the ship or aircraft has been used to commit any such act, so long as it remains under the control of the persons guilty of that act.

Article 18

A ship or aircraft may retain its nationality although it has become a pirate ship or aircraft. The retention or loss of nationality is determined by the law of the state from which such nationality was derived.

Article 19

On the high seas, or in any other place outside the jurisdiction of any state, every state may seize a pirate ship or aircraft, or a ship taken by piracy and under the control of pirates, and arrest the persons and seize the property on board. The courts of the state which carried out the seizure may decide upon the penalties to be imposed, and may also determine the action to be taken with regard to the ships, aircraft or property, subject to the rights of third parties acting in good faith.

Article 20

Where the seizure of a ship or aircraft on suspicion of piracy has been effected without adequate grounds, the state making the seizure shall be liable to the state the nationality of which is possessed by the ship or aircraft, for any loss or damage caused by the seizure.

Article 21

A seizure on account of piracy may only be carried out by warships or military aircraft, or other ships or aircraft on government service authorized to that effect.

Article 22

1. Except where acts of interference derive from powers conferred by treaty, a warship which encounters a foreign merchant ship on the high seas is not justified in boarding her unless there is reasonable ground for suspecting:

(a) That the ship is engaged in piracy; or
(b) That the ship is engaged in the slave trade; or
(c) That, though flying a foreign flag or refusing to show its flag, the ship is, in reality, of the same nationality as the warship.

2. In the cases provided for in sub-paragraphs (a), (b) and (c) above, the warship may proceed to verify the ship's right to fly its flag. To this end, it may send a boat under the command of an officer to the suspected ship. If suspicion remains after the documents have been checked, it may proceed to a further examination on board the ship, which must be carried out with all possible consideration.

3. If the suspicions prove to be unfounded, and provided that the ship boarded has not committed any act justifying them, it shall be compensated for any loss or damage that may have been sustained.

Notes

1. The basic principle of customary international law that "vessels on the high seas are subject to no authority except that of the State whose flag they fly" is stated and elaborated upon by the Permanent Court of International Justice in the *Lotus Case*.[53] Articles 8(1) and 9 of the High Seas Convention on the immunity of warships and other state ships not used for commercial purposes are reproduced in the 1982 Convention.[54] Some exceptions to the exclusive administrative jurisdiction of the flag state on the high seas exist. Smith comments on them as follows:

> The right of any ship to fly a particular flag must obviously be subject to verification by proper authority, and from this it follows that warships have a general right to verify the nationality of any merchant ship, which they may meet on the high seas. This "right of approach" (*vérification du pavillon* or *reconnaissance*) is the only qualification under customary law of the general principle which forbids any interference in time of peace with ships of another nationality upon the high seas. Any other act of interference (apart from the repression of piracy) must be justified under powers conferred by treaty. Provided that the merchant vessel responds by showing her flag the captain of the warship is not justified in boarding her or taking any further action, unless there is reasonable ground for suspecting that she is engaged in piracy or some other improper activity. . . . In the past the question of the right of approach has been the subject of some controversy and has occasionally given rise to friction. Under modern conditions the general use of wireless and other developments have made the matter one of very small importance.[55]

Slavery is not mentioned by Smith and it would seem that, subject to the effect of Article 22, customary international law gives no powers over foreign ships on the high seas in respect of it.[56] The 1982 Convention adds to the list of situations in which a right of visit is permitted by Article 22, High Seas Convention, cases in which there are reasonable grounds to suspect that the ship is operating a private radio station or is without a nationality (Art. 110(1)(c), (d)). The 1982 Convention (Art. 110(4), (5)) also allows the right of visit to be carried out *mutatis mutandis* by "military aircraft" and by "any other duly authorised ships or aircraft clearly marked and identifiable as being on government service." On the coastal state's right to visit ships in the exclusive economic zone under 1982 Convention, Art. 73, see below, p. 352. Other customary international law powers exist under the doctrines of hot pursuit[57] and the contiguous zone[58] and, possibly, for the purpose of self-defence.[59] As far as treaty exceptions are concerned, treaty powers of jurisdiction exist for the parties *inter se* in respect, *inter alia*, of fishing practices and conservation[60] and of interference with submarine cables.[61] The severe penalty in Article 22(3), which probably reflects customary international law,[62] was thought by the International Law Commission to be "justified in order to prevent the right of visit being abused."[63]

---

[53] See above, p. 212.
[54] Articles 95 and 96.
[55] *Loc. cit.* above, p. 284, n. 1, pp. 64–65.
[56] See Colombos, *loc. cit.* at p. 284, n. 1, above, pp. 457–463. On the uncertain position under the treaties on slavery, see Gutteridge, 6 I.C.L.Q. 449 (1957).
[57] See below, p. 334.
[58] See below, p. 331.
[59] See below, p. 657.
[60] See, *e.g.* Canada-U.S. Convention for the Preservation of the Halibut Fishery of the North Pacific Ocean and the Bering Sea 1953, Article II, U.S.T.I.A.S. 2900.
[61] See, *e.g.* Convention for the Protection of Submarine Cables 1884, Article X, 75 B.F.S.P. 356; 2 Malloy 1949.
[62] See Smith, *loc. cit.* at p. 284, n. 1, above, p. 65.
[63] Y.B.I.L.C., 1956, II, p. 284.

2. *Penal Jurisdiction in Collisions.* Article 11, which conflicts with the decision in the *Lotus Case*,[64] probably states the customary international law rule. Article 11 is reproduced verbatim in the 1982 Convention (Art. 97).

3. *Piracy.*[65] There is some doubt among writers whether, subject to the High Seas Convention, piracy *jure gentium* covers attacks by one ship upon another other than with intent to plunder (*animus furandi*).[66] The precise role of piracy *jure gentium* is also uncertain. According to one view, piracy is a crime under international law in respect of which all states are allowed jurisdiction.[67] According to another view, there is no international crime of piracy; instead international law authorises states to exercise criminal jurisdiction under their municipal law on a universality basis in respect of acts which come within the definition of *piracy jure gentium*.[68] A state may define piracy differently in its municipal law (*e.g.* the United Kingdom includes slave trading on the high seas[69]) from piracy *jure gentium*. It will, however, have the special jurisdiction allowed by international law only in respect of acts amounting to piracy *jure gentium*.

In its Commentary, the International Law Commission states that by "place outside the jurisdiction of any state" in Article 14, it "had chiefly in mind acts committed by a ship or aircraft on an island constituting *terra nullius* or on the shores of an unoccupied territory."[70] The extension of the crime to cover aircraft is an instance of "progressive development" of the law. Article 15 does not cover the hijacking of aircraft by the passengers or crew of the hijacked aircraft.

In the *Santa Maria* Incident,[71] in 1961, a Portuguese passenger vessel called the *Santa Maria* was seized in the Atlantic on the high seas by armed men who had boarded it as passengers. One member of the crew was killed and others injured. The men were supporters of General Delgado, a political opponent of President Salazar of Portugal. The ship was eventually handed over to Brazil and returned to Portugal. The men were given political asylum by Brazil. Were they pirates?[72]

The 1982 Convention (Arts. 100–107) repeats the rules concerning piracy in the High Seas Convention.

4. *Pirate Radio Stations.*[73] The 1982 Convention gives wide powers of enforcement jurisdiction over pirate radio stations on the high seas. Article 109(3)(4) read:

> 3. Any person engaged in unauthorised broadcasting[74] may be prosecuted before the court of:

---

[64] See above, p. 212. Essentially the same rule as that in Article 11 was included in the Brussels Convention on Penal Jurisdiction in Matters of Collision 1952, Article 1, U.K.T.S. 47 (1960); Cmnd. 1128; 53 A.J.I.L. 536 (1959).

[65] See Johnson, 43 Trans.Grot.Soc. 63 (1957).

[66] Contrast 2 Moore 953 ("A pirate is one who, without legal authority from any state, attacks a ship with intention to appropriate what belongs to it. The pirate is a sea brigand,") with Oppenheim, Vol. I, para. 272 (piracy is "every unauthorised act of violence against persons or goods committed on the open sea either by a pirate vessel against another vessel or by the mutinous crew or passengers against their own vessel").

[67] See, *e.g.* 2 Moore 951. On international crimes, see below, p. 376.

[68] See, *e.g.* Schwarzenberger (1950) 3 C.L.P. 263.

[69] Slave Trade Act 1824, s.9. And see *Cameron* v. *H.M. Advocate* [1971] S.C. 50.

[70] Y.B.I.L.C., 1956, II, p. 282.

[71] 4 Whiteman 665.

[72] See Frank, 36 N.Y.U.L.R. 389 (1961), reprinted in Mueller and Wise, *International Criminal Law* (1965), p. 218, and Green (1961) 37 B.Y.I.L. 496.

[73] See Hunnings, 14 I.C.L.Q. 410 (1965) and Van Panhuys and Van Emde Boas, 60 A.J.I.L. 303 (1966).

[74] "Unauthorised broadcasting" is defined as "the transmission of sound radio or television broadcasts from a ship or installation on the high seas intended for reception by the general public contrary to international regulations, but excluding the transmission of distress calls": Article 109(2).

(a) the flag State of the ship;
(b) the State of registry of the installation;
(c) the State of which the person is a national;
(d) any State where the transmissions can be received; or
(e) any State where authorized radio communication is suffering interference.

4. On the high seas, a State having jurisdiction in accordance with paragraph 3 may, in conformity with article 110 [above p. 329], arrest any person or ship engaged in unauthorised broadcasting and seize the broadcasting apparatus.

See also the European Agreement for the Prevention of Broadcasting from Stations outside National Waters 1965[75] which permits the exercise of criminal jurisdiction but does not give a right to visit.

(iv) THE CONTIGUOUS ZONE[76]

GENEVA CONVENTION ON THE TERRITORIAL SEA AND THE CONTIGUOUS ZONE 1958

See the references cited above p. 284, n.5

Article 24

1. In a zone of the high seas contiguous to its territorial sea, the coastal state may exercise the control necessary to:

(*a*) Prevent infringement of its customs, fiscal, immigration or sanitary regulations within its territory or territorial sea;
(*b*) Punish infringement of the above regulations committed within its territory or territorial sea.

2. The contiguous zone may not extend beyond twelve miles from the baseline from which the breadth of the territorial sea is measured.

3. Where the coasts of two states are opposite or adjacent to each other, neither of the two states is entitled, failing agreement between them to the contrary, to extend its contiguous zone beyond the median line every point of which is equidistant from the nearest points on the baselines from which the breadth of territorial seas of the two states is measured.

Notes

1. The International Law Commission's Commentary on its Draft Articles reads:

(1) International law accords States the right to exercise preventative or protective control for certain purposes over a belt of the high seas contiguous to their territorial sea. It is, of course, understood that this power of control does not change the legal status of the waters over which it is exercised. These waters are and remain a part of the high seas and are not subject to the sovereignty of the coastal State, which can exercise over them only such rights as are conferred on it by the present draft or are derived from international treaties.

(2) Many States have adopted the principle that in the contiguous zone the coastal State may exercise customs control in order to prevent attempted infringements of its

---

[75] E.T.S. No. 53; 634 U.N.T.S. 239; U.K.T.S. 1 (1968), Cmnd. 1497. In force 1967. On November 15, 1982, there were 15 contracting parties, including the U.K.
[76] See Fitzmaurice, *loc. cit.* at p. 284, n. 9, above, p. 108, and Oda, 11 I.C.L.Q. 131 (1962).

customs and fiscal regulations within its territory or territorial sea, and to punish infringements of those regulations committed within its territory or territorial sea. The Commission considered that it would be impossible to deny to States the exercise of such rights.

(3) Although the number of States which claim rights over the contiguous zone for the purpose of applying sanitary regulations is fairly small, the Commission considers that, in view of the connexion between customs and sanitary regulations, such rights should also be recognized for sanitary regulations.

(4) The Commission did not recognize special security rights in the contiguous zone. It considered that the extreme vagueness of the term "security" would open the way for abuses and that the granting of such rights was not necessary. The enforcement of customs and sanitary regulations will be sufficient in most cases to safeguard the security of the State. In so far as measures of self-defence against an imminent and direct threat to the security of the State are concerned, the Commission refers to the general principles of international law and the Charter of the United Nations.

(5) Nor was the Commission willing to recognize any exclusive rights of the coastal State to engage in fishing in the contiguous zone. The Preparatory Committee of the Hague Codification Conference found, in 1930, that the replies from Governments offered no prospect of an agreement to extend the exclusive fishing rights of the coastal State beyond the territorial sea. The Commission considered that in that respect the position has not changed.[77]

A proposal at Geneva to add "and violations of security" to Article 24(1)(a) was defeated.[78] On the right of self-defence, see below, p. 657. Note in this connection the practice of some states of having an aircraft carrier or other warship stationed offshore on the high seas as a "reminder" to a coastal state of its interest in events taking place within it. On the use of spy ships, see note 4, below. The reference to immigration regulations was added at Geneva. The International Law Commission had thought it unsupported by state practice and otherwise undesirable.[79] It also thought that the reference to sanitary regulations would cover immigration so far as the latter related to questions of public health.[80]

2. Article 24(1)(b) of the Territorial Sea Convention, which gives "police" jurisdiction to the coastal state after an offence has been committed in its territory or territorial sea, clearly must be read as giving a power of arrest. Does Article 24(1)(a), which applies before an offence is committed, do so too?[81] If not, what powers can be exercised under it?

3. Must a state claim a contiguous zone or does it have one by operation of law? Would the exercise of any powers justified by Article 24 be regarded as lawful in U.K. law by a British court without legislation?[82] Can a state that claims a territorial sea of 12 miles have a contiguous zone under the Convention? What does the 12 mile limit in Article 24 suggest was thought at Geneva to be the maximum permissible width of the territorial sea?

4. On January 23, 1968, the *Pueblo*, a U.S. "Navy intelligence collection auxiliary ship," was ordered to heave to by North Korean patrol ships off the coast of North Korea.[83] It was boarded and escorted into Wonsan. In December 1968, the crew of the *Pueblo* were returned to the United States after detention without trial and after the

---

[77] Y.B.I.L.C., 1956, II, pp. 294–295.
[78] *1958 Sea Conference Records*, Vol. II, p. 40. See also *ibid*. p. 117.
[79] Y.B.I.L.C., 1956, II, pp. 76–78.
[80] *Ibid*.
[81] See Fitzmaurice, *loc. cit.* at p. 284, n. 9, above, pp. 113–115. Contrast McDougal and Burke, *op. cit.* at p. 284, n. 1, above, pp. 621–630.
[82] See *R.* v. *Keyn*, above, p. 61.
[83] See *Keesing's Archives*, p. 23120A, and Rubin, 18 I.C.L.Q. 961 (1969).

U.S. had signed a document indicating that the *Pueblo* had been spying in North Korean territorial waters.[84] The body of the crew member who had died after being injured in the struggle during the capture of the *Pueblo* was also returned. Earlier, in February 1968, Secretary of State Rusk had sent this telegram to all United States diplomatic posts:

> The ship was seized slightly more than fifteen miles from the nearest land, Ung Do Island, which lies slightly seaward of a straight line across the mouth of Wonsan Bay. The geographic situation of Wonsan Bay is such as to warrant treating the bay as internal waters. The outer limits of the territorial waters would, therefore, be measured from a straight line across the mouth of Wonsan Bay or from Ung Do Island, to the extent measurement from the island increases the area within the territorial sea. . . .
>
> The United States Government has no official information concerning breadth of territorial sea claimed by North Korea, but we assume it claims twelve miles in line with claims of most other communist countries and in view of the position it took in the 1953 armistice talks. . . .
>
> The Pueblo was a commissioned vessel of the United States Navy and therefore entitled to the immunities recognized by article eight of the 1958 convention on the high seas.[85] Absolute immunity from any jurisdiction other than that of the flag state is, of course, the traditional rule of international law, and the fact that North Korea is not a party to the 1958 convention is irrelevant.
>
> The United States Government recognizes only the three-mile limit. North Korea has never alleged that the Pueblo was within three miles of the North Korean coast. Thus from the United States view of international law even if the Pueblo had been at the position alleged by North Korea (7·1 miles offshore), it would still have been on the high seas. Nonetheless, the Pueblo was under orders to stay at least thirteen miles from North Korea, *i.e.* at least one mile beyond waters presumably claimed by North Korea.
>
> Even if the Pueblo had been in the territorial waters of North Korea, its seizure would have been improper. On numerous occasions similar Soviet ships have intruded into United States territorial waters; we have warned them to leave and, when appropriate, have submitted protests through diplomatic channels. In the absence of immediate threat of armed attack (the Pueblo was armed with only two machine guns), escorting foreign naval vessels out of territorial waters is the strongest action a coastal state should take. The seizure of foreign war ships or other attacks upon them are much too dangerous and provocative acts to be permitted by international law. This restriction on the use of force by a coastal state is set forth in article twenty-three of the 1958 convention on the territorial sea, which authorizes, as the sole remedy, requiring a war ship to leave the territorial sea.[86]

Had North Korea violated international law? Had the United States?

5. The 1982 Convention (Art. 33) retains the contiguous zone and gives coastal states precisely the same powers as they have under the Territorial Sea Convention. The zone may, however, be up to 24 miles in width instead of 12. In the 12 miles beyond the limit of a 12 miles territorial sea, therefore, a coastal state may exercise powers that are additional to those (applying to different kinds of activities) that exist under the exclusive economic zone régime proposed by the 1982 Convention.[87]

---

[84] See 8 I.L.M. 199 (1969). This admission was later retracted: *ibid.*
[85] *Ed.* See above, p. 325.
[86] 62 A.J.I.L. 756 (1968).
[87] See below, p. 349.

(v) HOT PURSUIT[88]

THE I'M ALONE[89]

Canada v. United States

Interim and Final Reports of a Joint Commission. 1933 and 1935. 3 R.I.A.A. 1609; 29
A.J.I.L. 326 (1935)

In 1929, the *I'm Alone*, a British schooner registered in Canada was ordered to heave to
by the *Wolcott*, a United States coastguard vessel, on suspicion of smuggling liquor at
the time of prohibition in the United States when, according to the United States, she
was 10 miles of the Louisiana coast. She fled and was pursued by the *Wolcott* and, after
the *Wolcott's* gun had jammed, by the *Dexter*, a second United States coastguard vessel.
The *Dexter* and the *Wolcott* caught up with the *I'm Alone* more than 200 miles off the
coast of the United States. When the *I'm Alone* refused to heave to, she was fired upon
by the *Dexter* and sunk. The gunfire was aimed first above the water line. Later it was
aimed below it. The boatswain died and the schooner's cargo was lost. The United
States justified its action under the 1924 Convention between the United States and
Great Britain by which the latter agreed 'to raise no objection to the boarding of private
vessels under the British flag outside the limits of territorial waters by the authorities of
the United States" in order to check liquor smuggling. The power was not to be
"exercised at a greater distance from the coast of the United States than can be
traversed in one hour by the vessel suspected. . . ." Certain questions were put to two
Commissioners appointed under the 1924 Convention.

Joint Interim Report of the Commissioners

The first question is whether the Commissioners may enquire into the
beneficial or ultimate ownership of the *I'm Alone* or of the shares of the
corporation that owned the ship. If the Commissioners are authorized to make
this enquiry, a further question arises as to the effect of indirect ownership and
control by citizens of the United States upon the Claim; viz., whether it would
be an answer to the Claim under the Convention, or whether it would go to
mitigation of damages, or whether it would merely be a circumstance that
should actuate the claimant Government in refraining from pressing the claim,
in whole or in part. . . .

The Commissioners think they may enquire into the beneficial or ultimate
ownership of the *I'm Alone* and of the shares of the corporation owning the
ship; as well as into the management and control of the ship and the venture in
which it was engaged; and that this may be done as a basis for considering the
recommendations which they shall make. But the Commissioners reserve for
further consideration the extent to which, if at all, the facts of such ownership,
management and control may effect particular branches or phases of the claim
presented.

The second question relates to the right of hot pursuit. Further, it has two
aspects, and it is based upon the assumption that the averments in the Answer
[of the United States] with regard to the location and speed of the *I'm Alone* are
true. The question in its first aspect is whether the Government of the United

[88] See Poulantzas, *The Right of Hot Pursuit in International Law* (1969) and Williams (1939) 20
B.Y.I.L. 83.
[89] See Fitzmaurice (1936) 17 B.Y.I.L. 82.

States under the Convention has the right of hot pursuit where the offending vessel is within an hour's sailing distance of the shore at the commencement of the pursuit and beyond that distance at its termination. The question in its second aspect is whether the Government of the United States has the right of hot pursuit of a vessel when the pursuit commenced within the distance of twelve miles established by the revenue laws of the United States and was terminated on the high seas beyond that distance. . . .

As respects the question in its first aspect . . . the Commissioners are as yet not in agreement as to the proper answer, nor have they reached a final disagreement on the matter. The Commissioners, therefore, suggest that the proceeding go forward. . . .

The question in its second aspect need not be answered because the Government of the United States has now withdrawn so much of its answer as led to the propounding of that aspect of the question.

The third question is based upon the assumption that the United States Government had the right of hot pursuit in the circumstances and was entitled to exercise the rights under Article II of the Convention at the time when the *Dexter* joined the *Wolcott* in the pursuit of the *I'm Alone*. It is also based upon the assumption that the averments set forth in paragraph eight of the Answer are true. The question is whether, in the circumstances, the Government of the United States was legally justified in sinking the *I'm Alone*. . . .

On the assumptions stated in the question, the United States might, consistently with the Convention, use necessary and reasonable force for the purpose of effecting the objects of boarding, searching, seizing and bringing into port the suspected vessel; and if sinking should occur incidentally, as a result of the exercise of necessary and reasonable force for such purpose, the pursuing vessel might be entirely blameless. But the Commissioners think that, in the circumstances stated in paragraph eight of the Answer, the admittedly intentional sinking of the suspected vessel was not justified by anything in the Convention. . . .

Joint Final Report of the Commissioners

By their interim report the Commissioners found that the sinking of the vessel was not justified by anything in the Convention. The Commission now add that it could not be justified by any principle of international law. . . .

We find as a fact that, from September, 1928, down to the date when she was sunk, the *I'm Alone*, although a British ship of Canadian registry, was *de facto* owned, controlled, and at the critical times, managed, and her movements directed and her cargo dealt with and disposed of, by a group of persons acting in concert who were entirely, or nearly so, citizens of the United States, and who employed her for the purposes mentioned.[90] The possibility that one of the group may not have been of United States nationality we regard as of no importance in the circumstances of this case.

The Commissioners consider that, in view of the facts, no compensation ought to be paid in respect of the loss of the ship or the cargo.

The act of sinking the ship, however, by officers of the United States Coast Guard, was, as we have already indicated, an unlawful act; and the Commis-

---

[90] *Ed.* They were in fact led by one Hogan, a notorious New York gangster who was subsequently imprisoned under the U.S. liquor laws.

sioners consider that the United States ought formally to acknowledge its illegality, and to apologize to His Majesty's Canadian Government therefor; and, further, that as a material amend in respect of the wrong the United States should pay the sum of $25,000 to His Majesty's Canadian Government; and they recommend accordingly.

The Commissioners have had under consideration the compensation which ought to be paid by the United States to His Majesty's Canadian Government for the benefit of the captain and members of the crew, none of whom was a party to the illegal conspiracy to smuggle liquor into the United States and sell the same there. The Commissioners recommend that [a further sum of approximately $25,000] compensation be paid [under this heading]. . . .

Note

McNair states:

> [The British Law Officers] have repeatedly affirmed the right of "hot pursuit" of a ship which has committed an offence within territorial waters. The pursuit must be hot, that is, immediate, and it may even begin when the offending ship has reached the high seas.[91]

On this last point, McNair quotes an Opinion of 1891 as follows:

> In order to justify a seizure beyond the territorial waters it is necessary that the pursuit should have been undertaken immediately on the commission of the offence. In most cases it is obvious that such pursuit will, in fact, have been begun within the territorial waters. But cases may occur in which, though the offence was committed just within the limits of the territorial waters, the offender passed these limits before the pursuing vessel actually started in pursuit. It is a question of fact in each case whether the pursuit can fairly be described as immediate. If it were, a seizure in the open sea would not be unlawful, because, during the brief period that elapsed before the pursuing vessel got actually under way, the offender succeeded in passing out of the territorial water.[92]

On the degree of force that may be used to make an arrest, the Law Officers advised in 1852:

> We conceive the use of fire-arms in the case in question to have been wholly unjustifiable; a Cruizer can almost always capture a Fishing boat without having recourse to Arms, and we are of opinion that firing in such a case could (if at all) be justified only where resistance was threatened or offered or where escape would otherwise have been imminent and that then it should have been such as to disable the boat without, if it can be avoided, risking life.[93]

The Preparatory Committee of the Hague Codification Conference 1930 stated:

> With one exception, all the replies [of Governments] . . . recognise that a state is entitled to continue on the high seas a pursuit begun within its territorial waters. The only differences of opinion are as to whether the entry of the ship pursued into the territorial waters of another country merely suspends the pursuit or puts an end to it.[94]

---

[91] 1 McNair 253.
[92] *Ibid*. p. 255.
[93] *Ibid*. pp. 253–254.
[94] L.N.Doc. C.74, M. 39, 1939 V, p. 96.

GENEVA CONVENTION ON THE HIGH SEAS 1958

See the references above, p. 284, n. 6

Article 23

1. The hot pursuit of a foreign ship may be undertaken when the competent authorities of the coastal state have good reason to believe that the ship has violated the laws and regulations of that state. Such pursuit must be commenced when the foreign ship or one of its boats is within the internal waters or the territorial sea or the contiguous zone of the pursuing state, and may only be continued outside the territorial sea or the contiguous zone if the pursuit has not been interrupted. It is not necessary that, at the time when the foreign ship within the territorial sea or the contiguous zone receives the order to stop, the ship giving the order should likewise be within the territorial sea or the contiguous zone. If the foreign ship is within a contiguous zone, as defined in Article 24 of the Convention on the Territorial Sea and the Contiguous Zone, the pursuit may only be undertaken if there has been a violation of the rights for the protection of which the zone was established.

2. The right of hot pursuit ceases as soon as the ship pursued enters the territorial sea of its own country or of a third state.

3. Hot pursuit is not deemed to have begun unless the pursuing ship has satisfied itself by such practicable means as may be available that the ship pursued or one of its boats or other craft working as a team and using the ship pursued as a mother ship are within the limits of the territorial sea, or as the case may be within the contiguous zone. The pursuit may only be commenced after a visual or auditory signal to stop has been given at a distance which enables it to be seen or heard by the foreign ship.

4. The right of hot pursuit may be exercised only by warships or military aircraft, or other ships or aircraft on government service specially authorized to that effect.

5. Where hot pursuit is effected by an aircraft:

(a) The provisions of paragraphs 1 to 3 of this article shall apply *mutatis mutandis*;

(b) The aircraft giving the order to stop must itself actively pursue the ship until a ship or aircraft of the coastal state, summoned by the aircraft, arrives to take over the pursuit, unless the aircraft is itself able to arrest the ship. It does not suffice to justify an arrest on the high seas that the ship was merely sighted by the aircraft as an offender, if it was not both ordered to stop and pursued by the aircraft itself or other aircraft or ships which continue the pursuit without interruption.

6. The release of a ship arrested within the jurisdiction of a state and escorted to a port of that state for the purposes of an enquiry before the competent authorities, may not be claimed solely on the ground that the ship, in the course of its voyage, was escorted across a portion of the high seas, if the circumstances render this necessary.

7. Where a ship has been stopped or arrested on the high seas in circumstances which do not justify the exercise of the right of hot pursuit, it shall be compensated for any loss or damage that may have been thereby sustained.

Notes

1. Does "ship" in Article 23(1) include warship?[95] Can the hot pursuit of a ship be undertaken under the Convention when the violation of the local law has occurred not in the current passage but on some previous one? Can it be undertaken under the Convention where a violation is not by the ship but by a crew member or passenger on board? Note that a signal to stop made by radio is not sufficient for the purpose of Article 23(3). The International Law Commission stated:

> To prevent abuse, the Commission declined to admit orders given by wireless, as these could be given at any distance.[96]

This, it would seem, prevents a "signal" being given by radio after a ship has been detected by radar and hence may allow a ship which itself has radar sufficient time after detecting a coastguard or similar vessel by radar to escape to a place where hot pursuit cannot begin before a "signal" beginning it can be given.[97]

2. The 1982 Convention (Art. 111) repeats Article 23, High Seas Convention with alterations to allow for the right of hot pursuit in cases of violations of the coastal state's law and regulations applicable to the exclusive economic zone or continental shelf where the violations occur in or on those places. In the 1982 Convention, "other ships or aircraft" in government service must be "clearly marked and identifiable" as such as well as "authorised" to exercise the right of hot pursuit.

(vi) POLLUTION OF THE HIGH SEAS[98]

GENEVA CONVENTION ON THE HIGH SEAS 1958

See the references above, p. 284, n. 6

Article 24

Every state shall draw up regulations to prevent pollution of the seas by the discharge of oil from ships or pipelines or resulting from the exploitation and exploration of the seabed and its subsoil, taking account of existing treaty provisions on the subject.

Article 25

1. Every state shall take measures to prevent pollution of the seas from the dumping of radioactive waste, taking into account any standards and regulations which may be formulated by the competent international organisations.

2. All states shall co-operate with the competent international organisations in taking measures for the prevention of pollution of the seas or air-space above, resulting from any activities with radioactive materials or other harmful agents.

---

[95] See Article 8, High Seas Convention, above, p. 325.

[96] Y.B.I.L.C., 1956, II, p. 285.

[97] See the U.S. Coastguard memorandum, July 1957, 4 Whiteman 683 at p. 685.

[98] See Barros and Johnston, *The International Law of Pollution* (1974), pp. 200–293; Brown, *The Legal Regime of Hydrospace* (1971), Chaps. 4–7; Mendelson, in Sibthorp, ed., *The North Sea: Challenge and Opportunity* (1975), pp. 119–146; Mensah, in McKnight *et al.* eds., *Environmental Pollution Control* (1974), Chap. 9; Schachter and Serwer, 65 A.J.I.L. 84 (1971); and Teclaff, in Teclaff and Utton, eds., *International Environmental Law* (1974), Chap. 6.

Notes

1. *Oil*. The reference to "existing treaty provisions" in Article 24 is to the International Convention for the Prevention of Pollution of the Sea by Oil 1954.[99] The Convention applies to all sea-going ships of 500 tons or more except for naval auxiliaries, whaling ships and ships on the Great Lakes.[1] It prohibits the "discharge from any tanker, being a ship to which the Convention applies, of (a) oil; (b) any oil mixture, the oil in which fouls the surface of the sea."[2] A similar prohibition exists for ships other than tankers.[3] Any contravention "shall be an offence punishable under the laws of the territory in which the ship is registered."[4] These prohibitions extend to discharges within defined "prohibition zones" which, with certain exceptions either way, consists of the sea "within 50 miles from land."[5] The Convention was amended in 1962[6] to cover tankers of 150 tons and over[7] and to extend to certain other "prohibited zones" beyond 50 miles from land.[8] Further amendments were made in 1969 and 1971. The 1969 amendments[9] abandon the concept of "prohibited zones" and prohibit the discharge of oil or an "oily mixture" (redefined more strictly as "a mixture with *any* oil content") in any part of the sea unless certain stringent conditions as to the place, rate and quantity of the discharge are met. Their introduction follows the adoption by oil tankers of the "load on top" method of operating. By this, empty tankers do not discharge tank washings into the sea, but collect them in a slop tank. There the oil residue separates itself from the water. The water in the slop tank, which is an "oily mixture," is discharged consistently with the 1969 amendments and the next oil cargo is loaded on top of the oil residue that is left. Over 80 per cent. of tankers have come to use the "load on top" system since its introduction in the late 1960s. Operational oil pollution has been considerably reduced as a result. The 1971 amendments[10] impose new standards in the construction of oil tankers which should reduce the pollution consequent upon an accident and protect the Australian Great Barrier Reef.

The 1954 Convention as amended will be replaced by the International Convention for the Prevention of Pollution from Ships 1973[11] for the parties to the latter when the latter comes into force. The 1973 Convention incorporates the amendments to the 1954 Convention in one text and updates them in the light of new scientific knowledge. It also provides for an improved "tacit approval" procedure for technical amendments and is much wider in scope than the 1954 Convention, covering pollution caused by sewage and garbage and by other noxious or harmful substances discharged from a ship as well as oil.

2. *Radioactive waste*. Commenting upon Article 25 of the High Seas Convention, Bowett states:

Not the least of the difficulties here is the lack of scientific knowledge as to the effects of sea disposal, by various methods; given this uncertainty, it seems reasonable to

[99] U.K.T.S. 56 (1958), Cmnd. 595; 327 U.N.T.S. 3. The treaty entered into force in 1958. On August 21, 1982, there were 68 contracting parties, including the U.K.

[1] Article II.

[2] Article III.

[3] *Ibid*.

[4] *Ibid*.

[5] Article III and Annex 4.

[6] U.K.T.A. 59 (1967), Cmnd. 3354. The amendments came into force for all parties in 1967.

[7] Article II, as amended.

[8] Annex A, as amended.

[9] 9 I.L.M. 1 (1970). The 1969 amendments came into force for all contracting parties in 1978.

[10] 11 I.L.M. 267 (1972). The amendments are not yet in force. On August 21, 1982, the tanker construction amendments had been accepted by 25 states, including the U.K.; the Barrier Reef amendments had been accepted by 26 states but not by the U.K. 45 acceptances are needed in each case.

[11] Misc. 26 (1974), Cmnd. 5748; 12 I.L.M. 1319 (1973). On August 21, 1982, there were 13 contracting states, including the U.K. 15 are needed with the necessary tanker tonnage.

weight any rule against the would-be disposer of the waste, and Article 25 of the Geneva Convention seems to adopt this approach. Thus, when pollution does occur, and can be proved to have damaged the interests of other States or their nationals, the disposer-State may well be deemed to be in breach of a duty of prevention laid down in Article 25.[12]

Following the adoption of Article 25, an International Atomic Energy Authority Panel on Radioactive Waste Disposal into the Sea issued a series of recommendations, most of which concern the operation of nuclear powered ships.[13]

In 1959 the United States Atomic Energy Commission rejected a claim from a corporation in Texas for a licence to dispose of radio-active waste in the Gulf of Mexico at a point on the high seas equidistant from the United States and Mexico. The Commission said:

> . . . the Government of Mexico has indicated its legitimate concern with the porposed disposal project and has voiced its desire that the application be refused. The granting of the license under these circumstances will be considered by Mexicans to be at best an arbitrary, unilateral act by the United States.[14]

In 1966, a United States B-52 bomber collided in mid-air with a jet tanker that was refuelling it. As a result, four unarmed nuclear bombs were dropped; three fell on Spanish soil; the fourth landed in Spanish territorial waters and was recovered only with difficulty.[15]

In 1970, the United States disposed of nerve gas rockets embedded in concrete containers in the Atlantic below the high seas. The Secretary-General of the United Nations is reported as having characterised this action as contrary to the High Seas Convention[16] and General Assembly Resolution 2340 (XXII).[17] The United States is reported as having informed the United Nations Committee on Peaceful Uses of the Sea-bed and Ocean Floor that "experts had examined every conceivable alternative" but had not found any that was feasible.[18] The Committee unanimously expressed its concern at the practice of using the sea-bed and the ocean floor for dumping toxic, radio-active and other noxious materials.[19]

3. International concern for the marine environment has led to a number of multilateral treaties supplementing the High Seas Convention and the 1954 Convention. As well as the International Convention for the Prevention of Pollution from Ships 1973 (see note 1 above), the following conventions have been adopted:

> (i) the 1969 Intervention and Civil Liability Conventions (considered below);
> (ii) the Oslo Convention for the Prevention of Marine Pollution by Dumping from Ships and Aircraft 1972[20] (which applies to the North Sea and the North East Atlantic);
> (iii) the London Convention on the Prevention of Marine Pollution by Dumping of Wastes and Other Matter 1972[21] (which applies to the seas everywhere);

---

[12] *Op. cit.* at p. 284, n. 1, above, pp. 47–48. See also Hardy, 12 I.C.L.Q. 778 (1963).
[13] I.A.E.A., Radioactive Waste Disposal into the Sea, Safety Series No. 5, 1961.
[14] 4 Whiteman 613.
[15] *Keesings Archives*, p. 21393A.
[16] Article 25.
[17] December 18, 1967. This stresses the "importance of preserving the sea-bed and the ocean floor and the subsoil thereof . . . from actions and uses which might be detrimental to the common interests of mankind." See also G.A.Res. 2749 (XXV), para. 11, *loc. cit.* at p. 363, below. For the report, see 7 *U.N. Chronicle*, August-September 1970, p. 69.
[18] 5 *U.N. Law Reports* 1 (1970–71).   [19] *Ibid.* p. 2.
[20] U.K.T.S. 119 (1975), Cmnd. 6228; 11 I.L.M. 262 (1972). In force 1974. On August 6, 1981, there were 12 parties, including the U.K.
[21] Misc. 54 (1972), Cmnd. 5169; 11 I.L.M. 1291 (1972). In force 1975. On August 21, 1982, there were 48 parties, including the U.K.

(iv) the Paris Convention for the Prevention of Pollution from Land-based Sources 1974[22] (which concerns pollution of the sea from rivers, etc.);
(v) the Convention for the Protection of the Mediterranean Sea against Pollution 1976.[23]

INTERNATIONAL CONVENTION RELATING TO INTERVENTION ON THE HIGH SEAS IN CASES OF OIL POLLUTION CASUALTIES 1969[24]

U.K.T.S. 77 (1975), Cmnd. 6056; 9 I.L.M. 25 (1969)

Article 1

1. Parties to the present Convention may take such measures on the high seas as may be necessary to prevent, mitigate or eliminate grave and imminent danger to their coastline or related interests from pollution or threat of pollution of the sea by oil, following upon a maritime casualty or acts related to such a casualty, which may reasonably be expected to result in major harmful consequences.
2. However, no measures shall be taken under the present Convention against any warship or other ship owned or operated by a State and used, for the time being, only on government non-commercial service.

Article 2

For the purposes of the present Convention:
1. "maritime casualty" means a collision of ships, stranding or other incident of navigation, or other occurrence on board a ship or external to it resulting in material damage or imminent threat of material damage to a ship or cargo; . . .

Article 3

When a coastal State is exercising the right to take measures in accordance with Article 1, the following provisions shall apply:

(a) before taking any measures, a coastal State shall proceed to consultations with other States affected by the maritime casualty, particularly with the flag State or States;
(b) the coastal State shall notify without delay the proposed measures to any persons physical or corporate known to the coastal State, or made known to it during the consultations, to have interests which can reasonably be expected to be affected by those measures. The coastal State shall take into account any views they may submit; . . .
(d) in cases of extreme urgency requiring measures to be taken immediately, the coastal State may take measures rendered necessary by the urgency of the situation, without prior notification or consultation or without continuing consultations already begun; . . .

---

[22] 13 I.L.M. 352 (1974), Misc. 1 (1975), Cmnd. 5803. In force 1978. Seven parties on January 1, 1982, including the U.K.
[23] 15 I.L.M. 290 (1976). In force 1978. On February 15, 1982, there were 18 parties.
[24] In force 1975. On August 21, 1982, there were 42 contracting parties, including the U.K.

Article 5

1. Measures taken by the coastal State in accordance with Article 1 shall be proportionate to the damage actual or threatened to it.

2. Such measures shall not go beyond what is reasonably necessary to achieve the end mentioned in Article 1 and shall cease as soon as that end has been achieved; they shall not unnecessarily interfere with the rights and interests of the flag State, third States and of any persons, physical or corporate, concerned.

3. In considering whether the measures are proportionate to the damage, account shall be taken of:

(a) the extent and probability of imminent damage if those measures are not taken; and
(b) the likelihood of those measures being effective; and
(c) the extent of the damage which may be caused by such measures.

Article 6

Any Party which has taken measures in contravention of the provisions of the present Convention causing damage to others, shall be obliged to pay compensation to the extent of the damage caused by measures which exceed those reasonably necessary to achieve the end mentioned in Article 1.

Notes

1. The 1954 Convention is concerned with operational discharges. The Intervention Convention is concerned with discharges resulting from accidents at sea. The Convention was extended to cover "substances other than oil which may reasonably be expected to result in major harmful consequences" by the 1973 Protocol.[25]

2. The Convention was prompted by the *Torrey Canyon* incident, in 1967, in which the *Torrey Canyon*, a Liberian "supertanker" carrying over 119,000 tons of crude oil, negligently[26] became stranded on the Seven Stones on the high seas off the coast of Cornwall on its way to Milford Haven. Oil escaped in large quantities causing considerable pollution along the coasts of France and the United Kingdom. To prevent further escape of oil, the United Kingdom bombed the tanker from the air, apparently without protest from Liberia.

The British Government justified its conduct as follows:

> The overriding concern of the Government throughout has been to preserve the coasts from oil pollution and to adopt the course most likely to achieve this end. Neither legal nor financial considerations inhibited Government action at any stage.[27]

In 1969, the owners of the *Torrey Canyon*, a Liberian company, agreed to pay France and the United Kingdom £3 million in full settlement of their claims. It also agreed to make *ex gratia* payments in respect of private claims for damage.[28]

---

[25] Misc. 12 (1975), Cmnd. 6038; 13 I.L.M. 605 (1974). On December 31, 1981, there were 12 contracting states, including the U.K. Not in force. 15 ratifications are required.
[26] This was the conclusion of the Liberian Board of Investigation, 6 I.L.M. 480 (1967).
[27] Cmnd. 3246, p. 3. In 1969, eight states in the North Sea area, including the U.K., signed an Agreement for Co-operation in dealing with Pollution of the North Sea by Oil, U.K.T.S. 78 (1969), Cmnd. 4205; 9 I.L.M. 359 (1970), which entered into force in 1969. The U.K. has ratified it. For the power in English law to take action of the sort taken in the *Torrey Canyon* incident, see now the Prevention of Oil Pollution Act 1971, s.12.
[28] See the Attorney-General, *Hansard*, H.C., Vol. 791, col. 197. November 11, 1967.

3. In 1978, the worst case of oil pollution yet recorded occurred when the *Amoco Cadiz*, a Liberian registered tanker owned by a United States company, was wrecked on the Brittany coast and lost most of its cargo of 230,000 tons of crude oil. The incident, which was influential in the drafting of the 1982 Convention, led France to require that tankers keep seven miles from its coast in innocent passage through its territorial sea.

INTERNATIONAL CONVENTION ON CIVIL LIABILITY FOR OIL POLLUTION DAMAGE 1969[29]

U.K.T.S 106 (1975), Cmnd. 6183; 9 I.L.M. 45

Article 1

For the purposes of this Convention: . . .

3. "Owner" means the person or persons registered as the owner of the ship or, in the absence of registration, the person or persons owning the ship. However in the case of a ship owned by a State and operated by a company which in that State is registered as the ship's operator, "owner" shall mean such company. . . .

6. "Pollution damage" means loss or damage caused outside the ship carrying oil by contamination resulting from the escape or discharge of oil from the ship, wherever such escape or discharge may occur, and includes the costs of preventive measures and further loss or damage caused by preventive measures.

7. "Preventive measures" means any reasonable measures taken by any person after an incident has occurred to prevent or minimize pollution damage. . . .

Article 2

This Convention shall apply exclusively to pollution damage caused on the territory including the territorial sea of a Contracting State and to preventive measures taken to prevent or minimize such damage.

Article 3

1. Except as provided in paragraphs 2 and 3 of this Article, the owner of a ship at the time of an incident, or where the incident consists of a series of occurrences at the time of the first such occurrence, shall be liable for any pollution damage caused by oil which has escaped or been discharged from the ship as a result of the incident.

2. No liability for pollution damage shall attach to the owner if he proves that the damage:

   (a) resulted from an act of war, hostilities, civil war, insurrection or a natural phenomenon of an exceptional, inevitable and irresistible character, or
   (b) was wholly caused by an act or omission done with intent to cause damage by a third party, or

---

[29] The Convention entered into force in 1975. On August 21, 1982, there were 49 contracting parties, including the U.K. The Convention was amended (units of account provisions) by a 1976 Protocol, Misc. 26 (1977), Cmnd. 7028. On December 31, 1981, there were 14 contracting states, including the U.K. Not in force. Eight contracting parties *with the necessary tonnage* required.

(*c*) was wholly caused by the negligence or other wrongful act of any Government or other authority responsible for the maintenance of lights or other navigational aids in the exercise of that function.

3. If the owner proves that the pollution damage resulted wholly or partially either from an act or omission done with intent to cause damage by the person who suffered the damage or from the negligence of that person, the owner may be exonerated wholly or partially from his liability to such person.

Note
The Intervention Convention is known as the "public law" Convention; the Civil Liability Convention as the "private law" Convention. The latter imposes strict liability, subject to the exceptions allowed by Article 3, on the owner of any "seagoing vessel . . . actually carrying oil in bulk as cargo" (Art. 1(1)) that is registered under the law of a contracting party in respect of "pollution damage" in the territory or territorial sea of a contracting party. Claims must be brought in the courts of the contracting party in which the damage occurs (Art. 9). An owner must be insured to cover liability under the Convention in respect of vessels carrying 2,000 tons of oil or more (Art. 7). An owner may limit the extent of his liability (unless he has been guilty of "actual fault or privity") to 2,000 gold francs per ton of ship's tonnage (Art. 5). To meet the situation where the victim is unable to recover full compensation (i) because of such a limitation, or (ii) because Article 3(2) applies, or (iii) because of the default of the owner, the 1969 Convention was supplemented by the 1971 International Convention on the Establishment of an International Fund for Compensation for Oil Pollution Damage.[30] Victims may also have resort to the two compensation schemes set up by tanker owners—the Tanker Owners' Voluntary Agreement Concerning Liability for Oil Pollution 1969 (TOVALOP)[31] and the Contract Regarding an Interim Supplement to Tanker Liability for Oil Pollution 1971 (CRISTAL).[32]

CONVENTION ON THE LAW OF THE SEA 1982

Loc. cit. at p. 285, n. 16, above.

Article 192

States have the obligation to protect and preserve the marine environment.

Article 193

States have the sovereign right to exploit their natural resources pursuant to their environmental policies and in accordance with their duty to protect and preserve the marine environment.

Article 194

1. States shall take, individually or jointly as appropriate, all measures consistent with this Convention that are necessary to prevent, reduce and control pollution of the marine environment from any source, using for this purpose the best practicable means at their disposal and in accordance with their

[30] 11 I.L.M. 284 (1972). On August 21, 1982, there were 11 contracting states, including the U.K. In force 1978.
[31] 8 I.L.M. 497 (1969).
[32] 10 I.L.M. 137 (1971).

capabilities, and they shall endeavour to harmonize their policies in this connection.

2. States shall take all measures necessary to ensure that activities under their jurisdiction or control are so conducted as not to cause damage by pollution to other States and their environment, and that pollution arising from incidents or activities under their jurisdiction or control does not spread beyond the areas where they exercise sovereign rights in accordance with this Convention.

3. The measures taken pursuant to this Part shall deal with all sources of pollution of the marine environment. These measures shall include, *inter alia*, those designed to minimize to the fullest possible extent:

(a) the release of toxic, harmful, or noxious substances, especially those which are persistent, from land-based sources, from or through the atmosphere or by dumping.

(b) pollution from vessels, in particular measures for preventing accidents and dealing with emergencies, ensuring the safety of operations at sea, preventing intentional and unintentional discharges, and regulating the design, construction, equipment, operation and manning of vessels;

(c) pollution from installations and devices used in exploration or exploitation of the natural resources of the sea-bed and subsoil, in particular measures for preventing accidents and dealing with emergencies, ensuring the safety of operations at sea, and regulating the design, construction, equipment, operation and manning of such installations or devices;

(d) pollution from other installations and devices operating in the marine environment, in particular for preventing accidents and dealing with emergencies, ensuring the safety of operations at sea, and regulating the design, construction, equipment, operation and manning of such installations or devices.

4. In taking measures to prevent, reduce or control pollution of the marine environment, States shall refrain from unjustifiable interference with activities carried out by other States in the exercise of their rights and in pursuance of their duties in conformity with this Convention. . . .

Note

In keeping with the great concern over sea pollution apparent at the Stockholm Conference on the Environment,[33] the 1982 Convention contains a large number of detailed provisions on the protection of the marine environment.[34] In addition to the general provisions reprinted above, there are provisions on global and regional co-operation; technical assistance; monitoring and environmental assessment; and the development and enforcement of international and national law preventing pollution. It is also provided (Art. 235(1), (2)) that:

1. States are responsible for the fulfilment of their international obligations concerning the protection and preservation of the marine environment. They shall be liable in accordance with international law.

2. States shall ensure that recourse is available in accordance with their legal systems for prompt and adequate compensation or other relief in respect of damage caused by pollution of the marine environment by natural or juridical persons under their jurisdiction.

[33] See above, p. 204.
[34] Articles 192–238.

4. *THE EXCLUSIVE ECONOMIC ZONE*[35]

The exclusive economic zone has its roots in the concept of the exclusive fishing zone and the doctrine of the continental shelf. It combines and develops the two. The emergence of the concept of the exclusive fishing zone and its translation into the exclusive economic zone is considered in the following materials. The doctrine of the continental shelf is considered separately in section 5.

The exclusive fishing zone is a zone of the sea adjacent to a coastal state's territorial sea within which the coastal state has exclusive jurisdiction over fishing. The concept can be traced to the (then) extravagant 200-mile claims of certain Latin American states in the late 1940s to protect whaling and other fishing interests.[36] These were the subject of protest and were not thought to be lawful.[37] Then, as now, such claims were motivated by a genuine concern for conservation (international action not proving effective) as well as other national considerations. A turning point came with the failure of the 1958 Conference on the Law of the Sea and the supplementary 1960 Conference to agree upon a wider territorial sea than the traditional three-mile sea or upon fishing jurisdiction for coastal states beyond their territorial sea.[38] The majority view in 1958 was that, in the absence of agreement to the contrary, fishing beyond the limit of a lawful territorial sea was open to all states in accordance with "freedom of fishing" on the high seas. Unilateral action by Iceland and other states in the years that followed led gradually to an acceptance of a 12-mile[39] exclusive fishing zone by the time the *Fisheries Jurisdiction Cases* were decided.[40]

FISHERIES JURISDICTION CASE (MERITS)

United Kingdom *v.* Iceland

I.C.J. Reports 1974, p. 3

In 1958, following the Geneva Conference, Iceland declared a 12-mile exclusive fishing zone. The United Kingdom protested and protected British trawlers as they fished on the high seas within the zone in the first "Cod War." In 1961, the United Kingdom agreed by an exchange of notes[41] to the Icelandic claim, subject to a three-year phasing-out period. As to the area seawards of the 12-mile limit, the exchange of notes provided that Iceland

> will continue to work for the implementation of the Althing Resolution of May 5, 1959,[42] regarding the extension of fisheries jurisdiction around Iceland, but shall give

[35] See Extavour, *The Exclusive Economic Zone* (1981), and Phillips, 26 I.C.L.Q. 585 (1977).
[36] See Hollick, 71 A.J.I.L. 494 (1977).
[37] See Kunz, 50 A.J.I.L. 828 (1956).
[38] See 4 Whiteman 91–137.
[39] *i.e.* 12 miles as measured from the same baselines as those used for the territorial sea.
[40] A 1967 survey showed that exclusive fishing zones (mostly for 12 miles) were claimed by 33 states, including the U.K. (Fishery Limits Act 1964): Limits and Status of the Territorial Sea, Exclusive Zone, Fisheries Conservation Zones and the Continental Shelf, FAO Legislative Series No. 8, 1969, as revised. Other states had achieved the same result by claiming a 12-mile territorial sea. Most coastal states making such claims allowed other states to fish, permanently or for a phasing-out period, in the areas claimed where they could show that their fishermen had long done so.
[41] U.K.T.S. 17 (1961), Cmnd. 1328; 397 U.N.T.S. 275.
[42] By this, Iceland sought to extend its fishing zone to cover the whole of its continental shelf. The Althing is the Icelandic Parliament.

to the United Kingdom Government six months' notice of such extension and, in the case of a dispute in relation to such extension, the matter shall, at the request of either party, be referred to the International Court of Justice.

In 1971, Iceland gave notice of its intention to claim a 50-mile exclusive fisheries zone, this being approximately the width of its continental shelf. The United Kingdom again protested and in April 1972 filed an application with the Court, founding jurisdiction on the exchange of notes. In July 1972, Iceland made regulations carrying out its intent with effect from September. Thereupon, the United Kingdom sought, and in August obtained, interim measures of protection from the Court.[43] Pending the outcome of the case, Iceland was called upon to refrain from enforcing its 1972 regulations and the United Kingdom was called upon to limit its annual catch to 170,000 tons (it had asked for 180,000). When Iceland ignored the Court's order, the United Kingdom again protected its fishermen in the second "Cod War." In November 1973, an interim agreement[44] was reached by which United Kingdom trawlers were allowed to take 130,000 tons from the 50-mile zone for each of the next two years. In the meantime, in February 1973, the Court had found that it had jurisdiction to hear the application.[45] The Court ruled on the merits of the case in the present judgment in July 1974.

A parallel case, based upon similar facts and having the same outcome, was brought by the Federal Republic of Germany.[46]

Judgment of the Court

52. The 1960 Conference failed by one vote to adopt a text governing the two questions of the breadth of the territorial sea and the extent of fishery rights. . . . Two concepts have crystallized as customary law in recent years arising out of the general consensus revealed at that Conference. The first is the concept of the fishery zone, the area in which a State may claim exclusive fishery jurisdiction independently of its territorial sea; the extension of that fishery zone up to a 12-mile limit from the baselines appears now to be generally accepted. The second is the concept of preferential rights of fishing in adjacent waters in favour of the coastal State in a situation of special dependence on its coastal fisheries. . . .

53. . . . The Court is . . . aware of present endeavours, pursued under the auspices of the United Nations, to achieve in a third Conference on the Law of the Sea the further codification and progressive development of this branch of the law . . . the Court, as a court of law, cannot render judgment *sub specie legis ferendae*, or anticipate the law before the legislator has laid it down.

54. The concept of a 12-mile fishery zone, referred to in paragraph 52 above, as a *tertium genus* between the territorial sea and the high seas, has been accepted with regard to Iceland in the substantive provisions of the 1961 Exchange of Notes, and the United Kingdom has also applied the same fishery limit to its own coastal waters since 1964; therefore this matter is no longer in dispute between the Parties. . . .

58. State practice on the subject of fisheries reveals an increasing and widespread acceptance of the concept of preferential rights for coastal States, particularly in favour of countries or territories in a situation of special dependence on coastal fisheries. . . .

---

[43] *Fisheries Jurisdiction Case (Interim Protection)*, I.C.J. Rep. 1972, p. 12.
[44] U.K.T.S. 122 (1973), Cmnd. 5484.
[45] *Fisheries Jurisdiction Case (Jurisdiction)*, I.C.J. Rep. 1973, p. 3.
[46] *Fisheries Jurisdiction Case (Merits)*, I.C.J. Rep. 1974, p. 175.

59. There can be no doubt of the exceptional dependence of Iceland on its fisheries.[47] That exceptional dependence was explicitly recognized by the Applicant in the Exchange of Notes of 11 March 1961. . . .

60. The preferential rights of the coastal State come into play only at the moment when an intensification in the exploitation of fishery resources makes it imperative to introduce some system of catch-limitation and sharing of those resources, to preserve the fish stocks in the interests of their rational and economic exploitation. This situation appears to have been reached in the present case. . . .

62. . . . The characterization of the coastal State's rights as preferential implies a certain priority, but cannot imply the extinction of the concurrent rights of other States, and particularly of a State which, like the Applicant, has for many years been engaged in fishing in the waters in question, such fishing activity being important to the economy of the country concerned. . . .

67. Iceland's unilateral action thus constitutes an infringement of the principle enshrined in Article 2 of the 1958 Geneva Convention on the High Seas which requires that all States, including coastal States, in exercising their freedom of fishing, pay reasonable regard to the interests of other States. It also disregards the rights of the Applicant as they result from the Exchange of Notes of 1961. . . .

68. The findings stated by the Court in the preceding paragraphs suffice to provide a basis for the decision of the present case, namely: that Iceland's extension of its exclusive fishery jurisdiction beyond 12 miles is not opposable to the United Kingdom; that Iceland may on the other hand claim preferential rights in the distribution of fishery resources in the adjacent waters; that the United Kingdom also has established rights with respect to the fishery resources in question; and that the principle of reasonable regard for the interests of other States enshrined in Article 2 of the Geneva Convention on the High Seas of 1958 requires Iceland and the United Kingdom to have due regard to each other's interests, and to the interests of other States, in those resources. . . .

72. The most appropriate method for the solution of the dispute [between the parties] is clearly that of negotiation. Its objective should be the delimitation of the rights and interests of the Parties, the preferential rights of the coastal State on the one hand and the rights of the Applicant on the other, to balance and regulate equitably questions such as those of catch-limitation share allocations. . . .

75. The obligation to negotiate thus flows from the very nature of the respective rights of the Parties; to direct them to negotiate is therefore a proper exercise of the judicial function in this case. This also corresponds to the Principles and provisions of the Charter of the United Nations concerning peaceful settlement of disputes.[48]

78. In the fresh negotiations which are to take place on the basis of the present Judgment, the . . . task before [the parties] . . . will be to conduct their negotiations on the basis that each must in good faith pay reasonable regard to the legal rights of the other in the waters around Iceland outside the 12-mile limit, thus bringing about an equitable apportionment of the fishing resources

---

[47] *Ed.* Iceland imports almost all of the goods and commodities it needs. It pays for them by its exports, 80 per cent. of which are fish or fish products.

[48] *Ed.* See Article 33, Charter.

based on the facts of the particular situation, and having regard to the interests of other States which have established fishing rights in the area. It is not a matter of finding simply an equitable solution, but an equitable solution derived from the applicable law. . . .

79. For these reasons, the Court, by ten votes to four,[49] [held that Iceland's legislation was illegal; that it was not entitled to exclude U.K. fishing vessels unilaterally; that the two Governments were under an obligation to negotiate an equitable solution; and that the preferential rights of Iceland and the established rights of the U.K. should be taken into account in the negotiations].

Notes

1. Iceland declined to participate in the case, which was heard in its absence. In October 1975, contrary to the Court's judgment, Iceland extended its exclusive fishing zone unilaterally to 200 miles. The United Kingdom protested and, after unsuccessful negotiations, protected its trawlers during the third "Cod War" in the winter of 1975–76. Icelandic gunboats cut the warps of a number of British trawlers, collisions occurred, shots were fired, and diplomatic relations between Iceland and the United Kingdom were broken off.[50] The dispute was ended by an interim agreement[51] between the two states in June 1976 by which a small number of British trawlers were to be allowed to fish in Iceland's 200-mile zone for six months. After that, the matter was to be negotiated between Iceland and the European Communities. Such negotiations have not been successful and British trawlers to not fish within Iceland's 200-mile zone at present. In consequence, the Hull distant-waters fishing fleet has ceased to exist.

2. The Court limited itself to deciding that Iceland's claim was not opposable to the United Kingdom; although asked by the United Kingdom to rule on the general question whether a 50-mile exclusive fishing zone was valid *ergo omnes*, it declined to do so.[52] The reason for the Court's reluctance is not hard to find. With UNCLOS III already in session, it would have been a hazardous undertaking for the Court to have given judgment on such a contentious issue. (Witness the fate of the Court's initiative in proposing limited preferential rights for the coastal state.) What is remarkable is that soon after the Court's judgment the issue had been resolved in such a way that a 50-mile zone now seems modest.

CONVENTION ON THE LAW OF THE SEA 1982

Loc. cit. at p. 285, n. 16, above.

Article 55

The exclusive economic zone is an area beyond and adjacent to the territorial sea, subject to the specific legal régime established in this Part [Part V], under which the rights and jurisdiction of the coastal State and the rights and freedoms of other States are governed by the relevant provisions of this Convention.

[49] The judges in the majority were: Lachs, President; Judges Forster, Bengzon, Dillard, de Castro, Morozov, Jimenez de Aréchaga, Sir Humphrey Waldock, Nagendra Singh, and Ruda. Judges Gros, Petrén, Onyeama and Ignacio-Pinto dissented.

[50] It was estimated that 45 warps had been cut during the third "War" and that a similar number of collisions had occurred. Property damage on the British side was assessed at over £1 million.

[51] U.K.T.S. 73 (1976), Cmnd. 6545. Diplomatic relations were resumed after the agreement. It was estimated that it would yield about 15,000 tons of fish over the six months.

[52] The question was discussed by certain of the judges in their individual opinions: see Churchill, 24 I.C.L.Q. 82 at pp. 90–92 (1975).

Article 56

1. In the exclusive economic zone, the coastal State has:

(a) sovereign rights for the purpose of exploring and exploiting, conserving and managing the natural resources, whether living or non-living, of the waters superjacent to the sea-bed and of the sea-bed and subsoil, and with regard to other activities for the economic exploitation and exploration of the zone, such as the production of energy from the water, currents and winds;

(b) jurisdiction as provided for in the relevant provisions of this Convention with regard to:

   (i) the establishment and use of artificial islands, installations and structures;

   (ii) marine scientific research;

   (iii) the protection and preservation of the marine environment;

(c) other rights and duties provided for in this Convention.

2. In exercising its rights and performing its duties under this Convention in the exclusive economic zone, the coastal State shall have due regard to the rights and duties of other States and shall act in a manner compatible with the provisions of this Convention.

3. The rights set out in this article with respect to the sea-bed and subsoil shall be exercised in accordance with Part VI [on the continental shelf].

Article 57

The exclusive economic zone shall not extend beyond 200 nautical miles from the baselines from which the breadth of the territorial sea is measured.

Article 58

1. In the exclusive economic zone, all States, whether coastal or landlocked, enjoy, subject to the relevant provisions of this Convention, the freedoms referred to in article 87 of navigation and overflight and of the laying of submarine cables and pipelines, and other internationally lawful uses of the sea related to these freedoms, such as those associated with the operation of ships, aircraft and submarine cables and pipelines, and compatible with the other provisions of this Convention. . . .

3. In exercising their rights and performing their duties under this Convention in the exclusive economic zone, States shall have due regard to the rights and duties of the coastal State and shall comply with the laws and regulations adopted by the coastal State in accordance with the provisions of this Convention and other rules of international law in so far as they are not incompatible with this Part.

Article 59

In cases where this Convention does not attribute rights or jurisdiction to the coastal State or to other States within the exclusive economic zone, and a conflict arises between the interests of the coastal State and any other State or States, the conflict should be resolved on the basis of equity and in the light of all the relevant circumstances, taking into account the respective importance of the interests involved to the parties as well as to the international community as a whole.

Article 60

1. In the exclusive economic zone, the coastal State shall have the exclusive right to construct and to authorize and regulate the construction, operation and use of:

(a) artificial islands;

(b) installations and structures for the purposes provided for in article 56 and other economic purposes;

(c) installations and structures which may interfere with the exercise of the rights of the coastal State in the zone.

2. The coastal State shall have exclusive jurisdiction over such artificial islands, installations and structures, including jurisdiction with regard to customs, fiscal, health, safety and immigration laws and regulations. . . .

7. Artificial islands, installations and structures and the safety zones around them may not be established where interference may be caused to the use of recognised sea lanes essential to international navigation.

8. Artificial islands, installations and structures do not possess the status of islands. They have no territorial sea of their own, and their presence does not affect the delimitation of the territorial sea, the exclusive economic zone or the continental shelf.

Article 61

1. The coastal State shall determine the allowable catch of the living resources in its exclusive economic zone.

2. The coastal State, taking into account the best scientific evidence available to it, shall ensure through proper conservation and management measures that the maintenance of the living resources in the exclusive economic zone is not endangered by over-exploitation. As appropriate, the coastal State and competent international organisations, whether subregional, regional, or global, shall co-operate to this end.

3. Such measures shall also be designed to maintain or restore populations of harvested species at levels which can produce the maximum sustainable yield, as qualified by relevant environmental and economic factors, including the economic needs of coastal fishing communities and the special requirements of developing states, and taking into account fishing patterns, the interdependence of stocks and any generally recommended international minimum standards, whether subregional, regional or global. . . .

Article 62

1. The coastal State shall promote the objective of optimum utilization of the living resources in the exclusive economic zone without prejudice to article 61.

2. The coastal State shall determine its capacity to harvest the living resources of the exclusive economic zone. Where the coastal State does not have the capacity to harvest the entire allowable catch, it shall, through agreements or other arrangements and pursuant to the terms, conditions, laws and regulations referred to in paragraph 4, give other States access to the surplus of the allowable catch, having particular regard to the provisions of Articles 69 and 70,[53] especially in relation to the developing states mentioned therein.

[53] On the rights of land-locked states and states "with special geographical characteristics" (who together constituted about one third of the states at UNCLOS III). The latter are defined in 1982 Convention, Article 70(2).

3. In giving access to other States to its exclusive economic zone under this article, the coastal State shall take into account all relevant factors, including, *inter alia*, the significance of the living resources of the area to the economy of the coastal State concerned and its other national interests, the provisions of articles 69 and 70,[53] the requirements of developing countries in the subregion or region in harvesting part of the surplus and the need to minimize economic dislocation in States whose nationals have habitually fished in the zone or which have made substantial efforts in research and identification of stocks.

4. Nationals of other States fishing in the exclusive economic zone shall comply with the conservation measures and with the other terms and conditions established in the regulations of the coastal State. . . .

[Articles 64–67 make special provision for highly migratory species (*e.g.* tuna, swordfish), marine mammals (*e.g.* whales, seals), anadromous stocks (*e.g.* salmon), and catadromous species (*e.g.* eels)]

Article 73

1. The coastal state may, in the exercise of its sovereign rights to explore, exploit, conserve and manage the living resources in the exclusive economic zone, take such measures, including boarding, inspection, arrest and judicial proceedings, as may be necessary to ensure compliance with the laws and regulations adopted by it in conformity with this Convention. . . .

Article 74

1. The delimitation of the exclusive economic zone between States with opposite or adjacent coasts shall be effected by agreement on the basis of international law, as referred to in Article 38 of the Statute of the International Court of Justice, in order to achieve an equitable solution.

2. If no agreement can be reached within a reasonable period of time, the States concerned shall resort to the procedures provided for in Part XV [on the settlement of disputes].[54]

3. Pending agreement as provided for in paragraph 1, the States concerned, in a spirit of understanding and co-operation, shall make every effort to enter into provisional arrangements of a practical nature and, during this transitional period, not to jeopardize or hamper the reaching of the final agreement. Such arrangements shall be without prejudice to the final delimitation. . . .

Notes

1. It is clear that the international community is prepared to allow coastal states a 200-miles exclusive economic zone. A consensus to this effect quickly emerged at UNCLOS III and provision is accordingly made for such a zone in the 1982 Convention. In the *Continental Shelf (Tunisia v. Libya) Case*,[55] the International Court of Justice observed that the zone "may be regarded as part of modern international law." By 1978, 38 coastal states, from all political groupings, had made claims to 200-miles exclusive economic zones.[56] Another 23 had made claims to 200-miles exclusive fishing zones.[57]

[54] A state may declare at any time that it does not agree to compulsory arbitration in respect of disputes arising out of Article 74; submission to non-binding conciliation procedures is then compulsory in some cases: 1982 Convention, Article 298(1)(*a*).

[55] I.C.J. Reports 1982 at p. 74.

[56] FAO figures: see p. 288, n. 26 above. The states included Cuba, France, India, Madagascar, Mexico, New Zealand, Norway, Mozambique, and Democratic Yemen. The earliest claim was in 1974.

[57] *Ibid.* The states included Chile, Fiji, Gambia, Ireland, Japan, Netherlands, South Africa,

Indicative of the speed of events is the fact that the United Kingdom, which had fought a "war" over Iceland's claim to a 200-miles exclusive fishing zone just 12 months previously, claimed its own 200-miles exclusive fishing zone as of 1977.[58]

2. The 1982 Convention intentionally refrains from describing the exclusive economic zone as a part of the high seas. The zone is treated instead as an intermediate area of sea between the high seas and the territorial sea with a distinct régime of its own. This régime accords the coastal state (i) sovereign rights of exploitation of resources and (ii) ancillary and other powers of exclusive jurisdiction (1982 Convention, Art. 56). Although the position of the coastal state in an area previously regarded as being fully subject to the "freedom of the high seas" is thus greatly strengthened, it falls far short of sovereignty. In particular, states generally may continue to exercise within the zone freedom of navigation and overflight and other freedoms not covered by Article 56 of the 1982 Convention that form part of the established concept of "freedom of the high seas."[59] To this large extent, the 1982 Convention does not revert to Selden's idea of the closed sea in respect of the zone.[60]

3. The jurisdiction given to the coastal state by the 1982 Convention in its exclusive economic zone in respect of *fishing* is much wider than that indicated by the Court in the *Fisheries Jurisdiction Cases*. The obligations placed upon the coastal state to conserve fisheries are matched by rights of exploitation that make little concession to the interests of other states. In the *Fisheries Jurisdiction Cases*, Iceland would have been entitled, under Article 62, to reserve all of the allowable catch for Icelandic fishermen if, as is probable, they were capable of exploiting it. If they lacked that capacity, Article 62(3) would have applied to the advantage of the United Kingdom although not a developing, landlocked, or geographically disadvantaged state, since its nationals had "habitually fished in the zone." But the application of Article 62(3) depends on "agreements or other arrangements" (Art. 62(2)). Note also that disputes concerning a coastal state's sovereign rights over fisheries within its exclusive economic zone are not subject to compulsory arbitration or adjudication; *extreme* cases are subject to compulsory but non-binding *conciliation* (Art. 297(3)).

4. *Islands*. The 1982 Convention (Art. 121(3)) provides that an island may have an exclusive economic zone or a continental shelf with the following exceptions: "Rocks which cannot sustain human habitation or economic life of their own shall have no exclusive economic zone or continental shelf."[61] The meaning of "economic life" is obscure. An island such as Rockall would not qualify for an exclusive economic zone under this proposal. Such an island close to the mainland may, however, be taken into account when drawing baselines for an exclusive economic zone or continental shelf.[62]

5. Although Article 56 includes continental shelf (*i.e.* sea-bed and subsoil) resources within the actual resources of the exclusive economic zone, the 1982 Convention contains a separate régime for the continental shelf, based upon the 1958 Continental Shelf Convention, see below, p. 355. The two 1982 Convention régimes overlap, with

U.S.S.R., and the U.S. The EEC has adopted a 200 miles exclusive fishing zone *vis-à-vis* third states. In 1983, it agreed upon a fishing policy for its members *inter se*. See Gutteridge (1978) 49 B.Y.I.L. 202.

[58] Fishery Limits Act 1976. The Act allows certain states to fish within the 200-mile limit and in accordance with the Fishery Limits Act 1964. These include EEC states and the U.S.S.R.

[59] See those listed above, p. 320.

[60] See Ganz, *loc. cit.* at p. 285, n. 14, above, p. 53. Selden was a seventeenth-century English lawyer who argued unsuccessfully that the seas might be subjected to territorial sovereignty. The opposing view of Grotius, propounded when the Netherlands was the dominant maritime power, prevailed.

[61] Such rocks do have a territorial sea under the 1982 Convention (as under the Territorial Sea Convention) if they come within the definition of an island common to both texts: see above, p. 297.

[62] See the *English Channel Arbitration*, 18 I.L.M. 397, 434 (1979) (use of the Eddystone Rocks).

the same rules *within the 200-miles limit* about artificial structures, etc. (Arts. 60 and 80), the delimitation of boundaries (Arts. 74 and 83), and the publishing of charts (Arts. 75 and 84). The continental shelf régime alone applies to the exploitation of shelf resources *beyond the 200-miles limit*. The exploitation of shelf resources, including sedentary species (Art. 68), within the 200-miles limit is not subject to the conservation and sharing restrictions that apply under the exclusive economic zone régime applicable to fish.

5. THE CONTINENTAL SHELF[63]

THE TRUMAN PROCLAMATION ON THE CONTINENTAL SHELF 1945

4 Whiteman 756

Whereas the Government of the United States of America, aware of the long range world-wide need for new sources of petroleum and other minerals, holds the view that efforts to discover and make available new supplies of these resources should be encouraged; and. . . .

Whereas recognized jurisdiction over these resources is required in the interest of their conservation and prudent utilization when and as development is undertaken; and

Whereas it is the view of the Government of the United States that the exercise of jurisdiction over the natural resources of the subsoil and sea bed of the continental shelf by the contiguous nation is reasonable and just, since the effectiveness of measures to utilize or conserve these resources would be contingent upon cooperation and protection from the shore, since the continental shelf may be regarded as an extension of the land mass of the coastal nation and thus naturally appurtenant to it, since these resources frequently form a seaward extension of a pool or deposit lying within the territory, and since self-protection compels the coastal nation to keep close watch over activities off its shores which are of the nature necessary for utilization of these resources:

Now therefore, I, Harry S. Truman, President of the United States of America, do hereby proclaim the following policy of the United States of America with respect to the natural resources of the subsoil and sea bed of the continental shelf.

Having concern for the urgency of conserving and prudently utilizing its natural resources, the Government of the United States regards the natural resources of the subsoil and sea bed of the continental shelf beneath the high seas but contiguous to the coasts of the United States as appertaining to the United States, subject to its jurisdiction and control. In cases where the continental shelf extends to the shores of another state, or is shared with an adjacent state, the boundary shall be determined by the United States and the state concerned in accordance with equitable principles. The character as high seas of the waters above the continental shelf and the right to their free and unimpeded navigation are in no way thus affected.

Notes
1. The Truman Proclamation, which was the first of its kind, was quickly followed by similar declarations made by other states. By 1945, it had become technically possible to

[63] See Hurst, 34 Trans.Grot.Soc. 153 (1949); Lauterpacht (1950) 27 B.Y.I.L. 376; Gutteridge (1959) 35 B.Y.I.L. 102; Whiteman, 52 A.J.I.L. 69 (1958).

drill for oil and other mineral resources in the sea-bed from the sea and the Truman Proclamation was aimed at filling a gap in international law on the legal rights and duties of states arising from that possibility.

2. Geomorphologically, the continental shelf is the gently sloping platform of submerged land surrounding the continents and islands. Normally it extends to a depth of approximately 200 metres or 100 fathoms at which point the sea-bed falls away sharply.[64] In some places it continues beyond a depth of 200 metres. It varies in width from less than 5 miles (off the coast of California, for example), to 750 miles (below the Barents Sea). The continental shelf west of the United Kingdom has an outer limit at a depth of about 200 metres and extends to about 300 miles off Land's End. Shelves occupy about 7.5 per cent. of the total ocean area.

3. The status of the continental shelf doctrine in customary international law was considered by the Arbitrator, Lord Asquith, in the *Abu Dhabi Arbitration* in 1951.[65] In the light of the declarations then in existence, he concluded:

> . . . there are in this field so many ragged ends and unfilled blanks, so much that is merely tentative and exploratory, that in no form can the doctrine claim as yet to have assumed hitherto the hard lineaments or the definitive status of an established rule of international law.

GENEVA CONVENTION ON THE CONTINENTAL SHELF 1958

See the references above, p. 284, n. 7

Article 1

For the purpose of these articles, the term "continental shelf" is used as referring (*a*) to the seabed and subsoil of the submarine areas adjacent to the coast but outside the area of the territorial sea, to a depth of 200 metres or, beyond that limit, to where the depth of the superjacent waters admits of the exploitation of the natural resources of the said areas; (*b*) to the seabed and subsoil of similar submarine areas adjacent to the coasts of islands.

Article 2

1. The coastal state exercises over the continental shelf sovereign rights for the purpose of exploring it and exploiting its natural resources.

2. The rights referred to in paragraph 1 of this article are exclusive in the sense that if the coastal state does not explore the continental shelf or exploit its natural resources, no one may undertake these activities, or make a claim to the continental shelf, without the express consent of the coastal state.

3. The rights of the coastal state over the continental shelf do not depend on occupation, effective or notional, or on any express proclamation.

4. The natural resources referred to in these articles consist of the mineral and other non-living resources of the seabed and subsoil together with living organisms belonging to sedentary species, that is to say, organisms which, at the harvestable stage, either are immobile on or under the seabed or are unable to move except in constant physical contact with the seabed or the subsoil.

---

[64] This was the depth that the U.S. had in mind in the Truman Proclamation.
[65] 1 I.C.L.Q. 247 (1952); 18 I.L.R. 144 (1951). See now, however, the *North Sea Continental Shelf Cases*, above, p. 25.

Article 3

The rights of the coastal state over the continental shelf do not affect the legal status of the superjacent waters as high seas, or that of the airspace above those waters.

Article 4

Subject to its right to take reasonable measures for the exploration of the continental shelf and the exploitation of its natural resources, the coastal state may not impede the laying or maintenance of submarine cables or pipelines on the continental shelf.

Article 5

1. The exploration of the continental shelf and the exploitation of its natural resources must not result in any unjustifiable interference with navigation, fishing or the conservation of the living resources of the sea, nor result in any interference with fundamental oceanographic or other scientific research carried out with the intention of open publication.

2. Subject to the provisions of paragraphs 1 and 6 of this article, the coastal state is entitled to construct and maintain or operate on the continental shelf installations and other devices necessary for its exploration and the exploitation of its natural resources, and to establish safety zones around such installations and devices and to take in those zones measures necessary for their protection.

3. The safety zones referred to in paragraph 2 of this article may extend to a distance of 500 metres around the installations and other devices which have been erected, measured from each point of their outer edge. Ships of all nationalities must respect these safety zones.

4. Such installations and devices, though under the jurisdiction of the coastal state, do not possess the status of islands. They have no territorial sea of their own, and their presence does not affect the delimitation of the territorial sea of the coastal state.

5. Due notice must be given of the construction of any such installations, and permanent means for giving warning of their presence must be maintained. Any installations which are abandoned or disused must be entirely removed.

6. Neither the installations or devices, nor the safety zones around them, may be established where interference may be caused to the use of recognized sea lanes essential to international navigation.

7. The coastal state is obliged to undertake, in the safety zones, all appropriate measures for the protection of the living resources of the sea from harmful agents.

8. The consent of the coastal state shall be obtained in respect of any research concerning the continental shelf and undertaken there. Nevertheless, the coastal state shall not normally withhold its consent if the request is submitted by a qualified institution with a view to purely scientific research into the physical or biological characteristics of the continental shelf, subject to the proviso that the coastal state shall have the right, if it so desires, to participate or to be represented in the research, and that in any event the results shall be published.

Article 6

1. Where the same continental shelf is adjacent to the territories of two or more states whose coasts are opposite each other, the boundary of the continental shelf appertaining to such states shall be determined by agreement between them. In the absence of agreement, and unless another boundary line is justified by special circumstances, the boundary is the median line, every point of which is equidistant from the nearest points of the baselines from which the breadth of the territorial sea of each state is measured.

2. Where the same continental shelf is adjacent to the territories of two adjacent states, the boundary of the continental shelf shall be determined by agreement between them. In the absence of agreement, and unless another boundary line is justified by special circumstances, the boundary shall be determined by application of the principle of equidistance from the nearest points of the baselines from which the breadth of the territorial sea of each state is measured.

3. In delimiting the boundaries of the continental shelf, any lines which are drawn in accordance with the principles set out in pargraphs 1 and 2 of this article should be defined with reference to charts and geographical features as they exist at a particular date, and reference should be made to fixed permanent identifiable points on the land.

Article 7

The provisions of these articles shall not prejudice the right of the coastal state to exploit the subsoil by means of tunnelling irrespective of the depth of water above the subsoil.

Article 12

1. At the time of signature, ratification or accession, any state may make reservations to articles of the Convention other than to Articles 1 to 3 inclusive.

Notes

1. *The definition of the continental shelf.* The Convention clearly does not use a geomorphological definition. As the technical possibility of exploiting resources at depths greater than 200 metres has become a reality, so the question of the meaning of the phrase "adjacent to the coast" in Article 1 of the Convention has increased in importance. Is the middle of the Atlantic, which is certainly not continental shelf in a geomorphological sense, adjacent to *any* coast? Note that in the *North Sea Continental Shelf Cases*[66] the International Court of Justice stated:

> What confers the *ipso jure* title which international law attributes to the coastal State in respect of its continental shelf, is the fact that the submarine areas concerned may be deemed to be actually part of the territory over which the coastal State already has dominion—in the sense that, although covered with water, they are a prolongation or continuation of that territory, an extension of it under the sea. From this it would follow that whenever a given submarine area does not constitute a natural—or the most natural—extension of the land territory of a coastal State, even though that area may be closer to it than it is to the territory of any other State, it cannot be regarded as appertaining to that State—or at least it cannot be so regarded in the face of a competing claim by a State of whose land territory the submarine area concerned is to be regarded as a natural extension, even if it is less close to it.[67]

[66] Above, p. 25.   [67] I.C.J. Rep. 1969 at p. 31.

2. *No territorial sovereignty*. The Convention gives only limited rights to the coastal state in the continental shelf, not sovereignty. The Truman Proclamation and most others had not claimed sovereignty. In contrast, the claims of some Latin American states are to "national sovereignty."[68]

3. *Living resources*. The phrase "living organisms belonging to the sedentary species" was said at Geneva to include, *inter alia*, "coral, sponges, oysters, including pearl oysters, pearl shell, the sacred chank of India and Ceylon, the trocus and plants."[69] It probably also includes clams[70] and scallops. It excludes bottom fish, shrimps, prawns and, probably, octopuses. Crabs and lobsters have caused problems. The United Kingdom position has been expressed as follows:

> . . . lobsters swim and crabs do not. Therefore, crabs are within the Convention, and lobsters are not.[71]

The intention of at least one of the states sponsoring the text adopted was, however, to exclude all crustacea, including crabs.[72] In 1963, a dispute occurred between France and Brazil over the fishing of crawfish (*langoustes*) by Breton fishermen on the Brazilian continental shelf. It would seem that adult crawfish normally stay in rock holes or clamber about, but will swim if pursued. It is interesting that, although neither France nor Brazil were then parties to the Convention, both relied on their (differing) interpretations of Article 2(4) to support their claims in respect of freedom to fish for the crawfish.[73]

The inclusion in the Convention of living resources as well as mineral resources was probably an instance of "progressive development" rather than "codification." The Truman Proclamation is clearly concerned with mineral resources only and the customary international law position before the Convention was probably that claims to exploit living resources, such as pearls, sponges and oysters had to be based upon occupation.[74] In the *Continental Shelf (Tunisia* v. *Libya) Case*,[75] Tunisia, in the course of developing its continental shelf claim, argued that it had historic rights to the exploitation of fixed fisheries (to catch swimming species) and sponges in the waters off its coastline beyond its territorial sea. After noting that the juridical régime of "historic waters" had purposely been left for separate, later consideration when the 1958 Convention was being drafted and that UNCLOS III had not tackled the question either, the Court continued:

> "It seems clear that the matter continues to be governed by general international law which does not provide for a *single* 'régime' for 'historic waters' or 'historic bays,' but only for a particular régime for each of the concrete, recognized cases of 'historic waters' or 'historic bays.' It is clearly the case that, basically, the notion of historic

---

[68] See the claims made by Chile and Peru in 1947: 4 Whiteman 794–799. Such claims have been the subject of protests: *ibid*.

[69] Mr. Bailey (Australia), *1958 Sea Conference Records*, Vol. VI, p. 57.

[70] This is the U.S. view: 4 Whiteman 863.

[71] *Hansard*, H.C., Vol. 688, col. 277. January 28, 1964; 1964 B.P.I.L. 58–59 (but see the attitude taken by the U.K. on lobster fishing off the Bahamas: 4 Whiteman 863). The U.S. distinguishes between lobsters and crabs in the same way: 4 Whiteman 863. Zoologically, this clear cut distinction between lobsters and crabs is an oversimplification. France stated that it understood Article 2(4) to exclude all crustacea except for one kind of crab (*le crabe anatife*) when it ratified the Convention: see Hartingh, 11 *Annuaire Français* 725 (1965).

[72] See Mr. Bailey, Australia, *loc. cit.* at n. 69, above.

[73] A compromise was reached in 1964 allowing a limited number of French boats to fish for crawfish for the following five years. See Goldie, in Alexander, ed., *The Law of the Sea* (1967), pp. 286–287. See also Azzam, 13 I.C.L.Q. 1543 (1964). Zoologically, the crawfish, although sometimes known as the rock lobster, is not a lobster at all. On the U.S.-Japanese dispute over the king crab, see 4 Whiteman 864.

[74] Young, 55 AJ.I.L. 359 at pp. 360–362 (1961).

[75] I.C.J. Rep. 1982 at p. 74.

rights or waters and that of the continental shelf are governed by distinct legal régimes in customary international law. The first régime is based on acquisition and occupation, while the second is based on the existence of rights '*ipso facto* and *ab initio.*' No doubt both may sometimes coincide in part or in whole, but such co-incidence can only be fortuitous . . . it may be that Tunisia's historic rights and titles are more nearly related to the concept of the exclusive economic zone, which may be regarded as part of modern international law. . . ."

4. *Boundaries between States.* This is a matter that has generated much litigation because of the important economic consequences.[76] In the *North Sea Continental Shelf Cases*, the International Court of Justice ruled that Article 6(2) did not represent customary international law at least as far as lateral line delimitations between adjacent states (as opposed to median line delimitations between opposite states) were concerned. The Court then stated the rules that did apply, emphasising above all the need to achieve an equitable result.[77] The same approach was taken when applying custom in the *Continental Shelf (Tunisia v. Libya) Case*.[78] Here the Court commended the equidistance rule where "its application leads to an equitable solution," but this was not the case on the facts. On the meaning of equity, the Court said:

71. Equity as a legal concept is a direct emanation of the idea of justice. The Court whose task is by definition to administer justice is bound to apply it. In the course of the history of legal systems the term "equity" has been used to define various legal concepts. It was often contrasted with the rigid rules of positive law, the severity of which had to be mitigated in order to do justice. In general, this contrast has no parallel in the development of international law; the legal concept of equity is a general principle directly applicable as law. Moreover, when applying positive international law, a court may choose among several possible interpretations of the law the one which appears, in the light of the circumstances of the case, to be closest to the requirements of justice. Application of equitable principles is to be distinguished from a decision *ex aequo et bono*. The Court can take such a decision only on condition that the Parties agree (Art. 38, para. 2, of the Statute), and the Court is then freed from the strict application of legal rules in order to bring about an appropriate settlement. The task of the Court in the present case is quite different: it is bound to apply equitable principles as part of international law, and to balance up the various considerations which it regards as relevant in order to produce an equitable result. While it is clear that no rigid rules exist as to the exact weight to be attached to each element in the case, this is very far from being an exercise of discretion or conciliation; nor is it an operation of distributive justice.[79]

Commenting upon its reliance upon the "natural prolongation" factor in the *North Sea Cases*, the Court indicated that this was a factor that, while important, was subservient to the overall need to satisfy equitable principles and, in any event, might, as on the facts of the *Tunisia v. Libya* case, not be helpful in a particular geological situation.[80] The Court also emphasised that "each continental shelf case in dispute should be considered and judged on its own merits, having regard to its peculiar circumstances," and that, consequently "no attempt should be made . . . to overconceptualize the application of

---

[76] See, in addition to the cases cited below, the *Aegean Sea Continental Shelf Case*, I.C.J. Rep. 1978, p. 3 (no judgment on merits) and the *Gulf of Maine Case* between Canada and the U.S.A. over the boundary between the fisheries zones and continental shelf areas in the Gulf of Maine that is now pending before the I.C.J.

[77] See the passage from the judgment quoted at p. 28–29, above.

[78] I.C.J. Rep. 1982, p. 18. Neither state was a party to the Continental Shelf Convention.

[79] *Ibid.* p. 60. The Court rejected a Tunisian argument based in part upon its relative poverty *vis-à-vis* Libya; such economic considerations could not be taken into account: *ibid.* p. 77.

[80] In that case, the area of shelf in issue was the "natural prolongation" of a land mass common to both states.

the principles and rules relating to the continental shelf."[81] In the *English Channel Arbitration*,[82] the Court of Arbitration was asked to delimit the continental shelves of the United Kingdom and France in English Channel (West of Selsey Bill) and in the South Western Approaches. In contrast with the two I.C.J. cases, the case was decided on the basis of Continental Shelf Convention, Article 6(2),[83] to which both states were parties. In interpreting that provision, the Court observed:

> 68. Article 6 . . . does not formulate the equidistance principle and "special circumstances" as two separate rules. The rule there stated in each of the two cases is a single one, a combined equidistance-special circumstances rule. . . .
>
> 70. The Court does not overlook that under Article 6 the equidistance principle ultimately possesses an obligatory force which it does not have in the same measure under the rules of customary law; for Article 6 makes the application of the equidistance principle a matter of treaty obligation for Parties to the Convention. But the combined character of the equidistance-special circumstances rule means that the obligation to apply the equidistance principle is always one qualified by the condition "unless another boundary line is justified by special circumstances." . . . In short, the role of the "special circumstances" condition in Article 6 is to ensure an equitable delimitation; and the combined "equidistance-special circumstances rule," in effect, gives particular expression to a general norm that, failing agreement, the boundary between States abutting on the same continental shelf is to be determined on equitable principles. . . .
>
> 97. In short, this Court considers that the appropriateness of the equidistance method or any other method for the purpose of effecting an equitable delimitation is a function or reflection of the geographical and other relevant circumstances of each particular case. The choice of the method or methods of delimitation in any given case, whether under the 1958 Convention or customary law, has therefore to be determined in the light of those circumstances and of the fundamental norm that the delimitation must be in accordance with equitable principles. Furthermore, in appreciating the appropriateness of the equidistance method as a means of achieving an equitable solution, regard must be had to the difference between a "lateral" boundary between "adjacent" States and a "median" boundary between "opposite" States.[84]

In the last analysis, therefore, both the 1958 Convention rule and customary international law require an equitable solution. *cf.* Articles 74 and 83, 1982 Convention, referred to above, p. 352, and below, p. 363. The difficulty with such an approach is, as Bowett points out,[85] that, since different states will have different views of what equity requires, it reduces the changes of settling boundary disputes without litigation.

The *English Channel Arbitration* had to consider the effect of the Scilly and Channel Islands on the boundary between the United Kingdom and French shelves. In the case of the former, "[w]hat equity calls for is an appropriate abatement of the disproportionate effects" of a full application (favouring the U.K.) of the equidistance method. Taking a lead from examples of state practice "in which only partial effect has been given to offshore islands situated outside the territorial sea of the mainland," the Court accorded a "half effect" to the Scilly Islands.[86] The Channel Islands presented the problem of islands on the wrong side of the median line and "wholly detached geographically from

---

[81] *Ibid.* p. 92.

[82] 18 I.L.M. 397 (1979), including both the 1977 Award and the 1978 interpretative decision. The Court of Arbitration was composed of Castren, President; Briggs, Gros, Ustor and Waldock. See Bowett (1978) 49 B.Y.I.L. 1 and Colson, 72 A.J.I.L. 95 (1978).

[83] The Court held that Article 6(2) applied to the dispute subject to the French reservations to it.

[84] *Ibid.* pp. 421, 426–427.

[85] *Loc. cit.* at n. 82 above, p. 6.

[86] *Ibid.* p. 455.

the United Kingdom."[87] The solution adopted by the Court, in its search for a "more equitable balance" than would have resulted from the arguments put by either party, was to give the Channel Islands a continental shelf of 12 miles from its territorial sea baselines as an enclave within the French continental shelf.

The United Kingdom has reached agreement by treaty, very largely on the basis of the equidistance method of delimitation, with three of the states—Norway,[88] the Netherlands[89] and Denmark[90]—with which it shares the continental shelf in the North Sea. The whole of the North Sea is less than 200 metres deep except for the Norwegian Trough just off the coast of Norway. The Trough has, in effect, been ignored by Norway and the United Kingdom in the division of the area between them.

6. Provision is made by the Continental Shelf Act 1964 for the granting of licences for the exploration and exploitation of oil and natural gas in the United Kingdom continental shelf.

7. *Tunnelling.* The Convention does not affect tunnelling through the subsoil of the continental shelf from the territory of the coastal state. Colombos suggests that "the subsoil under the bed of the sea may be considered capable of occupation" and that it would "be unreasonable to withold recognition of the right of a State to drive mines or build tunnels in the subsoil, even when they extend considerably beyond the three-mile limit of territorial waters, provided that they do not affect or endanger the surface of the sea."[91] He also suggests that "in the case of a tunnel between two different States, the territorial property and jurisdiction of that part of the tunnel which runs under the bed of the high seas would have to be regulated by agreement between the two States chiefly concerned."[92] Tunnelling for mining purposes beyond the three-mile limit has occurred in Cornwall, for example, under the Cornwall Submarine Mines Act 1858. Section 2 states that "all mines and minerals lying below low-water mark under the open sea adjacent to, but not being part of the county of Cornwall, are vested in Her Majesty the Queen in right of her Crown as part of the soil and territorial possessions of the Crown."

LAW OF THE SEA CONVENTION 1982

Loc. cit. at p. 285, n. 16, above.

Article 76

1. The continental shelf of a coastal State comprises the sea-bed and subsoil of the submarine areas that extend beyond its territorial sea throughout the natural prolongation of its land territory to the outer edge of the continental margin, or to a distance of 200 nautical miles from the baselines from which the breadth of the territorial sea is measured where the outer edge of the continental margin does not extend up to that distance. . . .

2. The continental shelf of a coastal State shall not extend beyond the limits provided for in paragraphs 4 to 6.

3. The continental margin comprises the submerged prolongation of the land mass of the coastal State, and consists of the sea-bed and subsoil of the shelf, the slope and the rise. It does not include the deep ocean floor with its oceanic ridges or the subsoil thereof.

4. (*a*) For the purposes of this Convention, the coastal State shall establish the outer edge of the continental margin wherever the margin extends beyond 200

[87] *Ibid.* p. 444.
[88] U.K.T.S. 71 (1965), Cmnd. 2757; 551 U.N.T.S. 213.
[89] U.K.T.S. 23 (1967), Cmnd. 3253.
[90] U.K.T.S. 35 (1967), Cmnd. 3278; 592 U.N.T.S. 207.
[91] *Op. cit.* at p. 284, n. 1, above, p. 69.   [92] *Ibid.*

nautical miles from the baselines from which the breadth of the territorial sea is measured, by either:

    (i) a line delineated in accordance with paragraph 7 by reference to the outermost fixed points at each of which the thickness of sedimentary rocks is at least 1 per cent. of the shortest distance from such point to the foot of the continental slope; or

    (ii) a line delineated in accordance with paragraph 7 by reference to fixed points not more than 60 nautical miles from the foot of the continental slope.

(*b*) In the absence of evidence to the contrary, the foot of the continental slope shall be determined as the point of maximum change in the gradient at its base.

5. The fixed points comprising the line of the outer limits of the continental shelf on the sea-bed, drawn in accordance with paragraph 4(*a*)(i) and (ii), either shall not exceed 350 nautical miles from the baselines from which the breadth of the territorial sea is measured or shall not exceed 100 nautical miles from the 2,500 metre isobath, which is a line connecting the depth of 2,500 metres.

6. Notwithstanding the provisions of paragraph 5, on submarine ridges, the outer limit of the continental shelf shall not exceed 350 nautical miles from the baselines from which the breadth of the territorial sea is measured. This paragraph does not apply to submarine elevations that are natural components of the continental margin, such as its plateaux, rises, caps, banks and spurs.[93]

Notes

1. The "continental slope" is the steep slope with which the shelf proper terminates; the "continental rise" is the less sharply sloping area between the "slope" and the deep sea-bed. Unlike the 1958 Convention, the 1982 Convention does not define the shelf in terms of "exploitability." It also differs in providing that the shelf extends a distance of 200 miles from the coast whether it reaches that distance in nature or not. The 1982 Convention retains an advantage, however, for the naturally favoured state in that the shelf extends beyond that distance in law to the "outer edge" of the continental shelf *if* geomorphologically that point is more than 200 miles out. This was an advantage which such states have under the 1958 Convention and which they were not prepared to surrender; its inclusion was for them an essential part of the package in the 1982 Convention. Even so, the advantage is limited in two respects. First, no shelf may in law extend beyond the 350 miles or (subject to Article 76(6)) the "2500 metres depth plus 100 miles" limits set in Article 76(5). Article 76(6) concerns the role of submarine ridges that geomorphologically are not "natural components of the continental margin" but rise from the deep sea-bed. The shallower depths that these cause cannot be used to extend the "margin" into an area that is really a part of the deep sea-bed. Second, Article 82(1) of the 1982 Convention provides that a state shall make "payments or contributions in kind" in respect of the exploitation of shelf resources more than 200 miles from its coast. These payments or contributions go to the International Sea-Bed Authority for distribution "on the basis of equitable sharing criteria, taking into account the interests and needs of developing states, particularly the least developed and the land-locked among them." (Art. 82(4)). Payments commence after five years of produc-

[93] For further details of the rules for drawing the outer limits of the shelf beyond 200 miles, see Article 76(7) (Straight lines not exceeding 60 miles connecting fixed points to be used). A Commission on the Limits of the Continental Shelf is to "make recommendations to coastal states on matters related to the establishment of the outer limits" on the basis of "information on the limits . . . beyond 200 nautical miles" which the coastal state is obliged to submit to it; limits set by the state on the basis of these recommendations are "final and binding" (Art. 76(8)).

tion and increase from one per cent. to seven per cent. in the following years (Art. 82(2)).

2. In other respects, the 1982 Convention mostly follows the 1958 Convention. Articles 2, 3, 4, and 7 of the latter are repeated in Articles 77, 78(1), 79(2) and 87 respectively of the former. The rules concerning artificial structures, etc., in Article 5 of the 1958 Convention re-appear (by virtue of Article 80 of the 1982 Convention) with modifications in Article 60 of the 1982 Convention, above, p. 351, although there is no full equivalent of Article 5(1) of the 1958 Convention. Article 6 of the 1958 Convention is replaced by a different rule in Article 83 of the 1982 Convention. The latter is identical to Article 74 of the 1982 Convention, above, p. 353, and subject to the same exclusion of compulsory arbitration.

3. Had the continental shelf been limited in the 1982 Convention to 200 miles from the coast in all cases, it would have been possible (and simpler) to have merged the continental shelf régime totally with that of the exclusive economic zone. As it is, a separate régime is retained for the *whole* of the continental shelf. In fact, the régime (which is largely that of the Continental Shelf Convention) does not differ greatly from that of the exclusive economic zone in the jurisdiction it gives to the coastal state.[94]

4. *Islands.* As noted earlier,[95] islands have a continental shelf in the 1982 Convention unless they are just "rocks which cannot sustain human habitation or economic life of their own."[96]

6. *THE DEEP SEA-BED*[97]

DECLARATION OF PRINCIPLES GOVERNING THE SEA-BED AND THE OCEAN FLOOR, AND THE SUBSOIL THEREOF, BEYOND THE LIMITS OF NATIONAL JURISDICTION 1970[98]

G.A.Res. 2749 (XXV), December 17, 1970. 10 I.L.M. 230 (1970)

The General Assembly . . .

Affirming that there is an area of the sea-bed and the ocean floor, and the subsoil thereof, beyond the limits of national jurisdiction, the precise limits of which are yet to be determined,

Recognizing that the existing legal régime of the high seas does not provide substantive rules for regulating the exploration of the aforesaid area and the exploitation of its resources, . . .

Solemnly declares that:

1. The sea-bed and ocean floor, and the subsoil thereof, beyond the limits of national jurisdiction (hereinafter referred to as the area), as well as the resources of the area, are the common heritage of mankind.

2. The area shall not be subject to appropriation by any means by States or persons, natural or juridical, and no State shall claim or exercise sovereignty or sovereign rights over any part thereof.

3. No State or person, natural or juridical, shall claim, exercise or acquire rights with respect to the area or its resources incompatible with the international régime to be established and the principles of this Declaration.

---

[94] See Phillips, *loc. cit.* at p. 346, n. 35, above, pp. 612–615.
[95] p. 378.   [96] 1982 Convention, Article 121(3).
[97] See Andrassy, *International Law and the Resources of the Sea* (1970); Brown, *loc. cit.* at p. 338, n. 98, above; Friedmann, *loc. cit.* at p. 284, n. 1, above; Henkin, *Law for the Sea's Mineral Resources* (1968); Young, 62 A.J.I.L. 641 (1968).
[98] The resolution was adopted by 104 votes to 0, with 14 abstentions.

4. All activities regarding the exploration and exploitation of the resources of the area and other related activities shall be governed by the international régime to be established.

5. The area shall be open to use exclusively for peaceful purposes by all States whether coastal or land-locked, without discrimination, in accordance with the international régime to be established.

6. States shall act in the area in accordance with the applicable principles and rules of international law including the Charter of the United Nations and the [1970] Declaration on Principles of International Law concerning Friendly Relations and Co-operation among States [Appendix III, below] in the interests of maintaining international peace and security and promoting international co-operation and mutual understanding.

7. The exploration of the area and the exploitation of its resources shall be carried out for the benefit of mankind as a whole, irrespective of the geographical location of States, whether land-locked or coastal, and taking into particular consideration the interests and needs of the developing countries.

8. The area shall be reserved exclusively for peaceful purposes, without prejudice to any measures which have been or may be agreed upon in the context of international negotiations undertaken in the field of disarmament and which may be applicable to a broader area. One or more international agreements shall be concluded as soon as possible in order to implement effectively this principle and to constitute a step towards the exclusion of the sea-bed, the ocean floor and the subsoil thereof from the arms race.

9. On the basis of the principles of this Declaration, an international régime applying to the area and its resources and including appropriate international machinery to give effect to its provisions shall be established by an international treaty of a universal character, generally agreed upon. The régime shall, *inter alia*, provide for the orderly and safe development and rational management of the area and its resources and for expanding opportunities in the use thereof and ensure the equitable sharing by States in the benefits derived therefrom, taking into particular consideration the interests and needs of the developing countries, whether land-locked or coastal.

Notes
1. The exploitation[99] of the mineral resources of the deep sea-bed is now a practicable (though expensive) proposition. Interest centres upon

> . . . the hard minerals found in the so-called manganese nodules. The nodules themselves are strange potato-shaped little pieces of rock scattered over thousands of square miles of sea-bed, under 12,000 to 20,000 feet of water. They contain a score or more of minerals, but the ones of greatest value, taking into account their relative percentage in the ore, are manganese, copper, nickel and cobalt.[1]

Manganese nodules are to be found in the Pacific, Atlantic, and Indian Oceans and elsewhere in the seas of the world. At the moment, most attention would seem to be concentrated on an area of the sea-bed of the North Pacific, between the United States mainland and Hawaii. A number of international consortia composed of companies from developed states (U.S.A., Canada, France, F.R.G., Italy, Japan, Netherlands, and the U.K.) have made substantial investments in research and development and will

[99] Unless otherwise apparent, this term is used to include exploration and exploitation in this section.
[1] Ely, 10 *International Lawyer* 537 (1976).

be ready to begin production when this proves economically worthwhile, probably in the 1990s.

2. The United Nations has had the question of the legal régime of the deep sea-bed under discussion since 1967. It was not long before the analogy with "freedom of fishing" on the high seas, with each state controlling its own nationals, was abandoned (but see now the U.K. Deep Sea Mining (Temporary Provisions) Act 1981 and similar legislation, below, p. 369) in favour of the idea of an international régime. Even developed states preferred the security that a limited international régime would offer their national undertakings[2] to the hazards of a "free for all." In 1969, the General Assembly, by a majority,[3] declared a moratorium on sea-bed exploitation "beyond the limits of national jurisdiction" pending the establishment of an international régime. Similarly, the 1970 Declaration rules out the possibility of a "free for all" and indicates some principles upon which an international régime should be based. Above all, it establishes, in a text that attracted no dissent, the principle that the resources of the deep sea-bed are "the common heritage of mankind." They are, that is, to be used to benefit all states, not just those with the technology and capital to recover them. The understanding in 1970 was that a share of the profits from deep sea-bed mining should, in accordance with this principle, be distributed among developing states. The emergence of a new area in which there were no vested interests was seen to offer a good opportunity of progress towards a more equitable international economic order. What the 1970 Declaration did not do was to indicate whether the mining should be done by national undertakings under the aegis of an international body or by the international body itself. This, and other details, could only be formulated in a Convention.

CONVENTION ON THE LAW OF THE SEA 1982

Loc. cit. at p. 285, n. 16 above

Article 135

Neither this Part [XI] nor any rights granted or exercised pursuant thereto shall affect the legal status of the waters superjacent to the Area[4] or that of the air space above those waters.

Article 136

The Area and its resources[5] are the common heritage of mankind.

Article 137

1. No state shall claim or exercise sovereignty or sovereign rights over any part of the Area or its resources, nor shall any State or natural or juridical

---

[2] This term is used to include public and private undertakings at the national level, including consortia of companies of different nationalities.

[3] G.A. Resn. 2574D (XXIV), G.A.O.R., 24th Session, Supp. 30. The Resolution was adopted by 62 votes to 28, with 28 absentions.

[4] *Ed.* The "area" is the "sea-bed and ocean floor and subsoil thereof beyond the limits of national jurisdiction" (1982 Convention, Art. 1(1)), *i.e.* the area beyond the edge of the "continental margin": see above, p. 362.

[5] *Ed.* 1982 Convention, Article 133, reads:

   For the purposes of this Part:

   (a) "resources" means all solid, liquid or gaseous mineral resources *in situ* in the Area at or beneath the sea-bed, including polymetallic nodules;

   (b) resources, when recovered from the Area, are referred to as "minerals."

The definition of "resources" is very generally phrased to allow for the future discovery in commercial quantities of resources other than "polymetallic" (or manganese) nodules.

person appropriate any part thereof. No such claim or exercise of sovereignty or sovereign rights nor such appropriation shall be recognised.

2. All rights in the resources of the Area are vested in mankind as a whole, on whose behalf the Authority shall act. These resources are not subject to alienation. The minerals recovered from the Area, however, may only be alienated in accordance with this Part and the rules, regulations and procedures of the Authority.

3. No State or natural or juridical person shall claim, acquire or exercise rights with respect to the minerals recovered from the Area except in accordance with this Part. Otherwise, no such claim, acquisition or exercise of such rights shall be recognised. . . .

Article 140

1. Activities in the Area shall . . . be carried out for the benefit of mankind as a whole, irrespective of the geographical location of States, whether coastal or land-locked, and taking into particular consideration the interests and needs of developing States and of peoples who have not attained full independence or other self-governing status recognized by the United Nations in accordance with General Assembly resolution 1514 (XV)[6] and other relevant General Assembly resolutions.

2. The Authority shall provide for the equitable sharing of financial and other economic benefits derived from activities in the Area through any appropriate mechanism, on a non-discriminatory basis, in accordance with article 160, paragraph $2(f)(i)$.[7]

Article 141

The Area shall be open to use exclusively for peaceful purposes by all States, whether coastal or land-locked, without discrimination and without prejudice to the other provisions of this Part. . . .

Article 150

Activities in the Area shall . . . be carried out in such a manner as to foster healthy development of the world economy and balanced growth of international trade, and to promote international co-operation for the over-all development of all countries, especially developing States, and with a view to ensuring:

(a) the development of the resources of the Area;

(b) orderly, safe and rational management of the resources of the Area . . .

(d) participation in revenues by the Authority and the transfer of technology to the Enterprise and developing States as provided for in this Convention; . . .

(f) the promotion of just and stable prices remunerative to producers and fair to consumers for minerals derived both from the Area and from other sources, and the promotion of long-term equilibrium between supply and demand;

---

[6] *Ed.* Above, p. 95.

[7] *Ed.* This gives the Authority power to make regulations for "equitable sharing," "taking into particular consideration the interests and needs of developing states and peoples who have not attained full independence or other self-governing status."

(g) the enhancement of opportunities for all States Parties, irrespective of their social and economic systems or geographical location, to participate in the development of the resources of the Area and the prevention of monopolization of activities in the Area;

(h) the protection of developing countries from adverse effects on their economies or on their export earnings resulting from a reduction in the price of an affected mineral, or in the volume of exports of that mineral, to the extent that such reduction is caused by activities in the Area . . .

(i) the development of the common heritage for the benefit of mankind as a whole . . .

Article 153

1. Activities in the Area shall be organized, carried out and controlled by the Authority on behalf of mankind as a whole in accordance with this article as well as other relevant provisions of this Part and the relevant Annexes, and the rules, regulations and procedures of the Authority.

2. Activities in the Area shall be carried out: . . .

(a) by the Enterprise, and

(b) in association with the Authority by States Parties, or state enterprises or natural or juridical persons which possess the nationality of States Parties or are effectively controlled by them or their nationals, when sponsored by such States, or any group of the foregoing which meets the requirements provided in this Part and in Annex III. . . .

Notes

1. The 1982 Convention provisions on the deep sea-bed establish the "international régime" referred to in the 1970 Declaration (above). They seek to accommodate the different interests of developed and developing states. The Convention adopts the idea of the 1970 Declaration that the deep sea-bed and its resources are "the common heritage of mankind" not open to claims of sovereignty or sovereign rights. This was not controversial. The problem was to take the matter further and to devise a system for the exploitation of resources that was both consistent with this idea and meets the demands of developed and developing states alike. Developing states pressed for a system by which exploitation would be conducted by an international body—the Authority (see below)—and not by states or national undertakings. Developed states preferred the idea by which exploitation would be by states or national undertakings subject to a system of registration or, at most, licensing. The system of "parallel access" adopted in the Convention is a compromise between the two approaches, although one that leans mostly towards the approach of the developing states. Under Article 153 of the 1982 Convention, control of all sea-bed activities is placed firmly in the hands of the Authority, which may exploit resources itself or contract with a national undertaking to do so. Only national undertakings that meet the (i) nationality or control and (ii) sponsorship requirements of Article 153(2)(b) and Annex III to the 1982 Convention (linking the undertaking with a contracting party) are eligible for a contract.[8] An applicant for a contract is required to specify a "site" for exploration and/or exploitation[9] which "shall cover a total area, which need not be a single continuous area, sufficiently large and of sufficient estimated commercial value to allow two mining

[8] Article 4(2) of the Annex III to the Convention makes particular provision for partnerships and consortia of entities from more than one state.

[9] Prospecting, as opposed to exploration, needs no contract and may be carried out by more than one prospector in the same area simultaneously: Article 2, *ibid*.

operations."[10] The Authority selects half of the "site" as a "reserved Site" for exploration and exploitation by the Authority or by a developing state.[11] Exclusive rights to the remaining half are then allocated to the applicant.[12] Under the contract, the undertaking agrees to close control (including, *e.g.* site inspection) by the Authority of its activities and accepts the technology transfer obligations in the Convention.[13] Overall production levels are controlled by the Convention (to protect land-based metal producers) and detailed provision is made for the financial terms of contracts, with payments to be made by the contractor for distribution to developing states.[14] Contracts provide for security of tenure; they may not be terminated except for serious breach of a fundamental term, etc.[15]

2. The Convention (Arts. 156–188) provides for an *International Sea-Bed Authority*, with its seat in Jamaica, to have overall responsibility for the operation of the system. All states that become parties to the Convention will be members of the Authority. The Assembly, which will be composed of representatives of all member states, will be the policy making organ. It will take decisions by a two-third majority. The Council, which will be composed of 36 Member States elected by the Assembly to represent various interest groups, will be the executive organ. Decisions will be taken by a two-thirds or three-quarters majority vote or by consensus, depending upon the subject. The Council will work through an Economic Planning Commission and a Legal and Technical Commission. Exploitation undertaken by the Authority will be conducted by a separate body called the Enterprise. The Authority will be financed mainly by contributions from Member States on the scale of their contributions to the United Nations and by funds generated by the activities of the Enterprise. Provision is made for the compulsory settlement of deep sea-bed disputes either by judicial settlement (by reference to the International Tribunal for the Law of the Sea) or by commercial arbitration.

3. Provision is made for a review of the operation of the deep sea-bed régime every five years (Art. 154) and for a review conference 15 years after commercial production has begun (Art. 155) to consider whether the régime requires amending. Amendments would require ratification by two-thirds of the parties.

4. Dissatisfaction with the régime for the deep sea-bed led the United States, which continues to support an international sea-bed régime in principle, to vote against the adoption of the 1982 Convention and to declare that it will not become a signatory. In particular, the United States expressed its concern that it would be asked to finance (in proportion to its large contribution to the UN budget) the activities of a "supranational mining company called the Enterprise" that would compete with American mining interests and that "could eventually monopolise production of sea-bed minerals"; that United States companies would be obliged to sell their technology to the Enterprise, possibly posing a security threat in some cases; that the Convention "insulates land-based producers from competition with seabed mining"; that the Authority could discriminate against United States applicants in the selection of contractors; that in the Council of the Authority "the Soviet Union and its allies have three guaranteed seats, but the United States must compete with its allies for any representation"; and that the Convention "imposes revenue sharing obligations on seabed mining corporations

---

[10] Article 8, *ibid.*

[11] Article 9, *ibid.* A developing state that is a contracting party or any undertaking meeting the requirements of Article 153(2)(*b*) may apply for a contract for a reserved site; the Authority may develop such a site by itself or as a joint venture with a state or national undertaking: *ibid.*

[12] The Authority must allow applications if production limits, anti-monopoly rules, etc., permit: Articles 6, 7, *ibid.*

[13] As to the latter, see Article 144 and Article 5, Annex III.

[14] Article 15 (production policies) and Article 13 (financial terms), Annex III.

[15] Article 18, Annex III.

which would significantly increase the costs of seabed mining."[16] Another criticism was of the absence of any protection for pre-Convention investment. This last problem has now been resolved by arrangements made at UNCLOS III.[17] States and national undertakings that had spent 30 million on sea-bed activities by 1983 will be recognised as pioneer investors. As such, they will be able to explore, but not exploit, the deep sea-bed pending the Convention's entry into force and will then have priority over other applicants, but not the Enterprise, in the allocation of exploitation contracts. So far six consortia from western industrialised states (out of an agreed allocation of eight for such states) have been recognised under these arrangements. Are all of the United States objections listed above consistent with the basic idea that the deep sea-bed resources are the "common heritage of mankind" in which all nations would share?

5. If the United States remains true to its present position (but Governments sometimes change), the question will arise whether the Convention régime can succeed without its participation. If *any* state that has unilateral national deep sea-bed mining legislation of the kind that is already in force in some states, see below, p. 372, fails to become a party, it will be necessary to determine the relationship between the Convention's international régime and that state's national régime.[18] Would paragraph 4 of the 1970 Declaration (all activities to be governed by the international régime to be established), above, p. 364, affect the legality of a national régime, as a matter of customary law? See the arguments of the Group of 77 and the United States spokesman at UNCLOS III, below, p. 372. If national regimes may co-exist with the international one in the Convention, a system of reciprocity of the sort included in, for example, the United Kingdom Act, s.3, for national régimes would be sensible. Would an arrangement such as that in the United Kingdom Act for a Deep Sea Mining Levy be sufficient to meet the requirements of the "common heritage of mankind" principle in the 1970 Declaration?

DEEP SEA MINING (TEMPORARY PROVISIONS) ACT 1981[19]

(1981, c. 53)

1.—(1) Subject to the following provisions of this Act, a person to whom this section applies shall not explore for the hard mineral resources of any part of the deep sea bed unless he holds an exploration licence granted under section 2 below in respect of that part of the deep sea bed or is the agent or employee of the holder of that licence (acting in his capacity as such).

(2) Subject to the following provisions of this Act, a person to whom this section applies shall not exploit the hard mineral resources of any part of the deep sea bed unless he holds an exploitation licence granted under section 2 below in respect of that part of the deep sea bed or is the agent or employee of the holder of that licence (acting in his capacity as such).

---

[16] Testimony of Ambassador James L. Malone before the Subcommittee on Oceanography of the House of Merchant Marine and Fisheries Committee, April 28, 1981, quoted in Oxman, 76 A.J.I.L. 9 (1982). The testimony to the same Committee by Ambassador Elliott L. Richardson (a former head of the U.S. delegation to UNCLOS III) disagrees with many of these comments (no discrimination against U.S. applicants; provision for membership of Council virtually guarantees the U.S. a place; technology transfer provisions not burdensome and contain security guarantee), quoted *ibid*. p. 11, n. 27.

[17] Resolution II, which was approved with the Convention.

[18] The state that has national legislation and wants to ratify the Convention but has not done so by the time that the Convention enters into force presents only a temporary problem which co-operation and the arrangements for pioneer investments, above, will largely solve.

[19] See Henderson, 132 N.L.J. 627 (1982).

(3) Any person who contravenes subsection (1) or (2) above shall be guilty of an offence. . . .

(4) This section applies to any person who—

> (*a*) is a citizen of the United Kingdom and Colonies, a Scottish firm or a body incorporated under the law of any part of the United Kingdom; and
>
> (*b*) is resident in any part of the United Kingdom.

(5) Her Majesty may by Order in Council extend the application of this section—

> (*a*) to all citizens of the United Kingdom and Colonies, Scottish firms and bodies incorporated under the law of any part of the United Kingdom who are resident outside the United Kingdom or to such citizens, firms and bodies who are resident in any country specified in the Order;
>
> (*b*) to bodies incorporated under the law of any of the Channel Islands, the Isle of Man, any colony or an associated state.

(6) In this Act—

"deep sea bed" means that part of the bed of the high seas in respect of which sovereign rights in relation to the natural resources of the sea bed are neither exercisable by the United Kingdom nor recognised by Her Majesty's Government in the United Kingdom as being exercisable by another Sovereign Power or, in a case where disputed claims are made by more than one Sovereign Power, by one or other of those Sovereign Powers;

"hard mineral resources" means deposits of nodules containing (in quantities greater than trace) at least one of the following elements, that is to say, manganese, nickel, cobalt, copper, phosphorus and molybdenum; . . .

(7) In any proceedings, a certificate issued by the Secretary of State certifying that sovereign rights are not exercisable in relation to any part of the sea bed by the United Kingdom or by any other Sovereign Power shall be conclusive as to that fact: . . .

2.—(1) In this Act—

"exploration licence" means a licence authorising the licensee to explore for the hard mineral resources of such part of the deep sea bed as may be specified in the licence; and

"exploitation licence" means a licence authorising the licensee to exploit the hard mineral resources of such part of the deep sea bed as may be specified in the licence.

(2) Subject to subsection (4) and section 3 below, the Secretary of State may on payment of such fee as may with the consent of the Treasury be prescribed grant to such persons as he thinks fit exploration or exploitation licences; and in determining whether to grant a licence in any case he shall have regard to any relevant factors including in particular the desirability of keeping an area or areas of the deep sea bed free from deep sea bed mining operations so as to provide an area or areas for comparison with licensed areas in assessing the effects of such operations.

(3) An exploration or an exploitation licence shall be granted for such period as the Secretary of State thinks fit and shall contain such terms and conditions as

he thinks fit and, in particular but without prejudice to the generality of the foregoing, a licence may include terms and conditions—

(a) relating to the safety, health or welfare of persons employed in the licensed operations or in the ancillary operations;

(b) relating to the processing or other treatment of any hard mineral resources won in pursuance of the licence which is carried out by or on behalf of the licensee on any ship;

(c) relating to the disposal of any waste material resulting from such processing or other treatment;

(d) requiring plans, returns, accounts or other records with respect to any matter connected with any licensed area or licensed operations or ancillary operations to be furnished to the Secretary of State;

(e) requiring samples of any hard mineral resources discovered or won in any licensed area, or assays of such samples, to be furnished to the Secretary of State;

(f) requiring any exploration or exploitation of the hard mineral resources of the licensed area to be diligently carried out;

(g) requiring the payment to the Secretary of State of such sums as may with the consent of the Treasury be prescribed at such times as may be prescribed; and

(h) permitting the transfer of the licence in prescribed cases or with the written consent of the Secretary of State.

(4) An exploration licence shall not be granted in respect of any period before 1st July 1981 and an exploitation licence shall not be granted in respect of any period before 1st January 1988.

(5) Where the Secretary of State has granted an exploration licence he shall not grant an exploitation licence in respect of any part of the licensed area otherwise than to the licensee except with the licensee's written consent. . . .

3.—(1) Where, in the opinion of Her Majesty, the law of any country contains provisions similar in their aims and effects to the provisions of this Act, Her Majesty may by Order in Council designate that country as a reciprocating country for the purposes of this Act.

(2) Where a person holds a licence or other authorisation issued and for the time being in force under the law of a reciprocating country for the exploration or exploitation of the hard mineral resources of any area of the deep sea bed specified in that authorisation (the "authorised area")—

(a) the Secretary of State shall not grant an exploration or exploitation licence in respect of any part of the authorised area; and

(b) if section 1 above applies to that person, he shall not be prohibited by that section from engaging in the exploration or, as the case may be, exploitation of the hard mineral resources of the authorised area. . . .

4.—(1) A person to whom section 1 above applies shall not intentionally interfere with any operations carried on in pursuance of an exploration or exploitation licence or a reciprocal authorisation.

(2) Any person who contravenes subsection (1) above shall be guilty of an offence. . . .

5.—(1) In determining whether to grant an exploration or exploitation licence the Secretary of State shall have regard to the need to protect (so far as reasonably practicable) marine creatures, plants and other organisms and their habitat from any harmful effects which might result from any activities to be authorised by the licence; and the Secretary of State shall consider any representations made to him concerning such effects.

(2) Without prejudice to section 2 (3) above, any exploration or exploitation licence granted by the Secretary of State shall contain such terms and conditions as he considers necessary or expedient to avoid or minimise any such harmful effects. . . .

7. It shall be the duty of the licensee to exercise his rights under the licence with reasonable regard to the interests of other persons in their exercise of the freedom of the high seas.

Notes

1. The Act, which entered into force in 1982, follows the pattern of the United States Deep Seabed Hard Mineral Resources Act 1980, 19 I.L.M. 1003 (1980), and the West German Act of Interim Regulation of Deep Seabed Mining 1980, 20 I.L.M. 1003 (1981). Similar legislation has since been enacted by France (1981), the U.S.S.R. (1982), and Japan (1982). The Act, like its counterparts, is intended as a temporary measure, pending the establishment of an international régime for deep sea mining. Provision is made for the repeal of the Act if "it appears to the Secretary of State for Industry that an international agreement on the law of the sea which has been adopted by a United Nations Conference on the Law of the Sea is to be given effect within the United Kingdom" (s.18(3)). Licences granted under the Act may be varied or revoked "to avoid conflict with any obligation of the United Kingdom arising out of any international agreement in force for the United Kingdom" (s.6(1)).

2. The Act is intended to provide a régime within which United Kingdom companies (and other U.K. nationals) may finance exploration and, as of 1988 (see s.2(4)), exploitation of the deep sea-bed with some security before the entry into force for the United Kingdom of the 1982 Convention. The Act requires the holder of an exploitation licence to pay the Secretary of State a Deep Sea Mining levy which will be an amount equal to 3·75 per cent. of the value of the actual mineral extracted (s.9). This will be paid into a Deep Sea Mining Fund, the contents of which will be transferred to the International Sea-Bed Authority for distribution in accordance with the 1982 Convention (s.10). The Act, which assumes that mining is lawful as an aspect of freedom of the high seas, provides for the recognition of licences granted by "reciprocating countries" (s.3) and imposes criminal sanctions on a basis of nationality jurisdiction (s.1) upon United Kingdom nationals who do not respect licences issued by such countries or by the United Kingdom (s.4). The Act provides for the duration of licences, environmental controls, and other terms and conditions of licences in general terms only; regulations have yet to be made under the Act that will fill in the details. So far, no licences have been issued under the United Kingdom legislation.

3. The legality of such legislation was challenged by the Group of 77 in a 1979 resolution which declared that:

(*a*) Any unilateral measures, legislation or agreement restricted to a limited number of States on sea-bed mining are unlawful and violate well-established and imperative rules of international law;

(*b*) Such unilateral acts will not be recognized by the international community, and that, these acts, being unlawful, will entail international responsibility on the part of States who commit them, and an investor will not have legal security for his investments in activities in pursuance of such acts.[20]

This had been preceded by a discussion of the matter at UNCLOS III in 1978 in which the legal arguments either way had been presented[21]:

MR. NANDAN (Fiji), speaking as Chairman of the Group of 77, . . . rejected the

---

[20] Quoted in Oxman, 74 A.J.I.L. 8 (1980). On the Group of 77, see below, p. 439, n. 84.

[21] *UNCLOS III Records*, Vol. IX, pp. 103–104. See also the U.S. Dept. of State response to the Deep Sea Ventures Inc. claim in 1974: 14 I.L.M. 51 (1975).

entire basis for such legislation, in particular the premise that the right to engage in mining of the resources of the sea-bed beyond the limits of national jurisdiction was a legal freedom of the high seas. There was no practice or custom, in the legal sense, or general treaty authorizing the exploitation of the sea-bed. The declaration contained in General Assembly resolution 2749 (XXV) [above, p. 363] expressly excluded the possibility of extending freedom of the high seas to the sea-beds and subjected exploration and exploitation of the sea-beds to the international régime to be established. The situation was therefore entirely different from that which applied to the exploitation of the traditional resources of the high seas, which was based on three centuries of custom and innumerable treaties.

. . . The Declaration . . . could not be ignored merely by saying that General Assembly resolutions were not binding and were only recommendations. The Declaration was a solemn pronouncement by the most representative organ of the international community declaring that the resources of the sea-bed beyond national jurisdiction were the common heritage of mankind, could be exploited only under an international régime, and could not be unilaterally appropriated. All States, by adopting the Declaration without dissent, had accepted the common heritage principle, the international character of the sea-bed and its resources, and the inevitable legal consequences, namely that unilateral exploitation was incompatible with those principles. . . . The Declaration was thus the embodiment of current international law with regard to the régime of the sea-beds.

. . . The Group of 77 could not accept that any rights might be acquired by any State, person or entity by virtue of such unilateral measures, or that they should seek recognition of such rights by the Conference. . . .

MR. RICHARDSON (United States of America) said that . . . his delegation had consistently maintained that the right to explore and exploit the sea-bed beyond the limits of national jurisdiction derived from the freedom of the high seas, which was enjoyed by all nations. Initiatives that a country might take beyond the limits of national jurisdiction could be limited only by provisions of international law. With regard to sea-bed mining, there did not exist, so far as his Government was aware, any restraints other than those which applied generally to the freedom of the high seas, including the prohibition of claims of sovereignty, the exclusive jurisdiction of States over their vessels and their nationals, and the duty to have reasonable regard for other users of the high seas. If States were to subscribe to a convention establishing an international authority entrusted with overseeing the sea-bed mining, they would then be subject to additional restraints, since they would have voluntarily accepted the alteration of their freedoms in the interest of establishing a stable legal régime to regulate the exploitation of ocean resources. But the United States could not accept the suggestion that, without its consent, other States would be able, by resolutions or statements, to deny or alter its rights under international law.

It had been stated that national jurisdiction in the matter under discussion was incompatible with General Assembly resolutions 2574 (XXIV) and 2749 (XXV). With regard to the former, he recalled that that "moratorium" resolution had been adopted by 62 votes for and 28 against, including that of the United States of America, with 28 abstentions. Thus, it could not be said that it had commanded unanimous support. Furthermore, his delegation, in explaining its negative vote, had stated that, as was the case with practically all General Assembly resolutions, that resolution, which purported to prescribe to States standards of conduct in the oceans, had no binding legal effect. On the other hand, the United States, along with 107 other countries, had voted for the Declaration of Principles Governing the Sea-Bed and Ocean Floor contained in General Assembly resolution 2749 (XXV) adopted without opposition, with 14 abstentions. That resolution, while it proclaimed that the resources of he sea-beds were the "common heritage of mankind," did not purport to prohibit access to them. It was even apparent from its text, and from the statements made at the time of its adoption, that the intention had not been to impose it as an interim deep sea-bed mining régime, rather it had been intended as a general basis for further negotiation of an internationally agreed régime.

CHAPTER 8

STATE RESPONSIBILITY

1. *INTRODUCTORY NOTE*

IN any legal system there must be liability for failure to observe obligations imposed by its rules. Such liability is known in international law as *responsibility*. The materials in this chapter directly concern the responsibility of states. Other international persons are, of course, responsible for violating their obligations also.

In municipal law, a division is made between civil and criminal liability and, within the former, between liability in contract and in tort. From a different standpoint, liability is based upon intentional or negligent conduct or arises without fault at all. There are also rules about such matters as imputability (*e.g.* rules about the liability of employers for the *ultra vires* actions of their employees), remedies and *locus standi*. Some of these divisions and rules exist in international law, but, as will be apparent from the extracts in section 2 of this chapter, the theory of state responsibility is not very well developed. The International Law Commission, after earlier uncompleted work that linked questions of responsibility generally with responsibility for the treatment of aliens in particular, has now adopted a different approach and is limiting itself for the time being to the codification of the rules concerning responsibility generally.[1] So far, it has adopted 34 draft articles[2] on state responsibility for internationally wrongful acts. These indicate when state responsibility arises (imputability, etc.). The Commission is now drafting a second set of articles on the consequences of the Commission of an internationally wrongful act (duty to make reparation, duty of non-recognition by other states, etc.).[3] It is possible that, when these are complete, the articles as a whole will form the basis of a law-making treaty.

Responsibility arises for the breach of any obligation owed under international law. A state is responsible, for example, if it fails to honour a treaty, if it violates the territorial sovereignty of another state, if it damages the territory or property of another state, if it employs armed force against another state, if it injures the diplomatic representatives of another state, or if it mistreats the nationals of another state. For some writers the term state responsibility has been used only in connection with the last of these examples. Although it is not used in this limited sense here, the only particular category of state responsibility dealt with in this chapter, in section 3, is, in fact, the treatment of aliens. Materials on other categories of responsibility are included elsewhere.

---

[1] For criticism of this approach see Lillich, 161 *Hague Recueil* 329, 373 *et seq.* (1978–III).

[2] For the text, see Y.B.I.L.C., 1979, II (Part II), p. 90, and *ibid.*, 1980, II (Part II), pp. 14, 70. The text is accompanied by the usual valuable commentary.

[3] See, most recently, the Third Report of the Special Rapporteur (Riphagen), UN Doc. A/CN.4/354 (1982).

2. *THE THEORY OF RESPONSIBILITY*[4]

(i) Its Existence[5]

I.L.C. DRAFT ARTICLES ON STATE RESPONSIBILITY

Loc. cit. at p. 374, n. 2, above.

Article 1

Every internationally wrongful act of a State entails the international responsibility of that State.

Article 2

Every State is subject to the possibility of being held to have committed an internationally wrongful act entailing its international responsibility.

Article 3

There is an internationally wrongful act of a State when:

(*a*) conduct consisting of an action or omission is attributable[6] to the State under international law; and

(*b*) that conduct constitutes a breach of an international obligation of the State.

Article 4

An act of a State may only be characterized as internationally wrongful by international law. Such characterization cannot be affected by the characterization of the same act as lawful by internal law.

Notes

1. As the International Law Commission's Commentary to the Draft Articles states, the principle in Article 1 is "one of the principles most strongly upheld by State practice and judicial decisions and most deeply rooted in the doctrine of international law."[7] In the *Chorzów Factory Case (Indemnity) (Merits)*,[8] the P.C.I.J. commented:

> . . . it is a principle of international law, and even a general conception of law, that any breach of an engagement involves an obligation to make reparation. In Judgment No. 8[9] . . . the Court has already said that reparation is the indispensable complement of a failure to apply a convention, and there is no necessity for this to be stated in the convention itself.

2. Article 2 is intended to make it clear that all states are responsible in law for their illegal acts; there are no exceptions based upon lack of capacity (as, for example, there are in the case of infants in municipal law). In particular, there is no exception for new states:

> States establish themselves as equal members of the international community as soon as they achieve an independent and sovereign existence. If it is the prerogative of sovereignty to be able to assert its rights, the counterpart of that prerogative is the duty to discharge its obligations.[10]

[4] See Borchard, 1 Z.A.O.R.V. 223 (1929); Cheng, *General Principles of Law as Applied by International Courts and Tribunals* (1953), Chaps. 6–10; Garcia Amador, 94 *Hague Recueil* 365 (1958–II). Among textbooks, see, in particular, Brownlie, Chap. XX and Schwarzenberger, Chaps. 31–36.

[5] In addition to the following extracts, see also those in subsection V on "Reparation," below, p. 395, and the extract from the *Corfu Channel Case*, below, p. 380.

[6] *Ed., i.e.* "imputable" in the terminology used in this Chapter.

[7] Y.B.I.L.C., 1973, II, p. 173.   [8] P.C.I.J. Rep., Series A. No. 17, at p. 29.

[9] *Chorzów Factory Case (Jurisdiction), ibid.* No. 9, p. 21.   [10] Y.B.I.L.C., 1973, II, p. 177.

3. Article 3 separates, in (a) and (b), what the Commission refers to as the "subjective" and "objective" elements of any internationally wrongful act. On Article 4, see above, pp. 57–60.

4. Elsewhere in its Draft Articles, the Commission defines the defences that a state may generally rely upon to deny responsibility. These are consent, reprisal, force majeure, distress, necessity and self defence (Arts. 29–34 respectively). The Commission also states that responsibility does not arise if the obligation is not in force for the state at the time of its act (Art. 18) or if local remedies are not exhausted (Art. 22).[11]

(ii) Civil and Criminal Responsibility

I.L.C. DRAFT ARTICLES ON STATE RESPONSIBILITY

Loc. cit. at p. 374, n. 2, above.

Article 19

1. An act of a State which constitutes a breach of an international obligation is an internationally wrongful act, regardless of the subject-matter of the obligation breached.

2. An internationally wrongful act which results from the breach by a State of an international obligation so essential for the protection of fundamental interests of the international community that its breach is recognized as a crime by that community as a whole, constitutes an international crime.

3. Subject to paragraph 2, and on the basis of the rules of international law in force, an international crime may result, *inter alia,* from:

(a) a serious breach of an international obligation of essential importance for maintenance of international peace and security, such as that prohibiting aggression;

(b) a serious breach of an international obligation of essential importance for safeguarding the right of self-determination of peoples, such as that prohibiting the establishment or maintenance by force of colonial domination;

(c) a serious breach on a widespread scale of an international obligation of essential importance for safeguarding the human being, such as those prohibiting slavery, genocide, *apartheid*;

(d) a serious breach of an international obligation of essential importance for the safeguarding and preservation of the human environment, such as those prohibiting massive pollution of the atmosphere or of the seas.

4. Any internationally wrongful act which is not an international crime in accordance with paragraph 2, constitutes an international delict.

Notes

1. The Draft Articles recognise that there may be both civil and criminal liability on the part of states in international law. As far as *civil* (or delictual) liability is concerned, international law does not distinguish between contractual and tortious liability. The breach of a treaty obligation is subject to the same rules on the burden of proof and reparation as a violation of a customary rule of international law. Some writers[12] refer to a breach of any international law obligation as an "international tort." When used in this sense, the term "tort" clearly has a wider meaning than it has at common law.

---

[11] On local remedies, see below, p. 464.
[12] See, *e.g.* Schwarzenberger, pp. 581–582.

2. The question whether states may be *criminally* liable has long been the subject of debate.[13] In reaching the conclusion that they can, the International Law Commission commented on state practice as follows:

It seems undeniable that today's unanimous and prompt condemnation of any direct attack on international peace and security is paralleled by almost universal disapproval on the part of States towards certain other activities. Contemporary international law has reached the point of condemning outright the practice of certain States in forcibly keeping other peoples under colonial domination or forcibly imposing internal régimes based on discrimination and the most absolute racial segregation, in imperilling human life and dignity in other ways, or in so acting as gravely to endanger the preservation and conservation of the human environment. The international community as a whole, and not merely one or other of its members, now considers that such acts violate principles formally embodied in the Charter and, even outside the scope of the Charter, principles which are now so deeply rooted in the conscience of mankind that they have become particularly essential rules of general international law. There are enough manifestations of the views of States to warrant the conclusion that in the general opinion, some of these acts genuinely constitute "international crimes," that is to say, international wrongs which are more serious than others and which as such, should entail more severe legal consequences . . . in adopting the designation "international crime," the Commission intends only to refer to "crimes" of the State, to acts attributable to the State as such. Once again it wishes to sound a warning against any confusion between the expression "international crime" as used in this article and similar expressions, such as "crime under international law," "war crime," "crime against peace," "crime against humanity," etc., which are used in a number of conventions and international instruments to designate certain henious individual crimes, for which those instruments require States to punish the guilty persons adequately, in accordance with the rules of their internal law. Once again, the Commission takes this opportunity of stressing that the attribution to the State of an internationally wrongful act characterized as an "international crime" is quite different from the incrimination of certain individuals-organs for actions connected with the commission of an "international crime" of the State, and that the obligation to punish such individual actions does not constitute the form of international responsibility specially applicable to a State committing an "international crime" or, in any case, the sole form of this responsibility.[14]

The Commission stressed that it had left for later examination the question of the rules and sanctions applicable to criminal responsibility. The Commission was influenced also by the I.C.J.'s pronouncement in the *Barcelona Traction Case* (para. 33).[15] Is there any indication in the Court's judgment whether it was thinking of civil or criminal liability? Compare the Court's pronouncement with its earlier statements in the South-West Africa Cases.[16]

(iii) THE BASIS FOR RESPONSIBILITY: RISK OR FAULT?[17]

Note

The question considered in this subsection is whether responsibility arises from the commission of the prohibited act alone or whether it arises only when this is accom-

---

[13] *International Law and the Use of Force by States* (1963), p. 154; Oppenheim, Vol. I, para. 156b; Schwarzenberger (1950) 3 C.L.P. 263.

[14] Y.B.I.L.C., 1976, II (Pt. II), pp. 109, 119. On individual criminal responsibility, see below, p. 555.

[15] Below p. 453.

[16] *Loc cit.* at p. 104, n. 17, above.

[17] See Lauterpacht, *Private Law Sources and Analogies of International Law* (1927), pp. 135–143.

panied by some degree of intention or negligence on the part of the actor. In other words, is there strict liability or must some degree of blameworthiness be attributable to the actor? The first possibility is called the "risk" or "objective" theory of responsibility; the second, the "fault" or "subjective" theory. With regard to the latter, the Roman law terms *dolus,* referring to intentional conduct, and *culpa,* referring to negligent conduct, are sometimes used. It will be apparent from the following extracts from international judicial and arbitral practice that authority can be found supporting either theory.[18] As in municipal law, it seems likely that the need for intention or negligence varies from one area of responsibility to another. State practice on this theoretical question is, so far as it is available, of little help.

HOME MISSIONARY SOCIETY CLAIM

U.S. *v.* Great Britain (1920)

American and British Claims Arbitration: Fromageot, President; Anderson, American Arbitrator; Fitzpatrick, British Arbitrator. 6 R.I.A.A. 42

Award of the Tribunal

In 1898 the collection of a tax newly imposed [by Great Britain] on the natives of the Protectorate [of Sierra Leone] and known as the "hut tax" was the signal for a serious and widespread revolt in the Ronietta district. The revolt broke out on April 27 and lasted for several days. . . .

In the course of the rebellion all [the claimant's] . . . missions were attacked, and either destroyed or damaged, and some of the missionaries were murdered. . . .

The contention of the United States Government before this Tribunal is that the revolt was the result of the imposition and attempted collection of the "hut tax"; that it was within the knowledge of the British Government that this tax was the object of deep native resentment; that in the face of the native danger the British Government wholly failed to take proper steps for the maintenance of order and the protection of life and property; that the loss of life and damage to property was the result of this neglect and failure of duty, and therefore that it is liable to pay compensation.

Now, even assuming that the "hut tax" was the effective cause of the native rebellion, it was in itself a fiscal measure in accordance not only with general usage in colonial administration, but also with the usual practice in African countries. . . .

It was a measure to which the British Government was perfectly entitled to resort in the legitimate exercise of its sovereignty, if it was required. . . .

Further, though it may be true that some difficulty might have been foreseen, there was nothing to suggest that it would be more serious than is usual and inevitable in a semi-barbarous and only partially colonized protectorate, and certainly nothing to lead to any apprehension of widespread revolt.

It is a well-established principle of international law that no government can be held responsible for the act of rebellious bodies of men committed in violation of its authority, where it is itself guilty of no breach of good faith, or of no negligence in suppressing insurrection. (Moore's *International Law Digest,*

[18] See also the *Neer Claim,* below, p. 401.

vol. VI, p. 956; VII, p. 957; Moore's *Arbitrations*, pp. 2991–92; British answer, p. 1.)

The good faith of the British Government cannot be questioned, and as to the conditions prevailing in the Protectorate there is no evidence to support the contention that it failed in its duty to afford adequate protection for life and property. . . .

The Tribunal decides that this claim must be dismissed.

CAIRE CLAIM

France *v.* Mexico (1929)

French-Mexican Claims Commission: Verzijl, Presiding Commissioner; Ayguesparsse, French Commissioner; Gonzalez Roa, Mexican Commissioner. 5 R.I.A.A. 516.
Translation

Caire, a French national, was killed in Mexico by Mexican soldiers after they had demanded money from him.

VERZIJL, PRESIDING COMMISSIONER

(4) Responsibility of Mexico for actions of individual military personnel, acting without orders or against the wishes of their commanding officers and independently of the needs and aims of the revolution. . . .

In approaching the examination of the questions indicated under 4 in the light of the general principles I have just outlined, I should like to make clear first of all that I am interpreting the said principles in accordance with the doctrine of the "objective responsibility" of the State, that is, the responsibility for the acts of the officials or organs of a State, which may devolve upon it even in the absence of any "fault" of its own. It is widely known that theoretical conceptions in this sphere have advanced a great deal in recent times, and that the innovating work of Dionisio Anzilotti in particular has paved the way for new ideas, which no longer rank the responsibility of the State for the acts of its officials as subordinate to the question of the "fault" attaching to the State itself. Without going into the question of whether these new ideas, which are perhaps too absolute, may require some modifications in the direction proposed by Dr. Karl Strupp,[19] I can say that I regard them as perfectly correct in that they tend to impute to the State, in international affairs, the responsibility for all the acts committed by its officials or organs which constitute offences from the point of view of the law of nations, whether the official or organ in question has acted within or exceeded the limits of his competence. "It is generally agreed," as M. Bourquin has rightly said, "that acts committed by the officials and agents of a State entail the international responsibility of that State, even if the perpetrator did not have specific authorisation. This responsibility does not find its justification in general principles—I mean those principles regulating the judicial organisation of the State. The act of an official is only

---

[19] In his work *Das Völkerrechtliche Delikt*, pp. 48 *et seq.* Strupp makes express exception for "Unterlassungsdelikte," that is, for the offences of a State consisting, not of some positive act of its organs or officials, but of an omission on their part.

judicially established as an act of State if such an act lies within the official's sphere of competence. The act of an official operating beyond his competence is not an act of State. It should not in principle, therefore, affect the responsibility of the State. If it is accepted in international law that the position is different, it is for reasons peculiar to the mechanism of international life; it is because it is felt that international relations would become too difficult, too complicated and too insecure if foreign States were obliged to take into account the often complex judicial arrangements that regulate competence in the internal affairs of a State. From this it is immediately clear that in the hypothesis under consideration the international responsibility of the State is purely *objective* in character, and that it rests on an idea of *guarantee,* in which the subjective notion of fault plays no part."

But in order to be able to admit this so-called objective responsibility of the State for acts committed by its officials or organs outside their competence, they must have acted at least to all appearances as competent officials or organs, or they must have used powers or methods appropriate to their official capacity. . . .

If the principles stated above are applied to the present case, and if it is taken into account that the perpetrators of the murder of M. J.-B. Caire were military personnel occupying the ranks of "mayor" and "capitán primero" aided by a few privates, it is found that the conditions of responsibility formulated above are completely fulfilled. The officers in question, whatever their previous record, consistently conducted themselves as officers in the brigade of the *Villista* general, Tomás Urbina; in this capacity they began by exacting the remittance of certain sums of money; they continued by having the victim taken to a barracks of the occupying troops; and it was clearly because of the refusal of M. Caire to meet their repeated demands that they finally shot him. Under these circumstances, there remains no doubt that, even if they are to be regarded as having acted outside their competence, which is by no means certain, and even if their superior officers issued a counter-order, these two officers have involved the responsibility of the State, in view of the fact that they acted in their capacity of officers and used the means placed at their disposition by virtue of that capacity.

On these grounds, I have no hesitation in stating that, in accordance with the most authoritative doctrine supported by numerous arbitral awards, the events of 11 December 1914, which led to the death of M. J.-B. Caire, fall within the category of acts for which international responsibility devolves upon the State to which the perpetrators of the injury are amenable.

CORFU CHANNEL CASE (MERITS)[20]

U.K. *v.* Albania

I.C.J. Reports 1949, p. 4

Judgment of the Court

On October 22nd, 1946, a squadron of British warships, the cruisers *Mauritius* and *Leander* and the destroyers *Saumarez* and *Volage,* left the port of

[20] See 2 Verzijl 22. For the part of the Court's judgment dealing with Albania's counter-claim, see above, p. 301.

Corfu and proceeded northwards through a channel previously swept for mines in the North Corfu Strait. . . . Outside the Bay of Saranda, *Saumarez* struck a mine and was heavily damaged. . . . Whilst towing the damaged ship, *Volage* struck a mine and was much damaged. . . .

Three weeks later, on November 13th, the North Corfu Channel was swept by British minesweepers and twenty-two mines were cut. . . .

In October, 1944, the North Corfu Channel was swept by the British Navy and no mines were found in the Channel thus swept. . . . In January and February, 1945, the Channel was check-swept by the British Navy with negative results. . . . It was in this swept Channel that the minefield was discovered on November 13th, 1946.

. . . the mining of *Saumarez* and *Volage* occurred in Albanian territorial waters, just at the place in the swept Channel where the minefield was found. . . .

Such are the facts upon which the Court must, in order to reply to the first question of the Special Agreement, give judgment as to Albania's responsibility for the explosions on October 22nd, 1946, and for the damage and loss of human life which resulted, and for the compensation, if any, due in respect of such damage and loss.

. . . the main position of the United Kingdom is to be found in its submission No. 2: that the minefield which caused the explosions was laid between May 15th, 1946, and October 22nd, 1946, by or with the connivance of the Albanian Government. . . .

In fact, although the United Kingdom government never abandoned its contention that Albania herself laid the mines, very little attempt was made by the Government to demonstrate this point. . . .

In these circumstances, the Court need pay no further attention to this matter.

The Court now comes to the second alternative argument of the United Kingdom Government, namely that the minefield was laid with the connivance of the Albanian Government. According to this argument, the minelaying operation was carried out by two Yugoslav warships at a date prior to October 22nd, but very near that date. This would imply collusion between the Albanian and the Yugoslav Governments, consisting either of a request by the Albanian Government to the Yugoslav Government for assistance, or of acquiescence by the Albanian authorities in the laying of the mines. . . .

The Court found that there was insufficient evidence to establish connivance.

Finally, the United Kingdom Government put forward the argument that, whoever the authors of the minelaying were, it could not have been done without the Albanian Government's knowledge.

It is clear that knowledge of the minelaying cannot be imputed to the Albanian Government by reason merely of the fact that a minefield discovered in Albanian territorial waters caused the explosions of which the British warships were the victims. It is true, as international practice shows, that a State on whose territory or in whose waters an act contrary to international law has occurred, may be called upon to give an explanation. It is also true that that State cannot evade such a request by limiting itself to a reply that it is ignorant of the circumstances of the act and of its authors. The state may, up to a certain point, be bound to supply particulars of the use made by it of the means of information and inquiry at its disposal. But it cannot be concluded from the mere fact of the control exercised by a State over its territory and waters that that State necessarily knew, or ought to have known, of any unlawful act perpetrated therein, nor yet that it necessarily knew, or should have known, the authors. This fact, by itself and apart from other circumstances, neither involves *prima facie* responsibility nor shifts the burden of proof.

On the other hand, the fact of this exclusive territorial control exercised by a State within its frontiers has a bearing upon the methods of proof available to establish the knowledge of that State as to such events. By reason of this exclusive control, the other State, the victim of a breach of international law, is often unable to furnish direct proof of facts giving rise to responsibility. Such a State should be allowed a more liberal recourse to inferences of fact and circumstantial evidence. This indirect evidence is admitted in all systems of law, and its use is recognized by international decisions. It must be regarded as of special weight when it is based on a series of facts linked together and leading logically to a single conclusion.

The Court must examine therefore whether it has been established by means of indirect evidence that Albania has knowledge of minelaying in her territorial waters independently of any connivance on her part in this operation. The proof may be drawn from inferences of fact, provided that they leave *no room* for reasonable doubt. . . .

From all facts and observations mentioned above, the court draws the conclusion that the laying of the minefield which caused the explosions on October 22nd, 1946, could not have been accomplished without the knowledge of the Albanian Government.

The obligations resulting for Albania from this knowledge are not disputed between the parties. Counsel for the Albanian government expressly recognized that [*translation*] "if Albania had been informed of the operation before the incidents of October 22nd, and in time to warn the British vessels and shipping in general of the existence of mines in the Corfu Channel, her responsibility would be involved. . . . "

The obligations incumbent upon the Albanian authorities consisted in notifying for the benefit of shipping in general, the existence of a minefield in Albanian territorial waters and in warning the approaching British warships of the imminent danger to which the minefield exposed them. Such obligations are based not on the Hague Convention of 1907, No. VIII, which is applicable in time of war, but on certain general and well-recognized principles, namely: elementary considerations of humanity, even more exacting in peace then in war; the principle of the freedom of maritime communication; and every State's obligation not to allow knowingly its territory to be used for acts contrary to the rights of other States.

In fact, Albania neither notified the existence of the minefield, nor warned the British warships of the danger they were approaching.

But Albania's obligation to notify shipping of the existence of mines in her waters depends on her having obtained knowledge of that fact in sufficient time before October 22nd; and the duty of the Albanian coastal authorities to warn the British ships depends on the time that elapsed between the moment that these ships were reported and the moment of the first explosion.

On this subject, the Court makes the following observations. As has already been stated, the parties agree that the mines were recently laid. It must be concluded that the minelaying, whatever may have been its exact date, was done at a time when there was a close Albanian surveillance over the Strait. If it be supposed that it took place at the last possible moment, *i.e.,* in the night of October 21st–22nd, the only conclusion to be drawn would be that a general notification to the shipping of all States before the time of the explosions would have been difficult, perhaps even impossible. But this would certainly not have prevented the Albanian authorities from taking, as they should have done, all necessary steps immediately to warn ships near the danger zone. When on October 22nd about 13.00 hours the British warships were reported by the look-out post at St. George's Monastery to the Commander of the Coastal Defences as approaching Cape Long, it was perfectly possible for the Albanian authorities to use the interval of almost two hours that elapsed before the explosion affecting *Saumarez* (14.53 hours or 14.55 hours) to warn the vessels of the danger into which they were running.

In fact, nothing was attempted by the Albanian authorities to prevent the disaster. These grave omissions involve the international responsibility of Albania. . . .

For these reasons, the Court, on the first question put by the Special Agreement of March 25th, 1948, by eleven votes to five,[21] gives judgment that the People's Republic of Albania is responsible under international law for the explosions which occurred on October 22nd, 1946, in Albanian waters, and for the damage and loss of human life which resulted therefrom.[22]

DISSENTING OPINION OF JUDGE KRYLOV. [Having found that it was not proven that Albania had connived in laying the mines or had knowledge of their presence, Judge Krylov continued:]

But it is perhaps the case that the Albanian authorities *ought to* have seen or heard the minelaying operation?

To answer that question in the affirmative would, in my opinion, be to found Albania's responsibility on the notion of *culpa.*

I employ this term, subject to a reservation. I consider that the terms of Roman law and of contemporary civil and criminal law may be used in international law, but with a certain flexibility and without making too subtle distinctions. There is no need to transfer the distinctions which we sometimes meet in certain systems of municipal law into the system of international law.

Is it then possible to found the international responsibility of Albania on the notion of *culpa?* Can it be argued that Albania failed to exercise the diligence required by international law to prevent the laying of mines in the Corfu Channel? Can it be asserted that international law involves an obligation for a coastal state to prevent the laying of mines in its territorial waters? I do not think so. However perfectly the coastal watch of a coastal State may be organized, the clandestine laying of mines cannot be considered impossible, especially, one might add, in peace time when the coastal guards are not in a state of instant readiness. But the history of maritime war provides plenty of examples of clandestine minelaying.

Here I have an observation to make. The responsibility of a State in consequence of an international delinquency presupposes, at the very least, *culpa* on

---

[21] Judge Zoričić, Winiarski, Badawi, Krylov, Krylov and Judge ad hoc Ečer dissented.
[22] The duty to make reparation for this responsibility was also acknowledged and damages were awarded in a separate judgment: *Corfu Channel Case (Assessment of Compensation),* I.C.J.Rep. 1949, p. 244.

the part of that State. One cannot found the international responsibility of a State on the argument that, the act of which the State is accused took place in its territory—terrestrial, maritime, or aerial territory. One cannot transfer the theory of risk, which is developed in the municipal law of some States into the domain of international law. In order to found the responsibility of the States recourse must be had to the notion of *culpa*. I refer to the famous English author, Oppenheim. In his work on international law, he writes that the conception of international delinquency presumes that the State acted "wilfully and maliciously," or in cases of acts of omission "with culpable negligence" (Vol. 1, para. 154). Mr. Lauterpacht, the editor of the 7th edition (1948), adds that one can discern among modern authors a definite tendency to reject the theory of absolute responsibility and to found the responsibility of States on the notion of *culpa* (p. 311).

In view of the foregoing and owing to the inadequacy of the evidence produced by the British, I am unable to reach the conclusion that Albania was responsible for the explosions which took place on October 22nd, 1946, in Albanian waters. One cannot condemn a State on the basis of probabilities. To establish international responsibility, one must have clear and indisputable facts. In the present case these facts are absent.

DISSENTING OPINION OF JUDGE AZEVEDO. The notion of *culpa* is always changing and undergoing a slow process of evolution; moving away from the classical elements of imprudence and negligence, it tends to draw nearer to the system of objective responsibility; and this has led certain present-day authors to deny that *culpa* is definitely separate, in regard to a theory based solely on risk.

Notes

1. Would Albania have been responsible if it had not known of the mines? What if it had known of them and had done its best to warn the British ships in time but had failed to make contact, perhaps because of fog or failure of radio communications?

2. Do the cases in this subsection support Strupp's view[23] that responsibility is subjective in the case of an omission, but objective in other cases?

3. Are these reasons that make strict liability more acceptable in international law than it is in municipal law?[24]

(iv) IMPUTABILITY[25]

(a) Generally

I.L.C. DRAFT ARTICLES ON STATE RESPONSIBILITY

Loc. cit. at p. 374, n. 2.

Article 5

For the purposes of the present articles, conduct of any State organ having that status under the internal law of that State shall be considered as an act of the

---

[23] See above, p. 379, n. 19.
[24] See Brownlie, p. 423.
[25] See Starke (1938) 19 B.Y.I.L. 104.

State concerned under international law, provided that organ was acting in that capacity in the case in question.

Article 6

The conduct of an organ of the State shall be considered as an act of that State under international law, whether that organ belongs to the constitutent, legislative, executive, judicial or other power, whether its functions are of an international or an internal character and whether it holds a superior or a subordinate position in the organization of the State.

Article 7

1. The conduct of an organ of a territorial governmental entity within a State shall also be considered as an act of that State under international law, provided that organ was acting in that capacity in the case in question.

2. The conduct of an organ of an entity which is not part of the formal structure of the State or a territorial governmental entity, but which is empowered by the internal law of that State to exercise elements of the governmental authority, shall also be considered as an act of the State under international law, provided that organ was acting in that capacity in the case in question.

Article 8

The conduct of a person or a group of persons shall also be considered as an act of the State under international law if

(a) it is established that such person or group of persons was in fact acting on behalf of that State; or

(b) such person or group of persons was in fact exercising elements of the governmental authority in the absence of the official authorities and in circumstances which justified the exercise of those elements of authority.

Article 9

The conduct of an organ which has been placed at the disposal of a State by another State or by an international organization shall be considered as an act of the former State under international law, if that organ was acting in the exercise of elements of the governmental authority of the State at whose disposal it has been placed.

Notes

1. Article 5 states a well established rule. Article 6 indicates that responsibility is not excluded in the case of low level officials. Similarly, in the *Massey Case*,[26] Commissioner Nielsen stated:

> To attempt by some broad classification to make a distinction between some "minor" or "petty" officials and other kinds of officials must obviously at times involve practical difficulties. Irrespective of the propriety of attempting to make any such distinction at all, it would seem that in reaching conclusions in any given case with

---

[26] *U.S.* v. *Mexico*, 4 R.I.A.A. 155, at p. 157 (1927). Van Vollenhoven, Presiding Commissioner, concurred.

respect to responsibility for acts of public servants, the most important considerations of which account must be taken are the character of the acts alleged to have resulted in injury to persons or to property, or the nature of functions performed whenever a question is raised as to their proper discharge.

2. A "territorial governmental entity" in Article 7 includes a local government organ and the government of a unit within a federal state. The rule in Article 7(2)

> . . . stems from, and is designed to cover, . . . the tendency within State communities, to set up more and more . . . "entities" . . . which are required under internal law to perform certain tasks in the interest of the community but which possess, in the eyes of the law, an organisation and a personality of their own, separate from those of the state. Among these various "entities"—whatever the régime by which they are governed—there are some whose particular characteristic is that the internal legal system confers upon them, to a greater or lesser extent, the exercise of certain elements of the governmental authority, usually of a regulatory or executive nature. The fact that an entity can be classified as public or private according to the criteria of a given legal system, the existence of a greater or lesser State participation in its capital or, more generally, in the ownership of its assets, and the fact that it is not subject to State control, or that it is subject to such control to a greater or lesser extent, and so on, do not emerge as decisive criteria for the purposes of attribution or non-attribution to the State of the conduct of its organs. The Commission has come to the conclusion that the most appropriate solution is to refer to the real common feature which these entities have: namely that they are empowered, if only exceptionally and to a limited extent, to exercise specified functions which are akin to those normally exercised by its organs of the State. Thus, for example, the conduct of an organ of a railway company to which certain police powers have been granted will be regarded as an act of State under international law if it falls within the exercise of those powers.[27]

Would the United Kingdom be responsible for the acts of the British National Oil Corporation (BNOC), a public corporation, in its dealings with foreign oil companies operating in the North Sea?

3. Article 8 covers two kinds of *de facto* state acts. Article 8(*a*) covers, first, the conduct of private individuals or groups of private individuals who, while remaining such, are employed as auxiliaries in the police or armed forces or sent as "volunteers" to neighbouring countries, and, second, the acts of persons employed to carry out certain missions in foreign territory.[28] The Commentary gives the acts of the crew in the *Zafiro Case*[29] and of the abductors in the *Eichmann*[30] and *Argoud*[31] *Cases* as examples of these two kinds of acts respectively. See also the *United States Diplomatic and Consular Staff in Tehran Case,* above, p. 276. Article 8(*b*) covers acts by private persons acting on their own initiative at a time of emergency for the defence of the realm or during a natural disaster.

4. The Commentary to Article 9 reads:

> As examples of situations in which application of the rule stated in article 9 might be entertained, reference was made in the Commission to the case in which certain conduct is engaged in by a detachment of police placed at the disposal of another State to deal with internal disturbances; by a section of the health service or some other unit placed under the orders of another country to assist in overcoming an

---

[27] Commentary, Y.B.I.L.C., 1974, II, pp. 281–282. *cf.* the problem which arises in respect of state immunity, above, Chap. 6.
[28] *Ibid.* p. 283.
[29] Below, p. 391.
[30] Above, p. 223.
[31] Above, p. 229, n. 66.

epidemic or the consequences of a natural disaster; by officials of a State or of an international organization appointed by another State to administer in its territory a public service which its own officials are unable, in certain circumstances, to administer; by judicial organs appointed in particular cases to act as judicial organs of another State; and so on. Specific instances were cited: for example, that of the United Kingdom Privy Council acting as the highest court of appeals for New Zealand and that of judicial organs of Nigeria appointed to serve also as Chief Justices of Botswana and Uganda and as President of the Court of Appeal of the Gambia. It was pointed out that Nigeria has also placed some of its civil servants at the disposal of other African States to take temporary charge of organizing the civil service of the beneficiary State.[32]

The Commission considered that the acts of the armed contingents of one state stationed in another state or employed in military operations there would not be covered.

(b) *Liability for ultra vires acts*

I.L.C. DRAFT ARTICLES ON STATE RESPONSIBILITY

Loc. cit. at p. 374, n. 2.

Article 10

The conduct of an organ of a State, of a territorial governmental entity empowered to exercise elements of the governmental authority, such organ having acted in that capacity, shall be considered as an act of the State under international law even if, in the particular case, the organ exceeded its competence according to international law or contravened instructions concerning its activity.

Notes

1. The Commentary to Article 10 gives the following reason for the rule:

In the opinion of the Commission there is no need to reopen the discussion on the basic criterion which has been affirmed in diplomatic practice and in the decisions of international tribunals in this century, *i.e.* the criterion of the attribution to the State, as a subject of international law, of the acts and omissions of its organs which have acted in that capacity, even when they have contravened the provisions of municipal law concerning their activity. This criterion is based on the need for clarity and security in international relations which seems to be the dominant theme in modern international life. In international law, the State must recognize that it acts whenever persons or groups of persons whom it has instructed to act in its name in a given area of activity appear to be acting effectively in its name. Even when in so doing those persons or groups exceed the formal limits of their competence according to municipal law or contravene the provisions of that law or of administrative ordinances or internal instructions issued by their superiors, they are nevertheless acting, even though improperly, within the scope of the discharge of their functions. The State cannot take refuge behind the notion that, according to the provisions of its legal system, those actions or omissions ought not to have occurred or ought to have taken a different form. They have nevertheless occurred and the State is therefore obliged to assume responsibility for them and to bear the consequences provided for in international law.[33]

[32] *Ibid.* p. 288.
[33] Y.B.I.L.C., 1975, II, p. 67.

2. Article 10 does not limit responsibility to cases of apparent exercise of authority (so that a state would not be liable where it is manifest that the action is *ultra vires*). There are instances of state practice and arbitral decisions supporting such a limitation. In correspondence in the *American Bible Society Case* in 1885 the United States Secretary of State (Bayard) wrote:

> . . . it is a rule of international law that sovereigns are not liable . . . for damages to a foreigner when arising from the misconduct of agents acting out of the range not only of their real but of their apparent authority.[34]

See also the *Caire Case,* above, p. 379. The Commission rejected this limitation:

> In justification of this conclusion it has been argued that if the lack of competence of the organ was manifest at the time when the organ acted, the injured party could and should have been aware of it and, in consequence, been able to prevent the illicit act from taking place. . . . On the other hand, in the majority of cases at least, the fact of knowing that the organ engaging in unlawful conduct is either exceeding its competence, or contravening its instructions, will not enable the victim of such conduct to escape its harmful consequences. We are, then, faced with a dilemma. Either we simply include the limitation ruling out attribution to the State of the conduct of organs acting in situations "manifestly" outside their competence, in which case we run the unpardonable risk of presenting the State with an easy loophole in particularly serious cases where its international responsibility ought to be affirmed; we formulate the limitation in question in the way proposed by several writers, who maintain that conduct of an organ acting outside its competence should not be attributable to the State if the organ's lack of competence was so manifest that the injured party ought to have been aware of it and could, *ipso facto, have avoided the injury.* But then we finish up by reducing the applicability of the limitation to such a small number of cases that, in the end, it would only weaken unnecessarily the force of the basic rule which it is essential to confirm in the most positive fashion. In conclusion, the Commission is of the opinion that, however worded, the limitation to exclude from qualification as acts of the State the actions of organs in situations of "manifest" lack of competence has no place in the rule defined in the present article.[35]

One of the "writers" to whom the Commission refers is Meron,[36] who proposes responsibility for:

1. An act committed within the scope of the official's apparent authority.

2. An act committed outside the scope of the official's apparent authority, if the commission of the act was made possible through means put at the official's disposal by the state. However, a state is not responsible if the alien could, in consequence of the apparent lack of authority of the official, avoid the damage.

3. On liability for *ultra vires* "administrative practices" under the European Convention on Human Rights, see below, p. 490.

UNION BRIDGE COMPANY CLAIM

U.S. *v.* Great Britain (1924)

American and British Claims Arbitration: Fromageot, President; Olds, American arbitrator; Mitchell-Innes, British arbitrator. 6 R.I.A.A. 138

In 1899, shortly after the outbreak of war between Great Britain and the Orange Free State, the claimant company delivered material to Port Elizabeth under contract with

[34] 6 Moore 743.
[35] Y.B.I.L.C., 1975, II, p. 69.   [36] (1957) 33 B.Y.I.L. 85, at p. 113.

the Government of the latter state. It claimed damages arising out of the removal of the material from Port Elizabeth to Bloemfontein without its consent by an agent of the British Government and its subsequent sale.

Award of the Tribunal

The material continued to lie at Port Elizabeth till August 1901, when . . . it was forwarded by the order of Mr. W. H. Harrison, the Storekeeper of the Cape Government Railways at Port Elizabeth, by rail to . . . Bloemfontein. . . . In our view the result of the evidence is that Mr. Harrison purported to act upon instructions given to him, shortly after the outbreak of war, when he was storekeeper at East London, to forward all bridge material intended for the Orange Free State railways, to the Imperial Military Railways, Bloemfontein. . . . In so forwarding this material, therefore, he made two mistakes, inasmuch as it (1) was neutral property; and (2) was intended for a road, and not a railway bridge. . . .

The consignment of the material to Bloemfontein was a wrongful interference with neutral property. It was certainly within the scope of Mr. Harrison's duty as Railway Storekeeper to forward material by rail, and he did so under instructions which fix liability on His Britannic Majesty's Government.

That liability is not affected either by the fact that he did so under a mistake as to the character and ownership of the material or that it was a time of pressure and confusion caused by war, or by the fact, which, on the evidence, must be admitted, that there was no intention on the part of the British authorities to appropriate the material in question. . . .

Note
Would the United Kingdom have been liable if Mr. Harrison had taken the materials home to build an ornamental bridge for himself in his garden?

YOUMANS CLAIM

U.S. *v.* Mexico (1926)

U.S. *v.* Mexican General Claims Commission: Van Vollenhoven, Presiding Commissioner; Fernández McGregor, Mexican Commissioner; Nielsen, U.S. Commissioner.
4 R.I.A.A. 110

A mob gathered around a house in Mexico within which were 3 U.S. nationals. The local mayor was called.

Opinion of the Commission

The Mayor promptly went to the house, but was unable to quieten the mob. He then returned to his office and ordered José Maria Mora, *Jefe de la Tropa de la Seguridad Pública,* who held the rank of Lieutenant in the forces of the State of Michoacán, to proceed with troops to quell the riot and put an end to the attack upon the Americans. The troops, on arriving at the scene of the riot, instead of dispersing the mob, opened fire on the house, as a consequence of which Arnold was killed. . . . Connelly and Youmans were forced to leave, and as they did so they were killed by the troops and members of the mob. . . .

11. The claim made by the United States is predicated [*inter alia*] on the

failure of the Mexican Government to exercise due diligence to protect the father of the claimant from the fury of the mob at whose hands he was killed. . . . In connection with the contention with respect to the failure of the authorities to protect Youmans from the acts of the mob, particular emphasis is laid on the participation of soldiers which is asserted to be in itself a ground of liability. In behalf of the respondent Government it is contended that . . . even if it were assumed that the soldiers were guilty of such participation, the Mexican Government should not be held responsible for the wrongful acts of ten soldiers and one officer of the State of Michoacán, who, after having been ordered by the highest official in the locality to protect American citizens, instead of carrying out orders given them acted in violation of them in consequence of which the Americans were killed. . . .

13. With respect to the question of responsibility for the acts of soldiers there are citations in the Mexican Government's brief of extracts from a discussion of a subcommittee of the League of Nations Committee of Experts for the Progressive Codification of International Law.[37] The passage quoted, which deals with the responsibility of a State for illegal acts of officials resulting in damages to foreigners, begins with a statement relative to the acts of an official accomplished "outside the scope of his competency, that is to say, if he has exceeded his powers." An illegal act of this kind, it is stated in the quotation, is one that can not be imputed to the State. Apart from the question whether the acts of officials referred to in this discussion have any relation to the rule of international law with regard to responsibility for acts of soldiers, it seems clear that the passage to which particular attention is called in the Mexican Government's brief is concerned solely with the question of the authority of an officer as defined by domestic law to act for his Government with reference to some particular subject. Clearly it is not intended by the rule asserted to say that no wrongful act of an official acting in the discharge of duties entrusted to him can impose responsibility on a Government under international law because any such wrongful act must be considered to be "outside the scope of his competency." If this were the meaning intended by the rule it would follow that no wrongful acts committed by an official could be considered as acts for which his Government could be held liable. We do not consider that any of these passages from the discussion of the subcommittee quoted in the Mexican brief are at variance with the view which we take that the action of the troops in participating in the murder at Angangueo imposed a direct responsibility on the Government of Mexico.

14. Citation is also made in the Mexican brief to an opinion rendered by Umpire Lieber in which effect is evidently given to the well-recognized rule of international law that a Government is not responsible for malicious acts of soldiers committed in their private capacity. Awards have repeatedly been rendered for wrongful acts of soldiers acting under the command of an officer. . . . Certain cases coming before the international tribunals may have revealed some uncertainty whether the acts of soldiers should properly be regarded as private acts for which there was no liability on the State, or acts for which the State should be held responsible. But we do not consider that the participation of the soldiers in the murder at Angangueo can be regarded as acts

[37] *Ed.* The reference is to the report of the sub-committee, which is reprinted in 20 A.J.I.L., Sp. Supp. 176 (1926).

of soldiers committed in their private capacity when it is clear that at the time of the commission of these acts the men were on duty under the immediate supervision and in the presence of a commanding officer. Soldiers inflicting personal injuries or committing wanton destruction or looting always act in disobedience of some rules laid down by superior authority. There could be no liability whatever for such misdeeds if the view were taken that any acts committed by soldiers in contravention of instructions must always be considered as personal acts.

The Commission awarded compensation.

Notes
1. Would there have been liability under (i) the I.L.C. or (ii) Meron's approach?
2. To what extent might liability for *ultra vires* acts depend upon the character of the actor?[38] Might there, for example, be particularly strict liability for the *ultra vires* acts of soldiers as opposed to civil servants?
3. Are the rules concerning responsibility for *ultra vires* acts based upon fault or risk?

ZAFIRO CLAIM

Great Britain *v.* U.S. (1925)

American and British Claims Arbitration: Nerincx, President; Pound, American Arbitrator; FitzPatrick, British Arbitrator. 6 R.I.A.A. 160

The case arose out of looting during the Spanish-American War of 1898 at Cavite in the Philippines. The *Zafiro* was a privately owned ship, with a Chinese crew. It was being used during the war by the United States as a supply ship, with its master and crew being placed under the command of a United States naval officer.

Award of the Tribunal

It is well settled that we must distinguish between soldiers or sailors under the command of officers, on the one hand, and, on the other hand, bodies of straggling and marauding soldiers not under the command of an officer, or marauding sailors not under command or control of officers. Hayden's case, 3 Moore, International Arbitrations, 2985; case of Terry and Angus, Id. 2993; Mexican Claims, Id. 2996–7. These cases draw a very clear line between what is done by order or in the presence of an officer and what is done without the order or presence of an officer. But it is not necessary that an officer be on the very spot. . . .

In the case before us, we think the officers were not actually present at the houses when the looting was done. . . . After the matter was drawn to the attention of the naval officers, the vessel was searched and the articles found on board were returned to the claimants. But the damage had been done. Moreover, Captain Whitton's statement that he "stopped anything he saw coming on board" gives the impression that he did not stop with sufficient promptitude the taking of things on land before they could come on board, after he found that plundering was going on. Without regard to this point, however, we feel that there was no effective control of the Chinese crew at the time when the real damage took place. When the *Zafiro* was tied up alongside the

---

[38] See Brownlie, p. 435; Schwarzenberger, pp. 615–617.

company's wharf, where the houses were, the naval officer and the merchant captain went off to look at the Spanish batteries, leaving the crew in charge of the first mate. The latter gave half of the crew leave to go ashore. Captain Whitton says significantly: "You know what Chinese are, especially these times." To let this crew go ashore where these houses were, with no one in charge of them, at a time when plunder and pillage were certain—and plunder and pillage by the Filipinos had been observed by all the officers—seems to us to have been highly culpable.

It was said in argument that a government is not responsible for what its sailors do when on shore leave. But we cannot agree that letting this Chinese crew go ashore uncontrolled at the time and place in question was like allowing shore leave to sailors in a policed port where social order is maintained by the ordinary agencies of government. Here the Spaniards had evacuated Cavite, and no one was in control except as the Navy controlled its own men. The nature of the crew, the absence of a régime of civil or military control ashore, and the situation of the neutral property, were circumstances calling for diligence on the part of those in charge of the Chinese crew to see to it that they were under control when they went ashore in a body. . . .

We think it clear that not all of the damage was done by the Chinese crew of the *Zafiro*. The evidence indicates that an unascertainable part was done by Filipino insurgents, and makes it likely that some part was done by the Chinese employees of the company. But we do not consider that the burden is on Great Britain to prove exactly what items of damage are chargeable to the *Zafiro*. As the Chinese crew of the Zafiro are shown to have participated to a substantial extent and the part chargeable to unknown wrongdoers cannot be identified, we are constrained to hold the United States liable for the whole.

In view, however, of our finding that a considerable, though unascertainable, part of the damage is not chargeable to the Chinese crew of the *Zafiro,* we hold that interest on the claims should not be allowed.

Note

Who was responsible in international law for the actions of the Palestinian Arab guerillas in the Dawson's field hijacking?[39]

(c) *Absence of Liability for the Acts of Private Persons, Organs of Other States, and International Organisations*

I.L.C. DRAFT ARTICLES ON STATE RESPONSIBILITY

Loc. cit. at p. 374, n. 2, above.

Article 11

1. The conduct of a person or a group of persons not acting on behalf of the State shall not be considered as an act of the State under international law.

2. Paragraph 1 is without prejudice to the attribution to the State of any other conduct which is related to that of the persons or groups of persons referred to in that paragraph and which is to be considered as an act of the State by virtue of articles 5 to 10. [above, pp. 384–387]

[39] For the facts of the case, see above p. 239. See Brownlie, 7 I.C.L.Q. 712 (1958).

Article 12

1. The conduct of an organ of a State acting in that capacity, which takes place in the territory of another State or in any other territory under its jurisdiction, shall not be considered as an act of the latter State under international law.

2. Paragraph 1 is without prejudice to the attribution to a State of any other conduct which is related to that referred to in that paragraph and which is to be considered as an act of that State by virtue of articles 5 to 10.

Article 13

The conduct of an organ of an international organization acting in that capacity shall not be considered as an act of a State under international law by reason only of the fact that such conduct has taken place in the territory of that State or in any other territory under its jurisdiction.

(d) Liability for the Acts of Insurrectionaries

I.L.C. DRAFT ARTICLES ON STATE RESPONSIBILITY

Loc. cit. at p. 374, n. 2, above.

Article 14

1. The conduct of an organ of an insurrectional movement, which is established in the territory of a State or in any other territory under its administration, shall not be considered as an act of that State under international law.

2. Paragraph 1 is without prejudice to the attribution to a State of any other conduct which is related to that of the organ of the insurrectional movement and which is to be considered as an act of that State by virtue of articles 5 to 10. [above, pp. 384–387]

3. Similarly, paragraph 1 is without prejudice to the attribution of the conduct of the organ of the insurrectional movement to that movement in any case in which such attribution may be made under international law.

Article 15

1. The act of an insurrectional movement which becomes the new government of a State shall be considered as an act of that State. However, such attribution shall be without prejudice to the attribution to that State of conduct which would have been previously considered as an act of the State by virtue of articles 5 to 10.

2. The act of an insurrectional movement whose action results in the formation of a new State in part of the territory of a pre-existing State or in a territory under its administration shall be considered as an act of the new State.

Notes[40]

1. The lack of responsibility of a State for the acts of *unsuccessful* revolutionaries was explained by the Umpire (Ralston) in the *Sambaggio Case*,[41] in which a claim by an

[40] See Akehurst (1968–69) 43 B.Y.I.L. 49.   [41] *Italy* v. *Venezuela*, 10 R.I.A.A. 499 (1903).

Italian national for compensation for damage caused by unsuccessful revolutionaries in Venezuela was rejected:

> Governments are responsible, as a general principle, for the acts of those they control. But the very existence of a flagrant revolution presupposes that a certain set of men have gone temporarily or permanently beyond the power of the authorities; and unless it clearly appears that the government has failed to use promptly and with appropriate force its constituted authority, it can not reasonably be said that it should be responsible for a condition of affairs created without its volition. When we bear in mind that for six months previous to the taking complained of in the present case a bloody and determined revolution demanding the entire resources of the Government to quell it had been raging throughout the larger part of Venezuela, it can not be determined generally that there was such neglect on the part of the Government as to charge it with the offences of the revolutionists whose acts are now in question.
>
> We find ourselves therefore obliged to conclude, from the standpoint of general principle, that, save under the exceptional circumstances indicated, the Government should not be held responsible for the acts of revolutionists.
>
>   (a) Revolutionists are not the agents of government, and a natural responsibility does not exist.
>   (b) Their acts are committed to destroy the government, and no one should be held responsible for the acts of an enemy attempting his life.
>   (c) The revolutionists were beyond governmental control, and the Government can not be held responsible for injuries committed by those who have escaped its restraint.[42]

2. In the *Gelbtrunk Claim*,[43] the Tribunal emphasised *volenti non fit injuria:*

> The principle which I hold to be applicable to the present case may be thus stated: A citizen or subject of one nation who, in the pursuit of commercial enterprise, carries on trade within the territory and under the protection of the sovereignty of a nation other than his own is to be considered as having cast in his lot with the subjects or citizens of the State in which he resides and carries on business. Whilst on the one hand he enjoys the protection of that State, so far as the police regulations and other advantages are concerned, on the other hand he becomes liable to the political vicissitudes of the country in which he thus has a commercial domicile in the same manner as the subjects or citizens of that State are liable to the same. The State to which he owes national allegiance has no right to claim for him as against the nation in which he is resident any other or different treatment in case of loss by war—either foreign or civil—revolution, insurrection, or other internal disturbance caused by organised military force or by soldiers, than that which the latter country metes out to its own subjects or citizens.

BOLIVAR RAILWAY COMPANY CLAIM

Great Britain *v.* Venzuela (1903)

British-Venezuelan Mixed Claims Commission: Plumley, Umpire; Harrison, British Commissioner; Grisanti, Venezuelan Commissioner. 9 R.I.A.A. 445

Claims were brought by the above company arising out of the revolution in Venezuela that brought Castro to power in 1899. Claims in respect of contractual obligations

---

[42] *Ibid.* p. 513.
[43] *U.S.* v. *Salvador*, 1902 U.S.For.Rel. 876, 877–878. See also the *Home Missionary Society Claim*, above, p. 378.

incurred by both the old and the new governments were successful on the basis indicated in the following extract. Claims that were adjudged to have resulted from such obligations incurred by an unsuccessful revolution against Castro immediately after his assumption of power were not allowed.

Opinion of the Umpire

If the personal responsibility of General Castro in this matter were the question for decision, it might be possible to hold him responsible for the second revolution as growing out of the revolution he had led. Such, however, is not the ground on which successful revolutions are charged, through the government, with responsibility. Responsibility comes because it is the same nation. Nations do not die when there is a change of their rulers or in their forms of government. These are but expressions of a change of national will. "The king is dead; long live the king!" has typified this thought for ages. The nation is responsible for the debts contracted by its titular government, and that responsibility continues through all changing forms of government until the obligation is discharged. The nation is responsible for the obligations of a successful revolution from its beginning, because in theory, it represented ab initio a changing national will, crystallizing in the finally successful result. . . . success demonstrates that from the beginning it was registering the national will.

(v) REPARATION[44]

CHORZÓW FACTORY CASE (INDEMNITY) (MERITS)

Germany *v.* Poland (1928)

P.C.I.J. Reports, Series A, No. 17, pp. 47–48

The case concerned the expropriation by Poland of a factory at Chorzów contrary, as the Court had held,[45] to the Geneva Convention of 1922 between Germany and Poland on Upper Silesia. In this judgment the Court ruled upon a claim by Germany for an indemnity for the damage caused by the illegal expropriation.

Judgment of the Court

The essential principle contained in the actual notion of an illegal act—a principle which seems to be established by international practice and in particular by the decisions of arbitral tribunals—is that reparation must, as far as possible, wipe out all the consequences of the illegal act and re-establish the situation which would, in all probability, have existed if that act had not been committed. Restitution in kind, or, if this is not possible, payment of a sum corresponding to the value which a restitution in kind would bear; the award, if need be, of damages for loss sustained which would not be covered by restitution in kind or payment in place of it—such are the principles which should serve to determine the amount of compensation due for an act contrary to international law.

This conclusion particularly applies as regards the Geneva Convention, the object of which is to provide for the maintenance of economic life in Upper

[44] See Mann (1978) 48 B.Y.I.L. 1.
[45] *Certain German Interests in Polish Upper Silesia Case,* P.C.I.J.Rep., Series A, No. 7 (1926).

Silesia on the basis of respect for the *status quo*. The dispossession of an industrial undertaking—the expropriation of which is prohibited by the Geneva Convention—then involves the obligation to restore the undertaking and, if this be not possible, to pay its value at the time of the indemnification, which value is designed to take the place of restitution which has become impossible. To this obligation, in virtue of the general principles of international law, must be added that of compensating loss sustained as the result of the seizure. The impossibility, on which the Parties are agreed, of restoring the Chorzów factory could therefore have no other effect but that of substituting payment of the value of the undertaking for restitution; it would not be in conformity either with the principles of law or with the wish of the Parties to infer from that agreement that the question of compensation must henceforth be dealt with as though an expropriation properly so called was involved.

SCHWARZENBERGER, INTERNATIONAL LAW

3rd ed., 1957, pp. 653, 658. Footnotes omitted

International judicial institutions have slowly groped their way towards the articulate formulation of the rule that the commission of an international tort entails the duty to make reparation. For a considerable period, they tended to limit redress for breaches of international law to monetary compensation for actual injury or damage suffered. The fact that, in State practice, other forms of reparation, such as apologies and ceremonial honours to an insulted flag, were familiar occurrences did not necessarily constitute evidence of the existence of a comprehensive rule on reparation. Satisfaction, as this kind of reparation was termed, was explicable as an agreed form of redress and alternative to the application of reprisals or resort to war. . . .

If restitution in kind is not possible, two subsidiary forms of reparation are available: satisfaction and compensation. As international judicial practice permits monetary compensation to be awarded for other than material damage, it appears an unnecessary overcomplication to distinguish from it pecuniary satisfaction. Whether symbolical or excessive, any award of damages is a form of monetary compensation. This limits satisfaction to any non-monetary form of reparation which is not restitution in kind. Satisfaction has in common with restitution in kind, and in this differs from compensation, that it is of a non-monetary character. It differs from restitution in kind, and shares this feature with compensation, that it cannot lead to actual restoration of the *status quo ante*. The typical purpose of satisfaction is to repair breaches of international obligations in cases in which such a breach does not entail any actual damage or monetary compensation is either inappropriate or insufficient.

Notes

1. An example of "restitution in kind" is found in the *Martini Case*.[46] There the Tribunal ruled that proceedings in a case in the Venezuelan courts that was lost by the claimant company had been "manifestly unjust" and decided that "the Venezuelan Government is bound to recognise, by way of reparation, the annulment of the financial obligations imposed" by the Venezuelan courts on the claimant company. See also the

---

[46] *Italy* v. *Venezuela*, 2 R.I.A.A. 975, 1002 (1930). Translation.

Temple Case,[47] in which Thailand was ordered to return to Cambodia religious objects it had taken illegally from a temple in Cambodia. Brownlie[48] states that "it would seem that territorial disputes may be settled by specific restitution, although the declaratory form of the judgments of the International Court masks the element of "restitution."

2. "Restitution in kind," however, is exceptional.[49] Much more common as a means of "wiping out the consequences of the illegal act" is the award of monetary compensation. Rules about the award of such compensation in international law are far from clear. With respect to compensation for interference with property interests, the Tribunal in the *Norwegian Shipowners Claims*[50] stated:

> Just compensation implies a complete restitution of the *status quo ante,* based, not upon future gains of the United States or other powers, but upon the loss of profits of the Norwegian owners as compared with other owners of similar property.[51]

In that case, in assessing the compensation due to the Norwegian shipowners from the United States for the confiscation by the latter of their ships and contracts for the construction of ships during the First World War in a manner contrary to international law, the Tribunal stated that the "market value" of the property should be paid. Because of the special wartime circumstances, it decided that the actual market value was a distortion of the real market value. The Tribunal therefore ruled that the "value must be assessed *ex aequo et bono."*[52] Other examples of approaches taken by international tribunals to the question of monetary compensation for material injury to property interests and for injury to the person in cases concerning the treatment of aliens are found in Section 3 of this chapter.

As indicated by Schwarzenberger, monetary compensation has been awarded for non-material damage. In the *I'm Alone Case,* for example, the Commissioners recommended the payment by the United States of $25,000 "as a material amend in respect of the wrong" committed by the United States in sinking the *I'm Alone.*[53] The compensation was related to the indignity suffered by Canada by the unlawful sinking of a ship registered in Montreal; it was not related to the value of the ship or its cargo.

3. Schwarzenberger illustrates the forms that satisfaction may take by the *Borchgrave Case.*[54] There, in a case in which a Belgian national working at the Belgian Embassy in Madrid was found dead on the roadside in Spain in 1936, the Court listed the reparation sought by Belgium in diplomatic proceedings with Spain as follows: "In consequence, proceeding on the principles of international law relating to the responsibility of States, the Belgian Government demanded as reparation: (1) an expression of the Spanish Government's excuses and regrets; (2) transfer of the corpse to the port of embarcation with military honours; (3) the payment of an indemnity of one million Belgian francs in favour of the persons entitled; and (4) just punishment of the guilty." The forms of reparation listed under (1), (2) and (4) are clearly forms of satisfaction.[55] A declaration by a court or tribunal that a state has acted illegally may itself be sufficient satisfaction in some cases.[56]

---

[47] I.C.J.Rep. 1962, p. 6. See also the remedy sought by France in the *Savarkar Cáse*, above, p. 233, and the advice given by the Law Officers in the *Lawler Incident*, above, p. 233.

[48] Brownlie, p. 383.

[49] It was awarded in the *Texaco Case*, see below, p. 434, but not in the *B.P. Case*, see below p. 425, or the *Liamco* Case, see below, p. 426. All three were cases of expropriation contrary to an international contract.

[50] *Norway* v. *U.S.*, 1 R.I.A.A. 307 (1922).

[51] *Ibid.* p. 338.

[52] *Ibid.* p. 339.

[53] See above, p. 334. *cf.* the award of compensation for "moral" damage in the jurisprudence of the European Court of Human Rights, below, p. 482.

[54] *Belgium* v. *Spain*, P.C.I.J.Rep., Series A/B, No. 72, at p. 165 (1937).

[55] Note also the apology recommended in the *I'm Alone Case*, above, p. 334.

[56] See the *Corfu Channel Case*, above, p. 301 (on Albania's counter-claim).

3. *THE TREATMENT OF ALIENS*[57]

(i) INTRODUCTORY NOTE

The treatment of aliens (or, more accurately, the treatment of the nationals of other states) is as controversial a subject as any in international law. The controversy stems from a difference of approach between those states that consider that there is an "international minimum standard" of treatment which must be accorded to aliens by all states irrespective of how they treat their own nationals and those that argue that aliens may only insist upon "national treatment," *i.e.* treatment equal to that given by the state concerned to its own nationals.[58] Generally speaking, the older and economically developed states follow the "international minimum standard" approach while the newer and developing states favour "national treatment."[59] At the turn of the century, the latter states consisted mainly of Latin American states; more recently they have been joined by most of the post-colonial Afro-Asian states. Exceptionally, the U.S.S.R. and other developed communist states reject the "international minimum standard" approach also. The support for both points of view makes it difficult to determine many of the rules of international law in this area, although the Western developed States are becoming somewhat beleaguered in the particular area of expropriation.

Whether an "international minimum standard" or a "national treatment" rule applies, it is commonly agreed by states that international law does not control their treatment of aliens in every area of activity. Whereas, on either basis, states are limited in their treatment of aliens in the areas indicated in the materials in this section, in certain other areas states may at customary international law treat aliens *qua* aliens[60] in their discretion. For example, aliens may be, and commonly are, restricted in the ownership of property, participation in public life and the taking of employment. In the United Kingdom, an alien may not own a British ship, vote in a parliamentary election, or hold any public office (including that of policeman)[61]; he is also subject to the "nationality rule" in respect of permanent appointments in the civil service.[62]

Finally, there is a question of terminology. The term *denial of justice* is commonly used in the decisions of international tribunals and elsewhere.[63] According to the report of a Sub-Committee of the League of Nations Committee of Experts for the Progressive Codification of International Law[64] it has the following limited meaning: "*Denial of Justice* consists in refusing to allow foreigners easy access to the courts to defend those rights which the national law accords them. A refusal of the competent judge to exercise jurisdiction also constitutes a *denial of justice*." Commissioner Nielsen gave the term a

---

[57] See Amerasinghe, *State Responsibility for Injuries to Aliens* (1967); Borchard, *The Diplomatic Protection of Aliens Abroad* (1915); Dunn, *The Protection of Nationals (1932); Eagleton, The Responsibility of States in International Law* (1928); Freeman, *The International Responsibility of States for Denial of Justice* (1938); Jessup, *A Modern Law of Nations* (1946), Chap. V; Parry, 90 *Hague Recueil* 653 (1956–II).

[58] On the position of stateless persons, see below, p. 449.

[59] On the approach now adopted by developing states in the particular case of expropriation, see below, p. 422.

[60] Aliens may, as individuals, have some protection at customary international law on a human rights basis: see below, Chap. 9.

[61] Hood Phillips, *Constitutional and Administrative Law* (6th ed., 1979), p. 419.

[62] See Hepple, *Race, Jobs and the Law in Britain* (2nd ed., 1970), p. 270.

[63] See Fitzmaurice (1932) 13 B.Y.I.L. 93 and Lissitzyn, 30 A.J.I.L. 632 (1936).

[64] L.N.Doc. 1926 V. 3, p. 15; reprinted in 20 A.J.I.L. Sp.Supp. 177, at p. 202 (1926). The Sub-Committee Report was prepared by Guerrero.

much wider meaning in the *Neer Case*[65]: "I think it is useful and proper to apply the term denial of justice in a broader sense than that of a designation solely of a wrongful act on the part of the judicial branch of the government. I consider that a denial of justice may, broadly speaking, be properly regarded as the general ground of diplomatic intervention." A definition somewhere between these two extremes is that in the 1929 Harvard Draft Convention on the Responsibility of States for Damage done in their Territory to the Person or Property of Foreigners:

> Article 9. Denial of justice exists when there is a denial, unwarranted delay or obstruction of access to courts, gross deficiency in the administration of judicial or remedial process, failure to provide those guarantees which are generally considered indispensable to the proper administration of justice, or a manifestly unjust judgment. An error of a national court which does not produce manifest injustice is not a denial of justice.[66]

In view of its unsettled meaning the term is probably best avoided.

(ii) AN INJURY TO THE STATE

MAVROMMATIS PALESTINE CONCESSIONS CASE (JURISDICTION)

Greece *v.* U.K. (1924)

P.C.I.J. Reports, Series A, No. 2, p. 12

Judgment of the Court

In the case of the Mavrommatis concessions it is true that the dispute was at first between a private person and a State—*i.e.* between M. Mavrommatis and Great Britain. Subsequently, the Greek Government took up the case. The dispute then entered upon a new phase; it entered the domain of international law, and became a dispute between two States.

. . . It is an elementary principle of international law that a State is entitled to protect its subjects, when injured by acts contrary to international law committed by another State, from whom they have been unable to obtain satisfaction through the ordinary channels. By taking up the case of one of its subjects and by resorting to diplomatic action or international judicial proceedings on his behalf, a State is in reality asserting its own rights—its right to ensure, in the person of its subjects, respect for the rules of international law.

The question, therefore, whether the present dispute originates in an injury to a private interest, which in point of fact is the case in many international disputes, is irrelevant from this standpoint. Once a State has taken up a case on behalf of one of its subjects before an international tribunal, in the eyes of the latter the State is sole claimant.

---

[65] *U.S.* v. *Mexico*, 4 R.I.A.A. 60, at p. 64 (1926).
[66] 23 A.J.I.L. Sp.Supp. 133 (1929).

ADMINISTRATIVE DECISION NO. V

U.S. *v.* Germany (1924)

Mixed Claims Commission: Parker, Umpire; Anderson, American Commissioner;
Kiesselbalch, German Commissioner. 1924. 7 R.I.A.A. 119

Opinion of the Umpire

Ordinarily a nation will not espouse a claim on behalf of its national against another nation unless requested so to do by such national. When on such request a claim is espoused, the nation's absolute right to control it is necessarily exclusive. In exercising such control it is governed not only by the interest of the particular claimant but by the larger interests of the whole people of the nation and must exercise an untrammelled discretion in determining when and how the claim will be presented and pressed, or withdrawn or compromised, and the private owner will be bound by the action taken. Even if payment is made to the espousing nation in pursuance of an award, it has complete control over the fund so paid to and held by it and may, to prevent fraud, correct a mistake, or protect the national honor, at its election return the fund to the nation paying it or otherwise dispose of it. . . .

The Umpire agrees with the American Commissioner that the *control* of the United States over claims espoused by it before this Commission is complete. But the generally accepted theory formulated by Vattel, which makes the injury to the national an injury to the nation and internationally therefore the claim a national claim which may and should be espoused by the nation injured, must not be permitted to obscure the realities or blind us to the fact that the ultimate object of asserting the claim is to provide reparation for the private claimant. . . .

Notes

1. Is a state obliged to take up a national's case? Who decides on what terms to settle the case (if this question arises) if it does? Exceptionally, treaties allow individuals to bring claims against the parties to them.[67] Why should not customary international law allow them to bring claims against states in at least some cases?

2. A state is not obliged by international law to hand over to a claimant compensation received in his case; the question is one of municipal law. As far as English law is concerned, in *Rustomjee* v. *The Queen*,[68] Lush J. stated:

No doubt a duty arose as soon as the money was received to distribute that money amongst the persons towards whose losses it was paid by the Emperor of China; but then the distribution when made would be, not the act of an agent accounting to a principal, but the act of the sovereign in dispensing justice to her subjects. For any omission of that duty the sovereign cannot be held responsible.

The case concerned moneys paid to Great Britain by China by treaty as compensation for damage suffered by British nationals in China.

3. Consider whether, despite the theory that the injury is to the state and not to its national, the cases in this Section suggest that in practice tribunals commonly assess compensation by reference to the injury suffered by the latter.

---

[67] See above, p. 122.
[68] (1876) 1 Q.B.D. 487, at p. 497. See also *Civilian War Claimants' Association Ltd.* v. *The King* [1932] A.C. 14 (H.L.).

(iii) International Minimum Standard or National Treatment?

NEER CLAIM

U.S. *v.* Mexico (1926)

U.S.-Mexican General Claims Commission: for the Commissioners, see above, p. 389.
4 R.I.A.A. 60

In this case the United States claimed that Mexico had failed to exercise due diligence in finding and prosecuting the murderer of a United States national. In the course of rejecting the claim, the Commission indicated the standard that it would have to apply. The Commission was unanimous.

Opinion of the Commission

The Commission recognizes the difficulty of devising a general formula for determining the boundary between an international delinquency of this type and an unsatisfactory use of power included in national sovereignty. . . . Without attempting to announce a precise formula, it is in the opinion of the Commission possible . . . to hold (first) that the propriety of governmental acts should be put to the test of international standards, and (second) that the treatment of an alien, in order to constitute an international delinquency, should amount to an outrage, to bad faith, to wilful neglect of duty, or to an insufficiency of governmental action so far short of international standards that every reasonable and impartial man would readily recognize its insufficiency. Whether the insufficiency proceeds from deficient execution of an intelligent law or from the fact that the laws of the country do not empower the authorities to measure up to international standards is immaterial.

Notes
1. The great majority of arbitration awards are like that in the *Neer Claim* in supporting the view that international law requires states to treat nationals according to an "international minimum standard." In the *Chevreau Case*,[69] for instance, in which France claimed on behalf of a French national in respect of his arrest and treatment in detention by Great Britain, the Arbitrator (Beichmann) said: "The detained man must be treated in a manner fitting his station, and which conforms to the standard habitually practised among civilized nations."[70] The majority of arbitrators in such awards tend to be from developed states.
2. How persuasive is the argument that an alien who visits, takes up residence in, or does business in a foreign state must take conditions as he finds them? See the *Gelbtrunk Claim*, above, p. 394.
3. Might the "national treatment" approach work to the advantage of the alien in some cases?

---

[69] *France v. Great Britain*, 2 R.I.A.A. 1113 (1931). English translation in 27 A.J.I.L. 153 (1933).
[70] 27 A.J.I.L., at p. 160 (1933). See also the extracts from the *Roberts Claim*, below, p. 412. On the other hand, see, in the context of the protection of resident aliens against injury in war, revolution, etc., the *Gelbtrunk Claim*, above, p. 394.

PREPARATORY STUDY CONCERNING A DRAFT DECLARATION ON RIGHTS AND DUTIES OF STATES

Memorandum submitted by the U.N. Secretary-General, U.N.Doc. A/CN. 4/2, p. 71

Early discussion in the International Law Commission on a Draft Declaration on Rights and Duties of States was based upon a Panamanian draft upon which governments were asked to comment. Article 7 of that draft reads in part: "Foreigners may not claim rights different from, or more extensive than, those enjoyed by nationals." The following is the response by the United Kingdom Government to that Article. The sentence was finally omitted from the Commission's Draft Declaration on the separate ground that the question should be dealt with in the course of codifying the law of state responsibility.

The second sentence of this article is not in accord with existing international law, as His Majesty's Government apprehend it. There is much international authority for the existence of a minimum international standard, with which States are obliged to comply in their treatment of foreigners, whether or not they do so in the treatment of their nationals. If, and in so far as international law develops so as to limit the domestic jurisdiction of States in the treatment of their nationals to such an extent that every treatment of a national, which falls below the international standard, is a breach of international law (and therefore a matter on which other States may intervene), then the existing principle of international law with regard to the "international standard" will apply to both nationals and foreigners. Unless and until that position is reached, His Majesty's Government consider that the doctrine of the minimum international standard, with regard to the treatment of foreigners, remains part of international law and that agreement to abolish that doctrine will not be attained.

Notes

1. At the Hague Codification Conference in 1930 the following text on the particular question of injury to aliens at the hands of private persons was rejected by 23 votes to 17:

A state is only responsible for damage caused by private persons to the persons or property of foreigners if it has manifestly failed to take such preventive or punitive measures as in the circumstances might reasonably be expected of it had the persons injured been its own nationals.

A text on the same question favouring an international minimum standard was then adopted by 21 votes to 17.[71] On the other hand, Article 9 of the 1933 Montevideo Convention on Rights and Duties of States,[72] which would still represent the view of most developing states, reads in part:

Nationals and foreigners are under the same protection of the law and the national authorities and the foreigners may not claim rights other or more extensive than those of the nationals.

2. For a robust, Victorian statement favouring the international minimum standard in the administration of justice, note that of Lord Palmerston (Foreign Secretary) in 1850:

We shall be told, perhaps, as we have already been told, that if the people of the country are liable to have heavy stones placed upon their breasts, and police officers

[71] See Hackworth, 24 A.J.I.L. 500 at pp. 513–514 (1930).
[72] See above, p. 80. There are 16 parties to the Convention, including the United States. See, however, the United States reservation, 4 Malloy 4810.

to dance upon them; if they are liable to have their heads tied to their knees, and to be left for hours in that state; or to be swung like a pendulum and to be bastinadoed as they swing, foreigners have no right to be better treated then the natives, and have no business to complain if the same things are practised upon them. We may be told this, but this is not my opinion, nor do I believe it is the opinion of any reasonable man.[73]

3. In 1957, the International Law Commission debated the Second Report on State Responsibility of its Special Rapporteur (Garcia Amador).[74] The Rapporteur proposed in his Report the following draft article:

> *Article 5.* 1. The State is under a duty to ensure to aliens the enjoyment of the same civil rights, and to make available to them the same individual guarantees as are enjoyed by its nationals. These rights and guarantees shall not, however, in any case be less then the "fundamental human rights" recognized and defined in comtemporary international instruments.

This ambitious proposal would, in a sense, have married the international minimum standard and national treatment approaches. Its human rights basis, which would have made substantial inroads upon the domestic jurisdiction of states, was too far out of line with state practice to have had any real hope of approval. Despite redrafting, it was felt to be impracticable for purposes of codification and not pursued further. Since then the Commission has changed its approach and, as indicated earlier,[75] is concentrating upon the codification of the general principles of responsibility. The particular subject of responsibility for the treatment of aliens has been left to one side for the time being.

(iv) ADMISSION AND EXPULSION[76]

(a) *Of Aliens*

REPORT ON ADMISSION TO LOUISIANA

Report by J. Dodson, Queen's Advocate, to the Foreign Secretary, August 4, 1843.
2 *McNair* 105

. . . the purport of the Act in question [a Louisiana State Statute] is to prohibit free persons of colour from entering the State of Louisiana by sea, and of punishing them with great severity in case of their arrival within the territory contrary to the tenor of this inhospitable law.

The provisions of this extraordinary and illiberal Act are calculated to operate with peculiar harshness as regards the free coloured subjects of Her Majesty; and I therefore think that Her Majesty's Government would be justified in making a representation against it, in the shape of a remonstrance to the Government of the United States. Whether Her Majesty's Government would have a right to go further and insist upon the repeal of this specimen of Louisianian legislation, may be a matter not altogether free from doubt, but upon the best consideration I have been able to give the subject, I incline to think that Great Britain does not possess such right. It cannot be denied that every independent State or nation is entitled to admit or exclude from its

---

[73] H.C.Debs., 3rd Series, CXII, Col. 387; 6 B.D.I.L. 290.
[74] Y.B.I.L.C., 1957, II, p. 104. The debate was a famous one, in which nationals from developing and developed states put their different points of view most forcefully: *ibid.* Vol. I, pp. 155 *et seq.*   [75] See above, p. 374.
[76] See Goodwin-Gill, *International Law and the Movement of Persons between States* (1978) and Plender, *International Migration Law* (1972).

territories the subjects and citizens of foreign States, unless it has entered into any engagement by treaty on the subject, in which case the treaty must of course prescribe the rule to be observed.

Note

In *Att.-Gen. for Canada* v. *Cain,*[77] the Judicial Committee of the Privy Council said:

One of the rights possessed by the supreme power in every State is the right to refuse to permit an alien to enter that State, to annex what conditions it pleases to the permission to enter it, and to expel or deport from the State, at pleasure, even a friendly alien, especially if it considers his presence in the State opposed to its peace, order, and good government, or to its social or material interests.

DR. BREGER'S CASE

Letter of December 15, 1961, from the U.S. Department of State to a Congressman.
8 Whiteman 861

As to Dr. Breger's expulsion from the Island of Rhodes in 1938, it may be pointed out that under generally accepted principles of international law, a state may expel an alien whenever it wishes, provided it does not carry out the expulsion in an arbitrary manner, such as by using unnecessary force to effect the expulsion or by otherwise mistreating the alien or by refusing to allow the alien a reasonable opportunity to safeguard property. In view of Dr. Breger's statement to the effect that he was ordered by the Italian authorities to leave the Island of Rhodes within six months, it appears doubtful that international liability of the Italian Government could be based on the ground that he was not given enough time to safeguard his property.

Notes

1. On November 20, 1949, in *Palgrave Brown's Case,* a British student who had been awarded a Hungarian State scholarship to study for a year in Hungary was informed, within two weeks of his arrival in Budapest, that he must leave the country by December 12, 1949. No reasons were given. In the House of Commons, a Minister of State at the Foreign Office, in reply to a question stated:

It is, of course, within the rights of the Hungarian Government to expel any foreigner from their country and there seems, therefore, to be no legal ground for an official protest. My right hon. Friend nevertheless deplores their arbitrary expulsion, at the shortest notice, without specifying a reason, of a British student to whom they had just awarded a State Scholarship for one year.[78]

2. In the *Boffolo Claim,*[79] in which an Italian was expelled from Venezuela for publishing an article, *inter alia,* criticising the judiciary, the Umpire (Ralston) said:

(1) A State possesses the general right of expulsion; but, (2) Expulsion should only be resorted to in extreme instances, and must be accomplished in the manner least injurious to the person affected. (3) The country exercising the power must, when occasion demands, state the reason of such expulsion before an international tribunal, and an inefficient reason or none being advanced, accept the consequences. (4) In the present case the only reasons suggested to the Commission would be contrary to the Venezuelan constitution, and as this is a country not of despotic power, but of

[77] [1906] A.C. 542 at p. 546.
[78] *Hansard,* H.C., Vol. 460, cols. 154–155. January 19, 1949; 8 Whiteman 854.
[79] *Italy* v. *Venezuela,* 10 R.I.A.A. 528, at p. 537 (1903).

fixed laws, restraining, among other things, the acts of its officials, these reasons (whatever good ones may in point of fact have existed) can not be accepted by the umpire as sufficient.

In *Ben Tillet's Case*,[80] in which a British dock leader who had gone to Belgium to support dockers' activities there was expelled from that country, the Arbitrator stated that "the right of a State to exclude from its territory foreigners when their dealings or presence appears to compromise its security cannot be contested."

3. Goodwin-Gill[81] suggests that there are substantive as well as procedural limitations upon the power to expel aliens:

State practice accepts that expulsion is justified:

(*a*) for entry in breach of law;
(*b*) for breach of the conditions of admission;
(*c*) for involvement in criminal activities;
(*d*) in the light of political and security considerations.

In determining whether its interests are adversely affected by the continuing presence of the alien, or whether there is a threat to "ordre public," the expelling State enjoys under international law a fairly wide margin of appreciation.

"Ordre public" remains a "general legal conception," the content of which is determined by law. Whether or not reasons of "ordre public" exist is open to impartial adjudication in the light of the prescribed function of expulsion and of the international obligations which each State owcs.

The principle of good faith and the requirement of justification, or "reasonable cause," demand that due consideration be given to the interests of the individual, including his basic human rights, his family, property, and other connections with the State of residence, and his legitimate expectations. These must be weighed against the competing claims of "ordre public."

4. On the expulsion of refugees, see the 1951 Convention relating to the Status of Refugees.[82] Although there is no duty to admit a refugee, contracting parties "shall not expel a refugee lawfully in their territory save on grounds of national security or public order" (Art. 32(1)). Further, a refugee, whether lawfully or unlawfully present, must not be returned "to the frontiers of territories where his life or freedom would be threatened on account of his race, religion, nationality, membership of a particular social group or political opinion." (Art. 33(1)).[83] It is arguable that the Convention now states rules of customary international law.[84]

5. With regard to the deportation of stateless persons, British practice has been expressed as follows:

---

[80] *Great Britain* v. *Belgium*, 6 B.D.I.L. 147 (1898).
[81] *Op. cit.* at p. 403, n. 76, above, p. 262. As to procedure, he suggests that the expulsion must be in accordance with the local law and not arbitrary: *ibid.* p. 263.
[82] 189 U.N.T.S. 150; U.K.T.S. 39 (1954), Cmd. 9171. In force 1954. On December 31, 1981, there were 89 parties, including the U.K. See also the 1967 Protocol, 606 U.N.T.S. 267, Cmnd. 3906, to which there were 87 parties on the same date, including the U.K. A refugee is defined, Article 1A(2), as amended by Article 1A(2), 1967 Protocol, as a person who "owing to well-founded fear of being persecuted for reasons of race, religion, nationality, membership of a particular social group or political opinion, is outside the country of his nationality and is unable or, owing to such fear, is unwilling to avail himself of the protection of that country, or who, not having a nationality and being outside the country of his former habitual residence is unable or, owing to such fear, is unwilling to return to it."
[83] This is unless he is reasonably suspected of being a security risk or, having been finally convicted of a particularly serious crime, constitutes a danger to the community: Article 33(2).
[84] See Goodwin-Gill, *op. cit.* at p. 403, n. 76, above, p. 141.

H.M. Government observe the principle that an alien should not be deported except to the country of which he is a national. Accordingly, it is not the practice to deport stateless aliens resident in the United Kingdom.[85]

6. The admission and expulsion of aliens is regulated by a number of bilateral and multilateral treaties. The 1962 Anglo-Japanese Treaty of Commerce, Establishment and Navigation,[86] for example, reads:

Nationals of one High Contracting Party shall be accorded, with respect to entry into, residence in and departure from any territory of the other, treatment not less favourable than that accorded to the nationals of any other foreign country.

See also the European Covention on Establishment 1955.[87] The European Communities allow freedom of movement for employment for nationals of member states.[88]

7. In a press release dated May 21, 1951,[89] the United States Department of State expressed its concern "over the continued denial by Chinese Communist authorities of exit permits to certain Americans, including a number of Shanghai businessmen, some of whom have been endeavouring for over a year to leave China." It continued: "Arbitrary refusal to permit aliens to depart from a country is of course a violation of the elementary principles of international law and practice."

(b) *Of Nationals*[90]

R. v. IMMIGRATION OFFICER, ex p. THAKRAR

[1974] Q.B. 684. Court of Appeal

The applicant was born in Uganda of Indian parents. When, in 1972, Uganda expelled all Asian nationals who had not taken Ugandan citizenship, most of the applicant's family went to India. The applicant went to Austria where he stayed for a year before flying to London, to join a brother. When the immigration authorities, acting under the Immigration Act 1971, refused him admission, he sought in this application for *certiorari, mandamus,* and *habeas corpus* to establish his right of admission under international law (and hence United Kingdom law) as a British protected person. The Court of Appeal found that, although born a British protected person, he had registered as a Ugandan national and so he lost his British status. The following extracts are on the international law argument put to the Court. The appeal was unanimously dismissed.

LORD DENNING M.R. Sir Dingle Foot, on behalf of Pravinlal [Thakrar], raises this fundamental point: let us assume for the time being that Pravinlal is, as he asserts, a British protected person. Sir Dingle says that as such he is a British national just as much as a citizen of the United Kingdom and Colonies. As a British national, if he is expelled from the land where he is living, he is entitled as of right to come into the United Kingdom. This right, says Sir Dingle, is given by international law: and international law, he says, is part of the law of the land. It is incorporated into it and is to be enforced by the courts unless it is

---

[85] L.N.O.J. 1934, p. 373. This remains British practice.
[86] U.K.T.S. 17 (1963), Cmnd. 1979, Art. 3(1).
[87] U.K.T.S. 1 (1971), Cmnd. 4573. In force 1965. On February 15, 1982, there were 11 parties, including the U.K.
[88] See Hartley, *E.E.C. Immigration Law* (1978), and Wyatt and Dashwood, *The Substantive Law of the E.E.C.* (1980), Chap. 13.
[89] 8 Whiteman 874.
[90] This subject, which does not properly come within this section, is dealt with here for convenience.

excluded by Parliament. To support this claim in international law, Sir Dingle Foot quoted *Oppenheim's International Law,* 8th ed. (1955), vol. 1, 645–646: "The home state of expelled persons is bound to receive them on the home territory."

To support his assertion that international law is part of the law of the land, Sir Dingle quoted Sir William Blackstone in his *Commentaries,* 17th ed. (1830), Book IV, p. 67, and Lord Mansfield in *Heathfield* v. *Chilton* (1767) 4 Burr. 2016. They said that the law of nations is "part of the law of the land." But they were speaking of the law of nations, and then only of that part of it which was universally accepted and known for certain, such as the immunity of ambassadors. They were not speaking of rules which were not universally accepted or known for certain. In my opinion, the rules of international law only become part of our law in so far as they are accepted and adopted by us. I would follow the words of Lord Atkin in *Chung Chi Cheung* v. *The King* [1939] A.C. 160, 167–168.[91]

Test it by reference to the very point we have to consider here: the mass expulsion of Asians from Uganda. International law has never had to cope with such a problem. None of the jurists, so far as I can discover, has considered it. The statement in *Oppenheim* is all very well when one is considering a home state which is a *self-contained* country with no overseas territories or protectorates. If one of its citizens goes to a foreign country and is expelled from it, the home state may well be bound to accept him on his home territory if he has nowhere else to go. But that rule does not apply when the home state is an outgoing country with far-flung commitments abroad, such as the United Kingdom has or recently did have. Take the class of persons with whom we are here concerned—British protected persons. They are said to be British nationals, but they are not British subjects. These number, or used to number, many millions. They were not born here. They have never lived here. They live thousands of miles away in countries which have no connection with England except that they were once British protectorates. Is it to be said that by international law every one of them has a right if expelled to come into these small islands? Surely not. This country would not have room for them. It is not as if it was only one or two coming. They come not in single files "but in battalions." Mass expulsions have never hitherto come within the cognisance of international law. To my mind, there is no rule of international law by which we may have recourse. There is no rule by which we are bound to receive them.

Even in regard to self-contained countries, however, the rule of international law is only a rule between two states. It is not a rule as between an individual and a state. The expelling state—if it had a good case—might call upon the home state to receive the person whom it expelled. But the individual could not pray the rule in aid for his own benefit. Moreover, the rule would only apply if he had nowhere else to go. If he went to Austria, as Pravinlal did, the rule would not apply to him; or, if he could go to India, where his wife and children are, the rule would not apply to him. So even that rule of international law would not avail Pravinlal here.

ORR L.J. . . . it is common ground (see *per* Lord Atkin in *Chung Chi Cheung* v. *The King* [1939] A.C. 160, 167–168) that a rule of international law

[91] Above, p. 64. Lord Denning takes a different view: see *Trendtex Trading Corp.* v. *Central Bank of Nigeria,* above, p. 258.

cannot be treated as incorporated into English municipal law where to do so would be inconsistent with the provisions of a statute. In the present case it is, in my judgment, clear beyond any doubt that the right which the applicant claims under international law is in conflict with the opening words of section 3(1) of the Immigration Act, 1971, which provides as follows: "Except as otherwise provided by or under this Act, where a person is not a patrial—(a) he shall not enter the United Kingdom unless given leave to do so. . . ." . . . Before this court Mr. Slynn claimed that the obligation is owed, not to the individual expelled, but towards all other states and is restricted to the receiving of a national who has nowhere else to go. . . . On the whole of the argument I have not been satisfied that the obligation under international law goes beyond these limits and I am inclined, although it is unnecessary to decide the point, to accept Mr. Slynn's contention that the rule came into being as a necessary corollary of the recognition by international law of a state's right not to accept aliens into its territory if it does not wish to do so.

Lawton L.J. delivered a concurring judgment.

Notes[92]

1. When Kenya and Uganda became independent, some East African Asians chose (as, exceptionally, the constitutional arrangements for independence allowed them to do) to remain citizens of the United Kingdom and colonies or British protected persons[93] and not to take the nationality of the newly independent state. This possibility was provided because of the fears of such persons for the treatment that they would receive within the new states; it was understood that as United Kingdom citizens or protected persons they would have a right of entry into the United Kingdom if need be. By the Commonwealth Immigrants Act 1968 (now the Immigration Act 1971), United Kingdom citizens and British protected persons who did not, mainly by birth or ancestry, have certain defined ties with the United Kingdom lost their right of entry into the United Kingdom in English law and were made the subject of a system of controlled entry. In consequence, a large number of East African Asians who *voluntarily* left Kenya and Uganda after the 1968 Act came into force were refused entry. When, in 1972, Uganda *expelled* all East African Asians who were not Ugandan nationals, the United Kingdom acknowledged and acted upon an international law obligation to admit them. The Lord Chancellor (Lord Hailsham) stated:

> If I may now turn to the position in international law more generally, the Attorney General, acting in his capacity as the professional legal advisor to the Government, and not, as quite improperly suggested, instigated by his political colleagues, advised us that in international law a State is under a duty as between other States to accept in its territories those of its nationals who have nowhere else to go. If a citizen of the United Kingdom is expelled, as I think illegally from Uganda, and is not accepted for settlement elsewhere, we could be required by any State where he then was to accept him.[94]

---

[92] See Akehurst, 38 M.L.R. 72 (1975) and Sharma & Wooldridge, 23 I.C.L.Q. 397 (1974). For the *Eastern African Cases* under the European Convention on Human Rights, see below, p. 491.

[93] Under the British Nationality Act 1981, the status of citizen of the U.K. and Colonies is abolished. The Act provides for three kinds of citizenship: British citizenship (based on links with the U.K.); British Dependent Territories citizenship (links with existing colonies, etc.); and British Overseas citizenship (links with former colonies, etc., such as Uganda). The status of a British Protected Person remains. Persons within all of these categories are British nationals for international law purposes.

[94] *Hansard*, H.L., Vol. 335, col. 497. September 14, 1972.

Was this an instance of state practice with the Court of Appeal might have been expected to have taken into account in formulating the extent of the international law duty to admit expelled nationals? Was the refusal to admit East African Asians who had *voluntarily* left Kenya and Uganda a breach of customary international law? In *Van Duyn* v. *Home Office*,[95] the European Court of Justice stated that "it is a principle of international law . . . that a State is precluded from refusing to its own nationals the right of entry or residence." To whom is this duty owed? All states?[96]

2. On the *expulsion* of nationals, Weiss states:

> As between national and State of nationality the question of the right of sojourn is not a question of international law. It may, however, become a question bearing on the relations between States. The expulsion of nationals forces other States to admit aliens, but, according to the accepted principles of international law, the admission of aliens is in the discretion of each State. . . . It follows that the expulsion of a national may only be carried out with the consent of the State to whose territory he is to be expelled, and that the State of nationality is under a duty towards other States to receive its nationals back on its territory.[97]

See also Article 13 of the Universal Declaration of Human Rights 1948,[98] Article 12 of the International Covenant on Civil and Political Rights 1966,[99] and Article 2 of the 4th Protocol to the European Convention on Human Rights.[1]

3. In 1976, the British Government withdrew the passports of United Kingdom citizens who had fought as mercenaries in the Angolan war of independence. "The Foreign Office said that these will not be returned, and that future applications will be refused unless the men sign a declaration they they will not work as mercenaries."[2] Can a state prevent its nationals from leaving its territory (a) generally or (b) for certain purposes?[3] Are Russian restrictions on emigration to Israel consistent with international law?[4]

(v) THE ADMINISTRATION OF JUSTICE

HAGUE CODIFICATION CONFERENCE: THE BRITISH GOVERNMENT'S REPLY

L.N.Doc. C. 75, M. 69, 1929. V, pp. 44, 49

In preparation for the Hague Codification Conference of 1930, governments were asked by the Conference Preparatory Committee to reply to certain "Points" on state responsibility. The following is the British reply to Point IV on "acts relating to the operation of tribunals."

Courts capable of administering justice effectively for the protection and enforcement of the rights of private persons constitute a necessary part of the machinery of a State.

---

[95] [1974] E.C.R. 1337. The statement was made in the context of freedom of movement for employment, not expulsion from another state.

[96] See Goodwin-Gill, *op. cit.* p. 403, no. 76, above, p. 137.

[97] *Nationality and Statelessness in International Law* (2nd ed., 1979), pp. 45–46. Footnote omitted.

[98] Below, p. 534.

[99] *Loc. cit.* at p. 541, below.

[1] Below, p. 478. [2] *The Times*, February 20, 1976.

[3] See Torovsky, 4 Jo.I.C.J. 63 (1962–63). On the law concerning passports, see Turack, *The Passport in International Law* (1972). On the United Kingdom position, see Williams, 23 I.C.L.Q. 642 (1974).

[4] For an account of the facts, see Schroeter, *The Last Exodus* (1974).

1. The State is responsible if it refuses to give foreigners access to these courts for the protection and enforcement of their rights.

2. If the decisions of the courts are inconsistent with the treaty obligations or the international duties of the State, the State is responsible.

3. A State is responsible if it is established that there has been unconscionable delay on the part of the courts.

4. If the courts of justice established by a State give erroneous decisions which can be shown to be prompted by ill will against foreigners as such, or as nationals of a particular country, the State is responsible. It has failed to organise courts of justice capable of administering justice effectively for the protection and enforcement of the rights of such foreigners and is bound to make reparation.

5. The State is not responsible merely because a decision given in the courts is erroneous. But an erroneous decision on the part of a court of justice may engage the responsibility of the State if it is:

(a) so erroneous that no properly constituted court could honestly have arrived at such a decision;
(b) due to corruption;
(c) due to pressure from the executive organs of the Government;
(d) caused by procedure so faulty as to exclude all reasonable hope of just decisions.

The above enumeration is not intended to be exhaustive.

Note

As stated above an erroneous decision of a municipal court in interpreting its own municipal law is not by itself a violation of international law. See, for example, the Law Officers' Report in *Mr. Lindsay's Case*:

> There is no evidence of any corrupt judicial proceeding. The Judge may have been wrong in his law, the jury inconsistent in their finding of facts—I should rather incline to the opinion, as at present advised, that such was the case; but such untoward incidents in the administration of justice are not confined to the Courts of Portugal, or even unknown to those of this country. It is to be hoped that these miscarriages as to law and facts, if such they be, will be corrected by the Court of Appeal to which Mr. Lindsay has resorted.
>
> . . . there is at present no adequate ground for any interference, strictly speaking, on the part of Her Majesty's Government; . . .[5]

POPE CASE

8 Whiteman 709

This extract is from a 1958 United States Department of State Memorandum on "Legal Problems Involved in the Detention and Trial of Allan L. Pope in Indonesia." Pope, an American national, was tried by an Indonesian tribunal for offences arising out of acts committed while he was employed by rebels against the Indonesian Government. He was represented at his trial by an Indonesian lawyer chosen by the Indonesian Government and accepted by him. He was found guilty and sentenced to death.

. . . The right to the assistance of counsel . . . has been considered to be one of the fundamental rights protected by an international standard. The deriva-

[5] 6 B.D.I.L. 289 (1862).

tive or corollary implications of this right are a subject of difference among States. Some of these implications, though, seem clearly necessary for effective exercise of the right to the assistance of counsel. For example, this right implies the assistance of a diligent and effective counsel capable of conducting an adequate defense. Similarly, the right of the accused to counsel should include the opportunity of securing counsel of his choice, where the accused has the financial capability to make such a choice. The right to counsel also implies the right that his counsel should be in a position to prepare adequately a defense and to insure fair conduct of the trial. This should mean that at some point the accused's counsel has a right to access to his client prior to the trial and the opportunity to confer privately with him.

As a necessary implication of the right to the assistance of counsel, the United States has maintained that its nationals are entitled to the opportunity of choosing their own counsel in foreign courts, while the United States has secured this right to all persons in American courts. The choice of counsel, however, is not an unrestricted one, but is subject to a reasonable exercise of the police power by a State in prescribing the qualifications for the appearance of counsel in its courts. In terms of his procedural rights under international law, an alien is not entitled to demand the assistance of counsel, foreign or national, who otherwise would not be entitled to appear in the courts of that country. . . . The more difficult question is the point at which an alien prisoner is entitled to the assistance of counsel during pre-trial detention. In all countries, even the United States,[6] there is a certain period of time during which the authorities are permitted to question a prisoner without allowing him the assistance of counsel. At some point, however, denial of the assistance of counsel during pre-trial detention prejudices the right to make an effective defense and enjoy the advocacy of counsel at trial, as all defense efforts require some preparation. Thus, at the point where the reasonable objectives of a foreign government in investigating the crime have been completed, the United States would appear to be justified in requesting that its nationals be permitted the assistance of counsel, so that an adequate period of time is provided for preparation of a defense. . . .

The United States has maintained that private communication with its nationals is essential to their effective protection. The purpose of a visit by a consular or diplomatic officer is to determine whether an alien prisoner is receiving decent, sanitary, and humane treatment during his detention and the investigation of his alleged crime. Frequently prisoners are unwilling to complain of maltreatment in the presence of their captors. Likewise, a visit from American authorities provides an alien prisoner with an opportunity to enjoy or safeguard other procedural rights protected by international law, such as the right to the assistance of counsel for his defense.

Note

With regard to communication with a consular officer, it was stated in the *Chevreau Claim*[7] that in customary international law:

> [i]n cases of arrest . . . the arrested person . . . [must be] given an opportunity . . . to communicate with the consul of his country if he requests it.

[6] *Ed.* But now see *Miranda* v. *Arizona*, 384 U.S. 436 (1966).

[7] *France* v. *Great Britain*, 2 R.I.A.A. 1113, at p. 1123 (1931). Translation in 27 A.J.I.L. 153, at p. 160 (1933).

In the *Firth Case,* Mrs. Firth, a British subject employed by the British Embassy in Warsaw, was arrested in 1949 on espionage charges. Poland, acting in accordance with Polish law applicable to all Polish and foreign defendants alike, refused to allow the British consul access to her until five days before the trial. The United Kingdom protested against "this violation of international usage."[8]

ROBERTS CLAIM

U.S. *v.* Mexico (1926)

U.S.-Mexican General Claims Commission: for the Commissioners, see above, p. 389.
4 R.I.A.A.77

Opinion of the Commission

1. This claim is presented by the United States of America in behalf of Harry Roberts, an American citizen who, it is alleged in the Memorial, was arbitrarily and illegally arrested by Mexican authorities, who held him prisoner for a long time in contravention of Mexican law and subjected him to cruel and inhumane treatment throughout the entire period of confinement. . . .

6. The Commission is not called upon to reach a conclusion whether Roberts committed the crime with which he was charged.[9] The determination of that question rested with the Mexican judiciary, and it is distinct from the question whether the Mexican authorities had just cause to arrest Roberts and to bring him to trial. Aliens of course are obliged to submit to proceedings properly instituted against them in conformity with local laws. In the light of the evidence presented in the case the Commission is of the opinion that the Mexican authorities had ample grounds to suspect that Harry Roberts had committed a crime and to proceed against him as they did. The Commission therefore holds that the claim is not substantiated with respect to the charge of illegal arrest.

7. In order to pass upon the complaint with reference to an excessive period of imprisonment, it is necessary to consider whether the proceedings instituted against Roberts while he was incarcerated exceeded reasonable limits within which an alien charged with crime may be held in custody pending the investigation of the charge against him. Clearly there is no definite standard prescribed by international law by which such limits may be fixed. Doubtless an examination of local laws fixing a maximum length of time within which a person charged with crime may be held without being brought to trial may be useful in determining whether detention has been unreasonable in a given case. The Mexican Constitution of 1917, provides by its Article 20, section 8, that a person accused of crime "must be judged within four months if he is accused of a crime the maximum penalty for which may not exceed two years' imprisonment, and within one year if the maximum penalty is greater." From the judicial records presented by the Mexican Agent it clearly appears that there was a failure of compliance with this constitutional provision, since the proceedings were instituted on May 17, 1922, and that Roberts had not been brought to trial on December 16, 1923, the date when he was released. It was contended by the Mexican Agency that the delay was due to the fact that the accused repeatedly refused to name counsel to defend him, and that as a result of such refusal on his

---

[8] *Hansard*, H.C., Vol. 467, col. 30. July 11, 1949; 8 Whiteman 881.
[9] *Ed*. The crime was "assault upon a house." It was alleged that Roberts had, with other armed men, surrounded a house with a view to committing a crime therein.

part proceedings were to his advantage suspended in order that he might obtain satisfactory counsel to defend him. We do not consider that this contention is sound. There is evidence in the record that Roberts constantly requested the American Consul at Tampico to take steps to expedite the trial. . . . It was the duty of the Mexican Judge under Article 20, section 9, of the Mexican Constitution to appoint counsel to act for Roberts from the time of the institution of the proceedings against him. The Commission is of the opinion that preliminary proceedings could have been completed before the lapse of a year after the arrest of Roberts. Even though it may have been necessary to make use of rogatory letters to obtain the testimony of witnesses in different localities, it would seem that that could have been accomplished at least within six or seven months from the time of the arrest. In any event, it is evident in the light of provisions of Mexican law that Roberts was unlawfully held a prisoner without trial for at least seven months. . . . The Commission holds that an indemnity is due on the ground of unreasonably long detention.

8. With respect to the charge of ill-treatment of Roberts, it appears from evidence submitted by the American Agency that the jail in which he was kept was a room thirty-five feet long and twenty-feet wide with stone walls, earthen floor, straw roof, a single window, a single door and no sanitary accommodations, all the prisoners depositing their excrement in a barrel kept in a corner of the room; that thirty or forty men were at times thrown together in this single room; that the prisoners were given no facilities to clean themselves; that the room contained no furniture except that which the prisoners were able to obtain by their own means; that they were afforded no opportunity to take physical exercise; and that the food given them was scarce, unclean, and of the coarsest kind. The Mexican Agency did not present evidence disproving that such conditions existed in the jail. It was stated by the Agency that Roberts was accorded the same treatment as that given to all other persons, and with respect to the food Roberts received, it was observed in the Answer that he was given "the food that was believed necessary, and within the means of the municipality." All of the details given by Roberts in testimony which accompanies the Memorial with respect to the conditions of the jail are corroborated by a statement of the American Consul at Tampico who visited the jail. Facts with respect to equality of treatment of aliens and nationals may be important in determining the merits of a complaint of mistreatment of an alien. But such equality is not the ultimate test of the propriety of the acts of authorities in the light of international law. That test is, broadly speaking, whether aliens are treated in accordance with ordinary standards of civilization. We do not hesitate to say that the treatment of Roberts was such as to warrant an indemnity on the ground of cruel and inhumane imprisonment.

JANES CLAIM[10]

U.S. v. Mexico (1926)

U.S.-Mexican General Claims Commission: for the Commissioners, see above, p. 389.

4 R.I.A.A. 82

Opinion of the Commission

1. Claim is made by the United States of America in this case for losses and damages amounting to $25,000.00, which it is alleged in the Memorial were

[10] See Brierly (1928) 9 B.Y.I.L. 42.

"suffered on account of the murder, on or about July 10, 1918, at a mine near El Tigre, Sonora, Mexico, of Byron Everett Janes," an American citizen. The claim is presented, as stated in the Memorial, "on behalf of [the deceased's wife and children] . . .

17. Carbajal, the person who killed Janes, was well known in the community where the killing took place. Numerous persons witnessed the deed. The slayer, after killing his victim, left on foot. There is evidence that a Mexican police magistrate was informed of the shooting within five minutes after it took place. The official records with regard to the action taken to apprehend and punish the slayer speak for themselves. Eight years have elapsed since the murder, and it does not appear from the records that Carbajal has been apprehended at this time. Our conclusions to the effect that the Mexican authorities did not take proper steps to apprehend and punish the slayer of Janes is based on the record before us consisting of evidence produced by both Governments.

19. . . . At times international awards have held that, if a State shows serious lack of diligence in apprehending and/or punishing culprits, its liability is a derivative liability, assuming the character of some kind of complicity with the perpetrator himself and rendering the State responsible for the very consequences of the individual's misdemeanor. . . . The reasons upon which such finding of complicity is usually based in cases in which a Government could not possibly have prevented the crime, is that the non-punishment must be deemed to disclose some kind of approval of what has occurred, especially so if the Government has permitted the guilty parties to escape or has remitted the punishment by granting either pardon or amnesty.

20. A reasoning based on presumed complicity may have some sound foundation in cases of non-prevention where a Government knows of an *intended* injurious crime, might have averted it, but for some reason constituting its liability did not do so. The present case is different; it is one of non-repression. Nobody contends either that the Mexican Government might have prevented the murder of Janes, or that it acted in any other form of connivance with the murderer. The international delinquency in this case is one of its own specific type, separate from the private delinquency of the culprit. The culprit is liable for having killed or murdered an American national; the Government is liable for not having measured up to its duty of diligently prosecuting and properly punishing the offender. . . . The damage caused by the culprit is the damage caused to Janes' relatives by Janes' death; the damage caused by the Government's negligence is the damage resulting from the non-punishment of the murderer. If the murderer had not committed his delinquency—if he had not slain Janes—Janes (but for other occurrences) would still be alive and earning the livelihood for his family; if the Government had not committed its delinquency—if it had apprehended and punished Carbajal—Janes' family would have been spared indignant neglect and would have had an opportunity of subjecting the murderer to a civil suit. Even if the non-punishment were conceived as some kind of approval—which in the Commission's view is doubtful—still approving of a crime has never been deemed identical with being an accomplice to that crime; and even if non-punishment of a murderer really amounted to complicity in the murder, still it is not permissible to treat this derivative and remote liability not as an attenuate form of responsibility, but as just as serious as if the Government had perpetrated the killing with its own hands. The results of the old conception are unsatisfactory in two directions. If

the murdered man had been poor, or if, in a material sense, his death had meant little to his relatives, the satisfaction given these relatives should be confined to a small sum, though the grief and the indignity suffered may have been great. On the other hand, if the old theory is sustained and adhered to, it would, in cases like the present one, be to the pecuniary benefit of a widow and her children if a Government did *not* measure up to its international duty of providing justice, because in such a case the Government would repair the pecuniary damage caused by the killing, whereas she practically never would have obtained such reparation if the State had succeeded in apprehending and punishing the culprit. . . .

23. Once this old theory, however, is thrown off, we should take care not to go to the opposite extreme. It would seem a fallacy to sustain that, if in case of non-punishment by the Government it is not liable for the crime itself, then it can only be responsible, in a punitive way, to a sister Government, not to a claimant. There again, the solution in other cases of improper governmental action shows the way out. It shows that, apart from reparation or compensation for material losses, claimants always have been given substantial satisfaction for serious dereliction of duty on the part of a Government. . . . The indignity done the relatives of Janes by non-punishment in the present case is, as that in other cases of improper governmental action, a damage directly caused to an individual by a Government. If this damage is different from the damage caused by the killing, it is quite as different from the wounding of the national honor and national feeling of the State of which the victim was a national. . . .

26. Giving careful consideration to all elements involved, the Commission holds that an amount of $12,000, without interest, is not excessive as satisfaction for the personal damage caused the claimants by the non-apprehension and non-punishment of the murderer of Janes.

Note
See also the *Noyes Claim*, below p. 418.

(vi) DETENTION AND PHYSICAL INJURY TO THE PERSON OR TO PROPERTY

QUINTANILLA CLAIM

Mexico *v*. U.S. (1926)

U.S.-Mexican General Claims Commission: for the Commissioners, see above p. 389.
4 R.I.A.A. 101

Opinion of the Commission

1. This claim is presented by the United Mexican States against the United States in behalf of F. Quintanilla and M. I. Perez de Quintanilla, Mexican nationals, father and mother of Alejo Quintanilla, a young man, who was killed on or about July 16, 1922, not far from Edinburg, Hidalgo County, Texas, U.S.A. On July 15, 1922, about 5 p.m., said Alejo Quintanilla in a lonely spot had lassoed a girl of fourteen years, Agnes Casey, who was on horseback, and thrown her from the horse; she screamed, and the young Mexican fled. She told the occurrence to her father, Tom Casey with whom Quintanilla had been employed some time before; the father the next morning went to lodge his

complaint with the authorities, first to Edinburg (the County seat), where he did not find the sheriff, and then to Donna, where he found the deputy sheriff, one Sam A. Bernard. According to the record, this deputy sheriff with three other men, whose names are not mentioned, went to Quintanilla's house, took him from it, and the deputy sheriff with one Walter Weaver placed him in a motor car and drove with him, first to Casey's house, where they put on a new tire, and then in the direction of Edinburg to take him to the county jail. On July 18, 1922, about noon, Quintanilla's corpse was found near the side of this road, some three miles from Edinburg, traces showing that he had been taken there in a motor car. Bernard and Weaver were accused by the Mexican Consul at Hidalgo, Texas, and were accordingly arrested, but released on bail; Bernard's appointment as a deputy sheriff was cancelled by his sheriff on July 22, 1922. The public prosecutor made investigations and submitted the case to the Grand Jury, but the Grand Jury deferred it from 1922 to 1923, from 1923 to 1924, and never took action upon it. . . .

2. It appears from the record that Quintanilla was taken into custody on July 16, 1922, by a deputy sheriff of the State of Texas, to put him at the disposal of the judicial officers; it is left uncertain whether this official was provided with any authorization to take Quintanilla from his house and arrest him. The United States Government never reported what this deputy sheriff did with Quintanilla after he had taken him under custody. The young man apparently never reached the county jail. The deputy sheriff may have changed his mind and set him at liberty, and after that Quintanilla may have been murdered by an unknown person. An enemy of Quintanilla may have come up and taken him from the car. The companion of the deputy sheriff, who was not an official, may have killed Quintanilla; or the two custodians may have acted in self-defence. The United States Government has been silent on all of this. The only thing the record clearly shows is that Quintanilla was taken into custody by a State official, and that he never was delivered to any jail. The first question before this Commission, therefore, is whether under international law these circumstances present a case for which a Government must be held liable.

3. The Commission does not hesitate to answer in the affirmative. The most notable parallel in international law relates to war prisoners, hostages, and interned members of a belligerent army and navy. . . . The case before this Commission is analogous. A foreigner is taken into custody by a state official. It would go too far to hold that the Government is liable for everything which may befall him. But it has to account for him. The Government can be held liable if it is proven that it has treated him cruelly, harshly, unlawfully; so much the more it is liable if it can say only that it took him into custody—either in jail or in some other place and form—and that it ignores what happened to him.

4. The question then arises whether this duty to account for a man in Governmental custody is modified by the fact that the custodian himself is accused of having killed his prisoner and, as an accused, can not be made to testify against himself. The two things clearly are separate. If the Government is obligated to state what happened to the man in its custody, its officials are bound to inform their Governments. It might be that the custodians themselves perish in a calamity together with the men in their custody, and therefore can not furnish any information. But if they are alive, and are silent, the Government has to bear the consequences. The Commission holds, therefore, that

under international law . . . the respondent Government is liable for the damages originating in this act of a State official and resulting in injustice.

Note

In the *Turner Claim*,[11] the United States-Mexican General Claims Commission, in finding Mexico responsible for the death of a United States national who became ill while detained contrary to Mexican law in a Mexican jail pending trial, said:

> Though there is no convincing proof that his death was caused by his treatment in prison, there can be no doubt but that, if at liberty, he would have been able to take better measures for restoring his health than he could do either in prison, or in a prison hospital. If having a man in custody obligates a government to account for him, having a man in *illegal* custody doubtless renders a government liable for dangers and disasters which would not have been his share, or in a less degree, if he had been at liberty.

THE OESLNER AND SELLERS CASE

8 Whiteman 880

On July 31, 1949, two American students on a bicycling holiday in Europe accidentally entered the Soviet Zone of Germany. They were arrested and detained for eight weeks, including two weeks in solitary confinement, before being released. They were not charged with any offence. The following is an extract from a United States note of October 9, 1949, to the U.S.S.R.

. . . two American students, in Europe as tourists, whose identity and harmless purposes could never have been long in doubt, have been treated as criminals, subject to long incarceration, and not allowed to communicate with their families or their government. This treatment the United States Government finds to be in shocking contravention to the most elementary standards of international decency. The reaction of the Soviet authorities to the incursion of a pair of youthful bicyclists is the more astonishing as they can scarcely have been considered to be a serious threat to the security of the ample Soviet occupation army in Germany. . . .

The Government of the United States raises the most energetic protest against such actions by the Soviet authorities in Germany, and expects that those Soviet officials who are responsible for these acts will be punished. The Government of the United States further insists that the elementary rights of its citizens be observed in the future in accordance with the international comity which governs the conduct of all civilized states.

HARVARD DRAFT CONVENTION ON THE INTERNATIONAL RESPONSIBILITY OF STATES FOR INJURIES TO ALIENS 1961

55 A.J.I.L. 548 (1961)

Article 9

1. Deliberate destruction of or damage to the property of an alien is wrongful, unless it was required by circumstances of urgent necessity not reasonably admitting of any other course of action.

---

[11] *U.S. v. Mexico*, 4 R.I.A.A. 278, at p. 281 (1927).

2. A destruction of the property of an alien resulting from the judgment of a competent tribunal or from the action of the competent authorities of the State in the maintenance of public order, health, or morality shall not be considered wrongful, provided there has not been:

(a) a clear and discriminatory violation of the law of the State concerned;

(b) a violation of any provision of Articles 6 to 8 of this Convention;

(c) an unreasonable departure from the principles of justice recognized by the principal legal systems of the world; or

(d) an abuse of the powers specified in this paragraph for the purpose of depriving an alien of his property.

Notes

1. The Harvard Draft Convention is, like its predecessors,[12] an unofficial document prepared under the auspices of the Harvard Law School. The purpose of the draft Convention "is to codify with some particularity the standards established by international law for the protection of aliens and thereby to obviate, as far as possible, the necessity of looking to customary international law."[13] In some respects, it engages in "progressive development" rather than "codification" (in the terminology of the International Law Commission).

2. The explanatory note to Article 9 reads:

The Convention distinguishes a destruction of property or the damaging of property from an uncompensated taking of property or the deprivation of the use or enjoyment of property.[14] . . . Examples of destruction of or damage to property which would be wrongful under this Article would be: the deliberate burning by the police of a car owned by an alien; or physical damage to mercantile premises owned by an alien enterprise resulting from the intentional acts of employees of the State, whether such persons were acting under orders of higher authority or on their own initiative but within the scope of their function.

There is excepted from the scope of wrongful destruction of or damage to property such action as was required by circumstances of urgent necessity. The classic example of such destruction or damage is the tearing down of buildings in order to prevent the spread of fire. The destruction of property in actual combat operations during an international conflict or the destruction or damaging of property of an alien in order to interdict its use by the enemy typify legitimate destruction of property in time of war.[15]

(vii) PROTECTION OF ALIENS

NOYES CLAIM

U.S. *v.* Panama (1933)

General Claims Arbitration: Van Heeckeren, Presiding Commissioner; Root, U.S. Commissioner; Alfaro, Panamanian Commissioner. 6 R.I.A.A. 308

Opinion of the Commission

In this case a claim is made against the Republic of Panama by the United States of America on behalf of Walter A. Noyes, who was born, and has ever

[12] See, *e.g.* the Harvard Draft Convention on Jurisdiction with Respect to Crime 1935, above, p. 211.

[13] 55 A.J.I.L. 547 (1961). The two *rapporteurs* were Professors Sohn and Baxter.

[14] *Ed.* The latter is dealt with in Article 10 of the Draft Convention, see below, p. 423.

[15] 55 A.J.I.L. 551–552 (1961).

remained, an American citizen. The sum of $1,683 is claimed as an indemnity for the personal injuries and property losses sustained by Mr. Noyes through the attacks made upon him on June 19, 1927, in, and in the neighborhood of, the village of Juan Díaz, situated not far from Panama City. The claim is based upon an alleged failure to provide to the claimant adequate police protection, to exercise due diligence in the maintenance of order and to take adequate measures to apprehend and punish the aggressors. . . .

The village of Juan Díaz has only a small population, but on June 19, 1927, several hundreds of adherents of the party then in control of the Government had gathered there for a meeting. The police on the spot had not been increased for the occasion; it consisted of the usual three policemen stationed there. In the course of the day the authorities in Panama City learned that the crowd in Juan Díaz had become unruly under the influence of liquor. The chief of the police, General Pretelt, thereupon drove thither with reinforcements. . . .

At about 3.00 p.m. the claimant passed through the village in his automobile, on his return to Panama City from a trip to the Tapia River bridge. In the center of the village a crowd blocked the road and Mr. Noyes stopped and sounded his horn, whereupon the crowd slowly opened. Whilst he was progressing very slowly through it, he had to stop again, because somebody lurched against the car and fell upon the running-board. Thereupon members of the crowd smashed the windows of the car and attacked Mr. Noyes, who was stabbed in the wrist and hurt by fragments of glass. A police officer who had been giving orders that gangway should be made for the automobile, but who had not before been able to reach the car, then sprang upon the running-board and remained there, protecting the claimant and urging him to get away as quickly as possible. He remained with Mr. Noyes, until the latter had got clear of the crowd. At some distance from Juan Díaz the claimant was further attacked by members of the same crowd, who pursued him in a bus and who forced him to drive his car off the road and into a ditch. He was then rescued by General Pretelt who, having come from the opposite direction, had, after reaching the plaza of the village, returned upon his way in order to protect Mr. Noyes against his pursuers.

The facts related above show that in both instances the police most actively protected the claimant against his assailants and that in the second instance the protection was due to the fact, that the authorities sent reinforcements from Panama City upon learning that the conditions in Juan Díaz rendered assistance necessary. The contention of the American Agent however is, that the Panamanian Government incurred a liability under international law, because its officials had not taken the precaution of increasing for that day the police force at Juan Díaz, although they knew some time in advance that the meeting would assemble there.

The mere fact that an alien has suffered at the hands of private persons an aggression, which could have been averted by the presence of a sufficient police force on the spot, does not make a government liable for damages under international law. There must be shown special circumstances from which the responsibility of the authorities arises: either their behavior in connection with the particular occurrence, or a general failure to comply with their duty to maintain order, to prevent crimes or to prosecute and punish criminals.

There were no such circumstances in the present case. Accordingly a lack of protection has not been established. . . .

The claim is disallowed.

Note

See also the *Janes Case*, above, p. 413.

TEXAS CATTLE CLAIMS

American-Mexican Claims Commission[16] (1948). 8 Whiteman 749

Opinion of the Commission

These claims, commonly known as the Texas cattle claims, arose during the period from the close of the American Civil War to about 1878. The principal ground of complaint, as presented by the claimant government, relates to raids from Mexico and thefts of cattle and horses of American citizens in Texas. The claims are 462 in number. The total amount claimed is $53,275,890.50. . . .

It appearing from the record that the raids during the period in question were systematic and continuous and not isolated sporadic incidents; that they were openly and notoriously organized in Mexico; that the Mexican authorities failed to take steps to prevent them or to prevent in Mexico the open traffic in stolen Texas livestock; that, on the contrary, high Mexican Military officials and other officials were implicated in such raids and were profiting therefrom; and that, although the Mexican Government was aware of this condition of affairs and of the nature of the action necessary to put an end to such condition, it neglected, for a period of several years to take the necessary action, it seems clear that the raids which took place during the period in question were made possible by the conduct of the Mexican Government. Each raid was not an isolated raid but was a part of a general lawless condition which, throughout said period, was permanent and, as noted, was made possible by the action of the Mexican authorities. It follows, therefore, in the opinion of this Commission, that, if a claimant proves that his losses were caused by a raid or raids from Mexico during the period in question he will thereby have established liability on the part of the Mexican Government for the same.

The general legal grounds, therefore, on which this Commission holds the Mexican Government liable are: (1) active participation of Mexican officials in the depredations; (2) permitting the use of Mexican territory as a base for wrongful operations against the United States and the citizens thereof, thus encouraging the wrongful acts; (3) negligence, over a long period of years, to prosecute criminals or otherwise to discourage or prevent the raids; and (4) failure to co-operate with the Government of the United States in the matter of terminating the condition in question.

Notes

1. In the *Mallen Case*,[17] where a Mexican consul had been injured by a private person in Texas, the United States-Mexican General Claims Commission stated:

[16] This was a U.S. national commission appointed to distribute moneys handed over to the U.S. by Mexico. It was required to decide "in accordance with the applicable principles of international law, justice and equity": Section 5 of the Settlement of U.S. Mexican Claims Act 1942. On "lump sum" settlement agreements, see below, p. 440.

[17] *U.S.* v. *Mexico*, 4 R.I.A.A. 173 (1927).

6. The question has been raised whether consuls are entitled to a "special protection" for their persons. The answer depends upon the meaning given these two words. If they should indicate that, apart from prerogatives extended to consuls either by treaty or by unwritten law, the Government of their temporary residence is bound to grant them other prerogatives not enjoyed by common residents (be it citizens or aliens), the answer is in the negative. But if "special protection" means that in executing the laws of the country, especially those concerning police and penal law, the Government should realize that foreign Governments are sensitive regarding the treatment accorded their representatives, and that therefore the Government of the consul's residence should exercise greater vigilance in respect to their security and safety, the answer as evidently shall be in the affirmative. . . . In this second sense it was rightly stated by the Committee of Jurists appointed by the League of Nations on the Corfu difficulties, in a report adopted on March 13, 1924: "The recognized public character of a foreigner and the circumstances in which he is present in its territory, entail upon the State a corresponding duty of special vigilance on his behalf." (*American Journal of International Law* 18, 1924, p. 543.)

2. On April 2, 1970, the West German Ambassador to Guatemala, Count von Spreti, was kidnapped in Guatemala City by the "Revolutionary Armed Forces," an extreme left wing guerrilla organisation. The organisation demanded the release of certain prisoners. Despite West German appeals, the Guatemalan Government refused the demand and Count von Spreti was found murdered on April 5. The West German Government withdrew its *charge d'affaires* from Guatemala in protest. It is reported as saying that the Guatemalan Government had "shown itself unable to give accredited diplomatic representatives necessary security,"[18] Had Guatemala violated international law? Note that earlier in 1970 the Guatemalan Government had released other prisoners in response to other kidnappings.

3. The Convention on the Prevention and Punishment of Crimes against Internationally Protected Persons, including Diplomatic Agents 1973[19] provides:

Article 2

1. The intentional commission of:

(*a*) a murder, kidnapping or other attack upon the person or liberty of an internationally protected person;

(*b*) a violent attack upon the official premises, the private accommodation or the means of transport of an internationally protected person likely to endanger his person or liberty;

(*c*) a threat to commit any such attack;

(*d*) an attempt to commit any such attack; and

(*e*) an act constituting participation as an accomplice in any such attack shall be made by each State Party a crime under its internal law.

2. Each State Party shall make these crimes punishable by appropriate penalties which take into account their grave nature.

3. Paragraphs 1 and 2 of this article in no way derogate from the obligations of States Parties under international law to take all appropriate measures to prevent other attacks on the person, freedom or dignity of an internationally protected person.

Article 3

1. Each State Party shall take such measures as may be necessary to establish its jurisdiction over the crimes set forth in article 2 in the following cases:

[18] *Keesing's Archives*, p. 23906.
[19] 13 I.L.M. 42 (1974); Misc. 19 (1975), Cmnd. 6176. In force 1977. On December 31, 1981, there were 54 contracting parties including the U.K. See the Internationally Protected Persons Act 1978. See Rozakis, 23 I.C.L.Q. 32 (1974) and Wood, *ibid*. 791.

(a) when the crime is committed in the territory of that State or on board a ship or aircraft registered in that State;

(b) when the alleged offender is a national of that State;

(c) when the crime is committed against an internationally protected person as defined in article 1 who enjoys his status as such by virtue of functions which he exercises on behalf of that State.

Each State Party shall likewise take such measures as may be necessary to establish its jurisdiction over these crimes in cases where the alleged offender is present in its territory and it does not extradite him pursuant to article 8 to any of the States mentioned in paragraph 1 of this article.

3. This Convention does not exclude any criminal jurisdiction exercised in accordance with internal law.

An "internationally protected person" includes heads of state and their accompanying families and any representative or official of a State or any official who, at the time when and in the place where a crime against him, his official premises, his private accommodation or his means of transport is committed, is entitled pursuant to international law to special protection from any attack on his person, freedom or dignity, as well as members of his family forming part of his household.[20]

4. On the special duty to protect the premises of diplomatic missions and agents, see above, p. 274.

(viii) EXPROPRIATION[21]

Note

Expropriation, or the compulsory taking of private property by the state, is a phenomenon that has become especially important in international law with the spread of socialism and the emergence of the post-colonial state. If the typical nineteenth century case was the occasional taking of the property of a single foreigner in the context of a particular project or dispute, today it is the general expropriation of foreign property or of foreign property in certain areas of the economy as part of a concerted plan to improve a state's economy, usually by non-capitalist means. It is normally in this last context that the twentieth century term "nationalisation" is used. This is not a term of art in international law.[22] It usually connotes the retention of ownership and use of the property by the state. Unfortunately, the political differences between capitalist and communist or socialist states coupled with the economic differences between developed and developing states have led to a situation in which there is little agreement on the rules on expropriation, as the following extracts show. Whereas it is generally agreed that expropriation may occur, developed states suggest that it must occur in accordance with an "international minimum standard" set by international law while developing states deny that this is so. In their opinion, the circumstances and conditions of expropriation are matters to be left largely to the expropriating state to regulate in its discretion under its law.

---

[20] Article 1.

[21] Among the extensive literature, see Brownlie, 162 *Hague Recueil* 255 (1979–I); Dolzer, 75 A.J.I.L. 553 (1981); Fatouros, *Government Guarantees to Foreign Investors* (1962); Friedmann, *Expropriation in International Law* (1953); Jimenez de Aréchega, 11 N.Y.U.J.I.L.P., p. 179 (1978); Lillich, ed., *The Valuation of Nationalised Property in International Law*, 3 vols. (1972–5); Schwarzenberger, *Foreign Investments and International Law* (1969); White, *Nationalisation of Foreign Property* (1961); Wortley, *Expropriation in Public International Law* (1959).

[22] Nor is it in English law: *Benin* v. *Whimster* [1976] Q.B. 297 (C.A.).

RESOLUTION ON PERMANENT SOVEREIGNTY OVER NATURAL RESOURCES 1962[23]

G.A. Resolution 1803 (XVII), G.A.O.R., 17th Session, Supp. 17, p. 15

The General Assembly

Declares that:

1. The right of peoples and nations to permanent sovereignty over their natural wealth and resources must be exercised in the interest of their national development and of the well-being of the people of the State concerned; . . .

3. In cases where authorization is granted, the capital imported and the earnings on that capital shall be governed by the terms thereof, by the national legislation in force, and by international law. The profits derived must be shared in the proportions freely agreed upon, in each case, between the investors and the recipient State, due care being taken to ensure that there is no impairment, for any reason, of that State's sovereignty over its natural wealth and resources;

4. Nationalization, expropriation or requistioning shall be based on grounds or reasons of public utility, security or the national interest which are recognized as overriding purely individual or private interests, both domestic and foreign. In such cases the owner shall be paid appropriate compensation in accordance with the rules in force in the State taking such measures in the exercise of its sovereignty and in accordance with international law. In any case where the question of compensation gives rise to a controversy, the national jurisdiction of the State taking such measures shall be exhausted. However, upon agreement by sovereign States and other parties concerned, settlement of the dispute should be made through arbitration or international adjudication; . . .

8. Foreign investment agreements freely entered into by, or between, sovereign States shall be observed in good faith; States and international organizations shall strictly and conscientiously respect the sovereignty of peoples and nations over their natural wealth and resources in accordance with the Charter and the principles set forth in the present resolution.

Notes

1. The resolution was adopted by 87 votes to 2, with 12 abstentions. France and South Africa voted against it; the Soviet bloc and some other states abstained.

2. The Resolution, which was considered in the *Texaco Case*, below, p. 434, "to reflect the state of customary international law" (para. 87), recognises the right to expropriate foreign property. But it does not indicate what amounts to expropriation. The 1961 Harvard Draft Convention, see above, p. 417, regards not only the taking of title to property but also various other—and often equally destructive—forms of interference with property rights as giving rise to responsibility under its expropriation provision (Art. 10).[24] The Explanatory Note to the Draft Convention states:

There are a variety of methods by which an alien natural or juridical person may have the use or enjoyment of his property limited by State action, even to the extent of the State's forcing the alien to dispose of his property at a price representing only a fraction of what its value would be had not the alien's use of it been subjected to interference by the State.

. . . A State may make it impossible for an alien to operate a factory which he owns by blocking the entrances on the professed ground of maintaining order. It may,

---

[23] See Gess, 13 I.C.L.Q. 398 (1964) and O'Keefe, 8 Jo.W.T.L. 239 (1974).
[24] On the meaning of "taking," see Christie (1962) 38 B.Y.I.L. 307.

through its labor legislation and labor courts, designedly set the wages of local employees of the enterprise at a prohibitively high level. If technical personnel are needed from outside the country, entry visas may be denied them. Essential replacement parts or machinery may be refused entrance, or allocations of foreign exchange may deliberately be denied with the purpose of making it impossible to import the requisite machinery. Any one of these measures . . . could make it impossible for the alien owner to use or enjoy his property. More direct interferences may also be imagined. The alien may simply be forbidden to employ a certain portion of a building which he occupies, either on a wholly arbitrary basis or on the authority of some asserted requirement of the local law. A government, while leaving ownership of an enterprise in the alien owner, might appoint conservators, managers, or inspectors who might interfere with the free use by the alien of its premises and its facilities. Or, simply by forbidding an alien to sell his property, a government could effectively deprive that property of its value.

Whether an interference with the use, enjoyment, or disposal of property constitutes a "taking" or a "taking of use" will be dependent upon the duration of the interference. Although a restriction on the use of property may purport to be temporary, there obviously comes a stage at which an objective observer would conclude that there is no immediate prospect that the owner will be able to resume the enjoyment of his property. Considerable latitude has been left to the adjudicator of the claim to determine what period of interference is unreasonable and when the taking therefore ceases to be temporary.

The unreasonableness of an interference with the use, enjoyment, or disposal of property must be determined in conformity with the general principles of law recognized by the principal legal systems of the world. No attempt has been made to particularize on the expression used in the text, since the matter seems one best worked out by international tribunals.[25]

The following instances of British practice are of interest in this connection. In 1964, the Indonesian Government took the following action against British commercial interests:

> Under Presidential Decree No. 6 of 1964, dated November 26, 1964, all British-owned commercial interests in Indonesia, including estates, industrial enterprises and commercial agencies, were placed under complete and direct Indonesian management and control. This comprehensive Decree, however, was only the culminating point of a series of discriminatory measures introduced by the Indonesian authorities in the months following September 16, 1963, the day on which Malaysia came into being. . . .
>
> The control exercised over British interests initially varied from complete take-over, as in the case of the firm called Pemanukan and Tjiasem Lands who ran 21 rubber and tea estates in Java, to small security teams posted at manufacturing enterprises. The differences in approach and timing, as well as in the degree of harassment and take-over were due to the varying circumstances of each firm, the labour pressures brought against them, the personalities involved, the capacity of the British staff to resist take-over attempts, and the emotional or economic significance of the interests attacked.[26]

In a note[27] to the Indonesian Government dated July 20, 1965, the British Government stated:

---

[25] 55 A.J.I.L., pp. 558–559 (1961).
[26] 1964 B.P.I.L., pp. 194–195. *cf.* Judge Sir Gerald Fitzmaurice's assessment of the facts in the *Barcelona Traction Case, loc. cit.* at p. 453, below, p. 106 ("disguised expropriation"). See also Judge Gros, *ibid.* p. 274.
[27] *Ibid.* p. 200.

. . . in view of the complete inability of British enterprises and plantations to exercise and enjoy any of their rights of ownership in relation to their properties in Indonesia, Her Majesty's Government have concluded that the Indonesian Government have expropriated this property.

In 1964 also, the Chancellor of the Exchequer was questioned in Parliament about a Burmese profits tax which rose to 99 per cent. on profits above £22,000. He agreed that "such excessive taxation really amounts to *de facto* expropriation without compensation."[28]

3. Nor does the 1962 Resolution specify what is property within the rules on expropriation. The 1961 Harvard Draft Convention defines it as comprising "all movable and immovable property, whether tangible or intangible, including industrial, literary, and artistic property, as well as rights and interests in any property" (Art. 10(7)). The definition excludes contractual rights; these are regarded as being subject to a different rule, see below, p. 433. The 1962 Resolution contains a separate paragraph (para. 8) on foreign investment agreements. But in the *Anglo-Iranian Oil Co. Case*, the claimant United Kingdom Government argued[29]:

The Government of the United Kingdom does not consider it necessary to elaborate the proposition that rights acquired by foreign nationals by virtue of concessionary contracts are property rights and that as such they are entitled to the same protection as international law grants to the property rights of foreigners.

Note also that in the *Shufeldt Claim*, the Arbitrator, in awarding compensation for the premature termination by Guatemala by legislative decree of a concession contract for the exploitation of chicle, stated:

There cannot be any doubt that property rights are created under and by virtue of a contract.[30]

4. On the requirement of a public purpose, which the Resolution affirms ("public utility," etc.), the World Court stated in the *Certain German Interests in Polish Upper Silesia Case*[31] that "expropriation for reasons of public utility, judicial liquidation and similar measures" was permissible in international law. From the context, the Court can probably be taken to mean that expropriations not justifiable in the public interest are illegal. The 1974 Charter on Economic Rights and Duties of States, below p. 429, does not specify a public purpose requirement. Developed states, however, continue to insist upon it.

Public purpose considerations were relevant in the *BP Case* (1974).[32] In 1971, Libya nationalised the property, rights and assets under an oil concession contract of British Petroleum, a British company in which the British Government then held 49 per cent. of the shares. The British Government protested to Libya that its action infringed international law for the following reasons[33]:

---

[28] *Ibid.* p. 202.

[29] *Anglo-Iranian Oil Co. Case*, I.C.J. Pleadings, p. 83. The U.K. took the generally accepted view that a state can only expropriate an alien's property that is within its territory: *ibid.* p. 81.

[30] *U.S.* v. *Guatemala*, 2 R.I.A.A. 1083, at p. 1097 (1930).

[31] P.C.I.J. Rep., Series A, No. 7, p. 22 (1926).

[32] 53 I.L.R. 297.

[33] *Ibid.* p. 317. *cf.* the terms of the U.S. protest at one of several 1973 Libyan nationalisations, which it thought to be motivated by political opposition to U.S. policies in the Middle East and U.S. protest at the Arab oil boycott: "Under established principles of international law, measures taken against the rights and property of foreign nationals which are arbitrary, discriminatory, or based on considerations of political reprisal and economic coercion are invalid and not entitled to recognition by other states": quoted in Von Mehren and Kourides, 75 A.J.I.L. 476, 486 (1981).

An act of nationalisation is not legitimate in international law unless it satisfies the following requirements:
(i) it must be for a public purpose related to the internal needs of the taking State; and
(ii) it must be followed by the payment of prompt, adequate and effective compensation.
Nationalisation measures which are arbitrary or discriminatory or which are motivated by considerations of a political nature unrelated to the internal well being of the taking state are, by a reference to those principles, illegal and invalid.

In this case, the nationalisation was not accompanied by that of property held by other foreign oil companies under concession contracts (or even property held by British Petroleum itself under other concessions). The reason for the nationalisation was the refusal of the United Kingdom shortly before the nationalisation to intervene to prevent Iran from forcibly occupying the Tunb Islands in the Persian Gulf.[34] The islands were the territory of the trucial state of Ras Al-Khaymah (now within the United Arab Emirates) which at the time of the occupation was still a state entitled by treaty to protection from the United Kingdom. The treaty of protection expired the day following the occupation. The dispute was referred to arbitration by British Petroleum under the contract.[35] The sole arbitrator held[36]:

> The BP Nationalisation Law, and the actions taken thereunder by the Respondent, do constitute a fundamental breach of the BP Concession as they amount to a total repudiation of the agreement and the obligations of the Respondent thereunder, and, on the basis of rules of applicable systems of law too elementary and voluminous to require or permit citation, the Tribunal so holds. Further, the taking by the Respondent of the property, rights and interests of the Claimant clearly violates public international law as it was made for purely extraneous political reasons and was arbitrary and discriminatory in character. Nearly two years have now passed since the nationalisation, and the fact that no offer of compensation has been made indicates that the taking was also confiscatory.

Did the arbitrator suppose that there was a public purpose requirement?
In the *Liamco Case* (1977),[37] the arbitrator held that there was no separate public purpose requirement in international law:

> As to the contention that the said measures were politically motivated and not in pursuance of a legitimate public purpose, it is the general opinion in international theory that the public utility principle is not a necessary requisite for the legality of a nationalization. This principle was mentioned by Grotius and other later publicists, but now there is no international authority, from a judicial or any other source, to support its application to nationalization. . . .

---

[34] Libya justified the nationalisation thus in the Security Council: S.C.O.R. 1610th meeting, p. 20. December 9, 1971.

[35] Libya declined to appoint an arbitrator or otherwise participate in the proceedings. As in the *Texaco Case*, below, p. 434, a sole arbitrator (Judge Lagergren, President of the Court of Appeals of West Sweden) was appointed. The arrangements for arbitration and the provisions in the concession on the law of the contract and its stabilisation were the same as in that case.

[36] 53 I.L.R. 329. The arbitrator awarded the claimant damages, but not the restitution that it had claimed.

[37] 20 I.L.M. 1, 58–59 (1981). The sole arbitrator was Dr. Mahamssani, a Lebanese lawyer. Libya did not participate in the proceedings. See also, denying the existence of a public purpose requirement, Weston, *loc. cit.* at p. 430, n. 37, above, pp. 439–440. Garcia Amador argues for such a requirement on the ground that "[a]ny other view would condone and even facilitate the abusive exercise of the power to expropriate and give legal sanction to manifestly arbitrary acts of expropriation": Y.B.I.L.C., 1959, II, p. 15.

However, political motivation may take the shape of discrimination as a result of political retaliation. . . .

It is clear and undisputed that non-discrimination is a requisite for the validity of a lawful nationalisation. This is a rule well established in international legal theory and practice (V. White . . . [*op.cit.* at p. 422, n. 21, above] pp. 119 *et seq*). Therefore, a purely discriminatory nationalisation is illegal and wrongful.

The *Liamco Case* was very similar on its facts to the *Texaco Case*, below, p. 434, with a United States oil company complaining of Libya's nationalisation of property contrary to the terms of an oil concession contract. The company claimed in part that the nationalisation (i) had been effected as "part of an overall program of political retaliation against those nations including the United States whose politics were contrary to those of the new Libyan regime" and (ii) was discriminatory against "selected foreign companies." After examining evidence of Libyan policy and practice, the arbitrator concluded that the nationalisation was not discriminatory because "Libya's motive for nationalisation was its desire to preserve the ownership of its oil. . . . The political motive [complained of] was not the predominant motive for nationalisation, and . . . such motive per se does not constitute a sufficient proof of a purely discriminatory measure."[38]

5. The 1962 Resolution does not list non-discrimination as a separate international law requirement of a valid expropriation. Developed states insist that discrimination against foreigners vitiates an expropriation. See, *e.g.* the United Kingdom and United States protests against the Libyan nationalisations, above, pp. 424–426. In the *Anglo-Iranian Oil Co. Case*,[39] the United Kingdom submitted that a "measure of expropriation or nationalisation . . . becomes unlawful in international law, if in effect it is exclusively or primarily directed against foreigners as such, and it cannot be shown that, but for the measure of expropriation or nationalisation, public interests of vital importance would suffer." On the basis of the above submission, the United Kingdom challenged the legality of the Iranian Oil Nationalisation Act 1951. That Act "resolved that the oil industry throughout all parts of the country, without exception, be nationalised. . . . " In fact, the "oil industry" consisted only of the Anglo-Iranian Oil Co.[40] When can a state nationalise an industry that is wholly owned by foreign interests consistently with the British submission in the *Anglo-Iranian Oil Co. Case*? The arbitrator in the *Liamco Case*, above, had no doubt that a non-discrimination requirement exists. He seemed to assume that it applied to discrimination against particular foreign companies and against companies of a particular nationality as well as foreign companies generally. The requirement is not mentioned in the 1974 Charter, below, p. 429. Baade[41] argues against such a requirement:

Since states are free to decide with whom to trade, they must also be free to decide with whom to stop dealing—subject, of course, to as yet unexpired treaty obligations. . . . Discrimination can be dictated by a number of reasons: preferences based on consideration of foreign policy, military alliances, and the like; ethnic or cultural preferences or aversions; retaliation; or, more importantly for present purposes, decolonization in fact as well as in law. Independence would seem an empty gesture or even a cruel hoax to many a new country if it were prevented from singling out the

[38] *Ibid.* p. 60. The arbitrator nonetheless awarded the claimant compensation (not restitution as it had claimed) because the nationalisation of concession rights, although not by itself unlawful, created an obligation to compensate for the premature termination of the concession contract: *ibid.* p. 85. On the measure of compensation, see below, p. 439. Note that in the *Texaco Case*, below, p. 434, allegations of political motivation for the nationalisations were not examined; it was neither thought necessary nor, in Libya's absence, appropriate to do so.
[39] *Anglo-Iranian Oil Co. Case*, I.C.J. Pleadings, p. 81.
[40] A small concession owned partly by a Russian company was understood to have stopped working.
[41] In Miller & Stanger, eds., *Essays on Expropriation* (1967), p. 24. Footnotes omitted.

key investments of the former colonial power for nationalization. There is no support in law or reason for the proposition that a taking that meets other relevant tests of legality is illegal under international law merely because it is discriminatory.

6. In a note from the United States Secretary of State Hull to the Mexican Government in 1940 on the expropriation by Mexico of foreign oil interests it was stated:

> . . . the right to expropriate property is coupled with and conditioned on the obligation to make adequate, effective and prompt compensation. The legality of an expropriation is in fact dependent upon the observance of this requirement.[42]

A requirement of "prompt, adequate and effective" compensation is used in a number of bilateral treaties of commerce.[43] It is not found in so many words in judicial and arbitral practice which, although supporting a requirement of compensation in almost every case, uses terms such as "fair,"[44] "full"[45] and "just."[46] One of the more detailed statements is found in the *Goldenberg Case*,[47] which concerned compensation for property requisitioned for military purposes during war:

> However, if international law allows a state to derogate for public purposes (*utilité publique*) from the principle of respect for the private property of aliens, the property expropriated or requisitioned must be paid for on equitable terms as quickly as possible.

Some indication of the United Kingdom's understanding of the meaning of the terms used in the formula is found in its memorial in the *Anglo-Iranian Oil Co. Case*[48]:

> . . . it is clear that the nationalisation of the property of foreigners, even if not unlawful on any other ground, becomes an unlawful confiscation unless provision is made for compensation which is adequate, prompt and effective. By "adequate" compensation is meant "the value of the undertaking at the moment of dispossession, plus interest to the day of judgment"—*per* the Permanent Court of International Justice in the *Chorzów Factory* (Claim for Indemnity) (Merits) *Case,* Series A, No. 17. . . . There have, in fact, been pronouncements that prompt compensation means immediate payment in cash. Thus, in the arbitration between the United States and Norway relating to the requisitioning of contracts for the building of ships in the United States, it was held: "The Tribunal is of opinion that full compensation should have been paid . . . at the latest on the day of the effective taking" (Scott, *Hague Court Reports,* Second Series (1932) at p. 77). The Government of the United Kingdom is, however, prepared to admit that deferred payment may be interpreted as satisfying the requirement of payment in accordance with the rules of international law if:
> (a) the total amount to be paid is fixed promptly;
> (b) allowance for interest for late payment is made;
> (c) the guarantees that the future payments will in fact be made are satisfactory, so that the person to be compensated may, if he so desires, raise the full sum at once on the security of the future payments. . . .
> The third requirement is summed up in the word "effective" and means that the recipient of the compensation must be able to make use of it. He must, for instance, be able, if he wishes, to use it to set up a new enterprise to replace the one that has

---

[42] 3 Hackworth 662.

[43] See, *e.g.* the Anglo-Iranian Treaty of 1959, Cmnd. 698, Article 15.

[44] *Chorzów Factory Case (Indemnity) (Merits)*, P.C.I.J.Rep., Series A, No. 17, p. 46 (1928).

[45] Dissenting opinion of Judge Carneiro in the *Anglo-Iranian Oil Co. Case*, I.C.J.Rep. 1952, p. 93 at p. 162.

[46] *Upton Claim*, 9 R.I.A.A. 234 (1903).

[47] *Germany* v. *Roumania*, 2 R.I.A.A. 903, at p. 909 (1928). Translation.

[48] *Anglo-Iranian Oil Co. Case*, I.C.J. Pleadings, pp. 105–106.

been expropriated or to use it for such other purposes as he wishes. Monetary compensation which is in blocked currency is not effective because, where the person to be compensated is a foreigner, he is not in a position to use it or to obtain the benefit of it. The compensation therefore must be freely transferrable from the country paying it and, so far as that country's restrictions are concerned, convertible into other currencies.

7. Developed states still keep to the Hull compensation formula (which appears in various permutations) and accordingly condition the legality of an expropriation upon the payment of compensation complying with it.[49] See, *e.g.* the United Kingdom protest in the *BP case,* above, p. 426. When the 1962 Resolution was being debated, the United States repeatedly said that it understood "appropriate compensation" (para. 4) as incorporating the "international minimum standard" of the Hull formula.[50] In truth, the use of such a general and undefined phrase probably was an exercise in evasion. It is significant that the following amendment[51] to paragraph 4 proposed by the U.S.S.R., although defeated, received 28 votes[52].

The question of compensation to the owners shall in such cases be decided in accordance with the national law of the country taking these measures in the exercise of its sovereignty.

In the light of later United Nations Resolutions, the significance of the "appropriate compensation" sentence in paragraph 4 lies in its reference to "international law" as the law (together with national law) governing the payment of compensation. In the *Liamco Case*[53] the arbitrator, applying general principles of law, and relying upon the principle of equity in particular, concluded that it was "just and reasonable to adopt the formula of 'equitable compensation' as a measure . . . . of damages with the classical formula of 'prior, adequate and effective compensation' remaining as a maximum and practical guide for such assessment."

8. *Treaty obligations.* Expropriation contrary to a treaty obligation clearly engages responsibility. In the *Chorzów Factory Case (Indemnity) (Merits),* the Court commented upon Poland's action in taking property contrary to the 1922 Geneva Convention between Germany and Poland as follows:

The action of Poland which the Court has judged to be contrary to the Geneva Convention is not an expropriation—to render which lawful only the payment of fair compensation would have been wanting; it is a seizure of property, rights and interests which could not be expropriated even against compensation, save under the exceptional conditions fixed by Article 7 of the said Convention.[54]

CHARTER OF ECONOMIC RIGHTS AND DUTIES OF STATES 1974[55]

G.A. Resolution 3281 (XXIX). 14 I.L.M. 251 (1975).

Article 2

1. Every State has and shall freely exercise full permanent sovereignty,

---

[49] This last point is important in respect of remedies; restitution of the property may be obtained if the expropriation (and not just the failure to pay compensation) is illegal. See Schwebel, 53 Proc. A.S.I.L. 266, at pp. 272–273 (1959). On restitution in expropriation cases, see above, p. 397, n. 49.

[50] See, *e.g.* UN Doc. A/C.2/SR. 835, para. 10.   [51] UN Doc. A/C.2/L670.

[52] The full vote was 28 to 39, with 21 absentions: UN Doc. A/C.2/SR.858, para. 41.

[53] 20 I.L.M. at 86 (1981).

[54] P.C.I.J. Rep., Series A, No. 17, p. 46. On expropriation in breach of an international contract, see below, p. 433.

[55] The Charter was adopted by 120 votes to six, with 10 abstentions. The states voting against were Belgium, Denmark, the F.R.G., Luxembourg, the U.K. and the U.S. The abstaining states were Austria, Canada, France, Ireland, Israel, Italy, Japan, the Netherlands, Norway,

including possession, use and disposal, over all its wealth, natural resources and economic activities.

2. Each State has the right:

(a) To regulate and exercise authority over foreign investment within its national jurisdiction in accordance with its laws and regulations and in conformity with its national objectives and priorities. No State shall be compelled to grant preferential treatment to foreign investment;

(b) To regulate and supervise the activities of transnational corporations within its national jurisdiction and take measures to ensure that such activities comply with its laws, rules and regulations and conform with its economic and social policies. Transnational corporations shall not intervene in the internal affairs of a host State. Every State should, with full regard for its sovereign rights, co-operate with other States in the exercise of the right set forth in this subparagraph;

(c) To nationalize, expropriate or transfer ownership of foreign property in which case appropriate compensation should be paid by the State adopting such measures, taking into account its relevant laws and regulations and all circumstances that the State considers pertinent. In any case where the question of compensation gives rise to a controversy, it shall be settled under the domestic law of the nationalizing State and by its tribunals, unless it is freely and mutually agreed by all States concerned that other peaceful means be sought on the basis of the sovereign equality of States and in accordance with the principle of free choice of means.

Notes

1. The Charter was prepared by the United Nations Conference on Trade and Development (UNCTAD), an organ of the General Assembly whose function is primarily "to promote international trade . . . particularly trade between countries at different stages of development, between developing countries and between countries with different systems of economic and social organisation."[56] The Charter sets out economic rights and duties of states over the whole spectrum of international trade, including the right to engage without discrimination in international trade; the right to participate fully in the international decision-making process in the solution of world economic, financial and monetary problems; and the duty to co-operate in the expansion of world trade. Only the Article on expropriation is printed above.

and Spain. A separate vote was taken on Article 2(2)(c). The majority in favour of it was 104 to 16, with six abstentions. The votes against were by the six states that later voted against the Charter as a whole and by nine of the 10 states that later abstained on the Charter as whole plus Sweden (instead of Israel). The six states that abstained on Article 2(2)(c) were Australia, Barbados, Finland, Israel, New Zealand and Portugal. An amendment to Article 2(2)(c) which would have replaced the present wording by "to nationalise, expropriate, or requisition foreign property for a public purpose, provided that just compensation in the light of all the relevant circumstances shall be paid" was proposed by a group of western states in the Second Committee: U.N.Doc. A/C.2/L.1404. It was defeated by 87 votes to 19, with 11 abstentions. On the Charter, see Browner and Tepe, 9 *International Lawyer* 295 (1975); De Waart, 24 Neth. I.L.R. 304 (1977); Fatouros and Meagher, 12 N.Y.U.J.I.L.P. 653 (1980); Jain, 19 Indian J.I.L. 544 (1979); McWhinney, 14 C.Y.I.L. 57 (1976); Weston, 75 A.J.I.L. 437 (1981) and White, 24 I.C.L.Q. 542 (1975).

[56] G.A. Resn. 1995 (XIX), G.A.O.R., 19th Session, Supp. 15, p. 1.

2. The Charter was preceded by General Assembly Resolution 3171 (XXVIII)[57] of 1973 and by the Declaration on the Establishment of a New International Economic Order 1974[58] which follow the same pattern on expropriation. In Resolution 3171 (XXVIII), the Assembly

> 3. *Affirms* that the application of the principle of nationalization carried out by States, as an expression of their sovereignty in order to safeguard their natural resources, implies that each State is entitled to determine the amount of possible compensation and the mode of payment, and that any disputes which might arise should be settled in accordance with the national legislation of each State carrying out such measures.

The 1974 Declaration contains a similar provision. Para. 4(*e*) states the principle of:

> "Full permanent sovereignty of every State over its natural resources and economic activities. In order to safeguard these resources, each State is entitled to exercise effective control over them and their exploitation with means suitable to its own situation, including the right to nationalization or transfer of ownership to its nationals, this right being an expression of the full permanent sovereignty of the State. No State may be subjected to economic, political or any other type of coercion to prevent the free and full exercise of this inalienable right."

3. Clearly the 1974 Charter favours the view of developing states, although, in the opinion of Jimenez de Aréchaga,[59] a former President of the I.C.J. and distinguished Uruguayan international lawyer, not to the point where the question of compensation ceases to be regulated by international law at all:

> The *travaux préparatoires* of the Charter . . . show that . . . paragraph 2(*c*) is not based on a position which denies the existence of any obligation to pay compensation. This position, originally adopted by the working group which drafted the Chapter, was abandoned during discussion. . . . The text as finally adopted not only imposes the duty to pay "appropriate compensation" . . . it also provides that such compensation shall be determined by "taking into account . . . all circumstances that the State considers pertinent."
>
> The following exemplify factors which should be taken into account: whether the initial investment has been recovered, whether there has been undue enrichment as a result of a colonial situation, whether the profits obtained have been excessive, the contribution of the enterprise to the economic and social development of the country, its respect for labour laws and its reinvestment policies. Failure to pay taxes would not, in and of itself determine the amount of compensation due, but it would constitute a credit which may be set off by the expropriating State *vis-à-vis* the expropriated company at the moment of payment. For this reason or similar ones, there may be cases where, in fact, the indemnity is minimal or nonexistent; but, this would not signify legally the nonpayment of compensation. . . .
>
> Thus, it is clear that the basic features of Article 2, paragraph 2(*c*)—the recognition of an international duty to pay compensation and the determination of the amount

---

[57] 68 A.J.I.L. 381 (1974). The Resolution was adopted by 108 votes to one, with 16 abstentions. The vote on paragraph 3 was 86 to 11, with 28 abstentions. The states voting against were, predictably 11 of the developed states that later voted against or abstained in respect of Article 2(2)(*c*), Charter of Economic Rights and Duties of States, above, n. 55, including the U.K. and the U.S. The 28 abstaining states consisted of such states also and some developing states as well.

[58] G.A. Resn. 3201 (S-VI), 13 I.L.M. 715 (1974). The Declaration was adopted without a vote. The F.R.G., France, Japan, the U.K. and the U.S. made reservations to it: *ibid.* 744 *et seq.* (1974).

[59] *Loc. cit.* at p. 422, n. 21, above, pp. 183–187. Some footnotes omitted. *cf.* Brownlie, *loc. cit.* at p. 422, n. 21, above, pp. 268–269.

due in light of the particular circumstances of each case—are rooted in equitable considerations. . . .

However, this interpretation of the Charter provision has been widely criticized, especially by writers from industrialized countries. The main criticism . . . is "the absence of any references in article 2 to the applicability of international law to the treatment of foreign investment." . . . [60] Other critics have concluded that the only obligation "is to grant such compensation, if any, as it is subjectively thought to be 'appropriate,' considering only local law and 'circumstances,' to which international law is not necessarily 'pertinent.'"[61] . . . It is true that Article 2, paragraph 2(c) does not include the provision of . . . Resolution 1803 requiring . . . the payment of appropriate compensation ". . . in accordance with international law." . . .

Article 2 of the Charter also refers to the application by the expropriating State of its laws and regulations and to its appreciation of all pertinent circumstances. It is perfectly legitimate to accept this determination as the one to be made in the first instance since under the local remedies rule national law and local remedies must be applied and exhausted. But the requirement of Article 2, paragraph 2(c) for the payment of an "appropriate compensation" remains.

Thus, if a nationalizing State, in application of its laws and in its appreciation of the circumstances, were to offer compensation which was not considered "appropriate" by the other interested State (and not just by the individual party), the subjective determination by the host State would not be final. The State of nationality of the expropriated owner would become authorized under the existing rules of international law to take up the case of its national and to make a claim on its behalf, based on the host State's noncompliance with the international duty to pay "appropriate compensation."

On this interpretation, the 1974 Charter does not apply a "Calvo Clause" approach to expropriation.[62]

4. The value of the 1974 Charter as evidence of custom is a matter of dispute. In the *Texaco Case*, below, p. 434, the arbitrator considered that Article 2 was put forward *de lege ferenda* and not as a statement of current law. In any event, he considered that the opposition to it was of sufficient size and significance to deny it the status of custom.[63] Brownlie states[64]:

It is fairly clear that the Charter does not purport to be a declaration of pre-existing principles and overall it has a strong programmatic, political and didactic flavour. Nonetheless, there can be little doubt that Article 2, paragraph 2(c), is regarded by many States as an emergent principle, a statement of presently applicable rules.

5. The World Court has yet to decide on the merits a case of expropriation at customary international law. Given that there is no doctrine of *non liquet* in international law, how do you think that the Court, with its diverse membership, would rule on the question of compensation? Might it be likely to formulate a rule couched in equitable terms?[65]

6. When disputes arising out of expropriations are settled by negotiations, states on both sides of the argument agree to compensation of a compromise kind.[66] The United

[60] Statement by the delegate of Canada, 29 U.N. G.A.O.R., C.2 (1649th mtg.) 446, U.N. Doc.A/C.2/SR. 1649 (1974).

[61] Browner & Tepe, [*loc. cit.* at p. 430, n. 55, above], p. 305.

[62] See, *contra*, Lillich, 69 A.J.I.L. 359 (1975). On "Calvo" clauses, see below, p. 468.

[63] In the *Liamco Case*, Resolution 1803 and the 1974 Charter were both said to be "evidence of the recent dominant trend of international opinion": 20 I.L.M. 53 (1981).

[64] *Loc. cit.* at p. 422, n. 21, above, p. 268.   [65] *cf.* Dolzer, *loc. cit.* at p. 422, n. 21, above.

[66] See, *e.g.* the 1958 settlement between the U.K. and Egypt after the nationalisation of the Suez Canal Co., printed in Lauterpacht, ed., *The Suez Canal Settlement*, 1960, p. 3. The I.C.J. has classified such agreements as *sui generis* and as not providing a guide to custom (at least as far as lifting the "corporate veil" is concerned): *Barcelona Traction Case*, I.C.J.Rep. 1970, at p. 40.

Kingdom and other developed states have also made a number of bilaterals treaties[67] incorporating the "international minimum standard" approach. Such states may also make insurance provision for their nationals.

(ix) BREACH OF CONTRACT[68]

JALAPA RAILROAD AND POWER CO. CLAIM

American Mexican Claims Commission (1948). 8 Whiteman 908

This was a claim by a United States company for money due under a contract with the Mexican state of Veracruz. The contract would seem to have been governed by Mexican law. On the nature of the Commission, see above, p. 420, n. 16.

Opinion of the Commission

On January 30, 1926, the State Legislature of Veracruz authorized the Governor to negotiate a contract for the purchase, on behalf of the State, of claimant's properties [railway and electric light properties] for a sum not to exceed 2,000,000 pesos. Such contract was entered into with the approval of the Federal Government on May 28, 1926. The consideration for the sale was 1,800,000 pesos to be paid in monthly instalments of 100,000 pesos each, with interest at 6 per cent. annually. By Clause 12 of the contract 5 per cent. of the Federal tax on petroleum (which was one-half of the State's participation in such tax) was pledged to the payment of the purchase price of claimant's property. . . .

On November 28, 1931, the Legislature of the State of Veracruz issued a decree declaring Clause 12 of the contract of May 28, 1926, between claimant and the State to be void and of no value. The decree contains no statement as to the reasons underlying such action. . . .

It is not disputed that the Veracruz Government acquired physical possession and title to claimant's property under the aforesaid contract and that said property has been forever lost to claimant. Also, there is no dispute as to the purchase price or as to the amount of the payments made thereunder.

In the circumstances, the issue for determination is whether the breach of contract alleged to have resulted from the nullification of clause twelfth of the contract was an ordinary one involving no international responsibility or whether said breach was effected arbitrarily by means of a governmental power illegal under international law. . . .

The proof clearly establishes that the contract for the sale of the property was made pursuant to the decree of the Legislature of Veracruz dated February 2, 1926, as aforesaid. The Governor was expressly authorized to pledge the funds derived from the Federal tax on petroleum by the decree of said Legislature dated September 3, 1925. The Governor reported to the Legislature in his annual report of 1926 that the State had acquired claimant's property and that it was receiving the income therefrom. Partial payments on account of the purchase price had also been made by the State to claimant prior to November

---

[67] See, *e.g.* the U.K.-Sri Lanka 1980 Agreement for the Promotion and Protection of Investments, Article 5, U.K.T.S. 14 (1981), Cmnd. 8186. See Dolzer, *loc. cit.* at p. 422, n. 21, above, p. 565.

[68] See Jennings (1961) 37 B.Y.I.L. 156 and Mann, 54 A.J.I.L. 572 (1960).

28, 1931, when clause twelfth was nullified, and for some time thereafter. Under these circumstances, the 1931 decree of the same Legislature, nullifying the pledge of the funds received from the petroleum tax for the payment of the purchase price, was clearly not an ordinary breach of contract. Here the Government of Veracruz stepped out of the role of contracting party and sought to escape vital obligations under its contract by exercising its superior governmental power. Such action under international law has been held to be a confiscatory breach of contract and to constitute a denial of justice.

Notes

1. What if the exercise of "governmental power" in the *Jalapa Claim* had not been directed at the contract with the claimant in particular but had been a measure devaluing the Mexican *peso* as a matter of general economic policy which had the effect of reducing the value of the amount due to the claimant under the contract? Would Mexico have been responsible then?

2. Would Mexico have been responsible if Veracruz had simply refused to pay for the properties purchased? Note that in the nineteenth century, when attitudes in this area of law were being formed, states that one would have thought would have favoured the protection of the alien contractor showed themselves to be unsympathetic towards the plight of their nationals who had made contracts with foreign states and had "burnt their fingers." Thus, in 1858, the British Government was advised by a Law Officer against "international intervention on behalf of persons who enter into commercial speculations with foreign Governments." The Law Officer continued:

> Such persons are contractors "with notice," and speculate at their own risk; unless and until they have suffered a denial or flagrant perversion of justice or some other gross wrong, they are not, in my opinion, entitled to any peculiar favour or support.[69]

TEXACO v. LIBYA[70]

Texaco Overseas Petroleum Co. and California Asiatic Oil Co. v. *Libya* (1977) 53 I.L.R. 389; 17 I.L.M. 1 (1978)

In 1973 and 1974, Libya nationalised all of the properties, rights, assets and interests of the two claimant United States companies under certain concession contracts made between Libya and the claimants for the exploitation of oil in Libya. Each contract (clause 16) provided that "the contractual rights expressly created by this concession shall not be altered except by mutual consent of the parties." Each indicated the law of the contract (clause 28):

> "This concession shall be governed by and interpreted in accordance with the law of Libya and such rules and principles of international law as may be relevant but only to the extent that such rules and principles are not inconsistent with and do not conflict with the laws of Libya."

The contracts provided for the reference of any dispute arising under them to "two arbitrators, one of whom shall be appointed by each such party, and an Umpire who

---

[69] 2 McNair 202.
[70] See Bowett, 37 C.L.J. 5 (1978); Fatouros, 74 A.J.I.L. 134 (1980); Von Mehren and Kourides, *loc. cit.* at p. 425, n. 33 above; Varma, 18 Col. Jo. Trans. Law 259 (1979); White, 30 I.C.L.Q. 1 (1981). See also Benton, 11 Houston L.R. 924 (1974). On international contracts generally, see Asante, 28 I.C.L.Q. 401 (1979); Friedmann, *op. cit.* at p. 422, n. 21 above, pp. 200–210; Hyde, 105 *Hague Recueil* 267 (1962–II); Lalive, 13 I.C.L.Q. 987 (1964); McNair (1957) 33 B.Y.I.L. 1; Mann (1958) 35 B.Y.I.L. 34; Schwebel, *loc. cit.* at p. 429, n. 49 above.

shall be appointed by the Arbitrators" (*ibid.*). In the event of either party failing to appoint an arbitrator, a sole arbitrator was to be appointed by the President of the I.C.J. (*ibid.*). In this case, Professor Dupuy, a French international lawyer, was appointed as a sole arbitrator after Libya had failed to act. Libya did not participate in the proceedings at any stage, except by way of a memorandum to the President of the I.C.J. objecting to the proceedings.

The arbitrator held that the concessions were international contracts and that the law applying to them was that chosen by the parties in Clause 28. In the following extract, the arbitrator indicates more fully when a contract between a state and an alien may be characterised as an international one, and what the consequences of such a characterisation are. He then considers whether the contracts are binding under the applicable law and whether the Libyan nationalisation measures in breach of the contracts can be justified on other grounds.

Award of the arbitrator

40. The internationalization of contracts entered into between States and foreign private persons can result in various ways . . .

41. . . . it is accepted that the reference made by the contract, in the clause concerning the governing law, to the general principles of law leads to this result. . . .

In the present dispute, general principles of law have a subsidiary role in the governing law clause and apply in the case of lack of conformity between the principles of Libyan law and the principles of international law. . . . Now, these principles of international law must, in the present case, be the standard for the application of Libyan law since it is only if Libyan law is in conformity with international law that it should to applied. Therefore, the reference which is made mainly to the principles of international law and secondarily, to the general principles of law must have as a consequence the application of international law to the legal relations between the parties. . . .

42. International arbitration case law confirms that the reference to the general principles of law is always regarded to be a sufficient criterion for the internationalization of a contract.[71]

It should be noted that the invocation of the general principles of law does not occur only when the municipal law of the contracting state is not suited to petroleum problems. . . . It is also justified by the need for the private contracting party to be protected against unilateral and abrupt modifications of the legislation in the contracting State: it plays, therefore, an important role in the contractual equilibrium intended by the parties. . . .

44. . . . Another process for the internationalization of a contract consists in inserting a clause providing that possible differences which may arise in respect of the interpretation and the performance of the contract shall be submitted to arbitration.

. . . It is . . . unquestionable that the reference to international arbitration is sufficient to internationalize a contract, in other words, to situate it within a specific legal order—the order of the international law of contracts.

45. . . . A third element of the internationalization of the contracts in dispute

---

[71] *Ed.* The abitrator cited the following cases: the *Lena Goldfields Arbitration* (1930) 5 A.D. 3, 426; the *Abu Dhabi Arbitration, loc. cit.* at p. 42, above; the *Qatar Case* (1953) 20 I.L.R. 534; and the *Sapphire Case* (1963) 35 I.L.R. 136. See also the *Aramco Case* (1963) 27 I.L.R. 117.

results from the fact that it takes on a dimension of a new category of agreements between States and private persons: economic development agreements. . . .

Several elements characterize these agreements: in the first place, their subject matter is particularly broad: they are not concerned only with an isolated purchase or performance, but tend to bring to developing countries investments and technical assistance. . . . Thus, they assume a real importance in the development of the country where they are performed. . . .

In the second place, the long duration of these contracts implies close co-operation between the State and the contracting party and requires permanent installations as well as the acceptance of extensive responsibilities by the investor.

Finally, because of the purpose of the co-operation in which the contracting party must participate with the State and the magnitude of the investments to which it agreed, the contractual nature of this type of agreement is reinforced. . . . The investor must in particular be protected against legislative uncertainties, that is to say the risks of the municipal law of the host country being modified, or against any government measures which would lead to an abrogation or rescission of the contract. Hence, the insertion, as in the present case, of so-called stabilization clauses: these clauses tend to remove all or part of the agreement from the internal law and to provide for its correlative submission to *sui generis* rules . . . or to a system which is properly an international law system. . . .

46. The Tribunal must specify the meaning and the exact scope of internationalization of a contractual relationship so as to avoid any misunderstanding: . . . to say that international law governs contractual relations between a State and a foreign private party neither means that the latter is assimilated to a State nor that the contract entered into with it is assimilated to a treaty.[72] . . .

47. . . . stating that a contract between a State and a private person falls within the international legal order means that for the purposes of interpretation and performance of the contract, it should be recognized that a private contracting party has specific international capacities. But, unlike a State, the private person has only a limited capacity and his quality as a subject of international law does enable him only to invoke, in the field of international law, the rights which he derives from the contract.

The arbitrator next applied the law of the contracts in clause 28 and held that the concessions were binding. This was because both Libyan and international law accepted that contracts were binding (*pacta sunt servanda*).

53. The Tribunal must now rule on the point whether . . . the defendant Government has, or has not, breached its obligations arising from the contracts it executed. For this purpose, this Tribunal should examine the various reasons which could be envisaged in order to justify the defendant Government's behavior. . . .

After rejecting the possibility that Libya could be excused from its obligations in accordance with the law applicable to administative contracts (so that the obligations could be altered or terminated unilaterally by the state),[73] the arbitrator considered an

---

[72] *Ed. cf.* The *Anglo-Iranian Oil Co. Case*, below, p. 567.
[73] The arbitrator held that (i) the concessions were not administrative contracts under Libyan law and (ii) the theory of administrative contracts was not a part of international law. French in origin, it was not a general principle of law found in all of the main kinds of legal systems.

argument based upon "the concept of sovereignty and the nature of measures of nationalisation."

59. . . . the right of a State to nationalize is unquestionable today. It results from international customary law. . . . Territorial sovereignty confers upon the State an exclusive competence to organize as it wishes the economic structures of its territory and to introduce therein any reforms which may seem to be desirable to it. . . .

61. . . . It is clear from an international point of view that it is not possible to criticize a nationalization measure concerning nationals of the State concerned, or any measure affecting aliens in respect of whom the State concerned has made no particular commitment to guarantee and maintain their position. On the assumption that the nationalizing State has concluded with a foreign company a contract which stems from the municipal law of that State and is completely governed by that law the resolution of the new situation created by nationalization will be subject to the legal and administrative provisions then in force.

62. But the case is totally different where the State has concluded with a foreign contracting party an internationalized agreement. . . .

71. . . . the recognition by international law of the right to nationalize is not sufficient ground to empower a State to disregard its commitments, because the same law also recognizes the power of a State to commit itself internationally, especially by accepting the inclusion of stablization clauses in a contract entered into with a foreign private party. . . .

73. Thus, in respect of the international law of contracts, a nationalization cannot prevail over an internationalized contract, containing stabilization clauses, entered into between a State and a foreign private company. . . .

The arbitrator then considered, thirdly and finally, whether "resolutions concerning natural resources and wealth adopted by the General Assembly" justified Libya's conduct.

On the basis of the circumstances of adoption . . . and by expressing an *opinio juris communis,* Resolution 1803 (XVII)[74] seems to this Tribunal to reflect the state of customary law existing in this field. . . . The consensus by a majority of States belonging to the various representative groups indicates without the slightest doubt universal recognition of the rules therein incorporated, *i.e.* with respect to nationalization and compensation the use of the rules in force in the nationalizing State, but all this in conformity with international law.

88. While Resolution 1803 (XVII) appears to a large extent as the expression of a real general will, this is not at all the case with respect to the other Resolutions mentioned above.[75] . . . In particular, as regards the Charter of Economic Rights and Duties of States, several factors contribute to denying legal value to those provisions of the document which are of interest in the instant case.

—In the first place, Article 2 of this Charter must be analyzed as a political rather than as a legal declaration concerned with the ideological strategy of development and, as such, supported only by non-industrialized States.

—In the second place, this Tribunal notes that in the draft submitted by the

[74] *Ed.* Above, p. 423.
[75] *Ed.* Resolutions 3171 (XXVIII), 3201 (S-VI), and 3281 (XXIX), above, pp. 429, 431.

Group of 77 to the Second Commission . . . the General Assembly was invited to adopt the Charter "as a first measure of codification and progressive development" within the field of the international law of development. However, because of the opposition of several States, this description was deleted from the text submitted to the vote of the Assembly. . . .

The absence of any connection between the procedure of compensation and international law and the subjection of this procedure solely to municipal law cannot be regarded by this Tribunal except as a *de lege ferenda* formulation, which even appears *contra legem* in the eyes of many developed countries.[76] Similarly, several developing countries, although having voted favorably on the Charter of Economic Rights and Duties of States as a whole, in explaining their votes regretted the absence of any reference to international law. . . .

90. The argument of the Libyan Government . . . is also negated by a complete analysis of the whole text of the Charter of Economic Rights and Duties of States.

Analyzing the scope of these various provisions, Ambassador Castañeda, who chaired the Working Group charged with drawing up the Charter of Economic Rights and Duties of States, formally stated that the principle of performance in good faith of international obligations laid down in Chapter I(j) of the Charter applies to all matters governed by it, including, in particular, matters referred to in Article 2. Following his analysis, this particularly competent and eminent scholar concluded as follows[77]:

> "The Charter accepts that international law may operate as a factor limiting the freedom of the State should foreign interests be affected, even though Article 2 does not state this explicitly. This stems legally from the provisions included in other Articles of the Charter which should be interpreted and applied jointly with those of Article 2."

The arbitrator, having found no justification for Libya's acts, held that the appropriate remedy was *restitutio in integrum,* as claimed by the concessionaires, so that Libya was "legally bound to perform" the contracts. In fact, the claimants subsequently accepted an offer of compensation in full settlement of their claim.[78]

Notes

1. Most contracts between states and aliens are governed by municipal law—normally, but not always,[79] the municipal law of the contracting states. Nonetheless, many are governed by some other system of law as indicated or understood by the parties. The contract in the *Texaco Case* was typical of such "international contracts."

2. Did the arbitrator in the case consider that *all three* of the features that he lists

---

[76] *Ed.* Earlier, the Arbitrator had examined the voting record of the 1974 Charter and similar resolutions and concluded that they "were supported by a majority of states but not by any of the developed countries with market economies which carry on the largest part of international trade" (para. 86).

[77] *Ed.* 20 *Annuaire Français* 31, 54 (1974). Translation in Award. Chapter I(j) reads "Economic as well as political and other relations among States shall be governed, *inter alia*, by the following principles . . . (j) Fulfillment in good faith of international obligations." Article 32(2), 1974 Charter states that "[i]n their interpretation and application, the provisions of the present Charter are interrelated and each provision should be construed in the context of other provisions."

[78] See 17 I.L.M. 2 (1978).

[79] See, *e.g. R.* v. *International Trustee for the Protection of Bondholders Aktiengesellschaft* [1937] A.C. 500 (H.L.).

(paras. 41–45) need to be present for a contract to be regarded as an international one? Are they totally distinct characteristics, or do they overlap? Would it be correct to regard resort to arbitration under the contract as the equivalent of the exhaustion of local remedies[80] prior diplomatic protection by the national state of the contracting alien? How does the arbitrator's statement on the nationalisation of non-international contracts (para. 61) square with the approach to arbitrary breaches in the *Jalapa Case*, above p. 433?

3. The western writers who have advocated the theory of international contracts have not agreed on the legal system which gives an international contract its validity. In the *Texaco Case*, the arbitrator held that the particular contracts in the case were "in the domain of international law" (para. 35). Other views are that an international contract is *sui generis*, with a special legal system consisting solely of the terms of the contract itself[81] or that it is subject to a system of law consisting of the general principles of law recognised by civilised nations.[82] Such writers are agreed, however, that the effect of the internationalisation of a contract is to take the contract out of the municipal law system of the contracting state and to subject it to the basic legal principle that agreements are binding (*pacta sunt servanda*) and to whatever other stabilising clauses the contract contains. On this view, the internationalisation of a contract defeats the power of expropriation and the alien party is able to enforce his contractual rights through international arbitration under the contract. To this extent, in the opinion of the arbitrator in the *Texaco Case*, the individual contractor is a subject of international law.

The situation is viewed differently by developing states. Jiménez de Aréchaga[83] writes:

". . . the countries of the Group of 77[84] would not classify investment agreements between states and private foreign companies as international agreements. . . . "They did not have international status, because private companies [are] not subjects of international law."[85] . . .

"The rights represented by a concession or a contract are no more exempt from expropriation than are mines or factories. . . . Such a cancellation . . . would be subject to the payment of "appropriate compensation" in accordance with Article 2, paragraph 2(e) [1974 Charter]. . . . This does not mean that stabilisation clauses have no legal effect. . . . The amount of the indemnity would have to be much higher than in normal cases because . . . [of the concept of good faith . . . in Chapter I, subparagraph (j), Charter[86]]. For instance, there would be a duty to compensate for the prospective gains (*lucrum cessans*) to be obtained . . . during the period that the concession has still to run [as well as for the tangible assets lost].[87] After the exhausting of local remedies, there would be an international responsibility for expropriation of contractual rights, enforced by diplomatic protection, just as in any other case of expropriation which is not accompanied by an appropriate indemnification."

4. A study of recent practice shows that, because of the increasing power of oil producing states, the majority of oil contracts made since 1970 are governed by the law of the contracting state and subject to the jurisdiction of its courts.[88] To the extent that

---

[80] On the local remedies rule, see below, p. 464.
[81] See *Texaco Case*, 53 I.L.R. at 446.
[82] See McNair, *loc. cit.* at p. 434, n. 70 above, p. 19.
[83] *Loc. cit.* at p. 422, n. 21 above, pp. 189–192.
[84] The Group of 77 (now numbering over 100) emerged as a political unit in the UN in the 1960s and represents the developing states' point of view.
[85] 29 U.N. G.A.O.R. C.2 (1638th Meeting) 382, 383, U.N.Doc. A/C.2/SR, 1638 (1974).
[86] For text, see p. 438, n. 77 above.
[87] Compensation for *lucrum cessans* was awarded in the *Liamco Case*, above, p. 426.
[88] See Kuusi, *The Host State and the Transnational Corporation* (1979), pp. 140–145.

this practice continues, the theory of international contracts espoused by western international lawyers and followed in the *Texaco Case* will become less important.

(x) PROCEDURES FOR SETTLING DISPUTES

Notes

1. Since 1945, mixed claims commissions, from the extensive jurisprudence of which most of the cases in this chapter are taken, have been replaced as the predominant means of settling disputes concerning the treatment of aliens by the "lump sum settlement" agreement.[89] By such agreements, one state agrees by treaty to pay another a "lump sum" in full satisfaction of outstanding claims by the nationals of the latter against the former. The latter then arranges itself for the distribution of the settlement sum, typically by a national claims commission which normally adjudicates upon claims in accordance with international law. Settlements between the United Kingdom and East European states arising out of the nationalisations of the late 1940s, for example, have been reached in this way, the "lump sum" being distributed by the Foreign Claims Commission.[90] Such settlements are invariably of a compromise character so that claims are not fully met.[91]

2. In respect of investment disputes, available methods of settlement have been supplemented by the Convention on the Settlement of Investment Disputes between States and Nationals of Other States 1965.[92] This establishes an International Centre for the Settlement of Investment Disputes (in Washington D.C.). Conciliation and arbitration facilities are available through the Centre to settle cases between contracting parties and companies of the nationality of a contracting party where both sides consent.[93]

(xi) NATIONALITY OF CLAIMS[94]

(a) *The General Rule*

PANEVEZYS-SALDUTISKIS CASE[95]

Estonia *v.* Lithuania (1939)

P.C.I.J. Reports, Series A/B, No. 76

Judgment of the Court

. . . In taking up the case of one of its nationals, by resorting to diplomatic action or international judicial proceedings on his behalf, a State is in reality

[89] See Lillich, *International Claims: Their Adjudication by National Commissions* (1962), and Lillich and Weston, *International Claims: Their Settlement by Lump Sum Agreements*, 2 Vols. (1975).

[90] On British practice generally, see Lillich, *International Claims: Post-war British Practice*, (1967).   [91] See Lillich, *op. cit.* at n. 89, above, pp. 133–139.

[92] U.K.T.S. 25 (1967), Cmnd. 3255; 575 U.N.T.S. 159; 4 I.L.M. 532 (1965). The Convention came into force on October 14, 1966. On June 30, 1982, there were 81 contracting parties. These included France, the U.K. and the U.S. among developed states and most African and some Asian developing states. No Latin American states were parties.

[93] See Rodley, 4 C.Y.I.L. 43 (1966); Schwarzenberger, *Foreign Investments and International Law* (1969), Chap. 9; Starke, in Starke, *ed.*, *The Protection and Encouragement of Private Foreign Investment* (1966), Chap. 1; Amerasinghe, 11 *International Lawyer* 45 (1977); Baker and Ryans, 10 Jo.W.T.L. 65 (1976); Sutherland, 28 I.C.L.Q. 367 (1979); O'Keefe, 34 Y.B.W.A. 286 (1980).

[94] See Hurst (1926) 7 B.Y.I.L. 163; Joseph, *Nationality and Diplomatic Protection: The Commonwealth of Nations* (1969); Leigh, 20 I.C.L.Q. 453 (1971); Sinclair (1950) 27 B.Y.I.L. 124.

[95] See also the *Barcelona Traction Case*, below, p. 453.

asserting its own right, the right to ensure in the person of its nationals respect for the rules of international law. This right is necessarily limited to intervention on behalf of its own nationals because, in the absence of a special agreement, it is the bond of nationality between the State and the individual which alone confers upon the State the right of diplomatic protection, and it is as a part of the function of diplomatic protection that the right to take up a claim and to ensure respect for the rules of international law must be envisaged. Where the injury was done to the national of some other State, no claim to which such injury may give rise falls within the scope of the diplomatic protection which a State is entitled to afford nor can it give rise to a claim which that State is entitled to espouse.

1930 HAGUE CONVENTION ON CERTAIN QUESTIONS RELATING TO THE CONFLICT OF NATIONALITY LAWS[96]

179 L.N.T.S. 89

Article 1

It is for each State to determine under its own law who are its nationals. This law shall be recognised by other States in so far as it is consistent with international conventions, international custom, and the principles of law generally recognised with regard to nationality. . . .

Article 2

Any question as to whether a person possesses the nationality of a particular State shall be determined in accordance with the law of that State.

Article 3

Subject to the provisions of the present Convention, a person having two or more nationalities may be regarded as its national by each of the States whose nationality he possesses.

Article 4

A State may not afford diplomatic protection to one of its nationals against a State whose nationality such person also possesses.

Article 5

Within a third State, a person having more than one nationality shall be treated as if he had only one. Without prejudice to the application of its law in matters of personal status and of any conventions in force, a third State shall, of the nationalities which any such person possesses, recognise exclusively in its territory either the nationality of the country in which he is habitually and principally resident, or the nationality of the country with which in the circumstances he appears to be in fact most closely connected.

[96] The Convention entered into force on July 1, 1937. On December 31, 1981, there were 19 parties, including the U.K.

Notes

1. In the *Nationality Decrees in Tunis and Morocco Case,*[97] the Permanent Court of International Justice stated:

> Thus, in the present state of international law, questions of nationality are . . . in principle within the reserved domain [of a state's domestic jurisdiction].

2. The British Digest of International Law[98] states:

> There is today a strong current of international legal thinking to the effect that, apart from the case of concessions of territory or in very special circumstances, international recognition need not be accorded to the nationality of a State conferred on the recipient *not at his request or without his consent,* unless, by both parentage and permanent domicile, he has a genuine connexion with that State. (*cf. Weis, Nationality and Statelessness in International Law* (1956), pp. 110–113; Jones, *British Nationality Law and Practice* (1947), p. 15; Fitzmaurice, *Recueil des Cours,* 1957, II, pp. 198–201).

NOTTEBOHM CASE[99]

Liechtenstein *v.* Guatemala

I.C.J. Reports 1955, p. 4

Judgment of the Court

By the application filed on December 17th 1951, the Government of Liechtenstein instituted proceedings before the Court in which it claimed restitution and compensation on the ground that the Government of Guatemala had "acted towards the person and property of Mr. Friedrich Nottebohm, a citizen of Liechtenstein, in a manner contrary to international law."[1] In its Counter-Memorial, the Government of Guatemala contended that this claim was inadmissible on a number of grounds, and one of its objections to the admissibility of the claim related to the nationality of the person for whose protection Liechtenstein had seised the Court. . . .

Guatemala has referred to a well-established principle of international law, which it expressed in Counter-Memorial, where it is stated that "it is the bond of nationality between the State and the individual which alone confers upon the State the right of diplomatic protection." . . .

Nottebohm was born at Hamburg on September 16th, 1881. He was German by birth, and still possessed German nationality when, in October 1939, he applied for naturalization in Liechtenstein.

In 1905 he went to Guatemala. He took up residence there and made that country the headquarters of his business activities. . . . After 1905 he sometimes went to Germany on business and to other countries for holidays. He continued to have business connections in Germany. He paid a few visits to a

---

[97] P.C.I.J.Rep., Series B, No. 4, p. 24 (1923).

[98] 5 B.D.I.L. 25. Italics added.

[99] See Jones, 5 I.C.L.Q. 230 (1956); Kunz, 54 A.J.I.L. 536 (1960); 2 Verzijl 210.

[1] *Ed.* The Court was asked to "adjudge and declare that the Government of Guatemala in arresting, detaining, expelling and refusing to readmit Mr. Nottebohm and in seizing and retaining his property without compensation acted in breach of their obligations under international law": I.C.J.Rep. 1955, pp. 6–7.

brother who had lived in Liechtenstein since 1931. Some of his other brothers, relatives and friends were in Germany, others in Guatemala. He himself continued to have his fixed abode in Guatemala until 1943, that is to say, until the occurrence of the events which constitute the basis of the present dispute. . . .

The Liechtenstein Law of January 4th, 1934, lays down the conditions for the naturalization of foreigners. . . . The Law specifies certain mandatory requirements, namely, that the applicant for naturalization should prove: (1) "that the acceptance into the Home Corporation (*Heimatverband*) of a Liechtenstein commune has been promised to him in case of acquisition of the nationality of the State (2) that he will lose his former nationality as a result of naturalization, although this requirement may be waived under stated conditions. It further makes naturalization conditional upon compliance with the requirement of residence for at least three years in the territory of the Principality, although it is provided that "this requirement can be dispensed with in circumstances deserving special consideration and by way of exception." In addition, the applicant for naturalization is required to submit a number of documents, such as . . . , if he is not a resident in the Principality, proof that he has concluded an agreement with the Revenue authorities. . . . The Law further provides for the payment by the applicant of a naturalization fee. . . .

On October 9th, 1939, Nottebohm, "resident in Guatemala since 1905 (at present residing as a visitor with his brother, Hermann Nottebohm, in Vaduz)," applied for admission as a national of Liechtenstein. . . . He sought dispensation from the condition of three years' residence as prescribed by law, without indicating the special circumstances warranting such waiver. . . .

Lastly, he requested "that naturalization proceedings be initiated and concluded before the Government of the Principality and before the Commune of Mauren without delay. . . .

A certificate of nationality has . . . been produced . . . to the effect that Nottebohm was naturalized by Supreme Resolution of the Reigning Prince dated October 13th, 1939.

Having obtained a Liechtenstein passport, Nottebohm had it visaed by the Consul General of Guatemala in Zurich on December 1st, 1939, and returned to Guatemala at the beginning of 1940, where he resumed his former business activities. . . .

In order to decide upon the admissibility of the Application, the Court must ascertain whether the nationality conferred on Nottebohm by Liechtenstein by means of a naturalization which took place in the circumstances which have been described, can be validly invoked as against Guatemala, whether it bestows upon Liechtenstein a sufficient title to the exercise of protection in respect of Nottebohm as against Guatemala and therefore entitles it to seise the Court of a claim relating to him. In this connection, Counsel for Liechtenstein said: "the essential question is whether Mr. Nottebohm, having acquired the nationality of Liechtenstein, that acquisition of nationality is one which must be recognised by other States." This formulation is accurate, subject to the twofold reservation that, in the first place, what is involved is not recognition for all purposes but merely for the purposes of the admissibility of the Application, and, secondly, that what is involved is not recognition by all States but only by Guatemala.

The Court does not propose to go beyond the limited scope of the question which it has to decide, namely whether the nationality conferred on Nottebohm can be relied upon as against Guatemala in justification of the proceedings instituted before the Court. . . .

In order to establish that the Application must be held to be admissible, Liechtenstein has argued that Guatemala formerly recognized the naturalization which it now challenges and cannot therefore be heard to put forward a contention which is inconsistent with its former attitude. . . .

The Court considered and rejected this contention on the evidence. It dismissed part of the evidence as irrelevant because it referred to "the control of aliens in Guatemala and not to the exercise of diplomatic protection."

It is for Liechtenstein, as it is for every sovereign State, to settle by its own legislation the rules relating to the acquisition of its nationality, and to confer that nationality by naturalization granted by its own organs in accordance with that legislation. It is not necessary to determine whether international law imposes any limitations on its freedom of decision in this domain. Furthermore, nationality has its most immediate, its most far-reaching and, for most people, its only effects within the legal system of the State conferring it. Nationality serves above all to determine that the person upon whom it is conferred enjoys the rights and is bound by the obligations which the law of the State in question grants to or imposes on its nationals. This is implied in the wider concept that nationality is within the domestic jurisdiction of the State.

But the issue which the Court must decide is not one which pertains to the legal system of Liechtenstein. It does not depend on the law or on the decision of Liechtenstein whether that State is entitled to exercise its protection in the case under consideration. To exercise protection, to apply to the Court, is to place oneself on the plane of international law. It is international law which determines whether a State is entitled to exercise protection and to seise the Court. . . .

International practice provides many examples of acts performed by States in the exercise of their domestic jurisdiction which do not necessarily or automatically have international effect, which are not necessarily and automatically binding on other States or which are binding on them only subject to certain conditions: this is the case, for instance, of a judgment given by the competent court of a State which it is sought to invoke in another State. . . .

International arbitrators have decided . . . numerous cases of dual nationality, where the question arose with regard to the exercise of protection. They have given their preference to the real and effective nationality, that which accorded with the facts, that based on stronger factual ties between the person concerned and one of the States whose nationality is involved. Different factors are taken into consideration, and their importance will vary from one case to the next: the habitual residence of the individual concerned is an important factor, but there are other factors such as the centre of his interests, his family ties, his participation in public life, attachment shown by him for a given country and inculcated in his children, etc.

Similarly, the courts of third States, when they have before them an individual whom two other States hold to be their national, seek to resolve the conflict by having recourse to international criteria and their prevailing tendency is to prefer the real and effective nationality.

The same tendency prevails in the writings of publicists and in practice. This notion is inherent in the provisions of Article 3, paragraph 2, of the Statute of the Court.[2] National laws reflect this tendency when, *inter alia,* they make naturalization dependent on conditions indicating the existence of a link, which may vary in their purpose or in their nature but which are essentially concerned with this idea. The Liechtenstein Law of January 4th, 1934, is a good example.

The practice of certain States which refrain from exercising protection in favour of a naturalized person when the latter has in fact, by his prolonged absence, severed his links with what is no longer for him anything but his nominal country, manifests the view of these States that, in order to be capable of being invoked against another State, nationality must correspond with the factual situation. A similar view is manifested in the relevant provisions of the bilateral nationality treaties concluded between the United States of America and other States since 1868, such as those sometimes referred to as the Bancroft Treaties, and in the Pan-American Convention, signed at Rio de Janeiro on August 13th, 1906, on the status of naturalized citizens who resume residence in their country of origin.

The character thus recognized on the international level as pertaining to nationality is in no way inconsistent with the fact that international law leaves it to each State to lay down the rules governing the grant of its own nationality. The reason for this is that the diversity of demographic conditions has thus far made it impossible for any general agreement to be reached on the rules relating to nationality, although the latter by its very nature affects international relations. It has been considered that the best way of making such rules accord with the varying demographic conditions in different countries is to leave the fixing of such rules to the competence of each State. On the other hand, a State cannot claim that the rules it has thus laid down are entitled to recognition by another State unless it has acted in conformity with this general aim of making the legal bond of nationality accord with the individual's genuine connection with the State which assumes the defence of its citizens by means of protection as against other States.

The requirement that such a concordance must exist is to be found in the studies carried on in the course of the last thirty years upon the initiative and under the auspices of the League of Nations and the United Nations. It explains the provision which the Conference for the Codification of International Law, held at The Hague in 1930, inserted in Article I of the Convention relating to the Conflict of Nationality Laws. . . . [3] In the same spirit, Article 5 of the Convention refers to criteria of the individual's genuine connections for the purpose of resolving questions of dual nationality which arise in third States.

According to the practice of States, to arbitral and judicial decisions and to the opinions of writers, nationality is a legal bond having as its basis a social fact of attachment, a genuine connection of existence, interests and sentiments, together with the existence of reciprocal rights and duties. It may be said to constitute the juridical expression of the fact that the individual upon whom it is conferred, either directly by the law or as the result of an act of the authorities, is in fact more closely connected with the population of the State conferring nationality than with that of any other State. Conferred by a State, it only entitles that State to exercise protection *vis-à-vis* another State, if it constitutes a

[2] *Ed.* See Appendix I, below.
[3] *Ed.* See above, p. 441.

translation into juridical terms of the individual's connection with the State which has made him its national.

Diplomatic protection and protection by means of international juridical proceedings constitute measures for the defence of the rights of the State. . . .

Since this is the character which nationality must present when it is invoked to furnish the State which has granted it with a title to the exercise of protection and to the institution of international judicial proceedings, the Court must ascertain whether the nationality granted to Nottebohm by means of naturalization is of this character or, in other words, whether the factual connection between Nottebohm and Liechtenstein in the period preceding, contemporaneous with and following his naturalization appears to be sufficiently close, so preponderant in relation to any connection which may have existed between him and any other State, that it is possible to regard the nationality conferred upon him as real and effective, as the exact juridical expression of a social fact of a connection which existed previously or came into existence thereafter.

Naturalization is not a matter to be taken lightly. To seek and to obtain it is not something that happens frequently, in the life of a human being. It involves his breaking of a bond of allegiance and his establishment of a new bond of allegiance. It may have far-reaching consequences and involve profound changes in the destiny of the individual who obtains it. It concerns him personally, and to consider it only from the point of view of its repercussions with regard to his property would be to misunderstand its profound significance. In order to appraise its international effect, it is impossible to disregard the circumstances in which it was conferred, the serious character which attaches to it, the real and effective, and not merely the verbal preference of the individual seeking it for the country which grants it to him.

At the time of his naturalization does Nottebohm appear to have been more closely attached by his tradition, his establishment, his interests, his activities, his family ties, his intentions for the near future to Liechtenstein than to any other State? . . .

The essential facts are as follows:

At the date when he applied for naturalization Nottebohm had been a German national from the time of his birth. He had always retained his connections with members of his family who had remained in Germany and he had always had business connections with that country. His country had been at war for more than a month, and there is nothing to indicate that the application for naturalization then made by Nottebohm was motivated by any desire to dissociate himself from the Government of his country.

He had been settled in Guatemala for 34 years. He had carried on his activities there. It was the main seat of his interests. He returned there shortly after his naturalization, and it remained the centre of his interests and of his business activities. He stayed there until his removal as a result of war measures in 1943. He subsequently attempted to return there, and he now complains of Guatemala's refusal to admit him. There, too, were several members of his family who sought to safeguard his interests.

In contrast, his actual connections with Liechtenstein were extremely tenuous. No settled abode, no prolonged residence in that country at the time of his application for naturalization: the application indicates that he was paying a visit there and confirms the transient character of this visit by its request that the naturalization proceedings should be initiated and concluded without delay. No intention of settling there was shown at that time or realized in the ensuing weeks, months or years—on the contrary, he returned to Guatemala very shortly after his naturalization and showed every intention of remaining there. If Nottebohm went to Liechtenstein in 1946, this was because of the refusal of Guatemala to admit him. No indication is given of the grounds warranting the waiver of the condition of residence, required by the 1934 Nationality Law, which waiver was implicitly granted to him. There is no allegation of any economic interests or of any activities exercised or to be exercised in Liechtenstein and no manifestation of any intention whatsoever to transfer all or some of his interests and business activities to Liechtenstein. It is unnecessary in this connection to attribute much importance to the promise to pay the taxes levied at the time of his naturalization. The only links to be discovered between the Principality and Nottebohm are the short sojourns already referred to and the presence in Vaduz of one of his brothers: but his brother's presence is referred to in his application for naturalization only as a reference to his good conduct. Furthermore, other members of his family have asserted Nottebohm's desire to spend his old age in Guatemala.

These facts clearly establish, on the one hand, the absence of any bond of attachment between Nottebohm and Liechtenstein and, on the other hand, the existence of a long-standing and close connection between him and Guatemala, a link which his naturalization in no way weakened. That naturalization was not based on any real prior connection with Liechtenstein, nor did it in any way alter the manner of life of the person upon whom it was conferred in exceptional circumstances of speed and accommodation. In both respects, it was lacking in the genuineness requisite to an act of such importance, if it is to be entitled to be respected by a State in the position of Guatemala. It was granted without regard to the concept of nationality adopted in international relations.

Naturalization was asked for not so much for the purpose of obtaining a legal recognition of Nottebohm's membership in fact in the population of Liechtenstein, as it was to enable him to substitute for his status as a national of a belligerent State that of a national of a neutral State, with the sole aim of thus coming within the protection of Liechtenstein but not of becoming wedded to its traditions, its interests, its way of life or of assuming the obligations—other than fiscal obligations—and exercising the rights pertaining to the status thus acquired.

Guatemala is under no obligation to recognise a nationality granted in such circumstances. Liechtenstein consequently is not entitled to extend its protection to Nottebohm *vis-à-vis* Guatemala and its claim must, for this reason, be held to be inadmissible. . . .

For these reasons, THE COURT, by eleven votes to three,[4] Holds that the claim submitted by the Government of the Principality of Liechtenstein is inadmissible.

Notes
1. Nottebohm had lost his German nationality upon taking that of Liechtenstein. What state could have protected him against Guatemala in accordance with the

[4] The judges in the majority were President Hackworth; Vice-President Badawi; Judges Basdevant, Zoričić, Hsu Mo, Armand-Ugon, Kojevnikov, Sir Muhammad Zafrulla Khan, Moreno Quintana and Cordova; Judge ad hoc Garcia Bauer. Judges Klaestad and Read and Judge ad hoc Guggenheim dissented.

"genuine connection" requirement insisted upon by the Court? Could Liechtenstein have protected Nottebohm against any state? Could Guatemala ever have protected him?

2. How important do you think it was in the *Nottebohm Case* that Nottebohm's nationality was a "nationality of convenience"? Suppose he had been a Liechtenstein national by birth who had emigrated to Guatemala?

3. Should there be a "genuine connection" requirement, or should international law allow a state to protect any of its nationals without question? The Court supported its "genuine connection" requirement largely by reference to practice concerning dual nationality. Might that be a special case? Note that the requirement had an immediate impact upon the rule concerning the nationality of ships in the 1958 High Seas Convention.[5]

4. The Rules regarding International Claims issued by the British Foreign and Commonwealth Office in 1971,[6] which state the rules applying when a United Kingdom national seeks the protection of the British Government, read in part:

Rule I

Her Majesty's Government will not take up the claim unless the claimant is a United Kingdom national and was so at the date of the injury.

Comment

(1) International law requires that for a claim to be sustainable the claimant must be a national of the state which is presenting the claim both at the time when the injury occurred and continuously thereafter up to the date of formal presentation of the claim. In practice however it is sufficient to prove nationality at the date of injury and of presentation of the claim.

(2) The term "United Kingdom national" includes the following categories: . . .

    (vii) companies incorporated under the law of the United Kingdom or of any territory for which the United Kingdom is internationally responsible.

Rule II

Where the claimant has become or ceases to be a United Kingdom national after the date of the injury, Her Majesty's Government may in an appropriate case take up his claim in concert with the Government of the country of his former or subsequent nationality.

Rule XI

Where the prospective claimant has died since the date of the injury to him or his property, his personal representatives may seek to obtain relief or compensation for the injury on behalf of his estate. Such a claim is not to be confused with a claim by a dependant of a deceased person for damages for his death.

Comment

Where the personal representatives are of a different nationality from that of the original claimant, the rules set out above would probably be applied, just as if it were a case of a single claimant who had changed his national status.

Why should international law require that the claimant be a national at the time of the injury and when the claim is formally presented?

---

[5] See above, p. 324.
[6] Copy provided by the Foreign Office.

5. As to the exceptional cases in which a state may protect a person who is not its national, see above, p. 117, n. 47.

6. The position of stateless persons was indicated in the *Dickson Car Wheel Company Case*:

> A State . . . does not commit an international delinquency in inflicting an injury upon an individual lacking nationality, and consequently, no State is empowered to intervene or complain on his behalf either before or after the injury.[7]

FLEGENHEIMER CLAIM

Italian-United States Conciliation Commission: Sauser-Hall, Matturri, Sorrentino. 1958. 25 I.L.R. 91

Under the 1947 Peace Treaty between the Allied Powers and Italy, claims could be brought against Italy on behalf of "United Nations nationals" in certain cases arising out of the Second World War concerning property rights. In this case, brought by the United States, the Commission found that the claimant was not a United States national and hence not a "United Nations national" within the meaning of the Peace Treaty. The claim was therefore not admissible. Although its decision was based upon this finding, the Commission did consider an Italian argument that assumed that the claimant was a United States national and relied upon the absence of a "genuine connection" of the kind required by the *Nottebohm Case*. Note that the claimant was not a national of any other state. He had been a national of Germany, but had forfeited his German nationality in 1940 under German law.

Opinion of the Commission

The Commission is of the opinion that it is doubtful that the International Court of Justice intended to establish a rule of general international law in requiring, in the *Nottebohm Case,* that there must exist an effective link between the person and the State in order that the latter may exercise its right of diplomatic protection in behalf of the former. The Court itself restricted the scope of its Decision by affirming that the acquisition of nationality in a State must be recognized by all other States,

> subject to the twofold reservation that, in the first place, what is involved is not recognition for all purposes but merely for the purposes of the admissibility of the Application, and, secondly, that what is involved is not recognition by all States but only by Guatemala.

The Court further clarified its thought by affirming:

> The Court does not propose to go beyond the limited scope of the question which it has to decide, namely, whether the nationality conferred on Nottebohm can be relied upon as against Guatemala in justification of the proceedings instituted before the Court. (*I.C.J. Reports,* 1955, p. 17.)

The Court has thus distinctly affirmed the relative nature of its decision, cannot be opposed to the Government of the United States in this dispute.

The theory of effective or active nationality was established, in the Law of Nations, and above all in international private law, for the purpose of settling conflicts between two national States, or two national laws, regarding persons simultaneously vested with both nationalities, in order to decide which of them

---

[7] *U.S.* v. *Mexico*, 4 R.I.A.A. 669 at p. 678 (1931).

is to be dominant, whether that described as nominal, based on legal provisions of a given legal system, or that described as effective or active, equally based on legal provisions of another legal system, but confirmed by elements of fact (domicile, participation in the political life, the center of family and business interests, etc.). . . .

Application thereof was made in cases of dual nationality, like the *Canevaro Case*[8] . . .

The Commission referred also to the 1930 Hague Convention.[9]

The theory of effective or active nationality was nevertheless limited in its application by the principle of the unopposability of the nationality of a third State, which, in an international dispute caused by a person with multiple nationalities, permits the dismissal of the nationality of the third State, even when it should be considered as predominant in the light of the circumstances; this was the decision rendered on June 8, 1932, by the Arbitral Tribunal in the *Salem Case*,[10] disputed between the United States and Egypt, when this latter country invoked the Persian nationality which the claimant possessed, besides Egyptian nationality, to obtain a rejection of the claim of the United States. . . .

But when a person is vested with only one nationality, which is attributed to him or her either *jure sanguinis* or *jure soli,* or by a valid naturalization entailing the positive loss of the former nationality, the theory of effective nationality cannot be applied without the risk of causing confusion. It lacks a sufficiently positive basis to be applied to a nationality which finds support in a state law. There does not in fact exist any criterion of proven effectiveness for disclosing the effectiveness of a bond with a political collectivity, and the persons by the thousands who, because of the facility of travel in the modern world, possess the positive legal nationality of a State, but live in foreign States where they are domiciled and where their family and business center is located, would be exposed to non-recognition, at the international level, of the nationality with which they are undeniably vested by virtue of the laws of their national State, if this doctrine were to be generalized.

(b) *Protection in Cases of Dual Nationality*

CANEVARO CASE

Italy *v.* Peru (1912)

Permanent Court of Arbitration: Renault, Fusinato, Calderon. 11 R.I.A.A. 397.
Translation in 6 A.J.I.L. 746 (1912)

The Tribunal was asked whether Italy could claim on behalf of Raphael Canevaro who had both Italian and Peruvian nationality.

Award of the Tribunal

And whereas, as a matter of fact, Raphael Canevaro has on several occasions acted as a Peruvian citizen, both by running as a candidate for the Senate, where none are admitted except Peruvian citizens and where he went to defend his election, and also especially by accepting the office of Consul General of the

---

[8] *Ed.* See below.
[9] See above, p. 441.
[10] *Ed.* See below, p. 451.

Netherlands, after soliciting the authorization of the Peruvian Government and then of the Peruvian Congress;

And whereas, under these circumstances, whatever Raphael Canevaro's status may be in Italy with respect to his nationality, the Government of Peru has a right to consider him as a Peruvian citizen and to deny his status as an Italian claimant.

SALEM CASE

Egypt *v.* U.S. (1932)

Arbitral Tribunal: Simons; Nielsen, Amercan member; Badawi, Egyptian member. 2 R.I.A.A. 1161

Award of the Tribunal[11]

The principle of the so-called "effective nationality" the Egyptian Government referred to does not seem to be sufficiently established in international law. It was used in the famous *Canevaro* case; but the decision of the Arbitral Tribunal appointed at that time has remained isolated. In spite of the *Canevaro* case, the practice of several governments, for instance the German, is that if two powers are both entitled by international law to treat a person as their national, neither of these powers can raise a claim against the other in the name of such person (Borchard, 1. c., p. 588). Accordingly the Egyptian Government need not refer to the rule of "effective nationality" to oppose the American claim if they can only bring evidence that Salem was an Egyptian subject and that he acquired the American nationality without the express consent of the Egyptian Government.

. . . In the opinion of the Arbitral Court the Egyptian Government is unable to bring such evidence. Indeed from the circumstances it must be assumed that Salem was not an Egyptian subject but a Persian subject when he acquired American nationality. . . .

It is beside the point to ask whether Salem lost his Persian nationality or not by the acquisition of American nationality. . . . Whatever may be the true interpretation, the Egyptian Government cannot set forth against the United States the eventual continuation of the Persian nationality of George Salem; the rule of international law being that in a case of dual nationality a third power is not entitled to contest the claim of one of the two powers whose national is interested in the case by referring to the nationality of the other power. (*Cf. MacKenzie* v. *Germany,* 1922, Opinions of the Mixed Claims Commission, United States and Germany, p. 628.)[12]

Note

Could Italy have brought its claim against Peru in the *Canevaro* Case according to the Tribunal in the *Salem* Case? Could Peru have claimed against Italy?

[11] Nielsen dissenting.
[12] *Ed*. 20 A.J.I.L. 595 (1926).

MERGÉ CLAIM

Italian-United States Conciliation Commission: Yanguas Messia, Matturri, Sorrentino. 1955.
22 I.L.R. 443

As in the *Flegenheimer Claim* (above, p. 449, the United States brought this claim under the 1947 Italian Peace Treaty. In this case the problem was that the claimant was of both United States and Italian nationality. Having determined that the treaty, which permitted claims on behalf of "United Nations nationals," contained no provisions governing the case of dual nationality," the Commission decided that the question whether the United States could bring the claim against Italy must be decided according to "the general principles of international law."

Opinion of the Commission

(1) The rules of the Hague Convention of 1930[13] and the customary law manifested in international precedents and in the legal writings of the authors attest the existence and the practice of two principles in the problem of diplomatic protection in dual nationality cases. The first of these, specifically referring to the scope of diplomatic protection, as a question of public international law, is based on the sovereign equality of the States in the matter of nationality and bars protection in behalf of those who are simultaneously also nationals of the defendant State. The second of the principles had its origin in *private* international law, in those cases, that is, in which the courts of a third State had to resolve a conflict of nationality laws. Thus, the principle of effective nationality was created with relation to the individual. But decisions and legal writings, because of its evident justice, quickly transported it to the sphere of *public* international law.

(2) It is not a question of adopting one nationality to the exclusion of the other. Even less when it is recognized by both Parties that the claimant possesses the two nationalities. The problem to be explained is, simply, that of determining whether diplomatic protection can be exercised in such cases.

(3) . . . The Commission is of the opinion that no irreconcilable opposition between the two principles exists; in fact, to the contrary, it believes that they complement each other reciprocally. The principle according to which a State cannot protect one of its nationals against a State which also considers him its national and the principle of effective, in the sense of dominant, nationality, have both been accepted by the Hague Convention (Articles 4 and 5) and by the International Court of Justice (Advisory Opinion of April 11, 1949,[14] and the *Nottebohm* decision of April 6, 1955). If these two principles were irreconcilable, the acceptance of both by the Hague Convention and by the International Court of Justice would be incomprehensible. . . .

(5) The principle, based on the sovereign equality of States, which excludes diplomatic protection in the case of dual nationality, must yield before the principle of effective nationality whenever such nationality is that of the claiming State. But it must not yield when such predominance is not proved, because the first of these two principles is generally recognized and may constitute a criterion of practical application for the elimination of any possible uncertainty.

(6) The question of dual nationality obviously arises only in cases where the

[13] *Ed*. See above, p. 441.
[14] *Ed. Reparation Case*, above, p. 114.

claimant was in possession of both nationalities at the time the damage occurred and during the whole of the period comprised between the date of the Armistice (September 3, 1943) and the date of the coming into force of the Treaty of Peace (September 15, 1947). In view of the principles accepted, it is considered that the Government of the United States of America shall be entitled to protect its nationals before this Commission in cases of dual nationality, United States and Italian, whenever the United States nationality is the effective nationality. In order to establish the prevalence of the United States nationality in individual cases, habitual residence can be one of the criteria of evaluation, but not the only one. The conduct of the individual in his economic, social, political, civic and family life, as well as the closer and more effective bond with one of the two States must also be considered.

The Commission applied this test to the facts before it and found that the claimant failed to satisfy it.

Notes
1. Did the Commission prefer the approach taken in the *Canevaro* Case or that taken in the *Salem* Case? Which approach *should* be preferred?
2. The Rules regarding International Claims issued by the British Foreign and Commonwealth Office in 1971[15] read:

Rule III

Where the claimant is a dual national, Her Majesty's Government may take up his claim but will usually prefer to do so jointly with the other government entitled to do so. Her Majesty's Government will not normally take up his claim as a United Kingdom national if the respondent state is the state of his second nationality, but may do so if the respondent state has, in the circumstances which gave rise to the injury, treated the claimant as a United Kingdom national.

(c) *Protection of Companies and Shareholders*

BARCELONA TRACTION, LIGHT AND POWER CO. CASE[16]

Belgium *v.* Spain

I.C.J. Reports 1970, p. 3

The company concerned was established under Canadian law in 1911 in connection with the development of electricity supplies in Spain. In 1948, it was declared bankrupt by a Spanish court and, at about the same time, other steps were taken by Spanish authorities injuring it. Canada intervened on its behalf to begin with but later withdrew. At all relevant times, 88 per cent. of the shares in the company were, Belgium claimed, owned by Belgian nationals. Belgium brought this claim in respect of the injury to its nationals who were shareholders resulting from the injury to the company. Spain objected that since the injury was to the company, not the shareholders, Belgium lacked *locus standi* to bring the claim. In a judgment in 1964,[17] the Court joined this preliminary objection to the merits.

[15] See above p. 448.
[16] See Briggs, 65 A.J.I.L. 327 (1971); Higgins, 11 Virg. Jo. I.L. 327 (1971); Lillich, 65 A.J.I.L. 522 (1971).
[17] I.C.J.Rep. 1964, p. 6.

Judgment of the Court

33. When a State admits into its territory foreign investments or foreign nationals, whether natural or juristic persons, it is bound to extend to them the protection of the law and assumes obligations concerning the treatment to be afforded them. These obligations, however, are neither absolute nor unqualified. In particular, an essential distinction should be drawn between the obligations of a State towards the international community as a whole, and those arising *vis-à-vis* another State in the field of diplomatic protection. By their very nature the former are the concern of all States. In view of the importance of the rights involved, all States can be held to have a legal interest in their protection; they are obligations *erga omnes*.

34. Such obligations derive, for example, in contemporary international law, from the outlawing of acts of aggression, and of genocide, as also from the principles and rules concerning the basic rights of the human person including protection from slavery and racial discrimination. Some of the corresponding rights of protection have entered into the body of general international law (*Reservations to the Convention on the Prevention and Punishment of the Crime of Genocide, Advisory Opinion, I.C.J. Reports* 1951, p. 23); others are conferred by international instruments of a universal or quasi-universal character.

35. Obligations the performance of which is the subject of diplomatic protection are not of the same category. It cannot be held, when one such obligation in particular is in question, in a specific case, that all States have a legal interest in its observance. In order to bring a claim in respect of the breach of such an obligation, a State must first establish its right to do so, for the rules on the subject rest on two suppositions:

> The first is that the defendant State has broken an obligation towards the national State in respect of its nationals. The second is that only the party to whom an international obligation is due can bring a claim in respect of its breach. (*Reparation for Injuries Suffered in the Service of the United Nations, Advisory Opinion, I.C.J. Reports* 1949, pp. 181–182).

In the present case it is therefore essential to establish whether the losses allegedly suffered by Belgian shareholders in Barcelona Traction were the consequence of the violation of obligations of which they were the beneficiaries. In other words: has a right of Belgium been violated on account of its nationals' having suffered infringement of their rights as shareholders in a company not of Belgian nationality?

36. Thus it is the existence or absence of a right, belonging to Belgium and recognized as such by international law, which is decisive for the problem of Belgium's capacity. . . .

38. In this field international law is called upon to recognize institutions of municipal law that have an important and extensive role in the international field. . . .

41. . . . The concept and structure of the [limited liability] company are founded on and determined by a firm distinction between the separate entity of the company and that of the shareholder, each with a distinct set of rights. The separation of property rights as between company and shareholder is an important manifestation of this distinction. So long as the company is in existence the shareholder has no right to the corporate assets. . . .

44. Notwithstanding the separate corporate personality, a wrong done to the

company frequently causes prejudice to its shareholders. But the mere fact that damage is sustained by both company and shareholder does not imply that both are entitled to claim compensation. . . . Thus whenever a shareholder's interests are harmed by an act done to the company, it is to the latter that he must look to institute appropriate action; for although two separate entities may have suffered from the same wrong, it is only one entity whose rights have been infringed. . . .

47. The situation is different if the act complained of is aimed at the direct rights of the shareholder as such. It is well known that there are rights which municipal law confers upon the latter distinct from those of the company, including the right to any declared dividend, the right to attend and vote at general meetings, the right to share in the residual assets of the company on liquidation. Whenever one of his direct rights is infringed, the shareholder has an independent right of action. . . .

48. The Belgian Government claims that shareholders of Belgian nationality suffered damage in consequence of unlawful acts of the Spanish authorities and, in particular, that the Barcelona Traction shares, though they did not cease to exist, were emptied of all real economic content. It accordingly contends that the shareholders had an independent right to redress, nothwithstanding the fact that the acts complained of were directed against the company as such. Thus the legal issue is reducible to the question of whether it is legitimate to identify an attack on company rights, resulting in damage to shareholders, with the violation of their direct rights. . . .

50. In turning now to the international legal aspects of the case, the Court must, as already indicated, start from the fact that the present case essentially involves factors derived from municipal law—the distinction and the community between the company and the shareholder—which the Parties, however widely their interpretations may differ, each take as the point of departure of their reasoning. If the Court were to decide the case in disregard of the relevant institutions of municipal law it would, without justification, invite serious legal difficulties. It would lose touch with reality, for there are no corresponding institutions of international law to which the Court could resort. Thus the Court has, as indicated, not only to take cognizance of municipal law but also to refer to it. It is to rules generally accepted by municipal legal systems which recognize the limited company whose capital is represented by shares, and not to the municipal law of a particular State, that international law refers. In referring to such rules, the Court cannot modify, still less deform them.

51. On the international plane, the Belgian Government has advanced the proposition that it is inadmissible to deny the shareholders' national State a right of diplomatic protection merely on the ground that another State possesses a corresponding right in respect of the company itself. In strict logic and law this formulation of the Belgian claim to *jus standi* assumes the existence of the very right that requires demonstration. In fact the Belgian Government has repeatedly stressed that there exists no rule of international law which would deny the national State of the shareholders the right of diplomatic protection for the purpose of seeking redress pursuant to unlawful acts committed by another State against the company in which they hold shares. This, by emphasizing the absence of any express denial of the right, conversely implies the admission that there is no rule of international law which expressly confers such a right on the shareholders' national State.

52. International law may not, in some fields, provide specific rules in particular cases. In the concrete situation, the company against which allegedly unlawful acts were directed is expressly vested with a right, whereas no such right is specifically provided for the shareholder in respect of those acts. Thus the position of the company rests on a positive rule of both municipal and international law. As to the shareholder, while he has certain rights expressly provided for him by municipal law . . . . , appeal can, in the circumstances of the present case, only be made to the silence of international law. Such silence scarcely admits of interpretation in favour of the shareholder.

53. It is quite true, as was recalled in the course of oral argument in the present case, that concurrent claims are not excluded in the case of a person who, having entered the service of an international organization and retained his nationality, enjoys simultaneously the right to be protected by his national State and the right to be protected by the organization to which he belongs. This however is a case of one person in possession of two separate bases of protection, each of which is valid (*Reparation for Injuries Suffered in the Service of the United Nations, Advisory Opinion, I.C.J. Reports* 1949, p. 185). There is no analogy between such a situation and that of foreign shareholders in a company which has been the victim of a violation of international law which has caused them damage. . . .

55. The Court will now examine other grounds on which it is conceivable that the submission by the Belgian Government of a claim on behalf of shareholders in Barcelona Traction may be justified. . . .

The Court then refers to municipal law again and the practice of "lifting the veil" for some purposes to take account of the identity of persons behind the company.

58. In accordance with the principle expounded above, the process of lifting the veil, being an exceptional one admitted by municipal law in respect of an institution of its own making, is equally admissible to play a similar role in international law. It follows that on the international plane also there may in principle be special circumstances which justify the lifting of the veil in the interest of shareholders. . . .

64. . . . In this connection two particular situations must be studied: the case of the company having ceased to exist and the case of the company's national State lacking capacity to take action on its behalf.

65. As regards the first of these possibilities the Court observes that . . . Barcelona Traction has lost all its assets in Spain, and was placed in receivership in Canada, a receiver and manager having been appointed. It is common ground that from the economic viewpoint the company has been entirely paralyzed. . . .

66. It cannot however, be contended that the corporate entity of the company has ceased to exist, or that it has lost its capacity to take corporate action. . . . It has not become incapable in law of defending its own rights and the interests of the shareholders. In particular, a precarious financial situation cannot be equated with the demise of the corporate entity, which is the hypothesis under consideration: the company's status in law is alone relevant, and not its economic condition, nor even the possibility of its being "practically defunct"— a description on which argument has been based but which lacks all legal precision. Only in the event of the legal demise of the company are the shareholders deprived of the possibility of a remedy available through the

company; it is only if they became deprived of all such possibility that an independent right of action for them and their government could arise.

67. In the present case, Barcelona Traction is in receivership in the country of incorporation. Far from implying the demise of the entity or of its rights, this much rather denotes that those rights are preserved for so long as no liquidation has ensued. Though in receivership, the company continues to exist. Moreover, it is a matter of public record that the company's shares were quoted on the stock-market at a recent date.

68. . . . The Court is thus not confronted with the first hypothesis contemplated in paragraph 64, and need not pronounce upon it.

69. The Court will now turn to the second possibility, that of the lack of capacity of the company's national State to act on its behalf. The first question which must be asked here is whether Canada—the third apex of the triangular relationship—is, in law, the national State of Barcelona Traction.

70. In allocating corporate entities to States for purposes of diplomatic protection, international law is based, but only to a limited extent, on an analogy with the rules governing the nationality of individuals. The traditional rule attributes the right of diplomatic protection of a corporate entity to the State under the laws of which it is incorporated and in whose territory it has its registered office. These two criteria have been confirmed by long practice and by numerous international instruments. This notwithstanding, further or different links are at times said to be required in order that a right of diplomatic protection should exist. Indeed, it has been the practice of some States to give a company incorporated under their law diplomatic protection solely when it has its seat (*siège social*) or management or centre of control in their territory, or when a majority or a substantial proportion of the shares has been owned by nationals of the State concerned. Only then, it has been held, does there exist between the corporation and the State in question a genuine connection of the kind familiar from other branches of international law. However, in the particular field of the diplomatic protection of corporate entities, no absolute test of the "genuine connection" has found general acceptance. Such tests as have been applied are of a relative nature, and sometimes links with one State have had to be weighed against those with another. In this connection reference has been made to the *Nottebohm* case.[18] . . . However, given both the legal and factual aspects of protection in the present case the Court is of the opinion that there can be no analogy with the issues raised or the decision given in that case.

71. In the present case, it is not disputed that the company was incorporated in Canada and has its registered office in that country. The incorporation of the company under the law of Canada was an act of free choice. Not only did the founders of the company seek its incorporation under Canadian law but it has remained under that law for a period of over 50 years. It has maintained in Canada its registered office, its accounts and its share registers. Board meetings were held there for many years; it has been listed in the records of the Canadian tax authorities. Thus a close and permanent connection has been established, fortified by the passage of over half a century. This connection is in no way weakened by the fact that the company engaged from the very outset in commercial activities outside Canada, for that was its declared object. Barcelona Traction's links with Canada are thus manifold.

---

[18] *Ed.* See above, p. 442.

72. Furthermore, the Canadian nationality of the company has received general recognition. Prior to the institution of proceedings before the Court, three other governments apart from that of Canada (those of the United Kingdom, the United States and Belgium) made representations concerning the treatment accorded to Barcelona Traction by the Spanish authorities. The United Kingdom Government intervened on behalf of bondholders and of shareholders. Several representations were also made by the United States Government, but not on behalf of the Barcelona Traction company as such. . . .

73. Both Governments acted at certain stages in close co-operation with the Canadian Government. . . .

74. As to the Belgian Government, its earlier action was also undertaken in close co-operation with the Canadian Government. The Belgian Government admitted the Canadian character of the company in the course of the present proceedings. It explicitly stated that Barcelona Traction was a company of neither Spanish nor Belgian nationality but a Canadian company incorporated in Canada. The Belgian Government has even conceded that it was not concerned with the injury suffered by Barcelona Traction itself, since that was Canada's affair. . . .

76. In sum, the record shows that from 1948 onwards the Canadian Government made to the Spanish Government numerous representations which cannot be viewed otherwise than as the exercise of diplomatic protection in respect of the Barcelona Traction company. Therefore this was not a case where diplomatic protection was refused or remained in the sphere of fiction. It is also clear that over the whole period of its diplomatic activity the Canadian Government proceeded in full knowledge of the Belgian attitude and activity.

77. It is true that at a certain point the Canadian Government ceased to act on behalf of Barcelona Traction, for reasons which have not been fully revealed, though a statement made in a letter of 19 July 1955 by the Canadian Secretary of State for External Affairs suggests that it felt the matter should be settled by means of private negotiations.[19] The Canadian Government has nonetheless retained its capacity to exercise diplomatic protection; no legal impediment has prevented it from doing so: no fact has arisen to render this protection impossible. It has discontinued its action of its own free will.

78. The Court would here observe that, within the limits prescribed by international law, a State may exercise diplomatic protection by whatever means and to whatever extent it thinks fit, for it is its own right that the State is asserting. Should the natural or legal persons on whose behalf it is acting consider that their rights are not adequately protected, they have no remedy in international law. All they can do is to resort to municipal law, if means are available, with a view to furthering their cause or obtaining redress. The municipal legislator may lay upon the State an obligation to protect its citizens abroad, and may also confer upon the national a right to demand the performance of that obligation, and clothe the right with corresponding sanctions.

---

[19] *Ed.* "By late 1951 the Canadian Secretary of State for External Affairs told the Spanish Consul in Canada that 'Canadian interests in this case are so slight that it is of little interest to us' ": *Barcelona Traction Case (Preliminary Objections)*, Separate Opinion of Judge Wellington Koo, I.C.J.Rep. 1970, at pp. 61–62. Altogether, there were 12 judgments delivered in the case.

However, all these questions remain within the province of municipal law and do not affect the position internationally.

79. The State must be viewed as the sole judge to decide whether its protection will be granted, to what extent it is granted, and when it will cease. It remains in this respect a discretionary power the exercise of which may be determined by considerations of a political or other nature, unrelated to the particular case. Since the claim of the State is not identical with that of the individual or corporate person whose cause is espoused, the State enjoys complete freedom of action. Whatever the reasons for any change of attitude, the fact cannot in itself constitute a justification for the exercise of diplomatic protection by another government, unless there is some independent and otherwise valid ground for that. . . .

81. The cessation by the Canadian Government of the diplomatic protection of Barcelona Traction cannot, then, be interpreted to mean that there is no remedy against the Spanish Government for the damage done by the allegedly unlawful acts of the Spanish authorities. . . . Therefore there is no substance in the argument that for the Belgian Government to bring a claim before the Court represented the only possibility of obtaining redress for the damage suffered by Barcelona Traction and, through it, by its shareholders. . . .

83. The Canadian Government's right of protection in respect of the Barcelona Traction company remains unaffected by the present proceedings. The Spanish Government has never challenged the Canadian nationality of the company, either in the diplomatic correspondence with the Canadian Government or before the Court. Moreover it has unreservedly recognized Canada as the national State of Barcelona Traction in both written pleadings and oral statements made in the course of the present proceedings. Consequently, the Court considers that the Spanish Government has not questioned Canada's right to protect the company. . . .

92. Since the general rule on the subject does not entitle the Belgian Government to put forward a claim in this case, the question remains to be considered whether nonetheless, as the Belgian Government has contended during the proceedings, considerations of equity do not require that it be held to possess a right of protection . . . a theory has been developed to the effect that the State of the shareholders has a right of diplomatic protection when the State whose responsibility is invoked is the national State of the company. Whatever the validity of this theory may be, it is certainly not applicable to the present case, since Spain is not the national State of Barcelona Traction.

93. On the other hand, the Court considers that, in the field of diplomatic protection as in all other fields of international law, it is necessary that the law be applied reasonably. It has been suggested that if in a given case it is not possible to apply the general rule that the right of diplomatic protection of a company belongs to its national State, considerations of equity might call for the possibility of protection of the shareholders in question by their own national State. This hypothesis does not correspond to the circumstances of the present case.

94. In view, however, of the discretionary nature of diplomatic protection, considerations of equity cannot require more than the possibility for some protector State to intervene, whether it be the national State of the company, by virtue of the general rule mentioned above, or, in a secondary capacity, the national State of the shareholders who claim protection. In this connection,

account should also be taken of the practical effects of deducing from considerations of equity any broader right of protection for the national State of the shareholders. It must first of all be observed that it would be difficult on an equitable basis to make distinctions according to any quantitative test: it would seem that the owner of 1 per cent. and the owner of 90 per cent. of the share-capital should have the same possibility of enjoying the benefit of diplomatic protection. The protector State may, of course, be disinclined to take up the case of the single small shareholder, but it could scarcely be denied the right to do so in the name of equitable considerations. In that field, protection by the national State of the shareholders can hardly be graduated according to the absolute or relative size of the shareholding involved. . . .

96. The Court considers that the adoption of the theory of diplomatic protection of shareholders as such, by opening the door to competing diplomatic claims, could create an atmosphere of confusion and insecurity in international economic relations. The danger would be all the greater inasmuch as the shares of companies whose activity is international are widely scattered and frequently change hands. It might perhaps be claimed that, if the right of protection belonging to the national States of the shareholders were considered as only secondary to that of the national State of the company, there would be less danger of difficulties of the kind contemplated. However, the Court must state that the essence of a secondary right is that it only comes into existence at the time when the original right ceases to exist. As the right of protection vested in the national State of the company cannot be regarded as extinguished because it is not exercised, it is not possible to accept the proposition that in case of its non-exercise the national States of the shareholders have a right of protection secondary to that of the national State of the company. Furthermore, study of factual situations in which this theory might possibly be applied gives rise to the following observations.

97. The situations in which foreign shareholders in a company wish to have recourse to diplomatic protection by their own national State may vary. It may happen that the national State of the company simply refuses to grant it its diplomatic protection, or that it begins to exercise it (as in the present case) but does not pursue its action to the end. It may also happen that the national State of the company and the State which has committed a violation of international law with regard to the company arrive at a settlement of the matter, by agreeing on compensation for the company, but that the foreign shareholders find the compensation insufficient. Now, as a matter of principle, it would be difficult to draw a distinction between these three cases so far as the protection of foreign shareholders by their national State is concerned, since in each case they may have suffered real damage. Furthermore, the national State of the company is perfectly free to decide how far it is appropriate for it to protect the company, and is not bound to make public the reasons for its decision. To reconcile this discretionary power of the company's national State with a right of protection falling to the shareholders' national State would be particularly difficult when the former State has concluded, with the State which has contravened international law with regard to the company, an agreement granting the company compensation which the foreign shareholders find inadequate. If, after such a settlement, the national State of the foreign shareholders could in its turn put forward a claim based on the same facts, this would be likely to introduce into the negotiation of this kind of agreement a lack of security which would be

contrary·to the stability which it is the object of international law to establish in international relations.

98. It is quite true, as recalled in paragraph 53, that international law recognizes parallel rights of protection in the case of a person in the service of an international organization. Nor is the possibility excluded of concurrent claims being made on behalf of persons having dual nationality, although in that case lack of a genuine link with one of the two States may be set up against the exercise by that State of the right of protection. It must be observed, however, that in these two types of situation the number of possible protectors is necessarily very small, and their identity normally not difficult to determine. In this respect such cases of dual protection are markedly different from the claims to which recognition of a general right of protection of foreign shareholders by their various national States might give rise.

99. It should also be observed that the promoters of a company whose operations will be international must take into account the fact that States have, with regard to their nationals, a discretionary power to grant diplomatic protection or to refuse it. When establishing a company in a foreign country, its promoters are normally impelled by particular considerations; it is often a question of tax or other advantages offered by the host State. It does not seem to be in any way inequitable that the advantages thus obtained should be balanced by the risks arising from the fact that the protection of the company and hence of its shareholders is thus entrusted to a State other than the national State of the shareholders.

100. In the present case, it is clear from what has been said above that Barcelona Traction was never reduced to a position of impotence such that it could not have approached its national State, Canada, to ask for its diplomatic protection, and that, as far as appeared to the Court, there was nothing to prevent Canada from continuing to grant its diplomatic protection to Barcelona Traction if it had considered that it should do so.

101. For the above reasons, the Court is not of the opinion that, in the particular circumstances of the present case, *jus standi* is conferred on the Belgian Government by considerations of equity. . . .

103. Accordingly, the Court rejects the Belgian Government's claim by fifteen votes to one, twelve votes of the majority being based on the reasons set out in the present Judgment.[20]

Notes

1. *The Protection of Companies.*[21] The Barcelona Traction Company continues legally in existence, although it did not trade, until 1980 when it was dissolved under Canadian law. It would seem to have been understood by states before the *Nottebohm Case* that they could protect any company having their nationality according to their law. In 1911, for example, when it became known that the Government of Siam, in interpreting a treaty between Siam and the United Kingdom guaranteeing "British subjects" national treatment in respect of land in Siam, was of a mind to treat British companies, to which the treaty undoubtedly extended, differently from other

---

[20] The judges in the majority were President Bustamante y Rivero; Vice-President Koretsky; Judges Sir Gerald Fitzmaurice, Tanaka, Jessup, Morelli, Padilla Nervo, Forster, Gros, Ammoun, Bengzon, Petrén, Lachs and Onyeama; Judge ad hoc Armand-Ugon. The dissenting judge was Judge ad hoc Riphagen. The three judges in the majority who did not concur in the reasoning of the Court were Judges Tanaka, Jessup and Gros.

[21] See Beckett, 17 Trans.Grot.Soc. 175 (1932) and Harris, 18 I.C.L.Q. 275 (1969).

British subjects because non-British interests were incorporating British companies in order to take advantage of its terms, the Foreign Office responded in the following terms: "The Siamese Government could not be permitted to maintain that a company, duly incorporated as British, was really foreign and that His Majesty's Government had no right to protect it."[22] Is this attitude supported by the *Barcelona Traction Case?* Note that the Rules regarding International Claims[23] issued by the British Foreign and Commonwealth Office after that case read:

Rule IV

Her Majesty's Government may take up the claim of a corporation or other juridical person which is created and regulated by the law of the United Kingdom or of any territory for which Her Majesty's Government is internationally responsible.

Comment

This rule rests on the principle that a juridical person (such as a company, corporation or other association having a legal personality distinct from its members), has the nationality of that country whose law has formally created it, which regulates its constitution, and under whose law it can be wound up or dissolved. This principle was endorsed by the International Court of Justice in the *Barcelona Traction Case (Belgium v. Spain)* in 1970. Certain states determine nationality of a corporation by different tests—(a) the place of central administration (*siège social*) or (b) the place of effective control (to determine which the residence of the majority of shareholders as well as of the directors may be taken into account). The International Court however said that not one of these tests of "genuine connexion" has found general international acceptance.

In determining whether to exercise its right of protection, Her Majesty's Government may however consider whether the company has in fact a real and substantial connexion with the United Kingdom.

2. *Protection of Shareholders.*[24] Do you find the reasons given by the Court for rejecting the argument for a secondary power of protection on the part of the national state of shareholders in a foreign company when the national state of the company will not act convincing? Should the case be regarded as indicating one situation in which the general rule of protection in international law, leaving the interests of individuals as a discretionary matter in the hands of their national state, can lead to injustice? The Court suggests in its judgment (para. 99) that the promoters of companies should take into account the risk of non-protection as well as considerations such as tax advantage. Is the Court also suggesting that persons thinking of investing in foreign companies should bear in mind the same factor?

In 1925, in the *Romano-Americana Case,*[25] the United States sought compensation from the United Kingdom for the destruction in 1916 of the assets in Roumania of a Roumanian subsidiary company of an American parent company. The assets had been destroyed by "the Roumanian authorities with the collaboration of certain British Officers acting under instructions from the British Government"[26] to prevent them coming into the hands of the enemy. In denying responsibility, the United Kingdom argued: ". . . it will be found upon examination that the cases in which the right of a Government to intervene on behalf of the shareholders of such a corporation for the

---

[22] 5 B.D.I.L. 510, at p. 511.
[23] See above, p. 448.
[24] See Jones (1949) 26 B.Y.I.L. 225.
[25] 5 Hackworth 840.
[26] *Ibid.* p. 841.

purpose of establishing a claim against another Government, has been admitted, are few in number and exhibit certain marked characteristics, none of which are present in the case now under consideration. Cases of this kind fall, generally speaking into two classes: (1) where the action of the Government against whom the claim is made has, in law or in fact, put an end to the Company's existence, or by confiscating its property, has compelled it to suspend operations; (2) where by special agreement between the two Governments a right to compensation has been accorded to the shareholders. . . . The first class, so far from being an exception to the general rule, is in fact an example of its application; for it is not until a company has ceased to have an active existence or has gone into liquidation that the interest of its shareholders ceases to be merely the right to share in the company's profits and becomes a right to share in its actual surplus assets."[27] The United States later discontinued its claim against the United Kingdom and took up its case against Roumania, which eventually agreed to pay compensation. Is the British argument consistent with the Court's judgment?[28]

In 1938, in the *Mexican Eagle Co. Case,*[29] Mexico expropriated the assets of an oil company registered in Mexico the shares in which were almost entirely foreign owned. When Mexico protested at British intervention on behalf of the substantial British interests in the company, the United Kingdom replied: "If the doctrine were admitted that a government can first make the operation of foreign interests in its territories depend upon their incorporation under local law, and then plead such incorporation as the justification for rejecting foreign diplomatic intervention, it is clear that the means would never be wanting whereby foreign governments could be prevented from exercising their undoubted right under international law to protect the commercial interests of their nationals abroad." Eventually arrangements for the payment of compensation were made. Does the Court's judgment leave open the possibility that the British argument here would be acceptable to it? Or would the same considerations that prevented the Court from allowing a secondary power of protection to the national state of shareholders on a basis of equity defeat this argument too?

The Rules regarding International Claims[30] issued by the British Foreign and Commonwealth Office after the *Barcelona Traction Case* read:

Rule V

Where a United Kingdom national has an interest, as a shareholder or otherwise, in a company incorporated in another state, and that company is injured by the acts of a third state, Her Majesty's Government may normally take up his claim only in concert with the government of the state in which the company is incorporated. But exceptionally, as where the company is defunct, there may be independent intervention.

Rule VI

Where a United Kingdom national has an interest, as a shareholder or otherwise, in a company incorporated in another state and of which it is therefore a national, and that state injures the company, Her Majesty's Government may intervene to protect the interests of that United Kingdom national.

---

[27] *Ibid.* p. 843.
[28] Note also that in 1889, in the *Delagoa Bay Case*, Great Britain and the U.S. successfully intervened to protect Anglo-American shareholders in a Portuguese company on the ground that the Portuguese company was "practically defunct": 81 B.F.S.P. 691 (1888–89). Was *this* consistent with the Court's judgment?
[29] Cmd. 5758, p. 9.
[30] See above, p. 448

Comment

In some cases the state of incorporation of a company does not possess the primary national interest in the company. Thus a company may be created for reasons of legal or economic advantage under the law of one state, when nearly all the capital is owned by nationals of another. In such circumstances the state in which the company is incorporated may have little interest in protecting it, while the state to which the national who owns the capital belongs has considerable interest in so doing. In the *Barcelona Traction Case* the International Court of Justice denied the existence under customary international law of an inherent right for the national state of shareholders in a foreign company to exercise diplomatic protection. But the majority of the Court accepted the existence of a right to protect shareholders in the two cases described in Rules V and VI—when the company is defunct, and where the state in which the company is incorporated, although theoretically the legal protector of the company, itself causes injury to the company.

Where the capital in a foreign company is owned in various proportions by nationals of several states, including the United Kingdom, it is unusual for Her Majesty's Government to make representations unless the states whose nationals hold the bulk of the capital will support them in making representations.

(xii) Exhaustion of Local Remedies[31]

AMBATIELOS ARBITRATION

Greece *v.* U.K. (1956)

Commission of Arbitration: Alfaro, President; Bagge, Bourquin, Spiropoulos, Thesiger.
12 R.I.A.A. 83; 23 I.L.R. 306 (1956)

In 1919, Ambatielos, a Greek national, agreed to buy a number of ships from the United Kingdom. On the British side, negotiations were conducted by a Major Laing. In this arbitration, Greece brought claims on behalf of Ambatielos arising out of the contract. The claims were rejected by the Tribunal, *inter alia,* on the ground of non-exhaustion of local remedies.

Award of the Commission

The rule thus invoked by the United Kingdom Government is well established in international law. Nor is its existence contested by the Greek Government. It means that the State against which an international action is brought for injuries suffered by private individuals has the right to resist such an action if the persons alleged to have been injured have not first exhausted all the remedies available to them under the municipal law of that State. The defendant State has the right to demand that full advantage shall have been taken of all local remedies before the matters in dispute are taken on the international level by the State of which the persons alleged to have been injured are nationals.

In order to contend successfully that international proceedings are inadmissible, the defendant State must prove the existence, in its system of internal law, of remedies which have not been used. The views expressed by writers and in judicial precedents, however, coincide in that the existence of remedies which

---

[31] See Head, 5 C.Y.I.L. 142 (1967); Law, *The Local Remedies Rule in International Law* (1961); Meron (1959) 35 B.Y.I.L. 83; Mummery, 58 A.J.I.L. 389 (1964).

are obviously ineffective is held not to be sufficient to justify the application of the rule. Remedies which could not rectify the situation cannot be relied upon by the defendant State as precluding an international action.

The Greek Government contends that in the present case the remedies which English law offered to Mr. Ambatielos were ineffective and that, accordingly, the rule is not applicable.

The ineffectiveness of local remedies may result clearly from the municipal law itself. That is the case, for example, when a Court of Appeal is not competent to reconsider the judgment given by a Court of first instance on matters of fact, and when, failing such reconsideration, on redress can be obtained. . . .

Furthermore, however, it is generally considered that the ineffectiveness of available remedies, without being legally certain, may also result from circumstances which do not permit any hope of redress to be placed in the use of those remedies. But in a case of that kind it is essential that such remedies, if they had been resorted to, would have proved to be *obviously futile*. . . .

If the rule of exhaustion of local remedies is relied upon against the action of the claimant State, what is the test to be applied by an international tribunal for the purpose of determining the applicability of the rule?

As the arbitrator ruled in the *Finnish Vessels* Case of 9th May, 1934,[32] the only possible test is to assume the truth of the facts on which the claimant State bases its claim. . . .

In the Ambatielos Case, failure to use certain means of appeal is . . . relied upon by the United Kingdom Government, but reliance is also placed on the failure of Mr. Ambatielos to adduce before Mr. Justice Hill evidence which it is now said would have been essential to establish his claims. There is no doubt that the exhaustion of local remedies requires the use of the means of procedure which are essential to redress the situation complained of by the person who is alleged to have been injured. . . .

The rule requires that "local remedies" shall have been exhausted before an international action can be brought. These "local remedies" include not only reference to the courts and tribunals, but also the use of the procedural facilities which municipal law makes available to litigants before such courts and tribunals. It is the whole system of legal protection, as provided by municipal law, which must have been put to the test before a State, as the protector of its nationals, can prosecute the claim on the international plane. . . .

It is clear, however, that [this view] . . . cannot be strained too far. Taken literally, it would imply that the fact of having neglected to make use of some means of procedure—even one which is not important to the defence of the action—would suffice to allow a defendant State to claim that local remedies have not been exhausted, and that, therefore, an international action cannot be brought. This would confer on the rule of the prior exhaustion of local remedies a scope which is unacceptable.

In the view of the Commission the non-utilisation of certain means of procedure can be accepted as constituting a gap in the exhaustion of local remedies only if the use of these means of procedure were essential to establish the claimant's case before the municipal courts. . . .

---

[32] See below, p. 468.

As regards Claim A [for compensation for breach of contract], the questions of the non-exhaustion of local remedies thus raised are:

(1) In the 1922 proceedings Mr. Ambatielos failed to call (as he could have done) the witnesses who, as he now says, were essential to establish his case. . . .

It is not possible for the Commission to decide on the evidence before it the question whether the case would have been decided in favour of Mr. Ambatielos if Major Laing had been heard as a witness. The Commission has not heard the witnesses called before Mr. Justice Hill and cannot solely on the documentary evidence put before the Commission form an opinion whether the testimony of Major Laing would have been successful in establishing the claim of Mr. Ambatielos before Mr. Justice Hill. The Commission cannot put itself in the postion of Mr. Justice Hill in this respect.

The test as regards the question whether the testimony of Major Laing was essential must therefore be what the claimant Government in this respect has contended, viz. that the testimony of Major Laing would have had the effect of establishing the claim put forward by Mr. Ambatielos before Mr. Justice Hill.

Under English Law Mr. Ambatielos was not precluded from calling Major Laing as a witness.

In so far as concerns Claim A, the failure of Mr. Ambatielos to call Major Laing as a witness at the hearing before Mr. Justice Hill must therefore be held to amount to non-exhaustion of the local remedy available to him in the proceedings before Mr. Justice Hill.

It may be that the decision of Mr. Ambatielos not to call Major Laing as a witness, with the result that he did not exhaust local remedies, was dictated by reasons of expediency—quite understandable in themselves—in putting his case before Mr. Justice Hill. This, however, is not the question to be determined. The Commission is not concerned with the question as to whether he was right or wrong in acting as he did. He took his decision at his own risk.

(2) The second question as to non-exhaustion raised by the United Kingdom Government is the failure of Mr. Ambatielos to make use of or exhaust his appellate rights. . . .

Ambatielos instituted appeal proceedings in the Court of Appeal but did not continue with them after that Court had refused him leave to call Major Laing in evidence before it. He did not appeal against the Court of Appeal's decision on this question.

The refusal of the Court of Appeal to give leave to adduce the evidence of Major Laing did not, of course, in itself prevent this general appeal from being proceeded with.

The Greek Government argues by way of explanation that to proceed with the general appeal once the decision of the Court of Appeal not to admit the Laing evidence had been given would have been futile because the Laing evidence was essential to enable the Court to arrive at a decision favourable to Mr. Ambatielos.

The reason why Mr. Ambatielos was not allowed to call Major Laing in the Court of Appeal was, in the words of Lord Justice Scrutton, that "One of the principal rules which this Court adopts is that it will not give leave to adduce further evidence which might have been adduced with reasonable care at the trial of the action."

Accordingly, the failure of Mr. Ambatielos to exhaust the local remedy before Mr. Justice Hill, by not calling Major Laing as a witness, is the reason why it was futile for him to prosecute his appeal.

It would be wrong to hold that a party who, by failing to exhaust his opportunities in the Court of first instance, has caused an appeal to become futile should be allowed to rely on this fact in order to rid himself of the rule of exhaustion of local remedies.

It may be added that Mr. Ambatielos did not submit to the Court of Appeal any argument suggesting, or any evidence to show, that any illegal or improper manoeuvres by his opponents had prevented him from calling Major Laing or producing any documents.

In so far as concerns the appeal to the House of Lords, it is of course unlikely that that Court would have differed from the decision of the Court of Appeal, refusing to allow Major Laing to be called as a witness in the latter Court. If it is held that such an appeal would *not* have been obviously futile, the failure of Mr. Ambatielos to appeal to the House of Lords must be regarded as a failure to exhaust local remedies. If, on the other hand, it is held that an appeal to the House of Lords *would* have been obviously futile, Mr. Ambatielos must likewise be held to have lost his hope of a successful appeal, by reason of his failure to call Major Laing.

Arbitrators Alfaro and Spiropoulos dissented from the Commission's ruling on the question of local remedies.

Notes

1. Is there any indication in the arbitrators' award whether responsibility arises only upon the unsuccessful exhaustion of local remedies or whether it arises instead before and independently of their exhaustion upon the commission of the act being questioned?[33] The answer to this question has practical significance in connection with the rule concerning the nationality of claims that requires the claimant to have been a national of the state acting for him at the time that the claim arises and when the claim is brought.

2. In the *Aerial Incident of 27 July 1955 Case*,[34] Israel argued, correctly it is believed, as follows: ". . . it is universally recognised that the rule regarding exhaustion of local remedies is inapplicable to a case of a direct injury caused by one State to another. . . . The rule . . . applies solely to the case of so-called diplomatic protection. . . ." Any extension of the application of the rule to cover, for example, a case of violation of territorial sovereignty would conflict with the principle *par in parem non habet imperium, non habet jurisdictionem*.

3. *Kinds of Remedies.* The 1961 Harvard Draft Convention on the International Responsibility of States for Injuries to Aliens calls upon a claimant to employ "all administrative, arbitral, or judicial remedies" available to him.[35] The European Commission of Human Rights has ruled that an appeal for clemency is not a remedy for the purposes of the rule.[36] In the *Salem Case*,[37] Egypt argued that local remedies had not been exhausted because the claimant had available "the right to *recours en requête civile* against the decision of the Mixed Court of Appeal at Alexandria. . . ."[38] The Tribunal

---

[33] See Fawcett (1954) 31 B.Y.I.L. 452 and Article 22, I.L.C. Draft Articles on State Responsibility, *loc. cit.* at p. 374, n. 2 above.

[34] *I.C.J. Pleadings, Aerial Incident of 27 July 1955 Case*, pp. 530–531. See also the comment by Read above, p. 207–208, on the *Trail Smelter Case*.

[35] Draft Article 19, 55 A.J.I.L. 577.

[36] Application 458/59, 3 Y.B.E.C.H.R. 234 (1960).

[37] *Egypt* v. *U.S.*, 2 R.I.A.A. 1161 (1932).

[38] *Ibid.* p. 1177.

rejected the argument because "the *recours en requête civile* is no regular legal remedy but intends to re-open a process which has already been closed by a judgment of last resort."[39] It continued: "As a rule it is sufficient if the claimant has brought his suit up to the highest instance of the national judiciary."[40] In the *Nielsen Case*[41] the European Commission of Human Rights expressly disagreed and ruled that the extraordinary remedy in the case before it—recourse to the Danish Special Court of Revision—had to be exhausted to satisfy the rule.

Would the British Parliamentary Commissioner[42] be a local remedy for the purposes of the rule?

4. *Effective Remedies*. In the *Finnish Ships Arbitration*,[43] the arbitrator was asked to decide whether the local remedies rule had been exhausted by Finland in seeking compensation from Great Britain for the use by the latter of Finnish ships requisitioned during the First World War. Finland had sought compensation before the Admiralty Transport Arbitration Board but had been unsuccessful because the Arbitration Board had found as a fact that, although used during the War by Great Britain, the ships had been requisitioned by or on behalf of Russia (which then had sovereignty over Finland) and not, as required by the British legislation concerning compensation, by Great Britain. The Arbitrator ruled that Finland's failure to appeal to the Court of Appeal did not mean that it had not exhausted local remedies. Such an appeal would have been "obviously futile" because the Court of Appeal could not have reversed the Board's crucial finding of fact; it could only have considered questions of law. In the *Panevezys-Saldutiskis Railway Case*,[44] the P.C.I.J. said: "There can be no need to resort to the municipal court if . . . the result must be a repetition of a decision already given." Since 1966, the House of Lords has been free to reverse its own decisions where "the interests of justice so require."[45] Does this mean that an alien should now always take his case to the House of Lords to satisfy the local remedies rule?[46]

In the *El Oro Mining and Railway Co. Case*,[47] the British-Mexican Claims Commission took jurisdiction despite the presence of a "Calvo" clause.[48] The claimant went to the local courts, but the case was undecided after nine years. The Commission was of the opinion that "nine years by far exceeds the limit of the most liberal allowance that may be made."[49] There was, as a result, a denial of justice that excused the claimant company from its obligation not to resort to the Commission. It is arguable that such a delay in deciding a case would render a remedy ineffective for the purposes of the exhaustion of local remedies rule.

In the *Robert E. Brown Case*,[50] the Tribunal rejected a claim of non-exhaustion of local remedies by reference to "the frequently quoted language of an American Secretary of State: 'A claimant in a foreign State is not required to exhaust justice in

---

[39] *Ibid.* p. 1189.
[40] *Ibid.*
[41] Application 343/57, 2 Y.B.E.C.H.R. 413, at p. 436 (1958–59) and *Second Cyprus Case, ibid.* p. 186.
[42] See de Smith, *Constitutional and Administrative Law* (4th ed., 1981) pp. 627–633.
[43] *Finland* v. *Great Britain*, 3 R.I.A.A. 1479 (1934).
[44] *Estonia* v. *Lithuania*, P.C.I.J.Rep., Series A/B, No. 76, p. 18 (1939). *cf.* the *Vagrancy Cases*, Eur. Court H.R., Series A, Vol. 12. Judgment of June 18, 1971.
[45] *Practice Statement* [1966] 1 W.L.R. 1234.
[46] On the position under the European Convention on Human Rights, see below, p. 479, n. 36. Note that the defence of Act of State will still be available against him in some cases, thus preventing any claim in the British courts: see de Smith, *op. cit.* at n. 42, above, pp. 130–136.
[47] *Great Britain* v. *Mexico* 5 R.I.A.A. 191 (1931).
[48] A "Calvo" clause is a clause in a contract between a state and an alien whereby the latter agrees to resort to local remedies only and not invoke the protection of the state of which it is a national. Calvo was an Argentinian international lawyer. See Shea, *The Calvo Clause* (1955).
[49] *Ibid.* p. 198.
[50] *U.S.* v. *Great Britain* 6 R.I.A.A. 120, 129 (1923).

such State when there is no justice to exhaust.'" The Tribunal found this to be so in the case before it: "All three branches of the Government [of the South African Republic] conspired to ruin his [the claimant's] enterprise. . . . The judiciary, at first recalcitrant, was at length reduced to submission and brought into line with a determined policy of the Executive. . . ." Should the absence of counsel, the right to cross examine, etc.— *i.e.* other aspects of a fair trial as spelt out in the "international minimum standard" (which, according to one view, applies to the treatment of aliens)—also excuse a claimant from the need to exhaust local remedies?

The Rules regarding International Claims issued by the British Foreign and Commonwealth Office[51] in 1971 read:

Rule VII

Her Majesty's Government will not normally take up a claim of a United Kingdom national against another state until all the legal remedies available to him in the state concerned (*i.e.* municipal remedies) have been exhausted.

Comment

Failure to exhaust the local remedies will not constitute a bar to a claim if it is clearly established that in the circumstances of the case an appeal to a higher municipal tribunal would have had no effect. A claimant in another state is not required to exhaust justice in that state where there is no justice to exhaust.

Rule VIII

If in exhausting these municipal remedies the claimant has met with prejudice or obstruction, which are a denial of justice, Her Majesty's Government may intervene on his behalf to secure redress of injustice.

5. Note that the requirement of the exhaustion of local remedies is sometimes dispensed with by treaty. For example, claims heard by the United States-Mexican General Claims Commission, extracts from many of which are included in this chapter, did not have to satisfy the rule.[52]

---

[51] See above, p. 448.
[52] See Article V, U.S.-Mexican General Claims Convention 1923, 4 R.I.A.A., p. 11.

CHAPTER 9

HUMAN RIGHTS

1. *INTRODUCTION*[1]

INTERNATIONAL law rules framed in terms of the protection of human rights against state interference are very largely a post-1945 phenomenon. Before then individuals were seen mostly as aliens and nationals, not as individuals. Some protection was afforded to them as aliens,[2] but the treatment of nationals was regarded as being within the domestic jurisdiction of sovereign states. By the nineteenth century, most European writers recognised an exception in the case of humanitarian intervention, although state practice shows that intervention by a state on that ground was usually justified on other grounds at the same time.[3] After the First World War, efforts were made to protect minority groups by treaty,[4] but no protection of individuals generally, on a natural law or other basis, was attempted. Events in Europe in the 1930s and in the Second World War focused attention upon this wider question and the guarantee of human rights became one of the purposes for which the Allied Powers fought.[5] It was therefore no surprise when the realisation and protection of human rights became one of the purposes of the United Nations[6] and when the Charter imposed obligations upon members to this end.[7] The Charter was followed by the Universal Declaration on Human Rights 1948[8] and a still growing number of multilateral treaties concluded through the United Nations. At a regional level, the European Convention on Human Rights 1950,[9] the European Social Charter[10] and the American Convention on Human Rights[11] have been adopted; all three are now in force. There are also over 100 International Labour Organisation Conventions in force, some dating from before 1945,[12] and the four Geneva "Red Cross" Conventions of 1949.[13] The Final Act of the

---

[1] See Bilder, (1969) Wisc.L.R. 171; Dominguez, Rodley, Wood and Falk, *Enhancing Global Human Rights* (1979); Dowrick, ed., *Human Rights* (1979); Eide and Schou, eds., *International Protection of Human Rights* (1968); Ezejiofor, *Protection of Human Rights under the Law* (1964); Lauterpacht, *International Law and Human Rights* (1950); Lillich and Newman, *International Human Rights* (1979); Luard, ed., *The International Protection of Human Rights* (1967); McDougal, Lasswell and Chen, *Human Rights and World Public Order* (1980); Moskowicz, *International Concern with Human Rights* (1974); Sohn and Buergenthal, *International Protection of Human Rights* (1973).

[2] See above, Chap. 8.

[3] On the question whether there is a right of humanitarian intervention now, see the contrasting views in Lillich, ed., *Humanitarian Intervention and the United Nations* (1973), and Moore, ed., *Law and Civil War in the Modern World* (1974) (articles by Brownlie and Lillich). Those who argue for such a right claim that a state may intervene, by force if necessary, to prevent serious and large-scale violations of basic human rights (normally the right of life) by another state regardless of the nationality of the victims.

[4] See Oppenheim, Vol. I, paras. 340 (b)-(c).

[5] See the UN Declaration of January 1, 1942, 36 A.J.I.L., Supp. 191 (1942).

[6] Article 1, UN Charter, below, Appendix I.

[7] Articles 55–56, *ibid.*

[8] See below, p. 534.

[9] See below, p. 471.   [10] See below, p. 471, n. 22.   [11] See below, p. 483.

[12] See Jenks, *Human Rights and International Labour Standards* (1960) and *ibid. Social Justice in the Law of Nations* (1970).

[13] See Draper, *The Red Cross Conventions* (1958). Each Convention had 151 parties on December 31, 1981, including the U.K. See also the 1977 Protocols I and II to the Genevra Conventions, 16 I.L.M. 1391 (1977). In force 1978, 19 (Protocol I) and 17 (Protocol II) parties on December 31, 1981. The U.K. was not a party.

Conference on Security and Co-operation in Europe 1975 (the Helsinki Declaration)[14] has important sections on human rights.

International law has some rules concerning the responsibility of individuals for infringements of human rights also. The long-established law of war crimes[15] and the more recent law concerning crimes against humanity[16] and genocide[17] are the primary examples.

2. EUROPEAN CONVENTION ON HUMAN RIGHTS 1950[18]

Note

The Convention was drafted under the auspices of the Council of Europe, an international organisation composed of 21 West European States which was formed in 1949 as the result of the first post-war attempt at unifying Europe. The impetus for the Convention came from the need to define more closely the obligations of members of the Council concerning "human rights,"[19] especially in the face of the threat from the rival, communist East European bloc, and also from the wish to prevent a recurrence of conditions which Europe had then recently witnessed. It was believed that the Convention would serve as an alarm that would bring violations of human rights to the attention of the international community in time for it to take action to suppress them. In practice, this function of the Convention, which imagines large-scale violations of human rights, has largely remained dormant.[20] The Convention has instead been used primarily to raise questions of isolated weaknesses in legal systems that basically conform to its requirements and which are representative of the "common heritage of political traditions, ideals, freedom and the rule of law" to which the Preamble to the Convention refers. Most commonly such questions have concerned the administration of criminal justice, although the jurisprudence of the Strasbourg authorities is increasingly exploring other areas, such as torture or inhuman treatment, etc., respect for family and private life, freedom of speech and trade union rights. The Convention is concerned mainly with civil and political rights.[21] Economic, social and cultural rights are protected by a later treaty—the European Social Charter 1961.[22]

---

[14] 14 I.L.M. 1292 (1975). The declaration is not binding in law: see Russell, 70 A.J.I.L. 242 (1976). See also Buergenthal, ed., *Human Rights, International Law and the Helsinki Accord* (1977).

[15] See below, p. 555.

[16] See below, p. 560.

[17] See below, p. 561.

[18] See Beddard, *Human Rights in Europe* (2nd ed., 1980); Fawcett, *The Application of the European Convention on Human Rights* (1969); Jacobs, *The European Convention on Human Rights* (1975); Nedjati, *Human Rights under the European Convention* (1978); Robertson, *Human Rights in Europe* (2nd ed., 1977).

[19] See Articles 1 and 3, Council of Europe Statute 1949, U.K.T.S. 51 (1949), Cmnd. 7778; 87 U.N.T.S. 103.

[20] It did apply in the *Greek Case,* 12 Y.B.E.C.H.R., volume on *The Greek Case* (1969); CM Resolution DH (70) 1. In 1967, the "Regime of the Colonels," which had taken power by revolution, suspended the Greek Constitution and detained its opponents. State applications were brought against it by Denmark, the Netherlands, Norway and Sweden. The Committee of Ministers confirmed the opinion of the Commission that the Regime had tortured persons contrary to Article 3 and that breaches of nine other Articles of the Convention had occurred. Greece withdrew from the Council and denounced the Convention in 1970. Following the overthrow of the Colonels, Greece returned to the fold in 1974. See also the cases against Turkey, below, p. 480.

[21] The rights to family life and education are, however, included.

[22] U.K.T.S. 38 (1965), Cmnd. 2643; 529 U.N.T.S. 89. In force 1965. On December 31, 1981, there were 13 parties including the U.K.

EUROPEAN CONVENTION ON HUMAN RIGHTS 1950[23]

E.T.S. No. 5; U.K.T.S. 70 (1950), Cmd. 8969

Article 1

The High Contracting Parties shall secure to everyone within their jurisdiction[24] the rights and freedoms defined in Section I of this Convention.

Article 2

(1) Everyone's right to life shall be protected by law. No one shall be deprived of his life intentionally save in the execution of a sentence of a court following his conviction of a crime for which this penalty is provided by law.[25]

(2) Deprivation of life shall not be regarded as inflicted in contravention of this Article when it results from the use of force which is no more than absolutely necessary:

(*a*) in defence of any person from unlawful violence;

(*b*) in order to effect a lawful arrest or to prevent the escape of a person lawfully detained;

(*c*) in action lawfully taken for the purpose of quelling a riot or insurrection.

Article 3

No one shall be subjected to torture or to inhuman or degrading treatment or punishment.

Article 4

(1) No one shall be held in slavery or servitude.

(2) No one shall be required to perform forced or compulsory labour.

(3) For the purpose of this Article the term—forced or compulsory labour—shall not include:

(*a*) any work required to be done in the ordinary course of detention imposed according to the provisions of Article 5 of this Convention or during conditional release from such detention;

(*b*) any service of a military character or, in case of conscientious objectors in countries where they are recognised, service exacted instead of compulsory military service;

---

[23] In force 1953. On October 31st, 1982, there were 21 parties. They were Austria, Belguim, Cyprus, Denmark, the F.R.G., Greece, Iceland, Ireland, Italy, Liechtenstein, Luxembourg, Malta, The Netherlands, Norway, Portugal, Spain, Sweden, Switzerland, Turkey and the U.K. The Convention is open only to Council of Europe members. All such members are now parties.

[24] *Ed.* Individuals, whether nationals or aliens, are within a state's "jurisdiction" if they are under its actual authority and responsibility, whether they are on its territory or abroad: *Cyprus* v. *Turkey*, 2 D.R.E.C.H.R. 125 (1975). Decn. admiss. Consequently, applications against Turkey in respect of its treatment of individuals in that part of Cyprus occupied by Turkey were admissible. Note, however, the special rule for non-metropolitan territories in Art. 63, below, p. 491, n. 91.

[25] Does Art. 2 prohibit capital punishment? If not does it set any limits on the type of offence for which it can be prescribed? Is Art. 3 relevant in this connection?

(*c*) any service exacted in case of an emergency or calamity threatening the life or well-being of the community;

(*d*) any work or service which forms part of normal civic obligations.

Article 5[26]

(1) Everyone has the right to liberty and security of person.

No one shall be deprived of his liberty save in the following cases and in accordance with a procedure prescribed by law;

(*a*) the lawful detention of a person after conviction by a competent court;

(*b*) the lawful arrest or detention of a person for non-compliance with the lawful order of a court or in order to secure the fulfilment of any obligation prescribed by law;

(*c*) the lawful arrest or detention of a person effected for the purpose of bringing him before the competent legal authority on reasonable suspicion of having committed an offence or when it is reasonably considered necessary to prevent his committing an offence or fleeing after having done so;

(*d*) the detention of a minor by lawful order for the purpose of educational supervision or his lawful detention for the purpose of bringing him before the competent legal authority;

(*e*) the lawful detention of persons for the prevention of the spreading of infectious diseases, of persons of unsound mind, alcoholics or drug addicts or vagrants[27];

(*f*) the lawful arrest or detention of a person to prevent his effecting an unauthorised entry into the country or of a person against whom action is being taken with a view to deportation or extradition.

(2) Everyone who is arrested shall be informed promptly, in a language which he understands, of the reasons for his arrest and of any charge against him.

(3) Everyone arrested or detained in accordance with the provisions of paragraph 1(*c*) of this Article shall be brought promptly before a judge or other officer authorised by law to exercise judicial power and shall be entitled to trial within a reasonable time or to release pending trial. Release may be conditioned by guarantees to appear for trial.

(4) Everyone who is deprived of his liberty by arrest or detention shall be entitled to take proceedings by which the lawfulness of his detention shall be decided speedily by a court and his release ordered if the detention is not lawful.

---

[26] *Ed*. The "right to liberty" in Art. 5 concerns "individual liberty in its classic sense, that is to say the physical liberty of the person"; it is not to do with freedom of movement, as to which see Art. 2 of the Fourth Protocol, below, p. 478: *Engel Case*, Eur. Court H.R., Series A, Vol. 22, Judgment of June 8, 1976. The distinction between the two is not always easy to make. Confinement of a soldier to an unlocked room in barracks during off duty hours was not within Art. 5; detention in a locked cell therein during off and on duty hours was: *ibid*. The restriction of a suspected Mafia member to a small island where he was subject to constant surveillance was controlled by Art. 5; his later transfer and restriction to a mainland village and subjection only to a daily reporting obligation was not: *Guzzardi Case*, *ibid*. Vol. 39, Judgment of November 6, 1980. Although Art. 5 applies to the disciplinary detention of servicemen, the state is allowed more discretion in this context than in the detention of civilians: *Engel Case*, above.

[27] *Ed*. The terms used in Article 5(1)(*e*) have an autonomous, Convention meaning; the characterisation of a person in municipal law as a vagrant, for example, will not be conclusive of his Convention status. See the *Vagrancy Cases*, below, p. 479 (vagrants) and the *Winterwerp Case*, below, p. 506 (persons of unsound mind).

(5) Everyone who has been the victim of arrest or detention in contravention of the provisions of this Article shall have an enforceable right to compensation.

Article 6

(1) In the determination of his civil rights and obligations or of any criminal charge[28] against him, everyone is entitled to a fair and public hearing within a reasonable time by an independent and impartial tribunal established by law. Judgment shall be pronounced publicly but the press and public may be excluded from all or part of the trial in the interests of morals, public order or national security in a democratic society, where the interests of juveniles or the protection of the private life of the parties so require, or to the extent strictly necessary in the opinion of the court in special circumstances where publicity would prejudice the interests of justice.

(2) Everyone charged with a criminal offence shall be presumed innocent until proved guilty according to law.

(3) Everyone charged with a criminal offence has the following minimum rights:

(*a*) to be informed promptly, in a language which he understands and in detail, of the nature and cause of the accusation against him;

(*b*) to have adequate time and facilities for the preparation of his defence;

(*c*) to defend himself in person or through legal assistance of his own choosing or, if he has not sufficient means to pay for legal assistance, to be given it free when the interests of justice so require;

(*d*) to examine or have examined witnesses against him and to obtain the attendance and examination of witnesses on his behalf under the same conditions as witnesses against him;

(*e*) to have the free assistance of an interpreter if he cannot understand or speak the language used in court.

Article 7

(1) No one shall be held guilty of any criminal offence on account of any act or omission which did not constitute a criminal offence under national or international law at the time when it was committed. Nor shall a heavier penalty be imposed than the one that was applicable at the time the criminal offence was committed.

---

[28] In the *Engel Case, loc. cit.* at p. 473, n. 26, above, the Court held that military disciplinary proceedings may in some cases be subject to Art. 6 as involving the determination of a "criminal charge." The Court confirmed that the concept of a "criminal" charge was an autonomous Convention one—although only in a special, "one way" sense. If a state classified an offence as "criminal," it would be such for the purposes of Art. 6. If it classified it as "disciplinary," it might nonetheless be "criminal" for the purposes of Art. 6. When deciding whether an offence was "criminal" in this latter situation, three factors were relevant: (1) the classification of the offence in the local law (disciplinary or disciplinary *and* criminal); (2) the nature of the offence, so that one (*e.g.* absence without leave) to do primarily with the operation of the armed forces would be disciplinary rather than "criminal;" and (3) the nature of the punishment, so that an offence which might result in deprivation of a person's liberty to any significant extent would in principle be "criminal." In the *Campbell and Fell Case*, 14 D.R.E.C.H.R. 186 (1979), which is now before the Court, the Commission expressed the opinion in its 1982 report that Art. 6 applied to disciplinary proceedings before prison boards of visitors in cases where the possible penalty was the substantial loss of remission.

(2) This Article shall not prejudice the trial and punishment of any person for any act or omission which, at the time when it was committed, was criminal according to the general principles of law recognised by civilised nations.

Article 8

(1) Everyone has the right to respect for his private and family life, his home and his correspondence.

(2) There shall be no interference by a public authority with the exercise of this right except such as is in accordance with the law and is necessary in a democratic society in the interests of national security, public safety or the economic well-being of the country, for the prevention of disorder or crime, for the protection of health or morals, or for the protection of the rights and freedoms of others.

Article 9

(1) Everyone has the right to freedom of thought, conscience and religion; this right includes freedom to change his religion or belief and freedom, either alone or in community with others and in public or private, to manifest his religion or belief, in worship, teaching, practice and observance.

(2) Freedom to manifest one's religion or beliefs shall be subject only to such limitations as are prescribed by law and are necessary in a democratic society in the interests of public safety, for the protection of public order, health or morals, or for the protection of the rights and freedoms of others.

Article 10

(1) Everyone has the right to freedom of expression. This right shall include freedom to hold opinions and to receive and impart information and ideas without interference by public authority and regardless of frontiers. This Article shall not prevent States from requiring the licensing of broadcasting, television or cinema enterprises.

(2) The exercise of these freedoms, since it carries with it duties and responsibilities, may be subject to such formalities, conditions, restrictions or penalties as are prescribed by law and are necessary in a democratic society, in the interests of national security, territorial integrity or public safety, for the prevention of disorder or crime, for the protection of health or morals, for the protection of the reputation or rights of others, for preventing the disclosure of information received in confidence, or of maintaining the authority and impartiality of the judiciary.

Article 11

(1) Everyone has the right to freedom of peaceful assembly and to freedom of association with others, including the right to form and to join trade unions for the protection of his interests.

(2) No restrictions shall be placed on the exercise of these rights other than such as are prescribed by law and are necessary in a democratic society in the interests of national security or public safety, for the prevention of disorder or crime, for the protection of health or morals or for the protection of the rights and freedoms of others. This Article shall not prevent the imposition of lawful

restrictions on the exercise of these rights by members of the armed forces, of the police or of the administration of the State.

Article 12

Men and women of marriageable age have the right to marry and to found a family, according to the national laws governing the exercise of this right.

Article 13

Everyone whose rights and freedoms as set forth in this Convention are violated shall have an effective remedy before a national authority notwithstanding that the violation has been committed by persons acting in an official capacity.

Article 14

The enjoyment of the rights and freedoms set forth in this Convention shall be secured without discrimination on any ground such as sex, race, colour, language, religion, political or other opinion, national or social origin, association with a national minority, property, birth or other status.

Article 15

(1) In time of war or other public emergency threatening the life of the nation any High Contracting Party may take measures derogating from its obligations under this Convention to the extent strictly required by the exigencies of the situation, provided that such measures are not inconsistent with its other obligations under international law.

(2) No derogation from Article 2, except in respect of deaths resulting from lawful acts of war, or from Articles 3, 4 (para. 1) and 7 shall be made under this provision.

(3) Any High Contracting Party availing itself of this right of derogation shall keep the Secretary-General of the Council of Europe fully informed of the measures which it has taken and the reasons therefor. It shall also inform the Secretary-General of the Council of Europe when such measures have ceased to operate and the provisions of the Convention are again fully executed.

Article 16

Nothing in Articles 10, 11 and 14 shall be regarded as preventing the High Contracting Parties from imposing restrictions on the political activity of aliens.

Article 17

Nothing in this Convention may be interpreted as implying for any State, group or person any right to engage in any activity or perform any act aimed at the destruction of any of the rights and freedoms set forth herein or at their limitation to a greater extent than is provided for in the Convention.[29]

---

[29] *Ed*. Acting under Art. 17, the European Commission of Human Rights declared inadmissible an application from the West German Communist Party alleging that government action banning it was contrary to Arts. 9, 10 and 11 of the Convention: A.250/57, 1 Y.B.E.C.H.R. 222 (1955–57).

Article 18

The restrictions permitted under this Convention to the said rights and freedoms shall not be applied for any purpose other than those for which they have been prescribed.

FIRST PROTOCOL TO THE CONVENTION 1952[30]

E.T.S. No., 9; U.K.T.S. 46 (1954), Cmd. 9221

Article I

Every natural or legal person is entitled to the peaceful enjoyment of his possessions. No one shall be deprived of his possessions except in the public interest[31] and subject to the conditions provided for by law and by the general principles of international law.

The preceding provisions shall not, however, in any way impair the right of a State to enforce such laws as it deems necessary to control the use of property in accordance with the general interest or to secure the payment of taxes or other contributions or penalties.[32]

Article II

No person shall be denied the right to education. In the exercise of any functions which it assumes in relation to education and to teaching, the State shall respect the right of parents to ensure such education and teaching in conformity with their own religious and philosophical convictions.[33]

---

[30] On December 31, 1981 all of the parties to the Convention, with the exception of Spain and Switzerland, were parties to the Protocol, which entered into force in 1954.

[31] In A.3039/67, 10 Y.B.E.C.H.R. 506 (1967), the Commission declared inadmissible the application of certain debenture holders whose stock was to be compulsorily purchased by the British Government in the course of re-organisation of the British steel industry in 1967. On the question whether the taking was "in the public interest," the Commission stated that that requirement "is one of the clauses of exception in the Convention similar to those in 8 to 11" in the interpretation of which it had always allowed a "margin of appreciation" to the contracting party concerned. See Gilmour (1968) *Public Law* 62. On the "margin of appreciation" doctrine, see the *Sunday Times Case*, below, p. 519, and p. 531, below.

[32] *Ed.* On Art. 1, see Peukert, 2 H.R.L.J. 37 (1981).

[33] In the *Kjeldsen, Busk Madsen and Pedersen Case* (the *Danish Sex Education Case*), Eur. Court H.R. Series A, Vol. 23, Judgment of December 7, 1976, the Court held the system of compulsory sex education in Danish schools was not contrary to Art. 2, First Protocol. The judgment confirms that Art. 2 applies to education in state, as well as private, schools. In the *Campbell and Cosans Case* below, p. 492, the Court held, by six votes to one, that the applicants' right to respect for their "philosophical convictions" in the state's education of their children had been infringed by the system of corporal punishment in Scottish schools. The Court considered that "conviction" meant more than opinions or ideas, which were protected by Art. 10. A conviction was more akin to a "belief" (*cf.* Art. 9), and denoted "views that attain a certain level of cogency, seriousness, cohesion and importance." "Philosophical convictions" were "such convictions as are worthy of respect in a 'democratic society' . . . and are not incompatible with human dignity." Judge Sir Vincent Evans dissented. In his opinion, for which he found support in the *travaux préparatoires*, Art. 2 was concerned with the idealogical indoctrination of children in class and not with the organisation or administration of schools. He pointed out that parents also held "convictions" about mixed sex schools, mixed ability classes, and independent schools. He also considered that the case came within the British reservation to Art. 2.

Article III

The High Contracting Parties undertake to hold free elections at reasonable intervals by secret ballot, under conditions which will ensure the free expression of the opinion of the people in the choice of the legislature.

FOURTH PROTOCOL TO THE CONVENTION 1963[34]

E.T.S. No. 46; Misc. 6 (1964), Cmnd. 2309

Article 1

No one shall be deprived of his liberty merely on the ground of inability to fulfil a contractual obligation.

Article 2

1. Everyone lawfully within the territory of a state shall, within that territory, have the right to liberty of movement and freedom to choose his residence.
2. Everyone shall be free to leave any country, including his own.
3. No restrictions shall be placed on the exercise of these rights other than such as are in accordance with law and are necessary in a democratic society in the interests of national security or public safety, for the maintenance of *ordre public*, for the prevention of crime, for the protection of health or morals, or for the protection of the rights and freedoms of others.
4. The rights set forth in paragraph 1 may also be subject, in particular areas, to restrictions imposed in accordance with law and justified by the public interest in a democratic society.

Article 3

1. No one shall be expelled, by means either of an individual or of a collective measure, from the territory of the State of which he is a national.
2. No one shall be deprived of the right to enter the territory of the State of which he is a national.

Article 4

Collective expulsion of aliens is prohibited.

Notes
1. The Convention is enforced by means of state and individual applications to the European Commission of Human Rights in Strasbourg.[35] The Commission, which is part-time, consists of a number of members equal to the number of parties to the Convention, with, in practice, one national from each contracting party (Art. 20). The members are independent experts, and usually lawyers. Applications are first considered at the admissibility stage, when they are examined to see whether local remedies have been exhausted and whether they have been brought "within a period of six

---

[34] In force 1968. On December 31, 1981, there were 11 contracting parties. The U.K. was not a party.
[35] For an account of the procedure followed by the Commission at the admissibility stage, see Mikaelsen, *European Protection of Human Rights*, 1980.

months from the date on which the final decision was taken" (Art. 26).[36] *Individual* applications must meet certain other admissibility requirements in Article 27. Thus, an individual application will be rejected if it is "incompatible with the provisions of the present Convention," *i.e.* for the most part, if the facts do not bring the case within the scope of a right in the Convention.[37] It will be rejected as "manifestly ill-founded" if a right as defined in the Convention is in issue but the facts show no evidence of a breach of it, *i.e.* no prima facie breach. An individual application may also be rejected under Article 27 if it is anonymous, an abuse of the right of petition, or "is substantially the same as a matter which has already been examined by the Commission or has already been submitted to another procedure of international investigation or settlement[38] and if it contains no relevant new information." The decision to reject a state or individual application is final. This being so, and the final word as to the interpretation of the Convention resting with the European Court of Human Rights,[39] not the Commission, there is a strong case for arguing that the Commission should be reluctant to reject an application on a ground that involves its interpretation of the meaning of the guarantee.

2. Applications[40] by *states* under *Article* 24 have been few in number. In 1956–57, two cases[41] were brought by Greece against the United Kingdom concerning British action in Cyprus during the emergency situation there. After the settlement of the Cyprus Question in 1959, they were terminated by agreement between the parties and with the consent of the Committee of Ministers of the Council of Europe without final decisions being reached. In 1960, Austria brought a case against Italy[42] concerning criminal proceedings in the Italian Courts against six youths in respect of the death of an Italian customs official in a German-speaking area of Italy in the South Tyrol. In 1963, the Committee of Ministers decided that no violation of the Convention had occurred. The case is mainly important because of Italy's argument that Austria had no standing to bring the claim for the reason that although the alleged breach had taken place after *Italy* had become bound by the Convention, it had occurred before *Austria* had become bound by it. The Commission rejected this argument. It ruled that Article 24 did not require reciprocity in this sense and that in bringing a claim under it a state is not to be seen as enforcing its own rights "but rather as bringing before the Commission an alleged violation of the public order of Europe."[43] This last ruling was confirmed in the state applications brought against Greece in 1967.[44] In 1971 and 1972, Ireland made two applications against the United Kingdom concerning Northern Ireland which resulted in the judgment of the Court in *Ireland* v. *United Kingdom*.[45] More recently, Cyprus

---

[36] The Commission has taken "local remedies" to mean those required at customary international law, see above p. 464, and has developed a substantial jurisprudence applying the requirement. Only "effective" remedies need be exhausted. The Commission takes the view, for example, that there is no need to resort to the House of Lords or even the Court of Appeal if counsel advises that an appeal would be pointless. There is no need to resort to a court at all if a legal aid certificate is refused for lack of a prima facie case. The Commission has developed the idea of a continuing violation, see the *De Becker Case*, below, p. 592, which overcomes the six months requirement in some cases.

[37] *e.g.* where the application concerns the right to work, which is not protected at all, or the right to jury trial, which is not included in the Art. 6 guarantee of a fair trial.

[38] *Ed.*, *e.g.* under the UN Covenant system, see below, p. 551.

[39] *Vagrancy Cases*, Eur. Court H.R., Series A, Vol. 12, Judgment of June 18, 1971. The Court may rule on a question of admissibility in a case that reaches it. In the *Van Oosterwijck Case*, below, p. 515, the Court held, contrary to the decision of the Commission, that local remedies had not been exhausted.

[40] The term "application" has come to be used in connection with both Art. 24 and Art. 25 instead of "petition."

[41] See 2 Y.B.E.C.H.R. 174 (1958–59).

[42] See *ibid*. 740 (1963).

[43] 4 *ibid*. 116, at p. 140 (1961).

[44] See the *Greek Case*, above, p. 471, n. 20.

[45] See below, p. 483.

brought three applications against Turkey arising out of the Turkish Invasion of Cyprus in 1974. The Committee of Ministers upheld the Commission's opinion in respect of two of these applications that Turkey had infringed various Articles in the Convention and urged further inter-communal talks[46]; the third is still pending.[47] Finally, Denmark, France, the Netherlands, Norway and Sweden have brought a claim against Turkey in respect of its domestic situation.[48] Although, for political reasons, *state* applications will always be less numerous than *individual* applications, they are potentially more useful in two respects: (1) they may concern a violation of rights defined in the Convention even though there has, at the time, been no "victim" of it and (2) they may concern *any* provision of the Convention, whether one guaranteeing a right or not. They are also not subject to Article 27.

3. An individual may not bring an application against a state unless it has made a declaration under Article 25 accepting the right of individuals to petition against it. On October 31, 1982, the following 17 states had made such declarations: Austria, Belgium, Denmark, France, Federal Republic of Germany, Iceland, Ireland, Italy, Liechtenstein, Luxembourg, The Netherlands, Norway, Portugal, Spain, Sweden, Switzerland and the United Kingdom. Four had no time limit. The remainder were valid for two to five years. The United Kingdom's declaration was first made on January 14, 1966.[49] It applies only to violations occurring as of that date. It was renewed most recently for five years from January 14, 1981. Whereas applications in respect of the Isle of Man and the British Virgin Islands had previously been allowed, this is no longer the case under the 1981 declaration. In no other case has a state with a declaration with a time limit failed to renew it, wholly or in part.

In 1981, 404 individual applications were registered.[50] By the end of October 1982, the Commission had registered 10,100 altogether. By the end of 1981, altogether 255 applications had been admitted for consideration on the merits. This was less than three per cent. of all applications received in which decisions as to admissibility had been taken.

The Commission may grant legal aid in appropriate cases.[51]

4. If a state or individual application is admitted for consideration on the merits, a fact finding inquiry is conducted by the Commission on the basis of written and oral pleadings by the parties (who include at this stage any individual applicant) (Art. 28). This may involve an on-the-spot visit by members of the Commission for which the Government concerned must provide the necessary facilities.[52] Having established the facts, the Commission acts as a conciliator, placing itself "at the disposal of the parties concerned with a view to securing a friendly settlement of the matter on the basis of respect for human rights as defined" in the Convention (*ibid.*) Friendly settlements had been obtained in 22 cases by the end of 1981.[53]

---

[46] See the Report of the Commission of July 10, 1976 and Committee of Ministers Resolution DH (79) 1, both in 4 E.H. Rts. Rep. 482.

[47] See 21 Y.B.E.C.H.R. 100 (1978). Decn. admiss.

[48] See C.E. Doc. C (82) 33.   [49] Cmnd. 2894, U.K.T.S. 8 (1966).

[50] Figures have remained constant at about this level recently. In 1981 most applications were against the U.K. (132), followed by the F.R.G. (109) and then Switzerland (31).

[51] It is means-tested and based on average legal aid payments in Council of Europe states. Legal aid is only available if and when a Government has been asked for its observations on the application; it is not available in respect of the making of the application. On the legal aid scheme, see the Addendum to the Commission's Rules of Procedure. See further, *The Presentation of an Application before the European Commission of Human Rights*, C.E. publication (1978). On legal aid before the Court, see the addendum to the Court's revised Rules. Costs may be allowed by the Court under Art. 50, see below, p. 482.

[52] The Commission visited Greece in the *Greek Case*, above, p. 471, n. 20. It left abruptly when it was not accorded all the facilities it sought. Turkey refused to allow the Commission all the facilities it sought in the *Cyprus* v. *Turkey Case*, above. The Commission has visited Broadmoor to examine conditions there.

[53] See, *e.g.* the *Amekrane Case*, below, p. 493.

5. If no friendly settlement is reached, the Commission drafts a report in which it states its findings of fact and expresses an opinion, which is not legally binding, on the existence of a breach of the Convention (Art. 31). The report is sent to the Committee of Ministers of the Council of Europe (*ibid.*).[54] It may be referred to the European Court of Human Rights within three months of being so sent. The Court is composed of a number of judges, who are part-time, equal to the number of members of the Council of Europe.[55] A case may be referred to the Court only if the defendant state has made a declaration under Article 46 accepting the Court's compulsory jurisdiction or if it agrees to the Court's jurisdiction ad hoc in a particular case. On October 31, 1982, 19 states had made declarations under Article 46.[56] Three were without any time limit. The others were for periods of two to five years. All declaration with time limits have been renewed so far. The current United Kingdom declaration is for five years from January 14, 1981. Cases may be referred to the Court by the Commission, a defendant state, a state bringing an application, or a contracting party whose national is an alleged victim.[57] In practice, most cases that reach the Court are referred to it by the Commission. An individual applicant may not seize the Court of his case. 46 cases had been referred to the Court by the end of 1981. Breaches of the Convention had been found in 22 of the 34 cases decided on the merits by then.

6. The question of the applicant's standing in proceedings brought before the Court, which sits in public, was raised in the *Lawless Case*.[58] There the Court, after confirming that the individual applicant could not initiate proceedings or plead his case (but see now the Court's revised Rules, below) before the Court, stated that

> it is in the interests of the proper administration of justice that the Court should have knowledge of and, if need be, take into consideration, the Applicant's point of view

since the proceedings were "upon issues which concern" him.[59] These views, the Court said, would become known to the Court through the Commission's report. In addition, the Commission, which does have standing before the Court,

> as defender of the public interest, is entitled of its own accord, even if it does not share them, to make known the Applicant's views to the Court as a means of throwing light on the points at issue.[60]

The Court could also hear the Applicant as a witness.[61]

In 1971, in the *Vagrancy Cases*,[62] the Court, over the objection of Belgium, the defendant state, permitted the applicant's lawyer, at the request of and under the control of the Commission, to make a short statement on some questions of fact which

---

[54] This consists of the Foreign Ministers (in practice their deputies) of Council of Europe members.

[55] No state may have more than one national on the Court. Until recently, each member of the Council has had a national on the Court. A Canadian judge has, however, been now appointed in respect of Leichtenstein.

[56] *i.e.* all of the parties to the Convention except Malta and Turkey.

[57] *e.g.* the U.K. could have seized the Court in the *Luedicke Case* (against the F.R.G.), Eur. Court, H.R., Series A. Vol. 28, Judgment of November 28, 1978, since the applicant was a U.K. citizen.

[58] Eur. Court H.R., Series A. Vol. 1, Judgment of November 14, 1960, on Preliminary Objections and Questions of Procedure. See Harris, 10 I.C.L.Q. 616 (1961) and Robertson (1960) 36 B.Y.I.L. 343.

[59] *Ibid.* p. 15.

[60] *Ibid.* p. 16. The Commission presents its views to the Court on the interpretation and application of the Convention as an institution established to "ensure the observance of the engagements undertaken by the High Contracting Parties." (Art. 19).

[61] *Ibid.*

[62] Eur. Court H.R., Series A. Judgment of November 18, 1970 (Question of Procedure).

the Commission thought would help the Court.[63] Since then, the applicant's lawyer has been allowed to argue on questions of law.[64] In 1983, the Court revised its Rules to allow the applicant to plead his own case.[65]

7. If the Court finds that a breach of the Convention has occurred, it has the following power to award "satisfaction" under Article 50:

> If the Court finds that a decision or a measure taken by a legal authority or any other authority of a High Contracting Party is completely or partially in conflict with the obligations arising from the present Convention, and if the internal law of the said Party allows only partial reparation to be made for the consequences of this decision or measure, the decision of the Court shall, if necessary, afford just satisfaction to the injured party.

Under Rule 47 *bis* of its Rules, the Court may rule upon the question of "satisfaction" when the issue of liability is being determined if the question is "ready for decision." Otherwise, separate proceedings are conducted before the Court (with the Commission participating) after the defendant state has had an opportunity to make reparation in accordance with the Court's judgment. In the exercise of its essentially secondary power under Article 50, the Court has made monetary awards in a number of cases, including the *Sunday Times Case*[66] (£22,000) and the *Young, James and Webster Case*[67] (£130,000 for the three applicants altogether). The award in the *Sunday Times Case* was wholly in respect of the costs of taking the case to Strasbourg. In the *Young, James and Webster Case,* the award was for costs, pecuniary loss (loss of earnings, etc.) and "moral damage" (*i.e.* injury to feelings, etc.). In the majority of cases, the Court has made only a declaratory judgment and has not awarded compensation under Article 50. So far, "satisfaction" has always taken the form of monetary compensation." The execution of the Court's judgments is the responsibility of the Committee of Ministers (Art. 54). So far, all judgments have been complied with, *i.e.* the required "satisfaction" has been paid or any offending law or practice has been changed.

8. If a case is not referred to the Court, the final decision is taken by the Committee of Ministers (Art. 32). There is no real hearing of the case before the Committee. Its decision, which is not reasoned, is taken on the basis of the Commission's report. The Commission and any individual applicant are not heard by the Committee, although the defendant (and any applicant) state may explain its position through its representative on the Committee. A decision that a breach has occurred must be taken by a two-thirds majority vote of the members of the Committee. In contrast with the Court, the Committee, which had decided 41 cases by January 1, 1982, has no power to award "just satisfaction."

9. The existence of alternative bodies competent to take a final decision in a case, which was provided for because states were not prepared to accept a Convention in which every case might finally be decided by a court, is not in the interests of the development of a consistent jurisprudence interpreting the Convention. The unsatisfactory nature of an arrangement whereby a case may be determined by the Committee of Ministers was illustrated in the *Huber Case.*[68] There, the Committee rejected[69] an eight to two majority decision by the Commission that Austria had detained the applicant contrary to Article 5(3). This was done after a discussion of the case in which the

---

[63] The Commission acted under Rule 29(1) of the Rules of Court which permitted its delegates to "have the assistance of any person of their choice." *cf.* Rule 29, revised Rules.

[64] *e.g.* the *Sunday Times Case, loc. cit.* at p. 519, below.

[65] Rule 30, revised Rules of Court.

[66] Below, p. 519.

[67] Below, p. 523.

[68] 14 Y.B.E.C.H.R. 572 (1971). Decn. admiss.

[69] CM Resolution DH (75) 2. *Cf.* the failure of the Committee of Ministers to make a finding of a violation of the Convention in the *Les Fourons Case*: CM Resolution DH (74) 1. See Jacobs *op cit.* at p. 470, n. 1, p. 268. On the *East African Asians Cases*, see below, p. 493.

Austrian representative explained his state's defence and in the absence of any hearing of the Commission or applicant. For the Committee to reject, in these circumstances, the considered and independent judgment of a clear majority of the Commission, arrived at after a full hearing of the facts and legal arguments of the parties, is scarcely what one would hope for in the administration of a human rights guarantee that protects the right to a fair trial.

10. It is interesting to compare the European Convention with another, more recent, regional human rights treaty, *viz.* the American Convention on Human Rights 1970.[70] This contains a comprehensive guarantee of civil, political, economic, social and cultural rights and provides for a compulsory system of individual applications, leading to a decision as to the breach of the Convention by an independent commission or, if the defendant state accepts its jurisdiction, by an international court.[71] Acceptance of the right of other Contracting Parties to bring complaints is optional.[72] The system of enforcement applies to economic, social and cultural rights as well as to civil and political ones.[73] See also the 1981 African Charter on Human and Peoples' Rights.[74]

IRELAND v. UNITED KINGDOM[75]

Eur. Court H.R., Series A, Judgment of January 18, 1978

Ireland lodged two applications against the United Kingdom arising out of events in Northern Ireland. The first application in 1971 was declared admissible in respect of claims under Articles 1, 3, 5, and 6 and under the last two of these Articles read in conjunction with Article 14. The second application in 1972 was withdrawn in the light of an undertaking given by the United Kingdom.

The claims in the first application that were admitted for consideration on the merits concerned the introduction and operation of the policy of internment and detention that applied in Northern Ireland between 1971 and 1975. Following an increase in I.R.A. activities, it was decided in 1971 to intern without trial persons suspected of serious terrorist activities but against whom there was not sufficient evidence to bring court proceedings. Powers to detain persons for questioning over a forty-eight hour period or longer were also brought into operation. Implementation of this policy, which was originally based upon regulations made under the Civil Authorities (Special Powers) Act (N.I.) 1922, began with "Operation Demetrius" on August 9, 1971. Some 350 persons were arrested, of whom 104 were released within 48 hours. Of those detained further, 12 were sent to unidentified centres for "interrogation in depth." This involved use of the "five techniques" described in the Court's judgment. Many more suspects were interned or detained for questioning in the following months. Of these, two more (making a total of 14) were subjected to the "five techniques." The claims admitted for consideration on their merits were mainly to the effect that the policy of internment and detention infringed Articles 5 and 6 and that persons interned or detained had been

---

[70] 9 I.L.M. 672 (1970). In force 1978. On December 31, 1981, there were 17 parties. The U.S.A. was not a party. On the Convention, see Frowein, 1 H.R.L.J. 44 (1980); Buergenthal, in *Miscellanea Van Der Meersch*, Vol. 1, 1972, p. 385; *ibid.* 76 A.J.I.L. 231 (1982) (on the Court); *ibid. Protecting Human Rights in the Americas* (1982); and the symposium articles in 30 American U.L.R. 1 (1980). See also Shelton, 2 H.R.L.J. 309 (1981). And see the American Declaration of the Rights and Duties of Man 1948, 43 A.J.I.L., Supp. 133 (1949).

[71] American Convention, Arts. 33–69.

[72] Art. 45, *ibid.*

[73] The guarantee of economic, social and cultural rights (Article 26) is very general and progressive; it may not be easily enforceable by the right of petition.

[74] OAU Doc. CAB/LEG/67/3/Rev. 5; Rev. I.C.J. No. 27, December 1981, p. 76. Not in force. No parties yet.

[75] See O'Boyle, 71 A.J.I.L. 674 (1977).

subjected to ill-treatment that constituted an "administrative practice" in violation of Article 3. The ill-treatment, it was alleged, had occurred at the unidentified interrogation centres where the "five techniques" were used and at other named interrogation centres, including Palace Barracks, where, it was alleged, more familiar forms of assault occurred. In support of its allegations, the Irish Government presented evidence relating to the treatment of 228 persons. The procedure agreed upon by the Commission and parties to handle this mass of evidence was for the Commission to concentrate on 16 "illustrative cases" selected by Ireland. The Commission heard oral as well as written evidence in these cases and received medical reports. The Commission had regard to another "forty-one cases" in respect of which it heard written (but not oral) evidence and received medical reports. It also took account of the remaining cases, but did not examine them in detail. For the Commission's report, see the Court's judgment, para. 147, below.

Following the Commission's report, Ireland referred the case to the Court. The following extract from the judgment, which concentrates mainly on the Article 3 claims, contains, first, passages from the Court's assessment of the facts (in which it relies very heavily upon the Commission's findings) and then the Court's application of the law to those facts.

Judgment of the Court

96. Twelve persons arrested on August 9, 1971 and two persons arrested in October 1971 . . . were submitted to a form of "interrogation in depth" which involved the combined application of the five particular techniques.

These . . . techniques consisted of:

(a) *wall-standing*: forcing the detainees to remain for periods of some hours in a "stress position," described by those who underwent it as being "spreadeagled against the wall, with their fingers put high above the head against the wall, the legs spread apart and the feet back, causing them to stand on their toes with the weight of the body mainly on the fingers";

(b) *hooding*: putting a black or navy coloured bag over the detainees' heads and, at least initially, keeping it there all the time except during interrogation:

(c) *subjection to noise*: pending their interrogations, holding the detainees in a room where there was a continuous loud and hissing noise;

(d) *deprivation of sleep*: pending their interrogations, depriving the detainees of sleep;

(e) *deprivation of food and drink*: subjecting the detainees to a reduced diet during their stay at the centre and pending interrogations. . . .

97. From the start, it has been conceded by the respondent Government that the use of the five techniques was authorised at "high level."[76] . . .

98. The two operations of interrogation in depth by means of the five techniques led to the obtaining of a considerable quantity of intelligence information, including the identification of 700 members of both I.R.A. factions and the discovery of individual responsibility for about 85 previously unexplained criminal incidents. . . .

100. . . . On November 16, 1971, the British Home Secretary announced that a . . . Committee had been set up under the chairmanship of Lord Parker

[76] *Ed.* See the Parker Report, Cmnd. 4901 (1972), pp. 1 and 13.

of Waddington to consider "whether, and if so in what respects, the procedures currently authorised for interrogation of persons suspected of terrorism and for their custody while subject to interrogation require amendment."

The Parker report,[77] . . . contained a majority and a minority opinion. The majority report concluded that the application of the techniques, subject to recommend safeguards against excessive use, need not be ruled out on moral grounds. On the other hand, the minority report by Lord Gardiner disagreed that such interrogation procedures were morally justifiable, even in emergency terrorist conditions. Both the majority and the minority considered the methods to be illegal under domestic law, although the majority confined their view to English law and to "some if not all the techniques."

101. The Parker report was published on March 2, 1972 . . . directives expressly prohibiting the use of the techniques, whether singly or in combination, were then issued to the security forces by the Government. . . .

102. At the hearing before the Court on February 8, 1977, the United Kingdom Attorney-General made the following declaration:

> "The Government of the United Kingdom have considered the question of the use of the 'five techniques' with the very great care and with particular regard to Article 3 of the Convention. They now give this unqualified undertaking, that the 'five techniques' will not in any circumstances be reintroduced as an aid to interrogation."

103. The Irish Government referred to the Commission 8 cases of persons submitted to the five techniques during interrogation at the unidentified centre or centres between August 11 and 17, 1971. . . . The Commission examined as illustrative the cases of T6 and T13. . . .

104. T6 and T13 were arrested on August 9, 1971. . . . they were medically examined on arrival. Thereafter, with intermittent periods of respite, they were subjected to the five techniques during four or possibly five days. . . .

The Commission was satisfied that T6 and T13 were kept at the wall for different periods totalling between twenty to thirty hours, but it did not consider it proved that the enforced stress position had lasted all the time they were at the wall. It stated in addition that the required posture caused physical pain and exhaustion. The Commission noted that, later on during his stay at the interrogation centre, T13 was allowed to take his hood off when he was alone in the room, provided that he turned his face to the wall. It was not found possible by the Commission to establish for what periods T6 and T13 had been without sleep, or to what extent they were deprived of nourishment and whether or not they were offered food but refused to take it.

The Commission found no physical injury to have resulted from the application of the five techniques as such, but loss of weight by the two case-witnesses and acute psychiatric symptoms developed by them during interrogation were recorded in the medical and other evidence. The Commission, on the material before it, was unable to establish the exact degree of any psychiatric after-effects produced on T6 and T13, but on the general level it was satisfied that some

---

[77] *Ed. Loc. cit.* at n. 76, above. See also the report of the Compton Committee, Cmnd. 4823 (1971).

psychiatric after-effects in certain of the fourteen persons subjected to the techniques could not be excluded.[78] . . .

107. T13 and T6 instituted civil proceedings in 1971 to recover damages for wrongful imprisonment and assault; their claims were settled in 1973 and 1975 respectively for £15,000 and £14,000. The twelve other individuals against whom the five techniques were used have all received in settlement of their civil claims compensation ranging from £10,000 to £25,000. . . .

110. [T2, T8, T12 and T15] . . . were all arrested early on September 20, 1971 and taken to Palace Barracks for interrogation. They were photographed and examined by an army doctor immediately after their arrest; apart from one small scar, no injuries were apparently found. The next day they were transferred together from Palace Barracks to Crumlin Road Prison. They all alleged that at various times they had been made to stand spreadeagled against a wall and had been severely beaten or otherwise physically ill-treated, particularly during interrogations. On their arrival at Crumlin Road, a prison doctor found contusions and bruising on three of the men; on September 23, another doctor found similar injuries on the fourth man. In the Commission's view, this medical evidence made "it highly probable that all the four received their injuries while at Palace Barracks."

Despite the absolute denials given in evidence by witnesses from the security forces at Palace Barracks, the Commission held the following facts, amongst others, to be established beyond reasonable doubt:

> The four men . . . were severely beaten by members of the security forces . . . The beating was not occasional but it was applied in a sort of scheme in order to make them speak. . . .

Each man instituted civil proceedings for damages and rejected the offer of £750 made in settlement of his claim. . . .

The Court then reviewed the evidence of ill-treatment of a non- "five techniques" kind at other named interrogation centres and restated as follows the conclusions reached by the Commission on the claims as a whole:

147. In its report, the Commission expressed the opinion: . . .

(iv) unanimously, that the combined use of the five techniques in the cases before it constituted a practice of inhuman treatment and of torture in breach of Article 3;
(v) unanimously, that violations of Article 3 occurred by inhuman, and in two cases degrading, treatment of
—T6, in an unidentified interrogation centre in August 1971,
—T2, T8, T12, T15, T9, T14 and T10 at Palace Barracks, Holywood, in September, October and November 1971,
—T16, T7 and T11, at various places in August, October and December 1971;
(vi) unanimously, that there had been at Palace Barracks, Holywood, in the autumn of 1971, a practice in connection with the interrogation of

---

[78] *Ed.* A study of 125 detainees who were interrogated by use of the "five techniques" and otherwise concludes that there were lasting physical or mental consequences in some cases and that all of the detainees studied suffered "a damaging personality change": Fields, *A Society on the Run* (1973).

prisoners by members of the RUC which was inhuman treatment in breach of Article 3 of the Convention; . . .

158. . . . the Irish Government indicated . . . that they were asking the Court to hold that there had been in Northern Ireland, from 1971 to 1974, a practice or practices in breach of Article 3 and to specify, if need be, where they had occurred. . . .

159. A practice incompatible with the Convention consists of an accumulation of identical or analogous breaches which are sufficiently numerous and inter-connected to amount not merely to isolated incidents or exceptions but to a pattern or system; a practice does not of itself constitute a violation separate from such breaches.

It is inconceivable that the higher authorities of a State should be, or at least should be entitled to be, unaware of the existence of such a practice. Furthermore, under the Convention those authorities are strictly liable for the conduct of their subordinates; they are under a duty to impose their will on subordinates and cannot shelter behind their inability to ensure that it is respected.

The concept of practice is of particular importance for the operation of the rule of exhaustion of domestic remedies. This rule, as embodied in Article 26 of the Convention, applies to State applications (Article 24), in the same way as it does to "individual" applications (Article 25), when the applicant State does no more than denounce a violation or violations allegedly suffered by "individuals" whose place, as it were, is taken by the State. On the other hand and in principle, the rule does not apply where [as here] the applicant State complains of a practice as such, with the aim of preventing its continuation or recurrence, but does not ask the Commission or the Court to give a decision on each of the cases put forward as proof or illustrations of that practice. . . .

160. In order to satisfy itself as to the existence or not in Northern Ireland of practices contrary to Article 3, the Court will not rely on the concept that the burden of proof is borne by one or other of the two Governments concerned. In the cases referred to it, the Court examines all the material before it, whether originating from the Commission, the Parties or other sources, and, if necessary, obtains material *proprio motu*. . . .

161. . . . To assess this evidence, the Court adopts the standard of proof "beyond reasonable doubt" but adds that such proof may follow from the coexistence of sufficiently strong, clear and concordant inferences or of similar unrebutted presumptions of fact. In this context, the conduct of the Parties when evidence is being obtained has to be taken into account. . . .

162. As was emphasised by the Commission, ill-treatment must attain a minimum level of severity if it is to fall within the scope of Article 3. The assessment of this minimum is, in the nature of things, relative; it depends on all the circumstances of the case, such as the duration of the treatment, its physical or mental effects and, in some cases, the sex, age and state of health of the victim, etc. . . .

166. . . . Although never authorised in writing in any official document, the five techniques were taught orally by the English Intelligence Centre to members of the RUC at a seminar held in April 1971. There was accordingly a practice.

167. The five techniques were applied in combination, with premeditation and for hours at a stretch; they caused, if not actual bodily injury, at least intense

physical and mental suffering to the persons subjected thereto and also led to acute psychiatric disturbances during interrogation. They accordingly fell into the category of inhuman treatment within the meaning of Article 3. The techniques were also degrading since they were such as to arouse in their victims feelings of fear, anguish and inferiority capable of humiliating and debasing them and possibly breaking their physical or moral resistance. . . .

In order to determine whether the five techniques should also be qualified as torture, the Court must have regard to the distinction, embodied in Article 3, between this notion and that of inhuman or degrading treatment.

In the Court's view, this distinction derives principally from a difference in the intensity of the suffering inflicted.

The Court considers in fact that, whilst there exists on the one hand violence which is to be condemned both on moral grounds and also in most cases under the domestic law of the Contracting States but which does not fall within Article 3 of the Convention, it appears on the other hand that it was the intention that the Convention, with its distinction between "torture" and "inhuman or degrading treatment," should by the first of these terms attach a special stigma to deliberate inhuman treatment causing very serious and cruel suffering.

Moreover, this seems to be the thinking lying behind Article 1 *in fine* of Resolution 3452 (XXX) adopted by the General Assembly of the United Nations on December 9, 1975 [for text, see below, p. 491]. . . .

Although the five techniques, as applied in combination, undoubtedly amounted to inhuman and degrading treatment, although their object was the extraction of confessions, the naming of others and/or information and although they were used systematically, they did not occasion suffering of the particular intensity and cruelty implied by the word torture as so understood. . . .

174. In so far as the Commission has found that a practice of inhuman treatment was followed in the autumn of 1971 [at Palace Barracks], for example in the cases of T2, T8, T12, T15 . . . the facts summarised above . . . bear out its opinion. The evidence before the Court reveals that, at the time in question, quite a large number of those held in custody at Palace Barracks were subjected to violence by members of the RUC. This violence, which was repeated violence occurring in the same place and taking similar forms, did not amount merely to isolated incidents; it definitely constituted a practice. It also led to intense suffering and to physical injury which on occasion was substantial; it thus fell into the category of inhuman treatment.[79]

. . . Admittedly, the acts complained of often occurred during interrogation and, to this extent, were aimed at extracting confessions, the naming of others and/or information, but the severity of the suffering that they were capable of causing did not attain the particular level inherent in the notion of torture as understood by the Court. . . .

The Court next examined the claims under Articles 5, 6, and 14 and held against Ireland on the ground that derogations from these Articles by the U.K. were properly made under Article 15. The Court then considered and rejected Ireland's claim under Article 1 to the effect that this required a contracting party to adopt laws prohibiting the violation of the rights guaranteed. In the course of doing so it made the following general comments on the scheme of the Convention:

---

[79] *Ed. cf.* the *Zeidler-Kormann Case*, 11 Y.B.E.C.H.R. 1020 (1968); a physical assault upon a prisoner may fall within Art. 3 if sufficiently serious (not in this case).

238. Article 1, together with Articles 14, 2 to 13 and 63, demarcates the scope of the Convention *ratione personae, materiae* and *loci*; it is also one of the many Articles that attest the binding character of the Convention. Article 1 is drafted by reference to the provisions contained in Section I and thus comes into operation only when taken in conjunction with them; a violation of Article 1 follows automatically from, but adds nothing to, a breach of those provisions; hitherto, when the Court has found such a breach, it has never held that Article 1 has been violated. . . .

239. . . . Unlike international treaties of the classic kind, the Convention comprises more than mere reciprocal engagements between contracting States. It creates, over and above a network of mutual, bilateral undertakings, objective obligations which, in the words of the Preamble, benefit from a "collective enforcement."[80] By virtue of Article 24, the Convention allows Contracting States to require the observance of those obligations without having to justify an interest deriving, for example, from the fact that a measure they complain of has prejudiced one of their own nationals. By substituting the words "shall secure" for the words "undertake to secure" in the text of Article 1, the drafters of the Convention also intended to make it clear that the rights and freedoms set out in Section I would be directly secured to anyone within the jurisdiction of the Contracting States (document H (61) 4, pp. 664, 703, 733 and 927). That intention finds a particularly faithful reflection in those instances where the Convention has been incorporated into domestic law. . . .

240. The problem in the present case is essentially whether a Contracting State is entitled to challenge under the Convention a law *in abstracto*.

The answer to this problem is to be found much less in Article 1 than in Article 24. Whereas, in order to be able to lodge a valid petition, a "person, non-governmental organisation or group of individuals" must, under Article 25, claim "to be the victim of a violation . . . of the rights set forth," Article 24 enables each Contracting State to refer to the Commission "any alleged breach of [any of] the provisions of the Convention by another [State]."

Such a "breach" results from the mere existence of a law which introduces, directs or authorises measures incompatible with the rights and freedoms safeguarded; this is confirmed unequivocally by the *travaux préparatoires* (document H (61) 4, pp. 384, 502, 703 and 706).

Nevertheless, the institutions established by the Convention may find a breach of this kind only if the law challenged pursuant to Article 24 is couched in terms sufficiently clear and precise to make the breach immediately apparent; otherwise, the decision of the Convention institutions must be arrived at by reference to the manner in which the respondent State interprets and applies *in concreto* the impugned text or texts. . . .

FOR THESE REASONS, THE COURT

On Article 3

1. *holds* unanimously that, although certain violations of Article 3 were not contested, a ruling should nevertheless be given thereon; . . .

---

[80] *Ed. cf. Austria* v. *Italy*, above, p. 479.

3. *holds* by sixteen votes to one[81] that the use of the five techniques in August and October 1971 constituted a practice of inhuman and degrading treatment, which practice was in breach of Article 3;

4. *holds* by thirteen votes to four[82] that the said use of the five techniques did not constitute a practice of torture within the meaning of Article 3; . . .

6. *holds* unanimously that there existed at Palace Barracks in the autumn of 1971 a practice of inhuman treatment, which practice was in breach of Article 3;

7. *holds* by fourteen votes to three[83] that the last-mentioned practice was not one of torture within the meaning of Article 3; . . .

Notes

1. In this case, which is politically the most important the Court has had to consider, the Court sat *en banc*. Although the Convention does not mention this possibility, the Court has provided in its revised Rules of Court (Rule 50) that a chamber dealing with a case which "raises one or more serious questions affecting the interpretation of the Convention" may relinquish jurisdiction in favour of the plenary Court. It must do this if the case might lead to a decision on such a question that is inconsistent with a previous ruling by the Court. About one-third of the cases have been referred to the plenary court.

2. In its judgment, the Court approved the rule that has been developed in the Commission's jurisprudence by which local remedies need not be exhausted in a state application where the act or acts claimed to be in breach of the Convention is or are shown to be in consequence of an "administrative practice" and where the practice is being challenged as such (see para. 159). This is why the United Kingdom was liable even though the persons detained were able to bring successful civil actions in the Northern Irish courts (see para. 107). In the *Greek Case*,[84] also in the context of Article 3, the Commission had explained the justification for the rule as follows:

> 24. The Convention does not in terms speak of administrative practices incompatible with it, but the notion is closely linked with the principle of the exhaustion of domestic remedies. The rule in Article 26 is based on the assumption, borne out by Article 13, that for a breach of a Convention provision there is a remedy available in the domestic system of law and administration, even if the provision is not directly incorporated in domestic law, and that that remedy is effective.

> 25. Where, however, there is a practice of non-observance of certain Convention provisions, the remedies prescribed will of necessity be side-stepped or rendered inadequate. Thus, if there was an administrative practice of torture or ill-treatment, judicial remedies prescribed would tend to be rendered ineffective by the difficulty of securing probative evidence, and administrative enquiries would either be not instituted or, if they were, would be likely to be half-hearted and incomplete. . . .

In *Donnelly* v. *United Kingdom*[85] the Commission held that the rule extended to individual applications under Article 25, as well as to state applications, so that local remedies do not have to be exhausted where the applicant is a "victim" of a violation of the Convention attributable to an "administrative practice" and the existence of the practice has rendered local remedies ineffective.

[81] Judge Sir Gerald Fitzmaurice dissented.
[82] Judges Zekia, O'Donoghue, Evrigenis, and Matscher dissented.
[83] Judges Evrigenis and O'Donoghue and one other (unknown) judge dissented.
[84] 12 Y.B.E.C.H.R. (1969), *The Greek Case*, p. 194. See further the Commission's Report in *Ireland* v. *U.K.*, 19 Y.B.E.C.H.R. 512, at pp. 752–768 (1976). See also Hannum and O'Boyle, 68 A.J.I.L. 440 (1974) and McGovern, 24 I.C.L.Q. 119 (1975).
[85] 16 Y.B.E.C.H.R. 212 at p. 262 (1973) and 19 *ibid.* 84 (1975).

3. The definition of torture in the United Nations Declaration on the Protection of all Persons from being subjected to Torture and Other Cruel, Inhuman or Degrading Treatment or Punishment,[86] from which the Court quotes, reads:

> *Article* 1. 1. For the purpose of this Declaration, torture means any act by which severe pain or suffering, whether physical or mental, is intentionally inflicted by or at the instigation of a public official on a person for such purposes as obtaining from him or a third person information or confession, punishing him for an act he has committed or is suspected of having committed, or intimidating him or other persons. It does not include pain or suffering arising only from, inherent in or incidental to lawful sanctions to the extent consistent with the Standard Minimum Rules for the Treatment of Prisoners.
>
> 2. Torture constitutes an aggravated and deliberate form of cruel inhuman or degrading treatment or punishment.

Article 2 of the Declaration explains the significance of classifying an act of torture, etc.:

> . . . Any act of torture or other cruel, inhuman or degrading treatment or punishment is an offence to human dignity and shall be condemned as a denial of the purposes of the Charter of the United Nations and as a violation of human rights and fundamental freedoms proclaimed in the Universal Declaration of Human Rights.

Is it claimed in Article 2 that torture, etc., is contrary to customary international law?[87]

4. It is remarkable that the Court, by a large majority, reached a different conclusion on the question whether torture had occurred from that reached *unanimously* by the Commission.[88] Note in this connection that, although the Court is not bound by the findings of fact of the Commission (see para. 160, judgment), it does not conduct its own full investigation into the facts of a case. Its position is similar to that of an appeal court in the United Kingdom which relies upon finding of fact by the trial court. The Court must always rely very heavily upon the report of the Commission in a case; such written or oral evidence on the facts as is given in proceedings before the Court is likely to be of a supplementary nature only. There was no new evidence before the Court in *Ireland* v. *United Kingdom* on the application of the "five techniques" and their effects.[89]

5. Does the fact that Article 3 is one of the provisions from which a state may not derogate under Article 15 suggest that "inhuman or degrading treatment or punishment" was not intended to include relatively modest forms of ill-treatment? What significance attaches to the classification of conduct as "torture" as opposed to "inhuman treatment," etc.? Might it affect the compensation (if any) awarded under Article 50? Does it affect the reputation of a state?

6. *The Tyrer Case.*[90] The applicant was a United Kingdom citizen resident in the Isle of Man. In 1972, when aged 15, he was sentenced by a juvenile court to three strokes of the birch for an assault occasioning actual bodily harm contrary to Manx law. The Convention extends to the Isle of Man as a result of a declaration made by the United Kingdom Government under Article 63 of the Convention.[91] The applicant complained that the birching he was given was contrary to Article 3. Although the applicant sought

---

[86] G.A. Resn. 3452 (XXX); G.A.O.R., 30th Session, Supp. 34, p. 91, December 9, 1975. The Declaration was adopted without a vote.

[87] See on this question, the *Filartiga Case*, below, p. 539.

[88] See 19 Y.B.E.C.H.R. 512, at p. 750 (1976) (Report of the Commission).

[89] See the separate opinion of Judge Zekia.

[90] Eur. Court H.R., Series A, Vol. 26, Judgment of April 25, 1978.

[91] Art. 63 permits the extension of the Convention to any territory "for whose international relations" a party is responsible, subject to any "local requirements."

to withdraw his application after it had been admitted for consideration on the merits, the Commission refused to permit this because it raised issues of a general character affecting the operation of the Convention. In its report on the case,[92] the Commission expressed the opinion, by fourteen votes to one, that the punishment was "degrading" contrary to Article 3 and referred the case to the Court. Confirming the Commission's opinion, the Court held, by six votes to one,[93] that the punishment was "degrading." The Court stated that for a punishment to be "degrading," the humiliation or debasement must be more than that which exists in the case of generally accepted forms of punishment imposed by courts for criminal offences. In the case of corporal punishment, factors that made it "degrading" were the institutionalised use of physical violence by one human being against another and the assault upon a person's dignity and physical integrity that this involved. The fact that, in this case, punishment was administered to the bare posterior of the applicant "aggravated to some extent the degrading character of the applicant's punishment but it was not the only or determining factor." The Court emphasised that it was not relevant that the birch was thought to be an effective deterrent in the Isle of Man; a punishment contrary to Article 3 was not permitted however effective it might be. The Court recalled that "the Convention is a living instrument which . . . must be interpreted in the light of present-day conditions." Accordingly, it could not but be influenced in this case "by the developments and commonly accepted standards in the penal policy of the Member States of the Council of Europe." No further birching case is likely to arise. The United Kingdom has notified the Committee of Ministers that the judgment has been brought to the attention of those who can pass a sentence of corporal punishment under Manx law and that they have been informed that such a punishment would be a breach of the Convention. The Committee has accepted that this is sufficient to fulfill the obligations of the United Kingdom arising out of the judgment: C.M. Resolution (78)39. In any event, the United Kingdom does not now accept the right of petition in respect of the Isle of Man: see above, p. 480.

7. *Campbell and Cosans Case.*[94] The applicants were parents who objected to the use of corporal punishment in Scottish state schools which their children attended. In neither case was the applicant's child in fact given such punishment. The Court accepted that, "provided it is sufficiently real and immediate, a mere threat of conduct prohibited by Article 3 may itself be in conflict with" it, so that, for example, "to threaten an individual with torture might in some circumstances constitute at least inhuman treatment." On the facts, the Court held unanimously that no breach of Article 3 had occurred. It did find a breach of Article 1, First Protocol: see above, p. 477, n. 33. In 1982, the United Kingdom agreed to a friendly settlement of another school caning case by which it paid £2,000 by way of compensation and costs.

8. In *A* v. *U.K.*,[95] a Broadmoor offender mental patient complained of a breach of Article 3 because of the conditions (cell conditions, clothing, lack of exercise and association with others) of his detention when placed in seclusion for five weeks on suspicion of having started a fire. A friendly settlement was reached by which the United Kingdom agreed to pay £500 compensation, without admitting liability. The United Kingdom also indicated that the intensive care unit within which the applicant had been detained had been renovated; that an additional secure hospital was being

[92] Report adopted on December 14, 1976.
[93] Judge Sir Gerald Fitzmaurice dissented.
[94] Eur. Court H.R. Series A, Vol. 48, Judgment of February 25, 1982.
[95] Friendly Settlement of July 6, 1980, 20 D.R.E.C.H.R. 5 (1980). See also the *Simon-Herold Case*, 14 Y.B.E.C.H.R. 352 (1971) Decn. admiss. (detention of a remand prisoner in a psychiatric ward when there is no reason to suppose that he is suffering from mental illness may constitute inhuman or degrading treatment or punishment, depending upon the conditions (friendly settlement reached on facts).

built to reduce pressure on space; and that new guidelines had been set for the treatment of patients segregated in seclusion.

9. *The Amekrane Case.*[96] Mohamed Amekrane, a Moroccan national and a Lieutenant-Colonel in the Moroccan Air Force, was a party to a plot to kill King Hassan of Morocco and to overthrow his government. When the plot failed, Amekrane fled at once, on August 16, 1972, from Morocco to Gibraltar where he requested political asylum. The request was refused and he was declared a prohibited immigrant. The Moroccan Government asked for his return and on August 17, 1972, Amekrane was handed over to its representatives at Gibraltar airport whence he was flown back to Morocco on a Moroccan Air Force plane. On his return, Amekrane was interrogated, tried and sentenced to death by military tribunal. He was executed by firing squad on January 15, 1973.

An application was made to Strasbourg on December 16, 1972, in the name of Amekrane, his wife and his two children in which a violation *inter alia* of Article 3 was alleged. It was claimed that the first applicant had been subjected to "inhuman treatment" because he was returned to Morocco when it was known that he would be prosecuted there for a political offence and sentenced to death if convicted.

The application was given precedence by the Commission[97] and declared admissible on October 11, 1973. In July 1974, a "friendly settlement" in the sense of Article 28 was reached with the assistance of the Commission by which the United Kingdom agreed to pay the applicants £37,500 in full and final settlement of their claims. The payment was made *ex gratia* and was understood by the United Kingdom as not implying any admission by it that the Convention had been violated.

The case is a remarkable one both because it is the first in which an application against the United Kingdom from an overseas territory has been declared admissible and because of the amount of compensation paid by the United Kingdom. £37,500 is by far the largest sum that a State has agreed to pay as part of a "friendly settlement." But then, as *The Times* said, the whole affair was "a sad episode from which the government of the time emerged with little credit and some justified opprobium."[98] There was no extradition treaty between Morocco and the United Kingdom and the case would appear to have been one of extradition in the guise of the application of the immigration laws.[99] The haste with which the matter had been dealt with had, moreover, effectively prevented Amekrane from questioning in the courts in Gibraltar the legality of his return. A particularly interesting question is whether the Commission would have found that the return of the first applicant for trial for a political offence amounted to "inhuman treatment" contrary to Article 3. It has on several occasions stated that the return of a fugitive from justice in such circumstances could violate the Convention[1] but has not yet found this to be so on the facts of any case.

10. In the *East African Asians Cases*,[2] in 1970 the Commission admitted for consideration on the merits *inter alia* under Article 3 the cases of 31 United Kingdom citizens or British protected persons who had been resident in Kenya or Uganda and who had been refused entry into the United Kingdom. In its decision as to admissibility, the Commission stated that "quite apart from any consideration of Article 14, discrimination based on race could, in certain circumstances, of itself amount to degrading treatment within the meaning of Article 3."[3] In its report on the merits of the

---

[96] 16 Y.B.E.C.H.R. 356 (1973). Decn. admiss. Report of the Commission adopted 19 July 1974.

[97] Rule 28, Rules of Procedure of the Commission.

[98] *The Times*, August 14, 1974, editorial.

[99] *Cf.* the case of Dr. Soblen in 1963, as to which see O'Higgins, 17 M.L.R. 521 (1964), and Thornberry, 12 I.C.L.Q. 414 (1962).

[1] See, *e.g.* A.1462/62, 5 Y.B.E.C.H.R. 256 (1962).

[2] 13 Y.B.E.C.H.R. 928 (1970), (25 cases); 30 C.D.E.C.H.R. 127 (1970) (6 cases).

[3] *Ibid.* p. 994.

case in 1973, the Commission expressed the opinion by eight votes to three that Article 3 had been violated in the case of the 25 applicants who were United Kingdom citizens. After much delay, and after all 31 applicants in the case had been admitted to the United Kingdom, the Committee of Ministers decided in 1977, that "no further action" was called for.[4] The Committee did not rule on the question whether Article 3 had been infringed.

WEMHOFF CASE[5]

Eur. Court H.R., Series A, Vol. 7. Judgment of June 27, 1968

The applicant, a West German national, was arrested on November 9, 1961, on suspicion of complicity in offences of breach of trust. The investigation of the case by the West Berlin Prosecutor's Office was completed on February 24, 1964. An indictment was filed on April 23, 1964, and on July 17, 1964, the applicant was committed for trial. The trial began in the Regional Court of Berlin on November 9, 1964, and the applicant was convicted on April 7, 1965, of a "particularly serious case of prolonged abetment to breach of trust" for which he was sentenced to six-and-a-half-years penal servitude. The period of time spent in detention pending trial was counted as a part of this sentence. The applicant's appeal against conviction was rejected on December 17, 1965. The applicant had remained in detention since he was first arrested. The case was very complicated. It involved 12 other accused and required the examination of a mass of bank accounts and transactions. The Commission admitted the application for consideration on its merits in respect of alleged violations by West Germany of Articles 5(3) and 6(1). In its report, the Commission expressed the opinion, by seven votes to three, that Article 5(3) had been violated because the applicant had not been brought to trial "within a reasonable time" and, unanimously, that there had been no violation of Article 6(1). The Commission referred the case to the Court.

Judgment of the Court

A. *As regards Article* 5(3) *of the Convention*

4. . . . As the word "reasonable" applies to the time within which a person is entitled to trial, a purely grammatical interpretation would leave the judicial authorities with a choice between two obligations, that of conducting the proceedings until judgment within a reasonable time or that of releasing the accused pending trial, if necessary against certain guarantees.

5. The Court is quite certain that such an interpretation would not conform to the intention of the High Contracting Parties. It is inconceivable that they should have intended to permit their judicial authorities, at the price of release of the accused, to protract proceedings beyond a reasonable time. This would, moreover, be flatly contrary to the provision in Article 6(1) cited above. . . .

Article 5, which begins with an affirmation of the right of everyone to liberty and security of person, goes on to specify the situations and conditions in which derogations from this principle may be made. . . . It is thus mainly in the light of the fact of the detention of the person being prosecuted that national courts, possibly followed by the European Court, must determine whether the time that has elapsed, for whatever reason, before judgment is passed on the accused

---

[4] CM Resolution DH (77) 2. There was no decision by the Committee on the question whether a breach of Art. 3 had occurred because it was not possible to obtain a 2/3rds majority either way.

[5] See Daintith and Wilkinson, 18 A.J.C.L. 326 (1970) and Harris (1970) 44 B.Y.I.L. 87.

has at some stage exceeded a reasonable limit, that is to say imposed a greater sacrifice than could, in the circumstances of the case, reasonably be expected of a person presumed to be innocent.

In other words it is the provisional detention of accused persons which must not, according to Article 5(3), be prolonged beyond a reasonable time. . . .

6. Another question relating to the interpretation of Article 5(3) . . . is that of the period of detention covered by the requirement of a "reasonable time. . . ."

The representative of the German Government expounded the reasons which led him to maintain the interpretation, accepted in the Commission's Report, that it is the time of appearance before the trial court that marks the end of the period with which Article 5(3) is concerned.

7. The Court cannot accept this restrictive interpretation. It is true that the English text of the Convention allows such an interpretation. . . .

But while the English text permits two interpretations the French version, which is of equal authority, allows only one. According to it the obligation to release an accused person within a reasonable time continues until that person has been "*jugée*," that is until the day of the judgment that terminates the trial. Moreover, he must be released "*pendant la procédure*," a very broad expression which indubitably covers both the trial and the investigation.

8. Thus confronted with two versions of a treaty which are equally authentic but not exactly the same the Court must, following established international law precedents, interpret them in a way that will reconcile them as far as possible. Given that it is a law-making treaty, it is also necessary to seek the interpretation that is most appropriate in order to realise the aim and achieve the object of the treaty, not that which would restrict to the greatest possible degree the obligations undertaken by the Parties. It is impossible to see why the protection against unduly long detention on remand which Article 5 seeks to ensure for persons suspected of offences should not continue up to delivery of judgment rather than cease at the moment the trial opens.

9. It remains to ascertain whether the end of the period of detention with which Article 5(3) is concerned is the day on which a conviction becomes final or simply that on which the charge is determined, even if only by a court of first instance.

The Court finds for the latter interpretation.

One consideration has appeared to it as decisive, namely that a person convicted at first instance, whether or not he has been detained up to this moment, is in the position provided for by Article 5(1)(a) which authorises deprivation of liberty "*after conviction.*" This last phrase cannot be interpreted as being restricted to the case of a final conviction, for this would exclude the arrest at the hearing of convicted persons who appeared for trial while still at liberty, whatever remedies are still open to them. Now, such a practice is frequently followed in many Contracting States and it cannot be believed that they intended to renounce it. It cannot be overlooked moreover that the guilt of a person who is detained during the appeal or review proceedings, has been established in the course of a trial conducted in accordance with requirements of Article 6. . . . A person who has cause to complain of the continuation of his detention after conviction because of delay in determining his appeal, cannot avail himself of Article 5(3) but could possibly allege a disregard of the "reasonable time" provided for by Article 6(1). . . .

10. The reasonableness of an accused person's continued detention must be assessed in each case according to its special features. The factors which may be taken into consideration are extremely diverse. Hence the possibility of wide differences in opinion in the assessment of the reasonableness of a given detention. . . .

13. The arrest warrant taken out in Wemhoff's name on 9th November 1961 was based on the fear that if he were left at liberty, he would abscond and destroy the evidence against him, in particular by communicating with persons who might be involved. . . . Both of these reasons continued to be invoked until 5th August 1963 in the decisions of the courts rejecting Wemhoff's many applications for release pending trial.

On that date, however, although the investigation had yet to be concluded, the Court of Appeal accepted that there was some doubt as to whether any danger of suppression of evidence still existed, but it considered that the other reason was still operative . . . , and the same reasoning was repeated in later decisions dismissing the Applicant's appeals.

14. With regard to the existence of a danger of suppression of evidence, the Court regards this anxiety of the German courts to be justified in view of the character of the offences of which Wemhoff was suspected and the extreme complexity of the case.

As to the danger of flight, the Court is of opinion that, while the severity of the sentence which the accused may expect in the event of conviction may legitimately be regarded as a factor encouraging him to abscond—though the effect of such fear diminishes as detention continues and, consequently, the balance of the sentence which the accused may expect to have to serve is reduced, nevertheless the possibility of a severe sentence is not sufficient in this respect. The German courts have moreover been careful to support their affirmations that a danger of flight existed by referring at an early stage in the proceedings to certain circumstances relating to the material position and the conduct of the accused. . . .

15. The Court wishes, however, to emphasise that the concluding words of Article 5(3) of the Convention show that, when the only remaining reasons for continued detention is the fear that the accused will abscond and thereby subsequently avoid appearing for trial, his release pending trial must be ordered if it is possible to obtain from him guarantees that will ensure such appearance.

It is beyond doubt that, in a financial case such as that in which Wemhoff was involved, an essential factor in such guarantees should have been the deposit by him of bail or the provision of security for a large amount. The positions successively taken up by him on this matter (statement of the facts, paras. 5 and 14)[6] are not such as to suggest that he would have been prepared to furnish such guarantees.

16. In these circumstances the Court could not conclude that there had been any breach of the obligations imposed by Article 5(3) unless the length of Wemhoff's provisional detention between 9th November 1961 and 7th April 1965 had been due either (a) to the slowness of the investigation, which was only

---

[6] *Ed.* In August 1962, the applicant offered to deposit 200,000 DM but withdrew the offer two days later, apparently before the Court had considered it. After his conviction, an offer of 100,000 DM was accepted by the Court, but then replaced by a much lower one which the Court could not accept.

completed at the end of February 1964, or (b) to the lapse of time which occurred either between the closing of the investigation and the preferment of the indictment (April 1964) or between then and the opening of the trial (9th November 1964) or finally (c) to the length of the trial (which lasted until 7th April 1965). It cannot be doubted that, even when an accused person is reasonably detained during these various periods for reasons of the public interest, there may be a violation of Article 5(3) if, for whatever cause, the proceedings continue for a considerable length of time.

17. On this point the Court shares the opinion of the Commission that no criticism can be made of the conduct of the case by the judicial authorities. The exceptional length of the investigation and of the trial are justified by the exceptional complexity of the case and by further unavoidable reasons for delay. . . .

B. *As regards Article 6(1) which gives to everyone the right to have his case heard within a reasonable time*

18. The Court is of opinion that the precise aim of this provision in criminal matters is to ensure that accused persons do not have to lie under a charge for too long and that the charge is determined.

There is therefore no doubt that the period to be taken into consideration in applying this provision lasts at least until acquittal or conviction, even if this decision is reached on appeal. There is furthermore no reason why the protection given to the persons concerned against the delays of the courts should end at the first hearing in a trial: unwarranted adjournments or excessive delays on the part of trial courts are also to be feared.

19. As regards the beginning of the period to be taken into consideration, the Court is of opinion that it must run from 9th November 1961, the date on which the first charges were levelled against Wemhoff and his arrest was ordered.

It was on that date that his right to a hearing within a reasonable time came into being so that the criminal charges could be determined.

20. The period to be taken into consideration in order to check whether Article 6(1) has been observed thus coincides in Wemhoff's case, for the greater part, with the period of his detention as covered by Article 5(3). The Court therefore, having found no failure on the part of the judicial authorities in their duty of particular diligence under that provision, must *a fortiori* accept that there has been no contravention of the obligation contained in Article 6(1) of the Convention. Even if the length of the review proceedings (Revision) is to be taken into account, it certainly did not exceed the reasonable limit.

For these reasons, the Court,

Holds, by six votes to one, that there has been no breach of Article 5(3) of the Convention;

Holds, unanimously, that there has been no breach of Article 6(1) of the Convention. . . .

INDIVIDUAL DISSENTING OPINION OF JUDGE ZEKIA. The legal system of a country, governing the provisions of the criminal law and procedure relating to pre-trial proceedings—such as preliminary enquiries, investigation and arraignment—as well as the presentation of a case to the court and the power of the court itself in reopening investigations, has a lot to do with the time taken in the conclusion of a trial. . . .

In [a common law system] . . . it is the police and the prosecution who conduct the enquiries and collect the evidence. They present the case to a court either for trial or—in indictable offences—for preliminary enquiries for the purpose of committal before the Assizes. Under [a civil law] . . . system the investigation is carried out by a judge and the trial of the accused is started after judicial investigations are closed and after the decision is taken for remitting the case before trial. . . .

While in the former system sufficient evidence to build up a prima facie case against the suspected person is normally expected to be available before he is charged and is taken into custody, in the latter case, i.e. continental system, it appears that the availability of such evidence at an early stage is not essential. Information to the satisfaction of the judicial officials seems to be sufficient for the arrest and detention of a suspect.

As a consequence of these basic divergences inherent in the two systems, suspected persons are, as a rule, kept in detention considerably longer on the continent than in the case of those in England or other countries where the system of common law prevails.

. . . My intention is neither to touch on the merits or demerits of either system. My digression from the track is to emphasise the fact that—if in England, a Member of the Council of Europe—the concept of "reasonable time" regarding the period of detention of an unconvicted person awaiting his trial does not allow us to stretch the time beyond six months even in an exceptionally difficult and complicated case, could we say that in the continent in a similar case, the period of detention might be six times longer and yet it could be considered as reasonable and therefore compatible with the Convention?

. . . it may fairly be inferred that the Governments signatories of the Convention, intended amongst other things, to set a common standard of right to liberty, the scope of which could not differ so vastly from one country to another. . . .

If a man, presumably innocent, is kept in custody for years, this is bound to ruin him. It is true in the case of Wemhoff that the trial ended with a conviction, but it might have ended with an acquittal as well. . . .

I believe that in all systems of law there exist always ways and means of avoiding unreasonably long delayed trials. . . .

Notes

1. In deciding that the "reasonable time" guarantee in Article 5(3) provided a basis for reviewing the *grounds* upon which a person detained pending trial under Article 5(1)(c) continues to be detained after his initial arrest as well as providing a means of control over the *length* of the procedure against a person detained pending trial, the Court clearly filled what would otherwise have been a significant gap in the Convention and made sense of an obscure text.

2. In the *Stögmuller Case*[7] the Court expressed the general test that should be applied in deciding whether the danger of the accused disappearing is too great to permit his release as follows:

> There must be a whole set of circumstances . . . which give reason to suppose that the consequences and hazards of flight will seem to him [the accused] to be a lesser evil than continued imprisonment.[8]

[7] Eur. Court H.R., Series A, Vol. 9, Judgment of November 10, 1969.   [8] *Ibid.* p. 44.

Apart from the dangers of flight and of the suppression of evidence, the Court also, in the *Matznetter Case*,[9] by four votes to three, accepted prevention of crime as a permissible ground for detention "in the special circumstances of the case." These would seem to have been that there was good reason to believe that the accused, if released, would have committed an offence or offences of the same and serious kind as those with which he was already charged, although there was no particular offence which could be identified at the time that the question of release arose as one which it was reasonably believed he would commit. Note that in English law magistrates have been judicially urged to refuse bail in such circumstances.[10] For one of several further cases applying Article 5(3), see the *Ringeisen Case*.[11]

3. In 1965, after proceedings in the *Wemhoff Case* were begun, the Federal Republic of Germany changed its law concerning detention pending trial so that now detention can normally not be for a period of more than six months.[12]

4. In the *Wemhoff Case*, four years and five months elapsed between the bringing of the application and the ruling by the European Court. In the *Stögmuller Case,* which was also concerned with the "reasonable time" guarantee in Article 5(3), the same process took seven years and three months. This was so even though both cases were given priority by the Commission. Local remedies had had to be exhausted in accordance with the rule in Article 26. How effective from the point of view of the applicant is the remedy available to him through Strasbourg when it operates on such a time scale, particularly in cases where time is of the essence of the complaint? What could be done to shorten proceedings at Strasbourg? Should the Commission, which bears the heaviest burden, be made a full-time body? Are delays to some extent inevitable in an international multilingual forum?[13] It is true, of course, that under the Convention as finally conceived, the primary purpose of state and individual applications is not to offer an international remedy for individual victims of violations of the Convention but to bring to light violations of an *inter-state* guarantee. Individuals are expected to benefit generally, through the containment of municipal law that that guarantee is aimed at achieving, rather than as individual claimants in particular cases. The result is nonetheless that the Convention is less useful than it might otherwise have been for the individual victim.

5. *Article 5(4).* The purpose of this provision is to ensure judicial consideration of administrative decisions by the police, mental institutions, etc., to detain someone. If the original decision is taken by a "court" that meets the requirements of Article 5(4), that provision does not require a further judicial hearing.[14] To qualify as a "court," an institution must be independent of the executive and the parties and offer appropriate procedural safeguards.[15] The latter are those necessary to do justice, bearing in mind that the issue is the deprivation of liberty. Compliance with all of the safeguards in Article 6, Convention is not required. In the case of a mental patient, Article 5(4) requires that a detained patient be allowed a remedy at the time of detention *and* continually thereafter at reasonable intervals because the patient's mental condition may improve.[16] To comply with Article 5(4), a remedy must allow a person to challenge the grounds for his detention as well as the legality of the procedures followed. Thus, in

---

[9] Eur. Court H.R., Series A, Vol. 10, Judgment of November 10, 1969.

[10] See, *e.g. R.* v. *Phillips* (1947) 32 Cr.App.R. 47.

[11] Below, p. 504.

[12] West German Code of Criminal Procedure, para. 121.

[13] In this connection, see the European Agreement relating to Persons participating in Proceedings of the European Commission and Court of Human Rights 1969, U.K.T.S. 44 (1971), Cmnd. 4699. The agreement entered into force in 1971. On December 31, 1981, there were 14 contracting parties, including the U.K.

[14] *Vagrancy Cases, loc. cit.* at p. 479, n. 39, above.

[15] *Ibid.*

[16] *Winterwerp Case, loc. cit.* at p. 506, n. 41, above.

X v. *U.K.*,[17] habeas corpus was not a sufficient remedy in the case of a released mental patient who wished to challenge a decision to recall him for detention when there were signs that his condition was deteriorating. This was because habeas corpus did not allow him to question the need for his detention.

NEUMEISTER CASE

Eur. Court H.R., Series A. Judgment of June 27, 1968

The applicant was an Austrian national accused of complicity with others in large scale tax evasion. He was arrested for a while in 1961 and again in 1962. The application concerned the second period of pre-trial detention which lasted for two years and two months. The applicant's trial began in 1964. It had not been completed when the European Court gave judgment in June 1968.[18] In its report, the Commission ruled, by eleven to two, that the applicant had not been brought to trial within a reasonable time in accordance with Article 5(3) and, by six to six (with the casting vote of the President), that his case had not been heard within a reasonable time in accordance with Article 6(1). The Commission referred the case to the Court.

Judgment of the Court

(a) *The question whether the length of Neumeister's detention exceeded the reasonable time laid down in Article 5(3) of the Convention. . . .*

8. What strikes one first when examining the circumstances surrounding Neumeister's second detention is that, while his arrest on 12th July 1962 had been provoked by the recent statements of his co-accused Rafael, the Applicant, who had already been the subject of a long investigation, was not interrogated again during the fifteen months which elapsed between his second arrest (12th July 1962) and the close of the investigation (4th November 1963). On 21st January 1963, it is true, he was confronted with Rafael, but this confrontation, which was interrupted after a few minutes, was not recommenced, contrary to what was to be inferred from the minutes.

Such a state of affairs called for particular attention on the part of the judicial authorities when examining the applications which Neumeister made to them with a view to obtaining his release pending trial.

10. The Court finds it understandable that the Austrian judicial authorities consider the danger of flight as having been much increased in July 1962 by the greater gravity of the criminal and civil penalties which Rafael's new statements must have caused Neumeister to fear.

The danger of flight cannot, however, be evaluated solely on the basis of such considerations. Other factors, especially those relating to the character of the person involved, his morals, his home, his occupation, his assets, his family ties and all kinds of links with the country in which he is being prosecuted may either confirm the existence of a danger of flight or make it appear so small that it cannot justify detention pending trial.

[17] Eur. Court H.R., Series A, Vol. 46, Judgment of November 5, 1981. Recourse to a Mental Health Review Tribunal did not satisfy Art. 5(4) either, because the tribunal could only make a recommendation to the Home Secretary. The U.K. was held to be in breach of Art. 5(4). The Mental Health (Amendment) Act 1982 brings U.K. laws into line with the Convention.

[18] Neumeister was convicted by the Regional Criminal Court of Vienna in July 1968; his conviction was confirmed on appeal by the Austrian Supreme Court in July 1971.

It should also be borne in mind that the danger of flight necessarily decreases as the time spent in detention passes by, for the probability that the length of detention on remand will be deducted from the period of imprisonment which the person concerned may expect if convicted, is likely to make the prospect seem less awesome to him and reduce his temptation to flee. . . .

12. The Court is of the opinion that in these circumstances the danger that Neumeister would avoid appearing at the trial by absconding was, in October 1962 in any event, no longer so great that it was necessary to dismiss as quite ineffective the taking of the guarantees which under Article 5(3) may condition a grant of provisional release in order to reduce the risks which it entails.

However, this was precisely the attitude of the Austrian judicial authorities when for the first time, on 26th October 1962, Neumeister proposed a bank guarantee of 200,000 or, if necessary, 250,000 schillings . . . , again when this offer was repeated on 12th July 1963 . . . and even when the offer of bail was increased by his lawyer on 6th November 1963 to one million schillings. . . .

13. The Court is not in a position to state an opinion as to the amount of security which could reasonably be demanded of Neumeister, and it does not reject the notion that the first offers could have been dismissed as insufficient. It notes however that the Austrian courts based their calculations mainly on the amount of loss resulting from the offences imputed to Neumeister and which he might be called upon to make good. . . .

14. This concern to fix the amount of the guarantee to be furnished by a detained person solely in relation to the amount of the loss imputed to him does not seem to be in conformity with Article 5(3) of the Convention. The guarantee provided for by that Article is designed to ensure not the reparation of loss but rather the presence of the accused at the hearing. Its amount must therefore be assessed principally by reference to him, his assets and his relationship with the persons who are to provide the security, in other words to the degree of confidence that is possible that the prospect of loss of the security or of action against the guarantors in case of his non-appearance at the trial will act as a sufficient deterrent to dispel any wish on his part to abscond.

15. For these reasons, the Court finds that Neumeister's continued provisional detention until 16th September 1964 constituted a violation of Article 5(3) of the Convention.

(b) *The question whether the proceedings against Neumeister lasted beyond the reasonable time laid down in Article 6(1) of the Convention.* . . .

18. . . . The Court notes that Neumeister was charged on 23rd February 1961. . . .

20. That more than seven years have already elapsed since the laying of charges without any determination of them having yet been made in a judgment convicting or acquitting the accused, certainly indicates an exceptionally long period which in most cases should be considered as exceeding the reasonable time laid down in Article 6(1).

Moreover, an examination of . . . the activities of the Investigating Judge between 12th July 1962 and the close of the investigation on 4th November 1963 . . . gives rise to serious disquiet. Not only was there during those fifteen months, as the Court has already noted (para. 8), no interrogation of Neumeister nor any confrontation of any importance with the other accused person whose statements are said to have caused the Applicant's second arrest, but between 24th June 1963 and 18th September of the same year, the Judge did not interrogate any of the numerous co-accused or any witness, nor did he proceed to any other measure of investigation.

Lastly, it is indeed disappointing that the trial was not able to commence before 9th November 1964, that is a year after the closing of the investigation, and even more disappointing that, following such a long investigation the trial court was compelled, after sitting for several months, to order further investigations which were not all caused by the statements of the accused Huber, who had remained silent until the trial. . . .

It is beyond doubt that the Neumeister case was of extraordinary complexity. . . . It is, for example, not possible to hold the Austrian judicial authorities responsible for the difficulties they encountered abroad in obtaining the execution of their numerous letters rogatory. . . . The need to wait for replies probably explains the delay in closing the investigation, despite the fact that no further measures of investigation remained to be conducted in Austria.

The course of the investigation would probably have been accelerated had the Applicant's case been severed from those of his co-accused, but nothing suggests that such a severance would here have been compatible with the good administration of justice. . . .

Neither does the Court believe that the course of the investigation would have been accelerated, if it had been allocated to more than one judge, even supposing that this had been legally possible. It also notes that, although the designated Judge could not in fact be relieved of the financial cases of which he had been seized before 1959, many other cases which would normally have fallen to him after this date were assigned to other judges. . . .

It should moreover be pointed out that a concern for speed cannot dispense those judges who in the system of criminal procedure in force on the continent of Europe are responsible for the investigation or the conduct of the trial from taking every measure likely to throw light on the truth or falsehood of the charges. . . .

For these reasons, the Court

Holds unanimously that there has been a breach of Article 5(3) of the Convention;

Holds by five votes to two that there has been no breach of Article 6(1) of the Convention as regards the length of the proceedings against the Applicant; . . .

Decides, accordingly, that the facts of the case disclose . . . a breach by the Republic of Austria of its obligations arising from the Convention.

INDIVIDUAL DISSENTING OPINION OF JUDGE ZEKIA. Although the investigation was closed on 4th November 1963 the trial did not begin until 9th November 1964 and for a period of fifteen months prior to 1st November 1963 there appears to be a marked slackness on the part of the investigating authorities. . . .

Notwithstanding the difficulties encountered in the preparation and presentation of the case I am unable to persuade myself—even after making certain allowances for the delays caused by the necessity for these long investigations and the difficulties of procuring evidence—that such a long interval and delay between the date Neumeister was originally charged and the date of the conclusion of his trial, the date of which is not yet known, could be considered as compatible with the letter and spirit of Article 6(1) of the Convention just cited.

In a democratic society to keep a man in suspense and in mental agony for seven years and over, in a state of uncertainty and not knowing what would befall him, with the consequential hardships to him and to his family in business and society, in my view, constitutes a clear violation of the right guaranteed to him under Article 6(1) referred to. Undoubtedly it is desirable and the administration of justice also demands it that a court should endeavour to get the truth and the whole truth specially in a criminal case, but extremely belated proceedings in this direction is highly questionable whether they defeat or serve the ends of justice. It would be better in such cases to rule in favour of the individual if there exists a doubt in the minds of the Court.

Notes

1. If an accused were not brought to trial within a year in an English court as a result of an administrative error, might the United Kingdom be liable under Article 5 or 6? What if the delay were due not to maladministration in a particular case but to a general overloading of the courts? Note the following passage in the *Konig Case*,[19] in which the Court found that proceedings in West German administrative courts lasting, in one instance, nearly 11 years infringed the "reasonable time" guarantee:

> ... the Court wishes to emphasise that it is not its function to express an opinion on the German system of procedure before administrative courts which. . . . enjoys a long tradition. Admittedly, the present system may appear complex on account of the number of courts and remedies but the Court is not unaware that the explanation for this situation is to be found in the eminently praiseworthy concern to reinforce the guarantees of individual rights. Should these efforts result in a procedural maze, it is for the State alone to draw the conclusions and, if need be, to simplify the system with a view to complying with Article 6, § 1 of the Convention.

How persuasive are Judge Zekia's dissenting opinions in the *Wemhoff* and *Neumeister Cases*? Might it be argued that the number of states signatories to the Convention with civil law systems of criminal investigation was sufficient to lead the Court justifiably to the conclusion that the provisions in Articles 5(3) and 6(1) concerning trial within a "reasonable time" must be read as intending to accommodate the essentials of those systems as well as of common law ones?[20] Is the possibility of making reservations[21] relevant? How important is the common standard that Judge Zekia argues for? Note that a somewhat similar problem may arise in a federal state, as it has in the United States, where a federal supreme court applying a federal bill of rights has to decide how tightly to control criminal proceedings in state courts.

2. In the *Delcourt Case*,[22] the Court confirmed that the general requirement of a "fair . . . hearing" in Article 6(1) includes in criminal cases a requirement of "equality of arms," *i.e.* procedural equality, of the parties. It is thus not limited in criminal cases to the specific rights listed in Article 6(3).[23] Might the general requirement also be violated

---

[19] *Loc. cit.* at p. 506, n. 39, below, para. 100. *cf.* the *Bucholz Case*, Eur. Court H.R. Series A. no. 42. Judgment of May 6, 1981 (duty to organise one's legal system so as to comply with the "reasonable time" guarantee, but a temporary backlog of cases does not involve a breach of Article 6(1), if reasonably prompt remedial action is taken).

[20] Note that the Court adopted this approach on another question of interpretation in the *Wemhoff Case* (judgment, para. 9), above, p. 434.

[21] Article 64(1) permits reservations to "any particular provision of the Convention to the extent that any law then in force in its territory is not in conformity" with it. "Reservations of a general character" are not permitted: *ibid.*

[22] Eur. Court H.R., Series A, Vol. 11, Judgment of January 17, 1970. In the same case the Court held that although a right of appeal is not guaranteed in criminal (or civil) cases, if one is provided the appeal proceedings must comply with Art. 6.

[23] In English law, the Crown has the right to stand by jurors until the jury panel is completely exhausted, but the defence does not: see *R.* v. *Chandler* [1964] 2 Q.B. 322 (C.C.A.). Is this consistent with the Convention?

by the admission of illegally or unfairly obtained confessions or other evidence or by the conviction of an accused after newspaper or similar comment that has prejudiced his trial? What about freedom from self-incrimination? Freedom from double jeopardy? Jury trial? Would exclusion of evidence on the ground of Crown privilege in a criminal or a civil case come within it? Note how much room for judicial lawmaking a general requirement such as this offers. What action can a particular Contracting Party take if it thinks that the Court is applying the Convention wrongly?

3. In English law it is possible for a person to be found guilty of the criminal offence of contempt in the face of the court without any hearing in the normal sense. In particular, he may be found guilty and committed to prison on the spot without any opportunity to prepare a defence or, depending upon the circumstances, to have legal representation. It is also possible for the House of Commons to convict a person of contempt of Parliament without his being heard in person or informed of the case against him. Might these be breaches of Article 6?[24] In the case of contempt of Parliament, a Select Committee recommended in 1967 that the procedural arrangements should be changed to ensure an accused a fair trial,[25] but Parliament has yet to take the necessary steps.

4. The right to free legal aid (Art. 6(1)(c)) is a right to *effective* legal aid. If an appointed lawyer fails to act, the state must cause him to do so or appoint another lawyer.[26] The "interests of justice" limitation does not require actual prejudice to the applicant; it is sufficient that "it appears plausible that in the particular circumstances" a qualified lawyer would have helped.[27]

RINGEISEN CASE[28]

Eur. Court H.R., Series A, Vol. 13. Judgment of July 16, 1971

In 1962, the applicant, an Austrian national, made a contract with a Mr. and Mrs. Roth for the purchase from them of land in the Austrian province of Upper Austria. In accordance with an Upper Austrian statute, the transaction needed the approval of an administrative tribunal because the land was agricultural. The tribunal refused to approve the transaction on the statutory ground that the land was going to be used by the applicant for speculative building. As a result, the transaction was, in accordance with the statute, null and void. The applicant appealed, as the statute allowed, to a higher tribunal which rejected the applicant's appeal. In its judgment, the Court rejected the applicant's complaints that the proceedings in his case in Austria had not been consistent with Article 6.[29] The following extract from the judgment is on the preliminary question whether Article 6 applied to the applicant's case in the first place. Were his "civil rights and obligations" being determined?

Judgment of the Court

For Article 6, paragraph (1), to be applicable to a case (contestation) it is *not* necessary that both parties to the proceedings should be private persons, which is the view of the majority of the Commission and of the Government. The

---

[24] See Harris (1966) Crim.L.R. 206.
[25] *Report of the Select Committee on Parliamentary Privilege*, H.C. 34 of 1967–68, paras. 162–189.
[26] *Artico Case*, Eur. Court H.R., Series A, Vol. 37, Judgment of May 13, 1980. The case (against Italy) confirms that the legal aid guarantee applies to appeal proceedings.
[27] *Ibid*. p. 18.
[28] See Harris (1974–75) 47 B.Y.I.L. 157.
[29] Another claim by the applicant—that he had been detained contrary to Article 5(3), Convention in criminal proceedings—was accepted by the Court.

wording of Article 6, paragraph (1), is far wider; the French expression "contestations sur (des) droits et obligations de caractère civil" covers all proceedings the result of which is decisive for private rights and obligations. The English text, "determination of . . . civil rights and obligations," confirms this interpretation.

The character of the legislation which governs how the matter is to be determined (civil, commercial, administrative law, etc.) and that of the authority which is invested with jurisdiction in the matter (ordinary court, administrative body, etc.) are therefore of little consequence.

In the present case, when Ringeisen purchased property from the Roth couple, he had a right to have the contract for sale which they had made with him approved if he fulfilled, as he claimed to do, the conditions laid down in the Act. Although it was applying rules of administrative law, the Regional Commission's decision was to be decisive for the relations in civil law ("de caractère civil") between Ringeisen and the Roth couple.[30]

Notes

1. It is clear from this passage that the Court accepted the view of the Commission[31] that the term "civil rights" in Article 6 refers to the distinction between private and public law found in civil law systems, but absent from common law ones,[32] and that Article 6, accordingly, applies only to the determination of private law rights and obligations and not to the determination of public law ones.[33] The Court, however, extended the scope of Article 6 as understood by the Commission in one important respect.[34] It established that a civil right or obligation is being *determined* not only when it is directly in issue between the parties to a case but also when an adjudication on a separate public law question is indirectly decisive for it.

2. In the *Le Compte Case*,[35] the Court confirmed its approach in the *Ringeisen Case* on this last point, but added:

> As regards the question whether the dispute related to the abovementioned right, the Court considers that a tenuous connection or remote consequences do not suffice for Article 6, § 1 . . . :civil rights and obligations must be the object—or one of the objects—of the *"contestation"* (dispute)[36]; the result of the proceedings must be directly decisive for such a right.

So, for example, in one case the Commission held that deportation proceedings against an individual were not subject to Article 6 just because a decision to deport would be decisive for his rights under a private law contract of employment; the latter "were not

---

[30] The Court's ruling on this point was unanimous.

[31] See, *e.g.* A.3134/67, 11 Y.B.E.C.H.R. 528, at p. 562 (1968).

[32] Briefly, it is the distinction between the law governing relations of private persons *inter se* and the law affecting the state: see Merryman, *The Civil Law Tradition* (1969), Chap. XIV. Note that there are signs in recent British cases that a separate body of public law is being developed.

[33] Other possible interpretations are that "civil rights and obligations" are those which happen to be determinable in a court of law in the legal system concerned; or all legal rights and obligations (or duties) other than those in criminal law; or "civil rights" in the sense of the Convention and other human rights documents. Which interpretation would a common lawyer tend to adopt from a reading of the text?

[34] The Commission had expressed the opinion, by seven votes to five, that Article 6 did not apply to the *Ringeisen Case*.

[35] Eur. Court H.R., Series A, Vol. 43, Judgment of June 23, 1981.

[36] *Ibid.* p. 21.

in any sense in themselves the subject of the proceedings," which was the individual's right to remain in the United Kingdom.[37] What if the proceedings in the case had been an appeal against the refusal to issue a work permit when the permit was a condition of the applicant's contract of employment? In the *Le Compte Case,* the applicants were Belgian doctors who had been suspended from medical practice by disciplinary tribunals for breaches of rules of professional conduct. The Court held that Article 6 had been infringed because the proceedings had not been conducted in public. Article 6 applied because the right to practise medicine in Belgium was a private law right. Although the disciplinary proceedings were a matter of public law, the outcome in this case was "directly decisive" for a private law right. Contrast the position, for example, if the doctors had been fined, not suspended. In one sense, an extension of the scope of Article 6 is very welcome. It is mostly in respect of the functioning of administrative tribunals and authorities that the need for a fair trial guarantee is at present most evident in Western Europe. On the other hand, it is arguable that the better approach would be to draft a new text in a protocol tailored to the specific needs of administrative law rather than to apply a text which will not always easily fit accepted procedures for decision-making by administrative authorities[38] and tribunals.

3. *The König Case.*[39] The applicant in this case brought against the Federal Republic of Germany was a doctor who had had his licence to run a private clinic and then his licence to practise medicine revoked by the competent authorities. In 1967 and 1971 he instituted proceedings in the West German administrative courts challenging these decisions. His first claim was rejected in 1976; the second was still pending in 1977. The Court held that the "reasonable time" guarantee in Article 6 had been infringed in respect of both proceedings. In the course of holding that the rights to continue (i) to run a medical clinic and (ii) to practice medicine were "civil rights," the Court confirmed that "civil rights" is an autonomous Convention concept; a doctrine of *renvoi* does not apply. So, in a particular case, a right that falls within the public law of the state concerned may be classified as a private law right at Strasbourg. The local law is not totally irrelevant, however; it necessarily provides the framework within which the Convention concept applies.[40]

In the *Winterwerp* case,[41] under Dutch law the applicant automatically lost his capacity to act in respect of his property when an order were made for his detention as being mentally disordered. The Court held that this infringed Article 6. Although there

---

[37] *X.* v. *U.K.*, 9 D.R.E.C. H.R. 224 (1977). Decn. admiss.

[38] The *Ringeisen Case* concerned administrative tribunals. A more difficult question is the application of Art. 6 to executive decision making. A minister could scarcely be required, for example, to follow Article 6 in taking a planning decision. In the *Kaplan Case*, Report of the Commission, July 17, 1981; C.M. Resolution DH (81), January 23, 1981 the Commission expressed the opinion that Article 6 guarantees a right to the judicial review of executive decisions before a body complying with its terms, but not a right of appeal to such a body. Which decisions are left to the executive and which are given over to a tribunal is left, it seems, to the State concerned. In the *Kaplan Case*, for example, the U.K. Secretary of State for Trade had the power by statute to decide whether the applicant was a fit or proper person to be a controller of an insurance company. If that power had been given to a tribunal under U.K. law, the tribunal would have been directly controlled by Article 6, whereas the Minister was not. In the *Sporrong and Lönnroth Case*, Eur. Court H.R., Series A, Vol. 52, Judgment of September 23, 1982, the Court held that Sweden had infringed Art. 6(1) by not providing the applicants with a remedy in the sense of that provision to challenge the procedural legality (*i.e.* it was a judicial review case) of planning decisions that were decisive for their property rights.

[39] Eur. Court H.R., Series A, Vol. 27, Judgment of June 28, 1978.

[40] Thus, in the *Konig Case*, it was relevant to the Court's characterisation of the rights involved as civil rights for Convention purposes that the medical profession was not a public service in West German law. Similarly, in a case coming from the U.K. the Court would look to the status of a doctor under the National Health Service.

[41] Euro. Court H.R., Series A, Vol. 33. Judgment of October 24, 1979.

was a hearing on the question of detention, it did not comply with Article 6 and, anyway, "that procedure was concerned solely with his deprivation of liberty . . . [not] the question of his civil capacity." The Court would not have been satisfied with evidence that the detention proceedings complied with Article 6; it would have been necessary for a hearing addressed to the very question of the applicant's civil capacity to have occurred and for that hearing to have been conducted in accordance with Article 6.

GOLDER CASE[42]

Eur. Court H.R., Series A, Vol. 18. Judgment of February 21, 1975

The applicant, a United Kingdom national, was serving a prison sentence at Parkhurst Prison in October 1969 when a disturbance occurred in which L., a prison guard, was assaulted. L. made a statement in which he identified the applicant as one of his assailants. The applicant was told that he might be prosecuted for assault. L. then made a second statement conceding that he might have been mistaken in his identification and another prison officer gave evidence to the effect that the applicant had taken no part in the disturbance. Thereupon, the applicant was returned to his cell, after twelve days in solitary confinement. No proceedings were brought against him. The applicant believed that L.'s first statement had been left on his record and that this was why he had been refused parole.[43] On March 20, 1970, he sought permission to communicate with a solicitor with a view to bringing proceedings in libel against L. Permission was refused under Rule 34(8) of the Prison Rules[44] which reads:

> A prisoner shall not be entitled under this Rule to communicate with any person in connection with any legal or other business, or with any person other than a relative or friend, except with the leave of the Secretary of State.

The Commission expressed the unanimous opinion in its report that Article 6(1) guaranteed a right of access to the courts and that the refusal of the Home Secretary to allow the applicant to communicate with a solicitor was a violation of that right. It also expressed the opinion, by seven votes to two, that Article 8 applied to the facts of the case and, by eight votes to one, that it had been violated by the same facts as constituted a violation of Article 6(1). The case was referred to the Court by the United Kingdom.

Judgment of the Court

Clearly, no one knows whether Golder would have persisted in carrying out his intention to sue Laird if he had been permitted to consult a solicitor. Furthermore, the information supplied to the Court by the Government gives reason to think that a court in England would not dismiss an action brought by a convicted prisoner on the sole ground that he had managed to cause the writ to be issued—through an attorney for instance—without obtaining leave from the Home Secretary. . . .

The fact nonetheless remains that Golder had made it most clear that he intended "taking civil action for libel"; it was for this purpose that he wished to contact a solicitor, which was a normal preliminary step in itself and in Golder's

---

[42] See Triggs, 50 Aust.L.J. 229 (1976) and Zellick, 38 M.L.R. 683 (1975).

[43] It is not clear whether the statement was on his record. Entries were made there indicating possible charges against him and marked "charges not proceeded with," The U.K. Government offered to expunge them (and did so) in 1971 during the Commission's hearing of the case.

[44] S.I. 1964 No. 388. See also Rules 33 and 37.

case probably essential on account of his imprisonment. . . . Without formally denying Golder his right to institute proceedings before a court, the Home Secretary did in fact prevent him from commencing an action at that time, 1970. Hindrance in fact can contravene the Convention just like a legal impediment.

It is true that—as the Government have emphasised—on obtaining his release Golder would have been in a position to have recourse to the courts at will, but in March and April 1970 this was still rather remote and hindering the effective exercise of a right may amount to a breach of that right, even if the hindrance is of a temporary character. . . .

28. . . . Article 6 § 1 does not state a right of access to the courts or tribunals in express terms. . . .

32. The clearest indications [in the text of Article 6 that the right may be inferred] are to be found in the French text, first sentence. In the field of *contestations civiles* (civil claims) everyone has a right to proceedings instituted by or against him being conducted in a certain way—*"équitablement"* (fairly), *"publiquement"* (publicly), *"dans un délai raisonnable"* (within a reasonable time), etc.—but also and primarily *"à ce que sa cause soit entendue"* (that his case be heard) not by any authority whatever but *"par un tribunal"* (by a court tribunal) within the meaning of Article 6 § 1 . . . The Government have emphasised rightly that in French *"cause"* may mean *"procès qui se plaide."* . . . This, however, is not the sole ordinary sense of this noun; it serves also to indicate by extension *"l'ensemble des intérêts à soutenir, à faire prévaloir"* . . . Similarly, the *"contestation"* (claim) generally exists prior to the legal proceedings and is a concept independent of them. As regards the phrase *"tribunal indépendant et impartial établi par la loi"* (independent and impartial tribunal established by law), it conjures up the idea of organisation rather than that of functioning, of institutions rather than of procedure.

The English text, for its part, speaks of an "independent and impartial tribunal established by law." Moreover, the phrase "in the determination of his civil rights and obligations," on which the Government have relied in support of their contention, does not necessarily refer only to judicial proceedings already pending: as the Commission have observed, it may be taken as synonymous with "wherever his civil rights and obligations are being determined" (paragraph 52 of the report). It too would then imply the right to have the determination of disputes relating to civil rights and obligations made by a court or "tribunal." . . .

34. As stated in Article 31 § 2 of the Vienna Convention [on the Law of Treaties[45]], the preamble to a treaty forms an integral part of the context. Furthermore, the preamble is generally very useful for the determination of the "object" and "purpose" of the instrument to be construed.

In the present case, the most significant passage in the Preamble to the European Convention is the signatory Governments declaring that they are "resolved, as the Governments of European countries which are like-minded and have a common heritage of political traditions, ideals, freedom and the rule of law, to take the first steps for the collective enforcement of certain of the Rights stated in the Universal Declaration" of 10th December 1948.

. . . The Court . . . considers, like the Commission, that it would be a

---

[45] *Ed.* Below, p. 598.

mistake to see in this reference a merely "more or less rhetorical reference," devoid of relevance for those interpreting the Convention. . . .

And in civil matters one can scarcely conceive of the rule of law without there being a possibility of having access to the courts.

35. Article 31 § 3(c) of the Vienna Convention indicates that account is to be taken, together with the context, of "any relevant rules of international law applicable in the relations between the parties." Among those rules are general principles of law and especially "general principles of law recognised by civilized nations." . . .

The principle whereby a civil claim must be capable of being submitted to a judge ranks as one of the universally "recognised" fundamental principles of law; the same is true of the principle of international law which forbids the denial of justice. . . .

Were Article 6 § 1 to be understood as concerning exclusively the conduct of an action which had already been initiated before a court, a Contracting State could, without acting in breach of that text, do away with its courts, or take away their jurisdiction to determine certain classes of civil actions and entrust it to organs dependent on the Government. Such assumptions, indissociable from a danger of arbitrary power, would have serious consequences which are repugnant to the aforementioned principles and which the Court cannot overlook. . . .

It would be inconceivable . . . that Article 6 § 1 should describe in detail the procedural guarantees afforded to parties in a pending lawsuit and should not first protect that which alone makes it in fact possible to benefit from such guarantees, that is, access to a court. . . .

36. Taking all the preceding considerations together, it follows that the right of access constitutes an element which is inherent in the right stated by Article 6 § 1. This is not an extensive interpretation forcing new obligations on the Contracting State: it is based on the very terms of the first sentence of Article 6 § 1 read in its context and having regard to the object and purpose of the Convention, a lawmaking treaty (see the Wemhoff judgment of 27th June 1968, Series A no. 7, p. 23, § 8), and to general principles of law.

. . . the Article embodies the "right to a court," of which the right of access, that is the right to institute proceedings before courts in civil matters, constitutes one aspect only. To this are added the guarantees laid down by Article 6 § 1 as regards both the organisation and composition of the court, and the conduct of the proceedings. In sum, the whole makes up the right to a fair hearing. . . .

38. . . . the right of access to the courts is not absolute. As this is a right which the Convention sets forth (see Articles 13, 14, 17 and 25) without, in the narrower sense of the term, defining, there is room, apart from the bounds delimiting the very content of any right, for limitations permitted by implication. . . .

39. The Government and the Commission have cited examples of regulations, and especially of limitations, which are to be found in the national law of states in matters of access to the courts, for instance regulations relating to minors and persons of unsound mind. Although it is of less frequent occurrence and of a very different kind, the restriction complained of by Golder constitutes a further example of such a limitation.

It is not the function of the court to elaborate a general theory of the limitations admissible in the case of convicted prisoners, nor even to rule *in abstracto* on the compatibility of Rules 33 § 2, 34 § 8 and 37 § 2 of the Prison Rules 1964 with the Convention. Seised of a case which has its origin in a petition presented by an individual, the Court is called upon to pronounce itself only on the point whether or not the application of those Rules in the present case violated the Convention to the prejudice of Golder. . . .

40. . . . Golder could justifiably wish to consult a solicitor with a view to instituting legal proceedings. It was not for the Home Secretary himself to appraise the prospects of the action contemplated; it was for an independent and impartial court to rule on any claim that might be brought. In declining to accord the leave which had been requested, the Home Secretary failed to respect, in the person of Golder, the right to go before a court as guaranteed by Article 6 § 1. . . .

43. [In respect of Article 8, the] . . . Home Secretary's refusal of the petition of 20 March 1970 had the direct and immediate effect of preventing Golder from contacting a solicitor by any means whatever, including that which in the ordinary way he would have used to begin with, correspondence. While there was certainly neither stopping nor censorship of any message, such as a letter, which Golder would have written to a solicitor—or vice-versa—and which would have been a piece of correspondence within the meaning of paragraph 1 of Article 8, it would be wrong to conclude therefrom, as do the Government, that this text is inapplicable. Impeding someone from even initiating correspondence constitutes the most far-reaching form of "interference" (paragraph 2 of Article 8) with the exercise of the "right to respect for correspondence;" . . . In any event, if Golder had attempted to write to a solicitor notwithstanding the Home Secretary's decision or without requesting the required permission, that correspondence would have been stopped and he could have invoked Article 8; one would arrive at a paradoxical and hardly equitable result, if it were considered that in complying with the requirements of the Prison Rules 1964 he lost the benefit of the protection of Article 8. . . .

44. In the submission of the Government, the right to respect for correspondence is subject, apart from interference covered by paragraph 2 of Article 8, to implied limitations resulting, *inter alia*, from the terms of Article 5 § 1(a): a sentence of imprisonment passed after conviction by a competent court inevitably entails consequences affecting the operation of other Articles of the Convention, including Article 8.

. . . that submission conflicts with the explicit text of Article 8. The restrictive formulation used at paragraph 2 ("There shall be no interference . . . except such as . . . ") leaves no room for the concept of implied limitations. . . .

45. The Government have submitted in the alternative that the interference complained of satisfied the explicit conditions laid down in paragraph 2 of Article 8. . . .

In order to show why the interference complained of by Golder was "necessary," the Government advanced the prevention of disorder or crime and, up to a certain point, the interests of public safety and the protection of the rights and freedoms of others. Even having regard to the power of appreciation left to the Contracting States, the Court cannot discern how these considerations, as they are understood "in a democratic society," could oblige the Home Secretary to prevent Golder from corresponding with a solicitor with a view to suing Laird for libel. . . .

FOR THESE REASONS, THE COURT,

1. *Holds* by nine votes to three that there has been a breach of Article 6 § 1;

2. *Holds* unanimously that there has been a breach of Article 8;

3. *Holds* unanimously that the preceding findings amount in themselves to adequate just satisfaction under Article 50.

Notes

1. The three judges who disagreed with the Court on the question of a right of access did so for various reasons, the most important of which are the following. All three disagreed with the conclusion drawn by the Court from the wording of Article 6. For Judges Zekia and Sir Gerald Fitzmaurice it was clear from the text that Article 6 controlled only the conduct of court proceedings and not the right to bring them. For Judge Verdross, the exceptional character of the Court's jurisdiction, allowing the Court to rule upon matters normally within the domestic jurisdiction of a State, was such that the Court was incorrect to infer a right of access which it could enforce against a State just from a series of "clues" scattered about the text; the Court's jurisdiction was to be "interpreted strictly."[46] All three judges also emphasised that Article 1 of the Convention requires States to secure to persons within their jurisdiction the rights and freedoms "defined" in the Convention. Could a right be said to be "defined" when it was not even mentioned? Judges Zekia and Sir Gerald Fitzmaurice stressed a second contextual point. Article 17 states that nothing in the Convention shall be taken as allowing a State to impose limitations upon the rights and freedoms guaranteed in the Convention to any greater extent than is provided for in the Convention. In their view, this meant *expressly* provided for, so that any right of access to the courts would have to be an unqualified one, which could not have been intended. The same two judges also pointed out that in other comparable international instruments[47] the right of access had been expressly included where it was thought appropriate to protect it.

Judge Sir Gerald Fitzmaurice criticised the Court's general approach to the interpretation of the Convention. For him the important point was not that this was a law-making treaty which should be interpreted in case of doubt in accordance with its object and purpose of protecting human rights. It was instead the fact that the Convention had "broken entirely new ground internationally, making heavy inroads on some of the most cherished preserves of governments in the sphere of their domestic jurisdiction or *domaine réserve*."[48] The various revolutionary features of the Convention were such as could justify even a somewhat restrictive interpretation of the Convention but, without going as far as that, they must be said, unquestionably, not only to justify, but positively to demand, a cautious and conservative interpretation.[49] This, however, is very much a minority view.[50] Building upon the *Wemhoff* and *Golder* judgments, the Court has developed in the last decade and more a strongly teleological interpretation of the Convention, preferring an interpretation favouring human rights where the text is ambiguous or obscure. See, *e.g.* the *Airey Case*, next note, and the *Young James and Webster Cases*, below, p. 523. In the same vein, the Court has also adopted a "dynamic"

---

[46] Judgment, p. 24.

[47] *e.g.* Article 8, Universal Declaration of Human Rights, below, p. 534, and Article 7, European Convention on Establishment 1956, U.K.T.S. 1 (1971), Cmnd. 4573.

[48] Judgment, p. 52.

[49] *Ibid.* p. 53.

[50] The different approaches of Judge Sir Gerald Fitzmaurice and most of the other judges may also be explained in terms of the different approaches to common law (more literal) and civil law (more teleological) judges to the interpretation of statutes. A teleological approach is more appropriate for a constitutional Bill of Rights, which is what the Convention, despite its international origins, is threatening to become. On the role of the Convention as the bill of rights for the European Communities, see Ghandi, *Legal Issues of European Interpretation 1981*, p. 1.

approach to the interpretation of the Convention, seeing its role as the protection of human rights in accordance with the changing perception of them in Western Europe as social values and attitudes evolve. See, *e.g.* the *Dudgeon and Marckx Cases*, below, pp. 517 and 513. See also the Court's "living instrument" dictum in the *Tyrer Case*, above, p. 491.

2. The Prison Rules were amended to take account of the *Golder Case*.[51] In the *Silver Case*,[52] the Court held unanimously (1) that the refusal by the Home Secretary to allow an applicant to write to a solicitor about possible civil proceedings against the Home Office was a breach of the right of access to the courts and (2) that the censorship of correspondence with solicitors (on matters other than possible litigation), M.P.s, members of their family and friends was a breach of Articles 8 and 13.[53] Rule 34(2), Prison Rules, limits the number of letters that a convicted prisoner may write or receive to one a week. Is this consistent with Art. 8?[54]

3. *Airey Case*.[55] In this case, the applicant was an indigent Irish wife whose marriage had broken down and whose husband was violent. Under Irish law, divorce is illegal, but the courts may grant an order for judicial separation. Applying the *Golder* case, the Court held, by five votes to two, that Ireland had infringed Article 8 by not providing legal aid to the applicant in such proceedings. In the Court's opinion, the right of access meant a right of *effective* access. The Court emphasized that it did not follow from its ruling that legal aid should be provided in all civil proceedings for indigent persons. The particular circumstances that meant that it was required in the present case were as follows:

> "It seems certain to the Court that the applicant would be at a disadvantage if her husband were represented by a lawyer and she were not. Quite apart from this eventuality, it is not realistic . . . to suppose that, in litigation of this nature, the applicant could effectively conduct her own case, despite the assistance which . . . the judge affords to parties acting in person.
>
> . . . litigation of this kind, in addition to involving complicated points of law, necessitates proof of adultery, unnatural practices or, as in the present case, cruelty; to establish the facts, expert evidence may have [to be] tendered and witnesses may have to be found, called and examined. What is more, marital disputes often entail an emotional involvement that is scarcely compatible with the degree of objectivity required by advocacy in court.[56]

The Court found corroboration for its view in the fact that in 'each of the 255 judicial separation proceedings initiated in Ireland in the period from January 1972 to December 1978, without exception, the petitioner was represented by a lawyer.' The Court was not persuaded by the argument that by its judgment it was imposing an economic burden on States and that in doing so it might be said to be going against the grain of a guarantee of civil and political (as opposed to economic and social) rights by requiring States to take positive action to improve the lot of their inhabitants rather than just to refrain from interference with their rights:

> Whilst the Convention sets forth what are essentially civil and political rights, many of them have implications of a social and economic nature. The Court therefore considers, like the Commission, that the mere fact that an interpretation of the Convention may extend into the sphere of social and economic rights should not be a

---

[51] Rule 37A, added by S.I. 1976 No. 503, and Home Office circular No. 45/75, para. 3(ii), quoted in Cohen and Taylor, *Prison Secrets* (1978), p. 43.

[52] Eur. Court H.R., Series A, Judgment of March 25, 1983.

[53] Standing Order 5, published by the Home Office in 1981, amended prison practice in these respects in anticipation of the Court's judgment.

[54] See Jacobs, *op. cit.* at p. 471, n. 18, above, pp. 138–141.

[55] Eur. Court H.R. Series A, Vol. 32, Judgment of October 9, 1979.

[56] *Ibid.* p. 13.

decisive factor against such an interpretation; there is no water-tight division separating that sphere from the field covered by the Convention.

Ireland ratified the Convention subject to a reservation in respect of the legal aid obligation in *criminal* cases expressly included in Article 6(3)(c). Clearly it did not anticipate any comparable obligation in *civil* cases. This is a situation in which states are increasingly likely to find themselves as the Court develops the meaning of the Convention.

4. The right of access is infringed if the applicant's waiver of his right to a trial in a criminal case against him is made under constraint.[57]

DUDGEON CASE

Eur. Court H.R., Series A, Vol. 45. Judgment of October 22, 1981

The applicant, a 35 year-old United Kingdom citizen resident in Northern Ireland, was a homosexual. In 1976, the police seized evidence concerning his homosexual activities from his flat while searching it lawfully for drugs. He was taken to a police station and questioned about his sexual life. Later it was decided not to prosecute and his papers were returned. The applicant complained that the existence of the law in Northern Ireland making buggery (Offences against the Person Act 1861) and "gross indecency" (Criminal Law Amendment Act 1885) between consenting males a criminal offence was a breach of his right to privacy, Article 8, Convention.

Judgment of the Court

41. . . . the maintenance in force of the impugned legislation constitutes a continuing interference with the applicant's right to respect for his private life (which includes his sexual life) within the meaning of Article 8 § 1. . . . either he respects the law and refrains from engaging—even in private with consenting male partners—in prohibited sexual acts to which he is disposed by reason of his homosexual tendencies, or he commits such acts and thereby becomes liable to criminal prosecution.

It cannot be said that the law in question is a dead letter in this sphere. It was, and still is, applied so as to prosecute persons with regard to private consensual homosexual acts involving males under 21 years of age . . . Although no proceedings seem to have been brought in recent years with regard to such acts involving only males over 21 years of age, apart from mental patients, there is no stated policy on the part of the authorities not to enforce the law in this respect. . . . Furthermore . . . there always remains the possibility of a private prosecution. . . .

Moreover, the police investigation in . . . 1976 showed that the threat hanging over him was real. . . .

49. There can be no denial that some degree of regulation of male homosexual conduct, as indeed of other forms of sexual conduct, by means of the criminal law can be justified as "necessary in a democratic society." . . . In practice there is legislation on the matter in all the member States of the Council of Europe, but what distinguishes the law in Northern Ireland from that existing

---

[57] *De Weer Case*, Eur. Court H.R., Series A, No. 35, Judgment of February 27, 1980. (Breach of Art. 6(1) when a Belgian butcher accused under a price control law was constrained to pay a small out of court fine to avoid shop closure pending trial, with serious financial loss.)

in the great majority of the member States is that it prohibits generally gross indecency between males and buggery whatever the circumstances. . . .

The Court then considered the meaning of "necessary," etc., following its approach in the *Sunday Times* and *Handyside* Cases, see below, p. 521.

As was illustrated by the *Sunday Times* judgment, the scope of the margin of appreciation is not identical in respect of each of the aims justifying restrictions on a right. . . . It is an indisputable fact, as the Court stated in the *Handyside* judgment, that "the view taken . . . of the requirements of morals varies from time to time and from place to place, especially in our era," and that "by reason of their direct and continuous contact with the vital forces of their countries, State authorities are in principle in a better position than the international judge to give an opinion on the exact content of those requirements" (p. 22, § 48).

However, . . . [t]he present case concerns a most intimate aspect of private life. Accordingly, there must exist particularly serious reasons before interferences on the part of the public authorities can be legitimate for the purposes of paragraph 2 of Article 8.

53. . . . According to the Court's case-law, a restriction on a Convention right cannot be regarded as "necessary in a democratic society"—two hallmarks of which are tolerance and broadmindedness—unless, amongst other things, it is proportionate to the legitimate aim pursued . . .

57. . . . the moral climate in Northern Ireland in sexual matters . . . is one of the matters which the national authorities may legitimately take into account in exercising their discretion. There is, the Court accepts, a strong body of opposition stemming from a genuine and sincere conviction shared by a large number of responsible members of the Northern Irish community that a change in the law would be seriously damaging to the moral fabric of society . . .

Whether this point of view be right or wrong, and although it may be out of line with current attitudes in other communities, its existence among an important sector of Northern Irish society is certainly relevant for the purposes of Article 8 § 2.

58. . . . Nevertheless, this cannot of itself be decisive as to the necessity for the interference with the applicant's private life resulting from the measures being challenged . . .

60. The Convention right affected by the impugned legislation protects an essentially private manifestation of the human personality . . .

As compared with the era when that legislation was enacted, there is now a better understanding, and in consequence an increased tolerance, of homosexual behaviour to the extent that in the great majority of the member States of the Council of Europe it is no longer considered to be necessary or appropriate to treat homosexual practices of the kind now in question as in themselves a matter to which the sanctions of the criminal law should be applied; the Court cannot overlook the marked changes which have occurred in this regard in the domestic law of the member States . . . In Northern Ireland itself, the authorities have refrained in recent years from enforcing the law in respect of private homosexual acts between consenting males over the age of 21 years capable of valid consent. . . . No evidence has been adduced to show that this has been injurious to moral standards in Northern Ireland or that there has been any public demand for stricter enforcement of the law.

It cannot be maintained in these circumstances that there is a "pressing social need" to make such acts criminal offences, there being no sufficient justification provided by the risk of harm to vulnerable sections of society requiring protection or by the effects on the public. On the issue of proportionality, the Court considers that such justifications as there are for retaining the law in force unamended are outweighed by the detrimental effects which the very existence of the legislative provisions in question can have on the life of a person of homosexual orientation like the applicant. Although members of the public who regard homosexuality as immoral may be shocked, offended or disturbed by the commission by others of private homosexual acts, this cannot on its own warrant the application of penal sanctions when it is consenting adults alone who are involved.

61. . . . "Decriminalisation" does not imply approval, and a fear that some sectors of the population might draw misguided conclusions in this respect from reform of the legislation does not afford a good ground for maintaining it in force with all its unjustifiable features. . . .

62. In the opinion of the Commission, the interference complained of by the applicant *can*, in so far as he is prevented from having sexual relations with young males under 21 years of age, be justified as necessary for the protection of the rights of others . . .

The Court has already acknowledged the legitimate necessity in a democratic society for some degree of control over homosexual conduct notably in order to provide safeguards against the exploitation and corruption of those who are specially vulnerable by reason, for example, of their youth. . . . However, it falls in the first instance to the national authorities to decide on the appropriate safeguards of this kind required for the defence of morals in their society and, in particular, to fix the age under which young people should have the protection of the criminal law. . . .

For these reasons the Court . . . holds by 15 votes to four that there is a breach of Article 8 . . .

Notes

1. Northern Irish law has been changed in response to the judgment.[58] Only two of the dissenting judges—Judge Zekia (Cypriot) and Walsh (Irish)—dissented on the ground that no breach of Article 8 had occurred. Both are nationals of states with laws similar to those in question in the case. The other two judges dissented on the ground that the applicant was not a "victim."[59]

2. The case, which is a good example of the Court's "dynamic" approach to the interpretation of the Convention (see above, p. 512), is of importance in recognising that the right to a personality is a part of the right to privacy in Article 8.[60] This was also the view of the Commission in the *Van Oosterwijck Case*.[61] There the applicant, a barrister, had been born a female in 1944. His status as a transexual having been medically confirmed, he underwent surgery on medical advice in the early 1970s by which he was given the physical characteristics of a male. Since then, the applicant had lived as a man but was unable, under Belgian law, to change his civil status from female to male because there had been no error when his status was registered at birth. This was

---

[58] Homosexual Offences (Northern Ireland) Order 1982.

[59] *cf.* the *Klass Case*, below, p. 516.

[60] *cf.* the U.S. constitutional right to privacy established in *Griswold* v. *Conn.* 381 U.S. 479 (1965).

[61] Report of the Commission of March 1, 1979, Eur. Court H.R., Series A, Vol. 40, Judgment of November 6, 1980.

embarrassing and humiliating since he needed his full birth certificate, which recorded him as female, for certain legal purposes (*e.g.* to sell land and to vote). The Commission expressed the unanimous opinion that the facts disclosed a breach of the right to respect for "private life" in Article 8, which the Commission defined as follows:

> The concept of private life contained in Article 8 is . . . wider than the definition given by numerous Anglo-Saxon and French writers, according to which it is the right to live, as far as one wishes, protected from publicity; for the Commission, "it comprises also to a certain degree the right to establish and to develop relationships with other human beings, especially in the emotional field for the development and fulfilment of one's own personality." . . .

The case was dismissed by the Court for non-exhaustion of local remedies without considering the merits. If the Commission's opinion were to be sustained, law reform would be required in several West European countries, including the United Kingdom.

3. In the *Bruggeman and Scheuten Case*,[62] the Commission was of the opinion that the right to respect for privacy (in the sense of the right to a personality) did not guarantee a pregnant woman the right to an abortion in her discretion. The Commission held that the 1976 West German abortion law, which only permits abortions to protect the life or physical or mental health of the mother or on eugenic grounds, was consistent with Article 8.

4. In the *Klass Case*,[63] the Court held that the West German law permitting the interception of postal and telephonic communications in national security cases was consistent with Article 8; although an "interference by a public authority" with the "right to respect for" a person's "private and family life . . . and his correspondence," it was justified as being necessary "in the interests of national security" and/or for "the prevention of disorder or crime." The Court accepted that some power of interception was permissible to prevent espionage and terrorism and, bearing in mind the "margin of appreciation" doctrine, concluded that the controls built into the West German system to prevent abuse were sufficient. Under that system, permission to intercept communications is given by a Government Minister applying certain criteria as to "reasonable suspicion," etc. An independent Commission, chaired by a person qualified for judicial office, reviews and may reverse the Minister's decisions. A Board composed of government and opposition members of parliament keeps a more general watch on the system. A person whose communications are intercepted must be told that this has happened afterwards if national security allows. He may challenge the legality of current or past interceptions in the courts (so far as he is aware of their occurrence). Although the Court stated that it was "in principle desirable to entrust supervisory control to a judge," the above safeguards were sufficient, at least in a national security context. There is no judicial control and little independent control of any kind in security or non-security cases in United Kingdom law. See *Malone* v. *Metropolitan Police Commr.* (*No. 2*) [1979] Ch. 344 (Ch.D.), a case which has been admitted on the merits at Strasbourg. An interesting aspect of the *Klass Case* was that the Court regarded the applicants as "victims" able to bring a claim under Article 25 even though their telephones had not been tapped. Whereas an applicant under Article 25 normally cannot challenge the validity of a law *in abstracto* (as a state can under Article 24) but has to show that the law "has been applied to his detriment," the position is different in a case in which "owing to the secrecy of the measures objected to, he cannot point to any concrete measure specifically affecting him."[64] In such a case the need to make the application procedure effective dictates that the "individual may, *under certain conditions*, claim to be the

---

[62] Report of the Commission, July 12, 1977; 10 D.R.E.C.H.R. 100. The case was not referred to the Court. The Committee of Ministers confirmed the Commission's opinion.

[63] Eur. Court H.R. Series A, No. 28, Judgment of September 6, 1978.

[64] *Ibid.* p. 18.

victim of a violation occasioned by the mere existence of secret measures or of legislation permitting secret measures. . . . " Moreover, the Court stated, the mere prospect that a telephone may be tapped is such as to inhibit conversation and thereby directly interfere with respect for privacy.

MARCKX CASE

Eur. Court H.R., Series A, Vol. 31. Judgment of June 13, 1979

The applicant, an unmarried Belgian national, claimed on behalf of her infant daughter and herself. She complained of the law in Belgium on (i) the maternal affiliation of an illegitimate child; (ii) his family relationships; and (iii) his patrimonial rights. Under Belgian law, an illegitimate child was only regarded as the child of his mother if the latter in her discretion formally recognized her maternity. If she did so, the affiliation was retroactive to the date of birth. In the case of a legitimate child, there was no such need or delay: affiliation was proved simply by the legally obligatory entry of the married mother's name on the birth certificate. As regards family relationships, an illegitimate child remained, even after recognition, in principle a stranger to his parents' families. Thus, for example, in the absence of his mother, it was his guardian rather than his grandparents who had the power to consent to his marriage. The reverse was true of legitimate children. Similarly, the patrimonial rights of an illegitimate child were in certain ways less than those of a legitimate child, both in respect of inheritance and of *inter vivos* gifts.

The Commission expressed the opinion in its report that *inter alia* Article 8 had been infringed both taken by itself and in conjunction with Article 14 and referred the case to the Court.

Judgment of the Court

31. . . . By guaranteeing the right to respect for family life, Article 8 presupposes the existence of a family. The Court concurs entirely with the Commission's established case-law on a crucial point, namely that Article 8 makes no distinction between the "legitimate" and the "illegitimate" family. Such a distinction would not be consonant with the word "everyone," and this is confirmed by Article 14 with its prohibition, in the enjoyment of the rights and freedoms enshrined in the Convention, of discrimination grounded on "birth". In addition, the Court notes that the Committee of Ministers of the Council of Europe regards the single woman and her child as one form of family no less than others (Resolution (70) 15 of 15 May 1970 . . .).

Article 8 thus applies to the "family life"[65] of the "illegitimate" family as it does to that of the "legitimate" family. Besides, it is not disputed that Paula Marckx assumed responsibility for her daughter Alexandra from the moment of her birth and has continuously cared for her, with the result that a real family life existed and still exists between them. . . .

By proclaiming in paragraph 1 the right to respect for family life, Article 8 signifies firstly that the State cannot interfere with the exercise of that right otherwise than in accordance with the strict conditions set out in para-

---

[65] *Ed*. Elsewhere in its judgment (para. 45), the Court indicated that it understood "family life" as including "at least the ties between near relatives, for instance those between grandparents and grandchildren, since such relatives may play a considerable part of family life."

graph 2. . . . the object of the Article is "essentially" that of protecting the individual against arbitrary interference by the public authorities. . . . Nevertheless, it does not merely compel the State to abstain from such interference: in addition to this primarily negative undertaking, there may be positive obligations inherent in an effective "respect" for family life.

This means, amongst other things, that when the State determines in its domestic legal system the régime applicable to certain family ties such as those between an unmarried mother and her child, it must act in a manner calculated to allow those concerned to lead a normal family life. As envisaged by Article 8, respect for family life implies in particular, in the Court's view, the existence in domestic law of legal safeguards that render possible as from the moment of birth the child's integration in his family. In this connection, the State has a choice of various means, but a law that fails to satisfy this requirement violates paragraph 1 of Article 8 without there being any call to examine it under paragraph 2. . . .

DISSENTING OPINION OF JUDGE SIR GERALD FITZMAURICE. It is abundantly clear (at least it is to me)—and the nature of the whole background against which the idea of the European Convention on Human Rights was conceived bears out this view—that the main, if not indeed the sole object and intended sphere of application of Article 8, was that of what I will call the 'domiciliary protection' of the individual. He and his family were no longer to be subjected to the four o'clock in the morning rat-a-tat on the door; to domestic intrusions, searches and questionings; to examinations, delayings and confiscation of correspondence; to the planting of listening devices (buggings); to restrictions on the use of radio and television; to telephone tapping and disconnection; to measures of coercion such as cutting off the electricity or water supply; to such abominations as children being required to report upon the activities of their parents, and even sometimes the same for one spouse against another—in short the whole gamut of fascist and communist inquisitorial practices such as had scarcely been known, at least in Western Europe, since the eras of religious intolerance and oppression, until (ideology replacing religion) they became prevalent again in many countries between the two world wars and subsequently. Such, and not the internal, domestic regulation of family relationships, was the object of Article 8, and it was for the avoidance of these horrors, tyrannies and vexations that 'private and family life . . . home and . . . correspondence' were to be respected, and the individual endowed with a right to enjoy that respect—not for the regulation of the civil status of babies.

Notes

1. Having established that Article 8 applied, the Court examined the complaints in turn. As far as the *affiliation* rules in Belgian law were concerned, the Court held that they infringed Article 8 taken by itself with respect to both the mother (by 10 votes to 5) and the daughter (by 12 votes to 3). Similarly, the Court held that Article 8 had been infringed when read with Article 14 with respect both to the mother (by 11 votes to 4) and the daughter (by 13 votes to 2). In doing so, the Court stated that while "support and encouragement of the traditional family is in itself legitimate or even praiseworthy," it could not be given at the expense of the 'illegitimate' family, which was equally protected by Article 8. The Convention "must be interpreted in the light of present-day conditions" and the Court could not "but be struck by the fact that the

domestic law of the great majority of the member states of the Council of Europe has evolved and is continuing to evolve, in company with the relevant international instruments, towards full jurisdictional recognition of the maxim *mater semper certa est.*"

On the question of *family relationships*, the Court held, by 12 votes to 3, that there had been a breach of Article 8 with respect to both applicants because the daughter was not in Belgian law regarded as a member of her mother's family. The Court held, by 13 votes to 2, that the same facts amounted to a breach of Article 8 as read with Article 14. Although "the tranquillity of 'legitimate' families may sometimes be disturbed if an 'illegitimate' child is included, in the eyes of the law, in his mother's family, on the same footing as a child born in wedlock," this was not sufficient to justify depriving such a child of "fundamental rights." Applying Article 8 to the *patrimonial rights* of the applicants, the Court held that there had been no breach of the Article taken by itself in respect of either the mother (by 9 votes to 6) or the daughter (unanimously). Article 8 did not mean that a State has to ensure that all children were entitled to a share in their parents' or other relatives' estates on intestacy or to a share in any gifts made by will or *inter vivos*; similarly, from the mother's standpoint, Article 8 did not prevent a State from imposing any limitation on her right to give property to her children. But when Article 8 was read in conjunction with Article 14, the position was different. The Court held, by 13 votes to 2, that these provisions taken together were infringed in respect both of the mother and of the daughter. Whereas the State was free to control or limit the rights of entitlement to property within the family subject to the obligation indicated above, there was no justifiable reason for distinguishing between 'legitimate' and 'illegitimate' families when doing so. The Court also held by 10 votes to 5, that there had been a breach of Article 1, First Protocol, when read with Article 14 as far as the mother was concerned.

2. The *Marckx* case is of importance beyond its immediate context of illegitimacy because of the almost unanimous ruling of the plenary Court that Article 8 has a positive private law aspect as well as a negative public law one. This was at once relied upon by a Chamber of the Court as the basis for a finding of a breach of Article 8 in the *Airey* case.[66] It *could* be used to require States to take steps to prevent invasions of privacy and family life by *private* persons (*e.g.* the press or private detectives) as well as refraining from interference itself. See also on this point, the *Young, James and Webster Case*, below p. 523.

SUNDAY TIMES CASE

Eur. Court H.R., Series A, Vol. 30. Judgment of April 26, 1979

Following the thalidomide tragedy, a lot of parents issued writs for negligence against Distillers, the British manufacturers. In 1972, while negotiations to settle the claims were pending, *The Sunday Times* planned the publication of an article which reviewed the evidence on the question whether Distillers had been negligent. The Attorney-General obtained an injunction from the Divisional Court preventing the publication of the article on the ground of contempt of court. The injunction was discharged by a unanimous Court of Appeal, but restored at the instruction of a unanimous House of Lords. The reasons given by their Lordships varied. Lords Reid, Morris, and Cross

---

[66] *Loc. cit.* at p. 512, n. 55, above. The Court stated:

In Ireland . . . husband and wife are . . . entitled . . . to petition for a decree of judicial separation; this amounts to recognition of the fact that the protection of their private or family life may sometimes necessitate their being relieved from the duty to live together.

Effective respect for private or family life obliges Ireland to make this means of protection effectively accessible, when appropriate, to anyone who may wish to have recourse thereto. However, it was not effectively accessible to the applicant . . . She has therefore been the victim of a violation of Art. 8.

emphasized the "prejudgment" principle (by which 'trial by newspaper' of issues that are the subject of court proceedings is not to be tolerated); Lords Diplock and Simon relied mainly on the "pressure" principle (by which it is contempt to bring pressure upon a person not to abandon or settle his case). All their Lordships were agreed that the proposed article was in contempt because it posed a real threat to the proper administration of justice. The injunction was eventually discharged in 1976 after almost all of the claims against the company had been settled.

The application was brought by the publisher, editor, and a group of journalists of *The Sunday Times*. The Commission expressed the opinion, by 8 votes to 5, that the injunction was a breach of Article 10. The case was referred to the Court by the Commission. The Court held that Article 10 had been infringed because the restriction, although "prescribed by law" and imposed for a legitimate purpose, was not "necessary in a democratic society" for the maintenance of the "authority . . . of the judiciary." The full Court reached this conclusion by 11 votes to 9.

Judgment of the Court

49. In the Court's opinion, the following are two of the requirements that flow from the expression "prescribed by law." Firstly, the law must be adequately accessible: the citizen must be able to have an indication that is adequate in the circumstances of the legal rules applicable to a given case. Secondly, a norm cannot be regarded as a "law" unless it is formulated with sufficient precision to enable the citizen to regulate his conduct: he must be able—if need be with appropriate advice—to foresee, to a degree that is reasonable in the circumstances, the consequences which a given action may entail. Those consequences need not be foreseeable with absolute certainty: experience shows this to be unattainable. Again, whilst certainty is highly desirable, it may bring in its train excessive rigidity and the law must be able to keep pace with changing circumstances. Accordingly, many laws are inevitably couched in terms which, to a greater or lesser extent, are vague and whose interpretation and application are questions of practice.

The Court, having confirmed that the term "law" in the above phrase included unwritten law such as the common law, concluded that although the English law of contempt was not as clear as it might be, the applicants "were able to foresee to a degree that was reasonable in the circumstances, a risk that publication of the draft article" might be contempt. The Court also held that the injunction could be justified as having an aim permitted by Article 10(2), *viz.* the maintenance of the authority . . . of the judiciary." More difficult was the question whether it was "necessary," etc., to achieve that aim:

59. . . . The Court has noted[67] that, whilst the adjective "necessary," within the meaning of Article 10 § 2, is not synonymous with "indispensable," neither has it the flexibility of such expressions as "admissible," "ordinary," "useful," "reasonable" or "desirable" and that it implies the existence of a "pressing social need. . . . "

In the second place, the Court has underlined that the initial responsibility for securing the rights and freedoms enshrined in the Convention lies with the individual Contracting States. Accordingly, "Article 10 § 2 leaves to the Contracting States a margin of appreciation. This margin is given both to the

---

[67] *Ed.* In the *Handyside Case*, Eur. Court H.R., Series A, Vol. 24, Judgment of December 7, 1976. The quotations and paraphrases in the remainder of the Court's judgment are from that case.

domestic legislator . . . and to the bodies, judicial amongst others, that are called upon to interpret and apply the laws in force. . . ."

"Nevertheless, Article 10 § 2 does not give the Contracting States an unlimited power of appreciation:" "The Court . . . is empowered to give the final ruling on whether a 'restriction' . . . is reconcilable with freedom of expression as protected by Article 10. . . ."

The Court has deduced from a combination of these principles that "it is in no way [its] task to take the place of the competent national courts but rather to review under Article 10 the decisions they delivered in the exercise of their power of appreciation. . . ."

This does not mean that the Court's supervision is limited to ascertaining whether a respondent State exercised its discretion reasonably, carefully and in good faith. Even a Contracting State so acting remains subject to the Court's control as regards the compatibility of its conduct with the engagements it has undertaken under the Convention. . . .

Again, the scope of the domestic power of appreciation is not identical as regards each of the aims listed in Article 10 § 2. The *Handyside* case[68] concerned the "protection of morals." The view taken by the Contracting States of the "requirements of morals," observed the Court, "varies from time to time and from place to place, especially in our era." Precisely the same cannot be said of the far more objective notion of the "authority" of the judiciary. The domestic law and practice of the Contracting States reveal a fairly substantial measure of common ground in this area. This is reflected in a number of provisions of the Convention, including Article 6, which have no equivalent as far as "morals" are concerned. Accordingly, here a more extensive European supervision corresponds to a less discretionary power of appreciation. . . .

60. Both the minority of the Commission and the Government attach importance to the fact that the institution of contempt of court is peculiar to common-law countries and suggest that the concluding words of Article 10 § 2 were designed to cover this institution which has no equivalent in many other member States of the Council of Europe.

However, even if this were so, the Court considers that the reason for the insertion of those words would have been to ensure that the general aims of the law of contempt of court should be considered legitimate aims under Article 10 § 2 but not to make that law the standard by which to assess whether a given measure was "necessary." . . .

62. It must now be decided whether the "interference" complained of corresponded to a "pressing social need," whether it was "proportionate to the legitimate aim pursued . . ."

63. . . . The speeches in the House of Lords emphasised above all the concern that the processes of the law may be brought into disrespect and the functions of the courts usurped either if the public is led to form an opinion on the subject-matter of litigation before adjudication by the courts or if the parties to litigation have to undergo "trial by newspaper." Such concern is in itself "relevant" to the maintenance of the authority of the judiciary." . . .

Nevertheless, the proposed *Sunday Times* article was couched in moderate

---

[68] *Ed.* In the *Handyside Case, loc. cit.* at p. 520, n. 87 above, the Court held that the conviction of the applicant for publication of "The Little Red Schoolbook" under the Obscene Publications Acts was justifiable under Article 10(2).

terms and did not present just one side of the evidence or claim that there was only one possible result at which a court could arrive . . . Accordingly, even to the extent that the article might have led some readers to form an opinion on the negligence issue, this would not have had adverse consequences for the "authority of the judiciary," especially since, as noted above, there had been a nationwide campaign in the meantime.

65. . . . Whilst . . . [the courts] are the forum for the settlement of disputes, this does not mean that there can be no prior discussion of disputes elsewhere, be it in specialised journals, in the general press or amongst the public at large. . . . Not only do the media have the task of imparting such information and ideas: the public also has a right to receive them. . . . The Court observes . . . that, following a balancing of the conflicting interests involved, an absolute rule was formulated by certain of the Law Lords to the effect that it was not permissable to prejudge issues in pending cases. . . . Whilst emphasising that it is not its function to pronounce itself on an interpretation of English law adopted in the House of Lords . . . the Court points out that it has to take a different approach. The Court is faced not with a choice between two conflicting principles but with a principle of freedom of expression [in Article 10] that is subject to a number of exceptions which must be narrowly interpreted . . . the Court has to be satisfied that the interference was necessary having regard to the facts and circumstances prevailing in the specific case before it. . . . the families of numerous victims of the tragedy, who were unaware of the legal difficulties involved, had a vital interest in knowing all the underlying facts and the various possible solutions. They could be deprived of this information, which was crucially important for them, only if it appeared absolutely certain that its diffusion would have presented a threat to the "authority of the judiciary."

66. The thalidomide disaster was a matter of undisputed public concern. . . . fundamental issues concerning protection against and compensation for injuries resulting from scientific developments were raised and many facets of the existing law on these subjects were called in question.

. . . the facts of the case did not cease to be a matter of public interest merely because they formed the background to pending litigation. By bringing to light certain facts, the article might have served as a brake on speculative and unenlightened discussion.

67. Having regard to all the circumstances of the case . . . the Court concludes that the interference complained of did not correspond to a social need sufficiently pressing to outweigh the public interest in freedom of expression within the meaning of the Convention. The Court therefore finds the reasons for the restraint imposed on the applicants not to be sufficient under Article 10 § 2. That restraint proves not to be proportionate to the legitimate aim pursued; it was not necessary in a democratic society for maintaining the authority of the judiciary.

Notes

1. In their joint dissenting opinion, the nine dissenting judges, who included Judge Sir Gerald Fitzmaurice, disagreed with the majority essentially on the question whether the injunction was "necessary" and on the latitude to be given to the defendant State under the "margin of appreciation" doctrine. They pointed out that the "authority and impartiality of the judiciary" exception allowed by Article 10(2) was inserted on the proposal of the United Kingdom when the Convention was drafted to take account of the common law of contempt which is "peculiar to the legal traditions of the common-

law countries . . . and . . . is unknown in the law of most of the member states." In the opinion of the dissenting judges, the conclusion of the majority that the "authority . . . of the judiciary" was a far more objective notion than that of "the protection of morals" (so that less discretion should be allowed to the defendant State) was erroneous. It was "by no means divorced from national circumstances and cannot be determined in a uniform way." Evidence for this was to be found in the different ways in which States went about protecting that authority. A State such as the United Kingdom that relied upon the law of contempt to protect it should be given sufficient latitude to apply it as national circumstances warranted or required.

2. *The Sunday Times* case is the first in which the Court has been called upon to consider whether a judgment applying a rule of common law complies with the Convention. Crucial to the Court's decision was its understanding of the difference between the approach that it could adopt under Article 10 and that open to the House of Lords at common law. Whereas it had to give priority to freedom of expression, the House of Lords could give equal weight between two competing freedoms. Even so, it is difficult to avoid the conclusion that had the House of Lords been applying Article 10 (and it is interesting to note that the Convention was not referred to by any of their Lordships) it would have found the injunction to have been "necessary" in the sense in which the Court interpreted that term. It would seem, moreover, that when applying the "margin of appreciation" doctrine in this context, the Court reduced it almost to vanishing point. It appears to have made its own assessment of the situation *de novo* and simply to have disagreed with that of the House of Lords.[69] It seems likely that the Court found confidence to do this in the lack of unanimity among English judges on the proper scope of the law of criminal contempt and its application in this case. Certainly it was affected by the fact, to which it refers, that the Phillimore Committee had suggested that the "prejudgment" principle should be reconsidered[70] and that the British Government White Paper[71] had not called in question this suggestion. The Contempt of Court Act 1981 was enacted partly to bring United Kingdom law into line with the Convention.[72]

3. Another part of the Court's judgment that is of interest is the passage (para. 49) on the meaning of "prescribed by law," which appears in several Articles of the Convention. The passage, which might well be mistaken for an extract from Dicey's Rule of Law, raises questions about the process of judicial law-making as well as the publication of legal rules. Would a decision changing the common law, and doing so retroactively in the usual way, state a rule which was "prescribed by law?" Would unpublished delegated legislation pass the Court's test?[73]

YOUNG JAMES AND WEBSTER CASES

Eur. Court H.R., Series A, Vol. 44. Judgment of August 13, 1981

In 1975, British Rail entered into a closed shop agreement with three rail trade unions, by which membership of one of them was a condition of employment. The three applicants, who were British Rail employees before the agreement was negotiated, refused to become members and were dismissed. All three objected to membership on

---

[69] This raises the question of the relationship between the Strasbourg authorities and local courts. (*cf.* the *Handyside Case, loc. cit.* at p. 521, n. 68, above, in which a court judgment applying statutory law was in issue). As the Court indicated (para. 59), it is not a court of appeal from national courts.

[70] Cmnd. 5794, para. 111.

[71] Cmnd. 7145, para. 43.

[72] It may not do so: see Bailey (1982) 45 M.L.R. 301, 306.

[73] See the well-known strictures by Scott LJ. in *Blackpool Corp.* v. *Locker* [1948] 1 K.B. 349 (C.A.).

the ground that no one should be compelled to join a trade union; Y. and W. objected also to the political activities of trade unions; Y objected further to the political affiliations of the specified trade unions. The Commission was of the opinion, by 14 to three, that the applicants' freedom of association, Article 11, Convention, had been infringed and referred the case to the Court.

Judgment of the Court

49. Under Article 1 of the Convention, each Contracting State "shall secure to everyone within [its] jurisdiction the rights and freedoms defined in . . . [the] Convention"; hence, if a violation of one of those rights and freedoms is the result of non-observance of that obligation in the enactment of domestic legislation, the responsibility of the State for that violation is engaged. Although the proximate cause of the events giving rise to this case was the 1975 agreement between British Rail and the railway unions, it was the domestic law in force at the relevant time[74] that made lawful the treatment of which the applicants complained. The responsibility of the respondent State for any resultant breach of the Convention is thus engaged on this basis. Accordingly, there is no call to examine whether, as the applicants argued, the State might also be responsible on the ground that it should be regarded as employer or that British Rail was under its control. . . .

51. A substantial part of the pleadings before the Court was devoted to the question whether Article 11 guarantees not only freedom of association, including the right to form and to join trade unions, in the positive sense, but also, by implication, a "negative right" not to be compelled to join an association or a union. . . .

52. The Court does not consider it necessary to answer this question on this occasion.

The Court recalls, however, that the right to form and to join trade unions is a special aspect of freedom of association . . . it adds that the notion of a freedom implies some measure of freedom of choice as to its exercise.

Assuming for the sake of argument that, for the reasons given in . . . the *travaux préparatoires*,[75] a general rule such as that in Article 20 § 2 of the Universal Declaration of Human Rights was deliberately omitted from, and so cannot be regarded as itself enshrined in, the Convention, it does not follow that the negative aspect of a person's freedom of association falls completely outside the ambit of Article 11 and that each and every compulsion to join a particular trade union is compatible with the intention of that provision. . . .

53. The Court emphasises . . . that . . . in the present case, it is not called upon to review the closed shop system as such in relation to the Convention or

---

[74] *Ed., i.e.* the Trade Union and Labour Relations Act 1974. This repealed the Industrial Relations Act 1971, which had prohibited most closed shops and protected the right not to join a union. Under the 1974 Act dismissal for refusal to join a union required by a closed shop agreement was lawful (not "unfair dismissal") except where the refusal was "on grounds of religious belief to being a member of any union whatsoever or on any reasonable grounds to being a member of a particular union" (First Schedule, Part II, 1974 Act).

[75] *Ed.* These stated that "[o]n account of the difficulties raised by the 'closed shop system' in certain countries, the Conference [of Senior Government Officials drafting the Convention] . . . considered that it was undesirable to introduce into the Convention a rule under which 'no one may be compelled to belong to an association' which features in [Article 20(2), Universal Declaration of Human Rights, below, p. 534]" 4 *Travaux Préparatoires*, p. 262.

to express an opinion on every consequence or form of compulsion which it may engender; it will limit its examination to the effects of that system on the applicants. . . .

55. The situation facing the applicants clearly runs counter to the concept of freedom of association in its negative sense.

Assuming that Article 11 does not guarantee the negative aspect of that freedom on the same footing as the positive aspect, compulsion to join a particular trade union may not always be contrary to the Convention.

However, a threat of dismissal involving loss of livelihood is a most serious form of compulsion and, in the present instance, it was directed against persons engaged by British Rail before the introduction of any obligation to join a particular trade union.

In the Court's opinion, such a form of compulsion, in the circumstances of the case, strikes at the very substance of the freedom guaranteed by Article 11. For this reason alone, there has been an interference with that freedom as regards each of the three applicants.

56. Another facet of this case concerns the restriction of the applicants' choice as regards the trade unions which they could join of their own volition. An individual does not enjoy the right to freedom of association if in reality the freedom of action or choice which remains available to him is either non-existent or so reduced as to be of no practical value.

. . . the applicants . . . would . . . have been dismissed if they had not become members of one of the specified unions.

57. Moreover . . . [t]he protection of personal opinion afforded by Articles 9 and 10 . . . is also one of the purposes of freedom of association as guaranteed by Article 11. Accordingly, it strikes at the very substance of this Article to exert pressure, of the kind applied to the applicants, in order to compel someone to join an association contrary to his convictions.

In this further respect, the treatment complained of—in any event as regards Mr. Young and Mr. Webster—constituted an interference with their Article 11 rights.

The Court next considered and rejected the argument that the restrictions could be justified under Article 11(2) as being "necessary," etc.

For these reasons, the Court . . . holds by 18 votes to three that there has been a breach of Article 11 of the Convention.

Notes
1. Would the Court have ruled in favour of the applicants if (i) they had been free to join a trade union of their choice[76] or (ii) they had become British Rail employees after the closed shop agreement had entered into force?

2. United Kingdom law has changed again since the case. The Employment Act 1982 makes it more difficult to establish new closed shop agreements and to dismiss employees "fairly" (and hence lawfully) for failure to join a trade union as required by a closed shop agreement.

3. The Court has interpreted Article 11 in three other cases. In the *National Union of Belgian Police Case*[77] the Court held that the words "for the protection of his interests"

---

[76] In fact, closed shop agreements nearly always require membership of a specified union or unions.

[77] Eur. Court H.R., Series A, Vol. 19, Judgment of October 27, 1975.

indicated that, as far as trade unions are concerned, Article 11 has a *functional* as well as an *organisational* side. Individuals, that is, are not only entitled to "form an join" trade unions, but have the right to expect that these be allowed such rights as are necessary to protect their members' interests effectively. These rights include the "right to be heard" by the employer, although this does not necessarily mean a right to be consulted by him; an employer may, as in the *Belgian Police Case*, limit the number of trade unions with which it consults. In the *Swedish Engine Drivers' Union Case*[78] the Court ruled that the right to conclude a collective agreement with an employer was also not in itself a necessary condition of effective trade union action; an employer may, as on the facts of that case, limit the number of trade unions with which it concludes such agreements. In the *Schmidt and Dahlström Case*[79] the Court held that Article 11 also did not require that benefits from a collective agreement negotiated by a trade union be made retroactive so that the failure to make them retroactive because of strike action was not a violation of any right to strike that Article 11 might contain. The Court has yet to rule on the question whether the right to strike or a more general right to take industrial action is necessary to effective trade union functioning and hence protected by Article 11.

4. The Court's judgment (para. 49) touches upon the important question whether the Convention makes a state responsible for conduct by private individuals that interferes with rights protected by it. How far does the Court go? Is it saying that a state would be liable if its law were such, for example, as to permit (i) a private detective to tap telephones contrary to Article 8 or (ii) the press to comment on pending criminal proceedings contrary to the fair trial guarantee in Article 6? (In the latter case, a balance would have to be struck between the right to a fair trial and freedom of speech (Article 10): see the *Sunday Times Case*, above, p. 519). How important was it in the present case that the United Kingdom Parliament had legislated since the Convention so as to legalise private action contrary to Article 11 which had previously been unlawful under United Kingdom law? See also on state responsibility for private action, the *Marckx Case*, above, p. 517.

5. Note that the Court was faced with a very clear statement of the intention of the draftsmen in the *travaux préparatoires*. While not contradicting it expressly, would it be correct to say that, in pursuance of its teleological approach to the interpretation of the Convention, as to which see above, p. 511, the Court largely subverts that expressed intention?

BELGIAN LINGUISTIC CASE (MERITS)

Eur. Court H.R., Series A, Vol. 6, Judgment of July 23, 1968

For the purpose of determining the language of instruction in its state and state supported schools, Belgium is divided territorially by law into unilingual and bilingual areas. In the former, which consist of Dutch, French and German speaking areas, the predominant language of the region is the language of instruction. In the latter, including six communes surrounding Brussels, special arrangements exist. In this case, the Court held, by eight votes to seven, that this system "does not comply with the requirements of Article 14 of the Convention read in conjunction with the first sentence of Article 2 of the Protocol, in so far as it prevents certain children, solely on the basis of the residence of their parents, from having access to the French-language schools existing in the six communes on the periphery of Brussels invested with a special status, of which Kraainem is one. . . ." On the other five questions put to the Court concerning the arrangements in other areas, no violation of the Convention was found. In the following extract from its judgment, the Court examines the meaning of Article 14 of the Convention.

[78] *Ibid.* Vol. 20, Judgment of February 6, 1976.
[79] *Ibid.* Vol. 21, Judgment of February 6, 1976.

Judgment of the Court

While it is true that this guarantee has no independent existence in the sense that under the terms of Article 14 it relates solely to "rights and freedoms set forth in the Convention," a measure which in itself is in conformity with the requirements of the Article enshrining the right or freedom in question may however infringe this Article when read in conjunction with Article 14 for the reason that it is of a discriminatory nature.

Thus, persons subject to the jurisdiction of a Contracting State cannot draw from Article 2 of the [First] Protocol the right to obtain from the public authorities the creation of a particular kind of educational establishment; nevertheless, a State which had set up such an establishment could not, in laying down entrance requirements, take discriminatory measures within the meaning of Article 14.

To recall a further example . . . Article 6 of the Convention does not compel States to institute a system of appeal courts. . . . However it would violate that Article, read in conjunction with Article 14, were it to debar certain persons from these remedies without a legitimate reason while making them available to others in respect of the same type of actions.

In such cases there would be a violation of a guaranteed right or freedom as it is proclaimed by the relevant Article read in conjunction with Article 14. It is as though the latter formed an integral part of each of the Articles laying down rights and freedoms. No distinctions should be made in this respect according to the nature of these rights and freedoms and of their correlative obligations, and for instance as to whether the respect due to the right concerned implies positive action or mere abstention. . . .

In spite of the very general wording of the French version ("sans distinction aucune"), Article 14 does not forbid every difference in treatment in the exercise of the rights and freedoms recognised. This version must be read in the light of the more restrictive text of the English version ("without discrimination"). In addition, and in particular, one would reach absurd results were one to give Article 14 an interpretation as wide as that which the French version seems to imply. One would, in effect, be led to judge as contrary to the Convention every one of the many legal or administrative provisions which do not secure to everyone complete equality of treatment in the enjoyment of the rights and freedoms recognised. . . .

. . . the Court, following the principles which may be extracted from the legal practice of a large number of democratic States, holds that the principle of equality of treatment is violated if the distinction has no objective and reasonable justification. The existence of such a justification must be assessed in relation to the aim and effects of the measure under consideration, regard being had to the principles which normally prevail in democratic societies. A difference of treatment in the exercise of a right laid down in the Convention must not only pursue a legitimate aim: Article 14 is likewise violated when it is clearly established that there is no reasonable relationship of proportionality between the means employed and the aim sought to be realised.

In attempting to find out in a given case, whether or not there has been an arbitrary distinction, the Court cannot disregard those legal and factual features which characterise the life of the society in the State which, as a Contracting Party, has to answer for the measure in dispute. In so doing it cannot assume the rôle of the competent national authorities, for it would thereby lose sight of the subsidiary nature of the international machinery of collective enforcement established by the Convention. The national authorities remain free to choose the measures which they consider appropriate in those matters which are governed by the Convention. Review by the Court concerns only the conformity of these measures with the requirements of the Convention.

In the present case the Court notes that Article 14, even when read in conjunction with Article 2 of the Protocol, does not have the effect of guaranteeing to a child or to his parent the right to obtain instruction in a language of his choice. The object of these two Articles, read in conjunction, is more limited: it is to ensure that the right to education shall be secured by each Contracting Party to everyone within its jurisdiction without discrimination on the ground, for instance, of language. This is the natural and ordinary meaning of Article 14 read in conjunction with Article 2. Furthermore, to interpret the two provisions as conferring on everyone within the jurisdiction of a State a right to obtain education in the language of his own choice would lead to absurd results, for it would be open to anyone to claim any language of instruction in any of the territories of the Contracting Parties.

Notes

1. The Court has taken the view that it is not necessary for the obligations which the Convention contains in respect of a right which it protects to be infringed for there to be a breach of the Article concerned *when read in conjunction with Article 14*. It is sufficient that the discrimination occurs within the area of the right protected. See, *e.g.* the Court's example concerning the right of appeal and Article 6.[80]

2. The Court held that there was a "legitimate aim" behind the language discrimination in the *Belgian Linguistics Case, viz.* the efficient instruction of children in schools. Similarly, in the *National Union of Belgian Police Case*,[81] the limitation of the right of consultation to the main and most representative trade unions had the "legitimate aim" of ensuring effective negotiations. The "proportionality" requirement was not met in the one situation in the *Belgian Linguistics Case* in which a breach of Article 14 was found, because it would have been possible to have devised another language instruction scheme for the region concerned that placed a lesser burden upon minority language children.

3. "Other status" in Article 14 has been held to include the status of illegitimacy,[82] or of being a category based trade union.[83]

LAWLESS CASE (MERITS)[84]

Eur. Court H.R., Series A, Vol. 3. Judgment of July 1, 1961

The Applicant, a national of the Republic of Ireland, was arrested and detained without trial for a period of five months in 1957 at a time when the activities of the Irish

---

[80] Contrast the opinion of Judge Sir Gerald Fitzmaurice in the *National Union of Belgian Police Case, loc. cit.* at p. 525, n. 77, above. In his view, a right is "set forth" for the purposes of Article 14 only insofar as its protection is made obligatory by the Convention. Thus, discrimination in the provision of the right of appeal cannot be the subject of complaint under Article 14 because the provision of a right of appeal is not obligatory under Article 6. What scope does such an approach leave for Article 14?

[81] *Loc cit.* at p. 525, n. 77, above.

[82] *Marckx Case, loc. cit.* at p. 517, above.

[83] *National Union of Belgian Police Case, loc. cit.* at p. 525, n. 77, above.

[84] See Robertson (1961) 37 B.Y.I.L. 536.

Republican Army were causing much violence. The European Court held that Ireland's action in the Applicant's case violated Article 5(1)(c) of the Convention. The question then arose, however, whether Article 15 of the Convention applied.

Judgment of the Court

28. Whereas, in the general context of Article 15 of the Convention, the natural and customary meaning of the words "other public emergency threatening the life of the nation" is sufficiently clear; whereas they refer to an exceptional situation of crisis or emergency which affects the whole population and constitutes a threat to the organised life of the community of which the State is composed; . . . whereas the existence at the time of a "public emergency threatening the life of the nation," was reasonably deduced by the Irish Government from a combination of several factors, namely; in the first place, the existence in the territory of the Republic of Ireland of a secret army engaged in unconstitutional activities and using violence to attain its purposes; secondly, the fact that this army was also operating outside the territory of the State, thus seriously jeopardising the relations of the Republic of Ireland with its neighbour; thirdly the steady and alarming increase in terrorist activities from the autumn of 1956 and throughout the first half of 1957;

29. Whereas, despite the gravity of the situation, the Government had succeeded, by using means available under ordinary legislation, in keeping public institutions functioning more or less normally, but whereas the homicidal ambush on the night of 3rd to 4th July 1957 in the territory of Northern Ireland near the border had brought to light, just before 12th July—a date, which, for historical reasons[85] is particularly critical for the preservation of public peace and order—the imminent danger to the nation caused by the continuance of unlawful activities in Northern Ireland by the IRA and various associated groups, operating from the territory of the Republic of Ireland;

30. Whereas, in conclusion, the Irish Government were justified in declaring that there was a public emergency in the Republic of Ireland threatening the life of the nation and were hence entitled, applying the provisions of Article 15, paragraph 1, of the Convention for the purposes for which those provisions were made, to take measures derogating from their obligations under the Convention; . . .

36. Whereas, however, considering, in the judgment of the Court, that in 1957 the application of the ordinary law had proved unable to check the growing danger which threatened the Republic of Ireland; whereas the ordinary criminal courts, or even the special criminal courts or military courts, could not suffice to restore peace and order; whereas, in particular, the amassing of the necessary evidence to convict persons involved in activities of the IRA and its splinter groups was meeting with great difficulties caused by the military, secret and terrorist character of those groups and the fear they created among the population; whereas the fact that these groups operated mainly in Northern Ireland, their activities in the Republic of Ireland being virtually limited to the preparation of armed raids across the border was an additional impediment to the gathering of sufficient evidence; whereas the sealing of the border would

---

[85] *Ed*. It is the day on which the anniversary of the Battle of the Boyne 1690, in which the protestant William of Orange defeated the catholic James II, is celebrated.

have had extremely serious repercussions on the population as a whole, beyond the extent required by the exigencies of the emergency; . . .

37. Whereas, moreover, the Offences against the State (Amendment) Act of 1940, was subject to a number of safeguards designed to prevent abuses in the operation of the system of administrative detention; whereas the application of the Act was thus subject to constant supervision by Parliament, which not only received precise details of its enforcement at regular intervals but could also at any time, by a Resolution, annul the Government's Proclamation which had brought the Act into force; whereas the Offences against the State (Amendment) Act 1940 provided for the establishment of a "Detention Commission" made up of three members, which the Government did in fact set up, the members being an officer of the Defence Forces and two judges; whereas any person detained under this Act could refer his case to that Commission whose opinion, if favourable to the release of the person concerned, was binding upon the Government; whereas, moreover, the ordinary courts could themselves compel the Detention Commission to carry out its functions; . . .

Whereas, therefore, it follows from the foregoing that the detention without trial provided for by the 1940 Act, subject to the above-mentioned safeguards, appears to be a measure strictly required by the exigencies of the situation within the meaning of Article 15 of the Convention;

38. Whereas, in the particular case of G.R. Lawless, there is nothing to show that the powers of detention conferred upon the Irish Government by the Offences against the State (Amendment) Act 1940, were employed against him, either within the meaning of Article 18 of the Convention, for a purpose other than that for which they were granted, or within the meaning of Article 15 of the Convention, by virtue of a measure going beyond what was strictly required by the situation at that time; . . .

47. Whereas the Court is called upon in the first instance, to examine whether, in pursuance of paragraph 3 of Article 15 of the Convention, the Secretary-General of the Council of Europe was duly informed both of the measures taken and of the reasons therefor; whereas the Court notes that a copy of the Offences against the State (Amendment) Act 1940, and a copy of the Proclamation of 5th July, published on 8th July 1957, bringing into force Part II of the aforesaid Act were attached to the letter of 20th July; that it was explained in the letter of 20th July that the measures had been taken in order "to prevent the commission of offences against public peace and order and to prevent the maintaining of military or armed forces other than those authorised by the Constitution"; that the Irish Government thereby gave the Secretary-General sufficient information of the measures taken and the reasons therefor; that, in the second place, the Irish Government brought this information to the Secretary-General's attention only twelve days after the entry into force of the measures derogating from their obligations under the Convention; and that the notification was therefore made without delay; whereas, in conclusion, the Convention does not contain any special provision to the effect that the Contracting State concerned must promulgate in its territory the notice of derogation addressed to the Secretary-General of the Council of Europe;

Whereas the Court accordingly finds that, in the present case, the Irish Government fulfilled their obligations as Party to the Convention under Article 15, paragraph 3, of the Convention;

THE COURT

Unanimously . . . [decided that Ireland was not in breach of the Convention by virtue of its valid derogation under Article 15.]

Notes

1. Derogations under Article 15 have been made from time to time by Greece, Ireland, Turkey and the United Kingdom (in respect of overseas territories and Northern Ireland).[86]

2. What would be the effect of failure to comply with Article 15(3)? Would the derogation be invalid? Or would there just be a breach of the particular treaty obligation in Article 15(3), of which a state could complain under Article 24?

3. Does Article 15 suggest any hierarchy of rights among those found in the Convention?

4. In their pleadings before the Court, the Irish Government in the *Lawless Case* argued that the decision whether there was a state of emergency in the sense of Article 15 was one for the Government concerned, save that the Court could intervene if it was shown that the Government had acted in bad faith in the sense of Article 18.[87] The Commission disagreed and argued that the Strasbourg authorities could decide themselves whether a state of emergency existed, save that it was prepared to allow a "margin of appreciation" (*i.e.* there would be, as it were, a presumption favouring the Government's assessment of the facts) in favour of the Government.[88] The applicant argued for a strict objective test.[89] Which approach did the Court adopt?

5. The Court followed the *Lawless Case* on Article 15 in *Ireland* v. *United Kingdom*.[90]

DECISION OF 8th NOVEMBER 1966

Court of First Instance of Brussels—12th Civil Chamber, Journal des Tribunaux, 1966, pp. 686–687. English translation in 9 Y.B.E.C.H.R. 746 (1966)

Judgment of the Court

Whereas the respondent claims to have applied the provisions of Section 41 of the Act of 2nd August 1963 on the use of languages in administrative matters, which provides that for documents required by law or regulation or addressed to their employees, "industrial, commercial or financial undertakings shall use the language of the region where their registered office or place or business is situated"; . . .

Whereas the rights referred to in Articles 10(1) and 14 of the Convention may be implemented in Belgium without the necessity for any special internal measures to that end, since they are expressed in terms specific enough to allow of immediate application . . .

Whereas, if the existing international rules—constituting a supranational legal instrument which, as a formal source of law is binding upon States—are not to be deprived of all utility, it must be remembered that, in the event of conflict between municipal and international law, international treaties must prevail inasmuch as, or in cases where (as in the present instance) they have been approved by a Belgian Act;

---

[86] See the *Yearbooks of the European Convention on Human Rights*.
[87] Eur. Court H.R., Series B, *Pleadings*, p. 444.
[88] *Ibid.* p. 392. On the "margin of appreciation" doctrine, see also p. 477, n. 31, above.
[89] *Ibid.*
[90] See above, p. 483.

Whereas, having regard to the authorities and leading cases cited below, it must be allowed that the said Convention confers subjective rights on the nationals of a Contracting State and guarantees their exercise, therein overriding and disregarding any other conflicting rules established, even subsequently, by national legislation . . .

Whereas it follows that Section 41(1) of the Belgian Act of 2nd August 1963 cannot be applied in this case in as much as, contrary to the provisions of Articles 10(1) and 14 of the European Convention for the Protection of Human Rights . . . the said Section 41 must be regarded as imposing the use of a specific language on industrial, commercial and financial undertakings for the drafting of their official documents;

Whereas it is accordingly useless for the respondent to invoke the application of the said provision of municipal law, since there is no reason why the plaintiffs (the undertaking) should not draw up the documents in question in French.

Notes

1. Would an English court faced with a similar conflict between a Westminster statute and the Convention have adopted the Belgian court's approach?[91] Did it matter in this case that the Belgian statute postdated the European Convention?

2. The Convention does not require that a party incorporate it as local law; only that the local law directly or indirectly protects the rights guaranteed. Incorporation, however, is a "particularly faithful reflection" of the intention of the draftsmen: *Ireland* v. *U.K.*, above, p. 483, para. 239, judgment. At present, the Convention is directly enforceable, to a greater or lesser extent, in the municipal law courts of most of the contracting parties.[92] Should the United Kingdom make the Convention a part of its municipal law too? How effective is the Convention likely to be in controlling the government of a Contracting Party in which the Convention is not enforceable in the local courts and which has not made declarations under Articles 25 and 46?

3. In a case[93] which raised a very similar issue to that dealt with by the Belgian court above, the Commission ruled that the application was manifestly unfounded in so far as it alleged violations of Articles 9, 10 and 14. Whether the two decisions can be reconciled or not, they suggest the following question: Are national courts which apply to the Convention as a part of their local law bound by the interpretation of it by the Commission or by the Court? Note in this connection the power of the Court of Justice of the European Communities to rule on questions of interpretation of the Communities Treaties and other laws before their application by the courts of member states.[94]

3. *THE UNITED NATIONS*[95]

Note

Articles 55 and 56 of the Charter impose upon the United Nations and its members legal obligations to "promote" respect for and observance of human rights. United Nations action under Article 55 has taken several forms. A large number of declarations and treaties have been adopted, mostly as a result of the work of the United Nations

---

[91] For recent English cases on the Convention, see above, pp. 72–73.
[92] See Beddard, 16 I.C.L.Q. 206 (1967); Drzemczewski, *The European Human Rights Convention in Domestic Law* (1983); and Golsong (1962) 38 B.Y.I.L. 445.
[93] A/2333/64, 8 Y.B.E.C.H.R. 338 (1965).
[94] See Article 177, E.E.C. Treaty 1957.
[95] See Carey, *U.N. Protection of Civil and Political Rights* (1970); Ganji, *International Protection of Human Rights* (1962); Henkin, 19 *Int.Org.* 504 (1965); McDougal and Bebr, 58 A.J.I.L. 603 (1964); Moskowitz, 6 Israel Y.B.H.R. 82 (1976); Schoenberg, 7 *ibid.* 22 (1977).

Commission on Human Rights (composed of representatives of 43 states). These indicate the meaning of human rights in the law of the United Nations and, so far as the treaties are concerned, impose obligations upon the Contracting Parties. The extent to which such declarations and treaties have had, or will have, an impact upon general international law is less clear.[96]

The materials in the remainder of this section are concerned exclusively with some of the declarations and treaties on human rights the United Nations has promoted. To put these in perspective, it should be noted that the United Nations, acting mainly through the General Assembly and the Security Council, has sometimes acted to protect human rights by means other than the adoption of treaties and other documents. Recent examples have concerned *apartheid* in South Africa, the exercise by South Africa of its powers as mandatory in South West Africa/Namibia and the rebellion in Southern Rhodesia.[97] In such cases jurisdiction has often been founded more upon the United Nations peace-keeping role than upon Articles 55 and 56. One potential stumbling block in the way of action in the form of discussion, investigation, recommendation or decision in such cases—the domestic jurisdiction clause in Article 2(7) of the Charter— has, despite the protests of the states accused, made little impact.[98]

The United Nations Commission on Human Rights now spends much of its time considering allegations of human rights violations in particular situations on the basis either of state initiatives or, more recently, of individual petitions.[99] In the former case, the Commission has sometimes, on the proposal of a member, appointed an ad hoc Working Group to investigate the situation and report back to the Commission. Three situations which the Commission has considered in this way are the conduct of Israel in occupied Arab territories; *apartheid* in South Africa and South-West Africa/Namibia; and the control of opposition within Chile. All three of these "defendant" states have been strongly criticised. The weakness of such a procedure is that, although attention may be focused beneficially on situations of real concern for protectors of human rights, politics clearly determine the choice and treatment of situations considered. There are also no mandatory powers to enter territory to conduct investigations or to hear witnesses and any recommendations made are not binding in law. In 1970, a procedure was established by which the Commission on Human Rights may deal with some of the thousands of petitions that reach the United Nations every year alleging violations of human rights. Until then, the practice had been to file them without comment on the basis that the United Nations lacked jurisdiction to examine them. In Resolution 1503 (XXVIII), ECOSOC authorised the Commission on Human Rights' Sub-Commission on the Prevention of Discrimination and Protection of Minorities (a body of eighteen *independent* experts) to appoint a working group to examine *in private* individual petitions received by the Secretary-General and to report to the Sub-Commission on those "which appear to reveal a consistent pattern of gross and reliably attested violations of human rights." Acting under Resolution 1503, the Sub-Commission has, after much procedural wrangling, referred several situations—including that in Uganda— to the Commission. The latter has not established any ad hoc working group of the sort used to investigate allegations of human rights violations resulting from state initiatives or acted in any other way on the situations referred to it. Instead the

---

[96] On the role of treaties as a material source of custom, see above, p. 32. On the role of General Assembly resolutions in the development of international law, see above, p. 50.

[97] See above, pp. 105, and below, p. 690.

[98] See Higgins, *The Development of International Law through the Political Organs of the United Nations* (1963), pp. 118–130. Attempts to have the meaning of Art. 2(7) in a human rights context elucidated by an advisory opinion of the I.C.J. have been unsuccessful.

[99] See the periodic reviews of the Commission's work in the Rev. I.C.J.; Carey, 66 A.J.I.L. 107 (1972); Liskofsky, 8 H.Rts.Jo. 883 (1975). On the UN Commission on Human Rights and the Disappeared, see Kramer and Weissbrodt, 3 H. Rts. Q. 18 (1981) and Reoch, (1982) 36 Y.B.W.A. 166.

Commission has discussed the situations in secret but taken no effective action.[1] So far, therefore, Resolution 1503 has proved ineffectual. It seems likely that the focus of attention in respect of individual complaints will increasingly become the work of the Human Rights Committee under the Optional Protocol to the Civil and Political Rights Covenant.

UNIVERSAL DECLARATION OF HUMAN RIGHTS 1948

G.A. Resolution 217A (III), G.A.O.R., 3rd Sess., Part I, Resolutions, p. 71

THE GENERAL ASSEMBLY proclaims

THIS UNIVERSAL DECLARATION OF HUMAN RIGHTS as a common standard of achievement for all peoples and all nations, to the end that every individual and every organ of society, keeping this Declaration constantly in mind, shall strive by teaching and education to promote respect for these rights and freedoms and by progressive measures, national and international, to secure their universal and effective recognition and observance, both among the peoples of Member States themselves and among the peoples of territories under their jurisdiction.

Article 1

All human beings are born free and equal in dignity and rights. They are endowed with reason and conscience and should act towards one another in a spirit of brotherhood.

Article 2

Everyone is entitled to all the rights and freedoms set forth in this Declaration, without distinction of any kind, such as race, colour, sex, language, religion, political or other opinion, national or social origin, property, birth or other status. Furthermore, no distinction shall be made on the basis of the political, jurisdictional or international status of the country or territory to which a person belongs, whether it be independent, trust, non-self-governing or under any other limitation of sovereignty.

Article 3

Everyone has the right of life, liberty and security of person.

Article 4

No one shall be held in slavery or servitude; slavery and the slave trade shall be prohibited in all their forms.

Article 5

No one shall be subjected to torture or to cruel, inhuman or degrading treatment or punishment.

---

[1] On the frustration of the Sub-Commission at the secrecy and lack of results of its work, see Anon, Rev. I.C.J., No. 27, December 1981.

Article 6

Everyone has the right to recognition everywhere as a person before the law.

Article 7

All are equal before the law and are entitled without any discrimination to equal protection of the law. All are entitled to equal protection against any discrimination in violation of this Declaration and against any incitement to such discrimination.

Article 8

Everyone has the right to an effective remedy by the competent national tribunals for acts violating the fundamental rights granted him by the constitution or by law.

Article 9

No one shall be subjected to arbitrary arrest, detention or exile.

Article 10

Everyone is entitled in full equality to a fair and public hearing by an independent and impartial tribunal, in the determination of his rights and obligations and of any criminal charge against him.

Article 11

1. Everyone charged with a penal offence has the right to be presumed innocent until proved guilty according to law in a public trial at which he has had all the guarantees necessary for his defence.

2. No one shall be held guilty of any penal offence on account of any act or omission which did not constitute a penal offence, under national or international law, at the time when it was committed. Nor shall a heavier penalty be imposed than the one that was applicable at the time the penal offence was committed.

Article 12

No one shall be subjected to arbitrary interference with his privacy, family, home or correspondence, nor to attacks upon his honour and reputation. Everyone has the right to the protection of the law against such interference or attacks.

Article 13

1. Everyone has the right to freedom of movement and residence within the borders of each state.

2. Everyone has the right to leave any country, including his own, and to return to his country.

Article 14

1. Everyone has the right to seek and to enjoy in other countries asylum from persecution.

2. This right may not be invoked in the case of prosecutions genuinely arising from non-political crimes or from acts contrary to the purposes and principles of the United Nations.

Article 15

1. Everyone has the right to a nationality.

2. No one shall be arbitrarily deprived of his nationality nor denied the right to change his nationality.

Article 16

1. Men and women of full age, without limitation due to race, nationality or religion, have the right to marry and to found a family. They are entitled to equal rights as to marriage, during marriage and at its dissolution.

2. Marriage shall be entered into only with the free and full consent of the intending spouses.

3. The family is the natural and fundamental group unit of society and is entitled to protection by society and the State.

Article 17

1. Everyone has the right to own property alone as well as in association with others.

2. No one shall be arbitrarily deprived of his property.

Article 18

Everyone has the right to freedom of thought, conscience and religion; this right includes freedom to change his religion or belief, and freedom, either alone or in community with others and in public or private, to manifest his religion or belief in teaching, practice, worship and observance.

Article 19

Everyone has the right to freedom of opinion and expression; this right includes freedom to hold opinions without interference and to seek, receive and impart information and ideas through any media and regardless of frontiers.

Article 20

1. Everyone has the right to freedom of peaceful assembly and association.

2. No one may be compelled to belong to an association.

Article 21

1. Everyone has the right to take part in the government of his country, directly or through freely chosen representatives.

2. Everyone has the right of equal access to public service in his country.

3. The will of the people shall be the basis of the authority of government; this

will shall be expressed in periodic and genuine elections which shall be by universal and equal suffrage and shall be held by secret vote or by equivalent free voting procedures.

Article 22

Everyone, as a member of society, has the right to social security and is entitled to realization through national effort and international co-operation and in accordance with the organization and resources of each State, of the economic, social and cultural rights indispensable for his dignity and the free development of his personality.

Article 23

1. Everyone has the right to work, to free choice of employment, to just and favourable conditions of work to protection against unemployment.

2. Everyone, without any discrimination, has the right to equal pay for equal work.

3. Everyone who works has the right to just and favourable remuneration ensuring for himself and his family an existence worthy of human dignity, and supplemented, if necessary, by other means of social protection.

4. Everyone has the right to form and to join trade unions for the protection of his interests.

Article 24

Everyone has the right to rest and leisure including reasonable limitation of working hours and periodic holidays with pay.

Article 25

Everyone has the right to a standard of living adequate for the health and well-being of himself and of his family, including food, clothing, housing and medical care and necessary social services, and the right to security in the event of unemployment, sickness, disability, widowhood, old age or other lack of livelihood in circumstances beyond his control.

2. Motherhood and childhood are entitled to special care and assistance. All children, whether born in or out of wedlock, shall enjoy the same social protection.

Article 26

1. Everyone has the right to education. Education shall be free, at least in the elementary and fundamental stages. Elementary education shall be compulsory. Technical and professional education shall be made generally available and higher education shall be equally accessible to all on the basis of merit.

2. Education shall be directed to the full development of the human personality and to the strengthening of respect for human rights and fundamental freedoms. It shall promote understanding, tolerance and friendship among all nations, racial or religious groups, and shall further the activities of the United Nations for the maintenance of peace.

3. Parents have a prior right to choose the kind of education that shall be given to their children.

Article 27

1. Everyone has the right freely to participate in the cultural life of the community, to enjoy the arts and to share in scientific advancement and its benefits.

2. Everyone has the right to the protection of the moral and material interests resulting from any scientific, literary or artistic production of which he is the author.

Article 28

Everyone is entitled to a social and international order in which the rights and freedoms set forth in the Declaration can be fully realized.

Article 29

1. Everyone has duties to the community in which alone the free and full development of his personality is possible.

2. In the exercise of his rights and freedoms, everyone shall be subject only to such limitations as are determined by law solely for the purpose of securing due recognition and respect for the rights and freedoms of others and of meeting the just requirements of morality, public order and the general welfare in a democratic society.

3. These rights and freedoms may in no case be exercised contrary to the purposes and principles of the United Nations.

Article 30

Nothing in this Declaration may be interpreted as implying for any State, group or person any right to engage in any acitivity or to perform any act aimed at the destruction of any of the rights and freedoms set forth herein.

Note

One of the first steps taken by the United Nations was the adoption by the General Assembly of the Universal Declaration of Human Rights, by 48 votes to none, with eight abstentions.[2] The Declaration contains a comprehensive list of civil, political, economic, social and cultural rights. According to Mrs. Eleanor Roosevelt, United States representative to the General Assembly and Chairman of the United Nations Commission on Human Rights during the drafting of the Declaration, it "is not, and does not purport to be a statement of law or of legal obligation"; it is instead, she continued, "a common standard of achievement for all peoples of all nations."[3] Despite this, the Declaration has undoubtedly had considerable impact in shaping subsequent treaties on human rights, and has been relied upon extensively by persons putting forward claims for fair treatment in terms of human rights; it has also had some impact upon the content of the constitutions of new states and upon decisions of municipal courts.[4] The status of the Declaration was considered in the *Filartiga Case* below.

[2] The abstaining states were, Byelorussia, Czechoslavakia, Poland, Saudi Arabia, South Africa, Ukraine, U.S.S.R. and Yugoslavia.
[3] 19 *U.S. Dept. of State Bull.* 751 (1948).
[4] See *Measures taken within the United Nations in the field of Human Rights* U.N.Doc. A/CONF. 32/5, pp. 28–30.

FILARTIGA v. PENA-IRALA[4a]

630 F. 2d. 876 (1980). 19 I.L.M. 966 (1980). U.S. Circuit Court of Appeals, 2nd. Circuit

The plaintiffs, a father and daughter, were Paraguayan citizens who entered the United States in 1978 and applied for political asylum there. Shortly after their arrival, they learnt of the illegal presence in the United States of the defendant, who was a Paraguayan citizen and the former head of police in Asuncion, Paraguay. The plaintiffs brought civil proceedings for damages in a United States federal district court alleging that he had wrongfully caused the death of their son and brother (also a Paraguayan citizen) in Paraguay in 1976 by torture in retaliation for the father's political opposition to the Paraguayan Government. The cause of action was stated as arising under "wrongful death statutes; the United Nations Charter; the Universal Declaration on Human Rights; the United Nations Declaration against Torture; the American Declaration of the Rights and Duties of Man; and other pertinent declarations, documents and practices constituting the customary international law of human rights and the law of nations." It was claimed that the court had jurisdiction under the United States Judiciary Act 1789 (28 U.S.C. § 1350) which establishes original federal district court jurisdiction over "all causes where an alien sues for a tort . . . [committed] in violation of the law of nations." In this judgment for the Court of Appeals, the plaintiffs appeal against the district court ruling that it did not have jurisdiction to hear the case was considered.

Kaufman, Circuit Judge. . . . A threshold question on the jurisdictional issue is whether the conduct alleged violates the law of nations. In light of the universal condemnation of torture in numerous international agreements, and the renunciation of torture as an instrument of official policy by virtually all of the nations of the world (in principle if not in practice), we find that an act of torture committed by a state official against one held in detention violates established norms of the international law of human rights, and hence the law of nations. . . .

The United Nations Charter . . . [Preamble, and Articles 55 and 56] makes it clear that in this modern age a state's treatment of its own citizens is a matter of international concern.

. . . although there is no universal agreement as to the precise extent of the "human rights and fundamental freedoms" guaranteed to all by the Charter, there is at present no dissent from the view that the guaranties include, at a bare minimum, the right to be free from torture. This prohibition has become part of customary international law, as evidenced and defined by the Universal Declaration of Human Rights . . . which states, in the plainest of terms, "no one shall be subjected to torture." The General Assembly has declared that the Charter precepts embodied in this Universal Declaration "constitute basic principles of international law." G.A. Res. 2625 (XXV) (Oct. 24, 1970).[5]

Particularly relevant is the [1975] Declaration on the Protection of All Persons from Being Subjected to Torture.[6] . . . This Declaration, like the

---

[4a] See Blum and Steinhardt, 22 Harvard I.L. J. 53 (1981); D'Zurilla, 56 Tul. L.R. 186 (1981); the articles in 10 Ga. J.I.C.L. 305 *et seq.* (1981); and the case notes in 75 A.J.I.L. 149 (1981) and 67 Virg. L.R. 1379 (1981).

[5] *Ed.* Appendix III below. Does Resolution 2625 really declare this?

[6] *Ed.* Above, p. 491.

Declaration of Human Rights before it, was adopted without dissent by the General Assembly. . . .

These U.N. declarations are significant because they specify with great precision the obligations of member nations under the Charter. . . . it has been observed that the Universal Declaration of Human Rights "no longer fits into the dichotomy of 'binding treaty' against 'non-binding pronouncement,' but is rather an authoritative statement of the international community." *E. Schwelb, Human Rights and the International Community* 70 (1964). Thus a Declaration creates an expectation of adherence, and "insofar as the expectation is gradually justified by State practice, a declaration may by custom become recognized as laying down rules binding upon the States." 34 U.N. ESCOR, *supra*. Indeed, several commentators have concluded that the Universal Declaration has become, *in toto*, a part of binding, customary international law. Nayar, . . . [19 Harv. Int. L.J. 813] at 816–17; Waldock, "Human Rights in Contemporary International Law and the Significance of the European Convention," *Int'l & Comp. L.Q.*, Supp. Publ. No. 11 at 15 (1965).

Turning to the act of torture, we have little difficulty discerning its universal renunciation in the modern usage and practice of nations. . . . The international consensus surrounding torture has found expression in numerous international treaties and accords. *E.g., American Convention on Human Rights*, Art. 5, . . . ; . . . European Convention for the Protection of Human Rights and Fundamental Freedoms, Art. 3. The substance of these international agreements is reflected in modern municipal—*i.e.* national—law as well. Although torture was once a routine concomitant of criminal interrogations in many nations, during the modern and hopefully more enlightened era it has been universally renounced. According to one survey, torture is prohibited, expressly or implicitly, by the constitutions of over fifty-five nations, including both the United States and Paraguay.

. . . United States diplomatic contacts confirm the universal abhorrence with which torture is viewed:

> In exchanges between United States embassies and all foreign states with which the United States maintains relations, it has been the Department of State's general experience that no government has asserted a right to torture its own nationals. Where reports of torture elicit some credence, a state usually responds by denial or, less frequently, by asserting that the conduct was unauthorized or constituted rough treatment short of torture.

Memorandum of the United States as *Amicus Curiae* at 16 n.34.

Having examined the sources from which customary international law is derived—the usage of nations, judicial opinions and the works of jurists—we conclude that official torture is now prohibited by the law of nations. The prohibition is clear and unambiguous, and admits of no distinction between treatment of aliens and citizens.

The Court then held that the district court did have jurisdiction under the 1789 Act to hear the case.

Note

The Court of Appeals did not rule upon the question whether the claim should be dismissed on the ground of *forum non conveniens*. The defendant was allowed to return to Paraguay before the Court of Appeal's judgment. In later proceedings, the federal district court gave judgment against him in default. A hearing on the question of damages was pending in 1982.

INTERNATIONAL COVENANT ON CIVIL AND POLITICAL RIGHTS 1966[7]

U.K.T.S. 6 (1977), Cmnd. 6702; 61 A.J.I.L. 870 (1967)

Article 1

1. All people have the right of self-determination. By virtue of that right they freely determine their political status and freely pursue their economic, social and cultural development.

2. All peoples may, for their own ends, freely dispose of their natural wealth and resources without prejudice to any obligations arising out of international economic co-operation, based upon the principle of mutual benefit, and international law. In no case may a people be deprived of its own means of subsistence.

3. The States Parties to the present Covenant, including those having responsibility for the administration of Non-Self-Governing and Trust Territories, shall promote the realization of the right of self-determination, and shall respect that right, in conformity with the provisions of the Charter of the United Nations.

Article 2

1. Each State Party to the present Covenant undertakes to respect and to ensure to all individuals within its territory and subject to its jurisdiction the rights recognized in the present Covenant, without distinction of any kind, such as race, colour, sex, language, religion, political or other opinion, national, or social origin, property, birth or other status.

2. Where not already provided for by existing legislative or other measures, each State Party to the present Covenant undertakes to take the necessary steps, in accordance with its constitutional processes and with the provisions of the present Covenant, to adopt such legislative or other measures as may be necessary to give effect to the rights recognized in the present Covenant.

3. Each State Party to the present Covenant undertakes:

(*a*) To ensure that any person whose rights or freedoms as herein recognized are violated shall have an effective remedy, notwithstanding that the violation has been committed by persons acting in an official capacity;

(*b*) To ensure that any person claiming such a remedy shall have his right thereto determined by competent judicial, administrative or legislative authorities, or by any other competent authority provided for by the legal system of the State, and to develop the possibilities of judicial remedy;

(*c*) To ensure that the competent authorities shall enforce such remedies when granted.

Article 3

The States Parties to the present Covenant undertake to ensure the equal right of men and women to the enjoyment of all civil and political rights set forth in the present Covenant.

[7] In force 1976. On December 31, 1981, there were 69 parties, including the U.K.

Article 4

1. In time of public emergency which threatens the life of the nation and the existence of which is officially proclaimed, the States Parties to the present Covenant may take measures derogating from their obligations under the present Covenant to the extent strictly required by the exigencies of the situation, provided that such measures are not inconsistent with their other obligations under international law and do not involve discrimination solely on the ground of race, colour, sex, language, religion or social origin.

2. No derogation from articles 6, 7, 8 (paragraphs 1 and 2), 11, 15, 16 and 18 may be made under this provision.

3. Any State Party to the present Covenant availing itself of the right of derogation shall immediately inform the other States Parties to the present Covenant, through the intermediary of the Secretary-General of the United Nations, of the provisions from which it has derogated and of the reasons by which it was actuated. A further communication shall be made, through the same intermediary, on the date on which it terminates such derogation.

Article 5

1. Nothing in the present Covenant may be interpreted as implying for any State, group or person any right to engage in any activity or perform any act aimed at the destruction of any of the rights and freedoms recognized herein or at their limitation to a greater extent than is provided for in the present Covenant.

2. There shall be no restriction upon or derogation from any of the fundamental human rights recognized or existing in any State Party to the present Covenant pursuant to law, conventions, regulations or custom on the pretext that the present Covenant does not recognize such rights or that it recognizes them to a lesser extent.

Article 6

1. Every human being has the inherent right to life. This right shall be protected by law. No one shall be arbitrarily deprived of his life.

2. In countries which have not abolished the death penalty, sentence of death may be imposed only for the most serious crimes in accordance with the law in force at the time of the commission of the crime and not contrary to the provisions of the present Covenant and to the Convention on the Prevention and Punishment of the Crime of Genocide. This penalty can only be carried out pursuant to a final judgment rendered by a competent court.

3. When deprivation of life constitutes the crime of genocide, it is understood that nothing in this article shall authorize any State Party to the present Covenant to derogate in any way from any obligation assumed under the provisions of the Convention on the Prevention and Punishment of the Crime of Genocide.

4. Anyone sentenced to death shall have the right to seek pardon or commutation of the sentence. Amnesty, pardon or commutation of the sentence of death may be granted in all cases.

5. Sentence of death shall not be imposed for crimes committed by persons below eighteen years of age and shall not be carried out on pregnant women.

6. Nothing in this article shall be invoked to delay or to prevent the abolition of capital punishment by any State Party to the present Covenant.

Article 7

No one shall be subjected to torture or to cruel, inhuman or degrading treatment or punishment. In particular, no one shall be subjected without his free consent to medical or scientific experimentation.

Article 8

1. No one shall be held in slavery; slavery and the slave-trade in all their forms shall be prohibited.

2. No one shall be held in servitude.

3. (a) No one shall be required to perform forced or compulsory labour;

(b) Paragraph 3(a) shall not be held to preclude, in countries where imprisonment with hard labour may be imposed as a punishment for a crime, the performance of hard labour in pursuance of a sentence to such punishment by a competent court;

(c) For the purpose of this paragraph the term "forced or compulsory labour" shall not include:

   (i) Any work or service, not referred to in subparagraph (b), normally required of a person who is under detention in consequence of a lawful order of a court, or of a person during conditional release from such detention;

  (ii) Any service of a military character and, in countries where conscientious objection is recognized, any national service required by law of conscientious objectors;

 (iii) Any service exacted in cases of emergency or calamity threatening the life or well-being of the community;

 (iv) Any work or service which forms part of normal civil obligations.

Article 9

1. Everyone has the right to liberty and security of person. No one shall be subjected to arbitrary arrest or detention. No one shall be deprived of his liberty except on such grounds and in accordance with such procedure as are established by law.

2. Anyone who is arrested shall be informed, at the time of arrest, of the reasons for his arrest and shall be promptly informed of any charges against him.

3. Anyone arrested or detained on a criminal charge shall be brought promptly before a judge or other officer authorized by law to exercise judicial power and shall be entitled to trial within a reasonable time or to release. It shall not be the general rule that persons awaiting trial shall be detained in custody, but release may be subject to guarantees to appear for trial, at any other stage of the judicial proceedings, and, should occasion arise, for execution of the judgment.

4. Anyone who is deprived of his liberty by arrest or detention shall be entitled to take proceedings before a court, in order that that court may decide

without delay on the lawfulness of his detention and order his release if the detention is not lawful.

5. Anyone who has been the victim of unlawful arrest or detention shall have an enforceable right to compensation.

Article 10

1. All persons deprived of their liberty shall be treated with humanity and with respect for the inherent dignity of the human person.

2. (a) Accused persons shall, save in exceptional circumstances, be segregated from convicted persons and shall be subject to separate treatment appropriate to their status as unconvicted persons;

(b) Accused juvenile persons shall be separated from adults and brought as speedily as possible for adjudication.

3. The penitentiary system shall comprise treatment of prisoners the essential aim of which shall be their reformation and social rehabilitation. Juvenile offenders shall be segregated from adults and be accorded treatment appropriate to their age and legal status.

Article 11

No one shall be imprisoned merely on the ground of inability to fulfil a contractual obligation.

Article 12

1. Everyone lawfully within the territory of a State shall, within that territory, have the right to liberty of movement and freedom to choose his residence.

2. Everyone shall be free to leave any country, including his own.

3. The above-mentioned rights shall not be subject to any restrictions except those which are provided by law, are necessary to protect national security, public order (*ordre public*), public health or morals or the rights and freedoms of others, and are consistent with the other rights recognized in the present Covenant.

4. No one shall be arbitrarily deprived of the right to enter his own country.

Article 13

An alien lawfully in the territory of a State Party to the present Covenant may be expelled therefrom only in pursuance of a decision reached in accordance with law and shall, except where compelling reasons of national security otherwise require, be allowed to submit the reasons against his expulsion and to have his case reviewed by, and be represented for the purpose before, the competent authority or a person or persons especially designated by the competent authority.

Article 14

1. All persons shall be equal before the courts and tribunals. In the determination of any criminal charge against him, or of his rights and obligations in a suit of law, everyone shall be entitled to a fair and public hearing of a competent, independent and impartial tribunal established by law. The Press and

the public may be excluded from all or part of a trial for reasons of morals, public order (*ordre public*) or national security in a democratic society, or when the interest of the private lives of the parties so requires, or the extent strictly necessary in the opinion of the court in special circumstances where publicity would prejudice the interests of justice; but any judgment rendered in a criminal case or in a suit at law shall be made public except where the interest of juvenile persons otherwise requires or the proceedings concern matrimonial disputes or the guardianship of children.

2. Everyone charged with a criminal offence shall have the right to be presumed innocent until proved guilty according to law.

3. In the determination of any criminal charge against him, everyone shall be entitled to the following minimum guarantees, in full equality:

(*a*) To be informed promptly and in detail in a language which he understands of the nature and cause of the charge against him;

(*b*) To have adequate time and facilities for the preparation of his defence and to communicate with counsel of his own choosing;

(*c*) To be tried without undue delay;

(*d*) To be tried in his presence, and to defend himself in person or through legal assistance of his own choosing; to be informed, if he does not have legal assistance, of this right; and to have legal assistance assigned to him, in any case where the interests of justice so require, and without payment by him in any such case if he does not have sufficient means to pay for it;

(*e*) To examine, or have examined, the witnesses against him and to obtain the attendance and examination of witnesses on his behalf under the same conditions as witnesses against him;

(*f*) To have the free assistance of an interpreter if he cannot understand or speak the language used in court;

(*g*) Not to be compelled to testify against himself or to confess guilt.

4. In the case of juvenile persons, the procedure shall be such as will take account of their age and the desirability of promoting their rehabilitation.

5. Everyone convicted of a crime shall have the right to his conviction and sentence being reviewed by a higher tribunal according to law.

6. When a person has by a final decision been convicted of a criminal offence and when subsequently his conviction has been reversed or he has been pardoned on the ground that a new or newly discovered fact shows conclusively that there has been a miscarriage of justice, the person who has suffered punishment as a result of such conviction shall be compensated according to law, unless it is proved that the non-disclosure of the unknown fact in time is wholly or partly attributable to him.

7. No one shall be liable to be tried or punished again for an offence for which he has already been finally convicted or acquitted in accordance with each country.

Article 15

1. No one shall be held guilty of any criminal offence on account of any act or omission which did not constitute a criminal offence, under national or international law, at the time when it was committed. Nor shall a heavier penalty be imposed than the one that was applicable at the time when the criminal offence was committed. If, subsequent to the commission of the offence, provision is

made by law for imposition of a lighter penalty, the offender shall benefit thereby.

2. Nothing in this article shall prejudice the trial and punishment of any person for any act or omission which, at the time when it was committed, was criminal according to the general principles of law recognized by the community of nations.

Article 16

Everyone shall have the right to recognition everywhere as a person before the law.

Article 17

1. No one shall be subjected to arbitrary or unlawful interference with his privacy, family, home or correspondence, nor to unlawful attacks on his honour and reputation.

2. Everyone has the right to the protection of the law against such interference or attacks.

Article 18

1. Everyone shall have the right to freedom of thought, conscience and religion. This right shall include freedom to have or to adopt a religion or belief of his choice, and freedom, either individually or in community with others and in public or private, to manifest his religion or belief in worship, observance, practice and teaching.

2. No one shall be subject to coercion which would impair his freedom to have or to adopt a religion or belief of his choice.

3. Freedom to manifest one's religion or beliefs may be subject only to such limitations as are prescribed by law and are necessary to protect public safety, order, health, or morals or the fundamental rights and freedoms of others.

4. The States Parties to the present Covenant undertake to have respect for the liberty of parents and, when applicable, legal guardians to ensure the religious and moral education of their children in conformity with their own convictions.

Article 19

1. Everyone shall have the right to hold opinions without interference.

2. Everyone shall have the right to freedom of expression; this right shall include freedom to seek, receive and impart information and ideas of all kinds, regardless of frontiers, either orally, in writing or in print, in the form of art, or through any other media of his choice.

3. The exercise of the rights provided for in paragraph 2 of this article carries with it special duties and responsibilities. It may therefore be subject to certain restrictions, but these shall only be such as are provided by law and are necessary:

(*a*) For respect of the rights or reputations of others;

(*b*) For the protection of national security or of public order (*ordre public*), or of public health or morals.

Article 20

1. Any propaganda for war shall be prohibited by law.

2. Any advocacy of national, racial or religious hatred that constitutes incitement to discrimination, hostility or violence shall be prohibited by law.

Article 21

The right of peaceful assembly shall be recognized. No restrictions may be placed on the exercise of this right other than those imposed in conformity with the law and which are necessary in a democratic society in the interests of national security or public safety, public order (*ordre public*), the protection of public health or morals or the protection of the rights and freedoms of others.

Article 22

1. Everyone shall have the right to freedom of association with others, including the right to form and join trade unions for the protection of his interests.

2. No restrictions may be placed on the exercise of this right other than those which are prescribed by law and which are necessary in a democratic society in the interests of national security or public safety, public order (*ordre public*), the protection of public health or morals or the protection of the rights and freedoms of others. This article shall not prevent the imposition of lawful restrictions on members of the armed forces and of the police in their exercise of this right.

3. Nothing in this article shall authorize States Parties to the International Labour Organisation Convention of 1948 concerning Freedom of Association and Protection of the Right to Organize to take legislative measures which would prejudice, or to apply the law in such a manner as to prejudice, the guarantees provided for in that Convention.

Article 23

1. The family is the natural and fundamental group unit of society and is entitled to protection by society and the State.

2. The right of men and women of marriageable age to marry and to found a family shall be recognized.

3. No marriage shall be entered into without the free and full consent of the intending spouses.

4. State Parties to the present Covenant shall take appropriate steps to ensure equality of rights and responsibilities of spouses as to marriage, during marriage and at its dissolution. In the case of dissolution, provision shall be made for the necessary protection of any children.

Article 24

1. Every child shall have, without any discrimination as to race, colour, sex, language, religion, national or social origin, property or birth, the right to such measures of protection as are required by his status as a minor, on the part of his family, society and the State.

2. Every child shall be registered immediately after birth and shall have a name.

3. Every child has the right to acquire a nationality.

Article 25

Every citizen shall have the right and the opportunity, without any of the distinctions mentioned in article 2 and without unreasonable restrictions:

(*a*) To take part in the conduct of public affairs, directly or through freely chosen representatives;

(*b*) To vote and to be elected at genuine periodic elections which shall be by universal and equal suffrage and shall be held by secret ballot, guaranteeing the free expression of the will of the electors;

(*c*) To have access, on general terms of equality, to public service in his country.

Article 26

All persons are equal before the law and are entitled without any discrimination to the equal protection of the law. In this respect, the law shall prohibit any discrimination and guarantee to all persons equal and effective protection against discrimination on any ground such as race, colour, sex, language, religion, political or other opinion, national or social origin, property, birth or other status.

Article 27

In those States in which ethnic, religious or linguistic minorities exist, persons belonging to such minorities shall not be denied the right, in community with the other members of their group, to enjoy their own culture, to profess and practice their own religion, or to use their own language.

Notes

1. The Universal Declaration has been followed by a series of treaties adopted within the United Nations. Chief among these are the two 1966 International Covenants on Civil and Political Rights and on Economic, Social and Cultural Rights (on the latter, see below, p. 553). The Covenant on Civil and Political Rights covers much of the same ground as the European Convention on Human Rights and its Protocols. Some rights are defined in greater detail than in the equivalent European text (*cf.* Article 14, Covenant and Article 6, European Convention, above, p. 474). Although the European Convention was based on an early draft of the Covenant (which explains the many textual similarities), the Covenant text was refined over a longer period of time and is geared to universal application. Some rights (*e.g.* the right to equality before the law (Article 26, Covenant), which concerns, for example, racial discrimination) are protected only by the Covenant, not the European Convention. As yet, there has been little interpretation of the Covenant,[8] although the "views" and "general comments" of the Human Rights Committee promise gradually to give it meaning. The extensive jurisprudence of the Strasbourg authorities may offer useful guidelines. The Covenant, however, will have to apply world-wide, rather than European, standards where relevant.

2. The system of implementation of the Covenant on Civil and Political Rights centres

---

[8] For a discussion of the meaning of the guarantee, see Henkin, ed., *The International Bill of Rights* (1981).

upon the Human Rights Committee.[9] This consists of 18 members elected from among the nationals of the contracting parties.[10] The members are independent experts; they do not represent their governments. They are nearly all lawyers. The parties to the Covenant "undertake to submit periodic reports on the measures they have adopted which give effect to the rights recognised herein and on the progress made in the enjoyment of those rights" (Art. 40(1)).[11] By mid-1982, 55 initial reports (due within a year of ratification) had been submitted, including that of the United Kingdom. Eight reports were overdue, some by several years. The Committee has decided that subsequent reports shall be submitted at five yearly intervals.[12] It has so far examined over 40 reports. Its practice is to consider the reports at public hearings to which the state whose report is being discussed is invited to send a representative. So far no state has refused to do so. The representative is questioned on the report and sometimes a supplementary written report is called for. The exchanges have been courteous, with the Committee emphasising that its role is to define the obligations in the Covenant and to encourage compliance rather than to criticise. Discussion is almost always in general terms; particular cases of alleged violations are seldom discussed. The Committee may make and transmit to the parties "general comments" upon their reports (Art. 40(4)). It has agreed "as a first step" and "without prejudice to the further consideration of the Committee's duties under Article 40(4)," that it should make the same comments of a general nature to all of the parties; it should not make general comments addressed to individual parties relating to their particular reports.[13] So far the comments made by the Committee have concerned the reporting process (*e.g.* on the length of reports) and the Committee's interpretation of the Covenant guarantee. Considerable, and to an impressive extent successful, efforts have been made to achieve harmonious relations within the Committee and to work by consensus. Nonetheless, a clear difference of opinion has emerged as to the power of the Committee to make "general comments." Members from western states have pressed for a more ambitious role than East European members have so far been prepared to allow. The "first step" described above is seen as a compromise between the two approaches. The same division is apparent in the questioning of state representatives, with more cross-examination of state representatives coming from the former group of members than the latter.

3. The Covenant also provides in Article 41 for an optional system of *state* applications. A contracting party *may*, on condition of reciprocity, accept the right of the other contracting parties to bring a claim to the Committee alleging a violation of the Covenant by it. So far 14 contracting parties (including the U.K.) have accepted it. A claim cannot be lodged unless a prescribed process of negotiation between the two parties has been completed without success. If satisfied that local remedies have been exhausted, the Committee "shall make available its good offices." The Committee must, within twelve months, submit a report indicating the facts and the solution reached or, if no solution has been reached, indicating just the facts and attaching to its reports the submission of the two parties. If no solution is reached, the Committee "may, with the prior consent of the States Parties concerned," appoint an ad hoc Conciliation Commission. If such a Commission is used by the parties and no settlement

[9] For a survey of its work, see Fischer, 76 A.J.I.L. 142 (1982); Nowak, 1 H.R.L.J. 136 (1980); *ibid.* 2 H.R.L.J. 168 (1981).

[10] Article 28. On July 28, 1982, the members were Mavrommatis (Greek), Chairman; Graefrath (G.D.R.), Prado Vallejo (Ecuador), Tomuschat (F.R.G.), Vice Chairmen; Aguilar (Venezuela), Al Douri (Iraq), Bouziri (Tunisia), Dieye (Senegal), Ermacora (Austria), Sir Vincent Evans (U.K.), Hanga (Romania), Herdocia Ortega (Nicaragua), Janča (Yugoslavia), Lallah (Mauritius), Movchan (U.S.S.R.), Opsahl (Norway), Sadi (Jordan), Tarnopolsky (Canada). Members are elected for renewable four-year periods.

[11] On the reporting system, see Nowak, 1 H.R.L.J. 136 (1980).

[12] G.A.O.R., 36th Session, Supp. 40, Annex V. The reporting period may be reduced if the Committee's workload permits.

[13] *Ibid.* Supp. 40, p. 84.

is reached through it, the Commission must make a report stating the facts and indicating "its views on the possibilities of an amicable settlement." The Report of the Commission is not binding. No state applications have been brought so far.

THE WEINBERGER CASE

1981 Report of the Human Rights Committee, G.A.O.R., 36th Session, Supp. 40, p. 114

Views of the Committee

11. With regard to the exhaustion of domestic remedies, the Committee has been informed by the Government of Uruguay in another case . . . that the remedy of *habeas corpus* is not applicable to persons arrested under prompt security measures. . . . an appeal was lodged on behalf of Ismael Weinberger with the Supreme Military Court on 19 August 1979. Up to date no final judgment has been rendered . . . more than four and a half years after his arrest on 25 February 1976. The Committee concludes that in accordance with article 5(2)(b) of the Optional Protocol, it is not barred from considering the case, as the application of the remedy is unreasonably prolonged.

12. The Committee therefore decides to base its views on the following facts which have either been essentially confirmed by the State party or are uncontested except for denials of a general character offering no particular information or explanation: Ismael Weinberger Weisz was arrested at his home in Montevideo, Uruguay, on 25 February 1976 without any warrant of arrest. He was held incommunicado at the prison of "La Paloma" in Montevideo for more than 100 days and could be visited by family members only 10 months after his arrest. During this period, he was most of the time kept blindfolded with his hands tied together. As a result of the treatment received during detention, he suffered serious physical injuries (one arm paralysed, leg injuries and infected eyes) and substantial loss of weight.

Ismael Weinberger was first brought before a judge and charged on 16 December 1976, almost 10 months after his arrest. On 14 August 1979, three and a half years after his arrest, he was sentenced to eight years of imprisonment by the Military judge of the Court of First Instance for "subversive association" . . . with aggravating circumstances of conspiracy against the Constitution. The concrete factual basis of this offence has not been explained by the Government of Uruguay, although the author of the communication claims that the true reasons were that his brother had contributed information on trade union activities to a newspaper opposed to the Government and his membership in a political party which had lawfully existed while the membership lasted. . . . Ismael Weinberger was not granted the assistance of a counsel during the first 10 months of his detention. Neither the alleged victim nor his counsel had the right to be present at the trial, the proceedings being conducted in writing. The judgment handed down against him was not made public.

Pursuant to *Acta Institucional No.* 4 of 1st September 1976, Ismael Weinberger is deprived of the right to engage in political activities for 15 years. . . .

14. The Human Rights Committee has considered whether acts and treatment, which are *prima facie* not in conformity with the Covenant, could for any reasons be justified under the Covenant in the circumstances. . . . The Covenant (Art. 4) allows national measures derogating from some of its provisions only in strictly defined circumstances, and the Government has not made any submissions of fact or law to justify such derogation. Moreover, some of the

facts referred to above raise issues under provisions from which the Covenant does not allow any derogation under any circumstances.

15. The Human Rights Committee is aware that under the legislation of many countries criminal offenders may be deprived of certain political rights. Accordingly, Article 25 of the Covenant only prohibits "unreasonable" restrictions. In no case, however, may a person be subjected to such sanctions solely because of his or her political opinion (Arts. 2(1) and 26). Furthermore, in the circumstances of the present case there is no justification for such a deprivation of all political rights for a period of 15 years.

16. The Human Rights Committee acting under Article 5(4) of the Optional Protocol to the International Covenant on Civil and Political Rights is of the view that these facts . . . disclose violations of the Covenant, in particular:

> of Articles 7 and 10(1) because of the severe treatment which Ismael Weinberger received during the first 10 months of his detention;
> of Article 9(3) because he was not brought promptly before a judge or other officer authorized by law to exercise judicial power and because he was not tried within a reasonable time;
> of Article 9(4) because recourse to *habeas corpus* was not available to him;
> of Article 14(1) because he had no fair and public hearing and because the judgment rendered against him was not made public;
> of Article 14(3) because he did not have access to legal assistance during the first 10 months of his detention and was not tried in his presence;
> of Article 15(1) because the penal law was applied retroactively against him;
> of Article 19(2) because he was detained for having disseminated information relating to trade union activities;
> of Article 25 because he is barred from taking part in the conduct of public affairs and from being elected for 15 years in accordance with *Acta Institucional No.* 4 of 1 September 1976.

17. The Committee, accordingly, is of the view that the State party is under an obligation to provide the victim with effective remedies, including his immediate release and compensation for the violations which he has suffered and to take steps to ensure that similar violations do not occur in the future.

Notes

1. 27 of the parties to the Covenant on Civil and Political Rights are parties also to its 1966 Optional Protocol.[14] By this, a party accepts the right of an individual to submit a "communication to the Human Rights Committee against it alleging a breach of the Convention." The overlap between the Protocol and the regional American and European Convention petition systems is the subject of a rule by which recourse may be had to each system in turn, but not simultaneously.[15]

2. The Human Rights Committee is competent to consider communications made under the Protocol subject to admissibility requirements similar to those in the European Convention on Human Rights, as to which see above, p. 478. Only communications made by or on behalf of a "victim" may be considered. In the *Mauritian Women Case*,[16] the Committee stated:

[14] Misc. 4(1976), Cmnd. 3320; 61 A.J.I.L. 887 (1967). In force 1976.

[15] Article 5(2)(*a*), Protocol. The Human Rights Committee will consider a claim "if it has been withdrawn from or is no longer being examined under . . . [another] procedure at the time that the Committee reaches a decision on the admissibility" on it: 1978 Report of the Human Rights Committee, G.A.O.R., 33rd Session, Supp. 40, p. 100.

[16] 1981 Report of the Human Rights Committee, G.A.O.R., 36th Session, Supp. 40, pp. 134, 139. See also the *Hartikainen* case, *ibid.* pp. 147, 152.

. . . no individual can in the abstract by way of an *actio popularis*, challenge a law or practice claimed to be contrary to the Covenant. If the law or practice has not already been concretely applied to the detriment of that individual, it must in any event be applicable in such a way that the alleged victim's risk of being affected is more than a theoretical possibility.

Accordingly, it rejected the claim of certain unmarried women to be victims of legislation discriminating against foreign husbands, but considered the claims of three women married to foreign husbands because it placed them under the constant threat that their husbands would be deported. A communication need not be made by the victim himself in all cases:

". . . the Committee may accept . . . a communication submitted on behalf of an alleged victim when it appears that he is unable to submit the communication himself. The Committee regards a close family connection as a sufficient link to justify an author acting on behalf of an alleged victim."[17]

3. The Committee considers both the admissibility and the merits of communications in private on the basis of written statements or explanations by the complainant and the defendant state. There is no provision for oral hearings. The Committee, which has described its role under the Protocol as "investigatory,"[18] is required to formulate its "views" on the question whether a breach has occurred and to send them to the state and complainant concerned (Art. 5(4)); they are also published as annexes to the Comittee's annual report. There is no conciliation stage comparable to that in the European Convention. The Committee's "views" are not binding, and there is no provision for a court or for any other body to take a binding decision.

4. So far, just over 100 communications have been submitted, almost entirely from nationals of the defendant state. Of these the Committee has declared 44 admissible; 31 have been declared inadmissible, or have been discontinued or suspended. Of the first 18 cases to have been considered on their merits, a breach of the Covenant has been found in all but two.[19] Fourteen of the proven cases had been brought against Uruguay. These all follow the pattern of the *Weinberger Case* on their facts.[20] When Uruguay did not respond fully to requests for information and legal argument in these cases, the Committee's approach was to accept as true allegations that were not denied or were denied only in very general terms.[21]

5. The *Lovelace*[22] and *Mauritian Women*[23] *Cases* are the other two in which breaches of the Convention have been found. In the first of these, Canada was found to be in breach of Article 27, Covenant because its law did not allow an Indian woman to return to her home Indian reserve when her marriage with a non-Indian had broken down. In the second, Mauritius was found to be in breach of Articles 2(1), 3 and 26 in relation to Articles 17(1) and 23(1), Covenant, with respect to the three of the complainants who were married to foreign husbands. This was because the possibility that those husbands

---

[17] *Loc. cit.* at p. 551, n. 15, above, p. 99.

[18] 1980 Report of the Human Rights Committee, G.A.O.R., 35th Session, Supp. 40, p. 84.

[19] For a review of the Committee's early jurisprudence, see Tomuschat, 1 H.R.L.J. 249 (1980).

[20] In one particularly bad case, the allegations were of "the application of electric shocks, the use of the 'submarino' (putting the detainee's head into foul water), insertion of bottles or barrels of automatic rifles into his anus and forcing him to remain standing, hooded and handcuffed and with a piece of wood thrust into his mouth, for several days and nights:" the *Motta Case, ibid.* p. 132, at p. 133.

[21] Note the individual opinion of Mr. Tomuschat in the *Motta Case*, above, n. 20, in which he expressed the opinion that the *victim* had not proved his case on one point because *his* allegations were not sufficiently concrete; the rule that "general explanations and statements are not sufficient . . . applies to both sides": *ibid.* at p. 137.

[22] 1981 Report of the Human Rights Committee, GAOR, 36th Session, Supp. 40, p. 166.

[23] *Ibid.* p. 134.

might be deported under Mauritian law when Mauritian men married to foreign wives did not face the same risk resulted in discrimination on the ground of sex. The two cases in which no breach was found were the *Hartikainen Case*[24] (no breach of Article 18 by Finland in respect of compulsory religious education in schools) and the *Maroufidou Case*[25] (no breach by Sweden of Article 13 by the deportation of an alien suspected of terrorism).

Notes on other UN Human Rights Treaties

1. The other main treaty is the 1966 International Covenant on Economic, Social and Cultural Rights.[26] This protects the economic, social and cultural rights listed in the Universal Declaration on Human Rights (Arts. 22–27), above, p. 537. The Covenant recognises that realisation of such rights, to a much greater extent than is the case with civil and political rights, is dependent upon economic resources. The guarantee is therefore a progressive one. By Article 2, Economic, Social and Cultural Rights Covenant, each party "undertakes to take steps . . . to the maximum of its available resources, with a view to achieving progressively the full realisation . . . of the rights in the Covenant." Contrast Article 2, Civil and Political Rights Covenant, above, p. 541.

2. The system of implementation for the Covenant on Economic, Social and Cultural Rights consists solely of a system of reports.[27] These are examined not by the *independent* Human Rights Committee but by ECOSOC. Reports are submitted on approximately one-third of the rights protected every two years. The first reports were submitted in 1977 and are being examined at present. ECOSOC has established a Working Group composed of 15 member states of the Council to conduct this examination. So far the Group has spent most of its time on procedural matters. According to one commentator[28]

"It has hardly made an encouraging start. The examination of reports has been cursory, superficial, and politicised. It has neither established standards for evaluating reports nor reached any conclusions regarding its examination of reports."

ECOSOC "may transmit to the UN Commission on Human Rights for study and general recommendation or as appropriate for information" the reports made by states (Art. 19). It may also "submit from time to time to the General Assembly reports with recommendations of a general nature" on the reports by states (Art. 21).

The absence of a system of petitions is consistent with the practice of I.L.O. in respect of the supervision of I.L.O. conventions[29] and of the European Social Charter.[30] It is thought to be neither feasible nor appropriate to implement a guarantee of economic, social and cultural rights by such a system. Is this so? Has the European Court of Human Rights in fact been implementing such rights in the recent trade union cases?[31]

3. The British Representative to the General Assembly (Lady Gaitskell) stated that: "her delegation believed that the effectiveness of the Covenants would lie in the strength of their implementation clause. . . . [32] Although acceptance of the substantive guarantee in the Covenants may by itself have some preventive or curative effect in

---

[24] *Ibid.* p. 147.
[25] *Ibid.* p. 160. In its "views" the Committee established that it is not competent to question the interpretation by the competent national authorities of national law unless "unless it is established that they have not interpreted and applied it in good faith or that it is evident that there has been an abuse of power": *ibid.* p. 165.
[26] U.K.T.S. 6 (1977), Cmnd. 6702: 6 I.L.M. 360. In force 1976. On December 31, 1981, there were 71 parties, including the U.K.
[27] Article 16, Covenant. See Schwelb, 1 H.Rts.Jo. 363 (1968).
[28] Anon., Rev. I.C.J. No. 27, December 1981, p. 26, at p. 28.
[29] See Landy, *The Effectiveness of International Supervision*, 1966.
[30] *Loc. cit.* at p. 471, n. 22.
[31] See above, p. 523.
[32] G.A.O.R., A/C.3/S.R. 1415, para. 25.

some states, it seems both likely that the above comment is substantially accurate and doubtful that the Covenants, even with the Optional Protocol to the Civil and Political Rights Covenant, will prove to have wholly effective enforcement procedures. The European Convention only began to come alive in the United Kingdom when the much more forceful right of individual petition in that Convention became applicable in 1966. The Covenant procedures, weak as they are, were the result of a compromise to meet a division of opinion between those states who, on grounds of domestic jurisdiction or for other reasons, opposed any form of investigative procedure in this context and those who sought a stronger one.[33]

4. A further important convention is the International Convention on the Elimination of all Forms of Racial Discrimination 1966 (CERD).[34] The Contracting Parties "undertake to prohibit and to eliminate racial discrimination in all its forms."[35] In 1966, in the *South-West Africa Cases*, Judge Tanaka, in his dissenting opinion, stated that "the norm of non-discrimination or non-separation on the basis of race has become a rule of customary international law."[36] Note also the *Barcelona Traction Case*,[37] the United Nations Declaration on the Elimination of all Forms of Racial Discrimination of November 20, 1963,[38] which formed the basis for CERD, and the Convention on the Suppression and Punishment of the Crime of Apartheid 1973.[39]

The system of enforcement in CERD is based upon the Committee on the Elimination of Racial Discrimination consisting of 18 members elected by the Contracting Parties from among their nationals and sitting in their personal capacity.[40] The Committee receives bi-ennial reports from Contracting Parties on the implementation of CERD and makes its own annual report, which is published, to the General Assembly which may contain such "suggestions and general recommendations" on the reports from the Contracting Parties as it thinks fit.[41] There is a *compulsory* system of interstate claims,[42] but so far no state has made an application. Any application brought by a state is referred to the other state for comment.[43] If this does not lead to a satisfactory negotiated outcome, either state may refer the matter back to the Committee which is then competent to conduct a fact-finding inquiry and to appoint an ad hoc Conciliation Commission.[44] The findings and recommendation that result from this process are not binding upon the states concerned. There is also provision for an *optional* system of individual applications.[45] Such an application is considered, together with any reply by the Contracting Parties concerned, by the Committee which may "forward its suggestions and recommendations, if any, to the State Party concerned and to the

---

[33] See Schwelb, 62 A.J.I.L. 827, at pp. 833–835 (1968). See also Sohn, 62 A.J.I.L. 909 (1968).

[34] U.K.T.S. 77 (1969), Cmnd. 4108; 60 A.J.I.L. 650 (1966). In force 1969. On December 31, 1981, there were 111 contracting parties, including the U.K. See Buergenthal, 12 Texas I.L.J. 187 (1977); Das, 4 H.Rts Jo. 213 (1971); Lerner, *The U.N. Convention on the Elimination of all Forms of Racial Discrimination* (2nd ed., 1980); Newman, 56 Calif.L.R. 1559 (1968); Schwelb, 15 I.C.L.Q. 996 (1966).

[35] Article 5, Convention.

[36] I.C.J.Rep. 1966, p. 293. This was an alternative argument put by the applicants. The Court found no need to consider it. Judge *ad hoc* Van Wyk rejected it (*ibid.* pp. 168–172, 193). Judge Padilla Nervo was sympathetic towards it (*ibid.* pp. 457 and 464).

[37] See above, p. 453.

[38] G.A.Res. 1904 (XVIII), G.A.O.R., 18th Session, Supp. 15; 58 A.J.I.L. 1081 (1964); 3 I.L.M. 164 (1964). The Resolution was adopted unanimously.

[39] 13 I.L.M. 51 (1974). In force 1976. 65 contracting parties on December 31, 1981. The U.K. not a party (or signatory).

[40] Article 8, Convention.

[41] Article 9, *ibid.*

[42] Article 11, *ibid.*

[43] *Ibid.*

[44] Article 13.

[45] Article 14. It comes into force when 10 Parties accept it; Costa Rica, Ecuador, Iceland, Italy, The Netherlands, Norway, Sweden and Uruguay had done so by July 1, 1982.

petitioner."[46] The Committee has no power to take a binding decision. Even so, the system of implementation is stronger than that in either of the Covenants. Article 22, providing for the compulsory reference of disputes to the International Court of Justice, was the subject of considerable disagreement. A large number of contracting parties, including most of the Soviet bloc, have made reservations to it.

5. Other United Nations human rights treaties include the 1949 Genocide Convention, below, p. 561, the 1951 Convention relating to the Status of Refugees,[47] the 1953 Convention on the Political Rights of Women,[48] the 1973 Convention on the Crime of Apartheid,[49] and the 1979 Convention the Elimination of Discrimination against Women.[50]

4. HUMAN RIGHTS AND INTERNATIONAL CRIMINAL LAW[51]

JUDGMENT OF THE NUREMBURG INTERNATIONAL MILITARY TRIBUNAL[52]

1946. 41 A.J.I.L. 172 (1947)

On August 8, 1946, the Governments of France, the United Kingdom, the United States and the U.S.S.R., "acting in the interests of all the United Nations and by their representatives duly authorized thereto," signed in London an Agreement for the Establishment of an International Military Tribunal.[53] The Tribunal was "for the trial of war criminals whose offences have no particular geographical location."[54] It was to operate in accordance with a Charter annexed to the Agreement. The Tribunal was composed of four members, one appointed by each of the signatory governments. The members were Lawrence L.J., President; Biddle, Nikitchenko and de Vabres. The alternate members were Birkett J., Parker, Volchov and Falco.

Judgment of the Tribunal

The individual defendants are indicted under Article 6 of the Charter, which is as follows:

Article 6. The Tribunal established by the Agreement referred to in Article 1 hereof for the trial and punishment of the major war criminals of the European Axis countries shall have the power to try and punish persons who, acting in the interests of the European Axis countries, whether as individuals or as members of organizations, committed any of the following crimes:

The following acts, or any of them, are crimes coming within the jurisdiction of the Tribunal for which there shall be individual responsibility:

(a) Crimes Against Peace: namely, planning, preparation, initiation or waging of a war of aggression, or a war in violation of international treaties, agreements or assurances, or participation in a common plan or conspiracy for the accomplishment of any of the foregoing:

[46] *Ibid.*
[47] 189 U.N.T.S. 137.
[48] 193 U.N.T.S. 135.
[49] 13 I.L.M. 50.
[50] 19 I.L.M. 33.
[51] On criminal responsibility in international law, see above, p. 376.
[52] See Goodhart, 58 *Juridical Review* 1 (1946); Wright, 41 A.J.I.L. 38 (1947); Woetzel, *The Nuremberg Trials in International Law* (1960).
[53] U.K.T.S. 4 (1945), Cmd. 6671; 5 U.N.T.S. 251; 39 A.J.I.L., Suppl. 257 (1945).
[54] *Ibid.* Art. 2.

(b) War Crimes: namely, violations of the laws or customs of war. Such violations shall include, but not be limited to, murder, ill-treatment or deportation to slave labour or for any other purpose of civilian population of or in occupied territory, murder or ill-treatment of prisoners of war or persons on the seas, killing of hostages, plunder of public or private property, wanton destruction of cities, towns or villages, or devastation not justified by military necessity:

(c) Crimes Against Humanity: namely, murder, extermination, enslavement, deportation, and other inhumane acts committed against any civilian population, before or during the war, or persecutions on political, racial, or religious grounds in execution of or in connection with any crime within the jurisdiction of the Tribunal whether or not in violation of the domestic law of the country where perpetrated.

Leaders, organizers, instigators, and accomplices, participating in the formulation or execution of a common plan or conspiracy to commit any of the foregoing crimes are responsible for all acts performed by any persons in execution of such plan.

The Law of the Charter

The jurisdiction of the Tribunal is defined in the Agreement and Charter, and the crimes coming within the jurisdiction of the Tribunal, for which there shall be individual responsibility, are set out in Article 6. The law of the Charter is decisive, and binding upon the Tribunal.

The making of the Charter was the exercise of the sovereign legislative power by the countries to which the German Reich unconditionally surrendered; and the undoubted right of these countries to legislate for the occupied territories has been recognized by the civilized world. The Charter is not an arbitrary exercise of power on the part of the victorious Nations, but in the view of the Tribunal, as will be shown, it is the expression of international law existing at the time of its creation; and to that extent is itself a contribution to international law.

The Signatory Powers created this Tribunal, defined the law it was to administer, and made regulations for the proper conduct of the Trial. In doing so, they have done together what any one of them might have done singly; for it is not to be doubted that any nation has the right to set up special courts to administer law. With regard to the constitution of the Court, all that the defendants are entitled to ask is to receive a fair trial on the facts and law.

The Charter makes the planning or waging of a war of aggression or a war in violation of international treaties a crime; and it is therefore not strictly necessary to consider whether and to what extent aggressive war was a crime before the execution of the London Agreement. But in view of the great importance of the questions of law involved, the Tribunal has heard full argument from the Prosecution and the Defence, and will express its view on the matter.

It was urged on behalf of the defendants that a fundamental principle of all law—international and domestic—is that there can be no punishment of crime without a pre-existing law. "*Nullem crimen sine lege, nulla poena sine lege.*" It was submitted that *ex post facto* punishment is abhorrent to the law of all civilized nations, that no sovereign power had made aggressive war a crime at the time that the alleged criminal acts were committed, that no statute had defined aggressive war, that no penalty had been fixed for its commission, and no court had been created to try and punish offenders.

In the first place, it is to be observed that the maxim *nullum crimen sine lege* is not a limitation of sovereignty, but is in general a principle of justice. To assert that it is unjust to punish those who in defiance of treaties and assurances have attacked neighboring states without warning is obviously untrue, for in such circumstances the attacker must know that he is doing wrong, and so far from it being unjust to punish him, it would be unjust if his wrong were allowed to go unpunished. Occupying the positions they did in the Government of Germany, the defendants or at least some of them must have known of the treaties signed by Germany, outlawing recourse to war for the settlement of international disputes, they must have known that they were acting in defiance of all international law when in complete deliberation they carried out their designs of invasion and aggression. On this view of the case alone, it would appear that the maxim has no application to the present facts.

This view is strongly reinforced by a consideration of the state of international law in 1939, so far as aggressive war is concerned. The General Treaty for the Renunciation of War of 27 August 1928, more generally known as the Pact of Paris or the Kellogg-Briand Pact, was binding on 63 nations, including Germany, Italy and Japan at the outbreak of war in 1939. . . . In the opinion of the Tribunal, the solemn renunciation of war as an instrument of national policy necessarily involves the proposition that such a war is illegal in international law; and that those who plan and wage such a war, with its inevitable and terrible consequences, are committing a crime in so doing. . . . But it is argued that the Pact does not expressly enact that such wars are crimes, or set up courts to try those who make such wars. To that extent the same is true with regard to the laws of war contained in the Hague Convention. The Hague Convention of 1907 prohibited resort to certain methods of waging war. . . . Many of these prohibitions had been enforced long before the date of the Convention; but since 1907 they have certainly been crimes, punishable as offenses against the law of war; yet the Hague Convention nowhere designates such practices as criminal, nor is any sentence prescribed, nor any mention made of a court to try and punish offenders. For many years past, however, military tribunals have tried and punished individuals guilty of violating the rules of land warfare laid down by this Convention. . . .

It was submitted that international law is concerned with the actions of sovereign States, and provides no punishment for individuals; and further, that where the act in question is an act of State, those who carry it out are not personally responsible, but are protected by the doctrine of the sovereignty of the State. In the opinion of the Tribunal, both these submissions must be rejected. That international law imposes duties and liabilities upon individuals as well as upon States has long been recognised. In the recent case of Ex Parte Quirin (1942 317 U.S. 1), before the Supreme Court of the United States, persons were charged during the war with landing in the United States for purposes of spying and sabotage. The late Chief Justice Stone, speaking for the Court, said:

> From the very beginning of its history this Court has applied the law of war as including that part of the law of nations which prescribes for the conduct of war, the status, rights, and duties of enemy nations as well as enemy individuals.

He went on to give a list of cases tried by the Courts, where individual offenders were charged with offenses against the laws of nations, and particularly the laws of war. Many other authorities could be cited, but enough has been said to show that individuals can be punished for violations of international law. Crimes against international law are committed by men, not by abstract entities, and only by punishing individuals who commit such crimes can the provisions of international law be enforced. . . .

It was also submitted on behalf of most of these defendants that in doing what they did they were acting under the orders of Hitler, and therefore cannot be held responsible for the acts committed by them in carrying out these orders. The Charter specifically provides in Article 8:

> The fact that the Defendant acted pursuant to order of his Government or of a superior shall not free him from responsibility, but may be considered in mitigation of punishment.

The provisions of this article are in conformity with the law of all nations. That a soldier was ordered to kill or torture in violation of the international law of war has never been recognized as a defense to such acts of brutality, though, as the Charter here provides, the order may be urged in mitigation of the punishment. The true test, which is found in varying degrees in the criminal law of most nations, is not the existence of the order, but whether moral choice was in fact possible.

The Law as to the Common Plan or Conspiracy

In the previous recital of the facts relating to aggressive war, it is clear that planning and preparation had been carried out in the most systematic way at every stage of history.

Planning and preparation are essential to the making of war. In the opinion of the Tribunal aggressive war is a crime under international law. The Charter defines this offense as planning, preparation, initiation, or waging of a war of aggression "or participation in a Common Plan or Conspiracy for the accomplishment . . . of the foregoing." . . .

The "Common Plan or Conspiracy" charged in the Indictment covers 25 years, from the formation of the Nazi Party in 1919 to the end of the war in 1945. . . .

The Prosecution says, in effect, that any significant participation in the affairs of the Nazi Party or Government is evidence of a participation in a conspiracy that is in itself criminal. Conspiracy is not defined in the Charter. But in the opinion of the Tribunal the conspiracy must be clearly outlined in its criminal purpose. It must not be too far removed from the time of decision and of action. The planning, to be criminal, must not rest merely on the declarations of a party program, in the 25 points of the Nazi Party, announced in 1920, or the political affirmations expressed in *Mein Kampf* in later years. The Tribunal must examine whether a concrete plan to wage war existed, and determine the participants in that concrete plan. . . .

In the opinion of the Tribunal, the evidence establishes the common planning to prepare and wage war by certain of the defendants. . . .

War Crimes and Crimes against Humanity

The evidence relating to War Crimes has been overwhelming . . .

. . . Prisoners of war were ill-treated and tortured and murdered, not only in defiance of the well-established rules of international law, but in complete disregard of the elementary dictates of humanity. Civilian populations in occupied territories suffered the same fate. Whole populations were deported to Germany for the purposes of slave labor upon defense works, armament production, and similar tasks connected with the war effort. Hostages were taken in very large numbers from the civilian populations in all the occupied countries, and were shot as suited the German purposes. Public and private property was systematically plundered and pillaged in order the enlarge the resources of Germany at the expense of the rest of Europe. Cities and towns and villages were wantonly destroyed without military justification or necessity. . . .

The Tribunal is of course bound by the Charter, in the definition which it gives both of War Crimes and Crimes against Humanity. With respect to War Crimes, however, as has already been pointed out, the crimes defined by Article 6, Section (b), of the Charter were already recognized as War Crimes under international law. They were covered by Articles 46, 50, 52, and 56 of the Hague Convention of 1907, and Articles 2, 3, 4, 46 and 51 of the Geneva Convention of 1929. That violation of these provisions constituted crimes for which the guilty individuals were punishable is too well settled to admit of argument. . . .

With regard to Crimes against Humanity there is no doubt whatever that political opponents were murdered in Germany before the war, and that many of them kept in concentration camps in circumstances of great horror and cruelty. The policy of terror was certainly carried out on a vast scale, and in many cases was organized and systematic. The policy of persecution, repression, and murder of civilians in Germany before the war of 1939, who were likely to be hostile to the Government, was most ruthlessly carried out. The persecution of Jews during the same period is established beyond all doubt. To constitute Crimes against Humanity, the acts relied on before the outbreak of war must have been in execution of, or in connection with, any crime within the jurisdiction of the Tribunal. The Tribunal is of the opinion that revolting and horrible as many of these crimes were, it has not been satisfactorily proved that they were done in execution of, or in connection with, any such crime. The Tribunal therefore cannot make a general declaration that the acts before 1939 were Crimes against Humanity within the meaning of the Charter, but from the beginning of the war in 1939 War Crimes were committed on a vast scale, which were also Crimes against Humanity; and insofar as the inhumane acts charged in the Indictment, and committed after the beginning of the war, did not constitute War Crimes, they were all committed in execution of, or in connection with, the aggressive war, and therefore constituted Crimes Against Humanity.

The Accused Organizations

The Tribunal then considered the nature of the responsibility of the German organisations that were indicted:

A criminal organization is analogous to a criminal conspiracy in that the essence of both is cooperation for criminal purposes. There must be a group bound together and organized for a common purpose. The group must be formed or used in connection with the commission of crimes denounced by the Charter. Since the declaration with respect to the organizations and groups will, as has been pointed out, fix the criminality of its members, that definition should exclude persons who had no knowledge of the criminal purposes or acts of the organization and those who were drafted by the State for membership, unless they were personally implicated in the commission of acts declared criminal by Article 6 of the Charter as members of the organization. Membership alone is not enough to come within the scope of these declarations.

Notes

1. After dealing with these general questions in the above part of its judgment, the Tribunal proceeded to review the cases of each of the indicted individuals and organisations. Of the twenty-two individuals indicted, three were acquitted; the remainder were found guilty on one or more of the counts in the indictment, which was based upon Article 6 of the Tribunal's Charter. Of those found guilty, twelve (including Goering, Von Ribbentrop, Keitel, Streicher and Bormann) were sentenced to death[55]; three (including Hess) were sentenced to life imprisonment; and four were sentenced to periods of ten to 20 years' imprisonment. Of the six organisations indicted, three were declared criminal, including the Gestapo and the SS. The Soviet judge dissented on some of the acquittals and on the refusal of the Tribunal to pass a death sentence on Hess.

2. *Did* the case infringe the principle *nullum crimen sine lege*? Consider the position with regard to crimes against humanity (which was the only offence of which Streicher, for example, was found guilty) in particular. With regard to the defence of superior orders,[56] what does the Tribunal mean when it says that the "true test . . . is . . . whether moral choice was in fact possible"? Could it be argued that the Tribunal violated the principle *nemo judex in sua propria causa*? Or that the trial was invalid because war criminals on the Allied side were not tried also?

3. Was the Tribunal an international tribunal or was it a municipal court established in Germany by the governments jointly exercising sovereignty therein for the time being?

4. In 1946, the General Assembly of the United Nations resolved that it "affirms the principles of international law recognised by the Charter of the Nuremburg Tribunal and the judgment of the Tribunal."[57] The Nuremberg Principles were later formulated by the International Law Commission[58] on the instruction of the General Assembly. The Commission understood its task as not requiring it to "express any appreciation of these principles as principles of international law but merely to formulate them." In 1963, the Lord Chancellor stated in Parliament that the United Kingdom took the view that the Nuremberg Principles "are generally accepted among states and have the status of customary international law."[59]

5. The Japanese war leaders were tried by a similar tribunal—the International Tribunal for the Far East.[60] Other war crimes tribunals established by the Allied Powers tried lesser offenders.[61]

6. The Convention of the Non-applicability of Statutory Limitations to War Crimes and Crimes against Humanity 1968[62] achieves what its title suggests for parties to it. Article IV reads:

> The States Parties to the present Convention undertake to adopt, in accordance with their respective constitutional processes, any legislative or other measures necessary to ensure that statutory or other limitations shall not apply to the prosecution and

[55] Goering committed suicide before the sentence could be carried out. Bormann was tried *in absentia* (a fair trial?)
[56] See Dinstein, *The Defence of "Obedience to Superior Orders" in International Law* (1965).
[57] G.A. Res. 95(1), G.A.O.R., *Resolutions*, First Session, Part II, p. 188.
[58] They are printed in Y.B.I.L.C., 1950, II, p. 195.
[59] *Hansard*, H.L., Vol. 253, col. 831. December 2, 1963; B.P.I.L. 1963, p. 212.
[60] See Horwitz, *The Tokyo Trial*, *Int.Conc.* No. 465 (1950).
[61] See Taylor, *Nuremberg Trials: War Crimes and International Law*, *Int.Conc.* No. 450 (1949).
[62] 8 I.L.M. 68 (1969). In force 1970. On December 31, 1981, there were 23 contracting parties, including most of the East European bloc. The U.K. was not a party. See Miller, 65 A.J.I.L. 476 (1971).

punishment of the crimes referred to in articles I and II of this Convention and that, where they exist, such limitations shall be abolished.

7. In 1971, the United Nations General Assembly reaffirmed that *apartheid* is a crime against humanity.[63] The International Convention on the Suppression and Punishment of the Crime of Apartheid 1973, Article 1, states the same.[64]

CONVENTION ON THE PREVENTION AND PUNISHMENT OF THE CRIME OF GENOCIDE 1948[65]

U.K.T.S. 58 (1970) Cmnd. 4421; 78 U.N.T.S. 277; 45 A.J.I.L., Supp., 6 (1951)

The *Contracting Parties,*

Having considered the declaration made by the General Assembly of the United Nations in its resolution 96(I) dated 11 December 1946 that genocide is a crime under international law, contrary to the spirit and aims of the United Nations and condemned by the civilized world;

Recognizing that at all periods of history genocide has inflicted great losses on humanity; and

Being convinced that, in order to liberate mankind from such an odious scourge, international co-operation is required;

Hereby agree as hereinafter provided:

Article I

The Contracting Parties confirm that genocide, whether committed in time of peace or in time of war, is a crime under international law which they undertake to prevent and punish.

Article II

In the present Convention, genocide means any of the following acts committed with intent to destroy, in whole or in part, a national, ethnical, racial or religious group, as such:

    (*a*) Killing members of the group;
    (*b*) Causing serious bodily or mental harm to members of the group;
    (*c*) Deliberately inflicting on the group conditions of life calculated to bring about its physical destruction in whole or in part;
    (*d*) Imposing measures intended to prevent births within the group;
    (*e*) Forcibly transferring children of the group to another group.

Article III

The following acts shall be punishable:

    (*a*) Genocide;
    (*b*) Conspiracy to commit genocide;
    (*c*) Direct and public incitement to commit genocide;
    (*d*) Attempt to commit genocide;
    (*e*) Complicity in genocide.

Article IV

Persons committing genocide or any of the other acts enumerated in Article III shall be punished, whether they are constitutionally responsible rulers, public officials or private individuals.

[63] G.A. Res. 2784 (XXVI). The resolution was adopted by 93 votes to 5, with 15 abstentions.
[64] 13 I.L.M. 50 (1974). In force 1976. On December 31, 1981, there were 65 contracting parties. The U.K. was not a party.
[65] The Convention was adopted unanimously by the General Assembly on December 9, 1948. In force 1951. On December 31, 1981, there were 86 contracting parties, including the U.K. The offence in Art. 2 was made an offence in English law by the Genocide Act 1969. See Kunz, 43 A.J.I.L. 738 (1949); Lemkin, 41 A.J.I.L. 145 (1947); Robinson, *The Genocide Convention. A commentary* (1960).

Article V

The Contracting Parties undertake to enact, in accordance with their respective Constitutions, the necessary legislation to give effect to the provisions of the present Convention and, in particular, to provide effective penalties for persons guilty of genocide or any of the other acts enumerated in Article III.

Article VI

Persons charged with genocide or any of the other acts enumerated in Article III shall be tried by a competent tribunal of the State in the territory of which the act was committed, or by such international penal tribunal as may have jurisdiction with respect to those Contracting Parties which shall have accepted its jurisdiction.

Article VII

Genocide and the other acts enumerated in Article III shall not be considered as political crimes for the purpose of extradition.

Article IX

Disputes between the Contracting Parties relating to the interpretation, application or fulfilment of the present Convention, including those relating to the responsibility of a State for genocide or any of the other acts enumerated in Article III, shall be submitted to the International Court of Justice at the request of any of the parties to the dispute.

Notes

1. The term "genocide" was coined by Lemkin, a private individual whose efforts played a large part in prompting the United Nations work on genocide.

2. Is the offence of genocide defined in the Convention the same in scope as that of crimes against humanity in the Charter of the Nuremberg International Military Tribunal? Does the Convention cover cultural genocide? Note how vague the concept of "complicity in genocide" is.

3. There is no "international penal tribunal" with jurisdiction to try persons for genocide or any other international crime.[66] In this situation, how satisfactory is Article VI? Should there be universal jurisdiction to try persons for genocide?[67]

4. The Convention probably reflects customary international law. Note that it was adopted unanimously in the General Assembly and that Resolution 96(I) of the General Assembly upon which it was based was adopted unanimously too. Note also the *Barcelona Traction Case.*[68]

5. 17 Contracting Parties have made reservations not accepting the rule of compulsory jurisdiction in Art. IX of the Convention, including most of the Soviet bloc.[69] Several states, including the United Kingdom, have objected to such reservations.[70] The reservation to Article IX by the Philippines states that:

> the Philippine Government does not consider said article to extend the concept of State responsibility beyond that recognised by the general principles of international law.[71]

What did the Philippines have in mind?

---

[66] See Bridge, 13 I.C.L.Q. 1255 (1964).
[67] Note the approach of the court in the *Eichmann Case*, above, p. 223.
[68] See above, p. 453, in paras. 33, 34.
[69] See U.N.Doc. ST/LEG/SER.D/4, pp. 66–69.
[70] *Ibid*. pp. 69–70.
[71] *Ibid*. p. 68.

CHAPTER 10

THE LAW OF TREATIES

1. *INTRODUCTORY NOTE*[1]

THE special importance of the law of treaties in international law scarcely needs emphasis. The treaty is the ubiquitous instrument through which all kinds of international transactions are conducted. It is also the closest analogy to legislation that international law has to offer. Although fast being challenged in this latter role by the General Assembly resolution, the multilateral treaty remains the best medium available at the moment for imposing binding rules of precision and detail in the new areas into which international law is expanding[2] and for codifying, clarifying and supplementing the customary law already in existence in more familiar settings.

Given the extent to which treaties have long been woven into the fabric of international law, it is more than a little disappointing to find that the law governing them is in no happier a position than that of most other areas of customary international law. Whereas some rules are clear, a high proportion of them are not. In this situation, the adoption of the Vienna Convention on the Law of Treaties[3] in 1969 is particularly welcome. Like a number of other law making treaties in recent years, it is based upon Draft Articles, supplemented by an invaluable Commentary, produced by the International Law Commission.[4] Like those Conventions also, it is a compound of codification and of progressive development of customary international law.

Although the Convention does not have retroactive effect,[5] the materials in this chapter are moulded around it. This is so because of the great impact that the Convention, which was adopted by 79 votes to 1, with 19 abstentions,[6] is already having in

---

[1] See Detter, *Essays on the Law of Treaties* (1967); Elias, *The Modern Law of Treaties* (1974); Sinclair, *The Vienna Convention on the Law of Treaties* (1973); and McNair, *Treaties*. The last of these is the standard work on the subject.

[2] See the extract from Friedmann's *The Changing Structure of International Law*, above, p. 19.

[3] U.K.T.S. No. 58 (1980), Cmnd. 7964; 8 I.L.M. 679 (1969); 63 A.J.I.L. 875 (1969). In force 1980. As at December 31, 1981, there were 40 contracting states, including the U.K. The Convention was adopted on May 22, 1969, by the United Nations Conference on the Law of Treaties held at Vienna in two sessions in 1968 and 1969. See *U.N. Conference on the Law of Treaties, First and Second Sessions, 1968 and 1969, Official Records*, U.N. Docs. A/Conf. 39/11 and Add. 1. (These are referred to in this chapter as *Treaty Conference Records*, 1968, 1969.)

[4] For the text of the Draft Articles and the Commentary, see Y.B.I.L.C., 1966, II, pp. 177–274; 61 A.J.I.L. 263–463 (1967). Also of great value are the reports presented to the I.L.C. by its four Special Rapporteurs, who were, in chronological order, Brierly, Lauterpacht, Fitzmaurice and Waldock. The reports are printed in the *Yearbooks* of the I.L.C. On the Vienna Conference and Convention, see Kearney and Dalton, 64 A.J.I.L. 495 (1970); Rosenne, *The Law of Treaties: A Guide to the Legislative History of the Vienna Convention* (1970); Sinclair, 19 I.C.L.Q. 47 (1970). See also Rosenne, 41 Washington L.R. 261 (1966).

[5] Art. 4 of the Convention reads: "Without prejudice to the application of any rules set forth in the present Convention to which treaties would be subject under international law independently of the Convention, the Convention applies only to treaties which are concluded by States after the entry into force of the present Convention with regard to such States." Does this mean that it does not apply to the Vienna Convention itself?

[6] *Treaty Conference Records*, 1969, pp. 206–207. France dissented. It objected to the provisions on *jus cogens* and the procedures providing for the settlement of disputes: *ibid.* p. 203. A lot of the abstentions were by members of the Soviet bloc who objected to the failure of the Convention to adopt the principle of universality of participation in multilateral law-making treaties. They felt that all states should be entitled to participate in such treaties: *ibid.*

reinforcing and advancing customary international law.[7] Most of the law of treaties is "lawyers' law" over which the political interests of states do not clash. In this situation, and although certain doctrinal legal disputes (*e.g.* that on treaty interpretation) exist, the common interest of states in having a coherent, detailed and workable set of rules for their day-to-day international transactions has enhanced the attractiveness of the rules conveniently set out in the Convention. Less certain is the likely effect of the solutions offered by the Convention to the relatively few politically controversial questions concerning the substantive rules of the law of treaties (*e.g.* those concerning the doctrines of "unequal treaties" and *jus cogens*).

2. GENERAL CONSIDERATIONS

McNAIR, THE FUNCTIONS AND DIFFERING LEGAL CHARACTER OF TREATIES

(1930) 11 B.Y.I.L. 100. Footnotes omitted

The internal laws of the modern state provide its members with a variety of legal instruments for the regulation of life within that community: the contract; the conveyance or assignment of immovable or movable property, which may be made for valuable consideration or may be a gift or an exchange; the gratuitous promise clothed in a particular form; the charter or private Act of Parliament creating a corporation; legislation, which may be constituent, such as a written constitution, fragmentary or complete, or may be declaratory of existing law, or create new law, or codify existing law with comparatively unimportant changes. Further, though rarely, we may find a constitutional document which closely resembles the international treaty itself, for instance, Magna Carta.

It would not be suggested that all these differing private law transactions are governed by rules of universal or even of general application, and yet such is the underlying assumption of international lawyers in dealing with the only and sadly overworked instrument with which international society is equipped for the purpose of carrying out its multifarious transactions. Thus, if international society wishes to enact a fundamental, organic, constitutional law, such as the Covenant of the League of Nations was intended to be and in large measure is in fact, it employs the treaty. If two states wish to put on record their adherence to the principle of the three-mile limit of territorial waters, as in the first article of the Anglo-American Liquor Convention of 1924, they use a treaty. If further they wish to enter into a bargain which derogates from that principle, again they use a treaty. If Denmark wishes to sell to the United States of America her West

pp. 204–208. The Soviet bloc was concerned, for example, with the position of East Germany, Mainland China, North Korea and North Vietnam, which were not invited to Vienna. The Vienna Convention itself is open "for signature by all States, Members of the United Nations or of any of the specialised agencies or of the International Atomic Energy Agency or parties to the Statute of the International Court of Justice, and by any other state invited by the General Assembly of the United Nations to become a party to the Convention. . ." (Convention, Art. 81). Some other abstentions were based on the inadequacy of the procedures providing for the settlement of disputes: *ibid.*

[7] Note the reliance already placed upon the Convention by the I.C.J. in the *Namibia Case*, above, p. 106, and the *Fisheries Jurisdiction Cases*, below, p. 624, and by the law officers of the Crown in 1971 in connection with the Simonstown Agreements. The law officers stated that the "rules of international law for the interpretation of treaties have recently been declared in the Vienna Convention . . . ": Cmnd. 4589, p. 15.

Indian possessions, as she did in 1916, or if Great Britain wishes to cede Heligoland to Germany in return for a recognition of certain British rights in Africa, as happened in 1890, they do so by treaty. Again, if the great European Powers are engaged upon one of their periodic resettlements and determine upon certain permanent dispositions to which they wish to give the force of "the public law of Europe," they must do it by treaty. And if it is desired to create an international organization such as the International Union for the Protection of Works of Art and Literature, which resembles the corporation of private law, it is done by treaty.

Note

The above extract serves to illustrate the variety of purposes for which treaties are used and to raise the question, with which the author was concerned, of the problems that result for the law of treaties in having a single body of rules that covers all types of treaties. The question is one that needs to be borne in mind when reading the materials in the remainder of this chapter.

VIENNA CONVENTION ON THE LAW OF TREATIES 1969

Loc. cit. at p. 563, n. 3, above

Article 1

The present Convention applies to treaties between States.

Article 2

1. For the purposes of the present Convention:

   (a) "treaty" means an international agreement concluded between States in written form and governed by international law, whether embodied in a single instrument or in two or more related instruments and whatever its particular designation; . . .

Article 3

The fact that the present Convention does not apply to international agreements concluded between States and other subjects of international law or between such other subjects of international law, or to international agreements not in written form, shall not affect:

   (*a*) the legal force of such agreements;
   (*b*) the application to them of any of the rules set forth in the present Convention to which they would be subject under international law independently of the Convention;
   (*c*) the application of the Convention to the relations of States as between themselves under international agreements to which other subjects of international law are also parties.

Article 5

The present Convention applies to any treaty which is the constituent instrument of an international organization and to any treaty adopted within an international organization without prejudice to any relevant rules of the organization.

Article 6

Every State possesses capacity to conclude treaties.

Notes

1. *Capacity to make treaties.* The Convention reflects customary international law in providing that *states* may make treaties. Capacity to make treaties is, in fact, valuable evidence of statehood.[8] According to the International Law Commission's Commentary, the term "state" is used in Article 6 "with the same meaning as in the Charter of the United Nations, the Statute of the Court, the Geneva Convention on Diplomatic Relations; *i.e.* it means a State for the purposes of international law."[9]

The International Law Commission's Draft Articles contained a second paragraph to Article 6 concerning *federal states* which read as follows:

> States members of a federal union may possess a capacity to conclude treaties if such capacity is admitted by the federal constitution and within the limits there laid down.[10]

The Commentary to it reads:

> More frequently, the treaty-making capacity is vested exclusively in the federal government, but there is no rule of international law which precludes the component States from being invested with the power to conclude treaties with third States. Questions may arise in some cases as to whether the component State concludes the treaty as an organ of the federal State or in its own right. But on this point also the solution must be sought in the provisions of the federal constitution.[11]

Examples of federal states in which units within the federation have the power to make treaties are the Federal Republic of Germany[12] and the U.S.S.R.[13] The final text of the Vienna Convention omitted this paragraph. The difficulty it presented, which was mentioned by several delegations from federal states, was that the Vienna Convention had been limited to treaties made by "states" and had excluded those made by other subjects of international law. It was therefore, it was thought, inconsistent to include a provision concerning units within a federal state which "even if the law conferred upon them a certain capacity to conclude international agreements . . . could not be assimilated in general to States. . . . "[14]

Occasionally *colonial and similar territories* on their way to independence have been recognised as having treaty-making powers. Some former British Colonies have been in this position.[15] Thus Australia, Canada, India, New Zealand and South Africa were

---

[8] See above, pp. 80 *et seq.*

[9] Y.B.I.L.C., 1966, II, p. 192. See on federal states, Di Marzo, 16 C.Y.B.I.L. 197 (1978).

[10] Y.B.I.L.C., 1966, II, p. 191.

[11] *Ibid.* p. 192.

[12] Art. 32(3) of the Bonn Constitution reads: "Insofar as the Länder have power to legislate, they may, with the consent of the Federal Government, conclude treaties with foreign states." Thus, for example, the *Länder* of Baden-Wurttemberg and Bavaria are parties with Austria and Switzerland to a "Convention for the Protection of Lake Constance against Pollution of 27th October, 1960," printed as Appendix 7 in *Fresh Water Pollution Control*, Council of Europe, 1966.

[13] See above, p. 86.

[14] Mr. Groepper (West Germany), *Treaty Conference Records* (1969), p. 8. See the discussion generally, *ibid.* pp. 6–15.

[15] See Fawcett, *The British Commonwealth in International Law* (1963), pp. 144 *et seq.*

invited to participate in the Peace Conference at Paris in 1919 and became parties to the Treaty of Versailles and founder members of the League of Nations.

The decision not to extend the Vienna Convention to treaties to which *public international organisations* are parties was explained by the International Law Commission in its Commentary as follows:

> Treaties concluded by international organisations have many special characteristics; and the Commissions considered that it would both unduly complicate and delay the drafting of the present articles if it were to attempt to include in them satisfactory provisions concerning treaties of international organisations.[16]

Article 3 of the Vienna Convention, however, recognises that at customary international law entities other than states may have the international personality necessary to allow them to make treaties.

Individuals have never been recognised as having the capacity to make treaties, whether with states, with other individuals, or with other international persons with treaty-making capacity. The question has in recent years been discussed in the context of agreements between large municipal law companies and states, particularly agreements for the exploitation of oil. The nearest that the International Court of Justice has come to considering the question was in the *Anglo-Iranian Oil Company Case*[17] in which it rejected an argument to the effect that a contract between Iran and the Anglo-Iranian Oil Company, a British company, was a treaty because of the part played by the United Kingdom Government in its negotiation. The Court stated:

> It is nothing more than a concessionary contract between a government and a foreign corporation.[18]

Was the Mandate for South West Africa a treaty?[19] Are declarations accepting the compulsory jurisdiction of the International Court of Justice?[20]

2. *Intention to create legal relations.* This requirement, which is found in the law of contract in municipal law, is not mentioned in the Vienna Convention. The International Law Commission's Fourth Special Rapporteur stated that:

> in so far as this [requirement] may be relevant in any case, the element of intention is embraced in the phrase "governed by international law."[21]

States not infrequently wish to reach an agreement as to policy without going to the extent of making it enforceable at law. The Cairo Declaration of 1943,[22] signed by Churchill, Roosevelt and Chiang Kai-shek is probably an example. The signatories state:

> It is their purpose that . . . all the territories Japan has stolen from the Chinese, such as Manchuria, Formosa and the Pescadores, shall be restored to the Republic of China.

When asked in Parliament in 1958 if it was still the Government's policy to give effect to the Declaration, the British Foreign Secretary described the Declaration in his reply as "merely a statement of common purpose,"[23] implying its lack of legal effect.[24] The

---

[16] Y.B.I.L.C., 1965, II, p. 187. See also Chiu, *The Capacity of International Organisations to Conclude Treaties* (1966). And see the *Reparation Case,* above, p. 114.

[17] I.C.J.Rep. 1952, p. 93.

[18] *Ibid.* p. 112. See further on such contracts, above, pp. 433 *et seq.*

[19] See the *Namibia Case* (para. 94) above, p. 107.

[20] See below, p. 720.

[21] Fourth Report on the Law of Treaties, Y.B.I.L.C., 1965, II, p. 12. On the law governing a treaty, see below, p. 568.

[22] 154 B.F.S.P. 363 (1949); 38 A.J.I.L., Suppl., 8 (1944).

[23] *Hansard*, H.C., Vol. 595, col. 1140. November 19, 1958.

[24] See 7 U.K.C.P.I.L., in 8 I.C.L.Q. 146 at p. 186 (1959).

Final Act of the Helsinki Conference on Security and Co-operation in Europe 1975[25] is another example. The Act was stated to be "not eligible for registration under Article 102 of the Charter of the United Nations."[26] It was understood during the Conference that the Act would not be binding in law.[27]

On the question whether intention to create legal relations is to be presumed when agreements are made between states, contrast the views of Fawcett[28] and Mann.[29]

3. *"Governed by international law."* The International Law Commission's Fourth Special Rapporteur stated in his First Report[30]:

> . . . The Commission felt in 1959 that the element of subjection to international law is so essential a part of an international agreement that it should be expressly mentioned in the definition. There may be agreements between States, such as agreements for the acquisition of premises for a diplomatic mission or for some purely commercial transaction, the incidents of which are regulated by the local law of one of the parties or by a private law system determined by reference to conflict of laws principles. Whether in such cases the two States are internationally accountable to each other at all may be a nice question; but even if that were held to be so, it would not follow that the basis of their international accountability was a treaty obligation. At any rate, the Commission was clear that it ought to confine the notion of an "international agreement" for the purposes of the law of treaties to one the whole formation and execution of which (as well as the obligation to execute) is governed by international law.

Article 2 of the Vienna Convention does not indicate the test to be used in determining whether an agreement between states is governed by international law. What should be the test? The intention of the parties? The subject-matter of the agreement? Should there be a presumption that an inter-state agreement which is intended to create legal relations is governed by international law?[31]

4. *Nomenclature.* The Vienna Convention adopts the term "treaty," not the term "agreement," as the generic term. In practice, a whole host of terms are used interchangeably with no legal significance turning upon the choice of one or another. The International Law Commission's Commentary reads:

> Thus, in addition to "treaty," "convention" and "protocol," one not infrequently finds titles such as "declaration," "charter," "covenant," "pact," "act," "statute," "agreement," "concordat," whilst names like "declaration," "agreement" and *"modus vivendi"* may well be found given both to formal and less formal types of agreements. As to the latter, their nomenclature is almost illimitable, even if some names such as "agreement," "exchange of notes," "exchange of letters," "memorandum of agreement," or "agreed minute" may be more common than others. It is true that some types of instruments are used more frequently for some purposes rather than others; it is also true that some titles are more frequently attached to some types of transaction rather than to others. But there is no exclusive or systematic use of nomenclature for particular types of transaction.[32]

"Exchange of notes" and "Exchange of letters" take the form of an exchange of correspondence between states that often reads not unlike the offer and acceptance

---

[25] 14 I.L.M. 1292 (1975).   [26] Final (unnumbered) clauses.

[27] Russell, 70 A.J.I.L. 242 at p. 246 (1977). And see Schachter, 71 *ibid.* p. 296. See generally on such documents, Johnson (1959) 35 B.Y.I.L. I.

[28] (1953) 30 B.Y.I.L. 381 at pp. 385–400 (no presumption).

[29] (1957) 33 B.Y.I.L. 20 at pp. 30–32 (there is a presumption). See also Widdows (1979) 50 B.Y.I.L. 117.

[30] Y.B.I.L.C., 1962, II, p. 32.

[31] See Mann (1944) 21 B.Y.I.L. 11 at pp. 22–28; *id.* 68 A.J.I.L. 490 (1974); and Widdows, *loc. cit.* at n. 29 above.

[32] Y.B.I.L.C., 1966, II, 188.

letters familiar to any student of the law of contract. A treaty may also take the form of a joint communiqué issued by Government Ministers to the press at the end of a meeting, provided the necessary intention to enter into legal relations is present.[33]

5. *Consideration*. Treaties do not require consideration in the sense of the common law of contract. Territory, for example, can be ceded by treaty without consideration.

LEGAL STATUS OF EASTERN GREENLAND

Denmark *v.* Norway (1933)

P.C.I.J. Reports, Series A/B, No. 53

In addition to claiming sovereignty over Greenland in this case on the basis of occupation (see the summary above, p. 162), Denmark also argued that Norway had recognised Danish sovereignty over the island by the "Ihlen Declaration." M. Ihlen was the Norwegian Foreign Minister. In conversations on July 14, 1919, with the Danish Minister accredited to Norway, the latter suggested to M. Ihlen that Denmark would raise no objection to any claim Norway might want to make at the Paris Peace Conference to Spitzbergen if Norway would not oppose the claim that Denmark was to make at the same Conference to the whole of Greenland. On July 22, 1919, M. Ihlen, in the course of further conversations with the Danish Minister, declared that "the Norwegian Government would not make any difficulty" concerning the Danish claim. These were the terms used as they were minuted by M. Ihlen for his government's own purposes. Denmark argued before the Court that this undertaking was binding upon Norway. Judge Anzilotti; agreed with the Court on this point.

Judgment of the Court

This declaration by M. Ihlen has been relied on by Counsel for Denmark as a recognition of an existing Danish sovereignty in Greenland. The Court is unable to accept this point of view. A careful examination of the words used and of the circumstances in which they were used, as well as of the subsequent developments, shows that M. Ihlen cannot have meant to be giving then and there a definitive recognition of Danish sovereignty over Greenland, and shows also that he cannot have been understood by the Danish Government at the time as having done so. In the text of M. Ihlen's minute, submitted by the Norwegian Government, which has not been disputed by the Danish Government, the phrase used by M. Ihlen is couched in the future tense: "ne fera pas de difficultés"; he had been informed that it was at the Peace Conference that the Danish Government intended to bring up the question: and two years later—when assurances had been received from the Principal Allied Powers—the Danish Government made a further application to the Norwegian Government to obtain the recognition which they desired of Danish sovereignty over all Greenland.

Nevertheless, the point which must now be considered is whether the Ihlen declaration—even if not constituting a definitive recognition of Danish sovereignty—did not constitute an engagement obliging Norway to refrain from occupying any part of Greenland.

. . . It is clear from the relevant Danish documents which preceded the Danish Minister's démarche at Christiania on July 14th, 1919, that the Danish

[33] *Aegean Sea Case*, I.C.J. Rep. 1978, p. 39. It does not matter that, as in that case, the communiqué is not signed or initialled.

attitude in the Spitzbergen question and the Norwegian attitude in the Greenland question were regarded in Denmark as interdependent, and this interdependence appears to be reflected also in M. Ihlen's minute of the interview. Even if this interdependence—which, in view of the affirmative reply of the Norwegian Government, in whose name the Minister for Foreign Affairs was speaking, would have created a bilateral engagement—is not held to have been established, it can hardly be denied that what Denmark was asking of Norway ("not to make any difficulties in the settlement of the [Greenland] question") was equivalent to what she was indicating her readiness to concede in the Spitzbergen question (to refrain from opposing "the wishes of Norway in regard to the settlement of this question"). What Denmark desired to obtain from Norway was that the latter should do nothing to obstruct the Danish plans in regard to Greenland. The declaration which the Minister for Foreign Affairs gave on July 22nd, 1919, on behalf of the Norwegian Government, was definitely affirmative: "I told the Danish Minister today that the Norwegian Government would not make any difficulty in the settlement of this question."

The Court considers it beyond all dispute that a reply of this nature given by the Minister of Foreign Affairs on behalf of his Government in response to request by the diplomatic representative of a foreign Power, in regard to a question falling within his province, is binding upon the country to which the Minister belongs. . . .

It follows that, as a result of the undertaking involved in the Ihlen declaration of July 22, 1919, Norway is under an obligation to refrain from contesting Danish sovereignty over Greenland as a whole, and *a fortiori* to refrain from occupying a part of Greenland.

DISSENTING OPINION OF JUDGE ANZILOTTI. No arbitral or judicial decision relating to the international competence of a Minister for Foreign Affairs has been brought to the knowledge of the Court; nor has this question been exhaustively treated by legal authorities. In my opinion, it must be recognized that the constant and general practice of States has been to invest the Minister for Foreign Affairs—the direct agent of the chief of the State—with authority to make statements on current affairs to foreign diplomatic representatives, and in particular to inform them as to the attitude which the government, in whose name he speaks, will adopt in a qiven question. Declarations of this kind are binding upon the State.

As regards the question whether Norwegian constitutional law authorized the Minister for Foreign Affairs to make the declaration, that is a point which, in my opinion, does not concern the Danish Government: it was M. Ihlen's duty to refrain from giving his reply until he had obtained any assent that might be requisite under the Norwegian laws.

Notes

1. Was there an oral treaty in the *Eastern Greenland Case*?[34] If not, why was M. Ihlen's declaration binding?

2. The Vienna Convention was limited to written treaties "in the interest of clarity and simplicity."[35] The International Law Commission's Commentary reads: "The

---

[34] See Garner, 27 A.J.I.L. 493 (1933); Hambro, *Festschrift Spiropoulos* (1957), p. 227; McNair, *Treaties*, p. 10.

[35] Y.B.I.L.C., 1966, II, p. 189.

restriction of the use of the term "treaty" in the draft articles to international agreements expressed in writing is not intended to deny the legal force of oral agreements under international law or to imply that some of the principles contained in later parts of the Commission's draft articles . . . may not have relevance in regard to oral agreements."[36]

3. On the relevance of non-compliance with municipal law requirements, see below, p. 610.

NUCLEAR TEST CASES

Australia *v*. France; New Zealand *v*. France

I.C.J. Reports 1974, pp. 253, 457.

For the facts, see above, p. 322. The Court found, by nine votes to six,[37] that "the claim of Australia no longer has any object and that the Court is therefore not called upon to give a decision thereon." The Court reached this conclusion because France had indicated its intention not to hold any further tests in the atmosphere in the South Pacific after its 1974 series of tests. It gave this undertaking by way of a series of unilateral public announcements in that year. The Court considered the legal significance of these statements in the following passage in the judgment in the Australian case. The companion case brought by New Zealand against France resulted in a similar ruling.

Judgment of the Court

34. . . . The first statement is contained in the communiqué issued by the Office of the President of the French Republic on 8 June 1974 . . .

The Office of the President of the Republic takes this opportunity of stating that in view of the stage reached in carrying out the French nuclear defence programme France will be in a position to pass on to the stage of underground explosions as soon as the series of tests planned for this summer is completed.

A copy of the communiqué was transmitted with a Note dated 11 June 1974 from the French Embassy in Canberra to the Australian Department of Foreign Affairs . . .

35. . . . At the hearing of 10 July 1974 in [. . . the New Zealand] case, the Attorney-General of New Zealand . . . stated that on 10 June 1974 the French Embassy in Wellington sent a Note to the New Zealand Ministry of Foreign Affairs, containing a [similar] passage . . .

37. The next statement to be considered . . . will be that made on 25 July at a press conference given by the President of the Republic, when he said:

. . . on this question of nuclear tests, you know that the Prime Minister has publicly expressed himself in the National Assembly in his speech introducing the Government's programme. He had indicated that French nuclear testing would continue. I had myself made it clear that this round of

---

[36] *Ibid*.

[37] The judges in the majority were President Lachs; Judges Forster, Gros, Bengzon, Petrén, Ignacio-Pinto, Morozov, Nagendra Singh, and Ruda. The dissenting judges were Judges Onyeama, Dillard, de Castro, Jiménez de Aréchaga, Sir Humphrey Waldock; Judge ad hoc Sir Garfield Barwick.

atmospheric tests would be the last, and so the members of the Government were completely informed of our intentions in this respect . . .

39. On 25 September 1974, the French Minister for Foreign Affairs, addressing the United Nations General Assembly, said:

We have now reached a stage in our nuclear technology that makes it possible for us to continue our programme by underground testing, and we have taken steps to do so as early as next year.

The French Minister of Defence made similar statements on French television and at a press conference.

43. It is well recognized that declarations made by way of unilateral acts, concerning legal or factual situations, may have the effect of creating legal obligations. Declarations of this kind may be, and often are, very specific. When it is the intention of the State making the declaration that it should become bound according to its terms, that intention confers on the declaration the character of a legal undertaking, the State being thenceforth legally required to follow a course of conduct consistent with the declaration. An undertaking of this kind, if given publicly, and with an intent to be bound, even though not made within the context of international negotiations, is binding. In these circumstances, nothing in the nature of a *quid pro quo* nor any subsequent acceptance of the declaration, nor even any reply or reaction from other States, is required for the declaration to take effect, since such a requirement would be inconsistent with the strictly unilateral nature of the juridical act by which the pronouncement by the State was made.

44. Of course, not all unilateral acts imply obligation; but a State may choose to take up a certain position in relation to a particular matter with the intention of being bound—the intention is to be ascertained by interpretation of the act. When States make statements by which their freedom of action is to be limited, a restrictive interpretation is called for.

45. With regard to the question of form, it should be observed that this is not a domain in which international law imposes any special or strict requirements. Whether a statement is made orally or in writing makes no essential difference, for such statements made in particular circumstances may create commitments in international law, which does not require that they should be couched in written form . . .

46. One of the basic principles governing the creation and performance of legal obligations, whatever their source, is the principle of good faith. Trust and confidence are inherent in international co-operation, in particular in an age when this co-operation in many fields is becoming increasingly essential. Just as the very rule of *pacta sunt servanda* in the law of treaties is based on good faith, so also is the binding character of an international obligation assumed by unilateral declaration. Thus interested States may take cognizance of unilateral declarations and place confidence in them, and are entitled to require that the obligation thus created be respected . . .

49. Of the statements by the French Government now before the Court, the most essential are clearly those made by the President of the Republic. There can be no doubt, in view of his functions, that his public communications or statements, oral or written, as Head of State, are in international relations acts of the French State. His statements, and those of members of the French

Government acting under his authority . . . constitute a whole. Thus, in whatever form these statements were expressed, they must be held to constitute an engagement of the State, having regard to their intention and to the circumstances in which they were made . . .

51. In announcing that the 1974 series of atmospheric tests would be the last, the French Government conveyed to the world at large, including the Applicant, its intention effectively to terminate these tests. It was bound to assume that other States might take note of these statements and rely on their being effective. The validity of these statements and their legal consequences must be considered within the general framework of the security of international intercourse, and the confidence and trust which are so essential in the relations among States. It is from the actual substance of these statements, and from the circumstances attending their making, that the legal implications of the unilateral act must be deduced. The objects of these statements are clear and they were addressed to the international community as a whole, and the Court holds that they constitute an undertaking possessing legal effect. . . . It is true that the French Government has consistently maintained, for example in a Note dated 7 February 1973 from the French Ambassador in Canberra to the Prime Minister and Minister for Foreign Affairs of Australia, that it "has the conviction that its nuclear experiments have not violated any rule of international law," nor did France recognize that it was bound by any rule of international law to terminate its tests, but this does not affect the legal consequences of the statements examined above. The Court finds that the unilateral undertaking resulting from these statements cannot be interpreted as having been made in implicit reliance on an arbitrary power of reconsideration. The Court finds further that the French Government has undertaken an obligation the precise nature and limits of which must be understood in accordance with the actual terms in which they have been publicly expressed.

DISSENTING OPINION OF JUDGE SIR GARFIELD BARWICK. . . . Nothing is found as to the duration of the obligation although nothing said in the Judgment would suggest that it is of a temporary nature. There are apparently no qualifications of it related to changes in circumstances or to the varying needs of French security. . . .

. . . The Judgment finds an intention to enter into a binding legal obligation after giving the warning that statements limiting a State's freedom of action should receive a restrictive interpretation . . . I regret to say that I am unable to do so. There seems to be nothing, either in the language used or in the circumstances of its employment, which in my opinion would warrant, and certainly nothing to compel, the conclusion that those making the statements were intending to enter into a solemn and far-reaching international obligation. . . . I would have thought myself that the more natural conclusion to draw from the various statements was that they were statements of policy. . . .

Note

Although the undertakings in the *Nuclear Tests Cases* could not by any stretch of the imagination be seen as other than unilateral, the cases are most conveniently dealt with in conjunction with the law of treaties. The undertakings were quite different from that in the *Eastern Greenland* case in being made in public, not in the context of negotiations, and without a *quid pro quo*. There seems little evidence to support the rule stated by the Court whereby a state may be bound by a unilateral public pronouncement intended by it to be binding without more.[38] If there is such a rule—and it remains to be seen whether the Court's judgment will act as a catalyst in this regard—it is submitted that further by way of evidence of intent should be required than was present on the facts of the *Nuclear Tests Cases*.

3. *THE MAKING OF TREATIES*[39]

(i) NOTE ON THE TREATY-MAKING POWER IN MUNICIPAL LAW[40]

Each state is left free by international law to make its own constitutional arrangements for the exercise of its treaty-making power. In the *United Kingdom*, the making of treaties is a prerogative power of the Crown. It is the Crown which issues full powers or other authority to negotiate and sign treaties and which ratifies treaties if this is called for. Approval by Parliament is not required.[41] British practice since 1890 concerning treaties of cession comes close to establishing an exception to this rule. McNair concludes from this practice that

> it is unlikely that the Crown will agree to cede any territory without being sure that Parliament would approve, or, if in doubt, without inserting a clause making the cession dependent upon Parliamentary approval.[42]

The Crown will occasionally, in its discretion, insert provisions in treaties making their entry into force conditional upon Parliament approval.[43] In 1924, the British Government announced the "Ponsonby Rule," as follows:

> It is the intention of His Majesty's Government to lay on the Table of both Houses of Parliament every Treaty, when signed, for a period of 21 days, after which the Treaty will be ratified and published and circulated in the Treaty Series. In the case of important Treaties, the Government will, of course, take an opportunity of submitting them to the House for discussion within this period. . . . But this means secret Treaties and secret clauses of Treaties will be rendered impossible. . . . There are, of course, international conventions of a purely technical character which are not subject to ratification, and there is no reason to alter the procedure with regard to them.[44]

The rule does not affect the position in law. The laying of a treaty before Parliament before ratification is only "to enable Parliament to discuss treaties requiring ratification before ratification [occurs]," it is not legally required. The Rule was discontinued after a change of government in the same year. It was re-introduced in 1929 and has normally applied ever since. It was not complied with in the case of the 1939 Treaty of Mutual Assistance between France, Turkey and the United Kingdom.[45] The Prime Minister explained:

> . . . in view of the exceptional circumstance of the present case, it is desired that the Anglo-French-Turkish Treaty should be ratified as soon as possible.[46]

---

[38] See Rubin, 71 A.J.I.L. 1 (1977). See also Franck, 69 A.J.I.L. 612 (1975).
[39] See generally, Blix, *Treaty-Making Power* (1960); Holloway, *Modern Trends in Treaty Law* (1967); Jones, *Full Powers and Ratification* (1949).
[40] On the status of treaties in municipal law, see above, Chap. 3.
[41] On the need, however, for parliamentary legislation if a treaty binding upon the U.K. in international law is to have effect in the municipal law of the U.K., see above, p. 68.
[42] McNair, *Treaties*, p. 97.
[43] See the examples given by McNair, *ibid.* pp. 97–98.
[44] *Hansard*, H.C., Vol. 171, cols 2003–2004. April 1, 1924.
[45] U.K.T.S. 4 (1940), Cmd. 6165; 213 B.F.S.P. 200; 200 L.N.T.S. 173.
[46] *Hansard*, H.C. Vol. 352, col. 1407. October 25, 1939.

The Rule has not been applied to the Declaration made by the United Kingdom accepting the compulsory jurisdiction of the International Court of Justice because there is no requirement of ratification.[47]

The *United States* Constitution, Article II, Section 2, states that the President "shall have power by and with the advice and consent of the Senate to make treaties, provided two-thirds of the Senators present concur. . . . " Distinct from "treaties" are "executive agreements." These are treaties in an international law sense but differ from "treaties" in United States constitutional law in that they are made by the President alone; they are not subject to approval by the United States Senate. There is no express provision for executive agreements in the Constitution; the power to make them is implied.[48]

(ii) THE TREATY-MAKING POWER IN INTERNATIONAL LAW[49]

McNAIR, THE LAW OF TREATIES

2nd ed., 1961, pp. 15–21. Some footnotes omitted

The following are the forms in which treaties are usually cast . . .

(*a*) *Treaties in the form of agreements between states.* Instances of this practice can be found in . . . the Treaty of Versailles and other Peace Treaties which concluded the First World War . . .

(*b*) *Treaties in the form of agreements between heads of state,* which may perhaps be described as historically the oldest, and, in practice, the most orthodox, form in the case of treaties of an important character. . . .

(*c*) *Agreements in the form of inter-governmental agreements.* This form is now becoming increasingly common, as a purusal of the United Nations Treaty Series will show. It is in keeping with the general tendency towards informality. For the United Kingdom it means that no intervention on the part of Her Majesty is required and no use of the Great Seal, and Full Powers are issued by the Secretary of State for Foreign Affairs under his own signature and seal of office. It has become the regular form for agreements made between the Commonwealth countries; its convenience in such cases is manifest. . . .

Most Exchanges of Notes, now very common, fall into the category of inter-governmental agreements.

It is broadly true to say that the United Kingdom Government prefers to reserve the inter-governmental form for agreements of secondary importance or of a non-political character, but that is becoming increasingly difficult. . . .

(*d*) *Agreements expressed as made between Departments, or ministers, or other subordinate organs or agencies of Governments.* The following extract from the *Laws and Practices concerning the Conclusions of Treaties*[50] states the practice of the United Kingdom in this matter:

6. As regards inter-departmental agreements (*i.e.* agreements concluded directly between the Government Departments of different States) these agreements are, generally speaking, arrangements which concern matters of private law rather than matters of an international legal character (*e.g.* arrangements for, or in connexion with, the purchase of goods, or for the sale on a commercial basis of materials or supplies) and are not such as would be normally registrable

---

[47] *Hansard*, H.C., Vol. 578, cols. 1145–1146. November 27, 1957.
[48] On the definition of executive agreements, see [1973] *U.S. D.I.L.* 185.
[49] See Parry, 36 Trans.Grot.Soc. 149 (1950).
[50] U.N. ST/LEG/SER.B/3 at p. 121.

under Article 102 of the Charter of the United Nations. An example of such an agreement is the Agreement of 29 August 1949 between the United Kingdom Minister of Food and the Norwegian Director of Fisheries regarding the landings of fresh white fish in the United Kingdom from Norwegian fishing vessels. This Agreement was signed, on the one part, by an Assistant Secretary to the Ministry of Food on behalf of the Minister of Food and, on the other part, by the Norwegian Director of Fisheries.

What is important, is that this practice must not be allowed to obscure the fact that the real contracting parties are States. . . .

It is, however, necessary in view of the complexity and variety of organs, central or local, through which functions of government (including sometimes commercial activities) are discharged in the modern State, to be alert to the difference between an organ or agency of the central Government and capable of binding it, on the one hand, and, on the other, an organ, whether local or not, which possesses a legal personality distinct from the State itself and has no such capacity. It is believed that it is true only of an organ or agency of the central Government to say that its agreements bind the State; but the precise relation of certain departments to the central Government varies greatly in different States, and every case requires separate consideration upon its facts.

VIENNA CONVENTION ON THE LAW OF TREATIES 1969

Loc. cit. at p. 563, n. 3, above

Article 7

1. A person is considered as representing a State for the purpose of adopting or authenticating the text of a treaty or for the purpose of expressing the consent of the State to be bound by a treaty if:

   (*a*) he produces appropriate full powers[51]; or
   (*b*) it appears from the practice of the States concerned or from other circumstances that their intention was to consider that person as representing the State for such purposes and to dispense with full powers.

2. In virtue of their functions and without having to produce full powers, the following are considered as representing their State:

   (*a*) Heads of State, Heads of Government and Ministers for Foreign Affairs,[52] for the purpose of performing all acts relating to the conclusion of a treaty;
   (*b*) heads of diplomatic missions, for the purpose of adopting the text of a treaty between the accrediting State and the State to which they are accredited;

---

[51] *Ed.* The term "full powers" is defined in Art. 2(1)(*c*) of the Convention as "a document emanating from the competent authority of a State designating a person or persons to represent the State for negotiating, adopting or authenticating the text of a treaty, for expressing the consent of the State to be bound by a treaty, or for accomplishing any other act with respect to a treaty."

[52] *Ed.* See the *Eastern Greenland Case*, above, p. 569.

(c) representatives accredited by States to an international conference or to an international organization or one of its organs, for the purpose of adopting the text of a treaty in that conference, organization or organ.

Note

The International Law Commission's Commentary reads:

. . . the production of full powers is the fundamental safeguard to the representatives of the States concerned of each other's qualifications to represent their State for the purpose of performing the particular act in question;
. . . it is for the States to decide whether they may safely dispense with the production of full powers. In earlier times the production of full powers was almost invariably requested; and it is still common in the conclusion of more formal types of treaty. But a considerable proportion of modern treaties are concluded in simplified form, when more often than not the production of full powers is not required.[53]

Article 8

An act relating to the conclusion of a treaty performed by a person who cannot be considered under Article 7 as authorized to represent a State for that purpose is without legal effect unless afterwards confirmed by that State.

Note

The International Law Commission's Commentary reads:

Such cases [of acting without authority] are not, of course, likely to happen frequently, but instances have occurred. . . . In 1951 a convention concerning the naming of cheeses concluded at Stresa was signed by a delegate on behalf of Norway and Sweden, whereas it appears that he had authority to do so only from the former country. In both these instances the treaty was subject to ratification and was in fact ratified. A further case, in which the same question may arise, and one more likely to occur in practice, is where an agent has authority to enter into a particular treaty, but goes beyond his full powers by accepting unauthorised extensions or modifications of it. An instance of such a case was Persia's attempt, in discussions in the Council of the League, to disavow the Treaty of Erzerum of 1847 on the ground that the Persian representative had gone beyond his authority in accepting a certain explanatory note when exchanging ratifications.
. . . Where there is no authority to enter into a treaty, it seems clear, on principle, that the State must be entitled to disavow the act of its representative, and the article so provides. On the other hand, it seems equally clear that, notwithstanding the representative's original lack of authority, the State may afterwards endorse his act and thereby establish its consent to be bound by the treaty. It will also be held to have done so by implication if it invokes the provisions of the treaty or otherwise acts in such a way as to appear to treat the act of its representative as effective.[54]

Article 9

1. The adoption of the text of a treaty takes place by the consent of all the States participating in its drawing up except as provided in paragraph 2.

2. The adoption of the text of a treaty at an international conference takes place by the vote of two-thirds of the States present and voting, unless by the same majority they shall decide to apply a different rule.

[53] Y.B.I.L.C., 1966, II, p. 193.
[54] *Ibid.* p. 194. See also Article 46, below, p. 610.

Note

The International Law Commission's Commentary reads:

> In former times the adoption of the text of a treaty almost always took place by the agreement of all the States participating in the negotiations and unanimity could be said to be the general rule. The growth of the practice of drawing up treaties in large international conferences or within international organisations has, however, led to so normal a use of the procedure of majority vote that, in the opinion of the Commission, it would be unrealistic to lay down unanimity as the general rule for the adoption of the texts of treaties drawn up at conferences or within organizations. Unanimity remains the general rule for bilateral treaties and for treaties drawn up between few States. But for other multilateral treaties a different general rule must be specified, although, of course, it will always be open to the States concerned to apply the rule of unanimity in a particular case if they should so decide. . . .
>
> The Commission considered the further case of treaties like the Genocide Convention or the Convention on the Political Rights of Women, which are actually drawn up within an international organisation. Here, the voting rule for adopting the text of the treaty must clearly be the voting rule applicable in the particular organ in which the treaty is adopted. This case is, however, covered by the general provision in . . . [Art. 5, Vienna Convention] regarding the application of the rules of an international organisation, and need not receive mention in the present article.[55] On the attempt to adopt the 1982 Law of the Sea Convention by consensus, see above, p. 286.

Article 11

The consent of a State to be bound by a treaty may be expressed by signature, exchange of instruments constituting a treaty, ratification, acceptance, approval or accession, or by any other means if so agreed.[56]

Article 12

1. The consent of a State to be bound by a treaty is expressed by the signature of its representative when:

(*a*) the treaty provides that signature shall have that effect;

(*b*) it is otherwise established that the negotiating States[57] were agreed that signature should have that effect; or

(*c*) the intention of the State to give that effect to the signature appears from the full powers of its representative or was expressed during the negotiation.

2. For the purposes of paragraph 1:

(*a*) the initialling of a text constitutes a signature of the treaty when it is established that the negotiating States so agreed;

(*b*) the signature *ad referendum* of a treaty by a representative, if confirmed by his State, constitutes a full signature of the treaty.

---

[55] *Ibid.*

[56] *Ed.* Art. 2(1)(*b*) reads: " 'ratification,' 'acceptance,' 'approval' and 'accession' mean in each case the international act so named whereby a State establishes on the international plane its consent to be bound by a treaty."

[57] *Ed.* Art. 2(1)(*e*) reads: "'negotiating State' means a State which took part in the drawing up and adoption of the text of the treaty."

Article 13

The consent of States to be bound by a treaty constituted by instruments exchanged between them is expressed by that exchange when:

(*a*) the instruments provide that their exchange shall have that effect; or
(*b*) it is otherwise established that those States were agreed that the exchange of instruments should have that effect.[58]

Article 14

1. The consent of a State to be bound by a treaty is expressed by ratification when:

(*a*) the treaty provides for such consent to be expressed by means of ratification;
(*b*) it is otherwise established that the negotiating States were agreed that ratification should be required;
(*c*) the representative of the State has signed the treaty subject to ratification; or
(*d*) the intention of the State to sign the treaty subject to ratification appears from the full powers of its representative or was expressed during the negotiation.

2. The consent of a State to be bound by a treaty is expressed by acceptance or approval under conditions similar to those which apply to ratification.

Note
The International Law Commission's Commentary reads:

The modern institution of ratification[59] in international law developed in the course of the nineteenth century. Earlier, ratification had been an essentially formal and limited act by which, after a treaty had been drawn up, a sovereign confirmed, or finally verified, the full powers previously issued to his representative to negotiate the treaty. It was then not an approval of the treaty itself but a confirmation that the representative had been invested with authority to negotiate it and, that being so, there was an obligation upon the sovereign to ratify his representative's full powers, if these had been in order. Ratification came, however, to be used in the majority of cases as the means of submitting the treaty-making power of the executive to parliamentary control, and ultimately the doctrine of ratification underwent a fundamental change. It was established that the treaty itself was subject to subsequent ratification by the State before it become binding. Furthermore, this development took place at a time when the great majority of international agreements were formal treaties. Not unnaturally, therefore, it came to be the opinion that the general rule is that ratification is necessary to render a treaty binding.
. . . Meanwhile, however, the expansion of intercourse between States, especially in economic and technical fields, led to an ever-increasing use of less formal types of international agreements, amongst which were exchanges of notes, and these agreements are usually intended by the parties to become binding by signature alone. On the other hand, an exchange of notes or other informal agreement, though employed for its ease and convenience, has sometimes expressly been made subject to ratification because of constitutional requirements in one or the other of the contracting States.

[58] *Ed*. See Weinstein (1952) 29 B.Y.I.L. 205.
[59] *Ed*. On ratification, see Blix (1953) 30 B.Y.I.L. 352

. . . The general result of these developments has been to complicate the law concerning the conditions under which treaties need ratification in order to make them binding. The controversy which surrounds the subject is, however, largely theoretical. The more formal types of instrument include, almost without exception, express provisions on the subject of ratification, and occasionally this is so even in the case of exchanges of notes or other instruments in simplified form. Moreover, whether they are of a formal or informal type, treaties normally either provide that the instrument shall be ratified or, by laying down that the treaty shall enter into force upon signature or upon a specified date or event, dispense with ratification. Total silence on the subject is exceptional, and the number of cases that remain to be covered by a general rule is very small. But, if the general rule is taken to be that ratification is necessary unless it is expressly or impliedly excluded, large exceptions qualifying a rule have to be inserted in order to bring it into accord with modern practice, with the result that the number of cases calling for the operation of the general rule is small. Indeed, the practical effect of choosing either that version of the general rule, or the opposite rule that ratification is unnecessary unless expressly agreed upon by the parties, is not very substantial. . . .

. . . Acceptance has become established in treaty practice during the past twenty years as a new procedure for becoming a party to treaties[60] . . . on the international plane, "acceptance" is an innovation which is more one of terminology than of method. If a treaty provides that it shall be open for signature "subject to acceptance," the process on the international plane is like "signature subject to ratification" . . .

. . . "Signature subject to acceptance" was introduced into treaty practice principally in order to provide a simplified form of "ratification" which would allow the government a further opportunity to examine the treaty when it is not necessarily obliged to submit it to a State's constitutional procedure for obtaining ratification. . . .

. . . The observations in the preceding paragraph apply *mutatis mutandis* to "approval," whose introduction into the terminology of treaty-making is even more recent than that of "acceptance."[61]

Article 15

The consent of a State to be bound by a treaty is expressed by accession when:

(*a*) the treaty provides that such consent may be expressed by that State by means of accession;

(*b*) it is otherwise established that the negotiating States were agreed that such consent may be expressed by that State by means of accession; or

(*c*) all the parties have subsequently agreed that such consent may be expressed by that State by means of accession.

Note

The International Law Commission's Commentary reads:

Accession is the traditional method by which a State, in certain circumstances, becomes a party to a treaty of which it is not a signatory . . .

Divergent opinions have been expressed in the past as to whether it is legally possible to accede to a treaty which is not yet in force and there is some support for the view that it is not possible. However, an examination of the most recent treaty

[60] *Ed.* See Liang, 44 A.J.I.L. 342 (1950).
[61] Y.B.I.L.C., 1966, II, pp. 197–198.

practice shows that in practically all modern treaties which contain accession clauses the right to accede is made independent of the entry into force of the treaty, either expressly by allowing accession to take place before the date fixed for the entry into force of the treaty, or impliedly by making the entry into force of the treaty conditional on the deposit, *inter alia*, of instruments of accession.[62]

Article 16

Unless the treaty otherwise provides, instruments of ratification, acceptance, approval or accession establish the consent of a State to be bound by a treaty upon:

(*a*) their exchange between the contracting States;
(*b*) their deposit with the depositary; or
(*c*) their notification to the contracting States or to the depositary, if so agreed.

Note

The International Law Commission's Commentary reads:

The point of importance is the moment at which the consent to be bound is established and in operation with respect to contracting States. In the case of exchange of instruments there is no problem; it is the moment of exchange. In the case of the deposit of an instrument with a depositary, the problem arises whether the deposit by itself establishes the legal nexus between the depositing State and other contracting States or whether the legal nexus arises only upon their being informed by the depositary. The Commission considered that the existing general rule clearly is that the act of deposit by itself establishes the legal nexus.[63]

Article 18

A State is obliged to refrain from acts which would defeat the object and purpose of a treaty when:

(*a*) it has signed the treaty or has exchanged instruments constituting the treaty subject to ratification, acceptance or approval, until it shall have made its intention clear not to become a party to the treaty; or
(*b*) it has expressed its consent to be bound by the treaty, pending the entry into force of the treaty and provided that such entry into force is not unduly delayed.

Note

The International Law Commission's Commentary reads:

That an obligation of good faith to refrain from acts calculated to frustrate the object of the treaty attaches to a State which has signed a treaty subject to ratification appears to be generally accepted.[64]

---

[62] *Ibid.* p. 199.
[63] *Ibid.* p. 201.
[64] *Ibid.* p. 202.

(iii) RESERVATIONS[65]

RESERVATIONS TO THE CONVENTION ON GENOCIDE CASE

Advisory Opinion. I.C.J. Reports 1951, p. 15

The Genocide Convention 1948[66] contains no reservations clause. A number of states made reservations and some doubt arose as to their effect. The General Assembly of the United Nations requested the opinion of the I.C.J. on the following questions: "In so far as concerns the Convention on the Prevention and Punishment of the Crime of Genocide in the event of a State ratifying or acceding to the Convention subject to a reservation made either on ratification or on accession, or on signature followed by ratification:

    I Can the reserving State be regarded as being a party to the Convention while still maintaining its reservations if the reservation is objected to by one or more of the parties to the Convention but not by others?

    II If the answer to Question I is in the affirmative, what is the effect of the reservation as between the reserving State and:

      (*a*) The parties which object to the reservation?

      (*b*) Those which accept it?

    III What would be the legal effect as regards the answer to Question I if an objection to a reservation is made:

      (*a*) By a signatory which has not yet ratified?

      (*b*) By a State entitled to sign or accede but which has not yet done so?"

Opinion of the Court

It is well established that in its treaty relations a State cannot be bound without its consent, and that consequently no reservation can be effective against any State without its agreement thereto. It is also a generally recognized principle that a multilateral convention is the result of an agreement freely concluded upon its clauses and that consequently none of the contracting parties is entitled to frustrate or impair, by means of unilateral decisions or particular agreements, the purpose and *raison d'être* of the convention. To this principle was linked the notion of the integrity of the convention as adopted, a notion which in its traditional concept involved the proposition that no reservation was valid unless it was accepted by all the contracting parties without exception, as would have been the case if it had been stated during the negotiations.

This concept, which is directly inspired by the notion of contract, is of undisputed value as a principle. However, as regards the Genocide Convention, it is proper to refer to a variety of circumstances which would lead to a more flexible application of this principle. Among these circumstances may be noted the clearly universal character of the United Nations under whose auspices the Convention was concluded, and the very wide degree of participation envisaged by Article XI of the Convention. Extensive participation in conventions of this type has already given rise to greater flexibility in the international practice concerning multilateral conventions. More general resort

---

[65] See Anderson, 13 I.C.L.Q. 450 (1964); Bishop, 103 *Hague Recueil* 245 (1961–II); Bowett (1976–7) 48 B.Y.I.L. 67; Fitzmaurice, 2 I.C.L.Q. 1 (1953); Gamble, 74 A.J.I.L. 372 (1980); Szucki, 20 German Y.B.I.L. 277 (1977); Tomuschat, 27 Z.A.O.R.V. 463 (1967).

[66] See above, p. 561.

to reservations, very great allowance made for tacit assent to reservations, the existence of practices which go so far as to admit that the author of reservations which have been rejected by certain contracting parties is nevertheless to be regarded as a party to the convention in relation to those contracting parties that have accepted the reservations—all these factors are manifestations of a new need for flexibility in the operation of multilateral conventions.

It must also be pointed out that although the Genocide Convention was finally approved unanimously, it is nevertheless the result of a series of majority votes. The majority principle, while facilitating the conclusion of multilateral conventions, may also make it necessary for certain States to make reservations. This observation is confirmed by the great number of reservations which have been made of recent years to multilateral conventions.

In this state of international practice, it could certainly not be inferred from the absence of an article providing for reservations in a multilateral convention that the contracting States are prohibited from making certain reservations. Account should also be taken of the fact that the absence of such an article or even the decision not to insert such an article can be explained by the desire not to invite a multiplicity of reservations. The character of a multilateral convention, its purpose, provisions, mode of preparation and adoption, are factors which must be considered in determining, in the absence of any express provision on the subject, the possibility of making reservations, as well as their validity and effect. . . .

The Court recognizes that an understanding was reached within the General Assembly on the faculty to make reservations to the Genocide Convention and that it is permitted to conclude therefrom that States becoming parties to the Convention gave their assent thereto. It must now determine what kind of reservations may be made and what kind of objections may be taken to them.

. . . The origins of the Convention show that it was the intention of the United Nations to condemn and punish genocide as "a crime under international law" involving a denial of the right of existence of entire human groups, a denial which shocks the conscience of mankind and results in great losses to humanity, and which is contrary to moral law and to the spirit and aims of the United Nations (Resolution 96 (1) of the General Assembly, December 11th 1946). The first consequence arising from this conception is that the principles underlying the Convention are principles which are recognized by civilized nations as binding on States, even without any conventional obligation. A second consequence is the universal character both of the condemnation of genocide and of the co-operation required "in order to liberate mankind from such an odious scourge" (Preamble to the Convention). The Genocide Convention was therefore intended by the General Assembly and by the contracting parties to be definitely universal in scope. It was in fact approved on December 9th, 1948, by a resolution which was unanimously adopted by fifty-six States.

The objects of such a convention must also be considered. The Convention was manifestly adopted for a purely humanitarian and civilizing purpose. . . . In such a convention the contracting States do not have any interests of their own; they merely have, one and all, a common interest, namely, the accomplishment of those high purposes which are the *raison d'être* of the convention. Consequently, in a convention of this type one cannot speak of individual advantages or disadvantages to States, or of the maintenance of a perfect contractual balance between rights and duties. . . .

The object and purpose of the Genocide Convention imply that it was the intention of the General Assembly and of the States which adopted it that as many States as possible should participate. The complete exclusion from the Convention of one or more States would not only restrict the scope of its application, but would detract from the authority of the moral and humanitarian principles which are its basis. It is inconceivable that the contracting parties readily contemplated that an objection to a minor reservation should produce such a result. But even less could the contracting parties have intended to sacrifice the very object of the Convention in favour of a vain desire to secure as many participants as possible. The object and purpose of the Convention thus limit both the freedom of making reservations and that of objecting to them. It follows that it is the compatibility of a reservation with the object and purpose of the Convention that must furnish the criterion for the attitude of a State in making the reservation on accession as well as for the appraisal by a State in objecting to the reservation. . . .

. . . it has been argued that there exists a rule of international law subjecting the effect of a reservation to the express or tacit assent of all the contracting parties. . . .

It does not appear . . . that the conception of the absolute integrity of a convention has been transformed into a rule of international law. The considerable part which tacit assent has always played in estimating the effect which is to be given to reservations scarcely permits one to state that such a rule exists, determining with sufficient precision the effect of objections made to reservations. In fact, the examples of objections made to reservations appear to be too rare in international practice to have given rise to such a rule. It cannot be recognised that the report which was adopted on the subject by the Council of the League of Nations on June 17th, 1927, has had this effect. . . .

. . . It must also be pointed out that there existed among the American States members both of the United Nations and of the Organisation of American States, a different practice which goes so far as to permit a reserving State to become a party irrespective of the nature of the reservations or of the objections raised by other contracting States. The preparatory work of the Convention contains nothing to justify the statement that the contracting States implicitly had any definite practice in mind. Nor is there any such indication in the subsequent attitude of the contracting States: neither the reservations made by certain States nor the position adopted by other States towards those reservations permit the conclusion that assent to one or the other of these practices had been given. Finally, it is not without interest to note, in view of the preference generally said to attach to an established practice, that the debate on reservations to multilateral treaties which took place in the Sixth Committee at the fifth session of the General Assembly reveals a profound divergence of views, some delegations being attached to the idea of the absolute integrity of the Convention, others favouring a more flexible practice which would bring about the participation of as many States as possible.

It results from the foregoing considerations that Question I, on account of its abstract character, cannot be given an absolute answer. The appraisal of a reservation and the effect of objections that might be made to it depend upon the particular circumstances of each individual case.

. . . the Court will now examine Question II. . . .

. . . As no State can be bound by a reservation to which it has not consented, it necessarily follows that each State objecting to it will or will not, on the basis of its individual apraisal within the limits of the criterion of the object and purpose stated above, consider the reserving States to be a party to the Convention. In the ordinary course of events, such a decision will only affect the relationship between the State making the reservation and the objecting State; on the other hand, as will be pointed out later, such a decision might aim at the complete exclusion from the Convention in a case where it was expressed by the adoption of a position on the jurisdictional plane.

The disadvantages which result from this possible divergence of views—which an article concerning the making of reservations could have obviated—are real; they are mitigated by the common duty of the contracting States to be guided in their judgment by the compatibility or incompatibility of the reservation with the object and purpose of the Convention. . . .

It may be that the divergence of views between parties as to the admissibility of a reservation will not in fact have any consequences. On the other hand, it may be that certain parties who consider that the assent given by other parties to a reservation is incompatible with the purpose of the Convention, will decide to adopt a position on the jurisdictional plane in respect of this divergence and to settle the dispute which thus arises either by special agreement or by the procedure laid down in Article IX of the Convention.

Finally, it may be that a State, whilst not claiming that a reservation is incompatible with the object and purpose of the Convention, will nevertheless object to it, but that an understanding between that State and the reserving State will have the effect that the Convention will enter into force between them, except for the clauses affected by the reservation. . . .

. . . [On Question III] it is inconceivable that a State, even if it has participated in the preparation of the Convention, could, before taking one or the other of the two courses of action provided for becoming a party to the Convention [i.e. signature or accession], exclude another State. Possessing no rights which derive from the Convention, that State cannot claim such a right from its status as a Member of the United Nations or from the invitation to sign which has been addressed to it by the General Assembly.

The case of a signatory State is different. . . .

As distinct from the latter States, signatory States have taken certain of the steps necessary for the exercise of the right of being a party. Pending ratification, the provisional status created by signature confers upon the signatory a right to formulate as a precautionary measure objections which have themselves a provisional character. These would disappear if the signature were not followed by ratification, or they would become effective on ratification.

For these reasons,

the Court is of opinion,

in so far as concerns the Convention on the Prevention and Punishment of the Crime of Genocide, in the event of a State ratifying or acceding to the Convention subject to a reservation made either on ratification or on accession, or on signature followed by ratification,

On Question I:

by seven votes to five,

that a State which has made and maintained a reservation which has been objected to by one or more of the parties to the Convention but not by others, can be regarded as being a party to the Convention if the reservation is compatible with the object and purpose of the Convention; otherwise, that State cannot be regarded as being a party to the Convention.

On Question II:

by seven votes to five,

(a) that if a party to the Convention objects to a reservation which it considers to be incompatible with the object and purpose of the Convention, it can in fact consider that the reserving State is not a party to the Convention;

(b) that if, on the other hand, a party accepts the reservation as being compatible with the object and purpose of the Convention, it can in fact consider that the reserving State is a party to the Convention.

On Question III:

by seven votes to five,[67]

(a) that an objection to a reservation made by a signatory State which has not yet ratified the Convention can have the legal effect indicated in the reply to Question I only upon ratification. Until that moment it merely serves as a notice to the other State of the eventual attitude of the signatory State;

(b) that an objection to a reservation made by a State which is entitled to sign or accede but which has not yet done so, is without legal effect.

Notes

1. The problem raised in the *Reservations Case* concerns only multilateral treaties. In the case of a bilateral treaty, a proposed reservation is, in effect, a counter offer which the other party can accept or reject. In 1927, the League of Nations adopted the following approach to reservations with regard to multilateral treaties:

> In order that any reservation whatever may be validly made in regard to a clause of the treaty, it is essential that this reservation should be accepted by all the contracting parties, as would have been the case if it had been put forward in the course of the negotiations. If not, the reservation, like the signature to which it is attached, is null and void.[68]

In contrast, in 1932 the Pan American Union proposed a different approach:

> With respect to the juridical status of treaties ratified with reservations, which have not been accepted, the Governing Board of the Pan American Union understands that:
> 1. The treaty shall be in force, in the form in which it was signed, as between those countries which ratify it without reservations, in the terms in which it was originally drafted and signed.
> 2. It shall be in force as between the Governments which ratify it with reservations and the signatory States which accept the reservations in the form in which the treaty may be modified by said reservations.

---

[67] On all three questions, the judges in the majority were President Basdevant; Judges Hackworth, Winiarski, Zoričić, de Visscher, Klaestad and Badawi Pasha. The dissenting judges were Vice-President Guerrero; Judges Alvarez, Sir Arnold McNair, Read and Hsu Mo.

[68] Report of the L.N. Committee of Experts for the Progressive Codification of International Law, 8 L.N.O.J. 880 at p. 881 (1927).

3.   It shall not be in force between a Government which may have ratified with reservations and another which may have already ratified, and which does not accept such reservations.[69]

Clearly, the Court preferred the latter approach. In a joint dissenting opinion, Judges Guerrero, Sir Arnold McNair, Read and Hsu Mo thought that the League of Nations approach was consistent with customary international law. They accepted that some states might operate a different rule *inter se*, as had the states within the Pan American Union. On the Court's classification of reservations into those that are "compatible" and those that are "incompatible" with the "object and purpose" of a convention, they concluded: "It propounds a new rule for which we can find no legal basis."[70] As to the significance of the intended universality of the Genocide Convention, they stated:

While it was undoubtedly true that the representatives of the governments, in drafting and adopting the Genocide Convention, wished to see as many States become parties to it as possible, it was certainly not their intention to achieve universality at any price. There is no evidence to show that they desired to secure wide acceptance of the Convention even at the expense of the integrity or uniformity of its terms, irrespective of the wishes of those States which have accepted all the obligations under it.[71]

2. In 1951, the International Law Commission expressed disagreement with the Court's Opinion.[72] Faced with this conflict, the General Assembly, in a resolution[73] adopted on January 12, 1952, noted both the Court's Opinion and the view of the Commission and requested the Secretary-General, who had previously continued the League of Nations practice, to follow the Court's Opinion as depositary for the Genocide Convention, and, as depositary of future multilateral conventions,

(i)   to continue to act as depositary in connexion with the deposit of documents containing reservations or objections, without passing upon the legal effect of such documents; and
(ii) to communicate the text of such documents relating to reservations or objections to all States concerned, leaving it to each State to draw legal consequences from such communications.

In 1959, the Assembly extended this second request to *all* multilateral conventions for which the Secretary-General acted as depositary, whenever concluded.[74]

VIENNA CONVENTION ON THE LAW OF TREATIES 1969

Loc. cit. at p. 563, n. 3, above

Article 19

A State may, when signing, ratifying, accepting approving, or acceding to a treaty, formulate a reservation unless:
(*a*) the reservation is prohibited by the treaty;
(*b*) the treaty provides that only specified reservations, which do not include the reservation in question, may be made; or

[69] *Reservations to Multilateral Conventions*, U.N.Doc. A/1372, p. 11. The 1932 P.A.U. approach has been changed by a new set of O.A.S. standards in line with the Vienna Convention on the Law of Treaties: [1973] *U.S. D.I.L.* 179.
[70] I.C.J. Rep. 1951, p. 42.   [71] *Ibid.* p. 46.
[72] Y.B.I.L.C., 1951, II, pp. 125–131.
[73] G.A.Resn. 598 (VI), G.A.O.R., 6th Session, Supp. 20, p. 84.
[74] G.A.Resn. 1452B (XIV), G.A.O.R., 14th Session, Supp. 16, p. 56.

(c) in cases not falling under sub-paragraphs (a) and (b), the reservation is incompatible with the object and purpose of the treaty.

Article 20

1. A reservation expressly authorized by a treaty does not require any subsequent acceptance by the other contracting States unless the treaty so provides.

2. When it appears from the limited number of the negotiating States and the object and purpose of a treaty that the application of the treaty in its entirety between all the parties is an essential condition of the consent of each one to be bound by the treaty, a reservation requires acceptance by all the parties.

3. When a treaty is a constituent instrument of an international organization and unless it otherwise provides, a reservation requires the acceptance of the competent organ of that organization.

4. In cases not falling under the preceding paragraphs and unless the treaty otherwise provides:

(a) acceptance by another contracting State of a reservation constitutes the reserving State a party to the treaty in relation to that other State if or when the treaty is in force for those States;

(b) an objection by another contracting State to a reservation does not preclude the entry into force of the treaty as between the objecting and reserving States unless a contrary intention is definitely expressed by the objecting State;

(c) an act expressing a State's consent to be bound by the treaty and containing a reservation is effective as soon as at least one other contracting State has accepted the reservation.

5. For the purposes of paragraphs 2 and 4 and unless the treaty otherwise provides, a reservation is considered to have been accepted by a State if it shall have raised no objection to the reservation by the end of a period of twelve months after it was notified of the reservation or by the date on which it expressed its consent to be bound by the treaty, whichever is later.

Article 21

1. A reservation established with regard to another party in accordance with articles 19, 20 and 23:

(a) modifies for the reserving State in its relations with that other party the provisions of the treaty to which the reservation relates to the extent of the reservation; and

(b) modifies those provisions to the same extent for that other party in its relations with the reserving State.

2. The reservation does not modify the provisions of the treaty for the other parties to the treaty *inter se*.

3. When a State objecting to a reservation has not opposed the entry into force of the treaty between itself and the reserving State, the provisions to which the reservation relates do not apply as between the two States to the extent of the reservation.

Article 22

1. Unless the treaty otherwise provides, a reservation may be withdrawn at any time and the consent of a State which has accepted the reservation is not required for its withdrawal.

2. Unless the treaty otherwise provides, an objection to a reservation may be withdrawn at any time.

3. Unless the treaty otherwise provides, or it is otherwise agreed:

(*a*) the withdrawal of a reservation becomes operative in relation to another contracting State only when notice of it has been received by that State;

(*b*) the withdrawal of an objection to a reservation becomes operative only when notice of it has been received by the State which formulated the reservation.

Article 23

1. A reservation, an express acceptance of a reservation and an objection to a reservation must be formulated in writing and communicated to the contracting States and other States entitled to become parties to the treaty.

2. If formulated when signing the treaty subject to ratification, acceptance or approval, a reservation must be formally confirmed by the reserving State when expressing its consent to be bound by the treaty. In such a case the reservation shall be considered as having been made on the date of its confirmation.

3. An express acceptance of, or an objection to, a reservation made previously to confirmation of the reservation does not itself require confirmation.

4. The withdrawal of a reservation or of an objection to a reservation must be formulated in writing.

Notes

1. Basically, the Convention follows the Pan American Union approach, rather than that of the League of Nations. It substantially incorporates the International Law Commission's Draft Articles, except for Article 21(3). The Commission had proposed, partly to discourage reservations, that an objection would preclude entry into force of a treaty between the two states concerned unless a contrary intention were expressed by the objecting state.[75] At the suggestion of the U.S.S.R., which argued for complete freedom for states to make reservations, the contrary approach was adopted at Vienna.[76] The United Kingdom Government regards the Convention rules as stating custom.[77]

2. In its Commentary to its Draft Articles, the International Law Commission stated: "The majority of reservations relate to the particular point which a particular State for one reason or another finds difficult to accept, and the effect of the reservation on the general integrity of the treaty is often minimal; and the same is true even if the reservation in question relates to a comparatively important provision of the treaty, so long as the reservation is not made by more than a few States. In short, the integrity of the treaty would only be materially affected if a reservation of a somewhat substantial kind were to be formulated by a number of States. This might, no doubt, happen; but even then the treaty itself would remain the master agreement between the other

[75] Draft Articles. Art. 17(4)(*b*).   [76] See *Treaty Conference Records*, (1969), pp. 30–35.
[77] Dept. of Trade Memorandum to the House of Commons Select Committee on European Legislation, 1978, printed in U.K.M.I.L. 1978; (1978) 49 B.Y.I.L. 378. The Memorandum contains a useful summary of the law. On the effect of objections to reservations under the Convention, see the *English Channel Arbitration*, 18 I.L.M. 397, 417 *et seq*. (1979).

participating States. What is essential to ensure both the effectiveness and the integrity of the treaty is that a sufficient number of States should become parties to it, accepting the great bulk of its provisions. . . . But when today the number of the negotiating States may be upwards of one hundred States with very diverse cultural, economic and political conditions, it seems necessary to assume that the power to make reservations without the risk of being totally excluded by the objection of one or even of a few States may be a factor in promoting a more general acceptance of multilateral treaties. Moreover, the failure of negotiating States to take the necessary steps to become parties to multilateral treaties appears a greater obstacle to the development of international law through the medium of treaties than the possibility that the integrity of such treaties may be unduly weakened by the liberal admission of reserving States as parties to them. The Commission also considered that, in the present era of change and of challenge to traditional concepts, the rule calculated to promote the widest possible acceptance of whatever measure of common agreement can be achieved and expressed in a multilateral treaty may be the one most suited to the immediate needs of the inter-national community."[78] Clearly, the Commission had changed its mind since 1951.

3. A reservation is defined in Article 2(1)(*d*) of the Convention as "a unilateral statement, however phrased or named, made by a State, when signing, ratifying, accepting, approving or acceding to a treaty, whereby it purports to exclude or to modify the legal effect of certain provisions of the treaty in their application to that State."[79]

4. The concept of the "object and purpose" of a treaty is used in both Articles 19 and 20. What different role does it serve in each?

5. Probably the most controversial reservations to the Genocide Convention are those made by a number of states not accepting Article IX of the Convention which provides for the compulsory jurisdiction of the International Court of Justice in disputes arising under the Convention.[80] Objections to them have been registered by a number of states.[81] What would be the effect of such reservations under the Vienna Convention?

6. Suppose that states A, B and C make a treaty by which they undertake to develop a new aeroplane and the treaty provides that "development costs will be shared by the contracting parties equally." The treaty has no provision on reservations. D accedes to the treaty but makes its accession subject to the reservation that it will not regard itself as bound if its share of the costs of the venture rises above a stated level. A objects to this reservation but does not say that the treaty has no effect between A and D; B expressly accepts the reservation; C makes no response. Is D a party to the treaty according to the Vienna Convention? If so, what are its relations with A, B and C? Who decides these questions?

7. For an example of a treaty provision prohibiting a certain kind of reservation, see Article 64 of the European Convention on Human Rights 1950.[82] Note also the "mathematical" test used in Article 20 of the Racial Discrimination Convention for determining whether a reservation is incompatible with its "object and purpose."[83]

---

[78] Y.B.I.L.C., 1966, II, pp. 205–206. See Boyle, 29 I.C.L.Q. 498 (1980)

[79] For criticism of the characterisation of a reservation as "unilateral," see Brownlie, p. 587. On interpretative declarations or "understandings," see below, p. 600.

[80] See above, p. 562.

[81] See above, p. 562.

[82] Art. 64(1) permits reservations other than those "of a general character."

[83] Art. 20 states that a reservation is "incompatible" if at least two thirds of the contracting parties object to it.

(iv) Entry into Force

VIENNA CONVENTION ON THE LAW OF TREATIES 1969

Loc. cit. at p. 563, n. 3, above

Article 24

1. A treaty enters into force in such a manner and upon such date as it may provide or as the negotiating States may agree.

2. Failing any such provision or agreement, a treaty enters into force as soon as consent to be bound by the treaty has been established for all the negotiating States.

3. When the consent of a State to be bound by a treaty is established on a date after the treaty has come into force, the treaty enters into force for that State on that date, unless the treaty otherwise provides.

4. The provisions of a treaty regulating the authentication of its text, the establishment of the consent of States to be bound by the treaty, the manner or date of its entry into force, reservations, the functions of the depositary and other matters arising necessarily before the entry into force of the treaty apply from the time of the adoption of its text.

Note
The Vienna Convention provides that for its purposes "contracting State" means "a State which has consented to be bound by the treaty, whether or not the treaty has entered into force" (Art. 2(1)(*f*)) and that "party" means "a State which has consented to be bound by the treaty and for which the treaty is in force" (Art. 2(1)(*g*)).

4. OBSERVANCE AND APPLICATION OF TREATIES

(i) Pacta Sunt Servanda

VIENNA CONVENTION ON THE LAW OF TREATIES 1969

Loc. cit. at p. 563, n. 3, above

Article 26

Every treaty in force is binding upon the parties to it and must be performed by them in good faith.

Note
The International Law Commission's Commentary reads:

Pacta sunt servanda—the rule that treaties are binding on the parties and must be performed in good faith—is the fundamental principle of the law of treaties. There is much authority in the jurisprudence of international tribunals for the proposition that in the present context the principle of good faith is a legal principle which forms an integral part of the rule *pacta sunt servanda*. Thus, speaking of certain valuations to be made under Articles 95 and 96 of the Act of Algeciras, the Court said in the *Case concerning Rights of Nationals of the United States of America in Morocco* (Judgment of 27 August 1952)[84]: "The power of making the valuation rests with the

---
[84] I.C.J.Rep. 1952, p. 212.

Customs authorities, but it is a power which must be exercised reasonably and in good faith." Similarly, the Permanent Court of International Justice, in applying treaty clauses prohibiting discrimination against minorities, insisted in a number of cases, that the clauses must be so applied as to ensure the absence of discrimination in fact as well as in law; in other words, the obligation must not be evaded by a merely literal application of the clauses. Numerous precedents could also be found in the jurisprudence of arbitral tribunals. To give only one example, in the *North Atlantic Coast Fisheries Arbitration* the Tribunal, dealing with Great Britain's right to regulate fisheries in Canadian waters in which she had granted certain fishing rights to United States nationals by the Treaty of Ghent, said[85]: " . . . from the Treaty results an obligatory relation whereby the right of Great Britain to exercise its right of sovereignty by making regulations is limited to such regulations as are made in good faith, and are not in violation of the Treaty."[86]

(ii) RELATION WITH INTERNAL LAW

VIENNA CONVENTION ON THE LAW OF TREATIES 1969

Loc. cit. at p. 563, n. 3, above

Article 27

A party may not invoke the provisions of its internal law as justification for its failure to perform a treaty. This rule is without prejudice to Article 46.[87]

Note
See to the same effect the 1949 Draft Declaration on Rights and Duties of States, above, p. 57.

(iii) NON-RETROACTIVITY

VIENNA CONVENTION ON THE LAW OF TREATIES 1969

Loc. cit. at p. 563, n. 3, above

Article 28

Unless a different intention appears from the treaty or is otherwise established, its provisions do not bind a party in relation to any act or fact which took place or any situation which ceased to exist before the date of the entry into force of the treaty with respect to that party.

Note
In the *De Becker Case*,[88] the applicant alleged a violation by Belgium of Article 10 of the European Convention on Human Rights. He had been convicted in 1947 of a criminal offence and sentenced to life imprisonment and to the forfeiture for life of certain civil rights in accordance with the Belgian Penal Code (Article 123 sexies) including the right to participate in the running of a newspaper. The European Commission of Human Rights rejected the argument put by Belgium that the application was

---

[85] (1910) Reports of International Arbitral Awards, Vol. XI, p. 188.
[86] Y.B.I.L.C., 1966, II, p. 211.
[87] See below, p. 610.
[88] 2 Y.B.E.C.H.R. 214 (1958–59).

inadmissible *ratione temporis* because the sentence had been imposed before Belgium became a party to the Convention. It stated:

> whereas it should be pointed out in the first place that the judgment of the Brussels Military Court . . . was delivered prior to 14th June, 1955, on which date the Convention came into force in respect of Belgium; whereas, moreover, the subsequent entry into force of the Convention cannot have invalidated retrospectively the forfeiture of rights complained of for all the preceding period, since the Convention, according to the generally recognised rules of international law, did not take effect retrospectively; whereas it follows that the Applicant cannot legally claim, for the period in question, to have been the victim of a violation of the rights guaranteed by the Convention, even if the state of affairs complained of is of a permanent nature; Whereas it should nevertheless be noted that any person to whom the provisions of Article 123 sexies of the Belgian Penal Code are applied, is, in accordance with the very terms of that Article, deprived *ipso facto* and for life of the rights in question; that De Becker thus finds himself permanently deprived of the rights enumerated in Article 123 sexies and, in the event of an infringement of the provisions of the said Article, he may at any time be convicted under Article 123 nonies; . . . Whereas it therefore appears that the Applicant finds himself in a continuing situation in respect of which he claims to be the victim of a violation of the right to freedom of expression guaranteed by Article 10 of the Convention and that the Application, insofar as it concerns this continuing situation extending after 14th June, 1955, is consequently not inadmissible *ratione temporis*[89];

Article 28 of the Vienna Convention is consistent with such a ruling since the applicant's "situation" continued to exist after 1955.

What if a national of State A has his property confiscated by State B the day before a treaty between A and B comes into effect which makes such a confiscation illegal? Is State B liable under the treaty?

(iv) TERRITORIAL APPLICATION

VIENNA CONVENTION ON THE LAW OF TREATIES 1969

Loc. cit. at p. 563, n. 3, above

Article 29

Unless a different intention appears from the treaty or is otherwise established, a treaty is binding upon each party in respect of its entire territory.

Note

A question arises as to the territorial application of treaties made by a stated with overseas possessions and other territories for whose international affairs it is responsible. The International Law Commission's Fourth Special Rapporteur on the Law of Treaties reported that "the general understanding today clearly is that, in the absence of any territorial clause or other indication of a contrary intention, a treaty is presumed to apply to all the territories for which the contracting States are internationally responsible."[90] Thus treaties made by the British Government apply to overseas territories for which the United Kingdom is internationally responsible unless the treaty indicates otherwise. For an example of a "territorial clause," see Article 63, European Convention on Human Rights 1950.[91]

[89] *Ibid.* pp. 233–234.
[90] Third Report, Y.B.I.L.C., 1964, II, p. 15.
[91] See above, p. 491, n. 91.

(v) INCONSISTENT TREATIES

VIENNA CONVENTION ON THE LAW OF TREATIES 1969

Loc. cit. at p. 563, n. 3, above

Article 30

1. Subject to Article 103 of the Charter of the United Nations,[92] the rights and obligations of States parties to successive treaties relating to the same subject-matter shall be determined in accordance with the following paragraphs.

2. When a treaty specifies that it is subject to, or that it is not to be considered as incompatible with, an earlier or later treaty, the provisions of that other treaty prevail.

3. When all the parties to the earlier treaty are parties also to the later treaty but the earlier treaty is not terminated or suspended in operation under Article 59,[93] the earlier treaty applies only to the extent that its provisions are compatible with those of the later treaty.

4. When the parties to the later treaty do not include all the parties to the earlier one:

(*a*) as between States parties to both treaties the same rule applies as in paragraph 3;

(*b*) as between a State party to both treaties and a State party to only one of the treaties, the treaty to which both States are parties governs their mutual rights and obligations.

5. Paragraph 4 is without prejudice to Article 41,[94] or to any question of the termination or suspension of the operation of a treaty under Article 60[95] or to any question of responsibility which may arise for a State from the conclusion or application of a treaty the provisions of which are incompatible with its obligations towards another State under another treaty.

Notes

1. Imagine that States A and B make a treaty in which each undertakes not to allow any foreign military bases on its territory. States B and C make a treaty the following year in which B agrees that C shall establish a foreign base on B's territory. A learns of the treaty between B and C and protests, whereupon B refuses to allow C to establish the promised base. Has C a good claim to reparation under Article 30 of the Vienna Convention from B? What if B had ignored the protest? Would A then have had a good claim for reparation against B? Could either A or C insist upon specific performance?[96]

2. Imagine that States D, E, and F agree by treaty to apply certain conservation measures when fishing for halibut and cod on the high seas. Later, D and E, but not F, become parties with a large number of other states, including G, to a halibut treaty by which fishing practices aimed at the conservation of halibut are agreed upon which are

---

[92] *Ed.* Appendix I, below.
[93] *Ed.* See below, p. 613.
[94] *Ed.* See below, p. 609.
[95] *Ed.* See below, p. 619.
[96] It seems likely that specific performance is a "general principle of law" in the sense of Article 38(1)(*c*), Statute of the I.C.J., Appendix I, below. On its extensive use in civil law systems, see Schlesinger, *Comparative Law* (3rd ed., 1970), pp. 451 *et seq.*

less strict than those in the earlier treaty between D, E, and F. Which rules as to the conservation of halibut and cod apply in the relations between D and E and D and F under Article 30? Which rules concerning halibut apply in the relations between D and G under Article 30?

3. Imagine that the Security Council, acting under Articles 41 and 25 of the United Nations Charter,[97] imposed in 1970 upon the members of the United Nations a legally binding obligation to refrain from supplying military weapons to State B, a United Nations member. State A, a United Nations member, has a treaty with State B that entered into force in 1972 that requires each state to supply the other with military weapons on request. State B now makes a request under the treaty. What is State A's legal position under the Vienna Convention? Would it matter if the treaty had entered into force in 1962? Or if State B was not a member of the United Nations?

5. *TREATY INTERPRETATION*[98]

FITZMAURICE, THE LAW AND PROCEDURE OF THE INTERNATIONAL COURT OF JUSTICE: TREATY INTERPRETATION AND CERTAIN OTHER TREATY POINTS

(1951) 28 B.Y.I.L. 1. Some footnotes omitted

. . . There are today three main schools of thought on the subject, which could conveniently be called the "intentions of the parties" or "founding fathers" school; the "textual" or "ordinary meaning of the words" school; and the "teleological" or "aims and objects" school. The ideas of these three schools are not necessarily exclusive of one another, and theories of treaty interpretation can be constructed (and are indeed normally held) compounded of all three. However, each tends to confer the primacy on one particular aspect of treaty interpretation, if not to the exclusion, certainly to the subordination of the others. . . . For the "intentions" school, the prime, indeed the only legitimate, object is to ascertain and give effect to the intentions, or presumed intentions, of the parties. . . . For the "meaning of the text" school, the prime object is to establish what the text means according to the ordinary or apparent signification of its terms: the approach is therefore through the study and analysis of the text. For the "aims and objects" school, it is the general purpose of the treaty itself that counts, considered to some extent as having, or as having come to have, an existence of its own, independent of the original intentions of the framers. The main object is to establish this general purpose, and construe the particular clauses in the light of it: hence it is such matters as the general tenor and atmosphere of the treaty, the circumstances in which it was made, the place it has come to have in international life, which for this school indicate the approach to interpretation. It should be added that this last, the teleological, approach has its sphere of operation almost entirely in the field of general multilateral conventions, particularly those of the social, humanitarian, and

---

[97] Appendix I, below.

[98] See Bos, 27 Neth. I.L.R. 3 (1980); Fitzmaurice (1957) 33 B.Y.I.L. 203; Lauterpacht (1949) 26 B.Y.I.L. 48; McDougal, 61 A.J.I.L. 992 (1967); McDougal and Miller, *The Interpretation of Agreements and World Public Order*, 1967; Merrills (1968–69) Aust. Y.B.I.L. 55; Rosenne, 5 Col. Jo. of Trans. Law 205 (1966); Stone, 1 *Sydney L.R.* 344 (1953–55).

law-making type.[99] All three approaches are capable, in a given case, of producing the same result in practice; but equally (even though the differences may, on analysis, prove to be more of emphasis and methodology than principle) they are capable of leading to radically divergent results.

INTERPRETATION OF PEACE TREATIES CASE (SECOND PHASE)

Advisory Opinion. I.C.J. Reports 1950, p. 221

The three 1947 Peace Treaties between the Allied Powers, on the one hand, and Bulgaria, Hungary and Romania, on the other, provided for commissions to hear disputes concerning the "interpretation or execution of the treaty" where they could not be resolved by negotiation. The commissions were to consist of three members. The two parties to the dispute were to appoint a member each; the parties were then to agree upon a third. If they could not agree, the third member was to be appointed by the Secretary-General of the United Nations. Disputes arose over the human rights guarantees in the treaties which could not, the United Kingdom and the United States claimed, be settled by negotiation. Bulgaria, Hungary and Romania refused to appoint members to the commissions. The General Assembly asked the Court whether the Secretary-General could appoint the third member of a commission when one party had failed to appoint its member and, if so, whether a commission consisting of the third member and the appointee of the other party could hear a dispute. The Court answered the first question in the negative, so that the second question did not arise. In the course of its opinion, the Court made the following comments on treaty interpretation.

Opinion of the Court

. . . the Governments of Bulgaria, Hungary and Romania are under an obligation to appoint their representatives to the Treaty Commissions, and it is clear that refusal to fulfil a treaty obligation involves international responsibility. Nevertheless, such a refusal cannot alter the conditions contemplated in the Treaties for the exercise by the Secretary-General of his power of appointment. These conditions are not present in this case, and their absence is not made good by the fact that it is due to the breach of a treaty obligation. The failure of machinery for settling disputes by reason of the practical impossibility of creating the Commission provided for in the Treaties is one thing[1]; international responsibility is another. The breach of a treaty obligation cannot be remedied

---

[99] It may be useful to state briefly the main drawback of each method, if employed in isolation or pushed to an extreme. In the case of the "intentions" method, it is the element of unreality or fictitiousness frequently involved. There are so many cases in which the dispute has arisen precisely because the parties had no intentions on the point, or none that were genuinely common. To make the issue dependent on them involves either an abortive search or an artificial construction that does *not* in fact represent their intentions. The "textual" method suffers from the subjective elements involved in the notions of "clear" or "ordinary" meaning, which may be differently understood and applied according to the point of view of the individual judge. There may also be cases where the parties intended a term to be understood in a specialised sense, different from its ordinary one, but failed to make this clear on the face of the text. The teleological method, finally, is always in danger of "spilling over" into judicial legislation: it may amount, not to interpreting but, in effect, to amending an instrument in order to make it conform better with what the judge regards as its true purposes.

[1] *Ed.* For an example of a procedure for establishing a commission that would have avoided the difficulty in this case, see the Annex to the Vienna Convention on the Law of Treaties, below, p. 631.

by creating a Commission which is not the kind of Commission contemplated by the Treaties. It is the duty of the Court to interpret the Treaties, not to revise them.

The principle of interpretation expressed in the maxim: *Ut res magis valeat quam pereat*, often referred to as the rule of effectiveness, cannot justify the Court in attributing to the provisions for the settlement of disputes in the Peace Treaties a meaning which, as stated above, would be contrary to their letter and spirit.

Notes

1. The Court thus refused to apply the principle of effectiveness, according to which a treaty should be interpreted to give effect to its object and purpose, in such a way as to override the clear meaning of the text. At this point it parted company from the teleological approach.

2. The principle has been applied by the Court in a less extreme form in several cases. In the *Ambatielos Case*,[2] Greece and the United Kingdom had replaced one bilateral commercial treaty between them by another. A Declaration accompanying the new treaty provided for the arbitration of "claims based upon the provisions of the [old treaty]." The question arose whether, as argued by Greece, the Declaration applied to claims arising during the currency of the old treaty which were brought after the new treaty had been made as well as to such claims brought before it had been made. The Court ruled in favour of Greece:

> If the United Kingdom Government's interpretation were accepted, claims based on the Treaty of 1886, but brought after the conclusion of the Treaty of 1926 would be left without solution. They would not be subject to arbitration under either Treaty, although the provision on whose breach the claim was based might appear in both and might thus have been in force without a break since 1886. The Court cannot accept an interpretation which would have a result obviously contrary to the language of the Declaration and to the continuous will of both Parties to submit all differences to arbitration of one kind or another.[3]

The principle has also been used where the meaning of the text is unclear to prefer an interpretation that gives some effect to a provision over one that does not. In the *Corfu Channel Case*,[4] the Special Agreement by which the case was referred to the Court asked, *inter alia*, "is there any duty to pay compensation?" Albania argued that this question required only an answer "yes" or "no"; it did not require the Court to assess the amount of compensation due. The Court rejected this argument. It noted that it had, in any event, in answer to another question in the Special Agreement, to say whether international responsibility existed. Since international responsibility carried with it under customary international law an obligation to compensate and since there was no obligation to compensate in the absence of international responsibility, on Albania's interpretation of the question, the answer to it would add nothing to what the parties would otherwise know. The British argument, that the question required the Court to assess compensation, was preferred in order to give the question meaning. The Court said:

> It would indeed be incompatible with the generally accepted rules of interpretation to admit that a provision of this sort occurring in a special agreement should be devoid of purport or effect.[5]

[2] I.C.J.Rep. 1952, p. 28.
[3] *Ibid*. p. 45.
[4] I.C.J.Rep. 1949, p. 4.
[5] *Ibid*. p. 24.

The principle has been most strikingly applied by the Court in the specialised field of the constitutional law of international organisations to infer powers which are not expressly given to the organisation concerned but which are consistent with its purposes. See, in particular, the *Reparation*[6] and *Certain Expenses*[7] *Cases*. See also the *South-West Africa Cases*.[8]

VIENNA CONVENTION ON THE LAW OF TREATIES 1969

Loc. cit. at p. 563, n. 3, above

Article 31

1. A treaty shall be interpreted in good faith in accordance with the ordinary meaning to be given to the terms of the treaty in their context and in the light of its object and purpose.

2. The context for the purpose of the interpretation of a treaty shall comprise in addition to the text, including its preamble and annexes:

(*a*) any agreement relating to the treaty which was made between all the parties in connexion with the conclusion of the treaty;

(*b*) any instrument which was made by one or more parties in connexion with the conclusion of the treaty and accepted by the other parties as an instrument related to the treaty.

3. There shall be taken into account, together with the context:

(*a*) any subsequent agreement between the parties regarding the interpretation of the treaty or the application of its provisions;

(*b*) any subsequent practice in the application of the treaty which establishes the agreement of the parties regarding its interpretation;

(*c*) any relevant rules of international law applicable in the relations between the parties.

4. A special meaning shall be given to a term if it is established that the parties so intended.

Notes

1. Which of the three approaches discussed by Fitzmaurice[9] is adopted in the Vienna Convention? Note that the "object and purpose" of a treaty is to be referred to in determining the meaning of the "terms of the treaty" and not as an independent basis for interpretation.

2. On the *principle of effectiveness*, the International Law Commission's Commentary reads:

> The Commission, however, took the view that, in so far as the maximum *ut res magis valeat quam pereat* reflects a true general rule of interpretation, it is embodied in [Article 31, Vienna Convention] . . . When a treaty is open to two interpretations one of which does and the other does not enable the treaty to have appropriate effects, good faith and the objects and purposes of the treaty demand that the former interpretation should be adopted.[10]

[6] See above, p. 114.
[7] See below, p. 698.
[8] See above, p. 104.
[9] See above, p. 595.
[10] Y.B.I.L.C., 1966, II, p. 219.

The Commission clearly thought that the text as it stands permits the use of the principle in the way it has been used by the World Court.[11] On the emphasis upon a 'dynamic' object and purpose approach in the interpretation of the European Convention on Human Rights, see above, p. 512.

3. *The Textual or "plain meaning" approach.* As stated by the International Law Commission in its Commentary, "the jurisprudence of the International Court contains many pronouncements from which it is permissible to conclude that the textual approach to treaty interpretation is regarded by it as established law."[12] See, for example the *Admissions Case*[13] and the *Competence Case*.[14] On the limits to a "purely grammatical" approach, see the *Aegean Sea Continental Shelf Case*, I.C.J. Rep. 1978, at p. 23.

4. Would the Optional Protocol of Signature concerning the Compulsory Settlement of Disputes[15] adopted at the 1958 Geneva Conference on the Law of the Sea concerning disputes arising under the four Conventions adopted at the Conference constitute part of the "context" that could be used in interpreting any of those Conventions under Article 31(2)? Would the Resolution on Nuclear Tests on the High Seas[16] adopted at the same Conference? Could the definition of "warship" in the High Seas Convention be used to interpret the same term in the Territorial Sea Convention?[17]

5. *Subsequent Practice.* Fitzmaurice[18] states that:

> . . . recourse to the subsequent conduct and practice of the parties in relation to the treaty is permissible, and may be desirable, as affording the best and most reliable evidence . . . as to what its correct interpretation is.

The role of such practice is demonstrated by the following extract from the *Competence of the I.L.O. with respect to Agricultural Labour Case*[19]:

> If there were any ambiguity, the Court might, for the purpose of arriving at the true meaning, consider the action which has been taken under the Treaty. The Treaty was signed in June 1919, and it was not until October 1921, that any of the Contracting Parties raised the question whether agricultural labour fell within the competence of the International Labour Organisation. During the intervening period the subject of agriculture had repeatedly been discussed and had been dealt with in one form and another.

What if both or all of the parties to a treaty act upon it in a way that is contrary to the clear meaning of the text over a lengthy period of time before such action is challenged by one of their number? Has the treaty, in effect, been revised informally?[20]

There would seem to be no reason to distinguish between subsequent practice by both or all of the parties jointly and such practice by both or all of them separately that is to the same effect. The value of practice showing the interpretation of just one or some of the parties, however, is less certain. The International Law Commission thought that only practice establishing the understanding of "the parties as a whole"[21] should be used. The phrase "agreement of the parties" in Article 31(3)(*b*) can probably be taken as reinforcing this view. Presumably, however, acquiescence is relevant so that the practice of one party of which the other parties have or can be deemed to have

[11] See above, p. 596.
[12] Y.B.I.L.C., 1966, II, p. 220.
[13] I.C.J. Reports 1948, p. 57.
[14] I.C.J. Reports 1950, p. 4.
[15] U.K.T.S. 60 (1963), Cmnd. 2112; 450 U.N.T.S. 169.
[16] See above, p. 322.
[17] See above, p. 308.
[18] *Loc. cit.* at p. 595, n. 98, above, p. 210.
[19] P.C.I.J.Rep., Series B, No. 2, pp. 39–40 (1922).
[20] See Fitzmaurice, (1957) 33 B.Y.I.L. 203 at p. 225.
[21] Commentary, Y.B.I.L.C., 1966, II, p. 222.

knowledge can, through lack of protest, establish the common interpretation of the parties. In the *Anglo-Iranian Oil Co. Case*,[22] the International Court of Justice relied, in interpreting the Iranian declaration accepting the compulsory jurisdiction of the Court, upon an Iranian law approving the declaration some months after it was signed and some months before it was ratified. The Court said:

> This clause . . . is . . . a decisive confirmation of the intention of the Government of Iran at the time when it accepted the compulsory jurisdiction of the Court. . . . It is contended that this evidence as to the intention of the Government of Iran should be rejected as inadmissible and that this Iranian law is a purely domestic instrument, unknown to other governments. The law is described as "a private document written only in the Persian language which was not communicated to the League or to any of the other States which had made declarations." The Court is unable to see why it should be prevented from taking this piece of evidence into consideration. The law was published in the Corpus of Iranian laws voted and ratified during the period from January 15, 1931, to January 15, 1933. It has thus been available for the examination of other governments during a period of about twenty years. The law was filed for the sole purpose of throwing light on a disputed question of fact, namely, the intention of the Government of Iran at the time when it signed the Declaration.[23]

Clearly, the burden of watchfulness placed by the Court's approach upon other parties to a treaty, particularly as their numbers grow, is a very great one.[24]

When France acceded to the Geneva Convention on the Continental Shelf 1958, it declared its understanding of the meaning of Articles 1 and 2 of the Convention,[25] to which no reservations are permitted. Such an "understanding" may qualify as an "instrument" in the sense of Article 31(2)(*b*), Vienna Convention. As such it would be a factor to be taken into account but would not be binding upon the other parties.[26]

There may be a difference between action by a party accepting an obligation and other action. Referring to declarations made by South Africa on its obligations under the Mandate for South-West Africa, the International Court of Justice in the *South West Africa Case* (1950)[27] said:

> Interpretations placed upon legal instruments by the parties to them, though not conclusive as to their meaning, have considerable probative value when they contain recognition by a party of its own obligations under an instrument.

6. As to the establishment of a *"special meaning"* of a term (Article 31(4)), Norway unsuccessfully argued in the *Eastern Greenland Case*[28] that "in the legislative and administrative acts of the XVIIIth century on which Denmark relies . . . the word 'Greenland' is used not in the geographical sense, but means only the colonies of the colonised area on the West coast." The Court stated:

> The geographical meaning of the word "Greenland" . . . must be regarded as the ordinary meaning of the word. If it is alleged by one of the Parties that some unusual or exceptional meaning is to be attributed to it, it lies on that Party to establish its contention.

7. *Particular rules and maxims.* McNair[29] states:

> From the time of Grotius onwards, if not before, successive generations of writers and, more recently, of arbitrators and judges, have elaborated rules for the in-

---

[22] I.C.J.Rep. 1952, p. 92.
[23] *Ibid.* p. 107. On the juridical nature of declarations accepting the compulsory jurisdiction of the Court, see below, p. 719.   [24] *cf.* above, p. 36.
[25] See above, p. 358, n. 71, on the Declaration concerning Article 2. The U.S. noted the declarations "without prejudice"; U.N.Doc. ST/LEG/SER.D/5, p. 389.
[26] On interpretative declarations generally, see McRae (1978) 49 B.Y.I.L. 155.
[27] I.C.J.Rep. 1950 at p. 135.
[28] P.C.I.J.Rep., Series A, No. 53, p. 49.   [29] *Treaties*, pp. 364–366.

terpretation of treaties, borrowing mainly from the private law of contract. One result . . . is that today for many of the so-called rules of interpretation that one party may invoke before a tribunal the adverse party can often . . . find another. . . . The many maxims and phrases . . . are merely prima facie guides to the intention of the parties and must always give way to contrary evidence of the intention of the parties in a particular case.

The Vienna Convention, adopting the scepticism voiced by McNair, refrains from attempting to codify the numerous rules and maxims of interpretation, many of which are familiar from municipal law, that undoubtedly exist. It remains true, however, that some of the rules and maxims thus frowned upon will be of help in many cases. This is true, for example, of the maxim *inclusio unius est exclusio alterius*, which was stated in the *Life Insurance Claims*[30] to be "a rule of both law and logic and applicable to the construction of treaties as well as municipal statutes and contracts." The comment on it by Lopes L.J. in *Colquhoun* v. *Brooks*[31] is, however, worth noting:

The exclusion is often the result of inadvertence or accident, and the maxim ought not to be applied, when its application, having regard to the subject matter to which it is to be applied, leads to inconsistency or injustice.

An example of a somewhat questionable principle is the principle of restrictive interpretation, whereby limitations upon a State's sovereignty are not to be presumed, which was relied on by the P.C.I.J. in the *Wimbledon Case*.[32] McNair states:

It is believed to be now of declining importance and the time may not be far distant when it will disappear from the books. It dates from an age in which treaties were interpreted not by legal tribunals, and not even much by lawyers but by statesmen and diplomats. . . .
   It is difficult to defend the rule on a basis of logic. Every treaty obligation limits the sovereign powers of a State. With rare exceptions a treaty imposes obligations on both parties . . . if a so-called rule of interpretation is applied to restrict the obligations of one party, a sovereign State, it reduces the reciprocal benefit or "consideration" due to the other party, also a sovereign State, which seems to me to be absurd.[33]

It may, on occasions, contradict the principle of effectiveness.[34] It could have been used, for example, in opposition to the Greek contention in the *Ambatielos Case*.[35]

VIENNA CONVENTION ON THE LAW OF TREATIES 1969

Loc. cit. at p. 563, n. 3, above

Article 32

Recourse may be had to supplementary means of interpretation, including the preparatory work of the treaty and the circumstances of its conclusion, in order to confirm the meaning resulting from the application of Article 31, or to determine the meaning when the interpretation according to Article 31:

[30] *U.S.* v. *Germany*, 7 R.I.A.A. 91 at p. 111 (1924).
[31] (1888) 21 Q.B.D. 52 at p. 65. See McNair, *Treaties*, p. 400.
[32] See above, p. 201.
[33] *Symbolae Verzijl*, p. 222 at pp. 235–236; reprinted in McNair, *Treaties*, Appendix A, p. 754 at p. 765.
[34] See above, p. 595.
[35] See above, p. 597.

(*a*) leaves the meaning ambiguous or obscure; or

(*b*) leads to a result which is manifestly absurd or unreasonable.

Notes

1. The preparatory work, or *travaux préparatoires*, of a treaty is purposely not defined in the Vienna Convention. The International Law Commission thought that "to do so might only lead to the possible exclusion of relevant evidence."[36] In general terms, it is the record of the drafting of a treaty. It includes records of negotiations between the states that participate in the drafting and, in some cases, records of the work of independent bodies of experts, such as the International Law Commission and the United Nations Commission on Human Rights. On a wide interpretation, it also includes such materials as unilateral statements by government spokesmen made prior to or at the time of the negotiations but not as a part of them. McNair[37] argues however, that evidence coming within this wider interpretation should not be admitted before international courts and tribunals: "Surely whatever value there may be in preparatory work is that it may afford evidence of the common intention of the parties."

At the Vienna Conference, the United States argued forcefully, but unsuccessfully, for a rule permitting the use of the preparatory work equally with the text in determining the parties' intention and not just as the supplementary aid proposed by the International Law Commission. It argued in part:

> . . . the restrictions upon the use of preparatory works expressed in Article 28 [Art. 32, Convention] do not, any more than the restrictions imposed upon the use of other circumstances, represent established practice. . . . Even in the *Lotus Case*,[38] which perhaps contains the most famous exposition of the alleged rule that "there is no occasion to have regard to preparatory work if the text of a convention is sufficiently clear in itself," the Court did in fact look at the *travaux*. . . . The habitual use of preparatory work by foreign offices needs no emphasis here.[39]

Opposition to this proposal, based upon doubt about the value of preparatory work, was voiced by the British delegate:

> . . . preparatory work was almost invariably confusing, unequal and partial: confusing because it commonly consisted of the summary records of statements made during the process of negotiations, and early statements on the positions of delegations might express the intention of the delegation at that stage, but bear no relation to the ultimate text of the treaty; unequal, because not all delegations spoke on any particular issue; and partial because it excluded the informal meetings between heads of delegations at which final compromises were reached and which were often the most significant feature of any negotiation.[40]

The French delegate also preferred the Commission's textual approach:

> It was much less hazardous and much more equitable when ascertaining the intention of the parties to rely on what they had agreed in writing, rather than to seek outside the text elements of intent which were far more unreliable, scattered as they were through incomplete or unilateral documents.[41]

---

[36] Commentary, Y.B.I.L.C., 1966, II, p. 223.

[37] *Treaties*, p. 421.

[38] P.C.I.J.Rep., Series A, No. 10 at p. 16 (1927).

[39] 62 A.J.I.L. 1021 (1968). The statement is also reported in *Treaty Conference Records*, (1968), p. 167. For another view favouring the use of preparatory work, see Lauterpacht, 48 Harv.L.R. 549 (1935) and *ibid. Development*, Chap. 7.

[40] *Treaty Conference Records* (1968), p. 178. On the use of preparatory work by the British courts, see *Fothergill* v. *Monarch Airlines*, above, p. 75.

[41] *Ibid*. p. 176.

Is it a good argument for the textual approach that "[t]he text adopted by the signatories is, with rare exceptions, the only and the most recent expression of their common intent"?[42] Is it a good argument in favour of allowing recourse to preparatory work in all cases to say that it does no harm to look at whatever evidence is available, and that, occasionally, it may help? It will be evident that much use is made of preparatory work in this case book. What impression do you have of its value for treaty interpretation from its use here? Is it helpful, for example, in deciding whether warships have a right of innocent passage through a foreign territorial sea under the Territorial Seas Convention?[43] Or whether the conduct of scientific studies of the high seas is permitted by Article 2 of the High Seas Convention?[44] If the United States delegate is correct in his assertion as to the "habitual use of preparatory work by foreign offices," is that use evidence of state practice which is relevant in looking for a rule of customary international law?

In the *Employment of Women Case*,[45] the Court referred to the preparatory work of a treaty to confirm the clear meaning of its text. Could it do this under the Vienna Convention? What would a court do if the preparatory work, resorted to for purposes of confirmation, contradicts the clear meaning of the text?

In the *Territorial Jurisdiction of the International Commission of the River Oder Case*,[46] the Permanent Court of International Justice ruled that part of the preparatory work of the Treaty of Versailles 1919—the minutes of the Conference Committee on Ports, Waterways and Railways—could not be admitted in evidence before it for the purpose of interpreting the Treaty because not all of the parties to the case had participated in the drafting of the Treaty. The Court stated:

> . . . three of the Parties concerned in the present case did not take part in the work of the Conference which prepared the Treaty of Versailles; . . . accordingly, the record of this work cannot be used to determine, in so far as they are concerned, the import of the Treaty; . . . this consideration applies with equal force in regard to the passages previously published from this record and to the passages which have been reproduced for the first time in the written documents relating to the present case . . .

It thus refused to accept the distinction argued for by Poland in this case between preparatory work that had already been made public before presentation in the written proceedings in a case, which Poland thought should be admitted, and other preparatory work. The Vienna Convention contains no express limitation upon the use of the preparatory work in the sense of the ruling in the *Oder Case* and the International Law Commission's Commentary shows that none was intended:

> The Commission doubted, however, whether this ruling reflected . . . actual practice . . . in the case of multilateral treaties. . . . Moreover, . . . [a] State acceding to a treaty . . . is perfectly entitled to request to see the *travaux préparatoires*, if it wishes, before acceding.[47]

How acceptable would the rule in the *Oder Case* be in interpreting the United Nations Charter the number of parties to which is more than twice the original fifty who participated in its drafting?

2. Note that "the circumstances of" the "conclusion" of a treaty (Article 32) are, like the preparatory work, only a "supplementary means of interpretation." They were

---

[42] Huber, *Annuaire de l'Institut de Droit International* (1952), I, p. 199, Translation.
[43] See above, p. 308.
[44] See above, p. 320.
[45] P.C.I.J.Rep., Series A/B, No. 50 (1932).
[46] P.C.I.J.Rep., Series A, No. 23 (1929).
[47] Y.B.I.L.C., 1966, II, p. 223. See also Lauterpacht, *Development,* p. 137, and Rosenne, 12 I.C.L.Q. 1378 (1963).

understood by the International Law Commission's Fourth Special Rapporteur as being "both the contemporary circumstances and the historical context in which the treaty was concluded."[48] An example of reliance upon background circumstances is found in the *Anglo-Iranian Oil Co. Case*[49] where the International Court of Justice had to decide whether "treaties and conventions" in the Iranian declaration accepting the compulsory jurisdiction of the Court referred to treaties and conventions made before the declaration came into force as well as to those made afterwards. The Court noted:

> At the time when the Declaration was signed in October 1930 the Government of Iran considered all capitulatory treaties[50] as no longer binding, but was uncertain as to the legal effect of its unilateral denunciations. It is unlikely that the Government of Iran in such circumstances, should have been willing, on its own initiative, to agree that disputes relating to such treaties might be submitted for adjudication . . . by virtue of a general clause in the Declaration.[51]

VIENNA CONVENTION ON THE LAW OF TREATIES 1969

Loc. cit. at p. 563, n. 3, above

Article 33

1. When a treaty has been authenticated in two or more languages, the text is equally authoritative in each language, unless the treaty provides or the parties agree that, in case of divergence, a particular text shall prevail.

2. A version of the treaty in a language other than one of those in which the text was authenticated shall be considered an authentic text only if the treaty so provides or the parties so agree.

3. The terms of the treaty are presumed to have the same meaning in each authentic text.

4. Except where a particular text prevails in accordance with paragraph 1, when a comparison of the authentic texts discloses a difference of meaning which the application of Articles 31 and 32 does not remove, the meaning which best reconciles the texts, having regard to the object and purpose of the treaty, shall be adopted.

Notes[52]

1. The International Law Commission's Commentary reads:

> The phenonmenon of treaties drawn up in two or more languages has become extremely common and, with the advent of the United Nations, general multilateral treaties drawn up, or finally expressed, in five different languages have become quite numerous. When a treaty is plurilingual, there may or may not be a difference in the status of the different language versions for the purpose of interpretation. Each of the versions may have the status of an authentic text of the treaty; or one or more of them may be merely an "official text," that is a text which has been signed by the negotiating states but not accepted as authoritative; or one or more of them may be merely an "official translation," that is a translation prepared by the parties or an individual government or by an organ of an international organization. Today the majority of more formal treaties contain an express provision determining the status of the different language versions. If there is no such provision, it seems to be

---

[48] Y.B.I.L.C., 1966, II, p. 59.   [49] I.C.J.Rep. 1952, p. 93.
[50] *Ed.* On capitulatory regimes, see above, p. 11, n. 36.
[51] I.C.J.Rep. 1952, p. 105.
[52] See Hardy (1961) 37 B.Y.I.L. 72.

generally accepted that each of the versions in which the text of the treaty was "drawn" up is to be considered authentic, and therefore authoritative for purpose of interpretation. Few plurilingual treaties containing more than one or two articles are without some discrepancy between the texts. The different genius of the languages, the absence of a complete consensus *ad idem*, or lack of sufficient time to co-ordinate the texts may result in minor or even major discrepancies in the meaning of the texts. In that event the plurality of the texts may be a serious additional source of ambiguity or obscurity in the terms of the treaty. On the other hand, when the meaning of terms is ambiguous or obscure in one language but it is clear and convincing as to the intentions of the parties in another, the plurilingual character of the treaty facilitates interpretations of the text the meaning of which is doubtful.[53]

2. In the *Mavromatis Palestine Concessions Case*,[54] the Court had to interpret the phrases "public control" and "*contrôle public*" in the equally authentic English and French texts of the Palestine Mandate. The Court stated its approach as follows:

. . . where two versions possessing equal authority exist one of which appears to have a wider bearing than the other, it is bound to adopt the more limited interpretation which can be made to harmonise with both versions and which, as far as it goes, is doubtless in accordance with the common intention of the Parties. In the present case this conclusion is indicated with especial force because the question concerns an instrument laying down the obligations of Great Britain in her capacity as Mandatory for Palestine and because the original draft of this instrument was probably made in English.[55]

Is the *Wemhoff Case* consistent with this?[56] In the *Standard Oil Company Tankers Case*,[57] the Tribunal stated in interpreting a provision of the Treaty of Versailles 1919, of which the English and French texts are equally authentic, ". . . there is a notable discrepancy in these texts, for while the English stipulates that due regard shall be had to any "legal or equitable interests," which corresponds to very clear and well-known conceptions of English and American law, of which equity is a form, the French employs the infinitely vaguer phrase of "droits et intérêts légitimes," which corresponds to no definite legal idea . . . therefore everything points to the conclusion that the French phrase is merely the translation of the English, in which alone the expression employed has legal sense, and which makes clear the general tenor of the articles." The Tribunal then applied the English text.[58]

6. THIRD STATES[59]

FREE ZONES OF UPPER SAVOY AND THE DISTRICT OF GEX CASE

France *v.* Switzerland (1932)

P.C.I.J. Reports, Series A/B, No. 46

The facts of this case were nothing if not complicated. One of the many territorial problems that had to be dealt with at the Congress of Vienna in 1815 after the defeat of Napoleon was the future of Switzerland. On March 20, 1815, the powers participating in the Congress, who included France but not Switzerland, made a Declaration stating that if Switzerland "acceded to the stipulations contained in the present instrument, an

[53] Y.B.I.L.C., 1966, II, pp. 224–225.   [54] P.C.I.J.Rep., Series A, No. 2 (1926).
[55] *Ibid*. p. 19.   [56] See above, p. 494.
[57] *U.S.* v. *Reparation Commission*, 2 R.I.A.A. 777 at p. 792 (1926).
[58] See also the *German Reparations Case*, 1 R.I.A.A. 429, 439 (1924).
[59] See Jiménez de Aréchaga, 50 A.J.I.L. 338 (1956).

Act shall be prepared containing the acknowledgment and the guarantee, on the part of all the Powers, of the perpetual neutrality of Switzerland in her new frontiers." One of the "stipulations" was that territory in the District of Gex on the French side of the proposed border between France and Switzerland and in the immediate vicinity of Geneva, which was to be just on the Swiss side of the border, should be linked with Geneva as a single economic unit. This was thought necessary partly because of the dependence of Geneva upon the District of Gex for food and other supplies. To this end, the Declaration stated, France would not levy customs duties upon goods crossing into Switzerland from the District of Gex. Switzerland acceded to the Declaration, whereupon a second Declaration was made by the same Powers at Vienna on November 20, 1815, acknowledging the "perpetual neutrality of Switzerland." Somewhat similar arrangements were also made concerning territory in the District of Savoy which was then in the State of Sardinia and later in France. The areas on the French and, originally, the Sardinian sides of the border with Switzerland in which these arrangements applied were known as the free zones.

As a result of changed circumstances, the justification for the zones had, arguably, disappeared by the time of the First World War. France wanted to end them and, on its initiative, Article 435 of the Treaty of Versailles 1919 provided that the parties to the Treaty, who included France, but not Switzerland, agreed that the zones were "no longer consistent with present conditions, and that it is for France and Switzerland to come to an agreement together with a view to settling between themselves the status of these territories . . . " Subsequently, the two states negotiated a treaty on the question which, although approved by the Swiss Diet, failed because it was rejected by a plebiscite of the Swiss people. Thereupon, France purported to abolish the zones unilaterally. In the present case, the Court was asked to decide whether Article 435 had abrogated the zones or had created for Switzerland an obligation to abrogate them. The Court by six votes to five ruled, as a matter of construction of Article 435, that it had done neither. It also made the following comments on the question of third state rights and duties. The zones are still in existence.

Judgment of the Court

It follows from the foregoing that Article 435, paragraph 2, as such, does not involve the abolition of the free zones. But, even were it otherwise, it is certain that, in any case, Article 435 of the Treaty of Versailles is not binding upon Switzerland, who is not a Party to that Treaty, except to the extent to which that country accepted it. The extent is determined by the note of the Federal Council of May 5th, 1919, an extract from which constitutes Annex I of the said Article. It is by that instrument, and by it alone, that Switzerland has acquiesced in the provision of Article 435; and she did so under certain conditions and reservations, set out in the said note, which states, *inter alia*: "The Federal Council would not wish that its acceptance of the above wording [*scil*. Article 435, paragraph 2, of the Treaty of Versailles] should lead to the conclusion that it would agree to the suppression of a system intended to give neighbouring territory the benefit of a special régime which is appropriate to the geographical and economical situation and which has been well tested" . . .

On the question of the legal effect of the two Declarations of 1815 the Court stated:

It follows from all the foregoing that the creation of the Gex zone forms part of a territorial arrangement in favour of Switzerland, made as a result of an agreement between that country and the Powers, including France, which agreement confers on this zone the character of a contract to which Switzerland is a Party.

It also follows that no accession by Switzerland to the Declaration of November 20th was necessary and, in fact, no such accession was sought: it has never been contended that this Declaration is not binding owing to the absence of any accession by Switzerland.

The Court, having reached this conclusion simply on the basis of an examination of the situation of fact in regard to this case, need not consider the legal nature of the Gex zone from the point of view of whether it constitutes a stipulation in favour of a third Party.

But were the matter also to be envisaged from this aspect, the following observations should be made:

It cannot be lightly presumed that stipulations favourable to a third State have been adopted with the object of creating an actual right in its favour. There is however nothing to prevent the will of sovereign States from having this object and this effect. The question of the existence of a right acquired under an instrument drawn between other States is therefore one to be decided in each particular case: it must be ascertained whether the States which have stipulated in favour of a third State meant to create for that State an actual right which the latter has accepted as such.

VIENNA CONVENTION ON THE LAW OF TREATIES 1969

Loc. cit. at p. 563, n. 3, above

Article 34

A treaty does not create either obligations or rights for a third State without its consent.

Article 35

An obligation arises for a third State from a provision of a treaty if the parties to the treaty intend the provision to be the means of establishing the obligation and the third State expressly accepts that obligation in writing.

Article 36

1. A right arises for a third State from a provision of a treaty if the parties to the treaty intend the provision to accord that right either to the third State, or to a group of States to which it belongs, or to all States, and the third State assents thereto. Its assent shall be presumed so long as the contrary is not indicated, unless the treaty otherwise provides.

2. A State exercising a right in accordance with paragraph 1 shall comply with the conditions for its exercise provided for in the treaty or established in conformity with the treaty.

Article 37

1. When an obligation has arisen for a third State in conformity with Article 35, the obligation may be revoked or modified only with the consent of the parties to the treaty and of the third State, unless it is established that they had otherwise agreed.

2. When a right has arisen for a third State in conformity with Article 36, the right may not be revoked or modified by the parties if it is established that the right was intended not to be revocable or subject to modification without the consent of the third State.

Article 38

Nothing in Articles 34 to 37 precludes a rule set forth in a treaty from becoming binding upon a third State as a customary rule of international law, recognized as such.

Notes

1. The general rule in Article 34 of the Vienna Convention, which is known by the maxim *pacta tertiis nec nocent nec prosunt*, undoubtedly reflects customary international law.

2. Commenting upon its Draft Article concerning *obligations* that, in substance, became Article 35 of the Vienna Convention, the International Law Commission acknowledged that the requirements in it are so strict that when they are met "there is, in effect, a second collateral agreement between the parties to the treaty, on the one hand, and the third state on the other; and that the juridical basis of the latter's obligation is not the treaty itself but the collateral agreement."[60]

3. Examples of third party rights are in the treaty provisions guaranteeing freedom of passage for ships through the Suez and Kiel Canals.[61] Note that in the case of the Hay-Pauncefote Treaty 1901 concerning the Panama Canal, in 1924 the United States Secretary of State took the position that "other nations . . . not being parties to the treaty have no rights under it."[62]

4. Some writers have suggested that certain types of treaties affecting third parties, including the international canal treaties referred to in the previous note, should be seen not as contracts having effect for third parties but rather as instruments intending to establish, and accepted by the international community as being able to establish, legal changes valid *ergo omnes*. Thus McNair[63] distinguishes "the predominantly contractual type of treaty whose main object is to create obligations (both rights and duties) *in personam*," on the one hand, from "dispositive or 'real' treaties" and "constitutive or semi-legislative treaties," on the other. "Dispositive" treaties are "treaties creating or affecting territorial rights, and resembling the conveyance of English and American private law. . . ." McNair gives as examples treaties of cession, boundary treaties and mandates. As to "constitutive" treaties, he has in mind international settlements or arrangements such as those neutralising Switzerland and guaranteeing passage through the Suez Canal, as well as treaties creating states, *e.g.* Belgium, or other entities, *e.g.* the United Nations, and endowing them with legal personality valid *ergo omnes*. McNair suggests that the effect of "dispositive" and "constitutive" treaties is best explained not in terms of contract but of "some inherent and distinctive juridical element in those treaties."[64] The International Law Commission decided against adopting such a distinction:

> It considered that the provision in . . . [Article 36, Vienna Convention], regarding treaties intended to create rights in favour of States generally, together with the process mentioned in the present article, furnish a legal basis for the establishment of treaty obligations and rights valid *ergo omnes*, which goes as far as is at present possible. Accordingly, it decided not to propose any special provision on treaties creating so-called objective régimes.[65]

5. What is the effect of Article 2(6) of the United Nations Charter[66] for states not members of the United Nations?[67]

---

[60] Y.B.I.L.C., 1966, II, p. 227.
[61] See above, pp. 201–203.   [62] 5 Hackworth 222.   [63] *Treaties*, p. 256.
[64] *Ibid*. p. 255.   [65] Y.B.I.L.C., 1966, II, p. 231.   [66] Appendix I, below.
[67] Contrast the views of Kelsen, *The Law of the United Nations* (1950), pp. 106–110, and Kunz, 41 A.J.I.L. 119 (1947).

7. AMENDMENT AND MODIFICATION

VIENNA CONVENTION ON THE LAW OF TREATIES 1969

Loc. cit. at p. 563, n. 3, above

Article 39

A treaty may be amended by agreement between the parties. The rules laid down in Part II apply to such an agreement except in so far as the treaty may otherwise provide.

Article 40

1. Unless the treaty otherwise provides, the amendment of multilateral treaties shall be governed by the following paragraphs.

2. Any proposal to amend a multilateral treaty as between all the parties must be notified to all the contracting States, each one of which shall have the right to take part in:

(*a*) the decision as to the action to be taken in regard to such proposals;
(*b*) the negotiation and conclusion of any agreement for the amendment of the treaty.

3. Every State entitled to become a party to the treaty shall also be entitled to become a party to the treaty as amended.

4. The amending agreement does not bind any State already a party to the treaty which does not become a party to the amending agreement; Article 30, paragraph 4(*b*) [above, p. 594] , applies in relation to such State.

5. Any State which becomes a party to the treaty after the entry into force of the amending agreement shall, failing an expression of a different intention by that State:

(*a*) be considered as a party to the treaty as amended; and
(*b*) be considered as a party to the unamended treaty in relation to any party to the treaty not bound by the amending agreement.

Article 41

1. Two or more of the parties to a multilateral treaty may conclude an agreement to modify the treaty as between themselves alone if:

(*a*) the possibility of such a modification is provided for by the treaty; or
(*b*) the modification in question is not prohibited by the treaty and,

    (i) does not affect the enjoyment by the other parties of their rights under the treaty or the performance of their obligations;
    (ii) does not relate to a provision, derogation from which is incompatible with the effective execution of the object and purpose of the treaty as a whole.

2. Unless in a case falling under paragraph 1(*a*) the treaty otherwise provides, the parties in question shall notify the other parties of their intention to conclude the agreement and of the modification to the treaty for which it provides.

8. *VALIDITY OF TREATIES*[68]

(i) NON-COMPLIANCE WITH MUNICIPAL LAW REQUIREMENTS

VIENNA CONVENTION ON THE LAW OF TREATIES 1969

Loc. cit. at p. 563, n. 3, above

Article 46

1. A state may not invoke the fact that its consent to be bound by a treaty has been expressed in violation of a provision of its internal law regarding competence to conclude treaties as invalidating its consent unless that violation was manifest and concerned a rule of its internal law of fundamental importance.

2. A violation is manifest if it would be objectively evident to any State conducting itself in the matter in accordance with normal practice and in good faith.

Article 47

If the authority of a representative to express the consent of a State to be bound by a particular treaty has been made subject to a specific restriction, his omission to observe that restriction may not be invoked as invalidating the consent expressed by him unless the restriction was notified to the other negotiating States prior to his expressing such consent.

Notes

1. Opinion has been divided on the question whether non-compliance with a requirement of municipal law concerning competence to make a treaty affects the validity of a State's consent. The International Law Commission's Commentary summarises the three different approaches as follows:

> Some jurists maintain that international law leaves it to the internal laws of each State to determine the organs and procedures by which the will of a State to be bound by a treaty shall be formed and expressed. . . . On this view, internal laws limiting the power of State organs to enter into treaties are to be considered part of international law so as to avoid, or at least render voidable, any consent to a treaty given on the international plane in disregard of a constitutional limitation. . . . If this view were to be accepted, it would follow that other States would not be entitled to rely on the authority to commit the State ostensibly possessed by a Head of State, Prime Minister, Foreign Minister, etc., under [Article 7, Vienna Convention] . . . they would have to satisfy themselves in each case that the provisions of the State's constitution are not infringed or take the risk of subsequently finding the treaty void. . . . Other jurists, while basing themselves on the incorporation of constitutional limitations into international law, recognise that some qualification of that doctrine is essential if it is not to undermine the security of treaties. . . . On this view, a State contesting the validity of a treaty, on constitutional grounds may invoke only those provisions of the constitution which are notorious. . . . A third group of jurists considers that international law leaves to each State the determination of the organs and procedures by which its will to conclude treaties is formed, and is itself concerned

---

[68] See Nahlik, 65 A.J.I.L. 736 (1971). Note that Art. 42(1) of the Vienna Convention reads: The validity of a treaty or of the consent of a State to be bound by a treaty may be impeached only through the application of the present Convention.

exclusively with the external manifestations of this will on the international plane. . . . In consequence, if an agent, competent under international law to commit the State, expresses the consent of the State to a treaty through one of the established procedures, the State is held bound by the treaty in international law. . . . Some of these writers modify the stringency of the rule in cases where the the other State is actually aware of the failure to comply with internal law or where the lack of constitutional authority is so manifest that the other State must be deemed to have been aware of it.[69]

2. In the *Eastern Greenland Case*,[70] Norway argued[71] that M. Ihlen was not competent under Norway's constitution to bind it on a matter such as that covered by the Ihlen declaration. Clearly the Court thought this to be irrelevant as far as international law was concerned. Similarly, in his report in the *Spanish Zones of Morocco Claims*,[72] M. Huber rejected a Spanish contention in respect of one of the claims—the *Rio-Martin* claim—that a treaty was not binding upon Spain because it had not been approved in a manner required by Moroccan law:

The *Rapporteur* finds it unnecessary to elucidate this point of Moroccan constitutional law. It is enough to point out that the aforementioned exchange of letters between the authorized agents of the two Governments manifestly establishes their shared desire to transfer to a house at Tetuan rights that the British Government held in respect of the house at Martin by the terms of a treaty still valid for the point at issue.

3. The Government of the Isle of Man has no treaty making power; treaties affecting the Isle of Man are made by the United Kingdom Government. Imagine that the Government of Isle of Man were to purport to make a treaty with State A for the purchase of wheat. Could the United Kingdom avoid the treaty under Article 46? Could State A?

4. The International Law Commission's Commentary reads:

. . . [Article 47] is confined to cases in which the defect of authority relates to the execution of an act by which a representative purports *finally* to establish his state's consent to be bound.[73]

Where a treaty signed by a representative in excess of his authority requires ratification, if the state ratifies it "it will necessarily be held to have endorsed the unauthorised act of its representative and, by doing so, to have cured the original defect of authority."[74]

(ii) ERROR

VIENNA CONVENTION ON THE LAW OF TREATIES 1969

Loc. cit. at p. 563, n. 3, above

Article 48

1. A State may invoke an error in a treaty as invalidating its consent to be bound by the treaty if the error relates to a fact or situation which was assumed by that State to exist at the time when the treaty was concluded and formed an essential basis of its consent to be bound by the treaty.

[69] Y.B.I.L.C., 1966, II, p. 240–241. See also Meron (1978) 49 B.Y.I.L. 175.
[70] P.C.I.J. Reports, Series A/B, No. 53 (1933).
[71] P.C.I.J.Rep., Series C, No. 62, pp. 566–568.
[72] *Great Britain* v. *Spain*, 2 R.I.A.A. 615 at p. 724 (1925). Translation.
[73] Y.B.I.L.C., 1966, II, p. 243.   [74] *Ibid*.

2. Paragraph 1 shall not apply if the State in question contributed by its own conduct to the error or if the circumstances were such as to put that State on notice of a possible error.

3. An error relating only to the wording of the text of a treaty does not affect its validity; Article 79 then applies.

Notes

1. Error, or mistake, plays a much less important part in the law of treaties in international law than it does in the law of contract in municipal law. The considerable care generally attendant upon the conclusion of treaties, together with, in some cases, the publicity and political scrutiny afforded to their drafting help to make this so. In practice, the International Law Commission points out, almost all the recorded instances in which errors of substance have been alleged, "concern geographical errors, mostly errors in maps."[75]

2. Does Article 45 distinguish between mutual and unilateral error? Or between error of fact and of law?

3. In the *Temple Case*,[76] the International Court of Justice was asked to rule that Cambodia, and not Thailand, had sovereignty over the Temple of Preah Vihear and that Thailand should both remove the armed guards and other persons it had placed in the Temple since 1954 and return sculptures and other objects it had taken therefrom. In 1904, the boundary between Cambodia (then a protectorate of France) and Thailand (then Siam) in the wild, remote and sparsely populated area of Preah Vihear was determined by a treaty between France and Siam. The treaty stated that it was to follow the watershed line and provided for the details to be worked out by a Mixed Franco-Siamese Commission. Surveys were conducted by technical experts for the Commission on the basis of which a map [the Annex I map] was prepared. This clearly placed the Temple in Cambodia. The map was never approved by the Commission which did not meet again after the map had been made. Cambodia relied upon the map. Thailand argued, *inter alia*, that the map embodied a material error because it did not follow the watershed line as required by the treaty. It argued this even though, as the Court found, the Siamese had received and accepted the map. The Court rejected Thailand's argument as follows:

> It is an established rule of law that the plea of error cannot be allowed as an element vitiating consent if the party advancing it contributed by its own conduct to the error, or could have avoided it, or if the circumstances were such as to put that party on notice of a possible error. The Court considers that the character and qualifications of the persons who saw the Annex I map on the Siamese side would alone make it difficult for Thailand to plead error in law. These persons included the members of the very Commission of Delimitation within whose competence this sector of the frontier had lain. . . . [77]

(iii) FRAUD AND CORRUPTION

VIENNA CONVENTION ON THE LAW OF TREATIES 1969

Loc. cit. at p. 563, n. 3, above

Article 49

If a State has been induced to conclude a treaty by the fraudulent conduct of another negotiating State, the State may invoke the fraud as invalidating its consent to be bound by the treaty.

[75] *Ibid.*   [76] I.C.J.Rep. 1962, p. 6.   [77] *Ibid.* p. 26.

Article 50

If the expression of a State's consent to be bound by a treaty has been procured through the corruption of its representative directly or indirectly by another negotiating State, the State may invoke such corruption as invalidating its consent to be bound by the treaty.

Note

Fraud and corruption, like error, are not very important in practice in the law of treaties. As to *fraud*, the International Law Commission stated:

Fraud is a concept found in most systems of law, but the scope of the concept is not the same in all systems. In International law, the paucity of precedents means that there is little guidance to be found either in practice or in the jurisprudence of international tribunals as to the scope to be given to the concept. In these circumstances, the Commission considered whether it should attempt to define fraud in the law of treaties. The Commission concluded, however, that it would suffice to formulate the general concept of fraud applicable in the law of treaties and to leave its precise scope to be worked out in practice and in the decisions of international tribunals.[78]

As to *corruption of a representative*, it stated:

The strong term "corruption" is used expressly in order to indicate that only acts calculated to exercise a substantial influence on the disposition of the representative to conclude the treaty may be invoked as invalidating the expression of consent which he has purported to give on behalf of his state. The Commission did not mean to imply that under the present article a small courtesy or favour shown to a representative in connection with the conclusion of a treaty may be invoked as a pretext for invalidating the treaty.[79]

(iv) COERCION

VIENNA CONVENTION ON THE LAW OF TREATIES 1969

Loc. cit. at p. 563, n. 3, above

Article 51

The expression of a State's consent to be bound by a treaty which has been procured by the coercion of its representative through acts or threats directed against him shall be without any legal effect.

Article 52

A treaty is void if its conclusion has been procured by the threat or use of force in violation of the principles of international law embodied in the Charter of the United Nations.

Notes

1. Coercion of a representative of a state is rare. Article 51 is directed at coercion of a representative personally and not at coercion of him through a threat of action against his state. An example of the exercise of both is reported to have occurred when

[78] Y.B.I.L.C., 1966, II, p. 244.
[79] *Ibid.* p. 245.

President Hacha of Czechoslovakia signed a treaty with Germany establishing a German protectorate over Bohemia and Moravia in Berlin at 2.00 a.m. on March 15, 1939. According to one report

> The German ministers [Goering and Ribbentrop] were pitiless. . . . They literally hunted Dr. Hacha and M. Chvalkovsky round the table on which the documents were lying, thrusting them continually before them, pushing pens into their hands, incessantly repeating that if they continued in their refusal, half of Prague would lie in ruins from bombing within two hours, and that this would be only the beginning.[80]

Consent obtained contrary to Article 51 is of no legal effect; the state whose representative has been coerced cannot regard it as otherwise. The International Law Commission thought

> that the use of coercion against the representative of a state for the purpose of procuring the conclusion of a treaty would be a matter of such gravity that the article should provide for the absolute nullity of a consent to a treaty so obtained.[81]

2. As to coercion of a state, the International Law Commission's Commentary reads:

> The traditional doctrine prior to the Covenant of the League of Nations was that the validity of a treaty was not affected by the fact that it had been brought about by the threat or use of force. However, this doctrine was simply a reflection of the general attitude of international law during that era towards the legality of the use of force for the settlement of international disputes. With the Covenant and the Pact of Paris there began to develop a strong body of opinion which held that such treaties should no longer be recognised as legally valid. The endorsement of the criminality of aggressive war in the Charters of the Allied Military Tribunals for the trial of the Axis war criminals, the clear-cut prohibition of the threat or use of force in Article 2(4) of the Charter of the United Nations, together with the practice of the United Nations itself, have reinforced and consolidated this development in the law. The Commission considers that these developments justify the conclusion that the invalidity of a treaty procured by the illegal threat or use of force is a principle which is *lex lata* in the international law of today. . . . Some members of the Commission expressed the view that any other forms of pressure, such as a threat to strangle the economy of a country, ought to be stated in the article as falling within the concept of coercion. The Commission, however, decided to define coercion in terms of a "threat or use of force in violation of the principles of the Charter,"[82] and considered that the precise scope of the acts covered by this definition should be left to be determined in practice by interpretation of the relevant provisions of the Charter . . . the phrase "violation of the principles of the Charter" has been chosen rather than "violation of the Charter," in order that the article should not appear to be confined in its application to Members of the United Nations. The Commission further considered that a treaty procured by a threat or use of force in violation of the principles of the Charter must be characterised as void, rather than as voidable at the instance of the injured party. Even if it were conceivable that after being liberated from the influence of a threat or of a use of force a state might wish to allow a treaty procured from it by such means, the Commission considered it essential that the treaty should be regarded in law as void *ab initio*. This would enable the state concerned to take its decision in regard to the maintenance of the treaty in a position of full legal equality with the other state. If, therefore, the treaty were maintained in force, it would in effect be by the conclusion of a new treaty and not by the recognition of the validity of a treaty

[80] Dispatch by M. Coulondre, the French Ambassador to Berlin, quoted in Shirer, *The Rise and Fall of the Third Reich* (Pan Books edition, 1964), p. 545.
[81] Y.B.I.L.C., 1966, II, p. 246.
[82] *Ed.* Note that in Article 52 this wording was changed to "in violation of the principles of *international law embodied* in the Charter. . . . " Italics added.

procured by means contrary to the most fundamental principles of the Charter of the United Nations.[83]

3. In the *Fisheries Jurisdiction Case (Jurisdiction)*,[84] the International Court of Justice stated:

The letter of 29 May 1972 addressed to the Registrar by the Minister for Foreign Affairs of Iceland contains the following statement: "The 1961 Exchange of Notes took place under extremely difficult circumstances, when the British Royal Navy had been using force to oppose the 12-mile fishery limit established by the Icelandic Government in 1958."

This statement could be interpreted as a veiled charge of duress purportedly rendering the Exchange of Notes void *ab initio*, and it was dealt with as such by the United Kingdom in its Memorial. There can be little doubt, as is implied in the Charter of the United Nations and recognized in Article 52 of the Vienna Convention on the Law of Treaties, that under contemporary international law an agreement concluded under the threat or use of force is void. It is equally clear that a court cannot consider an accusation of this serious nature on the basis of a vague general charge unfortified by evidence in its support. The history of the negotiations which led up to the 1961 Exchange of Notes reveals that these instruments were freely negotiated by the interested parties on the basis of perfect equality and freedom of decision on both sides. No fact has been brought to the attention of the Court from any quarter suggesting the slightest doubt on this matter.

4. If state A were to attack state B and to be utterly defeated by it, would a peace treaty between the two states by which A agreed (i) to cede to B territory belonging to A and (ii) to pay compensation for injuries suffered by the population of B during the fighting be void because of coercion? Is Article 75 of the Vienna Convention applicable:

The provisions of the present Convention are without prejudice to any obligation in relation to a treaty which may arise for an aggressor State in consequence of measures taken in conformity with the Charter of the United Nations with reference to that States's aggression?

On the present validity of title to territory based upon treaties that were made before the rule stated in Article 52 was established, see above, p. 179. Note that it is the acceptance of the treaty that must be coerced. A treaty, such as the 1979 Egyptian-Israeli Treaty of Peace, see above, p. 176, that is signed as a matter of choice is not invalid under Article 52 if, even though its terms may have been dictated or influenced by a prior use of force.

5. Soviet writers have for some years supported a doctrine of "unequal treaties." The Soviet International Law textbook[85] states:

The principle that international treaties must be observed does not extend to treaties which are imposed by force, and which are unequal in character . . .

Equal treaties are treaties concluded on the basis of the equality of the parties; unequal treaties are those which do not fulfil this elementary requirement. Unequal treaties are not legally binding; . . .

Treaties must be based upon the sovereign equality of the contracting parties.

Krylov[86] cites as examples of "unequal treaties" those establishing capitulatory regimes "by which an imperialist power imposes its will upon a weaker state . . ."[87] and the

[83] *Ibid.* pp. 246–247.
[84] I.C.J.Rep. 1973, p. 14. *U.K.* v. *Iceland.* On the claim of duress in respect of the U.S.-Iranian Hostages Settlement, *see* Redwine, 14 Vanderbilt J. Trans. L. 847 (1981).
[85] Kozhevnikov (Ed.), *International Law* (1961), p. 248.
[86] 70 *Hague Recueil* 407 (1947–I).
[87] *Ibid.* p. 434. Translation. On capitulatory regimes, see above, p. 11, n. 36.

Munich Agreement of 1938,[88] by which France, Italy and the United Kingdom agreed to the cession to Germany of Sudeten German territory in Czechoslovakia. The Soviet International Law textbook gives the Anglo-Egyptian Treaty of Alliance of 1936[89] as a further example because it "violated the elementary sovereign rights of the Egyptian people."[90] Article 52 does not incorporate the Soviet doctrine.[91] The "fundamental change of circumstances" rule[92] or the "clean slate" approach to state succession to treaties[93] might, however, be applicable in some cases. The Soviet doctrine has in recent years also received support from other writers.[94] At the Vienna Treaty Conference a Declaration on the Prohibition of Military, Political or Economic Coercion in the Conclusion of Treaties[95] was adopted by which the Conference

Solemnly condemns the threat or use of pressure in any form, whether military, political, or economic, by any state in order to coerce another State to perform any act relating to the conclusion of a treaty in violation of the principles of the sovereign equality of States and freedom of consent.

(v) JUS COGENS[96]

VIENNA CONVENTION ON THE LAW OF TREATIES 1969

Loc. cit. at p. 563, n. 3, above

Article 53

A treaty is void if, at the time of its conclusion, it conflicts with a peremptory norm of general international law. For the purposes of the present Convention, a peremptory norm of general international law is a norm accepted and recognized by the international community of States as a whole as a norm from which no derogation is permitted and which can be modified only by a subsequent norm of general international law having the same character.

Article 64[97]

If a new peremptory norm of general international law emerges, any existing treaty which is in conflict with that norm becomes void and terminates.

Notes

1. The International Law Commission's Commentary reads:

The view that in the last analysis there is no rule of international law from which states cannot at their own free will contract out has become increasingly difficult to sustain, although some jurists deny the existence of any rules of *jus cogens* in international

---

[88] Misc. No. 8 (1938), Cmd. 5848.
[89] U.K.T.S. 6 (1937), Cmd. 5360.
[90] *Op. cit.* at p. 14, n. 49, above, p. 281.
[91] On the meaning of "force" in Art. 2(4) of the UN Charter, see below, p. 641.
[92] See below, p. 623.
[93] See below, p. 637.
[94] For a statement typical of several made by Asian writers, see Sinha, 14 I.C.L.Q. 121 (1965).
[95] *Treaty Conference Records,* 1969, p. 168.
[96] See Mangallona, 51 Phil. L.J. 521 (1976); Scheuner, 27 Z.A.O.R. 520 (1967) at 29 *ibid.* p. 28 (1969); Schwarzenberger, 43 Texas L.R. 456 (1965), a shorter version of which is printed in (1965) 18 C.L.P. 191 ; Schwelb, 61 A.J.I.L. 946 (1967); Sztucki, *Jus Cogens and the Vienna Convention of the Law of Treaties* (1974); Verdross, 60 A.J.I.L. 55 (1966).
[97] Art. 64, which really contains a rule on termination, is included here for convenience.

law, since in their view even the most general rules still fall short of being universal. The Commission pointed out that the law of the Charter concerning the prohibition of the use of force in itself constitutes a conspicuous example of a rule in international law having the character of *jus cogens*. Moreover, if some governments in their comments have expressed doubts as to the advisability of this article unless it is accompanied by provision for independent adjudication, only one questioned the existence of rules of *jus cogens* in the international law of today. Accordingly the Commission concluded that in codifying the law of treaties it must start from the basis that today there are certain rules from which states are not competent to derogate at all by a treaty arrangement, and which may be changed only by another rule of the same character. . . . The emergence of rules having the character of *jus cogens* is comparatively recent, while international law is in process of rapid development. The Commission considered the right course to be to provide in general terms that a treaty is void if it conflicts with a rule of *jus cogens* and to leave the full content of this rule to be worked out in state practice and in the jurisprudence of international tribunals. Some members of the Commission felt that there might be advantage in specifying, by way of illustration, some of the most obvious and best settled rules of *jus cogens* in order to indicate by these examples the general nature and scope of the rule contained in the article. Examples suggested included (a) a treaty contemplating an unlawful use of force contrary to the principles of the Charter, (b) a treaty contemplating the performance of any other act criminal under international law, and (c) a treaty contemplating or conniving at the commission of acts, such as trade in slaves, piracy or genocide, in the suppression of which every state is called upon to co-operate. Other members expressed the view that, if examples were given, it would be undesirable to appear to limit the scope of the articles to cases involving acts which constitute crimes under international law; treaties violating human rights, the equality of states or the principle of self determination were mentioned as other possible examples.[98]

The Commission eventually decided against including any examples of rules of *jus cogens* partly because "the mention of some cases . . . might, even with the most careful drafting, lead to misunderstanding as to the position concerning other cases. . . ."[99]

2. Can the International Court of Justice's reference to *jus cogens* in the *North Sea Continental Shelf Cases*[1] be read as acceptance by the Court that there is such a concept in international law? How can a rule of *jus cogens* be changed? Rules of *jus cogens* are sometimes contrasted with rules of *jus dispositivum*, from which derogations are permitted by treaty. They are comparable with rules of public policy in municipal law.

3. Commenting upon the Vienna Conference, Sinclair states:

Even before the Conference began, . . . it was clear that the vast majority of international lawyers from the developing countries and from the Eastern European countries attached the highest importance to the concept that a treaty concluded in violation of an existing or new rule of *jus cogens* should be regarded as void and of no effect. . . . On the other hand, the majority of Western European governments had, in their written and other comments on the Commission's proposals, expressed considerable doubts about the desirability of introducing *de lege ferenda* such a vague, indeterminate and undefined ground of invalidity; and some, including the United Kingdom Government, had stressed in addition that the application of the *jus cogens* articles must be made subject to independent adjudication.[2]

[98] Y.B.I.L.C., 1966, II, pp. 247–248.
[99] *Ibid*. p. 248.
[1] See above, p. 26.
[2] *Loc. cit.* at p. 563, n. 1, above, p. 66.

It was partly because of doubt about the provisions on *jus cogens* that France voted against the adoption of the Convention:

> It was no doubt a lofty concept but it was liable to jeopardise the stability of treaty law, which was a necessary safeguard in inter-State relations. On that point, even . . . recourse to the International Court of Justice, could not make up for the lack of precision in the drafting of the texts. In consequence, the judge would be given such wide discretion that he would become an international legislature and that was not his proper function.[3]

9. TERMINATION OF, SUSPENSION OF AND WITHDRAWAL FROM TREATIES[4]

(i) IN ACCORDANCE WITH THE TREATY OR OTHERWISE BY CONSENT

VIENNA CONVENTION ON THE LAW OF TREATIES 1969

Loc. cit. at p. 563, n. 3, above

Article 54

The termination of a treaty or the withdrawal of a party may take place:

(*a*) in conformity with the provisions of the treaty; or
(*b*) at any time by consent of all the parties after consultation with the other contracting States.

Article 55

Unless the treaty otherwise provides, a multilateral treaty does not terminate by reason only of the fact that the number of the parties falls below the number necessary for its entry into force.

Article 56

1. A treaty which contains no provision regarding its termination and which does not provide for denunciation or withdrawal is not subject to denunciation or withdrawal unless:

(*a*) it is established that the parties intended to admit the possibility of denunciation or withdrawal; or
(*b*) a right of denunciation or withdrawal may be implied by the nature of the treaty.

2. A party shall not give less than twelve months' notice of its intention to denounce or withdraw from a treaty under paragraph 1.

Article 57

The operation of a treaty in regard to all the parties or to a particular party may be suspended:

---

[3] M. Hubert (France), *Treaty Conference Records* (1969), p. 203.
[4] Note generally that Art. 42(2) of the Vienna Convention reads:
The termination of a treaty, its denunciation or the withdrawal of a party, may take place only as a result of the application of the provisions of the treaty or of the present Convention. The same rule applies to suspension of the operation of a treaty.

(a) in conformity with the provisions of the treaty; or
(b) at any time by consent of all the parties after consultation with the other
contracting States.

Article 58

1. Two or more parties to a multilateral treaty may conclude an agreement to
suspend the operation of provisions of the treaty, temporarily and as between
themselves alone, if:

the possibility of such a suspension is provided for by the treaty; or
(b) the suspension in question is not prohibited by the treaty and:

(i) does not affect the enjoyment by the other parties of their rights under
the treaty or the performance of their obligations;
(ii) is not incompatible with the object and purpose of the treaty.

2. Unless in a case falling under paragraph 1(a) the treaty otherwise provides,
the parties in question shall notify the other parties of their intention to conclude
the agreement and of those provisions of the treaty the operation of which they
intend to suspend.

Article 59

A treaty shall be considered as terminated if all the parties to it conclude a later
treaty relating to the same subject-matter and:

(a) it appears from the later treaty or is otherwise established that the parties
intended that the matter should be governed by that treaty; or
(b) the provisions of the later treaty are so far incompatible with those of the
earlier one that the two treaties are not capable of being applied at the
same time.

2. The earlier treaty shall be considered as only suspended in operation if it
appears from the later treaty or is otherwise established that such was the
intention of the parties.

Note
The United Nations Charter is probably a treaty that allows the possibility of
withdrawal under Article 56(1)(a).[5] A treaty of political alliance would, probably be a
treaty covered by Article 56(1)(b).

(ii) MATERIAL BREACH[6]

VIENNA CONVENTION ON THE LAW OF TREATIES 1969

Loc. cit. at p. 563, n. 3, above

Article 60

1. A material breach of a bilateral treaty by one of the parties entitles the
other to invoke the breach as a ground for terminating the treaty or suspending
its operation in whole or in part.

[5] See 7 U.N.C.I.O., *Documents*, p. 324.
[6] See Sinha, *Unilateral Denunciation of Treaty because of Prior Violations of Obligations by
Other Party* (1966).

2. A material breach of a multilateral treaty by one of the parties entitles:

(*a*) the other parties by unanimous agreement to suspend the operation of the treaty in whole or in part or to terminate it either:
  (i) in the relations between themselves and the defaulting State or
  (ii) as between all parties;
(*b*) a party specially affected by the breach to invoke it as a ground for suspending the operation of the treaty in whole or in part in the relations between itself and the defaulting State;
(*c*) any party other than the defaulting State to invoke the breach as a ground for suspending the operation of the treaty in whole or in part with respect to itself if the treaty is of such a character that a material breach of its provisions by one party radically changes the position of every party with respect to the further performance of its obligations under the treaty.

3. A material breach of a treaty, for the purposes of this article, consist in:

(*a*) a repudiation of the treaty not sanctioned by the present Convention; or
(*b*) the violation of a provision essential to the accomplishment of the object or purpose of the treaty.

4. The foregoing paragraphs are without prejudice to any provision in the treaty applicable in the event of a breach.

5. Paragraphs 1 to 3 do not apply to provisions relating to the protection of the human person contained in treaties of a humanitarian character, in particular to provisions prohibiting any form of reprisals against persons protected by such treaties.

Notes

1. The International Law Commission's Commentary reads:

The great majority of jurists recognize that a violation of a treaty by one party may give rise to a right in the other party to abrogate the treaty or to suspend the performance of its own obligations under the treaty. . . . Opinion differs, however, as to the extent of the right to abrogate the treaty and the conditions under which it may be exercised. . . . State practice does not give great assistance in determining the true extent of this right or the proper conditions for its exercise. In many cases, the denouncing State has decided for quite other reasons to put an end to the treaty and, having alleged the violation primarily to provide a pretext for its action, has not been prepared to enter into a serious discussion of the legal principles involved. The other party has usually contested the denunciation primarily on the basis of the facts; and, if it has sometimes used language appearing to deny that unilateral denunciation is ever justified, this has usually appeared rather to be a protest against the one-sided and arbitrary pronouncements of the denouncing State than a rejection of the right to denounce when serious violations are established. . . . The Commission was agreed that a breach of a treaty, however serious, does not *ipso facto* put an end to the treaty, and also that it is not open to a State simply to allege a violation of the treaty and pronounce that treaty at an end. On the other hand, it considered that within certain limits and subject to certain safeguards the right of a party to invoke the breach of a treaty as a ground for terminating it or suspending its operation must be recognized. . . . Some authorities have in the past seemed to assume that any breach of any provision would suffice to justify the denunciation of the treaty. The Commission, however, was unanimous that the right to terminate or suspend must be limited to cases where the breach is of a serious character. It preferred the term "material" to "fundamental" to express the kind of breach which is required. The word "fundamental" might be understood as meaning that only the violation of a provision directly touching the central purposes of the treaty can ever justify the other party in terminating the treaty. But other provisions considered by a party to be essential to the effective execution of the treaty may have been very material in inducing it to enter into the treaty at all, even although these provisions may be of an ancillary character.[7]

2. Support for the view that only a material, as opposed to any, breach justifies the termination or suspension of a treaty is found in the *Tacna-Arica arbitration*.[8] By Article 3 of the Treaty of Ancon 1883 between Chile and Peru it was provided that the Peruvian provinces of Tacna and Arica, sovereignty over which was sought by both parties, were to remain in the possession of Chile, which had obtained possession of them by armed force, for ten years and that after that time a plebiscite would be held to determine their future. In 1922, after the parties had been unable to agree upon arrangements for the plebiscite, the question whether the plebiscite had still to be held was referred to arbitration. Peru alleged, *inter alia*, that "Chile by preventing the performance of Article 3 has discharged Peru from her obligations thereunder, and hence that a plebiscite should not now be held and that Chile should be regarded as a trespasser in the territory now in question since the year 1894."[9] Chile had prevented the holding of the plebiscite as envisaged in Article 3, Peru argued, by her policy of 'Chileanization" of the provinces by the introduction of Chilean nationals and by measures discriminating against Peruvians. The Arbitrator (President Coolidge, U.S.A.) rejected this argument on the facts:

> The Arbitrator is far from approving the course of Chilean administration and condoning the acts committed against Peruvians to which reference has been made, but finds no reason to conclude that a fair plebiscite in the present circumstances cannot be held under proper conditions or that a plebiscite should not be had. . . . It is manifest that if abuses of administration could have the effect of terminating such an agreement, it would be necessary to establish such serious conditions as the consequence of administrative wrongs as would operate to frustrate the purpose of the agreement, and, in the opinion of the Arbitrator, a situation of such gravity has not been shown.[10]

3. When is there a material breach under Article 60(3)(*b*) in the case of a law-making treaty with a number of provisions of roughly equal importance? Would, for example, a breach of Article 11 of the Geneva Convention on the High Seas concerning criminal jurisdiction in respect of collisions on the high seas[11] be one?

4. In the case of some treaties, the International Law Commission stated in its Commentary, "a breach by one party tends to undermine the whole regime of the treaty as between all the parties."[12] The Commission gave disarmament treaties as examples of such treaties and explained:

> In the case of a material breach of such a treaty the interests of an individual party may not be adequately protected by the rules contained in paragraphs 2(*a*) and (*b*). It could not suspend the performance of its own obligations under the treaty *vis-à-vis* the defaulting State without at the same time violating its obligations to the other parties. Yet, unless it does so, it may be unable to protect itself against the threat resulting from the arming of the defaulting State. In these cases, where a material breach of the treaty by one party radically changes the position of every party with

---

[7] Y.B.I.L.C., 1966, II, pp. 253–255.
[8] *Chile* v. *Peru*, 2 R.I.A.A. 921 (1925).
[9] *Ibid.* p. 929.
[10] *Ibid.* pp. 943–944.
[11] See above, p. 326.
[12] Y.B.I.L.C., 1966, II, p. 255.

respect to the further performance of its obligations, the Commission considered that any party must be permitted without first obtaining the agreement of the other parties to suspend the operation of the treaty with respect to itself generally in its relations with all the other parties. Paragraph 2(c) accordingly so provides.[13]

Would the Nuclear Test Ban Treaty 1963,[14] or a treaty limiting the number of whales that may be caught annually be other examples of such treaties? Would Article 60(2)(c) be available in respect of a material breach of the Genocide Convention?[15] (Would Article 60(2)(b) be available in the same case?) What is the effect for the other innocent parties if one innocent party acts under Article 60(2)(c)?

5. Paragraph 5 of Article 60 was added at Vienna. The provisions in the 1949 Geneva Red Cross Conventions[16] prohibiting reprisals against the persons protected by the Conventions were mentioned as coming within it.[17] Reference was also made to conventions concerning refugees, slavery, genocide, and human rights generally, although these do not contain provisions prohibiting reprisals in cases of breach.[18]

6. For an application of the rules on material breach, see the *Namibia Case*.[19]

(iii) SUPERVENING IMPOSSIBILITY OF PERFORMANCE

VIENNA CONVENTION ON THE LAW OF TREATIES 1969

Loc. cit. at p. 563, n. 3, above

Article 61

1. A party may invoke the impossibility of performing a treaty as a ground for terminating or withdrawing from it if the impossibility results from the permanent disappearance or destruction of an object indispensible for the execution of the treaty. If the impossibility is temporary, it may be invoked only as a ground for suspending the operation of the treaty.

2. Impossibility of performance may not be invoked by a party as a ground for terminating, withdrawing from or suspending the operation of a treaty if the impossibility is the result of a breach by that party either of an obligation under the treaty or of any other international obligation owed to any other party to the treaty.

Note

The International Law Commission's Commentary reads:

"State practice furnishes few examples of the termination of a treaty on this ground. But the types of cases envisaged . . . [include] the submergence of an island, the

---

[13] *Ibid.*
[14] See above, p. 322. See on this question, Schwelb, 58 A.J.I.L. 642, 663–669 (1964).
[15] See above, p. 561.
[16] See, *e.g.* Art. 46 of the Geneva Convention for the Amelioration of the Condition of the Wounded and Sick in Armed Forces in the Field, U.K.T.S. 39 (1958), Cmnd. 550, 75 U.N.T.S. 3: "Reprisals against the wounded, sick, personnel, buildings, or equipment protected by the Convention are prohibited."
[17] Mr. Ruegger (Switzerland), introducing the amendment: *Treaty Conference Records*, 1969, p. 112.
[18] *Ibid.*
[19] Above, p. 106. See also the *Appeal relating to the jurisdiction of the I.C.A.O. Council Case*, I.C.J.Rep. 1972, p. 46, at p. 67. For commentary, see Briggs, 68 A.J.I.L. 51 (1974).

drying up of a river or the destruction of a dam or hydro-electric installation indispensable for the execution of a treaty."[20]

On the position where a state party to a treaty ceases to exist, see below, p. 637.

(iv) FUNDAMENTAL CHANGE OF CIRCUMSTANCES[21]

VIENNA CONVENTION ON THE LAW OF TREATIES 1969

Loc. cit. at p. 563, n. 3, above

Article 62

1. A fundamental change of circumstances which has occurred with regard to those existing at the time of the conclusion of a treaty, and which was not foreseen by the parties, may not be invoked as a ground for terminating or withdrawing from the treaty unless:

(*a*) the existence of those circumstances constituted an essential basis of the consent of the parties to be bound by the treaty; and

(*b*) the effect of the change is radically to transform the extent of obligations still to be performed under the treaty.

2. A fundamental change of circumstances may not be invoked as a ground for terminating or withdrawing from a treaty:

(*a*) if the treaty establishes a boundary; or

(*b*) if the fundamental change is the result of a breach by the party invoking it either of an obligation under the treaty or of any other international obligation owed to any other party to the treaty.

3. If, under the foregoing paragraphs, a party may invoke a fundamental change of circumstances as a ground for terminating or withdrawing from a treaty it may also invoke the change as a ground for suspending the operation of the treaty.

Notes

1. The International Law Commission's Commentary reads:

Almost all modern jurists, however reluctantly, admit the existence in international law of the principle with which this article is concerned and which is commonly spoken of as the doctrine of *rebus sic stantibus*.[22] Just as many systems of municipal law recognise that, quite apart from any actual impossibility of performance, contracts may become inapplicable through a fundamental change of circumstances, so also treaties may become inapplicable for the same reason. Most jurists, however, at the same time enter a strong caveat as to the need to confine the scope of the doctrine within narrow limits and to regulate strictly the conditions under which it may be invoked; for the risks to the security of treaties which this doctrine presents in the absence of any general system of compulsory jurisdiction are obvious. The circum-

---

[20] Y.B.I.L.C., 1966, II, p. 256.

[21] See Briggs, 36 A.J.I.L. 89 (1942); *ibid.* 43 A.J.I.L. 762 (1949); Lissitzyn, 61 A.J.I.L. 895 (1967).

[22] *Ed.* The term *rebus sic stantibus* means literally "things remaining as they are." Reference is often made to the *clausula rebus sic stantibus, i.e.* to an express or implied clause in a treaty conditioning its validity upon the continuance of the circumstances existing at the time when it is made.

stances of international life are always changing and it is easy to allege that the changes render the treaty inapplicable. The evidence of the principle in customary law is considerable, but the International Court has not yet committed itself on the point. . . . The principle of *rebus sic stantibus* has not infrequently been invoked in State practice either *eo nomine* or in the form of a reference to a general principle claimed to justify the termination or modification of treaty obligations by reason of changed circumstances. Broadly speaking, it shows a wide acceptance of the view that a fundamental change of circumstances may justify a demand for the termination or revision of a treaty, but also shows a strong disposition to question the right of a party to denounce a treaty unilaterally on this ground.[23]

The Commission rejected the view that the rule should be limited to "so-called perpetual treaties," *i.e.* "treaties not making any provision for their termination."[24] Although cases of "supervening impossibility of performance," dealt with under Article 61, could be brought within Article 62, the International Law Commission "considered that juridically 'impossibility of performance' and 'fundamental change of circumstances' are distinct grounds for regarding a treaty as having been terminated, and should be kept separate."[25]

2. On the juridical basis of the rule, the International Law Commission's Commentary reads:

In the past the principle has almost always been presented in the guise of a tacit condition implied in every "perpetual" treaty that would dissolve it in the event of a fundamental change of circumstances. The Commission noted, however, that the tendency today was to regard the implied term as only a fiction by which it was attempted to reconcile the principle of the dissolution of treaties in consequence of a fundamental change of circumstances with the rule *pacta sunt servanda*. In most cases the parties gave no thought to the possibility of a change of circumstances and, if they had done so, would probably have provided for it in a different manner. Furthermore, the Commission considered the fiction to be an undesirable one since it increased the risk of subjective interpretations and abuse. For this reason, the Commission was agreed that the theory of an implied term must be rejected and the doctrine formulated as an objective rule of law by which, on grounds of equity and justice, a fundamental change of circumstances may, under certain conditions, be invoked by a party as a ground for terminating the treaty.[26]

How does the rule compare with that of frustration in the common law of contract? What does the Commission mean when it refers to an "objective rule of law"? Is the test in Article 62 one of reasonable forseeability, or what was actually forseen? Is it the foresight of *all* of the parties?

FISHERIES JURISDICTION CASE (JURISDICTION)

United Kingdom *v.* Iceland

I.C.J. Reports 1974, p. 3

For the facts, see above, p. 346.

Judgment of the Court

35. In his letter of 29 May 1972 to the Registrar, the Minister of Foreign Affairs of Iceland refers to "the changed circumstances resulting from the ever-increasing exploitation of the fishery resources in the seas surrounding Iceland."

[23] Y.B.I.L.C., 1966, II, pp. 257 *et seq.*
[24] *Ibid.* p. 259.   [25] *Ibid.* p. 256.   [26] *Ibid.* p. 258.

36. . . . the Government of Iceland is basing itself on the principle of termination of a treaty by reason of change of circumstances. International law admits that a fundamental change in the circumstances which determined the parties to accept a treaty, if it has resulted in a radical transformation of the extent of the obligations imposed by it, may, under certain conditions, afford the party affected a ground for invoking the termination or suspension of the treaty. This principle, and the conditions and exceptions to which it is subject, have been embodied in Article 62 of the Vienna Convention on the Law of Treaties, which may in many respects be considered as a codification of existing customary law on the subject of the termination of a treaty relationship on account of change of circumstances.

37. One of the basic requirements embodied in that Article is that the change of circumstances must have been a fundamental one. In this respect the Government of Iceland has, with regard to developments in fishing techniques, referred . . . to the increased exploitation of the fishery resources in the seas surrounding Iceland and to the danger of still further exploitation because of an increase in the catching capacity of fishing fleets. The Icelandic statements recall the exceptional dependence of that country on its fishing for its existence and economic development. . . .

38. The invocation by Iceland of its "vital interests," which were not made the subject of an express reservation to the acceptance of the jurisdictional obligation under the 1961 Exchange of Notes, must be interpreted, in the context of the assertion of changed circumstances, as an indication by Iceland of the reason why it regards as fundamental the changes which in its view have taken place in previously existing fishing techniques. This interpretation would correspond to the traditional view that the changes of circumstances which must be regarded as fundamental or vital are those which imperil the existence of vital development of one of the parties. . . .

If, as contended by Iceland, there have been any fundamental changes in fishing techniques in the waters around Iceland, those changes might be relevant for the decision on the merits of the dispute. . . . But the alleged changes could not affect in the least the obligation to submit to the Court's jurisdiction, which is the only issue at the present stage of the proceedings. It follows that the apprehended dangers for the vital interests of Iceland, resulting from changes in fishing techniques, cannot constitute a fundamental change with respect to the lapse or subsistence of the compromissory clause establishing the Court's jurisdiction. . . .

43. Moreover, in order that a change of circumstances may give rise to a ground for invoking the termination of a treaty it is also necessary that it should have resulted in a radical transformation of the extent of the obligations still to be performed. The change must have increased the burden of the obligations to be executed to the extent of rendering the performance something essentially different from that originally undertaken. In respect of the obligation with which the Court is here concerned, this condition is wholly unsatisfied; the change of circumstances alleged by Iceland cannot be said to have transformed radically the extent of the jurisdictional obligation which is imposed in the 1961 Exchange of Notes. . . . The present dispute is exactly of the character anticipated in the compromissory clause of the Exchange of Notes. Not only has the jurisdictional obligation not been radically transformed in its extent; it has remained precisely what it was in 1961.

44. In the United Kingdom Memorial it is asserted that there is a flaw in the Icelandic contention of change of circumstances: that the doctrine never operates so as to extinguish a treaty automatically or to allow an unchallengeable unilateral denunciation by one party; it only operates to confer a right to call for termination and, if that call is disputed, to submit the dispute to some organ or body with power to determine whether the conditions for the operation of the doctrine are present. In this connection the Applicant alludes to Articles 65 and 66 of the Vienna Convention on the Law of Treaties.

45. In the present case, the procedural complement to the doctrine of changed circumstances is already provided for in the 1961 Exchange of Notes, which specifically calls upon the parties to have recourse to the Court in the event of a dispute relating to Iceland's extension of fisheries jurisdiction. . . .

SEPARATE OPINION OF JUDGE SIR GERALD FITZMAURICE. 17. With regard to the question of "changed circumstances" I have nothing to add to what is stated in paragraphs 35–43 of the Court's Judgment, except to emphasize that in my opinion the only change that could possibly be relevant (if at all) would be some change relating directly to the, so to speak, operability of the jurisdictional clause itself[27]—not to such things as developments in fishery techniques or in Iceland's situation relative to fisheries. These would indeed be matters that would militate for, not against, adjudication. But as regards the jurisdictional clause itself, the only "change" that has occurred is the purported extension of Icelandic fishery limits. This however is the absolute *reverse* of the type of change to which the doctrine of "changed circumstances" relates, namely one never contemplated by the Parties: it is in fact the actual change they did contemplate, and specified as the one that would give rise to the obligation to have recourse to adjudication.

Note

See also the *Free Zones Case*, above p. 605.

(v) SEVERANCE OF DIPLOMATIC OR CONSULAR RELATIONS

VIENNA CONVENTION ON THE LAW OF TREATIES 1969

Loc. cit. at p. 563, n. 3, above

Article 63

The severence of diplomatic or consular relations between parties to a treaty does not affect the legal relations established between them by the treaty except in so far as the existence of diplomatic or consular relations is indispensable for the application of the treaty.

Note

The International Law Commission noted in its Commentary that:

the use of third states and even of direct channels as means for making necessary communications in case of severance of diplomatic relations are so common that the absence of the normal channels ought not to be recognised as a disappearance of a "means" or of an "object" indispensable for the execution of a treaty.[28]

---

[27] For instance if the character of the International Court itself had changed in the meantime so that it was no longer the entity the Parties had had in mind, *e.g.* if owing to developments in the United Nations, the Court had been converted into a tribunal of mixed law and conciliation, proceeding on a basis other than a purely juridical one.

[28] Y.B.I.L.C., 1966, II, p. 261.

Article 63 of the Vienna Convention differs from the Commission's Draft Article by the inclusion of the words "except in so far as" onwards. The severance of consular relations by the two parties to a treaty providing for a right of consular access to a detained national would presumably come within the stated exception.

(vi) Jus Cogens

See Article 64 of the Vienna Convention.[29]

10. *GENERAL PROVISIONS ON THE INVALIDITY, TERMINATION AND SUSPENSION OF TREATIES*

(i) Consequences of Invalidity, Termination or Suspension

VIENNA CONVENTION ON THE LAW OF TREATIES 1969

Loc. cit. at p. 563, n. 3, above

Article 69

1. A treaty the invalidity of which is established under the present convention is void. The provisions of a void treaty has no legal force.
2. If acts have nevertheless been performed in reliance on such a treaty:

(*a*) each party may require any other party to establish as far as possible in their mutual relations the position that would have existed if the acts had not been performed;
(*b*) acts performed in good faith before the invalidity was invoked are not rendered unlawful by reason only of the invalidity of the treaty.

3. In cases falling under articles 49, 50, 51 or 52, paragraph 2 does not apply with respect to the party to which the fraud, the act of corruption or the coercion is imputable.
4. In the case of the invalidity of a particular State's consent to be bound by multilateral treaty, the foregoing rules apply in the relations between that State and the parties to the treaty.

Article 70

1. Unless the treaty otherwise provides or the parties otherwise agree, the termination of a treaty under its provisions or in accordance with the present Convention:

(*a*) releases the parties from any obligation further to perform the treaty;
(*b*) does not affect any right, obligation or legal situation of the parties created through the execution of the treaty prior to its termination.

2. If a State denounces or withdraws from a multilateral treaty, paragraph 1 applies in the relations between that state and each of the other parties to the treaty from the date when such denunciation or withdrawal takes effect.

---

[29] Above, p. 616.

Article 71

1. In the case of a treaty which is void under Article 53 the parties shall:

(*a*) eliminate as far as possible the consequences of any act performed in reliance on any provision which conflicts with the peremptory norm of general international law; and

(*b*) bring their mutual relations into conformity with the peremptory norm of general international law.

2. In the case of a treaty which becomes void and terminates under Article 64, the termination of the treaty:

(*a*) releases the parties from any obligation further to perform the treaty;

(*b*) does not affect any right, obligation or legal situation of the parties created through the execution of the treaty prior to its termination; provided that those rights, obligations or situations may thereafter be maintained only to the extent that their maintenance is not in itself in conflict with the new peremptory norm of general international law.

Article 72

1. Unless the treaty otherwise provides or the parties otherwise agree, the suspension of the operation of a treaty under its provisions or in accordance with the present Convention:

(*a*) releases the parties between which the operation of the treaty is suspended from the obligation to perform the treaty in their mutual relations during the period of the suspension;

(*b*) does not otherwise affect the legal relations between the parties established by the treaty.

2. During the period of the suspension the parties shall refrain from acts tending to obstruct the resumption of the operation of the treaty.

Note

The International Law Commission's Commentary reads:

The Commission considered that the establishment of the nullity of a treaty on any of the grounds set forth in . . . [Articles 46–53 of the Vienna Convention] would mean that the treaty was void *ab initio* and not merely from the date when the ground was invoked. Only in the case of the treaty's becoming void and terminating under . . . [Article 64 of the Vienna Convention[30]] would the treaty not be invalid as from the very moment of its purported conclusion.[31]

This view is reflected in Article 69 of the Vienna Convention, as is the Commission's view that

where neither party was to be regarded as a wrongdoer in relation to the cause of nullity (*i.e.* where no fraud, corruption or coercion was imputable to either party), the legal position should be determined on the basis of taking account both of the invalidity of the treaty *ab initio* and of the good faith of the parties.[32]

Invalidity because of a rule of *jus cogens* is treated separately in Article 71.

---

[30] On *jus cogens*, see above, p. 616.
[31] Y.B.I.L.C., 1966, II, p. 265.   [32] *Ibid.*

(ii) Separability of Treaty Provisions

VIENNA CONVENTION ON THE LAW OF TREATIES 1969

Loc. cit. at p. 563, n. 3, above

Article 44

1. A right of a party, provided for in a treaty or arising under Article 56, to denounce, withdraw from or suspend the operation of the treaty may be exercised only with respect to the whole treaty unless the treaty otherwise provides or the parties otherwise agree.

2. A ground for invalidating, terminating, withdrawing from or suspending the operation of a treaty recognized in the present Convention may be invoked only with respect to the whole treaty except as provided in the following paragraphs or in Article 60.

3. If the ground relates solely to particular clauses, it may be invoked only with respect to those clauses where:

(*a*) the said clauses are separable from the remainder of the treaty with regard to their application;

(*b*) it appears from the treaty or is otherwise established that acceptance of those clauses was not an essential basis of the consent of the other party or parties to be bound by the treaty as a whole; and

(*c*) continued performance of the remainder of the treaty would not be unjust.

4. In cases falling under Articles 49 and 50 the State entitled to invoke the fraud or corruption may do so with respect either to the whole treaty or, subject to paragraph 3, to the particular clauses alone.

5. In cases falling under Articles 51, 52 and 53, no separation of the provision of the treaty is permitted.

Notes

1. There would seem to be little evidence in state practice or in judicial or arbitral decisions to indicate whether in the application of the rules concerning the invalidity, termination and suspension of treaties, the treaty must be regarded as a whole, so that if one provision of the treaty is found to be invalid the treaty as a whole is invalid, or whether the provision in question may be separated from the remainder, so that the validity or continued operation of the latter is not affected. One of the few pronouncements upon the subject is that by Judge Lauterpacht in his individual opinion in the *Norwegian Loans Case*.[33] The International Law Commission, whose view is reflected in Article 44 of the Vienna Convention, thought it was desirable to permit severance in appropriate cases, but that it was

> inappropriate that treaties between sovereign states should be capable of being invalidated, terminated or suspended in operation in their entirety even in cases where the ground of invalidity, termination or suspension may relate to quite secondary provisions in the treaty.[34]

[33] See below, p. 728.
[34] Commentary, Y.B.I.L.C., 1966, II, p. 238.

2. Article 44(3)(*c*) was added at Geneva to "ensure that the rule of separability laid down in [Article 44] . . . would not create the very kind of international friction which the Commission sought to avoid"[35] by it.

(iii) LOSS OF THE RIGHT TO INVOKE A GROUND FOR INVALIDATING, ETC., A TREATY

VIENNA CONVENTION ON THE LAW OF TREATIES 1969

Loc. cit. at p. 563, n. 3, above

Article 45

A State may no longer invoke a ground for invalidating, terminating withdrawing from or suspending the operation of a treaty under Articles 46 to 50 or Articles 60 to 62 if, after becoming aware of the facts:

(*a*) it shall have expressly agreed that the treaty is valid or remains in force or continues in operation, as the case may be; or

(*b*) it must by reason of its conduct be considered as having acquiesced in the validity of the treaty or in its maintenance in force or in operation, as the case may be.

(iv) SETTLEMENT OF DISPUTES

VIENNA CONVENTION ON THE LAW OF TREATIES 1969

Loc. cit. at p. 563, n. 3, above

Article 65

1. A party which, under the provisions of the present Convention, invokes either a defect in its consent to be bound by a treaty or a ground for impeaching the validity of a treaty, terminating it, withdrawing from it or suspending its operation, must notify the other parties of its claim. The notification shall indicate the measure proposed to be taken with respect to the treaty and the reasons therefor.

2. If, after the expiry of a period which, except in cases of special urgency, shall not be less than three months after the receipt of the notification, no party has raised any objection, the party making the notification may carry out in the manner provided in Article 67 the measure which it has proposed.

3. If, however objection has been raised by any other party, the parties shall seek a solution through the means indicated in Article 33 of the Charter of the United Nations.[36]

4. Nothing in the foregoing paragraphs shall affect the rights or obligations of the parties under any provisions in force binding the parties with regard to the settlement of disputes.

5. Without prejudice to Article 45,[37] the fact that a State has not previously made the notification prescribed in paragraph 1 shall not prevent it from making

---

[35] Mr. Kearney (U.S.), introducing the amendment, *Treaty Conference Records* (1968), p. 230.
[36] *Ed.* Appendix I, below.   [37] *Ed.* Above.

such notification in answer to another party claiming performance of the treaty or alleging its violation.

Article 66

If, under paragraph 3, of Article 65, no solution has been reached within a period of 12 months following the date on which the objection was raised, the following procedures shall be followed:

(a) any one of the parties to a dispute concerning the application or the interpretation of Article 53[38] or 64[39] may, by a written application, submit it to the International Court of Justice for a decision unless the parties by common consent agree to submit the dispute to arbitration;

(b) any one of the parties to a dispute concerning the application or the interpretation of any of the other articles in Part V[40] of the present Convention may set in motion the procedure specified in the Annex to the Convention by submitting a request to that effect to the Secretary-General of the United Nations.

Annex to the Convention

1. A list of conciliators consisting of qualified jurists shall be drawn up and maintained by the Secretary-General of the United Nations. To this end, every state which is a Member of the United Nations or a party to the present Convention shall be invited to nominate two conciliators, and the names of the persons so nominated shall constitute the list. . . .

2. When a request has been made to the Secretary-General under Article 66, the Secretary-General shall bring the dispute before a conciliation commission constituted as follows:

The state or states constituting one of the parties to the dispute shall appoint:

(a) one conciliator of the nationality of that state or of one of those states, who may or may not be chosen from the list referred to in paragraph 1; and

(b) one conciliator not of the nationality of that state or of any of those states, who shall be chosen from the list.

The state or states constituting the other party to the dispute shall appoint two conciliators in the same way. The four conciliators chosen by the parties shall be appointed within sixty days following the date on which the Secretary-General receives the request.

The four conciliators shall, within sixty days following the date of the last of their own appointments, appoint a fifth conciliator chosen from the list, who shall be chairman.

If the appointment of the chairman or of any of the other conciliators has not been made within the period prescribed above for such appointment, it shall be made by the Secretary-General within sixty days following the expiry of that period. . . .

3. . . . Decisions and recommendations of the Commission shall be made by a majority vote of the five members.

[38] *Ed.* See above, p. 616.
[39] *Ed.* Above, p. 616.   [40] *Ed.* Articles 42–72.

4. The Commission may draw the attention of the parties to the dispute to any measures which might facilitate an amicable settlement.

5. The Commission shall hear the parties, examine the claims and objections, and make proposals to the parties with a view to reaching an amicable settlement of the dispute.

6. The Commission shall report within twelve months of its constitution. Its report shall be deposited with the Secretary-General and transmitted to the parties to the dispute. The report of the Commission, including any conclusions stated therein regarding the facts or questions of law, shall not be binding upon the parties and it shall have no other character than that of recommendations submitted for the consideration of the parties in order to facilitate an amicable settlement of the dispute . . .

Note

There was considerable debate at the Vienna Conference on the question of the procedure to be established for the settlement of disputes arising under the Convention. Certain states, including the United Kingdom, wanted provision for compulsory judicial settlement. It was felt that the rules in the Convention on invalidity, termination and suspension could easily be abused in the absence of compulsory and binding settlement procedures. This feeling was particularly strong with regard to the questions of *jus cogens* and fraud. Other states, including the U.S.S.R., with its fundamental opposition to binding international settlement procedures independent of the control of the disputing parties, disagreed.[41] Eventually, "at the eleventh hour and in circumstances of high drama not fully revealed in the drab official records of the Conference,"[42] the compromise in Articles 65 and 66 and the Annex to the Convention was adopted. How satisfactory a guarantee against abuse of the Convention is it?[43] What if, in cases other than ones concerning *jus cogens*, the parties cannot agree upon a solution after exhausting the procedure provided for in Articles 65(3) and 66 and in the Annex? Has the claim invoking a defect in the claimant's consent, etc., failed?

11. REGISTRATION OF TREATIES[44]

See Article 102, United Nations Charter[45]

VIENNA CONVENTION ON THE LAW OF TREATIES 1969

Loc. cit. at p. 563, n. 3, above

Article 80

1. Treaties shall, after their entry into force, be transmitted to the Secretariat of the United Nations for registration or filing and recording, as the case may be, and for publication. . . .

---

[41] See, *e.g.* Mr. Khlestov (U.S.S.R.), in *Treaty Conference Records*, 1969, pp. 302–303. For a statement of the case for compulsory and binding settlement procedures, see Briggs, 61 A.J.I.L. 976 at pp. 983–988 (1970).

[42] Sinclair, *loc. cit.* at p. 563, n. 1, above, pp. 68–69.

[43] Note that France and Australia were influenced by the inadequacy—in their view—of the procedures for settlement when voting against the adoption of the Convention and abstaining respectively: *Treaty Conference Records* 1969, pp. 203–209.

[44] See Brandon (1952) 29 B.Y.I.L. 186; Brandon, 47 A.J.I.L. 49 (1953); Higgins, *The Development of International Law by the Political Organs of the United Nations* (1963), pp. 328–336; Lillich, 65 A.J.I.L. 771 (1971).   [45] See Appendix I, below.

Note

1. The purpose of Article 102 of the United Nations Charter, like that of its predecessor, Article 18 of the League of Nations Covenant,[46] is to give publicity to treaty relations and avoid secret treaties. This has, to a large extent,[47] been achieved. Treaties registered under Article 102 are published in the United Nations Treaty Series of which there are so far 950 volumes, covering the period 1946 to 1974.

2. The term "treaty" and "international agreement" in Article 102 have purposely been left undefined, "it being recognized that experience and practice will in themselves aid in giving definition to the terms of the Charter."[48] The Final Act of the Helsinki Conference on Security and Co-operation in Europe 1975, for example, was understood as not being eligible for registration since it was not binding in law.[49] At San Francisco it was thought that the word "agreement" must be understood as including "unilateral engagements of an international character which have been accepted by the state in whose favour such an engagement has been entered into."[50] On the basis of this interpretation, the Secretariat has, on its own initiative and with the approval of the General Assembly Sixth Committee, arranged[51] for the registration, *inter alia*, of declarations by new members of the United Nations accepting membership and declarations made under the "Optional Clause."[52] In respect of instruments submitted to it by Members, the Secretariat has taken the following position:

> . . . the Secretariat . . . follows the principle that it acts in accordance with the position of the Member State submitting an instrument for registration that so far as that party is concerned the instrument is a treaty or an international agreement within the meaning of Article 102. Registration of an instrument submitted by a Member State, therefore, does not imply a judgment by the Secretariat on the nature of the instrument, the status of a party, or any similar question. It is the understanding of the Secretariat that its action does not confer on the instrument the status of a treaty or an international agreement if it does not already have that status and does not confer on a party a status which it would not otherwise have.[53]

Thus, when, in 1957, Egypt submitted for registration a unilateral "Declaration on the Suez Canal and Agreements for its Operation,"[54] the Secretary-General replied that it would be registered on the understanding that Egypt thought that it came within Article 102. The Secretariat has, however, had occasion to indicate its views with regard to certain types of instrument and has suggested, for example, that "postal agreements (even though concluded for example, between the respective postmasters-general)" are within Article 102, but that agreements to which non-governmental international organisations (*e.g.* the International Patents Institute) are parties are not.[55] Clearly treaties between United Nations Members, on the one hand, and non-member states or public international organisations with treaty-making capacity, on the other, are covered. The International Law Commission Commentary reads:

---

[46] Art. 18 read: "Every treaty or international engagement entered into hereafter by any Member of the League shall be forthwith registered with the Secretariat and shall as soon as possible be published by it. No such treaty or international engagement shall be binding until so registered."

[47] It is known, however, that some treaties are not registered. This is true, for example, of a Franco-United States Agreement of September 6, 1960, on NATO Nuclear Weapons.

[48] G.A.O.R., 1st Session, Part II, Plenary, Annex 91, p. 1586.

[49] See Russell, *loc. cit.* at p. 471, n. 14, above, at p. 246.

[50] 13 U.N.C.I.O., *Documents*, p. 705.

[51] 5 *U.N. Repertory of Practice* 293.

[52] *Ibid.*

[53] U.N.Doc. ST/LEG/SER./A/105, November 1955, Prefatory Note.

[54] 265 U.N.T.S. 299.

[55] 5 *U.N. Repertory of Practice* 295–296.

Although the Charter obligation is limited to Member States, non-member States have in practice "registered" their treaties habitually with the Secretariat of the United Nations. Under Article 10 of the Regulations concerning the Registration and Publication of Treaties and International Agreements adopted by the General Assembly, the term used instead of "registration" when no Member of the United Nations is party to the agreement is "filing and recording," but in substance this is a form of voluntary registration.[56]

3. Could an unregistered treaty to which a member of the United Nations was a party be invoked by another party not a member of the United Nations before the International Court of Justice or an ad hoc arbitral tribunal?

12. *STATE SUCCESSION TO TREATIES*

VIENNA CONVENTION ON SUCCESSION OF STATES IN RESPECT OF TREATIES 1978[57]

Misc. No. 1 (1980), Cmnd. 7760; 72 A.J.I.L. 971 (1978)

Article 2

1. For the purposes of the present Convention: . . .

(*b*) "succession of States" means the replacement of one State by another in the responsibility for the international relations of territory; . . .

Article 8

1. The obligations or rights of a predecessor State under treaties in force in respect of a territory at the date of a succession of States do not become the obligations or rights of the successor State towards other States parties to those treaties by reason only of the fact that the predecessor State and the successor State have concluded an agreement providing that such obligations or rights shall devolve upon the successor State.

2. Notwithstanding the conclusion of such an agreement, the effects of a succession of States on treaties which, at the date of that succession of States, were in force in respect of the territory in question are governed by the present Convention.

Article 9

1. Obligations or rights under treaties in force in respect of a territory at the date of a succession of States do not become the obligations or rights of the successor State or of other States parties to those treaties by reason only of the fact that the successor State has made a unilateral declaration providing for the continuance in force of the treaties in respect of its territory.

---

[56] Y.B.I.L.C., 1966, II, p. 273.

[57] The Convention requires 15 parties to enter into force. On December 31, 1981, there were five. The U.K. was not a signatory and has not acceded. See on state succession, McNair, *Treaties*, Chap. 37, and O'Connell, *State Succession in Municipal and International Law*, Vol. II (1967). On the 1978 Convention, see Bello, 23 German Y.B.I.L. 296 (1978); Lavalle, 73 A.J.I.L. 407 (1979); Maloney, 19 Virg. Jo.I.L. 885 (1979).

2. In such a case, the effects of the succession of States on treaties which, at the date of that succession of States, were in force in respect of the territory in question are governed by the present Convention.

Article 10

1. When a treaty provides that, on the occurrence of a succession of States, a successor State shall have the option to consider itself a party to the treaty, it may notify its succession in respect of the treaty in conformity with the provisions of the treaty or, failing any such provisions, in conformity with the provisions of the present Convention.

2. If a treaty provides that, on the occurrence of a succession of States, a successor State shall be considered as a party to the treaty, that provision takes effect as such only if the successor State expressly accepts in writing to be so considered.

3. In cases falling under paragraph 1 or 2, a successor State which establishes its consent to be a party to the treaty is considered as a party from the date of the succession of States unless the treaty otherwise provides or it is otherwise agreed.

Article 11

A succession of States does not as such affect:

(a) a boundary established by a treaty; or
(b) obligations and rights established by a treaty and relating to the règime of a boundary.

Article 12

1. A succession of States does not as such affect:

(a) obligations relating to the use of any territory, or to restrictions upon its use established by a treaty for the benefit of any territory of a foreign State and considered as attaching to the territories in question;
(b) rights established by a treaty for the benefit of any territory and relating to the use, or to restrictions upon the use, of any territory of a foreign State and considered as attaching to the territories in question.

2. A succession of States does not as such affect:

(a) obligations relating to the use of any territory, or to restrictions upon its use, established by a treaty for the benefit of a group of States or of all States and considered as attaching to that territory;
(b) rights established by a treaty for the benefit of a group of States or of all States and relating to the use of any territory, or to restrictions upon its use, and considered as attaching to that territory.

3. The provisions of the present article do not apply to treaty obligations of the predecessor State providing for the establishment of foreign military bases on the territory to which the succession of States relates.

Article 15

When part of the territory of a State, or when any territory for the international relations of which a State is responsible, not being part of the territory of that State, becomes part of the territory of another State:

    (*a*) treaties of the predecessor State cease to be in force in respect of the territory to which the succession of States relates from the date of the succession of States; and

    (*b*) treaties of the successor State are in force in respect of the territory to which the succession of States relates from the date of the succession of States, unless it appears from the treaty or is otherwise established that the application of the treaty to that territory would be incompatible with the object and purpose of the treaty or would radically change the conditions for its operation.

Article 16

A newly independent State is not bound to maintain in force, or to become a party to, any treaty by reason only of the fact that at the date of the succession of States the treaty was in force in respect of the territory to which the succession of States relates.

Article 17

1. Subject to paragraphs 2 and 3, a newly independent State may, by a notification of succession, establish its status as a party to any multilateral treaty which at the date of the succession of States was in force in respect of the territory to which the succession of States relates.

2. Paragraph 1 does not apply if it appears from the treaty or is otherwise established that the application of the treaty in respect of the newly independent State would be incompatible with the object and purpose of the treaty or would radically change the conditions for its operation.

3. When, under the terms of the treaty or by reason of the limited number of the negotiating States and the object and purpose of the treaty, the participation of any other State in the treaty must be considered as requiring the consent of all the parties, the newly independent State may establish its status as a party to the treaty only with such consent.

Article 24

1. A bilateral treaty which at the date of a succession of States was in force in respect of the territory to which the succession of States relates is considered as being in force between a newly independent State and the other State party when:

    (*a*) they expressly so agree; or

    (*b*) by reason of their conduct they are to be considered as having so agreed.

2. A treaty considered as being in force under paragraph 1 applies in the relations between the newly independent State and the other State party from the date of the succession of States, unless a different intention appears from their agreement or is otherwise established.

Notes

1. The Convention is based upon Draft Articles prepared by the International Law Commission.[58]

2. The problem of state succession to treaties has most commonly arisen in the past in cases of total or partial annexation by one existing state of territory belonging to another. More recently, attention has focused upon the consequences of the emergence of new states in the post-colonial era. The view adopted in the Convention (Article 16) is that a new state starts with a "clean slate" in respect of multilateral and bilateral treaty rights and obligations of its predecessor except for those concerning boundary and other territorial régimes for which a "clean slate" rule would be too disruptive (Articles 11 and 12).[59] A new state is entitled to take up its predecessor's rights and obligations under multilateral treaties but, with the exception mentioned, is not obliged to do so. The continuance of bilateral treaties is a matter of agreement between the parties. These provisions, which reflect the viewpoint of newly independent states more than that of older states, are best seen as an instance of progressive development rather than codification. It is noticeable that none of the former colonial powers, nor the U.S.A. or the U.S.S.R., signed or have so far acceded to the Convention.

3. For an example of a *devolution agreement* (Article 8), see that between the United Kingdom and Malaya in 1957.[60] More than 20 such agreements, mostly between France and the United Kingdom, on the one side, and their former territories, on the other, have been recorded.[61] What is the legal effect of such agreements for the parties to them and for other states? A similar number of new states have made *unilateral declarations* (Article 9), mostly following the pattern of that made by Tanganyika (1961)[62] or that made by Gambia (1965).[63]

4. When States merge or separate, the Convention provides in Articles 31 and 34, respectively, that treaties remain in force for the territory concerned. This is not so where the parties agree otherwise or if the result would be inconsistent with the object and purpose of the treaty or would radically change the conditions for its operation.

---

[58] The Commentary to the I.L.C. Draft Articles makes it clear that Article 16 is to be read subject to Articles 11 and 12: *ibid*. p. 214.

[59] *Ibid*. 1969, II, p. 55.

[60] *Ibid*. p. 54.

[61] For the Draft Articles and the I.L.C. Commentary, see Y.B.I.L.C., 1974, II (Part One), pp. 174 *et seq*.

[62] *Ibid*. p. 63.

[63] *Ibid*. p. 64. On the Lesotho Declaration of this sort, see *Molefi* v. *Legal Adviser* [1971] A.C. 182 (P.C.).

CHAPTER 11

THE USE OF FORCE BY STATES[1]

1. *THE UNILATERAL USE OF FORCE BY STATES*

(i) THE LAW BEFORE 1945

BRIERLY, INTERNATIONAL LAW AND RESORT TO ARMED FORCE

4 Cam.L.J. 308 (1932)

THE relation of war to the international system was stated by W. E. Hall in a well-known passage of his treatise in these words: "International law has no alternative but to accept war, independently of the justice of its origin, as a relation which the parties to it may set up if they choose, and to busy itself only in regulating the effects of the relation."[2] This view, which came to be more or less generally accepted by international lawyers in the course of the nineteenth century, marked the definite abandonment of the claim of the classical jurists to distinguish between *bellum iustum* and *bellum iniustum*, and it was in a sense an admission that international law had so far failed in the primary task of all legal systems, that of establishing and maintaining a distinction between the legal and the illegal use of force. But it had the great merit of candour, and it brought the theory of the law into accord with what had always been and still remained the facts of international practice.

Notes

1. Brierly is here stating the position as it stood at the beginning of this century. Paradoxically, at the same time that international law condoned war it controlled resort to armed force short of war by the law of reprisals[3] and governed its conduct by the laws of war.[4]

---

[1] See Bowett, *Self-Defence in International Law* (1958); Brownlie, *International Law and the Use of Force by States* (1963); Falk, *Legal Order in a Violent World* (1968); Higgins, *The Development of International Law through the Political Organs of the U.N.* (1963), pp. 167–239; McDougal and Feliciano, *Law and Minimum World Order: Legal Regulation of International Coercion* (1961); Murphy, *The United Nations and the Control of International Violence* (1983); Schwarz, *Confrontation and Intervention in the Modern World* (1970); Stone, *Legal Controls of International Conflict* (2nd ed., 1959); Waldock, 81 *Hague Recueil* 451 (1952–II).

[2] *Ed. International Law* (8th ed.), p. 82.

[3] See the *Naulilaa Case*, above, p. 9.

[4] See mainly the Hague Conventions of 1899 and 1907, printed in Schindler, *The Laws of Armed Conflicts* (1973) (on the conduct of hostilities generally); the four 1949 Geneva Red Cross Conventions, *loc. cit.* at p. 232, n. 80, above (on the treatment of the injured, prisoners of war and civilians); and the two 1977 Protocols to the 1949 Conventions, 16 I.L.M. 1391 (1977) (supplementing and revising the 1949 Conventions in their application to international conflicts (Protocol I) and extending the protection afforded to victims in non-international conflicts (Protocol II)). See generally, Cassese, ed., *The New Humanitarian Law of Armed Conflict*, 2 Vols. (1979), Castren, *The Present Law of War and Neutrality* (1954); Draper, *The Red Cross Conventions* (1958); and Greenspan, *The Modern Law of Land Warfare* (1959).

2. On the question what amounts to war, McNair and Watts[5] state:

> War may begin, first, by a declaration of war . . . In the second place, a state of war will arise upon the commission of an act of force, under the authority of a State, which is done *animo belligerendi*, or which, being done *sine animo belligerendi*, the State against which it is directed expressly or impliedly elects to regard as creating a state of war . . . repelling force by force, while raising a presumption that the attacked State elects to regard war as having broken out, does not necessarily amount to such an election. So serious a matter as the existence of a state of war is not lightly to be implied. Furthermore, where leading political figures of a country engaged in hostilities refer to their country being "at war," caution must be exercised . . . since such references may prove to be more of emotional and political significance than legal.
>
> It will be apparent that the existence of a state of war depends upon the determination of the parties to the conflict, and can arise where only one of the parties to the conflict asserts the existence of a state of war, even if the other denies it or keeps silence. State practice has by and large accepted that for war to exist one at least of the contenders must so assert. Such a view . . . has enabled conflicts, even if militarily extensive as between the parties, to stay essentially limited rather than to entail the overall dislocation . . . which would accompany the escalation of those conflicts into a state of war. That so fundamental a concept of international law as war should depend upon the view of the parties involved—even of one of them alone—has been a principal reason for criticism and for the attraction of other, more objective, concepts such as the "threat or use of force" adopted in the Charter.

3. Although the question whether a state of war exists remains of significance in international law (see, *e.g.* the law of neutrality) and municipal law (*e.g.* concerning the status of aliens[6]), it is now exceptional for the parties to hostilities to regard themselves as legally at war. The importance of the question has also been reduced by the fact that (i) the United Nations Charter rule on the use of force (Art.2(4)), draws no distinction between war and armed force short of war and (ii) the 1949 Geneva Red Cross Conventions and the 1977 Protocols[7] apply to "all cases of declared war or of any other armed conflict which may arise between two or more of the High Contracting Parties, even if the state of war is not recognised by one of them."[8]

GENERAL TREATY FOR THE RENUNCIATION OF WAR 1928[9]

U.K.T.S. 29 (1929), Cmnd. 3410; 94 L.N.T.S. 57

The Signatory states . . .

Persuaded that the time has come when a frank renunciation of war as an instrument of national policy should be made to the end that the peaceful and friendly relations now existing between their peoples may be perpetuated;

Convinced that all changes in their relations with one another should be sought only be pacific means and be the result of a peaceful and orderly process,

[5] *The Legal Effects of War* (4th ed., 1966), pp. 7–8. Footnotes omitted. In the Falkland Islands "War," the U.K. studiously avoided any statement indicating that it regarded the conflict as war, and Argentina made no formal proclamation of war.
[6] See, *e.g. R.* v. *Bottrill, ex p. Kuechenmeister* [1947] K.B. 41.
[7] See above, n. 4.
[8] Art. 2, common to the four 1949 Conventions. See also Art. 1, Protocols I and II.
[9] The Treaty is sometimes known as the Pact of Paris or the Briand-Kellogg Pact (after the French Foreign Minister and U.S.A. Secretary of State respectively).

and that any signatory Power which shall hereafter seek to promote its national interests by resort to war should be denied the benefits furnished by this Treaty. . . .

Have decided to conclude a Treaty. . . .

Article I

The High Contracting Parties solemnly declare in the names of their respective peoples that they condemn recourse to war for the solution of international controversies, and renounce it as an instrument of national policy in their relations with one another.

Article II

The High Contracting Parties agree that the settlement or solution of all disputes or conflicts of whatever nature or of whatever origin they may be, which may arise among them, shall never be sought except by pacific means.

Notes

1. After the First World War, the League of Nations Covenant[10] imposed some limitations upon "resort to war." It was not until the General Treaty of 1928, however, that a comprehensive prohibition of war as an instrument of national policy was achieved. Somewhat ironically, 63 states, *i.e.* virtually the whole of the international community at that time, were parties to the Treaty when the Second World War started in 1939. The Treaty has never been terminated.[11] For practical purposes, it has been superseded by Article 2(4) of the United Nations Charter.

2. It has never been clear whether the Treaty prohibits armed force short of war as well as war. Thus, on the one hand, Bowett[12] states that the Pact only prohibits war "for under accepted terminology of international law (and without defending that terminology) measures involving the use of force but falling short of war are characterised as pacific; in this case Article 2 cannot be invoked as a reason for departing from the plain meaning of the terms of Article 1." Brownlie,[13] on the other hand, suggests that "the best guide to the meaning of the Pact is to be found by recourse to the subsequent practice of the parties" and concludes that this "leaves little room for doubt that it was understood to prohibit any substantial use of armed force." In 1934, the International Law Association resolved as follows:

A signatory state which threatens to resort to armed force for the solution of an international dispute or conflict is guilty of a violation of the Pact.[14]

In 1935, it was emphasised in the House of Lords by the Lord Chancellor (Viscount Sankey) that the members of the Association "were expressing . . . their own views: they did not necessarily represent the opinions of lawyers in all their own countries, still less the opinions of their Governments."[15]

3. The treaty does not mention self-defence. In a reply to a communication from a United States spokesman during the drafting of the treaty, the British Foreign Secretary stated:

---

[10] Articles 15 and 16, U.K.T.S. 4 (1919), Cmd. 153.
[11] There are now 63 parties. Barbados and Fiji have deposited notification of succession to the treaty following their independence.
[12] *Op. cit.* at p. 638, n. 1, above p. 136.
[13] *Op. cit.* at p. 638, n. 1, above p. 87.
[14] *Report of the 38th Conference of the International Law Association*, Budapest (1934), p. 67.
[15] *Hansard*, H.L., 5th Series, Vol. 95, col. 1043. February 28, 1935.

I am entirely in accord with the views expressed by Mr. Kellogg in his speech of April 28 that the proposed treaty does not restrict or impair in any way the right of self-defence. . . . [16]

(ii) THE LAW AS OF 1945

(a) *The Use of Force in International Relations*

See Article 2(3)(4), United Nations Charter[17] and the 1970 Declaration on Principles of International Law concerning Friendly Relations and Co-operation among States in accordance with the Charter of the United Nations, Section on the Principle on the Use of Force.[18]

Notes

1. Although phrased in terms of "members" of the United Nations, Article 2(4) is commonly understood to state a rule of customary international law applying to all states.

2. The extent of the prohibition in Article 2(4) is not clear from the text. The Security Council and the General Assembly, being political rather than judicial bodies, have not spent much time debating the legal basis for their action in particular cases so that there is not a great deal to be found in their practice on the meaning of Article 2(4). This is particularly so since the attention of representatives has usually been focused on questions of jurisdiction under Article 39 (Is there a breach of the peace, etc.?) and not upon questions of compliance with Article 2(4). Some more precise meaning has been given to Article 2(4) by the 1970 Declaration on Principles of International Law, Appendix III, below, although that too is vaguely worded in places.[19] The Declaration was adopted by consensus and can be taken to reflect the views of the United Nations membership as a whole on the legal meaning of the principles in the Charter upon which it elaborates. The International Law Commission regards serious breaches of the rules on international peace and security such as Article 2(4) as giving rise to the criminal responsibility of states in international law.[20]

3. *Force.* Article 2(4) prohibits the use of armed force, whether amounting to war or not. It probably does not prohibit political pressure (*e.g.* the refusal to ratify a treaty or the severance of diplomatic relations) or economic pressure (*e.g.* a trade boycott or the blocking of a bank account). As far as the latter is concerned, a proposal by Brazil during the drafting of Article 2(4) that states should be required to refrain from "economic measures" was rejected.[21] It is not wholly clear, however, whether this was because it was intended not to prohibit economic force or because the term "force" in Article 2(4) was thought sufficient to cover it without specific mention. In the opinion of Goodrich, Hambro and Simons,[22]

It seems reasonable to conclude that while various forms of economic and political coercion may be treated as threats to the peace, as contrary to certain of the declared

---

[16] Cmd. 3153, p. 10. See also the Suez Statement by the Lord Chancellor in 1956, below, p. 667.

[17] Appendix I, below.

[18] Appendix II, below. This is referred to hereafter as the 1970 Declaration on Principles of International Law.

[19] On the Declaration, see Arangio-Ruiz, *The UN Declaration on Friendly Relations and the System of Sources of International Law*, 1979, and Rosenstock, 65 A.J.I.L. 713 (1971). On its drafting, see Hazard, 58 A.J.I.L. 952 (1964); Houben, 61 *ibid.* 703 (1967); Lee, 14 I.C.L.Q. 1296 (1965) and McWhinney, 60 A.J.I.L. (1966).

[20] See Art. 19(3), Draft Articles on State Responsibility, above, p. 376.

[21] 6 U.N.C.I.O., *Documents* 335.

[22] *Charter of the United Nations* (3rd ed., 1969), p. 49. See also Delanis, 12 Vanderbilt J. Trans. L. 101 (1979).

purposes and principles of the Organisation, or as violating agreements entered into or recognised principles of international law, they are not to be regarded as coming necessarily under the prohibition of Article 2(4), which is to be understood as directed against the use of armed force."

The matter was purposely not clarified in the 1970 Declaration. This just refers to "force" in the Section on the Principle on the Use of Force because of disagreement between mainly Western states, who argued that only armed force was prohibited, and East European and most (but not all) developing states, who claimed that "all forms of pressure, including those of a political and economic character, which have the effect of threatening the territorial integrity or political independence of any state" were prohibited.[23] The Western states were, however, prepared to admit, no doubt with the Arab oil boycott of 1973/4 in mind,[24] "that this was not to say that all forms of economic and political pressure which threatened the territorial integrity and political independence of another state were permissible; they might well constitute illegal intervention."[25] In fact, the Section of the 1970 Declaration on the Principle of Non-Intervention, which is distinct from the Section on the Use of Force, prohibits economic coercion (but without defining it).

An armed attack by State A against State D is clearly a breach of Article 2(4). If State T intervenes by armed force to assist State A, it too is directly in breach of Article 2(4). If it intervenes in the same way to assist State D, the right of collective self defence below, p. 659, may justify its conduct. If State T assists State A in its attack upon State D by providing it with military or other equipment, training facilities, land bases, etc., then State T is probably indirectly engaged in the "use of force" contrary to Article 2(4).[26]

4. *Threat of force.* The ultimatum issued by France and the United Kingdom to Egypt and Israel in 1956, see below, p. 667, would be a "threat of force." Would another be the threat made by the Soviet Premier, Mr. Khruschchev, in 1960 after the *U-2 Incident*, when he reportedly stated:

> Those countries that have bases on their territories should note most carefully the following: if they allow others to fly from their base to our territory we shall hit at those bases.[27]

---

[23] U.N. Doc. A/AC.125/SR.114 (1970).

[24] In late 1973 (just after the *Yom Kippur War*) and early 1974, the Arab oil-producing states, led by Saudi Arabia, imposed an embargo on the supply of oil to the U.S. and other states (including all of the EEC countries) which they claimed were supporting Israel. The purpose was to cause those states to change their Middle East policies. For differing views on the legality of the embargo, which had a devastating economic effect, see the essays in Lillich, ed., *Economic Coercion and the New International Economic Order* (1976), and Paust and Blaustein, ed., *The Arab Oil Weapon* (1977).

[25] U.K. representative (Mr. Sinclair), U.N. Doc. A/AC.125/SR.25 (1966). On the possibility that economic coercion may be a "threat to the peace" giving rise to jurisdiction under Charter Art. 39, see below p. 677.

[26] This last situation is not specifically mentioned in the 1970 Declaration. The Section in the Declaration on the Principle on the Use of Force, paras. 8 and 9, prohibits intervention in a *civil war* to assist rebels, by such "indirect aggression"; it would seem that assistance of the same sort to a third state is as much the "use of force" as this and is otherwise a breach of Art. 2(4). In any event, such assistance to a third state is contrary to the Principle of Non-Intervention in the 1970 Declaration. On the limited UN practice concerning aid to third states, see Higgins, *op. cit.* p. 638, n. 1, above, p. 189.

[27] 5 Whiteman 714–715. On the *U-2 Incident*, see above, p. 185. See also on "threats of force," UN Secretary-General *Report on the Question of Defining Aggression*, U.N. Doc. A/2211, p. 52: " . . . the threat to use force is not always made in so crude and open a form [as an ultimatum]. There are sometimes veiled threats which may be very effective, but are difficult to detect."

5. *Against the territorial integrity or political independence of any state or in any manner, etc.* Article 2(4) prohibits an armed attack by State A against State D that *either* deprives State D of the whole or a part of its territory (see, *e.g.* the invasion of Poland by Germany in 1939 and of Manchuria by Japan in 1931, p. 88, above, respectively) *or* brings State D under State A's political control (see, *e.g.* the *Afghanistan case*, below, p. 652). A claim to sovereignty by State A over territory occupied by D cannot be pursued by armed force (see, *e.g.* the *Falkland Islands case*, below, p. 661, and the Iraq-Iran war[28]), but armed force can be used against an occupier by way of self-defence (see, again, the *Falkland Islands case*).[28a] An armed attack by one state upon another in furtherance of the principle of self-determination is not permitted, despite the emphasis placed upon that principle in recent years.[29]

The words "territorial integrity" (and "political independence") could be read as words of limitation, with a distinction being drawn between "integrity" (to do with annexation or permanent occupation or control) and "inviolability" (to do with trespass). Bowett[30] supports this limited reading on the basis in part that "the phrase having been included, it must be given its plain meaning." It was relied upon in the *Corfu Channel Case* by the United Kingdom when it argued that *Operation Retail*, in which the Corfu Channel in Albanian territorial waters was mineswept by the United Kingdom after British ships had been damaged by mines in it, was not contrary to Article 2(4): Kingdom after British ships had been damaged by mines in it, was not contrary to Article 2(4);

> But our action . . . threatened neither the territorial integrity nor the political independence of Albania. Albania suffered thereby neither territorial loss nor [loss to] any part of its political independence.[31]

Although this argument was not specifically considered in the judgment, the Court's condemnation of *Operation Retail* is not in sympathy with it.[32] Brownlie[33] argues convincingly against such a limited interpretation as follows:

> The conclusion warranted by the *travaux préparatoires* is that the phrase under discussion was not intended to be restrictive but, on the contrary, to give more specific guarantees to small states and that it cannot be interpreted as having a qualifying effect.
> . . . The phrase "political independence and territorial integrity" has been used on many occasions to epitomize the *total* of legal rights which a state has. Moreover, it is difficult to accept a "plain meaning" which permits evasion of obligations by means

---

[28] In 1980, Iraq attacked Iran in order, it claimed, to regain territory in the area of the Shatt al-Arab waterway which it had conceded to Iran by a 1975 treaty of reconciliation between the two states. See Amin, 31 I.C.L.Q. 167 (1982).

[28a] See Feinberg, 15 Israel L.R. 160 (1980), who takes the view expressed above. See, however, Jennings, *op. cit.* at p. 151, n. 1, p. 72, who argues that force can be used to recover territory if the claim to sovereignty of the state using force is justified. In that case, there is no use of force against the "territorial integrity" of another state.

[29] On the *Invasion of Goa Case* in which India, not the inhabitants of Goa, took the initiative to incorporate Goa into India, see above, p. 172. On the disagreement among states on the question whether a state can help a "people" that has engaged in its own war of national liberation: see below, p. 649.

[30] *Loc. cit.* at p. 638, n. 1, p. 152. The same author also points out (pp. 150–151) that Article 2(4) can be interpreted as requiring *either* a "specific intent," so that "the use or threat of force contravenes this obligation only where intended to jeopardise the political independence or territorial integrity of another state," *or* only that armed force must not be used with this result. The latter interpretation is the one that would appear to be followed in practice.

[31] *Corfu Channel Case*, Pleadings, Vol. III, p. 296.

[32] See the passage from the judgment, above, p. 301.

[33] *Op. cit.* at p. 638, n. 1 above, p. 268.

of a verbal profession that there is no intention to infringe territorial integrity and which was not intended by the many delegations which approved the text. Lastly, if there is an ambiguity the principle of effectiveness should be applied.

See also the 1970 Declaration, 4th and 5th paras. of the Section on the Principle on the Use of Force which support this wider interpretation. Even if the words "territorial integrity" were to be read restrictively, the final phrase of Article 2(4) nonetheless indicates that the paragraph, taken as a whole, contains a general prohibition on the use of armed force as "an instrument of national policy" (in the words of the Briand-Kellogg Pact). One of the "purposes of the United Nations" is to "maintain international peace and security" (Charter, Art.1(1)). The use of armed force in international relations by way of reprisal[34] or otherwise (*e.g.* to persuade a state to a certain course of conduct) is contrary to this "purpose." This is so whether the armed force is used in the territory of another state (see the facts of the *Naulilaa* case, above, p. 9) or not (*e.g.* the use of force against a ship or aircraft[35] outside the state of registration). The only justification for the use of force by one state against another under the legal regime of the Charter is self-defence, see below, p. 655, or participation in United Nations enforcement action, see below, p. 674.[36] Otherwise the interest in international peace and security prevails.

BOWETT, REPRISALS INVOLVING RECOURSE TO ARMED FORCE

66 A.J.I.L. 1 (1972). Some footnotes omitted

Few propositions about international law have enjoyed more support than the proposition that, under the Charter of the United Nations, the use of force by way of reprisals is illegal. . . .

It cannot be doubted that a total outlawry of armed reprisals, such as the drafters of the Charter intended, presupposed a degree of community cohesiveness and, with it, a capacity for collective action to suppress any resort to unlawful force which has simply not been achieved. Not surprisingly, as states have grown increasingly disillusioned about the capacity of the Security Council to afford them protection against what they would regard as illegal and highly injurious conduct directed against them,[37] they have resorted to self-help in the form of reprisals and have acquired the confidence that, in so doing, they will not incur anything more than a formal censure from the Security Council. The law on reprisals is, because of its divorce from actual practice, rapidly degenerating to a stage where its normative character is in question.

. . . To take what is now perhaps the classic case, let us suppose that guerrilla activity from State A, directed against State B, eventually leads to a military action within State A's territory by which State B hopes to destroy the guerrilla bases from which the previous attacks have come and to discourage further attacks. Clearly, this military action cannot strictly be regarded as self-defence

---

[34] The 1970 Declaration expressly prohibits reprisals: para. 6 of the Section on the Principle on the Use of Force.

[35] These would presumably not be "territory" for the purposes of Art. 2(4). *cf.* the facts of the *Gulf of Tonkin Incident*, below, p. 661. In that case, the retaliation was justified as self-defence.

[36] On humanitarian intervention as a third claimed exception, see above, p. 470, n. 3.

[37] *Ed. cf.* Fitzmaurice, above, p. 8.

in the context of the previous guerrilla activities: they are past, whatever damage has occurred as a result cannot now be prevented and no new military action by State B can really be regarded as a defence against attacks in the past. But if one broadens the context and looks at the whole situation between these two states, cannot it be said that the destruction of the guerrilla bases represents a proper, proportionate means of defence—for the security of the state *is* involved—against future and (given the whole context of past activities) certain attacks? The reply that this constitutes an argument of "anticipatory" self-defence which is no longer permitted under the Charter, since Article 51 requires an actual "armed attack," is scarcely adequate. It was never the intention of the Charter to prohibit anticipatory self-defence and the traditional right certainly existed in relation to an "imminent" attack. Moreover, the rejection of an anticipatory right is, in this day and age, totally unrealistic and inconsistent with general state practice.[38]

In fact, the records of the Security Council are replete with cases where states have invoked self-defence in this broader sense but where the majority of the Council have rejected this classification and regarded their action as unlawful reprisals. . . .

Weighing the advantages against the disadvantages . . . it would seem that the approach of the Security Council in assessing whether a case for lawful self-defence has been made out has been somewhat unrealistic. To confine this assessment to the incident and its immediate "cause," without regard to the broader context of the past relations between the parties and events arising therefrom, is to ignore the difficulties in which states may be placed, especially in relation to guerrilla activities. The result is not only that the Council finds itself being accused of being "one-sided" but it may also be forced to characterize as reprisals (and therefore illegal) action which, on a broader view of self-defence, might be regarded as legitimate. Or, even worse, the Council characterizes such action as an unlawful reprisal but, realizing the difficulties faced by the "defendant" state, does not make any formal condemnation and thus appears to be condoning action which it holds is illegal. . . .

Recent practice, particularly in the context of the Arab-Israel confrontation, suggests that not only have states like Israel, the United States and the United Kingdom not abandoned their wider view of self-defence—based upon the "accumulation of events" theory—despite the Security Council's rejection of the theory, but, even more striking, Israel has relied less and less on a self-defence argument and has taken action which is openly admitted to be a reprisal. The Beirut raid of December 28, 1968,[39] is the obvious example of an

---

[38] Pakistan justified the entry of her troops into Kashmir in 1948 on this basis before the Security Council, an argument opposed only by India. Israel's invasion of Sinai in October 1956 and June 1967 rested on the same argument. The O.A.S. has used the same argument in relation to the blockade of Cuba during the 1962 missile crisis. Several states have expressed the same argument in the Sixth Committee in connection with the definition of aggression and the UN itself invoked the principle of anticipatory self-defence to justify action by O.N.U.C. in Katanga in December 1961, and December 1963. Following the invasion of Czechoslovakia by the U.S.S.R. in 1968, it is permissible to assume that the U.S.S.R. now shares this view for there certainly existed no "armed attack."

[39] *Ed.* 13 civil airplanes valued at over $40 million were destroyed while on the ground at Beirut airport in Lebanon by Israeli commandos. There was no loss of life. The raid was in

action not really defended on the basis of self-defence at all. Indeed, even as a reprisal, the motivation for reprisals seems to have shifted from that of punishment for previous acts to deterrence of future possible acts.[40] . . . It cannot be expected that the Security Council will ever accept this justification. But there is clearly some evidence that certain reprisals will, even if not accepted as justified, at least avoid condemnation. This shift in argument from self-defence to reprisals may in part be due to the realization that the self-defence argument is unlikely to be accepted in any event. It may in larger part be due to a growing feeling that not only do reprisals offer a more effective means of checking military and strategic gains by the other party but also that they will meet with no more than a formal condemnation by the Council, and that effective sanctions under Chapter VII are not to be feared. Obviously, if this trend continues, we shall achieve a position in which, while reprisals remain illegal *de jure*, they become accepted *de facto*. Indeed, it may be that the more relevant distinction today is not between self-defence and reprisals but between reprisals which are likely to be condemned and those which, because they satisfy some concept of "reasonableness," are not.

Notes

1. On reprisals in international law, see the *Naulilaa Case*, above, p. 9. One of the cases to which Bowett refers in which the Security Council rejected a claim of self-defence in the "broader sense" was the *Harib Fort Incident*.[41] In 1964, the Yemen brought a complaint against the United Kingdom before the Security Council resulting from the following situation. In 1963 and 1964, the British Government had complained to the Security Council of a large number of shooting incidents on the Yemeni-South Arabian border and of aerial raids into South Arabian territory from the Yemen. In three raids in March 1964, bedouin and their flocks had been attacked from the air. Thereupon, on March 28, 1964, British military aircraft bombed Harib Fort in the Yemen after having first dropped leaflets advising people to leave the area. The Yemen claimed that 25 people were killed, but this figure was disputed. The British representative justified this action as follows:

26. There is, in existing law, a clear distinction to be drawn between two forms of self-help. One, which is of a retributive or punitive nature, is termed "retaliation" or "reprisals"; the other, which is expressly contemplated and authorized by the Char-

retaliation for an attack on December 26 on an El Al airplane at Athens airport by Palestine guerrillas. The airplane was damaged and a passenger—an Israeli—killed. The Security Council condemned Israel "for its premeditated military action in violation of its obligations under the Charter" and considered that Lebanon was entitled to "appropriate redress for the destruction it has suffered": S.C. Resn. 262 (1968), S.C.O.R., 23rd Year, *Resolutions and Decisions*, p. 12. Adopted unanimously. See Falk, 63 A.J.I.L. 415 (1969) and Blum, 64 *ibid*. 73 (1970).

[40] The Israeli Chief of Staff, General Yetzhak Bar Lev, was reported to have stated the purpose as being "to make clear to the other side that the price they must pay for terrorist activities can be very high"; see *New York Times*, January 5, 1969, Sec. 4, p. 1. However, Ambassador Rosenne, in the Security Council, did raise the justification of self-defence (see Doc. S/PV. 1460, pp. 22–23). *Ed*. The 1982 Israeli invasion of the Lebanon, leading to the departure of P.L.O. forces that had been attacking Israel from Lebanese bases is yet another "accumulation of events" case. *cf*. also the Israeli attack in 1981 upon a nuclear reactor in Iraq. This was condemned by the Security Council as a "clear violation" of Art. 2(4): S.C. Resn. 487 (1981), 18 *UN Chronicle*, August 1981, p. 68.

[41] S.C.O.R. 19th Yr., 1106th–1111th Meetings, April 2nd–8th, 1964. *cf*. the *Gulf of Tonkin Incident* discussed below, p. 661, under self-defence.

ter, is self-defence against armed attack. . . . It is clear that the use of armed force to repel or prevent an attack—that is, legitimate action of a defensive nature—may sometimes have to take the form of a counter-attack. . . .

28. The fact that some of these aggressive acts from the Yemen have fortunately, in recent weeks, not resulted in loss of life or very serious damage is quite beside the point.[42] In the past lives have been lost as the result of these actions, and far inside Federation territory. This naturally caused great alarm among the people concerned.

29. . . . It indeed would be a strange legal doctrine which deprived the people of the Federation of any right to be defended, or deprived those responsible for defending them from taking appropriate measures of a preventive nature.[43]

30. It is therefore necessary to emphasize once more that the fort at Harib was not merely a military installation, but was known to be a centre for aggressive action against the Federation. To destroy the fort with the minimum use of force was therefore a defensive measure which was proportionate and confined to the necessities of the case.

31. It has no parallel with acts of retaliation or reprisals, which have as an essential element the purposes of vengeance or retribution. It is this latter use of force which is condemned by the Charter, and not the use of force for defensive purposes such as warding off future attacks.[44]

The Security Council adopted a resolution in which it

1. *Condemns* reprisals as incompatible with the purposes and principles of the United Nations;
2. *Deplores* the British military action at Harib on 28 March 1964;
3. *Deplores* all attacks and incidents which have occurred in the area.[45]

2. Bowett lists as factors which the practice of the Security Council suggests are relevant to the question whether a reprisal is "reasonable" and hence unlikely to be condemned, the proportionality between the reprisal and the earlier illegal act that causes it; whether the reprisal is against civilians or the armed forces; whether it is one against human life or property; whether the state against whom it is taken has provoked the reprisal; whether the reprisal jeopardises the chances of a peaceful settlement by its timing; and whether, at least in the guerrilla context, the state taking the reprisal has exhausted all practical measures for the defence of its territory within its own borders.[46]

3. In May/June 1977, Rhodesia entered Mozambique territory and attacked bases used by terrorists against it up to a distance of sixty miles from the border. It justified its action on grounds of "hot pursuit." The Security Council condemned the action.[47] The invocation of the doctrine of "hot pursuit" across a *land* border[48] would appear to have been misguided.[49] The question must be whether it could be justified as a reprisal or an act of anticipatory self-defence.

---

[42] *Ed.* Two camels were killed and two tents were burnt: U.N.Doc. S/5618.

[43] *Ed.* The U.K. was acting under a treaty of protection with the Federation.

[44] S.C.O.R., 19th Year, 1106th Meeting, April 2, 1964.

[45] *Ibid.* 1111th Meeting, April 8. The resolution adopted by 9 votes to 0, with 2 abstentions.

[46] See also the guidelines suggested by Falk, *loc. cit.* at p. 646, n. 39, above, at pp. 439–440, which are discussed by Bowett. For the view that Art. 2(4) no longer serves any useful purpose, see Franck, 64 A.J.I.L. 809 (1970). See, in reply, Henkin 65 A.J.I.L. 544 (1971).

[47] S.C. Resn. 411 (1977), S.C.O.R., 32nd Year, *Resolutions and Decisions*, p. 9.

[48] On the right of "hot pursuit" at sea, see above, p. 334.

[49] See Luttig, 3 S.A.Y.B.I.L. 136 (1977) and Poulantzas, *The Right of Hot Pursuit in International Law* (1969), pp. 11–12. The statement by the U.K. Foreign Minister (Dr. Owen) on the matter is less clear: *Hansard*, H.C., Vol. 933, col. 378. June 15, 1977.

(b) *Intervention in Civil Wars*[50]

DECLARATION ON THE INADMISSIBILITY OF INTERVENTION IN THE DOMESTIC AFFAIRS OF STATES AND THE PROTECTION OF THEIR INDEPENDENCE AND SOVEREIGNTY 1965[51]

General Assembly Resolution 2131 (XX), G.A.O.R., 20th Session, Supp. 14, p. 11; 60 A.J.I.L. 662 (1966)

The General Assembly . . . solemnly declares: . . .

1. No state has the right to intervene, directly or indirectly, for any reason whatever, in the internal or external affairs of any other state. Consequently, armed intervention and all other forms of interference or attempted threats against the personality of the state or against its political, economic and cultural elements, are condemned.

2. No state may use or encourage the use of economic, political or any other type of measures to coerce another state in order to obtain from it the subordination of the exercise of its sovereign rights or to secure from it advantages of any kind. Also, no state shall organize, assist, foment, finance, incite or tolerate subversive, terrorist or armed activities directed towards the violent overthrow of the régime of another state, or interfere in civil strife in another state.

3. The use of force to deprive peoples of their national identity constitutes a violation of their inalienable rights and of the principle of non-intervention.

4. The strict observance of these obligations is an essential condition to ensure that nations live together in peace with one another, since the practice of any form of intervention not only violates the spirit and letter of the Charter of the United Nations but also leads to the creation of situations which threaten international peace and security.

5. Every state has an inalienable right to choose its political, economic, social and cultural systems, without interference in any form by another State.

Notes

1. Paragraphs 1, 2, 3, and 5 of the 1965 Declaration were incorporated almost verbatim into the 1970 Declaration on Principles of International Law, Appendix III, below.

2. Intervention covers a much wider field than intervention in civil wars (the sole subject of this section). The prohibition upon intervention in civil wars is just one aspect of a more general prohibition the limits of which have always been uncertain and are not well defined in the vague language of the 1965 and 1970 Declarations. Intervention is defined by Oppenheim as "dictatorial interference by a State in the affairs of another State for the purpose of maintaining or altering the actual condition of things."[52] In the

---

[50] See Falk, ed., *The International Law of Civil War* (1971); Farer, 142 *Hague Recueil* 291 (1974–II); Friedmann, *The Changing Structure of International Law* (1964), pp. 262–272; Leurdijk, Neth.I.L.R. 143 (1977); Luard, ed., *The International Regulation of Civil War* (1972); Moore, ed., *Law and Civil War in the Modern World* (1974); Stassen, 3 S.A.Y.B.I.L. 65 (1977).

[51] The Resolution was adopted by 109 to 0, with 1 abstention. The one abstaining state was the U.K., which accepted the "fundamental propositions set out in the resolution" but objected to the manner in which that resolution had been evolved and the imprecision of some of its language": 1967 B.P.I.L. 35, 36.

[52] Oppenheim, Vol. I, para. 134.

nineteenth century, it was often darkly associated with the armed intervention, on humanitarian or other grounds, by powerful European states in the affairs of their weaker brethren.[53] As the 1965 Declaration indicates, it also includes other more subtle, forms of influence or control. For example, intervention in the "external affairs" of another state (paragraph 1) may include a case in which "State A sought to persuade State B by threats or by other measures amounting to economic coercion not to enter an association with other States."[54] The Principle of Non-Intervention in the 1965 and 1970 Declarations overlaps with that on the Use of Force in Article 2(4) and the 1970 Declaration. An armed attack upon another State annexing its territory is the ultimate form of intervention. Assistance to rebels in a civil war is within both principles also.

3. *Aid to rebels.* Intervention in a civil war to aid rebels against the constitutional government of a state is contrary to the Principle of Non-Intervention in the 1965 and 1970 Declarations: see paragraphs 2 of each. Paragraphs 8 and 9 of the Section on the Principle on the Use of Force in the 1970 Declaration, and hence Article 2(4), also prohibit it.[55] There is disagreement over the question whether a state may intervene to assist a "people" fighting a war of national liberation, *i.e.* one to realise their right to self-determination, as to which see above, p. 95. Developing and Communist states take the view that the use of force by a colonial power to repress such action by a "people" is a breach of Article 2(4) and that a state may intervene to give "material" (*i.e.* troops, equipment, etc.) as well as "moral" assistance to the rebels.[56] Western states deny that Article 2(4) applies to an internal war and claim that the Principle of Non-Intervention prohibits "material assistance." The Section on the Principle of Self-Determination in the 1970 Declaration purposely avoids the issue by simply stating (para. 6) that "such peoples are entitled to seek and receive support" (undefined). *Cf.* the similarly equivocal wording of the 1974 General Assembly Resolution on the Definition of Aggression, Article 7, below, p. 678.

4. *Angola.* In January 1975, Portugal signed an agreement with the three independence parties—MPLA, FNLA, and UNITA—in its colony of Angola by which the colony obtained its independence at the end of the year. Disagreement between the three parties led to the establishment during 1975 of rival governments, by the MPLA on the one side and by the FNLA and UNITA on the other. Civil war broke out early in 1975 with the MPLA being supported by Cuban troops and U.S.S.R. military advisers and equipment, and the FNLA and UNITA having the assistance of South African troops and other forms of aid from the United States (until the United States Senate forbad it), China and Zaire. By March 1976, the MPLA was in control of the most important areas of Angola and the other side had retreated to fight a still continuing guerrilla war. Angola, under the MPLA Government, was admitted to the United Nations in December 1976. In March 1976, the Security Council condemned "South

---

[53] *cf.* the passage in the *Corfu Channel Case* judgment, above, p. 301.

[54] U.K. representative (Mr. Sinclair) in the 1967 Special Committee on Principles of International Law, etc., UN Doc. A/AC.125/SR.73, p. 22; 1967 B.P.I.L. 39.

[55] It is odd to describe "indirect aggression," which is the name given to conduct of the sort proscribed by paras. 8 and 9, as the "use of force" in the sense of Art. 2(4). It is really "aiding and abetting" in criminal law terms.

[56] A number of General Assembly resolutions support the latter part of this view. See, *e.g.* G.A. Res. 2908 (XXVII) (1972), which "urges all states . . . to provide moral and material assistance to all peoples struggling for their freedom and independence in the colonial Territories and to those living under alien domination—in particular to the national liberation movements of the Territories of Africa. . . . " The resolution was adopted by 99 votes to 5 (France, Portugal, South Africa, U.K., and the U.S.), with 23 abstentions. Aid to the Smith Government in Southern Rhodesia would not have qualified, as that Government was not fighting a war of national liberation. On wars of national liberation as the modern equivalent of the "just war," see Grahl-Madsen, 22 German Y.B.I.L. 255 (1979).

Africa's aggression against the People's Republic of Angola."[57] No such resolution was adopted in respect of U.S.S.R. and Cuban aid to the other side.

5. *Bangladesh.* Until 1971, Pakistan consisted of East and West Pakistan, with India between the two parts. In March 26, 1971, East Pakistan declared itself independent under the name of Bangladesh. The Pakistan army was initially successful in suppressing the rebellion, but in November 1971 rebel guerrilla forces launched a general offensive with considerable success. There was evidence to suggest that India, which by then had taken into its territory about one million refugees from East Pakistan, had given the guerrillas military assistance and Pakistani and Indian troops clashed in the border area. On December 3, 1971, Pakistan attacked India in the west. War was declared on both sides and fighting began in earnest in east and west. By December 17, 1971, Pakistan had surrendered on both fronts. Bangladesh has since received general recognition (including that of Pakistan) as an independent state. Was India entitled in law to give military assistance to the Bangladesh guerrillas? Was its refugee problem relevant? Was Pakistan entitled to attack India on December 3?

THE JORDANIAN CASE

5 Whiteman 1171–1173

On July 17, 1958, the British Prime Minister, Harold Macmillan . . . informed the House of Commons that King Hussein and the Prime Minister of Jordan had, on the previous day, made a request for the immediate dispatch of British forces to Jordan. In making the request, he said, the King and Prime Minister said that Jordan was faced with an imminent attempt by the United Arab Republic to create internal disorder and to overthrow the present regime in Jordan, on the pattern of recent events in Iraq. The communication received went on to say that Jordan's territorial integrity was threatened by the movement of Syrian forces towards her northern frontier and by the infiltration of arms across it and that a *coup d'etat* organized by the United Arab Republic would be attempted on July 17. The British Prime Minister stated that his information clearly showed that the apprehensions of the Jordan Government were well founded "and that an attempt was indeed being organized for today." He stated that the Government had accordingly decided to accede to the request of Jordan and that British forces were being sent by air to Jordan from Cyprus. As to the purpose, he stated that "this military assistance is to stabilise the situation in Jordan by helping the Jordanian Government to resist aggression and threats to the integrity and independence of their country." . . .

The British Prime Minister at the same time informed the House of Commons that this decision of Her Majesty's Government was being reported to the United Nations, and that it was being made clear there that if arrangements were made by the Security Council to protect the lawful Government of Jordan from external threat—"and so maintain international peace and security"—the British action would be brought to an end. . . .

---

[57] S.C. Resn. 387 (1976), S.C.O.R., 20th Year, *Resolutions and Decisions*, p. 11. The vote was by 9 to 0. France, Italy, Japan and the U.K. and the U.S. abstained; China did not participate in the vote. Stone suggests that the Western powers and China found unacceptable a resolution that did not also condemn the U.S.S.R. and Cuba: Stone, *Conflict through Consensus: United Nations Approaches to Aggression*, 1977, p. 215, n. 1. Such a resolution would almost certainly have been vetoed by the U.S.S.R.

Notes

1. *Aid to governments.* The intervention of states at the request of other states to help suppress internal uprisings has been a common feature of international relations since the Second World War. Insofar as an uprising is assisted or fomented by a third state, as was claimed in the *Jordanian case*, intervention at the request of the constitutional government may be seen as a lawful exercise of the right of collective self-defence against "indirect aggression" contrary to Article 2(4). The legality of intervention in the case of a purely internal disturbance is more a matter of debate. Writing in 1937, Garner[58] stated emphatically that there "is no rule of international law which forbids the government of one state from rendering assistance to the established legitimate government of another state with a view of enabling it to suppress an insurrection against its authority."

Twenty years later, Wright[59] wrote equally surely that international law:

"does not permit the use of force in the territory of another state on invitation either of the recognized or the insurgent government in times of rebellion, insurrection, or civil war. Since international law recognizes the right of revolution, it cannot permit other states to intervene to prevent it."

This last statement probably represents the majority view of writers today and is consistent with the "broad principle" in the 1965 and 1970 Declarations "that internal conflicts within the state are the concern of that state alone."[60] The United Kingdom supports a rule of non-intervention, save in the case of "temporary difficulties":

"His Government believed that . . . if a country was unfortunate enough to fall into a situation in which control of the country was divided between warring factions and if no outside interference had taken place, then any form of interference or any encouragement given to any party was prohibited by international law. Nevertheless, the United Kingdom did not consider that that rule in any way prejudiced the right of a legally constituted and internationally recognised Government to seek and receive from a friendly State assistance in preserving or restoring internal law and order. Of course, any Government which responded to such a request for assistance would have to satisfy itself that the response was proper, and it would have to expect its actions to come under the closest scrutiny of the international community. His Government believed, however, that it would be wrong to suggest by an unduly broad definition of 'civil strife' that there were no circumstances in which a Government in temporary difficulties could seek and receive assistance from a friendly State which it trusted to render aid with full respect for the territorial integrity and political independence of the recipient State.[61]

2. *The Hungarian Uprising.*[62] On October 23, 1956, demonstrations took place in Budapest against the Hungarian Government calling, *inter alia*, for Mr. Nagy to be brought into the Government. Fighting broke out and, at 2 a.m. on the 24th, Russian tanks appeared in Budapest. Nonetheless, at 8.13 a.m., it was announced that a new Government was to be formed under Mr. Nagy. At 9 a.m., it was announced that "the Government had applied for help to the Soviet formations stationed in Hungary [under the Warsaw Pact]." It is not clear when and by whom the application was made.[63] On November 1, Hungary denounced the Warsaw Pact after Mr. Nagy had unsuccessfully

---

[58] 31 A.J.I.L. 66, 68 (1937).

[59] 54 A.J.I.L. 521, 529 (1960).

[60] Bowett, in Moore, ed., *op. cit.* at p. 648, n. 50, above, at p. 41. For a general discussion, see Brownlie, *op. cit.* at p. 638, n. 1, above, pp. 312–317.

[61] U.K. representative (Mr. Sinclair) in the 1967 Special Committee on Principles of International Law, etc., UN Doc. A/AC.125/S/R.57, p. 5; 1967 B.P.I.L. 36.

[62] The following summary is based on the Report of the UN Special Committee on the Problem of Hungary, G.A.O.R., 11th Session, Supp. 18.

[63] It is not known when Mr. Nagy's Government actually took office.

demanded the withdrawal of new Soviet troops known to be entering Hungary. On the same day, Mr. Nagy broadcast a declaration of Hungarian neutrality and called for the assistance of other states to defend it. On November 4, Soviet troops again entered Budapest and overcame resistance in a few days. On the same day, Mr. Kadar announced that he had formed a Government in place of that of Mr. Nagy and that he had requested the second intervention of Soviet troops. Thereafter the uprising petered out. The United Nations Special Committee on the Problem of Hungary, which was not allowed into Hungary to investigate, found it impossible to reach any conclusion on the question whether any request for aid had been made at the beginning; it rejected the Soviet argument[64] that what the committee called a "spontaneous national uprising" had been fomented by ex-Nazi leaders and Western powers who had sent in arms. The case demonstrates one of the weaknesses of allowing intervention at the request of the constitutional government, viz. that of determining which is the constitutional government (if any can be found in the middle of a revolution) and whether it in fact made a request.

3. *The Czechoslovak Case.* In 1968, with the arrival of Mr. Dubcek and other new leaders in power by lawful means, the still communist Government of Czechoslovakia introduced certain reforms resulting, *inter alia*, in increased freedom of speech, that were significantly at variance with Czechoslovakia's previous policies. In August 1968, troops from the U.S.S.R. and other East European communist states entered Czechoslovakia. With the assistance of Russian advisers, the policies and composition of the Czech Government thereafter gradually changed, with the movement towards liberalisation being reversed. The U.S.S.R. first claimed that the Czech Government had requested the intervention, but this was strenuously denied by that Government. Later the intervention was explained by Mr. Brezhnev, in a speech in Poland, as follows:

> Socialist states stand for strict respect for the sovereignty of all countries. We resolutely oppose interference in the affairs of any states and the violations of their sovereignty.
>
> . . . The U.S.S.R. has always advocated that each socialist country determine the concrete forms of its development along the path of socialism by taking into account the specific nature of its national conditions. But it is well known, comrades, that there are common natural laws of socialist construction, deviation from which could lead to deviation from socialism as such. And when external and internal forces hostile to socialism try to turn the development of a given socialist country in the direction of restoration of the capitalist system, when a threat arises to the cause of socialism in that country—a threat to the security of the socialist commonwealth as a whole—this is no longer merely a problem for the country's people, but a common problem, the concern of all socialist countries.
>
> It is quite clear that an action such as military assistance to a fraternal country to end a threat to the socialist system is an extraordinary measure, dictated by necessity; it can be called forth only by the overt actions of enemies of socialism within the country and beyond its boundaries, actions that create a threat to the common interests of the socialist camp.[65]

This doctrine of limited sovereignty has become known as the "Brezhnev Doctrine."[66]

4. *The Afghanistan Case.*[67] In 1978, the non-aligned Daud Government was ousted by force by the more left-wing Taraki (later Amin) Government, which established

---

[64] G.A.O.R., 11th Session, Special Political Committee, 41st Meeting, p. 189.

[65] 20 *Current Digest of the Soviet Press*, No. 46, pp. 3–4; December 4, 1968.

[66] See further Tunkin, *loc. cit.* at p. 14, n. 49, above, p. 440. And see Butler, 65 A.J.I.L. 796 (1971). The U.K. regards the doctrine as "inconsistent with the sovereign equality of states in international law" and with the 1975 Helsinki Declaration: U.K.M.I.L. 1980; (1980) 51 B.Y.I.L. 366.   [67] See *Keesings Archives*, p. 30229.

closer links with the U.S.S.R. In 1979, this Government was overthrown by a new Soviet-backed Government led by President Karmal, an Afghanistan politician flown to Afghanistan to take office by the U.S.S.R. from virtual exile in Eastern Europe. The change of government was accompanied by an airlift into Kabul of 4000 U.S.S.R. troops. The U.S.S.R. claimed that the Afghanistan Government had requested U.S.S.R. intervention under a 1978 bilateral treaty of friendship[68] to protect Afghanistan from "armed incursions and provocations from outside." U.S.S.R. troops, now thought to number 100,000, remain in Afghanistan assisting the Afghan army in fighting guerilla opponents of the Karmal Government. A Security Council draft resolution which deplored the U.S.S.R. intervention and called for the withdrawal of U.S.S.R. troops was vetoed by the U.S.S.R.[69] A General Assembly resolution of January 14, 1980[70] re-affirmed that "respect for the sovereignty, territorial integrity and political independence of every state is a fundamental principle of the Charter" and strongly deplored "the recent armed intervention in Afghanistan which is inconsistent with that principle." The resolution appealed to all states "to refrain from any interference in the internal affairs of that country" and called for the "immediate, unconditional and total withdrawal of the foreign troops from Afghanistan." The General Assembly resolution is phrased in the terms of both the Use of Force and Non-Intervention Principles in the 1970 Declaration. What would the U.S.S.R. have to prove to establish that its intervention was lawful (i) in 1979 or (ii) now?

5. *The Dominican Republic case.*[71] On April 24, 1965, a revolution occurred against the Cabral Government. It was led by young military officers and members of the Dominican Revolutionary Party. Fighting broke out and the situation deteriorated to the point where the military junta which had replaced the Cabral Government in opposition to the rebels informed the United States Embassy that it was not able to guarantee the safety of United States nationals. In response to a request from the junta,[72] 400 United States marines were landed in the Republic on April 28 in order, President Johnson stated, to protect United States and other foreign nationals. This figure was later increased to over 20,000 troops. On May 2, President Johnson gave a different reason for the United States involvement, which anticipates the Brezhnev Doctrine:

". . . what began as a popular democratic revolution . . . very shortly . . . was taken over . . . by a band of communist conspirators . . . The American nation cannot . . . permit the establishment of another Communist Government in the Western Hemisphere . . . This was the unanimous view of all the American nations when, in January 1962, they declared . . . 'The Principles of communism are incompatible with the principles of the inter-American system.' . . . This is and this will be the common action and common purpose of the democratic forces of the hemisphere."[73]

6. *Vietnam.*[74] When the Japanese, who had taken Vietnam—a French colonial possession—from the French during the Second World War, were defeated, the

---

[68] For the terms of this treaty see, *ibid.* p. 29459. It provides for the parties to "consult each other and take by agreement appropriate measures to ensure the security, independence and territorial integrity of their countries."

[69] The vote, on January 7, 1980, was by 13 to 2 (G.D.R., U.S.S.R.).

[70] GA Res. ES-6/2. The vote was by 104 votes to 18, with 18 abstentions. The resolution has been repeated, see, most recently, GA Res.36/34 (1982).

[71] See Friedmann, 59 A.J.I.L. 857, 866–868 (1965); Meeker, 53 *U.S. Dept. of State Bull.* 60 (1965); and Thomas and Thomas, *The Dominican Republic Crisis* 1965 (1967).

[72] According to one U.S. source, the request was solicited by the U.S. Government: see Thomas and Thomas, *loc. cit.* at n. 71 above, pp. 75, n. 10, and 94.

[73] 52 *U.S. Dept. of State Bull.* 745–746 (1965).

[74] See Falk, ed., *The Vietnam War and International Law*, Vols. I–III (1968–72), and Schick, 17 I.C.L.Q. 953 (1968).

Vietnamese Communist-led nationalist movement, established itself as the effective government in the North, with Hanoi as its capital, and claimed to be the government of the whole of the one state of Vietnam. Attempts at a settlement between France, which had retaken possession of South Vietnam after the war, and Hanoi failed and by the end of 1946, fighting had broken out between French and Hanoi forces which only ended with the defeat of the French at Dien Bien Phu in 1954. In December 1946, France established a second Vietnamese Government based on Saigon. This Government also claimed to be the Government of the one state of Vietnam. After Dien Bien Phu, a Conference was held at Geneva in July 1954 to consider the future of French Indo-China (Cambodia, Laos and Vietnam). The outcome for Vietnam was a cease-fire agreement and certain provisions in the Final Declaration of the Conference.[75] The former temporarily divided Vietnam at the 17th Parallel; the latter provided for elections to be held, leading to a single Vietnamese state. The elections were not held because of Saigon opposition on the ground that conditions for the "free expression of the national will" did not exist. Thereafter, a guerrilla war against the Saigon Government developed. This was partly indigenous and partly aided by the north. The Saigon Government was given financial and military support by the United States to repel it. By 1965, Hanoi and American involvement was extensive and had reached the point where regular North Vietnamese troops were deployed in the south against American troops and the United States was bombing the north. A peace agreement was signed in 1973[76] by which the United States left Vietnam. Provision was made for South and North Vietnam to agree on reunification of Vietnam "step by step through peaceful means" (Art. 15). Within a year, the North had taken over the South by military action and the one Hanoi-based state of Vietnam was established which has since been admitted to the United Nations.

The United States justified its intervention as an exercise of the right of collective self-defence against an "armed attack" from the north. In 1966, it explained its case in a Memorandum[77] which read in part:

It has been asserted that the conflict in Vietnam is "civil strife" in which foreign intervention is forbidden. . . . Any such characterization is an entire fiction disregarding the actual situation in Vietnam. The Hanoi regime is anything but the legitimate government of a unified country in which the South is rebelling against lawful national authority.

The Geneva accords of 1954 provided for a division of Vietnam into two zones at the 17th parallel. Although this line of demarcation was intended to be temporary, it was established by international agreement, which specifically forbade aggression by one zone against the other.

The Republic of Vietnam in the South has been recognized as a separate international entity by approximately 60 governments the world over. It has been admitted as a member of a number of the specialized agencies of the United Nations. The United Nations General Assembly in 1957 voted to recommend South Vietnam for membership in the organization, and its admission was frustrated only by the veto of the Soviet Union in the Security Council.

In any event there is no warrant for the suggestion that one zone of a temporarily divided state—whether it be Germany, Korea, or Vietnam—can be legally overrun by armed forces from the other zone, crossing the internationally recognized line of demarcation between the two. Any such doctrine would subvert the international agreement establishing the line of demarcation, and would post grave dangers to international peace.

[75] Misc. 20 (1954), Cmnd. 9239.
[76] 67 A.J.I.L. 389 (1973).
[77] *Memorandum on the Legality of United States Participation in the Defence of Vietnam*, prepared by the Legal Adviser of the U.S. Dept. of State, 60 A.J.I.L. 565 (1966). See Falk, 75 Yale L.J. 1122 (1966).

The action of the United Nations in the Korean conflict of 1950 clearly established the principle that there is no greater license for one zone of a temporarily divided state to attack the other zone than there is for one state to attack another state. South Vietnam has the same right that South Korea had to defend itself and to organize collective defence against an armed attack from the North. . . .

There is nothing in the charter to suggest that United Nations members are precluded from participating in the defence of a recognized international entity against armed attack merely because the entity may lack some of the attributes of an independent sovereign state. Any such result would have a destructive effect on the stability of international engagements such as the Geneva accords of 1954 and on internationally agreed lines of demarcation.

7. *The Cyprus Case.*[78] Cyprus has a population which is four-fifths Greek Cypriot and one-fifth Turkish Cypriot. The United Nations Force in Cyprus (UNFICYP) was established there in 1964[79] to help keep the peace between the two communities. Following the overthrow of the Makarios Government in 1974 by a coup supported by Greece and resulting in the establishment of a Greek Cypriot junta, Turkey invaded the island in the same month. The Security Council called upon "all states to respect the sovereignty, independence and territorial integrity of Cyprus" and demanded "an immediate end to foreign military intervention" in Cyprus that was contrary to such respect.[80] In 1975, a Turkish Federated State of Cyprus was declared in the 36 per cent. of the island occupied by Turkish forces, north of a line running through Nicosia and Famagusta. The Federated State has its own constitution. It has not been recognised as an independent state by any state. Turkey claims that its intervention in 1974 was justified under the Treaty of Guarantee[81] made between Cyprus, Greece, Turkey, and the United Kingdom in 1959 when Cypriot independence was agreed. By this treaty, Cyprus undertook to "ensure the maintenance of its independence, territorial integrity and security, as well as respect for its constitution" (Art. 1). The three guaranteeing powers, who undertook to recognise and guarantee the independence, territorial integrity and security of Cyprus (Art. 2), agreed in the event of a breach of the treaty to consult to determine what representations or measures were necessary. Insofar as concerted action proved impossible, each of them reserved "the right to take action with the sole aim of establishing the state of affairs created" by the treaty (Art. 4). Could Turkey rely upon the treaty (supposing "action" includes the use of force and that tripartite consultation had occurred (it had not)) to justify its intervention in the face of Article 2(4) of the Charter or the Principle of Non-Intervention in the 1970 Declaration? Would Article 103 of the United Nations Charter, below, Appendix I, be relevant?

2. THE RIGHT OF SELF-DEFENCE

THE CAROLINE CASE[82]

29 B.F.S.P. 1137–1138; 30 B.F.S.P. 195–196

The case arose out of the Canadian Rebellion of 1837. The rebel leaders, despite steps taken by United States authorities to prevent assistance being given to them, managed

[78] See Polyviou, *Cyprus: The Tragedy and the Challenge* (1975), who argues the Greek Cypriot case.
[79] See below, p. 697.
[80] S.C. Resn. 353 (1974), S.C.O.R., 29th Year, *Resolutions and Decisions*, p. 7. See, most recently, S.C. Resn. 440 (1978), S.C.O.R. 29th Year, *ibid*. p. 11.
[81] Cmnd. 1093.
[82] See Jennings, 32 A.J.I.L. 82 (1938).

on December 13, 1837, to enlist at Buffalo in the United States the support of a large number of American nationals. The resulting force established itself on Navy Island in Canadian waters from which it raided the Canadian shore and attacked passing British ships. The force was supplied from the United States shore by an American ship, the *Caroline*. On the night of December 29–30, the British seized the *Caroline*, which was then in the American port of Schlosser, fired her and sent her over Niagara Falls. Two United States nationals were killed. The legality of the British acts was discussed in detail in correspondence in 1841–42 when the United Kingdom sought the release of a British subject, McLeod, who had been arrested in the United States on charges of murder and arson arising out of the incident.

MR. WEBSTER TO MR. FOX (April 24, 1841). It will be for . . . [Her Majesty's] Government to show a neccesity of self-defence, instant, over-whelming, leaving no choice of means, and no moment for deliberation. It will be for it to show, also, that the local authorities of Canada, even supposing the necessity of the moment authorized them to enter the territories of The United States at all, did nothing unreasonable or excessive; since the act, justified by the necessity of self-defence, must be limited by that necessity, and kept clearly within it. It must be shown that admonition or remonstrance to the person on board the *Caroline* was impracticable, or would have been unavailing; it must be shown that day-light could not be waited for; that there could be no attempt at discrimination between the innocent and the guilty; that it would not have been enough to seize and detain the vessel; but that there was a necessity, present and inevitable, for attacking her in the darkness of the night, while moored to the shore, and while unarmed men were asleep on board, killing some and wounding others, and then drawing her into the current, above the cataract, setting her on fire, and, careless to know whether there might not be in her the innocent with the guilty, or the living with the dead, committing her to a fate which fills the imagination with horror. A necessity for all this, the Government of The United States cannot believe to have existed.

LORD ASHBURTON TO MR. WEBSTER (July 28, 1842). It is so far satisfactory to perceive that we are perfectly agreed as to the general principles of inter-national law applicable to this unfortunate case. Respect for the inviolable character of the territory of independent nations is the most essential founda-tion of civilization. . . .

Notes

1. In his reply, Lord Ashburton made a remarkably good attempt at justifying the British action in accordance with the test formulated by Webster, which has commonly been accepted as indicating when the right of self-defence may be exercised.

2. *Anticipatory self-defence.* It was not doubted in the *Caroline Case* that the British Government was entitled to anticipate further attacks. It was argued before the Inter-national Military Tribunal at Nuremberg that the German invasion of Norway in 1941 was an act of self-defence in the face of an imminent Allied landing there. The Tribunal recalled that preventive action in foreign territory is justified only in the circumstances cited by Webster in the *Caroline Case* and found on the facts that there was no imminent threat of an Allied landing in Norway.[83] The International Military Tribunal for the Far East (the Tokyo Tribunal), when considering the legality of Japan's invasion of Dutch

[83] 41 A.J.I.L. 205 (1947).

territory in the Far East after the Netherlands had been the first of the two states to declare war, stated:

> The fact that the Netherlands, being fully appraised of the imminence of the attack, in self-defence declared war against Japan on 8th December and thus officially recognised the existence of a state of war which had been begun by Japan cannot change that war from a war of aggression on the part of Japan into something other than that.[84]

3. The International Military Tribunal at Nuremberg also stated in respect of Germany's argument of "self-defence":

> It was further argued that Germany alone could decide, in accordance with the reservations made by many of the Signatory Powers at the time of the conclusion of the Kellogg-Briand Pact, whether preventive action was a necessity, and that in making her decision her judgment was conclusive. But whether action taken under the claim of self-defence was in fact aggressive or defensive must ultimately be subject to investigation and adjudication if the international law is ever to be enforced.[85]

4. *Proportionality.* A Report made to the League of Nations in 1927 said:

> Legitimate defence implies the adoption of measures proportionate to the seriousness of the attack and justified by the seriousness of the danger.[86]

5. *The seizure of ships on the high seas in self defence.* In the case of the *Virginius*, in which the seizure of an American merchant vessel on the high seas by Spain on the ground that the vessel was being used to assist Cuban insurgents against Spain in time of peace was in issue, Great Britain stated:

> Much may be excused in acts done under the expectation of instant damage in self-defence by a nation as well as by an individual. But, after the capture of the *Virginius* and the detention of the crew was effected, no pretence of imminent necessity of self-defence could be alleged.[87]

The United States maintained that "any visitation, molestation, or detention of . . . [American] . . . vessels by force, or by the exhibition of force, on the part of a foreign power is in derogation of the sovereignty of the United States."[88] The 1958 Geneva Convention on the High Seas, Article 22(1), makes no provision for jurisdiction over vessels on the high seas on the basis of self-defence.[89] If the *Caroline Case* permits the seizure of a vessel in the waters of another state, it must *a fortiori* allow seizure on the high seas.

See Article 51, United Nations Charter.[90]

Notes

1. There is some uncertainty as to the effect of Article 51 upon the customary international law right of self-defence. Kelsen[91] reads Article 51 as meaning that for

---

[84] Judgment, pp. 994–995, quoted in Horwitz, *The Tokyo Trial*, Int.Conc. No. 465 (1950), p. 560.

[85] 41 A.J.I.L. 207 (1947).

[86] L.N.Doc. A. 14, 1927. V.V. Legal 1927. V. 14, pp. 60, 69; quoted in Brownlie, *op. cit.* at p. 638, n. 1, p. 261. Compare the *Naulilaa Case*, above, p. 9, on proportionality in the law of reprisals.

[87] Correspondence respecting the Capture of the *Virginius*, Parl. Papers, LXXVI, 1874, p. 85, Spain No. 3 (1874), p. 85. Some of the crew members were British subjects.

[88] 2 Moore 898.

[89] See above p. 328. See also the Cuban Quarantine, below, p. 659.

[90] Appendix I, below.   [91] *The Law of the United Nations* (1950), p. 914.

United Nations members the right of self-defence "has no other content than the one determined by Article 51." Bowett,[92] however, states:

> It is . . . fallacious to assume that members have only those rights which the Charter accords to them; on the contrary they have those rights which general international law accords to them except in so far as they have surrendered them under the Charter . . .
>
> Now the relevant obligation assumed by members is, *prima facie*, that contained in Art. 2(4) . . . As we have seen, the view of Committee I at San Francisco was that this prohibition left the right of self-defence unimpaired.[93]

The official British Government Commentary on the Charter reads:

> It was considered at the Dumbarton Oaks Conference that the right of self-defence was inherent in the proposals and did not need explicit mention in the Charter. But self-defence may be undertaken by more than one state at a time, and the existence of regional organisations made this right of special importance to some states, while special treaties of defence made its explicit recognition important to others. Accordingly the right is given to individual states or to combinations of states to act until the Security Council itself has taken the necessary measures.[94]

See also the explanation given by the Lord Chancellor in the *Suez Case*, below, p. 667, of the relationship between Article 2(4) and Article 51. If Article 51 indicates the full extent of the right of self-defence, a state cannot defend its nationals abroad (as in the *Suez Case*) on the basis of it, since there will have been no "armed attack" against it. See further on this point, the *Entebbe Incident*, below, p. 669.

2. Similarly, if Article 51 states the whole of the right of self-defence, there is some doubt as to whether the right of anticipatory self-defence survives. The argument for saying that it does not is based upon the use of the phrase "an armed attack occurs" in Article 51. Brownlie[95] states, for example, that "the ordinary meaning of the phrase precludes action which is preventative in character." In contrast, Bowett[96] argues:

> "The history of Art. 51 suggests . . . that the article should safeguard the right of self-defence, not restrict it . . . furthermore, it is a restriction [no right of anticipation] which bears no relation to the realities of a situation which may arise prior to an actual attack and call for self-defence immediately if it is to be of any avail at all. No state can be expected to await an initial attack which, in the present state of armaments, may well destroy the state's capacity for further resistance and so jeopardise its very existence."

Henkin[97] argues against a right of anticipatory self-defence as follows:

> "Nothing in . . . its drafting . . . suggests that the framers of the Charter intended something broader than the language implied . . . It was that mild, old-fashioned Second World War which persuaded all nations that for the future national interests will have to be vindicated, or necessary change achieved, as well as can be by political

---

[92] *Op. cit.* at p. 638, n. 1, p. 185.

[93] Committee I [of Commission I], commenting upon Art. 2(4), reported that "the use of arms in legitimate self-defence remains admitted and unimpaired." 6 U.N.C.I.O., Documents 459.

[94] Misc. 9 (1945), Cmd. 6666, p. 9.

[95] *Op. cit.* at p. 638, n. 1, above, p. 275.

[96] *Op. cit.* at p. 638, n. 1, above, pp. 188–192. *cf.* McDougal, 47 A.J.I.L. 597 (1973) and the Lord Chancellor in the *Suez Case*, below, p. 667. Bowett agrees that the Security Council has rejected the view of a number of states that anticipatory self-defence is permitted in an "accumulation of events" context (such as that in the *Caroline* case): see above, p. 644.

[97] *How Nations Behave*, (2nd ed., 1979), pp. 141–142.

means, but not by war and military self-help. They recognised the exception of self-defence in emergency, but limited to actual armed attack, which is clear, unambiguous, subject to proof, and not easily open to misinterpretation or fabrication. . . . It is precisely in the age of the major deterrent that nations should not be encouraged to strike first under pretext of prevention or pre-emption.

The argument that "anticipatory self-defence" is essential to United States defence is fallacious. The United States relies for its security on its retaliatory power, and primarily on its second strike capability. It does not expect that it would be able to anticipate an attack and it could not afford to be mistaken, to bring about total war by a "pre-emptive strike," if the Soviet Union were not in fact striking or preparing to strike. In all probability, then, only an actual take-off by Soviet planes or missiles would cause the United States to strike, and in that case the United States is not "anticipating" an armed attack, for the attack would have begun.

Henkin's last comment raises the question, when does an armed attack begin to "occur"? Before soldiers, aircraft or missiles cross the border? From the time that troops are massed or ships set sail? The wider the meaning, the less the divergence between the two views.

3. *Collective self-defence.* The right of collective self-defence is the basis for the North Atlantic Treaty and the Warsaw Pact, see below, p. 672. It was relied upon by the United States in Vietnam, see above, p. 654. Bowett[98] has suggested that collective self-defence "requires each participating state to be exercising an individual right of self-defence, based upon a violation of its own substantive rights." Goodrich, Hambro and Simons[99] disagree, taking the view, in the light of "the discussion at San Francisco and the practice of member states since then" that the right allows "one state to come to the assistance of another state that is exercising the right of self-defence, not on the basis of a special substantive interest, but rather on the basis of a general interest in peace and security."

4. *The Role of Security Council.* The right of self-defence is a temporary one in the scheme of Article 51, existing only until the Security Council acts. In practice, of course, such is the power of the "veto," that the Security Council may never act and the right of self-defence will be of unlimited duration. Who is to judge when the Council "has taken the measures necessary . . . [etc.]"? The British Commentary on the Charter reads:

> It will be for the Security Council to decide whether these measures have been taken and whether they are adequate for the purpose. In the event of the Security Council failing to take any action, or if such action as it does take is clearly inadequate, the right of self-defence could be invoked by any Member or group of Members as justifying any action they thought fit to take.[1]

Is there an obligation placed upon a Member of the United Nations exercising the right of self-defence to inform the Security Council *before* it does so? See further, the *Falkland Islands* War, below, p. 661.

5. *The Cuban Quarantine.* On October 22, 1962, President Kennedy announced the United States intention to impose a "strict quarantine on all offensive military equipment under shipment to Cuba."[2] The United States decided upon this policy after discovering that the U.S.S.R. was sending to Cuba missiles and other weapons and materials which could be seen as a threat to United States security. On October 23, at the suggestion of the United States, the Security Council met and discussed the proposed quarantine but took no action.[3] On the same day, the Council of the Organisation of American States adopted a resolution[4] recommending that

[98] *Op. cit.* p. 638, n. 1, above, p. 245.
[99] *Op. cit.* p. 641, above, p. 348.
[1] *Loc. cit.* at n. 94, above, p. 9.
[2] *Keesings Archives*, p. 19061.
[3] S.C.O.R., 17th Year, 1022nd–1025th Meetings.   [4] 47 *U.S. Dept. of State Bull.* 723.

member states, in accordance with Articles 6 and 8 of the Inter-American Treaty of Reciprocal Assistance[5] take all measures, individually and collectively, including the use of armed force, which they may deem necessary to ensure that the Government of Cuba cannot continue to receive from the Sino-Soviet powers military material and related supplies which may threaten the peace and security of the Continent and to prevent the missiles in Cuba with offensive capability from ever becoming an active threat to the peace and security of the Continent.

Following this, also on October 23, the United States President issued a Proclamation[6] which in part gave the following authorisation:

> Any vessel or craft which may be proceeding toward Cuba may be intercepted and may be directed to identify itself, its cargo, equipment and stores and its ports of call, to stop, to lie to, to submit to visit and search, or to proceed as directed. Any vessel which fails or refuses to respond to or to comply with directions shall be subject to being taken into custody.

It was intended that these powers would be exercised "within a reasonable distance of Cuba."[6] During the course of the "quarantine," a Lebanese ship under charter to the U.S.S.R. was boarded but allowed to proceed and a Soviet tanker was cleared after visual checking from alongside. Both incidents occurred on the high seas. Other ships heading for Cuba changed course of their own accord.[7] The operation was ended on November 21, 1962. Meeker (United States Deputy Legal Adviser) justified the United States action as follows:

> The quarantine was based on a collective judgment and recommendation of the American Republics made under the Rio Treaty. It was considered not to contravene Article 2, paragraph 4, because it was a measure adopted by a regional organisation in conformity with the provisions of Chapter VIII of the Charter.[8] The purposes of the Organisation and its activities were considered to be consistent with the purposes and principles of the United Nations as provided in Article 52. This being the case, the quarantine would no more violate Article 2, paragraph 4, than measures voted for by the Council under Chapter VII, by the General Assembly under Articles 10 and 11, or taken by United Nations members in conformity with Article 51.[9]

Did the United States have a good case on this ground?[10] Note that Meeker does not justify the quarantine on the basis of "self-defence."[11] Could he have done so? Note also the following comment by Dean Acheson, a former United States Secretary of State for Foreign Affairs:

> I must conclude that the propriety of the Cuban quarantine is not a legal issue. The power, position and prestige of the United States has been challenged by another state; and law simply does not deal with such questions of ultimate power—power that comes close to the source of sovereignty. I cannot believe that there are

---

[5] *Ed.* The "Rio Treaty," signed at Rio de Janeiro on September 2, 1947: 21 U.N.T.S. 77.

[6] Proclamation 3504, 57 A.J.I.L. 512 (1963).

[7] See Christol & Davis, 57 A.J.I.L. 525, at p. 530 (1963).

[8] *Ed.* Appendix I, below.

[9] 57 A.J.I.L. 515 (1963).

[10] See article cited in note 7 above and Wright, 57 A.J.I.L. 546 (1963).

[11] Note, however, the following passage in the President's broadcast on October 22: "We no longer live in a world where only the actual firing of weapons represents a sufficient challenge to a nation's security to constitute a maximum peril. Nuclear weapons are so destructive, and ballistic missiles so swift, that any substantially increased possibility of their use or any sudden change in their deployment may well be regarded as a threat to the peace." *Keesings Archives*, p. 19060.

principles of law that say we must accept destruction of our way of life. . . . The survival of states is not a matter of law.[12]

6. On August 2 and 4, 1964, North Vietnamese torpedo-boats attacked United States warships in the Gulf of Tonkin, but were beaten off. The attacks occurred on the high seas. In retaliation, on August 5, the United States bombed the base from which the torpedo-boats operated and an oil storage depot to great effect. The retaliatory measures were justified by the United States in terms of freedom of the high seas and the right of self-defence. The British representative to the Security Council supported this view:

> The latest attacks on the United States ships took place, according to the information we have been given, some sixty-five miles from land. It seems to my delegation in these circumstances that, having regard to the repeated nature of these attacks and their mounting scale, the United States Government has a right in accordance with international law, to take action directed to prevent the recurrence of such attacks on its ships. Preventive action in accordance with that aim is an essential right which is embraced by any definition of that principle of self-defence. It therefore seems to my delegation that the action taken by the United States Government is fully consistent with Article 51 of the Charter.[13]

The U.S.S.R. representative characterised the measures as an "act of aggression." No resolution was voted upon or adopted. Is the case any different from the *Harib Fort Case*, above, p. 646.

THE FALKLAND ISLANDS WAR[13a]

U.N. Doc. S/PV. 2346, p. 7; S/PV. 2360, pp. 21–22, 37–38; S/PV. 1362, pp. 103–107

On April 2, 1982, Argentine forces invaded the Falkland Islands. On the following day Argentina took possession by force of the island of South Georgia, some 800 miles to the east of the Falklands. The small British military garrison on the Falklands and the few troops sent to South Georgia surrendered on April 2nd and 3rd respectively after some fighting. Both Argentine actions were taken in pursuit of claims of sovereignty over these islands, as to which see above, p. 171. On April 1, the President of the Security Council, acting for the Council, had called upon Argentina and the United Kingdom "to refrain from the use or threat of force in the region."[14] On April 3, following the Argentine action the Security Council adopted Resolution 502,[15] which reads:

> The Security Council,
> Recalling the statement made by the President of the Security Council at the 2345th meeting of the Security Council on 1 April 1982 calling on the Governments of

---

[12] 57 *Proceedings of the A.S.I.L.* 14 (1963).

[13] 1964 B.P.I.L., p. 268.

[13a] See Fawcett, in Pearce, ed., *The Falkland Islands Dispute: International Dimensions* (1982), p. 5; *ibid.* 38 *The World Today* 203 (1982); Franck, 77 A.J.I.L. 109 (1983); Murphy, *op. cit.* at p. 638, n. 1, above, pp. 67–71. See also Calvert, *The Falkland Islands Crisis: the Rights and Wrongs* (1982); Honeywell and Pearce, *Falkland Islands/Malvinas: Whose Crisis?* (1982); Sunday Times Insight Team, *The Falklands War* (1982); *The Falklands Campaign—Digest of the Debates and Statements and Statements in the House of Commons*, H.M.S.O. (1982). And see the references at p. 171, n. 43, above.

[14] U.N. Doc. S/PV. 2345, p. 33.

[15] U.N. Doc. S/PV. 2346, p. 6 (text). The resolution was adopted by 10 votes (France, Guyana, Ireland, Japan, Jordan, Togo, Uganda, U.K., U.S.A., Zaire) to 1 (Panama), with 4 abstentions (China, Poland, Spain, U.S.S.R.).

Argentina and the United Kingdom of Great Britain and Northern Ireland to refrain from the use or threat of force in the region of the Falkland Islands,

Deeply disturbed at reports of an invasion on 2 April 1982 by armed forces of Argentina,

Determining that there exists a breach of the peace in the region of the Falkland Islands (Islas Malvinas),

1. Demands an immediate cessation of hostilities;

2. Demands an immediate withdrawal of all Argentine forces from the Falkland Islands (Islas Malvinas);

3. Calls on the Governments of Argentina and the United Kingdom to seek a diplomatic solution to their differences and to respect fully the purposes and principles of the Charter of the United Nations.

On April 5, a British military expedition (the Task Force) sailed for the South Atlantic. Economic sanctions were imposed against Argentina by the United Kingdom and the European Communities. The United States gave the United Kingdom logistical assistance. The Organisation of American States resolved that its members should support Argentina. On April 25, British troops recovered South Georgia by force. After diplomatic efforts to achieve a peaceful solution had failed, the Task Force landed on the Falklands on May 21. The Argentine garrison surrendered on June 14, 1982. The following extracts are from the debates in the Security Council in which arguments on the legality of the Argentinian action and the British response were put.

2346th Meeting on April 2

MR. ROCA (ARGENTINA). I wish to inform the Council that today the Government of Argentina has proclaimed the recovery of its national sovereignty over the territories of the Malvinas Islands, South Georgia Islands and South Sandwich Islands, in an act which responds to a just Argentine claim, an act of self-defence in response to the acts of aggression by the United Kingdom.[16]

2350th Meeting on April 3

MR. COSTA MENDEZ (ARGENTINA). Some delegations here have stated that my Government acted hastily. . . . [i]t seems difficult to describe my country as acting hastily when, with the greatest respect for peaceful solutions, it has borne with a situation of continued usurpation of its territory by a colonial Power for 150 years. Argentina has wisely, patiently and imaginatively negotiated on its long-standing claim but the United Kingdom has not given the slightest indication of being flexible nor made a single just proposal. Furthermore, we have been accused in this chamber of violating Article 2(3) and (4) of the United Nations Charter. No provision of the Charter can be taken to mean the legitimization of situations which have their origin in wrongful acts, in acts

---

[16] Ed. By "acts of aggression," Mr. Roca may have been referring to the events of 1833 or to an incident on South Georgia in which, in March 1982, employees of an Argentine company landed on the island to recover scrap metal under a commercial contract. The Commander of the British Antarctic Survey base at Grytviken lowered an Argentine flag which the men had raised and insisted that they obtain official landing permission. *H.M.S. Endurance*, a lightly armed ice-patrol vessel, was dispatched to the area. The Argentine Government denied the need for permission to land on Argentine territory, whereupon the British Government indicated that the men would be removed, by force if necessary, if such permission were not obtained. The matter was unresolved on April 2.

carried out before the Charter was adopted and which subsisted during its prevailing force. Today, in 1982, the purposes of the Organization cannot be invoked to justify acts carried out in the last century in flagrant violation of principles that are today embodied in international law.

... It speaks volumes that the terms [of the U.K. draft resolution] are absolutely identical to those put forward more than 22 years ago in this same chamber in the case of Goa, when Portugal was hanging on to its colonial power, which consumed it and gave rise to a new Portugal. That resolution sought to deny India its territorial rights, just as an attempt is being made here to deny my country its proper rights. That draft resolution was thrown out by the Council because it was merely a defence, an expression of continuing colonialism.

SIR ANTHONY PARSONS (U.K.) The Foreign Minister of Argentina ... referred to our manoeuvres, our evasive tactics, our procrastinations [in negotiations] over the years. Of course, I cannot accept these charges.

... I [also] understood him to say that ... Article 2, paragraphs 3 and 4 ... were not necessarily applicable to situations which arose before the Charter was adopted.

... this is an extremely dangerous doctrine. The world is distressingly full of crisis situations, which have from time to time exploded into hostility in every continent on the globe. A large number of those situations have their origins years, decades, centuries before the United Nations Charter was adopted in 1945. If the proposition were to be accepted that the use of force was valid for situations which originated before the Charter was adopted, by heaven I believe the world would be an infinitely more dangerous and flammable place than it already is....

The Foreign Minister of Argentina argued that the people of the Falkland Islands are not a population in international law. Those 1,800 or 1,900 people are not recent arrivals in the Islands. The vast majority of them were born there to families which had been settled there for four, five, six generations since the first half of the nineteenth century. In the judgment of my Government, whether they are 1,800 or 18,000 or 18 million, they are still entitled to the protection of international law and they are entitled to have their freely expressed wishes respected.

These have been the only objectives of my Government in that area for a very long time. I cannot believe that the international community takes the view that Britain in the 1980s has a "colonialist" or "imperialist" ambition in the South Atlantic.

Finally, it has also been argued that this was not an invasion because the Islands belong to Argentina, a proposition which of course my Government contests. But the fact is that the United Kingdom has been accepted by the United Nations—by the General Assembly, by the Committee of 24—as the Administering Authority. It therefore flies in the face of the facts and in the face of reason to suggest that this was not an armed invasion.

2360th Meeting on May 21

MR. ROS (ARGENTINA). It is known that under Article 51 of the Charter ... [t]here is a legal obligation to suspend self-defence once the Security Council "has taken measures necessary to maintain international peace and security." The determination of whether such measures have been effective must be reached objectively and cannot be left to the arbitrary judgment of the Government of the United Kingdom itself . . .

The exercise of self-defence which the United Kingdom is alleging could only have taken place in the absence of a resolution by the Security Council. But now the resolution has been adopted, and the response of the United Kingdom to the Council has been the reiterated violation of that resolution, which demands the cessation of hostilities. . . .

Self-defence can be used only to repel imminent and grave danger. In the existing circumstances, the United Kingdom could not allege any imminent and grave danger. Argentina had complied in regard to the cessation of hostilities and had not threatened the United Kingdom. . . .

The United Kingdom cannot claim self-defence of territorial integrity to justify its acts of aggression. It is Argentine territorial integrity which has been violated. . . .

SIR ANTHONY PARSONS (U.K.) The Argentine invasion was carried out by the use of force against the entirely peaceful population of the Falkland Islands, people who had threatened no one at any time. There was no question of self-defence by Argentina. It is clear, therefore, that the Argentine action was also contrary to the fourth paragraph of Article 2 of the Charter [as well as Article 2(3)]. This is the obligation to:

"refrain . . . from the . . . use of force . . . in any . . . manner inconsistent with the Purposes of the United Nations."

I need hardly remind this Council that the very first purpose of the United Nations is:

". . . to bring about by peaceful means . . . settlement of international disputes . . . "(Art. 1(1)). . . .

Indeed, by its first use of armed force, Argentina committed an act of aggression within the meaning of the definition suggested by the General Assembly in resolution 3314 (XXIX).[17] . . .

Having established that the Argentine use of force was illegal, it follows that the military occupation of the Falkland Islands was and is also illegal. This was made clear by the Declaration on Friendly Relations,[18] which was adopted by way of consensus in 1970 and which includes the following proposition:

"The territory of a State shall not be the object of military occupation resulting from the use of force in contravention of the provisions of the Charter."

As if that were not enough, the continued Argentine occupation is also clearly contrary to operative paragraph 2 of Security Council resolution 502 (1982).

A word on self-defence. . . . British territory has been invaded by Argentine armed forces. British nationals are being subjected to both military occupation and military government against their freely expressed wishes. Argentina is using force day by day to occupy British territory and to subjugate the Falkland Islanders. Resolution 502 (1982) has proved insufficient to bring about

---

[17] *Ed.* Below, p. 677.
[18] *Ed.* Appendix II, below.

withdrawal. Nothing could be clearer against that background than that the United Kingdom is fully entitled to take measures in exercise of its inherent right of self-defence, recognized by Article 51 of the Charter. If the Charter were otherwise, it would be a licence for the aggressor and a trap for the victim of aggression. The first use of force to settle disputes, to seize territory and to subjugate peoples is something which the Charter was intended to prevent.

2362nd Meeting on May 22

SIR ANTHONY PARSONS (U.K.) Under-Secretary Ros also argued that there is an obligation to suspend self-defence once the Security Council "has taken measures necessary to maintain international peace and security." . . .

The United Kingdom accepts that the determination, [whether such measures have been taken] must be an objective one. It must be reached in the light of all the relevant circumstances. . . .

By resolution 502 (1982) the Security Council demanded the immediate withdrawal of all Argentine forces from the Falkland Islands. Argentina did not withdraw any of its forces: it did quite the opposite . . . The resolution determined that there was a breach of the peace as a result of the Argentine invasion . . . The results of that invasion were Argentine occupation. Accordingly, the breach of the peace still subsisted despite the adoption of the resolution. How, then, can it seriously be maintained that resolution 502 (1982) amounted to a measure "necessary to maintain international peace and security"?

In my letter to the President of the Security Council dated 30 April I pointed out that the reference in Article 51 to measures necessary to maintain international peace could

". . . only be taken to refer to measures which are actually effective to bring about the stated objective. Clearly, the Security Council's decision in its resolution 502 (1982) has not proved effective. The United Kingdom's inherent right of self-defence is thus unimpaired."[19]

The argument of Under-Secretary Ros that the exercise of self-defence is not available because the Security Council adopted resolution 502 (1982) would lead to absurd results. A State which has committed an act of aggression is told to stop its aggression and to withdraw by the Security Council. That State does not heed the demand. The victim, according to Mr. Ros, would then be obliged to fold his arms and allow the aggressor to continue his aggression and to digest its fruits.

A further argument of the Under-Secretary was that "the United Kingdom could not allege any imminent and grave danger." The Argentine invasion of 2 April not only posed an imminent and grave danger but it was determined by the Security Council to have caused an actual breach of the peace. It flies in the face of reason that there was no imminent and grave danger. There was an actual and grave danger to the people of the Falkland Islands: that they would continue for ever to be governed by an alien régime which they most decidedly and unanimously did not want. . . .

[19] The U.K. representative had earlier stated that, in compliance with Art. 51, the U.K. "have meticulously informed the President of the Council of every step we are taking in this regard:" UN Doc. S/PV. 2360, p. 36.

Finally, the Under-Secretary argued that the United Kingdom had violated resolution 502 (1982) by dispatching the Royal Navy. He argued that this was contrary to operative paragraph 1 of the resolution 502 (1982) which demanded a cessation of hostilities. The resolution has to be read as a whole. The preamble makes clear that there had been an invasion of the Falklands on 2 April by armed forces of Argentina which had caused a breach of peace. It was to these hostilities by Argentina that operative paragraph 1 was directed. The Falkland Islands had been at peace before 2 April and had never threatened Argentina. We maintained only the smallest of garrisons there. Had Argentina complied with operative paragraph 1 by ceasing its hostilities against the people of the Falkland Islands on 3 April and had Argentina complied with the demand for the immediate withdrawal of all Argentine forces there would have been no need for the Royal Navy to exercise the United Kingdom's right of self-defence when it arrived off the Falkland Islands.

Notes

1. Resolution 502, which was drafted by the United Kingdom representative on the Council, was adopted under Article 40. This point was agreed when the question was raised whether the United Kingdom was eligible to vote upon it.[20] It would not have been eligible to do so if the resolution had been adopted under Chapter VI or Article 52(3) of the Charter instead of Chapter VII; see Article 27(3), Charter. Argentina, which happened not to be a member of the Security Council at the time, was allowed, in accordance with normal practice, to participate in the debate, but it had no vote. As a permanent member, the United Kingdom had not only the right to vote, but also had the advantage of the power of veto, which it exercised on June 4 to veto a draft resolution calling for a cease-fire in the fighting then occurring in the Falklands.[21]

2. The Argentine argument justifying the invasion despite Article 2(3) (4), is not convincing. The whole object of the Charter regime is to prohibit the unilateral use of armed force in the resolution of international disputes, not to approve it. *cf.* the reasoning in the *Corfu Channel Case*, above, p. 301, in favour of the Albanian counter-claim. In the context of territorial disputes, a state must use peaceful means to achieve possession, however good its claim to title. The one exception is the right of self-defence. It is interesting that the British response would have been too late to have been regarded as self-defence in United Kingdom criminal law. If, for example, D were to learn that squatters had broken into and were occupying his country cottage, and he were to go and eject them the next day (*i.e.* as soon as he could), this would not be an act of self-defence. Were the objections by Argentina in the Security Council to the British use of force couched in these terms? Or was the argument instead largely that the right to self-defence terminated once resolution 502 had been adopted and, therefore, the Security Council had taken the necessary "measures?" The Council debates support the view that there is a customary right of self-defence even though an attack is complete (in this case the garrison had surrendered) provided that the response is immediate and continuous. There is therefore no need to resort to general principles of law. Why did the United Kingdom emphasise the "purposes of the United Nations" rather than the "territorial integrity" part of Article 2(4) when condemning Argentina's action? How does the Falkland Islands situation differ from that of Goa, as to which, see above, p. 172?

---

[20] U.N. Doc. S/PV. 2350, pp. 81–85. The U.K. representative later referred to it as "a mandatory resolution under Article 40" which "it was not open to Argentina to purport to reject:" U.N.Doc. S/PV. 2360, p. 36.

[21] U.N. Doc. S/PV. 2373, p. 16. The vote was 9 to 2 (U.K. and U.S.A.), with 4 abstentions (France, Guyana, Jordan, Togo).

4. On May 2, 1982, a British submarine sank an Argentine Cruiser, the *General Belgrano*, with much loss of life, when it was just outside the 200 miles exclusion zone which the United Kingdom had declared around the Falkland Islands. The Ministry of Defence statement proclaiming the zone indicated that "these measures are without prejudice to the right of the United Kingdom to take additional measures which may be needed in the exercise of its right of self-defence under Article 51 of the UN Charter."[22] The cruiser was judged to be posing a threat to British warships in the area.

THE ANGLO-FRENCH INVASION OF SUEZ 1956[23]

Hansard, H.L., Vol. 199, cols. 1348–1359. November 1, 1956

In July 1956, Egypt nationalised the Suez Canal Company, a company in which there were considerable British and French interests, and took over the running of the Suez Canal. On October 29, 1956, Israel invaded Egyptian territory in the area of the Suez Canal Zone. On October 30, the United States placed before the Security Council a draft resolution calling for a cease-fire and calling upon member states not to assist Israel. The draft resolution was vetoed by France and the United Kingdom. The United Kingdom representative voted against the draft resolution on the ground that "for the moment there is no action that the Security Council can constructively take which would contribute to the twin objectives of stopping the fighting and safeguarding free passage through the Suez Canal.[24] During the debate, France and the United Kingdom issued a twelve-hour joint ultimatum to Egypt and Israel demanding that they call a cease-fire, withdraw their forces from the Suez Canal area and allow British and French troops to be stationed along the Canal. The ultimatum was not complied with and on October 31 British and French troops invaded the Suez Canal area. The following day, the British action was justified in the House of Lords.

THE LORD CHANCELLOR (VISCOUNT KILMUIR). The position is that the combined effect of the Pact of Paris, the Charter of the United Nations and the General Assembly's "Uniting for Peace" resolution of 1951[25] is that force may lawfully be used or threatened only, first, with the express authority of the United Nations (that is, of the Security Council), and, secondly, in self-defence. But self-defence undoubtedly includes a situation in which the lives of a State's nationals abroad are threatened and it is necessary to intervene on that territory for their protection. . . .

Now the tests of whether such intervention is necessary under customary international law are, first, whether there is an imminent danger of injury to nationals; secondly, whether there is a failure or inability on the part of the territorial sovereign to protect the nationals in question, and, thirdly, whether the measures of protection of the intervener are strictly confined to the object of protecting those nationals against injury. It has been argued that there is a great distinction between the protection of human lives and the protection of property. That is not a proposition to which I would give absolute concurrence. I take the view that if really valuable and internationally important foreign property is in danger of irreparable injury, through the breakdown of order, entry by a foreign State for the sole purpose of securing the safety of that

[22] *Keesings Archives*, p. 31709.
[23] See Wright, 51 A.J.I.L. 257 (1957).
[24] S.C.O.R., 11th Year, 749th Meeting, para. 11.
[25] *Ed*. See below, p. 691.

property is excusable. I take the view that, since we can show that the blocking of or interference with the Canal for a considerable period would cause—and here I disagree with one or two of your Lordships—irreparable damage and suffering to a number of nations, for which it would be difficult to see adequate compensation being afforded, our intervention is also justified by the danger to the Canal.

We have therefore three good grounds of intervention: the danger to our nationals (for example, to those at Ismailia); the danger to shipping in the Canal, which shipping carries many hundreds, at least, if not thousands, of people in their crews; and the danger to the enormously valuable installations of the Canal itself and the incalculable consequential effect on many nations if the Canal were blocked. . . . As a Government, we requested that the threat of these dangers should cease. Our request was refused, with the clear indication from Egypt that they would resist any British or French measures. Although the measures of protection which we are entitled to use are limited to what is necessary for their purpose—namely, the protection of our nationals, shipping and the Canal installations—they must clearly also be proportionate to the resistance offered to them. If the Egyptians say that they will resist with all their land, sea and air forces any attempt at intervention, then we are entitled to use such forces as will defeat that force which the Egyptians threaten to deploy. . . .

The next point, which was argued before your Lordships on the last occasion, is that if Article 51 of the Charter makes provision for self-defence in special circumstances, that was the only applicable rule. Again it is essential to remember that the right of individual self-defence was regarded as automatically excepted from both the Covenant of the League of Nations and the Pact of Paris without any mention of it, and clearly the same would have been true of the Charter of the United Nations had there been no Article 51. As your Lordships well know, Article 51 was not inserted in the Charter for the purpose of destroying the individual right of self-defence, but for the purpose of clarifying the position in regard to collective understandings for mutual self-defence, particularly the Pan-American Treaty, known as the Act of Chapultepec. These understandings were concerned with defence against external aggression and it was natural for Article 51 to be related to defence against attack.

. . . Article 51 must be read in the light that it is part of Chapter VII of the Charter and concerned with defence against grave breaches of the peace. It would be an entire misreading of the whole intention of Article 51 to interpret it as forbidding forcible self-defence in resistance to an illegal use of force not constituting an armed attack. In my view, it is equally clear that Article 51 does not cut down the customary right by restricting forcible self-defence in cases where the attack provoking it has actually been launched. I think that every one of your Lordships will appreciate that if that were done it would be a travesty of the purpose of the Charter, to compel a defending State to allow its opponent to deliver the first fatal blow. The same applies to the form of self-defence with which I am dealing today. . . .

Note

Following the deadlock in the Security Council, an Emergency Session of the General Assembly was convened under the "Uniting for Peace" Resolution[26] which

[26] See below, p. 691.

adopted a Resolution on November 2, 1956, in which the General Assembly called for a cease-fire.[27]

France and the United Kingdom accepted the cease-fire within a few days and fighting stopped for the most part on November 7. On the United Nations Emergency Force (UNEF) that was then established, see below p. 697.

THE ENTEBBE INCIDENT[28]

U.N.Doc. S/PV. 1939, pp. 27, 51–59, 92 and U.N.Doc. S/PV. 1941, pp. 31–32. Reprinted in 15 I.L.M. 1224 (1976)

On June 27, 1976, an Air France airliner bound for Paris from Tel Aviv was hijacked over Greece after leaving Athens airport. Two of the hijackers appear to have been West German nationals; the other two held Arab passports. The airliner was diverted to Entebbe airport in Uganda where the Jewish passengers (about 100) were separated from the others and the latter released. The hijackers demanded the release of about 50 Palestinian terrorists imprisoned in various countries. The evidence seems to suggest that Uganda did not take such steps as it might have done against the hijackers and, indeed, helped them, although Uganda denied this. On July 3, 1976, Israel flew transport aircraft and soldiers to Entebbe and rescued the hostages by force. The hijackers were killed during the operation, as were some Ugandan and Israeli soldiers. There was also extensive damage to Ugandan aircraft and the airport. The following is an extract from the Security Council debate on the matter in July 1976.

LT. COL. JUMA ORIS ABDULLAH (UGANDA). Uganda gave all the help and hospitality it was capable of giving to all the hostages. The response to this humanitarian gesture by Zionist Israel—the vehicle of imperialism—was to invade Uganda, once again living up to its record of barbarism and banditry. . . .

We call upon this Council unreservedly to condemn in the strongest possible terms Israel's barbaric, unprovoked and unwarranted aggression against the sovereign Republic of Uganda. Uganda demands full compensation from Israel for the damage to life and property caused during its invasion. . . .

MR. HERZOG (ISRAEL). Uganda violated a basic tenet of international law in failing to protect foreign nationals on its territory. Furthermore, it behaved in a manner which constituted a gross violation of the 1970 Hague Convention on the Suppression or Unlawful Seizure of Aircraft.[29] This Convention had been ratified by both Israel and Uganda. . . .

The right of a State to take military action to protect its nationals in mortal danger is recognized by all legal authorities in international law. In *Self Defence in International Law*, Professor Bowett states, on page 87, that the right of the State to intervene by the use or threat of force for the protection of its nationals suffering injuries within the territory of another State is generally admitted, both in the writings of jurists and in the practice of States. In the arbitration

---

[27] G.A. Resn. 997 (ES-1). The resolution was adopted by 64 votes to 5 (Australia, France, Israel, New Zealand and the U.K.) with 6 abstentions.

[28] See Akehurst, 5 Int. Rel. 3 (1977); Boyle, 29 Neth. I.L.R. 32 (1982); Krift, 4 Brooklyn J.I.L. 43 (1977); and Margo, 94 S.A.L.J. 306 (1977). For a full account of the incident, see Stevenson, 90 *Minutes at Entebbe*, 1976.

[29] *Ed.* See Article 6, above, p. 237.

between Great Britain and Spain in 1925, one of the series known as the Spanish Moroccan claims[30] Judge Huber, as Rapporteur of the Commission, stated:

> However, it cannot be denied that at a certain point the interest of a State in exercising protection over its nationals and their property can take precedence over territorial sovereignty, despite the absence of any conventional provisions. . . . It presupposes the inadequacy of any other means of protection against some injury, actual or imminent, to the persons or property of nationals and, moreover, an injury which results either from the acts of the territorial State and its authorities or from the acts of individuals or groups of individuals which the territorial State is unable, or unwilling, to prevent.

In the *Law of Nations*, 6th edition, p. 427, Brierly states as follows:

> Every effort must be made to get the United Nations to act. But, if the United Nations is not in a position to move in time and the need for instant action is manifest, it would be difficult to deny the legitimacy of action in defence of nationals which every responsible Government would feel bound to take if it had the means to do so; this is, of course, on the basis that the action was strictly limited to securing the safe removal of the threatened nationals.[31] . . .

The right of self-defence is enshrined in international law and in the Charter of the United Nations and can be applied on the basis of the classic formulation, as was done in the well-known Caroline Case, permitting such action where there is a

> necessity of self-defence, instant, overwhelming, leaving no choice of means and no moment for deliberation.

That was exactly the situation which faced the Government of Israel.

MR. OYONO (CAMEROON). The Security Council, which is responsible for international peace and security, must vigorously condemn this barbaric act which constitutes a flagrant violation of the norms of international law and flouts the spirit and letter of the United Nations Charter, Article 2, paragraph 4. . . .

In the spirit of the Charter, that prohibition means that Member States have an obligation to settle their international disputes by peaceful means in order to maintain international peace and security. I need hardly remind you that our Organization is not dedicated to anarchy or to the notion that might makes right, but is an organized community whose mutually accepted principles and rules must be scrupulously respected, and their violation adequately punished.

It is the corner-stone of our Organization that there can be no justification for the use of force against the sovereignty, independence or territorial integrity of a State, unless we wish to imperil international co-operation in its present form and indeed the very existence of States that do not yet possess modern, sophisticated systems of detection and deterrence.

MR. SCRANTON (UNITED STATES). Israel's action in rescuing the hostages necessarily involved a temporary breach of the territorial integrity of Uganda.

---

[30] *Ed. Loc. cit.* at p. 50, n. 22, above.
[31] *Ed.* O'Connell, *International Law*, Vol. I, (2nd ed). p. 303 is quoted to the same effect.

Normally, such a breach would be impermissible under the Charter of the United Nations. However, there is a well established right to use limited force for the protection of one's own nationals from an imminent threat of injury or death in a situation where the State in whose territory they are located is either unwilling or unable to protect them. The right, flowing from the right of self-defence, is limited to such use of force as is necessary and appropriate to protect threatened nationals from injury.

The requirements of this right to protect nationals were clearly met in the Entebbe case. Israel had good reason to believe that at the time it acted Israeli nationals were in imminent danger of execution by the hijackers. Moreover, the actions necessary to release the Israeli nationals or to prevent substantial loss of Israeli lives had not been taken by the Government of Uganda, nor was there a reasonable expectation such actions would be taken. In fact, there is substantial evidence that the Government of Uganda co-operated with and aided the hijackers. A number of the released hostages have publicly related how the Ugandan authorities allowed several additional terrorists to reinforce the original group after the plane landed, permitted them to receive additional arms and additional explosives, participated in guarding the hostages and according to some accounts, even took over sole custody of some or all of the passengers to allow the hijackers to rest. The ease and success of the Israeli effort to free the hostages further suggests that the Ugandan authorities could have overpowered the hijackers and released the hostages if they had really had the desire to do so. . . .

That Israel might have secured the release of its nationals by complying with the terrorists' demands does not alter these conclusions. No State is required to yield control over persons in lawful custody in its territory under criminal charges. Moreover, it would be a self-defeating and dangerous policy to release prisoners, convicted in some cases of earlier acts of terrorism, in order to accede to the demands of terrorists.

It should be emphasized that this assessment of the legality of Israeli actions depends heavily on the unusual circumstances of this specific case. In particular, the evidence is strong that, given the attitude of the Ugandan authorities, co-operation with or reliance on them in rescuing the passengers and crew was impracticable.

Notes

1. No resolution was adopted at the end of the debate. A United Kingdom/United States draft resolution[32] which limited itself to condemning hijacking and did not comment on the conduct of the parties did not receive the necessary votes for adoption and a draft resolution[33] proposed by Benin/Libya/Tanzania condemning Israel was not put to the vote.

2. By no means all writers agree with those quoted by the Israeli representative in the debate on the right to defend nationals abroad. Brownlie, for example, states:

" . . . it is very doubtful if the present form of intervention has any basis in the modern law. The instances in which states have purported to exercise it, and the terms in which it is delimited, show that it provides infinite opportunities for abuse. Forcible intervention is now unlawful. It is true that the protection of nationals presents particular difficulties and that a government faced with a deliberate

---

[32] U.N.Doc. S/12138; 15 I.L.M. 1226 (1976).
[33] U.N.Doc. S/12139; 15 I.L.M. 1227 (1976).

massacre of a considerable number of nationals in a foreign state would have cogent reasons of humanity for acting, and would also be under very great political pressure. The possible risks of denying the legality of action in a case of such urgency, an exceptional circumstance, must be weighed against the more calculable dangers of providing legal pretexts for the commission of breaches of the peace in the pursuit of national rather than humanitarian interests."[34]

3. Does the part of the Court's judgment in the *Corfu Channel Case* on intervention (above p. 304), support Brownlie? If there is a right to protect nationals abroad, how serious does the threat to their person have to be for it to arise? Is there any support for a right to intervene to protect the property of nationals abroad? On humanitarian intervention, see above, p. 470, n. 3.

4. On the United States attempt to rescue the hostages in Iran, see the *U.S. Diplomatic and Consular Staff case*, above, p. 276. The United States justified its action, in a report to the Security Council pursuant to Article 51, Charter, as being "in exercise of its inherent right of self-defence with the aim of extricating American nationals who are and remain the victims of the Iranian armed attack on our Embassy."[35] The Court did not rule upon legality of the rescue attempt.

NORTH ATLANTIC TREATY 1949[36]

U.K.T.S. 56 (1949), Cmd. 7789; 34 U.N.T.S. 243; 43 A.J.I.L., Supp. 159 (1949)

Article 1

The Parties undertake, as set forth in the Charter of the United Nations, to settle any international disputes in which they may be involved by peaceful means in such a manner that international peace and security, and justice, are not endangered, and to refrain in their international relations from the threat or use of force in any manner inconsistent with the purposes of the United Nations.

Article 2

The Parties will contribute toward the further development of peaceful and friendly international relations by strengthening their free institutions, by bringing a better understanding of the principles upon which these institutions are founded, and by promoting conditions of stability and well-being. They will seek to eliminate conflict in their international economic policies and will encourage economic collaboration between any or all of them.

Article 3

In order more effectively to achieve the objectives of this treaty, the Parties, separately and jointly, by means of continuous and effective self-help and mutual aid, will maintain and develop their individual and collective capacity to resist armed attack.

[34] *Op. cit.* at p. 638, n. 1 above p. 301.
[35] I.C.J. Reports 1979, at p. 18. See D'Angelo, 21 Virg. Jo.I.L. 21 (1982). *cf.* the *Mayaguez case* (rescue by U.S. troops by force of a U.S. merchant ship and its crew captured by Cambodia; justified as self-defence of nationals), [1975] U.S.D.I.L. 776. See Paust, 85 Yale L.J. 774 (1975–76).
[36] The treaty entered into force on August 24, 1949. On April 30, 1982, there were 16 contracting parties: Belgium, Canada, Denmark, F.R.G., France, Greece, Iceland, Italy, Luxembourg, the Netherlands, Norway, Portugal, Spain, Turkey, U.K. and U.S.

Article 4

The Parties will consult together whenever, in the opinion of any of them, the territorial integrity, political independence or security of any of the Parties is threatened.

Article 5

The Parties agree that an armed attack against one or more of them in Europe or North America shall be considered an attack against them all; and consequently they agree that, if such an armed attack occurs, each of them, in exercise of the right of individual or collective self-defence recognized by Article 51 of the Charter of the United Nations, will assist the Party or Parties so attacked by taking forthwith, individually, and in concert with the other Parties, such action as it deems necessary, including the use of armed force, to restore and maintain the security of the North Atlantic area.

Any such armed attack and all measures taken as a result thereof shall immediately be reported to the Security Council. Such measures shall be terminated when the Security Council has taken the measures necessary to restore and maintain international peace and security.

Article 6

For the purpose of Article 5 an armed attack on one or more of the Parties is deemed to include an armed attack on the territory of any of the Parties in Europe or North America, on the Algerian Departments of France, on the occupation force of any Party in Europe, on the islands under the jurisdiction of any Party in the North Atlantic area north of the Tropic of Cancer or on the vessels or aircraft in this area of any of the Parties.

Article 7

This treaty does not affect, and shall not be interpreted as affecting, in any way the rights and obligations under the Charter of the Parties which are members of the United Nations, or the primary responsibility of the Security Council for the maintenance of international peace and security.

Article 9

The Parties hereby establish a council on which each of them shall be represented, to consider matters concerning the implementation of this Treaty. . . .

Article 13

After the Treaty has been in force for twenty years, any Party may cease to be a Party one year after its notice of denunciation has been given. . . .

Notes

1. Should the North Atlantic Treaty Organisation (NATO) established by this treaty be regarded as a "regional arrangement" in the sense of Chapter VIII of the Charter or an exercise of the right of collective self-defence?[37]

[37] See Beckett, *The North Atlantic Treaty, The Brussels Treaty, and the Charter of the United Nations* (1950), and Goodhart, 79 *Hague Recueil* 183 (1951–II).

2. Extensive defence arrangements have been agreed upon by the members of NATO since 1949. In 1966, France withdrew from its commitments under these arrangements without seeking to denounce the North Atlantic Treaty itself.

3. Article 5 of the North Atlantic Treaty is paralleled in the East European counterpart to the Treaty—the Warsaw Pact 1955.[38] Article 4 of the Pact reads:

> In the event of armed attack in Europe on one or more of the Parties to the Treaty by any state or group of states, each of the Parties to the Treaty, in the exercise of its right to individual or collective self-defence in accordance with Article 51 of the Charter of the United Nations Organisation, shall immediately, either individually or in agreement with other Parties to the Treaty, come to the assistance of the state or states attacked with all such means as it deems necessary, including armed force. The Parties to the Treaty shall immediately consult concerning the necessary measures to be taken by them jointly in order to restore and maintain international peace and security.
>
> Measures taken on the basis of this Article shall be reported to the Security Council in conformity with the provisions of the Charter of the United Nations Organisation. These measures shall be discontinued immediately the Security Council adopts the necessary measures to restore and maintain international peace and security.

3. COLLECTIVE MEASURES THROUGH THE UNITED NATIONS

(i) ACTION UNDER CHAPTER VI

See Chapter VI, United Nations Charter, Appendix I below.

Note
Who can seise the Security Council of a situation or dispute under Chapter VI? What powers of action has the Security Council under Chapter VI?[39] Can it take decisions binding upon member states?

(ii) SECURITY COUNCIL ACTION UNDER CHAPTER VII: JURISDICTION

See Article 39, United Nations Charter, Appendix I, below.

THE SPANISH QUESTION

S.C.O.R., 1st Year, 1st Series, 47th Meeting, pp. 370–376, June 18, 1946

In April 1946, the representative of Poland in the Security Council, invoking Article 2(6), 34 and 35 of the Charter, raised before the Council the situation in Spain and submitted a draft resolution asking the Council to declare "that the existence and activities of the Franco regime in Spain have led to international friction and endangered international peace and security" and asking it to call upon, "in accordance with Articles 39 and 41 of the Charter, all Members of the United Nations who maintain diplomatic relations with the Franco Government to sever such relations immediately."

---

[38] 49 A.J.I.L., Supp. 194 (1955). The treaty entered into force on June 5, 1955. There are eight contracting parties: Albania, Bulgaria, Czechoslovakia, the G.D.R., Hungary, Poland, Romania and the U.S.S.R.

[39] On the Security Council's powers of investigation under Art. 34, see Kerley, 55 A.J.I.L. 892 (1961).

A Sub-Committee, which was appointed to determine whether the Franco régime had the effect attributed to it in the draft resolution, concluded: ". . . although the activities of the Franco regime do not at present constitute an existing threat to the peace within the meaning of Article 39 of the Charter and therefore the Security Council has no jurisdiction to direct or authorise enforcement measures under Article 40 or 42, nevertheless such activities do constitute a situation "likely to endanger the maintenance of international peace and security," within the meaning of Article 34 of the Charter. . . . The Security Council is therefore empowered by paragraph 1 of Article 36 to recommend procedures or methods of adjustment in order to improve the situation mentioned. . . ."[40] The representative of Poland, Mr. Lange on the Sub-Committee filed a reservation concerning this conclusion.[41] The question was discussed in the Security Council when the report was presented to it.

MR. LANGE (POLAND). The report of the Sub-Committee makes a distinction between a potential and an actual threat to peace, and then interprets Article 39 to mean that the term "threat to the peace" used there refers only to an actual threat and not to a potential threat. I find it impossible to make sense of such a distinction. Any threat to the peace is potential by nature. It may mature tomorrow, after tomorrow, or in five years. It is a question of time. If the threat to the peace is no longer potential, then we have to do with actual aggression.

. . . Under this narrow interpretation of Article 39, namely, that it does not cover a potential threat to the peace, the Security Council would be unable to act in such cases as that of Fascist Italy prior to the actual invasion of Ethiopia, or Nazi Germany prior to the actual dropping of bombs on Polish cities.

It would seem, moreover, that the sanctions enumerated in Article 41 clearly indicate that when Article 39 speaks of a threat to peace, it refers not only to an act of aggression which has already been committed or to a threat which might materialize in a few weeks or months, but to any threat, however potential. Otherwise such sanctions as the interruption of postal, telegraphic, radio and other means of communication and the severance of diplomatic relations would have no meaning. If the threat to the peace is so immediate that it is about to materialize into actual warfare, the only sanctions which have any meaning are military sanctions. Article 41, however, clearly sets out weaker forms of sanctions, and I think we have to keep this in mind in our interpretation of Article 39.

THE PRESIDENT (MR. PARODI, FRANCE). . . . [The representative of Poland's] reservation places a special interpretation on the recommendation contained in the report; he takes the recommendation to imply that the Security Council has no direct jurisdiction to act in cases where the threats to peace are only potential. Article 39 of the Charter contains the word "threat"; by itself, this word seems to me to imply necessarily a state of affairs which is no more than a virtual possibility. So long as there is no act of aggression and so long as there is only a threat, such a threat is perforce contingent, latent or, in other words, "potential." The French text of Article 34 of the Charter, however, contains the words "si . . . cette situation semble devoir menacer le maintien de la paix," and the English text speaks of a situation "likely to endanger . . .

---

[40] Report of the Sub-Committee on the Spanish Question, S.C.O.R., First Year, First Series, Sp. Supp., p. 5. The Sub-Committee was composed of representatives of Australia, Brazil, China, France and Poland.

[41] Ibid. p. 6.

peace." Consequently Article 34 of the Charter also refers to a threatening or dangerous situation.

If the two articles of the Charter referred to are compared, it seems to me that the report merely meant to say that we ought to rely on Article 39 or Article 34, according to whether the threat is more or less remote, or more or less imminent. The report relies on Article 34, because of its estimate of the facts and as a result of assessing the more or less imminent nature of the threat.

Notes

1. The Polish draft resolution failed to obtain a majority. The proposal to consider the matter under Chapter VI obtained a majority but was vetoed by the U.S.S.R. Consequently the Spanish Question was not debated.

2. More often than not, the Security Council acts under Chapter VII without discussing the question of jurisdiction under Article 39 at all, let alone deciding upon which part of Article 39—"breach of the peace," etc.—its jurisdiction is founded. There is in consequence little "case-law" defining its meaning.

3. *Threat to the peace*. This requires a threat to *international* peace, although this limitation has been reduced in significance in recent years by the Security Council's practice in respect of Southern Africa, in which it has characterised two essentially internal situations—those in Southern Rhodesia and South Africa—as threatening international peace and security because of the potential for international conflict resulting from the existence and policies of racist regimes surrounded or bordered by black Africa.[42] In the case of Southern Rhodesia, in its first resolution[43] on November 12, 1965, no mention was made by the Security Council of a threat to the peace. In the second,[44] on November 20, 1965, the Council [d]etermines that the situation resulting from the proclamation of independence by the illegal authorities in Southern Rhodesia is extremely grave . . . and that its continuance in time constitutes a threat to international peace and security." In the third,[45] on April 9, 1966, the Council, having noted in the preamble that there had developed a real threat of substantial supplies of oil reaching the illegal Government of Southern Rhodesia, thereby encouraging it and prolonging its life," "[d]etermines that the resulting situation constitutes a threat to the peace." In the fourth[46] on December 16, 1966, the Council "[a]cting in accordance with Articles 39 and 41 of the United Nations Charter, 1. *Determines* that the present situation in Southern Rhodesia constitutes a threat to internal peace and security." *Cf.* the similar development in the resolutions leading to the imposition of mandatory economic sanctions against South Africa, see below, p. 690. Bearing in mind the *Spanish Question case*, above, how imminent was the threat to the peace in either the Southern Rhodesian or South African cases? How far can the precedents they establish[47] be applied to other internal situations? To any government that provokes its neighbours, intentionally or otherwise? To any civil conflict that has repercussions for a neighbour

---

[42] See also the earlier precedent in the *Indonesian case*, in which the Security Council had, without resolving the basis for its jurisdiction, in 1947 acted under Chapter VII by calling for a cease-fire under Art. 40 in fighting between the Netherlands and the Government of Indonesia: S/459, S.C.O.R. 178th Meeting, p. 1839. The latter Government had been established as a stage in the process under Linggadti Agreement by which the former Dutch colony was to be converted into a part of a larger Netherlands federation. It was an internal matter insofar as the Republic was not a state in international law but it was not a straightforward colonial situation, with the Republic having signed the Linggadti Agreement and having been recognised as the *de jure or de facto* government by a number of states.

[43] Resolution 216, see below, p. 687.

[44] Resolution 217, see below, p. 688.

[45] Resolution 221, see below, p. 689.

[46] Resolution 232, see below, p. 690.

[47] For doubts as to their constitutionality, see Sohn (1978) 49 B.Y.I.L. 223, 228.

(*e.g.* Bangladesh, see above, p. 650)? Note that the Southern Rhodesian and South African cases indicate that jurisdiction under Article 39 is not co-terminous with a breach of Article 2(4). Note also that whereas all "acts of aggression" (at least under the General Assembly definition, see below) and "breaches of the peace" will be a breach of Article 2(4), a "threat to the peace" of the Southern Rhodesian or South African kind will not.[48] It has been suggested that economic or political coercion could amount to a "threat to the peace."[49]

4. *Breach of the peace.* A breach of the peace, which would seem to include any use of armed force, has, despite the evidence of much world conflict since 1945, rarely been found to have occurred. The only two cases are the *Korean* case, below, p. 682 and the *Falkland Islands* case.

RESOLUTION ON THE DEFINITION OF AGGRESSION 1974

General Assembly Resolution 3314 (XXIX), G.A.O.R. 29th Session, Supp. 21; 69 A.J.I.L. 480 (1975)

The General Assembly adopts the following definition of Aggression:

Article 1

Aggression is the use of armed force by a State against the sovereignty, territorial integrity or political independence of another State, or in any other manner inconsistent with the Charter of the United Nations, as set out in this Definition.

Explanatory note: In this Definition the term "State":

(*a*) Is used without prejudice to questions of recognition or to whether a State is a Member of the United Nations;
(*b*) Includes the concept of a "group of States" where appropriate.

Article 2

The first use of armed force by a State in contravention of the Charter shall constitute *prima facie* evidence of an act of aggression although the Security Council may, in conformity with the Charter, conclude that a determination that an act of aggression has been committed would not be justified in the light of other relevant circumstances, including the fact that the acts concerned or their consequences are not of sufficient gravity.

Article 3

Any of the following acts, regardless of a declaration of war, shall, subject to and in accordance with the provisions of Article 2, qualify as an act of aggression:

(*a*) The invasion or attack by the armed forces of a State of the territory of another State, or any military occupation, however temporary, resulting from such invasion or attack, or an annexation by the use of force of the territory of another State or part thereof;

---

[48] Other more immediate threats of the use of armed force (*e.g.* an ultimatum) will be.
[49] See Broms, *loc. cit.* at p. 679, n. 52, p. 386 (economic coercion) and Goodrich, Hambro and Simons, in the passage quoted above, p. 641 (economic and political coercion). Broms also suggests that economic coercion could be a breach of the peace.

(*b*) Bombardment by the armed forces of a State against the territory of another State or the use of any weapons by a State against the territory of another State;

(*c*) The blockade of the ports or coasts of a State by the armed forces of another State; . . .

(*e*) The use of armed forces of one State which are within the territory of another State with the agreement of the receiving State, in contravention of the conditions provided for in the agreement or any extension of their presence in such territory beyond the termination of the agreement;

(*f*) The action of a State in allowing its territory, which it has placed at the disposal of another State, to be used by that other State for perpetrating an act of aggression against a third State;

(*g*) The sending by or on behalf of a State of armed bands, groups, irregulars or mercenaries, which carry out acts of armed force against another State of such gravity as to amount to the acts listed above, or its substantial involvement therein.

Article 4

The acts enumerated above are not exhaustive and the Security Council may determine that other acts constitute aggression under the provisions of the Charter.

Article 5

1. No consideration of whatever nature, whether political, economic, military or otherwise, may serve as a justification for aggression.

2. A war of aggression is a crime against international peace. Aggression gives rise to international responsibility.

3. No territorial acquisition or special advantage resulting from aggression is or shall be recognized as lawful.

Article 6

Nothing in this Definition shall be construed as in any way enlarging or diminishing the scope of the Charter including its provisions concerning cases in which the use of force is lawful.

Article 7

Nothing in this Definition, and in particular Article 3, could in any way prejudice the right to self-determination, freedom and independence, as derived from the Charter, of peoples forcibly deprived of that right and referred to in the Declaration on Principles of International Law concerning Friendly Relations and Co-operation among States in accordance with the Charter of the United Nations, particularly peoples under colonial and racist régimes or other forms of alien domination; nor the right of these peoples to struggle to that end and to seek and receive support, in accordance with the principles of the Charter and in conformity with the above-mentioned Declaration.

Notes

1. The Resolution also refers to the following explanatory notes in the Report of the Special Committee on the Question of Defining Aggression.[50]

[50] G.A.O.R., 29th Session, Supp. 19.

1. With reference to Article 3, paragraph (b), the Special Committee agreed that the expression "any weapons" is used without making a distinction between conventional weapons, weapons of mass destruction and any other kind of weapon.

2. With reference to Article 5, paragraph 1, the Committee had in mind, in particular, the principle contained in the Declaration on Principles of International Law concerning Friendly Relations and Co-operation among States in accordance with the Charter of the United Nations according to which "No State or group of States has the right to intervene, directly or indirectly, for any reason whatever, in the internal or external affairs of any other State."

3. With reference to Article 5, paragraph 2, the words "international responsibility" are used without prejudice to the scope of this term.

4. With reference to Article 5, paragraph 3, the Committee states that this paragraph should not be construed so as to prejudice the established principles of international law relating to the inadmissibility of territorial acquisition resulting from the threat or use of force.

2. The question of the definition of aggression was the subject of debate within the United Nations for over 20 years. After a long period during which the Special Committee on the Question of Defining Aggression seemed to be doing no more than going through the motions, the spirit of dètente of the early 1970s led to the adoption of the present definition by the Committee and then by the General Assembly. In both cases adoption was by consensus, *i.e.* without a vote.[51] The definition has had a mixed reception.[52] It glosses over or avoids many disputed points in the interest of agreement.

3. The 1974 text contains elements of each of the two approaches to the definition of aggression that had been championed over the years of debate: the enumerative approach, by which all of the acts that constitute aggression are listed, and the general definition approach. The general definition in Article 1 follows the pattern of Article 2(4), Charter. Like Article 2(4), it is limited to armed force; despite the doubts of a number of states, it excludes economic aggression.[53] "The economic, ideological and other modes of aggression were carefully considered . . . but the result was an interpretation that they did not fall within the term 'aggression' as it had been used in the Charter."[54] Article 1 differs from Article 2(4) in that it does not control the *threat* of armed force. It seems unlikely that the reference to "sovereignty" adds anything to that to "political independence" in the definition. The reference to "recognition" in the explanatory note to Article 1 intended to protect entities such as North and South Korea whose status is disputed. Article 2 is a compromise between the priority principle preferred by some states (*e.g.* the U.S.S.R.) and an approach emphasising the intent and purpose of the alleged aggressor supported by others (*e.g.* the U.K.). "Other relevant circumstances" in Article 2 would include the intention of the state resorting to force, which might be to engage in individual or collective self-defence. To safeguard the interests of landlocked states, it was agreed that nothing in Article 3(c) "shall be construed as a justification for a State to block, contrary to international law, the routes of free access of a landlocked country to and from the sea.[55] It was also agreed that nothing in Article 3(d) "shall be construed as in any way prejudicing or diminishing the authority of a coastal state to enforce its national legislation in maritime zones within the limits of its national jurisdiction provided such exercise is not inconsistent with the

---

[51] On consensus, see above, p. 13.

[52] See Broms, 154 Hague Receuil 299 (1977-I); Brown-John, 15 C.Y.B.I.L. 301 (1977); Cassin *et al.*, 16 Harvard I.L.J. 589 (1975); Ferencz, *Defining International Aggression*, 2 Vols. (1975); Garvey, 17 Virg. Jo.I.L. 177 (1977); Stone, 71 A.J.I.L. 224 (1977); *ibid. Conflict through Consensus: UN Approaches to Aggression*, (1977).

[53] See, however, Stone, *loc. cit.* at n. 52 above, p. 230.

[54] Broms, *loc. cit.* at n. 52 above, p. 386.

[55] Report of the Sixth Committee of the General Assembly on the Question of Defining Aggression, December 6, 1974, U.N.Doc. A/9890, para. 9.

Charter of the United Nations."[56] This makes it clear that a coastal state is not committing aggression when, for example, it takes action in the enforcement of an exclusive fishing zone or in a *Torrey Canyon* situation.[57] Article 3(g) covers indirect aggression, but is not as extensive as the equivalent provision in the 1970 Declaration on Principles of International Law.[58] However, Article 4 indicates that the list in Article 3 is not exhaustive. Article 5(2) distinguishes between a "*war* of aggression" and "aggression" generally and characterises only the former as criminal. The understanding would seem to have been that a war of aggression results in individual criminal responsibility under international law (as at Nuremburg) but that other, lesser forms of aggression give rise only to state responsibility of a civil kind, with an obligation only to make reparation.[59] Article 6 has in mind, but carefully avoids defining, the right to self-defence.

4. The Resolution is intended to assist the General Assembly and the Security Council by clarifying a key concept (see its use in Arts. 1 and 39, Charter) in the United Nations scheme for the maintenance of international peace and security and which (like many others) is left undefined in the text of the Charter. Although a General Assembly resolution is not binding upon the Security Council, it has been suggested that the definition has had an effect upon Security Council practice; the concept has been referred to more frequently in draft resolutions and debate and has generally "gained more substance than before."[60] The first finding by the Security Council that "aggression" had occurred was made in 1976, when South Africa was condemned for its "aggression" against Angola.[61]

(iii) Security Council Action under Chapter VII: Powers

(a) *The Original Scheme*

See Articles 40–50, United Nations Charter, Appendix I, below.

Note

It was originally intended that action under Chapter VII involving the use of armed force, *i.e.* action under Article 42, would be effected by armed forces provided by member states in accordance with bilateral agreements between each of them and the Security Council under Article 43. With a view to arranging for such agreements, on April 30, 1947, the Military Staff Committee, having been requested by the Security Council "to examine from a military point of view the provisions contained in Article 43 of the Charter, and to submit the results of the Study and any recommendations to the Council in due course,"[62] presented a report in the form of the texts and, where

---

[56] *Ibid.* para. 10.
[57] See above, pp. 342, 346.
[58] See Appendix III, below. There is no equivalent to para. 9 of the Section on the Principle on the Use of Force.
[59] See Ferencz, *op. cit.* at p. 679, n. 52, above, Vol. II, p. 43. On the more recent I.L.C. proposals for criminal responsibility, see above, p. 376.
[60] Broms, *loc. cit.* at p. 679, n. 52, above, p. 383. The Resolution (para. 4) "calls the attention of the Security Council to the definition it contains and recommends its use under Article 39." The possibility of formally adopting the definition was considered within the Security Council but not pursued: *ibid.* p. 397, n. 137.
[61] See above, p. 649. The General Assembly has not been so reticent, see *e.g.* the General Assembly finding of aggression against Communist China in the Korean War, see below, p. 684.
[62] S.C.O.R., 1st Year, 1st Series, 23rd Meeting (February 16, 1946), p. 369.

agreement on one text had not proved possible, alternative texts of 41 numbered Articles, entitled "General Principles Governing the Organisation of the Armed Forces made available to the Security Council by Member Nations of the United Nations."[63] The report, although showing some common ground among the five permanent members, disclosed disagreements on a number of crucial matters. Most notably, there was disagreement as to the size of the total force to be made available by Members to the Council (the United States sought a much larger force than the U.S.S.R. and, to a lesser extent, China, France and United Kingdom), the contribution of each of the permanent members (China, France, the United Kingdom and the United States favoured contributions that would be in proportion in size and content to each member's national strength; the U.S.S.R. wanted all contributions to be equal in size and content, although exceptions might be permitted), the location of the force when not in service of the Council (China, France, the United Kingdom and the United States proposed that it should be based anywhere it was permitted to stay: the U.S.S.R. wanted national contingents to return to their own territory), and the provision of bases, rights of passage and other facilities and assistance (China, France, the United Kingdom and the United States sought the negotiation of general guarantees in such matters; the U.S.S.R. was of the opinion that they should be left for separate negotiation in respect of individual agreements under Article 43). The Security Council adopted, with amendments, the Articles on which agreement had been reached. It failed to reconcile the differences reflected in the report on the question of contributions by the permanent members and at that point terminated its discussion of the report. No further attempt at implementing Article 43 has occurred. No state has made an agreement with the Security Council under it.

As a result, what is left to the Security Council in accordance with the original plan is action (subject to the power of veto) under Articles 39, 40 and 41. It may make recommendations under Article 39, which are not binding. It may "call upon" the parties to comply with "provisional measures" (*e.g.* a cease fire) under Article 40. On the question whether measures under Article 40 are binding, Goodrich, Hambro and Simons[64] state:

> There would appear to be considerable agreement that the parties concerned are obligated to comply with resolutions specifically adopted under Article 40. . . .
> There is considerable less agreement as to whether these obligations are applicable, if the Council fails to cite Article 40 and/or fails to make a formal determination under Article 39 that a threat to the peace, [etc.] . . . exists.

Measures not involving the use of armed force may be required of members by a decision (binding under Art. 25) under Article 41 (see the economic sanctions imposed on Southern Rhodesia and South Africa, below, p. 690. A non-binding recommendation for voluntary measures of the same sort may be made, presumably (since Article 41 is expressed in wholly mandatory terms) under Article 39. Measures involving the use of armed force cannot be taken under Article 42 in the absence of Article 43 agreements. The *Southern Rhodesian case*, below, p. 687, however, seems to establish that the Security Council can *authorise* a member state to use force that would otherwise be illegal in order to assist the international community in maintaining international peace and security. Action in accordance with the Korean precedent, below, p. 682, although unlikely to occur again, demonstrates another way in which, if the political will is present, the United Nations may act to maintain international peace and security, *viz.* by recommendation under Article 39 on the basis of implied powers.

---

[63] S.C.O.R., 2nd Year, Special Supp. No. 1, p. 1.
[64] *Op. cit.* at p. 641, n. 22, above, p. 306.

(b) *The Korean Question*[65]

Note

Korea became part of Japan in 1910. In 1943, the Allied Powers agreed that it would become an independent state when the Second World War ended. In 1945, Japanese troops in Korea surrendered to the U.S.S.R. north of the 38th Parallel and to the United States south of it. As agreed at the Moscow Conference of December 1945, a Joint Commission composed of U.S.S.R. and U.S. representatives was then established to assist in the formation of a provisional Korean Government and, ultimately, of a Korean state. The Joint Commission soon found itself at loggerheads, and in September 1947, the question of Korea was submitted to the General Assembly by the United States. The U.S.S.R. denied the United Nations' competence to act on the ground that arrangements for Korea's future had been set in train by other means. Despite this, the General Assembly discussed the question and resolved that elections for a Korean national assembly should be held under supervision of the United Nations Temporary Commission on Korea which was established for this purpose. The Commission was not allowed into North Korea (*i.e.* north of the 38th Parallel) but it supervised and approved elections held in the South. A South Korean Government was established and, on December 12, 1948, approved by the General Assembly.

On June 25, 1950, North Korean armed forces crossed the 38th Parallel into South Korea and fighting broke out. The resulting crisis was immediately debated by the Security Council which adopted the following series of resolutions.

SECURITY COUNCIL RESOLUTION OF JUNE 25, 1950

S.C.O.R., 5th Year, *Resolution and Decisions*, pp. 4–5

The Security Council,

Recalling the finding of the General Assembly in its resolution of 21st October 1949 that the Government of the Republic of Korea is a lawfully established government having effective control and jurisdiction over that part of Korea where the United Nations Temporary Commission on Korea was able to observe and consult and in which the great majority of the people of Korea reside; and that this Government is based on elections which were a valid expression of the free will of the electorate of that part of Korea and which were observed by the Temporary Commission; and that this is the only such Government in Korea;

Mindful of the concern expressed by the General Assembly in its resolutions of 12 December 1948 and 21 October 1949 of the consequences which might follow unless Member States refrained from acts derogatory to the results sought to be achieved by the United Nations in bringing about the complete independence and unity of Korea; and the concern expressed that the situation described by the United Nations Commission on Korea in its report menaces the safety and well-being of the Republic of Korea and of the people of Korea and might lead to open military conflict there;

Noting with grave concern the armed attack upon the Republic of Korea by forces from North Korea,

Determines that this action constitutes a breach of the peace,

---

[65] See Bowett, *United Nations Forces* (1964); Chap. 3; Kelsen, *Recent Trends in the Law of the United Nations* (1950), a supplement to the same author's *The Law of the United Nations*, Chap. 2; Kunz, 45 A.J.I.L. 137 (1951); Stone, *op. cit.* at p. 638, n. 1, above, pp. 228–237.

I. Calls for the immediate cessation of hostilities; and calls upon the authorities of North Korea to withdraw forthwith their armed forces to the 38th parallel; . . .

III. Calls upon all Members to render every assistance to the United Nations in the execution of this resolution and to refrain from giving assistance to the North Korean authorities.[66]

SECURITY COUNCIL RESOLUTION OF JUNE 27, 1950

S.C.O.R., 5th Year, *Resolutions and Decisions*, p. 5

The Security Council . . .

Having noted from the report of the United Nations Commission for Korea that the authorities in North Korea have neither ceased hostilities nor withdrawn their armed forces to the 38th parallel, and that urgent military measures are required to restore international peace and security; and

Having noted the appeal from the Republic of Korea to the United Nations for immediate and effective steps to secure peace and security,

Recommends that the Members of the United Nations furnish such assistance to the Republic of Korea as may be necessary to repel the armed attack and to restore international peace and security in the area.[67]

SECURITY COUNCIL RESOLUTION OF JULY 7, 1950

S.C.O.R., 5th Year, *Resolutions and Decisions*, p. 5

The Security Council, . . .

1. Welcomes the prompt and vigorous support which governments and peoples of the United Nations have given to its Resolutions of 25 and 27 June 1950 to assist the Republic of Korea in defending itself against armed attack and thus to restore international peace and security in the area;

2. Notes that Members of the United Nations have transmitted to the United Nations offers of assistance for the Republic of Korea;

3. Recommends that all Members providing military forces and other assistance pursuant to the aforesaid Security Council resolutions make such forces and other assistance available to a unified command under the United States;

4. Requests the United States to designate the commander of such forces;

5. Authorizes the unified command at its discretion to use the United Nations flag in the course of operations against North Korean forces concurrently with flags of the various nations participating;

6. Requests the United States to provide the Security Council with reports as appropriate on the course of action taken under the unified command.[68]

---

[66] Adopted by 9 votes (China, Cuba, Ecuador, Egypt, France, India, Norway, U.K., U.S.A.,) to 0 with 1 abstention (Yugoslavia). The U.S.S.R. was absent.

[67] Adopted by 7 votes (China, Cuba, Ecuador, France, Norway, U.K., U.S.A.) to 1 (Yugoslavia), with 2 members abstaining (Egypt, India). The U.S.S.R. was absent. India later accepted the resolution.

[68] Adopted by 7 votes (China, Cuba, Ecuador, France, Norway, U.K., U.S.A.) to 0 with 3 abstentions (Egypt, India, Yugoslavia). The U.S.S.R. was absent.

Notes

1. The Secretary-General asked member states what assistance, if any, each would give to the Republic of Korea in accordance with the June 27 Resolution and received 53 replies which were interpreted by the Secretary-General as indicating support for the Resolution. "By the end of 1950, personnel, transport, commodities, supplies, funds, facilities and other assistance had been offered . . . by 39 Member States of the United Nations in accordance with the Security Council's resolution of 27 June 1950, by one non-member State [Italy] and by nine organisations."[69] Sixteen member states finally sent armed forces to Korea.[70]

2. The Security Council ceased to play an active part in the conduct of the war after the representative of the U.S.S.R. resumed his seat on August 1, 1950. By early October the United Nations force had pushed North Korean forces back to the 38th Parallel and the question was whether it should cross it. On October 7, the General Assembly, acting on a report from the U.N. Commission in Korea, passed a resolution[71] which, by implication, authorised it to do so. By late October, troops from mainland China had entered the war and in mid-November they achieved considerable success against the United Nations force. After the U.S.S.R. had vetoed a draft resolution condemning the Chinese action on November 30[72] the General Assembly became the organ effectively seised of the question. Wary of expanding the war unduly, the Assembly postponed consideration of a draft resolution[73] along the lines of that vetoed in the Security Council and, instead, on December 14, 1950, appointed a committee of three to "determine the basis on which a satisfactory cease-fire in Korea can be arranged.[74] After the committee had unsuccessfully made overtures to the Peking Government, a resolution[75] was adopted on February 1, 1951, finding that Communist China "by giving direct aid and assistance to those who were already committing aggression in Korea and by engaging in hostilities against United Nations forces" was "itself engaged in aggression" in Korea and calling upon it to "cause its forces and nationals in Korea to cease hostilities against the United Nations forces and to withdraw from Korea." The resolution also established an Additional Measures Committee "as a matter of urgency to consider additional measures to be employed to meet [the] aggression [in Korea] . . . "and a Good Offices Committee to continue to work for a cease-fire. In the absence of satisfactory progress by the latter, the former presented a report in accordance with which the Assembly recommended on May 18, 1951,[76] that "every State: (a) apply an embargo on the shipment to areas under the control of the Central People's Government of the People's Republic of China and of the North Korean authorities of . . . [war material] . . ." "By June 30th 1951, . . . [t]he Governments of thirty-one Member States and three non-member States reported that they had implemented the resolution."[77] Truce negotiations between the United Nations Command and a Chinese-North Korean delegation were begun in July 1951. Neither the General Assembly nor the Security Council were involved except that on December 3, 1952, the Assembly adopted a resolution[78] relating to the repatriation of war prisoners when that question had brought negotiations almost to a halt. "In actual fact, the armistice negotiations were conducted by the United Nations Command under

---

[69] *Yearbook of the United Nations* (1950), p. 226.
[70] Australia, Belgium, Canada, Colombia, Ethiopia, France, Greece, Luxembourg, Netherlands, New Zealand, Philippines, Thailand, Turkey, South Africa, U.K. and U.S.A.
[71] Resolution 376(V); G.A.O.R., 5th Session, Supp. 20, pp. 9–10.
[72] See S.C.O.R., 5th Year, 530th Meeting, p. 25.
[73] See G.A.O.R., 5th Session, Annexes, Agenda Item 76, p. 4.
[74] Resolution 384 (V); G.A.O.R., 5th Session, Supp. 20, p. 15.
[75] Resolution 498 (V); G.A.O.R., 5th Session, Supp. 20A, p. 1.
[76] Resolution 500 (V); G.A.O.R., 5th Session, Supp. 20A, p. 2.
[77] Annual Report of the Secretary-General on the work of the Organisation, July 1, 1950—June 30, 1951, G.A.O.R., 5th Session, Supp. No. 1, p. 53.
[78] Resolution 610 (VII); G.A.O.R., 7th Session, Supp. No. 20, p. 3.

instructions which in the final analysis were given by the United States government in Washington."[79] An armistice in Korea came into effect on July 27, 1953. Attempts at a political settlement of the Korean Question at the Geneva Conference in 1954 were unsuccessful.

3. In proposing the Security Council resolution of July 7, 1950, the representative of the United Kingdom said: "It is clear to all concerned that a unified command is essential if confusion is to be avoided. . . . Had the Charter come fully into force and had the agreement provided for in Article 43 of the Charter been concluded, we should, of course, have proceeded differently, and the action to be taken by the Security Council to repel the armed attack would no doubt have been founded on Article 42. As it is, however, the Council can naturally act only under Article 39, which enables the Security Council to recommend what measures should be taken to restore international peace and security. The necessary recommendations were duly made in the resolutions of 25 and 27 June, but in the nature of things they could only be recommendations to individual Members of the United Nations. It could not therefore be the United Nations or the Security Council which themselves appointed a United Nations commander. All the Security Council can do is to recommend that one of its members should designate the commander of the forces which individual members have now made available.[80]

4. The constitutionality of the Security Council resolutions of June-July 1950 is uncertain.[81] Is it relevant that neither North nor South Korea were members of the United Nations or that, arguably, neither were states? Does it matter that the U.S.S.R. was absent when they were adopted? On this last question, note that whereas there is a well established practice accepted by all the permanent members of the Security Council by which abstention by a permanent member does not "veto" a resolution[82] there is no such practice with regard to absence and the U.S.S.R. has consistently maintained that the Korean resolutions were invalid because of its absence. Although the U.S.S.R. was in violation of Article 28 in absenting itself from the Council, this would not justify the Security Council in acting in the U.S.S.R.'s absence even if the violation were regarded as a "material breach."[83] The "veto" power was given to permanent members because of their primary responsibility in fact to maintain international peace and security.[84] Could it have been intended that the Security Council should adopt resolutions such as the Korean ones without the participation of all the permanent members? Arguing from the text of the Charter, if Article 27 meant *all* the permanent members, should it not have said so, like Article 108? On the other hand, if it meant all the permanent members *present*, should it not have said that (compare Article 18(3))?[85] Of what significance is the fact that the Security Council has no quorum rule?[86] Would the Council be able to act in the absence of all of the permanent members?

GOODRICH, KOREA: COLLECTIVE MEASURES AGAINST AGGRESSION

International Conciliation, No. 494, October 1953, pp. 157–169. Some footnotes omitted

The day following the adoption of the 7th July resolution, President Truman announced that he had designated General Douglas MacArthur as "the Com-

---

[79] Goodrich, *op. cit.* below, p. 178.   [80] S.C.O.R., 5th Year, 476th Meeting, pp. 3–4.
[81] See the writers cited at p. 682, n. 65, above.
[82] The I.C.J. stated in the *Legal Consequences Case,* I.C.J.Rep. 1971, p. 22, that the practice "has been generally accepted by Members of the United Nations and evidences a general practice of that Organisation."
[83] See the *Peace Treaties Case*, below, p. 739. On "material breach" in the law of treaties, see above, p. 619.
[84] See the Four Power Statement, June 7, 1945, 11 U.N.C.I.O., *Documents* 711.
[85] See Kelsen, *Law of the United Nations*, (1950), pp. 240–244.   [86] See *ibid.* p. 244.

manding General of the military forces which the members of the United Nations placed under the unified command of the United States pursuant to the United Nations' assistance to the Republic of Korea in repelling the unprovoked armed attack against it." The United Nations Command with General Headquarters at Tokyo, was established by General MacArthur on 25th July, and the first report to the Security Council was made on that date. . . .

The arrangements made for the Unified Command and for the operational control of the armed forces of members and the Republic of Korea was such that the United Nations Command was practically identical with the Far East Command of the United States. . . .

The argument might be made that the United Nations force as thus constituted and as identified by the right to use the United Nations flag and other devices, was not in fact a United Nations force, but rather a United States force, with other national units placed at its disposal. In a sense this was true. And yet, considering all the circumstances—the inexperience and disintegrated condition of the Republic of Korea forces immediately after the attack, the incomparably greater contribution which the United States made, the lack of time for planning an entirely new organization and command structure, the availability of the Far East Command, and the pressing need of quick action—it would seem that no other real choice existed if effective use were to be made of the military forces available. Furthermore, the system worked with complete satisfaction to all members of the United Nations with armed forces in Korea in so far as the effective conduct of military operations was concerned. The difficulties which arose and which led to numerous complaints on the part of participating governments had to do not with the efficiency with which military operations were conducted but rather with the failure of the United States government to take into account sufficiently the views of other governments in giving political guidance to the field commander and effectively to implement the political directives given. . . .

In principle, since collective measures were being taken for purposes broadly defined in the Charter and resolutions of the United Nations organs and upon the recommendations of the Security Council and the General Assembly, and since they were being taken in varying degrees by many members of the United Nations, it was desirable that there should be a close correlation of action to purposes and that this correlation should be achieved through organs and procedures permitting the formulation and implementation of joint decisions. In practice, however, largely because of the dominant role taken by the United States in the collective action (roughly 90 per cent. of the non-Korean forces in the field) and its understandable insistence on the recognition of this role, it became extremely difficult to do this. In fact, it can be said that the major weakness of United Nations collective action in Korea, from the point of view of organization and procedure, has been the failure to develop adequate organs and procedures for giving political guidance to the military measures taken to coerce the North Korean authorities and later the Chinese Communists.

From June down to the latter part of September 1950, the problem was not critical since all members of the United Nations giving any measures of support to collective action in Korea were in agreement that North Korean armed forces must be withdrawn or driven back of the thirty-eighth parallel. Once the United Nations forces had achieved this minimum objective, however, there was need of a United Nations decision as to whether military operations should be continued north of the thirty-eighth parallel with a view to destroying the North Korean forces and freeing North Korea of Communist control. This would permit a solution of the Korean problem along the lines of the General Assembly's earlier recommendations regarding the establishment of an independent, democratic and united Korea. The position of the United States government was that the Security Council resolution of 27th June permitted, even if it did not require, such a course of action. Nevertheless it desired the confirmation of this view by a United Nations organ. The Security Council was no longer capable of giving adequate policy guidance as the result of the return of the Soviet representative. The General Assembly was asked to meet the need, which it did by its resolution of 7 October implicitly, if not explicitly, confirming the United States position.

While the General Assembly was thus able to meet the need for political guidance which arose at a particular juncture of events, and involved an important question of principle, it was not equipped either by composition or operating procedures to give continuous political guidance to the United Nations Command. And yet once United Nations forces crossed the thirty-eighth parallel this kind of guidance became increasingly necessary.

Note

On the question whether the force in Korea was a United Nations force, note the conclusion of Bowett[87]

> There can be no doubt that, in practice, the overwhelming majority of States involved in the Korean action were fully prepared to regard it as a United Nations action involving United Nations Forces.

Bowett refers to a number of facts indicating acceptance of this view of the nature of the force, including the use of the United Nations flag and the adoption of General Assembly Resolution 483 (V)[88] authorising the award of a "distinguishing ribbon or other insignia for personnel which had participated in Korea in the defence of the principles of the Charter of the United Nations." An alternative view, which avoids the problem of the constitutionality of the Security Council resolutions, is that the force was an exercise of the customary international law right of collective self-defence.[88a]

(c) *The Southern Rhodesian Question*[89]

SECURITY COUNCIL DEBATE

S.C.O.R., 21st Year, 1276th Meeting, pp. 5 *et seq.*, April 9, 1966

On November 12, 1965, the day after Southern Rhodesia's unilateral declaration of independence, the Security Council decided, in Resolution 216 (1965), "to condemn the unilateral declaration of independence made by the racist minority in Southern Rhodesia" and "to call upon all states not to recognise this illegal racist minority régime

---

[87] *Op. cit.* at p. 682, n. 65, above, p. 47.
[88] G.A.O.R., 5th Session, Supp. No. 20, p. 76.
[88a] See Stone, *op. cit.* at p. 638, n. 1, above, pp. 234–237.
[89] See Fawcett (1965–66) 41 B.Y.I.L. 103; Fenwick, 61 A.J.I.L. 753 (1967); Howell, 63 A.J.I.L. 771 (1969); McDougal and Reisman, 62 A.J.I.L. 1 (1968).

in Southern Rhodesia and to refrain from rendering any assistance" to it.[90] On November 20, it adopted Resolution 217 (1965) in which it called upon "all States to refrain from any action which would assist and encourage the illegal régime and, in particular, to desist from providing it with arms, equipment, and military materials, and to do their utmost in order to break all economic relations with Southern Rhodesia, including an embargo on oil and petroleum products."[91] In the following debate the United Kingdom sought further Security Council action.

19. [LORD CARADON (UNITED KINGDOM)] On November 20, 1965, in resolution 217 (1965), the Council called for an oil embargo against Rhodesia. My Government has taken action in response to that call. But as we meet here today an oil tanker, called the *Joanna V*, with a full cargo of oil, rides at anchor in the port of Beira. Another tanker, also with a full cargo of oil, called the *Manuela*, has recently been close to Beira—and I have a message about that ship to which I shall presently refer. The *Manuela* could still put in to Beira very soon. But it is not merely a matter of one or two ships. Other tankers may follow, and will surely do so unless we act now. If the oil carried by such ships is pumped through the pipeline to the refinery at Umtali, which has been closed since last December, then the normal system of supply of petroleum products to Rhodesia will start again. If the oil from these tankers, and others to follow, reaches Rhodesia, the oil embargo for which this Council called will be severely prejudiced, the illegal regime in Salisbury will be encouraged, the purposes so clearly stated and so widely accepted here in the United Nations will be most seriously frustrated.

20. I come therefore to this Council to seek your help and your authority to stop this happening. . . .

21. Without that authority, the United Kingdom Government has to face the defiance of the United Nations with its hands tied. The Royal Navy undoubtedly had the physical power to prevent the *Joanna V*, for instance, from entering Beira. But in this matter my Government has been anxious that at all times its actions should be lawful actions and that it should not risk acting in breach of the law of nations. One of the very purposes of the action we are, at considerable sacrifice to ourselves, taking against the illegal regime in Southern Rhodesia is to assert the rule of law and principles of the United Nations Charter. I therefore ask the Council now, by adopting the draft resolution [Resolution 221 (1966), below] I propose, to enable the United Kingdom to carry out without fear of illegality the responsibilities which in the Rhodesian situation are ours. I ask the Council, in furtherance of our common cause, and to meet the threat which I have described, to enable the United Kingdom Government to take within the law all steps, including the use of force as the situation may demand, to stop the arrival at Beira of ships taking oil to the rebel regime. . . .

69. MR. GOLDBERG (UNITED STATES OF AMERICA). . . . The question of intercepting vessels on the high seas, the question of arresting and detaining

---

[90] Resolution 216 (1965). S.C.O.R., 20th Year, *Resolutions and Decisions*, p. 8. Adopted by 10 votes (Bolivia, China, Ivory Coast, Jordan, Malaysia, Netherlands, U.S.S.R., U.K., U.S.A., Uruguay) to 0, with 1 abstention (France).

[91] Resolution 217 (1965), S.C.O.R., 20th Year, *Resolutions and Decisions*, p. 8. Adopted by the same votes as Resolution 216 (1965), above.

them, is a matter that has a long history in the field of international law. . . . We are asked in the Security Council, and it should be a matter of deep consideration and concern for all of us, to put our sanction upon what will be a rule of international law—that when this Council acts vessels on the high seas can be arrested and detained in the interest of the international law which we will be making here today, if we adopt the draft resolution as I hope we will do.

SECURITY COUNCIL RESOLUTION 221 (1966)

S.C.O.R., 21st Year, *Resolutions and Decisions*, p. 5

The Security Council,

Recalling its resolutions Nos. 216 of 12 November 1965 and 217 of 20 November 1965 and in particular its call to all States to do their utmost to break off economic relations with Southern Rhodesia, including an embargo on oil and petroleum products,

Gravely concerned at reports that substantial supplies of oil may reach Rhodesia as the result of an oil tanker having arrived at Beira and the approach of a further tanker which may lead to the resumption of pumping through the CPMR pipeline with the acquiescence of the Portuguese authorities,

Considering that such supplies will afford great assistance and encouragement to the illegal regime in Southern Rhodesia, thereby enabling it to remain longer in being,

1. Determines that the resulting situation constitutes a threat to the peace;

2. Calls upon the Portuguese Government not to permit oil to be pumped through the pipeline from Beira to Rhodesia;

3. Calls upon the Portuguese Government not to receive at Beira oil destined for Rhodesia;

4. Calls upon all States to ensure the diversion of any of their vessels reasonably believed to be carrying oil destined for Rhodesia which may be en route for Beira;

5. Calls upon the Government of the United Kingdom to prevent by the use of force if necessary the arrival at Beira of vessels reasonably believed to be carrying oil destined for Rhodesia, and empowers the United Kingdom to arrest and detain tanker known as the Joanna V upon her departure from Beira in the event her oil cargo is discharged there.[92]

Notes

1. "At 0720 hours G.M.T. on the morning of 10 April *H.M.S. Berwick* made contact with the tanker *Manuela* which was then 180 miles south of Beira. As the tanker made no reply to signal instructions, at 0802 hours G.M.T. a British naval officer with escort was put on board the tanker with written instructions to its master to divert from his course to Beira, and was followed by a British armed naval party. The ship's master reported that his instructions were to proceed to Beira to make good engine defects. He was then informed in writing that, in view of the United Nations resolution, the tanker could not be allowed to proceed to Beira and that the British Government had

---

[92] Adopted by 10 votes (Argentina, China, Japan, Jordan, Netherlands, New Zealand, Nigeria, Uganda, U.K., U.S.A.), to 0, with 5 abstentions (Bulgaria, France, Mali, U.S.S.R., Uruguay).

authority, if necessary, to use force to prevent this. . . . The master . . . agreed to proceed to Lourenco Marques."[93] The *Joanna V* left Beira without discharging oil. The *Joanna V* had been registered as a Greek ship, but its registration was cancelled by Greece on April 6.[94] Was the boarding of the Manuela (of Greek registration) lawful in international law? What effect has Article 22 of the 1958 Geneva Convention on the High Seas?[95] The "Beira patrol" was maintained by British warships until 1975.

2. On December 16, 1966, the Security Council imposed selective mandatory economic sanctions on Southern Rhodesia under Article 41 of the Charter and re-minded Members that failure to implement them would give rise to a violation of Article 25 of the Charter.[96] On May 29, 1968, the Council, "[g]ravely concerned that the measures taken by the Security Council have not been complied with by all States and that some States, contrary to resolution 232 (1966) of the Security Council and to their obligations under Article 25 of the Charter, have failed to prevent trade with the illegal regime in Southern Rhodesia. . . . Acting under Chapter VII of the United Nations Charter" imposed comprehensive and mandatory economic sanctions upon Southern Rhodesia.[97]

3. In 1979, the Security Council terminated its sanctions against Southern Rhodesia in the light of the agreement for Zimbabwe's independence.[98]

(d) *Economic sanctions against South Africa*

SECURITY COUNCIL RESOLUTION 418 (1977)

S.C.O.R., 32nd Year, *Resolutions and Decisions*, p. 5

The Security Council,

Recalling its resolution 392 (1976) of 19 June 1976, strongly condemning the South African Government for its resort to massive violence against and killings of the African people, including schoolchildren and students and others oppos-ing racial discrimination, and calling upon that Government urgently to end violence against the African people and to take urgent steps to eliminate *apartheid* and racial discrimination,

Recognizing that the military build-up by South Africa and its persistent acts of aggression against the neighbouring States seriously disturb the security of those States. . . .

Gravely concerned that South Africa is at the threshold of producing nuclear weapons,

Recalling its resolution 181 (1963) of 7 August 1963 and other resolutions concerning a voluntary arms embargo against South Africa,

Convinced that a mandatory arms embargo needs to be universally applied against South Africa in the first instance,

Acting therefore under Chapter VII of the Charter of the United Nations,

---

[93] Letter from the permanent representative of the U.K. to the Secretary-General, April 11, 1966, S.C.O.R., 21st year, Supp. for April-June 1966, p. 34.

[94] *Keesings Archives*, p. 21418. It was given provisional registration by Panama but this was withdrawn on April 12.

[95] See above, p. 328.

[96] Resolution 232 (1966). Adopted by 11 votes to 0, with 4 abstentions (Bulgaria, France, Mali, U.S.S.R.).

[97] Resolution 235 (1968). Adopted unanimously.

[98] S.C. Res. 460 (1979), 34th Year, *Resolutions and Decisions*, p. 15.

1. Determines, having regard to the policies and acts of the South African Government, that the acquisition by South Africa of arms and related *matériel* constitutes a threat to the maintenance of international peace and security;

2. Decides that all States shall cease forthwith any provision to South Africa of arms and related *matériel* of all types, including the sale or transfer of weapons and ammunition, military vehicles and equipment, para-military police equipment, and spare parts for the aforementioned and shall cease as well the provision of all types of equipment and supplies and grants of licensing arrangements for the manufacture or maintenance of the aforementioned;

3. Calls upon all States to review, having regard to the objectives of the present resolution, all existing contractual arrangements with and licences granted to South Africa relating to the manufacture and maintenance of arms, ammunition of all types and military equipment and vehicles, with a view to terminating them;

4. Further decides that all States shall refrain from any co-operation with South Africa in the manufacture and development of nuclear weapons; . . .

Note

In 1963, "convinced that the situation in South Africa [of conflict resulting from the policy of apartheid contrary to the principles of the Charter] is seriously disturbing international peace and security," the Security Council had "solemnly call[ed] upon all States to cease forthwith the shipment of arms, ammunition of all types, and military vehicles to South Africa.[99] In 1970, "convinced . . . that the . . . continued application of the policies of apartheid and the constant build-up of the South African military and police forces . . . constitutes a potential threat to international peace and security, the Council strengthened (no training of or co-operation with South African forces, no technical assistance, etc.) the 1963 voluntary arms embargo. In 1975 and 1976, the Western permanent members of the Council vetoed attempts to make the embargo mandatory under Chapter VII on the ground that there was no threat to the peace in the sense of Article 39. Strong action taken by the South African authorities against black opposition (the banning of black organisations, the arrest of their leaders and the closing of black newspapers) caused them to accept resolution 418 (1977). Like the more general sanctions imposed earlier against Southern Rhodesia see above, p. 690, these were adopted under Article 41 of the Charter. Resolution 418 (like the Southern Rhodesian resolutions previously) had been implemented in the United Kingdom by Orders in Council made under the United Nations Act 1946.[1]

(iv) THE ROLE OF THE GENERAL ASSEMBLY

See Articles 10–14, United Nations Charter, Appendix I, below.

UNITING FOR PEACE RESOLUTION[2]

Resolution 377 (V), November 3, 1950; G.A.O.R., 5th Session, Supp. 20, p. 10

The General Assembly

Reaffirming the importance of the exercise by the Security Council of its primary responsibility for the maintenance of international peace and security,

---

[99] S.C. Res. 181 (1963), S.C.O.R., 18th Year, *Resolutions and Decisions*, p. 9.
[1] See U.K.M.I.L. 1980; (1980) 51 B.Y.I.L. 475.
[2] See Andrassy, 50 A.J.I.L. 563 (1956); Reicher, 20 Col. Jo. Trans. L. 1 (1981); and Woolsey, 45 A.J.I.L. 129 (1951).

and the duty of the permanent members to seek unanimity and to exercise restraint in the use of the veto,

Reaffirming that the initiative in negotiating the agreements for armed forces provided for in Article 43 of the Charter belongs to the Security Council, and desiring to ensure that, pending the conclusion of such agreements, the United Nations has at its disposal means for maintaining international peace and security,

Conscious that failure of the Security Council to discharge its responsibilities on behalf of all the Member States, particularly those responsibilities referred to in the two preceding paragraphs, does not relieve Member States of their obligations or the United Nations of its responsibility under the Charter to maintain international peace and security,

Recognizing in particular that such failure does not deprive the General Assembly of its rights or relieve it of its responsibilities under the Charter in regard to the maintenance of international peace and security,

Recognizing that discharge by the General Assembly of its responsibilities in these respects calls for possibilities of observation which would ascertain the facts and expose aggressors; for the existence of armed forces which could be used collectively; and for the possibility of timely recommendation by the General Assembly to Members of the United Nations for collective action which, to be effective, should be prompt,

1. Resolves that if the Security Council, because of lack of unanimity of the permanent members, fails to exercise its primary responsibility for the maintenance of international peace and security in any case where there appears to be a threat to the peace, breach of the peace, or act of aggression, the General Assembly shall consider the matter immediately with a view to making appropriate recommendations to Members for collective measures, including in the case of a breach of the peace or act of aggression the use of armed force when necessary, to maintain or restore international peace and security. If not in session at the time, the General Assembly may meet in emergency special session within twenty-four hours of the request therefor. Such emergency special session shall be called if requested by the Security Council on the vote of any seven[3] members, or by a majority of the Members of the United Nations. . . .

7. Invites each Member of the United Nations to survey its resources in order to determine the nature and scope of the assistance it may be in a position to render in support of any recommendations of the Security Council or of the General Assembly for the restoration of international peace and security.

8. Recommends to the State Members of the United Nations that each Member maintain within its national armed forces elements so trained, organized and equipped that they could promptly be made available, in accordance with its constitutional processes, for service as a United Nations unit or units, upon recommendation by the Security Council or the General Assembly, without prejudice to the use of such elements in exercise of the right of individual or collective self-defence recognized in Article 51 of the Charter. . . .

Notes

1. The resolution was adopted by 52 votes to five with two abstentions.
2. The resolution established (i) a Peace Observation Commission with representa-

[3] *Ed*. Now nine.

tives of 14 Member States, "which could observe and report on the situation in any area where there exists international tension the continuance of which is likely to endanger the maintenance of international peace and security" at the instance of the General Assembly or the Security Council and subject to the consent of the state whose territory is to be entered and (ii) a Collective Measures Committee "to study and make a report to the Security Council and the General Assembly . . . on methods, including those in Section C[4] of the present resolution which might be used to maintain and strengthen international peace and security. . . ." A Balkan Sub-Commission of the Peace Observation Commission was established in 1952 which sent observers to Northern border areas of Greece at the request of Greece. Apart from this, the Peace Observation Commission has not been used. The Collective Measures Committee submitted three Reports in the period 1951–54. Both bodies are still formally in existence.

3. Introducing the resolution in the First Committee of the General Assembly the representative of the United States is reported as saying:

. . . the authors of the joint draft resolution (A/C.1/576), of which his country was one, had been inspired by the United Nations action in Korea, which had proved that the Organization could be an effective instrument for suppressing aggression. Nevertheless, if aggressors were to be deterred by fear of the United Nations, certain organizational weaknesses would have to be remedied. . . .

Five years had elapsed and, while the Security Council had in many respects served admirably the purposes for which it had been set up, experience had shown that it was impossible to rely solely on the Council. . . . The right of veto had already been used nearly fifty times; the Security Council had not established an adequate system of observation; it had not taken the initiative required of it in virtue of Article 43.[5]

The representative of the U.S.S.R. is reported as saying:

. . . it could be contended that the veto was no good; that it was an obstruction; that it doomed the Security Council to a palsied state, that it prevented the Council or the United Nations from taking measures to discharge their responsibilities. If that were so, however, common sense and elementary good faith would require, in accordance with Article 109 of the Charter, that steps be taken to abolish such a provision. But the sponsors of the joint proposal avoided that course, although they attached considerable significance to speeches attacking the principle of unanimity in the Security Council, which was said to be the source of all the sorrows, failures and fiascos which the United Nations had experienced. . . . The principal questions relating to implementation of measures for the maintenance of peace and security had remained unsolved, not because of the veto, but because of the position taken in the Security Council by the Anglo-American bloc, which had consistently tried to foist decisions designed for its own benefit, on the Security Council, decisions which consistently failed to take into consideration the interests of the United Nations and were designed to favour the American monopolists. That had been done by dint of the Anglo-American bloc's majority in the Security Council. There was no use in the veto if a majority could always be commanded. The advantage was always on the side of the majority, particularly when it had reached an understanding and had set forth an objective to which all members of the majority must submit, though perhaps not all of them sympathized with it.[6]

4. The General Assembly has acted under the Resolution on a number of occasions, including Korea (1950),[7] the Suez Question (1956), the Hungarian Uprising (1956),

[4] See paragraphs 7 and 8 of the Resolution.
[5] G.A.O.R., 5th Session, 1st Committee, 354th Meeting (October 9, 1950), p. 63.
[6] *Ibid.* 357th Meeting (October 10, 1950), p. 82.
[7] Petersen, 13 Int.Org. 219 (1959), who concludes that the Assembly did not act under the Resolution in the *Korean Case*.

Lebanon and Jordan (1958), the Congo Question (1960), the Middle East (1967), the Pakistan Civil War (Bangladesh) (1972), Afghanistan (1980), the Palestine Situation (1980, 1982), Namibia (1981) and the Question of Occupied Arab Territories (1982). In nearly all of these cases, an emergency special session, in accordance with paragraph 1, was necessary.

5. See further on the role of the General Assembly under Articles 11–14, Charter, the *Certain Expenses Case*, below, p. 698.

(v) THE DOMESTIC JURISDICTION LIMITATION[8]

See Article 2(7), United Nations Charter, Appendix I, below.

THE SPANISH QUESTION

S.C.O.R., 1st Year, 1st Series, 44th Meeting, pp. 317–319

For the background to this case, see above, p. 674.

MR EVATT (AUSTRALIA). At the San Francisco Conference, together with other colleagues sitting at this Council with me today, I had some share in the final drafting of Article 2, paragraph 7, and I should like to quote from the memorandum presented by my delegation to the First Committee of Commission I at that Conference:

"Once a matter is recognized as one of legitimate international concern, no exception to the general rule is needed to bring it within the powers of the Organization. The general rule itself ceases to apply as soon as the matter ceases to be one of domestic jurisdiction."

Therefore, the Security Council must determine that point. The Security Council has to look at the facts of this particular situation and ask itself whether the situation is essentially within the domestic jurisdiction of Spain.

What are the facts? The facts are that there is a situation the continuance of which, in the finding of the Sub-Committee, is likely to endanger the maintenance of international peace and security. That situation has already led to strong expression of concern and disapproval by various Governments and to the closing of a frontier. There is a record of past participation in the Second World War and of recent action hindering the victorious Allies in removing vestiges of Nazism. Various Governments, Members of the United Nations, have already broken off diplomatic relations and recognized a rival Government. All this is a matter of vital international concern. The situation, I submit, is the complete antithesis of an essentially domestic situation.

Then, as to the action proposed, the recommended measures are the breaking off of diplomatic relations by all Members of the United Nations. This is a form of action completely within the control of the various nations as it is within their sole discretion to adopt this measure. The matter of diplomatic relations with other countries belongs to the sphere of external and international relationships. Further, the termination of diplomatic relations is the normal action taken by nations to express their disapproval or to make their protest against the international actions of another nation. Again, the proposed action follows

---

[8] See Gilmour, 16 I.C.L.Q. 330 (1967); Goodrich, Hambro and Simons, *op. cit.* at p. 641, n. 22, above, pp. 60–73; Higgins, *op. cit.* at p. 638, n. 1, above, pp. 58–130.

directly from the decision taken in the course of international deliberations during the past year seeking to exclude Franco's Spain from membership in the United Nations. Inasmuch as the United Nations, which is the organized family of nations, has already denied membership to Franco's Spain, it is completely logical and consequential for it not to maintain diplomatic relations with a regime, which according to the United Nations' own decision can never become a member of that Organization.

Then, I turn to the purpose of the action in order to demonstrate that this matter is not essentially one of domestic concern. The object is to remove a danger to international peace and a cause of international friction. It is true that this international objective may be served by a withdrawal of the Franco regime, but how that change is to be brought about is entirely a matter for the Spanish Government and people. The United Kingdom, the United States of America and France, in favouring such a change last March, expressed the hope that Franco himself would peacefully withdraw. So long as he remains, there is likely to be an international situation of concern to the United Nations because in the view of the Sub-Committee it is one likely to endanger the maintenance of international peace and security. . . .

The argument, therefore, that the United Nations and the Security Council, or any other Members of the United Nations, cannot touch this matter because it only affects internal affairs in Spain is unsubstantiated and should be rejected.

Notes

1. The provision equivalent to Article 2(7) in the League of Nations Covenant was Article 15(8) which read:

> If the dispute between the parties is claimed by one of them, and is found by the Council, to arise out of a matter which by international law is solely within the domestic jurisdiction of that party, the Council shall so report, and shall make no recommendations as to its settlement.

In its Advisory Opinion in the *Nationality Decrees issued in Tunis and Morocco Case*[9] the P.C.I.J. was asked whether questions concerning the application to British subjects of nationality decrees made in Tunis and Morocco by France were matters of domestic jurisdiction in the sense of Article 15(8). The Court replied in the negative. It stated:

> The question whether a certain matter is or is not solely within the jurisdiction of a state is an essentially relative question; it depends upon the development of international relations. Thus, in the present state of international law, questions of nationality are, in the opinion of the Court, in principle within this reserved domain.
>
> For the purpose of the present opinion, it is enough to observe that it may well happen that, in a matter which, like that of nationality, is not, in principle, regulated by international law, the right of a state to use its discretion is nevertheless restricted by obligations which it may have undertaken towards other states. In such a case, jurisdiction which, in principle, belongs solely to the state, is limited by rules of international law. Article 15, paragraph 8, then ceases to apply as regards those states which are entitled to invoke such rules, and the dispute as to the question whether a state has or has not the right to take certain measures becomes in these circumstances a dispute of an international character and falls outside the scope of the exception contained in this paragraph.[10]

[9] P.C.I.J.Rep., Series B, No. 4 (1923).
[10] *Ibid*. p. 24.

2. Article 2(7) was inserted at the instance of the four sponsoring powers. Mr. Dulles (U.S.), speaking for them, explained:

. . . the four power amendment dealt with domestic jurisdiction as a basic principle, and not, as had been the case in the original Dumbarton Oaks Proposals and in Article 15 of the Covenant of the League of Nations, as a technical and legalistic formula designed to deal with the settlement of disputes by the Security Council. This change in concept had been caused, he explained, by the change in the character of the Organization as planned in the discussions at San Francisco. The scope of the Organization was now broadened to include functions which would enable the Organization to eradicate the underlying causes of war as well as to deal with crises leading to war. Under the Social and Economic Council the Organization would deal with economic and social problems. This broadening of the scope of the Organization constituted a great advance, but it also engendered special problems.

For instance, the question had been raised as to what would be the basic relation of the Organization to member states: would the Organization deal with the governments of the member states, or would the Organization penetrate directly into the domestic life and social economy of the member states? As provided in the amendment of the sponsoring governments, Mr. Dulles pointed out that this principle would require the Organization to deal with the governments. . . .

In reply to the contention that domestic jurisdiction should be determined in accordance with international law, Mr. Dulles again pointed out that international law was subject to constant change and therefore escaped definition. It would, in any case, be difficult to define whether or not a given situation came within the domestic jurisdiction of a state. In this era the whole internal life of a country was affected by foreign conditions.[11]

3. Objections to United Nations jurisdiction based upon Article 2(7) have been raised in connection with such subjects as the character or internal activities of national governments (including respect for human rights) and the administration and future of non-self-governing territories. When the General Assembly has decided to take jurisdiction in respect of a question despite the protests of the state concerned, that state has, on occasions, walked out. South Africa walked out during discussion of *apartheid*; France did so when Algeria was discussed; and the United Kingdom was not present when voting on a matter concerning Southern Rhodesia occurred (before 1965).

4. Goodrich, Hambro and Simon[12] comment upon practice concerning Article 2(7) as follows:

Ambiguity results from the fact that a permissive view with respect to what the Organization *may* do can be the result either of a restrictive definition of intervention or a restrictive interpretation of "essentially within the domestic jurisdiction." United Nations practice is conclusive, however, on one point, namely, that placing a matter on the agenda for discussion does not constitute intervention. With regard to discussion, the same would appear to be true, although some members have taken an opposing view. The argument for not regarding discussion as intervention is that only after discussion can a decision be taken as to the competence of the organ. But in practice it is difficult, if not impossible, to prevent discussion of substance at this preliminary stage, and it has not generally been done. On the question whether steps taken beyond discussion, such as establishing a commission of inquiry or making recommendations to the parties, constitute intervention, the record is not clear since the attitude adopted on this issue cannot usually be separated from the assessment made of the degree of international concern. It has been suggested, however, that a distinction can be made between a recommendation of a general nature addressed to all members and one that is directed to a particular state.

[11] U.N.C.I.O., *Documents* 507.
[12] *Op. cit.* at p. 641, n. 22, above pp. 67–68. See also Watson, 71 A.J.I.L. 60 (1977).

Generally speaking, fears expressed at San Francisco that Article 2(7) would be a serious limitation on the work of the United Nations have not been justified in practice.

(vi) Peace-Keeping Forces [13]

Note

It soon became apparent that the United Nations needed not only the capacity to conduct enforcement action against an aggressor, but also a peace-keeping, or policing, competence. In a situation in which tension is running high between adjoining states or where law and order has broken down within a state, a neutral United Nations police presence can be of great help in maintaining or restoring the peace. The first United Nations force of this kind was the UN Emergency Force (UNEF). This was established by the General Assembly in 1956 to supervise the cease-fire in the Middle East after the Suez Invasion.[14] In 1960, the UN Force in the Congo (ONUC) was formed by the Security Council at the request of the Republic of the Congo to help restore peace in its territory after civil war had broken out shortly after its independence.[15] Both of these forces have since been disbanded. The three United Nations peace-keeping forces now in operation are the United Nations Force in Cyprus (UNICYP), which was established by the Security Council in 1964 after fighting had broken out between Greek and Turkish Cypriots[16]; the United Nations Disengagement Observation Force (UNDOF), which patrols the buffer zone between Israel and Syria[17] and the United Nations Interim Force in the Lebanon (UNFIL), which polices the Israeli-Lebanese border.[18] The present practice is for the mandate of these forces to be renewed for a period of up to six months at a time.

Such forces may only operate on the territory of a state with its consent. For example, UNEF operated only on Egyptian soil; it was refused permission to enter Israel. When, just prior to the Six Day War in 1967, Egypt withdrew its consent, UNEF was withdrawn from the Middle East.[19] Peace-keeping forces are composed of military contingents of armed troops voluntarily made available by member states and acting under United Nations Command. UNEF consisted, at its peak, of about 6000 men from the armed forces of ten states. United Nations peace-keeping forces are required to remain impartial and to avoid action that may affect the claims of opposing parties. They may only use their arms in self-defence.

There is no Article in the United Nations Charter which expressly provides for peace-keeping forces. Their constitutionality was confirmed in the *Certain Expenses* Case, below.

---

[13] See Bowett, *op. cit.* at p. 682, n. 65, above; Higgins, *United Nations Peace-Keeping: Documents and Commentary*, 4 vols. (1969–81); Seyersted, *United Nations Forces in the Law of Peace and War* (1966).

[14] For a discussion of the legal aspects of UNEF see the UN Secretary-General's Report on UNEF, 1958, U.N. Doc. A/3943, G.A.O.R., 13th Session, Annexes, Agenda Item 65. See also, Lauterpacht, 22 Int. Org. 413 (1957) and Rosner, *The United Nations Emergency Force* (1963).

[15] See Miller, 55 A.J.I.L.1 (1961).

[16] See Stanger, *The United Nations Force in Cyprus* (1968).

[17] See above, p. 176.

[18] Established by the Security Council in 1978, S.C. Resn. 425 (1978), S.C.O.R., 33rd Year, *Resolutions and Decisions,* p. 5. In addition to the three peace-keeping forces, there are also two *unarmed* Military Observer Missions—the UN Truce Supervision Organisation (UNTSO) in the Middle East and the Military Observer Group in India and Pakistan (UNMOGIP).

[19] UNEF was re-established by the Security Council in 1973 to supervise the cease-fire after the *Yom Kippur* War. Plans by which it would have supervised the 1979 Egyptian-Israeli Peace Treaty arrangements were not pursued in the face of U.S.S.R. opposition. It ceased to exist when its mandate expired in 1979.

CERTAIN EXPENSES OF THE UNITED NATIONS CASE[20]

I.C.J. Reports 1962, p. 151

Certain members of the United Nations fell seriously behind in the payment of the financial contributions assessed to them by the General Assembly under Article 17 of the Charter because of their refusal to accept these assessments so far as they related to the financing of UNEF and ONUC on the ground that both of these forces were unconstitutional. The General Assembly requested the advice of the I.C.J. The Court's opinion comments upon the relationship of the General Assembly and the Security Council in the maintenance of peace as well as upon constitutionality of the two peace-keeping forces concerned.

Opinion of the Court

The question on which the Court is asked to give its opinion is whether certain expenditures which were authorized by the General Assembly to cover the costs of the United Nations operations in the Congo (hereinafter referred to as ONUC) and of the operations of the United Nations Emergency Force in the Middle East (herinafter referred to as UNEF), "constitute 'expenses of the Organization' within the meaning of Article 17, paragraph 2, of the Charter of the United Nations."

. . . On the previous occasions when the Court had to interpret the Charter of the United Nations, it has followed the principles and rules applicable in general to the interpretation of treaties, since it has recognised that the Charter is a multilateral treaty, albeit a treaty having certain special characteristics. In interpreting Article 4 of the Charter, the Court was led to consider "the structure of the Charter" and "the relations established by it between the General Assembly and the Security Council;" a comparable problem confronts the Court in the instant matter. The Court sustained its interpretation of Article 4 by considering the manner in which the organs concerned "have consistently interpreted the text" in their practice (*Competence of the General Assembly for the Admission of a State to the United Nations, I.C.J. Reports* 1950, pp. 8–9). . . .

Turning to paragraph 2 of Article 17, the Court observes that, on its face, the term "expenses of the Organization" means all the expenses and not just certain types of expenses which might be referred to as "regular expenses." An examination of other parts of the Charter shows the variety of expenses which must inevitably be included within the "expenses of the Organization" just as much as the salaries of staff or the maintenance of buildings. . . .

. . . it has been argued before the Court that one type of expenses, namely those resulting from operations from the maintenance of international peace and security, are not "expenses of the Organization" within the meaning of Article 17, paragraph 2, of the Charter, inasmuch as they fail to be dealt with exclusively by the Security Council, and more especially through agreements negotiated in accordance with Article 43 of the Charter.

The argument rests in part upon the view that when the maintenance of international peace and security is involved, it is only the Security Council which is authorized to decide on any action relative thereto. It is argued further that since the General Assembly's power is limited to discussing, considering, studying and recommending, it cannot impose an obligation to pay the expenses

[20] U.N.Doc. S/5653; 3 I.L.M. 545 (1964).

which result from the implementation of its recommendations. This argument leads to an examination of the respective functions of the General Assembly and of the Security Council under the Charter, particularly with respect to the maintenance of international peace and security. . . .

The responsibility conferred [by Art. 24] is "primary", not exclusive. This primary responsibility is conferred upon the Security Council, as stated in Article 24, "in order to ensure prompt and effective action." To this end, it is the Security Council which is given a power to impose an explicit obligation of compliance if for example it issues an order or command to an aggressor under Chapter VII. It is only the Security Council which can require enforcement by coercive action against an aggressor.

The Charter makes it abundantly clear, however, that the General Assembly is also to be concerned with international peace and security. . . . The word "measures" [in Art. 14] implies some kind of action, and the only limitation which Article 14 imposes on the General Assembly is the restriction found in Article 12, namely, that the Assembly should not recommend measures while the Security Council is dealing with the same matter unless the Council requests it to do so. Thus while it is the Security Council which, exclusively, may order coercive action, the functions and powers conferred by the Charter on the General Assembly are not confined to discussion, consideration, the initiation of studies and the making of recommendations; they are not merely hortatory. Article 18 deals with *"decisions"* of the General Assembly "on important questions." These "decisions" do indeed include certain recommendations, but others have dispositive force and effect. Among these latter decisions, Article 18 includes suspension of rights and privileges of membership, expulsion of Members "and budgetary questions." In connection with the suspension of rights and privileges of membership and expulsion from membership under Articles 5 and 6, it is the Security Council which has only the power to recommend and it is the General Assembly which decides and whose decision determines status; but there is a close collaboration between the two organs. Moreover, these powers of decision of the General Assembly under Articles 5 and 6 are specifically related to preventive or enforcement measures. . . .

The argument supporting a limitation on the budgetary authority of the General Assembly with respect to the maintenance of international peace and security relies especially on the reference to "action" in the last sentence of Article 11, paragraph 2. . . .

The Court considers that the kind of action referred to in Article 11, paragraph 2, is coercive or enforcement action. This paragraph, which applies not merely to general questions relating to peace and security, but also to specific cases brought before the General Assembly by a State under Article 35, in its first sentence empowers the General Assembly, by means of recommendations to States or to the Security Council, or to both, to organize peace-keeping operations, at the request, or with the consent, of the States concerned. This power of the General Assembly is a special power which in no way derogates from its general powers under Article 10 or Article 14 except as limited by the last sentence of Article 11, paragraph 2. This last sentence says that when "action" is necessary the General Assembly shall refer the question to the Security Council. The word "action" must mean such action as is solely within the province of the Security Council. It cannot refer to recommendations which the Security Council might make, as for instance under Article 38, because the General Assembly under Article 11 has a comparable power. The "action" which is solely within the province of the Security Council is that which is indicated by the title of Chapter VII of the Charter, namely "Action with respect to threats to the peace, breaches of the peace, and acts of aggression." If the word "action" in Article 11, paragraph 2, were interpreted to mean that the General Assembly could make recommendations only of a general character affecting peace and security in the abstract, and not in relation to specific cases, the paragraph would not have provided that the General Assembly may make recommendations on questions brought before it by States or by the Security Council. Accordingly, the last sentence of Article 11, paragraph 2, has no application where the necessary action is not enforcement action.

The practice of the Organization throughout its history bears out the foregoing elucidation of the term "action" in the last sentence of Article 11, paragraph 2. Whether the General Assembly proceeds under Article 11, or under Article 14, the implementation of its recommendations for setting up commissions or other bodies involves organizational activity—action—in connection with the maintenance of international peace and security. Such implementation is a normal feature of the functioning of the United Nations. . . .

The Court accordingly finds that the argument which seeks, by reference to Article 11, paragraph 2, to limit the budgetary authority of the General Assembly in respect of the maintenance of international peace and security, is unfounded.

It has further been argued before the Court that Article 43 of the Charter constitutes a particular rule, a *lex specialis*, which derogates from the general rule in Article 17, whenever an expenditure for the maintenance of international peace and security is involved. . . .

With reference to this argument, the Court will state at the outset that, for reasons fully expounded later in this Opinion, the operations known as UNEF and ONOC were not *enforcement* actions within the compass of Chapter VII of the Charter and that therefore Article 43 could not have any applicability to the cases with which the Court is here concerned. However, even if Article 43 were applicable, the Court could not accept this interpretation of its text for the following reasons.

There is nothing in the text of Article 43 which would limit the discretion of the Security Council in negotiating such agreements. It cannot be assumed that in every such agreement the Security Council would insist, or that any Member State would be bound to agree, that such State would bear the entire cost of the "assistance" which it would make available including, for example, transport of forces to the point of operation, complete logistical maintenance in the field, supplies, arms and ammunition, etc. If, during negotiations under the terms of Article 43, a Member State would be entitled (as it would be) to insist, and the Security Council would be entitled (as it would be) to agree, that some part of the expense should be borne by the Organization then such expense would form part of the expenses of the Organization and would fall to be apportioned by the General Assembly under Article 17. . . .

Moreover, an argument which insists that all measures taken for the maintenance of international peace and security must be financed through agreements concluded under Article 43, would seem to exclude the possibility that the Security Council might act under some other Article of the Charter. The Court cannot accept so limited a view of the powers of the Security Council under the

Charter. It cannot be said that the Charter has left the Security Council impotent in the face of an emergency situation when agreements under Article 43 have not been concluded.

Articles of Chapter VII of the Charter speak of "situations" as well as disputes, and it must lie within the power of the Security Council to police a situation even though it does not resort to enforcement action against a State. The costs of actions which the Security Council is authorized to take constitute "expenses of the Organization within the meaning of Article 17, paragraph 2."

. . . In determining whether the actual expenditures authorized constitute "expenses of the Organization within the meaning of Article 17, paragraph 2, of the Charter," the Court agrees that such expenditures must be tested by their relationship to the purposes of the United Nations in the sense that if an expenditure were made for the purpose which is not one of the purposes of the United Nations, it could not be considered an "expense of the Organization."

The purposes of the United Nations are set forth in Article I of the Charter. . . .

. . . These purposes are broad indeed, but neither they nor the powers conferred to effectuate them are unlimited. Save as they have entrusted the Organization with the attainment of these common ends, the Member States retain their freedom of action. But when the Organization takes action which warrants the assertion that it was appropriate for the fulfilment of one of the stated purposes of the United Nations, the presumption is that such an action is not *ultra vires* the Organization.

If it is agreed that the action in question is within the scope of the function of the Organization but it is alleged that it has been initiated or carried out in a manner not in conformity with the division of functions among the several organs which the Charter prescribes, one moves to the internal plane, to the internal structure of the Organization. If the action was taken by the wrong organ, it was irregular as a matter of that internal structure, but this would not necessarily mean that the expense incurred was not an expense of the Organization. Both national and international law contemplate cases in which the body corporate or politic may be bound, as to third parties, by an *ultra vires* act of an agent.

In the legal systems of States, there is often some procedure for determining the validity of even a legislative or governmental act, but no analogous procedure is to be found in the structure of the United Nations. Proposals made during the drafting of the Charter to place the ultimate authority to interpret the Charter in the International Court of Justice were not accepted; the opinion which the Court is in course of rendering is an *advisory* opinion. As anticipated in 1945, therefore, each organ must, in the first place at least, determine its own jurisdiction. If the Security Council, for example, adopts a resolution purportedly for the maintenance of international peace and security and if, in accordance with a mandate or authorization in such resolution, the Secretary-General incurs financial obligations, these amounts must be presumed to constitute "expenses of the Organization."

In considering the operations in the Middle East, the Court must analyze the functions of UNEF as set forth in resolutions of the General Assembly. Resolution 998 (ES-I) of 4 November 1956 requested the Secretary-General to submit a plan "for the setting up, with the consent of the nations concerned, of an emergency international United Nations Force to secure and supervise the cessation of hostilities in accordance with all the terms of" the General Assembly's previous resolution 997 (ES-I) of 2 November 1956. The verb "secure" as applied to such matters as halting the movement of military forces and arms into the area and the conclusion of a cease-fire, might suggest measures of enforcement, were it not that the Force was to be set up "with the consent of the nations concerned."

In his first report on the plan for an emergency international Force the Secretary-General used the language of resolution 998 (ES-I) in submitting his proposals. The same terms are used in General Assembly resolution 1000 (ES-I) of 5 November in which operative paragraph 1 reads:

"*Establishes* a United Nations Command for an emergency international Force to secure and supervise the cessation of hostilities in accordance with all the terms of General Assembly resolution 997 (ES-I) of 2 November 1956."

This resolution was adopted without a dissenting vote. In his second and final report on the plan for an emergency international Force of 6 November, the Secretary-General, in paragraphs 9 and 10, stated:

"While the General Assembly is enabled to *establish* the Force with the consent of those parties which contribute units to the Force, it could not request the Force to be *stationed* or *operate* on the territory of a given country without the consent of the Government of that country. This does not exclude the possibility that the Security Council could use such a Force within the wider margins provided under Chapter VII of the United Nations Charter. I would not for the present consider it necessary to elaborate this point further, since no use of the Force under Chapter VII, with the rights in relation to Member States that this would entail, has been envisaged.

10. The point just made permits the conclusion that the setting up of the Force should not be guided by the needs which would have existed had the measure been considered as part of an enforcement action directed against a Member country. There is an obvious difference between establishing the Force in order to secure the cessation of hostilities, with a withdrawal of forces, and establishing such a Force with a view to enforcing a withdrawal of forces."

Paragraph 12 of the Report is particularly important because in resolution 1001 (ES-I) the General Assembly, again without a dissenting vote, "*Concurs* in the definition of the functions of the Force as stated in paragraph 12 of the Secretary-General's report." Paragraph 12 reads in part as follows:

"the functions of the United Nations Force would be, when a cease-fire is being established, to enter Egyptian territory with the consent of the Egyptian Government, in order to help maintain quiet during and after the withdrawal of non-Egyptian troops, and to secure compliance with the other terms established in the resolution of 2 November 1956. The Force obviously should have no rights other than those necessary for the execution of its functions, in co-operation with local authorities. It would be more than an observers' corps, but in no way a military force temporarily controlling the territory in which it is stationed; nor, moreover, should the Force have military functions exceeding those necessary to secure peaceful conditions on the assumption that the parties to the conflict take all necessary steps for compliance with the recommendations of the General Assembly."

It is not possible to find in this description of the functions of UNEF . . . any evidence that the Force was to be used for purposes of enforcement. Nor can such evidence be found in the subsequent operations of the Force, operations which did not exceed the scope of the functions ascribed to it.

It could not therefore have been patent on the face of the resolution that the establishment of UNEF was in effect "enforcement action" under Chapter VII which, in accordance with the Charter, could be authorized only by the Security Council.

On the other hand, it is apparent that the operations were undertaken to fulfil a prime purpose of the United Nations, that is, to promote and to maintain a peaceful settlement of the situation. This being true, the Secretary-General properly exercised the authority given him to incur financial obligations of the Organization and expenses resulting from such obligations must be considered "expenses of the Organization within the meaning of Article 17, paragraph 2."

Apropos what has already been said about the meaning of the word "action" in Article 11 of the Charter, attention may be called to the fact that resolution 997 (ES-I), which is chronologically the first of the resolutions concerning the operations in the Middle East mentioned in the request for the advisory opinion, provides in paragraph 5:

"*Requests* the Secretary-General to observe and report promptly on the compliance with the present resolution to the Security Council *and* to the General Assembly, for such further *action as they may deem appropriate in accordance with the Charter.*" . . .

The Court notes that these "actions" may be considered "measures" recommended under Article 14, rather than "action" recommended under Article 11. The powers of the General Assembly stated in Article 14 are not made subject to the provisions of Article 11, but only of Article 12. Furthermore, as the Court has already noted, the word "measures" implies some kind of action. So far as concerns the nature of the situations in the Middle East in 1956, they could be described as "likely to impair . . . friendly relations among nations," just as well as they could be considered to involve "the maintenance of international peace and security." Since the resolutions of the General Assembly in question do not mention upon which article they are based, and since the language used in most of them imply reference to either Article 14 or Article 11, it cannot be excluded that they were based upon the former rather than the latter article. . . .

The Court concludes that, from year to year, the expenses of UNEF have been treated by the General Assembly as expenses of the Organization within the meaning of Article 17, paragraph 2, of the Charter.

The operations in the Congo were initially authorized by the Security Council in the resolution of 14 July 1960 which was adopted without a dissenting vote. The resolution, in the light of the appeal from the Government of the Congo, the report of the Secretary-General and the debate in the Security Council, was clearly adopted with a view to maintaining international peace and security. However, it is argued that that resolution has been implemented, in violation of provisions of the Charter inasmuch as under the Charter it is the Security Council that determines which States are to participate in carrying out decisions involving the maintenance of international peace and security, whereas in the case of the Congo the Secretary-General himself determined which States were to participate with their armed forces or otherwise. . . .

The Court then considered the subsequent Security Council resolutions authorising and supporting the Secretary-General's action.

In the light of such a record of reiterated consideration, confirmation, approval and ratification by the Security Council and by the General Assembly of the actions of the Secretary-General in implementing the resolution of 14 July 1960, it is impossible to reach the conclusion that the operations in question usurped or impinged upon the prerogatives conferred by the Charter on the Security Council. The Charter does not forbid the Security Council to act through instruments of its own choice: under Article 29 it "may establish such subsidiary organs as it deems necessary for the performance of its functions"; under Article 98 it may entrust "other functions" to the Secretary-General.

It is not necessary for the Court to express an opinion as to which article or articles of the Charter were the basis for the resolutions of the Security Council, but it can be said that the operations of ONUC did not include a use of armed force against a State which the Security Council, under Article 39, determined to have committed an act of aggression or to have breached the peace. The armed forces which were utilized in the Congo were not authorized to take military action against any State. The operation did not involve "preventive or enforcement measures" against any State under Chapter VII and therefore did not constitute "action" as that term is used in Article 11.

For the reasons stated, financial obligations which, in accordance with the clear and reiterated authority of both the Security Council and the General Assembly, the Secretary-General incurred on behalf of the United Nations, constitute obligations of the Organization for which the General Assembly was entitled to make provision under the authority of Article 17. . . .

For these reasons, the Court is of opinion, by nine votes to five,[21] that the expenditures authorised [by the General Assembly related to operations of UNEF and ONUC] . . . constitute "expenses of the Organisation" within the meaning of Article 17, paragraph 2, of the Charter of the United Nations.

Notes

1. Although the General Assembly adopted the Court's opinion,[22] a number of states, particularly France and the U.S.S.R., refused to pay their contributions and became subject to the suspension of voting rights in the General Assembly under Article 19. By the expedient of not dealing with matters that could not be disposed of without objection, the General Assembly survived the whole of the 19th Session (1964–65) without putting the matter to the test. Then, the United States which had, with good reason in law, been pressing for the application of Article 19, gave way and accepted that Article 19 would not be enforced in the existing situation. There seems little doubt that this was a serious setback to the authority of the United Nations over its members. Under arrangements adopted in 1973, contributions are assessed not on the basis used for ordinary contributions to the United Nations budget, but on a basis that increases the amount paid by permanent members of the Security Council and developed states.[23] A number of states remain in default of their payments in respect of particular forces.[24]

2. How widely did the Court apply the doctrine of implied powers? Did it look to see what was essential for the execution of the United Nations functions or what was consistent with them? Compare the *Reparation Case*, above, p. 114.

[21] The judges in the majority were Vice-President Alfaro; Judges Badawi, Wellington Koo, Spiropoulos, Sir Percy Spender, Sir Gerald Fitzmaurice, Tanaka, Jessup, Morelli. President Winiarski and Judges Basdevant, Moreno Quintana, Koretsky and Bustamante y Rivero dissented. [22] G.A.Res. 1854, G.A.O.R., 17th Session, Supp. 17, p. 54. [23] G.A. Resn. 3101. [24] See 19 *UN Chronicle*, May 1982, p. 65.

CHAPTER 12

ARBITRATION AND JUDICIAL SETTLEMENT OF DISPUTES[1]

1. *INTRODUCTORY NOTE*

As in municipal law, litigation in international law is very much a matter of last resort. The possible worsening of relations by unilateral recourse to law, the uncertainty of the outcome of legal proceedings,[2] and the embarrassment and finality of an adverse ruling by a body beyond one's control are considerations common to both systems which conspire to make this so.[3] If the cost of legal proceedings sometimes deters the plaintiff at the national level, the absence in most cases of compulsory jurisdiction is an even greater weapon for the defendant in international law. In international relations, most disputes are settled through negotiation between the parties or by third-party assistance in the form of good offices, conciliation or the conduct of fact-finding inquiries.[4] Such assistance is sometimes provided through the United Nations or other regional organisations such as the Organisation of African Unity or the Organisation of American States. This chapter is limited to the machinery for the settlement of disputes upon a basis of law, whether by arbitration or judicial settlement. This is so for reasons of space and because arbitral tribunals and courts necessarily apply international law so that their functioning is of particular interest to lawyers.

2. *ARBITRATION*[5]

INTERPRETATION OF ARTICLE 3, PARAGRAPH 2, OF THE TREATY OF LAUSANNE

Advisory Opinion. P.C.I.J. Reports, Series B, No. 12, at p. 26 (1925)

Opinion of the Court

If the word "arbitration" is taken in a wide sense, characterized simply by the binding force of the pronouncement made by a third Party to whom the

---

[1] See Anand, *International Courts and Contemporary Conflicts* (1974); *ibid. Studies in International Adjudication* (1969); Gillis Wetter, *The International Arbitral Process: Public and Private*, 5 Vols (1979); Grieves, *Supranationalism and International Adjudication* (1969); Jenks, *The Prospects of International Adjudication* (1964); Mosler and Bernhardt, ed., *Judicial Settlement of Disputes*, 1974; and Simpson and Fox, *International Arbitration* (1959). See also Katz, *The Relevance of International Adjudication* (1968).

[2] Paradoxically, some of the uncertainty of international law is, as Gross points out (in Gross, ed., *The Future of the International Court of Justice*, Vol. II (1976), p. 727 at p. 746), because so few cases are taken to court.

[3] *cf.* Fitzmaurice in *The Future of the International Court, loc. cit.* at n. 2, above, pp. 463–470.

[4] UN Charter, Art. 33, Appendix II, below. See Cot, *International Conciliation* (1967), Eng. trans. (by Myers) (1972); David Davies Memorial Institute of International Studies, *Report of a Study Group on the Peaceful Settlement of International Disputes* (1966); Lall, *Modern International Negotiations* (1966); Northedge and Donelan, *International Disputes* (1971); and Vallat, in *Cambridge Essays in International Law* (1965), p. 155. For an example of a fact-finding commission of inquiry, see the *Red Crusader Case*, 35 I.L.R. 485 (1967). The fact that negotiations are being actively pursued is not in international law a bar to recourse to judicial settlement or arbitration: *Aegean Sea Continental Shelf Case*, I.C.J. Rep. 1978, at p. 13. The I.C.J. may consider a case while it is pending in the Security Council: *U.S. Diplomatic and Consular Staff in Tehran Case, ibid.* 1980, at p. 22.

[5] See Sohn, 108 *Hague Recueil* 1 (1963–I). See also the I.L.C.'s Model Rules on Arbitral Procedure, Y.B.I.L.C., 1958, II, p. 83.

interested Parties have had recourse, it may well be said that the decision in question is an "arbitral award."

This term, on the other hand, would hardly be the right one, if the intention were to convey a common and more limited conception of arbitration, namely, that which has for its object the settlement of differences between States by *judges* of their own choice and *on the basis of respect for law* (Hague Convention for the pacific settlement of international disputes, dated October 18th, 1907, Article 37). It appears, in fact, that according to the arguments put forward on both sides before the Council, the settlement of the dispute in question depends, at all events for the most part, on considerations not of a legal character; moreover, it is impossible, properly speaking, to regard the Council, acting in its capacity of an organ of the League of Nations . . . as a tribunal of arbitrators.

Notes

1. Arbitration was defined by the International Law Commission as "a procedure for the settlement of disputes between States by a binding award on the basis of law and as a result of an undertaking voluntarily accepted."[6] Schwarzenberger states: "The only difference between arbitration and *judicial settlement* lies in the method of selecting the members of these judicial organs. While, in arbitration proceedings, this is done by agreement between the parties, judicial settlement presupposes the existence of a standing tribunal with its own bench of judges and its own rules of procedure which parties to a dispute must accept."[7]

2. Arbitration in recent times dates from the mixed claims commissions established under the Jay Treaty[8] of 1794 between Great Britain and the United States. One well known and successful instance of its use in the nineteenth century was the *Alabama Claims Arbitration*[9] of 1872, also between Great Britain and the United States. Resort to arbitration still occurs,[10] although it has in recent years been to a large extent replaced by the "lump-sum settlement agreement" in the important area of state responsibility for the treatment of aliens.[11] Note also the procedure for the arbitration of investment disputes between states and foreign companies introduced by the 1965 World Bank Convention.[12]

3. Arbitration tribunals may consist of a single arbitrator or they may be collegiate bodies.[13] Where the former is the case, the arbitrator is sometimes a dignitary (*e.g.* a Head of State) who may delegate his responsibilities to a person knowledgeable in international law.[14] If the tribunal is a collegiate body, it will usually be a mixed commission,[15] *i.e.* one upon which sit two or more arbitrators (commissioners, etc.) appointed in equal numbers by each of the parties separately plus an Umpire (or

---

[6] Y.B.I.L.C., 1953, II, p. 202.

[7] *Manual of International Law* (6th ed., 1976), p. 195.

[8] 1 Malloy 590.   [9] Moore, 1 *Int.Arb.* 495.

[10] On the increased resort to arbitration in the last decade, see Johnson (1980) 34 Y.B.W.A. 305. Recent examples are the *Beagle Channel Arbitration* (*Argentina v. Chile*) (1977), 17 I.L.M. 634 (1978), as to which see Shaw, 6 Int. Rel. 415 (1978), and the *English Channel Arbitration*, see above, p. 360. The award in the former case was accepted by Chile but not Argentina, the other party. Later recommendations by the Pope, called in as a mediator, met a similar fate.

[11] See above, p. 440. But note that the Iran-U.S. Claims Tribunal, established in 1981, is at present considering claims by the U.S. and its nationals against Iran and *vice versa*: see Fagre, 22 Harvard I.L.J. 443 (1981) and Suy, 29 A.J.C.L. 523 (1981).

[12] See above, p. 440.

[13] See Johnson (1953) 30 B.Y.I.L. 53.

[14] See, *e.g.* the *Clipperton Island Case*, above, p. 159.

[15] See, *e.g.* the Mexican Claims Commission by which several of the cases in Chap. 8 were decided.

Presiding Commissioner, etc.) appointed jointly by the parties or by the arbitrators appointed by them.

4. *The Permanent Court of Arbitration.* This was established in 1900 in accordance with the 1899 Hague Convention for the Pacific Settlement of International Disputes[16] and, later, the 1907 Convention of the same name.[17] Each party to either Convention selects up to four persons "of known competence in questions of international law" and "of the highest moral competence" to serve for a renewable period of six years as members of the Court.[18] Should the parties to a dispute decide to refer a case to the Court, under the 1907 Convention they appoint a tribunal from the members of the Court of any size and composition upon which they agree; in the absence of agreement to the contrary, the tribunal is established according to the following scheme: "Each party appoints two Arbitrators, of whom one only can be its national or chosen from among the persons selected by it as members of the Permanent Court. These Arbitrators together choose an Umpire. If the votes are equally divided, the choice of the Umpire is intrusted to a third Power, selected by the parties by common accord. If an agreement is not arrived at on this subject each party selects a different Power, and the choice of the Umpire is made in concert by the Powers thus selected. If, within two months' time, these two Powers cannot come to an agreement, each of them presents two candidates taken from the list of members of the Permanent Court, exclusive of the members selected by the parties and not being nationals of either of them. Drawing lots determines which of the candidates thus presented shall be Umpire."[19] Twenty-five cases have been referred to the Court (or, more accurately, an arbitral tribunal established through the machinery of the Court); of these, only two have been referred since 1945, despite efforts to remind states of the Court's existence. Why do you think this is so?[20]

3. *THE WORLD COURT*[21]

(i) ORGANISATION

See Articles 2–33, Statute of the International Court of Justice.[22]

Notes

1. The World Court, which is by far the most important international court,[23] is the name commonly given to the Permanent Court of International Justice and the present

---

[16] U.K.T.S. 9 (1901), Cd. 798. The Convention entered into force in 1900.

[17] U.K.T.S. 6 (1971), Cmnd. 4575. On March 1, 1982, there were 74 contracting parties, including the U.K., to one or both Conventions. The 1907 Convention revised the 1899 Convention in the light of the experience of the Court in its early cases.

[18] Art. 23, 1899 Convention; Art. 44, 1907 Convention.

[19] Art. 45. The 1899 Convention (Art. 24) imposes no restrictions upon the choice by a party of its two arbitrators.

[20] See Lillich, 161 *Hague Recueil* 358 (1978–III) and Schwarzenberger (1980) 34 Y.B.W.A. 329.

[21] See Rosenne, *The Law and Practice of the International Court*, 2 vols. (1965); *ibid. The World Court* (3rd rev. ed., 1973): *The Future of the International Court of Justice, loc. cit.* at p. 705, n. 3, above. See also, Prott, *The Latent Power of Culture and the International Judge,* 1979.

[22] See Appendix I, below. The I.C.J. Rules of Court were amended in 1972. For the revised text, see 11 I.L.M. 899 (1972). For commentary, see Jiménez de Aréchaga, 67 A.J.I.L. 1 (1973) and Rosenne, 8 Israel L.R. 197 (1973).

[23] The only other international courts are regional and limited in jurisdiction. See the American Court of Human Rights, above, p. 483, the European Court of Human Rights, above, p. 481, and the European Court of Justice of the European Communities. All three are competent to adjudicate upon inter-state claims brought under the treaties establishing them. On the proposed International Tribunal for the Law of the Sea, above p. 285.

International Court of Justice. The Permanent Court of International Justice was established in 1920 under the auspices of the League of Nations. In 1946, it was replaced by the International Court of Justice, which was made "the principal judicial organ of the United Nations" by Article 92 of the United Nations Charter. The International Court of Justice is organised in accordance with the Statute of the International Court of Justice which is a part of the United Nations Charter and which in most respects is identical with the Statute of its predecessor. The World Court has always had its seat at The Hague.

2. The members of the Court, with the states of which they are nationals, are: President Elias (Nigeria); Vice-President Sette-Camara (Brazil); Judges Lachs (Poland), Morozov (USSR), Singh (India), Ruda (Argentina), Mosler (FRG), Oda (Japan), Ago (Italy), El-Khani (Syria), Schwebel (U.S.), Sir Robert Jennings (U.K.), de Lacharrière (France), Mbaye (Senegal), Bedjaoui (Algeria).

3. Judges are elected by the Security Council and the General Assembly according to a complicated procedure (Statute, Arts. 4–14) in which a lot of political infighting occurs. In recent years, the balance of nationalities represented on the Court has changed with the nature of the international community.[24] The understanding now is that the 15 seats on the Court are distributed (in terms of nationalities and power blocs) in the same way as membership of the Security Council. This means, *inter alia*, that the Court should have a national of each of the five permanent members of the Security Council. This has been the case since 1945 save that there has been no Chinese judge (nationalist or communist) as of 1967 since when no candidate has been put forward.

4. The Court normally sits as a full court of 15 judges.[25] The Court gives a single, collegiate judgment. Individual judges in the majority may add their own separate judgments. Individual dissenting judges may give dissenting judgements.

ROSENNE, THE COMPOSITION OF THE COURT

in *The Future of the International Court of Justice, loc. cit.* at p. 705, n. 3, above, Vol. I, pp. 388–390

Provision for the recusal of judges in cases in which they have an interest is made in Articles 17 and 24, Statute of the Court.[26] The following extract concerns the particular problem that arises from the fact that Court members have increasingly had experience within the United Nations as representatives of their governments or in some other capacity and have thereby been involved in cases which later come to the Court. See further on the *S. W. Africa* and *Namibia* Cases, pp. 103 *et seq.* above.

This type of *ad hoc* disqualification is not based on personal interests which lead to personal bias in the exercise of the judicial function. . . . The problem is to avoid the suspicion of obvious political bias. . . .

The first indication of this problem occurred in *Anglo-Iranian Oil Co.* Here Sir Benegal Rau, who had been elected to the Court in 1951, had previously

---

[24] In 1920, there were 10 Judges from western Europe; two from Asia; two from South America; and one from the U.S. In the period immediately after the Second World War, Latin American representation rose to four; it has since fallen as Afro-Asian representation has increased. The number of western European judges has also declined, although it is still substantial. Two are members as nationals of permanent members of the Security Council. See Schwarzenberger, 36 Y.B.W.A. 241 (1982). See on the election process generally, Rosenne, in *The Future of the International Court of Justice, loc. cit.* at p 705, n. 3, above.

[25] The *Gulf of Maine Case*, now pending, has been referred to a Chamber: see Art. 26, Statute, Appendix III, below.

[26] See Appendix I, below.

been the representative of India on the Security Council when that body had been seised of the United Kingdom's complaint of failure by the Iranian Government to comply with the provisional measures indicated by the Court. Sir Benegal thought that he ought not to sit in this case, and the Court agreed with him. . . .

The next formal indication occurred in 1965, in *South West Africa*, when South Africa made an application concerning the composition of the Court as it existed after the election of 1963. After listening to the contentions of the parties in closed hearings the Court, by eight votes to six (the two judges *ad hoc* taking part), decided not to accede to that application. The assumption at the time that this application referred at least in part to Judge Padilla Nervo, elected in 1963, was subsequently confirmed in *Namibia*. Prior to his election he had twice been permanent representative of Mexico to the United Nations; he had also been the representative of Mexico on the Trusteeship Council (where the affairs of South West Africa had been discussed) as well as President of the General Assembly.

A third indication, and one of extreme gravity, occurred in *Namibia*. Here the written statement of South Africa contained a broad (and public) challenge to the participation in this case of the President, Sir Zafrulla Khan, and Judges Padilla Nervo and Morozov, on the basis of their previous involvement in the affairs of South West Africa as members of their countries' delegations to the United Nations. The President had also been President of the General Assembly, and Judge Morozov had been one of his country's representatives on the Security Council when it had discussed South West Africa, and had played an active part in drawing up some resolutions directly relevant in the advisory case. In a series of three separate orders, unanimous in the cases of the President and Judge Padilla Nervo, and adopted by ten votes to four in the case of Judge Morozov (the recused judges not taking part), these challenges were all rejected. No hearings took place on those challenges. In 1965 the order was unreasoned, and no indication was given of how the Court divided on the challenge. In 1971 these orders, too, were unreasoned, but the advisory opinion itself gives the reasons; and the third indicates how the Court divided regarding Judge Morozov. In this respect, the greater frankness of the 1971 process, by implication also extending to the 1965 decision as regards Judge Padilla Nervo, is to be welcomed and is certainly less maladroit. . . .

The Court reached the general conclusion that the previous activity of each of its three members in his former capacity of representative of his Government, did not attract the disqualification imposed by Article 17, paragraph 2, of the Statute. In the case of Judge Padilla Nervo, the Court found no reason to depart from its decision in 1965 after hearing the same contentions. In the other two cases, the Court found that the activities in United Nations organs of the Judges concerned prior to their election to the Court did not furnish grounds for treating them differently from Judge Padilla Nervo. In the case of Judge Morozov the Court also took into consideration his participation in the formulation of a certain Security Council resolution concerning the Pretoria trial of some South West Africans: this participation in the work of the United Nations as representative of his Government did not justify any different conclusions.

In these instances, the decision was reached by the Court after due deliberation. Another case is far less satisfactory. It relates to the non-participation of Judges Sir Zafrulla Khan (re-elected in 1964) in the second phase of *South West*

Africa. This has never been satisfactorily explained. The various inspired newspaper accounts of this incident give rise to the most serious misgivings, and these have become magnified by the 1971 decision on the participation of that judge in *Namibia*.

Namibia confirms that in this respect there need be no difference between contentions and advisory proceedings, although doubtless in course of time characteristic and conceptual differences could make their presence felt.

GROSS, THE INTERNATIONAL COURT OF JUSTICE: CONSIDERATION OF REQUIREMENTS FOR ENHANCING ITS ROLE IN THE INTERNATIONAL LEGAL ORDER

in *The Future of the International Court of Justice, loc. cit.* at p. 705, n. 3, above, Vol. I, pp. 61–64. Some footnotes omitted

The institution of judges *ad hoc* in contentious cases [under Article 31, Statute of the Court] and in advisory proceedings under Articles 68 of the Statute and . . . [89] of the [revised] Rules of Court[27] has been a matter of controversy between those who would suppress it for the sake of enhancing the impartiality of the Court[28] and those who, for a variety of reasons, would maintain it.[29] There are also those who, occupying a middle ground, assert that the abolition of judges *ad hoc* should be combined with the exclusion of "national" judges from the bench, that is, judges who are [members of the Court and] nationals of one or both parties before the Court.[30] In this view, the essential objective is equality between the parties; this can be achieved either by adding to the bench a judge *ad hoc* or by excluding the "national" judge. . . .

Fitzmaurice [has] attacked the system . . . arguing in particular two points: First, those who advocate its retention on the ground that it increases confidence in the Court argue from an impermissible premise that judges, particularly *ad hoc* judges, will necessarily espouse the view of their government. Secondly, once a case is terminated, a judge *ad hoc* may feel himself free of every obligation of confidence and may reveal to his government what had been said in the deliberations of the Court. This could have harmful consequences for the independence of judges, particularly if such revelations occurred shortly before elections to the Court.[31] . . .

The fact of the matter is that in every case where the majority of the Court gave a favourable judgment for the appointing state, the judge *ad hoc* concurred, and he dissented in nearly every case where the judgment went against it. Such voting alignments, even if the *ad hoc* judge is the only dissenting judge, as was the case in the recent *Barcelona Traction* judgment, do not necessarily reflect on the independence of the judges concerned. Even the majority of 14 in

---

[27] 11 I.L.M. 899 (1972).

[28] For a recent view, see F. L. Grieves, *Supranationalism and International Adjudication*, at p. 180 (1969).

[29] See Rosenne [in *The Future of the International Court of Justice, loc. cit.* at p. 705, n. 3, above, Vol. I], at pp. 202–205.

[30] Erik Castrén, "Revision de la Charte des Nations Unies," 7 *Revue Hellénique de Droit International* 20–34, at p. 32 (1954).

[31] *Ed. 45 Annuaire de l'Institut de droit international*, II, p. 444 (1954).

that case could be wrong, and, despite concurrence in the result, there was wide disparity in the actual reasoning of the various judges. . . .

It has often been observed that where two parties appoint judges *ad hoc,* their votes cancel each other out. In litigation where only one party appoints a judge *ad hoc*, the other party having a national as a titular judge, his vote could make a difference in marginal cases, but there have been no such cases.

The most constructive view on the role of judges *ad hoc* has been expressed in two forms. According to one, such judges, while not representing their own countries, "fulfil a useful function in supplying local knowledge and a national point of view."[32] The other sees the task of an *ad hoc* judge not so much in his influence upon the judgment as upon its formulation. It rests with such judges "to represent their countries' interests in the whole process through which the decision is produced and the reasons formulated. If the role of the judges *ad hoc* could be more accurately designated as that of assessors, the grant to them of the status of judge (with the right to vote) represents a concession to diplomatic susceptibilities."[33]

It is recognized on all sides that diplomatic susceptibilities and politico-psychological considerations are involved, and if one takes them seriously, then the system of judges *ad hoc* should be left alone. To the purist it will remain objectionable as a survival of the basic idea of arbitration in the system of international adjudication. . . .

Perhaps the system of judges *ad hoc* is dying a quiet death anyhow. And if states continue to select qualified persons who are not their nationals as judges *ad hoc* then the main argument against the system, that in some fashion such judges represent "their" governments on the Court, would lose much of its persuasiveness.

(ii) ACCESS IN CONTENTIOUS LITIGATION

See Articles 34–35, Statute of the International Court of Justice and Article 93 of the United Nations Charter.[34]

Notes

1. Three states that are not members of the United Nations—Liechtenstein, San Marino and Switzerland—are currently parties to the Statute of the Court under Article 93(2) of the Charter. The conditions set by the Security Council and the General Assembly for Switzerland were:

   (a) Acceptance of the provisions of the Statute of the International Court of Justice;
   (b) Acceptance of all the obligations of a Member of the United Nations under Article 94 of the Charter;
   (c) An undertaking to contribute to the expenses of the Court such equitable amount as the General Assembly shall assess from time to time after consultation with the Swiss Government.[34a]

Essentially the same conditions were set for each of the other two states.

---

[32] Informal Inter-Allied Committee, Report, para. 39; 39 A.J.I.L. Supp. 1 at 11 (1945). . . .
[33] *Ed*. Rosenne, *loc. cit.* at p. 705, n. 3, above, p. 204.
[34] See Appendix I, below.
[34a] G.A.Res. 91 (I), December 11, 1946.

2. As far as access to the Court for states not parties to the Statute is concerned, the Security Council, acting under Article 35(2), has resolved:

1. The International Court of Justice shall be open to a State which is not a party to the Statute of the International Court of Justice, upon the following condition, namely, that such State shall previously have deposited with the Registrar of the Court a declaration by which it accepts the jurisdiction of the Court, in accordance with the Charter of the United Nations and with the terms and subject to the conditions of the Statute and Rules of the Court, and undertakes to comply in good faith with the decision or decisions of the Court and to accept all the obligations of a Member of the United Nations under Article 94 of the Charter;

2. Such declaration may be either particular or general. A particular declaration is one accepting the jurisdiction of the Court in respect only of a particular dispute or disputes which have already arisen. A general declaration is one accepting the jurisdiction generally in respect of all disputes or of a particular class or classes of disputes which have already arisen or which may arise in the future. A State, in making such a general declaration, may, in accordance with Article 36, paragraph 2, of the Statute, recognize as compulsory, *ipso facto* and without special agreement, the jurisdiction of the Court, provided, however, that such acceptance may not, without explicit agreement, be relied upon *vis-à-vis* States parties to the Statute of the International Court of Justice.[35]

Particular declarations in the sense of this resolution were filed by Albania as respondent in the *Corfu Channel Case*[36] and Italy as claimant in the *Monetary Gold Case*[37] A number of general declarations have been filed in the past but there are none in operation now.[38] Before becoming a member of the United Nations, West Germany was a party to the *North Sea Continental Shelf Cases* on the basis of such a declaration.[39] In those cases, the question of the status of West Germany as a state was not raised by the other parties. Apparently for this reason the Court did not find it necessary to consider it (although presumably it would have done if one of the parties, with the agreement of the other, had been, for example, a company).[40]

3. Can the United Nations bring a claim in contentious litigation before the World Court? Can it have any part in proceedings in such litigation? Can a company or an individual? In 1954, the Institute of International Law resolved:

It is a matter of urgency to widen the terms of Article 34 of the Statute so as to grant access to the Court to international organisations of States of which at least a majority of the members of which are members of the United Nations or parties to the Statute of the Court.[41]

Rosenne suggests:

It is possible that the direct representation of the individuals concerned in the proceedings before the Court would have the effect, not only of stimulating public interest in the work of the Court, but also, and this may be more important, of enhancing its prestige and public confidence in the reality of international justice.[42]

---

[35] S.C. Resn. 9 (1946), October 15, 1946.
[36] See above, p. 380.
[37] I.C.J.Rep. 1954, p. 19.
[38] See *I.C.J. Yearbook* 1981–82, p. 43.
[39] *Pleadings*, Vol. I, pp. 6, 8.
[40] The Security Council Resolution states that "all questions as to the validity or the effect of a declaration" made in accordance with it are questions for decision by the Court.
[41] 45 *Annuaire*, II. p. 298.
[42] *The Law and Practice of the International Court* (1965), Vol. I, p. 291.

(iii) JURISDICTION IN CONTENTIOUS LITIGATION

See Article 36–37, Statute of the International Court of Justice.[43]

(a) *Jurisdiction under Article* 36(1)

ROSENNE, THE LAW AND PRACTICE OF THE INTERNATIONAL COURT

1965, Vol. I, pp. 333–334. Footnotes omitted

In practice, two generic types of agreement for referring a matter to the Court can be discerned. The classic method by which the parties refer a case to the Court is by a *special agreement* (*compromis*). This is an agreement whereby two or more States agree to refer a particular and defined matter to the Court for a decision. The distinguishing feature of the special agreement as a title of jurisdiction is that jurisdiction is conferred and the Court is seised of the defined issues of the concrete case by the mere notification to the Court of the agreement. Only if an agreement has that double effect can it be regarded as a true special agreement, as that expression is used in the Statute and Rules of Court, so as to lead to the application of the special procedure, reminiscent of the procedure of classical international arbitration, which those texts specify. During the period of the Permanent Court, eleven cases[44] were instituted by special agreement. Since 1947, the *Minquiers and Ecrehos* and *Frontier Land Cases* were instituted in this way; and in the *Corfu Channel Case* the subsequent special agreement replaced the Court's prorogated jurisdiction.

The more usual method of conferring jurisdiction under this head is by a compromissory clause in a multilateral or bilateral treaty.[45] The treaty may be one providing for the reference of a given dispute to the Court, a general treaty of peaceful settlement of disputes, or a treaty regulating some other topic and containing a compromissory clause. The effect of such a provision is to establish the jurisdiction of the Court, as between the parties, to the extent specified in the compromissory clause. This device also had its origin in arbitration, but the permanence of the International Court since 1922 has enabled it to make great headway, and there are now hundreds of sets of jurisdictional obligations of this character—bilateral and multilateral—in force between States.

CORFU CHANNEL CASE (PRELIMINARY OBJECTION)[46]

U.K. *v.* Albania

I.C.J. Reports 1948, p. 15

On May 22, 1947, the United Kingdom brought a claim against Albania before the Court by unilateral application in accordance with Article 40(1)[47] of the Statute and

---

[43] See Appendix I, below.
[44] *Ed.* There have since been another three.
[45] *Ed.* See, *e.g.* the *US Diplomatic and Consular Staff in Tehran Case*, above, p. 276. On the current status of the 1928 General Act of Arbitration, see Merrills (1980) 39 C.L.J. 137.
[46] See Waldock, 2 I.L.Q. 377 (1948).   [47] See Appendix I, below.

Article 35(2)[48] of the Rules of the Court. The United Kingdom argued that the Court had jurisdiction "under Article 36(1) of its Statute as being a matter, which is one specially provided for in the Charter of the United Nations, on the grounds: (a) that the Security Council of the United Nations, at the conclusion of proceedings in which it dealt with the dispute under Article 36 of the Charter, by a Resolution, decided to recommend both the Government of the United Kingdom and the Albanian Government to refer the present dispute to the International Court of Justice; (b) that the Albanian Government accepted the invitation of the Security Council under Article 32 of the Charter to participate in the discussion of the dispute and accepted the condition laid down by the Security Council, when conveying the invitation, that Albania accepts in the present case all the obligations which a Member of the United Nations would have to assume in a similar case; (c) that Article 25 of the Charter provides that the Members of the United Nations agree to accept and carry out the decisions of the Security Council in accordance with the present Charter."[49] Albania was informed of the application by the Court Registry and responded by a letter of July 2, 1947, the relevant terms of which are indicated in the following extract from the Court's Judgment. Later, when steps had been taken for the hearing of the case by the Court, Albania filed a document raising a preliminary objection to the jurisdiction of the Court.

Judgment of the Court

In support of its application, the Government of the United Kingdom invoked certain provisions of the Charter of the United Nations and of the Statute of the Court to establish the existence of a case of compulsory jurisdiction. The Court does not consider that it needs to express an opinion on this point, since, as will be pointed out, the letter of July 2, 1947, addressed by the Albanian Government to the Court, constitutes a voluntary acceptance of its jurisdiction.

The letter of July 2, 1947 . . . removes all difficulties concerning the question of the admissibility of the Application and the question of the jurisdiction of the Court.

With respect to the first point, the Albanian Government, while declaring on the one hand that it "would be within its rights in holding that the Government of the United Kingdom was not entitled to bring the case before the International Court by unilateral application, without first concluding a special agreement with the Albanian Government," states on the other hand, that "it is prepared notwithstanding this irregularity in the action taken by the Government of the United Kingdom, to appear before the Court." This language used by the Albanian Government cannot be understood otherwise than as a waiver of the right subsequently to raise an objection directed against the admissibility of the Application founded on the alleged procedural irregularity of that instrument.

The letter of July 2, 1947, is no less decisive as regards the question of the Court's jurisdiction. Not only does the Albanian Government, which had

---

[48] Art. 35(2): "When a case is brought before the Court by means of an application, the application must, as laid down in Art. 40, para. 1, of the Statute, indicate the party making it, the party against whom the claim is brought and the subject of the dispute. It must also, as far as possible, specify the provision on which the applicant founds the jurisdiction of the Court, state the precise nature of the claim and give a succinct statement of the facts and grounds on which the claim is based, these facts and grounds being developed in the Memorial, to which the evidence will be annexed."

[49] I.C.J.Rep. 1948, p. 17.

already certain obligations towards the Security Council by its telegram of January 24, 1947,[50] declare in that letter that it "fully accepts the recommendation of the Security Council" to the effect that the dispute should be referred to the Court in accordance with the provisions of the Court's Statute, but, after stating that it is "profoundly convinced of the justice of its case," it accepts in precise terms "the jurisdiction of the Court for this case." The letter of July 2, therefore, in the opinion of the Court, constitutes a voluntary and indisputable acceptance of the Court's jurisdiction.

While the consent of the parties confers jurisdiction on the Court, neither the Statute nor the Rules require that this consent should be expressed in any particular form.

The Albanian contention that the Application cannot be entertained because it has been filed contrary to the provisions of Article 40, paragraph 1, and of Article 36, paragraph 1, of the Court's Statute, is essentially founded on the assumption that the institution of proceedings by application is only possible where compulsory jurisdiction exists and that, where it does not, proceedings can only be instituted by special agreement.

This is a mere assertion which is not justified by either of the texts cited. Article 32, paragraph 2, of the Rules[51] does not require the Applicant, as an absolute necessity, but only "as far as possible," to specify in the application the provision on which he founds the jurisdiction of the Court. It clearly implies, both by its actual terms and by the reasons underlying it, that the institution of proceedings by application is not exclusively reserved for the domain of compulsory jurisdiction.

In submitting the case by means of an Application, the Government of the United Kingdom gave the Albanian Government the opportunity of accepting the jurisdiction of the Court. This acceptance was given in the Albanian Government's letter of July 2, 1947.

Besides, separate action of this kind was in keeping with the respective positions of the parties in proceedings where there is in fact a claimant, the United Kingdom, and a defendant, Albania. . . .

For these reasons . . . the Court, by 15 votes against 1,[52] rejects the Preliminary Objection submitted by the Albanian Government.

SEPARATE OPINION BY JUDGES BASDEVANT, ALVAREZ, WINIARSKI, ZORIČIĆ, DE VISSCHER, BADAWI AND KRYLOV. Whilst concurring in the judgment of the Court, we feel obliged to state that we should have wished the Court to have passed upon the merits of the claim of the Government of the United Kingdom to treat the present case as one falling within the compulsory jurisidiction of the Court . . . Under the regime of the Charter, the rule holds good that the jurisidiction of the International Court of Justice, as of the Permanent Court of International Justice before it, depends on the consent of the States parties to a dispute. But Article 36 of the Charter has made it possible for the Security Council to recommend the parties to refer their dispute to the

---

[50] *Ed.* It was in this telegram that Albania accepted the invitation of the Security Council under Article 32 of the Charter to participate in its discussions of the dispute.

[51] *Ed.* Now Rules of Court, Art. 35(2).

[52] The judges in the majority were President Guerrero; Vice-President Basdevant; Judges Alvarez, Fabela, Hackworth, Winiarski, Zoričić, de Visscher, Sir Arnold McNair, Klaestad, Badawi Pasha, Krylov, Read, Hsu Mo and Asevedo. Judge ad hoc Daxner dissented.

International Court of Justice in accordance with the provisions of the Court's Statute. The Security Council, for the first time, availed itself of this power on April 9, 1947. . . .

The arguments presented on behalf of the United Kingdom to establish that this was a new case of compulsory jurisdiction—which arguments the Agent and Counsel for the Albanian Government sought to refute—have not convinced us. In particular, having regard (1) to the normal meaning of the word recommendation, a meaning which this word has retained in diplomatic language, as is borne out by the practice of the Pan-American Conference, of the League of Nations, of the International Labour Organization, etc. (2) to the general structure of the Charter and of the Statute which founds the jurisdiction of the Court on the consent of States, and (3) to the terms used in Article 36, paragraph 3, of the Charter and to its object which is to remind the Security Council that legal disputes should normally be decided by judicial methods, it appears impossible to us to accept an interpretation according to which this Article, without explicitly saying so, has introduced more or less surreptitiously, a new case of compulsory jurisdiction. . . .

Notes

1. Just prior to the Court's ruling, the parties announced that they had reached agreement to submit the case to the Court by special agreement.

2. The doctrine relied upon by the Court to found its jurisdiction in this case is that of *forum prorogatum*. In the *Mavrommatis Case* (*Merits*), brought by Greece against the United Kingdom, the United Kingdom replied in its written argument to an issue raised by Greece that was not within the jurisdiction of the Court under the mandate for Palestine under which the case had been brought. The Court decided that it had jurisdiction in respect of the issue "in consequence of an agreement between the parties resulting from the written proceedings . . . "[53] In the *Rights of Minorities in Polish Upper Silesia Case*, in which Poland had first raised objections to jurisdiction in its second written pleadings (its rejoinder) after having argued the case on its merits in its first written pleadings (its counter-memorial), the Court said: "And there seems to be no doubt that the consent of a State to the submission of a dispute to the Court may not only result from an express declaration, but may also be inferred from acts conclusively establishing it. It seems hard to deny that the submission of arguments on the merits, without making reservations in regard to the question of jurisdiction, must be regarded as an unequivocal indication of the desire of a State to obtain a decision on the merits of a suit. . . . If, in a special case, the Respondent has, by an express declaration, indicated his desire to obtain a decision on the merits and his intention to abstain from raising the question of jurisdiction, it seems clear that he cannot, later on in the proceedings, go back upon that declaration."[54]

In the 1930s, in the course of revision of the Rules of Court by the Judges of the Permanent Court of International Justice, a proposal put forward by some of the Judges requiring an applicant state to indicate the basis for the Court's jurisdiction in its application was not adopted. Opposing the proposal, Judge Shücking is reported as saying: "It was not desirable to insist on the application containing a reference to the treaty clause upon which it was based. The institution of the *forum prorogatum* had been introduced into the procedure by the Court's practice, in particular in Judgment No. 12 [Series A, No. 15] and it was in the interests of the good administration of justice. If they now made it a necessary condition for the admissibility of an application that it

[53] P.C.I.J.Rep., Series A, No. 5, p. 27 (1925).
[54] *Ibid.* No. 15, pp. 24–25 (1928). See also the *Chorzow Factory Case* (*Indemnity*) (*Merits*), *ibid.*, No. 17, p. 37 (1928).

must specify the treaty clause, and if, in a given case, the applicant was unable to specify it, because no such clause existed, the Court would be compelled to reject the application *a limine*. But that would amount to abolishing the institution of the *forum prorogatum*. . . . "[55] The revised text of the Rules of Court requires that the basis for the Court's jurisdiction should be specified "as far as possible."[56]

3. In the *Anglo-Iranian Oil Co. Case*, brought by the United Kingdom against Iran, the United Kingdom, having first based the Court's jurisdiction on the Iranian declaration under Article 36(2), continued: "Alternatively, whether or not the Court has the right to exercise jurisdiction in this case by virtue of the . . . declaration of the Imperial Government of Persia [under Article 36(2) of the Statute], the Government of the United Kingdom expect that Iran, as a Member of the United Nations, one of the purposes of which is 'to bring about by peaceful means and in conformity with the principles of justice and international law, adjustment or settlement of international disputes or situations which might lead to a breach of the peace' . . . and mindful of the principle that 'legal disputes should as a general rule be referred . . . to the . . . Court . . .' will agree to appear before the Court voluntarily in order to hear and answer on their merits the arguments of the Government of the United Kingdom. (*Forum prorogatum*; *Corfu Channel Case* (Preliminary Objection) . . .)"[57] Iran declined to accept this invitation and objected to the Court's jurisdiction generally. Despite this, the Court, before giving judgment on Iran's objections to its jurisdiction, made an order at the request of the United Kingdom for interim measures of protection. When the Court later sustained Iran's objections to its jurisdiction, it stated that the order "ceases to be operative upon the delivery of this judgment" and "that the provisional measures lapse at the same time."[58]

4. In the *Monetary Gold Case,* the respondent states—France, the United Kingdom and the United States—indicated their willingness in the Washington Statement of April 25, 1951, to be brought before the Court by either Albania or Italy. In response, Italy filed an Application with the Court but then challenged the Court's jurisdiction. Rejecting Italy's objections, the Court stated, *inter alia*: "The Governmmments of France, the United Kingdom and the United States of America, and the Government of Italy, by their separate and successive acts—the adoption of the Washington Statement, in the one case, and in the other case, the deposit on May 19, 1953, of the Declaration of acceptance of the jurisdiction of the Court and the filing of the Application—have referred a case to the Court within the meaning of Article 36(1) of its Statute. They have thus conferred jurisdiction on the Court to deal with the questions submitted in the Application of the Italian Government."[59]

5. Applications relying on *forum prorogatum* have since been made in the *Treatment in Hungary of Aircraft of the U.S.A. Cases*[60] (applications by the United States against Hungary and the U.S.S.R. respectively), in three *Aerial Incident Cases*[61] (the United States against Czechoslovakia and the U.S.S.R. respectively) and the *Antarctica Cases*[62] (the United Kingdom v. Argentina and Chile respectively). In all of these cases, no basis for jurisdiction other than *forum prorogatum* was available. In each case the respondent state took no positive action and eventually the case was struck off the Court's list.

6. The wording "all matters specially provided for in the Charter of the United Nations" in Article 36(1) would seem to have no meaning; it was included at a time

[55] P.C.I.J.Rep., Series D, 2, Add. 3, p. 69.
[56] Now Rules of the Court of the I.C.J., Art. 35(2), above, p. 714.
[57] *I.C.J. Pleadings, Anglo-Iranian Oil Co. Case*, p. 17.
[58] I.C.J.Rep. 1952, p. 114.
[59] *Ibid.* 1954, p. 19, at p. 31. The Court declined to hear the case because it lacked jurisdiction on another ground (Albania was not a party to the proceedings).
[60] *Ibid.* pp. 99, 103.
[61] *Ibid.* 1956, pp. 6, 9; *ibid.* 1959, p. 276.
[62] *Ibid.* 1956, pp. 12, 15.

when it was hoped that the Charter would provide for the Court to have compulsory jurisdiction. There is no provision in the Charter as it was finally drafted to which the wording could be taken to refer, apart from Article 36(3) of the Charter, as to which see the Separate Opinion in the *Corfu Channel Case*, above.

(b) *Jurisdiction under Article 36(2)*[63]

UNITED KINGDOM DECLARATION ACCEPTING THE COMPULSORY JURISDICTION OF THE COURT

Misc. No. 4 (1969), Cmnd. 3872

I have the honour, by direction of Her Majesty's Principal Secretary of State for Foreign and Commonwealth Affairs, to declare on behalf of the Government of the United Kingdom of Great Britain and Northern Ireland that they accept as compulsory *ipso facto* and without special convention, on condition of reciprocity, the jurisdiction of the International Court of Justice, in conformity with paragraph 2 of Article 36 of the Statute of the Court, until such time as notice may be given to terminate the acceptance, over all disputes arising after the 24th of October, 1945, with regard to situations or facts subsequent to the same date, other than:

(i) any dispute which the United Kingdom
   (a) has agreed with the other Party or Parties thereto to settle by some other method of peaceful settlement; or
   (b) has already submitted to arbitration by agreement with any States which had not at the time of submission accepted the compulsory jurisdiction of the International Court of Justice:

(ii) disputes with the Government of any other country which is a member of the Commonwealth with regard to situations or facts existing before the 1st of January, 1969:

(iii) disputes in respect of which any other Party to the dispute has accepted the compulsory jurisdiction of the International Court of Justice only in relation to or for the purposes of the dispute; or where the acceptance of the Court's compulsory jurisdiction on behalf of any other Party to the dispute was deposited or ratified less than twelve months prior to the filing of the application bringing the dispute before the Court.

. . . The Government of the United Kingdom also reserve the right at any time, by means of a notification addressed to the Secretary-General of the United Nations, and with effect as from the moment of such notification, either to add to, amend or withdraw any of the foregoing reservations, or any that may hereafter be added. . . ."

Notes

1. The current United Kingdom Declaration, which came into force on January 1, 1969, differs in several respects form the 1963 Declaration[64] which it replaces. It applies to disputes arising after October 24, 1945, whereas the 1963 Declaration related to

---

[63] See Briggs, 93 *Hague Recueil* 224 (1958–I); Merrills (1979) 50 B.Y.I.L. 87; Waldock (1955–56) 32 B.Y.I.L. 244.
[64] Cmnd. 2248.

disputes arising after February 5, 1930. The Commonwealth reservation in the 1963 Declaration read: "disputes with the Government of any country which is a Member of the British Commonwealth of Nations, all of which disputes shall be settled in such manner as the Parties have agreed or shall agree," The 1969 Declaration omits the following reservations found in the 1963 Declaration: "disputes with regard to questions which by international law fall exclusively within the jurisdiction of the United Kingdom"; "disputes arising out of events occurring between September 3, 1939, and September 2, 1945"; and " . . . disputes arising out of, or having reference to, any hostilities, war, state of war, or belligerent or military occupation in which the Government of the United Kingdom are or have been involved."

2. Reservations (i)–(iii) in the United Kingdom declaration are not reservations expressly permitted by Article 36. In practice, however, it has been accepted that states may attach reservations to their declarations other than those referred to in Article 36(3).

3. "On condition of reciprocity" in the United Kingdom declaration refers to the *principle of reciprocity* which follows from the wording "in relation to any other state accepting the same obligation" in Article 36(2). According to this principle, a state accepts the Court's jurisdiction *vis-à-vis* any other state only in so far as that state has accepted it also. If state A makes a declaration subject to reservation X and state B makes one subject to reservation Y, the Court has jurisdiction to hear disputes between these two states only in so far as they are not covered by reservations X *or* Y. ". . . jurisdiction is conferred on the Court only to the extent to which the two declarations coincide in conferring it."[65] See further on the principle of reciprocity, the extracts from the three cases immediately below these notes.[66] The "reciprocity" provision in Article 36(3) is quite distinct and was introduced to cover the case where a state might only want to be bound by the Court's jurisdiction if a worthwhile number of other states were bound or if a state whose acceptance was particularly important to it was bound.

4. Note that reservation (iii) in the British declaration applies to the Egyptian declaration, by which the jurisdiction of the Court is accepted solely in connection with certain disputes concerning the Suez Canal.[67] Note also that the same reservation would have prevented Portugal bringing a case against the United Kingdom in the way that it brought the *Right of Passage Case*[68] against India. Portugal made its declaration, which was valid for one year and then became terminable upon notice (which has not yet been given) on December 19, 1955. It brought its application on December 22, 1955.

5. *Juridical character of a declaration.* In the *Anglo-Iranian Oil Co. Case (Jurisdiction)*, the Court stated:

> The Government of the United Kingdom has further argued that the Declaration would contain some superfluous words if it is interpreted as contended by Iran. It asserts that a legal text should be interpreted in such a way that a reason and a meaning can be attributed to every word in the text. It may be said that this principle should in general be applied when interpreting the text of a treaty. But the text of the Iranian Declaration is not a treaty text resulting from negotiations between two or more States. It is the result of unilateral drafting by the Government of Iran, which appears to have shown a particular degree of caution when drafting the text of the Declaration. It appears to have inserted, *ex abundanti cautela*, words which, strictly speaking, may seem to have been superfluous.[69]

---

[65] *Anglo-Iranian Oil Co. Case*, I.C.J.Rep. 1952, p. 93, at p. 103.
[66] The principle was also invoked successfully as it applied under the 1928 General Act in the *Aegean Sea Continental Shelf Case*, I.C.J.Rep. 1978, at p. 37. Turkey was allowed to rely upon a Greek reservation to the Act to exclude the Court's jurisdiction.
[67] See above, p. 203.
[68] See below, p. 721.
[69] I.C.J.Rep. 1952, at p. 105.

Dissenting from the Court's Judgment, Judge Read stated:

> I am unable to accept the contention that the principles of international law which govern the interpretation of treaties cannot be applied to the Persian Declaration, because it is unilateral. Admittedly it was drafted unilaterally. On the other hand, it was related, in express terms, to Article 36 of the Statute, and to the declarations of other States which had already deposited, or which might in the future deposit reciprocal declarations. It was intended to establish legal relationships with such States, consensual in their character, within the régime established by the provisions of Article 36.[70]

In the *Fisheries Jurisdiction Cases*[71] the Court referred to optional clause declarations as "treaty provisions."

In 1959 the International Law Commission, when considering what "agreements" were within the scope of its Draft Articles on the Law of Treaties, treated Declarations under the "Optional Clause"[72] as being within them and stated:

> any two declarations under the "Optional Clause" . . . in so far as they cover the same disputes or class of disputes, may be regarded as constituting jointly an agreement to have recourse to the Court in regard to the disputes specified, or if a dispute of that class arises between the parties.[73]

The final text of the I.L.C.'s commentary on its Draft Articles omits this passage, although it is not clear that this is because the opinion previously expressed in the passage quoted had been revised.

6. On December 31, 1981, there were 47 declarations under the "Optional Clause" that were in force.[74] France terminated its declaration in 1974 as a result of the *Nuclear Tests Cases*.[75] Twenty-one declarations were terminable upon notice[76]; three were terminable upon six months' notice; two were terminable upon one year's notice; seven were valid for five-year periods which were automatically renewed in the absence of notice to the contrary before their expiry; and one was valid for a single period of 10 years. Thirteen contained no time limit (and no provision for notice). If a declaration has no time limit, can it be terminated?[77] Note that in 1938, Paraguay, after it had withdrawn from the League of Nations because of action by the League concerning a dispute between Paraguay and Bolivia which the latter was threatening to bring before the Permanent Court of International Justice, denounced its declaration under Article 36(2) which contained no provision for termination. Six states, including Bolivia, questioned the legality of this action. The Court Registry continued to list the declaration with other declarations until the mid-1950s when it was omitted. Is a Declaration terminable upon notice one that is made for a "certain time" (Statute, Art. 36(3))?[78]

---

[70] *Ibid* p. 142.
[71] I.C.J.Rep. 1973 at p. 16.
[72] *i.e.* Art. 36(2).   [73] Y.B.I.L.C. 1959, II, p. 94, n. 28.
[74] They were by Australia, Austria, Barbados, Belgium, Botswana, Canada, Colombia, Costa Rica, Democratic Kampuchea, Denmark, Dominican Republic, Egypt, El Salvador, Finland, Gambia, Haiti, Honduras, India, Israel, Japan, Kenya, Liberia, Liechtenstein, Luxembourg, Malawi, Malta, Mauritius, Mexico, Netherlands, New Zealand, Nicaragua, Nigeria, Norway, Pakistan, Panama, the Philippines, Portugal, Somalia, Sudan, Swaziland, Sweden, Switzerland, Togo, Uganda, U.K., U.S. and Uruguay. Is there any discernible pattern of states? Note that none of the Soviet bloc are parties, consistent with their general opposition to compulsory settlement procedures outside of the control of sovereign states.
[75] As to which see above, p. 372.
[76] Some of these had originally been valid for a certain number of years (usually 5) after which they were stated to be terminable upon notice.
[77] The Court raised the question in the *Fisheries Jurisdiction Cases*, I.C.J.Rep. 1973, at pp. 15–16, but left it unanswered.
[78] See the *Right of Passage Cases*, below, p. 721.

7. The value for the state making it of a declaration terminable upon notice was demonstrated in 1954 when Australia withdrew its declaration of 1940, which had been valid for five years and then became terminable upon notice, and made a new one adding a reservation in respect of disputes concerning pearl fishing off the Australian coast. At the time it seemed likely that Japan might bring a claim against Australia with this subject-matter before the Court under the "Optional Clause." Note also the reservation recently added by Canada to its declaration (which is terminable upon notice). When giving notice of its 1970 legislation on arctic waters, which controversially extended its jurisdiction to control pollution in those waters and which brought an immediate protest from the United States, it terminated its declaration and made a new one with a new reservation excluding disputes about the legislation. Canada explained that its "new reservation . . . does not in any way reflect lack of confidence in the court but takes into account the limitations within which the court must operate and the deficiencies of the law which it must interpret and apply."[79]

8. The fact that a case comes within a reservation to an "optional clause" declaration so that the Court lacks jurisdiction under Article 36(2) does not affect the possibility of the Court having jurisdiction on some other basis (e.g. a jurisdiction clause in a treaty between the parties): *Appeal Relating to the Jurisdiction of the I.C.A.O. Council Case*.[80]

9. One measure of the utility of the "Optional Clause" as a basis for the Court's jurisdiction is the fact that the last case in which the Court found it had jurisdiction because of the "Clause"—the *Temple Case*[81]—was decided as long ago as 1962.

10. The Ugandan "Optional Clause" declaration (made in 1963) reads:

I hereby declare on behalf of the Government of Uganda that Uganda recognises as compulsory *ipso facto* and without special agreement, in relation to any other State accepting the same obligation, and on condition of reciprocity, the jurisdiction of the International Court of Justice in conformity with paragraph 2 of Article 36 of the Statute of the Court.[82]

There are no reservations. Would the Court have had jurisdiction to decide a case brought by the United Kingdom under the Optional Clause in respect of the expulsion of British nationals from Uganda in 1972, as to which, see above, p. 406?

RIGHT OF PASSAGE OVER INDIAN TERRITORY CASE (PRELIMINARY OBJECTIONS)

Portugal *v.* India

I.C.J. Reports 1957, p. 125

For the facts of the case, see p. 198, above.

Judgment of the Court

First Preliminary Objection . . .
The Third Condition of the Declaration of Portugal provides as follows:

(3) The Portuguese Government reserves the right to exclude from the scope of the present declaration, at any time during its validity, any given

---

[79] 9 I.L.M. 612 (1970). See MacDonald, 8 C.Y.I.L. 3 (1970).
[80] I.C.J.Rep. 1972, p. 46, at p. 53.
[81] I.C.J.Rep. 1961, p. 17. Judgment on preliminary objections.
[82] *Multilateral Treaties in respect of which the Secretary-General Performs Depository Functions*, 1982, U.N.Doc. ST/LEG/SER.E/1, p. 23.

category or categories of disputes, by notifying the Secretary-General of the United Nations and with effect from the moment of such notification.

In the first instance, the Government of India maintains that that Condition gives Portugal the right, by making at any time a notification to that effect, to withdraw from the jurisdiction of the Court a dispute which has been submitted to it prior to such a notification. . . .

[In the opinion of the Court] the words "with effect from the moment of such notification" cannot be construed as meaning that such a notification would have retroactive effect so as to cover cases already pending before the Court. Construed in their ordinary sense, these words mean simply that a notification under the Third Condition applies only to disputes brought before the Court after the date of the notification. Such an interpretation leads to the conclusion that no retroactive effect can properly be imputed to notifications made under the Third Condition. It is a rule of law generally accepted, as well as one acted upon in the past by the Court, that, once the Court has been validly seised of a dispute, unilateral action by the respondent State in terminating its Declaration, in whole or in part, cannot divest the Court of jurisdiction. In the *Nottebohm Case* the Court gave expression to that principle in the following words:

> An extrinsic fact such as the subsequent lapse of the Declaration, by reason of the expiry of the period or by denunciation, cannot deprive the Court of the jurisdiction already established. (I.C.J.Rep. 1953, p. 123.)[83]

That statement by the Court must be deemed to apply both to total denunciation, and to partial denunciation as contemplated in the Third Portuguese Condition. It is a rule of interpretation that a text emanating from a Government must, in principle, be interpreted as producing and as intended to produce effects in accordance with existing law and not in violation of it.

The second reason, contended for by the Government of India . . . is that it has introduced into the Declaration a degree of uncertainty as to reciprocal rights and obligations which deprives the acceptance of the compulsory jurisdiction of the court of all practical value. In particular, it was contended that, in consequence of the Third Condition, the other Signatories are in a continuous state of uncertainty as to their reciprocal rights and obligations which may change from day to day. . . .

As Declarations, and their alterations, made under Article 36 must be deposited with the Secretary-General, it follows that, when a case is submitted to the Court, it is always possible to ascertain what are, at that moment, the reciprocal obligations of the Parties in accordance with their respective Declarations. Under the existing system, Governments can rely upon being informed of any changes in the Declarations in the same manner as they are informed of total denunciations of the Declarations. It is true that during the interval between the date of a notification to the Secretary-General and its receipt by the Parties to the Statute, there may exist some element of uncertainty. However, such uncertainty is inherent in the operation of the system of the Optional

---

[83] In the *Nottebohm Case*, the declaration of the respondent Government, Guatemala, expired a month or so after the applicant Government, Liechtenstein, had seised the Court. Seisin of the Court is the formal institution of proceedings before it (by, *e.g.* a unilateral application under the optional clause).

Clause and does not affect the validity of the Third Condition contained in the Portuguese Declaration.

It must also be noted that, with regard to any degree of uncertainty resulting from the right of Portugal to avail itself at any time of its Third Condition of Acceptance, the position is substantially the same as that created by the right claimed by many Signatories of the Optional Clause, including India, to terminate their Declarations of Acceptance by simple notification without any obligatory period of notice. India did so on January 7th, 1956, when it notified the Secretary-General of the denunciation of its previous Declaration of Acceptance, for which it simultaneously substituted a new Declaration incorporating reservations which were absent from its previous Declaration. By substituting, on January 7th, 1956, a new Declaration for its earlier Declaration, India achieved, in substance, the object of Portugal's Third Condition. . . .

Finally, as the third reason for the invalidity of the Third Condition, it has been contended that that Condition offends against the basic principle of reciprocity underlying the Optional Clause inasmuch as it claims for Portugal a right which in effect is denied to other Signatories who have made a Declaration without appending any such condition. The Court is unable to accept that contention. It is clear that any reservation notified by Portugal in pursuance of its Third Condition becomes automatically operative against it in relation to other Signatories of the Optional Clause. If the position of the Parties as regards the exercise of their rights is in any way affected by the unavoidable interval between the receipt by the Secretary-General of the appropriate notification and its receipt by the other Signatories, that delay operates equally in favour of or against all Signatories and is a consequence of the system established by the Optional Clause.

Neither can the Court accept the view that the Third Condition is inconsistent with the principle of reciprocity inasmuch as it renders inoperative that part of paragraph 2 of Article 36, which refers to Declarations of Acceptance of the Optional Clause in relation to States accepting the "same obligation." It is not necessary that the "same obligation" should be irrevocably defined at the time of the deposit of the Declaration of Acceptance for the entire period of its duration. That expression means no more than that, as between States adhering to the Optional Clause, each and all of them are bound by such identical obligations as may exist at any time during which the Acceptance is mutually binding.

Second Preliminary Objection . . .

The Second Preliminary Objection of the Government of India is based on the allegation that—as the Portuguese Application of December 22nd, 1955, was filed before the lapse of such brief period as in the normal course of events would have enabled the Secretary-General of the United Nations, in compliance with Article 36, paragraph 4, of the Statute of the Court, to transmit copies of the Portuguese Declaration of Acceptance of December 19th, 1955, to the other Parties to the Statute—the filing of the Application violated the equality, mutuality and reciprocity to which India was entitled under the Optional Clause and under the express condition of reciprocity contained in its Declaration of February 28, 1940; that, in consequence the conditions necessary to entitle the Government of Portugal to invoke the Optional Clause against

India did not exist when that Application was filed; and that, as a result, the Court is without jurisdiction to entertain the Application.

The principle of reciprocity forms part of the system of the Optional Clause by virtue of the express terms both of Article 36 of the Statute and of most Declarations of Acceptance, including that of India. . . .

[In its Second Preliminary Objection] the Government of India has contended that, in filing its Application on December 22nd, 1955, the Government of Portugal did not act in conformity with the provisions of the Statute. The Court is unable to accept that contention. The Court considers that, by the deposit of its Declaration of Acceptance with the Secretary-General, the accepting State became a Party to the system of the Optional Clause in relation to the other declarant States, with all the rights and obligations deriving from Article 36. The contractual relation between the Parties and the compulsory jurisdiction of the Court resulting therefrom are established, "*ipso facto* and without special agreement*," by the fact of the making of the Declaration. Accordingly, every State which makes a Declaration of Acceptance must be deemed to take into account the possibility that, under the Statute, it may at any time find itself subjected to the obligations of the Optional Clause in relation to a new Signatory as the result of the deposit by that Signatory of a Declaration of Acceptance. A State accepting the jurisdiction of the Court must expect that an Application may be filed against it before the Court by a new declarant State on the same day on which that State deposits with the Secretary-General its Declaration of Acceptance. For it is on that very day that the consensual bond, which is the basis of the Optional Clause, comes into being between the States concerned. When India made its Declaration of Acceptance of February 28, 1940, it stated that it accepted the jurisdiction of the Court for a specified period "from to-day's date."

It has been contended by the Government of India that as Article 36 requires not only the deposit of the Declaration of Acceptance with the Secretary-General but also the transmission by the Secretary-General of a copy of the Declaration to the Parties to the Statute, the Declaration of Acceptance does not become effective until the latter obligation has been discharged. However, it is only the first of these requirements that concerns the State making the Declaration. The latter is not concerned with the duty of the Secretary-General or the manner of its fulfilment. The legal effect of a Declaration does not depend upon subsequent action or inaction of the Secretary-General. Moreover, unlike some other instruments, Article 36 provides for no additional requirement, for instance, that the information transmitted by the Secretary-General must reach the Parties to the Statute, or that some period must elapse subsequent to the deposit of the Declaration before it can become effective. Any such requirement would introduce an element of uncertainty into the operation of the Optional Clause system. The Court cannot read into the Optional Clause any requirement of that nature.

. . . The Court rejected the First and Second Preliminary Objections by 15 votes to 3. . . .[84]

---

[84] Judge ad hoc Chagla dissented with regard to both Objections. Vice-President Badawi dissented on the Second Objection. It is not clear precisely how the rest of the Court voted on these two Objections.

Note

The United Kingdom in its current declaration, above, p. 718, reserves the right to add new reservations to it with effect upon notification. Is this permissible?[85]

INTERHANDEL CASE

Switzerland *v.* U.S.A.

I.C.J. Reports 1959, p. 6

Switzerland brought this claim against the United States for the restitution of the assets of Interhandel, a Swiss company, in the United States. The property had been taken by the United States in 1942 on the ground that Interhandel was German, and so enemy, controlled. Switzerland disputed this and, after several years of negotiation, etc., in 1948 asked the United States to return Interhandel's property. On July 26, 1948, the United States refused to do so. After unsuccessful court proceedings in the United States, in 1957 Switzerland instituted proceedings under the Optional Clause.

Judgment of the Court

According to [the United States Second Preliminary Objection to the Court's jurisdiction] . . . the present dispute, even if it is subsequent to the date of the Declaration of the United States, arose before July 28th, 1948, the date of the entry into force of the Swiss Declaration. The argument set out in the Preliminary Objections is as follows:

> The United States Declaration, which was effective August 26th, 1946, contained the clause limiting the Court's jurisdiction to disputes "hereafter arising," while no such qualifying clause is contained in the Swiss Declaration which was effective July 28th, 1948. But the reciprocity principle . . . requires that as between the United States and Switzerland the Court's jurisdiction be limited to disputes arising after July 28th, 1948. . . . Otherwise, retroactive effect would be given to the compulsory jurisdiction of the Court.

In particular, it was contended with regard to disputes arising after August 26th, 1946, but before July 28th, 1948, that "Switzerland, as a Respondent, could have invoked the principle of reciprocity and claimed that, in the same way as the United States is not bound to accept the Court's jurisdiction with respect to disputes arising before its acceptance, Switzerland, too, could not be required to accept the Court's jurisdiction in relation to disputes arising before its acceptance."

Reciprocity in the case of Declarations accepting the compulsory jurisdiction of the Court enables a Party to invoke a reservation to that acceptance which it has not expressed in its own Declaration but which the other Party has expressed in its Declaration. For example, Switzerland, which has not expressed in its Declaration any reservation *ratione temporis*, while the United States has accepted the compulsory jurisdiction of the Court only in respect of disputes to August 26th, 1946, might, if in the position of Respondent, invoke by virtue of reciprocity against the United States the American reservation if the United States attempted to refer to the Court a dispute with Switzerland which had

---

[85] See Merrills, *loc. cit.* at p. 718, n. 63 above, p. 96.

arisen before August 26th, 1946. This is the effect of reciprocity in this connection. Reciprocity enables the State which has made the wider acceptance of the jurisdiction of the Court to rely upon the reservations to the acceptance laid down by the other Party. There the effect of reciprocity ends. It cannot justify a State in this instance, the United States in relying upon a restriction which the other Party, Switzerland, has not included in its own Declaration.

The Second Preliminary Objection must therefore be rejected. . . .

Notes

1. A reservation of the sort in issue here is a reservation *ratione temporis*. What if the declaration made by Switzerland had contained a reservation limiting that state's acceptance of the Court's jurisdiction to disputes arising after its declaration came into force on July 28, 1948? Assuming that the dispute in the case arose subsequent to the date of the United States declaration but before July 28, 1948, could the United States then have relied on the principle of reciprocity to better effect than it was able to do on the facts of the case as they actually were?

2. The United States also objected unsuccessfully to jurisdiction on the ground that the dispute had arisen before the United States acceptance of the Court's jurisdiction in 1946 in respect of "disputes arising hereafter." Although the United States had taken Interhandel's assets in 1942 and although the United States and Switzerland had disagreed over the enemy or non-enemy character of Interhandel before 1946, in the Court's opinion the dispute itself only arose when the United States refused Switzerland's request to return Interhandel's assets on July 26, 1948. Applying the United States *ratione temporis* reservation, the Court noted that "the facts and situation which have led to a dispute must not be confused with the dispute itself."[86] The United Kingdom declaration, above, p. 718, applies to disputes arising as of 1945, "with regard to situations or facts subsequent to the same date." Would such a formula have helped the United States in the *Interhandel* case?[87]

3. On the "self-judging" or "automatic" reservation aspect of the *Interhandel* case, see below, p. 730. The Court finally declined jurisdiction in the case because local remedies had not been *fully* exhausted.

NORWEGIAN LOANS CASE[88]

France v. Norway

I.C.J. Reports 1957, p. 9

France brought this claim against Norway under the "Optional Clause" on behalf of French holders of Norwegian bonds. Norway objected to the Court's jurisdiction on several grounds, including that discussed in the following extract from its judgment. Judge Lauterpacht reached the same decision as the Court, but for different reasons.

Judgment of the Court

The Court will at the outset direct its attention to the Preliminary Objections of the Norwegian Government. . . .

It will be recalled that the French Declaration accepting the compulsory jurisdiction of the Court contains the following reservation:

This declaration does not apply to differences relating to matters which are essentially within the national jurisdiction as understood by the Government of the French Republic.

---

[86] I.C.J.Rep. 1959, p. 22.   [87] See Greig, *International Law* (2nd ed., 1976), pp. 657–61.
[88] See Jennings, 7 I.C.L.Q. 349 (1958). On "automatic" reservations, see Crawford (1979) 50 B.Y.I.L. 63.

In the Preliminary Objections filed by the Norwegian Government it is stated:

> The Norwegian Government did not insert any such reservation in its own Declaration. But it has the right to rely upon the restrictions placed by France upon her own undertakings.

> Convinced that the dispute which has been brought before the Court by the Application of July 6th, 1955, is within the domestic jurisdiction, the Norwegian Government considers itself fully entitled to rely on this right. Accordingly, it requests the Court to decline, on grounds that it lacks jurisdiction, the function which the French Government would have it assume.

> . . . in the present case the jurisdiction of the Court depends upon the Declarations made by the Parties in accordance with Article 36, paragraph 2, of the Statute on condition of reciprocity; and that, since two unilateral declarations are involved, such jurisdiction is conferred upon the Court only to the extent to which the Declarations coincide in conferring it. A comparison between the two Declarations shows that the French Declaration accepts the Court's jurisdiction within narrower limits than the Norwegian Declaration; consequently the common will of the Parties, which is the basis of the Court's jurisdiction, exists within these narrower limits indicated by the French reservation. . . .

> In accordance with the condition of reciprocity to which acceptance of the compulsory jurisdiction is made subject in both Declarations and which is provided for in Article 36, paragraph 3, of the Statute, Norway, equally with France, is entitled to except from the compulsory jurisdiction of the Court disputes understood by Norway to be essentially within its national jurisdiction. . . .

> The Court does not consider that it should examine whether the French reservation is consistent with the undertaking of a legal obligation and is compatible with Article 36, paragraph 6, of the Statute which provides. . . .

> The validity of the reservation has not been questioned by the Parties. It is clear that France fully maintains its Declarations, including the reservation, and that Norway relies upon the reservation. . . .

> The Court considers that the Norwegian Government is entitled, by virtue of the condition of reciprocity, to invoke the reservation contained in the French Declaration of March 1st, 1949; that this reservation excludes from the jurisdiction of the Court the dispute which has been referred to it by the Application of the French Government; that consequently the Court is without jurisdiction to entertain the Application. . . .

> For these reasons, the Court, by twelve votes to three,[89] finds that it is without jurisdiction to adjudicate upon the dispute which has been brought before it by the Application of the Government of the French Republic of July 6th, 1955.

---

[89] The judges in the majority were President Hackworth; Vice-President Badawi; Judges Winiarski, Zoričić, Klaestad, Armand-Ugon, Kojevnikov, Sir Muhammad Zafrulla Khan, Sir Hersch Lauterpacht, Moreno Quintana, Córdova and Wellington Koo. Judges Guerrero, Basdevant and Read dissented.

INDIVIDUAL OPINION OF JUDGE LAUTERPACHT. . . . I consider that as the French Declaration of Acceptance excludes from the jurisdiction of the Court, "matters which are essentially within the national jurisdiction as understood by the Government of the French Republic"—it is for the reason of that latter qualification an instrument incapable of producing legal effects before this Court and of establishing its jurisdiction. This is so for the double reason that: (a) it is contrary to the Statute of the Court; (b) the existence of the obligation being dependent upon the determination by the Government accepting the Optional Clause, the Acceptance does not constitute a legal obligation. That Declaration of Acceptance cannot, accordingly, provide a basis for the jurisdiction of the Court. . . .

If that type of reservation is valid, then the Court is not in the position to exercise the power conferred upon it—in fact, the duty imposed upon it—under paragraph 6 of Article 36 of its Statute. . . . The French reservation lays down that if, with regard to that particular question, there is a dispute between the Parties as to whether the Court has jurisprudence according the matter shall be settled by a decision of the French Government. The French reservation is thus not only contrary to one of the most fundamental principles of international— and national—jurisprudence according to which it is within the inherent power of a tribunal to interpret the text establishing its jurisdiction. It is also contrary to a clear specific provision of the Statute of the Court as well as to the general Articles I and 92 of the Statute and of the Charter, respectively, which require the Court to function in accordance with its Statute.

Now what is the result of the fact that a reservation or part of it are contrary to the provisions of the Statute of the Court? The result is that that reservation or that part of it is invalid. Some examples may usefully illustrate that aspect of the question: What would be the position if in accepting—or purporting to accept— the obligations of Article 36 of the Statute, a State were to exclude the operation of paragraph 6 of that Article not only with regard to one reservation but with regard to all reservations or, generally, with regard to any disputed question of the jurisdiction of the Court?

What would be the position if the Declaration were to make it a condition that the oral proceedings of the Court shall be secret; or that its Judgment shall not be binding unless given by unanimity; or that it should contain no reasons; or that no Dissenting Opinion shall be attached; or that Judges of certain nationality or nationalities shall be excluded; or that, contrary to what is said in Article 38 of its Statute, the Court shall apply only treaties and custom in the sense that it shall not be authorized to apply general principles of law as recognized by civilised States and that if it is unable to base its decision on treaty or custom it shall pronounce a *non liquet*? . . .

In accepting the jurisdiction of the Court Governments are free to limit its jurisdiction in a drastic manner. As a result there may be little left in the Acceptance which is subject to the jurisdiction of the Court. This the Governments, as trustees of the interests entrusted to them, are fully entitled to do. Their right to append reservations which are not inconsistent with the Statute is no longer in question. But the question whether that little that is left is or is not subject to the jurisdiction of the Court must be determined by the Court itself. . . .

I arrive at the same conclusion on the second—and different—ground, namely, that having regard to the formulation of the reservation of national jurisdiction on the part of the French Government the Acceptance embodying the "automatic reservation" is invalid as lacking in an essential condition of validity of a legal instrument. . . . An instrument in which a party is entitled to determine the existence of its obligation is not a valid and enforceable legal instrument of which a court of law can take cognizance. It is not a legal instrument. It is a declaration of a political principle and purpose. . . .

If the clause of the Acceptance reserving to the declaring Government the right of unilateral determination is invalid, then there are only two alternatives open to the Court: it may either treat as invalid that particular part of the reservation or it may consider the entire Acceptance to be tainted with invalidity. (There is a third possibility—which has only to be mentioned in order to be dismissed—namely, that the clause in question invalidates not the Acceptance as a whole but the particular reservation. This would mean that the entire reservation of matters of national jurisdiction would be treated as invalid while the Declaration of Acceptance as such would be treated as fully in force).

International practice on the subject is not sufficiently abundant to permit a confident attempt at generalization and some help may justifiably be sought in applicable general principles of law as developed in municipal law. That general principle of law is that it is legitimate—and perhaps obligatory—to sever an invalid condition from the rest of the [contract or other legal] instrument and to treat the latter as valid provided that having regard to the intention of the parties and the nature of the instrument the condition in question does not constitute an essential part of the instrument. *Utile non debet per inutile vitiari*. The same applies also to provisions and reservations relating to the jurisdiction of the Court. It would be consistent with the previous practice of the Court that it should, if only possible, uphold its jurisdiction when such a course is compatible with the intention of the parties and that it should not allow its jurisdiction to be defeated as the result of remediable defects of expression which are not of an essential character. If that principle were applied to the case now before the Court this would mean that, while the French acceptance as a whole would remain valid, the limitation expressed in the words "as understood by the Government of the French Republic" would be treated as invalid and non-existent with the further result that Norway could not rely on it. The outcome of the interpretation thus adopted would be somewhat startling inasmuch as it would, in the present case, favour the very State which originally made that reservation and defeat the objection of the defendant State—an aspect of the question commented upon in another part of this Opinion. That fact need not necessarily be a decisive reason against the adoption of any such interpretation.

However, I consider that it is not open to the Court in the present case to sever the invalid condition from the Acceptance as a whole. For the principle of severance applies only to provisions and conditions which are not of the essence of the undertaking. Now an examination of the history of this particular form of the reservation of national jurisdiction shows that the unilateral right of determining whether the dispute is essentially within domestic jurisdiction has been regarded by the declaring State as one of the crucial limitations—perhaps the crucial limitation—of the obligation undertaken by the acceptance of the Optional Clause of Article 36 of the Statute. As is well known, that particular limitation is, substantially, a repetition of the formula adopted, after considerable discussion, by the Senate of the United States of America in giving its consent and advice to the acceptance, in 1946, of the Optional Clause by that country. That instrument is not before the Court and it would not be proper for me to comment upon it except to the extent of noting that the reservation in question was included therein having regard to the decisive importance attached to it and notwithstanding the doubts, expressed in various quarters, as to its consistency with the Statute. It will also be noted that some governments, such as those of India and the Union of South Africa, have attributed so much importance to that particular formation of the reservation that they cancelled their previous acceptance of the Optional Clause in order to insert, in a substituted Declaration of Acceptance, a clause reserving for themselves the right of unilateral determination. To ignore that clause and to maintain the binding force of the Declaration as a whole would be to ignore an essential and deliberate condition of the Acceptance.

Notes

1. Note that Norway was entitled to rely on France's reservation as if it read "as understood by the *Norwegian* Government." Since France had excluded cases concerning *its* domestic jurisdiction, Norway could do likewise. How did the Court manage to avoid ruling on the validity of the reservation? Could the Court have done so if France had been relying on it?

2. Judge Guerrero, who was the only other judge in the *Norwegian Loans Case* to express an opinion on the validity of the French Declaration, stated in his dissenting opinion: "By the fact that France reserves her right to determine herself the limit between her own national jurisdiction and the jurisdiction of the Court, France renders void her main undertaking, for the latter ceases to be compulsory if it is France and not the Court that holds the power to determine the limit between their respective jurisdictions. The reservation conflicts also with paragraph 6 of Article 36. . . . "[90] He did not "agree that the Court is without jurisdiction when its lack of jurisdiction is founded on the terms of a unilateral instrument which I consider to be contrary to the spirit and to the letter of the Statute and which, in my view, is, for that reason, null and void."[91]

3. In the *Interhandel Case*, brought by Switzerland against the United States, the Court was confronted with the same form of "domestic jurisdiction" reservation in the United States Declaration.[92] It did not, however, either when deciding not to order certain interim measures[93] or when upholding the United States objections to its jurisdiction,[94] find it necessary to comment on the validity of the reservation or the Declaration containing it even though the reservation was invoked by the United States at both stages. In deciding that it lacked jurisdiction, the Court ruled instead that Switzerland had not exhausted local remedies, thus making it unnecessary for the Court to consider the objection to its jurisdiction presented by the United States (and challenged by Switzerland) relying upon the reservation.

Several judges in their separate opinions at the Preliminary Objection stage did, however, consider the questions that the objection raised. In his opinion, Judge Lauterpacht elaborated upon the position he had taken in the *Norwegian Loans Case*. Judge Spender reached the same conclusions as Judge Lauterpacht. Judge Klaestad, the President of the Court, agreed that the reservation was contrary to Article 36(6). As to the effect of this, he stated:

> It appears from the debate in the United States Senate concerning the acceptance of the compulsory jurisdiction of the Court . . . that fear was expressed lest the Court

[90] I.C.J.Rep. 1957, p. 68. See Shihata, *The Power of the International Court to Determine its own Jurisdiction* (1965).
[91] *Ibid.* p. 70.
[92] See above, p. 725. And see on the case, Briggs, 53 A.J.I.L. 301 (1959) and *ibid.* p. 547.
[93] I.C.J.Rep. 1957, p. 105.
[94] *Ibid.* 1959, p. 6.

might assume jurisdiction in matters which are essentially within the domestic jurisdiction of the United States, particularly in matters of immigration and the regulation of tariffs and duties and similar matters. The navigation of the Panama Canal was also referred to. Such were the considerations underlying the acceptance of Reservation (b). It may be doubted whether the Senate was fully aware of the possibility that this Reservation might entail the nullity of the whole Declaration of Acceptance, leaving the United States in the same legal situation with regard to the Court as States which have filed no such Declarations. Would the Senate have accepted this Reservation if it had been thought that the United States would thereby place themselves in such a situation, taking back by means of the Reservation what was otherwise given by the acceptance of the Declaration? The debate in the Senate does not appear to afford sufficient ground for such a supposition.

For my part, I am satisfied that it was the true intention of the competent authorities of the United States to issue a real and effective Declaration accepting the compulsory jurisdiction of the Court, though—it is true—with far-reaching exceptions. That this view is not unfounded appears to be shown by the subsequent attitude of the United States Government. . . .

These considerations have led me to the conclusion that the Court, both by its Statute and by the Charter, is prevented from acting upon that part of the Reservation which is in conflict with Article 36, paragraph 6, of the Statute, but that this circumstance does not necessarily imply that it is impossible for the Court to give effect to the other parts of the Declaration of Acceptance which are in conformity with the Statute. Part (a) of the Fourth Preliminary Objection should therefore in my view be rejected.[95]

Judge ad hoc Carry stated that he agreed "generally" with Judge Klaestad's Opinion; he did not give a full judgment of his own. Judge Armand-Ugon reached the same conclusion as Judge Klaestad. As to the effect of the reservation's invalidity, he was of the opinion that it "does not imply that the acceptance of the Court's jurisdiction, given in the American Declaration, is altogether without value and to be considered as null and void in its entirety. . . . The way in which this Declaration was employed by the Government of the United States in . . . cases [which the U.S. has submitted to the Court] shows that the reservation . . . was not a determining factor at the time of its formulation and submission."[96] In his judgment with respect to interim measures, Judge Wellington Koo considered that the reservation was applicable at that stage and was valid.[97]

4. In the *Aerial Incident of July 27, 1955, Case*,[98] which was brought by the United States against Bulgaria, Bulgaria invoked the United States domestic jurisdiction reservation. The United States withdrew the case before the Court made any ruling on its jurisdiction.

5. On December 31, 1981, there were in force six declarations with "domestic jurisdiction" reservations of the "self-judging" or "automatic" kind: those of Liberia, Malawi, Mexico, Philippines, Sudan and the United States. France made a new declaration in 1959 omitting such a reservation.[99] Efforts to have the United States reservation (the Connally Amendment) altered have not yet borne fruit. On December 31, 1981, also, 12 states had reservations excluding "disputes with regard to questions which by international law fall exclusively within the jurisdiction of [the state making it]" or reservations to that effect. Some of them omit any reference to international law but, at the same time, do not add "self-judging" words. Are such reservations open to challenge too? Do they serve any purpose? The 1957 Declaration made by the United

---

[95] *Ibid.* pp. 77–78.
[96] *Ibid.* p. 93.
[97] *Ibid.* 1957, pp. 113–114.
[98] *Ibid.* 1960, p. 146.
[99] It has now terminated its declaration. The Philippines reservation was added in 1972.

Kingdom, contained a reservation in respect of ". . . any question which, in the opinion of the Government of the United Kingdom, affects the national security of the United Kingdom or any of its dependent territories."[1] Was this open to the same objections as those raised against the French and United States domestic jurisdiction reservations?

(iv) Interim Measures in Contentious Litigation[2]

See Article 41(1), Statute of the International Court of Justice.[3]

ANGLO-IRANIAN OIL CO. CASE (INTERIM MEASURES)

I.C.J. Reports 1951, p. 89

In this case the United Kingdom brought a claim against Iran in respect of the nationalisation by the latter of the Anglo-Iranian Oil Co. Before the Court ruled on Iran's objection to the Court's jurisdiction to hear the case, the Untied Kingdom asked the Court for interim measures of protection.

Judgement of the Court

Whereas the complaint made in the Application is one of an alleged violation of international law by the breach of the agreement for a concession of April 29th, 1933, and by a denial of justice which, according to the Government of the United Kingdom, would follow from the refusal of the Iranian Government to accept arbitration in accordance with that agreement, and whereas it cannot be accepted *a priori* that a claim based on such a complaint falls completely outside the scope of international jurisdiction;

Whereas the considerations stated in the preceding paragraph suffice to empower the Court to entertain the Request for interim measures of protection;

Whereas the indication of such measures in no way prejudges the question of the jurisdiction of the Court to deal with the merits of the case and leaves unaffected the right of the Respondent to submit arguments against such jurisdiction;

The Court, by ten votes to two,[4] indicated interim measures by which, *inter alia*, the Iranian and United Kingdom Governments were asked to ensure that the Anglo-Iranian Oil Company was able to continue functioning as it had before the nationalisation law.

Dissenting Opinion of Judges Winiarski and Badawi Pasha. In international law it is the consent of the parties which confers jurisdiction on the Court. . . . The power given to the Court by Article 41 is not unconditional; it is given for the purposes of the proceedings and is limited to those proceedings. If

---

[1] The reservation was omitted in a revised declaration in 1958.

[2] See Bernhardt, 20 Virg.Jo.I.L. 557 (1980); Dumbauld, *Interim Measures of Protection in International Controversies* (1932); Goldsworthy, 68 A.J.I.L. 258 (1974); Gross, 74 A.J.I.L. 395 (1900); Haver, 3 Calif. West.I.L.J. 515 (1981); and Mendelson (1972–73) 46 B.Y.I.L. 259.

[3] See below, Appendix I. See also Rule 66 of Rules of Court.

[4] The judges in the majority were President Basdevant; Vice-President Guerrero; Judges Alvarez, Hackworth, Zoričić, de Visscher, Sir Arnold McNair, Klaestad, Read, and Hsu Mo. Judges Winiarski and Badawi Pasha dissented.

there is no jurisdiction as to the merits, there can be no jurisdiction to indicate interim measures of protection. Measures of this kind in international law are exceptional in character to an even greater extent than they are in municipal law; they may easily be considered a scarcely tolerable interference in the affairs of a sovereign State. For this reason, too, the Court ought not to indicate interim measures of protection unless its competence, in the event of this being challenged, appears to the Court to be nevertheless reasonably probable.

Note
The main problem which has arisen in respect of the Court's power to indicate interim measures has been to identify the circumstances in which they can be indicated before the Court's jurisdiction has been established to hear the merits of a case. The difficulty has been to find a rule that properly takes account both of the fact that the Court may ultimately decide that it lacks jurisdiction to hear the case and of the fact that the parties' rights may be irreparably damaged before a decision as to jurisdiction is taken. The Court's judgment weighs the second of these more heavily than does the opinion of the two dissenting judges.

NUCLEAR TESTS CASES (INTERIM PROTECTION)

Australia *v.* France; New Zealand *v.* France

I.C.J. Reports 1973, pp. 99, 135

For the facts of these cases, see above, p. 322. Here too the applicant states sought interim measures while the question of jurisdiction was unresolved. The following extract is from the Australian case.

Judgment of the Court

13. Whereas on a request for provisional measures the Court need not, before indicating them, finally satisfy itself that it has jurisdiction on the merits of the case, and yet ought not to indicate such measures unless the provisions invoked by the Applicant appear, prima facie, to afford a basis on which the jurisdiction of the Court might be founded;

14. Whereas in its Application and oral observations the Government of Australia claims to found the jurisdiction of the Court on the following provisions:

(i) Article 17 of the above-mentioned General Act of 1928, read together with Article 36, paragraph 1, and 37 of the Statute of the Court;

(ii) Alternatively, Article 36, paragraph 2, of the Statute of the Court and the respective declarations of Australia and France made thereunder; . . .

17. Whereas the material submitted to the Court leads it to the conclusion, at the present stage of the proceedings, that the provisions invoked by the Applicant appear, prima facie, to afford a basis on which the jurisdiction of the Court might be founded; . . .

20. Whereas the power of the Court to indicate interim measures under Article 41 of the Statute has as its object to preserve the respective rights of the Parties pending the decision of the Court, and presupposes that irreparable prejudice should not be caused to rights which are the subject of dispute in

judicial proceedings and that the Courts' judgment should not be anticipated by reason of any initiative regarding the matters in issue before the Court;

21. Whereas it follows that the Court in the present case cannot exercise its power to indicate interim measures of protection unless the rights claimed in the Application, prima facie, appear to fall within the purview of the Court's jurisdiction;

22. Whereas the claims formulated by the Government of Australia in its Application are as follows:

(i) The right of Australia and its people, in common with other States and their peoples, to be free from atmospheric nuclear weapon tests by any country is and will be violated;

(ii) The deposit of radio-active fall-out on the territory of Australia and its dispersion in Australia's airspace without Australia's consent:
   (a) violates Australian sovereignty over its territory;
   (b) impairs Australia's independent right to determine what acts shall take place within its territory and in particular whether Australia and its people shall be exposed to radiation from artificial sources;

(iii) the interference with ships and aircraft on the high seas and in the superjacent airspace, and the pollution of the high seas by radioactive fall-out, constitute infringements of the freedom of the high seas;

23. Whereas it cannot be assumed *a priori* that such claims fall completely outside the purview of the Court's jurisdiction, or that the Governments of Australia may not be able to establish a legal interest in respect of these claims entitling the Court to admit the Application;
Accordingly,

THE COURT,
indicates, by 8 votes to 6,[5] . . . the following provisional measures:

The Governments of Australia and France should each of them ensure that no action of any kind is taken which might aggravate or extend the dispute submitted to the Court or prejudice the rights of the other Party in respect of the carrying out of whatever decision the Court may render in the case; and, in particular, the French Government should avoid nuclear tests causing the deposit of radio-active fall-out on Australian territory . . .

DISSENTING OPINION OF JUDGE FORSTER. Even when it considers that circumstances require the indication of provisional measures, the Court, before proceeding to indicate them, must satisfy itself that it has jurisdiction. Neither the provisional character of the measures nor the urgency of the requirement that they be indicated can dispense the judge from the necessity of ascertaining his jurisdiction *in limine litis*; especially when it is seriously and categorically contested by the State proceeded against, which is the case at present.

---

[5] The Court consisted of Vice-President Ammoun; Judges Forster, Gros, Bengzon, Petrén, Onyeama, Ignacio-Pinto, de Castro, Morozov, Jiménez de Aréchaga, Sir Humphrey Waldock, Nagendra Singh, Ruda; and Judge ad hoc Sir Garfield Barwick. Judges Jiménez de Aréchaga, Sir Humphrey Waldock, Nagendra Singh, and Judge ad hoc Sir Garfield Barwick were in the majority. Judges Forster, Gros, Petrén, and Ignacio-Pinto dissented. It is not clear how the other judges voted.

DISSENTING OPINION OF JUDGE GROS. A certain tendency has arisen to consider that the Orders . . . in the *Fisheries Jurisdiction* cases have, as it were, consolidated the law concerning provisional measures. But each case must be examined according to its own merits and, as Article 41 says, according to "the circumstances." Now the case of Iceland was entirely different in circumstances. The Court had developed an awareness of the existence of its own jurisdiction, the urgency was admitted, the reality and the precise definition of the dispute were not contested; finally, the right of the Applicant States which was protected by the Orders was recognized as being a right currently exercised, whereas the claim of Iceland constituted a modification of existing law. It suffices to enumerate these points to show that the situation is entirely different today; so far as the last point is concerned, the situation is now even the reverse, since the Applicants stand upon a claim to the modification of existing positive law when they ask the Court to recognize the existence of a rule forbidding the over-stepping of a threshold of atomic pollution.

DISSENTING OPINION OF JUDGE PETRÉN. In the present case, it appears from paragraph 13 of the Order that the Court has been guided by that precedent,[6] for it there expresses the opinion that it ought not to indicate interim measures unless the provisions invoked by the Applicant appear, prima facie, to afford a basis on which the jurisdiction of the Court might be founded. I can agree to this formula, which in my view signifies that for Article 41 of the Statute to be applicable it is not sufficient for a mere adumbration of proof, considered in isolation, to indicate the possibility of the Court's possessing jurisdiction: that there must also be a probability transpiring from an examination of the whole of the elements at the Court's disposal.

Notes

1. The indication of interim, or provisional, measures in the *Nuclear Tests Cases* was one of the reasons why France withdrew its declaration under the Optional Clause.[7]

2. In the *Fisheries Jurisdiction Cases*,[8] the Court had also indicated interim measures, stating that although it need not satisfy itself that it had jurisdiction, "it ought not to act under Article 41 . . . if the absence of jurisdiction on the merits is manifest." Although the Court would seem to have followed the same approach in the present case, the voting was much closer here and four dissenting judges in the present case who gave opinions had been in the majority in the *Fisheries Jurisdiction Cases*.

3. Interim measures are "indicated," not required, and are not binding in law.[9] In fact, in none of the three cases from which the above extracts are taken were they observed by the defendant state. The interim measures indicated in the *U.S. Diplomatic and Consular Staff in Tehran Case*[10] were not complied with either. Does this record suggest that the Court should be more cautious in exercising its jurisdiction to indicate interim measures? Or is it part of a more general problem of non-compliance?

---

[6] *Ed.* In the *Fisheries Jurisdiction Cases.*

[7] See *The Future of the International Court of Justice, loc. cit.* at p. 705, n. 3, above, Vol. 2, p. 771, n. 79.

[8] I.C.J.Rep. 1972, p. 12. The vote was by 14 votes to one.

[9] See Hambro, in Schätzel and Schlochauer, eds., *Festschrift für Hans Wehberg*, 1956, p. 152.

[10] I.C.J.Rep. 1979, p. 7.

(v) ADVISORY JURISDICTION[11]

See Article 96, United Nations Charter and Chapter IV, Statute of the International Court of Justice.[12]

Note

In addition to its jurisdiction to decide cases brought by states under Article 36 of its Statute, the World Court

> may give an advisory opinion on any legal question at the request of whatever body may be authorised by or in accordance with the Charter of the United Nations to make such a request.[13]

The General Assembly and the Security Council are authorised "by" the Charter[14] to request opinions. ECOSOC and the Trusteeship Council have been authorised "in accordance with" the Charter,[15] as have 13 of the 14 United Nations specialised agencies (the exception is the Universal Postal Union), the International Atomic Energy Authority (which is not a specialised agency), the Interim Committee of the General Assembly, the Committee for Applications for the Review of Judgments of the United Nations Administrative Tribunal, and the International Fund for Agricultural Development.

Although advisory opinions are not binding in law upon the requesting body, they have over the years usually been accepted and acted upon by it and by any state concerned. Whereas the record of formal acceptance of opinions remains good, that of compliance in fact has declined recently. Striking examples are the failure of the General Assembly to enforce the opinion given to it in the *Certain Expenses Case*[16] and the steadfast refusal of South Africa to fall in line with the opinions on South West Africa/Namibia.[17]

Occasionally, provision is made in advance for an opinion to be binding. The 1946 General Convention on the Privileges and Immunities of the United Nations provides that if a difference arises between the United Nations and a member a request for an advisory opinion should be made by an organ of the United Nations and that the opinion rendered by the Court "shall be accepted as decisive by the parties."[18]

States may not request advisory opinions,[19] but they are permitted, along with international organisations, to participate in proceedings before the Court.[20] Individuals and other entities have no *locus standi*.

Recourse to the Court for advisory opinions has declined since 1945. Whereas the Permanent Court of International Justice gave 27 opinions in 18 years, the International Court of Justice has so far given only 17. The kind of question put to the Court has also changed. Fewer concern disputes between states and more concern constitutional questions about the functioning of the requesting body.

---

[11] See Keith, *The Extent of the Advisory Jurisdiction of the International Court of Justice* (1971); Pomerance, *The Advisory Function of the International Court in the League and U.N. Eras* (1973); Pratap, *The Advisory Jurisdiction of the International Court* (1972); Rosenne, Vol. II, Ch. XIX–XXI; Szasz, in *The Future of the International Court of Justice, loc. cit.* at p. 705, n. 3, above, Vol. II, p. 499.

[12] Appendix I, below.   [13] Statute of the Court, Art. 65(1).

[14] UN Charter, Art. 96(1).

[15] UN Charter, Art. 96(2). The other "principal organ" of the UN—the Secretariat—has not been authorised.

[16] See above, p. 704.   [17] See above, pp. 103 *et. seq.*

[18] Article 30, U.K.T.S. 10 (1950), Cmd. 7891. *cf.* Article XII, Statute of the I.L.O. Administrative Tribunal.

[19] A state may, however, obtain a declaratory judgment in contentious litigation if the Court has jurisdiction under Article 36, Statute of the Court.

[20] Article 66, Statute of the Court.

CONDITIONS OF ADMISSION OF A STATE TO MEMBERSHIP IN THE UNITED NATIONS CASE

Advisory Opinion. I.C.J. Reports 1948, p. 57

Opinion of the Court

It has nevertheless been contended that the question put must be regarded as a political one and that, for this reason, it falls outside the jurisdiction of the Court. The Court cannot attribute a political character to a request which, framed in abstract terms, invites it to undertake an essentially judicial task, the interpretation of a treaty provision. It is not concerned with the motives which may have inspired this request, nor with the considerations which, in the concrete cases submitted for examination to the Security Council, formed the subject of the exchange of views which took place in that body. It is the duty of the Court to envisage the question submitted to it only in the abstract form which has been given to it; nothing which is said in the present opinion refers, either directly or indirectly, to concrete cases or to particular circumstances.

It has also been contended that the Court should not deal with a question couched in abstract terms. That is a mere affirmation devoid of any justification. According to Article 96 of the Charter and Article 65 of the Statute, the Court may give an advisory opinion on any legal question, abstract or otherwise.

Lastly, it has also been maintained that the Court cannot reply to the question put because it involves an interpretation of the Charter. Nowhere is any provision to be found forbidding the Court, "the principal judicial organ of the United Nations," to exercise in regard to Article 4 of the Charter, a multilateral treaty, an interpretative function which falls within the normal exercise of its judicial powers.

Accordingly, the Court holds that it is competent, on the basis of Article 96 of the Charter and Article 65 of the Statute, and considers that there are no reason why it should decline to answer the question put to it.

Note
See further on the meaning of a "legal question," the *Western Sahara Case*, below, p. 740.

EASTERN CARELIA CASE

Advisory Opinion. P.C.I.J. Reports, Series B, No. 5 (1923)

This request for an advisory opinion arose out of a dispute between Finland and Russia over Russian government of Eastern Carelia. This territory, which lies between the two states, was declared to be an "autonomous" part of Russia in Articles 10 and 11 of the Treaty of Dorpat 1920.[21] This was the treaty which had ended the war between Finland and Russia following the former's declaration of independence from the latter.[22] The precise nature and extent of Eastern Carelia's autonomy was not indicated in the Treaty but was set out in detail in a Declaration made by Russia when the Treaty was drafted. Finland complained to the Council of the League of Nations, of which organisation it was a member, that Russia was not respecting Eastern Carelian autonomy. It relied

[21] 3 L.N.T.S. 5.
[22] See above, p. 81.

heavily in its complaint upon the terms of the Declaration, which it contended was legally binding. Russia, which was not a member of the League and which declined an invitation to answer these allegations before the Council, claimed that the Treaty was not intended to control Russia's government of Eastern Carelia, which was a matter within its domestic jurisdiction. It also argued that the Declaration had been made for information purposes only and did not create any legal obligation. The Council referred to the Court the following question:

> Do Articles 10 and 11 of the Treaty of Peace between Finland and Russia, signed at Dorpat on October 14, 1920, and the annexed Declaration of the Russian Delegation regarding the autonomy of Eastern Carelia, constitute engagements of an international character which place Russia under an obligation to Finland as to the carrying out of the provisions contained therein?

Russia refused to participate in the proceedings in the case. The Court decided, by seven to four, not to give an opinion.

Opinion of the Court

It is well established in international law that no State can, without its consent, be compelled to submit its disputes with other States either to mediation or to arbitration, or to any other kind of pacific settlement. Such consent can be given once and for all in the form of an obligation freely undertaken, but it can, on the contrary, also be given in a special case apart from any existing obligation. The first alternative applies to the Members of the League who, having accepted the Covenant, are under the obligation resulting from the provisions of this pact dealing with the pacific settlement of international disputes. As concerns States not members of the League, the situation is quite different; they are not bound by the Covenant. The submission, therefore, of a dispute between them and a member of the League for solution according to the methods provided for in the Covenant, could take place only by virtue of their consent. Such consent, however, has never been given by Russia. . . . The Court therefore finds it impossible to give its opinion on a dispute of this kind.

It appears to the Court that there are other cogent reasons which render it very inexpedient that the Court should attempt to deal with the present question. The question whether Finland and Russia contracted on the terms of the Declaration as to the nature of the autonomy of Eastern Carelia is really one of fact. . . . The Court would, of course, be at a very great disadvantage in such an enquiry, owing to the fact that Russia refuses to take part in it. It appears now to be very doubtful whether there would be available to the Court materials sufficient to enable it to arrive at any judicial conclusion upon the question of fact: What did the parties agree to? The Court does not say that there is an absolute rule that the request for an advisory opinion may not involve some enquiry as to facts, but, under ordinary circumstances, it is certainly expedient that the facts upon which the opinion of the Court is desired should not be in controversy, and it should not be left to the Court itself to ascertain what they are.

. . . The question put to the Court is not one of abstract law, but concerns directly the main point of the controversy between Finland and Russia, and can only be decided by an investigation into the facts underlying the case. Answering the question would be substantially equivalent to deciding the dispute between the parties. The Court, being a Court of Justice, cannot, even in giving advisory opinions, depart from the essential rules guiding their activity as a court.

Notes

1. The question here was not (as in the extract from the *Admissions Case* above) whether the Court had jurisdiction to act (there was clearly a "legal question"), but whether it was proper to do so, bearing in mind the discretion given to the Court ("may give").

2. In the *Fisheries Jurisdiction Cases*,[23] the Court gave judgments in *contentious litigation* in the absence of the participation of Iceland. How does that compare with the Court's refusal to give an opinion here in the absence of Russia?

INTERPRETATION OF PEACE TREATIES CASE

Advisory Opinion. I.C.J. Reports 1950, p. 65

For the facts of the case, see the extract above, p. 596.

Opinion of the Court

Another argument that has been invoked against the power of the Court to answer the Questions put to it in this case is based on the opposition of the Governments of Bulgaria, Hungary and Roumania to the advisory procedure. The Court cannot, it is said, give the Advisory Opinion requested without violating the well-established principle of international law according to which no judicial proceedings relating to a legal question pending between States can take place without their consent.

. . . In the opinion of the Court, the circumstances of the present case are profoundly different from those . . . in the Eastern Carelia case . . . when . . . [the] Court declined to give an Opinion because it found that the question put to it was directly related to the main point of a dispute actually pending between two States, so that answering the question would be substantially equivalent to deciding the dispute between the parties, and that at the same time it raised a question of fact which could not be elucidated without hearing both parties.

. . . the present Request for an Opinion is solely concerned with the applicability to certain disputes of the procedure for settlement instituted by the Peace Treaties, and it is justifiable to conclude that it in no way touches the merits of those disputes. Furthermore, the settlement of these disputes is entrusted solely to the Commissions provided for by the Peace Treaties. Consequently, it is for these Commissions to decide upon any objections which may be raised to their jurisdiction in respect of any of these disputes, and the present Opinion in no way prejudges the decisions that may be taken on those objections. It follows that the legal position of the parties to these disputes cannot be in any way compromised by the answers that the Court may give to the Questions put to it.

[23] See above, p. 346.

WESTERN SAHARA CASE

Advisory Opinion. I.C.J. Reports 1975, p. 12

For the facts, see above p. 97.

Opinion of the Court

15. The questions submitted by the General Assembly . . . are by their very nature susceptible of a reply based on law; indeed, they are scarcely susceptible of a reply otherwise than on the basis of law. . . .

17. It is true that, in order to reply to the questions, the Court will have to determine certain facts, before being able to assess their legal significance.

However, a mixed question of law and facts is none the less a legal question within the meaning of Article 96, paragraph 1, of the Charter and Article 65, paragraph 1, of the Statute. . . .

18. . . . The view has been expressed that in order to be a "legal question" . . . a question must not be of a historical character, but must concern or affect existing rights or obligations . . . the references to "any legal question" . . . are not to be interpreted restrictively.

19. . . . It has undoubtedly been the usual situation for an advisory opinion of the Court to pronounce on existing rights and obligations, or on their coming into existence, modification or termination, or on the powers of international organs. However, the Court may also be requested to give its opinion on questions of law which do not call for any pronouncement of that kind, though they may have their place within a wider problem the solution of which could involve such matters. . . .

23. . . . In exercising this discretion [under Article 65], the International Court of Justice, like the Permanent Court of International Justice, has always been guided by the principle that, as a judicial body, it is bound to remain faithful to the requirements of its judicial character even in giving advisory opinions. . . . It has also said that the reply of the Court, itself an organ of the United Nations, represents its participation in the activities of the Organization and, in principle, should not be refused. By lending its assistance in the solution of a problem confronting the General Assembly, the Court would discharge its functions as the principal judicial organ of the United Nations. The Court has further said that only "compelling reasons" should lead it to refuse to give a requested advisory opinion. . . .

24. Spain has put forward a series of objections which in its view would render the giving of an opinion in the present case incompatible with the Court's judicial character. . . .

29. It is clear that Spain has not consented to the adjudication of the questions formulated in resolution 3292 (XXIX). . . .

30. In other respects, however, Spain's position in relation to the present proceedings find no parallel in the circumstances of the advisory proceedings concerning the *Status of Eastern Carelia* in 1923. In that case, one of the States concerned was neither a party to the Statute of the Permanent Court nor, at the time, a Member of the League of Nations, and lack of competence of the League to deal with a dispute involving non-member States which refused its intervention was a decisive reason for the Court's declining to give an answer. In the present case, Spain is a Member of the United Nations and has accepted the

provisions of the Charter and Statute; it has thereby in general given its consent to the exercise by the Court of its advisory jurisdiction. It has not objected, and could not validly object, to the General Assembly's exercise of its powers to deal with the decolonization of a non-self-governing territory and to seek an opinion on questions relevant to the exercise of those powers. In the proceedings in the General Assembly, Spain did not oppose the reference of the Western Sahara question as such to the Court's jurisdiction: it objected rather to the restriction of that reference to the historical aspects of that question. . . .

32. The Court . . . affirmed in . . . [the *Peace Treaties Case*] that its competence to give an opinion did not depend on the consent of the interested States, even when the case concerned a legal question actually pending between them. However, the Court . . . then under consideration from the *Status of Eastern Carelia* case and explained the particular grounds which led it to conclude that there was no reason requiring the Court to refuse to reply to the request. Thus the Court recognized that lack of consent might constitute a ground for declining to give the opinion requested if, in the circumstances of a given case, considerations of judicial propriety should oblige the Court to refuse an opinion. . . .

33. . . . An instance of this would be when the circumstances disclose that to give a reply would have the effect of circumventing the principle that a State is not obliged to allow its disputes to be submitted to judicial settlement without its consent. . . .

34. The situation existing in the present case is not, however, the one envisaged above. . . .

39. . . . The object of the General Assembly has not been to bring before the Court, by way of a request for advisory opinion, a dispute or legal controversy, in order that it may later, on the basis of the Court's opinion, exercise its powers and functions for the peaceful settlement of that dispute or controversy. The object of the request is an entirely different one: to obtain from the Court an opinion which the General Assembly deems of assistance to it for the proper exercise of its functions concerning the decolonization of the territory. . . .

42. Furthermore, the origin and scope of the dispute . . . are important in appreciating, from the point of view of the exercise of the Court's discretion, the real significance in this case of the lack of Spain's consent. The issue between Morocco and Spain regarding Western Sahara is not one as to the legal status of the territory today, but one as to the rights of Morocco over it at the time of colonization. The settlement of this issue will not affect the rights of Spain today as the administering Power, but will assist the General Assembly in deciding on the policy to be followed in order to accelerate the decolonization process in the territory. It follows that the legal position of the State which has refused its consent to the present proceedings is not "in any way compromised by the answers that the Court may give to the questions put to it" (*Interpretation of Peace Treaties with Bulgaria, Hungary and Romania, First Phase, I.C.J. Reports* 1950, p. 72).

44. . . . [Another] way in which Spain . . . has presented its opposition to the Court's pronouncing upon the questions posed in the request is to maintain that in this case the Court cannot fulfil the requirements of good administration of justice as regards the determination of the facts. . . .

47. The situation in the present case is entirely different from that with which the Permanent Court was confronted in the *Status of Eastern Carelia* case.

Mauritania, Morocco and Spain have furnished very extensive documentary evidence of the facts which they considered relevant to the Court's examination of the questions posed in the request, and each of these countries, as well as Algeria and Zaire, have presented their views on these facts and on the observations of the others. The Secretary-General has also furnished a dossier of documents concerning the discussion of the question of Western Sahara in the competent United Nations organs. The Court therefore considers that the information and evidence before it are sufficient to enable it to arrive at a judicial conclusion concerning the facts which are relevant to its opinion and necessary for replying to the two questions posed in the request.

48. The Court has been asked to state that it ought not to examine the substance of the present request, since the reply to the questions put to it would be devoid of purpose. Spain considers that the United Nations has already affirmed the nature of the decolonization process applicable to Western Sahara in accordance with General Assembly resolution 1514 (XV). . . .

72.. . . . The General Assembly has referred to its intention to "continue its discussion of this question" in the light of the Court's advisory opinion . . . an opinion given by the Court in the present proceedings will furnish the General Assembly with elements of a legal character relevant to its further treatment of the decolonization of Western Sahara.

73. In any event, to what extent or degree its opinion will have an impact on the action of the General Assembly is not for the Court to decide. The function of the Court is to give an opinion based on law, once it has come to the conclusion that the questions put to it are relevant and have a practical and contemporary effect and, consequently, are not devoid of object or purpose.

74. In the light of the considerations set out . . . above, the Court finds no compelling reason, in the circumstances of the present case, to refuse to comply with the request by the General Assembly for an advisory opinion.

Notes

1. In this case the Court confirmed in general terms what was implicit in the *Admissions Case, viz.* that a "legal question" is one to be answered on a basis of law. Such an answer is, in fact, the only kind that the Court, acting as a judicial institution,[24] can give; it cannot "pronounce on the political or moral duties" that states may have.[25] A "legal question" may be couched in abstract terms (as in the *Admissions Case*) or it may be phrased in terms of a concrete situation (as in this case). Would it be "legal," so that the Court would have jurisdiction, if it involved only the determination of the facts of a case and not also (as in this case) the application of law to the facts?

2. Does the Court adopt in this case the same reading of the main reason for the opinion in the *Eastern Carelia Case* as it had in the *Peace Treaties Case*? Note that the Court carefully avoids specifying the actual grounds on which it had distinguished the *Eastern Carelia Case* in the *Peace Treaties Case*. Would the Court have given an opinion if Spain had not been a member of the United Nations (as it was not until 1955)? In what circumstances might the Court have found that Spain would have been impleaded without its consent?

3. Despite the considerable discussion that occurred in this (as in many other cases) of the propriety of giving an opinion, there remains only one case—the *Eastern Carelia Case*—in which the Court has found it improper to do so (and none in which the question put has not been found to be a legal one).

[24] The situation is different where the Court decides a case *ex aequo et bono* under Article 36(2) of the Court.
[25] *Status of South West Africa Case*, I.C.J. Rep. 1950, p. 140.

(vi) THE FUTURE OF THE COURT[26]

ANAND, ROLE OF INTERNATIONAL ADJUDICATION

in *The Future of the Court, loc. cit.* at p. 705, n. 3, above, pp. 2–14.
Some footnotes omitted

Although it is unanimously accepted that a strong and respected international court is indispensable for the development of an effective international legal order, the International Court of Justice, the only permanent international court and the principal judicial organ of the United Nations, has been ignored and neglected by states Members of the United Nations . . . despite the vast expansion of the international society since the Second World War and a corresponding increase in international relations and the number of conflicts, there has been no proportionate increase in the work of the Court. . . . On the contrary there was a steep decline in the work of the Court after the first few years. So steep was the decline that for some time—from June 21, 1971 to August 30, 1971, to be specific—there was not a single case pending before the Court. . . .

Although the "clientele" of the International Court is much larger than that of its predecessor, the Permanent Court of International Justice, the states have not put so much faith in the new Court as they had in the old. Thus, while 42 states out of 68 members of the judicial community in 1934, *i.e.*, nearly 61 per cent., were bound by the "optional clause" of the Statute of the Permanent Court, in July 1972 only 46[27] out of 135 potential "clients" of the International Court of Justice, *i.e.* only 33 per cent., had accepted its compulsory jurisdiction. But even the latter figure is deceptive in the sense that most of the declarations accepting compulsory jurisdiction are riddled with wide and far-reaching reservations so that in many cases the states are left virtually free to accept or decline jurisdiction when an actual dispute arises.

A similar retrogressive tendency on the part of states . . . is evident in a series of important codification conventions. Provisions intended to make possible proceedings to adjudicate disputes before the International Court of Justice by unilateral application were excluded from the conventions, and an optional protocol was put in. This was done in the 1958 Geneva Convention on the Law of the Sea[28] and the Vienna Conventions on Diplomatic Relations of 1961[29] and Consular Relations of 1963 because this was the only way by which participation of the Soviet Union and other Socialist countries could be obtained. Several newly independent countries, as well as some states of Latin America, also preferred an optional provision to a compulsory jurisdiction clause. So far, however, only a small number of states has ratified these optional protocols. It is important to note that such important instruments as the International Covenants on Economic, Social and Cultural Rights and on Civil and Political Rights of December 16, 1966[30] do not provide for a reference of disputes

[26] See *The Future of the Court, loc. cit.* at p. 705, n. 3, above, *passim*; Cheng, 20 Y.B.W.A. 241 (1966); Partan, 18 Harvard I.L.J. 557 (1977); Prott (1979) 33 Y.B.W.A. 284; Rosenne (1963) 39 B.Y.I.L. 1.

[27] *Ed.* for a more recent figure, see above, p. 720.

[28] *Ed.* above, p. 284, n. 9. Note, however, the proposed International Tribunal for the Law of the Sea, above, p. 285.

[29] *Ed.* above, p. 264.   [30] *Ed.* above, p. 541.

between the parties to the International Court. Nor does the 1969 Vienna Convention on the Law of Treaties except in regard to *jus cogens* disputes (Articles 53 and 64).[31] The [1970] Declaration on Principles of International Law[32] does not contain any direct reference to the Court.

The reticence of states to make use of the Court in the settlement of their disputes is also reflected in the reluctance of the General Assembly and the Security Council as well as other authorized organs of the United Nations for clarification of numerous issues that come before them. . . .

Apart from the general international climate since the Second World War— the political and ideological division of the world society, tension between Communist and the non-Communist blocs, and revolutionary changes in some parts of the world—one of the most important reasons for the present crisis of confidence in the Court is said to be the vast expansion of the international society from the old "Hague Community" with little or no connection left with the so-called tradition of the Hague system and the lack of homogeneous continuity that the Hague system assumed. Implicit in the Hague tradition, it is said, was a deep faith in the rule of law, in the primacy and superiority of the judicial procedure in the settlement of international disputes, and the important role of the international courts in the establishment and maintenance of inter-national peace and security . . . Without denying some influence of different religious, cultural, ethical and legal traditions of various states on international law and relations, we agree with Professor Julius Stone that the diagnosis of the present position in terms of mere cultural difference obscures the real problems of conflicts of interests between Western states and the underdeveloped states of Asia and Africa.[33] . . . National interest, rightly or wrongly understood, rather than cultural traditions, seems to be the decisive factor in the determina-tion of policies toward international law and affairs . . . For better or worse, and despite different cultural traditions, "the new states have behaved very much like the older states, pursuing their national interests to the maximum extent compatible with the acceptance of the rules of international law." . . . [34]

It may be suggested that the present coolness towards the International Court is partly affected by structural deficiencies of the Court . . . It is, of course, possible to disagree with some of its decisions here and there, but generally speaking the quality and integrity of the Court's decisions are accepted by commentators as excellent. Judges, being human, are of course not infallible, but no judge has ever been accused of being swayed by considerations of personal gain. In spite of all the criticism against the *South-West Africa* case, there is no basis for any doubt about the independence of the Court as a whole. Indeed, it is entirely wrong and rash to denounce a legal institution on the basis of a single case. In any case, the Court seems to have regained confidence in the *Namibia* opinion. The impartiality of its decisions and the integrity of its judges are unquestionable.

But the newly independent countries of Asia and Africa have rightly been concerned that the composition of the Court has not kept pace with the

---

[31] *Ed.* above, pp. 630–632.

[32] See Appendix III, below.

[33] Julius Stone, "A Common Law for Mankind?" 1 *International Studies*, p. 430 (New Dehli, 1955–56).

[34] W. Friedmann, . . . 59 A.J.I.L., p. 858 (1965).

increasingly universal composition of the international community. . . . it is still thought to be Euro-centric and biased in favour of European states.[35] Not unreasonably they have been demanding modification of the situation by stricter compliance with Article 9 of the Statute or perhaps by increasing the number of judges to get a more adequate and equitable representation. The composition of the Court has changed through the years and it is at present similar to that of the Security Council. But this is not entirely satisfactory for the Asian-African states. Some of them believe that "the membership of the Court could not reflect the structure of the Council without also reflecting its impotence."[36] They question the validity of the informal understanding whereby a national of each of the permanent members of the Security Council is always included among the judges of the Court, since that practice has resulted in the politicization of elections to the Court.

It is submitted, however, that changes in the composition of the Court in recent years, brought about by the increasing influence of the newly-independent states in the United Nations, promise a much more optimistic picture although complete reform cannot be accomplished overnight. It may be said that even a modest increase in the already large body of fifteen judges may adversely affect the internal efficiency of the Court and should not be introduced too hastily. There is little doubt that the present membership of the Court can be readjusted to reflect more faithfully the increasingly heterogeneous membership of the United Nations. . . . the real dilemma of the Court is the dilemma of international law. The law created by a minority in another age under very different circumstances, it is felt, cannot guarantee the subjective rights of all states. During recent debates in the Sixth Committee [in 1970–71] on the role of the International Court of Justice, it was stressed time and again by countries of the third world that certain institutions of traditional international law "were the juridical expression of a few special political interests, of a particular social structure and of a certain state of international relations." . . .

It must be pointed out, however, that the International Court has not in its decisions ignored the developments and new trends in international law and organizations, although it has sometimes been blamed as being too cautious, conservative and static.[37] Even within the limited sphere of its activity, the International Court has done a remarkable job in building up a body of case-law which is evidence of a growing body of international law of the highest value. Through some of its very bold opinions, such as in *Reparation for Injuries Suffered in the Service of the United Nations* and *Certain Expenses of the United Nations* cases it has made a major contribution to the development of the "constitutional law" of the United Nations.

However, without denying the positive role of the International Court in the development of international law, it is also realized that the law-creating function of the Court is after all a limited function. Professor Kunz rightly

---

[35] It was pointed out in 1971 that of the 42 judges elected to the Court since its establishment, 17 had come from Europe, 14 from the American continent, eight from Asia and Australia, and three from Africa. . . . At present there are four West European, two East European, two Latin American, three Asian, three African and one U.S. judges on the bench of the Court.
[36] See Mtango (Tanzania), U.N.G.A.O.R., 26th sess, Sixth Committee A/C. 6/SR.1281, November 18, 1971, p. 21.
[37] See C. W. Jenks, *The Prospects of International Adjudication*, p. 237 (1964).

pointed out that courts are generally unfit and unequipped for changing the law, just as political agencies are unfit to give objective and impartial decision.[38] . . .

The Court is also in a dilemma. If it does not modify the law, "we have, in respect of the matters at issue, to live with a body of law no longer fully appropriate to contemporary needs, until we can secure agreed change in the law; if the second alternative is chosen, we have to live with a degree of uncertainty, ranging, according to circumstances, from inconvenience through confusion to chaos, until we can secure agreement on a generally acceptable rule of law."[39] Professor Gross also warns: "If the Court should indulge in judicial law-making and should make light of the consent of states to the law it might abruptly find itself in the position of a leader without a following."[40]

Notes

1. The limited use to which the Court has been put in recent years has been the subject of considerable discussion. In the past 10 years, the Court has decided on the merits of only four cases of contentious litigation: the *Fisheries Jurisdiction Cases* (two),[41] the *Continental Shelf (Tunisia)* v. *Libya) Case*[42] and the *U.S. Diplomatic and Consular Staff in Tehran Case*.[43] In the same period it has given four advisory opinions: in the *Western Sahara Case*,[44] the *WHO and Egypt Case*[45] and two United Nations Administrative Tribunal cases.[46] At present the Court has only the *Gulf of Maine (Canada* v. *U.S.) Case* and the *Continental Shelf (Libya* v. *Malta) Case* on its list. This represents a very small case load for a Court of full-time judges.

2. Although the small number of cases being referred to the World Court is disappointing, the following comment by Jennings is worth bearing in mind:

> It is a besetting weakness of lawyers—and not only of international lawyers—to think of law, and even sometimes to attempt to define law, as if it consisted only of rules suitable to be applied by courts in adversary proceedings between two parties. This distorted view of the role of law in a society is singularly inapt for international law which throughout its history has been employed much more as an instrument of diplomacy than of formal forensic confrontation. Naturally, courts and court-law are of great importance in international law; yet so also is that law which provides the frameworks, procedures and standards for international political decision; and it is certainly the further development of this latter kind of international law which presents the most urgent problem today.[47]

At the same time, as Jennings has pointed out elsewhere, progress in the provision for "international adjudication is not only desirable for the settlement of disputes according to law; it is also essential for the proper development of the law itself. For it is often forgotten that some aspects of law—*e.g.* rules concerning nullity and validity—cannot be adequately developed at all in the absence of courts with compulsory jurisdiction."[48]

---

[38] J. L. Kunz, "Compulsory International Adjudication and Maintenance of Peace," 36 A.J.I.L., p. 676 (1942).
[39] *Ed.* Jenks (1960) 38 B.Y.I.L. 35.
[40] *Ed.* Gross, in *The Future of the International Court of Justice, loc. cit.* at p. 705, n. 3, p. 82.
[41] Above, p. 346.
[42] Above, p. 359.
[43] Above, p. 276.
[44] Above, p. 97.
[45] I.C.J.Rep. 1980, p. 73.
[46] I.C.J.Rep. 1973, p. 166 and *ibid.* 1982, p. 325.
[47] 121 *Hague Recueil* 323, 327–328 (1967–II).
[48] (1964) 40 B.Y.I.L. 413.

3. Whereas the judgments and orders of the P.C.I.J. in contentious litigation were all complied with, the record of the I.C.J., particularly in the last decade, has been less satisfactory. The judgments in the *Corfu Channel Case*,[49] the *Fisheries Jurisdiction Cases* and the *U.S. Diplomatic and Consular Staff in Tehran Case* and the orders for interim measures in four cases[50] were not followed. The judgment in the *Right of Passage Case*[51] was soon negated by the Indian invasion of Goa.[52] On the power, as yet unexercised, of the Security Council to enforce decisions of the Court, see Article 94(2) of the Charter.[53]

4. A new problem confronting the Court is that of the "non-appearing" defendant.[54] Iceland boycotted the proceedings in the *Fisheries Jurisdiction Cases*. In four cases[55] since then the defendant state has not appeared.

---

[49] Above, p. 301.
[50] See above, p. 735.
[51] Above, p. 198.
[52] Above, p. 172.
[53] Appendix II, below. See Kerley, in *The Future of the International Court of Justice, loc. cit.* at p. 705, n. 3, above p. 276.
[54] See Fitzmaurice (1980) 51 B.Y.I.L. 89 and Sinclair, 30 I.C.L.Q. 338 (1981).
[55] The *Nuclear Tests Cases* above, p. 571; the *Pakistani Prisoners of War Case*, I.C.J.Rep. 1973, pp. 328, 347; the *Aegean Sea Continental Shelf Case*, above, p. 719, n. 66; and the *U.S. Diplomatic and Consular Staff Case*.

CHARTER OF THE UNITED NATIONS[1]

WE THE PEOPLES OF THE UNITED NATIONS DETERMINED to save succeeding generations from the scourge of war, which twice in our lifetime has brought, untold sorrow to mankind, and to reaffirm faith in fundamental human rights, in the dignity and worth of the human person, in the equal rights of men and women and of nations large and small, and to establish conditions under which justice and respect for the obligations arising from treaties and other sources of international law can be maintained, and to promote social progress and better standards of life in larger freedom,

AND FOR THESE ENDS to practise tolerance and live together in peace with one another as good neighbours, and to unite our strength to maintain international peace and security, and to ensure, by the acceptance of principles and the institution of methods, that armed force shall not be used, save in the common interest, and to employ international machinery for the promotion of the economic and social advancement of all peoples,

HAVE RESOLVED TO COMBINE OUR EFFORTS TO ACCOMPLISH THESE AIMS. Accordingly, our respective Governments, through representatives assembled in the city of San Francisco, who have exhibited their full powers found to be in good and due form, have agreed to the present Charter of the United Nations and do hereby establish an international organization to be known as the United Nations.

CHAPTER I

PURPOSES AND PRINCIPLES

Article 1

The Purposes of the United Nations are:

1. To maintain international peace and security, and to that end: to take effective collective measures for the prevention and removal of threats to the peace, and for the suppression of acts of aggression or other breaches of the peace, and to bring about by peaceful means, and in conformity with the principles of justice and international law, adjustment or settlement of international disputes or situations which might lead to a breach of the peace;

2. To develop friendly relations among nations based on respect for the principles of equal rights and self-determination of peoples, and to take other appropriate measures to strengthen universal peace;

3. To achieve international co-operation in solving international problems of an economic, social, cultural, or humanitarian character, and in promoting and encouraging respect for human rights and for fundamental freedoms for all without distinction as to race, sex, language, or religion; and

4. To be a centre for harmonising the actions of nations in the attainment of these common ends.

Article 2

The Organization and its Members, in pursuit of the Purposes stated in Article 1, shall act in accordance with the following Principles.

[1] See Appendix II for a list of United Nations members.

1. The Organization is based on the principle of the sovereign equality of all its Members.

2. All Members, in order to ensure to all of them the rights and benefits resulting from membership, shall fulfil in good faith the obligations assumed by them in accordance with the present Charter.

3. All Members shall settle their international disputes by peaceful means in such a manner that international peace and security, and justice, are not endangered.

4. All Members shall refrain in their international relations from the threat or use of force against the territorial integrity or political independence of any state, or in any other manner inconsistent with the Purposes of the United Nations.

5. All Members shall give the United Nations every assistance in any action it takes in accordance with the present Charter, and shall refrain from giving assistance to any state against which the United Nations is taking preventive or enforcement action.

6. The Organization shall ensure that states which are not Members of the United Nations act in accordance with these Principles so far as may be necessary for the maintenance of peace and security.

7. Nothing contained in the present Charter shall authorise the United Nations to intervene in matters which are essentially within the domestic jurisdiction of any state or shall require the Members to submit such matters to settlement under the present Charter; but this principle shall not prejudice the application of enforcement measures under Chapter VII.

Chapter II

MEMBERSHIP

Article 3

The original Members of the United Nations shall be the states which, having participated in the United Nations Conference on International Organization at San Francisco, or having previously signed the Declaration by United Nations on 1 January 1942, sign the present Charter and ratify it in accordance with Article 110.

Article 4

1. Membership in the United Nations is open to all other peace-loving states which accept the obligations contained in the present Charter and, in the judgment of the Organization, are able and willing to carry out these obligations.

2. The admission of any such state to membership in the United Nations will be effected by a decision of the General Assembly upon the recommendation of the Security Council.

Article 5

A Member of the United Nations against which preventive or enforcement action has been taken by the Security Council may be suspended from the exercise of the rights and privileges of membership by the General Assembly upon the recommendation of the Security Council. The exercise of these rights and privileges may be restored by the Security Council.

Article 6

A Member of the United Nations which has persistently violated the Principles contained in the present Charter may be expelled from the Organization by the General Assembly upon the recommendation of the Security Council.

CHAPTER III

ORGANS

Article 7

1. There are established as the principal organs of the United Nations: a General Assembly, a Security Council, an Economic and Social Council, a Trusteeship Council, an International Court of Justice, and a Secretariat.
2. Such subsidiary organs as may be found necessary may be established in accordance with the present Charter.

Article 8

The United Nations shall place no restrictions on the eligibility of men and women to participate in any capacity and under conditions of equality in its principal and subsidiary organs.

CHAPTER IV

THE GENERAL ASSEMBLY

Composition

Article 9

1. The General Assembly shall consist of all the Members of the United Nations.
2. Each Member shall have not more than five representatives in the General Assembly.

Functions and Powers

Article 10

The General Assembly may discuss any questions or any matters within the scope of the present Charter or relating to the powers and functions of any organs provided for in the present Charter, and, except as provided in Article 12, may make recommendations to the Members of the United Nations or to the Security Council or to both on any such questions or matters.

Article 11

1. The General Assembly may consider the general principles of co-operation in the maintenance of international peace and security, including the principles governing disarmament and the regulation of armaments, and may make recommendations with regard to such principles to the Members or to the Security Council or to both.
2. The General Assembly may discuss any questions relating to the maintenance of international peace and security brought before it by any Member of the United Nations, or by the Security Council, or by a state which is not a Member of the United Nations in accordance with Article 35, paragraph 2, and, except as provided in Article 12, may make recommendations with regard to any such questions to the state or states concerned or to the Security Council or to both. Any such question on which action is necessary shall be referred to the Security Council by the General Assembly either before or after discussion.

3. The General Assembly may call the attention of the Security Council to situations which are likely to endanger international peace and security.

4. The powers of the General Assembly set forth in this Article shall not limit the general scope of Article 10.

Article 12

1. While the Security Council is exercising in respect of any dispute or situation the functions assigned to it in the present Charter, the General Assembly shall not make any recommendation with regard to that dispute or situation unless the Security Council so requests.

2. The Secretary-General, with the consent of the Security Council, shall notify the General Assembly at each session of any matters relative to the maintenance of international peace and security which are being dealt with by the Security Council and shall similarly notify the General Assembly, or the Members of the United Nations if the General Assembly is not in session, immediately the Security Council ceases to deal with such matters.

Article 13

1. The General Assembly shall initiate studies and make recommendations for the purpose of:

a. promoting international co-operation in the political field and encouraging the progressive development of international law and its codification;

b. promoting international co-operation in the economic, social, cultural, educational, and health fields, and assisting in the realization of human rights and fundamental freedoms for all without distinction as to race, sex, language, or religion.

2. The further responsibilities, functions and powers of the General Assembly with respect to matters mentioned in paragraph 1(b) above are set forth in Chapters IX and X.

Article 14

Subject to the provisions of Article 12, the General Assembly may recommend measures for the peaceful adjustment of any situation, regardless of origin, which it deems likely to impair the general welfare or friendly relations among nations, including situations resulting from the violation of the provisions of the present Charter setting forth the Purposes and Principles of the United Nations.

Article 15

1. The General Assembly shall receive and consider annual and special reports from the Security Council; these reports shall include an account of the measures that the Security Council has decided upon or taken to maintain international peace and security.

2. The General Assembly shall receive and consider reports from the other organs of the United Nations.

Article 16

The General Assembly shall perform such functions with respect to the international trusteeship system as are assigned to it under Chapters XII and XIII, including the approval of the trusteeship agreements for areas not designated as strategic.

Article 17

1. The General Assembly shall consider and approve the budget of the Organization.

2. The expenses of the Organization shall be borne by the Members as apportioned by the General Assembly.

3. The General Assembly shall consider and approve any financial and budgetary arrangements with specialized agencies referred to in Article 57 and shall examine the administrative budgets of such specialized agencies with a view to making recommendations to the agencies concerned.

Voting

Article 18

1. Each member of the General Assembly shall have one vote.

2. Decisions of the General Assembly on important questions shall be made by a two-thirds majority of the members present and voting. These questions shall include: recommendations with respect to the maintenance of international peace and security, the election of the non-permanent members of the Security Council, the election of the members of the Economic and Social Council, the election of members of the Trusteeship Council in accordance with paragraph 1(c) of Article 86, the admission of new Members to the United Nations, the suspension of the rights and privileges of membership, the expulsion of Members, questions relating to the operation of the trusteeship system, and budgetary questions.

3. Decisions on other questions, including the determination of additional categories of questions to be decided by a two-thirds majority, shall be made by a majority of the members present and voting.

Article 19

A Member of the United Nations which is in arrears in the payment of its financial contributions to the Organization shall have no vote in the General Assembly if the amount of its arrears equals or exceeds the amount of the contributions due from it for the preceding two full years. The General Assembly may, nevertheless, permit such a Member to vote if it is satisfied that the failure to pay is due to conditions beyond the control of the Member.

Article 20

The General Assembly shall meet in regular annual sessions and in such special sessions as occasion may require. Special sessions shall be convoked by the Secretary-General at the request of the Security Council or of a majority of the Members of the United Nations.

Article 21

The General Assembly shall adopt its own rules of procedure. It shall elect its President for each session.

Article 22

The General Assembly may establish such subsidiary organs as it deems necessary for the performance of its functions.

CHAPTER V

THE SECURITY COUNCIL

Composition

Article 23[2]

1. The Security Council shall consist of fifteen[3] Members of the United Nations. The Republic of China, France, the Union of Soviet Socialist Republics, the United Kingdom of Great Britain and Northern Ireland, and the United States of America shall be permanent members of the Security Council. The General Assembly shall elect ten other Members of the United Nations to be non-permanent members of the Security Council, due regard being specially paid, in the first instance to the contribution of Members of the United Nations to the maintenance of international peace and security and to the other purposes of the Organization, and also to equitable geographical distribution.

2. The non-permanent members of the Security Council shall be elected for a term of two years. In the first election of the non-permanent members after the increase of the membership of the Security Council from eleven to fifteen, two of the four additional members shall be chosen for a term of one year. A retiring member shall not be eligible for immediate re-election.

3. Each member of the Security Council shall have one representative.

Functions and Powers

Article 24

1. In order to ensure prompt and effective action by the United Nations, its Members confer on the Security Council primary responsibility for the maintenance of international peace and security, and agree that in carrying out its duties under this responsibility the Security Council acts on their behalf.

2. In discharging these duties the Security Council shall act in accordance with the Purposes and Principles of the United Nations. The specific powers granted to the Security Council for the discharge of these duties are laid down in Chapters VI, VII, VIII and XII.

3. The Security Council shall submit annual and, when necessary, special reports to the General Assembly for its consideration.

Article 25

The Members of the United Nations agree to accept and carry out the decisions of the Security Council in accordance with the present Charter.

Article 26

In order to promote the establishment and maintenance of international peace and security with the least diversion for armaments of the world's human and economic resources, the Security Council shall be responsible for formulating, with the assistance of the Military Staff Committee referred to in Article 47, plans to be submitted to the

---

[2] As amended in 1965.
[3] Formerly eleven.

Members of the United Nations for the establishment of a system for the regulation of armaments.

Voting

Article 27[4]

1. Each member of the Security Council shall have one vote.
2. Decisions of the Security Council on procedural matters shall be made by an affirmative vote of nine[5] members.
3. Decisions of the Security Council on all other matters shall be made by an affirmative vote of nine[5] members including the concurring votes of the permanent members; provided that, in decisions under Chapter VI, and under paragraph 3 of Article 52, a party to a dispute shall abstain from voting.

Procedure

Article 28

1. The Security Council shall be so organized as to be able to function continuously. Each member of the Security Council shall for this purpose be represented at all times at the seat of the Organization.
2. The Security Council shall hold periodical meetings at which each of its members may, if it so desires, be represented by a member of the government or by some other specially designated representative.
3. The Security Council may hold meetings at such places other than the seat of the Organization as in its judgment will best facilitate its work.

Article 29

The Security Council may establish such subsidiary organs as it deems necessary for the performance of its functions.

Article 30

The Security Council shall adopt its own rules of procedure, including the method of selecting its President.

Article 31

Any Member of the United Nations which is not a member of the Security Council may participate, without vote, in the discussion of any question brought before the Security Council whenever the latter considers that the interests of that Member are specially affected.

Article 32

Any Member of the United Nations which is not a member of the Security Council or any state which is not a Member of the United Nations, if it is a party to a dispute under consideration by the Security Council, shall be invited to participate, without vote, in

---

[4] As amended in 1965.
[5] Formerly seven.

the discussion relating to the dispute. The Security Council shall lay down such conditions as it deems just for the participation of a state which is not a Member of the United Nations.

CHAPTER VI

PACIFIC SETTLEMENT OF DISPUTES

Article 33

1. The parties to any dispute, the continuance of which is likely to endanger the maintenance of international peace and security, shall, first of all, seek a solution by negotiation, enquiry, mediation, conciliation, arbitration, judicial settlement, resort to regional agencies or arrangements, or other peaceful means of their own choice.
2. The Security Council shall, when it deems necessary, call upon the parties to settle their dispute by such means.

Article 34

The Security Council may investigate any dispute, or any situation which might lead to international friction or give rise to a dispute, in order to determine whether the continuance of the dispute or situation is likely to endanger the maintenance of international peace and security.

Article 35

1. Any Member of the United Nations may bring any dispute, or any situation of the nature referred to in Article 34, to the attention of the Security Council or of the General Assembly.
2. A state which is not a Member of the United Nations may bring to the attention of the Security Council or of the General Assembly any dispute to which it is a party if it accepts in advance, for the purposes of the dispute, the obligations of pacific settlement provided in the present Charter.
3. The proceedings of the General Assembly in respect of matters brought to its attention under this Article will be subject to the provisions of Articles 11 and 12.

Article 36

1. The Security Council may, at any stage of a dispute of the nature referred to in Article 33 or of a situation of like nature, recommend appropriate procedures or methods of adjustment.
2. The Security Council should take into consideration any procedures for the settlement of the dispute which have already been adopted by the parties.
3. In making recommendations under this Article the Security Council should also take into consideration that legal disputes should as a general rule be referred by the parties to the International Court of Justice in accordance with the provisions of the Statute of the Court.

Article 37

1. Should the parties to a dispute of the nature referred to in Article 33 fail to settle it by the means indicated in that Article, they shall refer it to the Security Council.

2. If the Security Council deems that the continuance of the dispute is in fact likely to endanger the maintenance of international peace and security, it shall decide whether to take action under Article 36 or to recommend such terms of settlement as it may consider appropriate.

Article 38

Without prejudice to the provisions of Articles 33 to 37, the Security Council may, if all the parties to any dispute so request, make recommendations to the parties with a view to a pacific settlement of the dispute.

CHAPTER VII

ACTION WITH RESPECT TO THREATS TO THE PEACE, BREACHES OF THE PEACE, AND ACTS OF AGGRESSION

Article 39

The Security Council shall determine the existence of any threat to the peace, breach of the peace, or act of aggression and shall make recommendations, or decide what measures shall be taken in accordance with Articles 41 and 42, to maintain or restore international peace and security.

Article 40

In order to prevent an aggravation of the situation, the Security Council may, before making the recommendations or deciding upon the measures provided for in Article 39, call upon the parties concerned to comply with such provisional measures as it deems necessary or desirable. Such provisional measures shall be without prejudice to the rights, claims, or position of the parties concerned. The Security Council shall duly take account of failure to comply with such provisional measures.

Article 41

The Security Council may decide what measures not involving the use of armed force are to be employed to give effect to its decisions, and it may call upon the Members of the United Nations to apply such measures. These may include complete or partial interruption of economic relations and of rail, sea, air, postal, telegraphic, radio, and other means of communication, and the severance of diplomatic relations.

Article 42

Should the Security Council consider that measures provided for in Article 41 would be inadequate or have proved to be inadequate, it may take such action by air, sea, or land forces as may be necessary to maintain or restore international peace or security. Such action may include demonstrations, blockade, and other operations by air, sea, or land forces of Members of the United Nations.

Article 43

1. All Members of the United Nations, in order to contribute to the maintenance of international peace and security, undertake to make available to the Security Council, on its call and in accordance with a special agreement or agreements, armed forces,

assistance, and facilities, including rights of passage, necessary for the purpose of maintaining international peace and security.

2. Such agreement or agreements shall govern the numbers and types of forces, their degree of readiness and general location, and the nature of the facilities and assistance to be provided.

3. The agreement or agreements shall be negotiated as soon as possible on the initiative of the Security Council. They shall be concluded between the Security Council and Members or between the Security Council and groups of Members and shall be subject to ratification by the signatory states in accordance with their respective constitutional processes.

Article 44

When the Security Council has decided to use force it shall, before calling upon a Member not represented on it to provide armed forces in fulfilment of the obligations assumed under Article 43, invite that Member, if the Member so desires, to participate in the decisions of the Security Council concerning the employment of contingents of that Member's armed forces.

Article 45

In order to enable the United Nations to take urgent military measures, Members shall hold immediately available national airforce contingents for combined international enforcement action. The strength and degree of readiness of these contingents and plans for their combined action shall be determined, within the limits laid down in the special agreement or agreements referred to in Article 43, by the Security Council with the assistance of the Military Staff Committee.

Article 46

Plans for the application of armed force shall be made by the Security Council with the assistance of the Military Staff Committee.

Article 47

1. There shall be established a Military Staff Committee to advise and assist the Security Council on all questions relating to the Security Council's military requirements for the maintenance of international peace and security, the employment and command of forces placed at its disposal, the regulation of armaments, and possible disarmament.

2. The Military Staff Committee shall consist of the Chiefs of Staff of the permanent members of the Security Council or their representatives. Any Member of the United Nations not permanently represented on the Committee shall be invited by the Committee to be associated with it when the efficient discharge of the Committee's responsibilities requires the participation of that Member in its work.

3. The Military Staff Committee shall be responsible under the Security Council for the strategic direction of any armed forces placed at the disposal of the Security Council. Questions relating to the command of such forces shall be worked out subsequently.

4. The Military Staff Committee with the authorization of the Security Council and after consultation with appropriate regional agencies, may establish regional subcommittees.

Article 48

1. The action required to carry out the decisions of the Security Council for the maintenance of international peace and security shall be taken by all the Members of the United Nations or by some of them, as the Security Council may determine.

2. Such decisions shall be carried out by the Members of the United Nations directly and through their action in the appropriate international agencies of which they are members.

Article 49

The Members of the United Nations shall join in affording mutual assistance in carrying out the measures decided upon by the Security Council.

Article 50

If preventive or enforcement measures against any state are taken by the Security Council, any other state, whether a Member of the United Nations or not, which finds itself confronted with special economic problems arising from the carrying out of those measures shall have the right to consult the Security Council with regard to a solution of those problems.

Article 51

Nothing in the present Charter shall impair the inherent right of individual or collective self-defence if an armed attack occurs against a Member of the United Nations, until the Security Council has taken measures necessary to maintain international peace and security. Measures taken by Members in the exercise of this right of self-defence shall be immediately reported to the Security Council and shall not in any way affect the authority and responsibility of the Security Council under the present Charter to take at any time such action as it deems necessary in order to maintain or restore international peace and security.

CHAPTER VIII

REGIONAL ARRANGEMENTS

Article 52

1. Nothing in the present Charter precludes the existence of regional arrangements or agencies for dealing with such matters relating to the maintenance of international peace and security as are appropriate for regional action, provided that such arrangements or agencies and their activities are consistent with the Purposes and Principles of the United Nations.

2. The Members of the United Nations entering into such arrangements or constituting such agencies shall make every effort to achieve pacific settlement of local disputes through such regional arrangements or by such regional agencies before referring them to the Security Council.

3. The Security Council shall encourage the development of pacific settlement of local disputes through such regional arrangements or by such regional agencies either on the initiative of the states concerned or by reference from the Security Council.

4. This Article in no way impairs the application of Articles 34 and 35.

Article 53

1. The Security Council shall, where appropriate, utilize such regional arrangements or agencies for enforcement action under its authority. But no enforcement action shall be taken under regional arrangements or by regional agencies without the authorization of the Security Council, with the exception of measures against any enemy state, as defined in paragraph 2 of this Article, provided for pursuant to Article 107 or in regional arrangements directed against renewal of aggressive policy on the part of any such state, until such time as the Organization may, on request of the Governments concerned, be charged with the responsibility for preventing further aggression by such a state.

2. The term enemy state as used in paragraph 1 of this Article applies to any state which during the Second World War has been an enemy of any signatory of the present Charter.

Article 54

The Security Council shall at all times be kept fully informed of activities undertaken or in contemplation under regional arrangements or by regional agencies for the maintenance of international peace and security.

CHAPTER IX

INTERNATIONAL ECONOMIC AND SOCIAL CO-OPERATION

Article 55

With a view to the creation of conditions of stability and well-being which are necessary for peaceful and friendly relations among nations based on respect for the principle of equal rights and self-determination of peoples, the United Nations shall promote:

a. higher standards of living, full employment, and conditions of economic and social progress and development;

b. solutions of international economic, social, health, and related problems; and international cultural and educational co-operation; and

c. universal respect for, and observance of, human rights and fundamental freedoms for all without distinction as to race, sex, language, or religion.

Article 56

All Members pledge themselves to take joint and separate action in co-operation with the Organization for the achievement of the purposes set forth in Article 55.

Article 57

1. The various specialized agencies, established by intergovernmental agreement and having wide international responsibilities, as defined in their basic instruments, in economic, social, cultural, educational, health, and related fields, shall be brought into relationship with the United Nations in accordance with the provisions of Article 63.

2. Such agencies thus brought into relationship with the United Nations are hereinafter referred to as specialized agencies.

Article 58

The Organization shall make recommendations for the co-ordination of the policies and activities of the specialized agencies.

Article 59

The Organization shall, where appropriate, initiate negotiations among the states concerned for the creation of any new specialised agencies required for the accomplishment of the purposes set forth in Article 55.

Article 60

Responsibility for the discharge of the functions of the Organization set forth in this Chapter shall be vested in the General Assembly and, under the authority of the General Assembly, in the Economic and Social Council, which shall have for this purpose the powers set forth in Chapter X.

CHAPTER X

THE ECONOMIC AND SOCIAL COUNCIL

Composition

Article 61[6]

1. The Economic and Social Council shall consist of fifty-four[7] Members of the United Nations elected by the General Assembly.

2. Subject to the provisions of paragraph 3, eighteen[8] members of the Economic and Social Council shall be elected each year for a term of three years. A retiring member shall be eligible for immediate re-election.

3. At the first election after the increase in the membership of the Economic and Social Council from twenty-seven to fifty-four members, in addition to the members elected in place of the nine[8] members whose term of office expires at the end of that year, twenty-seven additional members shall be elected. Of these twenty-seven additional members, the term of office of nine[8] members so elected shall expire at the end of one year, and of nine[8] other members at the end of two years, in accordance with arrangements made by the General Assembly.

4. Each member of the Economic and Social Council shall have one representative.

Functions and Powers

Article 62

1. The Economic and Social Council may make or initiate studies and reports with respect to international economic, social, cultural, educational, health, and related matters and may make recommendations with respect to any such matters to the General Assembly, to the Members of the United Nations, and to the specialized agencies concerned.

2. It may make recommendations for the purpose of promoting respect for, and observance of, human rights and fundamental freedoms for all.

[6] As amended in 1973.
[7] Originally eighteen.
[8] Originally six.

3. It may prepare draft conventions for submission to the General Assembly, with respect to matters falling within its competence.

4. It may call, in accordance with the rules prescribed by the United Nations, international conferences on matters falling within its competence.

Article 63

1. The Economic and Social Council may enter into agreements with any of the agencies referred to in Article 57, defining the terms on which the agency concerned shall be brought into relationship with the United Nations. Such agreements shall be subject to approval by the General Assembly.

2. It may co-ordinate the activities of the specialized agencies through consultation with and recommendations to such agencies and through recommendations to the General Assembly and to the Members of the United Nations.

Article 64

1. The Economic and Social Council may take appropriate steps to obtain regular reports from the specialized agencies. It may make arrangements with the Members of the United Nations and with the specialized agencies to obtain reports on the steps taken to give effect to its own recommendations and to recommendations on matters falling within its competence made by the General Assembly.

2. It may communicate its observations on these reports to the General Assembly.

Article 65

The Economic and Social Council may furnish information to the Security Council and shall assist the Security Council upon its request.

Article 66

1. The Economic and Social Council shall perform such functions as fall within its competence in connexion with the carrying out of the recommendations of the General Assembly.

2. It may, with the approval of the General Assembly, perform services at the request of Members of the United Nations and at the request of specialized agencies.

3. It shall perform such other functions as are specified elsewhere in the present Charter or as may be assigned to it by the General Assembly.

Voting

Article 67

1. Each Member of the Economic and Social Council shall have one vote.

2. Decisions of the Economic and Social Council shall be made by a majority of the members present and voting.

Procedure

Article 68

The Economic and Social Council shall set up commissions in economic and social fields and for the promotion of human rights, and such other commissions as may be required for the performance of its functions.

Article 69

The Economic and Social Council shall invite any Member of the United Nations to participate, without vote, in its deliberations on any matter of particular concern to that Member.

Article 70

The Economic and Social Council may make arrangements for representatives of the specialized agencies to participate, without vote, in its deliberations and in those of the commissions established by it, and for its representatives to participate in the deliberations of the specialized agencies.

Article 71

The Economic and Social Council may make suitable arrangements for consultation with non-governmental organizations which are concerned with matters within its competence. Such arrangements may be made with international organizations and, where appropriate, with national organizations after consultation with the Member of the United Nations concerned.

Article 72

1. The Economic and Social Council shall adopt its own rules of procedure, including the method of selecting its President.

2. The Economic and Social Council shall meet as required in accordance with its rules, which shall include provision for the convening of meetings on the request of a majority of its members.

CHAPTER XI

DECLARATION REGARDING NON-SELF-GOVERNING TERRITORIES

Article 73

Members of the United Nations which have or assume responsibilities for the administration of territories whose peoples have not yet attained a full measure of self-government recognize the principle that the interests of the inhabitants of these territories are paramount, and accept as a sacred trust the obligation to promote to the utmost, within the system of international peace and security established by the present Charter, the well-being of the inhabitants of these territories, and, to this end:

a. to ensure, with due respect for the culture of the peoples concerned, their political, economic, social, and educational advancement, their just treatment, and their protection against abuses;

b. to develop self-government, to take due account of the political aspirations of the peoples, and to assist them in the progressive development of their free political institutions, according to the particular circumstances of each territory and its peoples and their varying stages of advancement;

c. to further international peace and security;

d. to promote constructive measures of development, to encourage research, and to co-operate with one another and, when and where appropriate, with specialized international bodies with a view to the practical achievement of the social, economic, and scientific purposes set forth in this Article; and

e. to transmit regularly to the Secretary-General for information purposes, subject to such limitation as security and constitutional considerations may require, statistical and other information of a technical nature relating to economic, social, and educational conditions in the territories for which they are respectively responsible other than those territories to which Chapters XII and XIII apply.

Article 74

Members of the United Nations also agree to their policy in respect of the territories to which this Chapter applies, no less than in respect of their metropolitan areas, must be based on the general principle of good neighbourliness, due account being taken of the interests and well-being of the rest of the world, in social, economic, and commercial matters.

CHAPTER XII

INTERNATIONAL TRUSTEESHIP SYSTEM

Article 75

The United Nations shall establish under its authority an international trusteeship system for the administration and supervision of such territories as may be placed thereunder by subsequent individual agreements. These territories are hereinafter referred to as trust territories.

Article 76

The basic objectives of the trusteeship system, in accordance with the Purposes of the United Nations laid down in Article 1 of the present Charter, shall be:

a. to further international peace and security;

b. to promote the political, economic, social, and educational advancement of the inhabitants of the trust territories, and their progressive development towards self-government or independence as may be appropriate to the particular circumstances of each territory and its peoples and the freely expressed wishes of the peoples concerned, and as may be provided by the terms of each trusteeship agreement;

c. to encourage respect for human rights and for fundamental freedoms for all without distinction as to race, sex, language, or religion, and to encourage recognition of the inter-dependence of the peoples of the world; and

d. to ensure equal treatment in social, economic, and commercial matters for all Members of the United Nations and their nationals, and also equal treatment for the latter in the administration of justice, without prejudice to the attainment of the foregoing objectives and subject to the provisions of Article 80.

Article 77

1. The trusteeship system shall apply to such territories in the following categories as may be placed thereunder by means of trusteeship agreements:

a. territories now held under mandate;

b. territories which may be detached from enemy states as a result of the Second World War; and

c. territories voluntarily placed under the system by states responsible for their administration.

2. It will be a matter for subsequent agreement as to which territories in the foregoing categories will be brought under the trusteeship system and upon what terms.

Article 78

The trusteeship system shall not apply to territories which have become Members of the United Nations, relationship among which shall be based on respect for the principle of sovereign equality.

Article 79

The terms of trusteeship for each territory to be placed under the trusteeship system, including any alteration or amendment, shall be agreed upon by the states directly concerned, including the mandatory powers in the case of territories held under mandate by a Member of the United Nations, and shall be approved as provided for in Articles 83 and 85.

Article 80

1. Except as may be agreed upon in individual trusteeship agreements, made under Articles 77, 79, and 81, placing each territory under the trusteeship system, and until such agreements have been concluded, nothing in this Chapter shall be construed in or of itself to alter in any manner the rights whatsoever of any states or any peoples or the terms of existing international instruments to which Members of the United Nations may respectively be parties.

2. Paragraph 1 of this Article shall not be interpreted as giving grounds for delay or postponement of the negotiation and conclusion of agreements for placing mandated and other territories under the trusteeship system as provided for in Article 77.

Article 81

The trusteeship agreement shall in each case include the terms under which the trust territory will be administered and designate the authority which will exercise the administration of the trust territory. Such authority hereinafter called the administering authority, may be one or more states or the Organization itself.

Article 82

There may be designated, in any trusteeship agreement, a strategic area or areas which may include part or all of the trust territory to which the agreement applies, without prejudice to any special agreement or agreements made under Article 43.

Article 83

1. All functions of the United Nations relating to strategic areas, including the approval of the terms of the trusteeship agreements and of their alteration or amendment, shall be exercised by the Security Council.

2. The basic objectives set forth in Article 76 shall be applicable to the people of each strategic area.

3. The Security Council shall, subject to the provisions of the trusteeship agreements and without prejudice to security considerations, avail itself of the assistance of the Trusteeship Council to perform those functions of the United Nations under the trusteeship system relating to political, economic, social, and educational matters in the strategic areas.

Article 84

It shall be the duty of the administering authority to ensure that the trust territory shall play its part in the maintenance of international peace and security. To this end the administering authority may make use of volunteer forces, facilities, and assistance from the trust territory in carrying out the obligations towards the Security Council undertaken in this regard by the administering authority, as well as for local defence and the maintenance of law and order within the trust territory.

Article 85

1. The functions of the United Nations with regard to trusteeship agreements for all areas not designated as strategic, including the approval of the terms of the trusteeship agreements and of their alteration or amendment, shall be exercised by the General Assembly.

2. The Trusteeship Council, operating under the authority of the General Assembly, shall assist the General Assembly in carrying out these functions.

CHAPTER XIII

THE TRUSTEESHIP COUNCIL

Composition

Article 86

1. The Trusteeship Council shall consist of the following Members of the United Nations.

   a. those Members administering trust territories;
   b. such of those Members mentioned by name in Article 23 as are not administering trust territories; and
   c. As many other Members elected for three-year terms by the General Assembly as may be necessary to ensure that the total number of members of the Trusteeship Council is equally divided between those Members of the United Nations which administer trust territories and those which do not.

2. Each member of the Trusteeship Council shall designate one specially qualified person to represent it therein.

Functions and Powers

Article 87

The General Assembly and, under its authority, and Trusteeship Council, in carrying out their functions, may:

   a. consider reports submitted by the administering authority;
   b. accept petitions and examine them in consultation with the administering authority;
   c. provide for periodic visits to the respective trust territories at times agreed upon with the administering authority; and
   d. take these and other actions in conformity with the terms of the trusteeship agreements.

Article 88

The Trusteeship Council shall formulate a questionnaire on the political, economic, social, and educational advancement of the inhabitants of each trust territory, and the administering authority for each trust territory within the competence of the General Assembly shall make an annual report to the General Assembly upon the basis of such questionnaire.

Voting

Article 89

1. Each member of the Trusteeship Council shall have one vote.
2. Decisions of the Trusteeship Council shall be made by a majority of the members present and voting.

Procedure

Article 90

1. The Trusteeship Council shall adopt its own rules of procedure, including the method of selecting its President.
2. The Trusteeship Council shall meet as required in accordance with its rules. which shall include provision for the convening of meetings on the request of a majority of its members.

Article 91

The Trusteeship Council shall, when appropriate, avail itself of the assistance of the Economic and Social Council and of the specialized agencies in regard to matters with which they are respectively concerned.

CHAPTER XIV

THE INTERNATIONAL COURT OF JUSTICE

Article 92

The International Court of Justice shall be the principal judicial organ of the United Nations. It shall function in accordance with the annexed Statute, which is based upon the Statute of the Permanent Court of International Justice and forms an integral part of the present Charter.

Article 93

1. All Members of the United Nations are *ipso facto* parties to the Statute of the International Court of Justice.
2. A state which is not a Member of the United Nations may become a party to the Statute of the International Court of Justice on conditions to be determined in each case by the General Assembly upon the recommendation of the Security Council.

Article 94

1. Each Member of the United Nations undertakes to comply with the decision of the International Court of Justice in any case to which it is a party.

2. If any party to a case fails to perform the obligations incumbent upon it under a judgment rendered by the Court, the other party may have recourse to the Security Council, which may, if it deems necessary, make recommendations or decide upon measures to be taken to give effect to the judgment.

Article 95

Nothing in the present Charter shall prevent Members of the United Nations from entrusting the solution of their differences to other tribunals by virtue of agreements already in existence or which may be concluded in the future.

Article 96

1. The General Assembly or the Security Council may request the International Court of Justice to give an advisory opinion on any legal question.

2. Other organs of the United Nations and specialized agencies, which may at any time be so authorized by the General Assembly, may also request advisory opinions of the Court on legal questions arising within the scope of their activities.

CHAPTER XV

THE SECRETARIAT

Article 97

The Secretariat shall comprise a Secretary-General and such staff as the Organization may require. The Secretary-General shall be appointed by the General Assembly upon the recommendation of the Security Council. He shall be the chief administrative officer of the Organization.

Article 98

The Secretary-General shall act in that capacity in all meetings of the General Assembly, of the Security Council, of the Economic and Social Council, and of the Trusteeship Council, and shall perform such other functions as are entrusted to him by these organs. The Secretary-General shall make an annual report to the General Assembly on the work of the Organization.

Article 99

The Secretary-General may bring to the attention of the Security Council any matter which in his opinion may threaten the maintenance of international peace and security.

Article 100

1. In the performance of their duties the Secretary-General and the staff shall not seek or receive instructions from any government or from any other authority external to the Organization. They shall refrain from any action which might reflect on their position as international officials responsible only to the Organization.

2. Each Member of the United Nations undertakes to respect the exclusively international character of the responsibilities of the Secretary-General and the staff and not to seek to influence them in the discharge of their responsibilities.

Article 101

1. The staff shall be appointed by the Secretary-General under regulations established by the General Assembly.

2. Appropriate staffs shall be permanently assigned to the Economic and Social Council, the Trusteeship Council, and, as required, to other organs of the United Nations. These staffs shall form a part of the Secretariat.

3. The paramount consideration in the employment of the staff and in the determination of the conditions of service shall be the necessity of securing the highest standards of efficiency, competence, and integrity. Due regard shall be paid to the importance of recruiting the staff on as wide a geographical basis as possible.

Chapter XVI

MISCELLANEOUS PROVISIONS

Article 102

1. Every treaty and every international agreement entered into by any Member of the United Nations after the present Charter comes into force shall as soon as possible be registered with the Secretariat and published by it.

2. No party to any such treaty or international agreement which has not been registered in accordance with the provisions of paragraph 1 of this Article may invoke that treaty or agreement before any organ of the United Nations.

Article 103

In the event of a conflict between the obligations of the Members of the United Nations under the present Charter and their obligations under any other international agreement, their obligations under the present Charter shall prevail.

Article 104

The Organization shall enjoy in the territory of each of its Members such legal capacity as may be necessary for the exercise of its functions and the fulfilment of its purposes.

Article 105

1. The Organization shall enjoy in the territory of each of its Members such privileges and immunities as are necessary for the fulfilment of its purposes.

2. Representatives of the Members of the United Nations and officials of the Organization shall similarly enjoy such privileges and immunities as are necessary for the independent exercise of their functions in connexion with the Organization.

3. The General Assembly may make recommendations with a view to determining the details of the application of paragraphs 1 and 2 of this Article or may propose conventions to the Members of the United Nations for this purpose.

CHAPTER XVII

TRANSITIONAL SECURITY ARRANGEMENTS

Article 106

Pending the coming into force of such special agreements referred to in Article 43 as in the opinion of the Security Council enable it to begin the exercise of its responsibilities under Article 42, the parties to the Four-Nation Declaration, signed at Moscow, 30 October 1943, and France, shall, in accordance with the provisions of paragraph 5 of that Declaration, consult with one another and as occasion requires with other Members of the United Nations with a view to such joint action on behalf of the Organization as may be necessary for the purpose of maintaining international peace and security.

Article 107

Nothing in the present Charter shall invalidate or preclude action, in relation to any state which during the Second World War has been an enemy of any signatory to the present Charter, taken or authorized as a result of that war by the Governments having responsibility for such action.

CHAPTER XVIII

AMENDMENTS

Article 108

Amendments to the present Charter shall come into force for all Members of the United Nations when they have been adopted by a vote of two-thirds of the members of the General Assembly and ratified in accordance with their respective constitutional processes by two-thirds of the Members of the United Nations, including all the permanent members of the Security Council.

Article 109[9]

1. A General Conference of the Members of the United Nations for the purpose of reviewing the present Charter may be held at a date and place to be fixed[10] by a two-thirds vote of the members of the General Assembly and by a vote of any ten members of the Security Council. Each Member of the United Nations shall have one vote in the conference.

2. Any alteration of the present Charter recommended by a two-thirds vote of the conference shall take effect when ratified in accordance with their respective constitutional processes by two-thirds of the Members of the United Nations including all the permanent members of the Security Council.

3. If such a conference has not been held before the tenth annual session of the General Assembly following the coming into force of the present Charter, the proposal to call such a conference shall be placed on the agenda of that session of the General Assembly, and the conference shall be held if so decided by a majority vote of the members of the General Assembly and by a vote of any seven members of the Security Council.

[9] As amended in 1968.
[10] Formerly seven.

CHAPTER XIX

RATIFICATION AND SIGNATURE

Article 110

1. The present Charter shall be ratified by the signatory states in accordance with their respective constitutional processes.

2. The ratifications shall be deposited with the Government of the United States of America, which shall notify all the signatory states of each deposit as well as the Secretary-General of the Organization when he has been appointed.

3. The present Charter shall come into force upon the deposit of ratifications by the Republic of China, France, the Union of Soviet and Socialist Republics, the United Kingdom of Great Britain and Northern Ireland, and the United States of America, and by a majority of the other signatory states. A protocol of the ratifications deposited shall thereupon be drawn up by the Government of the United States of America which shall communicate copies thereof to all the signatory states.

4. The states signatory to the present Charter which ratify it after it has come into force will become original Members of the United Nations on the date of the deposit of their respective ratifications.

Article 111

The present Charter, of which the Chinese, French, Russian, English, and Spanish texts are equally authentic, shall remain deposited in the archives of the Government of the United States of America. Duly certified copies thereof shall be transmitted by that Government to the Governments of the other signatory states.

In FAITH WHEREOF the representatives of the Governments of the United Nations have signed the present Charter.

DONE at the city of San Francisco the twenty-sixth day of June, one thousand nine hundred and forty-five.

STATUTE OF THE INTERNATIONAL COURT OF JUSTICE

Article 1

THE INTERNATIONAL COURT OF JUSTICE established by the Charter of the United Nations as the principal judicial organ of the United Nations shall be constituted and shall function in accordance with the provisions of the present Statute.

CHAPTER 1

ORGANIZATION OF THE COURT

Article 2

The Court shall be composed of a body of independent judges, elected regardless of their nationality from among persons of high moral character, who possess the qualifications required in their respective countries for appointment to the highest judicial offices, or are jurisconsults of recognized competence in international law.

Article 3

1. The Court shall consist of fifteen members, no two of whom may be nationals of the same state.

2. A person who for the purposes of membership in the Court could be regarded as a national of more than one state shall be deemed to be a national of the one in which he ordinarily exercises civil and political rights.

Article 4

1. The members of the Court shall be elected by the General Assembly and by the Security Council from a list of persons nominated by the national groups in the Permanent Court of Arbitration, in accordance with the following provisions.

2. In the case of Members of the United Nations not represented in the Permanent Court of Arbitration, candidates shall be nominated by national groups appointed for this purpose by their governments under the same conditions as those prescribed for members of the Permanent Court of Arbitration by Article 44 of the Convention of The Hague of 1907 for the pacific settlement of international disputes.

3. The conditions under which a state which is a party to the present Statute but is not a Member of the United Nations may participate in electing the members of the Court shall, in the absence of a special agreement, be laid down by the General Assembly upon recommendation of the Security Council.

Article 5

1. At least three months before the date of the election, the Secretary-General of the United Nations shall address a written request to the members of the Permanent Court of Arbitration belonging to the states which are parties to the present Statute, and to the members of the national groups appointed under Article 4, paragraph 2, inviting them to undertake, within a given time, by national groups, the nomination of persons in a position to accept the duties of a member of the Court.

2. No group may nominate more than four persons, not more than two of whom shall be of their own nationality. In no case may the number of candidates nominated by a group be more than double the number of seats to be filled.

Article 6

Before making these nominations, each national group is recommended to consult its highest court of justice, its legal faculties and schools of law, and its national academies and national sections of international academies devoted to the study of law.

Article 7

1. The Secretary-General shall prepare a list in alphabetical order of all the persons thus nominated. Save as provided in Article 12, paragraph 2, these shall be the only persons eligible.

2. The Secretary-General shall submit this list to the General Assembly and to the Security Council.

Article 8

The General Assembly and the Security Council shall proceed independently of one another to elect the members of the Court.

Article 9

At every election, the electors shall bear in mind not only that the persons to be elected should individually possess the qualifications required, but also that in the body as a whole the representation of the main forms of civilization and of the principal legal systems of the world should be assured.

Article 10

1. Those candidates who obtain an absolute majority of votes in the General Assembly and in the Security Council shall be considered as elected.

2. Any vote of the Security Council, whether for the election of judges or for the appointment of members of the conference envisaged in Article 12, shall be taken without any distinction between permanent and non-permanent members of the Security Council.

3. In the event of more than one national of the same state obtaining an absolute majority of the votes both of the General Assembly and of the Security Council, the eldest of these only shall be considered as elected.

Article 11

If, after the first meeting held for the purpose of the election, one or more seats remain to be filled, a second and, if necessary, a third meeting shall take place.

Article 12

1. If, after the third meeting, one or more seats still remain unfilled, a joint conference consisting of six members, three appointed by the General Assembly and three by the Security Council, may be formed at any time at the request of either the General Assembly or the Security Council, for the purpose of choosing by the vote of an absolute majority one name for each seat still vacant, to submit to the General Assembly and the Security Council for their respective acceptance.

2. If the joint conference is unanimously agreed upon any person who fulfils the required conditions, he may be included in its list, even though he was not included in the list of nominations referred to in Article 7.

3. If the joint conference is satisfied that it will not be successful in procuring an election, those members of the Court who have already been elected shall, within a period to be fixed by the Security Council, proceed to fill the vacant seats by selection from among those candidates who have obtained votes either in the General Assembly or in the Security Council.

4. In the event of an equality of votes among the judges, the eldest judge shall have a casting vote.

Article 13

1. The members of the Court shall be elected for nine years and may be re-elected; provided, however, that of the judges elected at the first election, the terms of five judges shall expire at the end of three years and the terms of five more judges shall expire at the end of six years.

2. The judges whose terms are to expire at the end of the above-mentioned initial periods of three and six years shall be chosen by lot to be drawn by the Secretary-General immediately after the first election has been completed.

3. The members of the Court shall continue to discharge their duties until their places have been filled. Though replaced, they shall finish any cases which they may have begun.

4. In the case of the resignation of a member of the Court, the resignation shall be addressed to the President of the Court for transmission to the Secretary-General. This last notification makes the place vacant.

Article 14

Vacancies shall be filled by the same method as that laid down for the first election, subject to the following provision: the Secretary-General shall, within one month of the occurrence of the vacancy, proceed to issue the invitations provided for in Article 5, and the date of the election shall be fixed by the Security Council.

Article 15

A member of the Court elected to replace a member whose term of office has not expired shall hold office for the remainder of his predecessor's term.

Article 16

1. No member of the Court may exercise any political or administrative function, or engage in any other occupation of a professional nature.
2. Any doubt on this point shall be settled by the decision of the Court.

Article 17

1. No member of the Court may act as agent, counsel, or advocate in any case.
2. No member may participate in the decision of any case in which he has previously taken part as agent, counsel, or advocate for one of the parties, or as a member of a national or international court, or of a commission of enquiry, or in any other capacity.
3. Any doubt on this point shall be settled by the decision of the Court.

Article 18

1. No member of the Court can be dismissed unless, in the unanimous opinion of the other members, he has ceased to fulfil the required conditions.
2. Formal notification thereof shall be made to the Secretary-General by the Registrar.
3. This notification makes the place vacant.

Article 19

The members of the Court, when engaged on the business of the Court, shall enjoy diplomatic privileges and immunities.

Article 20

Every member of the Court shall, before taking up his duties, make a solemn declaration in open court that he will exercise his powers impartially and conscientiously.

Article 21

1. The Court shall elect its President and Vice-President for three years; they may be re-elected.

2. The Court shall appoint its Registrar and may provide for the appointment of such other officers as may be necessary.

Article 22

1. The seat of the Court shall be established at The Hague. This, however, shall not prevent the Court from sitting and exercising its functions elsewhere whenever the Court considers it desirable.

2. The President and the Registrar shall reside at the seat of the Court.

Article 23

1. The Court shall remain permanently in session, except during the judicial vacations, the dates and duration of which shall be fixed by the Court.

2. Members of the Court are entitled to periodic leave, the dates and duration of which shall be fixed by the Court, having in mind the distance between The Hague and the home of each judge.

3. Members of the Court shall be bound, unless they are on leave or prevented from attending by illness or other serious reasons duly explained to the President, to hold themselves permanently at the disposal of the Court.

Article 24

1. If, for some special reason, a member of the Court considers that he should not take part in the decision of a particular case, he shall so inform the President.

2. If the President considers that for some special reason one of the members of the Court should not sit in a particular case, he shall give him notice accordingly.

3. If in any such case the member of the Court and the President disagree, the matter shall be settled by the decision of the Court.

Article 25

1. The full Court shall sit except when it is expressly provided otherwise in the present Statute.

2. Subject to the condition that the number of judges available to constitute the Court is not thereby reduced below eleven, the Rules of the Court may provide for allowing one or more judges, according to circumstances and in rotation, to be dispensed from sitting.

3. A quorum of nine judges shall suffice to constitute the Court.

Article 26

1. The Court may from time to time form one or more chambers, composed of three or more judges as the Court may determine, for dealing with particular categories of cases; for example, labour cases and cases relating to transit and communications.

2. The Court may at any time form a chamber for dealing with a particular case. The number of judges to constitute such a chamber shall be determined by the Court with the approval of the parties.

3. Cases shall be heard and determined by the chambers provided for in this Article if the parties so request.

Article 27

A judgment given by any of the chambers provided for in Articles 26 and 29 shall be considered as rendered by the Court.

Article 28

The chambers provided for in Articles 26 and 29 may, with the consent of the parties, sit and exercise their functions elsewhere than at The Hague.

Article 29

With a view to the speedy dispatch of business, the Court shall form annually a chamber composed of five judges which, at the request of the parties, may hear and determine cases by summary procedure. In addition, two judges shall be selected for the purpose of replacing judges who find it impossible to sit.

Article 30

1. The Court shall frame rules for carrying out its functions. In particular, it shall lay down rules of procedure.
2. The Rules of the Court may provide for assessors to sit with the Court or with any of its chambers, without the right to vote.

Article 31

1. Judges of the nationality of each of the parties shall retain their right to sit in the case before the Court.
2. If the Court includes upon the Bench a judge of the nationality of one of the parties, any other party may choose a person to sit as judge. Such person shall be chosen preferably from among those persons who have been nominated as candidates as provided in Articles 4 and 5.
3. If the Court includes upon the Bench no judge of the nationality of the parties, each of these parties may proceed to choose a judge as provided in paragraph 2 of this Article.
4. The provisions of this Article shall apply to the case of Articles 26 and 29. In such cases, the President shall request one or, if necessary, two of the members of the Court forming the chamber to give place to the members of the Court of the nationality of the parties concerned, and, failing such, or if they are unable to be present, to the judges specially chosen by the parties.
5. Should there be several parties in the same interest, they shall, for the purpose of the preceding provisions, be reckoned as one party only. Any doubt upon this point shall be settled by the decision of the Court.
6. Judges chosen as laid down in paragraphs 2, 3, and 4 of this Article shall fulfil the conditions required by Articles 2, 17 (paragraph 2), 20, and 24 of the present Statute. They shall take part in the decision on terms of complete equality with their colleagues.

Article 32

1. Each member of the Court shall receive an annual salary.
2. The President shall receive a special annual allowance.
3. The Vice-President shall receive a special allowance for every day on which he acts as President.

4. The judges chosen under Article 31, other than members of the Court, shall receive compensation for each day on which they exercise their functions.

5. These salaries, allowances, and compensation shall be fixed by the General Assembly. They may not be decreased during the term of office.

6. The salary of the Registrar shall be fixed by the General Assembly on the proposal of the Court.

7. Regulations made by the General Assembly shall fix the conditions under which retirement pensions may be given to members of the Court and to the Registrar, and the conditions under which members of the Court and the Registrar shall have their travelling expenses refunded.

8. The above salaries, allowances, and compensation shall be free of all taxation.

Article 33

The expenses of the Court shall be borne by the United Nations in such a manner as shall be decided by the General Assembly.

CHAPTER II

COMPETENCE OF THE COURT

Article 34

1. Only states may be parties in cases before the Court.

2. The Court, subject to and in conformity with its Rules, may request of public international organizations information relevant to cases before it, and shall receive such information presented by such organizations on their own initiative.

3. Whenever the construction of the constituent instrument of a public international organization or of an international convention adopted thereunder is in question in a case before the Court, the Registrar shall so notify the public international organization concerned and shall communicate to it copies of all the written proceedings.

Article 35

1. The Court shall be open to the states parties to the present Statute.

2. The conditions under which the Court shall be open to other states shall, subject to the special provisions contained in treaties in force, be laid down by the Security Council, but in no case shall such conditions place the parties in a position of inequality before the Court.

3. When a state which is not a Member of the United Nations is a party to a case, the Court shall fix the amount which that party is to contribute towards the expenses of the Court. This provision shall not apply if such state is bearing a share of the expenses of the Court.

Article 36

1. The jurisdiction of the Court comprises all cases which the parties refer to it and all matters specially provided for in the Charter of the United Nations or in treaties and conventions in force.

2. The states parties to the present Statute may at any time declare that they recognize as compulsory *ipso facto* and without special agreement, in relation to any other state accepting the same obligation, the jurisdiction of the Court in all legal disputes concerning:

a. the interpretation of a treaty;

b. any question of international law;

c. the existence of any fact which, if established, would constitute a breach of an international obligation;

d. the nature or extent of the reparation to be made for the breach of an international obligation.

3. The declarations referred to above may be made unconditionally or on condition of reciprocity on the part of several or certain states, or for a certain time.

4. Such declarations shall be deposited with the Secretary-General of the United Nations, who shall transmit copies thereof to the parties to the Statute and to the Registrar of the Court.

5. Declarations made under Article 36 of the Statute of the Permanent Court of International Justice and which are still in force shall be deemed, as between the parties to the present Statute, to be acceptances of the compulsory jurisdiction of the International Court of Justice for the period which they still have to run and in accordance with their terms.

6. In the event of a dispute as to whether the Court has jurisdiction, the matter shall be settled by the decision of the Court.

Article 37

Whenever a treaty or convention in force provides for reference of a matter to a tribunal to have been instituted by the League of Nations, or to the Permanent Court of International Justice, the matter shall, as between the parties to the present Statute, be referred to the International Court of Justice.

Article 38

1. The Court, whose function is to decide in accordance with international law such disputes as are submitted to it, shall apply:

a. international conventions, whether general or particular, establishing rules expressly recognized by the contesting states;

b. international custom, as evidence of a general practice accepted as law;

c. the general principles of law recognized by civilized nations;

d. subject to the provisions of Article 59, judicial decisions and the teachings of the most highly qualified publicists of the various nations, as subsidiary means for the determination of rules of law.

2. This provision shall not prejudice the power of the Court to decide a case *ex aequo et bono*, if the parties agree thereto.

CHAPTER III

PROCEDURE

Article 39

1. The official languages of the Court shall be French and English. If the parties agree that the case shall be conducted in French, the judgment shall be delivered in French. If the parties agree that the case shall be conducted in English, the judgment shall be delivered in English.

2. In the absence of an agreement as to which language shall be employed each party may, in the pleadings, use the language which it prefers; the decision of the Court shall

be given in French and English. In this case the Court shall at the same time determine which of the two texts shall be considered as authoritative.

3. The Court shall, at the request of any party, authorize a language other than French or English to be used by that party.

Article 40

1. Cases are brought before the Court, as the case may be, either by the notification of the special agreement or by a written application addressed to the Registrar. In either case the subject of the dispute and the parties shall be indicated.

2. The Registrar shall forthwith communicate the application to all concerned.

3. He shall also notify the Members of the United Nations through the Secretary-General, and also any other states entitled to appear before the Court.

Article 41

1. The Court shall have the power to indicate, if it considers that circumstances so require, any provisional measures which ought to be taken to preserve the respective rights of either party.

2. Pending the final decision, notice of the measures suggested shall forthwith be given to the parties and to the Security Council.

Article 53

1. Whenever one of the parties does not appear before the Court, or fails to defend its case, the other party may call upon the Court to decide in favour of its claim.

2. The Court must, before doing so, satisfy itself, not only that it has jurisdiction in accordance with Articles 36 and 37, but also that the claim is well founded in fact and law.

Article 55

1. All questions shall be decided by a majority of the judges present.

2. In the event of an equality of votes, the President or the judge who acts in his place shall have a casting vote.

Article 56

1. The judgment shall state the reasons on which it is based.

2. It shall contain the names of the judges who have taken part in the decision.

Article 57

If the judgment does not represent in whole or in part the unanimous opinion of the judges, any judge shall be entitled to deliver a separate opinion.

Article 58

The judgment shall be signed by the President and by the Registrar. It shall be read in open court, due notice having been given to the agents.

Article 59

The decision of the Court has no binding force except between the parties and in respect of that particular case.

Article 60

The judgment is final and without appeal. In the event of dispute as to the meaning or scope of the judgment, the Court shall construe it upon the request of any party.

Article 61

1. An application for revision of a judgment may be made only when it is based upon the discovery of some fact of such a nature as to be a decisive factor, which fact was, when the judgment was given, unknown to the Court and also to the party claiming revision, always provided that such ignorance was not due to negligence.

2. The proceedings for revision shall be opened by a judgment of the Court expressly recording the existence of the new fact, recognizing that it has such a character as to lay the case open to revision, and declaring the application admissible on this ground.

3. The Court may require previous compliance with the terms of the judgment before it admits proceedings in revision.

4. The application for revision must be made at latest within six months of the discovery of the new fact.

5. No application for revision may be made after the lapse of ten years from the date of the judgment.

Article 62

1. Should a state consider that it has an interest of a legal nature which may be affected by the decision in the case, it may submit a request to the Court to be permitted to intervene.

2. It shall be for the Court to decide upon this request.

Article 63

1. Whenever the construction of a covention to which states other than those concerned in the case are parties is in question, the Registrar shall notify all such states forthwith.

2. Every state so notified has the right to intervene in the proceedings; but if it uses this right, the construction given by the judgment will be equally binding upon it.

Article 64

Unless otherwise decided by the Court, each party shall bear its own costs.

CHAPTER IV

ADVISORY OPINIONS

Article 65

1. The Court may give an advisory opinion on any legal question at the request of whatever body may be authorized by or in accordance with the Charter of the United Nations to make such a request.

2. Questions upon which the advisory opinion of the Court is asked shall be laid before the Court by means of a written request containing an exact statement of the question upon which an opinion is required, and accompanied by all documents likely to throw light upon the question.

Article 66

The Registrar shall forthwith give notice of the request for an advisory opinion to all states entitled to appear before the Court.

2. The Registrar shall also, by means of a special and direct communication, notify any state entitled to appear before the Court or international organization considered by the Court, or, should it not be sitting, by the President, as likely to be able to furnish information on the question, that the Court will be prepared to receive, within a time limit to be fixed by the President, written statements, or to hear, at a public sitting to be held for the purpose, oral statements relating to the question.

3. Should any such state entitled to appear before the Court have failed to receive the special communication referred to in paragraph 2 of this Article, such state may express a desire to submit a written statement or to be heard; and the Court will decide.

4. States and organizations having presented written or oral statements or both shall be permitted to comment on the statements made by other states or organizations in the form, to the extent, and within the time limits which the Court, or, should it not be sitting, the President, shall decide in each particular case. Accordingly, the Registrar shall in due time communicate any such written statements to states and organizations having submitted similar statements.

Article 67

The Court shall deliver its advisory opinions in open court, notice having been given to the Secretary-General and to the representatives of Members of the United Nations, of other states and of international organizations immediately concerned.

Article 68

In the exercise of its advisory functions the Court shall further be guided by the provisions of the present Statute which apply in contentious cases to the extent to which it recognizes them to be applicable.

CHAPTER V

AMENDMENT

Article 69

Amendments to the present Statute shall be effected by the same procedure as is provided by the Charter of the United Nations for amendments to that Charter, subject however to any provisions which the General Assembly upon recommendation of the Security Council may adopt concerning the participation of states which are parties to the present Statute but are not Members of the United Nations.

Article 70

The Court shall have power to propose such amendments to the present statute as it may deem necessary, through written communications to the Secretary-General, for consideration in conformity with the provisions of Article 69.

MEMBERS OF THE UNITED NATIONS[1]

The date indicates the year of admission; no date is given for the 51 original members.

Afghanistan (1946)
Albania (1955)
Algeria (1962)
Angola (1976)
Antigua and Barbuda (1981)
Argentina
Australia
Austria (1955)
Bahamas (1973)
Bahrain (1971)
Bangladesh (1974)
Barbados (1966)
Belgium
Belize (1981)
Benin (formerly Dahomey) (1960)
Bhutan (1971)
Bolivia
Botswana (1966)
Brazil
Bulgaria (1955)
Burma (1948)
Burundi (1962)
Byleorussian S.S.R.
Cameroon (1960)
Canada
Cape Verde (1975)
Central African Republic (1960)
Chad (1960)
Chile
China
Colombia
Comoros (1975)
Congo (People's Republic of) (1960)
Costa Rica
Cuba
Cyprus (1960)
Czechoslovakia
Democratic Kampuchea (1955)
Democratic Yemen (1967)

Denmark
Djibouti (1977)
Dominica (1978)
Dominican Republic
Ecuador
Egypt
El Salvador
Equatorial Guinea (1968)
Ethiopia
Fiji (1970)
Finland (1955)
France
Gabon (1960)
Gambia (1965)
Germany, Democratic Republic (1973)
Germany, Federal Republic (1973)
Ghana (1957)
Greece
Grenada (1974)
Guatemala
Guinea (1958)
Guinea-Bissau (1974)
Guyana (1966)
Haiti
Honduras
Hungary (1955)
Iceland (1946)
India
Indonesia (1950)
Iran
Iraq
Ireland (1955)
Israel (1949)
Italy (1955)
Ivory Coast (1960)
Jamaica (1962)
Japan (1956)
Jordan (1955)
Kenya (1963)
Kuwait (1963)
Laos (1955)
Lebanon

Lesotho (1966)
Liberia
Libya (1955)
Luxembourg
Madagascar (1960)
Malawi (1964)
Malaysia (1957)
Maldives (1965)
Mali (1960)
Malta (1964)
Mauritania (1961)
Mauritius (1968)
Mexico
Mongolia (1961)
Morocco (1956)
Mozambique (1975)
Nepal (1955)
Netherlands
New Zealand
Nicaragua
Niger (1960)
Nigeria (1960)
Norway
Oman (1971)
Pakistan (1947)
Panama
Papua New Guinea (1975)
Paraguay
Peru
Philippines
Poland
Portugal (1955)
Qatar (1971)
Romania (1955)
Rwanda (1962)
St. Lucia (1979)
St. Vincent and the Grenadines (1980)
Samoa (1976)
São Tomé and Principe (1975)
Saudi Arabia
Senegal (1960)
Seychelles (1976)

[1] 157 members on September 31, 1982.

Sierra Leone (1961)

Singapore (1965)

Solomon Is. (1978)

Somalia (1960)

South Africa

Spain (1955)

Sri Lanka (1955)

Sudan (1956)

Suriname (1975)

Swaziland (1963)

Sweden (1946)

Syria

Tanzania (1964)

Thailand (1946)

Togo (1960)

Trinidad and Tobago
(1962)

Tunisia (1956)

Turkey

Uganda (1962)

Ukranian S.S.R.

U.S.S.R.

United   Arab   Emirates
(1971)

United Kingdom

United States

Upper Volta (1960)

Uruguay

Vanuatu (1981)

Venezuela

Vietnam (1977)

Yemen (1947)

Yugoslavia

Zaire (1960)

Zambia (1964)

Zimbabwe (1980)

GENERAL ASSEMBLY DECLARATION ON PRINCIPLES OF INTERNATIONAL LAW CONCERNING FRIENDLY RELATIONS AND CO-OPERATION AMONG STATES IN ACCORDANCE WITH THE CHARTER OF THE UNITED NATIONS 1970[1]

The General Assembly . . .

1. *Solemnly proclaims* the following principles:

The principle that States shall refrain in their international relations from the threat or use of force against the territorial integrity or political independence of any State, or in any other manner inconsistent with the purposes of the United Nations

Every State has the duty to refrain in its international relations from the threat or use of force against the territorial integrity or political independence of any State, or in any other manner inconsistent with the purposes of the United Nations. Such a threat or use of force constitutes a violation of international law and the Charter of the United Nations and shall never be employed as a means of settling international issues.

A war of aggression constitutes a crime against the peace for which there is responsibility under international law.

In accordance with the purposes and principles of the United Nations, States have the duty to refrain from propaganda for wars of aggression.

Every State has the duty to refrain from the threat or use of force to violate the existing international boundaries of another State or as a means of solving international disputes, including territorial disputes and problems concerning frontiers of States.

Every State likewise has the duty to refrain from the threat or use of force to violate international lines of demarcation, such as armistice lines, established by or pursuant to an international agreement to which it is a party or which it is otherwise bound to respect. Nothing in the foregoing shall be construed as prejudicing the positions of the parties concerned with regard to the status and effects of such lines under their special régimes or as affecting their temporary character.

States have a duty to refrain from acts of reprisal involving the use of force.

Every State has the duty to refrain from any forcible action which deprives peoples referred to in the elaboration of the principle of equal rights and self-determination of their right to self-determination and freedom and independence.

Every State has the duty to refrain from organizing or encouraging the organization of irregular forces or armed bands, including mercenaries, for incursion into the territory of another State.

Every State has the duty to refrain from organizing, instigating, assisting or participating in acts of civil strife or terrorist acts in another State or acquiescing in organized activities within its territory directed towards the commission of such acts, when the acts referred to in the present paragraph involve a threat or use of force.

The territory of a State shall not be the object of military occupation resulting from the use of force in contravention of the provisions of the Charter. The territory of a State shall not be the object of acquisition by another State resulting from the threat or use of force. No territorial acquisition resulting from the threat or use of force shall be recognized as legal. Nothing in the foregoing shall be construed as affecting:

---

[1] G.A. Resn. 2625 (XXV), October 24, 1970. The resolution was adopted by the General Assembly without a vote.

(a) Provisions of the Charter or any international agreement prior to the Charter régime and valid under international law; or

(b) The powers of the Security Council under the Charter.

All States shall pursue in good faith negotiations for the early conclusion of a universal treaty on general and complete disarmament under effective international control and strive to adopt appropriate measures to reduce international tensions and strengthen confidence among States.

All States shall comply in good faith with their obligations under the generally recognized principles and rules of international law with respect to the maintenance of international peace and security, and shall endeavour to make the United Nations security system based upon the Charter more effective.

Nothing in the foregoing paragraphs shall be construed as enlarging or diminishing in any way the scope of the provisions of the Charter concerning cases in which the use of force is lawful.

The principle that States shall settle their international disputes by peaceful means in such a manner that international peace and security and justice are not endangered

Every State shall settle its international disputes with other States by peaceful means, in such a manner that international peace and security, and justice, are not endangered.

States shall accordingly seek early and just settlement of their international disputes by negotiation, inquiry, mediation, conciliation, arbitration, judicial settlement, resort to regional agencies or arrangements or other peaceful means of their choice. In seeking such a settlement, the parties shall agree upon such peaceful means as may be appropriate to the circumstances and nature of the dispute.

The parties to a dispute have the duty, in the event of failure to reach a solution by any one of the above peaceful means, to continue to seek a settlement of the dispute by other peaceful means agreed upon by them.

States parties to an international dispute, as well as other States, shall refrain from any action which may aggravate the situation so as to endanger the maintenance of international peace and security, and shall act in accordance with the purposes and principles of the United Nations.

International disputes shall be settled on the basis of the sovereign equality of States and in accordance with the principle of free choice of means. Recourse to, or acceptance of, a settlement procedure freely agreed to by States with regard to existing or future disputes to which they are parties shall not be regarded as incompatible with sovereign equality.

Nothing in the foregoing paragraphs prejudices or derogates from the applicable provisions of the Charter, in particular those relating to the pacific settlement of international disputes.

The principle concerning the duty not to intervene in matters within the domestic jurisdiction of any State, in accordance with the Charter

No State or group of States has the right to intervene, directly or indirectly, for any reason whatever, in the international or external affairs of any other State. Consequently, armed intervention and all other forms of interference or attempted threats against the personality of the State or against its political, economic and cultural elements, are in violation of international law.

No State may use or encourage the use of economic, political or any other type of measures to coerce another State in order to obtain from it the subordination of the exercise of its sovereign rights and to secure from it advantages of any kind. Also, no State shall organize, assist, foment, finance, incite or tolerate subversive, terrorist or armed activities directed towards the violent overthrow of the régime of another State, or interfere in civil strife in another State.

The use of force to deprive peoples of their national identity constitutes a violation of their inalienable rights and of the principle of non-intervention.

Every State has an inalienable right to choose its political, economic, social and cultural systems, without interference in any form by another State.

Nothing in the foregoing paragraphs shall be construed as affecting the relevant provisions of the Charter relating to the maintenance of international peace and security.

The duty of States to co-operate with one another in accordance with the Charter

States have the duty to co-operate with one another, irrespective of the differences in their political, economic and social systems, in the various spheres of international relations, in order to maintain international peace and security and to promote international economic stability and progress, the general welfare of nations and international co-operation free from discrimination based on such differences.

To this end:

(a) States shall co-operate with other States in the maintenance of international peace and security;

(b) States shall co-operate in the promotion of universal respect for and observance of human rights and fundamental freedoms for all, and in the elimination of all forms of racial discrimination and all forms of religious intolerance;

(c) States shall conduct their international relations in the economic, social, cultural, technical and trade fields in accordance with the principles of sovereign equality and non-intervention;

(d) States Members of the United Nations have the duty to take joint and separate action in co-operation with the United Nations in accordance with the relevant provisions of the Charter.

States should co-operate in the economic, social and cultural fields as well as in the field of science and technology and for the promotion of international cultural and educational progress. States should co-operate in the promotion of economic growth throughout the world, especially that of the developing countries.

The principle of equal rights and self-determination of peoples

By virtue of the principle of equal rights and self-determination of peoples enshrined in the Charter, all peoples have the right freely to determine, without external interference, their political status and to pursue their economic, social and cultural development, and every State has the duty to respect this right in accordance with the provisions of the Charter.

Every State has the duty to promote, through joint and separate action, the realization of the principle of equal rights and self-determination of peoples, in accordance with the provisions of the Charter, and to render assistance to the United Nations in carrying out the responsibilities entrusted to it by the Charter regarding the implementation of the principle in order:

(a) To promote friendly relations and co-operation among States; and

(b) To bring a speedy end to colonialism, having regard to the freely expressed will of the peoples concerned;

and bearing in mind that subjection of peoples to alien subjugation, domination and exploitation constitutes a violation of the principle, as well as a denial of fundamental human rights, and is contrary to the Charter of the United Nations.

Every State has the duty to promote through joint and separate action universal respect for the observance of human rights and fundamental freedoms in accordance with the Charter.

The establishment of a sovereign and independent State, the free association or integration with an independent State or the emergence into any other political status freely determined by a people constitute modes of implementing the right of self-determination by that people.

Every State has the duty to refrain from any forcible action which deprives peoples referred to above in the elaboration of the present principle of their right to self-determination and freedom and independence. In their actions against and resistance to such forcible action in pursuit of the exercise of their right to self-determination, such peoples are entitled to seek and to receive support in accordance with the purposes and principles of the Charter of the United Nations.

The territory of a colony or other non-governing territory has, under the Charter of the United Nations, a status separate and distinct from the territory of the State administering it; and such separate and distinct status under the Charter shall exist until the people of the colony or non-self-governing territory have exercised their right of self-determination in accordance with the Charter, and particularly its purposes and principles.

Nothing in the foregoing paragraphs shall be construed as authorizing or encouraging any action which would dismember or impair, totally or in part, the territorial integrity or political unity of sovereign and independent States conducting themselves in compliance with the principle of equal rights and self-determination of peoples as described above and thus possessed of a government representing the whole people belonging to the territory without distinction as to race, creed or colour.

Every State shall refrain from any action aimed at the partial or total disruption of the national unity and territorial integrity of any other State or country.

The principle of sovereign equality of States

All States enjoy sovereign equality. They have equal rights and duties and are equal members of the international community, notwithstanding differences of an economic, social, political or other nature.

In particular, sovereign equality includes the following elements:

(a) States are juridically equal;
(b) Each State enjoys the rights inherent in full sovereignty;
(c) Each State has the duty to respect the personality of other States;
(d) The territorial integrity and political independence of the State are inviolable;
(e) Each State has the right freely to choose and develop its political, social, economic and cultural systems;
(f) Each State has the duty to comply fully and in good faith with its international obligations and to live in peace with other States.

The principle that States shall fulfil in good faith the obligations assumed by them in accordance with the Charter

Every State has the duty to fulfil in good faith the obligations assumed by it in accordance with the Charter of the United Nations.

Every State has the duty to fulfil in good faith its obligations under the generally recognized principles and rules of international law.

Every State has the duty to fulfil in good faith its obligations under international agreements valid under the generally recognized principles and rules of international law.

Where obligations arising under international agreements are in conflict with the obligations of Members of the United Nations under the Charter of the United Nations, the obligations under the Charter shall prevail.

2. *Declares* that:

In their interpretation and application the above principles are interrelated and each principle should be construed in the context of the other principles,

Nothing in this Declaration shall be construed as prejudicing in any manner the provisions of the Charter or the rights and duties of Member States under the Charter or the rights of peoples under the Charter taking into account the elaboration of these rights in this Declaration,

3. *Declares further* that:

The principles of the Charter which are embodied in this Declaration constitute basic principles of international law, and consequently appeals to all States to be guided by these principles in their international conduct and to develop their mutual relations on the basis of their strict observance.

INDEX